British Pharmacopoeia (Veterinary) 2017

British Pharmacopoeia (Veterinary) 2017

The British Pharmacopoeia Commission has caused this British Pharmacopoeia (Veterinary) 2017 to be prepared under regulation 317(3)(b) of the Human Medicines Regulations 2012 and, in accordance with regulation 317(4), the Ministers have arranged for it to be published. It has been notified in draft to the European Commission in accordance with Directive 98/34/EEC.

The monographs of the Eighth Edition of the European Pharmacopoeia (2013), as amended by Supplements 8.1 to 8.8, published by the Council of Europe are reproduced either in this edition of the British Pharmacopoeia (Veterinary) or in the associated edition of the British Pharmacopoeia.

see General Notices

Effective date: 1 January 2017

see Notices

London: The Stationery Office

In respect of Great Britain:

THE DEPARTMENT OF HEALTH

In respect of Northern Ireland:

THE DEPARTMENT OF HEALTH, SOCIAL SERVICES AND
PUBLIC SAFETY

© Crown Copyright 2016

Published by The Stationery Office on behalf of the Medicines and
Healthcare products Regulatory Agency (MHRA) except that:

European Pharmacopoeia monographs are reproduced with the permission
of the Council of Europe and are not Crown Copyright. These are
identified in the publication by a chaplet of stars.

This publication is a 'value added' product. If you wish to re-use the
Crown Copyright material from this publication, applications must be made
in writing, clearly stating the material requested for re-use, and the purpose
for which it is required. Applications should be sent to: Dr S Atkinson,
MHRA, 5th Floor, 151 Buckingham Palace Road, London SW1W 9SZ.

First Published 2016

ISBN 978 011 3230 204

British Pharmacopoeia Commission Office:
MHRA
151 Buckingham Palace Road
London SW1W 9SZ
Telephone: +44 (0)20 3080 6561
E-mail: bpcom@mhra.gsi.gov.uk
Web site: http://www.pharmacopoeia.com

Laboratory:
British Pharmacopoeia Commission Laboratory
Queen's Road
Teddington
Middlesex TW11 0LY
Telephone: +44 (0)20 8943 8960
E-mail: bpcrs@mhra.gsi.gov.uk
Web site: http://www.pharmacopoeia.com

Contents

Notices

Monographs of the European Pharmacopoeia are distinguished by a chaplet of stars against the title. The term European Pharmacopoeia, used without qualification, means the eighth edition of the European Pharmacopoeia comprising, unless otherwise stated, the main volume, published in 2013, as amended by any subsequent supplements and revisions.

Patents In this Pharmacopoeia certain drugs and preparations have been included notwithstanding the existence of actual or potential patent rights. In so far as such substances are protected by Letters Patent their inclusion in this Pharmacopoeia neither conveys, nor implies, licence to manufacture.

Effective dates New and revised monographs of national origin enter into force on 1 January 2017. The monographs are brought into effect under regulation 320(2) of the Human Medicines Regulations 2012.

Monographs of the European Pharmacopoeia have previously been published by the European Directorate for the Quality of Medicines & HealthCare in accordance with the Convention on the Elaboration of a European Pharmacopoeia and have been brought into effect under European Directives 2001/82/EC, 2001/83/EC and 2003/63/EC, as amended, on medicines for human and veterinary use.

Preface

The British Pharmacopoeia Commission has caused to be prepared under regulation 317(3)(b) of the Human Medicines Regulations 2012 a compendium, namely this British Pharmacopoeia (Veterinary) 2017, and, in accordance with regulation 317(4), the Ministers have arranged for it to be published. It is a companion volume to the British Pharmacopoeia 2017.

The British Pharmacopoeia (Veterinary) 2017 contributes significantly to the quality control of materials used in the practice of veterinary medicine. It contains publicly available, legally enforceable standards that provide an authoritative statement of the quality that a product, material or article is expected to meet at any time during its period of use. The Pharmacopoeial standards are designed to complement and assist the licensing and inspection processes and are part of the overall system for safeguarding animal and human health in the UK.

The British Pharmacopoeia Commission wishes to record its appreciation of the services of all those who have contributed to the preparation of this important work.

British Pharmacopoeia Commission

The British Pharmacopoeia Commission is appointed, on behalf of the Secretary of State for Health, by the Department of Health's Appointments Team who are responsible for appointments to all of the Advisory Bodies appointed under the Human Medicines Regulations 2012.

Under the terms of the Human Medicines Regulations 2012, the duties of the British Pharmacopoeia Commission are as follows:

   (a)   the preparation and publication of any new edition of the British Pharmacopoeia [regulations 317(1) and 317(4)];

   (b)   the preparation and publication of any compendium containing information relating to substances and articles which are or may be used in the practice of veterinary medicine or veterinary surgery [regulations 317(3)(b) and 317(4)];

   (c)   the preparation and publication of a list of names to be used as the headings to monographs in the British Pharmacopoeia [regulations 318(1) and 318(2)];

   (d)   the preparation of any amendments to the above publications [regulation 317(5)(a)].

Members of the British Pharmacopoeia Commission are appointed for a renewable term of 4 years and, under the requirements laid down by the Office of the Commissioner for Public Appointments, can serve for a maximum of 10 years.

In order to ensure that the British Pharmacopoeia Commission fulfils its duties under the Human Medicines Regulations 2012, the members also have the following duties:

   (1)   to frame clear and unequivocal technical advice in order to discharge the Commission's responsibilities both for the British Pharmacopoeia, the British Pharmacopoeia (Veterinary) and British Approved Names and as the national pharmacopoeial authority with respect to the European Pharmacopoeia;

   (2)   to develop clear policies for the preparation and publication of the British Pharmacopoeia and its related publications;

   (3)   to serve on one or more Expert Advisory Groups or Panels of Experts of the BP Commission, usually in the position of Chair or Vice-Chair;

   (4)   to approve new and revised text for inclusion in new editions of the British Pharmacopoeia and British Pharmacopoeia (Veterinary);

   (5)   to approve new and revised names for inclusion in new editions of British Approved Names and its annual supplements.

In addition to the duties listed above, the Chair of the British Pharmacopoeia Commission has the following additional duties:

(1) To chair all scheduled and unscheduled meetings;

(2) To carry out members appraisals in accordance with Department of Health policies and timelines;

(3) To participate in the process to appoint/re-appoint members of the British Pharmacopoeia Commission.

Expert Advisory Groups, Panels of Experts and Working Parties

Members of Expert Advisory Groups, Panels of Experts and Working Parties are appointed by the British Pharmacopoeia Commission.

The duties of the members are as follows:

(a) to collaborate in the preparation and revision of Monographs, Appendices and Supplementary Chapters for inclusion in the British Pharmacopoeia and British Pharmacopoeia (Veterinary);

(b) to collaborate in the preparation and revision of Monographs, Methods and General Chapters of the European Pharmacopoeia;

(c) to review reports from the British Pharmacopoeia Laboratory in terms of technical content and, where possible, provide independent experimental data to assist in decision making;

(d) to collaborate in the preparation and revision of the list of names to be used as titles for monographs of the British Pharmacopoeia and British Pharmacopoeia (Veterinary).

Members of Expert Advisory Groups, Panels of Experts and Working Parties are usually appointed for a renewable term of 4 years.

Code of Practice

Members of the British Pharmacopoeia Commission and its supporting Expert Advisory Groups, Panels of Experts and Working Parties are required to comply with a Code of Practice on Declaration of Interests in the Pharmaceutical Industry.

British Pharmacopoeia Commission

The Chair and members of the British Pharmacopoeia Commission are required to make a full declaration of interests on appointment and annually thereafter. They must also inform the BP Secretariat promptly of any changes to these interests during the year. These interests are published in the Medicines Advisory Bodies Annual Reports.

Relevant interests must be declared at meetings and are recorded in the Minutes.

Expert Advisory Groups, Panels of Experts and Working Parties

Chairs and members are required to make a full declaration of interests on appointment and to update the Secretariat if these interests change during their term of office. A record is kept of those experts who have declared specific interests, but these are not published.

Relevant interests must be declared at meetings and are recorded in the Minutes.

Membership of the British Pharmacopoeia Commission

The list below includes those members who served during the period 2015 to 2016.

Chair   **Professor Kevin M G Taylor** BPharm PhD FRPharmS
Professor of Clinical Pharmaceutics, UCL School of Pharmacy

Vice-Chair   **Professor Alastair Davidson** BSc PhD FRPharmS
Visiting Professor of Pharmaceutical Sciences, University of Strathclyde

Professor Matthew Almond[1] BSc DPhil DSc CChem FRSC PFHEA NTF
Professor of Chemistry Education and Dean of the Faculty of Arts, Humanities & Social Sciences, University of Reading

Dr Jon Beaman[1] BSc PhD MBA CChem MRSC
Head of Development Analytical Group, Pfizer UK

Dr Anna-Maria Brady[1] BSc PhD
Head of Biologicals and Administration, Veterinary Medicines Directorate

Professor Donald Cairns[2] BSc PhD MRPharmS CSci CChem FRSC
Head: School of Pharmacy and Life Sciences, Robert Gordon University, Aberdeen

Mr Barry Capon[2] CBE MA DL (*Lay representative*)
Non-executive Director, Norfolk and Suffolk NHS Foundation Trust

Dr Graham D Cook BPharm PhD MRPharmS
Senior Director, Process Knowledge/Quality by Design, Pfizer

Mr Andrew Coulson BVetMed MSc MRCVS
Member of the Royal College of Veterinary Surgeons; Non-Executive Director, Veterinary Medicines Directorate; former Superintending Inspector, Science & Research Group, The Home Office

Dr Alison Gleadle[1] BSc PhD (*Lay representative*)
Former Group Product Risk Director, Tesco Stores Ltd.

Mr Christopher Goddard[2] BSc DIS CSci EurChem CChem FRSC
Quality Control Technical Manager, Recipharm Limited

Dr Keith Helliwell[2] BPharm PhD
Senior Technical Adviser, William Ransom & Son PLC

Dr Rodney L Horder BPharm PhD MRPharmS
Former Divisional Vice President, European Quality and Regulatory Strategy, Abbott

---

[1] Appointed from 1 January 2016.

[2] Retired, 31 December 2015.

[1] Appointed from 1 January 2016.
[2] Retired, 31 December 2015.

Membership of Expert Advisory Groups, Panels of Experts and Working Parties

The Commission appointed the following Expert Advisory Groups, Panels of Experts and Working Parties to advise it in carrying out its duties. Membership has changed from time to time; the lists below include all who have served during the period 2015 to 2016.

EXPERT ADVISORY GROUPS

ABS: Antibiotics
R L Horder (*Chair*), G Cook (*Vice-Chair*), P Ellis, E Flahive, A Gibson, V Jaitely, W Mann, J Miller, B White, I R Williams

BIO: Biological and Biotechnological Products
L Tsang (*Chair*), P Varley (*Vice-Chair*), L Bisset*, A F Bristow*, C Burns, D H Calam, K Chidwick*, A Cook*, J Cook*, L Findlay*, S Gill, E Griffiths, C Jones*, A Kippen*, B Patel, A M Pickett*, T Pronce, L Randon, I Rees*, S Schepelmann*, D Sesardic, P Sheppard, P Stickings*, W J Tarbit, A H Thomas, R Thorpe, M Wadhwa*

HCM: Herbal and Complementary Medicines
E Williamson (*Chair*), L A Anderson (*Vice-Chair*), P Anderson, A Bligh, S Gibbons, K Helliwell, C Leon, R Middleton, B Moore, M Pires, M Rowan, K Strohfeldt-Venables, J Sumal*, C Welham, K Zhao (*Corresponding members* SS Handa, A Krauss, Z-T Wang)

MC1: Medicinal Chemicals
A G Davidson (*Chair*), D Cairns (*Vice-Chair*), M Ahmed, J C Berridge, M Broughton, A J Caws, P Fleming, A James, W J Lough, D Malpas

MC2: Medicinal Chemicals
G Cook (*Chair*), C T Goddard (*Vice-Chair*), J Cowie, D Edwards, A Gibson, J Lim, J Miller, P Murray, A Ruggiero, M Turgoose, N Wynne (*Corresponding members* M Brits, W Sherwin)

MC3: Medicinal Chemicals
V Fenton-May (*Chair*), E Williamson (*Vice-Chair*), M Almond, S Arkle, J Beach, J Beaman, C T Goddard, P Hampshire, W K L Pugh, B Rackstraw, R Torano, M Tubby, I R Williams

NOM: Nomenclature
J K Aronson (*Chair*), L Tsang (*Vice-Chair*), M Ahmed, B Granell-Villen, D Mehta, G P Moss, R Thorpe (*Corresponding members* R G Balocco Mattavelli, J S Robertson)

PCY: Pharmacy
R L Horder (*Chair*), B R Matthews (*Vice-Chair*), M Ahmed*, E Baker, J Beach, D Elder, B Granell-Villen, J Lim*, R Lowe, J MacDonald, J F McGuire, T Purewal, L Randon, K Taylor, S Wicks (*Corresponding member* J Churchill)

ULM: Unlicensed Medicines
M G Lee (*Chair*), V Fenton-May (*Vice-Chair*), G Bennett, S Branch, D Caulfield, W Goddard, N Hussain, S Jones, J Rothwell, M Santillo, J Smith, A Sully, P Weir

---

* Specialist member.

PANELS OF EXPERTS

BLP: Blood Products   K Chidwick, A R Hubbard, J More, P Varley

CX: Excipients   B R Matthews (*Chair*), C Mroz (*Vice-Chair*), C Cable, R Cawthorne, W Cook, D Deutsch, N Hussain

IGC: Inorganic and General Chemicals   C T Goddard (*Chair*), M Almond, S Atherton, S Boland, D Caulfield, P Henrys, G Lay

MIC: Microbiology   V Fenton-May (*Chair*), B Alexander, S Denyer, P Hargreaves, B R Matthews, P Newby

RAD: Radioactive Materials   J Ballinger, J Brain, D Graham, G Inwards, R D Pickett, R Smith, S Waters

VET: Veterinary Medicines   E Williamson (*Chair*), A Coulson (*Vice-Chair*), A Cairns, S Cockbill, D Evans, E Flahive, B Ward

VIP: Veterinary Immunological Products   A M Brady (*Chair*), R Banks, R Cooney, K Redhead, J Salt, R Woodland

WORKING PARTIES

AQbD: Analytical Quality by Design   G Cook (*Chair*), S Brown, S Ellison, M Hanna-Brown, S Jones, D Makohon, P Nethercote, E Razzano
(*Corresponding member* K Barnett)

DNA: Identification Techniques   K Helliwell (*Chair*), I Feavers, J Hawkins, E Mee, A Slater, E Williamson

MCS: Microscopy   E Williamson (*Chair*), R Arroo, R Fleck, K Helliwell, K MacLellan Gibson

Current British Pharmacopoeia Staff

ISO 9001
FS 27268

Current British Pharmacopoeia Laboratory Staff

K Courtney *(Laboratory Manager)*

C Balsa, K Busuttil, S Blundell, A Ciesluk, J Clements, C Galdino,
S Humphries, R Irlam, R Mannan, C Marcolan, A Murphy, M Nanasi,
A Panchal, E Sanderson, G Searle, N Vadukal, A Vasilaki, M Wallis,
S Wilson

ISO 9001
FS 27613

Current Staff of the Publisher of the British Pharmacopoeia

J Hook *(MD Public Sector EMEA)*

A Prince *(Client Services Director)*

N Billington *(Client Services Manager)*

A Hughes *(Account Manager)*

P Allard *(Project Manager)*

A Dampier, C Hackett, S Page, M Parka, N Pope, M Rainbird, P Relfe, C Spary, J Stoker, I Webb, T Wheeler

ISO 9001
FS 22428

Introduction

British Pharmacopoeia (Veterinary) 2017

The British Pharmacopoeia (Veterinary) 2017 supersedes the British Pharmacopoeia (Veterinary) 2016. The British Pharmacopoeia Commission has caused this edition to be prepared under regulation 317(3)(b) of the Human Medicines Regulations 2012 and, in accordance with regulation 317(4), the Ministers have arranged for it to be published. This empowers the British Pharmacopoeia Commission to prepare a compendium containing information relating to substances, combinations of substances and articles (whether veterinary medicinal products or not) which are or may be used in the practice of veterinary medicine or veterinary surgery. Under the terms of the Human Medicines Regulations 2012 it is an offence to sell or supply a medicinal product in the United Kingdom that is the subject of a monograph in the Pharmacopoeia if that product does not comply with the standards specified in the monograph.

The British Pharmacopoeia (Veterinary) 2017 is published as a companion volume to the British Pharmacopoeia 2017 and thus contains only those monographs for substances and preparations used exclusively or predominantly in veterinary medicine within the United Kingdom, together with such additional texts as are necessary to support them. It therefore follows that any reference to a monograph, appendix or reagent not contained within this edition is to be construed as a reference to the said monograph, appendix or reagent contained within the British Pharmacopoeia 2017.

This edition, together with the British Pharmacopoeia 2017, contains all the monographs reproduced from the 8th Edition of the European Pharmacopoeia as amended by Supplements 8.1 to 8.8. Users of the British Pharmacopoeia and British Pharmacopoeia (Veterinary) therefore benefit by finding within these two compendia all current pharmacopoeial standards for veterinary medicines used within the United Kingdom.

Effective Date The effective date for this edition is 1 January 2017.

National monographs omitted from this or earlier editions of the British Pharmacopoeia remain effective in accordance with Regulation 252(2)(c) of the Human Medicines Regulations 2012.

Implementation dates regarding European Pharmacopoeia publications are provided in Supplementary Chapter IV B: Dates of Implementation. European Pharmacopoeia monographs are identified by a chaplet of stars alongside the title.

Revisions A number (nine comprising eight technical revisions and one editorial revision) of national monographs have been amended by means of this edition. Of these monographs, those with major technical revisions are listed at the end of this Introduction. For the benefit of the reader this list indicates the section, or sections, of each monograph which has/have been revised.

The list of revisions appended to this Introduction is as comprehensive as practicable. However, to ensure that the reader uses the current standard, it is essential to refer to the full text of each individual monograph.

For those texts reproduced from the European Pharmacopoeia, the European Directorate for the Quality of Medicines & HealthCare (EDQM) database (see below, under Websites) provides information on revisions of the monographs or other texts on a historical basis, beginning from the 5th Edition of the European Pharmacopoeia.

Veterinary Vaccine Monographs

The BP veterinary vaccine monographs have been revised to align them with the VICH Guidelines 41 (Target Animal Safety: Examination of Live Veterinary Vaccines in Target Animals for Absence of Reversion to Virulence) and 44 (Target Animal Safety for Veterinary Live and Inactivated Vaccines). This has resulted in the deletion of six *in vivo* tests, in accordance with the BP Commission's policy relating to the '3Rs' (Replacement, Reduction, Refinement) as set out in the European Convention for the Protection of Vertebrate Animals used for Experimental and Other Scientific Purposes. In addition, the Storage statements have been omitted as the permitted shelf life is the responsibility of the registration (competent) authority.

Title Changes   One monograph title has been amended in this edition. This change is listed at the end of this Introduction.

The European Pharmacopoeia (Ph. Eur.) has agreed to remove the word "anhydrous" from the title of a number of Ph. Eur. monographs for pharmaceutical substances, with justified exceptions. These changes in title will be made in the 9th Edition of the European Pharmacopoeia, effective from 1 January 2017, and are included in the BP 2017. Where appropriate, the former title has been included in the monograph as a subsidiary title. Subsidiary titles have the same significance as the main title and are official titles. To harmonise with this approach, the word "anhydrous" has also been removed from the titles of affected BP monographs.

For some of these monographs, the new Ph. Eur. title for the anhydrous substance is the same as the BP 2016 title (Approved Synonym) for the corresponding hydrated substance. The titles of the affected BP monographs have been changed in line with the current Ph. Eur. titles and a statement has been added to these monographs to indicate the former title used in the UK.

The reason for these changes in title is to harmonise with the Ph. Eur. policy and to ensure that the BP names for these substances are consistent with the names used across Europe.

References to the new Ph. Eur. titles within BP monographs for formulated preparations have been included in this edition.

Stakeholders are encouraged to contact the relevant competent authority in relation to the management of the regulatory impact of these changes on Marketing Authorisations.

Omissions   Four monographs have been omitted from the British Pharmacopoeia (Veterinary) 2017. The list of omissions is appended at the end of this Introduction.

Infrared Reference Spectra   As with the previous edition, the reference spectra are placed in alphabetical order within this edition.

European Pharmacopoeia

Co-operation Agreement

As a consequence of the Co-operation Agreement with the European Directorate for the Quality of Medicines & Healthcare (EDQM) of the Council of Europe, the British Pharmacopoeia Commission is pleased to note the integration of European Pharmacopoeia texts for the British Pharmacopoeia 2016 in-year online updates and for this edition of the British Pharmacopoeia (Veterinary).

All monographs of the 8th Edition of the European Pharmacopoeia, as amended by Supplements 8.1 to 8.8, which are used in veterinary practice but not normally in human medicine in the United Kingdom, are reproduced in this edition of the British Pharmacopoeia (Veterinary). Each of these monographs is signified by a chaplet of stars alongside its title. Additionally, reference to the European Pharmacopoeia monograph number is included immediately below the title in italics in the form '*Ph. Eur. monograph xxxx*'. Where the title in the British Pharmacopoeia (Veterinary) is different from that in the European Pharmacopoeia, an approved synonym has been created (see Appendix XXI B (Vet)) and the European Pharmacopoeia title is included before the monograph number. The entire European Pharmacopoeia text is delineated by two horizontal lines bearing the symbol '*Ph. Eur.*'.

The European Pharmacopoeia texts have been reproduced in their entirety but, where deemed appropriate, additional statements of relevance to UK usage have been added (e.g. action and use statement, a list of British Pharmacopoeia (Veterinary) preparations). It should be noted, however, that in the event of doubt of interpretation in any text of the European Pharmacopoeia, the text published in English under the direction of the Council of Europe should be consulted.

Correspondence between the general methods of the European Pharmacopoeia and the appendices of the British Pharmacopoeia (Veterinary) is indicated in each appendix. A list is also provided at the beginning of the appendices section. This provides a full listing of the European Pharmacopoeia method texts with their British Pharmacopoeia and British Pharmacopoeia (Veterinary) equivalents.

Pharmacopoeial Requirements   Pharmacopoeial requirements for articles used in veterinary medicine are established on the same basis as those used in human medicine. A proper understanding of the basis upon which these requirements are established is essential for their application and advice is provided within the General Notices of the British Pharmacopoeia (Veterinary) and the Supplementary Chapters of the British Pharmacopoeia. It should be noted that no requirement of the Pharmacopoeia can be taken in isolation. A valid interpretation of any particular requirement depends upon it being read in the context of (i) the monograph as a whole, (ii) the specified method of analysis, (iii) the relevant General Notices and (iv) where appropriate, the relevant General Monograph(s).

Where a preparation that is the subject of a monograph in the British Pharmacopoeia is supplied for use in veterinary medicine, the standards of the British Pharmacopoeia apply, unless otherwise justified and authorised. Attention is drawn to the Notice permitting the designation British Pharmacopoeia (Veterinary) [BP (Vet)] to be used in place of the designation British Pharmacopoeia [BP] where a preparation complying with the British Pharmacopoeia is supplied for use in veterinary medicine with the approval of the competent authority.

British Pharmacopoeia Commission

Following a successful campaign run by the Department of Health's Appointments Team during the year, eight new members were appointed and eight were re-appointed with effect from 1st January 2016.

Code of Practice

Members of the British Pharmacopoeia Commission and its supporting Expert Advisory Groups, Panels of Experts and Working Parties are required to comply with a Code of Practice on Declaration of Interests in the pharmaceutical industry. Details of the Code are published on the website (www.pharmacopoeia.com).

Recommendations of the Triennial Review of the British Pharmacopoeia Commission

In 2015 the Department of Health conducted a Triennial Review of the British Pharmacopoeia Commission (BPC) to provide assurance to the Department and the public that the functions of the Commission are required and that it is operating effectively. The Triennial Review report, published in March 2015, made a number of minor recommendations. The majority of these recommendations have now been completed with the remaining two recommendations currently being addressed by the BPC Secretariat.

The full report of the Review can be found on the website at www.gov.uk/government/consultations/british-pharmacopoeia-commission-triennial-review.

Websites

British Pharmacopoeia Websites

The new British Pharmacopoeia website, www.pharmacopoeia.com, consolidated from the two previous websites and launched in August 2015, contains information relating to the British Pharmacopoeia and allows subscribers to access the British Pharmacopoeia 2017 and British Pharmacopoeia (Veterinary) 2017 online and British Approved Names publications.

Chromatograms for information to support new monographs published in the British Pharmacopoeia 2017 have been added to the example test results gallery to aid users of British Pharmacopoeia monographs. This service will increase year-on-year to allow users to examine chromatograms obtained during the practical evaluation of new monographs by the British Pharmacopoeia Commission Laboratory.

Following stakeholder feedback, a regular review schedule for draft texts has been introduced, with draft new and revised monographs being posted at the start of each quarter and available for comment for a period of three months thereafter. This will allow greater visibility of the BP's work programme and better enable stakeholders to contribute to monograph development for future editions.

Subscribers to the BP online will find that draft texts and example test results are also linked with relevant texts and directly accessible from the BP online content. Additionally, BPCRS products are also linked with relevant BP monographs and subscribers to the BP online will be able to purchase these directly from the BP online. BPCRS customers will continue to be able to make purchases through invoice or credit card orders.

An email subscription feature allows users to keep abreast with BP news. Additionally, users can subscribe to receive BPCRS updates, which are now posted monthly.

Access to previous editions of the BP is available as a BP archive product for purchase by new and existing BP online subscribers. The content of the archive starts from the BP 2014 onwards and will grow year-on-year as superseded editions are added to the archive.

A policy of continuous improvement allows the BP website to keep up to date and respond to users. Customers are therefore invited to provide the Secretariat with feedback on their experience.

European Pharmacopoeia Websites

https://extranet.edqm.eu/publications/recherches_sw.shtml For those texts reproduced from the European Pharmacopoeia, the EDQM website provides access to a database (the Knowledge database) containing information of various sorts related to monographs and intended to facilitate their proper use. Information is provided on chromatographic columns used in monograph development, suppliers of reagents and equipment that may be difficult to find for some users, the status of monographs (in development, adopted, published, under revision), revisions of the monographs on a historical basis, beginning from the 5th Edition of the European Pharmacopoeia as well as other useful information.

https://pharmeuropa.edqm.eu/home The European Pharmacopoeia Forum, Pharmeuropa, is published quarterly as an aid for the elaboration of monographs and as a vehicle for information on pharmacopoeial and related matters. Pharmeuropa is available as a free on-line publication.

Forward Look   **Electronic Updates** The British Pharmacopoeia 2017 online updates will be published on the website, www.pharmacopoeia.com, to enable users to keep up to date with monographs published in the European Pharmacopoeia. These updates will be integrated annually with the publication of the main edition of the British Pharmacopoeia.

Monograph Development The British Pharmacopoeia Commission will continue to collaborate with stakeholders to develop BP monographs for veterinary medicines, to ensure that the British Pharmacopoeia (Veterinary) continues to provide authoritative quality standards for veterinary preparations.

Acknowledgements   The British Pharmacopoeia Commission is greatly indebted to the members of its Expert Advisory Groups, Panels of Experts, in particular, the Panel of Experts on Veterinary Medicines, and Working Parties for their dedicated

enthusiasm and assistance in the preparation of this edition. The British Pharmacopoeia Commission is particularly grateful for the contribution of the following members whose term of office ended in 2015:
Professor Donald Cairns, Mr Barry Capon, Mr Christopher Goddard, Dr Keith Helliwell, Dr Lincoln Tsang, Mrs Josephine Turnball and Professor Elizabeth Williamson.

Close co-operation has continued with many organisations at home and overseas. These include the Veterinary Medicines Directorate, the Medicines and Healthcare products Regulatory Agency, the National Office of Animal Health, the Association of the British Pharmaceutical Industry, the European Pharmacopoeia Commission and the European Directorate for the Quality of Medicines & HealthCare, the Therapeutic Goods Administration (Australia), the Health Products and Food Branch of Health Canada, the United States Pharmacopeia, the Quality Assurance and Safety: Medicines Department of the World Health Organization (WHO) and the Health Sciences Authority of Singapore.

The British Pharmacopoeia Commission wishes to thank the European Directorate for the Quality of Medicines & HealthCare for their support and assistance in the reproduction of the European Pharmacopoeia texts and monographs. The British Pharmacopoeia Commission acknowledges the importance of the work of the European Pharmacopoeia (Ph. Eur.) Commission and its Groups of Experts and Working Parties. The British Pharmacopoeia Commission is also grateful for the generous contribution by the UK experts to the work of the Groups of Experts and Working Parties of the European Pharmacopoeia Commission.

The British Pharmacopoeia Commission also acknowledges and appreciates the advice of the publishing team at The Stationery Office, in particular, Ms Nichola Billington, Mr Colin Hackett, Mr Paul Allard, Mr Paul Relfe and Mr Ian Webb, in the production of this edition.

Omissions   The following monographs of the British Pharmacopoeia (Veterinary) 2016 are not included in the British Pharmacopoeia (Veterinary) 2017.

Immunological Products
Clostridium Novyi Alpha Antitoxin[1]
Clostridium Perfringens Antitoxins
Clostridium Perfringens Beta Antitoxin[1]
Clostridium Perfringens Epsilon Antitoxin[1]

Technical Changes   The following monographs in the British Pharmacopoeia (Veterinary) 2017 have been technically amended since the publication of the British Pharmacopoeia (Veterinary) 2016, or have had a significant editorial change. This list does not include revised monographs of the European Pharmacopoeia. An indication of the nature of the change or the section of the monograph that has been changed is given in *italic type* in the right hand column.

---

[1] Monograph suppressed by European Pharmacopoeia Commission on 1 January 2016.

Formulated Preparations: Specific Monographs

Piperonyl Butoxide   *Related substances*

Formulated Preparations: Specific Monographs

Meloxicam Injection   *Alkalinity; Related substances*

Immunological Products

Contagious Pustular Dermatitis Vaccine, Living	*Production (Safety); Safety (deleted); Storage (deleted)*
Louping-ill Vaccine	*Production (Safety); Safety (deleted); Storage (deleted)*
Lungworm (Dictyocaulus Viviparus) Oral Vaccine, Living	*Production (Safety); Batch testing; Safety (deleted); Storage (deleted)*
Newcastle Disease and Avian Infectious Bronchitis Vaccine, Living	*Definition; Production (Caution statement deleted); Safety (deleted); Storage (deleted)*
Ovine Enzootic Abortion Vaccine, Inactivated	*Production (Safety); Safety (deleted); Storage (deleted)*
Salmonella Dublin Vaccine, Living	*Production (Caution statement deleted); Safety; Storage (deleted)*

Changes in Title   The following list gives the alterations in the titles of monographs of the British Pharmacopoeia (Veterinary) 2016 that have been retained in the British Pharmacopoeia (Veterinary) 2017.

BRITISH PHARMACOPOEIA (VETERINARY) 2016	**BRITISH PHARMACOPOEIA (VETERINARY) 2017**

Medicinal and Pharmaceutical Substances

Anhydrous Lufenuron	Lufenuron

General Notices

CONTENTS OF THE GENERAL NOTICES

General Notices

Part I

The British Pharmacopoeia (Veterinary) comprises the entire text within this publication. The word 'official' is used in the Pharmacopoeia to signify 'of the Pharmacopoeia'. It applies to any title, substance, preparation, method or statement included in the general notices, monographs and appendices of the Pharmacopoeia. The abbreviation for British Pharmacopoeia (Veterinary) is BP (Vet).

European Pharmacopoeia
Monographs of the European Pharmacopoeia are reproduced in this edition of the British Pharmacopoeia (Veterinary) by incorporation of the text published under the direction of the Council of Europe (Partial Agreement) in accordance with the Convention on the Elaboration of a European Pharmacopoeia (Treaty Series No. 32 (1974) CMND 5763) as amended by the Protocol to the Convention (Treaty Series No MISC16 (1990) CMND 1133). They are included for the convenience of users of the British Pharmacopoeia (Veterinary). In cases of doubt or dispute reference should be made to the Council of Europe text.

Monographs of the European Pharmacopoeia are distinguished by a chaplet of stars against the title and by reference to the European Pharmacopoeia monograph number included immediately below the title in italics. The beginning and end of text from the European Pharmacopoeia are denoted by means of horizontal lines with the symbol '*Ph Eur*' ranged left and right, respectively.

The general provisions of the European Pharmacopoeia relating to different types of dosage form are included in the appropriate general monograph in that section of either the British Pharmacopoeia or the British Pharmacopoeia (Veterinary) entitled Monographs: Formulated Preparations. These general provisions apply to all veterinary dosage forms of the type defined, whether or not an individual monograph is included in the British Pharmacopoeia (Veterinary). In addition, the provisions of the European Pharmacopoeia General Monograph for Pharmaceutical Preparations apply to all veterinary dosage forms, whether or not an individual monograph is included in the British Pharmacopoeia (Veterinary).

Texts of the European Pharmacopoeia are governed by the General Notices of the European Pharmacopoeia. These are reproduced as Part III of these notices.

Part II

The following general notices apply to the statements made in the monographs of the British Pharmacopoeia (Veterinary) other than those reproduced from the European Pharmacopoeia and to the statements made in the appendices of the British Pharmacopoeia (Veterinary) other than when a method, test or other matter described in an appendix is invoked in a monograph reproduced from the European Pharmacopoeia.

Official Standards   The requirements stated in the monographs of the Pharmacopoeia apply to articles that are intended for veterinary medicinal use but not necessarily to articles that may be sold under the same name for other purposes. An article intended for veterinary medicinal use that is described by means of an official title must comply with the requirements of the relevant monograph. A formulated preparation must comply throughout its assigned shelf-life (period of validity). The subject of any other monograph must comply throughout its period of use.

A monograph is to be construed in accordance with any general monograph or notice or any appendix, note or other explanatory material that is contained in this edition and that is applicable to that monograph. All statements contained in the monographs, except where a specific general notice indicates otherwise and with the exceptions given below, constitute standards for the official articles. An article is not of Pharmacopoeial quality unless it complies with all of the requirements stated. This does not imply that a manufacturer is obliged to perform all the tests in a monograph in order to assess compliance with the Pharmacopoeia before release of a product. The manufacturer may assure himself that a product is of Pharmacopoeial quality by other means, for example, from data derived from validation studies of the manufacturing process, from in-process controls or from a combination of the two. Parametric release in appropriate circumstances is thus not precluded by the need to comply with the Pharmacopoeia. The general notice on Assays and Tests indicates that analytical methods other than those described in the Pharmacopoeia may be employed for routine purposes.

Requirements in monographs have been framed to provide appropriate limitation of potential impurities rather than to provide against all possible impurities. Material found to contain an impurity not detectable by means of the prescribed tests is not of Pharmacopoeial quality if the nature or amount of the impurity found is incompatible with good pharmaceutical practice.

The status of any statement given under the side-headings Definition, Production, Characteristics, Storage, Labelling or Action and use is defined within the general notice relating to the relevant side-heading. In addition to any exceptions indicated by one of the general notices referred to above, the following parts of a monograph do not constitute standards:
(a) a graphic or molecular formula given at the beginning of a monograph;
(b) a molecular weight; (c) a Chemical Abstracts Service Registry Number;
(d) any information given at the end of a monograph concerning impurities known to be limited by that monograph; (e) information in any annex to a

monograph. Any statement containing the word 'should' constitutes non-mandatory advice or recommendation.

The expression 'unless otherwise justified and authorised' means that the requirement in question has to be met, unless a competent authority authorises a modification or exemption where justified in a particular case. The term 'competent authority' means the national, supranational or international body or organisation vested with the authority for making decisions concerning the issue in question. It may, for example, be a licensing authority or an official control laboratory. For a formulated preparation that is the subject of monograph in the British Pharmacopoeia (Veterinary) any justified and authorised modification to, or exemption from, the requirements of the relevant general monograph of the European Pharmacopoeia is stated in the individual monograph. For example, the general monograph for Tablets requires that Uncoated Tablets, except for chewable tablets, disintegrate within 15 minutes; for Ampicillin Tablets a time of 45 minutes is permitted.

Additional statements and requirements applicable to the individual monographs of the British Pharmacopoeia are also included in many of the general monographs of the British Pharmacopoeia for formulated preparations. Such statements and requirements apply also to all monographs for that dosage form included in the British Pharmacopoeia (Veterinary) unless otherwise indicated in either a general monograph or an individual monograph of the British Pharmacopoeia (Veterinary).

Any additions to or modifications of the statements and requirements of the British Pharmacopoeia that are generally applicable to the individual monographs of the British Pharmacopoeia (Veterinary) are provided by means of a supplementary text introduced by a subsidiary heading together with an italicised statement. Thus there is, for example, a supplementary text entitled 'Tablets of the British Pharmacopoeia (Veterinary)' that relates only to the specific monographs for individual tablets that are contained in the British Pharmacopoeia (Veterinary).

Where a monograph on a biological substance or preparation refers to a strain, a test, a method, a substance, *etc.*, using the qualifications 'suitable' or 'appropriate' without further definition in the text, the choice of such strain, test, method, substance, *etc.*, is made in accordance with any international agreements or national regulations affecting the subject concerned.

Definition of Terms   Where the term 'about' is included in a monograph or test it should be taken to mean approximately (fairly correct or accurate; near to the actual value).

Where the term 'corresponds' is included in a monograph or test it should be taken to mean similar or equivalent in character or quantity.

Where the term 'similar' is included in a monograph or test it should be taken to mean alike though not necessarily identical.

Further qualifiers (such as numerical acceptance criteria) for the above terms are not included in the BP (Vet). The acceptance criteria for any individual case are set based on the range of results obtained from known reference samples, the level of precision of the equipment or apparatus used and the level of accuracy required for the particular application. The user should determine the variability seen in his/her own laboratory and set in-house acceptance criteria that he/she judges to be appropriate based on the local operating conditions.

Expression of Standards Where the standard for the content of a substance described in a monograph is expressed in terms of the chemical formula for that substance an upper limit exceeding 100% may be stated. Such an upper limit applies to the result of the assay calculated in terms of the equivalent content of the specified chemical formula. For example, the statement 'contains not less than 99.0% and not more than 101.0% of $C_{20}H_{24}N_2O_2$,HCl' implies that the result of the assay is not less than 99.0% and not more than 101.0%, calculated in terms of the equivalent content of $C_{20}H_{24}N_2O_2$,HCl.

Where the result of an assay or test is required to be calculated with reference to the dried, anhydrous or ignited substance, the substance free from a specified solvent or to the peptide content, the determination of loss on drying, water content, loss on ignition, content of the specified solvent or peptide content is carried out by the method prescribed in the relevant test in the monograph.

Temperature The Celsius thermometric scale is used in expressing temperatures.

Weights and Measures The metric system of weights and measures is employed; SI Units have generally been adopted. Metric measures are required to have been graduated at 20° and all measurements involved in the analytical operations of the Pharmacopoeia are intended, unless otherwise stated, to be made at that temperature. Graduated glass apparatus used in analytical operations should comply with Class A requirements of the appropriate International Standard issued by the International Organization for Standardization. The abbreviation for litre is 'L' throughout the Pharmacopoeia. In line with European Directive 80/181/EEC, the abbreviation 'l' is also permitted for use.

Atomic Weights The atomic weights adopted are the values given in the Table of Relative Atomic Weights 2001 published by the International Union of Pure and Applied Chemistry (Appendix XXV).

Constant Weight The term 'constant weight', used in relation to the process of drying or the process of ignition, means that two consecutive weighings do not differ by more than 0.5 mg, the second weighing being made after an additional period of drying or ignition under the specified conditions appropriate to the nature and quantity of the residue (1 hour is usually suitable).

Expression of Concentrations The term 'per cent' or more usually the symbol '%' is used with one of four different meanings in the expression of concentrations according to circumstances. In order that the meaning to be attached to the expression in each instance is clear, the following notation is used:

Per cent w/w (% w/w) (percentage weight in weight) expresses the number of grams of solute in 100 g of product.

Per cent w/v (% w/v) (percentage weight in volume) expresses the number of grams of solute in 100 mL of product.

Per cent v/v (% v/v) (percentage volume in volume) expresses the number of millilitres of solute in 100 mL of product.

Per cent v/w (% v/w) (percentage volume in weight) expresses the number of millilitres of solute in 100 g of product.

Usually the strength of solutions of solids in liquids is expressed as percentage weight in volume, of liquids in liquids as percentage volume in volume and of gases in liquids as percentage weight in weight.

When the concentration of a solution is expressed as parts per million (ppm), it means weight in weight, unless otherwise specified.

When the concentration of a solution is expressed as parts of dissolved substance in parts of the solution, it means parts by weight (g) of a solid in parts by volume (mL) of the final solution; or parts by volume (mL) of a liquid in parts by volume (mL) of the final solution; or parts by weight (g) of a gas in parts by weight (g) of the final solution.

When the concentration of a solution is expressed in molarity designated by the symbol M preceded by a number, it denotes the number of moles of the stated solute contained in sufficient Purified Water (unless otherwise stated) to produce 1 litre of solution.

Water Bath The term 'water bath' means a bath of boiling water, unless water at some other temperature is indicated in the text. An alternative form of heating may be employed providing that the required temperature is approximately maintained but not exceeded.

Reagents The reagents required for the assays and tests of the Pharmacopoeia are defined in appendices. The descriptions set out in the appendices do not imply that the materials are suitable for use in medicine.

Indicators Indicators, the colours of which change over approximately the same range of pH, may be substituted for one another but in the event of doubt or dispute as to the equivalence of indicators for a particular purpose, the indicator specified in the text is alone authoritative.

The quantity of an indicator solution appropriate for use in acid-base titrations described in assays or tests is 0.1 mL unless otherwise stated in the text.

Any solvent required in an assay or test in which an indicator is specified is previously neutralised to the indicator, unless a blank test is prescribed.

Caution Statements A number of materials described in the monographs and some of the reagents specified for use in the assays and tests of the Pharmacopoeia may be injurious to health unless adequate precautions are taken. The principles of good laboratory practice and the provisions of any appropriate regulations such as those issued in the United Kingdom in accordance with the Health and Safety at Work *etc.* Act (1974) should be observed at all times in carrying out the assays and tests of the Pharmacopoeia.

Attention is drawn to particular hazards in certain monographs by means of an italicised statement; the absence of such a statement should not however be taken to mean that no hazard exists.

Titles Subsidiary titles, where included, have the same significance as the main titles. An abbreviated title constructed in accordance with the directions given in Appendix XXI A has the same significance as the main title.

Titles that are derived by the suitable inversion of words of a main or subsidiary title, with the addition of a preposition if appropriate, are also official titles. Thus, the following are all official titles: Acepromazine Tablets, Tablets of Acepromazine; Levamisole Injection, Injection of Levamisole.

A title of a formulated preparation that includes the full nonproprietary name of the active ingredient or ingredients, where this is not included in the title of the monograph, is also an official title. For example, the title

Acepromazine Maleate Injection has the same significance as Acepromazine Injection and the title Diprenorphine Hydrochloride Injection has the same significance as Diprenorphine Injection.

Where the English title at the head of a monograph in the European Pharmacopoeia is different from that at the head of the text incorporated into the British Pharmacopoeia (Veterinary), an Approved Synonym has been created on the recommendation of the British Pharmacopoeia Commission. Approved Synonyms have the same significance as the main title and are thus official titles. A cumulative list of such Approved Synonyms is provided in Appendix XXI B (Vet).

Where the names of Pharmacopoeial substances, preparations and other materials occur in the text they are printed with capital initial letters and this indicates that materials of Pharmacopoeial quality must be used. Words in the text that name a reagent or other material, a physical characteristic or a process that is described or defined in an appendix are printed in italic type, for example, *methanol, absorbance, gas chromatography*, and these imply compliance with the requirements specified in the appropriate appendix.

Chemical Formulae When the chemical composition of an official substance is known or generally accepted, the graphic and molecular formulae, the molecular weight and the Chemical Abstracts Service Registry Number are normally given at the beginning of the monograph for information. This information refers to the chemically pure substance and is not to be regarded as an indication of the purity of the official material. Elsewhere, in statements of standards of purity and strength and in descriptions of processes of assay, it is evident from the context that the formulae denote the chemically pure substances.

Where the absolute stereochemical configuration is specified, the International Union of Pure and Applied Chemistry (IUPAC) *R/S* and *E/Z* systems of designation have been used. If the substance is an enantiomer of unknown absolute stereochemistry the sign of the optical rotation, as determined in the solvent and under the conditions specified in the monograph, has been attached to the systematic name. An indication of sign of rotation has also been given where this is incorporated in a trivial name that appears on an IUPAC preferred list.

All amino acids, except glycine, have the L-configuration unless otherwise indicated. The three-letter and one-letter symbols used for amino acids in peptide and protein sequences are those recommended by the Joint Commission on Biochemical Nomenclature of the International Union of Pure and Applied Chemistry and the International Union of Biochemistry. In the graphic formulae the following abbreviations are used:

Me	$-CH_3$	Bu^s	$-CH(CH_3)CH_2CH_3$
Et	$-CH_2CH_3$	Bu^n	$-CH_2CH_2CH_2CH_3$
Pr^i	$-CH(CH_3)_2$	Bu^t	$-C(CH_3)_3$
Pr^n	$-CH_2CH_2CH_3$	Ph	$-C_6H_5$
Bu^i	$-CH_2CH(CH_3)_2$	Ac	$-COCH_3$

Definition Statements given under the side-heading Definition constitute an official definition of the substance, preparation or other article that is the subject of the monograph. They constitute instructions or requirements and are mandatory in nature.

Certain medicinal or pharmaceutical substances and other articles are defined by reference to a particular method of manufacture. A statement that a substance or article *is* prepared or obtained by a certain method constitutes part of the official definition and implies that other methods are not permitted. A statement that a substance *may be* prepared or obtained by a certain method, however, indicates that this is one possible method and does not imply that other methods are proscribed.

Additional statements concerning the definition of formulated preparations are given in the general notice on Manufacture of Formulated Preparations.

Production Statements given under the side-heading Production draw attention to particular aspects of the manufacturing process but are not necessarily comprehensive. They constitute mandatory instructions to manufacturers. They may relate, for example, to source materials, to the manufacturing process itself and its validation and control, to in-process testing or to testing that is to be carried out by the manufacturer on the final product (bulk material or dosage form) either on selected batches or on each batch prior to release. These statements cannot necessarily be verified on a sample of the final product by an independent analyst. The competent authority may establish that the instructions have been followed, for example, by examination of data received from the manufacturer, by inspection or by testing appropriate samples.

The absence of a section on Production does not imply that attention to features such as those referred to above is not required. A substance, preparation or article described in a monograph of the Pharmacopoeia is to be manufactured in accordance with the principles of good manufacturing practice and in accordance with relevant international agreements and supranational and national regulations governing medicinal products.

Where in the section under the side-heading Production a monograph on a vaccine defines the characteristics of the vaccine strain to be used, any test methods given for confirming these characteristics are provided as examples of suitable methods. The use of these methods is not mandatory.

Additional statements concerning the production of formulated preparations are given in the general notice on Manufacture of Formulated Preparations.

Manufacture of Formulated Preparations Attention is drawn to the need to observe adequate hygienic precautions in the preparation and dispensing of pharmaceutical formulations. The principles of good pharmaceutical manufacturing practice should be observed.

The Definition in certain monographs for pharmaceutical preparations is given in terms of the principal ingredients only. Any ingredient, other than those included in the Definition, must comply with the general notice on Excipients and the product must conform with the Pharmacopoeial requirements.

The Definition in other monographs for pharmaceutical preparations is presented as a full formula. No deviation from the stated formula is permitted except those allowed by the general notices on Colouring Agents and Antimicrobial Preservatives. Where additionally directions are given under the side-heading Extemporaneous Preparation these are intended for the extemporaneous preparation of relatively small quantities for short-term supply and use. When so prepared, no deviation from the stated directions is permitted. If, however, such a pharmaceutical preparation is manufactured on a larger scale with the intention that it may be stored, deviations from the stated directions are permitted provided that the final product meets the following criteria:

(1) compliance with all of the requirements stated in the monograph;

(2) retention of the essential characteristics of the preparation made strictly in accordance with the directions of the Pharmacopoeia.

Monographs for yet other pharmaceutical preparations include both a Definition in terms of the principal ingredients and, under the side-heading Extemporaneous Preparation, a full formula together with, in some cases, directions for their preparation. Such full formulae and directions are intended for the extemporaneous preparation of relatively small quantities for short-term supply and use. When so prepared, no deviation from the stated formula and directions is permitted. If, however, such a pharmaceutical preparation is manufactured on a larger scale with the intention that it may be stored, deviations from the formula and directions stated under the side-heading Extemporaneous Preparation are permitted provided that any ingredient, other than those included in the Definition, complies with the general notice on Excipients and that the final product meets the following criteria:

(1) accordance with the Definition stated in the monograph;

(2) compliance with all of the requirements stated in the monograph;

(3) retention of the essential characteristics of the preparation made strictly in accordance with the formula and directions of the Pharmacopoeia.

In the manufacture of any official preparation on a large scale with the intention that it should be stored, in addition to following any instruction under the side-heading Production, it is necessary to ascertain that the product is satisfactory with respect to its physical and chemical stability and its state of preservation over the claimed shelf-life. This applies irrespective of whether the formula of the Pharmacopoeia and any instructions given under the side-heading Extemporaneous Preparation are followed precisely or modified. Provided that the preparation has been shown to be stable in other respects, deterioration due to microbial contamination may be inhibited by the incorporation of a suitable antimicrobial preservative. In such circumstances the label states appropriate storage conditions, the date after which the product should not be used and the identity and concentration of the antimicrobial preservative.

Freshly and Recently Prepared The direction, given under the side-heading Extemporaneous Preparation, that a preparation must be freshly prepared indicates that it must be made not more than 24 hours before it is issued for use. The direction that a preparation should be recently prepared indicates that deterioration is likely if the preparation is stored for longer than about 4 weeks at 15° to 25°.

Methods of Sterilisation The methods of sterilisation used in preparing the sterile materials described in the Pharmacopoeia are given in Appendix XVIII. For aqueous preparations, steam sterilisation (heating in an autoclave) is the method of choice wherever it is known to be suitable. Any method of sterilisation must be validated with respect to both the assurance of sterility and the integrity of the product and to ensure that the final product complies with the requirements of the monograph.

Water The term Water used without qualification in formulae for formulated preparations means either potable water freshly drawn direct from the public supply and suitable for drinking or freshly boiled and cooled Purified

Water. The latter should be used if the public supply is from a local storage tank or if the potable water is unsuitable for a particular preparation.

Excipients   Where an excipient for which there is a Pharmacopoeial monograph is used in preparing an official preparation it shall comply with that monograph. Any substance added in preparing an official preparation shall be innocuous, shall have no adverse influence on the therapeutic efficacy of the active ingredients and shall not interfere with the assays and tests of the Pharmacopoeia. Particular care should be taken to ensure that such substances are free from harmful organisms.

Colouring Agents   If in a monograph for a formulated preparation defined by means of a full formula a specific colouring agent or agents is prescribed, suitable alternatives approved in the country concerned may be substituted.

Antimicrobial Preservatives   When the term 'suitable antimicrobial preservative' is used it is implied that the preparation concerned will be effectively preserved according to the appropriate criteria applied and interpreted as described in the test for *efficacy of antimicrobial preservation* (Appendix XVI C). In certain monographs for formulated preparations defined by means of a full formula, a specific antimicrobial agent or agents may be prescribed; suitable alternatives may be substituted provided that their identity and concentration are stated on the label.

Characteristics   Statements given under the side-heading Characteristics are not to be interpreted in a strict sense and are not to be regarded as official requirements. Statements on taste are provided only in cases where this property is a guide to the acceptability of the material (for example, a material used primarily for flavouring). The status of statements on solubility is given in the general notice on Solubility.

   Solubility   Statements on solubility given under the side-heading Characteristics are intended as information on the approximate solubility at a temperature between 15° and 25°, unless otherwise stated, and are not to be considered as official requirements.

   Statements given under side-headings such as Solubility in ethanol express exact requirements and constitute part of the standards for the substances under which they occur.

   The following table indicates the meanings of the terms used in statements of approximate solubilities.

Descriptive term	Approximate volume of solvent in millilitres per gram of solute
very soluble	less than 1
freely soluble	from 1 to 10
soluble	from 10 to 30
sparingly soluble	from 30 to 100
slightly soluble	from 100 to 1000
very slightly soluble	from 1000 to 10,000
practically insoluble	more than 10,000

The term 'partly soluble' is used to describe a mixture of which only some of the components dissolve.

Identification   The tests described or referred to under the side-heading Identification are not necessarily sufficient to establish absolute proof of identity. They provide a means of verifying that the identity of the material being examined is in accordance with the label on the container.

Unless otherwise prescribed, identification tests are carried out at a temperature between 15° and 25°.

Reference spectra   Where a monograph refers to an infrared reference spectrum, this spectrum is provided in a separate section of the Pharmacopoeia. A sample spectrum is considered to be concordant with a reference spectrum if the transmission minima (absorption maxima) of the principal bands in the sample correspond in position, relative intensities and shape to those of the reference. Instrumentation software may be used to calculate concordance with a previously recorded reference spectrum.

When tests for infrared absorption are applied to material extracted from formulated preparations, strict concordance with the specified reference spectrum may not always be possible, but nevertheless a close resemblance between the spectrum of the extracted material and the specified reference spectrum should be achieved.

Assays and Tests   The assays and tests described are the official methods upon which the standards of the Pharmacopoeia depend. The analyst is not precluded from employing alternative methods, including methods of micro-analysis, in any assay or test if it is known that the method used will give a result of equivalent accuracy. Local reference materials may be used for routine analysis, provided that these are calibrated against the official reference materials. In the event of doubt or dispute, the methods of analysis, the reference materials and the reference spectra of the Pharmacopoeia are alone authoritative.

Where the solvent used for a solution is not named, the solvent is Purified Water.

Unless otherwise prescribed, the assays and tests are carried out at a temperature between 15° and 25°.

A temperature in a test for Loss on drying, where no temperature range is given, implies a range of $\pm$ 2° about the stated value.

Visual comparative tests, unless otherwise prescribed, are carried out using identical tubes of colourless, transparent, neutral glass with a flat base and an internal diameter of 16 mm; tubes with a larger internal diameter may be used but the volume of liquid examined must be increased so that the depth of liquid in the tube is not less than that obtained when the prescribed volume of liquid and tubes 16 mm in internal diameter are used. Equal volumes of the liquids to be compared are examined down the vertical axis of the tubes against a white background or, if necessary, against a black background. The examination is carried out in diffuse light.

Where a direction is given that an analytical operation is to be carried out 'in subdued light', precautions should be taken to avoid exposure to direct sunlight or other strong light. Where a direction is given that an analytical operation is to be carried out 'protected from light', precautions should be taken to exclude actinic light by the use of low-actinic glassware, working in a dark room or similar procedures.

For preparations other than those of fixed strength, the quantity to be taken for an assay or test is usually expressed in terms of the active ingredient. This means that the quantity of the active ingredient expected to be present and the quantity of the preparation to be taken are calculated from the strength stated on the label.

In assays the approximate quantity to be taken for examination is indicated but the quantity actually used must not deviate by more than 10% from that stated. The quantity taken is accurately weighed or measured and the result of the assay is calculated from this exact quantity. Reagents are measured and the procedures are carried out with an accuracy commensurate with the degree of precision implied by the standard stated for the assay.

In tests the stated quantity to be taken for examination must be used unless any divergence can be taken into account in conducting the test and calculating the result. The quantity taken is accurately weighed or measured with the degree of precision implied by the standard or, where the standard is not stated numerically (for example, in tests for Clarity and colour of solution), with the degree of precision implied by the number of significant figures stated. Reagents are measured and the procedures are carried out with an accuracy commensurate with this degree of precision.

The limits stated in monographs are based on data obtained in normal analytical practice; they take account of normal analytical errors, of acceptable variations in manufacture and of deterioration to an extent considered acceptable. No further tolerances are to be applied to the limits prescribed to determine whether the article being examined complies with the requirements of the monograph.

In determining compliance with a numerical limit, the calculated result of a test or assay is first rounded to the number of significant figures stated, unless otherwise prescribed. The last figure is increased by one when the part rejected is equal to or exceeds one half-unit, whereas it is not modified when the part rejected is less than a half-unit.

In certain tests, the concentration of impurity is given in parentheses either as a percentage or in parts per million by weight (ppm). In chromatographic tests such concentrations are stated as a percentage irrespective of the limit. In other tests they are usually stated in ppm unless the limit exceeds 500 ppm. In those chromatographic tests in which a secondary spot or peak in a chromatogram obtained with a solution of the substance being examined is described as corresponding to a named impurity and is compared with a spot or peak in a chromatogram obtained with a reference solution of the same impurity, the percentage given in parentheses indicates the limit for that impurity. In those chromatographic tests in which a spot or peak in a chromatogram obtained with a solution of the substance being examined is described in terms other than as corresponding to a named impurity (commonly, for example, as any (other) *secondary spot* or *peak*) but is compared with a spot or peak in a chromatogram obtained with a reference solution of a named impurity, the percentage given in parentheses indicates an impurity limit expressed in terms of a nominal concentration of the named impurity. In chromatographic tests in which a comparison is made between spots or peaks in chromatograms obtained with solutions of different concentrations of the substance being examined, the percentage given in parentheses indicates an impurity limit expressed in terms of a nominal concentration of the medicinal substance itself. In some monographs, in particular those for certain formulated preparations, the impurity limit is expressed in terms of a nominal concentration of the active moiety rather than of the medicinal substance itself. Where necessary for clarification the terms in which the limit is expressed are stated within the monograph.

In all cases where an impurity limit is given in parentheses, the figures given are approximations for information only; conformity with the requirements is determined on the basis of compliance or otherwise with the stated test.

The use of a proprietary designation to identify a material used in an assay or test does not imply that another equally suitable material may not be used.

Biological Assays and Tests   Methods of assay described as Suggested methods are not obligatory, but when another method is used its precision must be not less than that required for the Suggested method.

For those antibiotics for which the monograph specifies a microbiological assay the potency requirement is expressed in the monograph in International Units (IU) or other Units per milligram. The material is not of pharmacopoeial quality if the upper fiducial limit of error is less than the stated potency. For such antibiotics the required precision of the assay is stated in the monograph in terms of the fiducial limits of error about the estimated potency.

For other substances and preparations for which the monograph specifies a biological assay, unless otherwise stated, the precision of the assay is such that the fiducial limits of error, expressed as a percentage of the estimated potency, are within a range not wider than that obtained by multiplying by a factor of ten the square roots of the limits given in the monograph for the fiducial limits of error about the stated potency.

In all cases fiducial limits of error are based on a probability of 95% ($P = 0.95$).

Where the biological assay is being used to ascertain the purity of the material, the stated potency means the potency stated on the label in terms of International Units (IU) or other Units per gram, per milligram or per millilitre. When no such statement appears on the label, the stated potency means the fixed or minimum potency required in the monograph. This interpretation of stated potency applies in all cases except where the monograph specifically directs otherwise.

Where the biological assay is being used to determine the total activity in the container, the stated potency means the total number of International Units (IU) or other Units stated on the label or, if no such statement appears, the total activity calculated in accordance with the instructions in the monograph.

Wherever possible the primary standard used in an assay or test is the respective International Standard or Reference Preparation established by the World Health Organization for international use and the biological activity is expressed in International Units (IU).

In other cases, where Units are referred to in an assay or test, the Unit for a particular substance or preparation is, for the United Kingdom, the specific biological activity contained in such an amount of the respective primary standard as the appropriate international or national organisation indicates. The necessary information is provided with the primary standard.

Unless otherwise directed, animals used in an assay or a test are healthy animals, drawn from a uniform stock, that have not previously been treated with any material that will interfere with the assay or test. Unless otherwise stated, guinea-pigs weigh not less than 250 g or, when used in systemic toxicity tests, not less than 350 g. When used in skin tests they are white or light coloured. Unless otherwise stated, mice weigh not less than 17 g and not more than 22 g.

Certain of the biological assays and tests of the Pharmacopoeia are such that in the United Kingdom they may be carried out only in accordance with the Animals (Scientific Procedures) Act 1986. Instructions included in such assays and tests in the Pharmacopoeia, with respect to the handling of animals, are therefore confined to those concerned with the accuracy and reproducibility of the assay or test.

Reference Substances and Reference Preparations

Certain monographs require the use of a reference substance, a reference preparation or a reference spectrum. These are chosen with regard to their intended use as prescribed in the monographs of the Pharmacopoeia and are not necessarily suitable in other circumstances.

Any information necessary for proper use of the reference substance or reference preparation is given on the label or in the accompanying leaflet or brochure. Where no drying conditions are stated in the leaflet or on the label, the substance is to be used as received. No certificate of analysis or other data not relevant to the prescribed use of the product are provided. The products are guaranteed to be suitable for use for a period of three months from dispatch when stored under the appropriate conditions. The stability of the contents of opened containers cannot be guaranteed. The current lot is listed in the BP Laboratory website catalogue. Additional information is provided in Supplementary Chapter III E.

Chemical Reference Substances   The abbreviation BPCRS indicates a Chemical Reference Substance established by the British Pharmacopoeia Commission. The abbreviation CRS or EPCRS indicates a Chemical Reference Substance established by the European Pharmacopoeia Commission. Some Chemical Reference Substances are used for the microbiological assay of antibiotics and their activity is stated, in International Units, on the label or on the accompanying leaflet and defined in the same manner as for Biological Reference Preparations.

Biological Reference Preparations   The majority of the primary biological reference preparations referred to are the appropriate International Standards and Reference Preparations established by the World Health Organisation. Because these reference materials are usually available only in limited quantities, the European Pharmacopoeia has established Biological Reference Preparations (indicated by the abbreviation BRP or EPBRP) where appropriate. Where applicable, the potency of the Biological Reference Preparations is expressed in International Units. For some Biological Reference Preparations, where an international standard or reference preparation does not exist, the potency is expressed in European Pharmacopoeia Units.

Storage

Statements under the side-heading Storage constitute non-mandatory advice. The substances and preparations described in the Pharmacopoeia are to be stored under conditions that prevent contamination and, as far as possible, deterioration. Unless otherwise stated in the monograph, the substances and preparations described in the Pharmacopoeia are kept in well-closed containers and stored at a temperature not exceeding 25°. Precautions that should be taken in relation to the effects of the atmosphere, moisture, heat and light are indicated, where appropriate, in the monographs. Further precautions may be necessary when some materials are stored in tropical climates or under other severe conditions.

The expression 'protected from moisture' means that the product is to be stored in an airtight container. Care is to be taken when the container is opened in a damp atmosphere. A low moisture content may be maintained, if necessary, by the use of a desiccant in the container provided that direct contact with the product is avoided.

The expression 'protected from light' means that the product is to be stored either in a container made of a material that absorbs actinic light sufficiently to protect the contents from change induced by such light or in a container enclosed in an outer cover that provides such protection or stored in a place from which all such light is excluded.

The expression 'tamper-evident container' means a closed container fitted with a device that reveals irreversibly whether the container has been opened, whereas, the expression 'tamper-proof container' means a closed container in which access to the contents is prevented under normal conditions of use. The two terms are considered to be synonymous by the European Pharmacopoeia Commission.

Labelling The labelling requirements of the Pharmacopoeia are not comprehensive, and the provisions of regulations issued in accordance with the requirements of the territory in which the medicinal product is to be used should be met.

Licensed medicines intended for use within the United Kingdom must comply with the requirements of the current Veterinary Medicines Regulations and European Directive 2001/82/EC (as amended) in respect of their labelling and package leaflets, together with those regulations for the labelling of hazardous materials.

Best practice guidance on the labelling and packaging of veterinary medicines for use in the United Kingdom advises that certain items of information are deemed critical for the safe use of the medicine. Further information and guidance on the labelling of medicinal products can be found in Supplementary Chapter I G.

Such matters as the exact form of wording to be used and whether a particular item of information should appear on the primary label and additionally, or alternatively, on the package or exceptionally in a leaflet are, in general, outside the scope of the Pharmacopoeia. When the term 'label' is used in Labelling statements of the Pharmacopoeia, decisions as to where the particular statement should appear should therefore be made in accordance with relevant legislation.

The label of every official formulated preparation other than those of fixed strength also states the content of the active ingredient or ingredients expressed in the terms required by the monograph. Where the content of active ingredient is required to be expressed in terms other than the weight of the official medicinal substance used in making the formulation, this is specifically stated under the heading Labelling. Unless otherwise stated in the monograph, the content of the active ingredient is expressed in terms of the official medicinal substance used in making the formulation.

Action and Use The statements given under this side-heading in monographs are intended only as information on the principal pharmacological actions or the uses of the materials in veterinary medicine or pharmacy. It should not be assumed that the substance has no other action or use. The statements are not intended to be binding on prescribers or to limit their discretion.

Antibiotics Intended for Use in the Manufacture of Intramammary Infusions   Where a monograph for an antibiotic in the British Pharmacopoeia or in the British Pharmacopoeia (Veterinary) contains specific requirements relating to sterility or to abnormal toxicity for material intended for use in the manufacture of a parenteral dosage form, these requirements, together with any qualification, apply also to any material intended for use in the manufacture of an intramammary infusion.

Crude Drugs; Traditional Herbal and Complementary Medicines   *Herbal and complementary medicines are classed as medicines under European Directive 2001/83/EC as amended. It is emphasised that, although requirements for the quality of the material are provided in the monograph to assist the registration scheme by the UK Licensing Authority, the British Pharmacopoeia Commission has not assessed the safety or efficacy of the material in traditional use.*

Monograph Title   For traditional herbal medicines, the monograph title is a combination of the binomial name together with a description of use. Monographs for the material that has not been processed (the herbal drug) and the processed material (the herbal drug preparation) are published where possible. To distinguish between the two, the word 'Processed' is included in the relevant monograph title.

Definition   Under the heading Definition, the botanical name together with any synonym is given. Where appropriate, for material that has not been processed, information on the collection/harvesting and/or treatment/ drying of the whole herbal drug may be given. For processed materials, the method of processing, where appropriate, will normally be given in a separate section.

Characteristics   References to odour are included only where this is highly characteristic. References to taste are not included.

Control methods   Where applicable, the control methods to be used in monographs are:

(a) macroscopical and microscopical descriptions and chemical/ chromatographic tests for identification

(b) tests for absence of any related species

(c) microbial test to assure microbial quality

(d) tests for inorganic impurities and non-specific purity tests, including extractive tests, Sulfated ash and Heavy metals, where appropriate

(e) test for Loss on drying or Water

(f) wherever possible, a method for assaying the active constituent(s) or suitable marker constituent(s).

The macroscopical characteristics include those features that can be seen by the unaided eye or by the use of a hand lens. When two species/ subspecies of the same plant are included in the Definition, individual differences between the two are indicated where possible.

The description of the microscopical characteristics of the powdered drug includes information on the dominant or the most specific characters. Where it is considered to be an aid to identification, illustrations of the powdered drug may be provided.

The following aspects are controlled by the general monograph for Herbal Drugs: they are required to be free from moulds, insects, decay, animal matter and animal excreta. Unless otherwise prescribed the amount of foreign matter is not more than 2% w/w. Microbial contamination should be minimal.

In determining the content of the active constituents or the suitable marker substances measurements are made with reference to the dried or anhydrous herbal drug. In the tests for Acid-insoluble ash, Ash, Extractive soluble in ethanol, Loss on drying, Sulfated ash, Water, Water-soluble ash and Water-soluble extractive of herbal drugs, the calculations are made with reference to the herbal drug that has not been specifically dried unless otherwise prescribed in the monograph.

Homoeopathic Medicines

Homoeopathic medicines are classed as medicines under European Directive 2001/83/EC as amended. It is emphasised that, although requirements for the quality of the material are provided in the relevant monograph in order to assist the simplified registration scheme by the UK Licensing Authority, the British Pharmacopoeia Commission has not assessed the safety or efficacy of the material in use.

All materials used for the production of homoeopathic medicines, including excipients, must comply with European Pharmacopoeia or British Pharmacopoeia monographs for those materials. Where such European Pharmacopoeia or British Pharmacopoeia monographs do not exist, each material used for the production of homoeopathic medicines must comply with an official national pharmacopoeia of a Member State.

British Pharmacopoeia monographs for homoeopathic medicines apply to homoeopathic stocks and mother tinctures only, but may be prefaced by a section which details the quality requirements applicable to the principle component where there is no European Pharmacopoeia or British Pharmacopoeia monograph for the material. These monographs also include either general statements on the methods of preparation or refer to specific methods of preparation given in the European Pharmacopoeia. Homoeopathic stocks and mother tinctures undergo the further process referred to as potentisation. Potentisation is a term specific to homoeopathic medicine and is a process of dilution of stocks and mother tinctures to produce the final product.

Identification tests are established for the components in homoeopathic stocks and usually relate to those applied to the materials used in the production of the homoeopathic stocks. An assay is included for the principal component(s) where possible. For mother tinctures, an identification test, usually chromatographic, is established and, where applicable, an assay for the principle component(s); where appropriate, other tests, related to the solvent, dry matter or known adulterants, are included.

Specifications have not been set for final homoeopathic products due to the high dilution used in their preparation and the subsequent difficulty in applying analytical methodology.

Statements under Crude Drugs; Traditional Herbal and Complementary Medicines also apply to homoeopathic stocks and mother tinctures, when appropriate.

Part III

Monographs and other texts of the European Pharmacopoeia that are incorporated in this edition of the British Pharmacopoeia are governed by the general notices of the European Pharmacopoeia; these are reproduced below.

GENERAL NOTICES OF THE EUROPEAN PHARMACOPOEIA

1.1. GENERAL STATEMENTS

The General Notices apply to all monographs and other texts of the European Pharmacopoeia.

The official texts of the European Pharmacopoeia are published in English and French. Translations in other languages may be prepared by the signatory States of the European Pharmacopoeia Convention. In case of doubt or dispute, the English and French versions are alone authoritative.

In the texts of the European Pharmacopoeia, the word 'Pharmacopoeia' without qualification means the European Pharmacopoeia. The official abbreviation Ph. Eur. may be used to indicate the European Pharmacopoeia.

The use of the title or the subtitle of a monograph implies that the article complies with the requirements of the relevant monograph. Such references to monographs in the texts of the Pharmacopoeia are shown using the monograph title and reference number in *italics*.

A preparation must comply throughout its period of validity; a distinct period of validity and/or specifications for opened or broached containers may be decided by the competent authority. The subject of any other monograph must comply throughout its period of use. The period of validity that is assigned to any given article and the time from which that period is to be calculated are decided by the competent authority in light of experimental results of stability studies.

Unless otherwise indicated in the General Notices or in the monographs, statements in monographs constitute mandatory requirements. General chapters become mandatory when referred to in a monograph, unless such reference is made in a way that indicates that it is not the intention to make the text referred to mandatory but rather to cite it for information.

The active substances, excipients, pharmaceutical preparations and other articles described in the monographs are intended for human and veterinary use (unless explicitly restricted to one of these uses).

Quality systems The quality standards represented by monographs are valid only where the articles in question are produced within the framework of a suitable quality system. The quality system must assure that the articles consistently meet the requirements of the Pharmacopoeia.

Alternative methods The tests and assays described are the official methods upon which the standards of the Pharmacopoeia are based. With the agreement of the competent authority, alternative methods of analysis may be used for control purposes, provided that the methods used enable an unequivocal decision to be made as to whether compliance with the standards of the monographs would be achieved if the official methods were used. In the event of doubt or dispute, the methods of analysis of the Pharmacopoeia are alone authoritative.

Demonstration of compliance with the Pharmacopoeia

(1) An article is not of Pharmacopoeia quality unless it complies with all the requirements stated in the monograph. This does not imply that performance of all the tests in a monograph is necessarily a prerequisite for a manufacturer in assessing compliance with the Pharmacopoeia before release of a product. The manufacturer may obtain assurance that a product is of Pharmacopoeia quality on the basis of its design, together with its control strategy and data derived, for example, from validation studies of the manufacturing process.

(2) An enhanced approach to quality control could utilise process analytical technology (PAT) and/or real-time release testing (including parametric release) strategies as alternatives to end-product testing alone. Real-time release testing in circumstances deemed appropriate by the competent authority is thus not precluded by the need to comply with the Pharmacopoeia.

(3) Reduction of animal testing: the European Pharmacopoeia is dedicated to phasing out the use of animals for test purposes, in accordance with the 3Rs (Replacement, Reduction, Refinement) set out in the European Convention for the Protection of Vertebrate Animals used for Experimental and Other Scientific Purposes. In demonstrating compliance with the Pharmacopoeia as indicated above (1), manufacturers may consider establishing additional systems to monitor consistency of production. With the agreement of the competent authority, the choice of tests performed to assess compliance with the Pharmacopoeia when animal tests are prescribed is established in such a way that animal usage is minimised as much as possible.

Grade of materials Certain materials that are the subject of a pharmacopoeial monograph may exist in different grades suitable for different purposes. Unless otherwise indicated in the monograph, the requirements apply to all grades of the material. In some monographs, particularly those on excipients, a list of functionality-related characteristics that are relevant to the use of the substance may be appended to the monograph for information. Test methods for determination of one or more of these characteristics may be given, also for information.

General monographs Substances and preparations that are the subject of an individual monograph are also required to comply with relevant, applicable general monographs. Cross-references to applicable general monographs are not normally given in individual monographs.

General monographs apply to all substances and preparations within the scope of the Definition section of the general monograph, except where a preamble limits the application, for example to substances and preparations that are the subject of a monograph of the Pharmacopoeia.

General monographs on dosage forms apply to all preparations of the type defined. The requirements are not necessarily comprehensive for a given specific preparation and requirements additional to those prescribed in the general monograph may be imposed by the competent authority.

General monographs and individual monographs are complementary. If the provisions of a general monograph do not apply to a particular product, this is expressly stated in the individual monograph.

Validation of pharmacopoeial methods

The test methods given in monographs and general chapters have been validated in accordance with accepted scientific practice and current recommendations on analytical validation. Unless otherwise stated in the monograph or general chapter, validation of the test methods by the analyst is not required.

Implementation of pharmacopoeial methods

When implementing a pharmacopoeial method, the user must assess whether and to what extent the suitability of the method under the actual conditions of use needs to be demonstrated according to relevant monographs, general chapters and quality systems.

Conventional terms

The term 'competent authority' means the national, supranational or international body or organisation vested with the authority for making decisions concerning the issue in question. It may, for example, be a national pharmacopoeia authority, a licensing authority or an official control laboratory.

The expression 'unless otherwise justified and authorised' means that the requirements have to be met, unless the competent authority authorises a modification or an exemption where justified in a particular case.

Statements containing the word 'should' are informative or advisory.

In certain monographs or other texts, the terms 'suitable' and 'appropriate' are used to describe a reagent, micro-organism, test method etc.; if criteria for suitability are not described in the monograph, suitability is demonstrated to the satisfaction of the competent authority.

Medicinal product (a) Any substance or combination of substances presented as having properties for treating or preventing disease in human beings and/or animals; or (b) any substance or combination of substances that may be used in or administered to human beings and/or animals with a view either to restoring, correcting or modifying physiological functions by exerting a pharmacological, immunological or metabolic action, or to making a medical diagnosis.

Herbal medicinal product Any medicinal product, exclusively containing as active ingredients one or more herbal drugs or one or more herbal drug preparations, or one or more such herbal drugs in combination with one or more such herbal drug preparations.

Active substance Any substance intended to be used in the manufacture of a medicinal product and that, when so used, becomes an active ingredient of the medicinal product. Such substances are intended to furnish a pharmacological activity or other direct effect in the diagnosis, cure, mitigation, treatment or prevention of disease, or to affect the structure and function of the body.

Excipient (auxiliary substance). Any constituent of a medicinal product that is not an active substance. Adjuvants, stabilisers, antimicrobial preservatives, diluents, antioxidants, for example, are excipients.

Interchangeable methods

Certain general chapters contain a statement that the text in question is harmonised with the corresponding text of the Japanese Pharmacopoeia and/or the United States Pharmacopeia and that these texts are interchangeable. This implies that if a substance or preparation is found to comply with a requirement using an interchangeable method from one of these pharmacopoeias it complies with the requirements of the European Pharmacopoeia. In the event of doubt or dispute, the text of the European Pharmacopoeia is alone authoritative.

References to regulatory documents Monographs and general chapters may contain references to documents issued by regulatory authorities for medicines, for example directives and notes for guidance of the European Union. These references are provided for information for users for the Pharmacopoeia. Inclusion of such a reference does not modify the status of the documents referred to, which may be mandatory or for guidance.

1.2. OTHER PROVISIONS APPLYING TO GENERAL CHAPTERS AND MONOGRAPHS

Quantities In tests with numerical limits and assays, the quantity stated to be taken for examination is approximate. The amount actually used, which may deviate by not more than 10 per cent from that stated, is accurately weighed or measured and the result is calculated from this exact quantity. In tests where the limit is not numerical, but usually depends upon comparison with the behaviour of a reference substance in the same conditions, the stated quantity is taken for examination. Reagents are used in the prescribed amounts.

Quantities are weighed or measured with an accuracy commensurate with the indicated degree of precision. For weighings, the precision corresponds to plus or minus 5 units after the last figure stated (for example, 0.25 g is to be interpreted as 0.245 g to 0.255 g). For the measurement of volumes, if the figure after the decimal point is a zero or ends in a zero (for example, 10.0 mL or 0.50 mL), the volume is measured using a pipette, a volumetric flask or a burette, as appropriate; otherwise, a graduated measuring cylinder or a graduated pipette may be used. Volumes stated in microlitres are measured using a micropipette or microsyringe.

It is recognised, however, that in certain cases the precision with which quantities are stated does not correspond to the number of significant figures stated in a specified numerical limit. The weighings and measurements are then carried out with a sufficiently improved accuracy.

Apparatus and procedures Volumetric glassware complies with Class A requirements of the appropriate International Standard issued by the International Organisation for Standardisation.

Unless otherwise prescribed, analytical procedures are carried out at a temperature between 15 °C and 25 °C.

Unless otherwise prescribed, comparative tests are carried out using identical tubes of colourless, transparent, neutral glass with a flat base; the volumes of liquid prescribed are for use with tubes having an internal diameter of 16 mm, but tubes with a larger internal diameter may be used provided the volume of liquid used is adjusted *(2.1.5)*. Equal volumes of the liquids to be compared are examined down the vertical axis of the tubes against a white background, or if necessary against a black background. The examination is carried out in diffuse light.

Any solvent required in a test or assay in which an indicator is to be used is previously neutralised to the indicator, unless a blank test is prescribed.

Water-bath The term 'water-bath' means a bath of boiling water unless water at another temperature is indicated. Other methods of heating may be substituted provided the temperature is near to but not higher than 100 °C or the indicated temperature.

Drying and ignition to constant mass The terms 'dried to constant mass' and 'ignited to constant mass' mean that 2 consecutive weighings do not differ by more than 0.5 mg, the 2nd weighing following an additional period of drying or of ignition respectively appropriate to the nature and quantity of the residue.

Where drying is prescribed using one of the expressions 'in a desiccator' or '*in vacuo*', it is carried out using the conditions described in chapter *2.2.32. Loss on drying*.

Reagents The proper conduct of the analytical procedures described in the Pharmacopoeia and the reliability of the results depend, in part, upon the quality of the reagents used. The reagents are described in general chapter *4*. It is assumed that reagents of analytical grade are used; for some reagents, tests to determine suitability are included in the specifications.

Solvents Where the name of the solvent is not stated, the term 'solution' implies a solution in water.

Where the use of water is specified or implied in the analytical procedures described in the Pharmacopoeia or for the preparation of reagents, water complying with the requirements of the monograph *Purified water (0008)* is used, except that for many purposes the requirements for bacterial endotoxins (*Purified water in bulk*) and microbial contamination (*Purified water in containers*) are not relevant. The term 'distilled water' indicates purified water prepared by distillation.

The term 'ethanol' without qualification means anhydrous ethanol. The term 'alcohol' without qualification means ethanol (96 per cent). Other dilutions of ethanol are indicated by the term 'ethanol' or 'alcohol' followed by a statement of the percentage by volume of ethanol (C_2H_6O) required.

Expression of content In defining content, the expression 'per cent' is used according to circumstances with one of 2 meanings:

— per cent *m/m* (percentage, mass in mass) expresses the number of grams of substance in 100 g of final product;

— per cent *V/V* (percentage, volume in volume) expresses the number of millilitres of substance in 100 mL of final product.

The expression 'parts per million' (or ppm) refers to mass in mass, unless otherwise specified.

Temperature Where an analytical procedure describes temperature without a figure, the general terms used have the following meaning:

— in a deep-freeze: below −15 °C;

— in a refrigerator: 2 °C to 8 °C;

— cold or cool: 8 °C to 15 °C;

— room temperature: 15 °C to 25 °C.

1.3. GENERAL CHAPTERS

Containers Materials used for containers are described in general chapter *3.1*. General names used for materials, particularly plastic materials, each cover a range of products varying not only in the properties of the principal constituent but also in the additives used. The test methods and limits for materials depend on the formulation and are therefore applicable only for materials whose formulation is covered by the preamble to the specification. The use of materials with different formulations, and the test methods and limits applied to them, are subject to agreement by the competent authority.

The specifications for containers in general chapter *3.2* have been developed for general application to containers of the stated category, but in view of the wide variety of containers available and possible new developments, the publication of a specification does not exclude the use, in justified circumstances, of containers that comply with other specifications, subject to agreement by the competent authority.

Reference may be made within the monographs of the Pharmacopoeia to the definitions and specifications for containers provided in chapter *3.2*. *Containers*. The general monographs for pharmaceutical dosage forms may, under the heading Definition/Production, require the use of certain types of container; certain other monographs may, under the heading Storage, indicate the type of container that is recommended for use.

1.4. MONOGRAPHS

Titles Monograph titles are in English and French in the respective versions and there is a Latin subtitle.

Relative Atomic and The relative atomic mass (A_r) or the relative molecular mass (M_r) is shown,
Molecular Masses as and where appropriate, at the beginning of each monograph. The relative atomic and molecular masses and the molecular and graphic formulae do not constitute analytical standards for the substances described.

Chemical Abstracts CAS registry numbers are included for information in monographs, where
Service (CAS) applicable, to provide convenient access to useful information for users.
Registry Number CAS Registry Number® is a registered trademark of the American Chemical Society.

Definition Statements under the heading Definition constitute an official definition of the substance, preparation or other article that is the subject of the monograph.

Limits of content Where limits of content are prescribed, they are those determined by the method described under Assay.

Herbal drugs In monographs on herbal drugs, the definition indicates whether the subject of the monograph is, for example, the whole drug or the drug in powdered form. Where a monograph applies to the drug in several states, for example both to the whole drug and the drug in powdered form, the definition states this.

Production Statements under the heading Production draw attention to particular aspects of the manufacturing process but are not necessarily comprehensive. They constitute mandatory requirements for manufacturers, unless otherwise stated. They may relate, for example, to source materials; to the manufacturing process itself and its validation and control; to in-process testing; or to testing that is to be carried out by the manufacturer on the final article, either on selected batches or on each batch prior to release. These statements cannot necessarily be verified on a sample of the final article by an independent analyst. The competent authority may establish that the instructions have been followed, for example, by examination of data received from the manufacturer, by inspection of manufacture or by testing appropriate samples.

The absence of a Production section does not imply that attention to features such as those referred to above is not required.

Choice of vaccine strain, Choice of vaccine composition The Production section of a monograph may define the characteristics of a vaccine strain or vaccine composition. Unless otherwise stated, test methods given for verification of these characteristics are provided for information as examples of suitable methods. Subject to approval by the competent authority, other test methods may be used without validation against the method shown in the monograph.

Potential Adulteration Due to the increasing number of fraudulent activities and cases of adulteration, information may be made available to Ph. Eur. users to help detect adulterated materials (i.e. active substances, excipients, intermediate products, bulk products and finished products).

To this purpose, a method for the detection of potential adulterants and relevant limits, together with a reminder that all stages of production and sourcing are subjected to a suitable quality system, may be included in this section of monographs on substances for which an incident has occurred or that present a risk of deliberate contamination. The frequency of testing by manufacturers or by users (e.g. manufacturers of intermediate products, bulk products and finished products, where relevant) depends on a risk assessment, taking into account the level of knowledge of the whole supply chain and national requirements.

This section constitutes requirements for the whole supply chain, from manufacturers to users (e.g. manufacturers of intermediate products, bulk products and finished products, where relevant). The absence of this section does not imply that attention to features such as those referred to above is not required.

Characters The statements under the heading Characters are not to be interpreted in a strict sense and are not requirements.

Solubility In statements of solubility in the Characters section, the terms used have the following significance, referred to a temperature between 15 °C and 25 °C.

Descriptive term	Approximate volume of solvent in millilitres per gram of solute		
Very soluble	less than	1	
Freely soluble	from	1	to	10
Soluble	from	10	to	30
Sparingly soluble	from	30	to	100
Slightly soluble	from	100	to	1000
Very slightly soluble	from	1000	to	10 000
Practically insoluble	more than		10 000

The term 'partly soluble' is used to describe a mixture where only some of the components dissolve. The term 'miscible' is used to describe a liquid that is miscible in all proportions with the stated solvent.

Identification

Scope The tests given in the Identification section are not designed to give a full confirmation of the chemical structure or composition of the product; they are intended to give confirmation, with an acceptable degree of assurance, that the article conforms to the description on the label.

First and second identifications Certain monographs have subdivisions entitled 'First identification' and 'Second identification'. The test or tests that constitute the 'First identification' may be used in all circumstances. The test or tests that constitute the 'Second identification' may be used in pharmacies provided it can be demonstrated that the substance or preparation is fully traceable to a batch certified to comply with all the other requirements of the monograph.

Certain monographs give two or more sets of tests for the purpose of the first identification, which are equivalent and may be used independently. One or more of these sets usually contain a cross-reference to a test prescribed in the Tests section of the monograph. It may be used to simplify the work of the analyst carrying out the identification and the prescribed tests. For example, one identification set cross-refers to a test for enantiomeric purity while the other set gives a test for specific optical rotation: the intended purpose of the two is the same, that is, verification that the correct enantiomer is present.

Powdered herbal drugs Monographs on herbal drugs may contain schematic drawings of the powdered drug. These drawings complement the description given in the relevant identification test.

Tests and Assays

Scope The requirements are not framed to take account of all possible impurities. It is not to be presumed, for example, that an impurity that is not detectable by means of the prescribed tests is tolerated if common sense and good pharmaceutical practice require that it be absent. See also below under Impurities.

Calculation Where the result of a test or assay is required to be calculated with reference to the dried or anhydrous substance or on some other specified basis, the determination of loss on drying, water content or other property is carried out by the method prescribed in the relevant test in the monograph. The words 'dried substance' or 'anhydrous substance' etc. appear in parentheses after the result.

Where a quantitative determination of a residual solvent is carried out and a test for loss on drying is not carried out, the content of residual solvent is taken into account for the calculation of the assay content of the substance, the specific optical rotation and the specific absorbance. No further indication is given in the specific monograph.

Limits The limits prescribed are based on data obtained in normal analytical practice; they take account of normal analytical errors, of acceptable variations in manufacture and compounding and of deterioration to an extent considered acceptable. No further tolerances are to be applied to the limits prescribed to determine whether the article being examined complies with the requirements of the monograph.

In determining compliance with a numerical limit, the calculated result of a test or assay is first rounded to the number of significant figures stated, unless otherwise prescribed. The limits, regardless of whether the values are

expressed as percentages or as absolute values, are considered significant to the last digit shown (for example 140 indicates 3 significant figures).
The last figure of the result is increased by one when the part rejected is equal to or exceeds one half-unit, whereas it is not modified when the part rejected is less than a half-unit.

Indication of permitted limit of impurities The acceptance criteria for related substances are expressed in monographs either in terms of comparison of peak areas (comparative tests) or as numerical values. For comparative tests, the approximate content of impurity tolerated, or the sum of impurities, may be indicated in brackets for information only. Acceptance or rejection is determined on the basis of compliance or non-compliance with the stated test. If the use of a reference substance for the named impurity is not prescribed, this content may be expressed as a nominal concentration of the substance used to prepare the reference solution specified in the monograph, unless otherwise described.

Herbal drugs For herbal drugs, the sulfated ash, total ash, water-soluble matter, alcohol-soluble matter, water content, content of essential oil and content of active principle are calculated with reference to the drug that has not been specially dried, unless otherwise prescribed in the monograph.

Equivalents Where an equivalent is given, for the purposes of the Pharmacopoeia only the figures shown are to be used in applying the requirements of the monograph.

Culture media The culture media described in monographs and general chapters have been found to be satisfactory for the intended purpose. However, the components of media, particularly those of biological origin, are of variable quality, and it may be necessary for optimal performance to modulate the concentration of some ingredients, notably:

— peptones and meat or yeast extracts, with respect to their nutritive properties;
— buffering substances;
— bile salts, bile extract, deoxycholate, and colouring matter, depending on their selective properties;
— antibiotics, with respect to their activity.

Storage The information and recommendations given under the heading Storage do not constitute a pharmacopoeial requirement but the competent authority may specify particular storage conditions that must be met.

The articles described in the Pharmacopoeia are stored in such a way as to prevent contamination and, as far as possible, deterioration. Where special conditions of storage are recommended, including the type of container (see section 1.3. General chapters) and limits of temperature, they are stated in the monograph.

The following expressions are used in monographs under Storage with the meaning shown.

In an airtight container Means that the product is stored in an airtight container (3.2). Care is to be taken when the container is opened in a damp atmosphere. A low moisture content may be maintained, if necessary, by the use of a desiccant in the container provided that direct contact with the product is avoided.

Protected from light Means that the product is stored either in a container made of a material that absorbs actinic light sufficiently to protect the contents from change induced by such light, or in a container enclosed in an outer cover that provides such protection, or is stored in a place from which all such light is excluded.

Labelling In general, labelling of medicines is subject to supranational and national regulation and to international agreements. The statements under the heading Labelling are not therefore comprehensive and, moreover, for the purposes of the Pharmacopoeia only those statements that are necessary to demonstrate compliance or non-compliance with the monograph are mandatory. Any other labelling statements are included as recommendations. When the term 'label' is used in the Pharmacopoeia, the labelling statements may appear on the container, the package, a leaflet accompanying the package, or a certificate of analysis accompanying the article, as decided by the competent authority.

Warnings Materials described in monographs and reagents specified for use in the Pharmacopoeia may be injurious to health unless adequate precautions are taken. The principles of good quality control laboratory practice and the provisions of any appropriate regulations are to be observed at all times. Attention is drawn to particular hazards in certain monographs by means of a warning statement; absence of such a statement is not to be taken to mean that no hazard exists.

Impurities A list of all known and potential impurities that have been shown to be detected by the tests in a monograph may be given. See also chapter *5.10. Control of impurities in substances for pharmaceutical use.* The impurities are designated by a letter or letters of the alphabet. Where a letter appears to be missing, the impurity designated by this letter has been deleted from the list during monograph development prior to publication or during monograph revision.

Functionality-Related Characteristics of Excipients Monographs on excipients may have a section on functionality-related characteristics. The characteristics, any test methods for determination and any tolerances are not mandatory requirements; they may nevertheless be relevant for use of the excipient and are given for information (see also section 1.1. General statements).

Reference Standards Certain monographs require the use of reference standards (chemical reference substances, herbal reference standards, biological reference preparations, reference spectra). See also chapter *5.12. Reference standards.* The European Pharmacopoeia Commission establishes the official reference standards, which are alone authoritative in case of arbitration. These reference standards are available from the European Directorate for the Quality of Medicines & HealthCare (*EDQM*). Information on the available reference standards and a batch validity statement can be obtained via the EDQM website.

1.5. Abbreviations and symbols

A	Absorbance	mp	Melting point
$A_{1\,cm}^{1\,per\,cent}$	Specific absorbance	n_D^{20}	Refractive index
A_r	Relative atomic mass	Ph. Eur. U.	European Pharmacopoeia Unit
$[\alpha]_D^{20}$	Specific optical rotation	ppb	Parts per billion (micrograms per kilogram)
bp	Boiling point	ppm	Parts per million (milligrams per kilogram)
BRP	Biological Reference Preparation	R	Substance or solution defined under *4. Reagents*
CRS	Chemical Reference Substance		
d_{20}^{20}	Relative density	R_F	Retardation factor (see chapter *2.2.46*)
λ	Wavelength	R_{st}	Used in chromatography to indicate the ratio of the distance travelled by a substance to the distance travelled by a reference substance
HRS	Herbal reference standard		
IU	International Unit	RV	Substance used as a primary standard in volumetric analysis (chapter *4.2.1*)
M	Molarity		
M_r	Relative molecular mass		

Abbreviations used in the monographs on immunoglobulins, immunosera and vaccines

LD_{50}	The statistically determined quantity of a substance that, when administered by the specified route, may be expected to cause the death of 50 per cent of the test animals within a given period	Lo/10 dose	The largest quantity of a toxin that, in the conditions of the test, when mixed with 0.1 IU of antitoxin and administered by the specified route, does not cause symptoms of toxicity in the test animals within a given period
MLD	Minimum lethal dose	Lf dose	The quantity of toxin or toxoid that flocculates in the shortest time with 1 IU of antitoxin
L+/10 dose	The smallest quantity of a toxin that, in the conditions of the test, when mixed with 0.1 IU of antitoxin and administered by the specified route, causes the death of the test animals within a given period	$CCID_{50}$	The statistically determined quantity of virus that may be expected to infect 50 per cent of the cell cultures to which it is added
L+ dose	The smallest quantity of a toxin that, in the conditions of the test, when mixed with 1 IU of antitoxin and administered by the specified route, causes the death of the test animals within a given period	EID_{50}	The statistically determined quantity of virus that may be expected to infect 50 per cent of fertilised eggs into which it is inoculated
lr/100 dose	The smallest quantity of a toxin that, in the conditions of the test, when mixed with 0.01 IU of antitoxin and injected intracutaneously causes a characteristic reaction at the site of injection within a given period	ID_{50}	The statistically determined quantity of a virus that may be expected to infect 50 per cent of the animals into which it is inoculated
		PD_{50}	The statistically determined dose of a vaccine that, in the conditions of the test, may be expected to protect 50 per cent of the animals against a challenge dose of the micro-organisms or toxins against which it is active
Lp/10 dose	The smallest quantity of toxin that, in the conditions of the test, when mixed with 0.1 IU of antitoxin and administered by the specified route, causes paralysis in the test animals within a given period	ED_{50}	The statistically determined dose of a vaccine that, in the conditions of the test, may be expected to induce specific antibodies in 50 per cent of the animals for the relevant vaccine antigens
		PFU	Pock-forming units or plaque-forming units
		SPF	Specified-pathogen-free.

Collections of micro-organisms

ATCC American Type Culture Collection
10801 University Boulevard
Manassas, Virginia 20110-2209, USA

C.I.P. Collection de Bactéries de l'Institut Pasteur
B.P. 52, 25 rue du Docteur Roux
75724 Paris Cedex 15, France

IMI International Mycological Institute
Bakeham Lane
Surrey TW20 9TY, Great Britain

I.P. Collection Nationale de Culture de
Microorganismes (C.N.C.M.)
Institut Pasteur
25, rue du Docteur Roux
75724 Paris Cedex 15, France

NCIMB National Collection of Industrial and Marine
Bacteria Ltd
23 St Machar Drive
Aberdeen AB2 1RY, Great Britain

NCPF National Collection of Pathogenic Fungi
London School of Hygiene and Tropical
Medicine
Keppel Street
London WC1E 7HT, Great Britain

NCTC National Collection of Type Cultures
Central Public Health Laboratory
Colindale Avenue
London NW9 5HT, Great Britain

NCYC National Collection of Yeast Cultures
AFRC Food Research Institute
Colney Lane
Norwich NR4 7UA, Great Britain

NITE Biological Resource Center
Department of Biotechnology
National Institute of Technology and
Evaluation
2-5-8 Kazusakamatari, Kisarazu-shi, Chiba,
292-0818
Japan

S.S.I. Statens Serum Institut
80 Amager Boulevard, Copenhagen, Denmark

1.6. UNITS OF THE INTERNATIONAL SYSTEM (SI) USED IN THE PHARMACOPOEIA AND EQUIVALENCE WITH OTHER UNITS

International System Of Units (SI)

The International System of Units comprises 3 classes of units, namely base units, derived units and supplementary units[1]. The base units and their definitions are set out in Table 1.6-1.

The derived units may be formed by combining the base units according to the algebraic relationships linking the corresponding quantities. Some of these derived units have special names and symbols. The SI units used in the Pharmacopoeia are shown in Table 1.6-2.

Some important and widely used units outside the International System are shown in Table 1.6-3.

The prefixes shown in Table 1.6-4 are used to form the names and symbols of the decimal multiples and submultiples of SI units.

---

[1] *The definitions of the units used in the International System are given in the booklet "Le Système International d'Unités (SI)" published by the Bureau International des Poids et Mesures, Pavillion de Breteuil, F-92310 Sèvres.*

Notes

1. In the Pharmacopoeia, the Celsius temperature is used (symbol t). This is defined by the following equation:

$$t = T - T_0$$

where $T_0 = 273.15$ K by definition. The Celsius or centigrade temperature is expressed in degree Celsius (symbol °C). The unit 'degree Celsius' is equal to the unit 'kelvin'.

2. The practical expressions of concentrations used in the Pharmacopoeia are defined in the General Notices.

3. The radian is the plane angle between two radii of a circle that cut off on the circumference an arc equal in length to the radius.

4. In the Pharmacopoeia, conditions of centrifugation are defined by reference to the acceleration due to gravity (g):

$$g = 9.806\,65\ m \cdot s^{-2}$$

5. Certain quantities without dimensions are used in the Pharmacopoeia: relative density *(2.2.5)*, absorbance *(2.2.25)*, specific absorbance *(2.2.25)* and refractive index *(2.2.6)*.

6. The microkatal is defined as the enzymic activity that, under defined conditions, produces the transformation (e.g. hydrolysis) of 1 micromole of the substrate per second.

Table 1.6.-1. – *SI base units*

Quantity		Unit		Definition
Name	**Symbol**	**Name**	**Symbol**	
Length	l	metre	m	The metre is the length of the path travelled by light in a vacuum during a time interval of 1/299 792 458 of a second.
Mass	m	kilogram	kg	The kilogram is equal to the mass of the international prototype of the kilogram.
Time	t	second	s	The second is the duration of 9 192 631 770 periods of the radiation corresponding to the transition between the two hyperfine levels of the ground state of the caesium-133 atom.
Electric current	I	ampere	A	The ampere is that constant current which, maintained in two straight parallel conductors of infinite length, of negligible circular cross-section and placed 1 metre apart in vacuum would produce between these conductors a force equal to 2×10^{-7} newton per metre of length.
Thermodynamic temperature	T	kelvin	K	The kelvin is the fraction 1/273.16 of the thermodynamic temperature of the triple point of water.
Amount of substance	n	mole	mol	The mole is the amount of substance of a system containing as many elementary entities as there are atoms in 0.012 kilogram of carbon-12*.
Luminous intensity	I_v	candela	cd	The candela is the luminous intensity in a given direction of a source emitting monochromatic radiation with a frequency of 540×10^{12} hertz and whose energy intensity in that direction is 1/683 watt per steradian.

* When the mole is used, the elementary entities must be specified and may be atoms, molecules, ions, electrons, other particles or specified groups of such particles.

Table 1.6.-2. – *SI units used in the European Pharmacopoeia and equivalence with other units*

Quantity		Unit				Conversion of other units into SI units
Name	**Symbol**	**Name**	**Symbol**	**Expression in SI base units**	**Expression in other SI units**	
Wave number	ν	one per metre	1/m	m^{-1}		
Wavelength	λ	micrometre	μm	$10^{-6}m$		
		nanometre	nm	$10^{-9}m$		
Area	A, S	square metre	m^2	m^2		
Volume	V	cubic metre	m^3	m^3		$1\ mL = 1\ cm^3 = 10^{-6}\ m^3$
Frequency	ν	hertz	Hz	s^{-1}		
Density	ρ	kilogram per cubic metre	kg/m^3	$kg{\cdot}m^{-3}$		$1\ g/mL = 1\ g/cm^3 = 10^3\ kg{\cdot}m^{-3}$
Velocity	v	metre per second	m/s	$m{\cdot}s^{-1}$		
Force	F	newton	N	$m{\cdot}kg{\cdot}s^{-2}$		$1\ dyne = 1\ g{\cdot}cm{\cdot}s^{-2} = 10^{-5}\ N$ $1\ kp = 9.806\ 65\ N$
Pressure	p	pascal	Pa	$m^{-1}{\cdot}kg{\cdot}s^{-2}$	$N{\cdot}m^{-2}$	$1\ dyne/cm^2 = 10^{-1}\ Pa = 10^{-1}\ N{\cdot}m^{-2}$ $1\ atm = 101\ 325\ Pa = 101.325\ kPa$ $1\ bar = 10^5\ Pa = 0.1\ MPa$ $1\ mm\ Hg = 133.322\ 387\ Pa$ $1\ Torr = 133.322\ 368\ Pa$ $1\ psi = 6.894\ 757\ kPa$
Dynamic viscosity	η	pascal second	Pa·s	$m^{-1}{\cdot}kg{\cdot}s^{-1}$	$N{\cdot}s{\cdot}m^{-2}$	$1\ P = 10^{-1}\ Pa{\cdot}s = 10^{-1}\ N{\cdot}s{\cdot}m^{-2}$ $1\ cP = 1\ mPa{\cdot}s$
Kinematic viscosity	ν	square metre per second	m^2/s	$m^2{\cdot}s^{-1}$	$Pa{\cdot}s{\cdot}m^3{\cdot}kg^{-1}$ $N{\cdot}m{\cdot}s{\cdot}kg^{-1}$	$1\ St = 1\ cm^2{\cdot}s^{-1} = 10^{-4}\ m^2{\cdot}s^{-1}$
Energy	W	joule	J	$m^2{\cdot}kg{\cdot}s^{-2}$	$N{\cdot}m$	$1\ erg = 1\ cm^2{\cdot}g{\cdot}s^{-2} = 1\ dyne{\cdot}cm = 10^{-7}\ J$ $1\ cal = 4.1868\ J$
Power Radiant flux	P	watt	W	$m^2{\cdot}kg{\cdot}s^{-3}$	$N{\cdot}m{\cdot}s^{-1} =$ $J{\cdot}s^{-1}$	$1\ erg/s = 1\ dyne{\cdot}cm{\cdot}s^{-1} =$ $10^{-7}\ W = 10^{-7}\ N{\cdot}m{\cdot}s^{-1} = 10^{-7}\ J{\cdot}s^{-1}$
Absorbed dose (of radiant energy)	D	gray	Gy	$m^2{\cdot}s^{-2}$	$J{\cdot}kg^{-1}$	$1\ rad = 10^{-2}\ Gy$
Electric potential, electromotive force	U	volt	V	$m^2{\cdot}kg{\cdot}s^{-3}{\cdot}A^{-1}$	$W{\cdot}A^{-1}$	
Electric resistance	R	ohm	Ω	$m^2{\cdot}kg{\cdot}s^{-3}{\cdot}A^{-2}$	$V{\cdot}A^{-1}$	
Quantity of electricity	Q	coulomb	C	$A{\cdot}s$		
Activity of a radionuclide	A	becquerel	Bq	s^{-1}		$1\ Ci = 37{\cdot}10^9\ Bq = 37{\cdot}10^9\ s^{-1}$
Concentration (of amount of substance), molar concentration	c	mole per cubic metre	mol/m^3	$mol{\cdot}m^{-3}$		$1\ mol/L = 1\ M = 1\ mol/dm^3 = 10^3\ mol{\cdot}m^{-3}$
Mass concentration	ρ	kilogram per cubic metre	kg/m^3	$kg{\cdot}m^{-3}$		$1\ g/L = 1\ g/dm^3 = 1\ kg{\cdot}m^{-3}$

Table 1.6.-3. – *Units used with the International System*

Quantity	Unit		Value in SI units
	Name	**Symbol**	
Time	minute	min	1 min = 60 s
	hour	h	1 h = 60 min = 3600 s
	day	d	1 d = 24 h = 86 400 s
Plane angle	degree	°	$1° = (\pi/180)$ rad
Volume	litre	L	$1\ L = 1\ dm^3 = 10^{-3}\ m^3$
Mass	tonne	t	$1\ t = 10^3\ kg$
Rotational frequency	revolution per minute	r/min	$1\ r/min = (1/60)\ s^{-1}$

Table 1.6.-4. – *Decimal multiples and sub-multiples of units*

Factor	Prefix	Symbol	Factor	Prefix	Symbol
10^{18}	exa	E	10^{-1}	deci	d
10^{15}	peta	P	10^{-2}	centi	c
10^{12}	tera	T	10^{-3}	milli	m
10^9	giga	G	10^{-6}	micro	μ
10^6	mega	M	10^{-9}	nano	n
10^3	kilo	k	10^{-12}	pico	p
10^2	hecto	h	10^{-15}	femto	f
10^1	deca	da	10^{-18}	atto	a

Monographs

Medicinal and Pharmaceutical Substances

MEDICINAL AND PHARMACEUTICAL SUBSTANCES

Substances for Pharmaceutical Use

(Ph. Eur. monograph 2034)

Ph Eur _____

DEFINITION

Substances for pharmaceutical use are any organic or inorganic substances that are used as active substances or excipients for the production of medicinal products for human or veterinary use. They may be obtained from natural sources or produced by extraction from raw materials, fermentation or synthesis.

This general monograph does not apply to herbal drugs, herbal drugs for homoeopathic preparations, herbal drug preparations, extracts, or mother tinctures for homoeopathic preparations, which are the subject of separate general monographs (*Herbal drugs (1433)*, *Herbal drugs for homoeopathic preparations (2045)*, *Herbal drug preparations (1434)*, *Extracts (0765)*, *Mother tinctures for homoeopathic preparations (2029)*). It does not apply to raw materials for homoeopathic preparations, except where there is an individual monograph for the substance in the non-homoeopathic part of the Pharmacopoeia.

This general monograph does not apply to chemical precursors for radiopharmaceutical preparations which are the subject of a separate monograph (*Chemical precursors for radiopharmaceutical preparations (2902)*).

Where a substance for pharmaceutical use not described in an individual monograph of the Pharmacopoeia is used in a medicinal product prepared for the special needs of individual patients, the need for compliance with the present general monograph is decided in the light of a risk assessment that takes account of the available quality of the substance and its intended use.

Where medicinal products are manufactured using substances for pharmaceutical use of human or animal origin, the requirements of chapter *5.1.7. Viral safety* apply.

Substances for pharmaceutical use may be used as such or as starting materials for subsequent formulation to prepare medicinal products. Depending on the formulation, certain substances may be used either as active substances or as excipients. Solid substances may be compacted, coated, granulated, powdered to a certain fineness, or processed in other ways. A monograph is applicable to a substance processed with an excipient only where such processing is mentioned in the definition section of the monograph.

Substance for pharmaceutical use of special grade Unless otherwise indicated or restricted in the individual monographs, a substance for pharmaceutical use is intended for human and veterinary use, and is of appropriate quality for the manufacture of all dosage forms in which it can be used.

Polymorphism Individual monographs do not usually specify crystalline or amorphous forms, unless bioavailability is affected. All forms of a substance for pharmaceutical use comply with the requirements of the monograph, unless otherwise indicated.

PRODUCTION

Substances for pharmaceutical use are manufactured by procedures that are designed to ensure a consistent quality and comply with the requirements of the individual monograph or approved specification.

The manufacture of active substances must take place under conditions of good manufacturing practice.

The provisions of general chapter *5.10* apply to the control of impurities in substances for pharmaceutical use.

Whether or not it is specifically stated in the individual monograph that the substance for pharmaceutical use:
— is a recombinant protein or another substance obtained as a direct gene product based on genetic modification, where applicable, the substance also complies with the requirements of the general monograph *Products of recombinant DNA technology (0784)*;
— is obtained from animals susceptible to transmissible spongiform encephalopathies other than by experimental challenge, where applicable, the substance also complies with the requirements of the general monograph *Products with risk of transmitting agents of animal spongiform encephalopathies (1483)*;
— is a substance derived from a fermentation process, whether or not the micro-organisms involved are modified by traditional procedures or recombinant DNA (rDNA) technology, where applicable, the substance also complies with the requirements of the general monograph *Products of fermentation (1468)*.

If solvents are used during production, they are of suitable quality. In addition, their toxicity and their residual level are taken into consideration (*5.4*). If water is used during production, it is of suitable quality.

If substances are produced or processed to yield a certain form or grade, that specific form or grade of the substance complies with the requirements of the monograph. Certain functionality-related tests may be described to control properties that may influence the suitability of the substance and subsequently the properties of dosage forms prepared from it.

Powdered substances May be processed to obtain a certain degree of fineness (*2.9.35*).

Compacted substances Are processed to increase the particle size or to obtain particles of a specific form and/or to obtain a substance with a higher bulk density.

Coated active substances Consist of particles of the active substance coated with one or more suitable excipients.

Granulated active substances Are particles of a specified size and/or form produced from the active substance by granulation directly or with one or more suitable excipients.

If substances are processed with excipients, these excipients comply with the requirements of the relevant monograph or, where no such monograph exists, the approved specification.

Where active substances have been processed with excipients to produce, for example, coated or granulated substances, the processing is carried out under conditions of good manufacturing practice and the processed substances are regarded as intermediates in the manufacture of a medicinal product.

CHARACTERS

The statements under the heading Characters (e.g. statements about the solubility or a decomposition point) are not to be interpreted in a strict sense and are not requirements. They are given for information.

Where a substance may show polymorphism, this may be stated under Characters in order to draw this to the attention of the user who may have to take this characteristic into consideration during formulation of a preparation.

IDENTIFICATION

Where under Identification an individual monograph contains subdivisions entitled 'First identification' and 'Second identification', the test or tests that constitute the 'First identification' may be used in all circumstances. The test or tests that constitute the 'Second identification' may be used in pharmacies provided it can be demonstrated that the substance or preparation is fully traceable to a batch certified to comply with all the other requirements of the monograph.

Certain monographs give two or more sets of tests for the purpose of the first identification, which are equivalent and may be used independently. One or more of these sets usually contain a cross-reference to a test prescribed in the Tests section of the monograph. It may be used to simplify the work of the analyst carrying out the identification and the prescribed tests. For example, one identification set cross-refers to a test for enantiomeric purity while the other set gives a test for specific optical rotation: the intended purpose of the two is the same, that is, verification that the correct enantiomer is present.

TESTS

Polymorphism (5.9)

If the nature of a crystalline or amorphous form imposes restrictions on its use in preparations, the nature of the specific crystalline or amorphous form is identified, its morphology is adequately controlled and its identity is stated on the label.

Related substances

Unless otherwise prescribed or justified and authorised, organic impurities in active substances are to be reported, identified wherever possible, and qualified as indicated in Table 2034.-1 or in Table 2034.-2 for peptides obtained by chemical synthesis.

Table 2034.-1. – *Reporting, identification and qualification of organic impurities in active substances*

Use	Maximum daily dose	Report-ing threshold	Identification threshold	Qualification threshold
Human use or human and veterinary use	≤ 2 g/day	> 0.05 per cent	> 0.10 per cent or a daily intake of > 1.0 mg (whichever is the lower)	> 0.15 per cent or a daily intake of > 1.0 mg (whichever is the lower)
Human use or human and veterinary use	> 2 g/day	> 0.03 per cent	> 0.05 per cent	> 0.05 per cent
Veterinary use only	Not applicable	> 0.10 per cent	> 0.20 per cent	> 0.50 per cent

Table 2034.-2. – *Reporting, identification and qualification of organic impurities in peptides obtained by chemical synthesis*

Reporting threshold	Identification threshold	Qualification threshold
> 0.1 per cent	> 0.5 per cent	> 1.0 per cent

Specific thresholds may be applied for impurities known to be unusually potent or to produce toxic or unexpected pharmacological effects.

If the individual monograph does not provide suitable control for a new impurity, a suitable test for control must be developed and included in the specification for the substance.

The requirements above do not apply to biological and biotechnological products, oligonucleotides, products of fermentation and semi-synthetic products derived therefrom, to crude products of animal or plant origin or herbal products.

For active substances in a new application for a medicinal product for human use, the requirements of the guideline on the limits of genotoxic impurities and the corresponding questions and answers documents published on the website of the European Medicines Agency (or similar evaluation principles for non-European Union member states) must be followed.

Residual solvents

are limited according to the principles defined in chapter 5.4, using general method 2.4.24 or another suitable method. Where a quantitative determination of a residual solvent is carried out and a test for loss on drying is not carried out, the content of residual solvent is taken into account for calculation of the assay content of the substance, the specific optical rotation and the specific absorbance.

Microbiological quality

Individual monographs give acceptance criteria for microbiological quality wherever such control is necessary. Table 5.1.4.-2. – *Acceptance criteria for microbiological quality of non-sterile substances for pharmaceutical use* in chapter 5.1.4. *Microbiological quality of non-sterile pharmaceutical preparations and substances for pharmaceutical use* gives recommendations on microbiological quality that are of general relevance for substances subject to microbial contamination. Depending on the nature of the substance and its intended use, different acceptance criteria may be justified.

Sterility (2.6.1)

If intended for use in the manufacture of sterile dosage forms without a further appropriate sterilisation procedure, or if offered as sterile grade, the substance for pharmaceutical use complies with the test for sterility.

Bacterial endotoxins (2.6.14)

If offered as bacterial endotoxin-free grade, the substance for pharmaceutical use complies with the test for bacterial endotoxins. The limit and test method (if not gelation method A) are stated in the individual monograph. The limit is calculated in accordance with the recommendations in general chapter 5.1.10. *Guidelines for using the test for bacterial endotoxins*, unless a lower limit is justified from results from production batches or is required by the competent authority. Where a test for bacterial endotoxins is prescribed, a test for pyrogens is not required.

Pyrogens (2.6.8)

If the test for pyrogens is justified rather than the test for bacterial endotoxins and if a pyrogen-free grade is offered, the substance for pharmaceutical use complies with the test for pyrogens. The limit and test method are stated in the individual monograph or approved by the competent authority. Based on appropriate test validation for bacterial endotoxins and pyrogens, the test for bacterial endotoxins may replace the test for pyrogens.

Additional properties

Control of additional properties (e.g. physical characteristics, functionality-related characteristics) may be necessary for individual manufacturing processes or formulations. Grades (such as sterile, endotoxin-free, pyrogen-free) may be produced with a view to manufacture of preparations for parenteral administration or other dosage forms and appropriate requirements may be specified in an individual monograph.

ASSAY

Unless justified and authorised, contents of substances for pharmaceutical use are determined. Suitable methods are used.

LABELLING

In general, labelling is subject to supranational and national regulation and to international agreements. The statements under the heading Labelling therefore are not comprehensive and, moreover, for the purposes of the Pharmacopoeia only those statements that are necessary to demonstrate compliance or non-compliance with the monograph are mandatory. Any other labelling statements are included as recommendations. When the term 'label' is used in the Pharmacopoeia, the labelling statements may appear on the container, the package, a leaflet accompanying the package or a certificate of analysis accompanying the article, as decided by the competent authority.

Where appropriate, the label states that the substance is:
— intended for a specific use;
— of a distinct crystalline form;
— of a specific degree of fineness;
— compacted;
— coated;
— granulated;
— sterile;
— free from bacterial endotoxins;
— free from pyrogens;
— containing gliding agents.

Where applicable, the label states:
— the degree of hydration;
— the name and concentration of any excipient.

_____ _Ph Eur_

Acepromazine Maleate

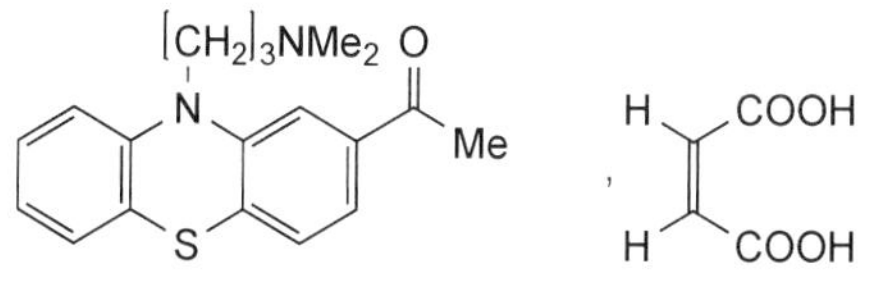

$C_{19}H_{22}N_2OS,C_4H_4O_4$ _442.5_   3598-37-6

Action and use

Dopamine receptor antagonist; neuroleptic.

Preparations

Acepromazine Injection

Acepromazine Tablets

DEFINITION

Acepromazine Maleate is 2-acetyl-10- (3-dimethylaminopropyl) phenothiazine hydrogen maleate. It contains not less than 98.5% and not more than 101.0% of $C_{19}H_{22}N_2OS,C_4H_4O_4$, calculated with reference to the dried substance.

CHARACTERISTICS

A yellow, crystalline powder.

Soluble in _water_; freely soluble in _chloroform_; soluble in _ethanol (96%)_; slightly soluble in _ether_.

IDENTIFICATION

A. Dissolve 20 mg in 2 mL of _water_, add 3 mL of 2M _sodium hydroxide_, extract with 5 mL of _cyclohexane_ and evaporate to dryness under reduced pressure. The _infrared absorption spectrum_ of the residue, Appendix II A, is concordant with the _reference spectrum_ of acepromazine _(RSV 01)_.

B. Complies with the test for _identification of phenothiazines_, Appendix III A, applying to the plate 1 µL of each solution and using _acepromazine maleate BPCRS_ for the preparation of solution (2).

C. Dissolve 0.2 g in a mixture of 3 mL of _water_ and 2 mL of 5M _sodium hydroxide_ and shake with three 3-mL quantities of _ether_. Add to the aqueous solution 2 mL of _bromine solution_, warm in a water bath for 10 minutes, heat to boiling, cool and add 0.25 mL to a solution of 10 mg of _resorcinol_ in 3 mL of _sulfuric acid_. A bluish black colour develops on heating for 15 minutes in a water bath.

TESTS

Acidity

pH of a 1.0% w/v solution, 4.0 to 4.5, Appendix V L.

Melting point

136° to 139°, Appendix V A.

Related substances

Complies with the test for _related substances in phenothiazines_, Appendix III A, but using a mixture of 75 volumes of n-_hexane_, 17 volumes of _butan-2-one_ and 8 volumes of _diethylamine_ as the mobile phase.

Loss on drying

When dried to constant weight at 105°, loses not more than 1.0% of its weight. Use 1 g.

Sulfated ash

Not more than 0.2%, Appendix IX A.

ASSAY

Dissolve 0.4 g in 50 mL of _acetic anhydride_ and carry out Method I for _non-aqueous titration_, Appendix VIII A, using _crystal violet solution_ as indicator. Each mL of 0.1M _perchloric acid VS_ is equivalent to 44.25 mg of $C_{19}H_{22}N_2OS,C_4H_4O_4$.

Alfaxalone

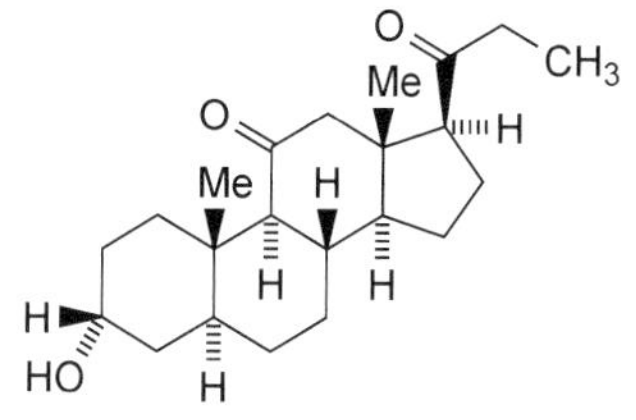

$C_{21}H_{32}O_3$ 332.5   _23930-19-0_

Action and use

Intravenous general anaesthetic.

DEFINITION

Alfaxalone is 3α-hydroxy-5α-pregnane-11, 20-dione. It contains not less than 95.0% and not more than 103.0% of $C_{21}H_{32}O_3$, calculated with reference to the dried substance.

of 25 volumes of *propan-2-ol R1* and 75 volumes of *carbon dioxide-free water* is usually suitable) and (c) a detection wavelength of 205 nm.

Calculate the content of $C_{21}H_{32}O_3$ in the substance being examined using the declared content of $C_{21}H_{32}O_3$ in *alfaxalone BPCRS*; peak areas or peak heights may be used irrespective of the symmetry factor.

Amitraz

$C_{19}H_{23}N_3$ 293.4 *33089-61-1*

Action and use
Topical parasiticide; acaricide.

Preparation
Amitraz Dip Concentrate (Liquid)

DEFINITION

Amitraz is *N*-methylbis (2,4-xylyliminomethyl) amine. It contains not less than 97.0% and not more than 101.0% of $C_{19}H_{23}N_3$, calculated with reference to the anhydrous substance.

CHARACTERISTICS

A white to buff powder.

Practically insoluble in *water*; decomposes slowly in *ethanol (96%)*; freely soluble in *acetone*.

IDENTIFICATION

The *infrared absorption spectrum*, Appendix II A, is concordant with the *reference spectrum* of amitraz *(RSV 04)*.

TESTS
Related substances
Carry out the method for *gas chromatography*, Appendix III B, using the following solutions.

0.010% w/v of *2,4-dimethylaniline*, 0.20% w/v of *form-2',4'-xylidide BPCRS* and 0.20% w/v of *N,N'-bis(2,4-xylyl)formamidine BPCRS* in *methyl acetate* (solution A)

Disperse 30 mg of *N-methyl-N'-(2,4-xylyl)formamidine hydrochloride BPCRS* in 5 mL of *methyl acetate*, add about 32 mg of *triethylamine*, mix with the aid of ultrasound for 2 minutes, filter, wash the filter with a small amount of *methyl acetate* and add sufficient *methyl acetate* to the combined filtrate and washings to produce 25 mL (solution B) (about 0.1% w/v of *N-methyl-N'-(2,4-xylyl)formamidine*).

(1) 5.0% w/v solution of the substance being examined in *methyl acetate*.

(2) A mixture of equal volumes of solution A and solution B.

CHROMATOGRAPHIC CONDITIONS

(a) Use a *fused silica capillary column* (10 m × 0.53 mm) bonded with a film (5 μm) of *poly [methyl(95)phenyl(5)]siloxane* (Chrompack CP-SIL 8 CB is suitable).

(b) Use *helium* as the carrier gas at 12 mL per minute.

(c) Use gradient conditions at an initial temperature of 125°, maintained at 125° for 5 minutes, increasing linearly to 270°

CHARACTERISTICS
A white to creamy white powder.

Practically insoluble in *water*; freely soluble in *chloroform*; soluble in *ethanol (96%)*; practically insoluble in *petroleum spirit (boiling range, 60° to 80°)*.

IDENTIFICATION

A. The *infrared absorption spectrum*, Appendix II A, is concordant with the *reference spectrum* of alfaxalone *(RSV 03)*.

B. Complies with the test for *identification of steroids*, Appendix III A, using *impregnating solvent II* and *mobile phase D*.

C. In the Assay, the chromatogram obtained with solution (2) shows a peak having the same retention time as the peak due to *alfaxalone BPCRS* in the chromatogram obtained with solution (1).

TESTS
Light absorption
Absorbance of a 0.20% w/v solution in *ethanol (96%)* at 235 nm, not more than 0.20, calculated with reference to the dried substance, Appendix II B.

Related substances
Carry out the method for *thin-layer chromatography*, Appendix III A, using *silica gel G* as the coating substance and a mixture of equal volumes of *ethyl acetate* and *toluene* as the mobile phase. Apply separately to the plate 10 μL of each of three solutions of the substance being examined in a mixture of equal volumes of *chloroform* and *methanol* containing (1) 5.0% w/v, (2) 0.15% w/v and (3) 0.050% w/v. After removal of the plate, dry it in a current of air until the solvent has evaporated, spray with a saturated solution of *cerium (IV) sulfate* in *sulfuric acid (50%)* and heat at 110° for 1 hour. Any *secondary spot* in the chromatogram obtained with solution (1) is not more intense than the spot in the chromatogram obtained with solution (2) (3%) and not more than one such spot is more intense than the spot in the chromatogram obtained with solution (3) (1%).

Loss on drying
When dried to constant weight at 105°, loses not more than 1.0% of its weight. Use 1 g.

Sulfated ash
Not more than 0.1%, Appendix IX A.

ASSAY
Carry out the method for *liquid chromatography*, Appendix III D, using the following solutions. For solution (1) dilute 25 mL of a solution in *propan-2-ol R1* containing 0.2% w/v of *alfaxalone BPCRS*, 0.01% w/v of *alfadolone acetate BPCRS* and 0.03% w/v of *betamethasone BPCRS* (internal standard) to 100 mL with *carbon dioxide-free water*. For solution (2) dilute 25 mL of a solution in *propan-2-ol R1* containing 0.2% w/v of the substance being examined to 100 mL with *carbon dioxide-free water*. For solution (3) dilute 25 mL of a solution in *propan-2-ol R1* containing 0.2% w/v of the substance being examined and 0.03% w/v of the internal standard to 100 mL with *carbon dioxide-free water*.

The chromatographic procedure may be carried out using (a) a stainless steel column (10 cm × 5 mm) packed with *octadecylsilyl silica gel for chromatography* (5 μm) (Spherisorb ODS 1 is suitable) and maintained at 60°, (b) as the mobile phase with a flow rate of 1 mL per minute a mixture of *propan-2-ol R1* and *carbon dioxide-free water* adjusted so that the *resolution factor* between the peaks due to alfadolone acetate (retention time about 5 minutes) and alfaxalone (retention time about 6 minutes) is more than 1.0 (a mixture at a rate of 5° per minute and maintained at 270° for 15 minutes.

(d) Use an inlet temperature of 230°.

(e) Use a flame ionisation detector at a temperature of 300°.

(f) Inject 1 µL of each of solutions (1) and (2).

In the chromatogram obtained with solution (2) the peaks following the solvent peak, in order of emergence, are due to 2,4-dimethylaniline, form-2′,4′-xylidide, N-methyl-N′-(2,4-xylyl)formamidine and N,N′-bis(2,4-xylyl)formamidine.

LIMITS

In the chromatogram obtained with solution (1):

the area of any peak corresponding to 2,4-dimethylaniline, form-2′,4′-xylidide, N-methyl-N′-(2,4-xylyl)formamidine and N,N′-bis(2,4-xylyl)formamidine is not greater than the area of the corresponding peak in the chromatogram obtained with solution (2) (0.1%, 2%, 1% and 2% respectively);

the area of any other secondary peak is not greater than the area of the peak due to 2,4-dimethylaniline in the chromatogram obtained with solution (2) (0.1%).

Water

Not more than 0.1% w/w, Appendix IX C, Method IA. Use 5 g and a mixture of equal volumes of *chloroform* and *2-chloroethanol* in place of *anhydrous methanol*.

Sulfated ash

Not more than 0.2%, Appendix IX A.

ASSAY

Carry out the method for *gas chromatography*, Appendix III B, using the following solutions.

Prepare a 2% v/v solution of *squalane* (internal standard) in *methyl acetate* (solution C).

(1) 0.15 g of the substance being examined in sufficient *methyl acetate* to produce 30 mL.

(2) 0.15 g of the substance being examined in 10 mL of solution C and add sufficient *methyl acetate* to produce 30 mL.

(3) 1.50% w/v solution of *amitraz BPCRS* in solution C and dilute 1 volume of this solution to 3 volumes with *methyl acetate*.

CHROMATOGRAPHIC CONDITIONS

(a) Use a fused silica capillary column (15 m × 0.53 mm) coated with a 1.5 µm film of methyl silicone gum (Chrompack CP-Sil 5 CB is suitable).

(b) Use *helium* as the carrier gas at 12 mL per minute.

(c) Use isothermal conditions maintained at 220°.

(d) Use an inlet temperature of 230°.

(e) Use a flame ionisation detector at a temperature of 300°.

(f) Inject 1 µL of each solution.

SYSTEM SUITABILITY

The assay is not valid unless, in the chromatogram obtained with solution (3), the *resolution factor* between the peaks corresponding to squalane and amitraz is at least 3.0.

LIMITS

Calculate the content of $C_{19}H_{23}N_3$ from the chromatograms obtained using the declared content of $C_{19}H_{23}N_3$ in *amitraz BPCRS*.

STORAGE

Amitraz should be kept in a well-closed container, which may contain paraformaldehyde, packed in separate sachets as a stabiliser.

IMPURITIES

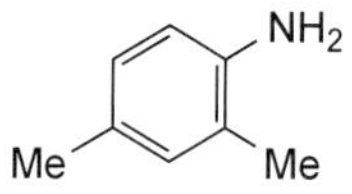

A. 2,4-dimethylaniline (2,4-xylidine),

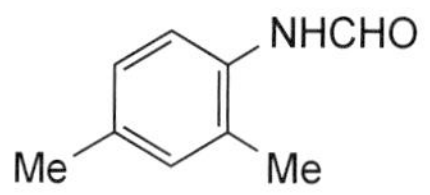

B. form-2′,4′-xylidide,

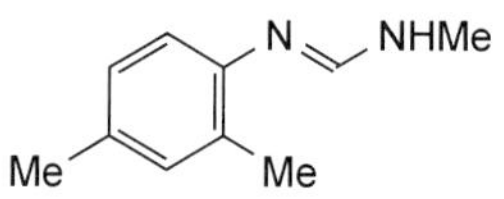

C. N-methyl-N′-(2,4-xylyl)formamidine,

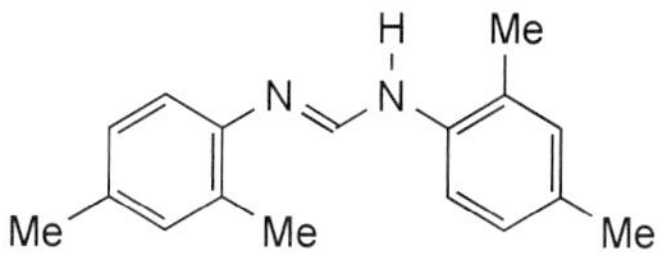

D. N,N′-bis(2,4-xylyl)formamidine.

Amprolium Hydrochloride

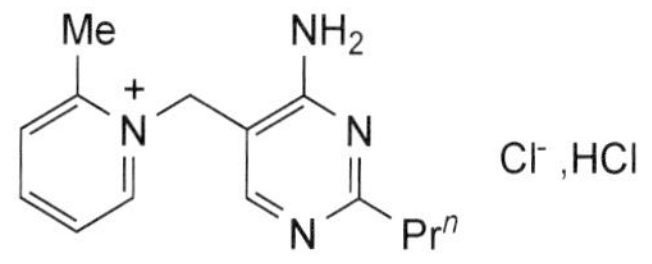

$C_{14}H_{19}ClN_4,HCl$ 315.3   *137-88-2*

Action and use

Antiprotozoal; prevention and treatment of coccidiosis (veterinary).

DEFINITION

Amprolium Hydrochloride is 1-(4-amino-2-propylpyrimidin-5-ylmethyl)-2-methylpyridinium chloride hydrochloride.

It contains not less than 97.5% and not more than 101.0% of $C_{14}H_{19}ClN_4,HCl$, calculated with reference to the dried substance.

CHARACTERISTICS

A white or almost white powder; odourless or almost odourless.

Freely soluble in *water*; slightly soluble in *ethanol (96%)*; very slightly soluble in *ether*; practically insoluble in *chloroform*.

IDENTIFICATION

A. The *infrared absorption spectrum*, Appendix II A, is concordant with the *reference spectrum* of amprolium hydrochloride *(RSV 07)*.

B. The *light absorption*, Appendix II B, in the range 230 to 350 nm of a 0.002% w/v solution in 0.1M *hydrochloric acid* exhibits two maxima, at 246 nm and 262 nm. The *absorbances* at the maxima are about 0.84 and about 0.80, respectively.

C. To 1 mg add 5 mL of *naphthalenediol reagent solution*; a deep violet colour is produced.

D. Yields the reactions characteristic of *chlorides*, Appendix VI.

TESTS
Picoline
Dissolve 1.5 g in 30 mL of *water* in a distillation flask, add 20 mL of a saturated solution of *potassium carbonate sesquihydrate*, connect the flask to a coarse-fritted aerator extending to the bottom of a 100-mL graduated cylinder containing 50 mL of 0.05M *hydrochloric acid*, and pass air, which has previously been passed through *sulfuric acid* and glass wool, through the system for 60 minutes. To 5 mL of the hydrochloric acid solution add sufficient 0.05M *hydrochloric acid* to produce 200 mL. The *absorbance* of the resulting solution at 262 nm is not greater than 0.52, Appendix II B.

Loss on drying
When dried to constant weight at 100° at a pressure not exceeding 0.7 kPa, loses not more than 1.0% of its weight. Use 1 g.

Sulfated ash
Not more than 0.1%, Appendix IX A.

ASSAY
Carry out Method I for *non-aqueous titration*, Appendix VIII A, using 0.3 g and *1-naphtholbenzein solution* as indicator. Each mL of 0.1M *perchloric acid VS* is equivalent to 15.77 mg of $C_{14}H_{19}ClN_4,HCl$.

Apramycin Sulfate
Apramycin Sulphate

$C_{21}H_{41}N_5O_{11},2\frac{1}{2}H_2SO_4$ 784.8   *41194-16-5*

Action and use
Aminoglycoside antibacterial.

Preparations
Apramycin Veterinary Oral Powder

Apramycin Premix

DEFINITION
Apramycin Sulfate is the sulfate of 4-*O*-[(2*R*,3*R*,4a*S*,6*R*,7*S*,8*R*,8a*R*)-3-amino-6-(4-amino-4-deoxy-α-D-glucopyranosyloxy)-8-hydroxy-7-methylaminoperhydropyrano[3,2-*b*]pyran-2-yl]-2-deoxystreptamine. It is produced by the growth of certain strains of *Streptomyces tenebrarius* or obtained by any other means. The potency is not less than 450 Units per mg, calculated with reference to the anhydrous substance.

CHARACTERISTICS
A light brown powder or granular material; hygroscopic.

Freely soluble in *water*; practically insoluble in *acetone*, in *ethanol (96%)*, in *ether* and in *methanol*.

IDENTIFICATION
A. Carry out the method for *thin-layer chromatography*, Appendix III A, using the following solutions in *water*.

(1) 0.1% w/v of the substance being examined.

(2) 0.07% w/v of *apramycin BPCRS*.

(3) 0.07% w/v of each of *apramycin BPCRS* and *tobramycin BPCRS*.

CHROMATOGRAPHIC CONDITIONS

(a) Use a silica gel F_{254} precoated plate (Merck silica gel 60 F_{254} plates are suitable).

(b) Use the mobile phase as described below.

(c) Apply 5 μL of each solution.

(d) Develop the plate to 10 cm.

(e) After removal of the plate, allow it to dry in a current of warm air, spray with a mixture of equal volumes of a 46% w/v solution of *sulfuric acid* and a 0.2% w/v solution of *naphthalene-1,3-diol* in *ethanol (96%)* and heat at 150° for 5 to 10 minutes.

MOBILE PHASE

20 volumes of *chloroform*, 40 volumes of 13.5M *ammonia* and 60 volumes of *methanol*, equilibrated for 1 hour before use.

SYSTEM SUITABILITY

The test is not valid unless the chromatogram obtained with solution (3) shows two clearly separated principal spots.

CONFIRMATION

The principal spot in the chromatogram obtained with solution (1) corresponds in colour and position to that in the chromatogram obtained with solution (2).

B. In the test for Related substances, the retention time of the principal peak in the chromatogram obtained with solution (1) corresponds to that of the principal peak in the chromatogram obtained with solution (2).

C. Yields reaction A characteristic of *sulfates*, Appendix VI.

TESTS
Sulfate
26.0 to 33.0% of SO_4, calculated with reference to the anhydrous substance, when determined by the following method. Dissolve 0.25 g in 100 mL of *water*, adjust to pH 11 with 13.5M *ammonia* and add 10 mL of 0.1M *barium chloride VS*. Titrate with 0.1M *disodium edetate VS* using 0.5 mg of *phthalein purple* as indicator; add 50 mL of *ethanol (96%)* when the colour of the solution begins to change and continue the titration until the violet-blue colour disappears. Each mL of 0.1M *barium chloride VS* is equivalent to 9.606 mg of SO_4.

Caerulomycin and dipyridyl derivatives
Dissolve 0.5 g in *water* in a 100 mL graduated flask, add 10 mL of *methanol* and dilute to 100 mL with *water*. Place 5 mL in a 25 mL graduated flask and add 5 mL of an acetate buffer prepared by dissolving 8.3 g of *anhydrous sodium acetate* in 25 mL of *water*, adding 12 mL of *glacial acetic acid* and diluting to 100 mL with *water*. Mix, add 1 mL of a 10% w/v solution of *hydroxylamine hydrochloride* in *water* and mix again. Add 5 mL of a 1% w/v solution of *ammonium iron(II) sulfate* and dilute to 25 mL with *water*. Measure the *absorbance* of the resulting solution at 520 nm, Appendix II B, using in the reference cell a solution obtained

by carrying out the same procedure without the substance being examined. The *absorbance* is not greater than that obtained by repeating the test using 5 mg of *2,2'-dipyridyl* dissolved in 10 mL of *methanol* and diluted to 100 mL with *water* and beginning at the words 'Place 5 mL in a 25 mL graduated flask...' (1%).

Related substances

Carry out the method for *liquid chromatography*, Appendix III D, using the following solutions in *water*.

(1) 0.50% w/v of the substance being examined.

(2) 0.35% w/v of *apramycin BPCRS*.

(3) Dilute 1 volume of solution (1) to 20 volumes.

(4) Dilute 1 volume of solution (3) to 50 volumes.

CHROMATOGRAPHIC CONDITIONS

(a) Use a column (25 cm × 4 mm) packed with fast cation-exchange polymeric beads (13 μm) with sulfonic acid functional groups (Dionex Fast Cation-1^R is suitable) and a stainless steel post-column reaction coil (380 cm × 0.4 mm) with internal baffles. Use in the reaction coil *ninhydrin reagent I* at a flow rate approximately the same as that for the mobile phase.

(b) Use gradient elution and the mobile phase described below.

(c) Use a flow rate of 0.8 mL per minute.

(d) Use a column temperature of 130°. Maintain the post-column reaction coil at the same temperature.

(e) Use a detection wavelength of 568 nm.

(f) Inject 20 μL of each solution.

MOBILE PHASE

Mobile phase A   A solution containing 1.961% w/v of *sodium citrate*, 0.08% v/v of *liquefied phenol* and 0.5% v/v of *thiodiglycol*, adjusted to pH 4.25 using *hydrochloric acid*.

Mobile phase B   A solution containing 4.09% w/v of *sodium chloride* and 3.922% w/v of *sodium citrate* with 0.08% v/v of *liquefied phenol*, adjusted to pH 7.4 with *hydrochloric acid*.

Equilibrate the column using a mixture containing 75% of mobile phase A and 25% of mobile phase B. After each injection elute for 3 minutes using the same mixture and then carry out a linear gradient elution for 6 minutes to 100% of mobile phase B. Elute for a further 21 minutes using 100% of mobile phase B, then step-wise re-equilibrate to a mixture of 75% of mobile phase A and 25% of mobile phase B and elute for at least 10 minutes.

SYSTEM SUITABILITY

The test is not valid unless, in the chromatogram obtained with solution (2), the *resolution factor* between the peaks due to compound A and 3-hydroxyapramycin, identified using the reference chromatogram supplied with *apramycin BPCRS*, is at least 0.8.

LIMITS

Multiply the areas of all the *secondary peaks* by 0.5. [NOTE: This is to ensure that the impurities are calculated relative to Apramycin Sulfate (which contains about 50% w/w of apramycin).]

In the chromatogram obtained with solution (1):

the areas of any peaks corresponding to 3-hydroxyapramycin, lividamine/2-deoxystreptamine (combined), compound A and compound B (identified using the reference chromatogram supplied with *apramycin BPCRS*) are not greater than 1.4, 1.0, 0.4 and 0.4 times respectively the area of the principal

peak in the chromatogram obtained with solution (3) (7%, 5%, 2% and 2% respectively);

the area of any other *secondary peak* is not greater than 0.4 times the area of the principal peak in the chromatogram obtained with solution (3) (2%);

the sum of the areas of all the *secondary peaks* is not greater than 3 times the area of the principal peak in the chromatogram obtained with solution (3) (15%).

Disregard any peak with an area less than the area of the peak in the chromatogram obtained with solution (4) (0.1%).

Sulfated ash

Not more than 1.0%, Appendix IX A, Method II. Use 1 g.

Water

Not more than 14.0% w/w, Appendix IX C. Use 0.2 g and 20 mL of a mixture containing 1 volume of *methanol* and 2 volumes of *formamide* as the solvent. The solvent mixture must be prepared at least 12 hours before use and should be stored in an airtight container.

ASSAY

Carry out the *microbiological assay of antibiotics*, Appendix XIV A, Method B. The precision of the assay is such that the fiducial limits of error are not less than 95% and not more than 105% of the estimated potency.

IMPURITIES

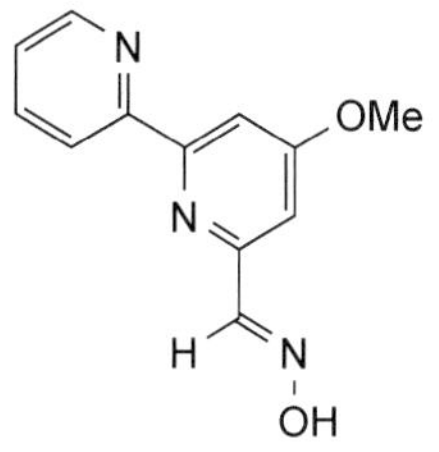

A. caerulomycin,

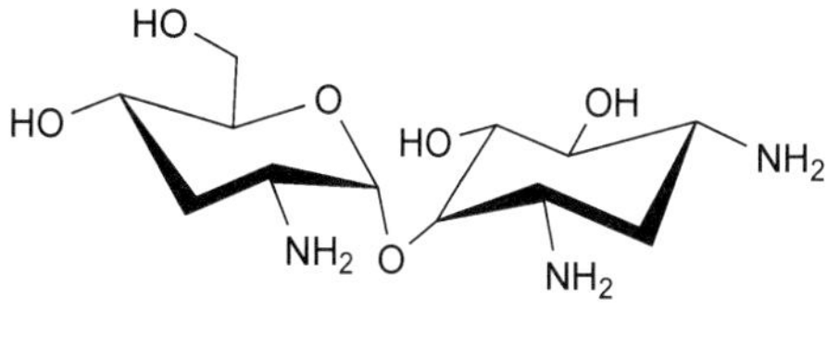

B. lividamine,

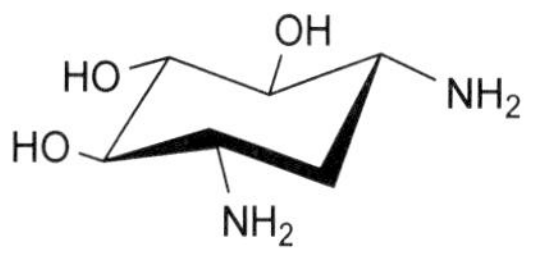

C. 2-deoxystreptamine,

D. 3-hydroxyapramycin; *R* = OH,

E. 'compound A',

F. 'compound B'.

Azaperone

*(Azaperone for Veterinary Use,
Ph Eur monograph 1708)*

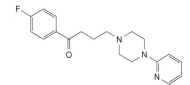

C₁₉H₂₂FN₃O   327.4   1649-18-9

$C_{19}H_{22}FN_3O$ 327.4   1649-18-9

Action and use

Dopamine receptor antagonist; neuroleptic (veterinary).

Preparation

Azaperone Injection

Ph Eur _____

DEFINITION

1-(4-Fluorophenyl)-4-[4-(pyridin-2-yl)piperazin-1-yl]butan-1-one.

Content

99.0 per cent to 101.0 per cent (dried substance).

CHARACTERS

Appearance

White or almost white powder.

Solubility

Practically insoluble in water, freely soluble in acetone and in methylene chloride, soluble in ethanol (96 per cent).

It shows polymorphism (*5.9*).

IDENTIFICATION

Infrared absorption spectrophotometry (*2.2.24*).

Preparation Discs.

Comparison azaperone CRS.

If the spectra obtained show differences, dissolve the substance to be examined and the reference substance separately in *acetone R*, evaporate to dryness and record new spectra using the residues.

TESTS

Appearance of solution

The solution is clear (*2.2.1*) and not more intensely coloured than reference solution Y₆ (*2.2.2, Method II*).

Dissolve 1.0 g in 25 mL of a 14 g/L solution of *tartaric acid R*.

Related substances

Liquid chromatography (*2.2.29*).

Test solution Dissolve 0.100 g of the substance to be examined in *methanol R* and dilute to 10.0 mL with the same solvent.

Reference solution (a) Dissolve 5.0 mg of *azaperone CRS* and 6.0 mg of *benperidol CRS* in *methanol R* and dilute to 200.0 mL with the same solvent.

Reference solution (b) Dilute 1.0 mL of the test solution to 100.0 mL with *methanol R*. Dilute 5.0 mL of the solution to 20.0 mL with *methanol R*.

Column:
— *size*: l = 0.10 m, Ø = 4.6 mm;
— *stationary phase*: base-deactivated octadecylsilyl silica gel for chromatography R (3 μm);
— *temperature*: 25 °C.

Mobile phase:
— *mobile phase A*: dissolve 1.4 g of *anhydrous sodium sulfate R* in 900 mL of *water R*, add 16.0 mL of *0.01 M sulfuric acid* and dilute to 1000 mL with *water R*;
— *mobile phase B*: methanol R;

Time (min)	Mobile phase A (per cent V/V)	Mobile phase B (per cent V/V)
0 - 15	95 → 20	5 → 80
15 - 20	20	80

Flow rate 1.5 mL/min.

Detection Spectrophotometer at 230 nm.

Injection 10 μL.

Relative retention With reference to azaperone (retention time = about 9 min): impurity A = about 0.9; impurity B = about 1.1; impurity C = about 1.15.

System suitability: reference solution (a):
— *resolution*: minimum 8.0 between the peaks due to azaperone and to benperidol.

Limits:
— *impurity A*: not more than the area of the principal peak in the chromatogram obtained with reference solution (b) (0.25 per cent);
— *unspecified impurities*: for each impurity, not more than 0.8 times the area of the principal peak in the chromatogram obtained with reference solution (b) (0.20 per cent);
— *sum of impurities B and C*: not more than 3 times the area of the principal peak in the chromatogram obtained with reference solution (b) (0.75 per cent);
— *total*: not more than 4 times the area of the principal peak in the chromatogram obtained with reference solution (b) (1.0 per cent);
— *disregard limit*: 0.2 times the area of the principal peak in the chromatogram obtained with reference solution (b) (0.05 per cent).

Loss on drying (*2.2.32*)

Maximum 0.5 per cent, determined on 1.000 g by drying *in vacuo* at 60 °C for 4 h.

Sulfated ash (*2.4.14*)

Maximum 0.1 per cent, determined on 1.0 g.

ASSAY

Dissolve 0.130 g in 70 mL of a mixture of 1 volume of *anhydrous acetic acid R* and 7 volumes of *methyl ethyl ketone R*. Titrate with *0.1 M perchloric acid*, using 0.2 mL of *naphtholbenzein solution R* as indicator.

1 mL of *0.1 M perchloric acid* is equivalent to 16.37 mg of $C_{19}H_{22}FN_3O$.

STORAGE

Protected from light.

IMPURITIES

Specified impurities A, B, C

A. 1-(2-fluorophenyl)-4-[4-(pyridin-2-yl)piperazin-1-yl]butan-1-one,

B. 4-[4-(pyridin-2-yl)piperazin-1-yl]-1-[4-[4-(pyridin-2-yl)piperazin-1-yl]phenyl]butan-1-one,

C. 4-hydroxy-1-[4-[4-(pyridin-2-yl)piperazin-1-yl]phenyl]butan-1-one.

———————————————————————— *Ph Eur*

Calcium Copperedetate

$C_{10}H_{12}CaCuN_2O_8,2H_2O$ 427.6

Action and use
Used in the treatment of copper deficiency.

Preparation
Calcium Copperedetate Injection

DEFINITION
Calcium Copperedetate is the dihydrate of calcium [ethylenediaminetetra-acetato(4-)-*N,N′,O,O′*]copper(II). It contains not less than 9.1% and not more than 9.7% of calcium, Ca, and not less than 14.4% and not more than 15.3% of copper, Cu, both calculated with reference to the dried substance.

CHARACTERISTICS
A blue, crystalline powder.

Freely soluble in *water*, the solution gradually precipitating the tetrahydrate; practically insoluble in *ethanol (96%)*.

IDENTIFICATION
A. Dissolve 0.2 g in 5 mL of *water* and add 1 mL of 6M *acetic acid* and 2 mL of *dilute potassium iodide solution*. The solution remains clear and deep blue.

B. Ignite 0.2 g, dissolve the residue in 3 mL of 2M *hydrochloric acid*, neutralise the solution with 5M *ammonia* and add 1 mL of 6M *acetic acid* and 2 mL of *dilute potassium iodide solution*. A white precipitate is produced and iodine is liberated, colouring the supernatant liquid brown.

C. Dissolve 0.5 g in 10 mL of *water*, acidify with 2M *hydrochloric acid*, add 25 mL of a 10% v/v solution of *mercaptoacetic acid* and filter. Make the filtrate alkaline with 5M *ammonia* and add 5 mL of a 2.5% w/v solution of *ammonium oxalate*. A white precipitate is produced which is soluble in *hydrochloric acid* but only sparingly soluble in 6M *acetic acid*.

TESTS
Lead
Not more than 25 ppm of Pb when determined by the following method. Dissolve 1.25 g in 10 mL of *hydrochloric acid*, dilute to 25 mL with *water* and determine by *atomic absorption spectrophotometry*, Appendix II D, measuring at 283.3 nm and using a lead hollow-cathode lamp as the radiation source and *lead standard solution (100 ppm Pb)*, diluted if necessary with *water*, to prepare the standard solutions.

Zinc
Not more than 200 ppm of Zn when determined by the following method. Dissolve 1.0 g in 20 mL of *hydrochloric acid*, dilute to 200 mL with *water* and determine by *atomic absorption spectrophotometry*, Appendix II D, measuring at 213.9 nm and using a zinc hollow-cathode lamp as the radiation source and *zinc standard solution (5 mg/mL Zn)* diluted if necessary with *water*, to prepare the standard solutions.

Loss on drying
When dried to constant weight at 105°, loses not more than 2.0% of its weight. Use 1 g.

ASSAY
For copper
Ignite 4 g at 600° to 700°, cool and heat the residue with 12 mL of a mixture of equal volumes of *hydrochloric acid* and *water* on a water bath for 15 minutes. Add 10 mL of *water*, filter and dilute the filtrate to 100 mL with *water* (solution A); reserve a portion for the Assay for calcium. To 25 mL of solution A add 25 mL of *water* and 10 mL of *bromine solution*, boil to remove the bromine, cool and add *dilute sodium carbonate solution* until a faint permanent precipitate is produced. Add 3 g of *potassium iodide* and 5 mL of 6M *acetic acid* and titrate the liberated iodine with 0.1M *sodium thiosulfate VS*, using *starch mucilage* as indicator, until only a faint blue colour remains; add 2 g of *potassium thiocyanate* and continue the titration until the blue colour disappears. Each mL of 0.1M *sodium thiosulfate VS* is equivalent to 6.354 mg of Cu.

For calcium
To 5 mL of solution A add 10 mL of *water* and 10 mL of a 10% v/v solution of *mercaptoacetic acid*, allow to stand until the precipitate has coagulated, dilute to 100 mL with *water*, add 5 mL of 5M *sodium hydroxide* and titrate with 0.05M *disodium edetate VS*, using *methyl thymol blue mixture* as indicator, until the solution becomes a full purple colour, adding the titrant slowly as the end point is approached. Each mL of 0.05M *disodium edetate VS* is equivalent to 2.004 mg of Ca.

Carprofen

(Carprofen for Veterinary Use,
Ph Eur monograph 2201)

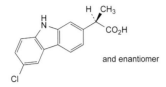

and enantiomer

$C_{15}H_{12}ClNO_2$ 273.7   53716-49-7

Action and use

Cyclo-oxygenase inhibitor; analgesic; anti-inflammatory.

Ph Eur

DEFINITION

(2RS)-2-(6-Chloro-9H-carbazol-2-yl)propanoic acid.

Content

98.5 per cent to 101.5 per cent (dried substance).

CHARACTERS

Appearance

White or almost white, crystalline powder.

Solubility

Practically insoluble in water, freely soluble in acetone, soluble in methanol, slightly soluble in 2-propanol.

It shows polymorphism (*5.9*).

IDENTIFICATION

Infrared absorption spectrophotometry (*2.2.24*).

Comparison carprofen CRS.

If the spectra obtained in the solid state show differences, dissolve the substance to be examined and the reference substance separately in *acetone R*, evaporate to dryness and record new spectra using the residues.

TESTS

Appearance of solution

The solution is clear (*2.2.1*) and not more intensely coloured than reference solution BY_3 (*2.2.2, Method II*).

Dissolve 1.0 g in *methanol R* and dilute to 25 mL with the same solvent.

Related substances

Liquid chromatography (*2.2.29*). *Carry out the test protected from light.*

Test solution Dissolve 50 mg of the substance to be examined in the mobile phase and dilute to 100.0 mL with the mobile phase.

Reference solution (a) Dissolve 2.5 mg of *carprofen for system suitability CRS* (containing impurity C) in the mobile phase and dilute to 10.0 mL with the mobile phase.

Reference solution (b) Dilute 1.0 mL of the test solution to 100.0 mL with the mobile phase. Dilute 1.0 mL of this solution to 10.0 mL with the mobile phase.

Column:
— *size*: l = 0.25 m, Ø = 4.6 mm;
— *stationary phase*: *end-capped polar-embedded octadecylsilyl amorphous organosilica polymer R* (5 μm).

Mobile phase Mix 30 volumes of a 1.36 g/L solution of *potassium dihydrogen phosphate R* adjusted to pH 3.0 with *phosphoric acid R* and 70 volumes of *methanol R2*.

Flow rate 1.3 mL/min.

Detection Spectrophotometer at 235 nm.

Injection 20 μL.

Run time 4 times the retention time of carprofen.

Retention time Carprofen = about 10 min.

System suitability: reference solution (a):
— *resolution*: minimum 1.5 between the peaks due to impurity C and carprofen.

Limits:
— *unspecified impurities*: for each impurity, not more than twice the area of the principal peak in the chromatogram obtained with reference solution (b) (0.20 per cent);
— *total*: not more than 5 times the area of the principal peak in the chromatogram obtained with reference solution (b) (0.5 per cent);
— *disregard limit*: the area of the principal peak in the chromatogram obtained with reference solution (b) (0.1 per cent).

Heavy metals (*2.4.8*)

Maximum 20 ppm.

Dissolve 1.0 g in *ethanol (96 per cent) R* and dilute to 20 mL with the same solvent. 12 mL of the solution complies with test B. Prepare the reference solution using *lead standard solution (1 ppm Pb) R*.

Loss on drying (*2.2.32*)

Maximum 0.5 per cent, determined on 1.000 g by drying in an oven at 105 °C for 2 h.

Sulfated ash (*2.4.14*)

Maximum 0.1 per cent, determined on 1.0 g.

ASSAY

Dissolve 0.200 g in 50 mL of *ethanol (96 per cent) R*. Add 1.0 mL of *0.1 M hydrochloric acid*. Titrate with *0.1 M sodium hydroxide*, determining the end-point potentiometrically (*2.2.20*). Read the volume added between the 2 points of inflexion.

1 mL of *0.1 M sodium hydroxide* is equivalent to 27.37 mg of $C_{15}H_{12}ClNO_2$.

STORAGE

Protected from light.

IMPURITIES

Other detectable impurities (the following substances would, if present at a sufficient level, be detected by one or other of the tests in the monograph. They are limited by the general acceptance criterion for other/unspecified impurities and/or by the general monograph Substances for pharmaceutical use (2034). It is therefore not necessary to identify these impurities for demonstration of compliance. See also 5.10. Control of impurities in substances for pharmaceutical use): A, B, C, D, E, F, G, H.

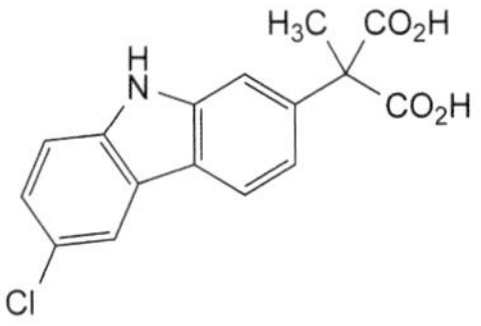

A. 2-(6-chloro-9H-carbazol-2-yl)-2-methylpropanedioic acid,

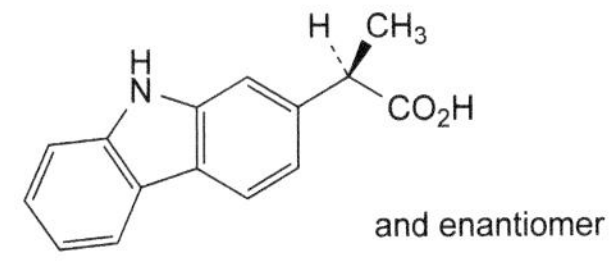

B. (2RS)-2-(9H-carbazol-2-yl)propanoic acid,

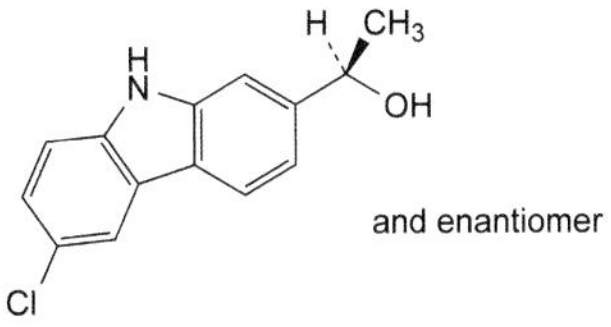

C. (1RS)-1-(6-chloro-9H-carbazol-2-yl)ethanol,

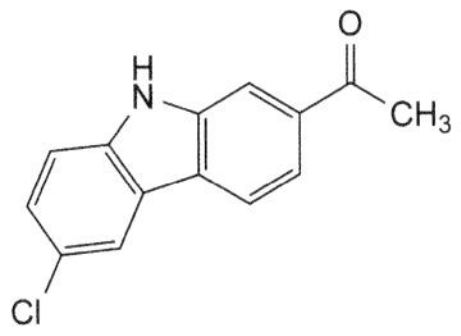

D. 1-(6-chloro-9H-carbazol-2-yl)ethanone,

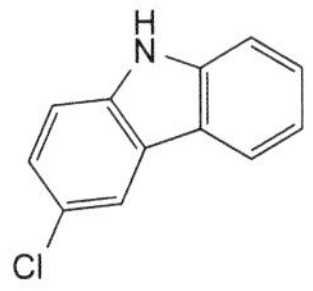

E. 3-chloro-9H-carbazole,

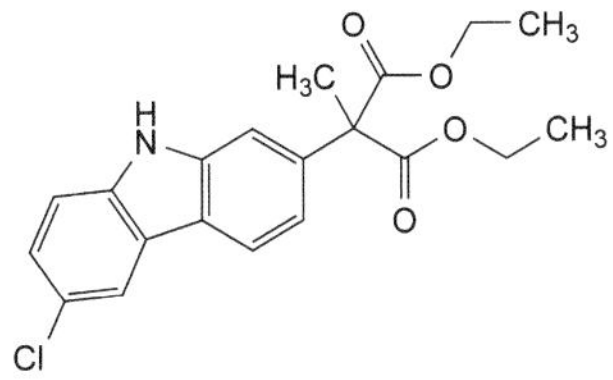

F. diethyl 2-(6-chloro-9H-carbazol-2-yl)-2-methylpropanedioate,

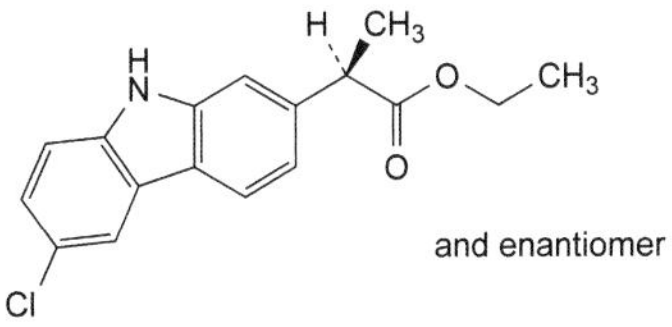

G. ethyl (2RS)-2-(6-chloro-9H-carbazol-2-yl)propanoate,

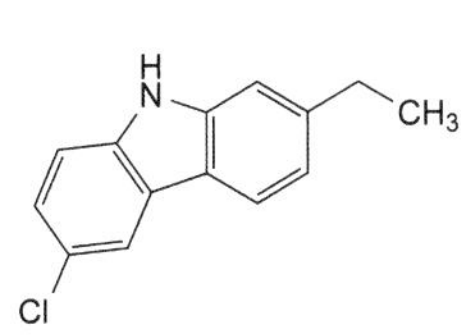

H. 6-chloro-2-ethyl-9H-carbazole.

Ph Eur

Cefalonium

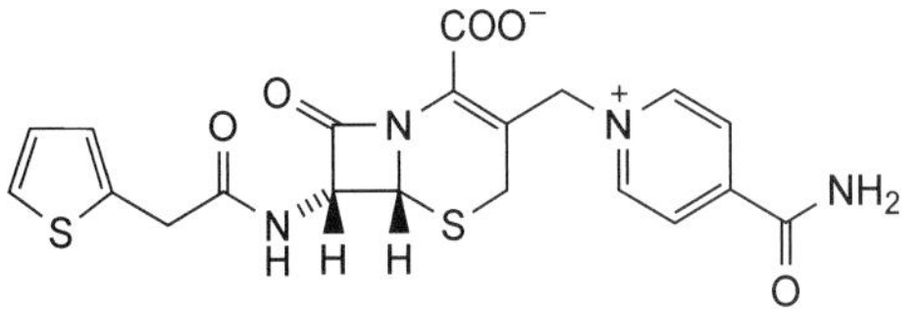

$C_{20}H_{18}N_4O_5S_2,2H_2O$ 494.5   *5575-21-3 (anhydrous)*

Action and use
Cephalosporin antibacterial.

Preparation
Cefalonium Intramammary Infusion (Dry Cow)

DEFINITION
Cefalonium is 3-(4-carbamoyl-1-pyridiniomethyl)-7-[(2-thienyl)acetamido]-3-cephem-4-carboxylate dihydrate.
It contains not less than 95.0% and not more than 103.5% of $C_{20}H_{18}N_4O_5S_2$, calculated with reference to the anhydrous substance.

CHARACTERISTICS
A white or almost white crystalline powder.

Very slightly soluble in *water* and in *methanol*; soluble in *dimethyl sulfoxide*; insoluble in *dichloromethane*, in *ethanol (96%)* and in *ether*. It dissolves in dilute acids and in alkaline solutions.

IDENTIFICATION
A. The *infrared absorption spectrum*, Appendix II A, is concordant with the *reference spectrum* of cefalonium *(RSV 09)*.

B. The *light absorption*, Appendix II B, in the range 220 to 350 nm of a 0.002% w/v solution in *water* exhibits two maxima, at 235 nm and at 262 nm. The *absorbance* at 235 nm is about 0.76 and at 262 nm is about 0.62.

TESTS
Specific optical rotation
Dissolve 0.25 g with the aid of gentle heat in sufficient *dimethyl sulfoxide* to produce 50 mL. Allow the solution to stand for 30 minutes before measurement of the optical rotation. The *specific optical rotation* of the resulting solution is -50 to -56, calculated with reference to the anhydrous substance, Appendix V F.

Related substances
Carry out the method for *thin-layer chromatography*, Appendix III A, using the following solutions in 8.3M *acetic acid*.

(1) 2.5% w/v of the substance being examined.

(2) 0.05% w/v of the substance being examined.

(3) 0.025% w/v of the substance being examined.

(4) 0.005% w/v of the substance being examined.

(5) 0.05% w/v of each of *cefalotin sodium EPCRS* and *isonicotinamide*.

CHROMATOGRAPHIC CONDITIONS

(a) Use as the coating *silica gel* F_{254}.

(b) Use the mobile phase as described below.

(c) Apply 4 µL of each solution.

(d) Develop the plate to 12 cm.

(e) After removal of the plate, allow it to dry in air and examine under *ultraviolet light (254 nm)*.

MOBILE PHASE

10 volumes of *glacial acetic acid*, 10 volumes of 1M *sodium acetate* and 30 volumes of *propan-2-ol.*

SYSTEM SUITABILITY

The test is not valid unless the chromatogram obtained with solution (5) shows two clearly separated spots.

LIMITS

Any *secondary spot* in the chromatogram obtained with solution (1) is not more intense than the spot in the chromatogram obtained with solution (2) (2%), not more than one such spot is more intense than the spot in the chromatogram obtained with solution (3) (1%) and not more than three such spots are more intense than the spot in the chromatogram obtained with solution (4) (0.2% each).

Sulfated ash

Not more than 0.2%, Appendix IX A.

Water

6.5 to 8.5% w/w, Appendix IX C. Use 0.5 g.

ASSAY

Measure the *absorbance* of a 0.002% w/v solution at the maximum at 262 nm, Appendix II B. Calculate the content of $C_{20}H_{18}N_4O_5S_2$ from the *absorbance* obtained using a 0.002% w/v solution of *cefalonium BPCRS* and from the declared content of $C_{20}H_{18}N_4O_5S_2$ in *cefalonium BPCRS.*

STORAGE

Cefalonium should be protected from light and stored at a temperature not exceeding 30°.

Cefalonium intended for use in the manufacture of either a parenteral dosage form or an intramammary infusion without a further appropriate sterilisation procedure complies with the following additional requirement.

Sterility

Complies with the *test for sterility*, Appendix XVI A.

IMPURITIES

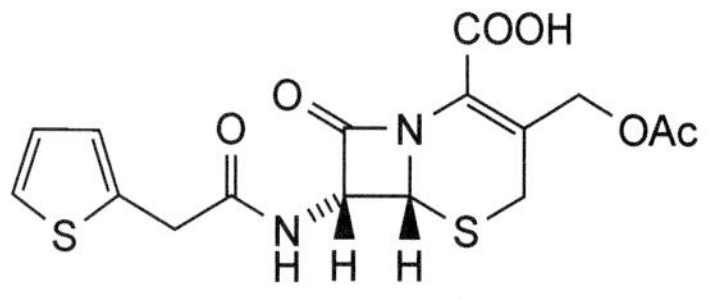

A. cefalotin,

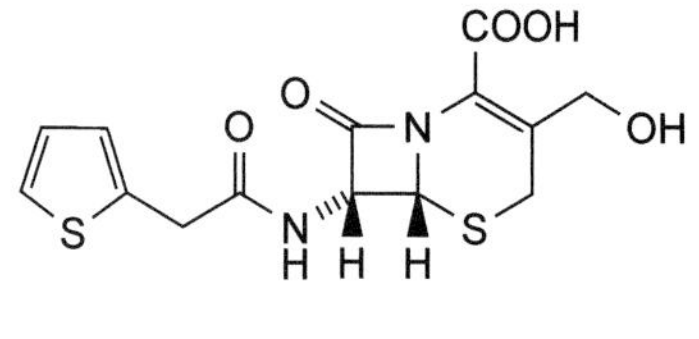

B. 3-hydroxymethyl-7β-(2-thienylacetamido)-3-cephem-4-carboxylic acid,

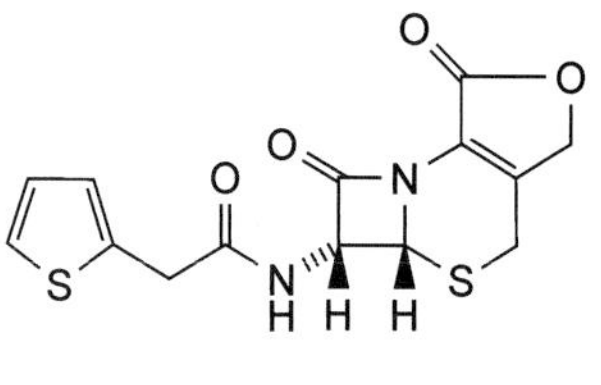

C. 3-hydroxymethyl-7β-(2-thienylacetamido)-3-cephem-4-carboxylic acid lactone,

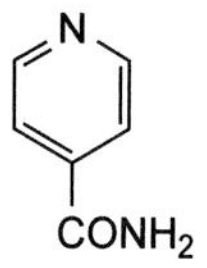

D. isonicotinamide.

Clazuril

(Clazuril for Veterinary Use, Ph Eur monograph 1714)

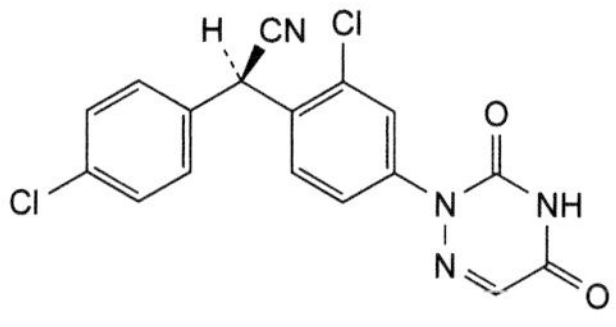

and enantiomer

$C_{17}H_{10}Cl_2N_4O_2$ 373.2   101831-36-1

Action and use

Treatment of coccidiosis; antiprotozoal (veterinary).

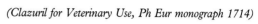

DEFINITION

(2RS)-[2-Chloro-4-(3,5-dioxo-4,5-dihydro-1,2,4-triazin-2(3H)-yl)phenyl](4-chlorophenyl)acetonitrile.

Content

99.0 per cent to 101.0 per cent (dried substance).

CHARACTERS

Appearance

White or light yellow powder.

Solubility

Practically insoluble in water, freely soluble in dimethylformamide, slightly soluble in ethanol (96 per cent) and in methylene chloride.

IDENTIFICATION

A. Melting point (*2.2.14*): 199 °C to 203 °C.

B. Infrared absorption spectrophotometry (*2.2.24*).

Comparison clazuril CRS.

TESTS

Related substances

Liquid chromatography (*2.2.29*).

Solvent mixture tetrahydrofuran R, water R (50:50 V/V).

Test solution Dissolve 20.0 mg of the substance to be examined in the solvent mixture and dilute to 20.0 mL with the solvent mixture.

Reference solution (a) Dissolve 5 mg of *clazuril for system suitability CRS* (containing impurities A, B, C, D, E, F, G, H and I) in the solvent mixture and dilute to 5.0 mL with the solvent mixture.

Reference solution (b) Dilute 1.0 mL of the test solution to 100.0 mL with the solvent mixture. Dilute 2.0 mL of this solution to 10.0 mL with the solvent mixture.

Column:

— *size:* l = 0.10 m, Ø = 4.6 mm;

— *stationary phase:* octadecylsilyl silica gel for chromatography R (3 µm);

— *temperature:* 35 °C.

Mobile phase:
— *mobile phase A*: mix 100 volumes of a 7.7 g/L solution of *ammonium acetate R* adjusted to pH 6.2 with a 10 per cent *V/V* solution of *anhydrous formic acid R*, 150 volumes of *acetonitrile R* and 750 volumes of *water R*;
— *mobile phase B*: mix 50 volumes of *water R*, 100 volumes of a 7.7 g/L solution of *ammonium acetate R* adjusted to pH 6.2 with a 10 per cent *V/V* solution of *anhydrous formic acid R* and 850 volumes of *acetonitrile R*;

Time (min)	Mobile phase A (per cent *V/V*)	Mobile phase B (per cent *V/V*)
0 - 20	100 → 0	0 → 100
20 - 25	0	100

Flow rate 1.0 mL/min.

Detection Spectrophotometer at 230 nm.

Injection 5 μL.

Identification of impurities Use the chromatogram supplied with *clazuril for system suitability CRS* and the chromatogram obtained with reference solution (a) to identify the peaks due to impurities A, B, C, D, E, F, G, H and I.

Relative retention With reference to clazuril (retention time = about 16 min): impurity A = about 0.6; impurity B = about 0.78; impurity C = about 0.80; impurity D = about 0.86; impurity E = about 0.9; impurity F = about 0.95; impurity G = about 0.98; impurity H = about 1.1; impurity I = about 1.2.

System suitability: reference solution (a):
— *peak-to-valley ratio*: minimum 1.5, where H_p = height above the baseline of the peak due to impurity G and H_v = height above the baseline of the lowest point of the curve separating this peak from the peak due to clazuril,
— the chromatogram obtained is similar to the chromatogram supplied with *clazuril for system suitability CRS*.

Limits:
— *correction factors*: for the calculation of contents, multiply the peak areas of the following impurities by the corresponding correction factor: impurity G = 1.4; impurity H = 0.8;
— *impurities A, B, C, D, E, F, G, H, I*: for each impurity, not more than the area of the principal peak in the chromatogram obtained with reference solution (b) (0.2 per cent);
— *unspecified impurities*: for each impurity, not more than the area of the principal peak in the chromatogram obtained with reference solution (b) (0.20 per cent);
— *total*: not more than 3 times the area of the principal peak in the chromatogram obtained with reference solution (b) (0.6 per cent);
— *disregard limit*: 0.25 times the area of the principal peak in the chromatogram obtained with reference solution (b) (0.05 per cent); disregard the peaks due to the solvents.

Loss on drying (*2.2.32*)
Maximum 0.5 per cent, determined on 1.000 g by drying in an oven at 105 °C for 4 h.

Sulfated ash (*2.4.14*)
Maximum 0.1 per cent, determined on 1.0 g.

ASSAY
Dissolve about 0.260 g in 35 mL of *tetrahydrofuran R* and add 35 mL of *water R*. Titrate with *0.1 M sodium hydroxide*,

determining the end-point potentiometrically (*2.2.20*). Carry out a blank titration.

1 mL of *0.1 M sodium hydroxide* is equivalent to 37.32 mg of $C_{17}H_{10}Cl_2N_4O_2$.

STORAGE
Protected from light.

IMPURITIES
Specified impurities A, B, C, D, E, F, G, H, I

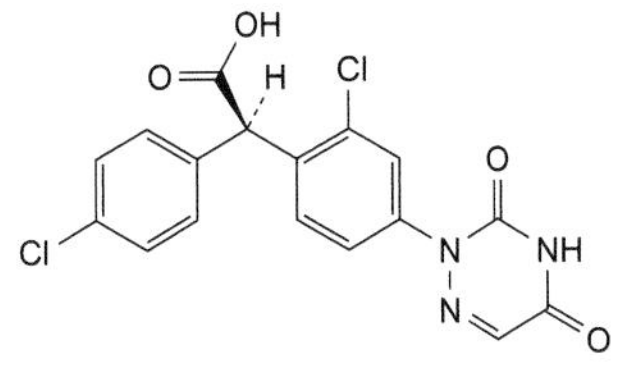

and enantiomer

A. (2*RS*)-[2-chloro-4-(3,5-dioxo-4,5-dihydro-1,2,4-triazin-2(3*H*)-yl)phenyl](4-chlorophenyl)acetic acid,

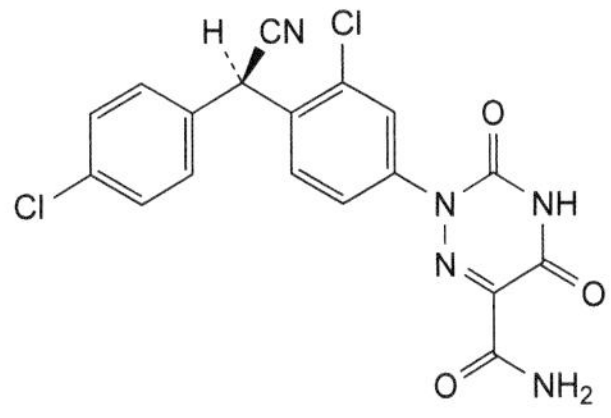

and enantiomer

B. 2-[3-chloro-4-[(*RS*)-(4-chlorophenyl)cyanomethyl]phenyl]-3,5-dioxo-2,3,4,5-tetrahydro-1,2,4-triazine-6-carboxamide,

and enantiomer

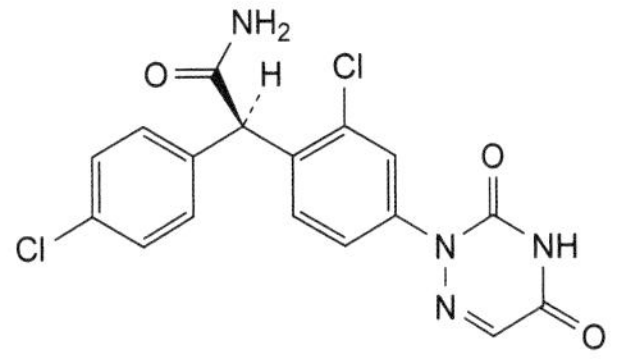

C. (2*RS*)-2-[2-chloro-4-(3,5-dioxo-4,5-dihydro-1,2,4-triazin-2(3*H*)-yl)phenyl]-2-(4-chlorophenyl)acetamide,

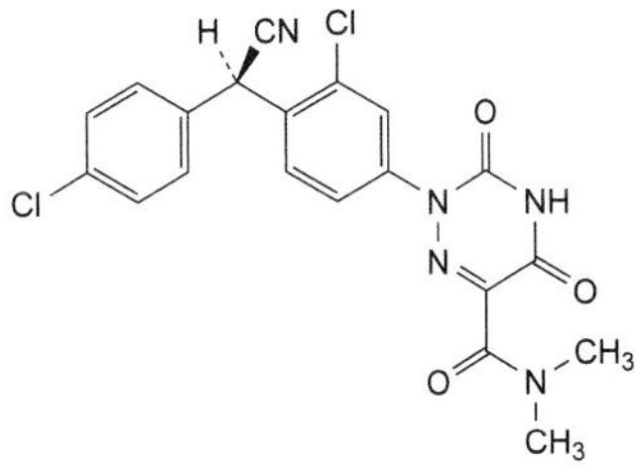

and enantiomer

D. 2-[3-chloro-4-[(*RS*)-(4-chlorophenyl)cyanomethyl]phenyl]-*N,N*-dimethyl-3,5-dioxo-2,3,4,5-tetrahydro-1,2,4-triazine-6-carboxamide,

and enantiomer

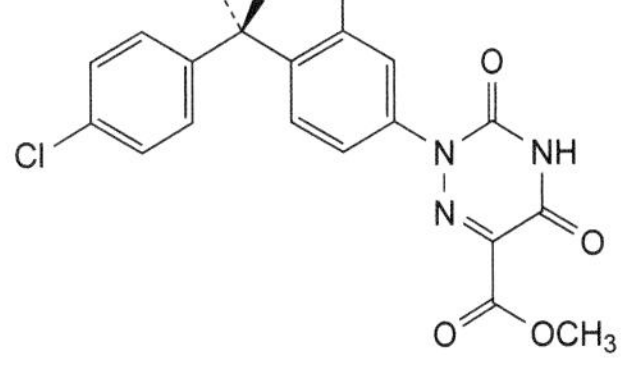

E. methyl 2-[3-chloro-4-[(*RS*)-(4-chlorophenyl)cyanomethyl]phenyl]-3,5-dioxo-2,3,4,5-tetrahydro-1,2,4-triazine-6-carboxylate,

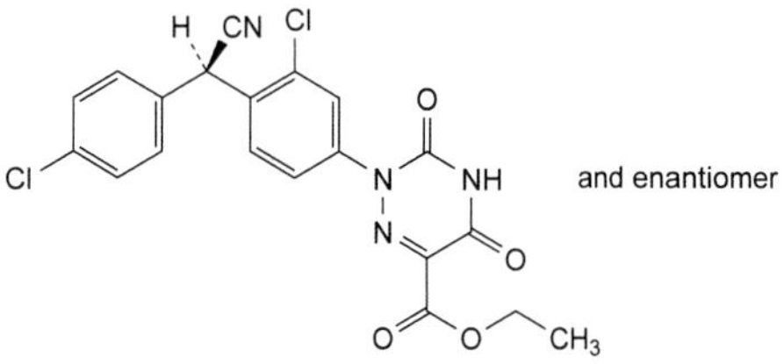

and enantiomer

F. ethyl 2-[3-chloro-4-[(RS)-
(4-chlorophenyl)cyanomethyl]phenyl]-3,5-dioxo-2,3,4,5-
tetrahydro-1,2,4-triazine-6-carboxylate,

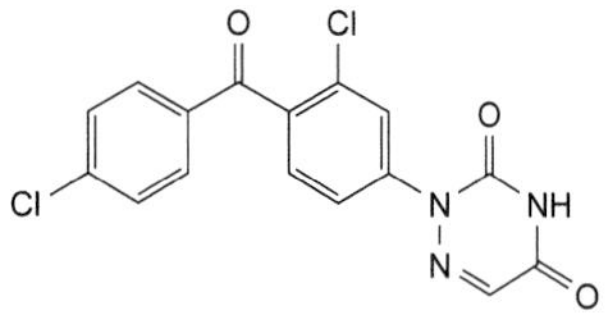

G. 2-[3-chloro-4-(4-chlorobenzoyl)phenyl]-1,2,4-
triazine3,5(2H,4H)-dione,

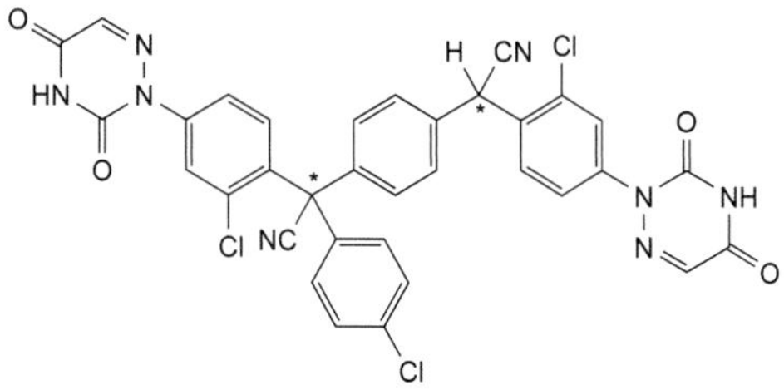

H. [2-chloro-4-(3,5-dioxo-4,5-dihydro-1,2,4-triazin-2(3H)-
yl)phenyl][4-[[2-chloro-4-(3,5-dioxo-4,5-dihydro-1,2,4-
triazin-2(3H)-
yl)phenyl]cyanomethyl]phenyl](4-chlorophenyl)acetonitrile,

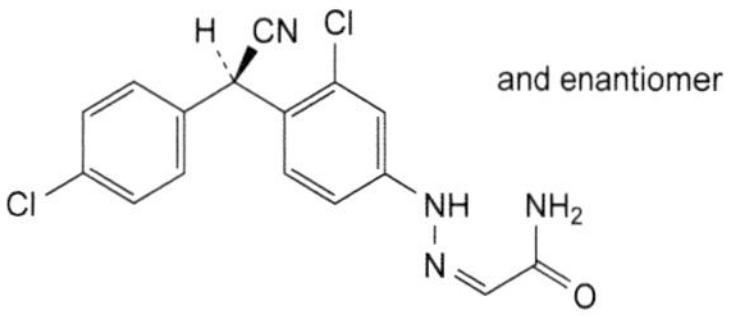

and enantiomer

I. (Z)-2-[[3-chloro-4-[(RS)-(4-chlorophenyl)cyanomethyl]
phenyl]diazanylidene]acetamide.

_____ *Ph Eur*

Cloprostenol Sodium

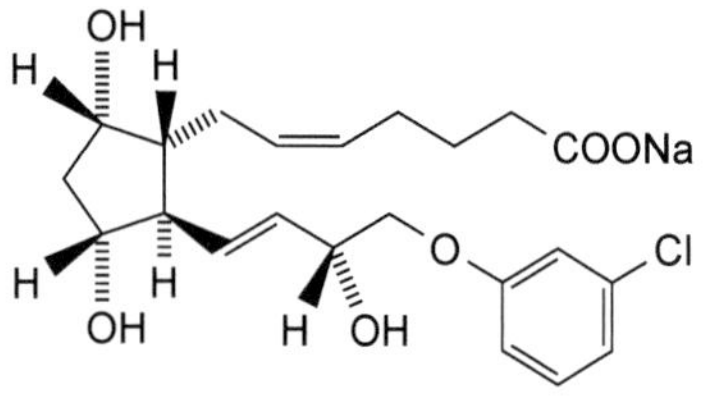

$C_{22}H_{28}ClNaO_6$ 446.9   *55028-72-3*

Action and use
Prostaglandin (PGF$_{2\alpha}$) analogue.

Preparation
Cloprostenol Injection

DEFINITION
Cloprostenol Sodium is ($\pm$)-(5Z)-7-(1R,3R,5S)-2-[(1E,3R)-
4-(3-chlorophenoxy)-3-hydroxybut-1-enyl]-3,5-
dihydroxycyclopentylhept-5-enoate. It contains not less than
97.5% and not more than 102.5% of $C_{22}H_{28}ClNaO_6$,
calculated with reference to the anhydrous substance.

CAUTION *Cloprostenol Sodium is extremely potent and
extraordinary care should be taken in any procedure in which it is
used.*

CHARACTERISTICS
A white or almost white, amorphous powder; hygroscopic.

Freely soluble in *water*, in *ethanol (96%)* and in *methanol*;
practically insoluble in *acetone*.

IDENTIFICATION
A. The *infrared absorption spectrum*, Appendix II A, is
concordant with the *reference spectrum* of cloprostenol sodium
(RSV 11).

B. Yields reaction A characteristic of *sodium salts*,
Appendix VI.

TESTS
Related substances
Carry out the method for *liquid chromatography*,
Appendix III D, using the following solutions in *absolute
ethanol*.

(1) 2.0% w/v of the substance being examined.

(2) 0.050% w/v of the substance being examined.

CHROMATOGRAPHIC CONDITIONS

(a) Use a stainless steel column (25 cm × 4.6 mm) packed
with *silica gel for chromatography* (5 µm) (Partisil is suitable).

(b) Use isocratic elution and the mobile phase described
below.

(c) Use a flow rate of 1.8 mL per minute.

(d) Use an ambient column temperature.

(e) Use a detection wavelength of 220 nm.

(f) Inject 5 µL of each solution.

(g) Allow the chromatography to proceed for twice the
retention time of the peak due to Cloprostenol.

MOBILE PHASE

1 volume of *glacial acetic acid*, 70 volumes of *absolute ethanol*
and 930 volumes of *hexane*.

LIMITS

In the chromatogram obtained with solution (1):

the sum of the areas of any *secondary peaks* is not greater than
the area of the principal peak in the chromatogram obtained
with solution (2) (2.5%).

Water
Not more than 3.0% w/w, Appendix IX C. Use 50 mg
dissolved in 1 mL of *absolute ethanol*.

ASSAY
Carry out the method for *liquid chromatography*,
Appendix III D, using the following solutions in *absolute
ethanol*.

(1) 0.08% w/v of the substance being examined.

(2) 0.08% w/v of *cloprostenol sodium BPCRS*.

CHROMATOGRAPHIC CONDITIONS

(a) Use a stainless steel column (25 cm × 4.6 mm) packed
with *silica gel for chromatography* (5 µm) (Partisil is suitable).

(b) Use isocratic elution and the mobile phase described
below.

(c) Use a flow rate of 1.8 mL per minute.

(d) Use an ambient column temperature.

(e) Use a detection wavelength of 220 nm.

(f) Inject 5 μL of each solution.

MOBILE PHASE

1 volume of *glacial acetic acid*, 100 volumes of *absolute ethanol* and 900 volumes of *hexane*.

DETERMINATION OF CONTENT

Calculate the content of $C_{22}H_{28}ClNaO_6$ from the chromatograms obtained and using the declared content of $C_{22}H_{28}ClNaO_6$ in *cloprostenol sodium BPCRS*.

STORAGE

Cloprostenol Sodium should be protected from light and moisture.

IMPURITIES

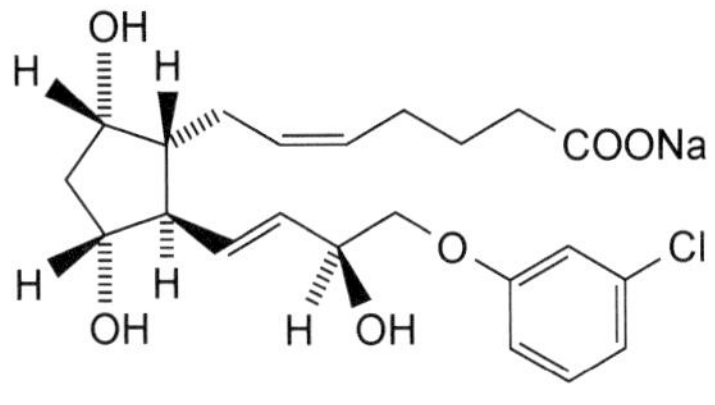

A. (±)-(5*Z*)-7-(1*R*,3*R*,5*S*)-2-[(1*E*,3*S*)-4-(3-chlorophenoxy)-3-hydroxybut-1-enyl]-3,5-dihydroxycyclopentylhept-5-enoate *(epimer)*,

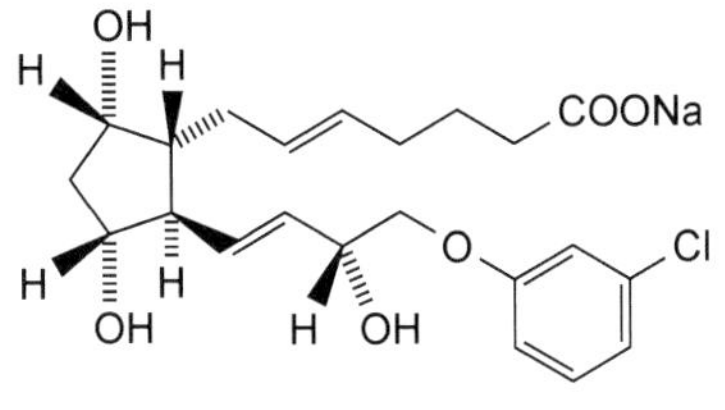

B. (±)-(5*E*)-7-(1*R*,3*R*,5*S*)-2-[(1*E*,3 *R*)-4-(3-chlorophenoxy)-3-hydroxybut-1-enyl]-3,5-dihydroxycyclopentylhept-5-enoate *(trans-isomer)*.

Closantel Sodium Dihydrate

(Closantel Sodium Dihydrate for Veterinary Use, Ph Eur monograph 1716)

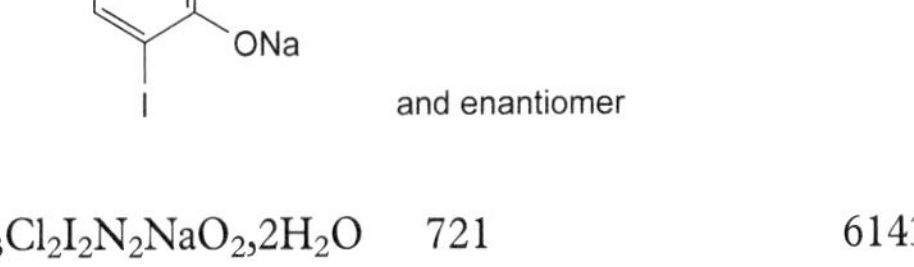

and enantiomer

$C_{22}H_{13}Cl_2I_2N_2NaO_2,2H_2O$ 721   61438-64-0

Action and use

Antihelminthic.

Ph Eur

DEFINITION

N-[5-Chloro-4-[(*RS*)-(4-chlorophenyl)cyanomethyl]-2-methylphenyl]-2-hydroxy-3,5-diiodobenzamide sodium salt dihydrate.

Content

98.5 per cent to 101.5 per cent (anhydrous substance).

CHARACTERS

Appearance

Yellow powder, slightly hygroscopic.

Solubility

Very slightly soluble in water, freely soluble in ethanol (96 per cent), soluble in methanol.

It shows polymorphism (*5.9*).

IDENTIFICATION

A. Infrared absorption spectrophotometry (*2.2.24*).

Preparation Discs without recrystallisation.

Comparison closantel sodium dihydrate CRS.

B. Dissolve 0.1 g in 2 mL of *ethanol (96 per cent) R*. The solution gives reaction (a) of sodium (*2.3.1*).

TESTS

Appearance of solution

The solution is clear (*2.2.1*) and not more intensely coloured than reference solution GY$_4$ (*2.2.2, Method II*).

Dissolve 0.50 g in *ethanol (96 per cent) R* and dilute to 50 mL with the same solvent.

Related substances

Liquid chromatography (*2.2.29*). *Prepare the solutions immediately before use and protect from light*.

Test solution Dissolve 0.100 g of the substance to be examined in *methanol R* and dilute to 10.0 mL with the same solvent.

Reference solution (a) Dissolve 10 mg of *closantel for system suitability CRS* (containing impurities A to J) in *methanol R* and dilute to 1.0 mL with the same solvent.

Reference solution (b) Dilute 1.0 mL of the test solution to 100.0 mL with *methanol R*. Dilute 5.0 mL of this solution to 25.0 mL with *methanol R*.

Column:
— *size*: *l* = 0.10 m, Ø = 4.6 mm,
— *stationary phase*: base-deactivated octadecylsilyl silica gel for chromatography R (3 μm),
— *temperature*: 35 °C.

Mobile phase:
— *mobile phase A*: to 100 mL of a 7.7 g/L solution of *ammonium acetate R* previously adjusted to pH 4.3 with *acetic acid R*, add 50 mL of *acetonitrile R* and 850 mL of *water R*;
— *mobile phase B*: to 100 mL of a 7.7 g/L solution of *ammonium acetate R* previously adjusted to pH 4.3 with *acetic acid R*, add 50 mL of *water R* and 850 mL of *acetonitrile R*;

Time (min)	Mobile phase A (per cent *V/V*)	Mobile phase B (per cent *V/V*)
0 - 2	50	50
2 - 22	50 → 20	50 → 80
22 - 27	20	80

Flow rate 1.5 mL/min.

Detection Spectrophotometer at 240 nm.

Injection 10 µL.

Relative retention With reference to closantel (retention time = about 16 min): impurity A = about 0.07; impurity B = about 0.48; impurity C = about 0.62; impurity D = about 0.65; impurity E = about 0.82; impurity F = about 0.89; impurity G = about 0.93; impurity H = about 1.13; impurity I = about 1.16; impurity J = about 1.55.

System suitability: reference solution (a):
— *resolution*: baseline separation between the peaks due to impurity G and closantel,
— the chromatogram obtained is similar to the chromatogram supplied with *closantel for system suitability CRS*.

Limits:
— *correction factors*: for the calculation of contents, multiply the peak areas of the following impurities by the corresponding correction factor: impurity A = 1.5; impurity B = 1.3;
— *impurity G*: not more than 2.5 times the area of the principal peak in the chromatogram obtained with reference solution (b) (0.5 per cent);
— *impurities F, H, I*: for each impurity, not more than 1.5 times the area of the principal peak in the chromatogram obtained with reference solution (b) (0.3 per cent);
— *impurities A, B, C, D, E, J*: for each impurity, not more than the area of the principal peak in the chromatogram obtained with reference solution (b) (0.2 per cent);
— *any other impurity*: for each impurity, not more than the area of the principal peak in the chromatogram obtained with reference solution (b) (0.2 per cent);
— *total*: not more than 7.5 times the area of the principal peak in the chromatogram obtained with reference solution (b) (1.5 per cent);
— *disregard limit*: 0.25 times the area of the principal peak in the chromatogram obtained with reference solution (b) (0.05 per cent).

Water *(2.5.12)*

4.8 per cent to 5.8 per cent, determined on 0.250 g.

Use a mixture of 1 volume of *dimethylformamide R* and 4 volumes of *methanol R* as the solvent.

ASSAY

Dissolve 0.500 g in 50 mL of a mixture of 1 volume of *anhydrous acetic acid R* and 7 volumes of *methyl ethyl ketone R*. Titrate with *0.1 M perchloric acid*, determining the end-point potentiometrically *(2.2.20)*.

1 mL of *0.1 M perchloric acid* is equivalent to 68.5 mg of $C_{22}H_{13}Cl_2I_2N_2NaO_2$.

STORAGE

In an airtight container, protected from light.

IMPURITIES

Specified impurities: A, B, C, D, E, F, G, H, I, J.

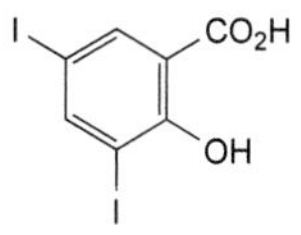

A. 2-hydroxy-3,5-diiodobenzoic acid,

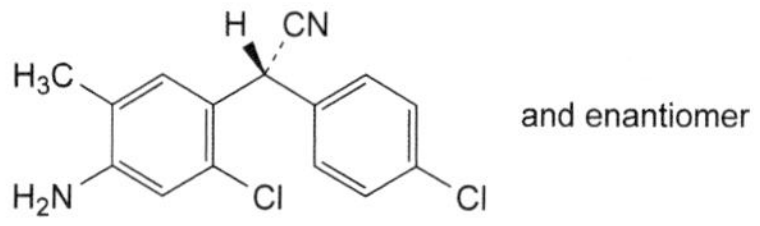

B. (2RS)-(4-amino-2-chloro-5-methylphenyl)(4-chlorophenyl)ethanenitrile,

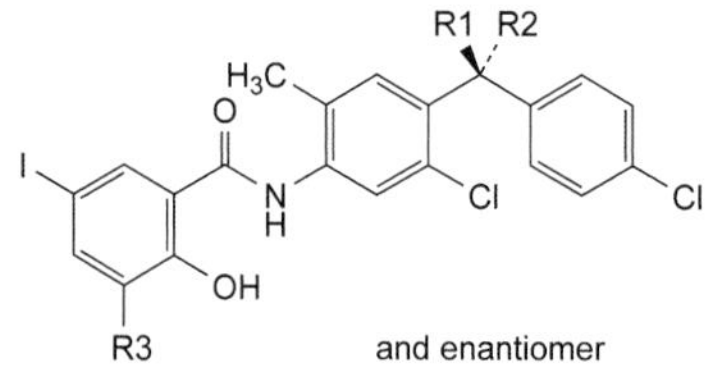

C. R1 = H, R2 = CO_2H, R3 = I: (2RS)-[2-chloro-4-[(2-hydroxy-3,5-diiodobenzoyl)amino]-5-methylphenyl](4-chlorophenyl)acetic acid,

D. R1 = H, R2 = $CONH_2$, R3 = I: N-[4-[(1RS)-2-amino-1-(4-chlorophenyl)-2-oxoethyl]-5-chloro-2-methylphenyl]-2-hydroxy-3,5-diiodobenzamide,

E. R1 = H, R2 = CN, R3 = Cl: 3-chloro-N-[5-chloro-4-[(RS)-(4-chlorophenyl)cyanomethyl]-2-methylphenyl]-2-hydroxy-5-iodobenzamide,

F. R1 + R2 = O, R3 = I: N-[5-chloro-4-(4-chlorobenzoyl)-2-methylphenyl]-2-hydroxy-3,5-diiodobenzamide,

G. R1 = H, R2 = C(=NH)OCH_3, R3 = I: methyl (2RS)-2-[2-chloro-4-[(2-hydroxy-3,5-diiodobenzoyl)amino]-5-methylphenyl]-2-(4-chlorophenyl)acetimidate,

H. R1 = H, R2 = CO-OCH_3, R3 = I: methyl (2RS)-[2-chloro-4-[(2-hydroxy-3,5-diiodobenzoyl)amino]-5-methylphenyl](4-chlorophenyl)acetate,

I. R1 = R3 = H, R2 = CN: N-[5-chloro-4-[(RS)-(4-chlorophenyl)cyanomethyl]-2-methylphenyl]-2-hydroxy-5-iodobenzamide,

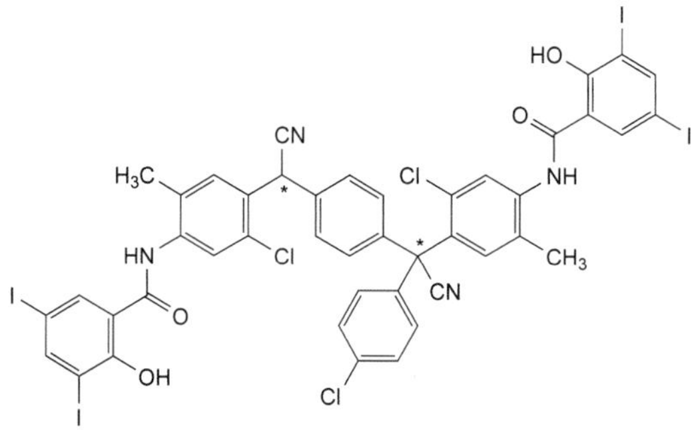

J. N-[5-chloro-4-[[4-[[2-chloro-4-[(2-hydroxy-3,5-diiodobenzoyl)amino]-5-methylphenyl]cyanomethyl]phenyl](4-chlorophenyl)cyanomethyl]-2-methylphenyl]-2-hydroxy-3,5-diiodobenzamide.

Cloxacillin Benzathine

$C_{16}H_{20}N_2,(C_{19}H_{18}ClN_3O_5S)_2$ 1112.1   *32222-55-2*

Action and use
Penicillin antibacterial.

Preparations
Cloxacillin Benzathine Intramammary Infusion (Dry Cow)

Ampicillin Trihydrate and Cloxacillin Benzathine Intramammary Infusion (Dry Cow)

DEFINITION
Cloxacillin Benzathine is *N,N'*-dibenzylethylenediammonium bis[(6*R*)-6-(3-*o*-chlorophenyl-5-methylisoxazole-4-carboxamido)penicillanate]. It contains not less than 92.0% of $C_{16}H_{20}N_2,(C_{19}H_{18}ClN_3O_5S)_2$ and not less than 20.0% and not more than 22.0% of benzathine, $C_{16}H_{20}N_2$, each calculated with reference to the anhydrous substance.

CHARACTERISTICS
A white or almost white powder.

Slightly soluble in *water*; freely soluble in *methanol*; slightly soluble in *ethanol (96%)* and in *propan-2-ol*.

IDENTIFICATION
A. The *infrared absorption spectrum*, Appendix II A, is concordant with the *reference spectrum* of cloxacillin benzathine *(RSV 12)*.

B. Shake 0.1 g with 1 mL of 1M *sodium hydroxide* for 2 minutes, add 2 mL of *ether*, shake for 1 minute and allow to separate. Evaporate 1 mL of the ether layer to dryness, dissolve the residue in 2 mL of *glacial acetic acid* and add 1 mL of *dilute potassium dichromate solution*. A golden yellow precipitate is produced.

C. Shake 50 mg with 10 mL of *water* and filter. To 5 mL of the filtrate add a few drops of *silver nitrate solution*. No precipitate is produced. Heat 50 mg with 2 mL of *alcoholic potassium hydroxide solution* on a water bath for 15 minutes, add 15 mg of *activated charcoal*, shake and filter. Acidify the filtrate with 2M *nitric acid*. The solution yields reaction A characteristic of *chlorides*, Appendix VI.

TESTS
Water
Not more than 5.0% w/w, Appendix IX C. Use 0.5 g.

ASSAY
For cloxacillin benzathine
To 60 mg add 40 mL of *methanol*, shake to dissolve, add 25 mL of 1M *sodium hydroxide* and allow to stand for 30 minutes. Add 27.5 mL of 1M *hydrochloric acid* and sufficient *water* to produce 100 mL, mix, transfer 20 mL of the solution to a stoppered flask, add 30 mL of 0.01M *iodine VS*, close the flask with a wet stopper and allow to stand for 15 minutes protected from light. Titrate the excess of iodine with 0.02M *sodium thiosulfate VS*, using *starch mucilage*, added towards the end of the titration, as indicator. Add a further 12 mg of the substance being examined to 10 mL of *water*, swirl to disperse, add 30 mL of 0.01M *iodine VS* and titrate immediately with 0.02M *sodium thiosulfate VS*, using *starch mucilage*, added towards the end of the titration, as indicator. The difference between the titrations represents the volume of 0.01M *iodine VS* equivalent to the total penicillins present. Calculate the content of $C_{16}H_{20}N_2,(C_{19}H_{18}ClN_3O_5S)_2$ from the difference obtained by carrying out the assay simultaneously using *cloxacillin benzathine BPCRS* and from the declared content of $C_{16}H_{20}N_2,(C_{19}H_{18}ClN_3O_5S)_2$ in *cloxacillin benzathine BPCRS*.

For benzathine
To 1 g add 30 mL of a saturated solution of *sodium chloride* and 10 mL of 5M *sodium hydroxide*, shake well, and extract with four 50 mL quantities of *ether*. Wash the combined extracts with three 10 mL quantities of *water*, extract the combined washings with 25 mL of *ether* and add the extract to the main ether solution. Evaporate the ether solution to low bulk, add 2 mL of *absolute ethanol* and evaporate to dryness. To the residue add 50 mL of *anhydrous acetic acid* and titrate with 0.1M *perchloric acid VS*, using 0.1 mL of *1-naphtholbenzein solution* as indicator. Repeat the operation without the substance being examined. The difference between the titrations represents the amount of perchloric acid required to neutralise the liberated base. Each mL of 0.1M *perchloric acid VS* is equivalent to 12.02 mg of $C_{16}H_{20}N_2$.

STORAGE
Cloxacillin Benzathine should be kept in an airtight container. If the material is sterile, the container should be sterile, tamper-evident and sealed so as to exclude micro-organisms.

LABELLING
The label states, where applicable, that the material is sterile.

Cloxacillin Benzathine intended for use in the manufacture of either a parenteral dosage form or an intramammary infusion without a further appropriate sterilisation procedure complies with the following additional requirement.

Sterility
Complies with the *test for sterility*, Appendix XVI A.

Cobalt Oxide

Co_3O_4 240.8   *1307-96-9*

Action and use
Used in the prevention of cobalt deficiency in ruminants.

DEFINITION
Cobalt Oxide consists of cobalt(II,III) oxide (tricobalt tetraoxide) with a small proportion of cobalt(III) oxide (dicobalt trioxide). It contains not less than 70.0% and not more than 75.0% of Co, calculated with reference to the substance ignited at about 600°.

CHARACTERISTICS
A black powder.

Practically insoluble in *water*. It dissolves in mineral acids and in solutions of the alkali hydroxides.

IDENTIFICATION
A. Dissolve 50 mg, with warming, in 5 mL of *hydrochloric acid* and add 10 mL of *water*. To 2 mL of the solution add 1 mL of 5M *sodium hydroxide*. A blue precipitate which becomes pink on warming is produced. Reserve the remainder of the solution for use in test B.

B. Neutralise 10 mL of the solution reserved in test A with 5M *sodium hydroxide* and add 0.5 mL of 6M *acetic acid* and 10 mL of a 10% w/v solution of *potassium nitrite*. A yellow crystalline precipitate is produced.

Loss on ignition

When ignited at about 600°, loses not more than 1.0% of its weight. Use 1 g.

ASSAY

Dissolve 0.1 g in 20 mL of *hydrochloric acid*, by repeated evaporation if necessary. Add 300 mL of *water*, 4 g of *hydroxylamine hydrochloride* and 25 mL of 13.5M *ammonia*. Warm to 80° and titrate with 0.05M *disodium edetate VS*, using *methyl thymol blue mixture* as indicator, until the colour changes from blue to purple. Each mL of 0.05M *disodium edetate VS* is equivalent to 2.946 mg of Co.

Decoquinate

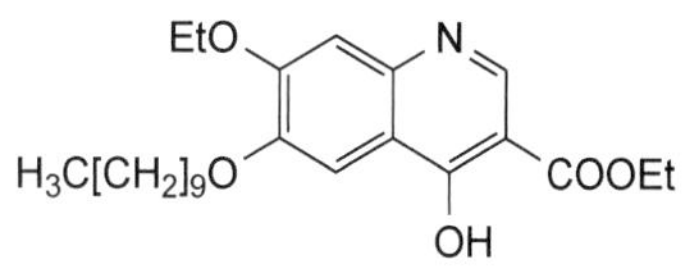

$C_{24}H_{35}NO_5$ 417.6 *18507-89-6*

Action and use

Antiprotozoal (veterinary).

Preparation

Decoquinate Premix

DEFINITION

Decoquinate is ethyl 6-decyloxy-7-ethoxy-4-hydroxyquinoline-3-carboxylate. It contains not less than 99.0% and not more than 101.0% of $C_{24}H_{35}NO_5$, calculated with reference to the dried substance.

CHARACTERISTICS

A cream to buff-coloured, microcrystalline powder; odourless or almost odourless.

Insoluble in *water*; very slightly soluble in *chloroform* and in *ether*; practically insoluble in *ethanol (96%)*.

IDENTIFICATION

A. The *infrared absorption spectrum*, Appendix II A, is concordant with the *reference spectrum* of decoquinate *(RSV 14)*.

B. The *light absorption*, Appendix II B, in the range 230 to 350 nm of the solution used in the test for Light absorption exhibits a well-defined maximum only at 265 nm.

TESTS

Light absorption

Dissolve 40 mg in 10 ml of hot *chloroform* and, keeping the solution warm, dilute slowly with 70 ml of *absolute ethanol*. Cool and dilute to 100 ml with *absolute ethanol*. Immediately dilute 10 ml to 100 ml with *absolute ethanol*. To 10 ml of the solution add 10 ml of 0.1M *hydrochloric acid* and dilute to 100 ml with *absolute ethanol*. The *absorbance* of the resulting solution at the maximum at 265 nm is 0.38 to 0.42, calculated with reference to the dried substance, Appendix II B.

Related substances

Carry out the method for *thin-layer chromatography*, Appendix III A, using the following solutions.

(1) 1.0% w/v of the substance being examined in *chloroform*, prepared with the aid of heat.

(2) 0.0050% w/v of *diethyl 4-decyloxy-3-ethoxyanilinomethylenemalonate BPCRS* in *chloroform*.

(3) 0.010% w/v of the substance being examined in *chloroform*.

CHROMATOGRAPHIC CONDITIONS

(a) Use as the coating *silica gel F_{254}* (Merck silica gel 60 F_{254} plates are suitable).

(b) Use the mobile phase as described below.

(c) Apply 10 µl of each solution.

(d) Develop the plate to 15 cm.

(e) After removal of the plate, dry in air and examine under *ultraviolet light (254 nm)*.

MOBILE PHASE

5 volumes of *anhydrous formic acid*, 10 volumes of *absolute ethanol* and 85 volumes of *chloroform*.

LIMITS

Any *secondary spot* corresponding to diethyl 4-decyloxy-3-ethoxyanilinomethylenemalonate in the chromatogram obtained with solution (1) is not more intense than the spot in the chromatogram obtained with solution (2) (0.5%) and any other *secondary spot* is not more intense than the spot in the chromatogram obtained with solution (3) (1%).

Loss on drying

When dried to constant weight at 105°, loses not more than 0.5% of its weight. Use 1 g.

Sulphated ash

Not more than 0.1%, Appendix IX A.

ASSAY

Dissolve 1 g in a mixture of 50 ml of *chloroform* and 50 ml of *anhydrous acetic acid* and carry out Method I for *non-aqueous titration*, Appendix VIII A, using *crystal violet solution* as indicator. Each ml of 0.1M *perchloric acid VS* is equivalent to 41.76 mg of $C_{24}H_{35}NO_5$.

Deltamethrin

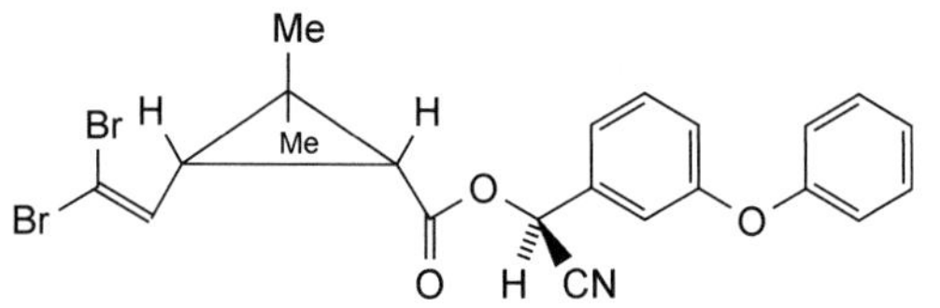

$C_{22}H_{19}Br_2NO_3$ 505.2 *52918-63-5*

Action and use

Insecticide (veterinary).

Preparation

Deltamethrin Pour-on

DEFINITION

Deltamethrin is (S)-α-cyano-3-phenoxybenzyl-(1R,3R)-3-(2,2-dibromovinyl)-2,2-dimethylcyclopropane carboxylate. It contains not less than 97.0% and not more than 101.0% of $C_{22}H_{19}Br_2NO_3$.

CHARACTERISTICS

A white to buff-coloured, crystalline powder.

Insoluble in *water*; soluble in *ethanol (96%)* and in *acetone*.

IDENTIFICATION

A. The *infrared absorption spectrum*, Appendix II A, is concordant with the *reference spectrum* of deltamethrin *(RSV 47)*.

B. In the test for Related substances, the principal spot in the chromatogram obtained with solution (2) corresponds to that in the chromatogram obtained with solution (5).

TESTS

Specific optical rotation

In a 4% w/v solution in *toluene*, +55.5 to +61.5, Appendix V F.

Becisthemic acid chloride

Not more than 0.2% when determined by the following method. Dissolve 2 g in 100 ml of *methanol* with moderate heating, if necessary, and cool. Titrate with 0.02M *potassium hydroxide VS* using a solution containing 0.8% w/v of *dimethyl yellow* and 0.08% w/v of *methylene blue* in *methanol* as indicator to a green end point. Each ml of 0.02M *potassium hydroxide VS* is equivalent to 6.329 mg of becisthemic acid chloride, $C_8H_9Br_2ClO$.

Becisthemic acid and becisthemic anhydride

Not more than 1% in total when determined by the following methods.

Becisthemic acid

Dissolve 2 g in 100 ml of *ethanol (96%)* with moderate heating. Cool in an ice-bath and immediately titrate with 0.02M *sodium hydroxide VS* using a 1% w/v solution of *1-naphtholbenzein* in *ethanol (96%)* solution as indicator to a green end point. Correct the volume of titrant for any contribution due to the becisthemic acid chloride content using the following expression:

$$V \times P_2/P_1$$

where V = titration volume obtained in the becisthemic acid chloride test,

P_1 = weight of sample used in the becisthemic chloride test,

P_2 = weight of sample used in this test.

Each ml of 0.02M *sodium hydroxide VS* is equivalent to 5.959 mg of becisthemic acid, $C_8H_{10}Br_2O_2$.

Becisthemic anhydride

To 1.0 g add 10 ml of 0.01M *aniline* in *cyclohexane* and 10 ml of *glacial acetic acid*. Stopper the flask and allow to stand at room temperature for 1 hour. Titrate with 0.01M *perchloric acid VS* using *crystal violet solution* as indicator. Repeat the procedure omitting the substance being examined. Correct the volume of titrant for any contribution due to twice the becisthemic acid chloride content calculated using the above formula. Each ml of 0.01M *perchloric acid VS* is equivalent to 5.779 mg of becisthemic anhydride, $C_{16}H_{18}Br_4O_3$.

Related substances

Carry out the method for *thin-layer chromatography*, Appendix III A, using the following solutions in *toluene*.

(1) 2.0% w/v of the substance being examined.

(2) 0.5% w/v of the substance being examined.

(3) 0.020% w/v of the substance being examined.

(4) 0.010% w/v of the substance being examined.

(5) 0.5% w/v of *deltamethrin BPCRS*.

CHROMATOGRAPHIC CONDITIONS

(a) Use a silica gel F_{254} precoated plate (Merck silica gel 60 F_{254} plates are suitable).

(b) Use the mobile phase as described below.

(c) Apply 10 µl of each solution.

(d) Develop the plate to 15 cm.

(e) After removal of the plate, dry in air and examine under *ultraviolet light (254 nm)*.

MOBILE PHASE

20 volumes of *di-isopropyl ether* and 80 volumes of *hexane*.

LIMITS

Any *secondary spot* in the chromatogram obtained with solution (1) is not more intense than the spot in the chromatogram obtained with solution (3) (1%) and not more than two such spots are more intense than the spot in the chromatogram obtained with solution (4) (0.5%).

ASSAY

Carry out the method for *liquid chromatography*, Appendix III D, using the following solutions in the mobile phase.

(1) 0.1% w/v of the substance being examined.

(2) 0.1% w/v of *deltamethrin BPCRS*.

(3) 0.1% w/v of *deltamethrin impurity standard BPCRS*.

CHROMATOGRAPHIC CONDITIONS

(a) Use a stainless steel column (25 cm × 4.6 mm) packed with *silica gel for chromatography* (5 µm) (Zorbax Sil is suitable).

(b) Use isocratic elution and the mobile phase described below.

(c) Use a flow rate of 1.3 ml per minute.

(d) Use an ambient column temperature.

(e) Use a detection wavelength of 278 nm.

(f) Inject 20 µl of each solution.

MOBILE PHASE

0.04 volume of *propan-2-ol*, 2 volumes of *acetonitrile*, 10 volumes of *dichloromethane* and 100 volumes of *hexane*.

SYSTEM SUITABILITY

The test is not valid unless, in the chromatogram obtained with solution (3), a peak due to (R)-deltamethrin appears immediately before the principal peak, as indicated in the reference chromatogram supplied with *deltamethrin impurity standard BPCRS*.

DETERMINATION OF CONTENT

Calculate the content of $C_{22}H_{19}Br_2NO_3$ using the declared content of $C_{22}H_{19}Br_2NO_3$ in *deltamethrin BPCRS*.

IMPURITIES

The impurities limited by the requirements of this monograph include:

— Becisthemic acid,

— Becisthemic anhydride,

— Becisthemic acid chloride.

Dembrexine Hydrochloride Monohydrate

(Dembrexine Hydrochloride Monohydrate for Veterinary Use, Ph Eur monograph 2169)

$C_{13}H_{18}Br_2ClNO_2,H_2O$ 433.6   *52702-51-9*

Ph Eur

DEFINITION

trans-4-[(3,5-Dibromo-2-hydroxybenzyl)amino]cyclohexanol hydrochloride monohydrate.

Content

98.0 per cent to 101.0 per cent (anhydrous substance).

CHARACTERS

Appearance

White or almost white, crystalline powder.

Solubility

Slightly soluble in water, freely soluble in methanol, slightly soluble in anhydrous ethanol.

IDENTIFICATION

A. Infrared absorption spectrophotometry *(2.2.24)*.

Comparison dembrexine hydrochloride monohydrate CRS.

B. It gives reaction (a) of chlorides *(2.3.1)*.

TESTS

Related substances

Liquid chromatography *(2.2.29)*. *Prepare the solutions immediately before use.*

Test solution Dissolve 25.0 mg of the substance to be examined in *methanol R* and dilute to 10.0 mL with the same solvent.

Reference solution (a) Dilute 1.0 mL of the test solution to 50.0 mL with *methanol R*. Dilute 1.0 mL of this solution to 10.0 mL with *methanol R*.

Reference solution (b) Dissolve 2.5 mg of *tribromophenol R* (impurity E) in *methanol R* and dilute to 50.0 mL with the same solvent. To 1.0 mL of this solution add 1.0 mL of the test solution and dilute to 10.0 mL with *methanol R*.

Blank solution Methanol R.

Column:
— *size*: l = 0.15 m, Ø = 4.0 mm;
— *stationary phase*: *end-capped octadecylsilyl silica gel for chromatography R* (5 µm);
— *temperature*: 40 °C.

Mobile phase:
— *mobile phase A*: dissolve 1.0 g of *potassium dihydrogen phosphate R* in 900 mL of *water R*, adjust to pH 7.4 with *0.5 M potassium hydroxide* and dilute to 1000 mL with *water R*; mix 80 volumes of this solution with 20 volumes of *methanol R*;
— *mobile phase B*: methanol R, acetonitrile R (20:80 *V/V*);

Time (min)	Mobile phase A (per cent *V/V*)	Mobile phase B (per cent *V/V*)
0 - 7	75	25
7 - 15	75 → 50	25 → 50
15 - 20	50	50
20 - 25	50 → 75	50 → 25
25 - 30	75	25

Flow rate 1.0 mL/min.

Detection Spectrophotometer at 250 nm.

Injection 10 µL.

Relative retention With reference to dembrexine (retention time = about 6 min): impurity A = about 2.3; impurity B = about 1.3.

System suitability: reference solution (b):
— *resolution*: minimum 2 between the peaks due to dembrexine and impurity E.

Limits:
— *impurities A, B*: for each impurity, not more than the area of the principal peak in the chromatogram obtained with reference solution (a) (0.2 per cent);
— *unspecified impurities*: for each impurity, not more than the area of the principal peak in the chromatogram obtained with reference solution (a) (0.2 per cent);
— *total*: not more than 2.5 times the area of the principal peak in the chromatogram obtained with reference solution (a) (0.5 per cent);
— *disregard limit*: 0.5 times the area of the principal peak in the chromatogram obtained with reference solution (a) (0.1 per cent); disregard any peak due to the blank.

Water *(2.5.12)*

3.5 per cent to 5.0 per cent, determined on 0.500 g.

Sulfated ash *(2.4.14)*

Maximum 0.1 per cent, determined on 1.0 g.

ASSAY

Dissolve 0.350 g in 40 mL of *methanol R*. Add 40 mL of *acetone R* and 1 mL of *0.1 M hydrochloric acid*. Carry out a potentiometric titration *(2.2.20)* using *0.1 M sodium hydroxide*. Read the volume added between the 2 points of inflexion.

1 mL of *0.1 M sodium hydroxide* is equivalent to 41.56 mg of $C_{13}H_{18}Br_2ClNO_2$.

IMPURITIES

Specified impurities A, B.

Other detectable impurities (the following substances would, if present at a sufficient level, be detected by one or other of the tests in the monograph. They are limited by the general acceptance criterion for other/unspecified impurities and/or by the general monograph *Substances for pharmaceutical use (2034)*. It is therefore not necessary to identify these impurities for demonstration of compliance. See also *5.10*. *Control of impurities in substances for pharmaceutical use)*: C, D, E.

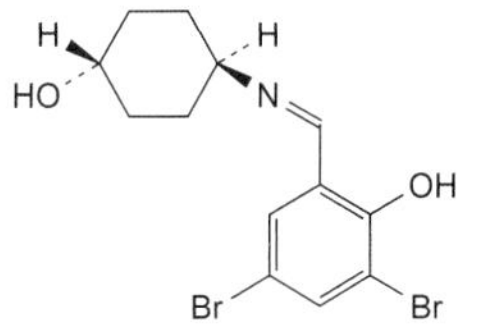

A. *trans*-4-[(3,5-dibromo-2-hydroxybenzylidene)amino]cyclohexanol,

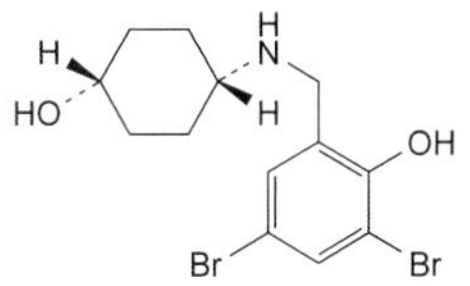

B. *cis*-4-[(3,5-dibromo-2-hydroxybenzyl)amino]cyclohexanol,

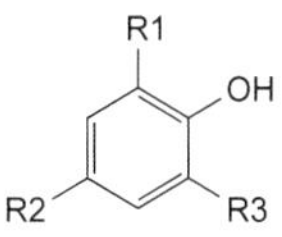

C. R1 = CHO, R2 = R3 = Br: 3,5-dibromo-2-hydroxybenzaldehyde,

D. R1 = CHO, R2 = R3 = H: 2-hydroxybenzaldehyde (salicylaldehyde),

E. R1 = R2 = R3 = Br: 2,4,6-tribromophenol.

_____ *Ph Eur*

Detomidine Hydrochloride

(Detomidine Hydrochloride for Veterinary Use, Ph. Eur. monograph 1414)

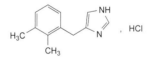

$C_{12}H_{15}ClN_2$ 222.7   *90038-01-0*

Action and use
Alpha$_2$-adrenoceptor agonist.

Ph Eur _____

DEFINITION
4-[(2,3-Dimethylphenyl)methyl]-1*H*-imidazole hydrochloride.

Content
99.0 per cent to 101.0 per cent (anhydrous substance).

CHARACTERS
Appearance
White or almost white, hygroscopic, crystalline powder.

Solubility
Soluble in water, freely soluble in ethanol (96 per cent), very slightly soluble in methylene chloride.

IDENTIFICATION
A. Infrared absorption spectrophotometry (*2.2.24*).

Comparison detomidine hydrochloride CRS.

If the spectra obtained show differences, dry the substance to be examined and the reference substance separately in an oven at 105 °C and record new spectra.

B. It gives reaction (a) of chlorides (*2.3.1*).

TESTS
Appearance of solution
The solution is clear (*2.2.1*) and colourless (*2.2.2, Method II*).

Dissolve 0.25 g in *water R* and dilute to 25 mL with the same solvent.

Related substances
Liquid chromatography (*2.2.29*).

Test solution Dissolve 25 mg of the substance to be examined in 20 mL of the mobile phase and dilute to 50.0 mL with the mobile phase.

Reference solution (a) Dilute 0.20 mL of the test solution to 100.0 mL with the mobile phase.

Reference solution (b) Dissolve 1 mg of *detomidine impurity B CRS* in the mobile phase and dilute to 100.0 mL with the mobile phase. Dilute 1.0 mL of the solution to 10.0 mL with reference solution (a).

Column:
— *size*: l = 0.15 m, Ø = 4.6 mm;
— *stationary phase*: *end-capped octylsilyl silica gel for chromatography R* (5 μm).

Mobile phase acetonitrile R1, 2.64 g/L solution of *ammonium phosphate R* (35:65 *V/V*).

Flow rate 1 mL/min.

Detection Spectrophotometer at 220 nm.

Injection 20 μL.

Run time 4 times the retention time of detomidine.

Identification of impurities Use the chromatogram obtained with reference solution (b) to identify the peak due to impurity B.

Relative retention With reference to detomidine (retention time = about 6 min): impurity B = about 2.1.

System suitability: reference solution (b):
— *resolution*: minimum 5.0 between the peaks due to detomidine and impurity B.

Calculation of percentage contents:
— for each impurity, use the concentration of detomidine in reference solution (a).

Limits:
— *unspecified impurities*: for each impurity, maximum 0.20 per cent;
— *total*: maximum 0.5 per cent;
— *reporting threshold*: 0.10 per cent.

Water (*2.5.12*)
Maximum 2.0 per cent, determined on 0.250 g.

Sulfated ash (*2.4.14*)
Maximum 0.1 per cent, determined on 1.0 g.

ASSAY
Dissolve 0.170 g in 50 mL of *ethanol (96 per cent) R*. Add 5.0 mL of *0.01 M hydrochloric acid*. Carry out a potentiometric titration (*2.2.20*), using *0.1 M sodium hydroxide*. Read the volume added between the 2 points of inflexion.

1 mL of *0.1 M sodium hydroxide* is equivalent to 22.27 mg of $C_{12}H_{15}ClN_2$.

STORAGE
In an airtight container.

IMPURITIES
Other detectable impurities (the following substances would, if present at a sufficient level, be detected by one or other of the tests in the monograph. They are limited by the general

acceptance criterion for other/unspecified impurities and/or by the general monograph *Substances for pharmaceutical use (2034)*. It is therefore not necessary to identify these impurities for demonstration of compliance. See also *5.10. Control of impurities in substances for pharmaceutical use)*: A, B, C.

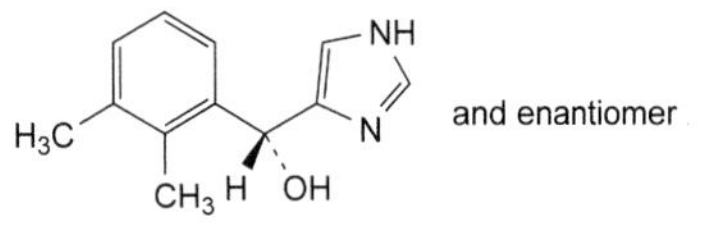

A. (*RS*)-(2,3-dimethylphenyl)(1*H*-imidazol-4-yl)methanol,

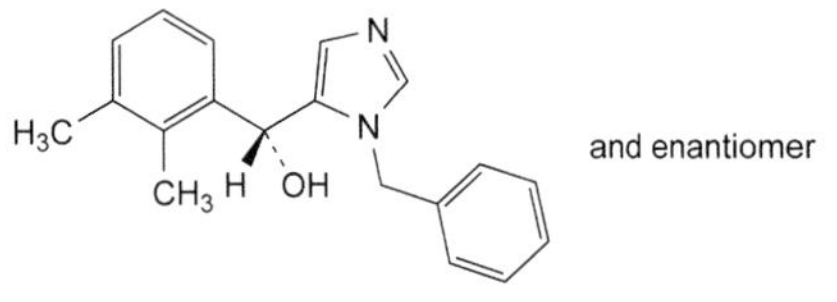

B. (*RS*)-(1-benzyl-1*H*-imidazol-5-yl)(2,3-dimethylphenyl)methanol,

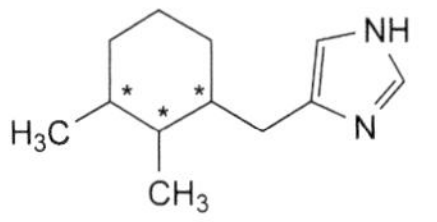

C. 4-[(2,3-dimethylcyclohexyl)methyl]-1*H*-imidazole.

Ph Eur

Diclazuril

(Diclazuril for Veterinary Use, Ph Eur monograph 1718)

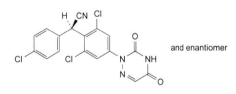

and enantiomer

$C_{17}H_9Cl_3N_4O_2$ 407.6   *101831-37-2*

Action and use

Antiprotozoal (veterinary); coccidiosis.

Ph Eur

DEFINITION

(*RS*)-(4-Chlorophenyl)[2,6-dichloro-4-(3,5-dioxo-4,5-dihydro-1,2,4-triazin-2(3*H*)-yl)phenyl]acetonitrile.

Content

99.0 per cent to 101.0 per cent (dried substance).

CHARACTERS

Appearance

White or light yellow powder.

Solubility

Practically insoluble in water, sparingly soluble in dimethylformamide, practically insoluble in alcohol and methylene chloride.

IDENTIFICATION

Infrared absorption spectrophotometry (*2.2.24*).

Comparison Ph. Eur. reference spectrum of diclazuril.

TESTS
Related substances

Liquid chromatography (*2.2.29*).

Test solution Dissolve 20.0 mg of the substance to be examined in *dimethylformamide R* and dilute to 20.0 mL with the same solvent.

Reference solution (a) Dissolve 5 mg of *diclazuril for system suitability CRS* in *dimethylformamide R* and dilute to 5.0 mL with the same solvent.

Reference solution (b) Dilute 1.0 mL of the test solution to 100.0 mL with *dimethylformamide R*. Dilute 5.0 mL of the solution to 20.0 mL with *dimethylformamide R*.

Column:
— *size*: *l* = 0.10 m, Ø = 4.6 mm,
— *stationary phase*: base-deactivated octadecylsilyl silica gel for chromatography *R* (3 μm),
— *temperature*: 35 °C.

Mobile phase:
— *mobile phase A*: mix 10 volumes of a 6.3 g/L solution of *ammonium formate R* adjusted to pH 4.0 with *anhydrous formic acid R*, 15 volumes of *acetonitrile R* and 75 volumes of *water R*,
— *mobile phase B*: mix 10 volumes of a 6.3 g/L solution of *ammonium formate R* adjusted to pH 4.0 with *anhydrous formic acid R*, 85 volumes of *acetonitrile R* and 5 volumes of *water R*,

Time (min)	Mobile phase A (per cent *V/V*)	Mobile phase B (per cent *V/V*)
0 - 20	100 → 0	0 → 100
20 - 25	0	100

Flow rate 1.0 mL/min.

Detection Spectrophotometer at 230 nm.

Injection 5 μL.

System suitability: reference solution (a):
— *peak-to-valley ratio*: minimum of 1.5, where H_p = height above the baseline of the peak due to impurity D and H_v = height above the baseline of the lowest point of the curve separating this peak from the peak due to diclazuril.

Limits:
— *correction factors*: for the calculation of contents, multiply the peak areas of the following impurities by the corresponding correction factor: impurity D = 1.9; impurity H = 1.4,
— *impurity D*: not more than 0.4 times the area of the principal peak in the chromatogram obtained with reference solution (b) (0.1 per cent),
— *any other impurity*: not more than the area of the principal peak in the chromatogram obtained with reference solution (b) (0.25 per cent),
— *total*: not more than 4 times the area of the principal peak in the chromatogram obtained with reference solution (b) (1.0 per cent),
— *disregard limit*: 0.2 times the area of the principal peak in the chromatogram obtained with reference solution (b) (0.05 per cent).

Loss on drying (*2.2.32*)

Maximum 0.5 per cent, determined on 1.000 g by drying in an oven at 105 °C for 4 h.

Sulfated ash (*2.4.14*)

Maximum 0.1 per cent, determined on 1.0 g.

ASSAY

Dissolve 0.150 g in 75 mL of *dimethylformamide R*. Carry out a potentiometric titration (*2.2.20*), using *0.1 M tetrabutylammonium hydroxide*. Read the volume added at the second inflexion point. Carry out a blank titration.

1 mL of *0.1 M tetrabutylammonium hydroxide* is equivalent to 20.38 mg of $C_{17}H_9Cl_3N_4O_2$.

STORAGE

Protected from light.

IMPURITIES

Specified impurities: A, B, C, D, E, F, G, H, I.

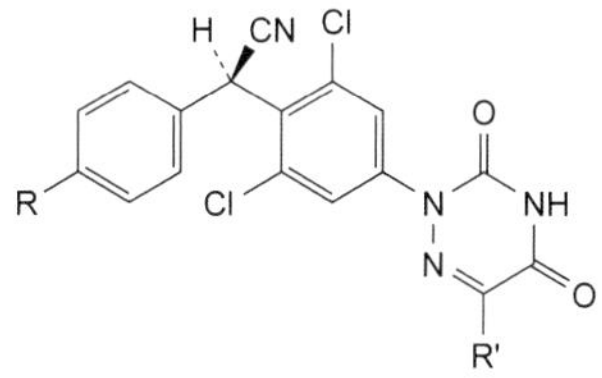

A. R = Cl, R' = CO_2H: 2-[3,5-dichloro-4-[(*RS*)-(4-chlorophenyl)cyanomethyl]phenyl]-3,5-dioxo-2,3,4,5-tetrahydro-1,2,4-triazine-6-carboxylic acid,

B. R = OH, R' = H: (*RS*)-[2,6-dichloro-4-(3,5-dioxo-4,5-dihydro-1,2,4-triazin-2(3*H*)-yl)phenyl](4-hydroxyphenyl)acetonitrile,

C. R = Cl, R' = $CONH_2$: 2-[3,5-dichloro-4-[(*RS*)-(4-chlorophenyl)cyanomethyl]phenyl]-3,5-dioxo-2,3,4,5-tetrahydro-1,2,4-triazine-6-carboxamide,

G. R = Cl, R' = CO-O-[CH_2]$_3$-CH_3: butyl 2-[3,5-dichloro-4-[(*RS*)-(4-chlorophenyl)cyanomethyl]phenyl]-3,5-dioxo-2,3,4,5-tetrahydro-1,2,4-triazine-6-carboxylate,

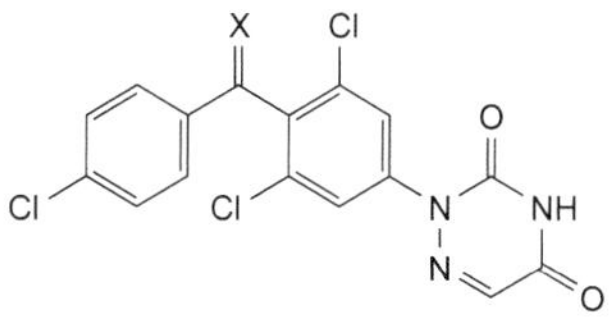

D. X = O: 2-[3,5-dichloro-4-(4-chlorobenzoyl)phenyl]-1,2,4-triazine-3,5(2*H*,4*H*)-dione,

F. X = H_2: 2-[3,5-dichloro-4-(4-chlorobenzyl)phenyl]-1,2,4-triazine-3,5(2*H*,4*H*)-dione,

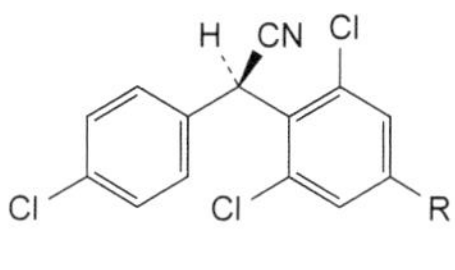

E. R = NH_2: (*RS*)-(4-amino-2,6-dichlorophenyl)(4-chlorophenyl)acetonitrile,

H. R = H: (*RS*)-(4-chlorophenyl)(2,6-dichlorophenyl)acetonitrile,

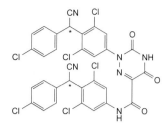

I. N,2-bis[3,5-dichloro-4-[(4-chlorophenyl)cyanomethyl]phenyl]-3,5-dioxo-2,3,4,5-tetrahydro-1,2,4-triazine-6-carboxamide.

Ph Eur

Difloxacin Hydrochloride Trihydrate

(Difloxacin Hydrochloride Trihydrate for Veterinary Use, Ph Eur monograph 2239)

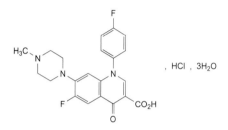

$C_{21}H_{20}ClF_2N_3O_3,3H_2O$ 490.0   *91296-86-5*

Action and use

Fluoroquinolone antibacterial.

Ph Eur

DEFINITION

6-Fluoro-1-(4-fluorophenyl)-7-(4-methylpiperazin1-yl)-4-oxo-1,4-dihydroquinoline-3-carboxylic acid hydrochloride trihydrate.

Content

99.0 per cent to 101.0 per cent (anhydrous substance).

CHARACTERS

Appearance

White or light yellow, crystalline powder.

Solubility

Slightly soluble in water and in methanol, very slightly soluble in methylene chloride.

It shows polymorphism (*5.9*).

IDENTIFICATION

A. Infrared absorption spectrophotometry (*2.2.24*).

Comparison difloxacin hydrochloride CRS.

If the spectra obtained in the solid state show differences, dissolve the substance to be examined and the reference substance separately in *methanol R*, evaporate to dryness and record new spectra using the residues.

B. Suspend 30 mg in 2 mL of *water R*, acidify with *dilute nitric acid R* and filter. The clear filtrate gives reaction (a) of chlorides (*2.3.1*).

C. Water (see Tests).

TESTS
Related substances
Liquid chromatography *(2.2.29)*.

Solvent mixture acetonitrile R, water R (50:50 V/V).

Solution A Dissolve 2.72 g of *potassium dihydrogen phosphate R* in 900 mL of *water R* and adjust to pH 2.5 with *phosphoric acid R*; dilute to 1000 mL with *water R*.

Test solution Dissolve 30.0 mg of the substance to be examined in 50.0 mL of the solvent mixture and dilute to 100.0 mL with mobile phase A.

Reference solution (a) Dissolve 6.0 mg of *difloxacin impurity G CRS* in *acetonitrile R* and dilute to 20.0 mL with the same solvent.

Reference solution (b) Mix 0.5 mL of reference solution (a), 1.0 mL of the test solution and 50 mL of the solvent mixture and dilute to 100.0 mL with mobile phase A.

Reference solution (c) Dissolve 3 mg of *sarafloxacin hydrochloride R* (impurity B) in 100.0 mL of solution A. Dilute 1.0 mL of the solution to 50.0 mL with the test solution.

Column:
— *size*: l = 0.15 m, Ø = 4.6 mm;
— *stationary phase*: end-capped octadecylsilyl silica gel for chromatography R (5 μm).

Mobile phase:
— *mobile phase A*: acetonitrile R, tetrahydrofuran R, solution A (5:5:90 V/V/V);
— *mobile phase B*: acetonitrile R, solution A, tetrahydrofuran R (5:35:60 V/V/V);

Time (min)	Mobile phase A (per cent V/V)	Mobile phase B (per cent V/V)
0 - 15	100	0
15 - 50	100 → 0	0 → 100
50 - 60	0	100

Flow rate 1.0 mL/min.

Detection Spectrophotometer at 325 nm.

Injection 30 μL of the test solution and reference solutions (b) and (c).

Identification of impurities Use the chromatogram obtained with reference solution (c) to identify the peak due to impurity B; use the chromatogram obtained with reference solution (b) to identify the peak due to impurity G.

Relative retention With reference to difloxacin (retention time = about 10 min): impurity B = about 1.2; impurity G = about 4.0.

System suitability: reference solution (c):
— *peak-to-valley ratio*: minimum 2.0, where H_p = height above the baseline of the peak due to impurity B and H_v = height above the baseline of the lowest point of the curve separating this peak from the peak due to difloxacin.

Limits:
— *impurity G*: not more than the area of the corresponding peak in the chromatogram obtained with reference solution (b) (0.5 per cent);
— *unspecified impurities*: for each impurity, not more than 0.2 times the area of the peak due to difloxacin in the chromatogram obtained with reference solution (b) (0.20 per cent);
— *total*: maximum 1.0 per cent;

— *disregard limit*: 0.1 times the area of the peak due to difloxacin in the chromatogram obtained with reference solution (b) (0.10 per cent).

Heavy metals *(2.4.8)*
Maximum 20 ppm.

Solvent mixture Dissolve 30 g of *propylene glycol R* in 30 mL of *methanol R*, add 4 g of *arginine R* and dilute to 100 mL with *water R*.

0.25 g complies with test H. Prepare the reference solution using 0.5 mL of *lead standard solution (10 ppm Pb) R*. The substance precipitates after addition of *buffer solution pH 3.5 R*. Dilute to 20 mL with *methanol R*; the substance re-dissolves completely.

Water *(2.5.12)*
8.0 per cent to 12.0 per cent, determined on 0.100 g, using a mixture of 20 volumes of *formamide R* and 25 volumes of *methanol R* as solvent.

Sulfated ash *(2.4.14)*
Maximum 0.1 per cent, determined on 1.0 g in a platinum crucible.

ASSAY
Dissolve 0.150 g in 5 mL of *anhydrous formic acid R* and add 50 mL of *acetic anhydride R*. Titrate with *0.1 M perchloric acid*, determining the end-point potentiometrically *(2.2.20)*. Read the volume added at the 2nd point of inflexion.

1 mL of *0.1 M perchloric acid* is equivalent to 21.79 mg of $C_{21}H_{20}ClF_2N_3O_3$.

IMPURITIES
Specified impurities G

Other detectable impurities (the following substances would, if present at a sufficient level, be detected by one or other of the tests in the monograph. They are limited by the general acceptance criterion for other/unspecified impurities and/or by the general monograph *Substances for pharmaceutical use (2034)*. It is therefore not necessary to identify these impurities for demonstration of compliance. See also *5.10. Control of impurities in substances for pharmaceutical use)*: A, B, C, D, E, F.

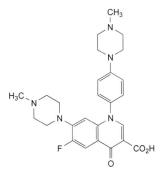

A. 6-fluoro-7-(4-methylpiperazin-1-yl)-1-[4-(4-methylpiperazin-1-yl)phenyl]-4-oxo-1,4-dihydroquinoline-3-carboxylic acid,

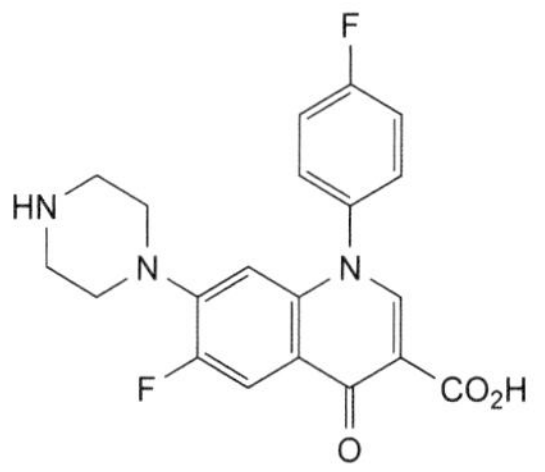

B. 6-fluoro-1-(4-fluorophenyl)-4-oxo-7-piperazin-1-yl-1,4-dihydroquinoline-3-carboxylic acid (sarafloxacin),

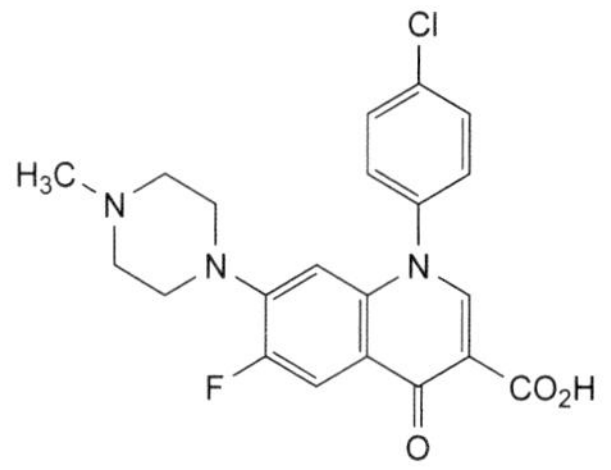

C. 1-(4-chlorophenyl)-6-fluoro-7-(4-methylpiperazin-1-yl)-4-oxo-1,4-dihydroquinoline-3-carboxylic acid,

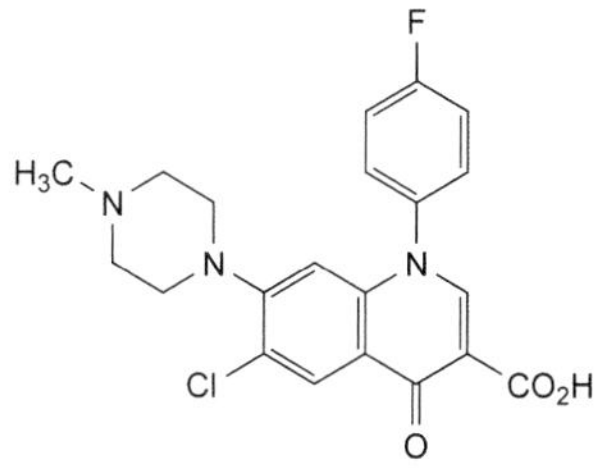

D. 6-chloro-1-(4-fluorophenyl)-7-(4-methylpiperazin-1-yl)-4-oxo-1,4-dihydroquinoline-3-carboxylic acid,

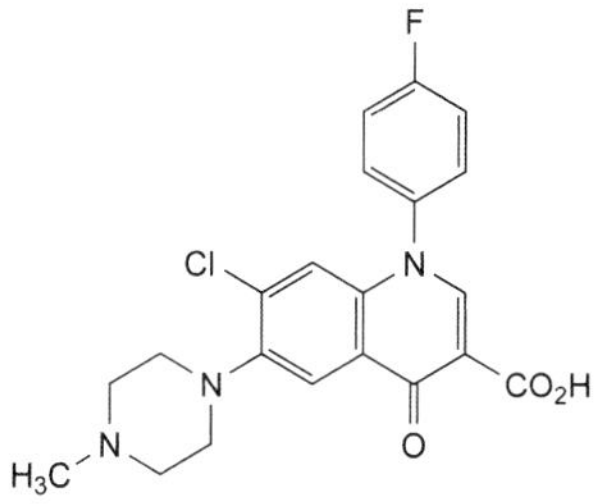

E. 7-chloro-1-(4-fluorophenyl)-6-(4-methylpiperazin-1-yl)-4-oxo-1,4-dihydroquinoline-3-carboxylic acid,

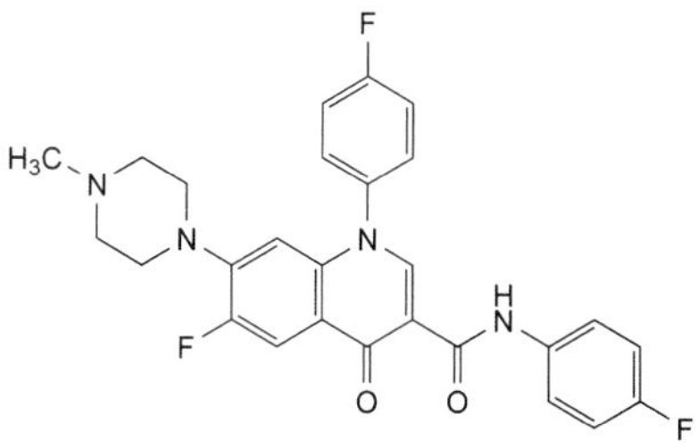

F. 6-fluoro-*N*,1-bis(4-fluorophenyl)-7-(4-methylpiperazin-1-yl)-4-oxo-1,4-dihydroquinoline-3-carboxamide,

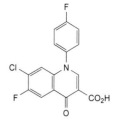

G. 7-chloro-6-fluoro-1-(4-fluorophenyl)-4-oxo-1,4-dihydroquinoline-3-carboxylic acid.

_____ *Ph Eur*

Dihydrostreptomycin Sulfate

Dihydrostreptomycin Sulphate

(Dihydrostreptomycin Sulfate for Veterinary Use, Ph Eur monograph 0485)

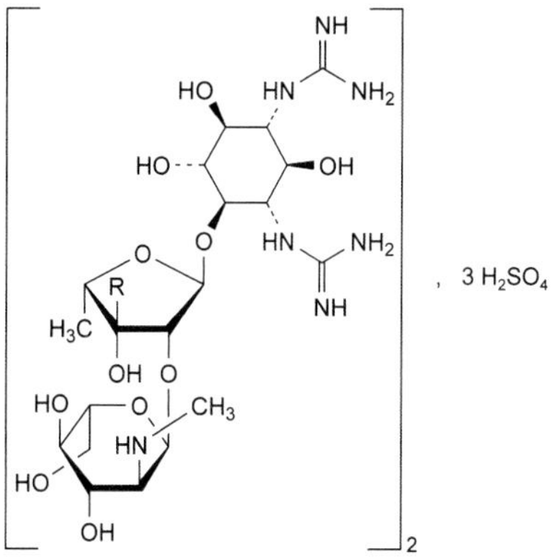

Compound	R	Molec. Formula	M_r
dihydrostreptomycin sulphate	CH_2OH	$C_{42}H_{88}N_{14}O_{36}S_3$	1461
streptomycin sulphate	CHO	$C_{42}H_{84}N_{14}O_{36}S_3$	1457

5490-27-7

Action and use
Aminoglycoside antibacterial.

Ph Eur _____

DEFINITION
Main compound Bis[*N*,*N'''*-[(1*R*,2*R*,3*S*,4*R*,5*R*,6*S*)-4-[[5-deoxy-2-*O*-[2-deoxy-2-(methylamino)-α-L-glucopyranosyl]-3-*C*-(hydroxymethyl)-α-L-lyxofuranosyl]oxy]-2,5,6-trihydroxycyclohexane-1,3-diyl]diguanidine] trisulfate.

Sulfate of a substance obtained by catalytic hydrogenation of streptomycin or by any other means.

Semi-synthetic product derived from a fermentation product.

Stabilisers may be added.

Content
— *sum of the percentage contents of dihydrostreptomycin sulfate and streptomycin sulfate*: 95.0 per cent to 102.0 per cent (dried substance);
— *streptomycin sulfate*: maximum 2.0 per cent (dried substance).

PRODUCTION

The method of manufacture is validated to demonstrate that the product, if tested, would comply with the following test.

Abnormal toxicity (2.6.9)

Inject into each mouse 1 mg dissolved in 0.5 mL of *water for injections R*.

CHARACTERS

Appearance

White or almost white, hygroscopic powder.

Solubility

Freely soluble in water, practically insoluble in acetone, in ethanol (96 per cent) and in methanol.

IDENTIFICATION

First identification A, E

Second identification B, C, D, E

A. Examine the chromatograms obtained in the assay.

Results The principal peak in the chromatogram obtained with the test solution is similar in retention time and size to the principal peak in the chromatogram obtained with reference solution (a).

B. Thin-layer chromatography (2.2.27).

Test solution Dissolve 10 mg of the substance to be examined in *water R* and dilute to 10 mL with the same solvent.

Reference solution (a) Dissolve the contents of a vial of *dihydrostreptomycin sulfate CRS* in 5.0 mL of *water R*.

Reference solution (b) Dilute 1.0 mL of reference solution (a) to 5.0 mL with *water R*.

Reference solution (c) Dissolve 10 mg of *kanamycin monosulfate CRS* and 10 mg of *neomycin sulfate CRS* in *water R*, add 2.0 mL of reference solution (a), mix thoroughly and dilute to 10 mL with *water R*.

Plate TLC silica gel plate R.

Mobile phase 70 g/L solution of *potassium dihydrogen phosphate R.*

Application 10 μL.

Development Over 2/3 of the plate.

Drying In a current of warm air.

Detection Spray with a mixture of equal volumes of a 2 g/L solution of *1,3-dihydroxynaphthalene R* in *ethanol (96 per cent) R* and a 460 g/L solution of *sulfuric acid R*; heat at 150 °C for 5-10 min.

System suitability: reference solution (c):
— the chromatogram shows 3 clearly separated spots.

Results The principal spot in the chromatogram obtained with the test solution is similar in position, colour and size to the principal spot in the chromatogram obtained with reference solution (b).

C. Dissolve 0.1 g in 2 mL of *water R* and add 1 mL of α-*naphthol solution R* and 2 mL of a mixture of equal volumes of *strong sodium hypochlorite solution R* and *water R*. A red colour develops.

D. Dissolve 10 mg in 5 mL of *water R* and add 1 mL of *1 M hydrochloric acid*. Heat in a water-bath for 2 min. Add 2 mL of a 5 g/L solution of α-*naphthol R* in *1 M sodium hydroxide* and heat in a water-bath for 1 min. A violet-pink colour is produced.

E. It gives reaction (a) of sulfates (2.3.1).

TESTS

Solution S

Dissolve 2.5 g in *carbon dioxide-free water R* and dilute to 10 mL with the same solvent.

Appearance of solution

Solution S is not more intensely coloured than intensity 5 of the range of reference solutions of the most appropriate colour (2.2.2, *Method II*). Allow to stand protected from light at about 20 °C for 24 h; solution S is not more opalescent than reference suspension II (2.2.1).

pH (2.2.3)

5.0 to 7.0 for solution S.

Specific optical rotation (2.2.7)

−83.0 to −91.0 (dried substance).

Dissolve 0.200 g in *water R* and dilute to 10.0 mL with the same solvent.

Related substances

Liquid chromatography (2.2.29).

Test solution Dissolve 50.0 mg of the substance to be examined in *water R* and dilute to 10.0 mL with the same solvent.

Reference solution (a) Dissolve the contents of a vial of *dihydrostreptomycin sulfate CRS* (containing impurities A, B and C) in 5.0 mL of *water R*.

Reference solution (b) Dilute 1.0 mL of the test solution to 100.0 mL with *water R*.

Reference solution (c) Dilute 5.0 mL of reference solution (b) to 50.0 mL with *water R*.

Reference solution (d) Dissolve 10 mg of *streptomycin sulfate CRS* in *water R* and dilute to 20 mL with the same solvent. Mix 0.1 mL of this solution with 1.0 mL of reference solution (a).

Reference solution (e) Dilute 1.0 mL of reference solution (a) to 100.0 mL with *water R*.

Column:
— *size*: l = 0.25 m, Ø = 4.6 mm;
— *stationary phase*: octadecylsilyl silica gel for chromatography R (5 μm);
— *temperature*: 45 °C.

Mobile phase Solution in *water R* containing 4.6 g/L of *anhydrous sodium sulfate R*, 1.5 g/L of *sodium octanesulfonate R*, 120 mL/L of *acetonitrile R1* and 50 mL/L of a 27.2 g/L solution of *potassium dihydrogen phosphate R* adjusted to pH 3.0 with a 22.5 g/L solution of *phosphoric acid R*.

Flow rate 1.0 mL/min.

Detection Spectrophotometer at 205 nm.

Injection 20 μL.

Run time 1.5 times the retention time of dihydrostreptomycin.

Identification of impurities Use the chromatogram supplied with *dihydrostreptomycin sulfate CRS* and the chromatogram obtained with reference solution (a) to identify the peaks due to streptomycin and impurities A, B and C.

Relative retention With reference to dihydrostreptomycin (retention time = about 57 min): impurity A = about 0.2; impurity B = about 0.8; streptomycin = about 0.9; impurity C = about 0.95.

System suitability:
— peak-to-valley ratio (a): minimum 1.1, where H_p = height above the baseline of the peak due to streptomycin and H_v = height above the baseline of the lowest point of the curve separating this peak from the peak due to impurity C in the chromatogram obtained with reference solution (d);

— peak-to-valley ratio (b): minimum 5, where H_p = height above the baseline of the peak due to impurity C and H_v = height above the baseline of the lowest point of the curve separating this peak from the peak due to dihydrostreptomycin in the chromatogram obtained with reference solution (d);

— the chromatogram obtained with reference solution (a) is similar to the chromatogram supplied with *dihydrostreptomycin sulfate CRS*.

Limits:

— *correction factor*: for the calculation of content, multiply the peak area of impurity A by 0.5;

— *impurity C*: not more than twice the area of the principal peak in the chromatogram obtained with reference solution (b) (2.0 per cent);

— *impurities A, B*: for each impurity, not more than the area of the principal peak in the chromatogram obtained with reference solution (b) (1.0 per cent);

— *any other impurity*: for each impurity, not more than the area of the principal peak in the chromatogram obtained with reference solution (b) (1.0 per cent);

— *total*: not more than 5 times the area of the principal peak in the chromatogram obtained with reference solution (b) (5.0 per cent);

— *disregard limit*: the area of the principal peak in the chromatogram obtained with reference solution (c) (0.1 per cent); disregard the peak due to streptomycin.

Heavy metals (*2.4.8*)

20 ppm.

1.0 g complies with test C. Prepare the reference solution using 2 mL of *lead standard solution (10 ppm Pb) R*.

Loss on drying (*2.2.32*)

Maximum 5.0 per cent, determined on 1.000 g by drying under high vacuum at 60 °C for 4 h.

Sulfated ash (*2.4.14*)

Maximum 1.0 per cent, determined on 1.0 g.

Bacterial endotoxins (*2.6.14*)

Less than 0.50 IU/mg, if intended for use in the manufacture of parenteral preparations without a further appropriate procedure for removal of bacterial endotoxins.

ASSAY

Liquid chromatography (*2.2.29*) as described in the test for related substances with the following modification.

Injection Test solution and reference solutions (a) and (e).

Calculate the percentage content of streptomycin sulfate using the chromatogram obtained with reference solution (e) and the declared content of *dihydrostreptomycin sulfate CRS*.

Calculate the percentage content of dihydrostreptomycin sulfate using the chromatogram obtained with reference solution (a) and the declared content of *dihydrostreptomycin sulfate CRS*.

STORAGE

In an airtight container, protected from light. If the substance is sterile, store in a sterile, airtight, tamper-proof container.

IMPURITIES

Specified impurities A, B, C

Other detectable impurities (the following substances would, if present at a sufficient level, be detected by one or other of the tests in the monograph. They are limited by the general acceptance criterion for other/unspecified impurities and/or by the general monograph Substances for pharmaceutical use (2034). It is therefore not necessary to identify these impurities for demonstration of compliance. See also *5.10. Control of impurities in substances for pharmaceutical use*): D.

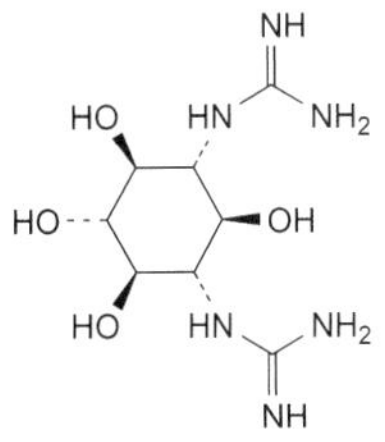

A. N,N'''-[(1R,2s,3S,4R,5r,6S)-2,4,5,6-tetrahydroxycyclohexane-1,3-diyl]diguanidine (streptidine),

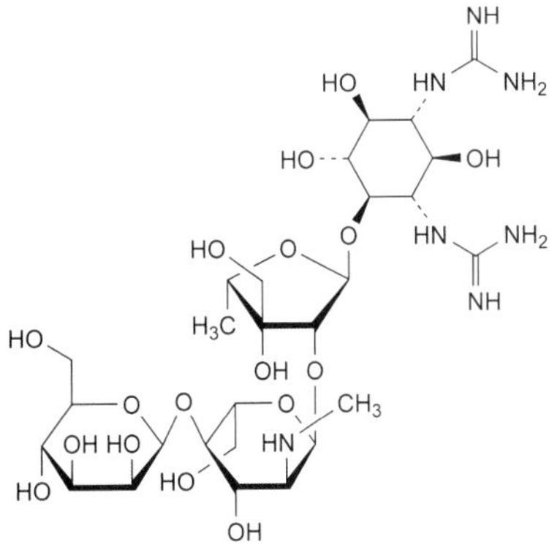

B. N,N'''-[(1S,2R,3R,4S,5R,6R)-2,4,5-trihydroxy-6-[[β-D-mannopyranosyl-(1→4)-2-deoxy-2-(methylamino)-α-L-glucopyranosyl-(1→2)-5-deoxy-3-C-(hydroxymethyl)-α-L-lyxofuranosyl]oxy]cyclohexane-1,3-diyl]diguanidine (dihydrostreptomycin B),

C. unknown structure,

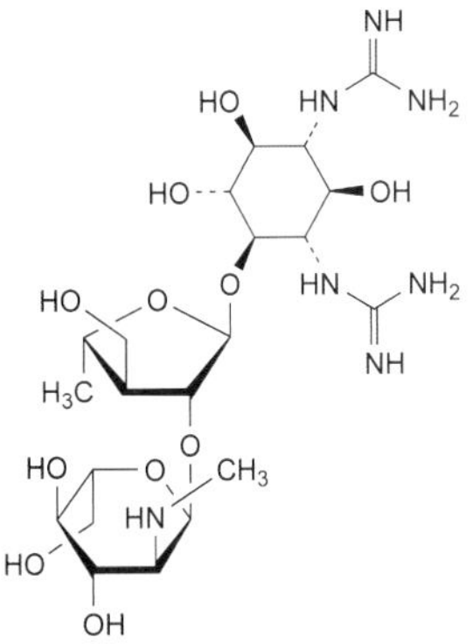

D. N,N'''-[(1R,2R,3S,4R,5R,6S)-4-[[3,5-dideoxy-2-O-[2-deoxy-2-(methylamino)-α-L-glucopyranosyl]-3-(hydroxymethyl)-α-L-arabinofuranosyl]oxy]-2,5,6-trihydroxycyclohexane-1,3-diyl]diguanidine (deoxydihydrostreptomycin).

Ph Eur

Dimpylate

$C_{12}H_{21}N_2O_3PS$ 304.4   *333-41-5*

Time (Minutes)	Temperature	Comment
0 - 1	35°	isothermal
1 - 15.5	35°→180°	linear increase 10°/minute
15.5 - 23.5	180°	isothermal
23.5 - 30.5	180°→250°	linear increase 10°/minute
30.5 – 40.5	250°	isothermal

Action and use
Insecticide.

DEFINITION
Dimpylate is *O,O*-diethyl *O*-(2-isopropyl-6-methylpyrimidin-4-yl)phosphorothioate. It contains not less than 95.0% and not more than 101.0% of $C_{12}H_{21}N_2O_3PS$, calculated with reference to the anhydrous substance.

It may contain suitable stabilisers such as antioxidants.

CHARACTERISTICS
A clear, yellowish brown, slightly viscous liquid.

Practically insoluble in *water*; miscible with *ethanol (96%)*, with *ether* and with most organic solvents.

IDENTIFICATION
A. The *infrared absorption spectrum*, Appendix II A, is concordant with the *reference spectrum* of dimpylate (*RSV 49*).

B. In the Assay, the chromatogram obtained with solution (1) shows a peak with the same retention time as the peak due to dimpylate in the chromatogram obtained with solution (3).

TESTS
Toluene
Not more than 1% v/v when determined by the test for *residual solvents*, Appendix VIII L.

Related substances
Carry out the method for *gas chromatography*, Appendix III B, using the following solutions. Solution (1) contains 0.5% w/v of the substance being examined in *dichloromethane*. Solution (2) contains 0.5% w/v of the substance being examined and 0.025% w/v of *diethyl phthalate* (internal standard) in *dichloromethane*. Solution (3) contains 0.0020% w/v of the substance being examined and 0.025% w/v of *diethyl phthalate* in *dichloromethane*. Solution (4) contains 0.5% w/v of *dimpylate for chromatography BPCRS* and 0.025% w/v of *diethyl phthalate* in *dichloromethane*. Solution (5) contains 0.012% v/v of *toluene* in *dichloromethane*.

The chromatographic procedure may be carried out using (a) a fused silica capillary column (15 m × 0.32 mm) coated with a 1 μm film of dimethyl silicone gum (SE-54 is suitable) fitted with a precolumn (0.2 m × 0.53 mm) coated with a 1 μm film of dimethyl silicone gum, the temperature programme described below with the inlet port at room temperature and the detector at 280° and (b) *hydrogen* as the carrier gas at a flow rate of 40 mL per minute and *nitrogen* as the make up gas with a flow rate of 50 mL per minute.

In the chromatogram obtained with solution (3) the retention time of the internal standard is about 18.5 minutes and of dimpylate, about 23 minutes. The test is not valid unless the chromatogram obtained with solution (4) closely resembles that supplied with *dimpylate for chromatography BPCRS*.

In the chromatogram obtained with solution (2) identify any peaks corresponding to 4-ethoxy-2-isopropyl-6-methylpyrimidine, *O,O,S*-triethyl phosphorothioate, 3-ethyl-2-isopropyl-6-methyl-4-oxo-3,4-dihydropyrimidine, tetraethyl thionopyrophosphate, tetraethyl dithionopyrophosphate and *O,O*-diethyl *O*-(2-isopropyl-6-methylpyrimidin-4-yl)phosphate from the chromatogram supplied with *dimpylate for chromatography BPCRS*. The area of any peak corresponding to 4-ethoxy-2-isopropyl-6-methylpyrimidine or 3-ethyl-2-isopropyl-6-methyl-4-oxo-3,4-dihydropyrimidine is not greater than 2.5 times the area of the peak due to dimpylate in the chromatogram obtained with solution (3) (1% of each), the area of any peak corresponding to *O,O,S*-triethyl phosphorothioate is not greater than 1.25 times the area of the peak due to dimpylate in the chromatogram obtained with solution (3) (0.5%), the area of any peak corresponding to tetraethyl thionopyrophosphate is not greater than 0.02 times the area of the peak due to dimpylate in the chromatogram obtained with solution (3) (0.02%, assuming a response factor of 0.4), the area of any peak corresponding to tetraethyl dithionopyrophosphate is not greater than 0.25 times the area of the peak due to dimpylate in the chromatogram obtained with solution (3) (0.2%, assuming a response factor of 0.5), the area of any peak corresponding to *O,O*-diethyl *O*-(2-isopropyl-6-methylpyrimidin-4yl)phosphate is not greater than 0.75 times the area of the peak due to dimpylate in the chromatogram obtained with solution (3) (0.3%) and the area of any other *secondary peak* is not greater than 0.5 times the area of the peak due to dimpylate in the chromatogram obtained with solution (3) (0.2%). Disregard any peak corresponding to toluene.

Water
Not more than 0.1% w/w, Appendix IX C. Use 2 g.

ASSAY
Carry out the method for *gas chromatography*, Appendix III B, using solutions in *4-methylpentan-2-one* containing (1) 0.2% w/v of the substance being examined, (2) 0.2% w/v of the substance being examined and 0.15% w/v of *diethyl phthalate* (internal standard) and (3) 0.2% w/v of *dimpylate BPCRS* and 0.15% w/v of *diethyl phthalate*.

The chromatographic procedure may be carried out using (a) a fused silica capillary column (15 m × 0.53 mm) coated with a 1.5 μm film of dimethyl silicone gum (SE-54 from J & W Scientific is suitable) at a temperature of 110° increasing linearly at a rate of 6° per minute to 215° with the inlet port at 250° and the detector at 250° and (b) *helium* as the carrier gas at a flow rate of 20 mL per minute with *nitrogen* as the make up gas with a flow rate of 10 mL per minute.

The assay is not valid unless, in the chromatogram obtained with solution (3), the *resolution factor* between the peaks due to dimpylate and the internal standard is at least 2.

Calculate the content of $C_{12}H_{21}N_2O_3PS$ from the chromatograms obtained and using the declared content of $C_{12}H_{21}N_2O_3PS$ in *dimpylate BPCRS*.

IMPURITIES

The impurities limited by the requirements of this monograph include:

A. Diethyl disulfide,

B. *O,O*-Diethyl chlorophosphorothioate,

C. 4-Ethoxy-2-isopropyl-6-methylpyrimidine,

D. *O,O,O*-Triethyl phosphorothioate,

E. *O,O,S*-Triethyl phosphorothioate,

F. 3-Ethyl-2-isopropyl-6-methyl-4-oxo-3,4-dihydropyrimidine,

G. 4-Hydroxy-2-isopropyl-6-methylpyrimidine,

H. Tetraethyl thionopyrophosphate,

I. Tetraethyl dithionopyrophosphate,

J. *O,O*-Diethyl *O*-(2-isopropyl-6-methylpyrimidin-4-yl)phosphate,

K. *O,O*-Diethyl *S*-(2-isopropyl-6-methylpyrimidin-4-yl)phosphorothiophate,

L. *O,S*-Diethyl *O*-(2-isopropyl-6-methylpyrimidin-4-yl)phosphorothiophate,

M. Bis(2-isopropyl-6-methylpyrimidin-4-yl) sulfide,

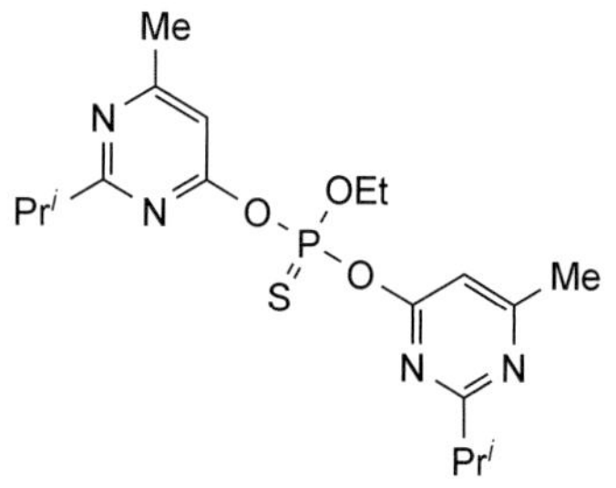

N. *O*-ethyl *O*,*O*-(2-isopropyl-6-methylpyrimidin-4-yl)phosphorothiophate.

Diprenorphine Hydrochloride

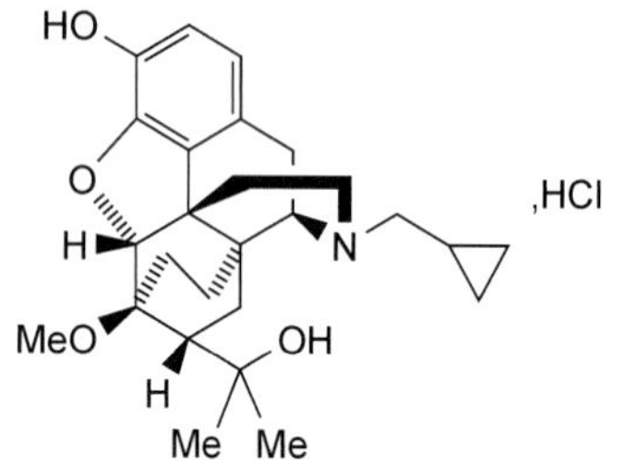

C$_{26}$H$_{35}$NO$_4$,HCl   462.1   *16808-86-9*

Action and use

Opioid receptor antagonist.

Preparation

Diprenorphine Injection

DEFINITION

Diprenorphine Hydrochloride is *N*-cyclopropylmethyl-7,8-dihydro-7α-(1-hydroxy-1-methylethyl)-6-*O*-methyl-6α,14α-ethanonormorphine hydrochloride. It contains not less than 98.5% and not more than 101.0% of C$_{26}$H$_{35}$NO$_4$,HCl, calculated with reference to the dried substance.

CHARACTERISTICS

A white or almost white, crystalline powder.

Sparingly soluble in *water*; slightly soluble in *ethanol (96%)*; very slightly soluble in *chloroform*; practically insoluble in *ether*.

IDENTIFICATION

A. The *infrared absorption spectrum*, Appendix II A, is concordant with the *reference spectrum* of diprenorphine hydrochloride *(RSV 18)*.

B. The *light absorption*, Appendix II B, in the range 230 to 350 nm of a 0.02% w/v solution in 0.1M *hydrochloric acid* exhibits a maximum only at 287 nm. The *absorbance* at the maximum is about 0.70.

C. The *light absorption*, Appendix II B, in the range 230 to 350 nm of a 0.02% w/v solution in 0.1M *sodium hydroxide* exhibits a maximum only at 301 nm. The *absorbance* at the maximum is about 1.1.

D. Yields reaction A characteristic of *chlorides*, Appendix VI.

TESTS

Acidity

pH of a 2.0% w/v solution, 4.5 to 6.0, Appendix V L.

Specific optical rotation

In a solution prepared by dissolving 0.5 g in sufficient *methanol* to produce 25 mL, -97.0 to -107.0, calculated with reference to the dried substance, Appendix V F.

Related substances

Carry out the method for *thin-layer chromatography*, Appendix III A, using *silica gel G* as the coating substance and a mixture of 1 volume of *water*, 5 volumes of *methanol*, 30 volumes of *butan-2-one*, 80 volumes of *acetone* and 100 volumes of *cyclohexane* as the mobile phase. Apply separately to the plate 20 μL of each of two solutions of the substance being examined in *methanol* containing (1) 2.0% w/v and (2) 0.020% w/v. Add at each point of application 10 μL of a mixture of 4 volumes of *methanol* and 1 volume of 13.5M *ammonia*. After removal of the plate, allow it to dry in air and spray with a 1% w/v solution of *iodine* in *methanol*. Any *secondary spot* in the chromatogram obtained with solution (1) is not more intense than the spot in the chromatogram obtained with solution (2) (1%).

Loss on drying

When dried to constant weight at 105°, loses not more than 2.0% of its weight. Use 1 g.

Sulfated ash

Not more than 0.1%, Appendix IX A.

ASSAY

Carry out Method I for *non-aqueous titration*, Appendix VIII A, using 0.5 g, adding 7 mL of *mercury(II) acetate solution* and using *crystal violet solution* as indicator. Each mL of 0.1M *perchloric acid VS* is equivalent to 46.21 mg C$_{26}$H$_{35}$NO$_4$,HCl.

STORAGE

Diprenorphine Hydrochloride should be protected from light.

Enilconazole

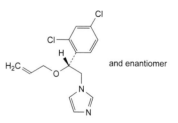

(Enilconazole for Veterinary Use, Ph Eur monograph 1720)

C$_{14}$H$_{14}$Cl$_2$N$_2$O   297.2   *35554-44-0*

Action and use

Antifungal.

Ph Eur _____

DEFINITION

1-[(2*RS*)-2-(2,4-Dichlorophenyl)-2-(prop-2-enyloxy)ethyl]-1*H*-imidazole.

Content

98.5 per cent to 101.5 per cent (dried substance).

CHARACTERS

Appearance

Clear, yellowish, oily liquid or solid mass.

Solubility

Very slightly soluble in water, freely soluble in ethanol (96 per cent), in methanol and in toluene.

IDENTIFICATION

Infrared absorption spectrophotometry (2.2.24).

Comparison enilconazole CRS.

TESTS

Optical rotation (2.2.7)

−0.10° to + 0.10°.

Dissolve 0.1 g in *methanol R* and dilute to 10 mL with the same solvent.

Related substances

Gas chromatography (2.2.28). *Prepare the solutions immediately before use and protect from light.*

Test solution Dissolve 0.100 g of the substance to be examined in *toluene R* and dilute to 100.0 mL with the same solvent.

Reference solution (a) Dissolve 10.0 mg of *enilconazole CRS* and 10.0 mg of *enilconazole impurity E CRS* in *toluene R* and dilute to 100.0 mL with the same solvent.

Reference solution (b) Dilute 5.0 mL of the test solution to 100.0 mL with *toluene R*. Dilute 1.0 mL of this solution to 10.0 mL with *toluene R*.

Column:
— *material*: fused silica;
— *size*: l = 25 m, Ø = 0.32 mm;
— *stationary phase*: chemically bonded *poly(dimethyl)(diphenyl)siloxane R* (film thickness 0.52 µm).

Carrier gas helium for chromatography R.

Flow rate 1.3 mL/min.

Split ratio 1:38.

Temperature:

	Time (min)	Temperature (°C)
Column	0 - 6.4	100 → 260
	6.4 - 14	260
Injection port		250
Detector		300

Detection Flame ionisation.

Injection 2 µL.

Identification of impurities Use the chromatogram obtained with reference solution (a) to identify the peak due to impurity E.

Relative retention With reference to enilconazole (retention time = about 10 min): impurity A = about 0.6; impurity B = about 0.7; impurity C = about 0.8; impurity D = about 0.9; impurity E = about 1.03; impurity F = about 1.1.

System suitability: reference solution (a):
— *resolution*: minimum 2.5 between the peaks due to enilconazole and impurity E.

Limits:
— *impurities A, B, C, D, E, F*: for each impurity, not more than twice the area of the principal peak in the chromatogram obtained with reference solution (b) (1.0 per cent), and not more than 1 such peak has an area greater than the area of the principal peak in the chromatogram obtained with reference solution (b) (0.5 per cent);

— *unspecified impurities*: for each impurity, not more than 0.4 times the area of the principal peak in the chromatogram obtained with reference solution (b) (0.20 per cent);
— *total*: not more than 4 times the area of the principal peak in the chromatogram obtained with reference solution (b) (2.0 per cent);
— *disregard limit*: 0.1 times the area of the principal peak in the chromatogram obtained with reference solution (b) (0.05 per cent).

Loss on drying (2.2.32)

Maximum 0.5 per cent, determined on 1.000 g by drying *in vacuo* at 40 °C for 4 h.

Sulfated ash (2.4.14)

Maximum 0.1 per cent, determined on 1.0 g.

ASSAY

Dissolve 0.230 g in 50 mL of a mixture of 1 volume of *anhydrous acetic acid R* and 7 volumes of *methyl ethyl ketone R*. Titrate with *0.1 M perchloric acid* using 0.2 mL of *naphtholbenzein solution R* as indicator.

1 mL of *0.1 M perchloric acid* is equivalent to 29.72 mg of $C_{14}H_{14}Cl_2N_2O$.

STORAGE

In an airtight container, protected from light.

IMPURITIES

Specified impurities A, B, C, D, E, F

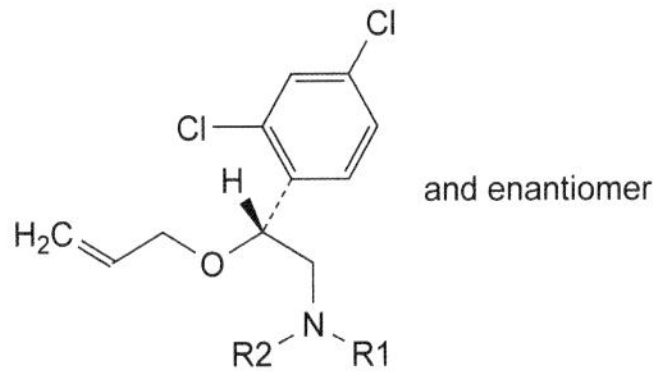

A. R1 = R2 = H: (2RS)-2-(2,4-dichlorophenyl)-2-(prop-2-enyloxy)ethanamine,

B. R1 = H, R2 = CH₂-CH=CH₂: N-[(2RS)-2-(2,4-dichlorophenyl)-2-(prop-2-enyloxy)ethyl]prop-2-en-1-amine,

C. R1 = CHO, R2 = H: N-[(2RS)-2-(2,4-dichlorophenyl)-2-(prop-2-enyloxy)ethyl]formamide,

D. R1 = CHO, R2 = CH₂-CH=CH₂: N-[(2RS)-2-(2,4-dichlorophenyl)-2-(prop-2-enyloxy)ethyl]-N-(prop-2-enyl)formamide,

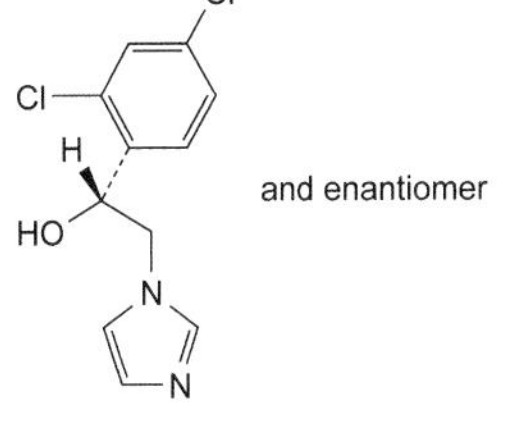

E. (1RS)-1-(2,4-dichlorophenyl)-2-(-1H-imidazol-1-yl)ethanol,

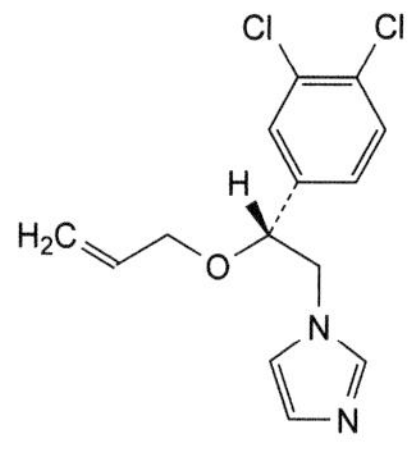

F. 1-[(2RS)-2-(3,4-dichlorophenyl)-2-(prop-2-enyloxy)ethyl]-1H-imidazole.

_____ *Ph Eur*

Enrofloxacin

(Enrofloxacin for Veterinary Use,
Ph Eur monograph 2229)

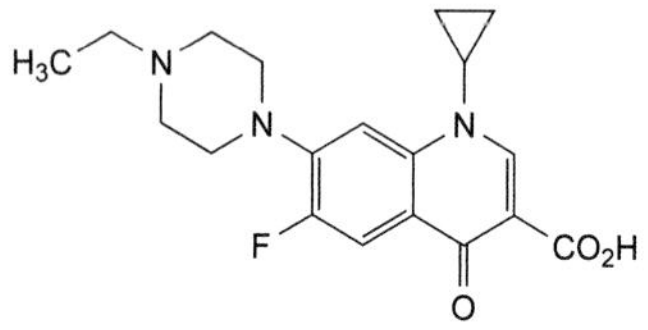

C₁₉H₂₂FN₃O₃   359.4   *93106-60-6*

Action and use
Fluoroquinolone antibacterial (veterinary).

Ph Eur _____

DEFINITION
1-Cyclopropyl-7-(4-ethylpiperazin-1-yl)-6-fluoro-4-oxo-1,4-dihydroquinoline-3-carboxylic acid.

Content
98.5 per cent to 101.5 per cent (dried substance).

CHARACTERS
Appearance
Pale yellowish or light yellow, crystalline powder.

Solubility
Practically insoluble in water, freely soluble in methylene chloride, slightly soluble in methanol.

IDENTIFICATION
Infrared absorption spectrophotometry (2.2.24).

Comparison enrofloxacin CRS.

TEST
Appearance of solution
The solution is not more opalescent than reference suspension II (2.2.1) and not more intensely coloured than reference solution GY₄ (2.2.2, Method II).

To 1.0 g of the substance to be examined add about 0.25 g of *potassium hydroxide R* and 7 mL of *water R*. Sonicate to dissolve and dilute to 10.0 mL with *water R*.

Impurity A
Thin-layer chromatography (2.2.27). *Prepare the solutions immediately before use.*

Solvent mixture methanol R, methylene chloride R (50:50 V/V).

Test solution Dissolve 0.100 g of the substance to be examined in the solvent mixture and dilute to 5.0 mL with the solvent mixture.

Reference solution Dissolve 5.0 mg of *ciprofloxacin impurity A CRS* (enrofloxacin impurity A) in the solvent mixture and dilute to 50.0 mL with the solvent mixture. Dilute 4.0 mL of this solution to 10.0 mL with the solvent mixture.

Plate TLC silica gel F_{254} *plate R* (2-10 μm).

Mobile phase butanol R, water R, anhydrous acetic acid R, ethyl acetate R (15:15:20:50 V/V/V/V).

Application 10 μL.

Development Over 3/4 of the plate.

Drying In air.

Detection Examine in ultraviolet light at 254 nm.

Results:
— *impurity A*: any spot due to impurity A is not more intense than the spot in the chromatogram obtained with the reference solution (0.2 per cent).

Related substances
Liquid chromatography (2.2.29).

Test solution Dissolve 50 mg of the substance to be examined in the mobile phase and dilute to 50.0 mL with the mobile phase.

Reference solution (a) Dissolve 10 mg of *enrofloxacin for system suitability CRS* (containing impurities B and C) and dilute to 10 mL with the mobile phase.

Reference solution (b) Dilute 1.0 mL of the test solution to 50.0 mL with the mobile phase. Dilute 1.0 mL of this solution to 10.0 mL with the mobile phase.

Column:
— *size*: l = 0.15 m, Ø = 4.6 mm;
— *stationary phase*: base-deactivated end-capped octadecylsilyl silica gel for chromatography R (5 μm);
— *temperature*: 40 °C.

Mobile phase Mix 15 volumes of *methanol R* and 85 volumes of a 2.9 g/L solution of *phosphoric acid R*, previously adjusted to pH 2.3 with *triethylamine R*.

Flow rate 1.5 mL/min.

Detection Spectrophotometer at 270 nm.

Injection 10 μL.

Run time 3 times the retention time of enrofloxacin.

Identification of impurities Use the chromatogram supplied with *enrofloxacin for system suitability CRS* and the chromatogram obtained with reference solution (a) to identify the peaks due to impurities B and C.

Relative retention With reference to enrofloxacin (retention time = about 16 min): impurity C = about 0.6; impurity B = about 0.8.

System suitability: reference solution (a):
— *resolution*: minimum 2.0 between the peaks due to impurity B and enrofloxacin.

Limits:
— *impurity B*: not more than 2.5 times the area of the principal peak in the chromatogram obtained with reference solution (b) (0.5 per cent);
— *impurity C*: not more than the area of the principal peak in the chromatogram obtained with reference solution (b) (0.2 per cent);
— *unspecified impurities*: for each impurity, not more than the area of the principal peak in the chromatogram obtained with reference solution (b) (0.20 per cent);
— *total*: not more than 5 times the area of the principal peak in the chromatogram obtained with reference solution (b) (1.0 per cent);

— *disregard limit*: 0.5 times the area of the principal peak in the chromatogram obtained with reference solution (b) (0.1 per cent).

Heavy metals (*2.4.8*)
Maximum 20 ppm.
Dissolve 1.5 g in a mixture of 5 mL of *2 M acetic acid* and 10 mL of *water R*. Filter. 12 mL of the filtrate after adding 2 mL of *water R* (instead of buffer solution) complies with test E. Prepare the reference solution using 12 mL of *lead standard solution (2 ppm Pb) R*.

Loss on drying (*2.2.32*)
Maximum 1.0 per cent, determined on 2.000 g by drying under high vacuum at 120 °C for 6 h.

Sulfated ash (*2.4.14*)
Maximum 0.1 per cent, determined on 1.0 g.

ASSAY
Dissolve 0.250 g in 100 mL of *anhydrous acetic acid R* and titrate with *0.1 M perchloric acid* determining the end-point potentiometrically (*2.2.20*).

1 mL of *0.1 M perchloric acid* is equivalent to 35.94 mg of $C_{19}H_{22}FN_3O_3$.

STORAGE
Protected from light.

IMPURITIES
Specified impurities A, B, C

Other detectable impurities (the following substances would, if present at a sufficient level, be detected by one or other of the tests in the monograph. They are limited by the general acceptance criterion for other/unspecified impurities and/or by the general monograph *Substances for pharmaceutical use (2034)*. It is therefore not necessary to identify these impurities for demonstration of compliance. See also *5.10. Control of impurities in substances for pharmaceutical use*): E, F, G.

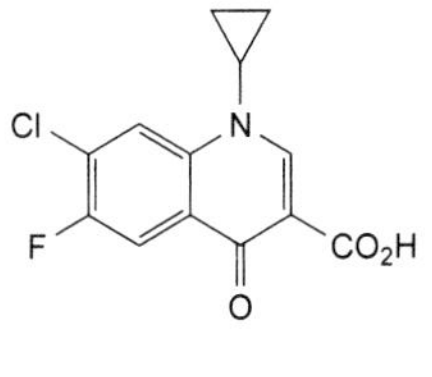

A. 7-chloro-1-cyclopropyl-6-fluoro-4-oxo-1,4-dihydroquinoline-3-carboxylic acid,

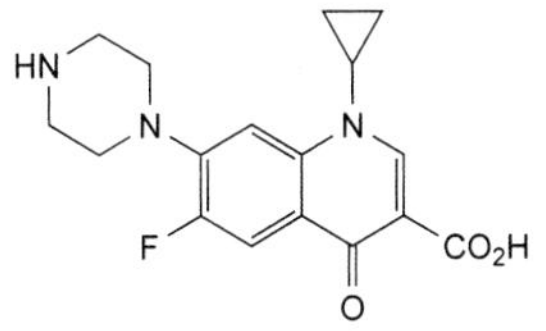

B. ciprofloxacin,

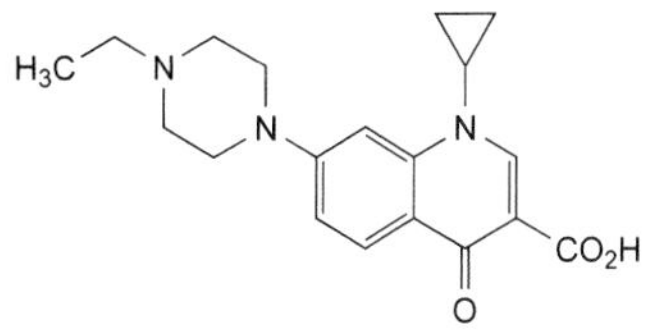

C. 1-cyclopropyl-7-(4-ethylpiperazin-1-yl)-4-oxo-1,4-dihydroquinoline-3-carboxylic acid,

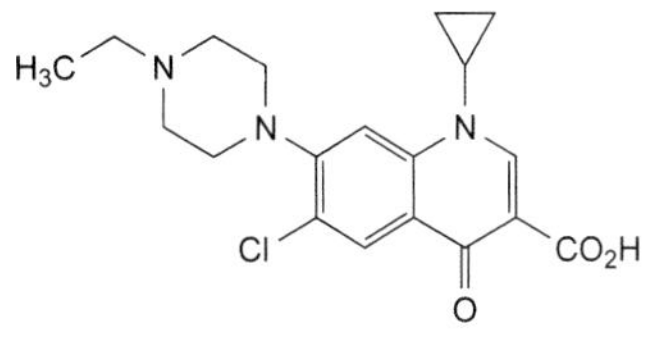

E. 6-chloro-1-cyclopropyl-7-(4-ethylpiperazin-1-yl)-4-oxo-1,4-dihydroquinoline-3-carboxylic acid,

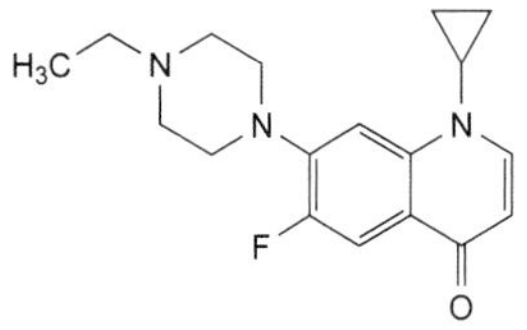

F. 1-cyclopropyl-7-(4-ethylpiperazin-1-yl)-6-fluoroquinolin-4(1*H*)-one,

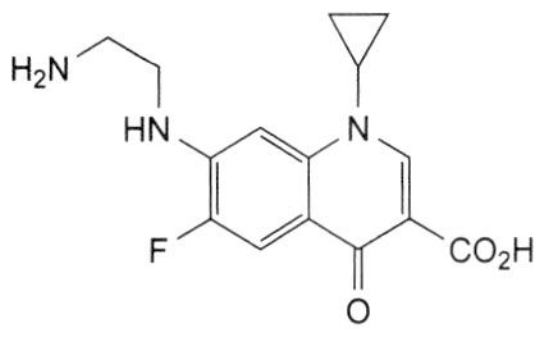

G. 7-[(2-aminoethyl)amino]-1-cyclopropyl-6-fluoro-4-oxo-1,4-dihydroquinoline-3-carboxylic acid.

_____ *Ph Eur*

Etamiphylline Camsilate

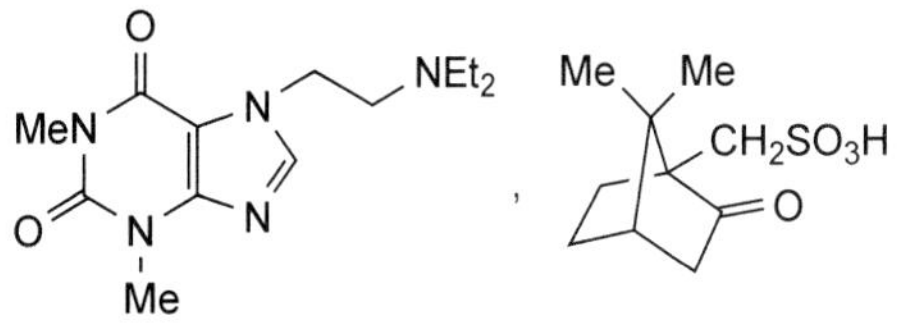

$C_{13}H_{21}N_5O_2,C_{10}H_{16}O_4S$ 511.6   *19326-29-5*

Action and use
Non-selective phosphodiesterase inhibitor (xanthine); treatment of reversible airways obstruction.

Preparations
Etamiphylline Injection
Etamiphylline Tablets

DEFINITION
Etamiphylline Camsilate is 7-(2-diethylaminoethyl)theophylline camphorsulfonate.
It contains not less than 98.0% and not more than 102.0% of $C_{13}H_{21}N_5O_2,C_{10}H_{16}O_4S$, calculated with reference to the

dried substance, when determined by both methods described under the Assay.

CHARACTERISTICS

A white or almost white powder.

Very soluble in *water*; soluble in *chloroform* and in *ethanol (96%)*; very slightly soluble in *ether*.

IDENTIFICATION

A. The *light absorption*, Appendix II B, in the range 230 to 350 nm of a 0.004% w/v solution exhibits a maximum only at 274 nm. The *absorbance* at 274 nm is about 0.70.

B. The *infrared absorption spectrum*, Appendix II A, is concordant with the *reference spectrum* of etamiphylline camsilate *(RSV 51)*.

C. Fuse 0.1 g with a pellet of *sodium hydroxide*, dissolve in *water* and neutralise with *hydrochloric acid*. The resulting solution yields reaction A characteristic of *sulfates*, Appendix VI.

TESTS

Melting point

202° to 206°, Appendix V A.

Acidity

pH of a 10% w/v solution, 3.9 to 5.4, Appendix V L.

Free etamiphylline

Not more than 2.0% w/w when determined by Method I for *non-aqueous titration*, Appendix VIII A, using 2 g dissolved in 75 mL of *acetic anhydride* and determining the end point potentiometrically. Each mL of 0.1M *perchloric acid VS* is equivalent to 27.93 mg of free etamiphylline.

Related substances

Carry out the method for *thin-layer chromatography*, Appendix III A, using *silica gel HF$_{254}$* as the coating substance and a mixture of 80 volumes of *chloroform*, 20 volumes of *ethanol (96%)* and 1 volume of 13.5M *ammonia* as the mobile phase. Apply separately to the plate 10 µL of each of two solutions of the substance being examined in *water* containing (1) 4.0% w/v and (2) 0.0080% w/v. After removal of the plate, allow it to dry in air and examine under *ultraviolet light (254 nm)*. Any *secondary spot* in the chromatogram obtained with solution (1) is not more intense than the spot in the chromatogram obtained with solution (2) (0.2%).

Loss on drying

When dried to constant weight at 105°, loses not more than 0.5% of its weight. Use 1 g.

Sulfated ash

Not more than 0.2%, Appendix IX A.

ASSAY

For camphorsulfonic acid

Dissolve 1 g in 25 mL of *methanol*, previously neutralised with 1M *sodium hydroxide VS*, and titrate with 0.1M *sodium hydroxide VS* using *thymol blue solution* as indicator. Each mL of 0.1M *sodium hydroxide VS* is equivalent to 51.16 mg of $C_{13}H_{21}N_5O_2,C_{10}H_{16}O_4S$.

For etamiphylline

Dissolve 0.15 g in 20 mL of 2M *hydrochloric acid*, add 12 mL of a 5% w/v solution of *silicotungstic acid* and allow to stand for 5 hours. Filter, wash the residue with 2M *hydrochloric acid* until the filtrate yields no precipitate with a 1% w/v solution of *quinine hydrochloride* and dry at 110°. Each g of residue is equivalent to 0.2830 g of $C_{13}H_{21}N_5O_2,C_{10}H_{16}O_4S$.

Ethopabate

$C_{12}H_{15}NO_4$ 237.3   59-06-3

Action and use

Antiprotozoal.

DEFINITION

Ethopabate is methyl 4-acetamido-2-ethoxybenzoate. It contains not less than 96.0% and not more than 101.0% of $C_{12}H_{15}NO_4$, calculated with reference to the dried substance.

CHARACTERISTICS

A white or pinkish white powder. It melts at about 148°.

Very slightly soluble in *water*; soluble in *chloroform* and in *methanol*; sparingly soluble in *ethanol (96%)*; slightly soluble in *ether*.

IDENTIFICATION

A. The *infrared absorption spectrum*, Appendix II A, is concordant with the *reference spectrum* of ethopabate *(RSV 20)*.

B. In the Assay, the retention time of the principal peak in the chromatogram obtained with solution (1) is the same as that of the principal peak in the chromatogram obtained with solution (2).

TESTS

Related substances

Carry out the method for *liquid chromatography*, Appendix III D, using the following solutions in a mixture of equal volumes of *methanol* and *water*. Solution (1) contains 0.040% w/v of the substance being examined. For solution (2) dilute 1 volume of solution (1) to 100 volumes. Solution (3) contains 0.040% w/v of *ethopabate BPCRS* and 0.010% w/v of *methyl 4-acetamido-2-hydroxybenzoate BPCRS*.

The chromatographic procedure may be carried out using (a) a stainless steel column (30 cm × 3.9 mm) packed with particles of silica the surface of which has been modified by chemically-bonded phenyl groups (10 µm) (Waters µBondapak phenyl is suitable), (b) 30 volumes of *acetonitrile*, 150 volumes of *methanol* and 450 volumes of 0.15M *sodium hexanesulfonate*, adjusted to pH 2.5 with *orthophosphoric acid*, as the mobile phase with a flow rate of 1 mL per minute and (c) a detection wavelength of 268 nm. Maintain the temperature of the column at 45°.

The test is not valid unless, in the chromatogram obtained with solution (3), the *resolution factor* between the peaks due to ethopabate and methyl 4-acetamido-2-hydroxybenzoate is at least 1.2.

In the chromatogram obtained with solution (1) the area of any peak eluting before the peak corresponding to methyl 4-acetamido-2-hydroxybenzoate (identified by the peak in the chromatogram obtained with solution (3)) is not greater than 0.1 times the area of the principal peak in the chromatogram obtained with solution (2) (0.1%); the area of any other *secondary peak* is not greater than the area of the principal peak in the chromatogram obtained with solution (2) (1%) and the sum of the areas of all the *secondary peaks* is not greater than twice the area of the principal peak in the chromatogram obtained with solution (2) (2%).

Loss on drying

When dried at 60° at a pressure of 2 kPa for 2 hours, loses not more than 1.0% of its weight. Use 1 g.

Sulfated ash

Not more than 0.1%, Appendix IX A.

ASSAY

Carry out the method for *liquid chromatography*, Appendix III D, using the following solutions in a mixture of equal volumes of *methanol* and *water*. Solution (1) contains 0.002% w/v of the substance being examined. Solution (2) contains 0.002% w/v of *ethopabate BPCRS*. Solution (3) contains 0.002% w/v of *ethopabate BPCRS* and 0.010% w/v of *methyl 4-acetamido-2-hydroxybenzoate BPCRS*.

The chromatographic conditions described under Related substances may be used.

The test is not valid unless, in the chromatogram obtained with solution (3), the *resolution factor* between the peaks due to ethopabate and methyl 4-acetamido-2-hydroxybenzoate is at least 1.2.

Calculate the content of $C_{12}H_{15}NO_4$ in the substance being examined using the declared content of $C_{12}H_{15}NO_4$ in *ethopabate BPCRS*.

IMPURITIES

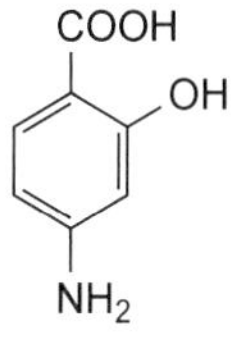

COOH
OH
NH$_2$

A. 4-aminosalicylic acid,

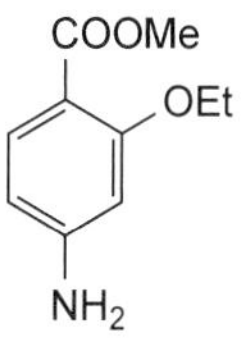

COOMe
OEt
NH$_2$

B. methyl 2-ethoxy-4-aminobenzoate,

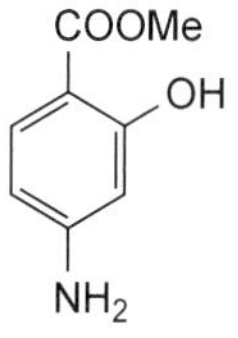

COOMe
OH
NH$_2$

C. methyl 2-hydroxy-4-aminobenzoate,

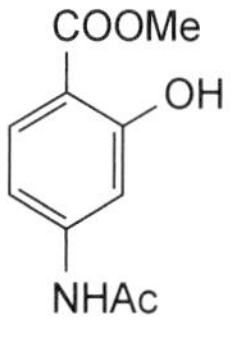

COOMe
OH
NHAc

D. methyl 4-acetamido-2-hydroxybenzoate,

COOEt
OEt
NHAc

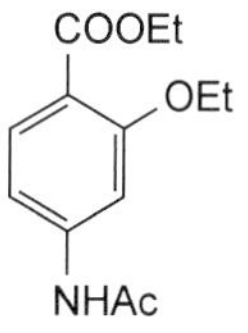

E. ethyl 4-acetamido-2-ethoxybenzoate.

Etorphine Hydrochloride

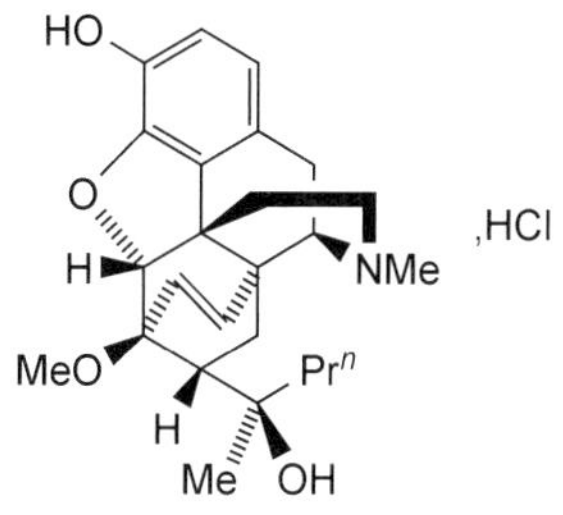

$C_{25}H_{33}NO_4,HCl$ 448.0   *13764-49-3*

Action and use

Opioid receptor agonist; analgesic.

Preparation

Etorphine and Acepromazine Injection

DEFINITION

Etorphine Hydrochloride is (6*R*,7*R*,14*R*)-7,8-dihydro-7-[(1*R*)-1-hydroxy-1-methylbutyl]-6-*O*-methyl-6,14-ethenomorphine hydrochloride. It contains not less than 98.0% and not more than 101.0% of $C_{25}H_{33}NO_4,HCl$, calculated with reference to the dried substance.

CAUTION *Etorphine Hydrochloride is extremely potent and extraordinary care should be taken in any procedure in which it is used. Any spillage on the skin should be washed off at once. In the case of accidental injection or absorption through broken skin or mucous membrane, a reversing agent should be injected immediately.*

CHARACTERISTICS

A white or almost white, microcrystalline powder.

Sparingly soluble in *water* and in *ethanol (96%)*; very slightly soluble in *chloroform*; practically insoluble in *ether*.

IDENTIFICATION

A. The light absorption, Appendix II B, in the range 230 to 350 nm of a 0.02% w/v solution in 0.1M *hydrochloric acid* exhibits a maximum only at 289 nm. The *absorbance* at the maximum is about 0.68.

B. The *light absorption*, Appendix II B, in the range 230 to 350 nm of a 0.02% w/v solution in 0.1M *sodium hydroxide* exhibits a maximum only at 302 nm. The *absorbance* at the maximum is about 1.2.

C. Carry out the method for *thin-layer chromatography*, Appendix III A, in subdued light using *silica gel GF$_{254}$* as the coating substance and a mixture of 10 volumes of *diethylamine*, 20 volumes of *ethyl acetate* and 70 volumes of *toluene* as the mobile phase. Apply separately to each half of the plate 1 µL of each of two solutions in *methanol* containing (1) 2.0% w/v of the substance being examined and (2) 1.8% w/v of *diprenorphine BPCRS*. Add at each point of application 10 µL of a mixture of 4 volumes of *methanol* and

1 volume of 13.5M *ammonia.* After removal of the plate, allow it to dry in air and examine under *ultraviolet light (254 nm).* Spray one half of the plate with a mixture of 5 volumes of *chloroplatinic acid solution,* 35 volumes of *dilute potassium iodide solution* and 60 volumes of *acetone.* Spray the other half of the plate with a mixture of 1 volume of *iron(III) chloride solution R1* and 1 volume of *dilute potassium hexacyanoferrate(III) solution.* The principal spot in the chromatogram obtained with solution (1) has an Rf value of about 1.15 relative to that of the spot in the chromatogram obtained with solution (2), absorbs ultraviolet light and yields a reddish violet colour with the iodoplatinate spray reagent and a blue colour with the iron—hexacyanoferrate spray reagent.

D. Yields reaction A characteristic of *chlorides,* Appendix VI.

TESTS

Acidity
pH of a 2.0% w/v solution, 4.0 to 5.5, Appendix V L.

Specific optical rotation
In a solution prepared by dissolving 0.5 g in sufficient *methanol* to produce 25 mL, -122 to -132, calculated with reference to the dried substance, Appendix V F.

Related substances
Carry out in subdued light the method for *thin-layer chromatography,* Appendix III A, using *silica gel G* as the coating substance and a mixture of 10 volumes of *diethylamine,* 20 volumes of *ethyl acetate* and 70 volumes of *toluene* as the mobile phase. Apply separately to the plate 20 μL of each of two solutions of the substance being examined in *methanol* containing (1) 2.0% w/v and (2) 0.020% w/v. Add at each point of application 10 μL of a mixture of 4 volumes of *methanol* and 1 volume of 13.5M *ammonia.* After removal of the plate, allow it to dry in air and spray with a 1% w/v solution of *iodine* in *methanol.* Any *secondary spot* in the chromatogram obtained with solution (1) is not more intense than the spot in the chromatogram obtained with solution (2) (1%).

Loss on drying
When dried to constant weight at 105°, loses not more than 4.0% of its weight. Use 1 g.

Sulfated ash
Not more than 0.1%, Appendix IX A.

ASSAY
Carry out Method I for *non-aqueous titration,* Appendix VIII A, using 0.5 g, adding 7 mL of *mercury(II) acetate solution* and using *crystal violet solution* as indicator. Each mL of 0.1M *perchloric acid VS* is equivalent to 44.80 mg of $C_{25}H_{33}NO_4,HCl$.

STORAGE
Etorphine Hydrochloride should be protected from light.

Febantel

(Febantel for Veterinary Use, Ph Eur monograph 2176)

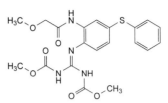

$C_{20}H_{22}N_4O_6S$ 446.5   58306-30-2

Action and use
Antihelminthic.

Ph Eur

DEFINITION
Dimethyl N,N'-[[[2-[(methoxyacetyl)amino]-4-(phenylsulfanyl)phenyl]imino]methylene]dicarbamate.

Content
97.5 per cent to 102.0 per cent (dried substance).

CHARACTERS
Appearance
White or almost white, crystalline powder.

Solubility
Practically insoluble in water, soluble in acetone, slightly soluble in anhydrous ethanol.

It shows polymorphism (*5.9*).

IDENTIFICATION
Infrared absorption spectrophotometry (*2.2.24*).

Comparison febantel CRS.

If the spectra obtained in the solid state show differences, dissolve the substance to be examined and the reference substance separately in *acetone R,* evaporate to dryness and record new spectra using the residues.

TESTS
Related substances
Liquid chromatography (*2.2.29*).

Solvent mixture acetonitrile R, tetrahydrofuran R (50:50 V/V).

Test solution (a) Dissolve 0.100 g of the substance to be examined in the solvent mixture and dilute to 10.0 mL with the solvent mixture.

Test solution (b) Dilute 5.0 mL of test solution (a) to 100.0 mL with the solvent mixture.

Reference solution (a) Dilute 1.0 mL of test solution (a) to 100.0 mL with the solvent mixture. Dilute 1.0 mL of this solution to 10.0 mL with the solvent mixture.

Reference solution (b) Dissolve 50.0 mg of *febantel CRS* in the solvent mixture and dilute to 10.0 mL with the solvent mixture. Dilute 5.0 mL of this solution to 50.0 mL with the solvent mixture.

Reference solution (c) Dissolve 5 mg of *febantel for system suitability CRS* (containing impurities A, B and C) in 1.0 mL of the solvent mixture.

Column:
— *size: l = 0.15 m, Ø = 4.0 mm;*
— *stationary phase: spherical end-capped octadecylsilyl silica gel for chromatography R1 (5 μm).*

Mobile phase Dissolve 6.8 g of *potassium dihydrogen phosphate R* in 1000 mL of *water for chromatography R*. Mix 350 mL of *acetonitrile R* with 650 mL of this solution.

Flow rate 1.0 mL/min.

Detection Spectrophotometer at 280 nm.

Injection 10 μL of test solution (a) and reference solutions (a) and (c).

Run time 1.5 times the retention time of febantel.

Elution order Impurity A, impurity B, impurity C, febantel.

Retention time Febantel = about 32 min.

System suitability: reference solution (c):
— *resolution*: minimum 3.0 between the peaks due to impurities A and B and minimum 4.0 between the peaks due to impurities B and C.

Limits:
— *impurities A, B, C*: for each impurity, not more than the area of the principal peak in the chromatogram obtained with reference solution (a) (0.1 per cent);
— *unspecified impurities*: for each impurity, not more than twice the area of the principal peak in the chromatogram obtained with reference solution (a) (0.20 per cent);
— *total*: not more than 5 times the area of the principal peak in the chromatogram obtained with reference solution (a) (0.5 per cent);
— *disregard limit*: 0.5 times the area of the principal peak in the chromatogram obtained with reference solution (a) (0.05 per cent).

Heavy metals (*2.4.8*)
Maximum 20 ppm.

1.0 g complies with test F. Prepare the reference solution using 2 mL of *lead standard solution (10 ppm Pb) R*.

Loss on drying (*2.2.32*)
Maximum 0.5 per cent, determined on 1.000 g by drying in an oven at 105 °C for 2 h.

Sulfated ash (*2.4.14*)
Maximum 0.1 per cent, determined on 1.0 g.

ASSAY
Liquid chromatography (*2.2.29*) as described in the test for related substances with the following modification.

Injection Test solution (b) and reference solution (b).

Calculate the percentage content of $C_{20}H_{22}N_4O_6S$ from the declared content of *febantel CRS*.

IMPURITIES
Specified impurities A, B, C

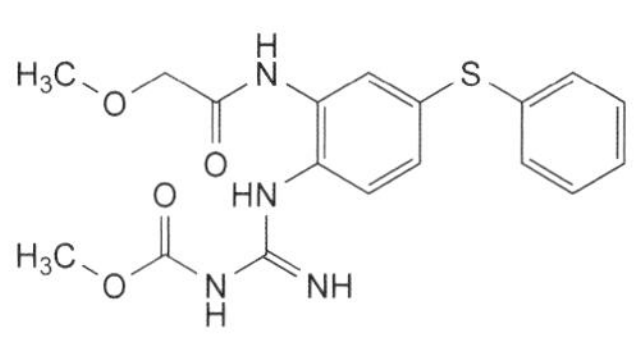

A. methyl [[2-[(methoxyacetyl)amino]-4-(phenylsulfanyl)phenyl]carbamimidoyl]carbamate,

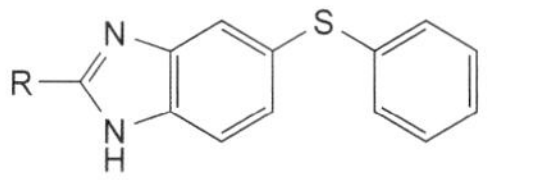

B. R = CH₂-OCH₃: 2-(methoxymethyl)-5-(phenylsulfanyl)-1*H*-benzimidazole,

C. R = NH-CO-OCH₃: methyl [5-(phenylsulfanyl)-1*H*-benzimidazol-2-yl]carbamate (fenbendazole).

_____ *Ph Eur*

Fenbendazole

(Fenbendazole for Veterinary Use, Ph Eur monograph 1208)

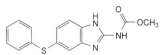

$C_{15}H_{13}N_3O_2S$ 299.4   *43210-67-9*

Action and use
Antihelminthic.

Preparations
Fenbendazole Granules
Fenbendazole Veterinary Oral Paste
Fenbendazole Veterinary Oral Suspension

Ph Eur _____

DEFINITION
Methyl [5-(phenylsulfanyl)-1*H*-benzimidazol-2-yl]carbamate.

Content
98.0 per cent to 101.0 per cent (dried substance).

CHARACTERS
Appearance
White or almost white powder.

Solubility
Practically insoluble in water, sparingly soluble in dimethylformamide, very slightly soluble in methanol.

IDENTIFICATION
Infrared absorption spectrophotometry (*2.2.24*).
Comparison fenbendazole CRS.

TESTS
Related substances
Liquid chromatography (*2.2.29*). *Prepare the solutions immediately before use. Keep the temperature of the autosampler at 10 °C.*

Test solution Dissolve 50.0 mg of the substance to be examined in 10.0 mL of *hydrochloric methanol R*.

Reference solution (a) Dissolve 50.0 mg of *fenbendazole CRS* in 10.0 mL of *hydrochloric methanol R*. Dilute 1.0 mL of the solution to 200.0 mL with *methanol R*. Dilute 5.0 mL of this solution to 10.0 mL with *hydrochloric methanol R*.

Reference solution (b) Dissolve 10.0 mg of *fenbendazole impurity A CRS* in 100.0 mL of *methanol R*. Dilute 1.0 mL of the solution to 10.0 mL with *hydrochloric methanol R*.

Reference solution (c) Dissolve 10.0 mg of *fenbendazole impurity B CRS* in 100.0 mL of *methanol R*. Dilute 1.0 mL of the solution to 10.0 mL with *hydrochloric methanol R*.

Reference solution (d) Dissolve 10.0 mg of *fenbendazole CRS* and 10.0 mg of *mebendazole CRS* in 100.0 mL of *methanol R*. Dilute 1.0 mL of the solution to 10.0 mL with *hydrochloric methanol R*.

Column:
— *size*: *l* = 0.25 m, Ø = 4.6 mm;
— *stationary phase: base-deactivated end-capped octadecylsilyl silica gel for chromatography R* (5 μm).

Mobile phase:
— *mobile phase A: anhydrous acetic acid R, methanol R, water R* (1:30:70 *V/V/V*);
— *mobile phase B: anhydrous acetic acid R, water R, methanol R* (1:30:70 *V/V/V*);

Time (min)	Mobile phase A (per cent *V/V*)	Mobile phase B (per cent *V/V*)
0 - 10	100 → 0	0 → 100
10 - 40	0	100

Flow rate 1.0 mL/min.

Detection Spectrophotometer at 280 nm.

Injection 10 μL.

Identification of impurities Use the chromatogram obtained with reference solution (b) to identify the peak due to impurity A; use the chromatogram obtained with reference solution (c) to identify the peak due to impurity B; use the chromatogram obtained with reference solution (d) to identify the peak due to mebendazole.

Relative retention With reference to fenbendazole (retention time = about 18 min): impurity A = about 0.2; impurity B = about 0.6; mebendazole = about 0.8.

System suitability Reference solution (d):
— *resolution*: minimum 1.5 between the peaks due to mebendazole and fenbendazole.

Limits:
— *impurity A*: not more than 2.5 times the area of the corresponding peak in the chromatogram obtained with reference solution (b) (0.5 per cent);
— *impurity B*: not more than 2.5 times the area of the corresponding peak in the chromatogram obtained with reference solution (c) (0.5 per cent);
— *unspecified impurities*: for each impurity, not more than twice the area of the principal peak in the chromatogram obtained with reference solution (a) (0.5 per cent);
— *total*: maximum 1.0 per cent;
— *disregard limit*: 0.4 times the area of the principal peak in the chromatogram obtained with reference solution (a) (0.10 per cent).

Heavy metals (*2.4.8*)
Maximum 20 ppm.

1.0 g complies with test C. Prepare the reference solution using 2 mL of *lead standard solution (10 ppm Pb) R*.

Loss on drying (*2.2.32*)
Maximum 1.0 per cent, determined on 1.000 g by drying in an oven at 105 °C for 3 h.

Sulfated ash (*2.4.14*)
Maximum 0.3 per cent, determined on 1.0 g.

ASSAY
Dissolve 0.200 g in 30 mL of *anhydrous acetic acid R*, warming gently if necessary. Cool and titrate with *0.1 M perchloric acid*, determining the end-point potentiometrically (*2.2.20*).

1 mL of *0.1 M perchloric acid* is equivalent to 29.94 mg of $C_{15}H_{13}N_3O_2S$.

STORAGE
Protected from light.

IMPURITIES
Specified impurities A, B

A. methyl (1*H*-benzimidazol-2-yl)carbamate,

B. methyl (5-chloro-1*H*-benzimidazol-2-yl)carbamate.

————————————————————————————————— *Ph Eur*

Fluanisone

$C_{21}H_{25}FN_2O_2$ 356.4   *1480-19-9*

Action and use
Dopamine receptor antagonist; neuroleptic.

DEFINITION
Fluanisone is 4′-fluoro-4-[4-(2-methoxyphenyl)piperazin-1-yl]-butyrophenone. It contains not less than 98.0% and not more than 101.0% of $C_{21}H_{25}FN_2O_2$, calculated with reference to the dried substance.

CHARACTERISTICS
White or almost white to buff-coloured crystals or powder; odourless or almost odourless. It exhibits polymorphism.

Practically insoluble in *water*; freely soluble in *chloroform*, in *ethanol (96%)*, in *ether* and in dilute solutions of organic acids.

IDENTIFICATION
A. The *infrared absorption spectrum*, Appendix II A, is concordant with the *reference spectrum* of fluanisone (*RSV 22*). If the spectra are not concordant, dissolve 0.1 g of the substance being examined in 3 ml of *dichloromethane* and evaporate the solvent at room temperature, scratching the side of the container occasionally with a glass rod and prepare a new spectrum of the residue.

B. The *light absorption*, Appendix II B, in the range 230 to 350 nm of a 0.002% w/v solution in a mixture of 9 volumes of *propan-2-ol* and 1 volume of 0.1M *hydrochloric acid* exhibits a well-defined maximum only at 243 nm. The *absorbance* at 243 nm is about 1.1.

C. Heat 0.5 ml of *chromic-sulphuric acid mixture* in a small test tube in a water bath for 5 minutes; the solution wets the side of the tube readily and there is no greasiness. Add 2 to 3 mg of the substance being examined and again heat in a water bath for 5 minutes; the solution does not wet the side of the tube and does not pour easily from the tube.

TESTS
Melting point
72° to 76°, Appendix V A.

Related substances
Carry out the method for *thin-layer chromatography*, Appendix III A, using the following solutions.
(1) 2.0% w/v of the substance being examined.
(2) 0.010% w/v of the substance being examined.
(3) 0.020% w/v of *4′-fluoro-4-chlorobutyrophenone BPCRS*.
(4) 0.010% w/v of *1-(2-methoxyphenyl)piperazine BPCRS*.

CHROMATOGRAPHIC CONDITIONS

(a) Use as the coating silica gel GF_{254} precoated plate (Merck silica gel 60 plates are suitable).

(b) Use the mobile phase as described below.

(c) Apply 10 µl of each solution.

(d) Develop the plate to 15 cm.

(e) After removal of the plate, dry in air and expose to iodine vapour for 15 minutes.

MOBILE PHASE

10 volumes of *ethanol (96%)* and 90 volumes of *chloroform.*

LIMITS

In the chromatogram obtained with solution (1):

any spots corresponding to 4′-fluoro-4-chlorobutyrophenone and 1-(2-methoxyphenyl)piperazine are not more intense than the spots in the chromatograms obtained with solutions (3) and (4) respectively (1% and 0.5%, respectively);

any other *secondary spot* in the chromatogram obtained with solution (1) is not more intense than the spot in the chromatogram obtained with solution (2) (0.5%).

Loss on drying

When dried to constant weight at 40° at a pressure not exceeding 0.7 kPa, loses not more than 0.5% of its weight. Use 1 g.

Sulphated ash

Not more than 0.1%, Appendix IX A.

ASSAY

Carry out Method I for *non-aqueous titration,* Appendix VIII A, using 0.15 g and *crystal violet solution* as indicator. Each ml of 0.1M *perchloric acid VS* is equivalent to 17.82 mg of $C_{21}H_{25}FN_2O_2$.

STORAGE

Fluanisone should be protected from light.

Flunixin Meglumine

(Flunixin Meglumine for Veterinary Use, Ph Eur monograph 1696)

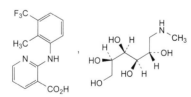

$C_{21}H_{28}F_3N_3O_7$ 491.5   *42461-84-7*

Action and use

Cyclo-oxygenase inhibitor; analgesic; anti-inflammatory.

Ph Eur

DEFINITION

2-[[2-Methyl-3-(trifluoromethyl)phenyl]amino]pyridine-3-carboxylic acid, 1-deoxy-1-(methylamino)-D-glucitol.

Content

99.0 per cent to 101.0 per cent (dried substance).

CHARACTERS

Appearance

White or almost white, crystalline powder.

Solubility

Freely soluble in water and in methanol, practically insoluble in acetone.

IDENTIFICATION

A. Specific optical rotation (*2.2.7*): −12.0 to −9.0 (dried substance), determined on solution S (see Tests).

B. Infrared absorption spectrophotometry (*2.2.24*).

Comparison flunixin meglumine CRS.

TESTS

Solution S

Dissolve 2.50 g in *carbon dioxide-free water R* and dilute to 50.0 mL with the same solvent.

Appearance of solution

Solution S is clear (*2.2.1*) and not more intensely coloured than reference solution Y_7 (*2.2.2, Method II*).

pH (*2.2.3*)

7.0 to 9.0 for solution S.

Related substances

Liquid chromatography (*2.2.29*).

Test solution Dissolve 50.0 mg of the substance to be examined in the mobile phase and dilute to 10.0 mL with the mobile phase.

Reference solution (a) Dissolve 5.0 mg of *flunixin impurity B CRS* in 1.0 mL of the test solution and dilute to 50.0 mL with the mobile phase.

Reference solution (b) Dissolve 5.0 mg of *2-chloronicotinic acid R* (impurity A) in the mobile phase and dilute to 50.0 mL with the mobile phase. To 2.0 mL of this solution add 2.0 mL of reference solution (a) and dilute to 20.0 mL with the mobile phase.

Reference solution (c) Dissolve 50 mg of *flunixin impurity C CRS* in the mobile phase and dilute to 100 mL with the mobile phase.

Column:

— *size:* l = 0.125 m, Ø = 4.0 mm,

— *stationary phase: octadecylsilyl silica gel for chromatography R* (5 µm).

Mobile phase Mix 300 volumes of *water R* and 700 volumes of *acetonitrile R*, and add 0.25 volumes of *phosphoric acid R*.

Flow rate 1.0 mL/min.

Detection Spectrophotometer at 254 nm.

Injection 10 µL.

Run time 5 times the retention time of flunixin.

Relative retention With reference to flunixin (retention time = about 3.1 min): impurity A = about 0.4; impurity C = about 0.6; impurity B = about 0.7; impurity D = about 4.2.

System suitability: reference solution (a):

— *resolution:* minimum 3.5 between the peaks due to impurity B and flunixin.

Limits:

— *correction factor:* for the calculation of content, multiply the peak area of impurity C by 1.9,

— *impurity A:* not more than the area of the corresponding peak in the chromatogram obtained with reference solution (b) (0.2 per cent),

— *impurity B*: not more than the area of the corresponding peak in the chromatogram obtained with reference solution (b) (0.2 per cent),

— *impurities C, D*: for each impurity, not more than the area of the peak due to flunixin in the chromatogram obtained with reference solution (b) (0.2 per cent),

— *any other impurity*: for each impurity, not more than the area of the peak due to flunixin in the chromatogram obtained with reference solution (b) (0.2 per cent),

— *total*: not more than 2.5 times the area of the peak due to flunixin in the chromatogram obtained with reference solution (b) (0.5 per cent),

— *disregard limit*: 0.25 times the area of the peak due to flunixin in the chromatogram obtained with reference solution (b) (0.05 per cent).

Loss on drying (*2.2.32*)
Maximum 0.5 per cent, determined on 1.000 g by drying in an oven at 105 °C for 4 h.

Sulfated ash (*2.4.14*)
Maximum 0.1 per cent, determined on 1.0 g.

ASSAY
Dissolve 0.175 g in 50 mL of *anhydrous acetic acid R*. Titrate with *0.1 M perchloric acid*, determining the end-point potentiometrically (*2.2.20*).

1 mL of *0.1 M perchloric acid* is equivalent to 24.57 mg of $C_{21}H_{28}F_3N_3O_7$.

IMPURITIES
Specified impurities: A, B, C, D.

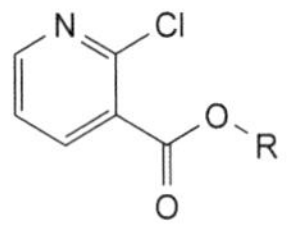

A. R = H: 2-chloropyridine-3-carboxylic acid,
C. R = C_2H_5: ethyl 2-chloropyridine-3-carboxylate,

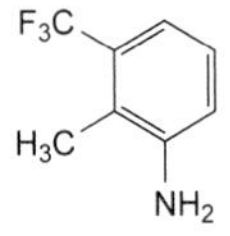

B. 2-methyl-3-(trifluoromethyl)aniline,

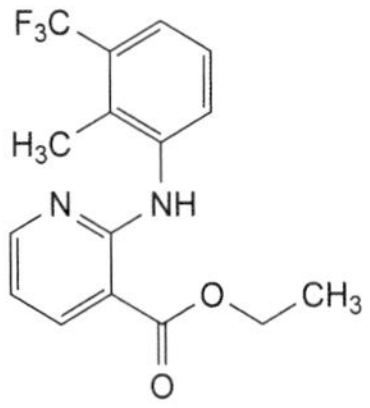

D. ethyl 2-[[2-methyl-3-(trifluoromethyl)phenyl]amino]pyridine-3-carboxylate.

_____ *Ph Eur*

Serum Gonadotrophin

(Equine Serum Gonadotrophin for Veterinary Use, Ph Eur monograph 0719)

Action and use
Equine serum gonadotrophin.

Preparation
Serum Gonadotrophin Injection

Ph Eur _____

DEFINITION
Equine serum gonadotrophin for veterinary use is a dry preparation of a glycoprotein fraction obtained from the serum or plasma of pregnant mares. It has follicle-stimulating and luteinising activities. The potency is not less than 1000 IU of gonadotrophin activity per milligram, calculated with reference to the anhydrous substance.

PRODUCTION
Equine serum gonadotrophin may be prepared by precipitation with alcohol (70 per cent *V/V*) and further purification by a suitable form of chromatography. It is prepared in conditions designed to minimise microbial contamination.

CHARACTERS
Appearance
White or pale grey, amorphous powder.

Solubility
Soluble in water.

IDENTIFICATION
When administered as prescribed in the assay it causes an increase in the mass of the ovaries of immature female rats.

TESTS
Water (*2.5.12*)
Maximum 10.0 per cent, determined on 80 mg.

Bacterial endotoxins (*2.6.14, method C*)
Less than 0.035 IU per IU of equine serum gonadotrophin, if intended for use in the manufacture of parenteral preparations without a further appropriate procedure for the removal of bacterial endotoxins.

ASSAY
The potency of equine serum gonadotrophin is estimated by comparing under given conditions its effect of increasing the mass of the ovaries of immature female rats with the same effect of the International Standard of equine serum gonadotrophin or of a reference preparation calibrated in International Units.

The International Unit is the activity contained in a stated amount of the International Standard, which consists of a mixture of a freeze-dried extract of equine serum gonadotrophin from the serum of pregnant mares with lactose. The equivalence in International Units of the International Standard is stated by the World Health Organization.

Use immature female rats of the same strain, 21 to 28 days old, differing in age by not more than 3 days and having masses such that the difference between the heaviest and the lightest rat is not more than 10 g. Assign the rats at random to 6 equal groups of not fewer than 5 animals. If sets of 6 litter mates are available, assign one litter mate from each set to each group and mark according to litter.

Choose 3 doses of the reference preparation and 3 doses of the preparation to be examined such that the smallest dose is sufficient to produce a positive response in some of the rats and the largest dose does not produce a maximal response in all the rats. Use doses in geometric progression: as an initial approximation total doses of 8 IU, 12 IU and 18 IU may be tried, although the dose will depend on the sensitivity of the animals used and may vary widely.

Dissolve separately the total quantities of the preparation to be examined and of the reference preparation corresponding to the doses to be used in sufficient of a sterile 9 g/L solution of *sodium chloride R* containing 1 mg/mL of *bovine albumin R* such that each single dose is administered in a volume of about 0.2 mL. Store the solutions at $5 \pm 3\ ^{\circ}C$.

Inject subcutaneously into each rat the dose allocated to its group. Repeat the injections 18 h, 21 h, 24 h, 42 h and 48 h after the first injection. Not less than 40 h and not more than 72 h after the last injection, euthanise the rats and remove the ovaries. Remove any extraneous fluid and tissue and weigh the 2 ovaries immediately. Calculate the results by the usual statistical methods, using the combined mass of the 2 ovaries of each animal as the response.

The estimated potency is not less than 80 per cent and not more than 125 per cent of the stated potency.

The confidence limits ($P = 0.95$) of the estimated potency are not less than 64 per cent and not more than 156 per cent of the stated potency.

STORAGE

In an airtight container, protected from light, at a temperature not exceeding 8 °C. If the substance is sterile, store in a sterile, airtight, tamper-proof container.

LABELLING

The label states the potency in International Units per milligram.

_____ *Ph Eur*

Levamisole

(*Levamisole for Veterinary Use, Ph. Eur. monograph 1728*)

C₁₁H₁₂N₂S   204.3   *14769-73-4*

Action and use

Immunostimulant; antihelminthic.

Ph Eur _____

DEFINITION

(6*S*)-6-Phenyl-2,3,5,6-tetrahydroimidazo[2,1-*b*]thiazole.

Content

98.5 per cent to 101.5 per cent (anhydrous substance).

CHARACTERS

Appearance

White or almost white powder.

Solubility

Slightly soluble in water, freely soluble in ethanol (96 per cent) and in methanol.

It shows polymorphism (*5.9*).

IDENTIFICATION

A. Specific optical rotation (see Tests).

B. Infrared absorption spectrophotometry (*2.2.24*).

Comparison Ph. Eur. reference spectrum of levamisole.

If the spectra show differences, dissolve the substance to be examined in *methylene chloride R*, evaporate to dryness and record a new spectrum using the residue.

TESTS

Solution S

Dissolve 2.50 g in *ethanol R* and dilute to 50.0 mL with the same solvent.

Appearance of solution

Solution S is clear (*2.2.1*) and not more intensely coloured than reference solution BY₆ (*2.2.2, Method II*).

Specific optical rotation (*2.2.7*)

−89 to −85 (anhydrous substance), determined on solution S.

Related substances

Liquid chromatography (*2.2.29*). *Prepare the solutions immediately before use, protect from light and keep below 25 °C.*

Test solution Dissolve 0.100 g of the substance to be examined in *methanol R* and dilute to 10.0 mL with the same solvent.

Reference solution (a) Dissolve 10 mg of *levamisole hydrochloride for system suitability CRS* (containing impurities A, B, C, D and E) in *methanol R*, add 0.1 mL of *concentrated ammonia R* and dilute to 1.0 mL with *methanol R.*

Reference solution (b) Dilute 1.0 mL of the test solution to 100.0 mL with *methanol R*. Dilute 5.0 mL of the solution to 25.0 mL with *methanol R.*

Column:
— *size*: $l = 0.10$ m, $\varnothing = 4.6$ mm,
— *stationary phase: base-deactivated octadecylsilyl silica gel for chromatography R* (3 μm).

Mobile phase:
— *mobile phase A*: dissolve 0.5 g of *ammonium dihydrogen phosphate R* in 90 mL of *water R*; adjust to pH 6.5 with a 40 g/L solution of *sodium hydroxide R* and dilute to 100 mL with *water R,*
— *mobile phase B*: *acetonitrile R.*

Time (min)	Mobile phase A (per cent *V/V*)	Mobile phase B (per cent *V/V*)
0 - 8	90 → 30	10 → 70
8 - 10	30	70

Flow rate 1.5 mL/min.

Detection Spectrophotometer at 215 nm.

Injection 10 μL.

Identification of impurities Use the chromatogram supplied with *levamisole hydrochloride for system suitability CRS* and the chromatogram obtained with reference solution (a) to identify the peaks due to impurities A, B, C, D and E.

Relative retention With reference to levamisole (retention time = about 3 min): impurity A = about 0.9; impurity B = about 1.4; impurity C = about 1.5; impurity D = about 1.6; impurity E = about 2.0.

System suitability: reference solution (a):
— the chromatogram obtained is similar to the chromatogram supplied with *levamisole hydrochloride for system suitability CRS.*

Limits:

— *correction factors*: for the calculation of content, multiply the peak areas of the following impurities by the corresponding correction factor: impurity A = 2.0; impurity B = 1.7; impurity C = 2.9; impurity D = 1.3; impurity E = 2.7;

— *impurities A, B, C, D, E*: for each impurity, not more than the area of the principal peak in the chromatogram obtained with reference solution (b) (0.2 per cent);

— *any other impurity*: not more than half the area of the principal peak in the chromatogram obtained with reference solution (b) (0.1 per cent);

— *total*: not more than 1.5 times the area of the principal peak in the chromatogram obtained with reference solution (b) (0.3 per cent);

— *disregard limit*: 0.25 times the area of the principal peak in the chromatogram obtained with reference solution (b) (0.05 per cent).

Water (*2.5.12*)

Maximum 0.5 per cent, determined on 1.00 g.

Sulfated ash (*2.4.14*)

Maximum 0.1 per cent, determined on 1.0 g.

ASSAY

Dissolve 0.150 g in 50 mL of a mixture of 1 volume of *anhydrous acetic acid R* and 7 volumes of *methyl ethyl ketone R*. Titrate with *0.1 M perchloric acid*, using 0.2 mL of *naphtholbenzein solution R* as indicator.

1 mL of *0.1 M perchloric acid* is equivalent to 20.43 mg of $C_{11}H_{12}N_2S$.

STORAGE

In an airtight container, protected from light.

IMPURITIES

Specified impurities A, B, C, D, E

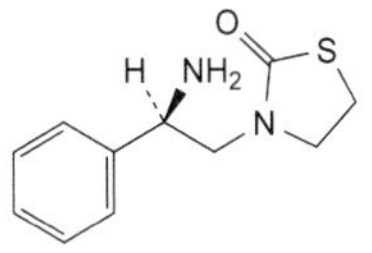

A. 3-[(2*RS*)-2-amino-2-phenylethyl]thiazolidin-2-one,

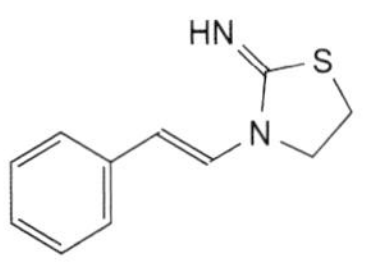

B. 3-[(*E*)-2-phenylethenyl]thiazolidin-2-imine,

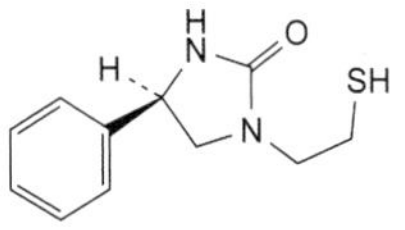

C. (4*RS*)-4-phenyl-1-(2-sulfanylethyl)imidazolidin-2-one,

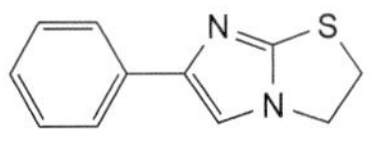

D. 6-phenyl-2,3-dihydroimidazo[2,1-*b*]thiazole,

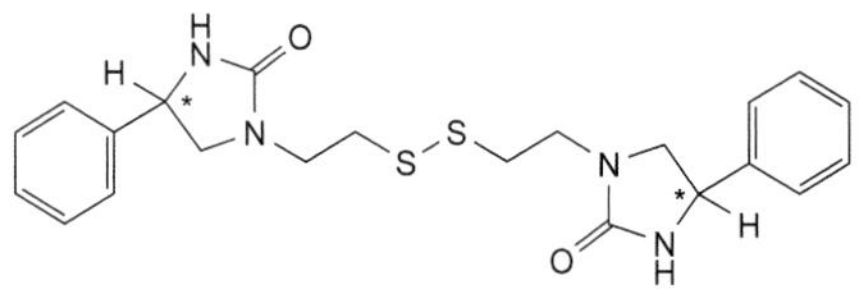

E. 1,1′-[(disulfane-1,2-diyl)bis(ethylene)]bis[(4*RS*)-4-phenylimidazolidin-2-one].

Ph Eur

Lufenuron

Anhydrous Lufenuron

(Lufenuron for Veterinary Use, Ph. Eur. monograph 2177)

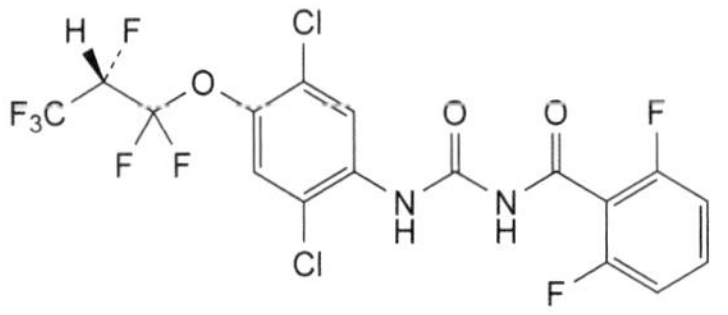

$C_{17}H_8Cl_2F_8N_2O_3$ 511.2   *103055-07-8*

Action and use

Ectoparasiticide.

Ph Eur

DEFINITION

1-[2,5-Dichloro-4-[(2*RS*)-1,1,2,3,3,3-hexafluoropropoxy]phenyl]-3-(2,6-difluorobenzoyl)urea.

Content

98.0 per cent to 102.0 per cent (dried substance).

CHARACTERS

Appearance

White or pale yellow powder.

Solubility

Practically insoluble in water, freely soluble in acetonitrile, soluble in anhydrous ethanol.

It shows polymorphism (*5.9*).

mp: about 172 °C.

IDENTIFICATION

Infrared absorption spectrophotometry (*2.2.24*).

Comparison lufenuron CRS.

If the spectra obtained in the solid state show differences, dissolve the substance to be examined and the reference substance separately in *2-propanol R*, evaporate to dryness and record new spectra using the residues.

TESTS

Related substances

Liquid chromatography (*2.2.29*).

Solvent mixture water R, acetonitrile R (30:70 V/V).

Test solution (a) Dissolve 40.0 mg of the substance to be examined in the solvent mixture by sonicating for about 10 min and dilute to 100.0 mL with the solvent mixture.

Test solution (b) Dilute 1.0 mL of test solution (a) to 10.0 mL with the solvent mixture.

Reference solution (a) Dilute 1.0 mL of test solution (b) to 100.0 mL with the solvent mixture.

Reference solution (b) Dissolve 7 mg of *lufenuron impurity G CRS* in test solution (a) and dilute to 50.0 mL with test solution (a).

Reference solution (c) Dissolve the contents of a vial of *lufenuron for peak identification CRS* (containing impurities B and C) in 1.0 mL of the solvent mixture.

Reference solution (d) Dissolve 40.0 mg of *lufenuron CRS* in the solvent mixture by sonicating for about 10 min and dilute to 100.0 mL with the solvent mixture. Dilute 1.0 mL of the solution to 10.0 mL with the solvent mixture.

Column:
— *size*: *l* = 0.25 m, Ø = 4.0 mm;
— *stationary phase*: *end-capped octadecylsilyl silica gel for chromatography R* (5 µm).

Mobile phase:
— *mobile phase A*: 0.01 per cent *V/V* of *phosphoric acid R*;
— *mobile phase B*: *acetonitrile R*;

Time (min)	Mobile phase A (per cent *V/V*)	Mobile phase B (per cent *V/V*)
0 - 5	30	70
5 - 15	30 → 10	70 → 90
15 - 17	10	90

Flow rate 1.0 mL/min.

Detection Spectrophotometer at 255 nm.

Injection 20 µL of test solution (a) and reference solutions (a), (b) and (c).

Identification of impurities Use the chromatogram supplied with *lufenuron for peak identification CRS* and the chromatogram obtained with reference solution (c) to identify the peaks due to impurities B and C.

Relative retention With reference to lufenuron (retention time = about 9 min): impurity B = about 0.3; impurity C = about 0.7; impurity G = about 0.9.

System suitability: reference solution (b):
— *resolution*: minimum 3.0 between the peaks due to impurity G and lufenuron.

Limits:
— *correction factors*: for the calculation of content, multiply the peak areas of the following impurities by the corresponding correction factor: impurity B = 1.3; impurity C = 1.3;
— *impurity C*: not more than 4 times the area of the principal peak in the chromatogram obtained with reference solution (a) (0.4 per cent);
— *impurity B*: not more than 3 times the area of the principal peak in the chromatogram obtained with reference solution (a) (0.3 per cent);
— *unspecified impurities*: for each impurity, not more than twice the area of the principal peak in the chromatogram obtained with reference solution (a) (0.20 per cent);
— *total*: not more than 10 times the area of the principal peak in the chromatogram obtained with reference solution (a) (1.0 per cent);
— *disregard limit*: the area of the principal peak in the chromatogram obtained with reference solution (a) (0.1 per cent).

Heavy metals (*2.4.8*)
Maximum 20 ppm.

Dissolve 1.0 g in 20 mL of a mixture of 15 volumes of *water R* and 85 volumes of *dioxan R*. 12 mL of the solution complies with test B. Prepare the reference solution using lead standard solution (1 ppm Pb) obtained by diluting *lead standard solution (100 ppm Pb) R* with a mixture of 15 volumes of *water R* and 85 volumes of *dioxan R*.

Loss on drying (*2.2.32*)
Maximum 0.5 per cent, determined on 1.000 g by drying in an oven at 105 °C.

Sulfated ash (*2.4.14*)
Maximum 0.1 per cent, determined on 1.0 g in a platinum crucible.

ASSAY
Liquid chromatography (*2.2.29*) as described in the test for related substances with the following modification.

Injection Test solution (b) and reference solution (d).

Calculate the percentage content of $C_{17}H_8Cl_2F_8N_2O_3$ from the declared content of *lufenuron CRS*.

IMPURITIES
Specified impurities B, C

Other detectable impurities (the following substances would, if present at a sufficient level, be detected by one or other of the tests in the monograph. They are limited by the general acceptance criterion for other/unspecified impurities and/or by the general monograph *Substances for pharmaceutical use (2034)*. It is therefore not necessary to identify these impurities for demonstration of compliance. See also 5.10. Control of impurities in substances for pharmaceutical use): A, D, E, F, G, H.

A. 2,6-difluorobenzamide,

B. 1-(2,5-dichloro-4-hydroxyphenyl)-3-(2,6-difluorobenzoyl)urea,

C. 1-[3-chloro-4-[(2RS)-1,1,2,3,3,3-hexafluoropropoxy]phenyl]-3-(2,6-difluorobenzoyl)urea,

D. 1-[2-chloro-4-[(2RS)-1,1,2,3,3,3-hexafluoropropoxy]phenyl]-3-(2,6-difluorobenzoyl)urea,

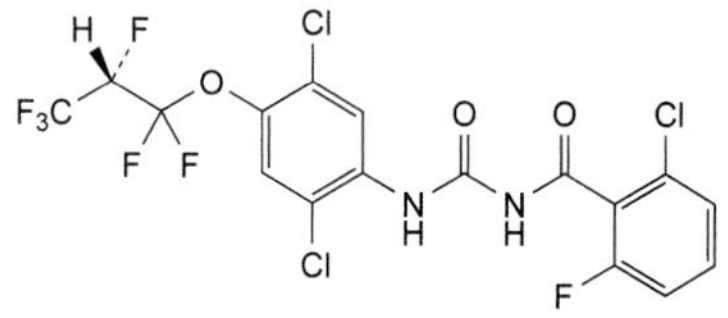

E. 1-(2-chloro-6-fluorobenzoyl)-3-[2,5-dichloro-4-[(2RS)-1,1,2,3,3,3hexafluoropropoxy]phenyl]urea,

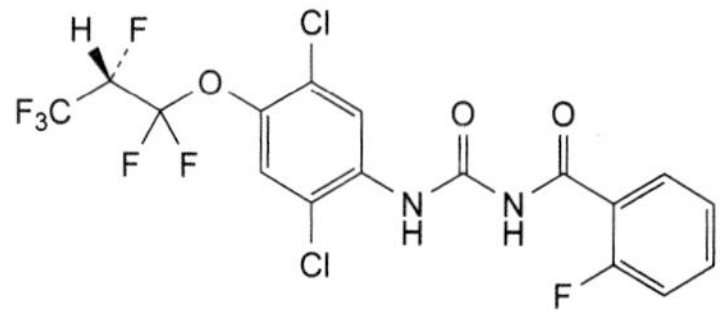

F. 1-[2,5-dichloro-4-[(2RS)-1,1,2,3,3,3-hexafluoropropoxy]phenyl]-3-(2-fluorobenzoyl)urea,

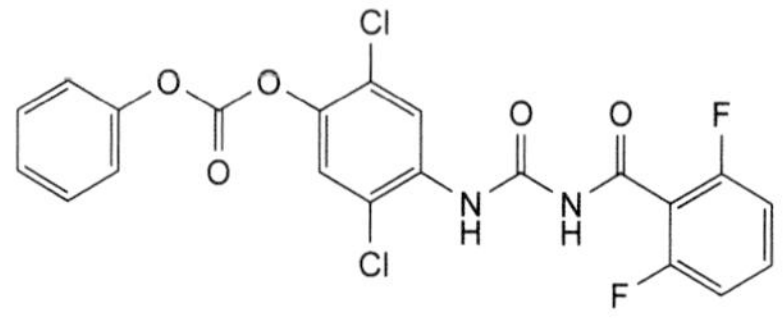

G. 2,5-dichloro-4-[[[(2,6-difluorophenyl)carbonyl]carbamoyl]amino]phenyl phenyl carbonate,

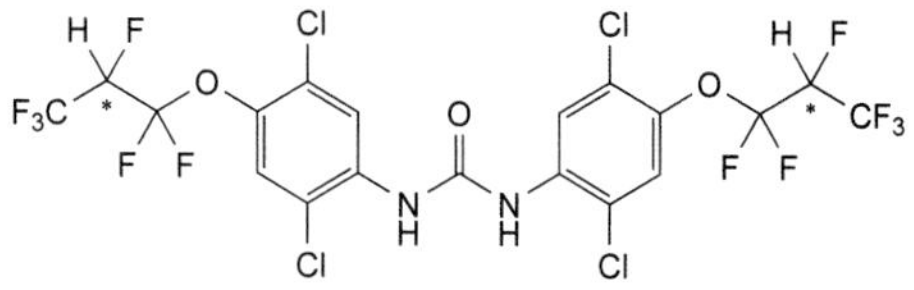

H. 1,3-bis[2,5-dichloro-4-(1,1,2,3,3,3-hexafluoropropoxy)phenyl]urea.

_____ *Ph Eur*

Marbofloxacin

(Marbofloxacin for Veterinary Use, Ph. Eur. monograph 2233)

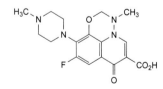

C$_{17}$H$_{19}$FN$_4$O$_4$ 362.4   *115550-35-1*

Action and use

Fluoroquinolone antibacterial.

Ph Eur _____

DEFINITION

9-Fluoro-3-methyl-10-(4-methylpiperazin-1-yl)-7-oxo-2,3-dihydro-7*H*-pyrido[3,2,1-*ij*][4,1,2]benzoxadiazine-6-carboxylic acid.

Content

99.0 per cent to 101.0 per cent (dried substance).

CHARACTERS

Appearance

Light yellow, crystalline powder.

Solubility

Slightly soluble in water, sparingly soluble or slightly soluble in methylene chloride, very slightly soluble in ethanol (96 per cent).

IDENTIFICATION

Infrared absorption spectrophotometry (*2.2.24*).

Comparison marbofloxacin CRS.

TESTS

Absorbance (*2.2.25*)

Maximum 0.20, determined at 450 nm. *Prepare the solution immediately before use.*

Dissolve 0.400 g in *0.1 M ammonium carbonate buffer solution pH 10.3 R* using sonication and dilute to 10.0 mL with the same buffer solution.

Related substances

Liquid chromatography (*2.2.29*). *Carry out the test protected from light.*

Solvent mixture methanol R, water R (23:77 V/V).

Test solution To 0.100 g of the substance to be examined add 80 mL of the solvent mixture, sonicate until dissolution and dilute to 100.0 mL with the solvent mixture.

Reference solution (a) Dilute 5.0 mL of the test solution to 100.0 mL with the solvent mixture. Dilute 1.0 mL of this solution to 50.0 mL with the solvent mixture.

Reference solution (b) Dissolve 10 mg of *marbofloxacin for peak identification CRS* (containing impurities A, B, C, D and E) in the solvent mixture and dilute to 10 mL with the solvent mixture.

Column:
— *size: l* = 0.15 m, Ø = 4.6 mm;
— *stationary phase:* end-capped polar-embedded octadecylsilyl amorphous organosilica polymer R (3.5 μm);
— *temperature:* 40 °C.

Mobile phase Mix 230 volumes of *methanol R* and 5 volumes of *glacial acetic acid R* with 770 volumes of a 2.70 g/L solution of *sodium dihydrogen phosphate R* containing 3.50 g/L of *sodium octanesulfonate R* and previously adjusted to pH 2.5 with *phosphoric acid R*.

Flow rate 1.2 mL/min.

Detection Spectrophotometer at 315 nm.

Injection 10 μL.

Run time 2.5 times the retention time of marbofloxacin.

Identification of impurities Use the chromatogram supplied with *marbofloxacin for peak identification CRS* and the chromatogram obtained with reference solution (b) to identify the peaks due to impurities A, B, C, D and E.

Relative retention With reference to marbofloxacin (retention time = about 33 min): impurity B = about 0.5; impurity A = about 0.7; impurity C = about 0.9; impurity D = about 1.3; impurity E = about 1.5.

System suitability: reference solution (b):
— *resolution:* minimum 1.5 between the peaks due to impurity C and marbofloxacin, and minimum 4.0 between the peaks due to marbofloxacin and impurity D.

Limits:
— *correction factor:* for the calculation of content, multiply the peak area of impurity E by 1.5;

— *impurities C, D, E*: for each impurity, not more than twice the area of the principal peak in the chromatogram obtained with reference solution (a) (0.2 per cent);

— *impurities A, B*: for each impurity, not more than the area of the principal peak in the chromatogram obtained with reference solution (a) (0.1 per cent);

— *unspecified impurities*: for each impurity, not more than twice the area of the principal peak in the chromatogram obtained with reference solution (a) (0.2 per cent);

— *total*: not more than 5 times the area of the principal peak in the chromatogram obtained with reference solution (a) (0.5 per cent);

— *disregard limit*: the area of the principal peak in the chromatogram obtained with reference solution (a) (0.1 per cent).

Heavy metals (*2.4.8*)
Maximum 20 ppm.

Dissolve 0.5 g in *dilute acetic acid R* and dilute to 30 mL with the same solvent. Adding 2 mL of *water R* instead of 2 mL of *buffer solution pH 3.5 R*, the filtrate complies with test E. Prepare the reference solution using 5 mL of *lead standard solution (2 ppm Pb) R*.

Loss on drying (*2.2.32*)
Maximum 0.5 per cent, determined on 1.000 g by drying at 105 °C for 4 h.

Sulfated ash (*2.4.14*)
Maximum 0.1 per cent, determined on 1.0 g in a platinum crucible.

ASSAY
Dissolve 0.300 g in 80 mL of *glacial acetic acid R*. Titrate with *0.1 M perchloric acid*, determining the end-point potentiometrically (*2.2.20*).

1 mL of *0.1 M perchloric acid* is equivalent to 36.24 mg of $C_{17}H_{19}FN_4O_4$.

STORAGE
Protected from light.

IMPURITIES
Specified impurities A, B, C, D, E

Other detectable impurities (the following substances would, if present at a sufficient level, be detected by one or other of the tests in the monograph. They are limited by the general acceptance criterion for other/unspecified impurities and/or by the general monograph *Substances for pharmaceutical use (2034)*. It is therefore not necessary to identify these impurities for demonstration of compliance. See also *5.10. Control of impurities in substances for pharmaceutical use*): F.

A. 6,7-difluoro-8-hydroxy-1-(methylamino)-4-oxo-1,4-dihydroquinoline-3-carboxylic acid,

B. 9,10-difluoro-3-methyl-7-oxo-2,3-dihydro-7*H*-pyrido[3,2,1-*ij*][4,1,2]benzoxadiazine-6-carboxylic acid,

C. 6,8-difluoro-1-(methylamino)-7-(4-methylpiperazin-1-yl)-4-oxo-1,4-dihydroquinoline-3-carboxylic acid,

D. 6-fluoro-8-hydroxy-1-(methylamino)-7-(4-methylpiperazin-1-yl)-4-oxo-1,4-dihydroquinoline-3-carboxylic acid,

E. 8-ethoxy-6-fluoro-1-(methylamino)-7-(4-methylpiperazin-1-yl)-4-oxo-1,4-dihydroquinoline-3-carboxylic acid,

F. 4-[6-carboxy-9-fluoro-3-methyl-7-oxo-2,3-dihydro-7*H*-pyrido[3,2,1-*ij*][4,1,2]benzoxadiazin-10-yl]-1-methylpiperazine 1-oxide.

Morantel Tartrate

*(Morantel Hydrogen Tartate for Veterinary Use,
Ph Eur monograph 1546)*

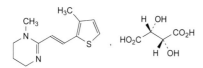

C$_{16}$H$_{22}$N$_2$O$_6$S   370.4   *26155-31-7*

Action and use
Antihelminthic.

Ph Eur

DEFINITION
1-Methyl-2-[(*E*)-2-(3-methylthiophen-2-yl)ethenyl]-1,4,5,6-
tetrahydropyrimidine hydrogen tartrate.

Content
98.5 per cent to 101.5 per cent (dried substance).

CHARACTERS
Appearance
White or pale yellow, crystalline powder.

Solubility
Very soluble in water and in ethanol (96 per cent), practically
insoluble in ethyl acetate.

IDENTIFICATION
First identification B

Second identification A, C, D

A. Melting point (*2.2.14*): 167 °C to 172 °C.

B. Infrared absorption spectrophotometry (*2.2.24*).

Comparison morantel hydrogen tartrate CRS.

C. Dissolve about 10 mg in 1 mL of a 5 g/L solution of
ammonium vanadate R. Evaporate to dryness. Add 0.1 mL of
sulfuric acid R. A purple colour is produced.

D. Dissolve about 10 mg in 1 mL of *0.1 M sodium hydroxide*.
Transfer to a separating funnel and shake with 5 mL of
methylene chloride R. Discard the organic layer. Neutralise the
aqueous layer with a few drops of *dilute hydrochloric acid R*.
The solution gives reaction (b) of tartrates (*2.3.1*).

TESTS
Solution S
Dissolve 0.25 g in *carbon dioxide-free water R* and dilute to
25.0 mL with the same solvent.

Appearance of solution
Solution S is clear (*2.2.1*) and not more intensely coloured
than reference solution GY$_6$ or Y$_6$ (*2.2.2, Method II*).

pH (*2.2.3*)
3.3 to 3.9 for solution S.

Related substances
Liquid chromatography (*2.2.29*). *Carry out the test protected
from light.*

Test solution Dissolve 50.0 mg of the substance to be
examined in the mobile phase and dilute to 100.0 mL with
the mobile phase.

Reference solution (a) Dilute 1.0 mL of the test solution to
100.0 mL with the mobile phase.

Reference solution (b) Dilute 2.0 mL of reference solution (a)
to 100.0 mL with the mobile phase.

Reference solution (c) Expose 10 mL of reference solution (a)
to daylight for 15 min before injection.

Reference solution (d) Dissolve 15.0 mg of *tartaric acid R* in
the mobile phase and dilute to 100.0 mL with the mobile
phase.

Column:
— *size*: *l* = 0.25 m, Ø = 4.6 mm;
— *stationary phase*: base-deactivated end-capped octadecylsilyl
   silica gel for chromatography R (5 μm).

Mobile phase To a mixture of 0.35 volumes of *triethylamine R*
and 85 volumes of *water R* adjusted to pH 2.5 with
phosphoric acid R, add 5 volumes of *tetrahydrofuran R* and
10 volumes of *methanol R*.

Flow rate 0.75 mL/min.

Detection Spectrophotometer at 226 nm.

Injection 20 μL.

Run time Twice the retention time of morantel.

System suitability: reference solution (c):
— *resolution*: minimum of 2 between the principal pcak and
   the preceding peak ((*Z*)-isomer).

Limits:
— *any impurity apart from the peak due to tartaric acid*: not
   more than 0.5 times the area of the principal peak in the
   chromatogram obtained with reference solution (a)
   (0.5 per cent);
— *total*: not more than the area of the principal peak in the
   chromatogram obtained with reference solution (a)
   (1 per cent);
— *disregard limit*: the area of the principal peak in the
   chromatogram obtained with reference solution (b)
   (0.02 per cent).

Heavy metals (*2.4.8*)
Maximum 20 ppm.

1.0 g complies with test C. Prepare the reference solution
using 2 mL of *lead standard solution (10 ppm Pb) R*.

Loss on drying (*2.2.32*)
Maximum 1.5 per cent, determined on 1.000 g by drying in
an oven at 105 °C.

Sulfated ash (*2.4.14*)
Maximum 0.1 per cent, determined on 1.0 g.

ASSAY
Dissolve 0.280 g in 40 mL of *anhydrous acetic acid R*. Titrate
with *0.1 M perchloric acid*, determining the end-point
potentiometrically (*2.2.20*).

1 mL of *0.1 M perchloric acid* is equivalent to 37.04 mg of
C$_{16}$H$_{22}$N$_2$O$_6$S.

STORAGE
Protected from light.

IMPURITIES

A. 1-methyl-2-[(*E*)-2-(4-methylthiophen-2-yl)ethenyl]-
1,4,5,6-tetrahydropyrimidine,

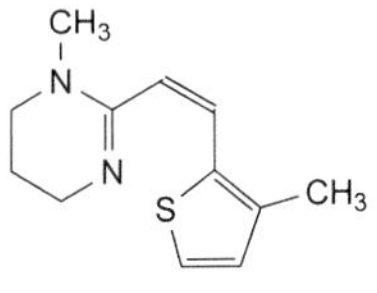

B. 1-methyl-2-[(*Z*)-2-(3-methylthiophen-2-yl)ethenyl]-1,4,5,6-tetrahydropyrimidine,

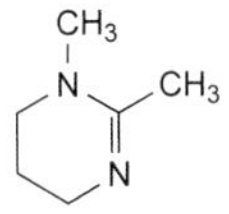

C. 1,2-dimethyl-1,4,5,6-tetrahydropyrimidine,

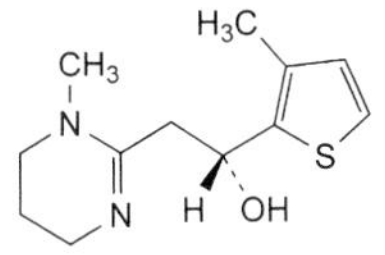

and enantiomer

D. (1*RS*)-2-(1-methyl-1,4,5,6-tetrahydropyrimidin-2-yl)-1-(3-methylthiophen-2-yl)ethanol,

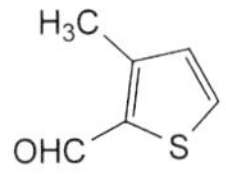

E. 3-methylthiophene-2-carbaldehyde.

Ph Eur

Moxidectin

*(Moxidectin for Veterinary Use,
Ph Eur monograph 1656)*

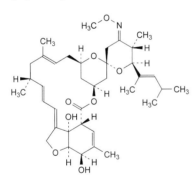

C₃₇H₅₃NO₈   640   *113507-06-5*

$C_{37}H_{53}NO_8$ 640   *113507-06-5*

Action and use

Antihelminthic; ectoparasiticide.

Preparation

Moxidectin Injection

Moxidectin Oral Solution

Moxidectin Oromucosal Gel

Moxidectin Pour-on

Ph Eur

DEFINITION

(2a*E*,2′*R*,4*E*,4′*E*,5′*S*,6*R*,6′*S*,8*E*,11*R*,15*S*,17a*R*,20*R*,20a*R*,20b*S*)-6′-[(1*E*)-1,3-Dimethylbut-1-enyl]-20,20b-dihydroxy-4′-(methoxyimino)-5′,6,8,19-tetramethyl-3′,4′,5′,6,6′,7,10,11,14,15,17a,20,20a,20b-tetradecahydrospiro[2*H*,17*H*-11,15-methanofuro[4,3,2-*pq*][2,6]benzodioxacyclooctadecine-13,2′-pyran]-17-one

((6*R*,23*E*,25*S*)-5*O*-demethyl-28-deoxy-25-[(1*E*)-1,3-dimethylbut-1-enyl]-6,28-epoxy-23-(methoxyimino)milbemycin B).

Semi-synthetic product derived from a fermentation product. It may contain suitable stabilisers such as antioxidants.

Content

92.0 per cent to 102.0 per cent (anhydrous substance).

CHARACTERS

Appearance

White or pale yellow, amorphous powder.

Solubility

Practically insoluble in water, very soluble in ethanol (96 per cent), slightly soluble in hexane.

IDENTIFICATION

Infrared absorption spectrophotometry *(2.2.24)*.

Comparison moxidectin CRS.

TESTS

Appearance of solution

The solution is clear *(2.2.1)* and not more intensely coloured than reference solution GY₅ *(2.2.2, Method II)*.

Dissolve 0.40 g in *benzyl alcohol R* and dilute to 20 mL with the same solvent.

Related substances

Liquid chromatography *(2.2.29)*.

A. *Test solution.* Dissolve 25.0 mg of the substance to be examined in *acetonitrile R* and dilute to 25.0 mL with the same solvent.

Reference solution (a) Dilute 1.0 mL of the test solution to 100.0 mL *acetonitrile R*.

Reference solution (b) Dissolve 5 mg of *moxidectin for system suitability CRS* (containing impurities A, B, C, D, E, F, G, H, I, J and K) in 5 mL of *acetonitrile R*.

Reference solution (c) Dissolve 25.0 mg of *moxidectin CRS* in *acetonitrile R* and dilute to 25.0 mL with the same solvent.

Column:
— *size*: *l* = 0.15 m, Ø = 3.9 mm;
— *stationary phase: end-capped octadecylsilyl silica gel for chromatography R* (4 μm);
— *temperature*: 50 °C.

Mobile phase Dissolve 7.7 g of *ammonium acetate R* in 400 mL of *water R*, adjust to pH 4.8 with *glacial acetic acid R* and add 600 mL of *acetonitrile R*.

Flow rate 2.5 mL/min.

Detection Spectrophotometer at 242 nm.

Injection 10 μL of the test solution and reference solutions (a) and (b).

Run time 2 times the retention time of moxidectin.

Identification of impurities Use the chromatogram supplied with *moxidectin for system suitability CRS* and the chromatogram obtained with reference solution (b) to identify the peaks due to impurities A, B, C, D, E + F and G.

Relative retention With reference to moxidectin (retention time = about 12 min): impurity A = about 0.5; impurity B = about 0.7; impurity C = about 0.75; impurity D = about 0.94; impurities E and F = about 1.3-1.5; impurity G = about 1.6.

System suitability: reference solution (b):
— *peak-to-valley ratio*: minimum 3.0, where H_p = height above the baseline of the peak due to impurity D and H_v = height above the baseline of the lowest point of

the curve separating this peak from the peak due to moxidectin.

Limits:
— *impurity D*: not more than 2.5 times the area of the principal peak in the chromatogram obtained with reference solution (a) (2.5 per cent);
— *sum of impurities E and F*: not more than 1.7 times the area of the principal peak in the chromatogram obtained with reference solution (a) (1.7 per cent);
— *impurities A, C, G*: for each impurity, not more than 1.5 times the area of the principal peak in the chromatogram obtained with reference solution (a) (1.5 per cent);
— *impurity B*: not more than 0.5 times the area of the principal peak in the chromatogram obtained with reference solution (a) (0.5 per cent);
— *any other impurity eluting before impurity G*: for each impurity, not more than 0.5 times the area of the principal peak in the chromatogram obtained with reference solution (a) (0.5 per cent);
— *disregard limit*: 0.1 times the area of the principal peak in the chromatogram obtained with reference solution (a) (0.1 per cent); disregard the peak due to the stabiliser (identify this peak, where applicable, by injecting a suitable reference solution).

B. *Test solution*. Dissolve 75.0 mg of the substance to be examined in *acetonitrile R* and dilute to 25.0 mL with the same solvent.

Reference solution (a) Dilute 1.0 mL of the test solution to 100.0 mL with *acetonitrile R*.

Reference solution (b) Dissolve 5 mg of *moxidectin for system suitability CRS* (containing impurities A, B, C, D, E, F, G, H, I, J and K) in 5 mL of *acetonitrile R*.

Column:
— *size*: l = 0.15 m, Ø = 3.9 mm;
— *stationary phase*: *end-capped octadecylsilyl silica gel for chromatography R* (4 μm);
— *temperature*: 35 °C.

Mobile phase Dissolve 3.8 g of *ammonium acetate R* in 250 mL of *water R*, adjust to pH 4.2 with *acetic acid R* and add 750 mL of *acetonitrile R*.

Flow rate 2.0 mL/min.

Detection Spectrophotometer at 242 nm.

Injection 10 μL.

Run time 10 times the retention time of moxidectin.

Identification of impurities Use the chromatogram supplied with *moxidectin for system suitability CRS* and the chromatogram obtained with reference solution (b) to identify the peaks due to impurities H + I, J and K.

Relative retention With reference to moxidectin (retention time = about 4 min): impurity G = about 1.4; impurities H and I = about 2.0; impurity J = about 2.2; impurity K = about 3.4.

System suitability: reference solution (b):
— *resolution*: baseline separation between the peaks due to impurities H + I and J.

Limits:
— *sum of impurities H and I*: not more than the area of the principal peak in the chromatogram obtained with reference solution (a) (1.0 per cent);
— *impurities J, K*: for each impurity, not more than 0.5 times the area of the principal peak in the chromatogram obtained with reference solution (a) (0.5 per cent);

— *any other impurity eluting after impurity G*: for each impurity, not more than 0.5 times the area of the principal peak in the chromatogram obtained with reference solution (a) (0.5 per cent);
— *disregard limit*: 0.1 times the area of the principal peak in the chromatogram obtained with reference solution (a) (0.1 per cent); disregard the peak due to the stabiliser (identify this peak, where applicable, by injecting a suitable reference solution).

Total of all impurities Calculate the sum of the impurities eluting from the start of the run to impurity G in test A, and from impurities H + I to the end of the run in test B. The total of all impurities is not more than 7.0 per cent.

Heavy metals (*2.4.8*)
Maximum 20 ppm.

It complies with test A with the following modifications.

Prescribed solution Dissolve 0.50 g in 20 mL of *ethanol (96 per cent) R*.

Test solution 12 mL of the prescribed solution.

Reference solution A mixture of 2 ml of the prescribed solution, 4 ml of *water R* and 6 ml of *lead standard solution (1 ppm Pb) R*.

Blank solution A mixture of 2 mL of the prescribed solution and 10 mL of *ethanol (96 per cent) R*.

Use a membrane filter (nominal pore size 0.45 μm).

Water (*2.5.12*)
Maximum 1.3 per cent, determined on 0.50 g.

Sulfated ash (*2.4.14*)
Maximum 0.2 per cent, determined on 1.0 g.

ASSAY
Liquid chromatography (*2.2.29*) as described in test A for related substances with the following modification.

Injection Test solution and reference solution (c).

Calculate the percentage content of $C_{37}H_{53}NO_8$ using the declared content of *moxidectin CRS*.

IMPURITIES
Specified impurities A, B, C, D, E, F, G, H, I, J, K

A. R1 = R2 = R3 = R4 = CH₃, R5 = R6 = H: 25-des[(1*E*)-1,3-dimethylbut-1-enyl]-25-[(1*E*)-1-methylprop-1-enyl]moxidectin,

B. R1 = R2 = R3 = R5 = R6 = CH₃, R4 = H: 24-desmethylmoxidectin,

C. R1 = R2 = R3 = R4 = R5 = CH₃, R6 = H: 25-des[(1*E*)-1,3-dimethylbut-1-enyl]-25-[(1*E*)-1-methylbut-1-enyl]moxidectin,

F. one of groups R1 to R6 is C_2H_5, the others are CH₃: x-desmethyl-x-ethylmoxidectin,

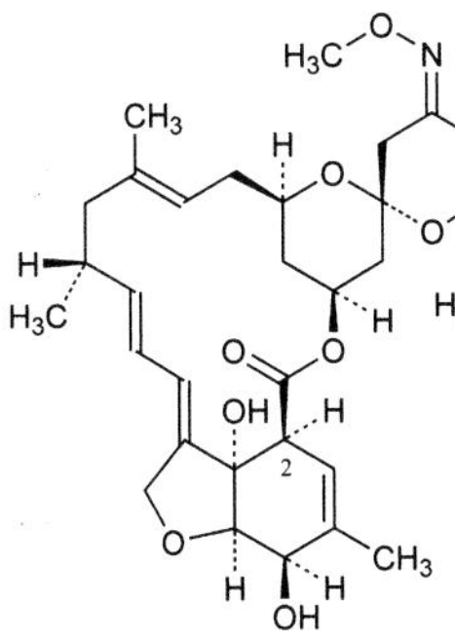

D. 2-*epi*-moxidectin,

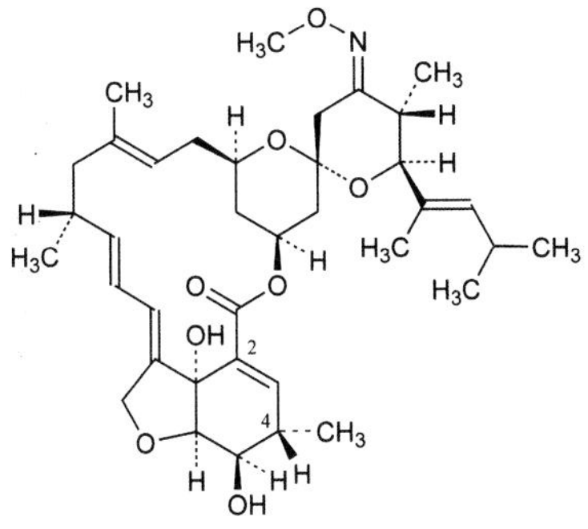

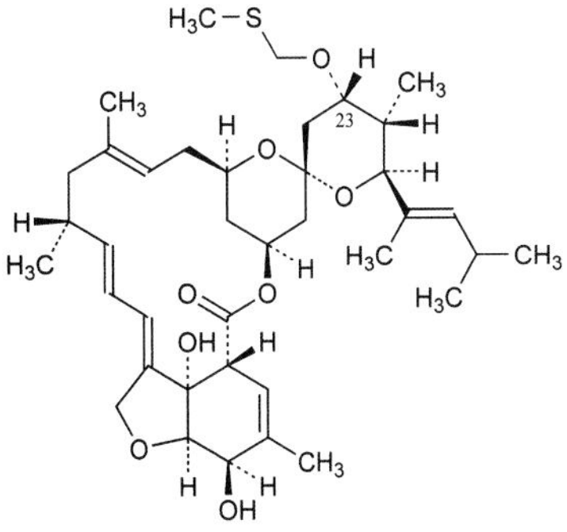

I. (23*S*)-23-des(methoxyimino)-23-
[(methylsulfanyl)methoxy]moxidectin,

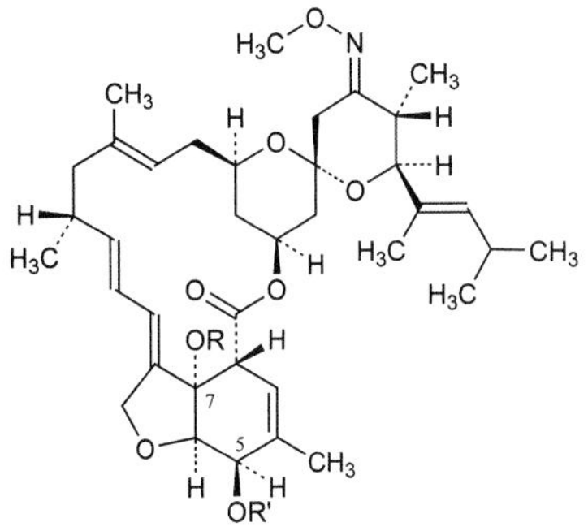

E. (4*S*)-2-dehydro-4-hydromoxidectin,

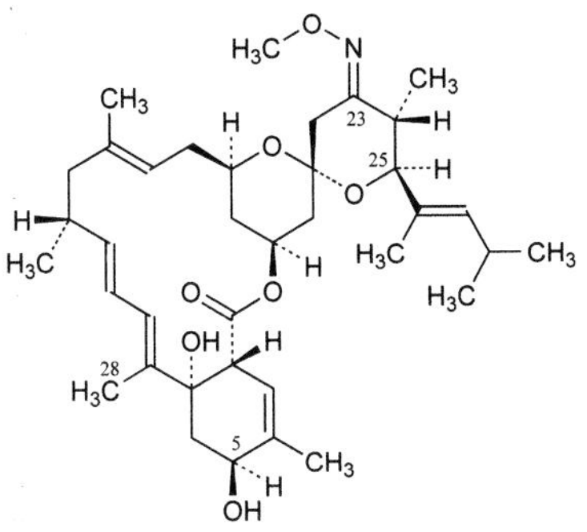

J. R = CH$_2$-S-CH$_3$, R′ = H: 7-*O*-
[(methylsulfanyl)methyl]moxidectin,
K. R = H, R′ = CO-C$_6$H$_4$-*p*NO$_2$: 5-*O*-
(4-nitrobenzoyl)moxidectin,

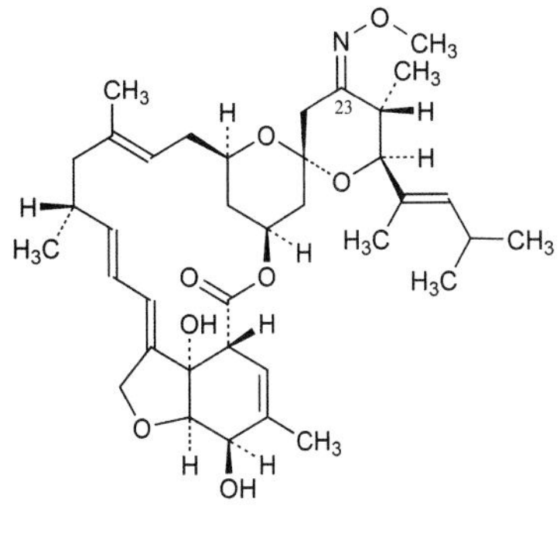

G. (23*E*,25*S*)-5*O*-desmethyl-28-deoxy-25-[(1*E*)-1,3-
dimethylbut-1-enyl]-23-(methoxyimino)milbemycin B,

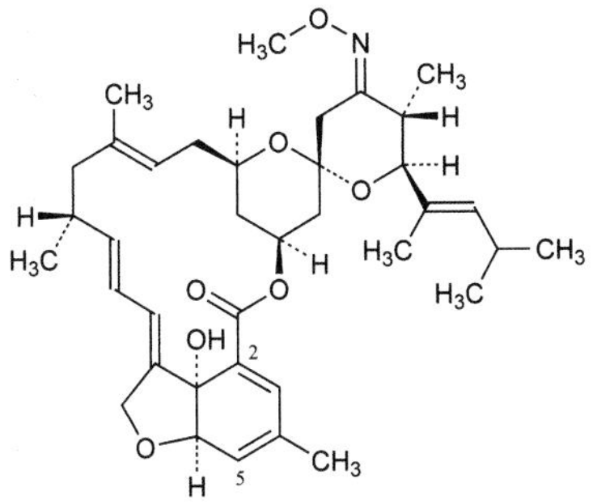

L. (23*Z*)-moxidectin.

Ph Eur

Nandrolone Laurate

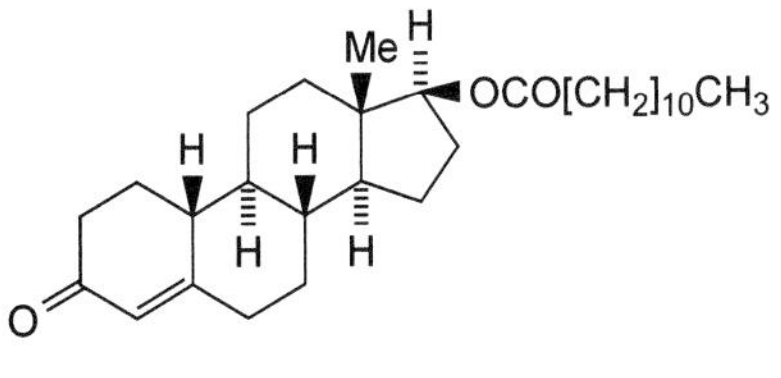

C$_{30}$H$_{48}$O$_3$ 456.7   *26490-31-3*

Action and use
Anabolic steroid; androgen.

Preparation
Nandrolone Laurate Injection

H. 2,5-didehydro-5-deoxymoxidectin,

DEFINITION

Nandrolone Laurate is 3-oxo-estr-4-en-17β-yl laurate. It contains not less than 97.0% and not more than 103.0% of $C_{30}H_{48}O_3$, calculated with reference to the dried substance.

CHARACTERISTICS

A white to creamy white, crystalline powder.

Practically insoluble in *water*; freely soluble in *chloroform*, in *ethanol (96%)*, in *ether*, in fixed oils and in esters of fatty acids.

IDENTIFICATION

A. The *infrared absorption spectrum*, Appendix II A, is concordant with the *reference spectrum* of nandrolone laurate *(RSV 30)*.

B. Carry out the method for *thin-layer chromatography*, Appendix III A, using the following solutions in *chloroform*.

(1) 0.5% w/v of the substance being examined.

(2) 0.5% w/v of *nandrolone laurate BPCRS*.

(3) Mix equal volumes of solutions (1) and (2).

CHROMATOGRAPHIC CONDITIONS

(a) Use as the coating *silica gel F_{254}* precoated plate the surface of which has been modified by chemically-bonded octadecylsilyl groups (Whatman KC 18F plates are suitable).

(b) Use the mobile phase as described below.

(c) Apply 5 µL of each solution.

(d) Develop the plate to 15 cm.

(e) After removal of the plate, dry in air until the odour of solvent is no longer detectable and heat at 100° for 10 minutes. Allow to cool and examine under *ultraviolet light (254 nm)*.

MOBILE PHASE

20 volumes of *water*, 40 volumes of *acetonitrile* and 60 volumes of *propan-2-ol*.

CONFIRMATION

The principal spot in the chromatogram obtained with solution (1) corresponds in position and colour to that in the chromatogram obtained with solution (2).

The principal spot in the chromatogram obtained with solution (3) appears as a single, compact spot.

C. *Melting point*, about 47°, Appendix V A.

TESTS

Specific optical rotation

In a 2% w/v solution in *1,4-dioxan*, +31 to +35, calculated with reference to the dried substance, Appendix V F.

Nandrolone

Carry out the method for *thin-layer chromatography*, Appendix III A, using the following solutions in *chloroform*.

(1) 1.50% w/v of the substance being examined.

(2) 0.030% w/v of *nandrolone BPCRS*.

CHROMATOGRAPHIC CONDITIONS

(a) Use as the coating *silica gel G*.

(b) Use the mobile phase as described below.

(c) Apply 1 µL of each solution.

(d) Develop the plate to 15 cm.

(e) After removal of the plate, dry in air until the solvent has evaporated, spray with a 10% v/v solution of *sulfuric acid* in *ethanol (96%)*, heat at 105° for 30 minutes and examine under *ultraviolet light (365 nm)*.

MOBILE PHASE

3 volumes of *acetone* and 7 volumes of *heptane*.

LIMITS

In the chromatogram obtained with solution (1):

Any spot corresponding to nandrolone is not more intense than the spot in the chromatogram obtained with solution (2) (2%).

Loss on drying

When dried over *phosphorus pentoxide* at a pressure not exceeding 0.7 kPa for 24 hours, loses not more than 0.5% of its weight. Use 1 g.

Sulfated ash

Not more than 0.1%, Appendix IX A.

ASSAY

Dissolve 10 mg in sufficient *absolute ethanol* to produce 100 mL, dilute 5 mL to 50 mL with *absolute ethanol* and measure the *absorbance* of the resulting solution at the maximum at 240 nm, Appendix II B. Calculate the content of $C_{30}H_{48}O_3$, taking 380 as the value of A(1%, 1 cm) at the maximum at 240 nm.

STORAGE

Nandrolone Laurate should be protected from light and stored at a temperature 2° and 8°.

Nitroxinil

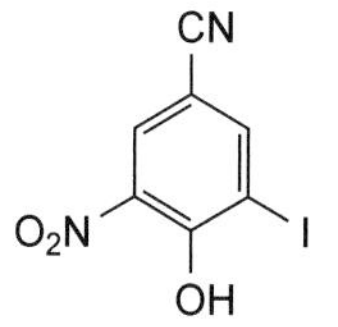

$C_7H_3IN_2O_3$ 290.0   *1689-89-0*

Action and use

Antihelminthic.

Preparation

Nitroxinil Injection

DEFINITION

Nitroxinil is 4-hydroxy-3-iodo-5-nitrobenzonitrile. It contains not less than 98.0% and not more than 101.0% of $C_7H_3IN_2O_3$, calculated with reference to the dried substance.

CHARACTERISTICS

A yellow to yellowish brown powder.

Practically insoluble in *water*; sparingly soluble in *ether*; slightly soluble in *ethanol (96%)*. It dissolves in solutions of alkali hydroxides.

IDENTIFICATION

A. The *infrared absorption spectrum*, Appendix II A, is concordant with the *reference spectrum* of nitroxinil *(RSV 31)*.

B. The *light absorption*, Appendix II B, in the range 220 to 350 nm of a 0.002% w/v solution in 0.01M *sodium hydroxide* exhibits maxima at 225 nm and at 271 nm. The *absorbance* at the maximum at 271 nm is about 1.3.

C. Heat with *sulfuric acid*; iodine vapour is evolved.

TESTS

Melting point

136° to 139°, Appendix V A.

Inorganic iodide

To 0.40 g add 0.35 g of N-*methylglucamine* and 10 mL of *water*, shake to dissolve and add sufficient *water* to produce 50 mL. To 10 mL of the resulting solution add 4 mL of 1M *sulfuric acid* and extract with three 10 mL quantities of *chloroform*. Add to the aqueous extract 1 mL of *hydrogen peroxide solution (100 vol)* and 1 mL of *chloroform*, shake for 2 minutes and allow to separate. Any purple colour produced in the chloroform layer is not more intense than that obtained in a solution prepared in the following manner. Add 2 mL of a 0.0026% w/v solution of *potassium iodide* to a mixture of 4 mL of 1M *sulfuric acid* and 8 mL of *water*, add 10 mL of *chloroform*, shake for 2 minutes, add to the aqueous layer 1 mL of *hydrogen peroxide solution (100 vol)* and 1 mL of *chloroform*, shake for 2 minutes and allow to separate (500 ppm of iodide).

Loss on drying

When dried to constant weight at 105°, loses not more than 1.0% of its weight. Use 1 g.

Sulfated ash

Not more than 0.1%, Appendix IX A.

ASSAY

Carry out the method for *oxygen-flask combustion for iodine*, Appendix VIII C, using 25 mg. Each mL of 0.02M *sodium thiosulfate VS* is equivalent to 0.9667 mg of $C_7H_3IN_2O_3$.

STORAGE

Nitroxinil should be protected from light.

Orbifloxacin

(Orbifloxacin for Veterinary Use, Ph Eur monograph 2259)

$C_{19}H_{20}F_3N_3O_3$ 395.4   *113617-63-3*

Ph Eur _____

DEFINITION

1-Cyclopropyl-7-[(3R,5S)-3,5-dimethylpiperazin-1-yl]-5,6,8-trifluoro-4-oxo-1,4-dihydroquinoline-3-carboxylic acid.

Content

99.0 per cent to 101.0 per cent (anhydrous substance).

CHARACTERS

Appearance

White or pale yellow, crystals or crystalline powder.

Solubility

Very slightly soluble in water, soluble in glacial acetic acid, practically insoluble in anhydrous ethanol.

It shows polymorphism (*5.9*).

IDENTIFICATION

Infrared absorption spectrophotometry (*2.2.24*).

Comparison   orbifloxacin CRS.

If the spectra obtained in the solid state show differences, dissolve 0.1 g of the substance to be examined and 0.1 g of the reference substance separately in 12 mL of *methanol R*. Heat to boiling while shaking. Filter the solutions and let

them cool slowly to room temperature. Filter under vacuum and wash the residues with cooled *methanol R*. Dry the residues under vacuum and record new spectra using the residues.

TESTS

Appearance of solution

The solution is clear (*2.2.1*) and not more intensely coloured than reference solution GY_4 (*2.2.2, Method II*).

Dissolve 0.4 g in a 4 g/L solution of *sodium hydroxide R* and dilute to 20 mL with the same solution.

Related substances

Liquid chromatography (*2.2.29*).

Buffer solution   Dissolve 5.9 g of *sodium citrate R* in 800 mL of *water R*, add 90 mL of *glacial acetic acid R* and mix. Adjust to pH 3.5 with a 240 g/L solution of *sodium hydroxide R* in *water R* and dilute to 1000 mL with *water R*.

Test solution   Dissolve 10 mg of the substance to be examined in the buffer solution and dilute to 50.0 mL with the buffer solution.

Reference solution (a)   Dilute 1.0 mL of the test solution to 50.0 mL with the buffer solution. Dilute 1.0 mL of this solution to 10.0 mL with the buffer solution.

Reference solution (b)   Dissolve 10.0 mg of *methyl 4-aminobenzoate R* in the buffer solution and dilute to 100.0 mL with the buffer solution. Mix 10.0 mL of the solution with 5.0 mL of the test solution and dilute to 50.0 mL with the buffer solution. Dilute 1.0 mL of this solution to 50.0 mL with the buffer solution.

Reference solution (c)   Dissolve the contents of a vial of *orbifloxacin impurity mixture CRS* (impurities A and D) in 1.0 mL of the buffer solution.

Reference solution (d)   Dilute 0.25 mL of reference solution (c) to 1.0 mL of the buffer solution.

Column:
— *size: l* = 33 mm, Ø = 4.6 mm;
— *stationary phase: base-deactivated octadecylsilyl silica gel for chromatography R* (3 μm).

Mobile phase   *dioxane R, methanol R, buffer solution* (4:11:86 *V/V/V*).

Flow rate   1 mL/min.

Detection   Spectrophotometer at 290 nm.

Injection   10 μL.

Run time   9 times the retention time of orbifloxacin.

Identification of the impurities   Use the chromatogram supplied with *orbifloxacin impurity mixture CRS* and the chromatogram obtained with reference solution (c) to identify the peaks due to impurities A and D.

Relative retention   With reference to orbifloxacin (retention time = about 2 min): impurity A = about 0.5; methyl 4-aminobenzoate = about 1.2; impurity D = about 2.5.

System suitability:
— *resolution:* minimum 2.0 between the peaks due to orbifloxacin and methyl 4-aminobenzoate in the chromatogram obtained with reference solution (b);
— *signal-to-noise ratio:* minimum 10 for the peak due to impurity A in the chromatogram obtained with reference solution (d).

Limits:
— *correction factors:* for the calculation of contents, multiply the peak areas of the following impurities by the

corresponding correction factor: impurity A = 2.8; impurity D = 1.4;

— *impurities A, D*: for each impurity, not more than the area of the principal peak in the chromatogram obtained with reference solution (a) (0.2 per cent);

— *unspecified impurities*: for each impurity, not more than the area of the principal peak in the chromatogram obtained with reference solution (a) (0.20 per cent);

— *total*: not more than twice the area of the principal peak in the chromatogram obtained with reference solution (a) (0.4 per cent);

— *disregard limit*: 0.5 times the area of the principal peak in the chromatogram obtained with reference solution (a) (0.10 per cent).

Water (*2.5.12*)

1.5 per cent to 2.9 per cent, determined on 0.250 g.

Sulfated ash (*2.4.14*)

Maximum 0.1 per cent, determined on 1.0 g.

ASSAY

Dissolve 0.300 g in 100 mL of *anhydrous acetic acid R*. Titrate with *0.1 M perchloric acid* determining the end-point potentiometrically (*2.2.20*).

1 mL of *0.1 M perchloric acid* is equivalent to 39.54 mg of $C_{19}H_{20}F_3N_3O_3$.

IMPURITIES

Specified impurities A, D.

Other detectable impurities (the following substances would, if present at a sufficient level, be detected by one or other of the tests in the monograph. They are limited by the general acceptance criterion for other/unspecified impurities and/or by the general monograph *Substances for pharmaceutical use (2034)*. It is therefore not necessary to identify these impurities for demonstration of compliance. See also *5.10. Control of impurities in substances for pharmaceutical use*): B, C, E, F, G.

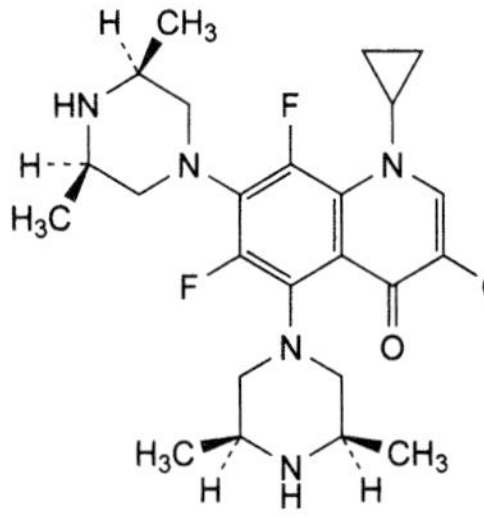

A. 1-cyclopropyl-5,7-bis[(3R,5S)-3,5-dimethylpiperazin-1-yl]6,8-difluoro-4-oxo-1,4-dihydroquinoline-3-carboxylic acid,

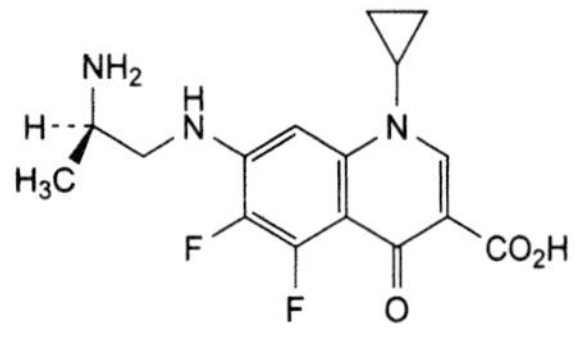

B. 7-[[(2R)-2-aminopropyl]amino]-1-cyclopropyl-5,6-difluoro-4-oxo-1,4-dihydroquinoline-3-carboxylic acid,

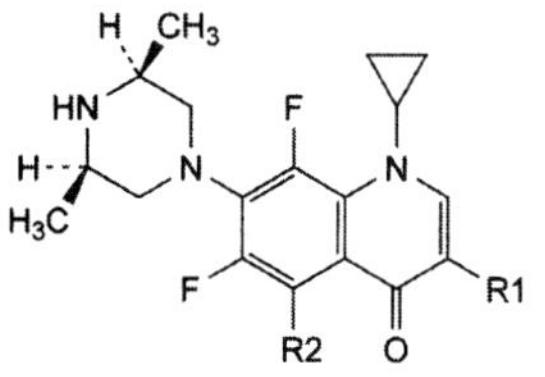

C. R1 = CO2H, R2 = H : 1-cyclopropyl-7-[(3R,5S)3,5-dimethylpiperazin-1-yl]-6,8-difluoro-4-oxo-1,4-dihydroquinoline-3-carboxylic acid,

G. R1 = H, R2 = F: 1-cyclopropyl-7-[(3R,5S)-3,5-dimethylpiperazin-1-yl]-5,6,8-trifluoroquinolin-4(1H)-one,

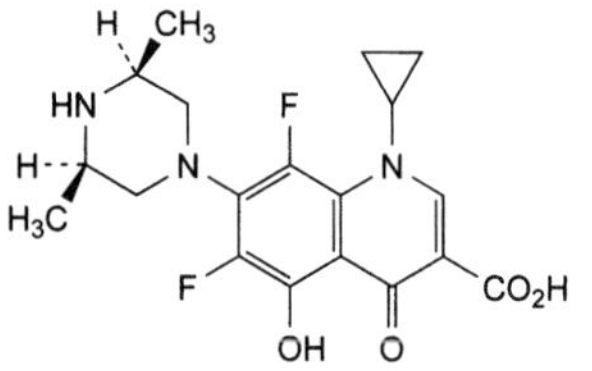

D. 1-cyclopropyl-7-[(3R,5S)-3,5-dimethylpiperazin-1-yl]-6,8-difluoro-5-hydroxy-4-oxo-1,4-dihydroquinoline-3-carboxylic acid,

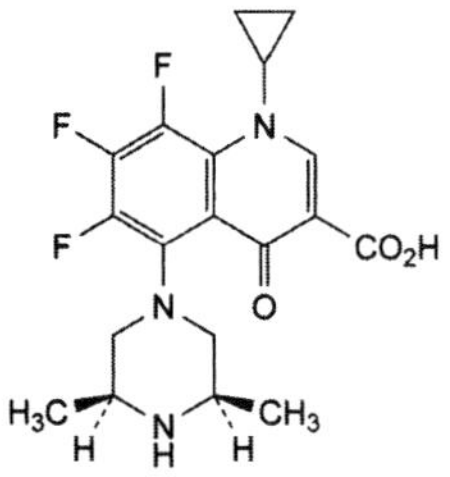

E. 1-cyclopropyl-5-[(3R,5S)-3,5-dimethylpiperazin-1-yl]-6,7,8-trifluoro-4-oxo-1,4-dihydroquinoline-3-carboxylic acid,

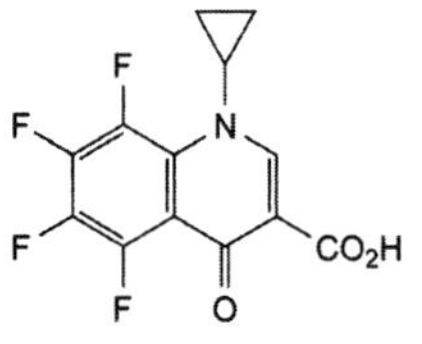

F. 1-cyclopropyl-5,6,7,8-tetrafluoro-4-oxo-1,4-dihydroquinoline-3-carboxylic acid.

Oxfendazole

(Oxfendazole for Veterinary Use,
Ph Eur monograph 1458)

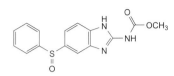

C$_{15}$H$_{13}$N$_3$O$_3$S   315.4   *53716-50-0*

Action and use
Antihelminthic.

Preparation
Oxfendazole Oral Suspension

Ph Eur _____

DEFINITION
Methyl [5-(phenylsulfinyl)-1*H*-benzimidazol-2-yl]carbamate.

Content
97.5 per cent to 100.5 per cent (dried substance).

CHARACTERS
Appearance
White or almost white powder.

Solubility
Practically insoluble in water, slightly soluble in ethanol
(96 per cent) and in methylene chloride.

It shows polymorphism (*5.9*).

IDENTIFICATION
Infrared absorption spectrophotometry (*2.2.24*).

Comparison oxfendazole CRS.

If the spectra obtained in the solid state show differences,
dissolve the substance to be examined and the reference
substance separately in *ethanol (96 per cent) R*, evaporate to
dryness and record new spectra using the residues.

TESTS
Related substances
Liquid chromatography (*2.2.29*).

Test solution Dissolve 25.0 mg of the substance to be
examined in the mobile phase and dilute to 100.0 mL with
the mobile phase.

Reference solution (a) Dilute 1.0 mL of the test solution to
100.0 mL with the mobile phase.

Reference solution (b) To 10 mL of the test solution add
0.25 mL of *strong hydrogen peroxide solution R* and dilute to
25 mL with the mobile phase.

Reference solution (c) Dissolve 5.0 mg of *fenbendazole CRS*
(impurity A) and 10.0 mg of *oxfendazole impurity B CRS* in
the mobile phase and dilute to 100.0 mL with the mobile
phase. Dilute 1.0 mL of the solution to 20.0 mL with the
mobile phase.

Reference solution (d) Dissolve 5 mg of *oxfendazole with
impurity D CRS* in the mobile phase and dilute to 20 mL
with the mobile phase (for identification of impurity D).

Column:
— *size: l* = 0.25 m, Ø = 4.6 mm;
— *stationary phase:* spherical *end-capped octadecylsilyl silica gel
  for chromatography R* (5 µm) with a specific surface area of
  350 m^2/g, a pore size of 10 nm and a carbon loading of
  14 per cent.

Mobile phase Mix 36 volumes of *acetonitrile R* and 64 volumes
of a 2 g/L solution of *sodium pentanesulfonate R* previously
adjusted to pH 2.7 with a 2.8 per cent *V/V* solution of
sulfuric acid R.

Flow rate 1 mL/min.

Detection Spectrophotometer at 254 nm.

Injection 20 µL.

Run time 4 times the retention time of oxfendazole.

Relative retention With reference to oxfendazole (retention
time = about 6.5 min): impurity C = about 0.7;
impurity B = about 1.5; impurity D = about 1.9;
impurity A = about 3.4.

System suitability: reference solution (b):
— *resolution:* minimum 4.0 between the peaks due to
  impurity C and oxfendazole.

Limits:
— *impurity B:* not more than the area of the corresponding
  peak in the chromatogram obtained with reference
  solution (c) (2.0 per cent);
— *impurity A:* not more than the area of the corresponding
  peak in the chromatogram obtained with reference
  solution (c) (1.0 per cent);
— *impurities C, D:* for each impurity, not more than the area
  of the principal peak in the chromatogram obtained with
  reference solution (a) (1.0 per cent);
— *unspecified impurities:* not more than 0.2 times the area of
  the principal peak in the chromatogram obtained with
  reference solution (a) (0.20 per cent);
— *total:* maximum 3.0 per cent;
— *disregard limit:* 0.1 times the area of the principal peak in
  the chromatogram obtained with reference solution (a)
  (0.10 per cent).

Loss on drying (*2.2.32*)
Maximum 0.5 per cent, determined on 1.000 g by drying in
an oven at 105 °C at a pressure not exceeding 0.7 kPa for
2 h.

Sulfated ash (*2.4.14*)
Maximum 0.2 per cent, determined on 1.0 g.

ASSAY
Dissolve 0.250 g in 3 mL of *anhydrous formic acid R*.
Add 40 mL of *anhydrous acetic acid R*. Titrate with *0.1 M
perchloric acid*, determining the end-point potentiometrically
(*2.2.20*).

1 mL of *0.1 M perchloric acid* is equivalent to 31.54 mg of
C$_{15}$H$_{13}$N$_3$O$_3$S.

STORAGE
Protected from light.

IMPURITIES
Specified impurities A, B, C, D

A. methyl [5-(phenylsulfanyl)-1*H*-benzimidazol-2-
yl]carbamate (fenbendazole),

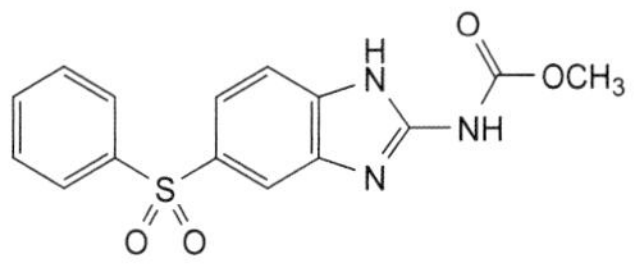

B. methyl [5-(phenylsulfonyl)-1*H*-benzimidazol-2-yl]carbamate,

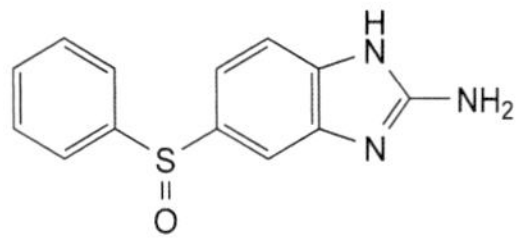

C. 5-(phenylsulfinyl)-1*H*-benzimidazol-2-amine,

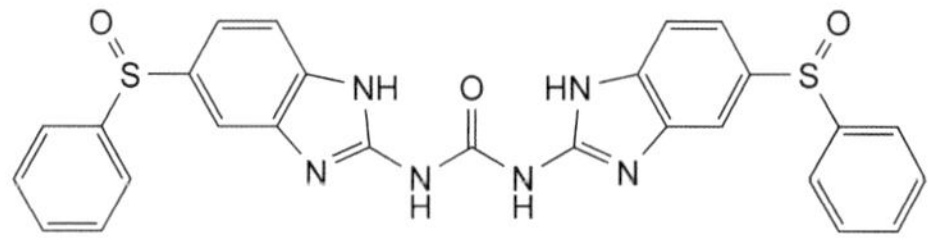

D. *N,N'*-bis[5-(phenylsulfinyl)-1*H*-benzimidazol-2-yl]urea.

———————— *Ph Eur*

Oxyclozanide

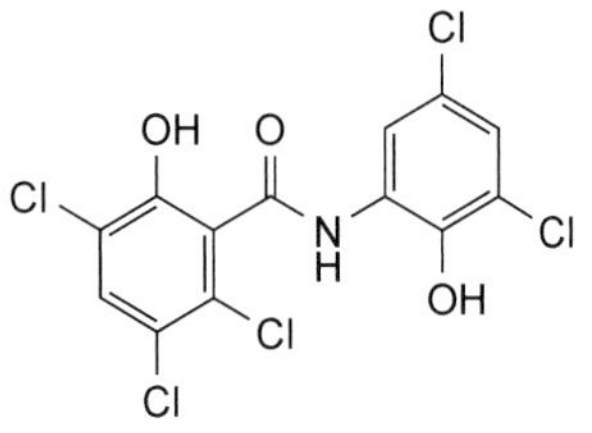

$C_{13}H_6Cl_5NO_3$ 401.5   *2277-92-1*

Action and use
Antihelminthic.

Preparation
Oxyclozanide Oral Suspension

DEFINITION
Oxyclozanide is 3,3′,5,5′,6-pentachloro-2′-hydroxysalicylanilide. It contains not less than 98.0% and not more than 101.0% of $C_{13}H_6Cl_5NO_3$, calculated with reference to the dried substance.

CHARACTERISTICS
A pale cream or cream coloured powder.

Very slightly soluble in *water*; freely soluble in *acetone*; soluble in *ethanol (96%)*; slightly soluble in *chloroform*.

IDENTIFICATION
A. The *infrared absorption spectrum*, Appendix II A, is concordant with the *reference spectrum* of oxyclozanide (*RSV 33*).

B. The *light absorption*, Appendix II B, in the range 250 to 350 nm of a 0.003% w/v solution in *acidified methanol* exhibits a maximum only at 300 nm. The *absorbance* at the maximum is about 0.76, Appendix II B.

C. *Melting point*, about 208°, Appendix V A.

TESTS
Ionisable chlorine
Dissolve 2 g in 100 mL of *methanol*, add 10 mL of 1.5M *nitric acid* and titrate with 0.1M *silver nitrate VS* determining the end point potentiometrically. Not more than 1.4 mL is required (0.25%).

Related substances
Carry out the method for *liquid chromatography*, Appendix III D, using the following solutions.

(1) 0.1% w/v of the substance being examined prepared by dissolving it in a suitable volume of *methanol* and slowly diluting with *water* containing 0.1% v/v *orthophosphoric acid* to give a solution containing about the same ratio of methanol to water as the mobile phase.

(2) Dilute 1 volume of solution (1) to 100 volumes with the mobile phase.

CHROMATOGRAPHIC CONDITIONS

(a) Use a stainless steel column (20 cm × 4.6 mm) packed with *octadecylsilyl silica gel for chromatography* (5 µm) (Hypersil ODS is suitable).

(b) Use isocratic elution and the mobile phase described below.

(c) Use a flow rate of 2 mL per minute.

(d) Use an ambient column temperature.

(e) Use a detection wavelength of 300 nm.

(f) Inject 20 µL of each solution.

MOBILE PHASE

A mixture of *methanol* and *water* containing 0.1% v/v of *orthophosphoric acid* (a mixture of 38 volumes of water and 62 volumes of methanol is usually suitable).

LIMITS

In the chromatogram obtained with solution (1):

the area of any *secondary peak* with a retention time less than that of the principal peak is not greater than one third of the area of the principal peak in the chromatogram obtained with solution (2) (0.3%);

the area of any *secondary peak* with a retention time greater than that of the principal peak is not greater than the area of the principal peak in the chromatogram obtained with solution (2) (1%).

Loss on drying
When dried to constant weight at 60° at a pressure not exceeding 0.7 kPa, loses not more than 1.0% of its weight. Use 1 g.

Sulfated ash
Not more than 0.2%, Appendix IX A.

ASSAY
Dissolve 0.25 g in 75 mL of *anhydrous pyridine* and pass a current of *nitrogen* through the solution for 5 minutes. Carry out Method II for *non-aqueous titration*, Appendix VIII A, maintaining a current of *nitrogen* through the solution throughout the titration, using 0.1M *tetrabutylammonium hydroxide VS* as titrant and determining the end point potentiometrically. Each mL of 0.1M *tetrabutylammonium hydroxide VS* is equivalent to 20.07 mg of $C_{13}H_6Cl_5NO_3$.

Piperonyl Butoxide

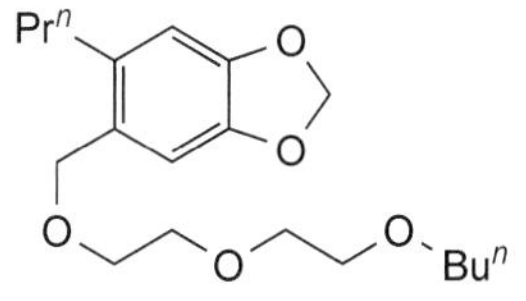

$C_{19}H_{30}O_5$ 338.4   *51-03-6*

Action and use
Insecticide.

DEFINITION
Piperonyl Butoxide is 5-[2-(2-butoxyethoxy)ethoxymethyl]-6-propyl-1,3-benzodioxole. It contains not less than 94.0% and not more than 102.0% of $C_{19}H_{30}O_5$.

CHARACTERISTICS
A colourless to light yellow, oily liquid.

Very slightly soluble in *water*; miscible with *ethanol (96%)*, with *ether* and with petroleum oils.

IDENTIFICATION
The *infrared absorption spectrum*, Appendix II A, is concordant with the *reference spectrum* of Piperonyl Butoxide *(RS 478)*.

TESTS
Refractive index
1.494 to 1.504, Appendix V E.

Weight per mL
1.050 to 1.065 g, Appendix V G.

Sulfated ash
Not more than 0.2%, Appendix IX A, Method II.

Related substances
Carry out the method for *gas chromatography*, Appendix III B, using the following solutions in n-*hexane*.

(1) 1.2% w/v of the substance being examined.

(2) Dilute 1 volume of solution (1) to 100 volumes and dilute 1 volume of the resulting solution to 10 volumes.

(3) Dilute 1 volume of solution (2) to 20 volumes.

(4) 0.16% w/v of *piperonyl butoxide impurity standard BPCRS*.

CHROMATOGRAPHIC CONDITIONS

(a) Use a fused silica capillary column (25 m × 0.32 mm) bonded with a 0.52-μm layer of 100% dimethylpolysiloxane (DB1 is suitable).

(b) Use *helium* as the carrier gas at 1 mL per minute.

(c) Use the temperature gradient described below.

(d) Use an inlet temperature of 250°.

(e) Use a flame ionisation detector at a temperature of 300°.

(f) Use a split ratio of 1:10.

(g) Inject 1 μL of each solution.

Time (Minutes)	Temperature °C	Comment
0-2	70	isothermal
2-45	70→285	linear gradient
45-60	285	isothermal

SYSTEM SUITABILITY

The test is not valid unless:

the chromatogram obtained with solution (4) closely resembles the reference chromatogram supplied with *piperonyl butoxide impurity standard BPCRS*;

in the chromatogram obtained with solution (3), the *signal-to-noise ratio* of the principal peak is at least 10;

the *resolution* between piperonyl butoxide and dipiperonyl methane is at least 2.

LIMITS

In the chromatogram obtained with solution (1):

determine the area of each *secondary peak* by *normalisation*:

dipiperonyl methane is not greater than 2.0%;

diethylene glycol butyl ether is not greater than 2.0%;

dipiperonyl ether is not greater than 1.5%;

dihydrosafrole is not greater than 50 ppm;

any other *secondary peak* is not greater than 0.5%;

the sum of all the *secondary peaks* is not greater than 2.5%.

Disregard any peak with an area less than the area of the principal peak in the chromatogram obtained with solution (2) (0.1%), with the exception of dihydrosafrole.

ASSAY
Carry out the method for *gas chromatography*, Appendix III B, using the following solutions in *hexane*.

(1) 0.16% w/v of the substance being examined.

(2) 0.16% w/v of *piperonyl butoxide BPCRS*.

(3) 0.16% w/v of *piperonyl butoxide impurity standard BPCRS*.

CHROMATOGRAPHIC CONDITIONS

The chromatographic conditions described under Related substances may be used.

SYSTEM SUITABILITY

The test is not valid unless the chromatogram obtained with solution (3) closely resembles the reference chromatogram supplied with *piperonyl butoxide impurity standard BPCRS* and the *resolution* between piperonyl butoxide and dipiperonyl methane is at least 2.0.

Determination of content

Calculate the content of $C_{19}H_{30}O_5$ using the declared content of $C_{19}H_{30}O_5$ in *piperonyl butoxide BPCRS*.

IMPURITIES

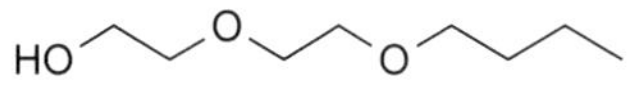

A. 2-(2-butoxyethoxy)ethanol (*diethylene glycol butyl ether*);

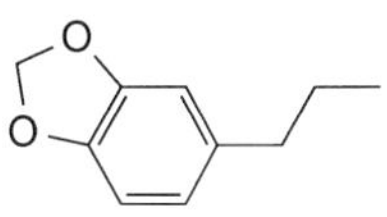

B. 5-propyl-1,3-benzodioxole, 1,2-methylendioxy-4-propylbenzene (*dihydrosafrole*);

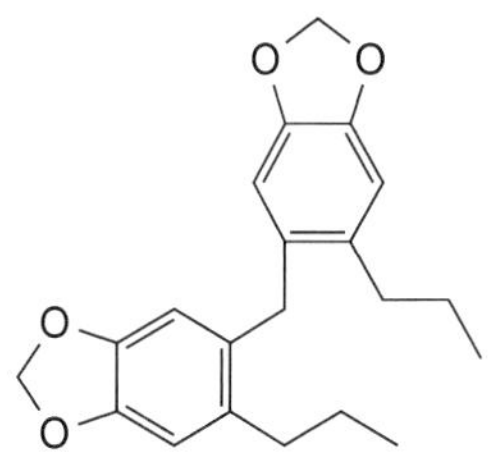

C. [1,1'- di-(6-propyl-benzo-[1,3]-dioxol-5-yl)methane] (*dipiperonyl methane*);

D. [di-((6-propyl-benzo-[1,3]dioxol-5-yl)methyl)ether] (*dipiperonyl ether*).

Potassium Selenate

K_2SeO_4 221.2 *7790-59-2*

Action and use
Used, with Alpha Tocopheryl Acetate, in the treatment of nutritional muscular dystrophy.

DEFINITION
Potassium Selenate contains not less than 97.0% and not more than 100.5% of K_2SeO_4, calculated with reference to the dried substance.

CHARACTERISTICS
Colourless crystals or a white, crystalline powder.

Freely soluble in *water*.

IDENTIFICATION
A. Yields the reactions characteristic of *potassium salts*, Appendix VI.

B. To a solution of 0.1 g in 3 mL of *water* add 1 mL of *hydrochloric acid* and 0.5 mL of *hydrazine hydrate* and boil. A red precipitate is produced.

C. Acidify 1 mL of a 1% w/v solution with 2M *hydrochloric acid* and add 0.15 mL of *barium chloride solution*. Wash the precipitate with *water* and boil with *hydrochloric acid*. Chlorine is evolved.

TESTS
Chloride
0.3 g complies with the *limit test for chlorides*, Appendix VII (170 ppm).

Selenite
Not more than 0.1%, calculated as SeO_3, when determined by the following method. Dissolve 2.0 g in 50 mL of *water*, add 50 mL of 9M *sulfuric acid*, 12 g of *disodium hydrogen orthophosphate* and 10 mL of 0.02M *potassium permanganate VS* and allow to stand for 20 minutes with occasional agitation. Titrate the excess of potassium permanganate with 0.1M *ammonium iron(II) sulfate VS*. Each mL of 0.02M *potassium permanganate VS* is equivalent to 6.348 mg of SeO_3.

Loss on drying
When dried to constant weight at 105°, loses not more than 0.1% of its weight. Use 1 g.

ASSAY
Dissolve 1 g in 60 mL of *water*, add 15 mL of *hydrochloric acid* and 5 mL of a 50% w/v solution of *hydrazine hydrate*, boil, heat on a water bath for 3 hours, and allow to stand overnight. Transfer the precipitated selenium to a weighed, sintered-glass crucible, wash with hot *water* until the washings are free from chloride ions, rinse with *absolute ethanol* and dry at 105° to constant weight. Correct for the amount of selenium present as selenite found in the test for selenite. Each mg of selenium is equivalent to 2.801 mg of K_2SeO_4.

Pyrethrum Flower
Dalmatian Insect Flowers

Preparation
Pyrethrum Extract

DEFINITION
Pyrethrum Flower is the dried flower heads of *Chrysanthemum cinerariaefolium* Vis. It contains not less than 1.0% of pyrethrins of which not less than half consists of pyrethrin I.

CHARACTERISTICS
Odour, faint but characteristic.

Macroscopical
Capitula occurring loose or compressed into masses; individual capitula more or less flattened, about 6 to 12 mm in diameter, and commonly with a short piece of stalk attached; receptacle almost flat, about 5 to 10 mm in diameter, without paleae, surrounded by an involucre of 2 or 3 rows of brownish yellow lanceolate bracts; ray florets number about 15 to 23, disc florets about 200 to 300; corollas of ligulate florets pale brownish and shrivelled, oblong, about 16 mm long with three rounded apical teeth, the central tooth frequently smaller than the two lateral ones; in the middle region of the corolla about 17 veins present; corollas of the disc florets tubular, yellow, with five short lobes, and enclosing five epipetalous, syngenesious stamens; each ray and disc floret has an inferior five-ribbed oblong ovary about 5 mm long with a filiform style and bifid stigma and surmounted by a membranous tubular calyx about 1 mm long; ovaries and lower part of the corollas covered with numerous scattered shining oil glands.

Microscopical
Loosely arranged large-celled sclereids of the receptacle with moderately thickened walls and few pits; fragments of the corollas of the florets, those of the ray florets showing puckered papillae on the inner epidermis and sinuous-walled cells with a striated cuticle on the outer epidermis, those of the tubular florets composed of cells with slightly thickened walls with papillae occurring only on the lobes; ovoid to spherical glandular trichomes each composed of a short, biseriate stalk and a biseriate head with two or four cells; covering trichomes twisted, T-shaped with moderately thickened walls; numerous pollen grains, spherical, 34 to 40 µm in diameter with three pores and a warty and spiny exine; groups of small rectangular sclereids, some containing prisms of calcium oxalate, from the involucral bracts, ovaries and basal region of the calyx; parenchymatous cells of the calyx and ovaries containing tabular or diamond-shaped crystals of calcium oxalate; occasional cells containing cluster crystals from the base of the corolla of the disc florets; portions of stigmas with papillose tips.

Acid-insoluble ash
Not more than 1.0%, Appendix XI K.

ASSAY
Transfer 12.5 g in *No. 1000 powder* to an apparatus for the *continuous extraction of drugs*, Appendix XI F, and extract with *aromatic-free petroleum spirit (boiling range, 40° to 60°)* for 7 hours. Evaporate the extract to about 40 mL and allow to stand overnight at 0° to 5°. Add 20 mL of 0.5M *ethanolic potassium hydroxide* and boil under a reflux condenser for 45 minutes. Transfer the solution to a beaker and wash the flask with sufficient hot *water*, adding the washings to the beaker, to produce a total volume of 200 mL. Boil until the volume is reduced to 150 mL, cool rapidly and transfer the

solution to a stoppered flask, washing the beaker with three 20 mL quantities of *water* and transferring any gummy residue to the flask. Add 1 g of diatomaceous earth (Filtercel is suitable) and 10 mL of *barium chloride solution*, swirl gently and add sufficient *water* to produce 250 mL. Stopper the flask, shake vigorously until the separating liquid is clear and filter the suspension through a filter paper (Whatman No. 1 is suitable).

For pyrethrin I

Transfer 200 mL of the filtrate to a separating funnel, rinsing the measuring vessel with two 5 mL quantities of *water*, and add 0.05 mL of *phenolphthalein solution R1*. Neutralise the solution by the drop wise addition of *hydrochloric acid* and add 1 mL of *hydrochloric acid* in excess. Add 5 mL of a saturated solution of *sodium chloride* and 50 mL of *aromatic-free petroleum spirit (boiling range, 40° to 60°)*, shake vigorously for 1 minute, allow to separate, remove and retain the lower layer. Filter the petroleum spirit extract through absorbent cotton into a second separating funnel containing 10 mL of *water*. Return the aqueous layer to the first separating funnel and repeat the extraction with 50 mL and then with 25 mL of *aromatic-free petroleum spirit (boiling range, 40° to 60°)*, reserving the aqueous layer for the assay of pyrethrin II, and filtering the petroleum spirit extracts through the same absorbent cotton into the second separating funnel. Shake the combined petroleum spirit extracts and water for about 30 seconds and allow to separate; remove the lower layer and add it to the aqueous liquid reserved for the assay of pyrethrin II. Wash the combined petroleum spirit extracts with a further 10 mL of *water*, adding the washings to the reserved aqueous liquid.

To the petroleum spirit extracts add 5 mL of 0.1M *sodium hydroxide*, shake vigorously for 1 minute, allow to separate and remove the clear lower layer, washing the stem of the separating funnel with 1 mL of *water*. Repeat the extraction by shaking for about 30 seconds with two quantities of 2.5 mL and 1.5 mL of 0.1M *sodium hydroxide* and add the extracts to the alkaline extract. Add to the flask 10 mL of *mercury(II) sulfate solution*, stopper, swirl and allow to stand in the dark at 25° ±0.5° for exactly 60 minutes after the addition of the mercury(II) sulfate solution. Add 20 mL of *acetone* and 3 mL of a saturated solution of *sodium chloride*, heat to boiling on a water bath, allow the precipitate to settle and decant the supernatant liquid through a filter paper (Whatman No. 1 is suitable), retaining most of the precipitate in the flask. Wash the precipitate with 10 mL of *acetone*, again boil, allow to settle and decant through the same filter paper. Repeat the washing and decanting with three 10 mL quantities of hot *chloroform*. Transfer the filter paper to the flask, add 50 mL of a cooled mixture of three volumes of *hydrochloric acid* and two volumes of *water*, 1 mL of *strong iodine monochloride reagent* and 6 mL of *chloroform*. Titrate with 0.01M *potassium iodate VS*, running almost all the required volume of titrant into the flask in one portion. Continue the titration, shaking the flask vigorously for 30 seconds after each addition of the titrant, until the chloroform is colourless. Repeat the operation without the extract; the difference between the titrations represents the amount of potassium iodate required. Each mL of 0.01M *potassium iodate VS* is equivalent to 5.7 mg of pyrethrin I.

For pyrethrin II

Transfer the combined aqueous liquids reserved in the Assay for pyrethrin I to a beaker, cover with a watch glass and evaporate to 50 mL within 35 to 45 minutes. Cool, washing the underside of the watch glass with not more than 5 mL of *water* and adding the washings to the beaker. Filter through absorbent cotton into a separating funnel, washing with successive quantities of 10, 7.5, 7.5, 5 and 5 mL of *water*. Saturate the aqueous liquid with *sodium chloride*, add 10 mL of *hydrochloric acid* and 50 mL of *ether*, shake for 1 minute, allow to separate, and remove the lower layer. Repeat the extraction successively with 50, 25 and 25 mL of *ether*. Wash the combined ether extracts with three 10 mL quantities of a saturated solution of *sodium chloride* and transfer the ether layer to a flask with the aid of 10 mL of *ether*. Remove the bulk of the ether by distillation and remove the remainder with a gentle current of air and dry the residue at 100° for 10 minutes, removing any residual acid fumes with a gentle current of air. Add 2 mL of *ethanol (96%)* previously neutralised to *phenolphthalein solution R1* and 0.05 mL of *phenolphthalein solution R1*, swirl to dissolve the residue, add 20 mL of *carbon dioxide-free water* and titrate rapidly with 0.02M *sodium hydroxide VS* until the colour changes to brownish pink and persists for 30 seconds, keeping the flask stoppered between additions of alkali. Repeat the operation using the aqueous liquid reserved for the repeat operation in the Assay for pyrethrin I. The difference between the titrations represents the volume of 0.02M *sodium hydroxide VS* required. Each mL of 0.02M *sodium hydroxide VS* is equivalent to 3.74 mg of pyrethrin II.

Ronidazole

$C_6H_8N_4O_4$	200.2	7681-76-7

Action and use

Antiprotozoal.

DEFINITION

Ronidazole is (1-methyl-5-nitroimidazol-2-yl)methyl carbamate. It contains not less than 98.5% and not more than 101.0% of $C_6H_8N_4O_4$, calculated with reference to the anhydrous substance.

CHARACTERISTICS

A white to yellowish brown powder; odourless or almost odourless.

Slightly soluble in *water*, in *chloroform* and in *ethanol (96%)*; very slightly soluble in ether.

IDENTIFICATION

A. The *infrared absorption spectrum*, Appendix II A, is concordant with the *reference spectrum* of ronidazole *(RSV 36)*.

B. The *light absorption*, Appendix II B, in the range 230 to 350 nm of a 0.002% w/v solution in 0.1M *methanolic hydrochloric acid* exhibits a maximum only at 270 nm. The *absorbance* at the maximum is about 0.64.

C. *Melting point*, about 167°, Appendix V A.

TESTS

Colour of solution

A 0.5% w/v solution in *methanol* is not more intensely coloured than *reference solution Y_6, Appendix IV B*, Method II.

(1-Methyl-5-nitroimidazol-2-yl)methanol

Carry out the method for *thin-layer chromatography*, Appendix III A, using *silica gel GF₂₅₄* as the coating substance and a mixture of 5 volumes of *glacial acetic acid*, 5 volumes of *methanol* and 80 volumes of *toluene* as the mobile phase. Apply separately to the plate 20 μL of each of two solutions in *acetone* containing (1) 1.0% w/v of the substance being examined and (2) 0.0050% w/v of *(1-methyl-5-nitroimidazol-2-yl)methanol BPCRS*. After removal of the plate, allow it to dry in air and examine under *ultraviolet light (254 nm)*. Any spot in the chromatogram obtained with solution (1) corresponding to (1-methyl-5-nitroimidazol-2-yl)methanol is not more intense than the spot in the chromatogram obtained with solution (2) (0.5%).

Water

Not more than 0.5% w/w, Appendix IX C. Use 5 g.

Sulfated ash

Not more than 0.1%, Appendix IX A.

ASSAY

Carry out Method I for *non-aqueous titration*, Appendix VIII A, using 0.3 g and determining the end point potentiometrically. Each mL of 0.1M *perchloric acid VS* is equivalent to 20.02 mg $C_6H_8N_4O_4$.

STORAGE

Ronidazole should be protected from light.

Selamectin

(Selamectin for Veterinary Use, Ph. Eur. monograph 2268)

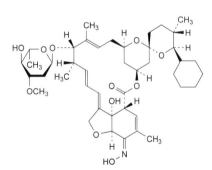

$C_{43}H_{63}NO_{11}$ 770   *165108-07-6*

Ph Eur

DEFINITION

(2aE,2′R,4E,5′S,6S,6′S,7S,8E,11R,15S,17aR,20Z,20aR,
20bS)-6′-cyclohexyl-7-[(2,6-dideoxy-3-O-methyl-α-L-*arabino*-hexopyranosyl)oxy]-20b-hydroxy-20-(hydroxyimino)-5′,6,8,19-tetramethyl-3′,4′,5′,6,6′,7,10,11,14,15,17a,20,20a,20b-tetradecahydrospiro[2H,17H-11,15-methanofuro[4,3,2-pq][2,6]benzodioxacyclooctadecine-13,2′-pyran]-17-one
((5Z,21R,25S)-25-cyclohexyl-4′-O-de(2,6-dideoxy-3-O-methyl-α-L-*arabino*-hexopyranosyl)-5-demethoxy-25-de(1-methylpropyl)-22,23-dihydro-5-(hydroxyimino)avermectin A₁ₐ).

Semi-synthetic product derived from a fermentation product.

Content

96.0 per cent to 102.0 per cent (anhydrous substance).

CHARACTERS

Appearance

White or almost white, hygroscopic powder.

Solubility

Practically insoluble in water, freely soluble in isopropyl alcohol, soluble in acetone and in methylene chloride, sparingly soluble in methanol.

IDENTIFICATION

Infrared absorption spectrophotometry (*2.2.24*).

Comparison selamectin CRS.

TESTS

Related substances

Liquid chromatography (*2.2.29*).

Solvent mixture water R, acetonitrile R (40:60 V/V).

Test solution Dissolve 25 mg of the substance to be examined in the solvent mixture and dilute to 50 mL with the solvent mixture.

Reference solution (a) Dilute 1.0 mL of the test solution to 100.0 mL with the solvent mixture.

Reference solution (b) Dissolve 2.5 mg of *selamectin for peak identification CRS* (containing impurities A, C and D) in the solvent mixture and dilute to 5 mL with the solvent mixture.

Reference solution (c) Dissolve the contents of a vial of *selamectin impurity B CRS* in 1.0 mL of reference solution (b).

Column:
— *size*: *l* = 0.15 m, Ø = 3.9 mm;
— *stationary phase*: end-capped octadecylsilyl silica gel for chromatography R (4 μm);
— *temperature*: 30 °C.

Mobile phase:
— *mobile phase A*: water R;
— *mobile phase B*: acetonitrile R;

Time (min)	Mobile phase A (per cent V/V)	Mobile phase B (per cent V/V)
0 - 28	40	60
28 - 45	40 → 20	60 → 80

Flow rate 2.0 mL/min.

Detection Spectrophotometer at 243 nm.

Injection 20 μL.

Identification of impurities Use the chromatogram supplied with *selamectin for peak identification CRS* and the chromatogram obtained with reference solution (c) to identify the peaks due to impurities A, B, C and D.

Relative retention With reference to selamectin (retention time = about 22 min): impurity A = about 0.2; impurity B = about 0.4; impurity C = about 0.5; impurity D = about 1.7.

System suitability Reference solution (c):
— *resolution*: minimum 2.5 between the peaks due to impurities B and C.

Limits:
— *correction factor*: for the calculation of content, multiply the peak area of impurity D by 1.5;
— *impurities A, B*: for each impurity, not more than twice the area of the principal peak in the chromatogram obtained with reference solution (a) (2.0 per cent);
— *impurities C, D*: for each impurity, not more than 1.5 times the area of the principal peak in the

chromatogram obtained with reference solution (a) (1.5 per cent);
— *any other impurity*: for each impurity, not more than the area of the principal peak in the chromatogram obtained with reference solution (a) (1.0 per cent);
— *total*: not more than 4 times the area of the principal peak in the chromatogram obtained with reference solution (a) (4.0 per cent);
— *disregard limit*: 0.2 times the area of the principal peak in the chromatogram obtained with reference solution (a) (0.2 per cent).

Heavy metals (*2.4.8*)
Maximum 20 ppm.

Dissolve 2.0 g in *ethanol (96 per cent) R* and dilute to 20.0 mL with the same solvent. 12 mL of the solution complies with test B. Prepare the reference solution using lead standard solution (2 ppm Pb) obtained by diluting *lead standard solution (100 ppm Pb) R* with *ethanol (96 per cent) R*. Filter the solution through a membrane filter (nominal pore size 0.45 μm). Compare the spots on the filters obtained with the different solutions. Any brownish-black colour in the spot from the test solution is not more intense than that in the spot from the reference solution.

Water (*2.5.12, Method A*)
Maximum 7.0 per cent, determined on 0.20 g.

Sulfated ash (*2.4.14*)
Maximum 0.1 per cent, determined on 1.0 g.

ASSAY
Liquid chromatography (*2.2.29*).

Test solution Dissolve 50.0 mg of the substance to be examined in the mobile phase and dilute to 250.0 mL with the mobile phase.

Reference solution Dissolve 50.0 mg of *selamectin CRS* in the mobile phase and dilute to 250.0 mL with the mobile phase.

Column:
— *size*: l = 0.15 m, Ø = 3.9 mm;
— *stationary phase*: end-capped octadecylsilyl silica gel for chromatography R (4 μm);
— *temperature*: 30 °C.

Mobile phase water R, acetonitrile R (20:80 *V/V*).

Flow rate 1.0 mL/min.

Detection Spectrophotometer at 243 nm.

Injection 20 μL.

Run time Twice the retention time of selamectin.

Retention time Selamectin = about 9 min.

Calculate the percentage content of $C_{43}H_{63}NO_{11}$ from the declared content of *selamectin CRS*.

STORAGE
In an airtight container.

IMPURITIES
Specified impurities A, B, C, D

A. (2a*E*,2′*R*,4*E*,4′*S*,5′*S*,6*S*,6′*R*,7*S*,8*E*,11*R*,15*S*,17a*R*,20*Z*, 20a*R*,20b*S*)-6′-cyclohexyl-7-[(2,6-dideoxy-3-*O*-methyl-α-L-*arabino*-hexopyranosyl)oxy]-4′,20b-dihydroxy-20-(hydroxyimino)-5′,6,8,19-tetramethyl-3′,4′,5′,6,6′,7,10,11,14,15,17a,20,20a,20b-tetradecahydrospiro[2*H*,17*H*-11,15-methanofuro[4,3,2-*pq*][2,6]benzodioxacyclooctadecine-13,2′-pyran]-17-one ((5*Z*,21*R*,23*S*,25*R*)-25-cyclohexyl-4′-*O*-de(2,6-dideoxy-3-*O*-methyl-α-L-*arabino*-hexopyranosyl)-5-demethoxy-25-de(1-methylpropyl)-22,23-dihydro-23-hydroxy-5-(hydroxyimino)avermectin A₁ₐ),

B. (2a*E*,2′*S*,4*E*,5′*S*,6*S*,6′*R*,7*S*,8*E*,11*R*,15*S*,17a*R*,20*Z*,20a*R*, 20b*S*)-6′-cyclohexyl-7-[(2,6-dideoxy-3-*O*-methyl-α-L-*arabino*-hexopyranosyl)oxy]-20b-hydroxy-20-(hydroxyimino)-5′,6,8,19-tetramethyl-5′,6,6′,7,10,11,14,15,17a,20,20a,20b-dodecahydrospiro[2*H*,17*H*-11,15-methanofuro[4,3,2-*pq*][2,6]benzodioxacyclooctadecine-13,2′-pyran]-17-one ((5*Z*,25*R*)-25-cyclohexyl-4′-*O*-de(2,6-dideoxy-3-*O*-methyl-α-L-*arabino*-hexopyranosyl)-5-demethoxy-25-de(1-methylpropyl)-5-(hydroxyimino)avermectin A₁ₐ),

C. (2a*E*,2′*R*,4*E*,5′*S*,6*S*,6′*S*,7*S*,8*E*,11*R*,15*S*,17a*R*,20*Z*,20a*R*, 20b*S*)-6′-cyclohexyl-7,20b-dihydroxy-20-(hydroxyimino)-5′,6,8,19-tetramethyl-3′,4′,5′,6,6′,7,10,11,14,15,17a,20,20a,20b-tetradecahydrospiro[2*H*,17*H*-11,15-methanofuro[4,3,2-*pq*][2,6]benzodioxacyclooctadecine-13,2′-pyran]-17-one ((5*Z*,21*R*,25*S*)-25-cyclohexyl-13-*O*-de[2,6-dideoxy-4-*O*-

(2,6-dideoxy-3-*O*-methyl-α-L-*arabino*-hexopyranosyl)-3-*O*-methyl-α-L-*arabino*-hexopyranosyl]-5-demethoxy-25-de(1-methylpropyl)-22,23-dihydro-5-(hydroxyimino)avermectin A$_{1a}$),

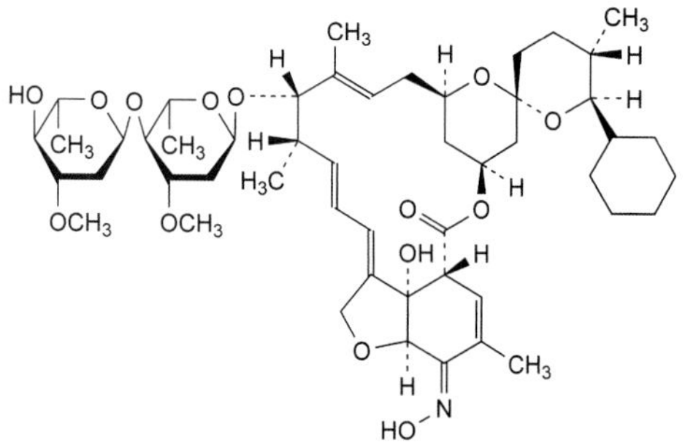

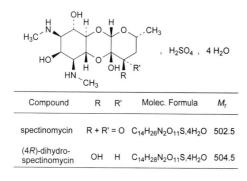

D. (2a*E*,2′*R*,4*E*,5′*S*,6*S*,6′*S*,7*S*,8*E*,11*R*,15*S*,17a*R*,20*Z*,20a*R*,
20b*S*)-6′-cyclohexyl-7-[(2,6-dideoxy-3-*O*-methyl-α-L-*arabino*-hexopyranosyl-(1→4)-2,6-dideoxy-3-*O*-methyl-α-L-*arabino*-hexopyranosyl)oxy]-20b-hydroxy-20-(hydroxyimino)-5′,6,8,19-tetramethyl-3′,4′,5′,6,6′,7,10,11,14,15,17a,20,20a,20b-tetradecahydrospiro[2*H*,17*H*-11,15-methanofuro[4,3,2-*pq*][2,6]benzodioxacyclooctadecine-13,2′-pyran]-17-one
((5*Z*,21*R*,25*S*)-25-cyclohexyl-5-demethoxy-25-de(1-methylpropyl)-22,23-dihydro-5-(hydroxyimino)avermectin A$_{1a}$).

_____ Ph Eur

Spectinomycin Sulfate Tetrahydrate

Spectinomycin Sulphate Tetrahydrate

(Spectinomycin Sulfate Tetrahydrate for Veterinary Use, Ph Eur monograph 1658)

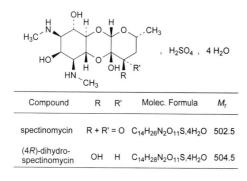

Compound	R	R'	Molec. Formula	M_r
spectinomycin	R + R' = O		$C_{14}H_{26}N_2O_{11}S,4H_2O$	502.5
(4R)-dihydro-spectinomycin	OH	H	$C_{14}H_{28}N_2O_{11}S,4H_2O$	504.5

Ph Eur _____

DEFINITION

Mixture of (2*R*,4a*R*,5a*R*,6*S*,7*S*,8*R*,9*S*,9a*R*,10a*S*)-4a,7,9-trihydroxy-2-methyl-6,8-bis(methylamino)decahydro-4*H*-pyrano[2,3-*b*][1,4]benzodioxin-4-one sulfate tetrahydrate (spectinomycin sulfate tetrahydrate) and (2*R*,4*R*,4a*S*,5a*R*,6*S*,7*S*,8*R*,9*S*,9a*R*,10a*S*)-2-methyl-6,8-bis(methylamino)decahydro-2*H*-pyrano[2,3-*b*][1,4]benzodioxine-4,4a,7,9-tetrol sulfate tetrahydrate ((4*R*)-dihydrospectinomycin sulfate tetrahydrate).

It is produced by *Streptomyces spectabilis* or by any other means.

Content

— *(4R)-dihydrospectinomycin sulfate*: maximum 2.0 per cent (anhydrous substance);
— *sum of the contents of spectinomycin sulfate and (4R)-dihydrospectinomycin sulfate*: 93.0 per cent to 102.0 per cent (anhydrous substance).

CHARACTERS

Appearance
White or almost white powder.

Solubility
Freely soluble in water, insoluble in ethanol (96 per cent).

IDENTIFICATION

A. Infrared absorption spectrophotometry (*2.2.24*).

Comparison spectinomycin sulfate tetrahydrate CRS.

B. Dilute 1.0 mL of solution S (see Tests) to 10 mL with *water R*. The solution gives reaction (a) of sulfates (*2.3.1*).

TESTS

Solution S
Dissolve 2.50 g in *carbon dioxide-free water R* and dilute to 25.0 mL with the same solvent.

Appearance of solution
Solution S is clear (*2.2.1*) and colourless (*2.2.2, Method II*).

pH (*2.2.3*)
3.8 to 5.6 for solution S.

Specific optical rotation (*2.2.7*)
+ 10.0 to + 14.0 (anhydrous substance).

Dissolve 2.50 g in an 8 mL/L solution of *concentrated ammonia R1* and dilute to 25.0 mL with the same solvent. Allow the solution to stand at room temperature for not less than 30 min and not more than 2 h prior to determination.

Related substances
Liquid chromatography (*2.2.29*). *In order to avoid the formation of anomers, prepare the solutions immediately before use.*

Test solution Dissolve 15.0 mg of the substance to be examined in the mobile phase and dilute to 100.0 mL with the mobile phase.

Reference solution (a) Dissolve 3 mg of *spectinomycin for system suitability CRS* in the mobile phase and dilute to 20 mL with the mobile phase.

Reference solution (b) Dilute 1.0 mL of the test solution to 100.0 mL with the mobile phase.

Reference solution (c) Dilute 3.0 mL of reference solution (b) to 10.0 mL with the mobile phase.

Column:
— *size: l* = 0.25 m, Ø = 4.6 mm;
— *stationary phase: octylsilyl silica gel for chromatography R* (5 μm);
— *temperature*: ambient and constant.

Mobile phase Dissolve 4.2 g of *oxalic acid R* and 2.0 mL of *heptafluorobutyric acid R* in *water R* and dilute to 1000 mL with *water R*; adjust to pH 3.2 with *sodium hydroxide solution R*; add 105 mL of *acetonitrile R* and mix; filter through a 0.45 μm filter and degas with *helium for chromatography R* for 10 min.

Flow rate 1.0 mL/min.

Post-column solution carbonate-free sodium hydroxide solution R diluted with *carbon dioxide-free water R* to obtain a final concentration of NaOH of 21 g/L. Degas the solution with *helium for chromatography R* for 10 min before use. Add it pulse-less to the column effluent using a 375 μL polymeric mixing coil.

Post-column flow rate 0.5 mL/min.

Detection Pulsed amperometric detection or equivalent with a gold indicator electrode having preferably a diameter of 1.4 mm or greater, a suitable reference electrode and a stainless steel counter electrode, held at + 0.12 V detection, + 0.70 V oxidation and −0.60 V reduction potentials respectively, with pulse durations according to the instrument used. Keep the detection cell at ambient and constant temperature. Clean the gold indicator electrode with an eraser and damp precision wipe prior to start-up of the system to enhance the detector sensitivity and increase the signal-to-noise ratio.

Injection 20 μL.

Run time 1.5 times the retention time of spectinomycin.

Identification of impurities Use the chromatogram supplied with *spectinomycin for system suitability CRS* and the chromatogram obtained with reference solution (a) to identify the peaks due to impurities A, D and E.

Relative retention With reference to spectinomycin (retention time = 11 min to 20 min): impurity A = about 0.5; impurity D = about 0.7; impurity E = about 0.9; (4R)-dihydrospectinomycin = about 1.3.

System suitability: reference solution (a):
— *resolution*: minimum 1.5 between the peaks due to impurity E and spectinomycin.

Limits:
— *correction factor*: for the calculation of content, multiply the peak area of impurity A by 0.4;
— *impurities A, E*: for each impurity, not more than the area of the principal peak in the chromatogram obtained with reference solution (b) (1.0 per cent);
— *impurity D*: not more than 4 times the area of the principal peak in the chromatogram obtained with reference solution (b) (4.0 per cent);
— *any other impurity*: for each impurity, not more than the area of the principal peak in the chromatogram obtained with reference solution (b) (1.0 per cent);
— *total*: not more than 6 times the area of the principal peak in the chromatogram obtained with reference solution (b) (6.0 per cent);
— *disregard limit*: the area of the principal peak in the chromatogram obtained with reference solution (c) (0.3 per cent); disregard the peak due to (4R)-dihydrospectinomycin.

Water (*2.5.12*)
12.0 per cent to 16.5 per cent, determined on 0.100 g.

Sulfated ash (*2.4.14*)
Maximum 1.0 per cent, determined on 1.0 g.

Bacterial endotoxins (*2.6.14*)
Less than 0.17 IU/mg, if intended for use in the manufacture of parenteral preparations without a further appropriate procedure for the removal of bacterial endotoxins. Prepare the solutions using a 0.42 per cent *m/m* solution of *sodium hydrogen carbonate R*.

ASSAY
Liquid chromatography (*2.2.29*) as described in the test for related substances with the following modifications.

Test solution Dissolve 40.0 mg of the substance to be examined in *water R* and dilute to 50.0 mL with the same solvent. Allow to stand for not less than 15 h and not more than 72 h (formation of anomers). Dilute 5.0 mL of this solution to 50.0 mL with the mobile phase.

Reference solution Dissolve 40.0 mg of *spectinomycin hydrochloride CRS* (containing (4R)-dihydrospectinomycin) in *water R* and dilute to 50.0 mL with the same solvent. Allow to stand for the same period of time as the test solution (formation of anomers). Dilute 5.0 mL of this solution to 50.0 mL with the mobile phase.

System suitability:
— *repeatability*: maximum relative standard deviation of 3.0 per cent for the principal peak after 6 injections of the reference solution.

Calculate the sum of the percentage contents of spectinomycin sulfate and (4R)-dihydrospectinomycin sulfate from the declared contents of $C_{14}H_{26}Cl_2N_2O_7$ and $C_{14}H_{28}Cl_2N_2O_7$ in *spectinomycin hydrochloride CRS*, applying a correction factor of 1.062.

STORAGE
In an airtight container. If the substance is sterile, store in a sterile, airtight, tamper-proof container.

IMPURITIES
Specified impurities A, D, E

Other detectable impurities (the following substances would, if present at a sufficient level, be detected by one or other of the tests in the monograph. They are limited by the general acceptance criterion for other/unspecified impurities and/or by the general monograph Substances for pharmaceutical use (2034). It is therefore not necessary to identify these impurities for demonstration of compliance. See also 5.10. *Control of impurities in substances for pharmaceutical use*): B, C, F, G.

A. 1,3-dideoxy-1,3-bis(methylamino)-*myo*-inositol (actinamine),

B. (2S,3RS,5R)-3-hydroxy-5-methyl-2-[[(1r,2R,3S,4r,5R,6S)-2,4,6-trihydroxy-3,5-bis(methylamino)cyclohexyl]oxy]tetrahydrofuran-3-carboxylic acid (actinospectinoic acid),

C. R1 = CH₃, R2 = R4 = H, R3 = OH:
(2R,4S,4aS,5aR,6S,7S,8R,9S,9aR,10aS)-2-methyl-6,8-bis(methylamino)decahydro-2H-pyrano[2,3-b][1,4]benzodioxine-4,4a,7,9-tetrol ((4S)-dihydrospectinomycin),

D. R1 = CH₃, R2 = H, R3 = R4 = OH:
(2R,3R,4S,4aS,5aR,6S,7S,8R,9S,9aR,10aS)-2-methyl-6,8-bis(methylamino)decahydro-2H-pyrano[2,3-b][1,4]benzodioxine-3,4,4a,7,9-pentol
(dihydroxyspectinomycin),

E. R1 = R4 = H, R2 + R3 = O:
(2R,4aR,5aR,6S,7R,8R,9S,9aR,10aS)-6-amino-4a,7,9-trihydroxy-2-methyl-8-(methylamino)decahydro-4H-pyrano[2,3-b][1,4]benzodioxin-4-one
(N-desmethylspectinomycin),

G. R1 = CH₃, R2 + R3 = O, R4 = OH:
(2R,3S,4aR,5aR,6S,7S,8R,9S,9aR,10aS)-3,4a,7,9-tetrahydroxy-2-methyl-6,8-bis(methylamino)decahydro-4H-pyrano[2,3-b][1,4]benzodioxin-4-one
(tetrahydroxyspectinomycin),

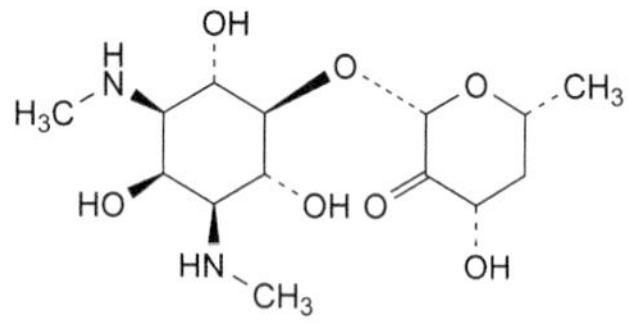

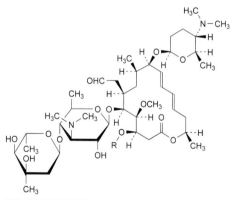

F. (2S,4S,6R)-4-hydroxy-6-methyl-2-[[(1r,2R,3S,4r,5R,6S)-2,4,6-trihydroxy-3,5-bis(methylamino)cyclohexyl]oxy]dihydro-2H-pyran-3(4H)-one (triol spectinomycin).

_____ *Ph Eur*

Spiramycin

(Ph. Eur. monograph 0293)

Compound	R	Molec Formula	M_r
Spiramycin I	H	$C_{43}H_{74}N_2O_{14}$	843.1
Spiramycin II	CO-CH₃	$C_{45}H_{76}N_2O_{15}$	885.1
Spiramycin III	CO-CH₂-CH₃	$C_{46}H_{78}N_2O_{15}$	899.1

8025-81-8

Action and use

Antibacterial.

Ph Eur _____

DEFINITION

Macrolide antibiotic produced by the growth of certain strains of *Streptomyces ambofaciens* or obtained by any other means. The main component is

(4R,5S,6S,7R,9R,10R,11E,13E,16R)-6-[[3,6-dideoxy-4-O-(2,6-dideoxy-3-C-methyl-α-L-*ribo*-hexopyranosyl)-3-(dimethylamino)-β-D-glucopyranosyl]oxy]-4-hydroxy-5-methoxy-9,16-dimethyl-7-(2-oxoethyl)-10-[[2,3,4,6-tetradeoxy-4-(dimethylamino)-D-*erythro*-hexopyranosyl]oxy]oxacyclohexadeca-11,13-dien-2-one (spiramycin I; 843). Spiramycin II (4-O-acetylspiramycin I) and spiramycin III (4-O-propanoylspiramycin I) are also present.

Potency

Minimum 4100 IU/mg (dried substance).

CHARACTERS

Appearance

White or slightly yellowish powder, slightly hygroscopic.

Solubility

Slightly soluble in water, freely soluble in acetone, in ethanol (96 per cent) and in methanol.

IDENTIFICATION

A. Ultraviolet and visible absorption spectrophotometry (2.2.25).

Test solution Dissolve 0.10 g of the substance to be examined in *methanol R* and dilute to 100.0 mL with the same solvent. Dilute 1.0 mL of this solution to 100.0 mL with *methanol R*.

Spectral range 220-350 nm.

Absorption maximum At 232 nm.

Specific absorbance at the absorption maximum About 340.

B. Thin-layer chromatography (2.2.27).

Test solution Dissolve 40 mg of the substance to be examined in *methanol R* and dilute to 10 mL with the same solvent.

Reference solution (a) Dissolve 40 mg of *spiramycin CRS* in *methanol R* and dilute to 10 mL with the same solvent.

Reference solution (b) Dissolve 40 mg of *erythromycin A CRS* in *methanol R* and dilute to 10 mL with the same solvent.

Plate TLC silica gel G plate R.

Mobile phase The upper layer of a mixture of 4 volumes of *2-propanol R*, 8 volumes of a 150 g/L solution of *ammonium acetate R* previously adjusted to pH 9.6 with *strong sodium hydroxide solution R*, and 9 volumes of *ethyl acetate R*.

Application 5 μL.

Development Over 3/4 of the plate.

Drying In air.

Detection Spray with *anisaldehyde solution R1* and heat at 110 °C for 5 min.

Results The principal spot in the chromatogram obtained with the test solution is similar in position, colour and size to the principal spot in the chromatogram obtained with reference solution (a). If in the chromatogram obtained with the test solution 1 or 2 spots occur with R_F values slightly higher than that of the principal spot, these spots are similar in position and colour to the secondary spots in the chromatogram obtained with reference solution (a) and differ from the spots in the chromatogram obtained with reference solution (b).

C. Dissolve 0.5 g in 10 mL of *0.05 M sulfuric acid* and add 25 mL of *water R*. Adjust to about pH 8 with *0.1 M sodium hydroxide* and dilute to 50 mL with *water R*. To 5 mL of this solution add 2 mL of a mixture of 1 volume of *water R* and 2 volumes of *sulfuric acid R*. A brown colour develops.

TESTS

pH (2.2.3)

8.5 to 10.5.

Dissolve 0.5 g in 5 mL of *methanol R* and dilute to 100 mL with *carbon dioxide-free water R*.

Specific optical rotation *(2.2.7)*
−80 to −85 (dried substance).

Dissolve 1.00 g in a 10 per cent *V/V* solution of *dilute acetic acid R* and dilute to 50.0 mL with the same acid solution.

Composition
Liquid chromatography *(2.2.29)* as described in the test for related substances.

Injection Test solution and reference solution (a).

Calculate the percentage content using the declared content of spiramycins I, II and III in *spiramycin CRS*.

Composition of spiramycins (dried substance):
— *spiramycin I*: minimum 80.0 per cent,
— *spiramycin II*: maximum 5.0 per cent,
— *spiramycin III*: maximum 10.0 per cent,
— *sum of spiramycins I, II and III*: minimum 90.0 per cent.

Related substances
Liquid chromatography *(2.2.29)*. *Prepare the solutions immediately before use.*

Solvent mixture methanol R, water R (30:70 *V/V*).

Test solution Dissolve 25.0 mg of the substance to be examined in the solvent mixture and dilute to 25.0 mL with the solvent mixture.

Reference solution (a) Dissolve 25.0 mg of *spiramycin CRS* in the solvent mixture and dilute to 25.0 mL with the solvent mixture.

Reference solution (b) Dilute 2.0 mL of reference solution (a) to 100.0 mL with the solvent mixture.

Reference solution (c) Dissolve 5 mg of *spiramycin CRS* in 15 mL of *buffer solution pH 2.2 R* and dilute to 25 mL with *water R*, then heat in a water-bath at 60 °C for 5 min and cool under cold water.

Blank solution The solvent mixture.

Column:
— *size*: l = 0.25 m, Ø = 4.6 mm;
— *stationary phase: end-capped polar-embedded octadecylsilyl amorphous organosilica polymer R* (5 µm) (polar-embedded octadecylsilyl methylsilica gel), with a pore size of 12.5 nm and a carbon loading of 15 per cent;
— *temperature*: 70 °C.

Mobile phase Mix 5 volumes of a 34.8 g/L solution of *dipotassium hydrogen phosphate R* adjusted to pH 6.5 with a 27.2 g/L solution of *potassium dihydrogen phosphate R*, 40 volumes of *acetonitrile R* and 55 volumes of *water R*.

Flow rate 1.0 mL/min.

Detection Spectrophotometer at 232 nm.

Injection 20 µL of the blank solution, the test solution and reference solutions (b) and (c).

Run time 3 times the retention time of spiramycin I.

Identification of spiramycins Use the chromatogram supplied with *spiramycin CRS* and the chromatogram obtained with reference solution (a) to identify the peaks due to spiramycins I, II and III.

Relative retention With reference to spiramycin I (retention time = 20 min to 30 min): impurity F = about 0.41; impurity A = about 0.45; impurity D = about 0.50; impurity G = about 0.66; impurity B = about 0.73; impurity H = about 0.87; spiramycin II = about 1.4; spiramycin III = about 2.0; impurity E = about 2.5.

If necessary adjust the composition of the mobile phase by changing the amount of acetonitrile.

System suitability: reference solution (c):
— *resolution*: minimum 10.0 between the peaks due to impurity A and spiramycin I.

Limits:
— *impurities A, B, D, E, F, G, H*: for each impurity, not more than the area of the principal peak in the chromatogram obtained with reference solution (b) (2.0 per cent);
— *any other impurity*: for each impurity, not more than the area of the principal peak in the chromatogram obtained with reference solution (b) (2.0 per cent);
— *total*: not more than 5 times the area of the principal peak in the chromatogram obtained with reference solution (b) (10.0 per cent);
— *disregard limit*: 0.05 times the area of the principal peak in the chromatogram obtained with reference solution (b) (0.1 per cent); disregard any peak due to the blank and the peaks due to spiramycins I, II and III.

Heavy metals *(2.4.8)*
Maximum 20 ppm.

1.0 g complies with test F. Prepare the reference solution using 2 mL of *lead standard solution (10 ppm Pb) R*.

Loss on drying *(2.2.32)*
Maximum 3.5 per cent, determined on 0.500 g by drying at 80 °C over *diphosphorus pentoxide R* at a pressure not exceeding 0.67 kPa for 6 h.

Sulfated ash *(2.4.14)*
Maximum 0.1 per cent, determined on 1.0 g.

ASSAY
Carry out the microbiological assay of antibiotics *(2.7.2)*.

STORAGE
In an airtight container.

IMPURITIES
Specified impurities A, B, D, E, F, G, H

Other detectable impurities (the following substances would, if present at a sufficient level, be detected by one or other of the tests in the monograph. They are limited by the general acceptance criterion for other/unspecified impurities and/or by the general monograph Substances for pharmaceutical use (2034). It is therefore not necessary to identify these impurities for demonstration of compliance. See also *5.10. Control of impurities in substances for pharmaceutical use)*: C.

A. R1 = H, R2 = OH, R3 = CH₂-CHO:
(4*R*,5*S*,6*S*,7*R*,9*R*,10*R*,11*E*,13*E*,16*R*)-6-[[3,6-dideoxy-3-(dimethylamino)-β-D-glucopyranosyl]oxy]-4-hydroxy-5-methoxy-9,16-dimethyl-7-(2-oxoethyl)-10-[[2,3,4,6-tetradeoxy-4-(dimethylamino)-β-D-*erythro*-hexopyranosyl]oxy]oxacyclohexadeca-11,13-dien-2-one (neospiramycin I),

B. R1 = H, R2 = osyl, R3 = CH₂-CH₂OH:
(4*R*,5*S*,6*S*,7*R*,9*R*,10*R*,11*E*,13*E*,16*R*)-6-[[3,6-dideoxy-4-*O*-
(2,6-dideoxy-3-*C*-methyl-α-L-*ribo*-hexopyranosyl)-3-
(dimethylamino)-β-D-glucopyranosyl]oxy]-4-hydroxy-7-
(2-hydroxyethyl)-5-methoxy-9,16-dimethyl-10-[[2,3,4,6-
tetradeoxy-4-(dimethylamino)-β-D-*erythro*-
hexopyranosyl]oxy]oxacyclohexadeca-11,13-dien-2-one
(spiramycin IV),

C. R1 = H, R2 = osyl, R3 = C(=CH₂)-CHO:
(4*R*,5*S*,6*S*,7*S*,9*R*,10*R*,11*E*,13*E*,16*R*)-6-[[3,6-dideoxy-4-*O*-
(2,6-dideoxy-3-*C*-methyl-α-L-*ribo*-hexopyranosyl)-3-
(dimethylamino)-β-D-glucopyranosyl]oxy]-7-
(1-formylethenyl)-4-hydroxy-5-methoxy-9,16-dimethyl-10-
[[2,3,4,6-tetradeoxy-4-(dimethylamino)-β-D-*erythro*-
hexopyranosyl]oxy]oxacyclohexadeca-11,13-dien-2-one
(17-methylenespiramycin I),

E. R1 = H, R2 = osyl, R3 = CH₂-CH₃:
(4*R*,5*S*,6*S*,7*S*,9*R*,10*R*,11*E*,13*E*,16*R*)-6-[[3,6-dideoxy-4-*O*-
(2,6-dideoxy-3-*C*-methyl-α-L-*ribo*-hexopyranosyl)-3-
(dimethylamino)-β-D-glucopyranosyl]oxy]-7-ethyl-4-hydroxy-
5-methoxy-9,16-dimethyl-10-[[2,3,4,6-tetradeoxy-4-
(dimethylamino)-β-D-*erythro*-
hexopyranosyl]oxy]oxacyclohexadeca-11,13-dien-2-one
(18-deoxy-18-dihydrospiramycin I or DSPM),

G. R1 = CO-CH₃, R2 = OH, R3 = CH₂-CHO:
(4*R*,5*S*,6*S*,7*R*,9*R*,10*R*,11*E*,13*E*,16*R*)-6-[[3,6-dideoxy-3-
(dimethylamino)-β-D-glucopyranosyl]oxy]-5-methoxy-9,16-
dimethyl-2-oxo-7-(2-oxoethyl)-10-[[2,3,4,6-tetradeoxy-4-
(dimethylamino)-β-D-*erythro*-
hexopyranosyl]oxy]oxacyclohexadeca-11,13-dien-4-yl acetate
(neospiramycin II),

H. R1 = CO-C₂H₅, R2 = OH, R3 = CH₂-CHO:
(4*R*,5*S*,6*S*,7*R*,9*R*,10*R*,11*E*,13*E*,16*R*)-6-[[3,6-dideoxy-3-
(dimethylamino)-β-D-glucopyranosyl]oxy]-5-methoxy-9,16-
dimethyl-2-oxo-7-(2-oxoethyl)-10-[[2,3,4,6-tetradeoxy-4-
(dimethylamino)-β-D-*erythro*-
hexopyranosyl]oxy]oxacyclohexadeca-11,13-dien-4-yl
propanoatate (neospiramycin III),

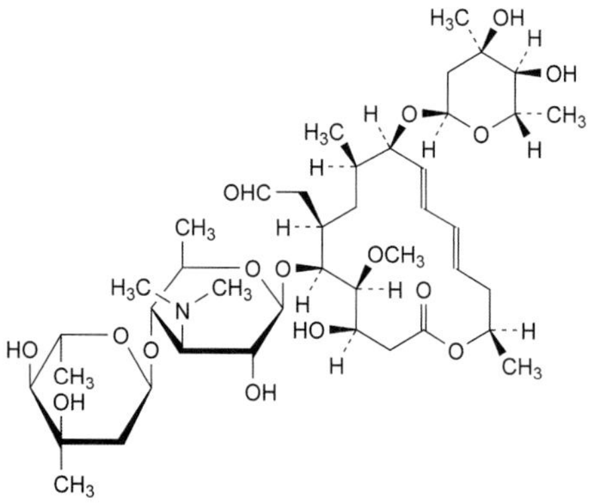

D. (4*R*,5*S*,6*S*,7*R*,9*R*,10*R*,11*E*,13*E*,16*R*)-6-[[3,6-dideoxy-4-
O-(2,6-dideoxy-3-*C*-methyl-α-L-*ribo*-hexopyranosyl)-3-
(dimethylamino)-β-D-glucopyranosyl]oxy]-10-[(2,6-dideoxy-
3-*C*-methyl-α-L-*ribo*-hexopyranosyl)oxy]-4-hydroxy-5-
methoxy-9,16-dimethyl-7-(2-oxoethyl)oxacyclohexadeca-
11,13-dien-2-one (spiramycin V),

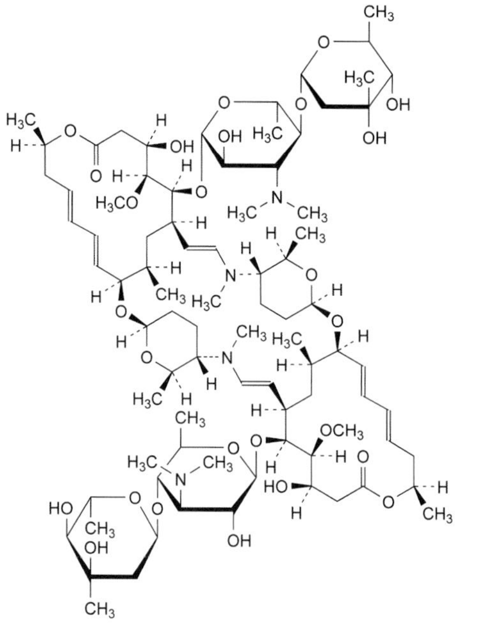

F. spiramycin dimer.

Ph Eur

Sulfadimidine

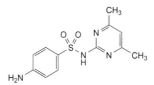

(Ph. Eur. monograph 0295)

C₁₂H₁₄N₄O₂S   278.3   *57-68-1*

Action and use
Sulfonamide antibacterial.

Preparation
Sulfadimidine Injection

Ph Eur

DEFINITION
4-Amino-*N*-(4,6-dimethylpyrimidin-2-yl)benzenesulfonamide.

Content
99.0 per cent to 101.0 per cent (dried substance).

CHARACTERS
Appearance
White or almost white powder or crystals.

Solubility
Very slightly soluble in water, soluble in acetone, slightly
soluble in ethanol (96 per cent). It dissolves in solutions of
alkali hydroxides and in dilute mineral acids.

IDENTIFICATION
First identification A.

Second identification B, C, D.

A. Infrared absorption spectrophotometry (*2.2.24*).

Comparison sulfadimidine CRS.

B. Thin-layer chromatography (*2.2.27*).

Solvent mixture concentrated ammonia R, methanol R
(4:96 *V/V*).

Test solution Dissolve 20 mg of the substance to be examined in 3 mL of the solvent mixture and dilute to 5.0 mL with the solvent mixture.

Reference solution Dissolve 20 mg of *sulfadimidine CRS* in 3 mL of the solvent mixture and dilute to 5.0 mL with the solvent mixture.

Plate TLC silica gel GF$_{254}$ plate R.

Mobile phase dilute ammonia R1, water R, nitromethane R, dioxan R (3:5:40:50 *V/V/V/V*).

Application 5 μL.

Development Over 2/3 of the plate.

Drying At 100-105 °C for 30 min.

Detection Examine in ultraviolet light at 254 nm.

Results The principal spot in the chromatogram obtained with the test solution is similar in position and size to the principal spot in the chromatogram obtained with the reference solution.

C. Place 3 g in a dry tube. Immerse the lower part of the tube, inclined at 45°, in a silicone-oil bath and heat to about 270 °C. The substance to be examined decomposes and a white or yellowish-white sublimate is formed which, after recrystallisation from *toluene R* and drying at 100 °C, melts (*2.2.14*) at 150 °C to 154 °C.

D. Dissolve about 5 mg in 10 mL of a 103 g/L solution of *hydrochloric acid R*. Dilute 1 mL of the solution to 10 mL with *water R*. The solution, without further acidification, gives the reaction of primary aromatic amines (*2.3.1*).

TESTS

Appearance of solution
The solution is not more intensely coloured than reference solution Y$_5$, BY$_5$ or GY$_5$ (*2.2.2, Method II*).

Dissolve 0.5 g in a mixture of 5 mL of *dilute sodium hydroxide solution R* and 5 mL of *water R*.

Acidity
To 1.25 g of the finely powdered substance to be examined, add 25 mL of *carbon dioxide-free water R*. Heat at about 70 °C for 5 min. Cool in iced water for about 15 min and filter. To 20 mL of the filtrate add 0.1 mL of *bromothymol blue solution R1*. Not more than 0.2 mL of *0.1 M sodium hydroxide* is required to change the colour of the indicator.

Related substances
Liquid chromatography (*2.2.29*).

Solvent mixture 40 g/L solution of *sodium hydroxide R, acetonitrile R, water R* (2.5:25:75 *V/V/V*).

Test solution Dissolve 50.0 mg of the substance to be examined in 41 mL of the solvent mixture and dilute to 50.0 mL with *water R*.

Reference solution (a) Dissolve 5 mg of *sulfacetamide sodium CRS* (impurity E) and 5 mg of *sulfaguanidine CRS* (impurity C) in 41 mL of the solvent mixture and dilute to 100.0 mL with *water R*.

Reference solution (b) Dilute 1.0 mL of the test solution to 100.0 mL with mobile phase B. Dilute 1.0 mL of this solution to 10.0 mL with mobile phase B.

Reference solution (c) Dissolve 20 mg of *sulfadimidine for peak identification CRS* (containing impurity G) in 16.4 mL of the solvent mixture and dilute to 20.0 mL with *water R*.

Column:
— *size*: *l* = 0.25 m, Ø = 4.6 mm;

— *stationary phase*: end-capped octylsilyl silica gel for chromatography R (5 μm);
— *temperature*: 35 °C.
Mobile phase:
— *mobile phase A*: mix 10 volumes of *acetonitrile R* and 90 volumes of a 0.6 per cent *V/V* solution of *acetic acid R* previously adjusted to pH 6.5 with a 250 g/L solution of *ammonia R*;
— *mobile phase B*: mix equal volumes of *acetonitrile R* and a 0.6 per cent *V/V* solution of *acetic acid R* previously adjusted to pH 6.5 with a 250 g/L solution of *ammonia R*;

Time (min)	Mobile phase A (per cent *V/V*)	Mobile phase B (per cent *V/V*)
0 - 25	100	0
25 - 35	100 → 0	0 → 100
35 - 45	0	100

Flow rate 1.3 mL/min.

Detection Spectrophotometer at 241 nm.

Injection 20 μL.

Identification of impurities Use the chromatogram supplied with *sulfadimidine for peak identification CRS* and the chromatogram obtained with reference solution (c) to identify the peak due to impurity G.

Relative retention With reference to sulfadimidine (retention time = about 20 min): impurity E = about 0.13; impurity C = about 0.15; impurity D = about 0.2; impurity G = about 1.7.

System suitability: reference solution (a):
— *resolution*: minimum 2.0 between the peaks due to impurities E and C.

Limits:
— *impurities C, D, G*: for each impurity, not more than the area of the principal peak in the chromatogram obtained with reference solution (b) (0.10 per cent);
— *unspecified impurities*: for each impurity, not more than 0.5 times the area of the principal peak in the chromatogram obtained with reference solution (b) (0.05 per cent);
— *total*: not more than 5 times the area of the principal peak in the chromatogram obtained with reference solution (b) (0.5 per cent);
— *disregard limit*: 0.3 times the area of the principal peak in the chromatogram obtained with reference solution (b) (0.03 per cent).

Heavy metals (*2.4.8*)
Maximum 20 ppm.

1.0 g complies with test D. Prepare the reference solution using 2 mL of *lead standard solution (10 ppm Pb) R*.

Loss on drying (*2.2.32*)
Maximum 0.5 per cent, determined on 1.000 g by drying in an oven at 105 °C.

Sulfated ash (*2.4.14*)
Maximum 0.1 per cent, determined on 1.0 g.

ASSAY
Dissolve 0.250 g in a mixture of 20 mL of *dilute hydrochloric acid R* and 50 mL of *water R*. Cool the solution in iced water. Carry out the determination of primary aromatic amino- nitrogen (*2.5.8*), determining the end-point electrometrically.

1 mL of *0.1 M sodium nitrite* is equivalent to 27.83 mg of $C_{12}H_{14}N_4O_2S$.

STORAGE

Protected from light.

IMPURITIES

Specified impurities C, D, G

Other detectable impurities (the following substances would, if present at a sufficient level, be detected by one or other of the tests in the monograph. They are limited by the general acceptance criterion for other/unspecified impurities and/or by the general monograph *Substances for pharmaceutical use (2034)*. It is therefore not necessary to identify these impurities for demonstration of compliance. See also *5.10. Control of impurities in substances for pharmaceutical use*): A, B, E, F.

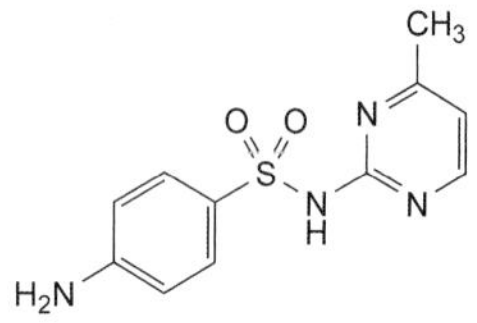

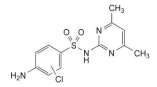

A. 4-amino-*N*-(4-methylpyrimidin-2-yl)benzenesulfonamide (sulfamerazine),

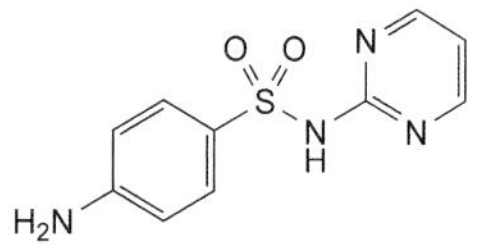

B. 4-amino-*N*-pyrimidin-2-ylbenzenesulfonamide (sulfadiazine),

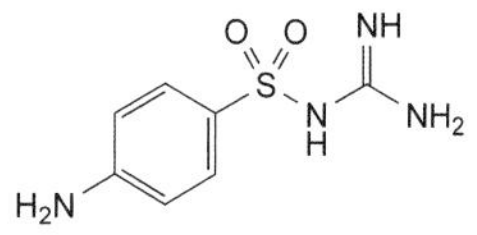

C. (4-aminophenylsulfonyl)guanidine (sulfaguanidine),

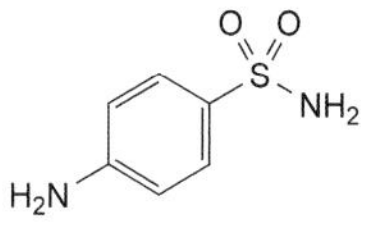

D. 4-aminobenzenesulfonamide (sulfanilamide),

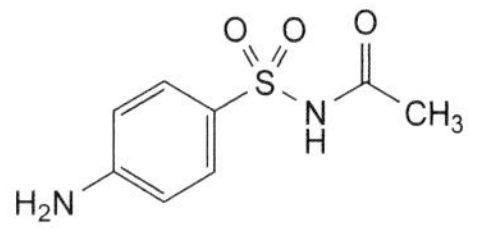

E. *N*-[(4-aminophenyl)sulfonyl]acetamide (sulfacetamide),

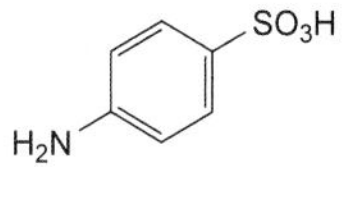

F. 4-aminobenzenesulfonic acid (sulfanilic acid),

G. 4-amino-2-chloro-*N*-(4,6-dimethylpyrimidin-2-yl)benzenesulfonamide or 4-amino-3-chloro-*N*-(4,6-dimethylpyrimidin-2-yl)benzenesulfonamide.

_____ Ph Eur

Sulfadimethoxine Sodium

(Sulfadimethoxine Sodium for Veterinary Use, Ph. Eur. monograph 2745)

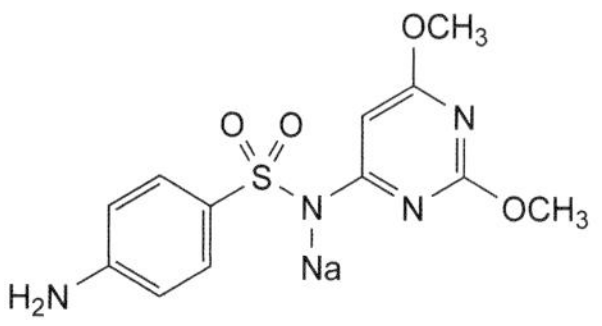

$C_{12}H_{13}N_4NaO_4S$ 332.3   *1037-50-9*

Action and use

Sulfonamide antibacterial.

Ph Eur _____

DEFINITION

Sodium [(4-aminophenyl)sulfonyl](2,6-dimethoxypyrimidin-4-yl)azanide.

Content

97.5 per cent to 102.0 per cent (anhydrous substance).

CHARACTERS

Appearance

White or almost white, crystalline powder, hygroscopic.

Solubility

Freely soluble in water, slightly soluble in ethanol (96 per cent), practically insoluble in methylene chloride.

IDENTIFICATION

A. Infrared absorption spectrophotometry (*2.2.24*).

Preparation Dissolve 1 g in 20 mL of *water R*; add 0.20 mL of *glacial acetic acid R*; filter the precipitate, wash with 1 mL of *water R* and dry at 105 °C for 2 h.

Comparison sulfadimethoxine CRS.

B. 2 mL of the filtrate obtained in identification test A gives reaction (a) of sodium (*2.3.1*).

TESTS

Appearance of solution

The solution is clear (*2.2.1*) and not more intensely coloured than reference solution BY_5 (*2.2.2, Method II*).

Dissolve 0.5 g in *water R* and dilute to 10 mL with the same solvent.

pH (*2.2.3*)

8.5 to 10.0.

Dissolve 0.2 g in *carbon dioxide-free water R* and dilute to 20 mL with the same solvent.

Related substances

Liquid chromatography (*2.2.29*).

Solution A Dissolve 6.0 g of *sodium dihydrogen phosphate R* in 950 mL of *water R*, adjust to pH 7.0 with *dilute sodium hydroxide solution R* and dilute to 1 L with *water R*.

Test solution Dissolve 22.0 mg of the substance to be examined in 76 mL of solution A and dilute to 100.0 mL with *methanol R*.

Reference solution (a) Dissolve 20.0 mg of *sulfadimethoxine CRS* in 25 mL of *methanol R* and dilute to 100.0 mL with solution A.

Reference solution (b) Dilute 2.0 mL of the test solution to 100.0 mL with mobile phase A. Dilute 1.0 mL of this solution to 10.0 mL with mobile phase A.

Reference solution (c) Dissolve 4 mg of *sulfadimethoxine for peak identification CRS* (containing impurities A and F) in 5 mL of *methanol R* and dilute to 20 mL with solution A.

Column:
— *size*: *l* = 0.25 m, Ø = 4.6 mm;
— *stationary phase*: *end-capped octadecylsilyl amorphous organosilica polymer R* (5 µm);
— *temperature*: 25 °C.

Mobile phase:
— *mobile phase A*: *methanol R*, solution A (25:75 *V/V*);
— *mobile phase B*: *methanol R*, *acetonitrile R*, solution A (25:35:40 *V/V/V*);

Time (min)	Mobile phase A (per cent *V/V*)	Mobile phase B (per cent *V/V*)
0 - 10	100	0
10 - 30	100 → 0	0 → 100
30 - 35	0	100

Flow rate 1.0 mL/min.

Detection Spectrophotometer at 254 nm.

Injection 10 µL of the test solution and reference solutions (b) and (c).

Identification of impurities Use the chromatogram supplied with *sulfadimethoxine for peak identification CRS* and the chromatogram obtained with reference solution (c) to identify the peaks due to impurities A and F.

Relative retention With reference to sulfadimethoxine (retention time = about 11 min): impurity F = about 0.4; impurity A = about 1.2.

System suitability:
— *resolution*: minimum 2.5 between the peaks due to sulfadimethoxine and impurity A in the chromatogram obtained with reference solution (c);
— *signal-to-noise ratio*: minimum 40 for the principal peak in the chromatogram obtained with reference solution (b).

Calculation of percentage contents:
— *correction factors*: multiply the peak areas of the following impurities by the corresponding correction factor: impurity A = 1.4; impurity F = 1.7;
— for each impurity, use the concentration of sulfadimethoxine in reference solution (b).

Limits:
— *impurities A, F*: for each impurity, maximum 0.2 per cent;
— *unspecified impurities*: for each impurity, maximum 0.20 per cent;
— *total*: maximum 0.5 per cent;
— *reporting threshold*: 0.10 per cent.

Heavy metals (*2.4.8*)

Maximum 20 ppm.

Solvent water R.

0.5 g complies with test H. Prepare the reference solution using 1 mL of *lead standard solution (10 ppm Pb) R*.

Water (*2.5.12*)

: maximum 5.0 per cent, determined on 0.200 g.

ASSAY

Liquid chromatography (*2.2.29*) as described in the test for related substances with the following modification.

Injection Test solution and reference solution (a).

Calculate the percentage content of $C_{12}H_{13}N_4NaO_4S$ taking into account the assigned content of *sulfadimethoxine CRS* and a conversion factor of 1.071.

STORAGE

In an airtight container, protected from light.

IMPURITIES

Specified impurities A, F

Other detectable impurities (the following substances would, if present at a sufficient level, be detected by one or other of the tests in the monograph. They are limited by the general acceptance criterion for other/unspecified impurities and/or by the general monograph *Substances for pharmaceutical use* (*2034*). It is therefore not necessary to identify these impurities for demonstration of compliance. See also *5.10. Control of impurities in substances for pharmaceutical use*): B, C, D, E.

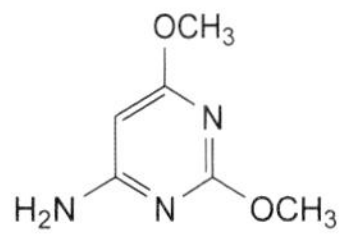

A. 2,6-dimethoxypyrimidin-4-amine,

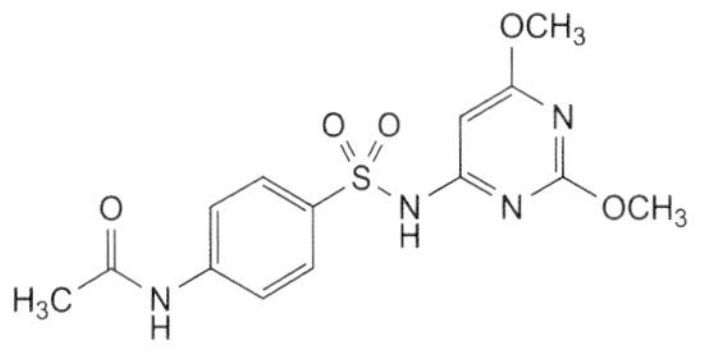

B. *N*-[4-[(2,6-dimethoxypyrimidin-4-yl)sulfamoyl]phenyl]acetamide,

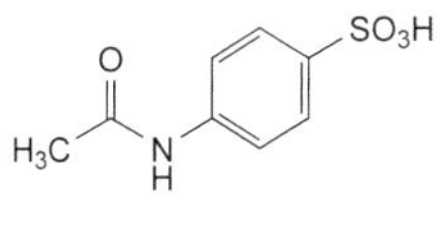

C. 4-(acetylamino)benzene-1-sulfonic acid,

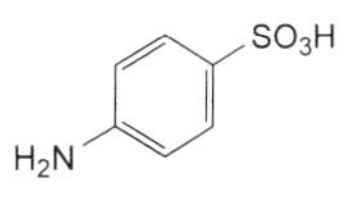

D. 4-aminobenzene-1-sulfonic acid (sulfanilic acid),

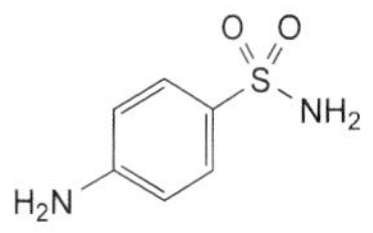

E. 4-aminobenzene-1-sulfonamide (sulfanilamide),

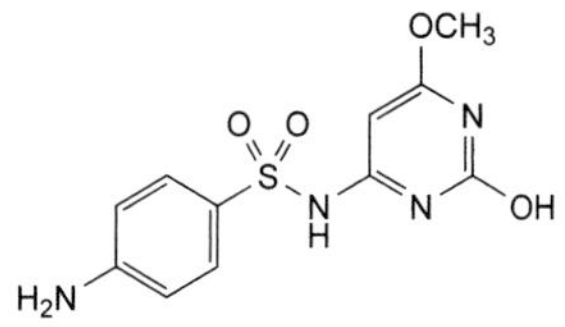

F. 4-amino-*N*-(2-hydroxy-6-methoxypyrimidin-4-yl)benzene-1-sulfonamide.

Ph Eur

Sulfamerazine

(*Ph. Eur. monograph 0358*)

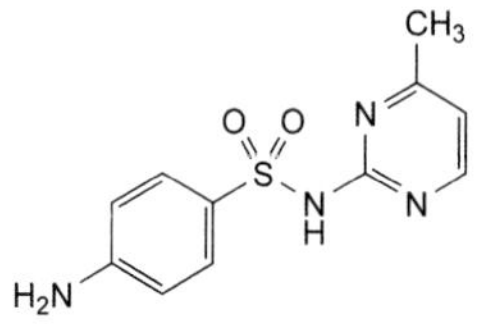

C₁₁H₁₂N₄O₂S   264.3   127-79-7

$C_{11}H_{12}N_4O_2S$ 264.3   127-79-7

Action and use
Sulfonamide antibacterial.

Ph Eur

DEFINITION
Sulfamerazine contains not less than 99.0 per cent and not more than the equivalent of 101.0 per cent of 4-amino-*N*-(4-methyl-2-pyrimidinyl)benzenesulfonamide, calculated with reference to the dried substance.

CHARACTERS
White, yellowish-white or pinkish-white, crystalline powder or crystals, very slightly soluble in water, sparingly soluble in acetone, slightly soluble in alcohol, very slightly soluble in methylene chloride. It dissolves in solutions of alkali hydroxides and in dilute mineral acids.

It melts at about 235 °C, with decomposition.

IDENTIFICATION
First identification A, B.

Second identification B, C, D.

A. Examine by infrared absorption spectrophotometry (*2.2.24*), comparing with the spectrum obtained with *sulfamerazine CRS*. Examine the substances as discs.

B. Examine the chromatograms obtained in the test for related substances. The principal spot in the chromatogram obtained with test solution (b) is similar in position, colour and size to the principal spot in the chromatogram obtained with reference solution (a).

C. Place 3 g in a dry tube. Incline the tube by about 45°, immerse the bottom of the tube in a silicone-oil bath and heat to about 270 °C. The substance decomposes, producing a white or yellowish-white sublimate which, after recrystallisation from *toluene R* and drying at 100 °C, melts (*2.2.14*) at 157 °C to 161 °C.

D. Dissolve about 20 mg in 0.5 mL of *dilute hydrochloric acid R* and add 1 mL of *water R*. The solution gives, without further addition of acid, the identification reaction of primary aromatic amines (*2.3.1*).

TESTS
Appearance of solution
Dissolve 0.8 g in a mixture of 5 mL of *dilute sodium hydroxide solution R* and 5 mL of *water R*. The solution is not more intensely coloured than reference solution Y₄, BY₄ or GY₄ (*2.2.2, Method II*).

Acidity
To 1.25 g, finely powdered, add 40 mL of *carbon dioxide-free water R* and heat at about 70 °C for 5 min. Cool for about 15 min in iced water and filter. To 20 mL of the filtrate add 0.1 mL of *bromothymol blue solution R1*. Not more than 0.2 mL of *0.1 M sodium hydroxide* is required to change the colour of the indicator.

Related substances
Examine by thin-layer chromatography (*2.2.27*) using *silica gel GF₂₅₄ R* as the coating substance.

Test solution (a) Dissolve 0.10 g of the substance to be examined in 3 mL of a mixture of 2 volumes of *concentrated ammonia R* and 48 volumes of *methanol R* and dilute to 5 mL with the same mixture of solvents.

Test solution (b) Dilute 1 mL of test solution (a) to 10 mL with a mixture of 2 volumes of *concentrated ammonia R* and 48 volumes of *methanol R*.

Reference solution (a) Dissolve 10 mg of *sulfamerazine CRS* in 3 mL of a mixture of 2 volumes of *concentrated ammonia R* and 48 volumes of *methanol R* and dilute to 5 mL with the same mixture of solvents.

Reference solution (b) Dilute 2.5 mL of test solution (b) to 50 mL with a mixture of 2 volumes of *concentrated ammonia R* and 48 volumes of *methanol R*.

Apply to the plate 5 μL of each solution. Develop over a path of 15 cm with a mixture of 3 volumes of *dilute ammonia R1*, 5 volumes of *water R*, 40 volumes of *nitromethane R* and 50 volumes of *dioxan R*. Dry the plate at 100 °C to 105 °C and examine in ultraviolet light at 254 nm. Any spot in the chromatogram obtained with test solution (a), apart from the principal spot, is not more intense that the spot in the chromatogram obtained with reference solution (b) (0.5 per cent).

Heavy metals (*2.4.8*)
1.0 g complies with test C for heavy metals (20 ppm). Prepare the reference solution using 2 mL of *lead standard solution (10 ppm Pb) R*.

Loss on drying (*2.2.32*)
Not more than 0.5 per cent, determined on 1.000 g by drying in an oven at 105 °C.

Sulfated ash (*2.4.14*)
Not more than 0.1 per cent, determined on 1.0 g.

ASSAY
Dissolve 0.2500 g in a mixture of 20 mL of *dilute hydrochloric acid R* and 50 mL of *water R*. Cool the solution in iced water. Carry out the determination of primary aromatic amino- nitrogen (*2.5.8*), determining the end-point electrometrically.

1 mL of *0.1 M sodium nitrite* is equivalent to 26.43 mg of $C_{11}H_{12}N_4O_2S$.

STORAGE
Store protected from light.

Ph Eur

Sulfametoxypyridazine

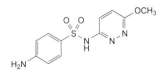

*(Sulfamethoxypyridazine for Veterinary Use,
Ph Eur monograph 0638)*

$C_{11}H_{12}N_4O_3S$ 280.3   *80-35-3*

Action and use
Sulfonamide antibacterial.

Ph Eur

DEFINITION
Sulfamethoxypyridazine for veterinary use contains not less than 99.0 per cent and not more than the equivalent of 101.0 per cent of 4-amino-*N*-(6-methoxypyridazin-3-yl)benzenesulfonamide, calculated with reference to the dried substance.

CHARACTERS
A white or slightly yellowish, crystalline powder, colouring slowly on exposure to light, practically insoluble in water, sparingly soluble in acetone, slightly soluble in alcohol, very slightly soluble in methylene chloride. It dissolves in solutions of alkali hydroxides and in dilute mineral acids.

It melts at about 180 °C, with decomposition.

IDENTIFICATION
First identification A, B

Second identification B, C, D

A. Examine by infrared absorption spectrophotometry (*2.2.24*), comparing with the spectrum obtained with *sulfamethoxypyridazine CRS*. Examine the substances prepared as discs.

B. Examine the chromatograms obtained in the test for related substances. The principal spot in the chromatogram obtained with test solution (b) is similar in position and size to the principal spot in the chromatogram obtained with reference solution (a).

C. Dissolve 0.5 g in 1 mL of a 40 per cent *V/V* solution of *sulfuric acid R*, heating gently. Continue heating until a crystalline precipitate appears (about 2 min). Cool and add 10 mL of *dilute sodium hydroxide solution R*. Cool again, add 25 mL of *ether R* and shake the solution for 5 min. Separate the ether layer, dry over *anhydrous sodium sulfate R* and filter. Evaporate the ether by heating in a water-bath. An oily residue is obtained which becomes crystalline on cooling; if necessary, scratch the wall of the container with a glass rod. The residue melts (*2.2.14*) at 102 °C to 106 °C.

D. Dissolve about 5 mg in 10 mL of *1 M hydrochloric acid*. Dilute 1 mL of the solution to 10 mL with *water R*. The solution, without further acidification, gives the reaction of primary aromatic amines (*2.3.1*).

TESTS
Appearance of solution
Dissolve 1.0 g in a mixture of 10 mL of *1 M sodium hydroxide* and 15 mL of *water R*. The solution is clear (*2.2.1*) and not more intensely coloured than reference solution Y_4 or BY_4 (*2.2.2, Method II*).

Acidity
To 1.25 g, finely powdered, add 25 mL of *carbon dioxide-free water R*. Heat at 70 °C for 5 min. Cool in iced water for about 15 min and filter. To 20 mL of the filtrate add 0.1 mL of *bromothymol blue solution R1*. Not more than 0.5 mL of *0.1 M sodium hydroxide* is required to change the colour of the indicator.

Related substances
Examine by thin layer chromatography (*2.2.27*), using *TLC silica gel GF₂₅₄ plate R*.

Test solution (a) Dissolve 0.10 g of the substance to be examined in *acetone R* and dilute to 5 mL with the same solvent.

Test solution (b) Dilute 1 mL of test solution (a) to 10 mL with *acetone R*.

Reference solution (a) Dissolve 20 mg of *sulfamethoxypyridazine CRS* in *acetone R* and dilute to 10 mL with the same solvent.

Reference solution (b) Dilute 2.5 mL of test solution (b) to 50 mL with *acetone R*.

Apply separately to the plate 5 μL of each solution. Develop over a path of 15 cm using a mixture of 1 volume of *dilute ammonia R1*, 9 volumes of *water R*, 30 volumes of *2-propanol R* and 50 volumes of *ethyl acetate R*. Dry the plate at 100-105 °C and examine in ultraviolet light at 254 nm. Any spot in the chromatogram obtained with test solution (a), apart from the principal spot, is not more intense than the spot in the chromatogram obtained with reference solution (b) (0.5 per cent).

Heavy metals (*2.4.8*)
1.0 g complies with test D for heavy metals (20 ppm). Prepare the reference solution using 2 mL of *lead standard solution (10 ppm Pb) R*.

Loss on drying (*2.2.32*)
Not more than 0.5 per cent, determined on 1.000 g by drying in an oven at 105 °C.

Sulfated ash (*2.4.14*)
Not more than 0.1 per cent, determined on 1.0 g.

ASSAY
Carry out the assay of primary aromatic amino-nitrogen (*2.5.8*), using 0.2500 g, determining the end-point electrometrically.

1 mL of *0.1 M sodium nitrite* is equivalent to 28.03 mg of $C_{11}H_{12}N_4O_3S$.

STORAGE
Protected from light.

Ph Eur

Sulfanilamide

(Ph. Eur. monograph 1571)

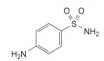

C₆H₈N₂O₂S   172.2   63-74-1

Action and use

Sulfonamide antibacterial.

Ph Eur

DEFINITION

Sulfanilamide contains not less than 99.0 per cent and not more than the equivalent of 101.0 per cent of 4-aminobenzenesulfonamide, calculated with reference to the dried substance.

CHARACTERS

White or yellowish-white crystals or fine powder, slightly soluble in water, freely soluble in acetone, sparingly soluble in alcohol, practically insoluble in methylene chloride. It dissolves in solutions of alkali hydroxides and in dilute mineral acids.

IDENTIFICATION

First identification B

Second identification A, C, D

A. Melting point *(2.2.14)*: 164.5 °C to 166.0 °C.

B. Examine by infrared absorption spectrophotometry *(2.2.24)*, comparing with the spectrum obtained with *sulfanilamide CRS*. Examine the substances prepared as discs.

C. Examine the chromatograms obtained in the test for related substances. The principal spot in the chromatogram obtained with test solution (a) is similar in position and size to the principal spot in the chromatogram obtained with reference solution (a).

D. Dissolve about 5 mg in 10 mL of *1 M hydrochloric acid*. Dilute 1 mL of the solution to 10 mL with *water R*. The solution, without further acidification, gives the reaction of primary aromatic amines *(2.3.1)*.

TESTS

Solution S

To 2.5 g add 50 mL of *carbon dioxide-free water R*. Heat at about 70 °C for about 5 min. Cool in iced water for about 15 min and filter.

Acidity

To 20 mL of solution S add 0.1 mL of *bromothymol blue solution R1*. Not more than 0.2 mL of *0.1 M sodium hydroxide* is required to change the colour of the indicator.

Related substances

Examine by thin-layer chromatography *(2.2.27)*, using a *TLC silica gel F₂₅₄ plate R*.

Test solution (a) Dissolve 20 mg of the substance to be examined in 3 mL of a mixture of 2 volumes of *concentrated ammonia R* and 48 volumes of *methanol R* and dilute to 5 mL with the same mixture of solvents.

Test solution (b) Dissolve 0.10 g of the substance to be examined in 0.5 mL of *concentrated ammonia R* and dilute to 5 mL with *methanol R*. If the solution is not clear, heat gently until dissolution is complete.

Reference solution (a) Dissolve 20 mg of *sulfanilamide CRS* in 3 mL of a mixture of 2 volumes of *concentrated ammonia R* and 48 volumes of *methanol R* and dilute to 5 mL with the same mixture of solvents.

Reference solution (b) Dilute 1.25 mL of test solution (a) to 50 mL with a mixture of 2 volumes of *concentrated ammonia R* and 48 volumes of *methanol R*.

Reference solution (c) Dissolve 20 mg of the substance to be examined and 20 mg of *sulfamerazine CRS* in 3 mL of a mixture of 2 volumes of *concentrated ammonia R* and 48 volumes of *methanol R* and dilute to 5 mL with the same mixture of solvents.

Apply to the plate 5 µL of each solution. Develop over a path corresponding to two-thirds of the plate height using a mixture of 3 volumes of *dilute ammonia R1*, 5 volumes of *water R*, 40 volumes of *nitromethane R* and 50 volumes of *dioxan R*. Dry the plate at 100 °C to 105 °C and examine in ultraviolet light at 254 nm. Any spot in the chromatogram obtained with test solution (b), apart from the principal spot, is not more intense than the spot in the chromatogram obtained with reference solution (b) (0.5 per cent). The test is not valid unless the chromatogram obtained with reference solution (c) shows two clearly separated principal spots.

Heavy metals *(2.4.8)*

12 mL of solution S complies with test A for heavy metals (20 ppm). Prepare the reference solution using *lead standard solution (1 ppm Pb) R*.

Loss on drying *(2.2.32)*

Not more than 0.5 per cent, determined on 1.000 g by drying in an oven at 105 °C.

Sulfated ash *(2.4.14)*

Not more than 0.1 per cent, determined on 1.0 g.

ASSAY

Carry out the determination of primary aromatic amino-nitrogen *(2.5.8)*, using 0.140 g and determining the end-point electrometrically.

1 mL of *0.1 M sodium nitrite* is equivalent to 17.22 mg of C₆H₈N₂O₂S.

STORAGE

Store protected from light.

Ph Eur

Sulfaquinoxaline

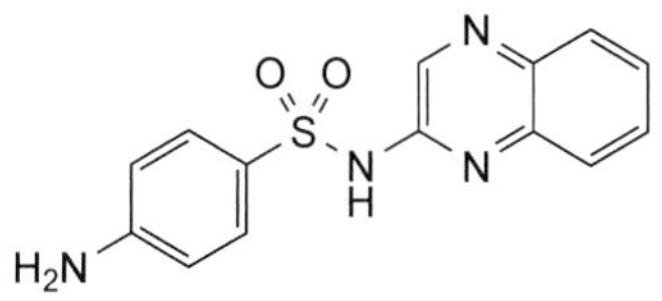

C₁₄H₁₂N₄O₂S   300.3   59-40-5

Action and use

Sulfonamide antibacterial.

DEFINITION

Sulfaquinoxaline is N^1-quinoxalin-2-ylsulfanilamide.

It contains not less than 98.0% and not more than 101.0% of C₁₄H₁₂N₄O₂S, calculated with reference to the dried substance.

CHARACTERISTICS

A yellow powder.

Practically insoluble in *water*; very slightly soluble in *ethanol (96%)*; practically insoluble in *ether*. It dissolves in aqueous solutions of alkalis.

IDENTIFICATION

A. The *infrared absorption spectrum*, Appendix II A, is concordant with the *reference spectrum* of sulfaquinoxaline *(RSV 41)*.

B. The *light absorption*, Appendix II B, in the range 230 to 350 nm of a 0.001% w/v solution in 0.01M *sodium hydroxide* exhibits a maximum only at 252 nm. The *absorbance* at 252 nm is about 1.1.

C. Yields the reaction characteristic of *primary aromatic amines*, Appendix VI, dissolving 4 mg in 2 mL of warm 2M *hydrochloric acid*. An orange-red precipitate is produced.

TESTS

Acidity

To 2 g add 100 mL of *water*, heat at 70° for 5 minutes, cool to 20° and filter. 50 mL of the filtrate requires for titration to pH 7.0 not more than 0.2 mL of 0.1M *sodium hydroxide VS*, Appendix V L.

Heavy metals

Dissolve the residue obtained in the test for Sulfated ash in 1 mL of 2M *hydrochloric acid* and dilute to 14 mL with *water*. 12 mL of the solution complies with *limit test A for heavy metals*, Appendix VII. Use *lead standard solution (2 ppm Pb)* to prepare the standard (20 ppm).

Related substances

Carry out the method for *thin-layer chromatography*, Appendix III A, using the following solutions.

(1) Dissolve 0.40 g of the substance being examined in 4 mL of 1M *sodium hydroxide* and add sufficient *methanol* to produce 100 mL.

(2) 0.012% w/v of N^1,N^2-*diquinoxalin-2-ylsulfanilamide BPCRS* in *methanol*.

(3) 0.0040% w/v of *sulfanilamide* in *methanol*.

CHROMATOGRAPHIC CONDITIONS

(a) Use a silica gel F_{254} precoated plate (Merck silica gel 60 F_{254} plates are suitable).

(b) Use the mobile phase as described below.

(c) Apply 5 μL of each solution.

(d) Develop the plate to 15 cm.

(e) After removal of the plate, allow it to dry in air until the solvent has evaporated and examine under *ultraviolet light (254 nm)*.

MOBILE PHASE

20 volumes of 18M *ammonia*, 40 volumes of *methanol* and 60 volumes of *chloroform*.

LIMITS

In the chromatogram obtained with solution (1):

any spot corresponding to N^1,N^2-diquinoxalin-2-ylsulfanilamide is not more intense than the spot in the chromatogram obtained with solution (2) (3%);

any other *secondary spot* is not more intense than the spot in the chromatogram obtained with solution (3) (1%).

Loss on drying

When dried to constant weight at 105°, loses not more than 1.0% of its weight. Use 1 g.

Sulfated ash

Not more than 0.1%, Appendix IX A. Ignite at 600° and use 1.5 g.

ASSAY

Dissolve 0.65 g in 10 mL of a mixture of equal volumes of 1M *sodium hydroxide* and *water*. Add 20 mL of *glycerol*, 20 mL of 9M *sulfuric acid* and 5 g of *potassium bromide*, cool in ice and titrate slowly with 0.1M *sodium nitrite VS*, stirring constantly and determining the end point electrometrically. Each mL of 0.1M *sodium nitrite VS* is equivalent to 30.03 mg of $C_{14}H_{12}N_4O_2S$.

STORAGE

Sulfaquinoxaline should be protected from light.

Sulfathiazole Sodium

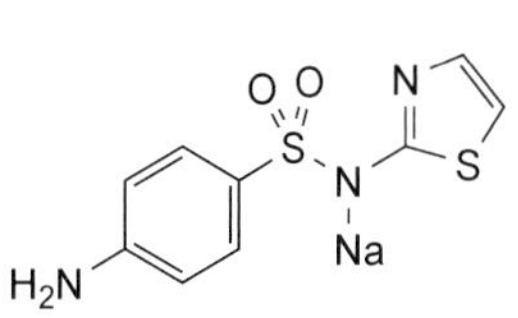

$C_9H_8N_3NaO_2S_2,1\frac{1}{2}H_2O$	304.3	*144-74-1 (anhydrous)*
$C_9H_8N_3NaO_2S_2,5H_2O$	367.4	*6791-71-5*

Action and use

Sulfonamide antibacterial.

DEFINITION

Sulfathiazole Sodium is the hydrated sodium salt of N^1-thiazol-2-yl sulfanilamide, either the sesquihydrate or the pentahydrate. It contains not less than 99.0% and not more than 101.0% of $C_9H_8N_3NaO_2S_2$, calculated with reference to the dried substance.

CHARACTERISTICS

A white or yellowish white, crystalline powder or granules.

Freely soluble in *water*; soluble in *ethanol (96%)*.

IDENTIFICATION

A. The *infrared absorption spectrum* of the dried substance, Appendix II A, is concordant with the *reference spectrum* of sulfathiazole sodium *(RSV 42)*.

B. Dissolve 1 g in 25 mL of *water* and add 2 mL of 6M *acetic acid*. The *melting point* of the precipitate, after washing with *water* and drying for 4 hours at 105°, is about 201°, Appendix V A.

C. The precipitate obtained in test B yields the reaction characteristic of primary aromatic amines, Appendix VI, giving an orange-red precipitate.

TESTS

Alkalinity

pH of a solution containing the equivalent of 1.0% w/v of the anhydrous substance, 9.0 to 10.0, Appendix V L.

Heavy metals

Dissolve a quantity containing the equivalent of 2.5 g of the anhydrous substance in 10 mL of *water*, add 15 mL of 2M *acetic acid*, shake for 30 minutes and filter. 12 mL of the resulting solution complies with *limit test A for heavy metals*, Appendix VII. Use *lead standard solution (2 ppm Pb)* to prepare the standard (20 ppm).

Related substances

Carry out the method for *thin-layer chromatography*, Appendix III A, using *silica gel H* as the coating substance and a mixture of 18 volumes of 10M *ammonia* and 90 volumes of *butan-1-ol* as the mobile phase. Apply separately to the plate 10 µL of each of two solutions in a mixture of 1 volume of 13.5M *ammonia* and 9 volumes of *ethanol (96%)* containing (1) 1.0% w/v of the substance being examined and (2) 0.0050% w/v of *sulfanilamide*. After removal of the plate, heat it at 105° for 10 minutes and spray with a 0.1% w/v solution of *4-dimethylaminobenzaldehyde* in *ethanol (96%)* containing 1% v/v of *hydrochloric acid*. Any *secondary spot* in the chromatogram obtained with solution (1) is not more intense than the spot in the chromatogram obtained with solution (2) (0.5%).

Loss on drying

When dried to constant weight at 105°, loses not less than 6.0% and not more than 10.0% of its weight (sesquihydrate) or not less than 22.0% and not more than 27.0% of its weight (pentahydrate).

ASSAY

Dissolve 0.5 g in a mixture of 75 mL of *water* and 10 mL of *hydrochloric acid*, add 3 g of *potassium bromide*, cool in ice and titrate slowly with 0.1M *sodium nitrite VS*, stirring constantly and determining the end point electrometrically. Each mL of 0.1M *sodium nitrite VS* is equivalent to 27.73 mg of $C_9H_8N_3NaO_2S_2$.

STORAGE

Sulfathiazole Sodium should be protected from light.

LABELLING

The label states whether the substance is the sesquihydrate or the pentahydrate.

of *dichloromethane*, evaporate to dryness and prepare a new spectrum of the residue.

B. Complies with the test for *identification of steroids*, Appendix III A, using *impregnating solvent III* and *mobile phase F*.

C. Dissolve 25 mg in 1 mL of *methanol*, add 2 mL of *semicarbazide acetate solution*, heat under a reflux condenser for 30 minutes and cool. The *melting point* of the resulting precipitate is about 218°, Appendix V A.

TESTS

Melting point
114° to 117°, Appendix V A.

Specific optical rotation
In a 1% w/v solution in *1,4-dioxan*, +86 to +91, calculated with reference to the dried substance, Appendix V F.

Loss on drying
When dried to constant weight at 105°, loses not more than 0.5% of its weight. Use 1 g.

Sulfated ash
Not more than 0.1%, Appendix IX A.

ASSAY

Dissolve 10 mg in sufficient *absolute ethanol* to produce 100 mL, dilute 5 mL to 50 mL with *absolute ethanol* and measure the *absorbance* of the resulting solution at the maximum at 240 nm, Appendix II B. Calculate the content of $C_{28}H_{36}O_3$ taking 395 as the value of A(1%, 1 cm) at the maximum at 240 nm.

STORAGE

Testosterone Phenylpropionate should be protected from light.

Testosterone Phenylpropionate

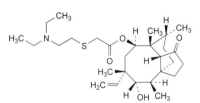

$C_{28}H_{36}O_3$ 420.6   *1255-49-8*

Action and use

Androgen.

DEFINITION

Testosterone Phenylpropionate is 3-oxo-androst-4-en-17β-yl 3-phenylpropionate. It contains not less than 97.0% and not more than 103.0% of $C_{28}H_{36}O_3$, calculated with reference to the dried substance.

CHARACTERISTICS

A white to almost white, crystalline powder.

Practically insoluble in *water*; sparingly soluble in *ethanol (96%)*.

IDENTIFICATION

A. The *infrared absorption spectrum*, Appendix II A, is concordant with the *reference spectrum* of testosterone phenylpropionate *(RSV 43)*. If the spectra are not concordant, dissolve the substances in the minimum volume

Tiamulin

(Tiamulin for Veterinary Use, Ph Eur monograph 1660)

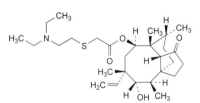

$C_{28}H_{47}NO_4S$ 493.8   *55297-95-5*

Action and use

Antibacterial.

Ph Eur _____

DEFINITION

(3a*S*,4*R*,5*S*,6*S*,8*R*,9*R*,9a*R*,10*R*)-6-Ethenyl-5-hydroxy-4,6,9,10-tetramethyl-1-oxodecahydro-3a,9-propano-3a*H*-cyclopentacycloocten-8-yl [[2-(diethylamino)ethyl]sulfanyl]acetate.

Semi-synthetic product derived from a fermentation product.

Content

96.5 per cent to 102.0 per cent (dried substance).

CHARACTERS

Appearance

Sticky, translucent yellowish mass, slightly hygroscopic.

Solubility

Practically insoluble in water, very soluble in methylene chloride, freely soluble in anhydrous ethanol.

IDENTIFICATION

Infrared absorption spectrophotometry (*2.2.24*).

Comparison Ph. Eur. reference spectrum of tiamulin.

TESTS

Appearance of solution

The solution is clear (*2.2.1*) and its absorbance (*2.2.25*) at 420 nm is not greater than 0.050.

Dissolve 2.5 g in 50 mL of *methanol R*.

Related substances

Liquid chromatography (*2.2.29*).

Ammonium carbonate buffer solution pH 100 Dissolve 10.0 g of *ammonium carbonate R* in *water R*, add 22 mL of *perchloric acid solution R* and dilute to 1000.0 mL with *water R*. Adjust to pH 10.0 with *concentrated ammonia R1*.

Solvent mixture acetonitrile R1, ammonium carbonate buffer solution pH 10.0 (50:50 *V/V*).

Test solution Dissolve 0.200 g of the substance to be examined in the solvent mixture and dilute to 50.0 mL with the solvent mixture.

Reference solution (a) Dissolve 0.250 g of *tiamulin hydrogen fumarate CRS* in the solvent mixture and dilute to 50.0 mL with the solvent mixture.

Reference solution (b) Dilute 1.0 mL of the test solution to 100.0 mL with the solvent mixture.

Reference solution (c) Dilute 0.1 mL of *toluene R* to 100 mL with *acetonitrile R*. Dilute 0.1 mL of this solution to 100.0 mL with the solvent mixture.

Column:
— *size*: *l* = 0.15 m, Ø = 4.6 mm;
— *stationary phase*: end-capped octadecylsilyl silica gel for chromatography R (5 μm);
— *temperature*: 30 °C.

Mobile phase acetonitrile R1, ammonium carbonate buffer solution pH 10.0, *methanol R1* (21:30:49 *V/V/V*).

Flow rate 1.0 mL/min.

Detection Spectrophotometer at 212 nm.

Injection 20 μL.

Run time 3 times the retention time of tiamulin.

Relative retention With reference to tiamulin (retention time = about 18 min): impurity A = about 0.22; impurity B = about 0.5; impurity C = about 0.66; impurity D = about 1.1; impurity F = about 1.6; impurity E = about 2.4.

System suitability: reference solution (a):
— baseline separation between the peaks due to tiamulin and impurity D.

Limits:
— *impurities A, B, C, D, E, F*: for each impurity, not more than the area of the principal peak in the chromatogram obtained with reference solution (b) (1.0 per cent);
— *any other impurity*: for each impurity, not more than 0.2 times the area of the principal peak in the chromatogram obtained with reference solution (b) (0.2 per cent);

— *total*: not more than 3 times the area of the principal peak in the chromatogram obtained with reference solution (b) (3.0 per cent);
— *disregard limit*: 0.1 times the area of the principal peak in the chromatogram obtained with reference solution (b) (0.1 per cent); disregard any peak present in the chromatogram obtained with reference solution (c).

Loss on drying (*2.2.32*)

Maximum 1.0 per cent, determined on 1.000 g by drying in an oven at 80 °C.

Bacterial endotoxins (*2.6.14, Method D*)

Less than 0.4 IU/mg, determined in a 1 mg/mL solution in *anhydrous ethanol R* (endotoxin free) diluted 1:40 with water for bacterial endotoxins test.

ASSAY

Liquid chromatography (*2.2.29*) as described in the test for related substances with the following modification.

Injection Test solution and reference solution (a).

Calculate the percentage content of $C_{28}H_{47}NO_4S$, from the declared content of *tiamulin hydrogen fumarate CRS*.

STORAGE

Protected from light.

IMPURITIES

Specified impurities A, B, C, D, E, F

Other detectable impurities (the following substances would, if present at a sufficient level, be detected by one or other of the tests in the monograph. They are limited by the general acceptance criterion for other/unspecified impurities and/or by the general monograph Substances for pharmaceutical use (2034). It is therefore not necessary to identify these impurities for demonstration of compliance. See also *5.10. Control of impurities in substances for pharmaceutical use*): *G, H, I, J, K, L, M, N, O, P, Q, R.*

A. R1 = R2 = H: (3a*S*,4*R*,5*S*,6*S*,8*R*,9*R*,9a*R*,10*R*)-6-ethenyl-5,8-dihydroxy-4,6,9,10-tetramethyloctahydro-3a,9-propano-3a*H*-cyclopentacycloocten-1(4*H*)-one (mutilin),

G. R1 = CO-CH₂OH, R2 = H: (3a*S*,4*R*,5*S*,6*S*,8*R*,9*R*,9a*R*,10*R*)-6-ethenyl-5-hydroxy-4,6,9,10-tetramethyl-1-oxodecahydro-3a,9-propano-3a*H*-cyclopentacycloocten-8-yl hydroxyacetate (pleuromutilin),

J. R1 = CO-CH₃, R2 = H: (3a*S*,4*R*,5*S*,6*S*,8*R*,9*R*,9a*R*,10*R*)-6-ethenyl-5-hydroxy-4,6,9,10-tetramethyl-1-oxodecahydro-3a,9-propano-3a*H*-cyclopentacycloocten-8-yl acetate (mutilin 14-acetate),

K. R1 = H, R2 = CO-CH₃: (3a*S*,4*R*,5*S*,6*S*,8*R*,9*R*,9a*R*,10*R*)-6-ethenyl-8-hydroxy-4,6,9,10-tetramethyl-1-oxodecahydro-3a,9-propano-3a*H*-cyclopentacycloocten-5-yl acetate (mutilin 11-acetate),

L. R1 = CO-CH₂-O-SO₂-C₆H₄-*p*CH₃, R2 = H: (3a*S*,4*R*,5*S*,6*S*,8*R*,9*R*,9a*R*,10*R*)-6-ethenyl-5-hydroxy-4,6,9,10-tetramethyl-1-oxodecahydro-3a,9-propano-3a*H*-cyclopentacycloocten-8-yl [[(4-methylphenyl)sulfonyl]oxy]acetate (pleuromutilin 22-tosylate),

M. R1 = R2 = CO-CH₃: (3aS,4R,5S,6S,8R,9R,9aR,10R)-6-
ethenyl-4,6,9,10-tetramethyl-1-oxodecahydro-3a,9-propano-
3aH-cyclopentacycloocten-5,8-diyl diacetate (mutilin 11,14-
diacetate),

P. R1 = CO-CH₂-O-SO₂-C₆H₅, R2 = H:
(3aS,4R,5S,6S,8R,9R,9aR,10R)-6-ethenyl-5-hydroxy-
4,6,9,10-tetramethyl-1-oxodecahydro-3a,9-propano-3aH-
cyclopentacycloocten-8-yl [(phenylsulfonyl)oxy]acetate,

B. R = CH₂-C₆H₅: 2-(benzylsulfanyl)-N,N-
diethylethanamine,

C. R = S-CH₂-CH₂-N(C₂H₅)₂: 2,2′-(disulfane-1,2-
diyl)bis(N,N-diethylethanamine),

O. R = H: 2-(diethylamino)ethanethiol,

D. (3aR,4R,6S,8R,9R,9aR,10R)-6-ethenylhydroxy-4,6,9,10-
tetramethyl-5-oxodecahydro-3a,9-propano-3aH-
cyclopentacycloocten-8-yl [[2-
(diethylamino)ethyl]sulfanyl]acetate,

E. (3aS,4R,6S,8R,9R,9aR,10R)-6-ethenyl-4,6,9,10-
tetramethyl-1,5-dioxodecahydro-3a,9-propano-3aH-
cyclopentacycloocten-8-yl [[2-
(diethylamino)ethyl]sulfanyl]acetate (11-oxotiamulin),

F. (1RS,3aR,4R,6S,8R,9R,9aR,10R)-6-ethenyl-1-hydroxy-
4,6,9,10-tetramethyl-5-oxodecahydro-3a,9-propano-3aH-
cyclopentacycloocten-8-yl [[2-
(diethylamino)ethyl]sulfanyl]acetate (1-hydroxy-11-
oxotiamulin),

H. (2E)-4-[(2RS)-2-[(3aS,4R,5S,6R,8R,9R,9aR,10R)-8-[[[2-
(diethylamino)ethyl]sulfanyl]acetyl]oxy]-5-hydroxy-4,6,9,10-
tetramethyl-1-oxodecahydro-3a,9-propano-3aH-
cyclopentacycloocten-6-yl]-2-hydroxyethoxy]-4-oxobut-2-
enoic acid (19,20-dihydroxytiamulin 20-fumarate),

I. (2E)-4-[[(3aS,4R,5S,6S,8R,9R,9aR,10R)-8-[[[2-
(diethylamino)ethyl]sulfanyl]acetyl]oxy]-6-ethenyl-1,5-
dihydroxy-4,6,9,10-tetramethyldecahydro-3a,9-propano-3aH-
cyclopentacycloocten-2-yl]oxy]-4-oxobut-2-enoic acid
(2,3-dihydroxytiamulin 2-fumarate),

N. (2E)-4-[2-[[(3aS,4R,5S,6S,8R,9R,9aR,10R)-6-ethenyl-5-
hydroxy-4,6,9,10-tetramethyl-1-oxodecahydro-3a,9-propano-
3aH-cyclopentacycloocten-8-yl]oxy]-2-oxoethoxy]-4-oxobut-
2-enoic acid (pleuromutilin 22-fumarate),

Q. (3aS,4R,5S,6S,8R,9R,10R)-6-ethenyl-2,5-dihydroxy-
4,6,9,10-tetramethyl-2,3,4,5,6,7,8,9-octahydro-3a,9-propano-
3aH-cyclopentacycloocten-8-yl [[2-
(diethylamino)ethyl]sulfanyl]acetate (3,4-didehydro-2-
hydroxytiamulin),

R. N-benzyl-N,N-dibutylbutan-1-aminium.

Tiamulin Hydrogen Fumarate

*(Tiamulin Hydrogen Fumarate for Veterinary use,
Ph Eur monograph 1659)*

$C_{32}H_{51}NO_8S$ 610   55297-96-6

Action and use
Antibacterial.

Ph Eur

DEFINITION
(3aS,4R,5S,6S,8R,9R,9aR,10R)-6-Ethenyl-5-hydroxy-
4,6,9,10-tetramethyl-1-oxodecahydro-3a,9-propano-3aH-
cyclopentacycloocten-8-yl [[2-
(diethylamino)ethyl]sulfanyl]acetate hydrogen
(E)-butenedioate.

Semi-synthetic product derived from a fermentation product.

Content
96.5 per cent to 102.0 per cent (dried substance).

CHARACTERS
Appearance
White or light yellow, crystalline powder.

Solubility
Soluble in water, freely soluble in anhydrous ethanol and
soluble in methanol.

IDENTIFICATION
Infrared absorption spectrophotometry (*2.2.24*).

Comparison tiamulin hydrogen fumarate CRS.

TESTS
pH (*2.2.3*)
3.1 to 4.1.

Dissolve 0.5 g in *carbon dioxide-free water R* and dilute to
50 mL with the same solvent.

Related substances
Liquid chromatography (*2.2.29*).

Ammonium carbonate buffer solution pH 100 Dissolve 10.0 g of
ammonium carbonate R in *water R*, add 22 mL of *perchloric
acid solution R* and dilute to 1000.0 mL with *water R*. Adjust
to pH 10.0 with *concentrated ammonia R1*.

Solvent mixture Ammonium carbonate buffer solution
pH 10.0, *acetonitrile R1* (50:50 *V/V*).

Test solution Dissolve 0.200 g of the substance to be
examined in the solvent mixture and dilute to 50.0 mL with
the solvent mixture.

Reference solution (a) Dissolve 0.200 g of *tiamulin hydrogen
fumarate CRS* in the solvent mixture and dilute to 50.0 mL
with the solvent mixture.

Reference solution (b) Dilute 1.0 mL of the test solution to
100.0 mL with the solvent mixture.

Reference solution (c) Dissolve 40.0 mg of *fumaric acid R* in
the solvent mixture and dilute to 50.0 mL with the solvent
mixture.

Reference solution (d) Dissolve 4 mg of *tiamulin for peak
identification CRS* (tiamulin hydrogen fumarate containing
impurities B, C, D, F, H and I) in the solvent mixture and
dilute to 1 mL with the solvent mixture.

Column:
— *size*: l = 0.15 m, Ø = 4.6 mm,
— *stationary phase*: end-capped octadecylsilyl silica gel for
  chromatography R (5 μm),
— *temperature*: 30 °C.

Mobile phase acetonitrile R1, ammonium carbonate buffer
solution pH 10.0, *methanol R1* (21:30:49 *V/V/V*).

Flow rate 1.0 mL/min.

Detection Spectrophotometer at 212 nm.

Injection 20 μL.

Run time 3 times the retention time of tiamulin.

Identification of impurities Use the chromatogram supplied
with *tiamulin for peak identification CRS* and the
chromatogram obtained with reference solution (d) to
identify the peaks due to impurities B and H.

Relative retention With reference to tiamulin (retention
time = about 18 min): impurity G = about 0.2;
impurity A = about 0.22; impurity H = about 0.23;
impurity I = about 0.3; impurity J = about 0.4;
impurity K = about 0.45; impurity B = about 0.5;
impurity L = about 0.65; impurity C = about 0.66;
impurity F = about 0.8; impurity M = about 0.85;
impurity D = about 1.1; impurity S = about 1.4;
impurity T = about 1.6; impurity E = 2.4.

System suitability: reference solution (a):
— baseline separation between the peaks due to tiamulin
  and impurity D.

Limits:
— *impurities B, H*: for each impurity, not more than
  1.5 times the area of the principal peak in the
  chromatogram obtained with reference solution (b)
  (1.5 per cent),
— *impurities A, C, D, E, F, G, I, J, K, L, M, S, T*: for each
  impurity, not more than the area of the principal peak in
  the chromatogram obtained with reference solution (b)
  (1.0 per cent),
— *any other impurity*: for each impurity, not more than
  0.2 times the area of the principal peak in the
  chromatogram obtained with reference solution (b)
  (0.2 per cent),
— *total*: not more than 3 times the area of the principal peak
  in the chromatogram obtained with reference solution (b)
  (3.0 per cent),
— *disregard limit*: 0.1 times the area of the principal peak in
  the chromatogram obtained with reference solution (b)
  (0.1 per cent); disregard any peak present in reference
  solution (c).

Loss on drying (*2.2.32*)
Maximum 0.5 per cent, determined on 1.000 g by drying in
an oven at 105 °C.

ASSAY
Liquid chromatography (*2.2.29*) as described in the test for
related substances with the following modification.

Injection Test solution and reference solution (a).

Calculate the percentage content of $C_{32}H_{51}NO_8S$ from the
declared content of *tiamulin hydrogen fumarate CRS*.

STORAGE
Protected from light.

IMPURITIES

Specified impurities A, B, C, D, E, F, G, H, I, J, K, L, M, S, T

Other detectable impurities (the following substances would, if present at a sufficient level, be detected by one or other of the tests in the monograph. They are limited by the general acceptance criterion for other/unspecified impurities and/or by the general monograph Substances for pharmaceutical use (2034). It is therefore not necessary to identify these impurities for demonstration of compliance. See also *5.10. Control of impurities in substances for pharmaceutical use*): N, O, P, Q, R.

A. R1 = R2 = H: (3a*S*,4*R*,5*S*,6*S*,8*R*,9*R*,9a*R*,10*R*)-6-ethenyl-5,8-dihydroxy-4,6,9,10-tetramethyloctahydro-3a,9-propano-3a*H*-cyclopentacycloocten-1(4*H*)-one (mutilin),

G. R1 = CO-CH₂OH, R2 = H: (3a*S*,4*R*,5*S*,6*S*,8*R*,9*R*,9a*R*,10*R*)-6-ethenyl-5-hydroxy-4,6,9,10-tetramethyl-1-oxodecahydro-3a,9-propano-3a*H*-cyclopentacycloocten-8-yl hydroxyacetate (pleuromutilin),

J. R1 = CO-CH₃, R2 = H: (3a*S*,4*R*,5*S*,6*S*,8*R*,9*R*,9a*R*,10*R*)-6-ethenyl-5-hydroxy-4,6,9,10-tetramethyl-1-oxodecahydro-3a,9-propano-3a*H*-cyclopentacycloocten-8-yl acetate (mutilin 14-acetate),

K. R1 = H, R2 = CO-CH₃: (3a*S*,4*R*,5*S*,6*S*,8*R*,9*R*,9a*R*,10*R*)-6-ethenyl-8-hydroxy-4,6,9,10-tetramethyl-1-oxodecahydro-3a,9-propano-3a*H*-cyclopentacycloocten-5-yl acetate (mutilin 11-acetate),

L. R1 = CO-CH₂-O-SO₂-C₆H₄-*p*CH₃, R2 = H: (3a*S*,4*R*,5*S*,6*S*,8*R*,9*R*,9a*R*,10*R*)-6-ethenyl-5-hydroxy-4,6,9,10-tetramethyl-1-oxodecahydro-3a,9-propano-3a*H*-cyclopentacycloocten-8-yl [[(4-methylphenyl)sulfonyl]oxy]acetate (pleuromutilin 22-tosylate),

M. R1 = R2 = CO-CH₃: (3a*S*,4*R*,5*S*,6*S*,8*R*,9*R*,9a*R*,10*R*)-6-ethenyl-4,6,9,10-tetramethyl-1-oxodecahydro-3a,9-propano-3a*H*-cyclopentacycloocten-5,8-diyl diacetate (mutilin 11,14-diacetate),

P. R1 = CO-CH₂-O-SO₂-C₆H₅, R2 = H: (3a*S*,4*R*,5*S*,6*S*,8*R*,9*R*,9a*R*,10*R*)-6-ethenyl-5-hydroxy-4,6,9,10-tetramethyl-1-oxodecahydro-3a,9-propano-3a*H*-cyclopentacycloocten-8-yl [(phenylsulfonyl)oxy]acetate,

T. R1 = CO-CH₂-[S-CH₂-CH₂-]₂N(C₂H₅)₂, R2 = H: (3a*S*,4*R*,5*S*,6*S*,8*R*,9*R*,9a*R*,10*R*)-6-ethenyl-5-hydroxy-4,6,9,10-tetramethyl-1-oxodecahydro-3a,9-propano-3a*H*-cyclopentacycloocten-8-yl [[2-[[2-(diethylamino)ethyl]sulfanyl]ethyl]sulfanyl]acetate,

B. R = CH₂-C₆H₅: 2-(benzylsulfanyl)-*N,N*-diethylethanamine,

C. R = S-CH₂-CH₂-N(C₂H₅)₂: 2,2′-(disulfane-1,2-diyl)bis(*N,N*-diethylethanamine),

O. R = H: 2-(diethylamino)ethanethiol,

D. (3a*R*,4*R*,6*S*,8*R*,9*R*,9a*R*,10*R*)-6-ethenylhydroxy-4,6,9,10-tetramethyl-5-oxodecahydro-3a,9-propano-3a*H*-cyclopentacycloocten-8-yl [[2-(diethylamino)ethyl]sulfanyl]acetate,

E. (3a*S*,4*R*,6*S*,8*R*,9*R*,9a*R*,10*R*)-6-ethenyl-4,6,9,10-tetramethyl-1,5-dioxodecahydro-3a,9-propano-3a*H*-cyclopentacycloocten-8-yl [[2-(diethylamino)ethyl]sulfanyl]acetate (11-oxotiamulin),

F. impurity of unknown structure with a relative retention of about 0.8,

H. (2*E*)-4-[(2*RS*)-2-[(3a*S*,4*R*,5*S*,6*R*,8*R*,9*R*,9a*R*,10*R*)-8-[[[[2-(diethylamino)ethyl]sulfanyl]acetyl]oxy]-5-hydroxy-4,6,9,10-tetramethyl-1-oxodecahydro-3a,9-propano-3a*H*-cyclopentacycloocten-6-yl]-2-hydroxyethoxy]-4-oxobut-2-enoic acid (19,20-dihydroxytiamulin 20-fumarate),

I. (2*E*)-4-[[(3a*S*,4*R*,5*S*,6*S*,8*R*,9*R*,9a*R*,10*R*)-8-[[[[2-(diethylamino)ethyl]sulfanyl]acetyl]oxy]-6-ethenyl-1,5-dihydroxy-4,6,9,10-tetramethyldecahydro-3a,9-propano-3a*H*-cyclopentacycloocten-2-yl]oxy]-4-oxobut-2-enoic acid (2,3-dihydroxytiamulin 2-fumarate),

N. (2*E*)-4-[2-[[(3a*S*,4*R*,5*S*,6*S*,8*R*,9*R*,9a*R*,10*R*)-6-ethenyl-5-hydroxy-4,6,9,10-tetramethyl-1-oxodecahydro-3a,9-propano-3a*H*-cyclopentacycloocten-8-yl]oxy]-2-oxoethoxy]-4-oxobut-2-enoic acid (pleuromutilin 22-fumarate),

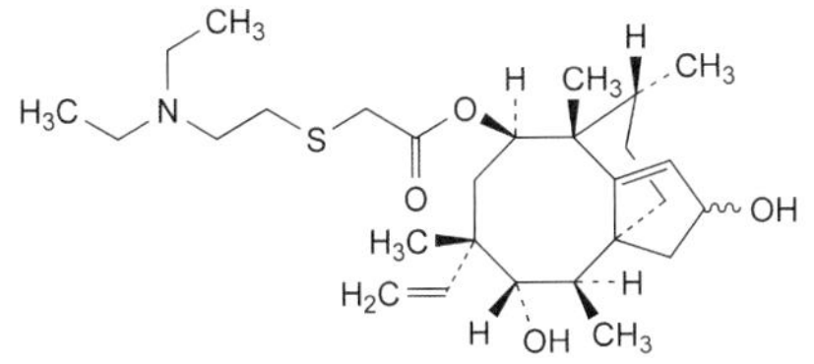

Q. (3a*S*,4*R*,5*S*,6*S*,8*R*,9*R*,10*R*)-6-ethenyl-2,5-dihydroxy-4,6,9,10-tetramethyl-2,3,4,5,6,7,8,9-octahydro-3a,9-propano-3a*H*-cyclopentacycloocten-8-yl [[2-(diethylamino)ethyl]sulfanyl]acetate (3,4-didehydro-2-hydroxytiamulin),

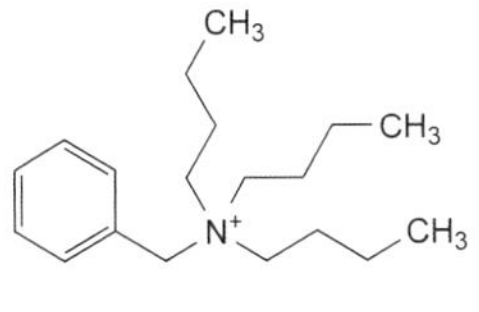

R. *N*-benzyl-*N*,*N*-dibutylbutan-1-aminium,

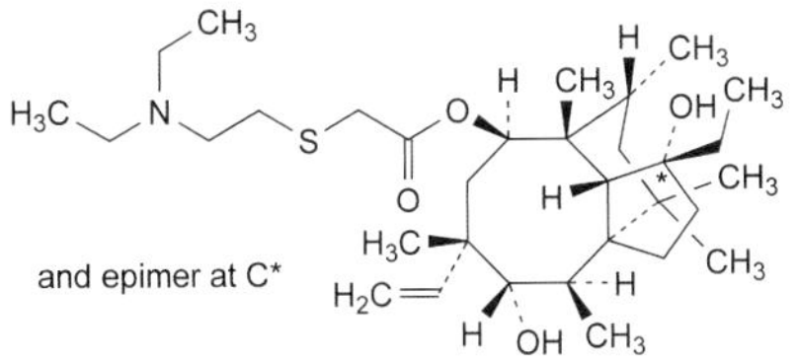

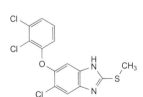

and epimer at C*

S. (1*RS*,3a*R*,4*R*,5*S*,6*S*,8*R*,9*R*,9a*R*,10*R*)-6-ethenyl-1-ethyl-1,5-dihydroxy-4,6,9,10,12,12-hexamethyldecahydro-3a,9-propano-3a*H*-cyclopentacycloocten-8-yl [[2-(diethylamino)ethyl]sulfanyl]acetate.

_____ *Ph Eur*

Triclabendazole

Triclabendazole for Veterinary Use

(Ph Eur monograph 2609)

$C_{14}H_9Cl_3N_2OS$ 359.7   68786-66-3

Action and use
Benzimidazole antihelminthic

Ph Eur _____

DEFINITION
5-Chloro-6-(2,3-dichlorophenoxy)-2-(methylsulfanyl)-1*H*-benzimidazole.

Content
99.0 per cent to 101.0 per cent (dried substance).

CHARACTERS
Appearance
White or almost white, crystalline powder.

Solubility
Practically insoluble in water, soluble in acetone, sparingly soluble in ethanol (96 per cent).

IDENTIFICATION
Infrared absorption spectrophotometry *(2.2.24)*.

Comparison triclabendazole CRS.

TESTS
Related substances
Liquid chromatography *(2.2.29)*. *Prepare the solutions protected from light.*

Test solution Dissolve 50.0 mg of the substance to be examined in 10 mL of *acetonitrile R* and dilute to 25.0 mL with the mobile phase.

Reference solution (a) Dilute 1.0 mL of the test solution to 50.0 mL with the mobile phase. Dilute 1.0 mL of this solution to 10.0 mL with the mobile phase.

Reference solution (b) Dissolve the contents of a vial of *triclabendazole for system suitability CRS* (impurities A, B and D) in 1.0 mL of the mobile phase.

Column:
— *size*: *l* = 0.25 m, Ø = 4.6 mm;
— *stationary phase*: *base-deactivated end-capped octadecylsilyl silica gel for chromatography R* (5 μm).

Mobile phase Dissolve 0.77 g of *ammonium acetate R* in 800 mL of *water for chromatography R*, add 1 mL of *triethylamine R* and mix; adjust to pH 4.5 with *glacial acetic acid R* and dilute to 1 L with *water for chromatography R*. Mix 40 volumes of this solution and 60 volumes of *acetonitrile R*.

Flow rate 1.0 mL/min.

Detection Spectrophotometer at 305 nm.

Injection 20 μL.

Run time 2.5 times the retention time of triclabendazole.

Identification of impurities Use the chromatogram supplied with *triclabendazole for system suitability CRS* and the chromatogram obtained with reference solution (b) to identify the peaks due to impurities A, B and D.

Relative retention With reference to triclabendazole (retention time = about 10 min): impurity A = about 0.6; impurity B = about 0.7; impurity D = about 1.9.

System suitability: reference solution (b):
— *resolution*: minimum 2.5 between the peaks due to impurities A and B.

Calculation of percentage contents:
— *correction factors*: multiply the peak areas of the following impurities by the corresponding correction factor: impurity A = 1.9; impurity D = 2.7;
— for each impurity, use the concentration of triclabendazole in reference solution (a).

Limits:
— *impurities A, D*: for each impurity, maximum 0.3 per cent;
— *unspecified impurities*: for each impurity, maximum 0.20 per cent;
— *total*: maximum 1.0 per cent;
— *reporting threshold*: 0.10 per cent.

Loss on drying *(2.2.32)*
Maximum 0.5 per cent, determined on 1.000 g by drying in an oven at 105 °C for 6 h.

Sulfated ash *(2.4.14)*
Maximum 0.1 per cent, determined on 1.0 g.

ASSAY

Dissolve 0.280 g in 50 mL of *anhydrous acetic acid R*. Allow to cool and titrate with *0.1 M perchloric acid*, determining the end-point potentiometrically (*2.2.20*).

1 mL of *0.1 M perchloric acid* is equivalent to 35.97 mg of $C_{14}H_9Cl_3N_2OS$.

STORAGE

Protected from light.

IMPURITIES

Specified impurities A, D

Other detectable impurities (the following substances would, if present at a sufficient level, be detected by one or other of the tests in the monograph. They are limited by the general acceptance criterion for other/unspecified impurities and/or by the general monograph *Substances for pharmaceutical use (2034)*. It is therefore not necessary to identify these impurities for demonstration of compliance. See also *5.10. Control of impurities in substances for pharmaceutical use*): B.

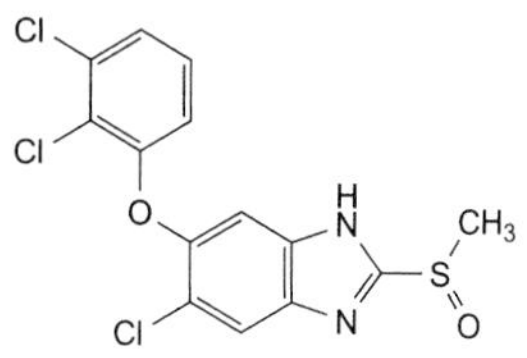

A. 5-chloro-6-(2,3-dichlorophenoxy)-2-(methylsulfinyl)-1*H*-benzimidazole,

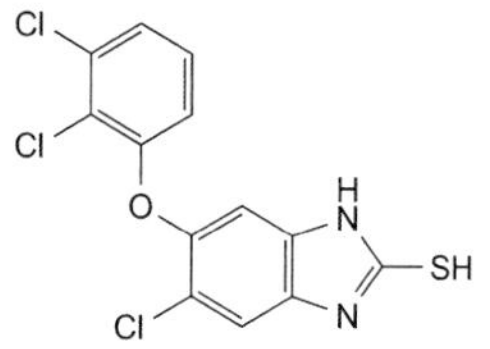

B. 5-chloro-6-(2,3-dichlorophenoxy)-1*H*-benzimidazole-2-thiol,

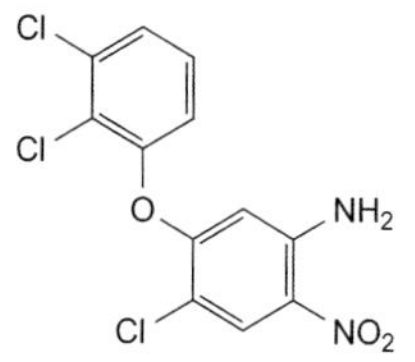

D. 4-chloro-5-(2,3-dichlorophenoxy)-2-nitroaniline.

Ph Eur

Tylosin

(Tylosin for Veterinary Use, Ph Eur monograph 1273)

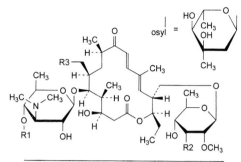

Name	Mol. Formula	R1	R2	R3
tylosin A	$C_{46}H_{77}NO_{17}$	osyl	OCH_3	CHO
tylosin B	$C_{39}H_{65}NO_{14}$	H	OCH_3	CHO
tylosin C	$C_{45}H_{75}NO_{17}$	osyl	OH	CHO
tylosin D	$C_{46}H_{79}NO_{17}$	osyl	OCH_3	CH_2OH

Action and use

Macrolide antibacterial.

Preparation

Tylosin Injection

Ph Eur

DEFINITION

Mixture of macrolide antibiotics produced by a strain of *Streptomyces fradiae* or by any other means. The main component of the mixture is (4*R*,5*S*,6*S*,7*R*,9*R*,11*E*,13*E*,15*R*,16*R*)-15-[[(6-deoxy-2,3-di-*O*-methyl-β-D-allopyranosyl)oxy]methyl]-6-[[3,6-dideoxy-4-*O*-(2,6-dideoxy-3-*C*-methyl-α-L-*ribo*-hexopyranosyl)-3-(dimethylamino)-β-D-glucopyranosyl]oxy]-16-ethyl-4-hydroxy-5,9,13-trimethyl-7-(2-oxoethyl)oxacyclohexadeca-11,13-diene-2,10-dione (tylosin A, M_r 916). Tylosin B (desmycosin, M_r 772), tylosin C (macrocin, M_r 902) and tylosin D (relomycin, M_r 918) may also be present. They contribute to the potency of the substance to be examined.

Potency

Minimum 900 IU/mg (dried substance).

CHARACTERS

Appearance

Almost white or slightly yellow powder.

Solubility

Slightly soluble in water, freely soluble in anhydrous ethanol and in methylene chloride. It dissolves in dilute solutions of mineral acids.

IDENTIFICATION

A. Infrared absorption spectrophotometry (*2.2.24*).

Comparison tylosin CRS.

B. Examine the chromatograms obtained in the test for composition.

Results The principal peak in the chromatogram obtained with the test solution is similar in retention time and size to the principal peak in the chromatogram obtained with reference solution (a).

C. Dissolve about 30 mg in a mixture of 0.15 mL of *water R*, 2.5 mL of *acetic anhydride R* and 7.5 mL of *pyridine R*. Allow to stand for about 10 min. No green colour develops.

TESTS

pH *(2.2.3)*

8.5 to 10.5.

Suspend 0.25 g in 10 mL of *carbon dioxide-free water R*.

Composition

Liquid chromatography *(2.2.29)*: use the normalisation procedure. *Prepare the solutions immediately before use.*

Solvent mixture acetonitrile *R*, water *R* (50:50 *V/V*).

Test solution Dissolve 20.0 mg of the substance to be examined in the solvent mixture and dilute to 100.0 mL with the solvent mixture.

Reference solution (a) Dissolve 2 mg of *tylosin phosphate for peak identification CRS* (containing tylosins A, B, C and D) in the solvent mixture and dilute to 10 mL with the solvent mixture.

Reference solution (b) Dissolve 2 mg of *tylosin CRS* and 2 mg of *tylosin D CRS* in the solvent mixture and dilute to 10 mL with the solvent mixture.

Column:
— *size*: l = 0.20 m, Ø = 4.6 mm;
— *stationary phase*: octadecylsilyl silica gel for chromatography *R* (5 µm);
— *temperature*: 35 °C.

Mobile phase Mix 40 volumes of *acetonitrile R* and 60 volumes of a 200 g/L solution of *sodium perchlorate R* previously adjusted to pH 2.5 using *1 M hydrochloric acid*.

Flow rate 1.0 mL/min.

Detection Spectrophotometer at 290 nm.

Injection 20 µL.

Retention time Tylosin A = about 12 min.

Identification of peaks Use the chromatogram supplied with *tylosin phosphate for peak identification CRS* and the chromatogram obtained with reference solution (a) to identify the peaks due to tylosins A, B, C and D.

System suitability: reference solution (b):
— *resolution*: minimum 2.0 between the peaks due to tylosins A and D.

Limits:
— *tylosin A*: minimum 80.0 per cent;
— *sum of tylosins A, B, C and D*: minimum 95.0 per cent.

Tyramine

Maximum 0.35 per cent and maximum 0.15 per cent, if intended for use in the manufacture of parenteral preparations.

In a 25.0 mL volumetric flask, dissolve 50.0 mg in 5.0 mL of a 3.4 g/L solution of *phosphoric acid R*. Add 1.0 mL of *pyridine R* and 2.0 mL of a saturated solution of *ninhydrin R* (about 40 g/L). Close the flask with a piece of aluminium foil and heat in a water-bath at 85 °C for 30 min. Cool the solution rapidly and dilute to 25.0 mL with *water R*. Mix and measure immediately the absorbance *(2.2.25)* of the solution at 570 nm using a blank solution as the compensation liquid. The absorbance is not greater than that of a standard prepared at the same time and in the same manner using 5.0 mL of a 35 mg/L solution of *tyramine R* in a 3.4 g/L solution of *phosphoric acid R*. If intended for use in the manufacture of parenteral preparations, the absorbance is not greater than that of a standard prepared at the same time and in the same manner using 5.0 mL of a 15 mg/L solution of *tyramine R* in a 3.4 g/L solution of *phosphoric acid R*.

Loss on drying *(2.2.32)*

Maximum 5.0 per cent, determined on 1.000 g by drying in an oven at 60 °C at a pressure not exceeding 0.7 kPa for 3 h.

Sulfated ash *(2.4.14)*

Maximum 3.0 per cent, determined on 1.0 g.

ASSAY

Carry out the microbiological assay of antibiotics *(2.7.2)*. Use *tylosin CRS* as the chemical reference substance.

STORAGE

Protected from light.

IMPURITIES

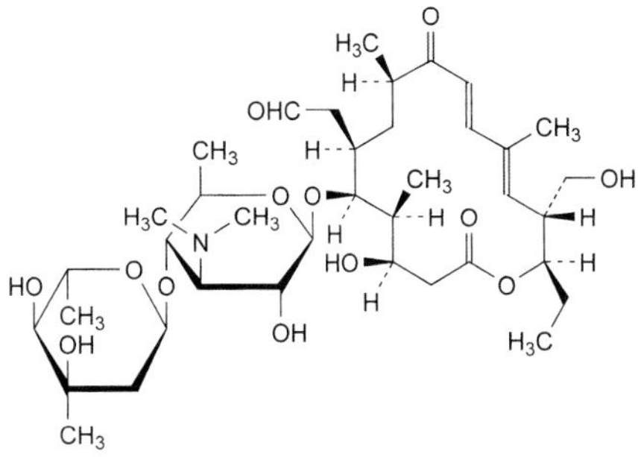

A. desmycinosyltylosin,

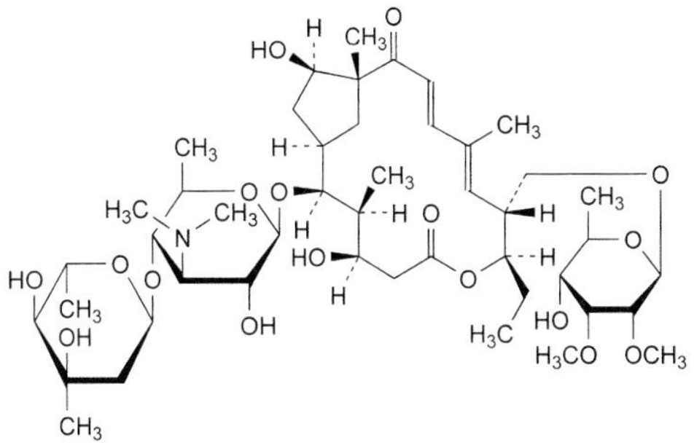

B. tylosin A aldol.

———————————————————— *Ph Eur*

Tylosin Phosphate

(Tylosin Phosphate Bulk Solution for Veterinary Use, Ph Eur monograph 1661)

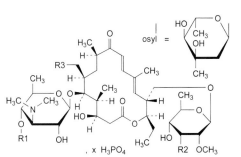

Tylosin	R1	R2	R3	Mol. Formula	M_r
A	osyl	OCH$_3$	CHO	C$_{46}$H$_{77}$NO$_{17}$	916
B	H	OCH$_3$	CHO	C$_{39}$H$_{65}$NO$_{14}$	772
C	osyl	OH	CHO	C$_{45}$H$_{75}$NO$_{17}$	902
D	osyl	OCH$_3$	CH$_2$OH	C$_{46}$H$_{79}$NO$_{17}$	918

Action and use

Macrolide antibacterial.

Ph Eur

DEFINITION

Solution of the dihydrogen phosphate of a mixture of macrolide antibiotics produced by a strain of *Streptomyces fradiae* or by any other means.

The main component is the phosphate of (4R,5S,6S,7R,9R,11E,13E,15R,16R)-15-[[(6-deoxy-2,3-di-*O*-methyl-β-D-allopyranosyl)oxy]methyl]-6-[[3,6-dideoxy-4-*O*-(2,6-dideoxy-3-*C*-methyl-α-L-*ribo*-hexopyranosyl)-3-(dimethylamino)-β-D-glucopyranosyl]oxy]-16-ethyl-4-hydroxy-5,9,13-trimethyl-7-(2-oxoethyl)oxacyclohexadeca-11,13-diene-2,10-dione (tylosin A phosphate).

The phosphates of tylosin B (desmycosin phosphate), tylosin C (macrocin phosphate) and tylosin D (relomycin phosphate) may also be present. The solution also contains sodium dihydrogen phosphate.

Potency

Minimum 800 IU per milligram of dry residue.
Tylosins A, B, C and D contribute to the potency.

CHARACTERS

Appearance

Yellow or brownish-yellow, viscous liquid.

Solubility

Miscible with water.

IDENTIFICATION

A. Ultraviolet and visible absorption spectrophotometry (*2.2.25*).

Test solution Dilute an amount of the preparation to be examined equivalent to 400 000 IU of tylosin phosphate to 100.0 mL with *water R*. Dilute 1.0 mL of this solution to 100.0 mL with *water R*.

Spectral range 230-350 nm.

Absorption maximum At 290 nm.

Absorbance at the absorption maximum Minimum 0.70.

B. Examine the chromatograms obtained in the test for composition.

Results The principal peak in the chromatogram obtained with the test solution is similar in retention time and size to the principal peak in the chromatogram obtained with reference solution (a).

C. Dilute an amount of the preparation to be examined equivalent to 400 000 IU of tylosin phosphate in 10 mL of *water R*. The solution gives reaction (a) of phosphates (*2.3.1*).

TESTS

pH (*2.2.3*)
5.5 to 6.5.

Dilute 1.0 g in 10 mL of *carbon dioxide-free water R*.

Composition

Liquid chromatography (*2.2.29*): use the normalisation procedure. *Prepare the solutions immediately before use.*

Test solution Dilute an amount of the preparation to be examined equivalent to 50 000 IU of tylosin phosphate to 200 mL with a mixture of equal volumes of *acetonitrile R* and *water R*.

Reference solution (a) Dissolve 2 mg of *tylosin phosphate for peak identification CRS* (containing tylosins A, B, C and D) in a mixture of equal volumes of *acetonitrile R* and *water R* and dilute to 10 mL with the same mixture of solvents.

Reference solution (b) Dissolve 2 mg of *tylosin CRS* and 2 mg of *tylosin D CRS* in a mixture of equal volumes of

acetonitrile R and *water R* and dilute to 10 mL with the same mixture of solvents.

Reference solution (c) Dilute 1.0 mL of reference solution (a) to 100.0 mL with a mixture of equal volumes of *acetonitrile R* and *water R*. Dilute 1.0 mL of this solution to 10.0 mL with a mixture of equal volumes of *acetonitrile R* and *water R*.

Column:
— *size*: *l* = 0.20 m, Ø = 4.6 mm;
— *stationary phase*: octadecylsilyl silica gel for chromatography *R* (5 μm);
— *temperature*: 35 °C.

Mobile phase Mix 40 volumes of *acetonitrile R* and 60 volumes of a 200 g/L solution of *sodium perchlorate R* previously adjusted to pH 2.5 using a 36.5 g/L solution of *hydrochloric acid R*.

Flow rate 1.0 mL/min.

Detection Spectrophotometer at 290 nm.

Injection 20 μL.

Run time 1.8 times the retention time of tylosin A.

Identification of tylosins Use the chromatogram supplied with *tylosin phosphate for peak identification CRS* and the chromatogram obtained with reference solution (a) to identify the peaks due to tylosins A, B, C and D.

Relative retention With reference to tylosin A (retention time = about 12 min): impurity A = about 0.35; tylosin C = about 0.5; tylosin B = about 0.6; tylosin D = about 0.85; impurity B = about 0.9.

System suitability: reference solution (b):
— *resolution*: minimum 2.0 between the peaks due to tylosin D and tylosin A.

Limits:
— *tylosin A*: minimum 80.0 per cent;
— *sum of tylosins A, B, C and D*: minimum 95.0 per cent;
— *disregard limit*: area of the principal peak in the chromatogram obtained with reference solution (c).

Tyramine

In a 25.0 mL volumetric flask, dissolve an amount of the preparation to be examined equivalent to 50 000 IU of tylosin phosphate in 5.0 mL of a 3.4 g/L solution of *phosphoric acid R*. Add 1.0 mL of *pyridine R* and 2.0 mL of a saturated solution of *ninhydrin R* (about 40 g/L). Close the flask with aluminium foil and heat in a water-bath at 85 °C for 20-30 min. Cool the solution rapidly and dilute to 25.0 mL with *water R*. Mix and measure immediately the absorbance (*2.2.25*) of the solution at 570 nm using a blank solution as the compensation liquid.

The absorbance is not greater than that of a standard prepared at the same time and in the same manner using 5.0 mL of a 35 mg/L solution of *tyramine R* in a 3.4 g/L solution of *phosphoric acid R*.

Phosphate

8.5 per cent to 10.0 per cent of PO_4, calculated with reference to the dry residue (see Assay).

Test solution Dissolve an amount of the preparation to be examined equivalent to 200 000 IU of tylosin phosphate in 50 mL of *water R*. Add 5.0 mL of *dilute sulfuric acid R* and dilute to 100.0 mL with *water R*. To 2.0 mL of this solution add successively, mixing after each addition, 10.0 mL of *water R*, 5.0 mL of *ammonium molybdate reagent R2*, 1.0 mL of *hydroquinone solution R* and 1.0 mL of a 200 g/L solution of *sodium metabisulfite R*. Allow to stand for at least 20 min and dilute to 50.0 mL with *water R*. Mix thoroughly.

Reference solution (a) To 1.0 mL of a standard solution containing 0.430 g/L of *potassium dihydrogen phosphate R* (corresponds to 300 ppm of PO_4) add successively, mixing after each addition, 10.0 mL of *water R*, 5.0 mL of *ammonium molybdate reagent R2*, 1.0 mL of *hydroquinone solution R* and 1.0 mL of a 200 g/L solution of *sodium metabisulfite R*. Allow to stand for at least 20 min and dilute to 50.0 mL with *water R*. Mix thoroughly.

Reference solution (b) Prepare as reference solution (a) but using 2.0 mL of the standard solution.

Reference solution (c) Prepare as reference solution (a) but using 5.0 mL of the standard solution.

Compensation liquid Prepare as reference solution (a) but omitting the standard solution.

Measure the absorbance *(2.2.25)* of the test solution and of the reference solutions at 650 nm. Draw a calibration curve with the absorbances of the 3 reference solutions as a function of the quantity of phosphate in the solutions and read from the curve the quantity of phosphate in the test solution. Determine the percentage content of PO_4, calculated with reference to the dry residue (see Assay).

ASSAY

Carry out the microbiological assay of antibiotics *(2.7.2)*. Use *tylosin CRS* as the reference substance. Calculate the potency from the mass of the dry residue and the activity of the solution.

Dry residue Dry 3.0 g of the preparation to be examined *in vacuo* at 60 °C for 3 h and weigh.

STORAGE

Protected from light, at a temperature of 2 °C to 8 °C.

LABELLING

The label states the concentration of the solution in International Units per milligram of preparation.

IMPURITIES

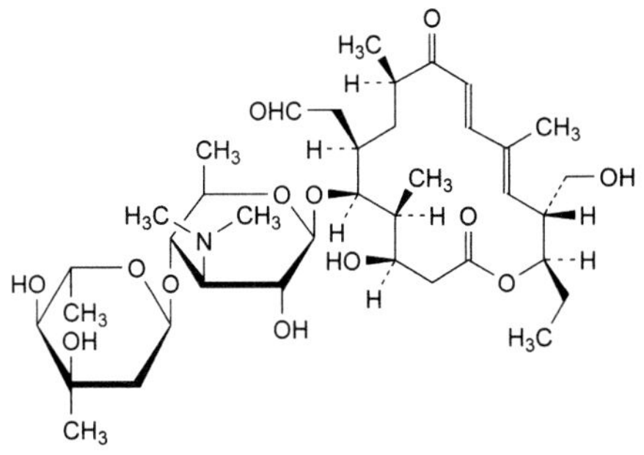

A. desmycinosyltylosin A,

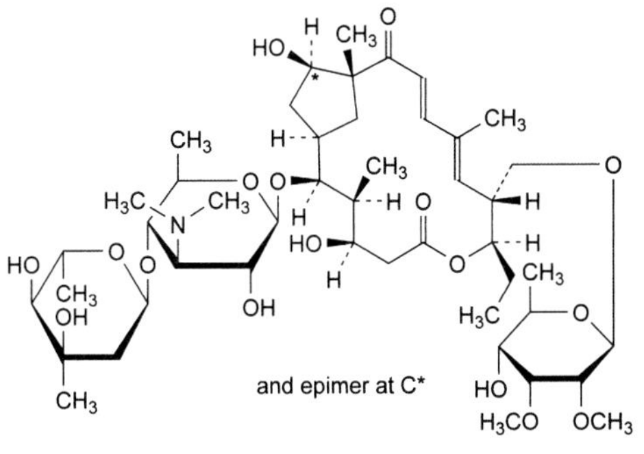

B. (1*R*,2*S*,3*S*,4*R*,8*R*,9*R*,10*E*,12*E*,15*R*,16*RS*)-9-[[(6-deoxy-2,3-di-*O*-methy-β-D-allopyranosyl)oxy]methyl]-2-[[3,6-

dideoxy-4-*O*-(2,6-dideoxy-3-*C*-methyl-α-L-*ribo*-hexopyranosyl)-3-(dimethylamino)-β-D-glucopyranosyl]oxy]-8-ethyl-4,16-dihydroxy-3,11,15-trimethyl-7-oxabicyclo[13.2.1]octadeca-10,12-diene-6,14-dione (tylosin A aldol).

_____ *Ph Eur*

Tylosin Tartrate

(Tylosin Tartrate for Veterinary Use, Ph Eur monograph 1274)

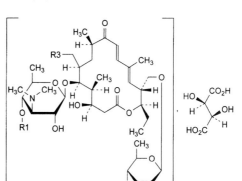

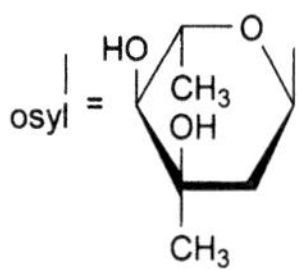

Tylosin	Mol. Form.	R1	R2	R3
A	$C_{46}H_{77}NO_{17}$	osyl	OCH_3	CHO
B	$C_{39}H_{65}NO_{14}$	H	OCH_3	CHO
C	$C_{45}H_{75}NO_{17}$	osyl	OH	CHO
D	$C_{46}H_{79}NO_{17}$	osyl	OCH_3	CH_2OH

Action and Use
Macrolide antibacterial.

Ph Eur _____

DEFINITION
Tartrate of a mixture of macrolide antibiotics produced by a strain of *Streptomyces fradiae* or by any other means. The main component of the mixture is (4*R*,5*S*,6*S*,7*R*,9*R*,11*E*,13*E*,15*R*,16*R*)-15-[[(6-deoxy-2,3-di-*O*-methyl-β-D-allopyranosyl)oxy]methyl]-6-[[3,6-dideoxy-4-*O*-(2,6-dideoxy-3-*C*-methyl-α-L-*ribo*-hexopyranosyl)-3-(dimethylamino)-β-D-glucopyranosyl]oxy]-16-ethyl-4-hydroxy-5,9,13-trimethyl-7-(2-oxoethyl)oxacyclohexadeca-11,13-diene-2,10-dione (tylosin A, tartrate M_r 1982). Tylosin B (desmycosin, tartrate M_r 1694), tylosin C (macrocin, tartrate M_r 1954) and tylosin D (relomycin, tartrate M_r 1986) may also be present. They contribute to the potency of the substance to be examined.

Potency
Minimum 800 IU/mg (dried substance).

CHARACTERS
Appearance
Almost white or slightly yellow, hygroscopic powder.

Solubility
Freely soluble in water and in methylene chloride, slightly soluble in anhydrous ethanol. It dissolves in dilute solutions of mineral acids.

IDENTIFICATION
A. Infrared absorption spectrophotometry *(2.2.24)*.

Comparison Ph. Eur. reference spectrum of tylosin tartrate.

B. Examine the chromatograms obtained in the test for composition.

Results The principal peak in the chromatogram obtained with the test solution is similar in retention time and size to the principal peak in the chromatogram obtained with reference solution (a).

C. Dissolve about 30 mg in a mixture of 0.15 mL of *water R*, 2.5 mL of *acetic anhydride R* and 7.5 mL of *pyridine R*. Allow to stand for about 10 min. A green colour is produced.

TESTS

pH (*2.2.3*)

5.0 to 7.2.

Dissolve 0.25 g in 10 mL of *carbon dioxide-free water R*.

Composition

Liquid chromatography (*2.2.29*): use the normalisation procedure. *Prepare the solutions immediately before use.*

Solvent mixture acetonitrile R, water R (50:50 V/V).

Test solution Dissolve 20.0 mg of the substance to be examined in the solvent mixture and dilute to 100.0 mL with the solvent mixture.

Reference solution (a) Dissolve 2 mg of *tylosin phosphate for peak identification CRS* (containing tylosins A, B, C and D) in the solvent mixture and dilute to 10 mL with the solvent mixture.

Reference solution (b) Dissolve 2 mg of *tylosin CRS* and 2 mg of *tylosin D CRS* in the solvent mixture and dilute to 10 mL with the solvent mixture.

Column:
— *size*: *l* = 0.20 m, Ø = 4.6 mm;
— *stationary phase*: octadecylsilyl silica gel for chromatography R (5 μm);
— *temperature*: 35 °C.

Mobile phase Mix 40 volumes of *acetonitrile R* and 60 volumes of a 200 g/L solution of *sodium perchlorate R* previously adjusted to pH 2.5 using *1 M hydrochloric acid*.

Flow rate 1.0 mL/min.

Detection Spectrophotometer at 290 nm.

Injection 20 μL.

Retention time Tylosin A = about 12 min.

Identification of peaks Use the chromatogram supplied with *tylosin phosphate for peak identification CRS* and the chromatogram obtained with reference solution (a) to identify the peaks due to tylosins A, B, C and D.

System suitability: reference solution (b):
— *resolution*: minimum 2.0 between the peaks due to tylosins A and D.

Limits:
— *tylosin A*: minimum 80.0 per cent;
— *sum of tylosins A, B, C and D*: minimum 95.0 per cent.

Tyramine

Maximum 0.35 per cent and maximum 0.15 per cent, if it is intended for use in the manufacture of parenteral preparations.

In a 25.0 mL volumetric flask, dissolve 50.0 mg in 5.0 mL of a 3.4 g/L solution of *phosphoric acid R*. Add 1.0 mL of *pyridine R* and 2.0 mL of a saturated solution of *ninhydrin R* (about 40 g/L). Close the flask with a piece of aluminium foil and heat in a water-bath at 85 °C for 30 min. Cool the solution rapidly and dilute to 25.0 mL with *water R*. Mix and measure immediately the absorbance (*2.2.25*) of the solution at 570 nm using a blank solution as the compensation liquid.

The absorbance is not greater than that of a standard prepared at the same time and in the same manner using 5.0 mL of a 35 mg/L solution of *tyramine R* in a 3.4 g/L solution of *phosphoric acid R*. If intended for use in the manufacture of parenteral preparations, the absorbance is not greater than that of a standard prepared at the same time and in the same manner using 5.0 mL of a 15 mg/L solution of *tyramine R* in a 3.4 g/L solution of *phosphoric acid R*.

Loss on drying (*2.2.32*)

Maximum 4.5 per cent, determined on 1.000 g by drying at 60 °C at a pressure not exceeding 0.7 kPa for 3 h.

Sulfated ash (*2.4.14*)

Maximum 2.5 per cent, determined on 1.0 g.

ASSAY

Carry out the microbiological assay of antibiotics (*2.7.2*). Use *tylosin CRS* as the chemical reference substance.

STORAGE

In an airtight container, protected from light.

IMPURITIES

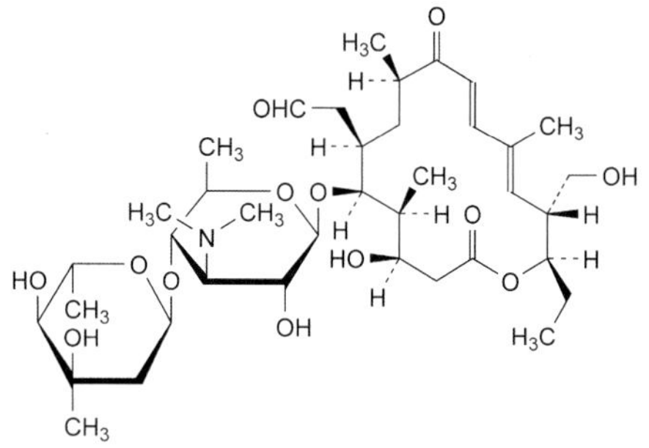

A. desmycinosyltylosin,

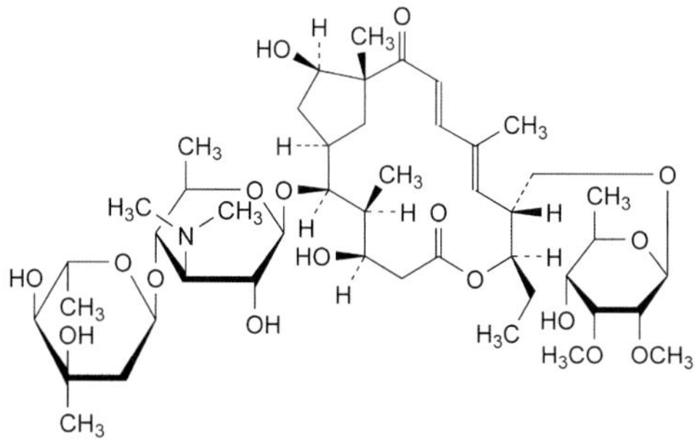

B. tylosin A aldol.

_____ *Ph Eur*

Valnemulin Hydrochloride

(Valnemulin Hydrochloride for Veterinary Use, Ph Eur monograph 2137)

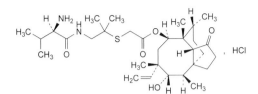

C$_{31}$H$_{53}$ClN$_2$O$_5$S   601   133868-46-9

Action and use
Antibacterial.

Ph Eur

DEFINITION

(3a*S*,4*R*,5*S*,6*S*,8*R*,9*R*,9a*R*,10*R*)-6-Ethenyl-5-hydroxy-4,6,9,10-tetramethyl-1-oxodecahydro-3a,9-propano-3a*H*-cyclopenta[8]annulen-8-yl [[2-[[(2*R*)-2-amino-3-methylbutanoyl]amino]-1,1-dimethylethyl]sulfanyl]acetate hydrochloride.

Semi-synthetic product derived from a fermentation product.

Content
96.0 per cent to 102.0 per cent (anhydrous substance).

CHARACTERS

Appearance
White or yellowish, amorphous powder, hygroscopic.

Solubility
Freely soluble in water and in anhydrous ethanol, practically insoluble in *tert*-butyl methyl ether.

IDENTIFICATION

A. Infrared absorption spectrophotometry *(2.2.24)*.

Comparison valnemulin hydrochloride CRS.

B. It gives reaction (a) of chlorides *(2.3.1)*.

TESTS

pH *(2.2.3)*
3.0 to 6.0.

Dissolve 2.0 g in *carbon dioxide-free water R* and dilute to 20 mL with the same solvent.

Specific optical rotation *(2.2.7)*
+ 15.5 to + 18.0 (anhydrous substance).

Dissolve 0.250 g in *water R* and dilute to 25.0 mL with the same solvent.

Related substances
Liquid chromatography *(2.2.29)*.

Phosphate buffer solution pH 25 Dissolve 8.0 g of *disodium hydrogen phosphate R* and 3.0 g of *potassium dihydrogen phosphate R* in *water for chromatography R* and dilute to 1000.0 mL with the same solvent. Adjust to pH 2.5 with *phosphoric acid R*.

Solvent mixture Mix equal volumes of *acetonitrile R1* and *water for chromatography R*.

Test solution Dissolve 0.100 g of the substance to be examined in the solvent mixture and dilute to 10.0 mL with the solvent mixture.

Reference solution (a) Dilute 1.0 mL of the test solution to 100.0 mL with the solvent mixture.

Reference solution (b) Dissolve 5 mg of *valnemulin impurity E CRS* and 5 mg of the substance to be examined in the solvent mixture and dilute to 25 mL with the solvent mixture.

Reference solution (c) Dissolve the contents of a vial of *valnemulin for peak identification CRS* (containing impurities A, B and C) in 1 mL of the solvent mixture.

Column:
— *size*: *l* = 0.15 m, Ø = 4.6 mm;
— *stationary phase*: octadecylsilyl silica gel for chromatography *R* (3 μm);
— *temperature*: 50 °C.

Mobile phase:
— *mobile phase A*: phosphate buffer solution pH 2.5, *water R* (25:75 *V/V*);
— *mobile phase B*: phosphate buffer solution pH 2.5, *acetonitrile R1* (25:75 *V/V*);

Time (min)	Mobile phase A (per cent *V/V*)	Mobile phase B (per cent *V/V*)
0 - 2	95 → 55	5 → 45
2 - 4.5	55 → 50	45 → 50
4.5 - 5.5	50 → 35	50 → 65
5.5 - 6.85	35	65
6.85 - 10	35 → 0	65 → 100
10 - 13	0	100
13 - 14	0 → 95	100 → 5
14 - 20	95	5

Flow rate 1.5 mL/min.

Detection Spectrophotometer at 200 nm.

Injection 5 μL.

Identification of impurities Use the chromatogram supplied with *valnemulin for peak identification CRS* and the chromatogram obtained with reference solution (c) to identify the peaks due to impurities A, B and C.

Relative retention With reference to valnemulin (retention time = about 7 min): impurity D = about 0.2; impurity A = about 0.7; impurity B = about 0.85; impurity E = about 0.9; impurity C = about 1.1.

System suitability: reference solution (b):
— *resolution*: minimum 1.5 between the peaks due to impurity E and valnemulin.

Limits:
— *correction factors*: for the calculation of content multiply the peak areas of the following impurities by the corresponding correction factor: impurity B = 3.2; impurity E = 4.2;
— *impurity A*: not more than 0.5 times the area of the principal peak in the chromatogram obtained with reference solution (a) (0.5 per cent);
— *impurity B*: not more than twice the area of the principal peak in the chromatogram obtained with reference solution (a) (2.0 per cent);
— *impurity C*: not more than the area of the principal peak in the chromatogram obtained with reference solution (a) (1.0 per cent);
— *any other impurity*: for each impurity, not more than 0.2 times the area of the principal peak in the chromatogram obtained with reference solution (a) (0.2 per cent);

— *total*: not more than 3 times the area of the principal peak in the chromatogram obtained with reference solution (a) (3.0 per cent);
— *disregard limit*: 0.1 times the area of the principal peak in the chromatogram obtained with reference solution (a) (0.1 per cent); disregard the peak due to the chloride ion.

Water (*2.5.12*)

Maximum 4.0 per cent, determined on 0.500 g.

ASSAY

Liquid chromatography (*2.2.29*).

Test solution Dissolve 40.0 mg of the substance to be examined in a mixture of equal volumes of *acetonitrile R1* and *water R* and dilute to 50.0 mL with the same mixture of solvents.

Reference solution Dissolve 50.0 mg of *valnemulin hydrogen tartrate CRS* in a mixture of equal volumes of *acetonitrile R1* and *water R* and dilute to 50.0 mL with the same mixture of solvents.

Column:
— *size*: l = 0.125 m, Ø = 4.6 mm;
— *stationary phase*: octadecylsilyl silica gel for chromatography R (3 µm);
— *temperature*: 45 °C.

Mobile phase Mix 43 volumes of *acetonitrile R1* and 57 volumes of a solution containing 0.94 g/L of *disodium hydrogen phosphate R* and 8.7 g/L of *potassium dihydrogen phosphate R* previously adjusted to pH 2.5 with *phosphoric acid R*.

Flow rate 1.2 mL/min.

Detection Spectrophotometer at 210 nm.

Injection 5 µL.

Run time 3 times the retention time of valnemulin (retention time = about 2.4 min).

Calculate the percentage content of $C_{31}H_{53}ClN_2O_5S$, using the declared content of *valnemulin hydrogen tartrate CRS* and by multiplying by 0.841.

STORAGE

In an airtight container, protected from light.

IMPURITIES

Specified impurities A, B, C.

Other detectable impurities (the following substances would, if present at a sufficient level, be detected by one or other of the tests in the monograph. They are limited by the general acceptance criterion for other/unspecified impurities and/or by the general monograph *Substances for pharmaceutical use* (*2034*). It is therefore not necessary to identify these impurities for demonstration of compliance. See also *5.10*. *Control of impurities in substances for pharmaceutical use*): D, E.

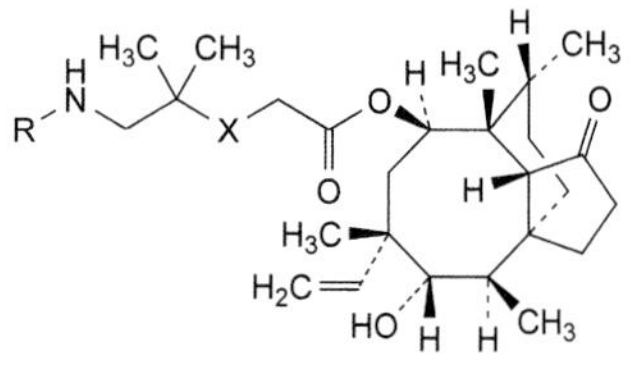

A. R = D-Val, X = SO: (3a*S*,4*R*,5*S*,6*S*,8*R*,9*R*,9a*R*,10*R*)-6-ethenyl-5-hydroxy-4,6,9,10-tetramethyl-1-oxodecahydro-3a,9-propano-3a*H*-cyclopenta[8]annulen-8-yl [[2-[[(2*R*)-2-amino-3-methylbutanoyl]amino]-1,1-dimethylethyl]sulfinyl]acetate (valnemulin sulfoxide),

B. R = H, X = S: (3a*S*,4*R*,5*S*,6*S*,8*R*,9*R*,9a*R*,10*R*)-6-ethenyl-5-hydroxy-4,6,9,10-tetramethyl-1-oxodecahydro-3a,9-propano-3a*H*-cyclopenta[8]annulen-8-yl [(2-amino-1,1-dimethylethyl]sulfanyl]acetate (dimethyl cysteaminyl pleuromulin),

C. R = D-Val-D-Val, X = S: (3a*S*,4*R*,5*S*,6*S*,8*R*,9*R*,9a*R*,10*R*)6-ethenyl-5-hydroxy-4,6,9,10-tetramethyl-1-oxodecahydro-3a,9-propano-3a*H*-cyclopenta[8]annulen-8-yl [[2-[[(2*R*)-2-[[(2*R*)-2-amino-3-methylbutanoyl]amino]-3-methylbutanoyl]amino]-1,1-dimethylethyl]sulfanyl]acetate (valyl-valneumulin),

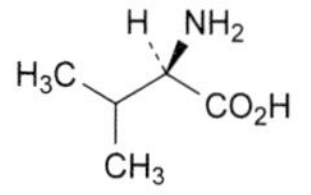

D. (2*R*)-2-amino-3-methylbutanoic acid (D-valine),

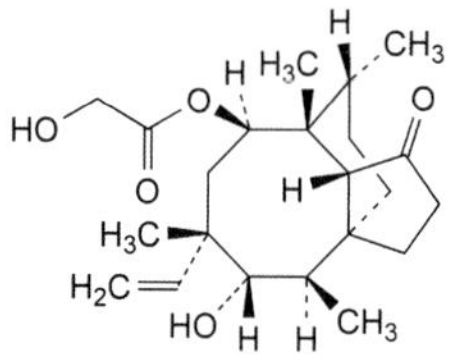

E. (3a*S*,4*R*,5*S*,6*S*,8*R*,9*R*,9a*R*,10*R*)6-ethenyl-5-hydroxy-4,6,9,10-tetramethyl-1-oxodecahydro-3a,9-propano-3a*H*-cyclopenta[8]annulen-8-yl 2-hydroxyacetate (pleuromulin).

Ph Eur

Vedaprofen

(Vedaprofen for Veterinary Use, Ph Eur monograph 2248)

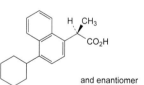

and enantiomer

$C_{19}H_{22}O_2$ 282.4   71109-09-6

Action and use

Cyclo-oxygenase inhibitor; analgesic; anti-inflammatory.

Ph Eur

DEFINITION

(2*RS*)-2-(4-Cyclohexyl-1-naphthyl)propanoic acid.

Content

98.5 per cent to 101.0 per cent (dried substance).

CHARACTERS

Appearance

White or almost white powder.

Solubility

Practically insoluble in water, freely soluble in acetone, soluble in methanol. It dissolves in dilute solutions of alkali hydroxides.

IDENTIFICATION

Infrared absorption spectrophotometry (*2.2.24*).

Comparison vedaprofen CRS.

TESTS

Appearance of solution

The solution is clear (2.2.1) and not more intensely coloured than reference solution Y_5 (2.2.2, Method II).

Dissolve 2.0 g in acetone R and dilute to 20.0 mL with the same solvent.

Related substances

Liquid chromatography (2.2.29).

Test solution Dissolve 25 mg of the substance to be examined in methanol R and dilute to 50.0 mL with the same solvent.

Reference solution (a) Dilute 1.0 mL of the test solution to 50.0 mL with methanol R. Dilute 1.0 mL of this solution to 10.0 mL with methanol R.

Reference solution (b) Dissolve the contents of a vial of vedaprofen impurity mixture CRS (impurities A, B and C) in 1.0 mL of reference solution (a).

Column:
— size: l = 0.10 m, Ø = 3.0 mm;
— stationary phase: octadecylsilyl silica gel for chromatography R (5 μm);
— temperature: 35 °C.

Mobile phase Dissolve 1.70 g of tetrabutylammonium hydrogen sulfate R in 1000 mL of a mixture of 20 volumes of water R and 80 volumes of methanol R.

Flow rate 0.4 mL/min.

Detection Spectrophotometer at 288 nm.

Injection 10 μL.

Run time 5 times the retention time of vedaprofen.

Identification of impurities Use the chromatogram supplied with vedaprofen impurity mixture CRS and the chromatogram obtained with reference solution (b) to identify the peaks due to impurities A, B and C.

Relative retention With reference to vedaprofen (retention time = about 6 min): impurity C = about 0.8; impurity A = about 1.8; impurity B = about 3.7.

System suitability: reference solution (b):
— resolution: minimum 2.0 between the peaks due to impurity C and vedaprofen.

Limits:
— correction factor: for the calculation of content, multiply the peak area of impurity B by 0.7;
— impurities A, B: for each impurity, not more than twice the area of the principal peak in the chromatogram obtained with reference solution (a) (0.4 per cent);
— unspecified impurities: for each impurity, not more than the area of the principal peak in the chromatogram obtained with reference solution (a) (0.20 per cent);
— total: not more than 2.5 times the area of the principal peak in the chromatogram obtained with reference solution (a) (0.5 per cent);
— disregard limit: 0.5 times the area of the principal peak in the chromatogram obtained with reference solution (a) (0.1 per cent).

Heavy metals (2.4.8)

Maximum 10 ppm.

Dissolve 1.0 g in a mixture of 15 volumes of water R and 85 volumes of acetone R and dilute to 20 mL with the same mixture of solvents. 12 mL of the solution complies with test B. Prepare the reference solution using lead standard solution (0.5 ppm Pb) obtained by diluting lead standard solution (100 ppm Pb) R with a mixture of 15 volumes of water R and 85 volumes of acetone R.

Loss on drying (2.2.32)

Maximum 0.5 per cent, determined on 1.000 g by drying in an oven at 105 °C.

Sulfated ash (2.4.14)

Maximum 0.3 per cent, determined on 0.500 g.

ASSAY

Dissolve 0.200 g in 50 mL of ethanol (96 per cent) R and add 1.0 mL of 0.1 M hydrochloric acid. Carry out a potentiometric titration (2.2.20), using 0.1 M sodium hydroxide. Read the volume added between the 2 points of inflexion.

1 mL of 0.1 M sodium hydroxide is equivalent to 28.24 mg of $C_{19}H_{22}O_2$.

IMPURITIES

Specified impurities A, B

Other detectable impurities (the following substances would, if present at a sufficient level, be detected by one or other of the tests in the monograph. They are limited by the general acceptance criterion for other/unspecified impurities and/or by the general monograph Substances for pharmaceutical use (2034). It is therefore not necessary to identify these impurities for demonstration of compliance. See also 5.10. Control of impurities in substances for pharmaceutical use): C, D.

A. R = CH_3: methyl (2RS)-2-(4-cyclohexyl-1-naphthyl)propanoate,

B. R = $C(CH_3)_3$: 1,1-dimethylethyl (2RS)-2-(4-cyclohexyl-1-naphthyl)propanoate,

C. R = H: (4-cyclohexyl-1-naphthyl)acetic acid,

D. R = CH_3: methyl (2RS)-2-(4-cyclohexyl-1-naphthyl)acetate.

Xylazine Hydrochloride

(Xylazine Hydrochloride for Veterinary Use, Ph Eur monograph 1481)

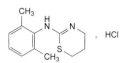

C₁₂H₁₇ClN₂S   256.8   23076-35-9

$C_{12}H_{17}ClN_2S$ 256.8   23076-35-9

Action and use
Analgesic.

Ph Eur _____

DEFINITION
N-(2,6-Dimethylphenyl)-5,6-dihydro-4H-1,3-thiazin-2-amine hydrochloride.

Content
98.0 per cent to 102.0 per cent (dried substance).

CHARACTERS
Appearance
White or almost white, crystalline powder, hygroscopic.

Solubility
Freely soluble in water, very soluble in methanol, freely soluble in methylene chloride.

It shows polymorphism (5.9).

IDENTIFICATION
A. Infrared absorption spectrophotometry (2.2.24).

Comparison xylazine hydrochloride CRS.

If the spectra obtained show differences, dissolve the substance to be examined and the reference substance separately in the minimum volume of *water R*, evaporate to dryness at 60 °C and at a pressure of 10-20 kPa, and record new spectra using the residues.

B. It gives reaction (b) of chlorides (2.3.1).

TESTS
Solution S
Dissolve 5.0 g in *carbon dioxide-free water R* prepared from *distilled water R*, heating at 60 °C if necessary; allow to cool and dilute to 50.0 mL with the same solvent.

Appearance of solution
Solution S is not more opalescent than reference suspension II (2.2.1) and is colourless (2.2.2, Method II).

pH (2.2.3)
4.0 to 5.5 for solution S.

Impurity A
Maximum 100 ppm.

Solution A Dissolve 0.25 g of the substance to be examined in *methanol R* and dilute to 10 mL with the same solvent. This solution is used to prepare the test solution.

Solution B Dissolve 50 mg of *2,6-dimethylaniline R* (impurity A) in *methanol R* and dilute to 100 mL with the same solvent. Dilute 1 mL of the solution to 100 mL with *methanol R*. This solution is used to prepare the reference solution.

Using 2 flat-bottomed tubes with an inner diameter of about 10 mm, place in the 1ˢᵗ tube 2 mL of solution A, and in the 2ⁿᵈ tube 1 mL of solution B and 1 mL of *methanol R*. To each tube add 1 mL of a freshly prepared 10 g/L solution of *dimethylaminobenzaldehyde R* in *methanol R* and 2 mL of

glacial acetic acid R and allow to stand at room temperature for 10 min. Compare the colours in diffused daylight, viewing vertically against a white background. Any yellow colour in the test solution is not more intense than that in the reference solution.

Related substances
Liquid chromatography (2.2.29). *Prepare the solutions immediately before use.*

Solvent mixture Mix 8 volumes of *acetonitrile R*, 30 volumes of *methanol R* and 62 volumes of a 2.72 g/L solution of *potassium dihydrogen phosphate R* adjusted to pH 7.2 with *dilute sodium hydroxide solution R*.

Test solution Dissolve 0.100 g of the substance to be examined in the solvent mixture and dilute to 20.0 mL with the solvent mixture.

Reference solution (a) Dissolve 5.0 mg of the substance to be examined, 5.0 mg of *2,6-dimethylaniline R* (impurity A) and 5.0 mg of *xylazine impurity C CRS* in *acetonitrile R* and dilute to 100.0 mL with the same solvent. Dilute 1.0 mL of this solution to 10.0 mL with the solvent mixture.

Reference solution (b) With the aid of ultrasound, dissolve the contents of a vial of *xylazine impurity mixture CRS* (impurities B and D) in 1.0 mL of the solvent mixture.

Column:
— *size:* l = 0.15 m, Ø = 3.9 mm;
— *stationary phase:* end-capped octylsilyl silica gel for chromatography with polar incorporated groups R (5 μm);
— *temperature:* 40 °C.

Mobile phase:
— *mobile phase A:* mix 30 volumes of *methanol R* and 70 volumes of a 2.72 g/L solution of *potassium dihydrogen phosphate R* adjusted to pH 7.2 with *dilute sodium hydroxide solution R*;
— *mobile phase B: methanol R, acetonitrile R* (30:70 V/V);

Time (min)	Mobile phase A (per cent V/V)	Mobile phase B (per cent V/V)
0 - 15	89 → 28	11 → 72
15 - 21	28	72

Flow rate 1.0 mL/min.

Detection Spectrophotometer at 230 nm.

Equilibration With a mixture of 28 volumes of mobile phase A and 72 volumes of mobile phase B for at least 30 min.

Injection 20 μL.

Identification of impurities Use the chromatogram supplied with *xylazine impurity mixture CRS* and the chromatogram obtained with reference solution (b) to identify the peaks due to impurities B and D; use the chromatogram obtained with reference solution (a) to identify the peaks due to impurities A and C.

Relative retention With reference to xylazine (retention time = about 8 min): impurity D = about 0.5; impurity A = about 0.8; impurity B = about 1.3; impurity C = about 2.2.

System suitability: reference solution (a):
— *resolution:* minimum 4.0 between the peaks due to impurity A and xylazine.

Calculation of percentage contents:
— for impurity C, use the concentration of impurity C in reference solution (a);
— for impurities other than C, use the concentration of xylazine in reference solution (a).

Limits:
— *impurities B, D*: for each impurity, maximum 0.2 per cent;
— *impurity C*: maximum 0.2 per cent;
— *unspecified impurities*: for each impurity, maximum 0.20 per cent;
— *sum of impurities other than B, C and D*: maximum 0.2 per cent;
— *reporting threshold*: 0.10 per cent; disregard any peak due to the blank.

Heavy metals (*2.4.8*)
Maximum 10 ppm.

12 mL of solution S complies with test A. Prepare the reference solution using 10 mL of *lead standard solution (1 ppm Pb) R*.

Loss on drying (*2.2.32*)
Maximum 0.5 per cent, determined on 1.000 g by drying in an oven at 105 °C for 2 h.

Sulfated ash (*2.4.14*)
Maximum 0.1 per cent, determined on 1.0 g.

ASSAY
Dissolve 0.200 g in 25 mL of *ethanol (96 per cent) R*.
Add 25 mL of *water R*. Titrate with *0.1 M sodium hydroxide*, determining the end-point potentiometrically (*2.2.20*).

1 mL of *0.1 M sodium hydroxide* is equivalent to 25.68 mg of $C_{12}H_{17}ClN_2S$.

STORAGE
In an airtight container, protected from light.

IMPURITIES
Specified impurities: A, B, C, D.

A. 2,6-dimethylaniline (2,6-xylidine),

B. *N,N′*-bis(2,6-dimethylphenyl)thiourea,

C. 2,6-dimethylphenyl isothiocyanate,

D. *N*-(2,6-dimethylphenyl)-*N′*-(3-hydroxypropyl)thiourea.

Monographs

Formulated Preparations

Attention is drawn to the General Notices of the British Pharmacopoeia (Veterinary) governing this section

FORMULATED PREPARATIONS: GENERAL MONOGRAPHS

The general provisions of the European Pharmacopoeia relating to a specific type of dosage form apply to all veterinary dosage forms of the type defined, whether or not an individual monograph is included in the British Pharmacopoeia (Veterinary). These provisions are reproduced in the general monographs listed below:

Capsules

Liquids for Cutaneous Application[†]

Ear Preparations

Extracts

Eye Preparations

Medicated Foams

Granules[⋆]

Preparations for Inhalation

Preparations for Irrigation

Oral Liquids[⋆]

Nasal Preparations

Parenteral Preparations[⋆]

Topical Powders[⋆]

Pressurised Pharmaceutical Preparations

Rectal Preparations

Topical Semi-solid Preparations

Sticks

Tablets[⋆]

Medicated Tampons

Tinctures

Transdermal Patches

Vaginal Preparations

Where a general monograph listed above includes additional statements and requirements applicable to the individual monographs of the British Pharmacopoeia, such statements, modified where appropriate as described below, apply unless otherwise indicated to any individual monograph for that dosage form in the British Pharmacopoeia (Veterinary).

[⋆]Where *justified and authorised, the requirements of the European Pharmacopoeia reproduced in the general monograph do not necessarily apply to formulated preparations for veterinary use.*

[†] *Where justified and authorised, the requirements of the European Pharmacopoeia reproduced in the general monograph do not necessarily apply to formulated preparations for systemic and veterinary use.*

Pharmaceutical Preparations

(Ph. Eur. monograph 2619)

Ph Eur _____

INTRODUCTION

This monograph is intended to be a reference source of standards in the European Pharmacopoeia on active substances, excipients and dosage forms, which are to be applied in the manufacture/preparation of pharmaceuticals, but not a guide on how to manufacture as there is specific guidance available covering methods of manufacture and associated controls.

It does not cover investigational medicinal products, but competent authorities may refer to pharmacopoeial standards when authorising clinical trials using investigational medicinal products.

DEFINITION

Pharmaceutical preparations are medicinal products generally consisting of active substances that may be combined with excipients, formulated into a dosage form suitable for the intended use, where necessary after reconstitution, presented in a suitable and appropriately labelled container.

Pharmaceutical preparations may be licensed by the competent authority, or unlicensed and made to the specific needs of patients according to legislation. There are 2 categories of unlicensed pharmaceutical preparations:
— extemporaneous preparations, i.e. pharmaceutical preparations individually prepared for a specific patient or patient group, supplied after preparation;
— stock preparations, i.e. pharmaceutical preparations prepared in advance and stored until a request for a supply is received.

In addition to this monograph, pharmaceutical preparations also comply with the General Notices and with the relevant general chapters of the Pharmacopoeia. General chapters are normally given for information and become mandatory when referred to in a general or specific monograph, unless such reference is made in a way that indicates that it is not the intention to make the text referred to mandatory but rather to cite it for information.

Where relevant, pharmaceutical preparations also comply with the dosage form monographs (e.g. *Capsules (0016)*, *Tablets (0478)*) and general monographs relating to pharmaceutical preparations (e.g. *Allergen products (1063)*, *Herbal teas (1435)*, *Homoeopathic preparations (1038)*, *Immunosera for human use, animal (0084)*, *Immunosera for veterinary use (0030)*, *Monoclonal antibodies for human use (2031)*, *Radiopharmaceutical preparations (0125)*, *Vaccines for human use (0153)*, *Vaccines for veterinary use (0062)*).

Where pharmaceutical preparations are manufactured/prepared using materials of human or animal origin, the general requirements of general chapters *5.1.7. Viral safety*, *5.2.6. Evaluation of safety of veterinary vaccines and immunosera* and *5.2.8. Minimising the risk of transmitting animal spongiform encephalophathy agents via human and veterinary medicinal products* apply, where appropriate.

ETHICAL CONSIDERATIONS AND GUIDANCE IN THE PREPARATION OF UNLICENSED PHARMACEUTICAL PREPARATIONS

The underlying principle of legislation for pharmaceutical preparations is that, subject to specific exemptions, no pharmaceutical preparation may be placed on the market without an appropriate marketing authorisation.

The exemptions from the formal licensing requirement allow the supply of unlicensed products to meet the special needs of individual patients. However, when deciding to use an unlicensed preparation all health professionals involved (e.g. the prescribing practitioners and/or the preparing pharmacists) have, within their area of responsibilities, a duty of care to the patient receiving the pharmaceutical preparation.

In considering the preparation of an unlicensed pharmaceutical preparation, a suitable level of risk assessment is undertaken.

The risk assessment identifies:
— the criticality of different parameters (e.g. quality of active substances, excipients and containers; design of the preparation process; extent and significance of testing; stability of the preparation) to the quality of the preparation; and
— the risk that the preparation may present to a particular patient group.

Based on the risk assessment, the person responsible for the preparation must ensure, with a suitable level of assurance, that the pharmaceutical preparation is, throughout its shelf-life, of an appropriate quality and suitable and fit for its purpose. For stock preparations, storage conditions and shelf-life have to be justified on the basis of, for example, analytical data or professional judgement, which may be based on literature references.

PRODUCTION

Manufacture/preparation must take place within the framework of a suitable quality system and be compliant with the standards relevant to the type of product being made. Licensed products must comply with the requirements of their licence. For unlicensed products a risk assessment as outlined in the section 'Ethical considerations and guidance in the preparation of unlicensed pharmaceutical preparations' is of special importance, as these products are not previously assessed by the competent authority.

Formulation

During pharmaceutical development or prior to manufacture/preparation, suitable ingredients, processes, tests and specifications are identified and justified in order to ensure the suitability of the product for the intended purpose. This includes consideration of the properties required in order to identify whether specific ingredient properties or process steps are critical to the required quality of the pharmaceutical preparation.

Active substances and excipients

Active substances and excipients used in the formulation of pharmaceutical preparations comply with the requirements of the relevant general monographs, e.g. *Substances for pharmaceutical use (2034), Essential oils (2098), Extracts (0765), Herbal drugs (1433), Herbal drug preparations (1434), Herbal drugs for homoeopathic preparations (2045), Mother tinctures for homoeopathic preparations (2029), Methods of preparation of homoeopathic stocks and potentisation (2371), Products of fermentation (1468), Products with risk of transmitting agents of animal spongiform encephalopathies (1483), Products of recombinant DNA technology (0784), Vegetable fatty oils (1579).*

In addition, where specific monographs exist, the quality of the active substances and excipients used complies with the corresponding monographs.

Where no specific monographs exist, the required quality must be defined, taking into account the intended use and the involved risk.

When physicochemical characteristics of active substances and functionality-related characteristics (FRCs) of excipients (e.g. particle-size distribution, viscosity, polymorphism) are critical in relation to their role in the manufacturing process and quality attributes of the pharmaceutical preparation, they must be identified and controlled.

Detailed information on FRCs is given in general chapter *5.15. Functionality-related characteristics of excipients.*

Microbiological quality

The formulation of the pharmaceutical preparation and its container must ensure that the microbiological quality is suitable for the intended use.

During development, it shall be demonstrated that the antimicrobial activity of the preparation as such or, if necessary, with the addition of a suitable preservative or preservatives, or by the selection of an appropriate container, provides adequate protection from adverse effects that may arise from microbial contamination or proliferation during the storage and use of the preparation. A suitable test method together with criteria for evaluating the preservative properties of the formulation are provided in general chapter *5.1.3. Efficacy of antimicrobial preservation.*

If preparations do not have adequate antimicrobial efficacy and do not contain antimicrobial preservatives they are supplied in single-dose containers, or in multidose containers that prevent microbial contamination of the contents after opening.

In the manufacture/preparation of non-sterile pharmaceutical preparations, suitable measures are taken to ensure their microbial quality; recommendations on this aspect are provided in general chapters *5.1.4. Microbiological quality of non-sterile pharmaceutical preparations and substances for pharmaceutical use* and *5.1.8. Microbiological quality of herbal medicinal products for oral use and extracts used in their preparation.*

Sterile preparations are manufactured/prepared using materials and methods designed to ensure sterility and to avoid the introduction of contaminants and the growth of micro-organisms; recommendations on this aspect are provided in general chapter *5.1.1. Methods of preparation of sterile products.*

Containers

A suitable container is selected. Consideration is given to the intended use of the preparation, the properties of the container, the required shelf-life, and product/container incompatibilities. Where applicable, containers for pharmaceutical preparations comply with the requirements for containers (3.2 and subsections) and materials used for the manufacture of containers (3.1 and subsections).

Stability

Stability requirements of pharmaceutical preparations are dependent on their intended use and on the desired storage time.

Where applicable, the probability and criticality of possible degradation products of the active substance(s) and/or reaction products of the active substance(s) with an excipient and/or the immediate container must be assessed. Depending on the result of this assessment, limits of degradation and/or reaction products are set and monitored in the pharmaceutical preparation. Licensed products require a stability exercise.

Methods used for the purpose of stability testing for all relevant characteristics of the preparation are validated as stability indicating, i.e. the methods allow the quantification of the relevant degradation products and physical characteristic changes.

TESTS

Relevant tests to apply in order to ensure the appropriate quality of a particular dosage form are described in the specific dosage form monographs.

Where it is not practical, for unlicensed pharmaceutical preparations, to carry out the tests (e.g. batch size, time restraints), other suitable methods are implemented to ensure that the appropriate quality is achieved in accordance with the risk assessment carried out and any local guidance or legal requirements.

Stock preparations are normally tested to a greater extent than extemporaneous preparations.

The following tests are applicable to many preparations and are therefore listed here.

Appearance
The appearance (e.g. size, shape and colour) of the pharmaceutical preparation is controlled.

Identity and purity tests
Where applicable, the following tests are carried out on the pharmaceutical preparation:
— identification of the active substance(s);
— identification of specific excipient(s), such as preservatives;
— purity tests (e.g. investigation of degradation products, residual solvents (*2.4.24*) or other related impurities, sterility (*2.6.1*));
— safety tests (e.g. safety tests for biological products).

Uniformity (*2.9.40* or *2.9.5*/*2.9.6*).

Pharmaceutical preparations presented in single-dose units comply with the test(s) as prescribed in the relevant specific dosage form monograph. If justified and authorised, general chapter 2.9.40 can be applicable only at the time of release. Special uniformity requirements apply in the following cases:
— for herbal drugs and herbal drug preparations, compliance with general chapter *2.9.40* is not required;
— for homoeopathic preparations, the provisions of general chapters *2.9.6* and *2.9.40* are normally not appropriate, however in certain circumstances compliance with these chapters may be required by the competent authority;
— for single- and multivitamin and trace-element preparations, compliance with general chapters *2.9.6* and *2.9.40* (*content uniformity only*) is not required;
— in justified and authorised circumstances, for other preparations, compliance with general chapters *2.9.6* and *2.9.40* may not be required by the competent authority.

Reference standards
Reference standards may be needed at various stages for quality control of pharmaceutical preparations. They are established and monitored taking due account of general chapter *5.12. Reference standards.*

ASSAY

Unless otherwise justified and authorised, contents of active substances and specific excipients such as preservatives are determined in pharmaceutical preparations. Limits must be defined and justified.

Suitable and validated methods are used. If assay methods prescribed in the respective active substance monographs are used, it must be demonstrated that they are not affected by the presence of the excipients and/or by the formulation.

Reference standards
See Tests.

LABELLING AND STORAGE
The relevant labelling requirements given in the general dosage form monographs apply. In addition, relevant European Union or other applicable regulations apply.

GLOSSARY
Formulation
The designing of an appropriate formula (including materials, processes, etc.) that will ensure that the patient receives the suitable pharmaceutical preparation in an appropriate form that has the required quality and that will be stable and effective for the required length of time.

Licensed pharmaceutical preparation
A medicinal product that has been granted a marketing authorisation by a competent authority. Synonym: authorised pharmaceutical preparation.

Manufacture
All operations of purchase of materials and products, Production, Quality Control, release, storage, distribution of medicinal products and the related controls.

Preparation (of an unlicensed pharmaceutical preparation)
The 'manufacture' of unlicensed pharmaceutical preparations by or at the request of pharmacies or other healthcare establishments (the term 'preparation' is used instead of 'manufacture' in order clearly to distinguish it from the industrial manufacture of licensed pharmaceutical preparations).

Reconstitution
Manipulation to enable the use or application of a medicinal product with a marketing authorisation in accordance with the instructions given in the summary of product characteristics or the patient information leaflet.

Risk assessment
The identification of hazards and the analysis and evaluation of risks associated with exposure to those hazards.

Unlicensed pharmaceutical preparation
A medicinal product that is exempt from the need of having a marketing authorisation issued by a competent authority but is made for specific patients' needs according to legislation.

Ph Eur

Glossary

A glossary of terms relating to formulated preparations is included in the British Pharmacopoeia.

Veterinary Liquid Preparations for Cutaneous Application

(Ph. Eur. monograph 1808)

Veterinary Liquid Preparations for Cutaneous Application comply with the requirements of the European Pharmacopoeia. These requirements are reproduced below.

Ph Eur _____

Unless otherwise justified and authorised, veterinary liquid preparations for cutaneous application comply with the requirements of the monograph on Liquid preparations for cutaneous application (0927). In addition to these requirements, the following statements apply to veterinary liquid preparations for cutaneous application.

DEFINITION

Veterinary liquid preparations for cutaneous application are liquid preparations intended to be applied to the skin to obtain a local and/or systemic effect. They are solutions, suspensions or emulsions which may contain one or more active substances in a suitable vehicle. They may be presented as concentrates in the form of wettable powders, pastes, solutions or suspensions, which are used to prepare diluted suspensions or emulsions of active substances. They may contain suitable antimicrobial preservatives, antioxidants and other excipients such as stabilisers, emulsifiers and thickeners.

Several categories of veterinary liquid preparations for cutaneous application may be distinguished:
— cutaneous foams (see *Liquid preparations for cutaneous application (0927)*);
— dip concentrates;
— pour-on preparations;
— shampoos (see *Liquid preparations for cutaneous application (0927)*);
— spot-on preparations;
— sprays;
— teat dips;
— teat sprays;
— udder-washes.

DIP CONCENTRATES

DEFINITION

Dip concentrates are preparations containing one or more active substances, usually in the form of wettable powders, pastes, solutions or suspensions, which are used to prepare diluted solutions, suspensions or emulsions of active substances. The diluted preparations are applied by complete immersion of the animal.

POUR-ON PREPARATIONS

DEFINITION

Pour-on preparations contain one or more active substances for the prevention and treatment of ectoparasitic and/or endoparasitic infestations of animals. They are applied in volumes which are usually greater than 5 mL by pouring along the animal's dorsal midline.

SPOT-ON PREPARATIONS

DEFINITION

Spot-on preparations contain one or more active substances for the prevention and treatment of ectoparasitic and/or endoparasitic infestations of animals. They are applied in volumes which are usually less than 10 mL, to a small area on the head or back, as appropriate, of the animal.

SPRAYS

DEFINITION

Sprays contain one or more active substances that are intended to be applied externally for therapeutic or prophylactic purposes. They are delivered in the form of an aerosol by the actuation of an appropriate valve or by means of a suitable atomising device that is either an integral part of the container or is supplied separately.

Sprays may be presented in pressurised containers (see *Pressurised pharmaceutical preparations (0523)*). When so presented, sprays usually consist of one or more active substances in a suitable vehicle held under pressure with suitable propellants or suitable mixtures of propellants. When otherwise presented, sprays are supplied in well-closed containers.

PRODUCTION

During the development and manufacture of a spray, measures are taken to ensure that the assembled product conforms to a defined spray rate and spray pattern.

TEAT DIPS

DEFINITION

Teat dips contain one or more disinfectant active substances, usually in the form of solutions into which the teats of an animal are dipped pre- and post-milking, as appropriate, to reduce the population of pathogenic micro-organisms on the surfaces. Teat dips may be supplied/presented as ready-to-use preparations or they may be prepared by dilution of teat dip concentrates. Pre- and post-milking teat dips often differ in formulation. Teat dips usually contain emollients to promote skin hydration, to soften the skin and allow healing of lesions that would otherwise harbour bacteria.

TEAT SPRAYS

DEFINITION

Teat sprays contain one or more disinfectant active substances, usually in the form of solutions which are sprayed onto the teats of an animal pre- and post-milking, as appropriate, to reduce the population of pathogenic micro-organisms on the surfaces. Teat sprays may be supplied/presented as ready-to-use preparations or they may be prepared by dilution of teat spray concentrates. Pre- and post-milking sprays often differ in formulation. Teat sprays usually contain emollients to promote skin hydration, to soften the skin and allow healing of lesions that would otherwise harbour bacteria.

UDDER-WASHES

DEFINITION

Udder-washes contain one or more disinfectant active substances, usually in the form of solutions which are sprayed onto the udder and teats of an animal to remove mud and faecal contamination before the application of teat dips or sprays. Udder-washes are usually prepared by the dilution either of concentrated preparations or of ready-to-use teat dips or teat sprays.

_____ *Ph Eur*

Liquid Preparations for Cutaneous Application of the British Pharmacopoeia (Veterinary)

In addition to the above requirements of the European Pharmacopoeia, the following statements apply to any dip concentrate that is the subject of an individual monograph in the British Pharmacopoeia (Veterinary).

DIP CONCENTRATES

DEFINITION
When diluted, Dip Concentrates are used for the prevention and treatment of ectoparasitic infestations of animals.
The diluted preparations are applied by complete immersion of the animal or, where appropriate, by spraying.

EXTRACTS

(Ph Eur monograph 0765)

Extracts comply with the requirements of the European Pharmacopoeia. These requirements are reproduced in the British Pharmacopoeia.

EYE PREPARATIONS

(Ph Eur monograph 1163)

Eye Preparations comply with the requirements of the European Pharmacopoeia. These requirements are reproduced in the British Pharmacopoeia.

Eye Preparations of the British Pharmacopoeia (Veterinary)

In addition to the requirements of the European Pharmacopoeia, the statements applicable to Eye Preparations of the British Pharmacopoeia apply to those eye ointments that are the subject of an individual monograph in the British Pharmacopoeia (Veterinary).

GRANULES

(Ph Eur monograph 0499)

Unless otherwise justified and authorised, Granules comply with the appropriate requirements of the European Pharmacopoeia. These requirements are reproduced in the British Pharmacopoeia.

INTRAMAMMARY INFUSIONS

intramammary injections

(Intramammary Preparations for Veterinary Use, Ph Eur monograph 0945)

Ph Eur _____

DEFINITION
Intramammary preparations for veterinary use are sterile preparations intended for introduction into the mammary gland via the teat canal. There are two main categories: those intended for administration to lactating animals, and those intended for administration to animals at the end of lactation or to non-lactating animals for the treatment or prevention of infection.

Intramammary preparations for veterinary use are solutions, emulsions or suspensions or semi-solid preparations containing one or more active substances in a suitable vehicle. They may contain excipients such as stabilising, emulsifying, suspending and thickening agents. Suspensions may show a sediment which is readily dispersed on shaking. Emulsions may show evidence of phase separation but are readily redispersed on shaking.

Unless otherwise justified and authorised, intramammary preparations for veterinary use are supplied in containers for use on one occasion only for introduction in a single teat canal of an animal.

If supplied in multidose containers, aqueous preparations contain a suitable antimicrobial preservative at a suitable concentration, except where the preparation itself has adequate antimicrobial properties. Precautions for administration and for storage between administrations must be taken.

Where applicable, containers for intramammary preparations for veterinary use comply with the requirements of *Materials used for the manufacture of containers* (*3.1* and subsections) and *Containers* (*3.2* and subsections).

PRODUCTION
During the development of a intramammary preparation for veterinary use, the formulation for which contains an antimicrobial preservative, the effectiveness of the chosen preservative shall be demonstrated to the satisfaction of the competent authority. A suitable test method together with criteria for judging the preservative properties of the formulation are provided in the text on *Efficacy of antimicrobial preservation (5.1.3)*.

Intramammary preparations for veterinary use are prepared using materials and methods designed to ensure sterility and to avoid the introduction of contaminants and the growth of micro-organisms; recommendations on this aspect are provided in the text on *Methods of preparation of sterile products (5.1.1)*.

In the manufacture of intramammary preparations for veterinary use containing dispersed particles, measures are taken to ensure a suitable and controlled particle size with regard to the intended use.

TESTS
Deliverable mass or volume
Squeeze out as much as possible of the contents of ten containers according to the instructions on the label.
The mean mass or volume does not differ by more than 10 per cent from the nominal mass or volume.

Sterility (*2.6.1*)

Intramammary preparations for veterinary use comply with the test for sterility; use the technique of membrane filtration or, in justified cases, direct inoculation of the culture media. Squeeze out the contents of ten containers and mix thoroughly. For each medium, use 0.5 g to 1 g (or 0.5 mL to 1 mL as appropriate) taken from the mixed sample.

STORAGE

Store in a sterile, airtight, tamper-proof container.

LABELLING

The label states:

— the name of the active substance(s) and the mass or number of International Units of the active substance(s) that may be delivered from the container using normal technique;

— whether the preparation is intended for use in a lactating animal or a non-lactating animal;

— in the case of multidose containers, the name of any added antimicrobial preservative.

_____ *Ph Eur*

Intramammary Infusions of the British Pharmacopoeia (Veterinary)

In addition to the above requirements of the European Pharmacopoeia, the following statements apply to those intramammary infusions that are the subject of an individual monograph in the British Pharmacopoeia (Veterinary).

DEFINITION

Intramammary Infusions intended for administration to lactating animals are described as Intramammary Infusions (Lactating Cow) and those intended for administration to animals at the end of lactation or during the non-lactating period for the prevention or treatment of infections during the dry period are described as Intramammary Infusions (Dry Cow).

PRODUCTION

Intramammary Infusions are prepared by dissolving or suspending the sterile medicaments in the sterilised vehicle using aseptic technique, unless a process of terminal sterilisation is employed.

When Intramammary Infusions are supplied in single-dose containers, these are sealed so as to exclude micro-organisms and are fitted with a smooth, tapered nozzle to facilitate the introduction of the infusion into the teat canal.

The containers are sterilised before being filled aseptically unless the intramammary infusion is to be subjected to a process of terminal sterilisation.

Sterility

Guidance to manufacturers on the number of containers to be tested is provided in the Annex to this monograph.

ANNEX

Guidance to manufacturers in performing the test for sterility

In determining the number of containers to be tested, the manufacturer should have regard to the environmental conditions of manufacture, the quantity (volume) of preparation per container and any other special considerations applying to the preparation concerned. With respect to intramammary infusions, 1% of the containers in a batch, with a minimum of three and a maximum of ten is considered a suitable number assuming that the preparation has been manufactured under appropriately validated conditions designed to exclude contamination.

INTRARUMINAL DEVICES

(Ph. Eur. monograph 1228)

Intranuminal Devises comply with the requirements of the European Pharmacopoeia. These requirements are reproduced below.

Ph Eur _____

The requirements of this monograph do not apply to preparation (sometimes known as boluses), such as large conventional tablets, capsules or moulded dosage forms which give immediate or prolonged release of the active substance(s). Such preparations comply with the relevant parts of the monographs on Capsules (0016) or Tablets (0478)

DEFINITION

Intraruminal devices are solid preparations each containing one or more active substances. They are intended for oral administration to ruminant animals and are designed to be retained in the rumen to deliver the active substance(s) in a continuous or pulsatile manner. The period of release of the active substance(s) may vary from days to weeks according to the nature of the formulation and/or the delivery device.

Intraruminal devices may be administered using a balling gun. Some intraruminal devices are intended to float on the surface of the ruminal fluid while others are intended to remain on the floor of the rumen or reticulum. Each device has a density appropriate for its intended purpose.

PRODUCTION

For continuous release, the intraruminal device is designed to release the active substance(s) at a defined rate over a defined period of time. This may be achieved by erosion, corrosion, diffusion, osmotic pressure or any other suitable chemical, physical or physico-chemical means.

For pulsatile-release, the intraruminal device is designed to release a specific quantity of active substance(s) at one or several defined intermediate times. This may be achieved by corrosion by ruminal fluids of the metallic elements of the intraruminal device which leads to sequential release of the constituent units which are usually in the form of tablets.

In the manufacture of intraruminal devices, measures are taken to ensure an appropriate release of the active substance(s).

In the manufacture, packaging, storage and distribution of intraruminal devices, suitable measures are taken to ensure their microbial quality; recommendations on this aspect are provided in the text on *5.1.4. Microbiological quality of non-sterile pharmaceutical preparations and substances for pharmaceutical use.*

TESTS

Uniformity of dosage units

Constituent tablet units of intraruminal devices comply with the test for uniformity of dosage units (*2.9.40*) or, where justified and authorised, with the tests for uniformity of content and/or uniformity of mass shown below. Herbal drugs and herbal drug preparations present in the dosage form are not subject to the provisions of this paragraph.

Uniformity of content (*2.9.6*)

Unless otherwise justified and authorised, constituent tablet units of intraruminal devices in which the active substances are present at levels less than 2 mg or less than 2 per cent of the total mass comply with test A for uniformity of content of single-dose preparations. If the preparation contains more than one active substance, the requirement applies only to those substances which correspond to the above conditions.

Uniformity of mass (*2.9.5*)

Unless otherwise justified and authorised, the constituent tablet units of intraruminal devices comply with the test for uniformity of mass. If the test for uniformity of content is prescribed for all active substances, the test for uniformity of mass is not required.

LABELLING

The label states:

— for continuous-release devices, the dose released per unit time;
— for pulsatile-release devices, the dose released at specified times.

Ph Eur

INTRAUTERINE PREPARATIONS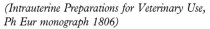

(Intrauterine Preparations for Veterinary Use, Ph Eur monograph 1806)

Intrauterine Preparations comply with the requirements of the European Pharmacopoeia. These requirements are reproduced below.

Ph Eur

DEFINITION

Intrauterine preparations for veterinary use are liquid, semi-solid or solid preparations intended for the direct administration to the uterus (cervix, cavity or fundus), usually in order to obtain a local effect. They contain 1 or more active substances in a suitable basis.

Where appropriate, containers for intrauterine preparations for veterinary use comply with the requirements for *Materials used for the manufacture of containers* (*3.1* and subsections) and *Containers* (*3.2* and subsections).

Several categories of intrauterine preparations for veterinary use may be distinguished:

— intrauterine tablets;
— intrauterine capsules;
— intrauterine solutions, emulsions and suspensions, concentrates for intrauterine solutions;
— tablets for intrauterine solutions and suspensions;
— semi-solid intrauterine preparations;
— intrauterine foams;
— intrauterine sticks.

PRODUCTION

During the development of an intrauterine preparation for veterinary use, the effectiveness of any added antimicrobial preservative shall be demonstrated to the satisfaction of the competent authority. A suitable test method together with criteria for judging the preservative properties of the formulation are provided under *Efficacy of antimicrobial preservation* (*5.1.3*).

In the manufacture, packaging, storage and distribution of intrauterine preparations for veterinary use, suitable measures are taken to ensure their microbial quality; recommendations on this aspect are provided in the text on *5.1.4*. *Microbiological quality of non-sterile pharmaceutical preparations and substances for pharmaceutical use*, see Table 5.1.4.-1. – Cutaneous use.

Sterile intrauterine preparations for veterinary use are prepared using materials and methods designed to ensure sterility and to avoid the introduction of contaminants and the growth of microorganisms; recommendations on this aspect are provided in the text on *Methods of preparation of sterile products* (*5.1.1*).

During development, it must be demonstrated that the nominal content can be withdrawn from the container of liquid and semi-solid intrauterine preparations for veterinary use presented in single-dose containers.

TESTS

Uniformity of dosage units

Single-dose intrauterine preparations for veterinary use comply with the test for uniformity of dosage units (*2.9.40*) or, where justified and authorised, with the tests for uniformity of content and/or uniformity of mass shown below. Herbal drugs and herbal drug preparations present in the dosage form are not subject to the provisions of this paragraph.

Uniformity of content (*2.9.6*)

Unless otherwise prescribed or justified and authorised, solid single-dose preparations with a content of active substance less than 2 mg or less than 2 per cent of the total mass comply with test A (intrauterine tablets) or test B (intrauterine capsules) for uniformity of content of single-dose preparations. If the preparation has more than 1 active substance, the requirement applies only to those substances which correspond to the above conditions.

Uniformity of mass (*2.9.5*)

Solid single-dose intrauterine preparations for veterinary use comply with the test for uniformity of mass of single-dose preparations. If the test for uniformity of content is prescribed or justified and authorised for all the active substances, the test for uniformity of mass is not required.

Dissolution

A suitable test may be carried out to demonstrate the appropriate release of the active substance(s) from solid single-dose intrauterine preparations for veterinary use, for example one of the tests described in *Dissolution test for solid dosage forms* (*2.9.3*).

When a dissolution test is prescribed, a disintegration test may not be required.

Sterility (*2.6.1*)

Sterile intrauterine preparations for veterinary use comply with the test for sterility. Applicators supplied with the preparation also comply with the test for sterility. Remove the applicator with aseptic precautions from its package and transfer it to a tube of culture medium so that it is completely immersed. Incubate and interpret the results as described in the test for sterility.

LABELLING

The label states:

— the name of any added antimicrobial preservative;
— where applicable, that the preparation is sterile.

INTRAUTERINE TABLETS

DEFINITION

Intrauterine tablets are solid preparations each containing a single dose of 1 or more active substances. They generally conform to the definition given in the monograph on *Tablets (0478)*.

A suitable applicator may be used for application into the uterus.

TESTS

Disintegration

Unless intended for prolonged local action, they comply with the test for disintegration of suppositories and pessaries (*2.9.2*). Examine the state of the tablets after 30 min, unless otherwise justified and authorised.

INTRAUTERINE CAPSULES

DEFINITION

Intrauterine capsules are solid, single-dose preparations. They are generally similar to soft capsules, differing only in their shape and size. Intrauterine capsules have various shapes, usually ovoid. They are smooth and have a uniform external appearance.

A suitable applicator may be used for application into the uterus.

TESTS

Disintegration

Unless intended for prolonged local action, they comply with the test for disintegration of suppositories and pessaries (*2.9.2*). Examine the state of the capsules after 30 min, unless otherwise justified and authorised.

INTRAUTERINE SOLUTIONS, SUSPENSIONS AND EMULSIONS CONCENTRATES FOR INTRAUTERINE SOLUTIONS

DEFINITION

Intrauterine solutions, suspensions and emulsions are liquid preparations. Concentrates for intrauterine solutions are intended for administration after dilution.

They may contain excipients, for example to adjust the viscosity of the preparation, to adjust or stabilise the pH, to increase the solubility of the active substance(s) or to stabilise the preparation. The excipients do not adversely affect the intended medical action, or, at the concentrations used, cause undue local irritation.

Intrauterine emulsions may show evidence of phase separation, but are readily redispersed on shaking. Intrauterine suspensions may show a sediment that is readily dispersed on shaking to give a suspension which remains sufficiently stable to enable a homogeneous preparation to be delivered.

They may be supplied in single-dose containers. The container is adapted to deliver the preparation to the uterus or it may be accompanied by a suitable applicator.

PRODUCTION

In the manufacture of intrauterine suspensions, measures are taken to ensure a suitable and controlled particle size with regard to the intended use.

TABLETS FOR INTRAUTERINE SOLUTIONS AND SUSPENSIONS

DEFINITION

Tablets intended for the preparation of intrauterine solutions and suspensions are single-dose preparations which are dissolved or dispersed in water at the time of administration. They may contain excipients to facilitate dissolution or dispersion or to prevent caking.

Tablets for intrauterine solutions or suspensions conform with the definition given in the monograph on *Tablets (0478)*.

After dissolution or dispersion, they comply with the requirements for intrauterine solutions or intrauterine suspensions, as appropriate.

TESTS

Disintegration (*2.9.1*)

Tablets for intrauterine solutions or suspensions disintegrate within 3 min using *water R* at 15-25 °C.

LABELLING

The label states:
— the method of preparation of the intrauterine solution or suspension;
— the conditions and duration of storage of the solution or suspension after reconstitution.

SEMI-SOLID INTRAUTERINE PREPARATIONS

DEFINITION

Semi-solid preparations for intrauterine use are ointments, creams or gels.

Semi-solid preparations for intrauterine use comply with the requirements of the monograph on *Semi-solid preparations for cutaneous application (0132)*.

They are often supplied in single-dose containers. The container is adapted to deliver the preparation to the uterus or it may be accompanied by a suitable applicator.

INTRAUTERINE FOAMS

DEFINITION

Intrauterine foams comply with the requirements of the monograph on *Medicated foams (1105)*.

They are supplied in multidose containers. The container is adapted to deliver the preparation to the uterus or it may be accompanied by a suitable applicator.

INTRAUTERINE STICKS

DEFINITION

Intrauterine sticks comply with the requirements of the monograph on *Sticks (1154)*. They often produce a foam when coming into contact with physiological fluids.

_____ Ph Eur

ORAL LIQUIDS

LIQUID PREPARATIONS FOR ORAL USE

(Ph Eur monograph 0672)

Unless otherwise justified and authorised, Oral Liquids comply with the appropriate requirements of the European Pharmacopoeia monograph for Liquid Preparations for Oral Use. These requirements are reproduced in the British Pharmacopoeia.

Oral Liquids of the British Pharmacopoeia (Veterinary)

In addition to the requirements of the European Pharmacopoeia, the statements applicable to Oral Liquids of the British Pharmacopoeia apply to any oral solution or oral suspension that is the subject of an individual monograph in the British Pharmacopoeia (Veterinary).

PARENTERAL PREPARATIONS

(Ph. Eur. monograph 0520)

Unless otherwise justified and authorised, Parenteral Preparations comply with the appropriate requirements of the European Pharmacopoeia. These requirements are reproduced in the British Pharmacopoeia or, where they apply to veterinary preparations only, below.

Ph Eur _____

The requirements of this monograph do not necessarily apply to products derived from human blood, to immunological preparations, or radiopharmaceutical preparations. Special requirements may apply to preparations for veterinary use depending on the species of animal for which the preparation is intended.

DEFINITION

Parenteral preparations are sterile preparations intended for administration by injection, infusion or implantation into the human or animal body.

Parenteral preparations may require the use of excipients, for example to make the preparation isotonic with respect to blood, to adjust the pH, to increase solubility, to prevent deterioration of the active substances or to provide adequate antimicrobial properties, but not to adversely affect the intended medicinal action of the preparation or, at the concentrations used, to cause toxicity or undue local irritation.

Containers for parenteral preparations are made as far as possible from materials that are sufficiently transparent to permit the visual inspection of the contents, except for implants and in other justified and authorised cases.

Where applicable, the containers for parenteral preparations comply with the requirements for *Materials used for the manufacture of containers* (*3.1* and subsections) and *Containers* (*3.2* and subsections).

Parenteral preparations intended for chronic use or total parenteral nutrition should have appropriate limits for specific components or elements, taking long-term toxicity into account.

Parenteral preparations are supplied in glass containers (*3.2.1*) or in other containers such as plastic containers (*3.2.2, 3.2.2.1 and 3.2.9*) and prefilled syringes. The tightness of the container is ensured by suitable means. Closures ensure a good seal, prevent the access of micro-organisms and other contaminants and usually permit the withdrawal of a part or the whole of the contents without removal of the closure. The plastic materials or elastomers (*3.2.9*) used to manufacture the closures are sufficiently firm and elastic to allow the passage of a needle with the least possible shedding of particles. Closures for multidose containers are sufficiently elastic to ensure that the puncture is resealed when the needle is withdrawn.

Several categories of parenteral preparations may be distinguished:
— injections;
— infusions;
— concentrates for injections or infusions;
— powders for injections or infusions;
— gels for injections;
— implants.

PRODUCTION

During the development of a parenteral preparation, the formulation for which contains an antimicrobial preservative, the effectiveness of the chosen preservative shall be demonstrated to the satisfaction of the competent authority. A suitable test method together with criteria for judging the preservative properties of the formulation are provided under *Efficacy of antimicrobial preservation (5.1.3)*.

Parenteral preparations are prepared using materials and methods designed to ensure sterility and to avoid the introduction of contaminants and the growth of micro-organisms. Recommendations on this aspect are provided in the text *Methods of preparation of sterile products (5.1.1)*.

Water used in the manufacture of parenteral preparations complies with the requirements of water for injections in bulk stated in the monograph *Water for injections (0169)*.

TESTS

Particulate contamination: sub-visible particles *(2.9.19)*
For preparations for human use, solutions for infusion or solutions for injection comply with the test.

In the case of preparations for subcutaneous or intramuscular injection, higher limits may be appropriate. Radiopharmaceutical preparations are exempt from these requirements. Preparations for which the label states that the product is to be used with a final filter are exempt from these requirements, providing it has been demonstrated that the filter delivers a solution that complies with the test.

For preparations for veterinary use, when supplied in containers with a nominal content of more than 100 mL and when the content is equivalent to a dose of more than 1.4 mL per kilogram of body mass, solutions for infusion or solutions for injection comply with the test for particulate contamination: sub-visible particles.

Sterility *(2.6.1)*
Parenteral preparations comply with the test for sterility.

STORAGE

In a sterile, airtight, tamper-proof container.

LABELLING

The label states:
— the name and concentration of any added antimicrobial preservative;
— where applicable, that the solution is to be used in conjunction with a final filter;
— where applicable, that the preparation is free from bacterial endotoxins or that it is apyrogenic.

INJECTIONS

DEFINITION

Injections are sterile solutions, emulsions or suspensions. They are prepared by dissolving, emulsifying or suspending the active substance(s) and any added excipients in water, in a suitable non-aqueous liquid, that may be non-sterile where justified, or in a mixture of these vehicles.

Solutions for injection, examined under suitable conditions of visibility, are clear and practically free from particles.

Emulsions for injection do not show any evidence of phase separation. Suspensions for injection may show a sediment which is readily dispersed on shaking to give a suspension which remains sufficiently stable to enable the correct dose to be withdrawn.

Multidose preparations Multidose aqueous injections contain a suitable antimicrobial preservative at an appropriate concentration except when the preparation itself has adequate antimicrobial properties. When a preparation for parenteral administration is presented in a multidose container, the precautions to be taken for its administration and more particularly for its storage between successive withdrawals are given.

Antimicrobial preservatives Aqueous preparations which are prepared using aseptic precautions and which cannot be terminally sterilised may contain a suitable antimicrobial preservative in an appropriate concentration.

No antimicrobial preservative is added when:
— the volume to be injected in a single dose exceeds 15 mL, unless otherwise justified;
— the preparation is intended for administration by routes where, for medical reasons, an antimicrobial preservative is not acceptable, such as intracisternally, epidurally, intrathecally or by any route giving access to the cerebrospinal fluid, or intra- or retro-ocularly.

Such preparations are presented in single-dose containers.

PRODUCTION
In the manufacture of injections containing dispersed particles, measures are taken to ensure a suitable and controlled particle size with regard to the intended use.

Single-dose preparations The volume of the injection in a single-dose container is sufficient to permit the withdrawal and administration of the nominal dose using a normal technique (*2.9.17*).

TESTS
Uniformity of dosage units
Single-dose suspensions for injection comply with the test for uniformity of dosage units (*2.9.40*) or, where justified and authorised, with the test for uniformity of content shown below. Herbal drugs and herbal drug preparations present in the dosage form are not subject to the provisions of this paragraph.

Uniformity of content (*2.9.6*)
Unless otherwise prescribed or justified and authorised, single-dose suspensions for injection with a content of active substance less than 2 mg or less than 2 per cent of the total mass comply with test A for uniformity of content of single-dose preparations. If the preparation contains more than one active substance, the requirement applies only to those substances that correspond to the above conditions.

Bacterial endotoxins - pyrogens
A test for bacterial endotoxins (*2.6.14*) is carried out or, where justified and authorised, the test for pyrogens (*2.6.8*). Recommendations on the limits for bacterial endotoxins are given in general chapter *5.1.10*.

Preparations for human use The preparation complies with a test for bacterial endotoxins (*2.6.14*) or with the test for pyrogens (*2.6.8*).

Preparations for veterinary use When the volume to be injected in a single dose is 15 mL or more and is equivalent to a dose of 0.2 mL or more per kilogram of body mass, the preparation complies with a test for bacterial endotoxins (*2.6.14*) or with the test for pyrogens (*2.6.8*).

Any preparation Where the label states that the preparation is free from bacterial endotoxins or apyrogenic, respectively, the preparation complies with a test for bacterial endotoxins (*2.6.14*) or with the test for pyrogens (*2.6.8*), respectively.

INFUSIONS
DEFINITION
Infusions are sterile, aqueous solutions or emulsions with water as the continuous phase. They are usually made isotonic with respect to blood. They are principally intended for administration in large volume. Infusions do not contain any added antimicrobial preservative.

Solutions for infusion, examined under suitable conditions of visibility, are clear and practically free from particles.

Emulsions for infusion do not show any evidence of phase separation.

PRODUCTION
In the manufacture of infusions containing dispersed particles, measures are taken to ensure a suitable and controlled particle size with regard to the intended use.

The volume of the infusion in the container is sufficient to permit the withdrawal and administration of the nominal dose using a normal technique (*2.9.17*).

TESTS
Bacterial endotoxins - pyrogens
They comply with a test for bacterial endotoxins (*2.6.14*) or, where justified and authorised, with the test for pyrogens (*2.6.8*). For the latter test inject 10 mL per kilogram of body mass into each rabbit, unless otherwise justified and authorised.

CONCENTRATES FOR INJECTIONS OR INFUSIONS
DEFINITION
Concentrates for injections or infusions are sterile solutions intended for injection or infusion after dilution. They are diluted to a prescribed volume with a prescribed liquid before administration. After dilution, they comply with the requirements for injections or for infusions.

TESTS
Bacterial endotoxins - pyrogens
They comply with the requirements prescribed for injections or for infusions, after dilution to a suitable volume.

POWDERS FOR INJECTIONS OR INFUSIONS
DEFINITION
Powders for injections or infusions are solid, sterile substances distributed in their final containers and which, when shaken with the prescribed volume of a prescribed sterile liquid rapidly form either clear and practically particle-free solutions or uniform suspensions. After dissolution or suspension, they comply with the requirements for injections or for infusions.

Freeze-dried products for parenteral administration are considered as powders for injections or infusions.

PRODUCTION
The uniformity of content and uniformity of mass of freeze-dried products for parenteral administration are ensured by the in-process control of the amount of the solution prior to freeze-drying.

TESTS
Uniformity of dosage units
Powders for injections or infusions comply with the test for uniformity of dosage units (*2.9.40*) or, where justified and authorised, with the tests for uniformity of content and/or uniformity of mass shown below. Herbal drugs and herbal drug preparations present in the dosage form are not subject to the provisions of this paragraph.

Uniformity of content (*2.9.6*)
Unless otherwise prescribed or justified and authorised, powders for injections or infusions with a content of active substance less than 2 mg or less than 2 per cent of the total mass, or with a unit mass equal to or less than 40 mg comply with test A for uniformity of content of single-dose preparations. If the preparation contains more than one active substance, the requirement applies only to those substances that correspond to the above conditions.

Uniformity of mass (*2.9.5*)
Powders for injections or infusions comply with the test for uniformity of mass of single-dose preparations. If the test for uniformity of content is prescribed for all the active substances, the test for uniformity of mass is not required.

Bacterial endotoxins - pyrogens
They comply with the requirements prescribed for injections or for infusions, after dissolution or suspension in a suitable volume of liquid.

LABELLING
The label states the instructions for the preparation of injections and infusions.

GELS FOR INJECTIONS
DEFINITION
Gels for injections are sterile gels with a viscosity suitable to guarantee a modified release of the active substance(s) at the site of injection.

IMPLANTS
DEFINITION
Implants are sterile, solid preparations of a size and shape suitable for parenteral implantation and release of the active substance(s) over an extended period of time. Each dose is provided in a sterile container.

TESTS
A suitable test is carried out to demonstrate the appropriate release of the active substance(s).

———————————————————— Ph Eur

Parenteral Preparations of the British Pharmacopoeia (Veterinary)

In addition to the requirements of the European Pharmacopoeia, the statements applicable to Parenteral Preparations of the British Pharmacopoeia, modified as stated below, apply to those injections and intravenous infusions that are the subject of an individual monograph in the British Pharmacopoeia (Veterinary).

DEFINITION
Parenteral Preparations prepared with an oily vehicle are suitable for intramuscular or subcutaneous administration only and are not given intravenously.

Veterinary Oral Pastes

Unless otherwise authorised and justified, Veterinary Oral Pastes comply with the requirements of the monograph on Oromucosal Preparations. In addition, the following statements apply to Veterinary Oral Pastes that are the subject of an individual monograph in the British Pharmacopoeia (Veterinary).

DEFINITION
Veterinary Oral Pastes are semi-solid preparations containing one or more active substances in a suitable vehicle. They are administered to the oral cavity and are intended to be swallowed for delivery of active substances to the gastrointestinal tract.

Veterinary Oral Pastes are presented in multi-dose containers which are designed to allow the accurate dosing of animals according to their bodyweight.

TESTS
Dissolution
A suitable test may be carried out to demonstrate the appropriate release of the active substance(s), for example, the test using Apparatus 2 described under *dissolution test for tablets and capsules*, Appendix XII B1.

Uniformity of mass of delivered doses from multi-dose containers
Veterinary Oral Pastes supplied in multi-dose containers comply with Appendix XII C2.

STORAGE
Veterinary Oral Pastes should be stored in airtight containers if they contain water or other volatile ingredients.

TOPICAL POWDERS
POWDERS FOR CUTANEOUS APPLICATION
(Ph Eur monograph 1166)

Unless otherwise justified and authorised, Topical Powders comply with the requirements of the European Pharmacopoeia monograph for Powders for Cutaneous Application. These requirements are reproduced in the British Pharmacopoeia.

Topical Powders of the British Pharmacopoeia (Veterinary)

In addition to the requirements of the European Pharmacopoeia, the statements applicable to Topical Powders of the British Pharmacopoeia apply to any dusting powder that is the subject of an individual monograph in the British Pharmacopoeia (Veterinary).

VETERINARY ORAL POWDERS

Unless otherwise justified and authorised, Veterinary Oral Powders comply with the requirements of the European Pharmacopoeia monograph for Oral Powders (1165). In addition to these requirements, reproduced in the British Pharmacopoeia, the following statements apply to those veterinary oral powders that are the subject of an individual monograph in the British Pharmacopoeia (Veterinary).

DEFINITION

Veterinary Oral Powders are finely divided powders that contain one or more active ingredients with or without excipients such as antimicrobial preservatives, dispersing, suspending or wetting agents and, where necessary, authorised flavouring agents and colouring matter. They are intended for oral administration, usually after dilution in the feed or drinking water. Veterinary Oral Powders may be in the form of soluble or wettable powders.

STORAGE

Veterinary Oral Powders should be stored in airtight containers.

Premixes

(Premixes for Medicated Feeding Stuffs for Veterinary Use, Ph Eur monograph 1037)

Premixes comply with the requirements of the European Pharmacopoeia monograph for Premixes for Medicated Feeding Stuffs for Veterinary Use. These requirements are reproduced below.

Ph Eur

DEFINITION

Mixtures of one or more active substances, usually in a suitable basis or vehicle, that are prepared to facilitate feeding the active substances to animals. They are used exclusively in the preparation of medicated feeding stuffs.

Premixes occur in granulated, powdered, semi-solid or liquid form. Used as powders or granules, they are free-flowing and homogeneous; any aggregates break apart during normal handling. Used in liquid form, they are homogeneous suspensions or solutions that may be obtained from thixotropic gels or structured liquids. The particle size and other properties are such as to ensure uniform distribution of the active substance(s) in the final feed. Unless otherwise justified and authorised, the instructions for use state that the concentration of a premix in granulated or powdered form is at least 0.5 per cent in the medicated feeding stuff.

PRODUCTION

In the manufacture, packaging, storage and distribution of premixes for medicated feeding stuffs for veterinary use, suitable measures are taken to ensure their microbial quality; recommendations on this aspect are provided in general chapter *5.1.4. Microbiological quality of non-sterile pharmaceutical preparations and substances for pharmaceutical use.*

Active substance

Unless already otherwise justified and authorised for existing premixes, an active substance intended for incorporation into a medicated premix:

— complies with the requirements of the relevant monograph of the European Pharmacopoeia;

— in the case of a fermentation product that is not the subject of a monograph of the European Pharmacopoeia, complies with the monograph *Products of fermentation (1468)*, notably with the section Down-stream processing.

TESTS

Loss on drying *(2.2.32)*

Unless otherwise justified and authorised, for premixes occurring in granulated or powdered form, maximum 15.0 per cent, determined on 3.000 g by drying in an oven at 105 °C for 2 h.

LABELLING

The label states the instructions for the preparation of the medicated feeding stuffs from the premix and the basic feed, including information on whether or not the premix can be granulated with the feed and the critical parameters (e.g. maximum temperature) that may be applied during the process.

Ph Eur

Premixes of the British Pharmacopoeia (Veterinary)

DEFINITION

Premixes may occur in pelletted form.

Veterinary Semi-solid Preparations for Oral Use

(Ph. Eur. monograph 2638)

Ph Eur

DEFINITION

Veterinary semi-solid preparations for oral use (usually pastes or gels) contain one or more active substances dissolved or dispersed in a suitable basis. They are administered to the oral cavity and are intended to be swallowed for delivery of active substances to the gastrointestinal tract.

Veterinary semi-solid preparations for oral use may contain suitable antimicrobial preservatives and other excipients such as dispersing, suspending, thickening, emulsifying, buffering, wetting, solubilising, stabilising, flavouring and sweetening agents.

Veterinary semi-solid preparations for oral use are usually supplied in multidose containers such as oral syringes, which are designed to allow the accurate dosing of animals according to their bodyweight.

Where applicable, containers for veterinary semi-solid preparations for oral use comply with the requirements described in *Materials used for the manufacture of containers (3.1 and subsections)* and *Containers (3.2 and subsections)*.

PRODUCTION

During the development of veterinary semi-solid preparations for oral use whose formulation contains an antimicrobial preservative, the need for and the efficacy of the chosen preservative shall be demonstrated to the satisfaction of the competent authority. A suitable test method together with criteria for judging the preservative properties of the formulation are provided in general chapter *5.1.3. Efficacy of antimicrobial preservation.*

In the manufacture, packaging, storage and distribution of veterinary semi-solid preparations for oral use, suitable measures are taken to ensure their microbiological quality; recommendations on this are provided in general chapter *5.1.4. Microbiological quality of non-sterile pharmaceutical preparations and substances for pharmaceutical use.*

TESTS

Dissolution

A suitable test may be carried out to demonstrate the appropriate release of the active substance(s).

Uniformity of mass of delivered doses from multidose containers (2.9.27)

Unless otherwise justified and authorised, the minimum and the maximum labelled doses are tested, where possible using the same container and dosing device.

Discharge once to waste in order to prime the system, if so stated on the label and depending on the type and shape of the container.

Unless otherwise justified and authorised, the preparation complies with the test.

STORAGE

If the preparation contains water or other volatile ingredients, store in an airtight container.

LABELLING

The label states:
— the name of any added antimicrobial preservative;
— if it is necessary to prime the dosing device before administration.

_____ *Ph Eur*

TABLETS

(Ph Eur monograph 0478)

Unless otherwise justified and authorised, Tablets comply with the appropriate requirements of the European Pharmacopoeia. These requirements are reproduced in the British Pharmacopoeia.

Tablets of the British Pharmacopoeia (Veterinary)

In addition to the requirements of the European Pharmacopoeia, the statements applicable to Tablets of the British Pharmacopoeia, modified as stated below, apply to those tablets that are the subject of an individual monograph in the British Pharmacopoeia (Veterinary).

DEFINITION

Tablets of the British Pharmacopoeia (Veterinary) are usually solid, right circular cylinders the end surfaces of which are flat or convex and the edges of which may be bevelled except that those that weigh 5 g or more are frequently elongated or biconical.

Disintegration

Apply test A or test B, Appendix XII A1, as appropriate. When using test B, test 6 tablets either by using two basket-rack assemblies in parallel or by repeating the procedure. To pass the test, all six of the tablets must have disintegrated.

FORMULATED PREPARATIONS: SPECIFIC MONOGRAPHS

Acepromazine Injection

Action and use
Dopamine receptor antagonist; neuroleptic.

DEFINITION
Acepromazine Injection is a sterile solution of Acepromazine Maleate in Water for Injections. The pH of the solution is adjusted to about 5 by the addition of Sodium Hydroxide.

The injection complies with the requirements stated under Parenteral Preparations and with the following requirements.

Content of acepromazine, $C_{19}H_{22}N_2OS$
92.5 to 107.5% of the stated amount.

IDENTIFICATION
A. To a volume containing the equivalent of 20 mg of acepromazine add 2 mL of *water* and 3 mL of 2M *sodium hydroxide*, extract with two 5 mL quantities of *cyclohexane* and evaporate to dryness under reduced pressure. The *infrared absorption spectrum* of the residue, Appendix II A, is concordant with the *reference spectrum* of acepromazine *(RSV 01)*.

B. Complies with the test for *identification of phenothiazines*, Appendix III A, applying to the plate 1 μL of each of the following solutions. For solution (1) extract a volume containing the equivalent of 20 mg of acepromazine with two 5 mL quantities of *chloroform* and use the combined extracts. Solution (2) is a solution of *acepromazine maleate BPCRS* in *chloroform* containing the equivalent of 0.2% w/v of acepromazine.

C. To 5 mg of the residue obtained in test A add 2 mL of *sulfuric acid*. A yellow colour is produced which becomes deep orange on warming for 2 minutes.

D. To a volume of the injection containing the equivalent of 25 mg of acepromazine add 2 mL of 5M sodium hydroxide and shake with three 3 mL quantities of ether. Add 2 mL of bromine solution to the aqueous solution, warm in a water bath for 10 minutes, heat to boiling and cool. Add 0.25 mL to a solution of 10 mg of resorcinol in 3 mL of sulfuric acid and heat for 15 minutes in a water bath. A bluish black colour develops.

TESTS
Acidity
pH, 4.5 to 5.5, Appendix V L.

ASSAY
To a volume containing the equivalent of 40 mg of acepromazine add 5 mL of 1M *sodium hydroxide* and extract with 50 mL quantities of *chloroform* until the chloroform extract is colourless. Wash the extracts with the same 10 mL of *water* and filter through a plug of absorbent cotton previously moistened with *chloroform*. Evaporate the combined extracts to dryness and dissolve the residue in 15 mL of *acetic anhydride*. Carry out Method I for *non-aqueous titration*, Appendix VIII A, using 0.02M *perchloric acid VS* as titrant and *crystal violet solution* as indicator. Each mL of 0.02M *perchloric acid VS* is equivalent to 6.529 mg of $C_{19}H_{22}N_2OS$.

STORAGE
Acepromazine Injection should be protected from light.

LABELLING
The strength is stated as the equivalent amount of acepromazine in a suitable dose-volume.

Acepromazine Tablets

Action and use
Dopamine receptor antagonist; neuroleptic.

DEFINITION
Acepromazine Tablets contain Acepromazine Maleate.

The tablets comply with the requirements stated under Tablets and with the following requirements.

Content of acepromazine, $C_{19}H_{22}N_2OS$
92.5 to 107.5% of the stated amount.

IDENTIFICATION
A. To a quantity of the powdered tablets containing the equivalent of 20 mg of acepromazine add 2 mL of *water* and 3 mL of 2M *sodium hydroxide*. Extract with two 5 mL quantities of *cyclohexane* and evaporate to dryness under reduced pressure. The *infrared absorption spectrum* of the residue, Appendix II A, is concordant with the *reference spectrum* of acepromazine *(RSV 01)*.

B. Complies with the test for *identification of phenothiazines*, Appendix III A, applying to the plate 1 μL of each of the following solutions. For solution (1) extract a quantity of the powdered tablets containing the equivalent of 20 mg of acepromazine with two 5 mL quantities of *chloroform*. Solution (2) is a solution of *acepromazine maleate BPCRS* in *chloroform* containing the equivalent of 0.2% w/v of acepromazine.

C. To a quantity of the powdered tablets containing the equivalent of 5 mg of acepromazine add 2 mL of *sulfuric acid*. A yellow colour is produced which becomes deep orange on warming for 2 minutes.

D. Dissolve as completely as possible a quantity of the powdered tablets containing the equivalent of 25 mg of acepromazine in a mixture of 3 mL of *water* and 2 mL of 5M *sodium hydroxide* and shake with three 3 mL quantities of *ether*. Add 2 mL of *bromine solution* to the aqueous solution, warm in a water bath for 10 minutes, heat to boiling and cool. Add 0.25 mL to a solution of 10 mg of *resorcinol* in 3 mL of *sulfuric acid* and heat for 15 minutes on a water bath. A bluish black colour develops.

TESTS
Related substances
Comply with the test for *related substances in phenothiazines*, Appendix III A, but using a mixture of 8 volumes of *diethylamine*, 17 volumes of *butan-2-one* and 75 volumes of n-*hexane* as the mobile phase and using the following solutions. For solution (1) shake a quantity of the powdered tablets containing the equivalent of 50 mg of acepromazine with 10 mL of *chloroform*, filter, evaporate to dryness and dissolve the residue in 5 mL of *methanol* containing 0.5% v/v of 13.5M *ammonia*. For solution (2) dilute 1 volume of solution (1) to 100 volumes with *methanol* containing 0.5% v/v of 13.5M *ammonia*.

ASSAY

Weigh and powder 20 tablets. To a quantity of the powder containing the equivalent of 60 mg of acepromazine add 5 mL of *water* and extract with three or more 50 mL quantities of *chloroform* or until the chloroform extract is colourless. Evaporate to dryness and dissolve the residue in 15 mL of *acetic anhydride*. Carry out Method I for *non-aqueous titration*, Appendix VIII A, using 0.02M *perchloric acid VS* as titrant and *crystal violet solution* as indicator. Each mL of 0.02M *perchloric acid VS* is equivalent to 6.529 mg of $C_{19}H_{22}N_2OS$.

LABELLING

The quantity of the active ingredient is stated in terms of the equivalent amount of acepromazine.

Albendazole Oral Suspension

Action and use
Benzimidazole antihelminthic.

DEFINITION

Albendazole Oral Suspension is a suspension of Albendazole in a suitable vehicle.

The oral suspension complies with the requirements stated under Oral Liquids and with the following requirements.

Content of albendazole, $C_{12}H_{15}N_3O_2S$
90.0 to 110.0% of the stated amount.

IDENTIFICATION

A. To a volume of oral suspension containing 25 mg of Albendazole add 50 mL of 0.1M *sodium hydroxide* and shake with the aid of ultrasound for 10 minutes. Dilute to 100 mL with the same solvent, filter through a 0.45-µm filter and dilute 1 volume of this solution to 10 volumes with the same solvent. The *light absorption*, Appendix II B, in the range 240 to 340 nm of the resulting solution exhibits a maximum at 308 nm, a minimum at 281 nm and a shoulder at 269 nm.

B. To a volume of oral suspension containing 25 mg of Albendazole add 50 mL of 0.1M *hydrochloric acid* and shake with the aid of ultrasound for 10 minutes. Dilute to 100 mL with the same solvent, filter through a 0.45-µm filter and dilute 1 volume of this solution to 10 volumes with the same solvent. The *light absorption*, Appendix II B, in the range 240 to 340 nm of the resulting solution exhibits a maximum at 292 nm, a minimum at 273 nm and a shoulder at 261 nm.

C. In the Assay, the chromatogram obtained with solution (1) shows a peak with the same retention time as the principal peak in the chromatogram obtained with solution (2).

TESTS
Acidity
pH, 4.5 to 5.5, Appendix V L.

Related substances
Carry out the method for *liquid chromatography*, Appendix III D, using the following solutions.

Solvent A   30% of mobile phase A and 70% of mobile phase B.

(1) Dilute a quantity of the oral suspension with 1% v/v solution of *methanolic sulfuric acid* to give a solution containing 1.0% w/v of Albendazole and dilute 1 volume of the resulting solution to 2 volumes with solvent A.

(2) Dilute 1 volume of solution (1) to 100 volumes with solvent A.

(3) Dissolve 25.0 mg of *albendazole BPCRS* and 25.0 mg of *oxibendazole BPCRS* in 5 mL of 1% v/v solution of *methanolic sulfuric acid* and dilute to 50 mL with solvent A.

CHROMATOGRAPHIC CONDITIONS

(a) Use a stainless steel column (25 cm × 4.6 mm) packed with *end-capped octadecylsilyl silica gel for chromatography* (5 µm) (Waters Symmetry is suitable).

(b) Use gradient elution and the mobile phase described below.

(c) Use a flow rate of 0.7 mL per minute.

(d) Use an ambient column temperature.

(e) Use a detection wavelength of 292 nm.

(f) Inject 20 µL of each solution.

MOBILE PHASE

Mobile phase A   0.015M *ammonium dihydrogen orthophosphate.*
Mobile phase B   *methanol.*

Time (Minutes)	Mobile phase A%	Mobile phase B%	Comment
0-3	100	0	isocratic
3-5	100→30	0→70	linear gradient
5-70	30	70	isocratic
70-72	30→100	70→0	linear gradient
72-80	100	0	re-equilibration

SYSTEM SUITABILITY

The test is not valid unless, in the chromatogram obtained with solution (3), the *resolution factor* between the two principal peaks is at least 7.0.

LIMITS

In the chromatogram obtained with solution (1):

the area of any *secondary peak* is not greater than the area of the principal peak in the chromatogram obtained with solution (2) (1%);

the sum of the areas of any *secondary peaks* is not greater than twice the area of the principal peak in the chromatogram obtained with solution (2) (2%).

Disregard any peak with an area less than 0.05 times the area of the principal peak in the chromatogram obtained with solution (2) (0.05%).

ASSAY

Carry out the method for *liquid chromatography*, Appendix III D, using the following solutions.

(1) Add 70 mL of 1% v/v solution of *methanolic sulfuric acid* to a quantity of the oral suspension containing 0.10 g of Albendazole, stir for 15 minutes, mix with the aid of ultrasound for 10 minutes and add sufficient 1% v/v solution of *methanolic sulfuric acid* to produce 100 mL. Allow to stand and dilute 5 volumes of the clear supernatant to 25 volumes with 1% v/v solution of *methanolic sulfuric acid*.

(2) 0.020% w/v of *albendazole BPCRS* in 1% v/v solution of *methanolic sulfuric acid*.

CHROMATOGRAPHIC CONDITIONS

The chromatographic conditions described under Related substances may be used.

DETERMINATION OF CONTENT

Determine the *weight per mL* of the oral suspension, Appendix V G, and calculate the content of $C_{12}H_{15}N_3O_2S$, weight in volume, using the declared content of $C_{12}H_{15}N_3O_2S$ in *albendazole BPCRS*.

Albendazole Oral Suspension with Minerals

Action and use
Benzimidazole antihelminthic.

DEFINITION
Albendazole Oral Suspension with Minerals is a suspension of Albendazole in a suitable vehicle containing cobalt and selenium.

The oral suspension complies with the requirements stated under Oral Liquids and with the following requirements.

Content of albendazole, $C_{12}H_{15}N_3O_2S$
95.0 to 105.0% of the stated amount.

Content of Co
90.0 to 110.0% of the stated amount.

Content of Se
90.0 to 115.0% of the stated amount.

IDENTIFICATION
A. To a volume of oral suspension containing of 25 mg of Albendazole add 50 mL of 0.1M *sodium hydroxide* and shake with the aid of ultrasound for 10 minutes. Dilute to 100 mL with the same solvent, filter through a 0.45-μm filter and dilute 1 volume of this solution to 10 volumes with the same solvent. The *light absorption*, Appendix II B, in the range 240 to 340 nm of the resulting solution exhibits a maximum at 308 nm, a minimum at 281 nm and a shoulder at 269 nm.

B. To a volume of oral suspension containing of 25 mg of Albendazole add 50 mL of 0.1M *hydrochloric acid* and shake with the aid of ultrasound for 10 minutes. Dilute to 100 mL with the same solvent, filter through a 0.45-μm filter and dilute 1 volume of this solution to 10 volumes with the same solvent. The *light absorption*, Appendix II B, in the range 240 to 340 nm of the resulting solution exhibits a maximum at 292 nm, a minimum at 273 nm and a shoulder at 261 nm.

C. In the Assay for albendazole, the chromatogram obtained with solution (1) shows a peak with the same retention time as the principal peak in the chromatogram obtained with solution (2).

D. In the Assay for cobalt, the oral suspension absorbs radiation at 240.7 nm.

E. In the Assay for selenium, the oral suspension absorbs radiation at 196.0 nm.

TESTS
Acidity
pH, 4.5 to 6.0, Appendix V L.

Related substances
Carry out the method for *liquid chromatography*, Appendix III D, using the following solutions.

Solvent A   30% of mobile phase A and 70% of mobile phase B.

(1) Dilute a quantity of the oral suspension with *methanolic sulfuric acid (1%)* to give a solution containing 1.0% w/v of Albendazole and dilute 1 volume to 2 volumes with solvent A.

(2) Dilute 1 volume of solution (1) to 100 volumes with solvent A.

(3) Dissolve 25.0 mg of *albendazole BPCRS* and 25.0 mg of *oxibendazole BPCRS* in 5 mL of 1% v/v solution of *methanolic sulfuric acid* and dilute to 50 mL with solvent A.

CHROMATOGRAPHIC CONDITIONS

(a) Use a stainless steel column (25 cm × 4.6 mm) packed with *end-capped octadecylsilyl silica gel for chromatography* (5 μm) (Waters Symmetry is suitable).

(b) Use gradient elution and the mobile phase described below.

(c) Use a flow rate of 0.7 mL per minute.

(d) Use ambient column temperature.

(e) Use a detection wavelength of 292 nm.

(f) Inject 20 μL of each solution.

MOBILE PHASE

Mobile phase A   0.015M *ammonium dihydrogen orthophosphate.*
Mobile phase B   *methanol.*

Time (Minutes)	Mobile phase A%	Mobile phase B%	Comment
0–3	100	0	isocratic
3–5	100→30	0→70	linear gradient
5–70	30	70	isocratic
70–72	30→100	70→0	linear gradient
72–80	100	0	re-equilibration

SYSTEM SUITABILITY

The test is not valid unless, in the chromatogram obtained with solution (3), the *resolution factor* between the two principal peaks is at least 7.0.

LIMITS

In the chromatogram obtained with solution (1):

the area of any *secondary peak* is not greater than the area of the principal peak in the chromatogram obtained with solution (2) (1%);

the sum of the areas of any *secondary peaks* is not greater than twice the area of the principal peak in the chromatogram obtained with solution (2) (2%).

Disregard any peak with an area less than 0.05 times the area of the principal peak in the chromatogram obtained with solution (2) (0.05%).

ASSAY
For albendazole
Carry out the method for *liquid chromatography*, Appendix III D, using the following solutions.

(1) Add 70 mL of 1% v/v solution of *methanolic sulfuric acid* to a quantity of the oral suspension containing 0.10 g of Albendazole, stir for 15 minutes, mix with the aid of ultrasound for 10 minutes and add sufficient 1% v/v solution of *methanolic sulfuric acid* to produce 100 mL. Allow to stand

and dilute 5 volumes of the clear supernatant to 25 volumes with 1% v/v solution of *methanolic sulfuric acid*.

(2) 0.020% w/v of *albendazole BPCRS* in 1% v/v solution of *methanolic sulfuric acid*.

CHROMATOGRAPHIC CONDITIONS

The chromatographic conditions described under Related substances may be used.

DETERMINATION OF CONTENT

Determine the *weight per mL* of the oral suspension, Appendix V G, and calculate the content of $C_{12}H_{15}N_3O_2S$, weight in volume, using the declared content of $C_{12}H_{15}N_3O_2S$ in *albendazole BPCRS*.

For cobalt

Add 5 mL of *hydrochloric acid* to a quantity of the oral suspension containing 2.5 mg of cobalt, heat in a water bath for 10 minutes, cool and add sufficient *water* to produce 100 mL. Mix thoroughly and filter. Carry out the method for *atomic absorption spectrophotometry*, Appendix II D, measuring at 240.7 nm and using *cobalt standard solution (100 ppm Co)*, diluted if necessary with *water*, to prepare the standard solution. Determine the *weight per mL* of the oral suspension, Appendix V G, and calculate the content of Co, weight in volume.

For selenium

Add 5 mL of *nitric acid* to a quantity of the oral suspension containing 2.5 mg of selenium, heat in a water bath for 15 minutes, cool and add sufficient *water* to produce 50 mL. Mix thoroughly and filter. Carry out the method for *atomic absorption spectrophotometry*, Appendix II D, measuring at 196.0 nm and using *selenium standard solution* (100 ppm Se), diluted if necessary with *water*, to prepare the standard solution. Determine the weight per mL of the oral suspension, Appendix V G, and calculate the content of Se, weight in volume.

Amitraz Dip Concentrate (Liquid)

Action and use
Topical parasiticide; acaricide.

DEFINITION

Amitraz Dip Concentrate (Liquid) contains Amitraz in a suitable emulsifiable vehicle. It may contain a suitable stabilising agent.

The dip concentrate complies with the requirements stated under Veterinary Liquid Preparations for Cutaneous Application and with the following requirements.

Content of amitraz, $C_{19}H_{23}N_3$
94.0 to 106.0% of the stated amount.

IDENTIFICATION

A. In the test for Related substances, the principal spot in the chromatogram obtained with solution (2) corresponds to that in the chromatogram obtained with solution (3).

B. In the Assay, the chromatogram obtained with solution (1) shows a peak with the same retention time as the peak due to amitraz in the chromatogram obtained with solution (3).

Related substances
Carry out the method for *thin-layer chromatography*, Appendix III A, using the following solutions.

(1) Dilute the dip concentrate with *toluene* to produce a solution containing 5.0% w/v of Amitraz.

(2) Dilute 1 volume of solution (1) to 10 volumes with *toluene*.

(3) 0.5% w/v of *amitraz BPCRS* in *toluene*.

(4) 0.10% w/v of *amitraz BPCRS* in *toluene*.

(5) 0.005% w/v of *2,4-dimethylaniline* in *toluene*.

CHROMATOGRAPHIC CONDITIONS

(a) Use as the coating *silica gel HF$_{254}$*.

(b) Use the mobile phase as described below.

(c) Stand the plate to a depth of 3.5 cm in a solution prepared by dissolving 35 g of *acetamide* in 100 ml of *methanol*, adding 100 ml of *triethylamine* and diluting to 250 ml with *methanol* before standing the plate in a stream of cold air for about 30 seconds. Immediately apply separately to the plate, at a level 1 cm below the top of the impregnated zone, 2 μl of each solution.

(d) Develop the plate to 15 cm.

(e) After removal of the plate, dry in air and examine under *ultraviolet light (254 nm)* (visualisation 1). Expose the plate to the vapour of hydrochloric acid until the coating is impregnated. Expose to the vapour of nitrogen dioxide (prepared by the action of nitric acid on zinc) for 10 minutes, remove any excess nitrogen dioxide with air and spray with a 0.5% w/v solution of N-*(1-naphthyl) ethylenediamine dihydrochloride* in *methanol (50%)* (visualisation 2).

MOBILE PHASE

2 volumes of *triethylamine*, 3 volumes of *ethyl acetate* and 5 volumes of *cyclohexane*.

LIMITS

Using method of visualisation 1, in the chromatogram obtained with solution (1):

any *secondary spot* is not more intense than the spot in the chromatogram obtained with solution (4) (2%).

Using method of visualisaion 2, in the chromatogram obtained with solution (1):

any spot corresponding to 2,4-dimethylaniline is not more intense than the spot in the chromatogram obtained with solution (5) (0.1%)

Water
Not more than 0.15% w/v, Appendix IX C, Method I A. Use 5 ml of the dip concentrate and a mixture of equal volumes of *chloroform* and *2-chloroethanol* in place of anhydrous methanol.

ASSAY

Carry out the method for *gas chromatography*, Appendix III B. Prepare a 2% v/v solution of *squalane* (internal standard) in *methyl acetate* (solution A).

(1) Dissolve a quantity of the dip concentrate containing 0.15 g of Amitraz in sufficient *methyl acetate* to produce 30 ml.

(2) Dissolve a quantity of the dip concentrate containing 0.15 g of Amitraz in 10 ml of solution A and add sufficient *methyl acetate* to produce 30 ml.

(3) Dissolve 0.15 g of *amitraz BPCRS* in 10 ml of solution A and add sufficient *methyl acetate* to produce 30 ml.

CHROMATOGRAPHIC CONDITIONS

(a) Use a fused silica capillary column (15 m × 0.53 mm) coated with a film (1.5 μm) of methyl silicone gum (Chrompack CP-Sil 5 CB is suitable).

(b) Use *helium* as the carrier gas at 12 ml per minute.

(c) Use isothermal conditions maintained at 220°.

(d) Use an inlet temperature of 230°.

(e) Use a flame ionisation detector at a temperature of 300°.

(f) Inject 1 μl of each solution.

SYSTEM SUITABILITY

The assay is not valid unless, in the chromatogram obtained with solution (3), the *resolution factor* between the peaks corresponding to squalane and amitraz is at least 3.0.

DETERMINATION OF CONTENT

Calculate the content of $C_{19}H_{23}N_3$ in the dip concentrate using the declared content of $C_{19}H_{23}N_3$ in *amitraz BPCRS*.

Amoxicillin Oily Injections

Action and use
Penicillin antibacterial.

DEFINITION
Amoxicillin Oily Injections are sterile suspensions of Amoxicillin Trihydrate in oily vehicles appropriate to their intended use. Injections intended for use as long acting preparations are described as Amoxicillin Oily Injection (Long Acting).

The injections comply with the requirements stated under Parenteral Preparations and with the following requirements.

Content of amoxicillin, $C_{16}H_{19}N_3O_5S$
90.0 to 105.0% of the stated amount.

CHARACTERISTICS
A white or almost white, oily suspension.

IDENTIFICATION
Extract a quantity containing the equivalent of 0.25 g of amoxicillin with three 20-mL quantities of *petroleum spirit (boiling range, 120° to 160°)* and discard the extracts. Wash the residue with *ether* and dry in a current of air. The residue complies with the following tests.

A. The *infrared absorption spectrum*, Appendix II A, is concordant with the *reference spectrum* of amoxicillin trihydrate *(RSV 05)*.

B. Carry out the method for *thin-layer chromatography*, Appendix III A, using the following solutions.

(1) Dissolve a quantity of the residue in sufficient *sodium hydrogen carbonate solution* to produce a solution containing the equivalent of 0.25% w/v of amoxicillin.

(2) 0.25% w/v of *amoxicillin trihydrate BPCRS* in *sodium hydrogen carbonate solution*.

(3) 0.25% w/v of each of *amoxicillin trihydrate BPCRS* and *ampicillin trihydrate BPCRS* in *sodium hydrogen carbonate solution*.

CHROMATOGRAPHIC CONDITIONS

(a) Use a *TLC silica gel silanised plate* (Merck silanised silica gel 60 F_{254s} (RP-18) plates are suitable).

(b) Use the mobile phase as described below.

(c) Apply 1 μL of each solution.

(d) Develop the plate to 15 cm.

(e) After removal of the plate allow it to dry in air, expose to iodine vapour until spots appear and examine in daylight.

MOBILE PHASE

10 volumes of *acetone* and 90 volumes of a 15.4% w/v solution of *ammonium acetate* adjusted to pH 5.0 with *glacial acetic acid*.

SYSTEM SUITABILITY

The test is not valid unless the chromatogram obtained with solution (3) shows two clearly separated spots.

CONFIRMATION

The principal spot in the chromatogram obtained with solution (1) is similar in position, colour and size to that in the chromatogram obtained with solution (2).

TESTS
Pyrogens
The requirement for Pyrogens does not apply to Amoxicillin Oily Injections.

ASSAY
Carry out the method for *liquid chromatography*, Appendix III D, using the following solutions.

(1) Shake a quantity of the injection containing the equivalent of 60 mg of amoxicillin with 15 mL of *petroleum spirit (boiling range, 120° to 160°)*, centrifuge and discard the supernatant liquid. Repeat the extraction twice using a further 15 mL of *petroleum spirit (boiling range, 120° to 160°)* each time. Dissolve the residue in 20 mL of *ether*, centrifuge, discard the supernatant liquid and allow the residue remaining to dry in air until the solvents have evaporated. Dissolve the dried residue in mobile phase A, add sufficient mobile phase A to produce 100 mL, mix and filter (Whatman GF/C filter paper is suitable).

(2) 0.070% w/v of *amoxicillin trihydrate BPCRS* in mobile phase A.

(3) 0.0004% w/v of *cefadroxil BPCRS* and 0.003% w/v of *amoxicillin trihydrate BPCRS* in mobile phase A.

CHROMATOGRAPHIC CONDITIONS

(a) Use a stainless steel column (25 cm × 4.6 mm) packed with *octadecylsilyl silica gel for chromatography* (5 μm) (Hypersil 5 ODS is suitable).

(b) Use isocratic elution and the mobile phase described below.

(c) Use a flow rate of 1 mL per minute.

(d) Use an ambient column temperature.

(e) Use a detection wavelength of 254 nm.

(f) Inject 50 μL of each solution.

MOBILE PHASE

8 volumes of mobile phase B and 92 volumes of mobile phase A.

Mobile phase A 1 volume of *acetonitrile* and 99 volumes of a 25% v/v solution of 0.2M *potassium dihydrogen orthophosphate* adjusted to pH 5.0 with 2M *sodium hydroxide*.

Mobile phase B 20 volumes of *acetonitrile* and 80 volumes of a 25% v/v solution of 0.2M *potassium dihydrogen orthophosphate* adjusted to pH 5.0 with 2M *sodium hydroxide*.

SYSTEM SUITABILITY

The Assay is not valid unless, in the chromatogram obtained with solution (3), the *resolution factor* between the peaks due to amoxicillin and cefadroxil is at least 2.0. If necessary, adjust the composition of the mobile phase to achieve the required resolution.

DETERMINATION OF CONTENT

Calculate the content of $C_{16}H_{19}N_3O_5S$ in the injection from the chromatograms obtained and from the declared content of $C_{16}H_{19}N_3O_5S$ in *amoxicillin trihydrate BPCRS*.

LABELLING

The label states (1) the quantity of active ingredient in terms of the equivalent amount of amoxicillin in a suitable dose-volume; (2) where appropriate, that the preparation is Amoxicillin Oily Injection (Long Acting).

Amoxicillin Veterinary Oral Powder

Action and use

Penicillin antibacterial.

DEFINITION

Amoxicillin Veterinary Oral Powder is a mixture of Amoxicillin Trihydrate, Lactose Monohydrate or other suitable diluent and a stabilising agent.

The veterinary oral powder complies with the requirements stated under Veterinary Oral Powders and with the following requirements.

Content of amoxicillin, $C_{16}H_{19}N_3O_5S$

90.0 to 110.0% of the stated amount.

IDENTIFICATION

A. Carry out the method for *thin-layer chromatography*, Appendix III A, using the following solutions.

(1) Dissolve a quantity of the veterinary oral powder containing the equivalent of 0.25 g of amoxicillin in sufficient *sodium hydrogen carbonate solution* to produce 100 mL.

(2) 0.25% w/v of *amoxicillin trihydrate BPCRS* in *sodium hydrogen carbonate solution*.

(3) 0.25% w/v of each of *amoxicillin trihydrate BPCRS* and *ampicillin trihydrate BPCRS* in *sodium hydrogen carbonate solution*.

CHROMATOGRAPHIC CONDITIONS

(a) Use a *TLC silica gel silanised plate* (Merck silanised silica gel 60 F_{254s} (RP-18) plates are suitable).

(b) Use the mobile phase as described below.

(c) Apply 1 μL of each solution.

(d) Develop the plate to 15 cm.

(e) After removal of the plate allow it to dry in air, expose it to iodine vapour until spots appear and examine in daylight.

MOBILE PHASE

10 volumes of *acetone* and 90 volumes of a 15.4% w/v solution of *ammonium acetate* adjusted to pH 5.0 with *glacial acetic acid*.

SYSTEM SUITABILITY

The test is not valid unless the chromatogram obtained with solution (3) shows two clearly separated spots.

CONFIRMATION

The principal spot in the chromatogram obtained with solution (1) is similar in position, colour and size to that in the chromatogram obtained with solution (2).

B. Shake a quantity of the veterinary oral powder containing the equivalent of 0.5 g of amoxicillin with 5 mL of *water* for 5 minutes, filter, wash the residue first with *absolute ethanol* and then with *ether* and dry at a pressure not exceeding 0.7 kPa for 1 hour. Suspend 10 mg of the residue in 1 mL of

water and add 2 mL of a mixture of 2 mL of *cupri-tartaric solution R1* and 6 mL of *water*. A magenta colour is produced immediately.

C. Dissolve 0.1 mL of *aniline* in a mixture of 1 mL of *hydrochloric acid* and 3 mL of *water*. Cool the solution in ice and add 1 mL of a freshly prepared 20% w/v solution of *sodium nitrite*. Add the resulting mixture drop wise to a cold solution of 0.1 g of the residue obtained in test B in 2 mL of 5M *sodium hydroxide*. The solution becomes deep cherry-red and a copious dark brown precipitate is produced.

ASSAY

Carry out the method for *liquid chromatography*, Appendix III D, using the following solutions.

(1) Add 80 mL of mobile phase A to a quantity of the veterinary oral powder containing the equivalent of 60 mg of amoxicillin and shake for 15 minutes. Mix with the aid of ultrasound for 1 minute, add sufficient mobile phase A to produce 100 mL, mix and filter (Whatman GF/C filter paper is suitable).

(2) 0.070% w/v of *amoxicillin trihydrate BPCRS* in mobile phase A.

(3) 0.0004% w/v of *cefadroxil BPCRS* and 0.003% w/v of *amoxicillin trihydrate BPCRS* in mobile phase A.

CHROMATOGRAPHIC CONDITIONS

(a) Use a stainless steel column (25 cm × 4.6 mm) packed with *octadecylsilyl silica gel for chromatography* (5 μm) (Hypersil 5 ODS is suitable).

(b) Use isocratic elution and the mobile phase described below.

(c) Use a flow rate of 1 mL per minute.

(d) Use an ambient column temperature.

(e) Use a detection wavelength of 254 nm.

(f) Inject 50 μL of each solution.

MOBILE PHASE

8 volumes of mobile phase B and 92 volumes of mobile phase A.

Mobile phase A 1 volume of *acetonitrile* and 99 volumes of a 25% v/v solution of 0.2M *potassium dihydrogen orthophosphate* adjusted to pH 5.0 with 2M *sodium hydroxide*.

Mobile phase B 20 volumes of *acetonitrile* and 80 volumes of a 25% v/v solution of 0.2M *potassium dihydrogen orthophosphate* adjusted to pH 5.0 with 2M *sodium hydroxide*.

SYSTEM SUITABILITY

The Assay is not valid unless, in the chromatogram obtained with solution (3), the *resolution factor* between the peaks due to amoxicillin and cefadroxil is at least 2.0. If necessary, adjust the composition of the mobile phase to achieve the required resolution.

DETERMINATION OF CONTENT

Calculate the content of $C_{16}H_{19}N_3O_5S$ in the veterinary oral powder from the chromatograms obtained and from the declared content of $C_{16}H_{19}N_3O_5S$ in *amoxicillin trihydrate BPCRS*.

LABELLING

The quantity of active ingredient is stated in terms of the equivalent amount of amoxicillin.

Amoxicillin Tablets

Action and use
Penicillin antibacterial.

DEFINITION
Amoxicillin Tablets contain Amoxicillin Trihydrate.
The tablets comply with the requirements stated under Tablets and with the following requirements.

Content of amoxicillin, $C_{16}H_{19}N_3O_5S$
90.0 to 110.0% of the stated amount.

IDENTIFICATION
A. Carry out the method for *thin-layer chromatography*, Appendix III A, using the following solutions.

(1) Dissolve a quantity of the powdered tablets containing the equivalent of 0.25 g of amoxicillin in sufficient *sodium hydrogen carbonate solution* to produce 100 mL.

(2) 0.25% w/v of *amoxicillin trihydrate BPCRS* in *sodium hydrogen carbonate solution.*

(3) 0.25% w/v of each of *amoxicillin trihydrate BPCRS* and *ampicillin trihydrate BPCRS* in *sodium hydrogen carbonate solution.*

CHROMATOGRAPHIC CONDITIONS

(a) Use a *TLC silica gel silanised plate* (Merck silanised silica gel 60 F_{254s} (RP-18) plates are suitable).

(b) Use the mobile phase as described below.

(c) Apply 1 μL of each solution.

(d) Develop the plate to 15 cm.

(e) After removal of the plate allow it to dry in air, expose it to iodine vapour until spots appear and examine in daylight.

MOBILE PHASE

10 volumes of *acetone* and 90 volumes of a 15.4% w/v solution of *ammonium acetate* adjusted to pH 5.0 with *glacial acetic acid.*

SYSTEM SUITABILITY

The test is not valid unless the chromatogram obtained with solution (3) shows two clearly separated spots.

CONFIRMATION

The principal spot in the chromatogram obtained with solution (1) is similar in position, colour and size to that in the chromatogram obtained with solution (2).

B. Shake a quantity of the powdered tablets containing the equivalent of 0.5 g of amoxicillin with 5 mL of *water* for 5 minutes, filter, wash the residue first with *absolute ethanol* and then with *ether* and dry at a pressure not exceeding 0.7 kPa for 1 hour. Suspend 10 mg of the residue in 1 mL of *water* and add 2 mL of a mixture of 2 mL of *cupri-tartaric solution R1* and 6 mL of *water*. A magenta colour is produced immediately.

C. Dissolve 0.1 mL of *aniline* in a mixture of 1 mL of *hydrochloric acid* and 3 mL of *water*. Cool the solution in ice and add 1 mL of a freshly prepared 20% w/v solution of *sodium nitrite*. Add the resulting mixture drop wise to a cold solution of 0.1 g of the residue obtained in test B in 2 mL of 5M *sodium hydroxide*. The solution becomes deep cherry-red and a copious dark brown precipitate is produced.

ASSAY
Weigh and powder 20 tablets. Carry out the method for *liquid chromatography*, Appendix III D, using the following solutions.

(1) Add 80 mL of mobile phase A to a quantity of the powdered tablets containing the equivalent of 60 mg of amoxicillin and shake for 15 minutes. Mix with the aid of ultrasound for 1 minute, add sufficient mobile phase A to produce 100 mL, mix and filter (Whatman GF/C filter paper is suitable).

(2) 0.070% w/v of *amoxicillin trihydrate BPCRS* in mobile phase A.

(3) 0.0004% w/v of *cefadroxil BPCRS* and 0.003% w/v of *amoxicillin trihydrate BPCRS* in mobile phase A.

CHROMATOGRAPHIC CONDITIONS

(a) Use a stainless steel column (25 cm × 4.6 mm) packed with *octadecylsilyl silica gel for chromatography* (5 μm) (Hypersil 5 ODS is suitable).

(b) Use isocratic elution and the mobile phase described below.

(c) Use a flow rate of 1 mL per minute.

(d) Use an ambient column temperature.

(e) Use a detection wavelength of 254 nm.

(f) Inject 50 μL of each solution.

MOBILE PHASE

8 volumes of mobile phase B and 92 volumes of mobile phase A.

Mobile phase A   1 volume of *acetonitrile* and 99 volumes of a 25% v/v solution of 0.2M *potassium dihydrogen orthophosphate* adjusted to pH 5.0 with 2M *sodium hydroxide*.

Mobile phase B   20 volumes of *acetonitrile* and 80 volumes of a 25% v/v solution of 0.2M *potassium dihydrogen orthophosphate* adjusted to pH 5.0 with 2M *sodium hydroxide*.

SYSTEM SUITABILITY

The Assay is not valid unless, in the chromatogram obtained with solution (3), the *resolution factor* between the peaks due to amoxicillin and cefadroxil is at least 2.0. If necessary, adjust the composition of the mobile phase to achieve the required resolution.

DETERMINATION OF CONTENT

Calculate the content of $C_{16}H_{19}N_3O_5S$ in the tablets from the chromatograms obtained and from the declared content of $C_{16}H_{19}N_3O_5S$ in *amoxicillin trihydrate BPCRS*.

LABELLING
The quantity of active ingredient is stated in terms of the equivalent amount of amoxicillin.

Ampicillin Sodium and Cloxacillin Sodium Intramammary Infusion (Lactating Cow)

Ampicillin and Cloxacillin Intramammary Infusion (LC)

Action and use
Penicillin antibacterial.

DEFINITION
Ampicillin Sodium and Cloxacillin Sodium Intramammary Infusion (Lactating Cow) is a sterile suspension of Ampicillin Sodium and Cloxacillin Sodium in a suitable vehicle containing suitable suspending agents.

The intramammary infusion complies with the requirements stated under Intramammary Infusions and with the following requirements.

Content of ampicillin, $C_{16}H_{19}N_3O_4S$
90.0 to 110.0% of the stated amount.

Content of cloxacillin, $C_{19}H_{18}ClN_3O_5S$
90.0 to 110.0% of the stated amount.

IDENTIFICATION

A. Carry out the method for *thin-layer chromatography*, Appendix III A, using the following solutions.

(1) Extract a quantity of the infusion containing the equivalent of 50 mg of ampicillin with three 15-mL quantities of *petroleum spirit (boiling range, 120° to 160°)*. Discard the extracts, wash the residue with 10 mL of *ether* and dry in a current of air. Dissolve the residue in 50 mL of *phosphate buffer pH 7.0*, shake well, filter and use the filtrate.

(2) 0.1% w/v of *anhydrous ampicillin BPCRS* in *phosphate buffer pH 7.0*.

CHROMATOGRAPHIC CONDITIONS

(a) Use a *TLC silica gel plate* (Merck silica gel 60 plates are suitable). Impregnate the plate by spraying it with a 0.1% w/v solution of *disodium edetate* in a 5% w/v solution of *sodium dihydrogen orthophosphate*, allow the plate to dry in air and heat at 105° for 1 hour.

(b) Use the mobile phase as described below.

(c) Apply 1 μL of each solution.

(d) Develop the plate to 15 cm.

(e) After removal of the plate allow it to dry, heat at 105° for 10 to 15 minutes and spray with a mixture of 100 volumes of *starch mucilage*, 6 volumes of *glacial acetic acid* and 2 volumes of a 1% w/v solution of *iodine* in a 4% w/v solution of *potassium iodide*.

MOBILE PHASE

5 volumes of *butan-1-ol*, 10 volumes of a 0.1% w/v solution of *disodium edetate* in a 5% w/v solution of *sodium dihydrogen orthophosphate*, 30 volumes of *glacial acetic acid* and 50 volumes of *butyl acetate*.

CONFIRMATION

The principal spot in the chromatogram obtained with solution (1) corresponds to that in the chromatogram obtained with solution (2).

B. Carry out the method for *thin-layer chromatography*, Appendix III A, using the following solutions.

(1) Extract a quantity of the infusion containing the equivalent of 0.130 g of cloxacillin with three 15-mL quantities of *petroleum spirit (boiling range, 120° to 160°)*. Discard the extracts, wash the residue with 10 mL of *ether* and dry in a current of air. Dissolve the residue in 50 mL of *phosphate buffer pH 7.0*, shake well, filter and use the filtrate.

(2) 0.28% w/v of *cloxacillin sodium BPCRS* in *phosphate buffer pH 7.0*.

CHROMATOGRAPHIC CONDITIONS

(a) Use a *TLC silica gel F_{254} silanised plate* (Merck plates are suitable).

(b) Use the mobile phase as described below.

(c) Apply 1 μL of each solution.

(d) Develop the plate to 15 cm.

(e) After removal of the plate allow it to dry, heat at 105° for 10 to 15 minutes and spray with a mixture of 100 volumes of *starch mucilage*, 6 volumes of *glacial acetic acid* and 2 volumes

of a 1% w/v solution of *iodine* in a 4% w/v solution of *potassium iodide*.

MOBILE PHASE

1 volume of *formic acid*, 30 volumes of *acetone* and 70 volumes of 0.05M *potassium hydrogen phthalate* that has been adjusted first to pH 6.0 with 5M *sodium hydroxide* and then to pH 9.0 with 0.1M *sodium hydroxide*.

CONFIRMATION

The principal spot in the chromatogram obtained with solution (1) corresponds to that in the chromatogram obtained with solution (2).

C. Extract a quantity containing the equivalent of 50 mg of ampicillin with three 15-mL quantities of *petroleum spirit (boiling range, 120° to 160°)*. Discard the extracts, wash the residue with 10 mL of *ether* and dry the residue at 55°. The residue produces an intense, persistent yellowish orange colour when introduced into a non-luminous Bunsen burner flame on a platinum wire moistened with *hydrochloric acid*.

TESTS
Water
Not more than 1.0% w/w, Appendix IX C. Use 1.5 g and a mixture of 70 volumes of *chloroform* and 30 volumes of *anhydrous methanol* as the solvent.

ASSAY
Express, as far as possible, weigh and mix the contents of 10 containers. Extract a quantity of the mixed contents containing the equivalent of 50 mg of ampicillin with three 15-mL quantities of *petroleum spirit (boiling range, 120° to 160°)* previously saturated with ampicillin sodium and cloxacillin sodium. Discard the extract, wash the residue with *ether* previously saturated with ampicillin sodium and cloxacillin sodium, dry in a current of air, dissolve in *water* and dilute to 100 mL with *water*. Centrifuge and use the clear supernatant liquid (solution A).

For ampicillin
Dilute 2 mL of solution A to 50 mL with *buffered copper sulfate solution pH 5.2*, transfer 10 mL to a stoppered test tube and heat in a water bath at 75° for 30 minutes. Rapidly cool to room temperature, dilute to 20 mL with *buffered copper sulfate solution pH 5.2* and measure the *absorbance* of the resulting solution at the maximum at 320 nm, Appendix II B, using in the reference cell a solution prepared by diluting 2 mL of solution A to 100 mL with *buffered copper sulfate solution pH 5.2*. Calculate the content of $C_{16}H_{19}N_3O_4S$ in a container of average content from the *absorbance* obtained by carrying out the operation at the same time using 2 mL of a solution prepared by dissolving 50 mg of *anhydrous ampicillin BPCRS* in 100 mL of *water*, diluting to 50 mL with *buffered copper sulfate solution pH 5.2* and beginning at the words 'transfer 10 mL...' and from the declared content of $C_{16}H_{19}N_3O_4S$ in *anhydrous ampicillin BPCRS*.

For cloxacillin
Dilute 2 mL of solution A to 100 mL with 1M *hydrochloric acid*. Measure the *absorbance* of the resulting solution at the maximum at 350 nm, Appendix II B, at 20° after exactly 12 minutes using 1M *hydrochloric acid* in the reference cell. Calculate the content of $C_{19}H_{18}ClN_3O_5S$ in a container of average content from the *absorbance* obtained by carrying out the operation at the same time using 2 mL of a solution prepared by dissolving 0.14 g of *cloxacillin sodium BPCRS* in 100 mL of *water* and from the declared content of $C_{19}H_{17}ClN_3NaO_5S$ in *cloxacillin sodium BPCRS*. Each mg of

$C_{19}H_{17}ClN_3NaO_5S$ is equivalent to 0.9520 mg of $C_{19}H_{18}ClN_3O_5S$.

LABELLING

The label states the quantity of Ampicillin Sodium in terms of the equivalent amount of ampicillin and the quantity of Cloxacillin Sodium in terms of the equivalent amount of cloxacillin.

Ampicillin Trihydrate and Cloxacillin Benzathine Intramammary Infusion (Dry Cow)

Ampicillin and Cloxacillin Intramammary Infusion (DC)

DEFINITION

Ampicillin Trihydrate and Cloxacillin Benzathine Intramammary Infusion (Dry Cow) is a sterile suspension of Ampicillin Trihydrate and Cloxacillin Benzathine in a suitable vehicle, containing suitable suspending agents.

The intramammary infusion complies with the requirements stated under Intramammary Infusions and with the following requirements.

Content of ampicillin, $C_{16}H_{19}N_3O_4S$

90.0 to 110.0% of the stated amount.

Content of cloxacillin, $C_{19}H_{18}ClN_3O_5S$

90.0 to 110.0% of the stated amount.

IDENTIFICATION

A. Extract a quantity containing the equivalent of 0.25 g of ampicillin with three 15-mL quantities of *petroleum spirit (boiling range, 120° to 160°)*. Discard the extracts, wash the residue with 10 mL of *ether* and dry in a current of air. Shake with 10 mL of *chloroform* and filter. Retain the filtrate. Wash the residue with two 5-mL quantities of *chloroform* and dry at room temperature at a pressure of 2 kPa. The *infrared absorption spectrum* of the residue, Appendix II A, is concordant with the *reference spectrum* of ampicillin trihydrate *(RSV 06)*.

B. Wash the filtrate obtained in test A with two 5-mL quantities of *water*, dry the chloroform layer with *anhydrous sodium sulfate*, filter and dilute the filtrate to 20 mL with *chloroform*. The *infrared absorption spectrum* of the resulting solution, Appendix II A, is concordant with the *reference spectrum* of cloxacillin benzathine *(RSV 12)*.

TESTS

Water

Not more than 3.0% w/w, Appendix IX C. Use 1.5 g and a mixture of 70 volumes of *chloroform* and 30 volumes of *anhydrous methanol* as the solvent.

ASSAY

Express, as far as possible, weigh and mix the contents of 10 containers. Extract a quantity of the mixed contents containing the equivalent of 60 mg of ampicillin with three 15-mL quantities of *petroleum spirit (boiling range, 120° to 160°)* previously saturated with ampicillin trihydrate and cloxacillin benzathine. Discard the extracts, wash the residue with *ether* previously saturated with ampicillin trihydrate and cloxacillin benzathine, dry in a current of air, dissolve in 50 mL of *methanol* and dilute to 100 mL with *water*. Centrifuge and use the clear supernatant liquid (solution A).

For ampicillin

Dilute 2 mL of solution A to 50 mL with *buffered copper sulfate solution pH 5.2*, transfer 10 mL to a stoppered test tube and heat in a water bath at 75° for 30 minutes. Rapidly cool to room temperature, dilute to 20 mL with *buffered copper sulfate solution pH 5.2* and measure the *absorbance* of the resulting solution at the maximum at 320 nm, Appendix II B, using in the reference cell the unheated buffered solution of the infusion. Calculate the content of $C_{16}H_{19}N_3O_4S$ in a container of average content from the *absorbance* obtained by carrying out the operation at the same time using 2 mL of a solution prepared by dissolving 60 mg of *anhydrous ampicillin BPCRS* in 100 mL of a 50% v/v solution of *methanol*, diluting to 50 mL with *buffered copper sulfate solution pH 5.2*, and beginning at the words 'transfer 10 mL...' and from the declared content of $C_{16}H_{19}N_3O_4S$ in *anhydrous ampicillin BPCRS*.

For cloxacillin

Dilute 2 mL of solution A to 100 mL with 1M *hydrochloric acid*. Measure the *absorbance* of the resulting solution at the maximum at 350 nm, Appendix II B, at 20° after exactly 12 minutes, using 1M *hydrochloric acid* in the reference cell. Calculate the content of $C_{19}H_{18}ClN_3O_5S$ in a container of average content from the *absorbance* obtained by carrying out the operation at the same time using 2 mL of a solution prepared by dissolving 0.165 g of *cloxacillin benzathine BPCRS* in 100 mL of a 50% v/v solution of *methanol* and from the declared content of $C_{19}H_{18}ClN_3O_5S$ in *cloxacillin benzathine BPCRS*.

LABELLING

The label states the quantity of Ampicillin Trihydrate in terms of the equivalent amount of ampicillin and the quantity of Cloxacillin Benzathine in terms of the equivalent amount of cloxacillin.

Apramycin Veterinary Oral Powder

Action and use

Aminoglycoside antibacterial.

DEFINITION

Apramycin Veterinary Oral Powder contains Apramycin Sulfate.

The veterinary oral powder complies with the requirements stated under Veterinary Oral Powders and with the following requirements.

CHARACTERISTICS

Light brown, granular powder.

IDENTIFICATION

A. Carry out the method for *thin-layer chromatography*, Appendix III A, using the following solutions.

(1) Dissolve a quantity of the veterinary oral powder containing the equivalent of 60 mg of apramycin in *water* and dilute to 100 mL.

(2) 0.06% w/v of *apramycin BPCRS* in *water*.

(3) 0.06% w/v of each of *apramycin BPCRS* and *tobramycin BPCRS* in *water*.

CHROMATOGRAPHIC CONDITIONS

(a) Use a silica gel F_{254} precoated plate (Merck silica gel 60 F_{254} plates are suitable).

(b) Use the mobile phase as described below.

(c) Apply 5 μL of each solution.

(d) Develop the plate to 10 cm.

(e) After removal of the plate, allow it to dry in air for 10 minutes, heat at 100° for 10 minutes, spray with *sodium hypochlorite solution* whilst hot and cool for 5 minutes. Spray with *absolute ethanol,* heat at 100° for 5 to 10 minutes, or until an area of the plate below the line of application gives at most a faint blue colour with one drop of a 1% w/v solution of *potassium iodide* containing 1% w/v *soluble starch,* and spray with the potassium iodide-starch solution.

MOBILE PHASE

20 volumes of *chloroform,* 40 volumes of 13.5M *ammonia* and 60 volumes of *methanol,* equilibrated for 1 hour before use.

SYSTEM SUITABILITY

The test is not valid unless the chromatogram obtained with solution (3) shows two clearly separated principal spots.

CONFIRMATION

The principal spot in the chromatogram obtained with solution (1) corresponds to that in the chromatogram obtained with solution (2).

B. In the test for Related substances, the retention time of the principal peak in the chromatogram obtained with solution (1) corresponds to that of the principal peak in the chromatogram obtained with solution (2).

C. Yields reaction A characteristic of *sulfates,* Appendix VI.

TESTS
Related substances
Carry out the method for *liquid chromatography,* Appendix III D, using the following solutions in *water.*

(1) Dissolve a quantity of the oral powder containing the equivalent of 0.3 g of apramycin and dilute to 100 mL.

(2) 0.30% w/v of *apramycin BPCRS.*

(3) Dilute 1 volume of solution (1) to 20 volumes.

(4) Dilute 1 volume of solution (3) to 50 volumes.

CHROMATOGRAPHIC CONDITIONS

(a) Use a column (25 cm × 4 mm) packed with fast cation-exchange polymeric beads (13 μm) with sulfonic acid functional groups (Dionex Fast Cation-1^R is suitable) and a stainless steel post-column reaction coil (380 cm × 0.4 mm) with internal baffles. Use in the reaction coil *ninhydrin reagent I* at a flow rate approximately the same as that for the mobile phase.

(b) Use gradient elution and the mobile phase described below.

(c) Use a flow rate of 0.8 mL per minute.

(d) Use a column temperature of 130°. Maintain the post-column reaction coil at the same temperature.

(e) Use a detection wavelength of 568 nm.

(f) Inject 20 μL of each solution.

MOBILE PHASE

Mobile phase A   A solution containing 1.961% w/v of *sodium citrate,* 0.08% v/v of *liquefied phenol* and 0.5% v/v of *thiodiglycol,* adjusted to pH 4.25 using *hydrochloric acid.*

Mobile phase B   A solution containing 4.09% w/v of *sodium chloride* and 3.922% w/v of *sodium citrate* with 0.08% v/v of *liquefied phenol,* adjusted to pH 7.4 with *hydrochloric acid.*

Equilibrate the column using a mixture containing 75% of mobile phase A and 25% of mobile phase B. After each injection elute for 3 minutes using the same mixture and then carry out a linear gradient elution for 6 minutes to

100% of mobile phase B. Elute for a further 21 minutes using 100% of mobile phase B, then step-wise re-equilibrate to a mixture of 75% of mobile phase A and 25% of mobile phase B and elute for at least 10 minutes.

SYSTEM SUITABILITY

The test is not valid unless, in the chromatogram obtained with solution (2), the *resolution factor* between compound A and 3-hydroxyapramycin, identified as indicated in the reference chromatogram supplied with *apramycin BPCRS,* is at least 0.8.

LIMITS

Multiply the areas of all the *secondary peaks* by 0.5. [NOTE: This is to ensure that the impurities are calculated relative to Apramycin Sulfate (which contains about 50% w/w of apramycin).]

In the chromatogram obtained with solution (1):

the areas of any peaks corresponding to 3-hydroxyapramycin, lividamine/2-deoxystreptamine (combined), compound A and compound B (identified as indicated in the reference chromatogram supplied with *apramycin BPCRS*) are not greater than 1.4, 1.0, 0.4 and 0.4 times respectively the area of the principal peak in the chromatogram obtained with solution (3) (7%, 5%, 2% and 2% respectively);

the area of any other *secondary peak* is not greater than 0.4 times the area of the principal peak in the chromatogram obtained with solution (3) (2%);

the sum of the areas of all the *secondary peaks* is not greater than 3 times the area of the principal peak in the chromatogram obtained with solution (3) (15%).

Disregard any peak with an area less than the area of the peak in the chromatogram obtained with solution (4) (0.1%).

ASSAY

Carry out the *microbiological assay of antibiotics,* Appendix XIV A, Method B. The precision of the assay is such that the fiducial limits of error are not less than 95% and not more than 105% of the estimated potency.

Calculate the content of apramycin in the veterinary oral powder taking each 1000 Units found to be equivalent to 1 mg of apramycin. The upper fiducial limit of error is not less than 97.0% and the lower fiducial limit of error is not more than 110.0% of the stated content.

LABELLING

The quantity of active ingredient is stated in terms of the equivalent amount of apramycin.

IMPURITIES

The impurities limited by the requirements of this monograph include those listed under Apramycin Sulfate.

Apramycin Premix

Action and use
Aminoglycoside antibacterial.

DEFINITION

Apramycin Premix contains Apramycin Sulfate.

The premix complies with the requirements stated under Premixes and with the following requirements.

CHARACTERISTICS

Light brown granules.

IDENTIFICATION

A. Carry out the method for *thin-layer chromatography*, Appendix III A, using the following solutions.

(1) Shake a quantity of the premix containing the equivalent of 60 mg of apramycin with 60 mL of 0.1M *sodium hydrogen carbonate* at 60°, cool, dilute to 100 mL, filter and use the filtrate.

(2) 0.06% w/v of *apramycin BPCRS* in *water*.

(3) 0.06% w/v of each of *apramycin BPCRS* and *tobramycin BPCRS* in *water*.

CHROMATOGRAPHIC CONDITIONS

(a) Use a silica gel F_{254} precoated plate (Merck silica gel 60 F_{254} plates are suitable).

(b) Use the mobile phase as described below.

(c) Apply 5 µL of each solution.

(d) Develop the plate to 10 cm.

(e) After removal of the plate, allow it to dry in air for 10 minutes, heat at 100° for 10 minutes, spray with *sodium hypochlorite solution* whilst hot and cool for 5 minutes. Spray with *absolute ethanol*, heat at 100° for 5 to 10 minutes, or until an area of the plate below the line of application gives at most a faint blue colour with one drop of a 1% w/v solution of *potassium iodide* containing 1% w/v *soluble starch*, and spray with the potassium iodide-starch solution.

MOBILE PHASE

20 volumes of *chloroform*, 40 volumes of 13.5M *ammonia* and 60 volumes of *methanol*, equilibrated for 1 hour before use.

SYSTEM SUITABILITY

The test is not valid unless the chromatogram obtained with solution (3) shows two clearly separated principal spots.

CONFIRMATION

The principal spot in the chromatogram obtained with solution (1) corresponds to that in the chromatogram obtained with solution (2).

B. In the test for Related substances, the retention time of the principal peak in the chromatogram obtained with solution (1) corresponds to that of the principal peak in the chromatogram obtained with solution (2).

C. Yields reaction A characteristic of *sulfates*, Appendix VI.

TESTS

Related substances

Carry out the method for *liquid chromatography*, Appendix III D, using the following solutions.

(1) Shake a quantity of the premix containing the equivalent of 3 mg of apramycin per mL in a 5% w/v solution of *sodium chloride* and centrifuge for 5 minutes at 4000 revolutions per minute. Filter the supernatant liquid using filters of nominal pore size of 5 µm and 0.45 µm.

(2) 0.30% w/v of *apramycin BPCRS* in *water*.

(3) Dilute 1 volume of solution (1) to 20 volumes with *water*.

(4) Dilute 1 volume of solution (3) to 50 volumes with *water*.

CHROMATOGRAPHIC CONDITIONS

(a) Use a column (25 cm × 4 mm) packed with fast cation-exchange polymeric beads (13 µm) with sulfonic acid functional groups (Dionex Fast Cation-1^R is suitable) and a stainless steel post-column reaction coil (380 cm × 0.4 mm) with internal baffles. Use in the reaction coil *ninhydrin reagent I* at a flow rate approximately the same as that for the mobile phase.

(b) Use gradient elution and the mobile phase described below.

(c) Use a flow rate of 0.8 mL per minute.

(d) Use a column temperature of 130°. Maintain the post-column reaction coil at the same temperature.

(e) Use a detection wavelength of 568 nm.

(f) Inject 20 µL of each solution.

MOBILE PHASE

Mobile phase A   A solution containing 1.961% w/v of *sodium citrate*, 0.08% v/v of *liquefied phenol* and 0.5% v/v of *thiodiglycol*, adjusted to pH 4.25 using *hydrochloric acid*.

Mobile phase B   A solution containing 4.09% w/v of *sodium chloride* and 3.922% w/v of *sodium citrate* with 0.08% v/v of *liquefied phenol*, adjusted to pH 7.4 with *hydrochloric acid*.

Equilibrate the column using a mixture containing 75% of mobile phase A and 25% of mobile phase B. After each injection elute for 3 minutes using the same mixture and then carry out a linear gradient elution for 6 minutes to 100% of mobile phase B. Elute for a further 21 minutes using 100% of mobile phase B, then step-wise re-equilibrate to a mixture of 75% of mobile phase A and 25% of mobile phase B and elute for at least 10 minutes.

SYSTEM SUITABILITY

The test is not valid unless, in the chromatogram obtained with solution (2), the *resolution factor* between compound A and 3-hydroxyapramycin, identified as indicated in the reference chromatogram supplied with *apramycin BPCRS*, is at least 0.8.

LIMITS

Multiply the areas of all the *secondary peaks* by 0.5. [*NOTE*: This is to ensure that the impurities are calculated relative to Apramycin Sulfate (which contains about 50% w/w of apramycin).]

In the chromatogram obtained with solution (1):

the areas of any peaks corresponding to 3-hydroxyapramycin, lividamine/2-deoxystreptamine (combined), compound A and compound B (identified as indicated in the reference chromatogram supplied with *apramycin BPCRS*) are not greater than 1.4, 1.0, 0.4 and 0.4 times respectively the area of the principal peak in the chromatogram obtained with solution (3) (7%, 5%, 2% and 2% respectively);

the area of any other *secondary peak* is not greater than 0.4 times the area of the principal peak in the chromatogram obtained with solution (3) (2%);

the sum of the areas of all the *secondary peaks* is not greater than 3 times the area of the principal peak in the chromatogram obtained with solution (3) (15%).

Disregard any peak with an area less than the area of the peak in the chromatogram obtained with solution (4) (0.1%).

ASSAY

To about 5 g of the premix, accurately weighed, add 250 mL of a solution containing 0.6% w/v of *sodium hydroxide* and 0.745% w/v of *ethylenediaminetetra-acetic acid* in *water*. Shake for 1 hour and allow to stand for 15 minutes. Decant the supernatant liquid and dilute to concentrations equivalent to the solutions of the Standard Preparation with the pH 8.0 buffer and carry out the *microbiological assay of antibiotics*, Appendix XIV A, Method B. The precision of the assay is such that the fiducial limits of error are not less than 95% and not more than 105% of the estimated potency.

Calculate the content of apramycin in the premix taking each 1000 Units found to be equivalent to 1 mg of apramycin.

The upper fiducial limit of error is not less than 97.0% and the lower fiducial limit of error is not more than 110.0% of the stated content.

STORAGE

Apramycin Premix should be stored in a dry place.

LABELLING

The quantity of active ingredient is stated in terms of the equivalent amount of apramycin.

IMPURITIES

The impurities limited by the requirements of this monograph include those listed under Apramycin Sulfate.

Azaperone Injection

Action and use

Dopamine receptor antagonist; neuroleptic (veterinary).

DEFINITION

Azaperone Injection is a sterile solution of Azaperone in Water for Injections.

The injection complies with the requirements stated under Parenteral Preparations and with the following requirements.

Content of azaperone, $C_{19}H_{22}FN_3O$

90.0 to 110.0% of the stated amount.

CHARACTERISTICS

A clear, yellow solution.

IDENTIFICATION

A. To a volume containing 80 mg of Azaperone add 5 mL of 0.5M *sulfuric acid* and 20 mL of *water*. Extract the solution with 50 mL of *ether*, make the aqueous phase alkaline with 1M *sodium hydroxide* and extract with 50 mL of *ether*. Wash the ether extracts with two 10 mL-quantities of *water*, shake with *anhydrous sodium sulfate*, filter and evaporate to dryness. The *infrared absorption spectrum* of the residue, Appendix II A, is concordant with the *reference spectrum* of azaperone *(RSV 08)*.

B. The *light absorption*, Appendix II B, in the range 230 to 350 nm of a 2-cm layer of the solution obtained in the Assay exhibits maxima at 242 nm and at 312 nm. The *absorbances* at the maxima are about 1.1 and about 0.38, respectively.

TESTS

Acidity

pH, 3.5 to 5.0, Appendix V L.

Related substances

Carry out in subdued light the method for *thin-layer chromatography*, Appendix III A, using a silica gel F_{254} precoated plate (Merck silica gel 60 F_{254} plates are suitable) and a mixture of 1 volume of *ethanol (96%)* and 9 volumes of *chloroform* as the mobile phase. Apply separately to the plate 10 µL of each of the following two solutions. For solution (1) dissolve the extracted residue obtained in Identification test A in sufficient *chloroform* to produce a solution containing 1% w/v of Azaperone. For solution (2) dilute 1 volume of solution (1) to 100 volumes with *chloroform*. After removal of the plate allow it to dry in air and examine under *ultraviolet light (254 nm)*. Any *secondary spot* in the chromatogram obtained with solution (1) is not more intense than the spot in the chromatogram obtained with solution (2) (1%).

ASSAY

To a volume containing 0.4 g of Azaperone add 25 mL of 0.5M *sulfuric acid* and sufficient *water* to produce 250 mL. Mix, transfer 10 mL of the solution to a separating funnel containing 10 mL of 0.05M *sulfuric acid* and shake with 20 mL of *ether*. Wash the ether layer with two 10 mL quantities of 0.05M *sulfuric acid*. Make the combined acid extract and washings alkaline with 5 mL of 1M *sodium hydroxide*, add 50 mL of *ether*, shake and allow to separate. Extract the aqueous layer with 50 mL of *ether*. Wash the two ether solutions, in succession, with a 20 mL quantity of *water* and extract each of the two ether solutions, in succession, with two 20 mL quantities and one 5 mL quantity of 0.25M *sulfuric acid*. Combine the acid extracts and add sufficient 0.25M *sulfuric acid* to produce 100 mL. To 5 mL of the resulting solution add 5 mL of *methanol* and sufficient 0.25M *sulfuric acid* to produce 100 mL. Measure the *absorbance* of the resulting solution at the maximum at 242 nm, Appendix II B. Dissolve 40 mg of *azaperone BPCRS* in sufficient *methanol* to produce 250 mL, dilute 5 mL of the resulting solution to 100 mL with 0.25M *sulfuric acid* and measure the *absorbance* at 242 nm. Calculate the content of $C_{19}H_{22}FN_3O$ in the injection from the absorbances obtained using the declared content of $C_{19}H_{22}FN_3O$ in *azaperone BPCRS*.

STORAGE

Azaperone Injection should be protected from light.

Calcium Borogluconate Injection

DEFINITION

Calcium Borogluconate Injection is a sterile solution of Calcium Gluconate and Boric Acid in Water for Injections.

The injection complies with the requirements stated under Parenteral Preparations and with the following requirements.

Content of calcium, Ca

95.0 to 105.0% of the stated amount.

Content of boric acid, H_3BO_3

Not more than 2.3 times the stated content of calcium.

IDENTIFICATION

A. To 1 mL add sufficient *water* to produce a solution containing about 0.75% w/v of calcium and add 0.05 mL of *iron(III) chloride solution R1*. An intense yellow or yellowish green colour is produced.

B. Yields the reactions characteristic of *calcium salts*, Appendix VI.

C. To 1 mL add 0.15 mL of *sulfuric acid* and 5 mL of *methanol* and ignite. The mixture burns with a flame tinged with green.

Acidity

pH of the injection, diluted if necessary with *carbon dioxide-free water* to contain 1.5% w/v of calcium, 3.0 to 4.0, Appendix V L.

ASSAY

For calcium

Dilute a quantity containing the equivalent of 45 mg of calcium to about 50 mL with *water*. Titrate with 0.05M *disodium edetate VS* to within a few mL of the expected end point, add 4 mL of a 40% w/v solution of *sodium hydroxide* and 10 mg of *solochrome dark blue mixture* and continue the titration until the colour changes from pink to blue. Each mL of 0.05M *disodium edetate VS* is equivalent to 2.004 mg of Ca.

For boric acid

Dilute a quantity containing 0.1 g of Boric Acid to 50 mL with *water*, add 3 g of D-*mannitol* and titrate with 0.1M *sodium hydroxide VS* using *phenolphthalein solution R1* as indicator. Each mL of 0.1M *sodium hydroxide VS* is equivalent to 6.183 mg of H_3BO_3.

STORAGE

Calcium Borogluconate Injection should be protected from light. It may be supplied in containers of *glass type III*, Appendix XIX B.

LABELLING

The strength is stated as the amount of calcium in a suitable dose-volume. The label also states the proportion of boric acid present.

Calcium Copperedetate Injection

Action and use

Used in the treatment of copper deficiency.

DEFINITION

Calcium Copperedetate Injection is a sterile suspension of Calcium Copperedetate, with suitable stabilising and dispersing agents, in an oil-in-water emulsion.

The injection complies with the requirements stated under Parenteral Preparations and with the following requirements.

Content of copper, Cu

92.0 to 108.0% of the stated amount.

CHARACTERISTICS

Macroscopical   A blue, opaque, viscous suspension.

Microscopical   When diluted with *glycerol* and examined microscopically, cubic crystals 10 to 30 μm in diameter are visible, but large plate-like crystals are absent.

IDENTIFICATION

Ignite 1 g and dissolve the residue by warming in 10 mL of a mixture of equal volumes of *hydrochloric acid* and *water*, filter if necessary. The solution complies with the following tests.

A. Neutralise 2 mL of the solution with 5M *ammonia*, and add 1 mL of 6M *acetic acid* and 2 mL of *potassium iodide solution*. A white precipitate is produced and iodine is liberated, colouring the supernatant liquid brown.

B. To 5 mL of the solution add 25 mL of a 10% v/v solution of *mercaptoacetic acid* and filter. Make the filtrate alkaline with 5M *ammonia* and add 5 mL of a 2.5% w/v solution of *ammonium oxalate*. A white precipitate is produced which is soluble in *hydrochloric acid* but only sparingly soluble in 6M *acetic acid*.

ASSAY

Evaporate a quantity containing the equivalent of 0.13 g of copper to dryness, ignite at 600° to 700°, cool and heat the residue with 5 mL of a mixture of equal volumes of *hydrochloric acid* and *water* on a water bath for 15 minutes. Add 5 mL of *water*, filter and wash the residue with about 20 mL of *water*. Combine the filtrate and the washings, add 10 mL of *bromine water*, boil to remove the bromine, cool and add *dilute sodium carbonate solution* until a faint permanent precipitate is produced. Add 3 g of *potassium iodide* and 5 mL of 6M *acetic acid* and titrate the liberated iodine with 0.1M *sodium thiosulfate VS*, using *starch mucilage*

as indicator, until only a faint blue colour remains; add 2 g of *potassium thiocyanate* and continue the titration until the blue colour disappears. Each mL of 0.1M *sodium thiosulfate VS* is equivalent to 6.354 mg of Cu.

LABELLING

The strength is stated as the equivalent amount of copper in a suitable dose-volume.

Cefalonium Intramammary Infusion (Dry Cow)

Action and use

Cephalosporin antibacterial.

DEFINITION

Cefalonium Intramammary Infusion (Dry Cow) is a sterile suspension of Cefalonium in a suitable non-aqueous vehicle, containing suitable suspending agents.

The intramammary infusion complies with the requirements stated under Intramammary Infusions and with the following requirements.

Content of anhydrous cefalonium, $C_{20}H_{18}N_4O_5S_2$

90.0 to 112.0% of the stated amount.

IDENTIFICATION

A. In the Assay, the retention time of the principal peak in the chromatogram obtained with solution (1) corresponds to that of the principal peak in the chromatogram obtained with solution (2).

B. To a quantity of the intramammary infusion containing the equivalent of 20 mg of anhydrous cefalonium add a few drops of *sulfuric acid (80% v/v)* containing 1% v/v of *nitric acid* and mix. A pale green colour is produced which immediately changes to dark green.

TESTS

Related substances

Carry out the method for *liquid chromatography*, Appendix III D, using the following solutions prepared immediately before use and stored in a refrigerator between injections.

(1) Disperse a quantity of the intramammary infusion containing the equivalent of 0.10 g of anhydrous cefalonium in 50 mL of *petroleum spirit (boiling range, 60° to 80°)*, add 100 mL of 0.1M *hydrochloric acid* and shake vigorously by hand for 5 minutes and then mechanically for 30 minutes, filter and use the lower layer.

(2) Dilute 2 volumes of solution (1) to 100 volumes with 0.1M *hydrochloric acid*.

(3) 0.0020% w/v of *isonicotinamide* in 0.1M *hydrochloric acid*.

(4) 0.0050% w/v of each of *cefalonium BPCRS* and *isonicotinamide* in 0.1M *hydrochloric acid*.

CHROMATOGRAPHIC CONDITIONS

(a) Use a stainless steel column (10 cm × 4.6 mm) packed with particles of silica the surface of which has been modified with chemically-bonded hexylsilyl groups (Spherisorb S5 C6 is suitable).

(b) Use isocratic elution and the mobile phase described below.

(c) Use a flow rate of 2 mL per minute.

(d) Use an ambient column temperature.

(e) Use a detection wavelength of 262 nm.

(f) Inject 10 µL of each solution.

(g) For solution (1), allow the chromatography to proceed for at least 3.5 times the retention time of the principal peak.

MOBILE PHASE

3 volumes of *acetonitrile* and 97 volumes of a pH 3.4 solution containing 5 volumes of 0.1M *sodium acetate* and 95 volumes of 0.1M *acetic acid*.

SYSTEM SUITABILITY

The test is not valid unless, in the chromatogram obtained with solution (4), the *resolution factor* between the two principal peaks is at least 10.

LIMITS

In the chromatogram obtained with solution (1):

the area of any peak corresponding to isonicotinamide is not greater than the area of the principal peak in the chromatogram obtained with solution (3) (2%);

the area of any other *secondary peak* is not greater than half the area of the principal peak in the chromatogram obtained with solution (2) (1%).

ASSAY

Express, as far as possible, weigh and mix the contents of 10 containers. Carry out the method for *liquid chromatography*, Appendix III D, using the following solutions prepared immediately before use and stored in a refrigerator between injections.

(1) Disperse a quantity of the mixed contents of the 10 containers containing the equivalent of 75 mg of anhydrous cefalonium in 50 mL of *petroleum spirit (boiling range, 60° to 80°)*, add 100 mL of 0.1M *hydrochloric acid* and shake vigorously by hand for 5 minutes and then mechanically for 30 minutes. Filter the lower layer and dilute 10 mL of the filtrate to 100 mL with 0.1M *hydrochloric acid*.

(2) 0.0075% w/v of *cefalonium BPCRS* in 0.1M *hydrochloric acid*.

CHROMATOGRAPHIC CONDITIONS

The chromatographic conditions described under Related substances may be used.

DETERMINATION OF CONTENT

Calculate the content of $C_{20}H_{18}N_4O_5S_2$ in a container of average content using the declared content of $C_{20}H_{18}N_4O_5S_2$ in *cefalonium BPCRS*.

STORAGE

Cefalonium Intramammary Infusion (Dry Cow) should be stored at a temperature not exceeding 30°. It should not be allowed to freeze.

LABELLING

The quantity of active ingredient is stated in terms of the equivalent amount of anhydrous cefalonium.

Chlortetracycline Veterinary Oral Powder

Chlortetracycline Soluble Powder

Action and use
Tetracycline antibacterial.

DEFINITION

Chlortetracycline Veterinary Oral Powder is a mixture of Chlortetracycline Hydrochloride and Lactose Monohydrate or other suitable diluent.

The veterinary oral powder complies with the requirements stated under Veterinary Oral Powders and with the following requirements.

Content of chlortetracycline hydrochloride, $C_{22}H_{23}ClN_2O_8,HCl$
90.0 to 110.0% of the stated amount.

IDENTIFICATION

A. Carry out the method for *thin-layer chromatography*, Appendix III A, using the following solutions.

(1) Extract a quantity of the oral powder containing 10 mg of Chlortetracycline Hydrochloride with 20 mL of *methanol* and centrifuge.

(2) 0.05% w/v of *chlortetracycline hydrochloride BPCRS* in *methanol*.

(3) 0.05% w/v of each of *chlortetracycline hydrochloride BPCRS*, *tetracycline hydrochloride BPCRS* and *metacycline hydrochloride BPCRS* in *methanol*.

CHROMATOGRAPHIC CONDITIONS

(a) Use *silica gel H* as the coating. Adjust the pH of a 10% w/v solution of *disodium edetate* to 8.0 with 10M *sodium hydroxide* and spray the solution evenly onto the plate (about 10 mL for a plate 100 mm × 200 mm). Allow the plate to dry in a horizontal position for at least 1 hour. At the time of use, dry the plate in an oven at 110° for 1 hour.

(b) Use the mobile phase as described below.

(c) Apply 1 µL of each solution.

(d) Develop the plate to 15 cm.

(e) After removal of the plate, allow it to dry in a current of air and examine under *ultraviolet light (365 nm)*.

MOBILE PHASE

6 volumes of *water*, 35 volumes of *methanol* and 59 volumes of *dichloromethane*.

SYSTEM SUITABILITY

The test is not valid unless the chromatogram obtained with solution (3) shows three clearly separated spots.

CONFIRMATION

The principal spot in the chromatogram obtained with solution (1) corresponds to that in the chromatogram obtained with solution (2).

B. To a quantity of the oral powder containing 10 mg of Chlortetracycline Hydrochloride add 20 mL of warm *ethanol (96%)*, allow to stand for 20 minutes, filter and evaporate to dryness on a water bath. A 0.1% w/v solution of the residue in *phosphate buffer pH 7.6*, when heated at 100° for 1 minute, exhibits a strong blue fluorescence in ultraviolet light.

Tetracycline hydrochloride and 4-epichlortetracycline hydrochloride
Not more than 8.0% and 6.0% respectively, determined as described under the Assay. Inject separately solutions (1) and (4).

ASSAY

Carry out the method for *liquid chromatography*, Appendix III D, using the following solutions.

(1) Mix a quantity of the oral powder containing 25 mg of Chlortetracycline Hydrochloride with 50 mL of 0.01M *hydrochloric acid*, shake for 10 minutes, dilute to 100 mL with 0.01M *hydrochloric acid* and filter (GF/C paper is suitable).

(2) 0.025% w/v of *chlortetracycline hydrochloride BPCRS* in 0.01M *hydrochloric acid*.

(3) 0.025% w/v of each of *chlortetracycline hydrochloride BPCRS* and *4-epichlortetracycline hydrochloride EPCRS* in 0.01M *hydrochloric acid*.

(4) 0.002% w/v of *tetracycline hydrochloride BPCRS* and 0.0015% w/v of *4-epichlortetracycline hydrochloride EPCRS* in 0.01M *hydrochloric acid*.

CHROMATOGRAPHIC CONDITIONS

(a) Use a stainless steel column (25 cm × 4.6 mm) packed with *end-capped octadecylsilyl silica gel for chromatography* (10 μm) (Nucleosil C18 is suitable).

(b) Use isocratic elution and the mobile phase described below.

(c) Use a flow rate of 2 mL per minute.

(d) Use a column temperature of 40°.

(e) Use a detection wavelength of 355 nm.

(f) Inject 20 μL of each solution.

MOBILE PHASE

20 volumes of *dimethylformamide* and 80 volumes of 0.1M *oxalic acid* the pH of which has been adjusted to 2.2 with *triethylamine*.

SYSTEM SUITABILITY

The Assay is not valid unless, in the chromatogram obtained with solution (3), the *resolution factor* between the two principal peaks is at least 1.5.

DETERMINATION OF CONTENT

Calculate the content of $C_{22}H_{23}ClN_2O_8,HCl$ in the oral powder using the declared content of $C_{22}H_{23}ClN_2O_8,HCl$ in *chlortetracycline hydrochloride BPCRS*.

Chlortetracycline Tablets

Action and use
Tetracycline antibacterial.

DEFINITION
Chlortetracycline Tablets contain Chlortetracycline Hydrochloride.

The tablets comply with the requirements stated under Tablets and with the following requirements.

Content of chlortetracycline hydrochloride, $C_{22}H_{23}ClN_2O_8,HCl$
95.0 to 110.0% of the stated amount.

IDENTIFICATION
A. Carry out the method for *thin-layer chromatography*, Appendix III A, using the following solutions.

(1) Extract a quantity of the powdered tablets containing 10 mg of Chlortetracycline Hydrochloride with 20 mL of *methanol* and centrifuge.

(2) 0.05% w/v of *chlortetracycline hydrochloride BPCRS* in *methanol*.

(3) 0.05% w/v of each of *chlortetracycline hydrochloride BPCRS, tetracycline hydrochloride BPCRS* and *metacycline hydrochloride BPCRS* in *methanol*.

CHROMATOGRAPHIC CONDITIONS

(a) Use *silica gel H* as the coating. Adjust the pH of a 10% w/v solution of *disodium edetate* to 8.0 with 10M *sodium hydroxide* and spray the solution evenly onto the plate (about 10 mL for a plate 100 mm × 200 mm). Allow the plate to dry in a horizontal position for at least 1 hour. At the time of use, dry the plate in an oven at 110° for 1 hour.

(b) Use the mobile phase as described below.

(c) Apply 1 μL of each solution.

(d) Develop the plate to 15 cm.

(e) After removal of the plate, allow it to dry in a current of air and examine under *ultraviolet light (365 nm)*.

MOBILE PHASE

6 volumes of *water*, 35 volumes of *methanol* and 59 volumes of *dichloromethane*.

SYSTEM SUITABILITY

The test is not valid unless the chromatogram obtained with solution (3) shows three clearly separated spots.

CONFIRMATION

The principal spot in the chromatogram obtained with solution (1) corresponds to that in the chromatogram obtained with solution (2).

B. To a quantity of the powdered tablets containing 10 mg of Chlortetracycline Hydrochloride add 20 mL of warm *ethanol (96%)*, allow to stand for 20 minutes, filter and evaporate to dryness on a water bath. A 0.1% w/v solution of the residue in *phosphate buffer pH 7.6*, when heated at 100° for 1 minute, exhibits a strong blue fluorescence in ultraviolet light.

TESTS
Tetracycline hydrochloride and 4-epichlortetracycline hydrochloride
Not more than 8.0% and 6.0% respectively, determined as described under Assay. Inject separately solutions (1) and (4).

Dissolution
Comply with the requirements for Monographs of the British Pharmacopoeia in the *dissolution test for tablets and capsules*, Appendix XII B1.

TEST CONDITIONS

(a) Use Apparatus 2, rotating the paddle at 50 revolutions per minute.

(b) Use 900 mL of 0.1M *hydrochloric acid*, at a temperature of 37°, as the medium.

PROCEDURE

After 45 minutes withdraw a 10 mL sample of the medium and filter. Measure the *absorbance* of the filtered sample, suitably diluted with the dissolution medium if necessary, at the maximum at 266 nm, Appendix II B, using 0.1M *hydrochloric acid* in the reference cell.

DETERMINATION OF CONTENT

Calculate the total content of chlortetracycline hydrochloride, $C_{22}H_{23}ClN_2O_8,HCl$, in the medium taking 346 as the value of A(1%, 1 cm) at the maximum at 266 nm.

ASSAY
Weigh and powder 20 tablets. Carry out the method for *liquid chromatography*, Appendix III D, using the following solutions.

(1) Mix a quantity of the powdered tablets containing 25 mg of Chlortetracycline Hydrochloride with 50 mL of 0.01M *hydrochloric acid*, shake for 10 minutes, dilute to 100 mL with 0.01M *hydrochloric acid* and filter (GF/C paper is suitable).

(2) 0.025% w/v of *chlortetracycline hydrochloride BPCRS* in 0.01M *hydrochloric acid*.

(3) 0.025% w/v of each of *chlortetracycline hydrochloride BPCRS* and *4-epichlortetracycline hydrochloride EPCRS* in 0.01M *hydrochloric acid*.

(4) 0.002% w/v of *tetracycline hydrochloride BPCRS* and 0.0015% w/v of *4-epichlortetracycline hydrochloride EPCRS* in 0.01M *hydrochloric acid*.

CHROMATOGRAPHIC CONDITIONS

(a) Use a stainless steel column (25 cm × 4.6 mm) packed with *end-capped octadecylsilyl silica gel for chromatography* (10 μm) (Nucleosil C18 is suitable).

(b) Use isocratic elution and the mobile phase described below.

(c) Use a flow rate of 2 mL per minute.

(d) Use a column temperature of 40°.

(e) Use a detection wavelength of 355 nm.

(f) Inject 20 μL of each solution.

MOBILE PHASE

20 volumes of *dimethylformamide* and 80 volumes of 0.1M *oxalic acid* the pH of which has been adjusted to 2.2 with *triethylamine*.

SYSTEM SUITABILITY

The assay is not valid unless, in the chromatogram obtained with solution (3), the *resolution factor* between the two principal peaks is at least 1.5.

DETERMINATION OF CONTENT

Calculate the content of $C_{22}H_{23}ClN_2O_8,HCl$ in the tablets using the declared content of $C_{22}H_{23}ClN_2O_8,HCl$ in *chlortetracycline hydrochloride BPCRS*.

Cloprostenol Injection

Action and use
Prostaglandin ($PGF_{2\alpha}$) analogue.

DEFINITION
Cloprostenol Injection is a sterile solution of Cloprostenol Sodium in Water for Injections.

The injection complies with the requirements stated under Parenteral Preparations and with the following requirements.

Content of cloprostenol, $C_{22}H_{29}ClO_6$
90.0 to 110.0% of the stated amount.

IDENTIFICATION
In the Assay, the chromatogram obtained with solution (1) shows a peak with the same retention time as the peak due to cloprostenol in the chromatogram obtained with solution (2).

Related substances
Carry out the method for *liquid chromatography*, Appendix III D, using the following solutions.

(1) Dilute the injection, if necessary, in *absolute ethanol* to contain the equivalent of 0.009% w/v of cloprostenol.

(2) 0.00018% w/v of *cloprostenol sodium BPCRS* in *absolute ethanol*.

(3) Dissolve 5 mg of *hydrocortisone acetate BPCRS* and 2.5 mg of *cloprostenol sodium BPCRS* in *absolute ethanol* and dilute to 10 mL with the mobile phase.

CHROMATOGRAPHIC CONDITIONS

(a) Use a stainless steel column (25 cm × 5 mm) packed with *base-deactivated octadecylsilyl silica gel for chromatography* (Waters Symmetry ODS is suitable).

(b) Use isocratic elution and the mobile phase described below.

(c) Use a flow rate of 1.8 mL per minute.

(d) Use an ambient column temperature.

(e) Use a detection wavelength of 220 nm.

(f) Inject 20 μL of each solution.

(g) For solutions (1) and (2) allow the chromatography to proceed for 1.5 times the retention time of the principal peak.

MOBILE PHASE

270 volumes of *acetonitrile* and 730 volumes of a solution containing 0.24% w/v of *sodium dihydrogen orthophosphate* the pH of which has been adjusted to 2.5 with *orthophosphoric acid*.

SYSTEM SUITABILITY

The test is not valid unless, in the chromatogram obtained with solution (3), the *resolution factor* between the peak due to hydrocortisone acetate (retention time about 25 minutes) and that of cloprostenol (retention time about 35 minutes) is at least 6.

LIMITS

In the chromatogram obtained with solution (1) the sum of the areas of any *secondary peaks* is not more than 1.25 times the area of the principal peak in the chromatogram obtained with solution (2) (2.5%).

ASSAY
Carry out the method for *liquid chromatography*, Appendix III D, using the following solutions.

(1) Dilute the injection, if necessary, in *absolute ethanol* to contain the equivalent of 0.009% w/v of cloprostenol.

(2) 0.009% w/v of *cloprostenol sodium BPCRS* in *absolute ethanol*.

(3) Dissolve 5 mg of *hydrocortisone acetate BPCRS* and 2.5 mg of *cloprostenol sodium BPCRS* in *absolute ethanol* and dilute to 10 mL with the mobile phase.

CHROMATOGRAPHIC CONDITIONS

The chromatographic conditions described under Related substances may be used.

SYSTEM SUITABILITY

The test is not valid unless, in the chromatogram obtained with solution (3), the *resolution factor* between the peak due to hydrocortisone acetate (retention time about 25 minutes) and that of cloprostenol (retention time about 35 minutes) is at least 6.

DETERMINATION OF CONTENT

Calculate the content of $C_{22}H_{29}ClO_6$ in the injection using the declared content of $C_{22}H_{29}ClO_6$ in *cloprostenol sodium BPCRS*.

STORAGE
Cloprostenol Sodium Injection should be protected from light.

LABELLING
The quantity of active ingredient is stated in terms of the equivalent amount of cloprostenol in a suitable dose-volume.

Cloxacillin Benzathine Intramammary Infusion (Dry Cow)

Cloxacillin Intramammary Infusion (DC)

Action and use
Penicillin antibacterial.

DEFINITION
Cloxacillin Benzathine Intramammary Infusion (Dry Cow) is a sterile suspension of Cloxacillin Benzathine in a suitable non-aqueous vehicle containing suitable suspending agents.

The intramammary infusion complies with the requirements stated under Intramammary Infusions and with the following requirements.

Content of cloxacillin, $C_{19}H_{18}ClN_3O_5S$
90.0 to 110.0% of the stated amount.

IDENTIFICATION
Extract a quantity of the infusion containing the equivalent of 75 mg of cloxacillin with three 15-mL quantities of *petroleum spirit (boiling range, 120° to 160°)*, discard the extracts, wash the residue with *ether* and dry in a current of air. The residue obtained complies with the following tests.

A. The *infrared absorption spectrum*, Appendix II A, is concordant with the *reference spectrum* of cloxacillin benzathine *(RSV 12)*.

B. Shake 50 mg with 1 mL of 1M *sodium hydroxide* for 2 minutes, add 2 mL of *ether*, shake for 1 minute and allow to separate. Evaporate 1 mL of the ether layer to dryness, dissolve the residue in 2 mL of *glacial acetic acid* and add 1 mL of *dilute potassium dichromate solution*. A golden yellow precipitate is produced.

Water
Not more than 2.0% w/w, Appendix IX C. Use 3 g and a mixture of 70 volumes of *chloroform* and 30 volumes of *anhydrous methanol* as solvent.

ASSAY
Express, as far as possible, weigh and mix the contents of 10 containers. Extract a quantity of the mixed contents containing the equivalent of 80 mg of cloxacillin, with three 15 mL quantities of *petroleum spirit (boiling range, 120° to 160°)* previously saturated with *cloxacillin benzathine*. Discard the extract, wash the residue with *ether* previously saturated with *cloxacillin benzathine*, dry in a current of air, dissolve in 25 mL of *methanol* and dilute to 50 mL with *water*. Dilute 2 mL to 100 mL with *buffered copper sulfate solution pH 2.0*, transfer 10 mL to a stoppered test tube and heat in a water bath at 70° for 20 minutes. Rapidly cool to room temperature, dilute to 20 mL with *absolute ethanol* and measure the *absorbance* of the resulting solution at the maximum at 338 nm, Appendix II B, using in the reference cell 10 mL of the unheated buffered solution of the substance being examined, diluted to 20 mL with *absolute ethanol*.

Calculate the content of $C_{19}H_{18}ClN_3O_5S$ in a container of average content from the *absorbance* obtained by carrying out the procedure simultaneously using 2 mL of a solution prepared by dissolving 105 mg of *cloxacillin benzathine BPCRS* in 50 mL of a mixture of equal volumes of *methanol* and *water* and from the declared content of $C_{19}H_{18}ClN_3O_5S$ in *cloxacillin benzathine BPCRS*.

LABELLING
The quantity of active ingredient is stated in terms of the equivalent amount of cloxacillin.

Cloxacillin Sodium Intramammary Infusion (Lactating Cow)

Cloxacillin Intramammary Infusion (LC)

Action and use
Penicillin antibacterial.

DEFINITION
Cloxacillin Sodium Intramammary Infusion (Lactating Cow) is a sterile suspension of Cloxacillin Sodium in a suitable non-aqueous vehicle containing suitable suspending and dispersing agents.

The intramammary infusion complies with the requirements stated under Intramammary Infusions and with the following requirements.

Content of cloxacillin, $C_{19}H_{18}ClN_3O_5S$
90.0 to 110.0% of the stated amount.

IDENTIFICATION
Extract a quantity containing the equivalent of 75 mg of cloxacillin with three 15-mL quantities of *petroleum spirit (boiling range, 120° to 160°)*. Discard the extracts, wash the residue with *ether* and dry in a current of air. The residue obtained complies with the following tests.

A. The *infrared absorption spectrum*, Appendix II A, is concordant with the *reference spectrum* of cloxacillin sodium *(RSV 13)*.

B. Yields the reactions characteristic of *sodium salts*, Appendix VI.

Water
Not more than 1.0% w/w, Appendix IX C. Use 3 g and a mixture of 70 volumes of *chloroform* and 30 volumes of *anhydrous methanol* as the solvent.

ASSAY
Express, as far as possible, weigh and mix the contents of 10 containers. Carry out the method for *liquid chromatography*, Appendix III D, using the following solutions.

(1) Extract a quantity of the mixed contents of the 10 containers containing the equivalent of 50 mg of cloxacillin with 15 mL of *petroleum spirit (boiling range, 120° to 160°)*, centrifuge and discard the supernatant liquid. Repeat the extraction with a further two 15-mL quantities of *petroleum spirit (boiling range, 120° to 160°)*. Shake the residue with 20 mL of *ether*, centrifuge and dry in a current of air until the solvents have evaporated. Dissolve the final residue in sufficient of the mobile phase to produce 50 mL and dilute 5 volumes of the resulting solution to 50 volumes with mobile phase.

(2) 0.011% w/v of *cloxacillin sodium BPCRS* in the mobile phase.

(3) 0.01% w/v of each of *cloxacillin sodium BPCRS* and *flucloxacillin sodium BPCRS* in the mobile phase.

CHROMATOGRAPHIC CONDITIONS

(a) Use a stainless steel column (25 cm × 4.6 mm) packed with *octadecylsilyl silica gel for chromatography* (5 μm) (Hypersil 5 ODS is suitable).

(b) Use isocratic elution and the mobile phase described below.

(c) Use a flow rate of 1 mL per minute.

(d) Use an ambient column temperature.

(e) Use a detection wavelength of 225 nm.

(f) Inject 20 μL of each solution.

MOBILE PHASE

25 volumes of *acetonitrile* and 75 volumes of a 0.27% w/v solution of *potassium dihydrogen orthophosphate* adjusted to pH 5.0 with 2M *sodium hydroxide*.

SYSTEM SUITABILITY

The test is not valid unless, in the chromatogram obtained with solution (3), the *resolution factor* between the first peak (cloxacillin) and the second peak (flucloxacillin) is at least 2.5.

DETERMINATION OF CONTENT

Calculate the content of $C_{19}H_{18}ClN_3O_5S$ in a container of average content weight using the declared content of $C_{19}H_{17}ClN_3NaO_5S$ in *cloxacillin sodium BPCRS*. Each mg of $C_{19}H_{17}ClN_3NaO_5S$ is equivalent to 0.9520 mg of $C_{19}H_{18}ClN_3O_5S$.

LABELLING

The quantity of active ingredient is stated in terms of the equivalent amount of cloxacillin.

Co-trimazine Injection

Trimethoprim and Sulfadiazine Injection

Action and use

Dihydrofolate reductase inhibitor + sulfonamide antibacterial.

DEFINITION

Co-trimazine Injection is a sterile suspension in Water for Injections containing Trimethoprim and Sulfadiazine in the proportion one part to five parts.

PRODUCTION

Co-trimazine Injection is prepared by the addition, with aseptic precautions, of sterile Trimethoprim to a solution of sulfadiazine sodium previously sterilised by *filtration*.
The solution of sulfadiazine sodium is prepared by the interaction of Sulfadiazine and Sodium Hydroxide.

The injection complies with the requirements stated under Parenteral Preparations and with the following requirements.

Content of trimethoprim, $C_{14}H_{18}N_4O_3$

90.0 to 110.0% of the stated amount.

Content of sulfadiazine, $C_{10}H_{10}N_4O_2S$

90.0 to 110.0% of the stated amount.

CHARACTERISTICS

A suspension of an almost white solid in a pale straw-coloured solution.

IDENTIFICATION

A. The light absorption, Appendix II B, in the range 250 to 325 nm of the solution obtained in the Assay for trimethoprim exhibits a maximum only at 271 nm.

B. Carry out the method for *thin-layer chromatography*, Appendix III A, using the following solutions.

(1) Ensure that the injection is homogeneous by gently inverting the container several times. To 2.5 mL of the well mixed injection add 4 mL of *hydrochloric acid* and dilute to 50 mL with 1.4M *methanolic ammonia*.

(2) 2.0% w/v of *sulfadiazine BPCRS* in 1.4M *methanolic ammonia*.

(3) 0.4% w/v of *trimethoprim BPCRS* in 1.4M *methanolic ammonia*.

CHROMATOGRAPHIC CONDITIONS

(a) Use as the coating silica gel F_{254}.

(b) Use the mobile phase as described below.

(c) Apply 1 µL of each solution.

(d) Develop the plate to 15 cm.

(e) After removal of the plate, dry in air and examine under *ultraviolet light (254 nm)*.

MOBILE PHASE

5 volumes of *water*, 15 volumes of *dimethylformamide* and 75 volumes of *ethyl acetate*.

CONFIRMATION

In the chromatogram obtained with solution (1):

one of the principal spots in the chromatogram obtained with solution (1) corresponds to the principal spot in the chromatogram obtained with solution (2);

the other principal spot corresponds to the principal spot in the chromatogram obtained with solution (3).

C. To 5 mL of the filtrate obtained in the Assay for sulfadiazine add 10 mL of *water* and 5 mL of *thiobarbituric acid-citrate buffer*, mix and heat on a water bath for 30 minutes. A pink colour is produced.

Alkalinity

pH, 10.0 to 10.5, Appendix V L.

ASSAY

For trimethoprim

Extract the chloroform solution reserved in the Assay for sulfadiazine with three quantities, of 100, 50 and 50 mL, of 1M *acetic acid* and dilute the combined extracts to 500 mL with 1M *acetic acid*. To 5 mL add 35 mL of 1M *acetic acid* and sufficient *water* to produce 200 mL and measure the *absorbance* of the resulting solution at the maximum at 271 nm, Appendix II B. Calculate the content of $C_{14}H_{18}N_4O_3$ taking 204 as the value of A(1%, 1 cm) at the maximum at 271 nm.

For sulfadiazine

Disperse the trimethoprim evenly throughout the injection by gently inverting the container several times, avoiding the formation of foam. Transfer a quantity of the injection containing the equivalent of 2 g of Sulfadiazine to a separating funnel containing 50 mL of 0.1M *sodium hydroxide* and extract with two quantities, of 100 mL and 50 mL, of *chloroform*, washing the extract with the same 25 mL quantity of 0.1M *sodium hydroxide*. Reserve the combined chloroform extracts for the Assay for trimethoprim.

Dilute the combined aqueous solutions and washings to 250 mL with *water*, filter and dilute 5 mL of the filtrate to 200 mL with *water*. Dilute 10 mL of this solution to 100 mL with *water*. To 3 mL of the resulting solution add 1 mL of 2M *hydrochloric acid* and 1 mL of a 0.1% w/v solution of *sodium nitrite* and allow to stand for 2 minutes. Add 1 mL of a 0.5% w/v solution of *ammonium sulfamate* and allow to stand for 3 minutes. Add 1 mL of a 0.1% w/v solution of N-*(1-naphthyl)ethylenediamine dihydrochloride*, allow to stand for 10 minutes, add sufficient *water* to produce 25 mL and measure the *absorbance* of the resulting solution at 538 nm, Appendix II B. Repeat the operation using 3 mL of a solution prepared by dissolving 0.2 g of *sulfadiazine BPCRS* in 50 mL of 0.1M *sodium hydroxide*, adding sufficient *water* to produce 200 mL, diluting 5.0 mL of the resulting solution to 250 mL with *water* and beginning at the words 'add 1 mL of 2M *hydrochloric acid* ...'. Calculate the content of $C_{10}H_{10}N_4O_2S$ in the injection from the absorbances obtained using the declared content of $C_{10}H_{10}N_4O_2S$ in *sulfadiazine BPCRS*.

When trimethoprim and sulfadiazine injection is prescribed or demanded, Co-trimazine Injection shall be dispensed or supplied.

Co-trimazine Veterinary Oral Powder

Trimethoprim and Sulfadiazine Veterinary Oral Powder

Action and use

Dihydrofolate reductase inhibitor + sulfonamide antibacterial.

DEFINITION

Co-trimazine Veterinary Oral Powder consists of Trimethoprim and Sulfadiazine in the proportion of one part to five parts mixed with suitable wetting, dispersing and suspending agents.

The veterinary oral powder complies with the requirements stated under Veterinary Oral Powders and with the following requirements.

Content of trimethoprim, $C_{14}H_{18}N_4O_3$

92.5 to 107.5% of the stated amount.

Content of sulfadiazine, $C_{10}H_{10}N_4O_2S$

92.5 to 107.5% of the stated amount.

IDENTIFICATION

Carry out the method for *thin-layer chromatography*, Appendix III A, using the following solutions.

(1) Shake a quantity of the powder containing 0.2 g of Sulfadiazine with sufficient 1.4M *methanolic ammonia* to produce 100 mL, centrifuge and use the supernatant liquid.

(2) Shake a quantity of the powder containing 0.2 g of Trimethoprim with sufficient 1.4M *methanolic ammonia* to produce 100 mL, centrifuge and use the supernatant liquid.

(3) 0.2% w/v solution of *sulfadiazine BPCRS* in 1.4M *methanolic ammonia*.

(4) 0.2% w/v solution of *trimethoprim BPCRS* in 1.4M *methanolic ammonia*.

(5) Mix equal volumes of solutions (3) and (5).

CHROMATOGRAPHIC CONDITIONS

(a) Use as the coating *silica gel GF$_{254}$*.

(b) Use the mobile phase as described below.

(c) Apply 5 μL of each solution.

(d) Develop the plate to 15 cm.

(e) After removal of the plate, dry in a current of air, spray with a 0.1% w/v solution of *4-dimethylaminobenzaldehyde* in a mixture of 1 mL of *hydrochloric acid* and 100 mL of *ethanol (96%)*, allow to dry and spray with *dilute potassium iodobismuthate solution*.

MOBILE PHASE

5 volumes of *water*, 15 volumes of *dimethylformamide* and 75 volumes of *ethyl acetate*.

SYSTEM SUITABILITY

The test is not valid unless the chromatogram obtained with solution (5) shows two clearly separated spots.

CONFIRMATION

The spot in the chromatogram obtained with solution (1) with an Rf value of about 0.7 corresponds to the principal spot in the chromatogram obtained with solution (3) and the spot in the chromatogram obtained with solution (2) with an Rf value of about 0.3 corresponds to the principal spot in the chromatogram obtained with solution (4).

ASSAY

For trimethoprim

Extract the combined chloroform extracts from the Assay for sulfadiazine with four 50-mL quantities of a 5% v/v solution of 6M *acetic acid*. Wash the combined aqueous extracts with 5 mL of *chloroform*, discard the chloroform layer and dilute to 250 mL with a 5% v/v solution of 6M *acetic acid*. Dilute 20 mL to 100 mL with *water*. Determine the *absorbance* of the resulting solution at the maximum at 271 nm, Appendix II B, and calculate the content of $C_{14}H_{18}N_4O_3$ taking 204 as the value of A(1%, 1 cm) at the maximum at 271 nm.

For sulfadiazine

Transfer a quantity of the powder containing 0.125 g of Sulfadiazine to a separating funnel containing 20 mL of 0.1M *sodium hydroxide* and extract with four 50-mL quantities of *chloroform*. Wash each chloroform extract with the same two 10-mL quantities of 0.1M *sodium hydroxide*. Combine the aqueous washings and the aqueous layer from the separating funnel and reserve the combined chloroform extracts for the Assay for trimethoprim. Dilute the combined aqueous solutions to 250 mL with *water*, filter and dilute 10 mL of the filtrate to 200 mL with *water*. To 2 mL of the resulting solution add 0.5 mL of 4M *hydrochloric acid* and 1 mL of a 0.1% w/v solution of *sodium nitrite* and allow to stand for 2 minutes. Add 1 mL of a 0.5% w/v solution of *ammonium sulfamate* and allow to stand for 3 minutes. Add 1 mL of a 0.1% w/v solution of *N-(1-naphthyl)-ethylenediamine dihydrochloride*, allow to stand for 10 minutes and dilute to 25 mL with *water*. Measure the *absorbance* of the resulting solution at the maximum at 538 nm, Appendix II B, using in the reference cell a solution prepared at the same time and in the same manner using 2 mL of *water* and beginning at the words 'add 0.5 mL of 4M *hydrochloric acid*...'. Calculate the content of $C_{10}H_{10}N_4O_2S$ from the *absorbance* obtained by repeating the operation with 2 mL of a 0.0025% w/v solution of *sulfadiazine BPCRS* in 0.0005M *sodium hydroxide* and beginning at the words 'add 0.5 mL of 4M *hydrochloric acid* ...'.

When trimethoprim and sulfadiazine veterinary oral powder is prescribed or demanded, Co-trimazine Veterinary Oral Powder shall be dispensed or supplied.

Co-trimazine Tablets

Trimethoprim and Sulfadiazine Tablets

Action and use

Dihydrofolate reductase inhibitor + sulfonamide antibacterial.

DEFINITION

Co-trimazine Tablets contain Trimethoprim and Sulfadiazine in the proportion one part to five parts.

The tablets comply with the requirements stated under Tablets and with the following requirements.

Content of trimethoprim, $C_{14}H_{18}N_4O_3$

92.5 to 107.5% of the stated amount.

Content of sulfadiazine, $C_{10}H_{10}N_4O_2S$

92.5 to 107.5% of the stated amount.

IDENTIFICATION

Comply with the test described under Co-trimazine Oral Suspension using solutions prepared in the following manner as solutions (1) and (2). For solution (1) shake a quantity of the finely powdered tablets containing 0.2 g of Sulfadiazine with sufficient 1.4M *methanolic ammonia* to produce 100 mL, centrifuge and use the supernatant liquid. For solution (2) shake a quantity of the finely powdered tablets containing 0.2 g of Trimethoprim with sufficient 1.4M *methanolic ammonia* to produce 100 mL, centrifuge and use the supernatant liquid.

ASSAY

Weigh and finely powder 20 tablets.

For trimethoprim

Carry out the Assay for trimethoprim described under Co-trimazine Veterinary Oral Powder.

For sulfadiazine

Carry out the Assay for sulfadiazine described under Co-trimazine Veterinary Oral Powder using a quantity of the powdered tablets containing 0.125 g of Sulfadiazine. Repeat the operation using 2 mL of a 0.0025% w/v solution of *sulfadiazine BPCRS* in 0.0005M *sodium hydroxide* beginning at the words 'add 0.5 mL of 4M *hydrochloric acid* . . .'. Calculate the content of $C_{10}H_{10}N_4O_2S$ in the oral suspension from the absorbances obtained using the declared content of $C_{10}H_{10}N_4O_2S$ in *sulfadiazine BPCRS*.

When trimethoprim and sulfadiazine tablets are prescribed or demanded, Co-trimazine Tablets shall be dispensed or supplied.

Decoquinate Premix

Action and use

Antiprotozoal (veterinary).

DEFINITION

Decoquinate Premix contains Decoquinate.

The premix complies with the requirements stated under Premixes and with the following requirements.

Content of decoquinate, $C_{24}H_{35}NO_5$

95.0 to 105.0% of the stated amount.

IDENTIFICATION

Carry out the method for *thin-layer chromatography*, Appendix III A, using the following solutions.

(1) Heat a quantity containing 0.1 g of Decoquinate with 40 mL of *chloroform* for 20 minutes on a water bath under a reflux condenser, cool and filter.

(2) 0.25% w/v of *decoquinate BPCRS* in *chloroform*.

CHROMATOGRAPHIC CONDITIONS

(a) Use as the coating *silica gel GF₂₅₄*.

(b) Use the mobile phase as described below.

(c) Apply 10 µL of each solution.

(d) Develop the plate to 15 cm.

(e) After removal of the plate, dry in air and examine under *ultraviolet light (254 nm)*.

MOBILE PHASE

30 volumes of *ethanol (96%)* and 70 volumes of *chloroform*.

CONFIRMATION

The principal spot in the chromatogram obtained with solution (1) corresponds in position and colour to that in the chromatogram obtained with solution (2).

ASSAY

Heat a quantity containing 0.2 g of Decoquinate with 50 mL of *chloroform* in an apparatus for the *continuous extraction of drugs*, Appendix XI F, for eight reflux cycles. Cool and add sufficient *chloroform* to produce 100 mL. Dilute 5 mL to 100 mL with *absolute ethanol*. To 5 mL add 10 mL of 0.1M *hydrochloric acid* and dilute to 100 mL with *absolute ethanol*. Measure the *absorbance* of the resulting solution at the maximum at 265 nm, Appendix II B. Dissolve 50 mg of *decoquinate BPCRS* in 10 mL of hot *chloroform* and, keeping the solution warm, add slowly 70 mL of *absolute ethanol*. Cool, dilute to 100 mL with *absolute ethanol* and immediately dilute 10 mL to 100 mL with *absolute ethanol*. To 10 mL of the resulting solution add 10 mL of 0.1M *hydrochloric acid* and dilute to 100 mL with *absolute ethanol*. Calculate the content of $C_{24}H_{35}NO_5$ in the premix from the absorbances obtained using the declared content of $C_{24}H_{35}NO_5$ in *decoquinate BPCRS*.

Deltamethrin Pour-on

Action and use

Insecticide (veterinary).

DEFINITION

Deltamethrin Pour-on is a *pour-on solution*. It contains Deltamethrin in a suitable, oily vehicle.

The pour-on complies with the requirements stated under Veterinary Liquid Preparations for Cutaneous Application and with the following requirements.

Content of deltamethrin, $C_{22}H_{19}Br_2NO_3$

90.0 to 110.0% of the stated amount.

IDENTIFICATION

In the Assay, the chromatogram obtained with solution (1) shows a peak with the same retention time as the peak in the chromatogram obtained with solution (2).

ASSAY

Carry out the method for *liquid chromatography*, Appendix III D, using the following solutions.

(1) Mix a weighed quantity of the preparation being examined containing 30 mg of Deltamethrin with sufficient *hexane* to produce 100 mL. Dilute 1 volume to 4 volumes with *hexane*.

(2) 0.0075% w/v of *deltamethrin BPCRS* in *hexane*.

(3) 0.0075% w/v of *deltamethrin impurity standard BPCRS* in *hexane*.

CHROMATOGRAPHIC CONDITIONS

(a) Use a stainless steel column (25 cm × 4.6 mm) packed with particles of silica the surface of which has been modified with chemically-bonded nitro-phenyl groups (5 µm) (Nucleosil-NO2 is suitable).

(b) Use isocratic elution and the mobile phase described below.

(c) Use a flow rate of 2 mL per minute.

(d) Use an ambient column temperature.

(e) Use a detection wavelength of 230 nm.

(f) Inject 20 µL of each solution.

MOBILE PHASE

hexane containing 0.25% v/v of *propan-2-ol*.

SYSTEM SUITABILITY

The test is not valid unless, in the chromatogram obtained with solution (3), a peak due to (R)-deltamethrin appears immediately before the principal peak, as indicated in the reference chromatogram supplied with *deltamethrin impurity standard BPCRS*.

DETERMINATION OF CONTENT

Determine the *weight per mL* of the preparation, Appendix V G, and calculate the content of $C_{22}H_{19}Br_2NO_3$, weight in volume, using the declared content of $C_{22}H_{19}Br_2NO_3$ in *deltamethrin BPCRS*.

Diprenorphine Injection

Action and use
Opioid receptor antagonist.

DEFINITION

Diprenorphine Injection is a sterile solution of Diprenorphine Hydrochloride in Water for Injections containing Methylthioninium Chloride (methylene blue). The pH is adjusted to about 4.

The injection complies with the requirements stated under Parenteral Preparations and with the following requirements.

Content of diprenorphine, $C_{26}H_{35}NO_4$
90.0 to 110.0% of the stated amount.

IDENTIFICATION

Carry out the method for *thin-layer chromatography*, Appendix III A, in subdued light using *silica gel GF$_{254}$* as the coating substance and a mixture of 10 volumes of *diethylamine*, 20 volumes of *ethyl acetate* and 70 volumes of *toluene* as the mobile phase. Apply separately to each half of the plate 10 µL of each of the following solutions. For solution (1) add 3 mL of 5M *ammonia* to a volume containing the equivalent of 0.5 mg of diprenorphine, mix and extract with two 5 mL quantities of *chloroform*. Combine the chloroform extracts, shake with 1 g of *anhydrous sodium sulfate*, filter, evaporate to dryness using a rotary evaporator and dissolve the residue in 0.4 mL of *chloroform*. Solution (2) contains 0.115% w/v of *diprenorphine BPCRS* in *chloroform*. Add to each point of application of solution (2) 10 µL of a mixture of 4 volumes of *methanol* and 1 volume of 13.5M *ammonia*. After removal of the plate, allow it to dry in air and examine under *ultraviolet light (254 nm)*. Spray one half of the plate with a mixture of 5 volumes of *chloroplatinic acid solution*, 35 volumes of *dilute potassium iodide solution* and 60 volumes of *acetone*. Spray the other half of the plate with a mixture of 1 volume of *iron(III) chloride solution R1* and 1 volume of *dilute potassium hexacyanoferrate(III) solution*. The spot in the chromatogram obtained with solution (1) corresponds in position, quenching and colour to that in the chromatogram obtained with solution (2).

TESTS
Acidity
pH, 3.5 to 4.5, Appendix V L.

ASSAY

For an injection containing the equivalent of more than 0.1% w/v of diprenorphine Dissolve 50 mg of *phenolphthalein* (internal standard) in sufficient *methanol* to produce 20 mL (solution A). Carry out the method for *gas chromatography*, Appendix III B, using the following solutions. For solution (1) add 2 mL of solution A to 2 mL of a 0.30% w/v solution of *diprenorphine BPCRS* in *methanol* and evaporate the solvent using a rotary evaporator. To the dried residue add 1 mL of a mixture of 8 volumes of *dimethylformamide*, 2 volumes of N,O-*bis(trimethylsilyl)acetamide* and 1 volume of

trimethylchlorosilane and allow to stand for 30 minutes. Prepare solution (2) in a similar manner to solution (3) but omitting the addition of solution A. For solution (3) add 2 mL of 5M *ammonia* to a volume containing the equivalent of 6 mg of diprenorphine and extract with three 7 mL quantities of *chloroform*. To the combined extracts add 2 mL of solution A, shake with 2 g of *anhydrous sodium sulfate*, filter and evaporate the filtrate to dryness using a rotary evaporator; treat the dried residue as described for solution (1).

The chromatographic procedure may be carried out using a glass column (1.5 m × 4 mm) packed with *acid-washed, silanised, diatomaceous support* (80 to 100 mesh) coated with 2% w/w of *methyl silicone gum* (SE 30 is suitable) and maintained at 245°.

Calculate the content of $C_{26}H_{35}NO_4$ using the declared content of $C_{26}H_{35}NO_4$ in *diprenorphine BPCRS*.

For an injection containing the equivalent of 0.1% w/v or less of diprenorphine Carry out the Assay described above, but dissolving 50 mg of *phenolphthalein* (internal standard) in sufficient *methanol* to produce 100 mL (solution A) and using the following solutions. For solution (1) add 2 mL of solution A to 5 mL of a 0.027% w/v solution of *diprenorphine BPCRS* in *methanol* and evaporate the solvent using a rotary evaporator; to the dried residue add 1 mL of a mixture of 8 volumes of *dimethylformamide*, 2 volumes of N,O-*bis(trimethylsilyl)acetamide* and 1 volume of *trimethylchlorosilane* and allow to stand for 30 minutes. Prepare solution (2) in a similar manner to solution (3) but omitting the addition of solution A. For solution (3) add 2 mL of 5M *ammonia* to a volume containing the equivalent of 1.36 mg of diprenorphine and extract with three 10 mL quantities of *chloroform*; to the combined extracts add 2 mL of solution A, shake with 3 g of *anhydrous sodium sulfate*, filter and evaporate the filtrate to dryness; treat the dried residue as described for solution (1).

LABELLING

The quantity of active ingredient is stated in terms of the equivalent amount of diprenorphine in a suitable dose-volume.

STORAGE

Diprenorphine Injection should be protected from light.

Etamiphylline Injection

Action and use
Non-selective phosphodiesterase inhibitor (xanthine); treatment of reversible airways obstruction.

DEFINITION

Etamiphylline Injection is a sterile solution of Etamiphylline Camsilate in Water for Injections.

The injection complies with the requirements stated under Parenteral Preparations and with the following requirements.

Content of etamiphylline camsilate, $C_{13}H_{21}N_5O_2,C_{10}H_{16}O_4S$
95.0 to 105.0% of the stated amount.

IDENTIFICATION

Prepare a quantity of the residue as described in the Assay. The residue complies with the following tests.

A. The *infrared absorption spectrum*, Appendix II A, is concordant with the *reference spectrum* of etamiphylline (*RSV 19*).

B. Yields the reactions characteristic of *xanthines*, Appendix VI.

TESTS

Acidity

pH, 3.9 to 5.4, Appendix V L.

Related substances

Carry out the method for *thin-layer chromatography*, Appendix III A, using the following solutions.

(1) Dilute the injection with sufficient *water* to produce a solution containing 3.5% w/v of Etamiphylline Camsilate.

(2) Dilute 1 volume of solution (1) to 500 volumes with *water*.

CHROMATOGRAPHIC CONDITIONS

(a) Use as the coating *silica gel HF$_{254}$*.

(b) Use the mobile phase as described below.

(c) Apply 10 µl of each solution.

(d) Develop the plate to 15 cm.

(e) After removal of the plate, allow it to dry in air and examine under *ultraviolet light (254 nm)*.

MOBILE PHASE

1 volume of 13.5M *ammonia*, 20 volumes of *ethanol (96%)* and 80 volumes of *chloroform*.

LIMITS

Any *secondary spot* in the chromatogram obtained with solution (1) is not more intense than the spot in the chromatogram obtained with solution (2) (0.2%).

ASSAY

To a volume containing 0.7 g of Etamiphylline Camsilate add 15 mL of *water*, make alkaline with 5M *ammonia* and extract with three 25-mL quantities of *chloroform*, washing each extract with the same 5-mL quantity of *water*. Evaporate the combined extracts to dryness, dissolve the residue in 25 mL of *water* and titrate with 0.05M *sulfuric acid VS* using *bromocresol green solution* as indicator. Each mL of 0.05M *sulfuric acid VS* is equivalent to 51.16 mg of $C_{13}H_{21}N_5O_2,C_{10}H_{16}O_4S$.

Etamiphylline Tablets

Action and use

Non-selective phosphodiesterase inhibitor (xanthine); treatment of reversible airways obstruction.

DEFINITION

Etamiphylline Tablets contain Etamiphylline Camsilate. They are coated.

The tablets comply with the requirements stated under Tablets and with the following requirements.

Content of etamiphylline camsilate, $C_{13}H_{21}N_5O_2,C_{10}H_{16}O_4S$

95.0 to 105.0% of the stated amount.

IDENTIFICATION

Prepare a quantity of the residue as described in the Assay. The residue complies with the following tests.

A. The *infrared absorption spectrum*, Appendix II A, is concordant with the *reference spectrum* of etamiphylline (*RSV 19*).

B. Yields the reactions characteristic of *xanthines*, Appendix VI.

Related substances

Carry out the method for *thin-layer chromatography*, Appendix III A, using the following solutions.

(1) Shake a quantity of the powdered tablets containing 0.2 g of Etamiphylline Camsilate with 5 mL of *methanol* and centrifuge.

(2) Dilute 1 volume of solution (1) to 500 volumes with *methanol*.

CHROMATOGRAPHIC CONDITIONS

(a) Use as the coating *silica gel HF$_{254}$*.

(b) Use the mobile phase as described below.

(c) Apply 10 µL of each solution.

(d) Develop the plate to 15 cm.

(e) After removal of the plate, allow it to dry in air and examine under *ultraviolet light (254 nm)*.

MOBILE PHASE

1 volume of 13.5M *ammonia*, 20 volumes of *ethanol (96%)* and 80 volumes of *chloroform*.

LIMITS

Any *secondary spot* in the chromatogram obtained with solution (1) is not more intense than the spot in the chromatogram obtained with solution (2) (0.2%).

ASSAY

Weigh and powder 20 tablets. Dissolve a quantity of the powder containing 0.5 g of Etamiphylline Camsilate in 30 mL of *water*, make alkaline with 5M *ammonia* and extract with three 25-mL quantities of *chloroform*, washing each chloroform extract with the same 5-smL quantity of *water*. Evaporate the combined chloroform extracts to dryness, dissolve the residue in 25 mL of *water* and titrate with 0.05M *sulfuric acid VS* using *bromocresol green solution* as indicator. Each mL of 0.05M *sulfuric acid VS* is equivalent to 51.16 mg of $C_{13}H_{21}N_5O_2,C_{10}H_{16}O_4S$.

Etorphine and Acepromazine Injection

Action and use

Opioid receptor agonist; analgesic.

DEFINITION

Etorphine and Acepromazine Injection is a sterile solution of Etorphine Hydrochloride and Acepromazine Maleate in Water for Injections containing a suitable antimicrobial preservative. The pH is adjusted to about 4.

The injection complies with the requirements stated under Parenteral Preparations and with the following requirements.

Content of etorphine hydrochloride, $C_{25}H_{33}NO_4,HCl$

0.22 to 0.27% w/v.

Content of acepromazine maleate, $C_{19}H_{22}N_2OS,C_4H_4O_4$

0.90 to 1.10% w/v.

CHARACTERISTICS

A clear, yellow solution.

IDENTIFICATION

A. The *light absorption*, Appendix II B, in the range 230 to 350 nm of a solution prepared by diluting a volume of the injection containing 10 mg of Acepromazine Maleate to 500 mL with *water* exhibits well-defined maxima at 242 nm and at 280 nm. The *absorbances* at the maxima are about 1.1 and about 0.85, respectively.

B. Carry out the method for *thin-layer chromatography*, Appendix III A, in subdued light using *silica gel GF$_{254}$* as the coating substance and *ethyl acetate* as the mobile phase and applying separately to each half of the plate 10 μL of each of two solutions containing (1) the injection being examined and (2) 0.09% w/v of *diprenorphine BPCRS* in *chloroform*. Add to each point of application 10 μL of a mixture of 4 volumes of *methanol* and 1 volume of 13.5M *ammonia*. After removal of the plate, allow it to dry in air and examine under *ultraviolet light (254 nm)*. Spray one half of the plate with a mixture of 5 volumes of *chloroplatinic acid solution*, 35 volumes of *dilute potassium iodide solution* and 60 volumes of *acetone*. Spray the other half of the plate with a mixture of 1 volume of *iron(III) chloride solution R1* and 1 volume of *dilute potassium hexacyanoferrate(III) solution*. The principal spot in the chromatogram obtained with solution (1) has an Rf value of about 1.15 relative to that of the spot in the chromatogram obtained with solution (2), absorbs ultraviolet light and yields a reddish violet colour with the iodoplatinate spray reagent and a blue colour with the iron-hexacyanoferrate spray reagent.

TESTS
Acidity
pH, 3.5 to 4.5, Appendix V L.

ASSAY
For etorphine hydrochloride
Dissolve 46 mg of *diprenorphine BPCRS* (internal standard) in sufficient *methanol* to produce 10 mL (solution A). Carry out the method for *gas chromatography*, Appendix III B, using the following solutions. For solution (1) add 1 mL of solution A to 2 mL of the injection and 2 mL of 5M *ammonia*, extract with three 7-mL quantities of *chloroform*, shake the combined extracts with 2 g of *anhydrous sodium sulfate*, filter and evaporate the filtrate to a small volume using a rotary evaporator. Transfer the contents to a stoppered test tube with the aid of 2 mL of *chloroform* and evaporate to dryness. To the residue add 1 mL of a mixture of 8 volumes of *dimethylformamide*, 2 volumes of N,O-*bis(trimethylsilyl)- acetamide* and 1 volume of *trimethylchlorosilane* and allow to stand for 15 minutes. For solution (2) treat a volume of the injection containing 4.9 mg of Etorphine Hydrochloride in a similar manner but omitting the addition of solution A. Protect the solutions from light during preparation and subsequent use.

The chromatographic procedure may be carried out using a glass column (1.5 m × 4 mm) packed with *acid-washed, silanised diatomaceous support* (80 to 100 mesh) coated with 2% w/w of methyl silicone gum (SE 30 is suitable) and maintained at 245°.

Calculate the content of $C_{25}H_{33}NO_4$ using the declared content of $C_{26}H_{35}NO_4$ in *diprenorphine BPCRS* assuming that the trimethylsilyl derivatives of equal weights of etorphine and diprenorphine have the same response in the flame ionisation detector and hence calculate the content of $C_{25}H_{33}NO_4,HCl$ taking each mg of $C_{25}H_{33}NO_4$ to be equivalent to 1.089 mg of $C_{25}H_{33}NO_4,HCl$.

For acepromazine maleate
Protect the solutions from light throughout the Assay. To 1 mL add sufficient *ethanol (96%)* to produce 100 mL. Measure the *absorbance*, Appendix II B, of the resulting solution at the maximum at 370 nm. Calculate the content of $C_{19}H_{22}N_2OS,C_4H_4O_4$ taking 46.1 as the value of A(1%, 1 cm) at the maximum at 370 nm.

STORAGE
Etorphine and Acepromazine Injection should be protected from light.

Fenbendazole Granules

Action and use
Antihelminthic.

DEFINITION
Fenbendazole Granules contain Fenbendazole mixed with suitable diluents.

The granules comply with the requirements stated under Granules and with the following requirements.

Content of fenbendazole, $C_{15}H_{13}N_3O_2S$
95.0 to 105.0% of the stated amount.

IDENTIFICATION
A. In the Assay, the retention time of the principal peak in the chromatogram obtained with solution (1) is the same as that of the principal peak in the chromatogram obtained with solution (2).

B. Carry out the method for thin-layer chromatography, Appendix III A, using the following solutions.

(1) Mix with the aid of ultrasound a quantity of the powdered granules containing 80 mg of Fenbendazole with 80 mL of 0.1M *methanolic hydrochloric acid* for 90 minutes, cool, dilute to 100 mL with 0.1M *methanolic hydrochloric acid*, mix, filter through a 0.4-μm filter (Whatman GF/C is suitable) and use the filtrate.

(2) 0.08% w/v of *fenbendazole BPCRS* in 0.1M *methanolic hydrochloric acid*.

CHROMATOGRAPHIC CONDITIONS

(a) Use a TLC silica gel F$_{254}$ plate (Merck silica gel F$_{254}$ plates are suitable).

(b) Use the mobile phase as described below.

(c) Apply 5 μL of each solution.

(d) Develop the plate to 10 cm.

(e) After removal of the plate, dry in air for 10 minutes, heat at 100° for 5 minutes and examine under *ultraviolet light (254 nm and 365 nm)*.

MOBILE PHASE

2.5 volumes of *water*, 6.5 volumes of *acetone*, 26 volumes of 13.5M *ammonia* and 65 volumes of *toluene*.

CONFIRMATION

By each method of visualisation the principal spot in the chromatogram obtained with solution (1) corresponds to that in the chromatogram obtained with solution (2).

TESTS
Related impurities A, B and 1
Carry out the method for *liquid chromatography*, Appendix III D, using the following solutions.

(1) Mix, with the aid of ultrasound, a quantity of the powdered granules containing 0.1 g of Fenbendazole with 50 mL of 0.1M *methanolic hydrochloric acid* for 30 minutes, cool, dilute to 100 mL with *methanol (65%)*, mix and filter through a glass-fibre filter (Whatman GF/C is suitable).

(2) Dilute 1 volume of a 0.001% w/v solution of *fenbendazole impurity A EPCRS* (methyl (1*H*-benzimidazol-2-yl)carbamate) in 0.1M *methanolic hydrochloric acid* to 2 volumes with *methanol (65%)*.

(3) Dilute 1 volume of a 0.001% w/v solution of *fenbendazole impurity B EPCRS* (methyl (5-chloro-1*H*-benzimidazol-2-yl)carbamate) in 0.1M *methanolic hydrochloric acid* to 2 volumes with *methanol (65%)*.

(4) Dilute 1 volume of a 0.0010% w/v solution of *fenbendazole impurity 1 BPCRS* (5-phenylthio)-2-aminobenzimidazole) in 0.1M *methanolic hydrochloric acid* to 2 volumes with *methanol (65%)*.

(5) Dilute 1 volume of a solution containing 0.002% w/v each of *fenbendazole impurity A EPCRS, fenbendazole impurity B EPCRS, fenbendazole impurity 1 BPCRS* and *0.20% w/v of fenbendazole BPCRS* in 0.1M *methanolic hydrochloric acid* to 2 volumes with *methanol (65%)*.

CHROMATOGRAPHIC CONDITIONS

(a) Use a stainless steel column (25 cm × 4.6 mm) packed with *octadecylsilyl silica gel for chromatography* (5 μm) (Nucleosil C18 is suitable).

(b) Use isocratic elution and the mobile phase described below.

(c) Use a flow rate of 1 mL per minute.

(d) Use an ambient column temperature.

(e) Use a detection wavelength of 280 nm.

(f) Inject 20 μL of each solution.

MOBILE PHASE

350 volumes of a 0.5% w/v solution of *sodium dihydrogen orthophosphate* and 650 volumes of *methanol* containing 1.88 g of *sodium hexanesulfonate*, the pH of which has been adjusted to 3.5 with *orthophosphoric acid*.

SYSTEM SUITABILITY

The test is not valid unless the chromatogram obtained with solution (5) closely resembles the reference chromatogram supplied with *fenbendazole BPCRS*.

LIMITS

In the chromatogram obtained with solution (1):

the areas of any peaks corresponding to fenbendazole impurity A, fenbendazole impurity B and fenbendazole impurity 1 (5-(phenylthio)-2-aminobenzimidazole) are not greater than the areas of the corresponding peaks in the chromatograms obtained with solutions (2), (3) and (4) respectively (0.5% each).

ASSAY

Carry out the method for *liquid chromatography*, Appendix III D, using the following solutions.

(1) Mix with the aid of ultrasound a quantity of the powdered granules containing 0.1 g of Fenbendazole with 50 mL of 0.1M *methanolic hydrochloric acid* for 30 minutes, cool, dilute to 100 mL with *methanol (65%)*, mix, filter through a glass-fibre filter (Whatman GF/C is suitable). Dilute 5 volumes of the resulting solution to 50 volumes with 0.1M *hydrochloric acid* in *methanol (85%)*.

(2) 0.01% w/v of *fenbendazole BPCRS* in a mixture of 1 volume of 0.1M *hydrochloric acid* and 1 volume of *methanol (85%)*.

CHROMATOGRAPHIC CONDITIONS

The chromatographic procedure described under Related substances may be used.

DETERMINATION OF CONTENT

Calculate the content of $C_{15}H_{13}N_3O_2S$ in the granules using the declared content of $C_{15}H_{13}N_3O_2S$, in *fenbendazole BPCRS*.

IMPURITIES

The impurities limited by the requirements of this monograph include impurities A and B listed under Fenbendazole and the following:

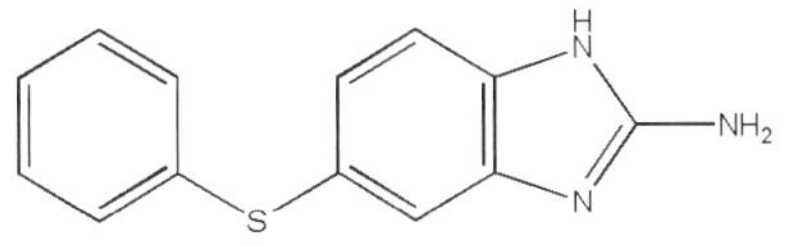

1. (5-phenylthio)-2-aminobenzimidazole.

Fenbendazole Oral Suspension

Action and use
Antihelminthic.

DEFINITION

Fenbendazole Oral Suspension is an aqueous suspension of Fenbendazole.

The oral suspension complies with the requirements stated under Oral Liquids and with the following requirements.

Content of fenbendazole, $C_{15}H_{13}N_3O_2S$
95.0 to 105.0% of the stated amount.

IDENTIFICATION

In the Assay, the retention time of the principal peak in the chromatogram obtained with solution (1) is the same as that of the principal peak in the chromatogram obtained with solution (2).

TESTS
Related impurities A, B and 1
Carry out the method for *liquid chromatography*, Appendix III D, using the following solutions.

(1) Mix with the aid of ultrasound, a quantity of the oral suspension containing 0.1 g of Fenbendazole with 50 mL of 0.1M *methanolic hydrochloric acid* for 30 minutes, cool, dilute to 100 mL with *methanol (65%)*, mix and filter through a glass-fibre filter (Whatman GF/C is suitable).

(2) Dilute 1 volume of a 0.001% w/v solution of *fenbendazole impurity A EPCRS* (methyl (1*H*-benzimidazol-2-yl)carbamate) in 0.1M *methanolic hydrochloric acid* to 2 volumes with *methanol (65%)*.

(3) Dilute 1 volume of a 0.001% w/v solution of *fenbendazole impurity B EPCRS* (methyl(5-chloro-1*H*-benzimidazol-2-yl)carbamate) in 0.1M *methanolic hydrochloric acid* to 2 volumes with *methanol (65%)*.

(4) Dilute 1 volume of a 0.001% w/v solution of *fenbendazole impurity 1 BPCRS* ((5-phenylthio)-2-aminobenzimidazole) in 0.1M *methanolic hydrochloric acid* to 2 volumes with *methanol (65%)*.

(5) Dilute 1 volume of a solution containing 0.002% w/v each of *fenbendazole impurity A EPCRS, fenbendazole impurity B EPCRS, fenbendazole impurity 1 BPCRS* and 0.20% w/v of *fenbendazole BPCRS* in 0.1M *methanolic hydrochloric acid* to 2 volumes with *methanol (65%)*.

CHROMATOGRAPHIC CONDITIONS

(a) Use a stainless steel column (25 cm × 4.6 mm) packed with *octadecylsilyl silica gel for chromatography* (5 μm) (Nucleosil C18 is suitable).

(b) Use isocratic elution and the mobile phase described below.

(c) Use a flow rate of 1 mL per minute.

(d) Use an ambient column temperature.

(e) Use a detection wavelength of 280 nm.

(f) Inject 20 μL of each solution.

MOBILE PHASE

350 volumes of a 0.5% w/v solution of *sodium dihydrogen orthophosphate* and 650 volumes of *methanol* containing 1.88 g of *sodium hexanesulfonate*, the pH of which has been adjusted to 3.5 with *orthophosphoric acid*.

SYSTEM SUITABILITY

The test is not valid unless the chromatogram obtained with solution (5) closely resembles the reference chromatogram supplied with *fenbendazole BPCRS*.

LIMITS

In the chromatogram obtained with solution (1):

the area of any peak corresponding to fenbendazole impurity A (methyl (1*H*-benzimidazol-2-yl)carbamate) is not greater than the area of the corresponding peak in the chromatogram obtained with solution (2), (0.5%);

the area of any peak corresponding to fenbendazole impurity B (methyl(5-chloro-1*H*-benzimidazol-2-yl)carbamate) is not greater than the area of the corresponding peak in the chromatogram obtained with solution (3) (0.5%);

the area of any peak corresponding to fenbendazole impurity 1 ((5-phenylthio)-2-aminobenzimidazole) is not greater than the area of the corresponding peak in the chromatogram obtained with solution (4) (0.5%).

ASSAY

Carry out the method for *liquid chromatography*, Appendix III D, using the following solutions.

(1) Mix with the aid of ultrasound a quantity of the oral suspension containing 0.1 g of Fenbendazole with 50 mL of 0.1M *methanolic hydrochloric acid* for 30 minutes, cool, dilute to 100 mL with *methanol (65%)*, mix and filter through a glass-fibre filter (Whatman GF/C is suitable). Dilute 5 volumes of the resulting solution to 50 volumes with 0.1M *hydrochloric acid* in *methanol (85%)*.

(2) 0.01% w/v of *fenbendazole BPCRS* in a mixture of 1 volume of 0.1M *hydrochloric acid* and 1 volume of *methanol (85%)*.

CHROMATOGRAPHIC CONDITIONS

The chromatographic conditions described under Related substances may be used.

SYSTEM SUITABILITY

The test is not valid unless the chromatogram obtained with solution (5) closely resembles the reference chromatogram supplied with *fenbendazole BPCRS*.

DETERMINATION OF CONTENT

Calculate the content of $C_{15}H_{13}N_3O_2S$ in the oral suspension from the chromatogram obtained and using the declared content of $C_{15}H_{13}N_3O_2S$ in *fenbendazole BPCRS*.

IMPURITIES

The impurities limited by the requirements of this monograph include impurities A and B listed under Fenbendazole and the following:

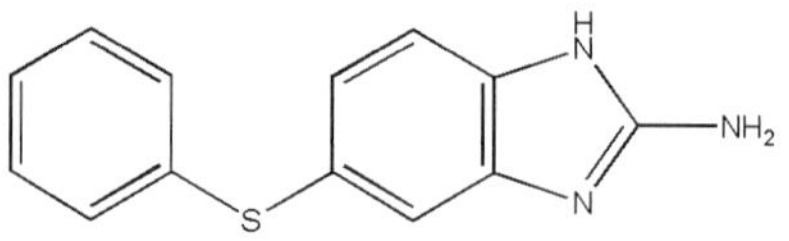

1. (5-phenylthio)-2-aminobenzimidazole.

Fenbendazole Veterinary Oral Paste

Fenbendazole Veterinary Paste

Action and use

Antihelminthic.

DEFINITION

Fenbendazole Veterinary Oral Paste contains Fenbendazole finely dispersed in a suitable basis.

The veterinary oral paste complies with the requirements stated under Veterinary Oral Pastes and with the following requirements.

Content of fenbendazole, $C_{15}H_{13}N_3O_2S$

95.0 to 105.0% of the stated amount.

IDENTIFICATION

In the Assay, the retention time of the principal peak in the chromatogram obtained with solution (1) is the same as that of the principal peak in the chromatogram obtained with solution (2).

TESTS

Related impurities A, B and 1

Carry out the method for *liquid chromatography*, Appendix III D, using the following solutions.

(1) Mix with the aid of ultrasound, a quantity of the oral paste containing 0.1 g of Fenbendazole with 50 mL of 0.1M *methanolic hydrochloric acid* for 30 minutes, cool, dilute to 100 mL with *methanol (65%)*, mix, filter through a glass-fibre filter (Whatman GF/C is suitable).

(2) Dilute 1 volume of a 0.001% w/v solution of *fenbendazole impurity A EPCRS* (methyl (1*H*-benzimidazole-2-yl)carbamate) in 0.1M *methanolic hydrochloric acid* to 2 volumes with *methanol (65%)*.

(3) Dilute 1 volume of a 0.001% w/v solution of *fenbendazole impurity B EPCRS* (methyl (5-chloro-1*H*-benzimidazole-2-yl)carbamate) in 0.1M *methanolic hydrochloric acid* to 2 volumes with *methanol (65%)*.

(4) Dilute 1 volume of a 0.001% w/v solution of *fenbendazole impurity 1 BPCRS*((5-phenylthio)-2-aminobenzimidazole) in 0.1M *methanolic hydrochloric acid* to 2 volumes with *methanol (65%)*.

(5) Dilute 1 volume of a solution containing 0.002% w/v each of *fenbendazole impurity A EPCRS, fenbendazole impurity B EPCRS, fenbendazole impurity 1 BPCRS* and 0.20% w/v of *fenbendazole BPCRS* in 0.1M *methanolic hydrochloric acid* to 2 volumes with *methanol (65%)*.

CHROMATOGRAPHIC CONDITIONS

(a) Use a stainless steel column (25 cm × 4.6 mm) packed with *octadecylsilyl silica gel for chromatography* (5 μm) (Nucleosil C18 is suitable).

(b) Use isocratic elution and the mobile phase described below.

(c) Use a flow rate of 1 mL per minute.

(d) Use an ambient column temperature.

(e) Use a detection wavelength of 280 nm.

(f) Inject 20 μL of each solution.

MOBILE PHASE

350 volumes of a 0.5% w/v solution of *sodium dihydrogen orthophosphate* and 650 volumes of *methanol* containing 1.88 g of *sodium hexanesulfonate*, the pH of which has been adjusted to 3.5 with *orthophosphoric acid*

SYSTEM SUITABILITY

The test is not valid unless the chromatogram obtained with solution (5) closely resembles the reference chromatogram supplied with *fenbendazole BPCRS*.

LIMITS

In the chromatogram obtained with solution (1):

the area of any peaks corresponding to fenbendazole impurity A (methyl (1*H*-benzimidazol-2-yl)carbamate), fenbendazole impurity B (methyl (5-chloro-1*H*-benzimidazol-2-yl)carbamate) and fenbendazole impurity 1 ((5-phenylthio)-2-aminobenzimidazole) are not greater than the areas of the corresponding peaks in the chromatograms obtained with solutions (2), (3) and (4) respectively (0.5% each).

ASSAY

Carry out the method for *liquid chromatography*, Appendix III D, using the following solutions.

(1) Mix with the aid of ultrasound a quantity of the oral paste containing 0.1 g of Fenbendazole with 50 mL of 0.1M *methanolic hydrochloric acid* for 30 minutes, cool, dilute to 100 mL with *methanol* (65%), mix, filter through a glass-fibre filter (Whatman GF/C is suitable). Dilute 5 volumes of the resulting solution to 50 volumes with 0.1M *hydrochloric acid* in *methanol* (85%).

(2) 0.01% w/v of *fenbendazole BPCRS* in a mixture of 1 volume of 0.1M *hydrochloric acid* and 1 volume of *methanol* (85%).

CHROMATOGRAPHIC CONDITIONS

The chromatographic conditions described under Related impurities A, B and 1 may be used.

DETERMINATION OF CONTENT

Calculate the content of $C_{15}H_{13}N_3O_2S$ in the veterinary oral paste from the chromatograms obtained and using the declared content of $C_{15}H_{13}N_3O_2S$ in *fenbendazole BPCRS*.

IMPURITIES

The impurities limited by the requirements of this monograph include impurities A and B listed under Fenbendazole and the following:

1. (5-phenylthio)-2-aminobenzimidazole.

Serum Gonadotrophin Injection

Action and use
Equine serum gonadotrophin.

DEFINITION
Serum Gonadotrophin Injection is a sterile solution of Serum Gonadotrophin in Water for Injections. It is prepared by dissolving Serum Gonadotrophin for Injection in the requisite amount of Water for Injections immediately before use.

The injection complies with the requirements stated under Parenteral Preparations.

STORAGE
Serum Gonadotrophin Injection should be used immediately after preparation.

SERUM GONADOTROPHIN FOR INJECTION

DEFINITION
Serum Gonadotrophin for Injection is a sterile material consisting of Serum Gonadotrophin with or without excipients. It is supplied in a sealed container.

The contents of the sealed container comply with the requirements for Powders for Injections or Infusions stated under Parenteral Preparations and with the following requirements.

Potency
For each container tested, the estimated potency is not less than 80% and not more than 125% of the stated potency

CHARACTERISTICS
A white or pale grey, amorphous powder.

Soluble in *water*.

IDENTIFICATION
Causes enlargement of the ovaries of immature female rats when administered as directed in the Assay.

TESTS
Clarity, colour and acidity or alkalinity of solution
A solution containing 5000 IU per mL is *clear*, Appendix IV A, Method I, and *colourless*, Appendix IV B, Method I, and has a pH of 6.0 to 8.0, Appendix V L.

Water
Not more than 10.0% w/w, Appendix IX C. Use 80 mg.

Bacterial endotoxins
Carry out the *test for bacterial endotoxins*, Appendix XIV C, using Method C. Dissolve the contents of the sealed container in *water BET* to give a solution containing 1000 IU of serum gonadotrophin per mL (solution A). The endotoxin limit concentration of solution A is 35 IU of endotoxin per mL. Carry out the test using a suitable dilution of solution A as described under Method C.

ASSAY
Carry out the Assay described under Serum Gonadotrophin. The fiducial limits of error are not less than 64% and not more than 156% of the stated potency.

STORAGE
The sealed container should be protected from light and stored at a temperature not exceeding 8°.

Griseofulvin Premix

Action and use
Antifungal.

DEFINITION
Griseofulvin Premix contains Griseofulvin. The particles of Griseofulvin are generally up to 5 μm in maximum dimension, although larger particles, which may occasionally exceed 30 μm, may be present.

The premix complies with the requirements stated under Premixes and with the following requirements.

Content of griseofulvin, $C_{17}H_{17}ClO_6$
90.0 to 110.0% of the stated amount.

IDENTIFICATION
A. Shake a quantity of the premix containing 0.1 g of Griseofulvin with 10 mL of *chloroform*. Centrifuge, decant the supernatant liquid, dry with *anhydrous sodium sulfate* and evaporate the chloroform. The *infrared absorption spectrum* of the residue, Appendix II A, is concordant with the *reference spectrum* of griseofulvin *(RSV 24)*.

B. Shake a quantity of the premix containing 80 mg of Griseofulvin with 150 mL of *ethanol (96%)*. Dilute to 200 mL with *ethanol (96%)* and centrifuge. Dilute 2 mL of the supernatant liquid to 100 mL with *ethanol (96%)*. The *light absorption* of the resulting solution, Appendix II B, in the range 240 to 350 nm, exhibits two maxima at 291 nm and at 325 nm and a shoulder at 250 nm.

C. Dissolve 5 mg of the residue obtained in test A in 1 mL of *sulfuric acid* and add 5 mg of powdered *potassium dichromate*. A wine red colour is produced.

Related substances
Carry out the method for *gas chromatography*, Appendix III B, using the following solutions. Dissolve 50 mg of *9,10-diphenylanthracene* (internal standard) in sufficient *chloroform* to produce 50 mL (solution A).

(1) Add 60 mL of *chloroform* to a quantity of the premix containing 50 mg of Griseofulvin, heat at 60° with shaking for 20 minutes, cool and dilute to 100 mL with *chloroform*. Centrifuge and evaporate 20 mL of the supernatant liquid to about 1 mL.

(2) Prepare solution (2) in the same manner as solution (1) but adding 1 mL of solution A before diluting to 100 mL with *chloroform*.

(3) Dissolve 5 mg of *griseofulvin BPCRS* in *chloroform*, add 2 mL of solution A and sufficient *chloroform* to produce 200 mL. Evaporate 20 mL of the solution to about 1 mL.

CHROMATOGRAPHIC CONDITIONS

(a) Use a glass column (1 m × 4 mm) packed with *acid-washed, silanised diatomaceous support* (100 to 120 mesh) coated with 1% w/w of cyanopropylmethyl phenylmethyl silicone fluid (OV 225 is suitable).

(b) Use *nitrogen* as the carrier gas at a flow rate of 50 to 60 mL per minute.

(c) Use isothermal conditions maintained at 250°.

(d) Use an inlet temperature of 270°.

(e) Use a flame ionisation detector at a temperature of 300°.

(f) Inject a suitable volume of each solution.

(g) For solution (1), allow the chromatography to proceed for 3 times the retention time of griseofulvin.

When the chromatograms are recorded under the prescribed conditions the retention time of griseofulvin is about

11 minutes. The retention times relative to griseofulvin are: dechlorogriseofulvin, about 0.6; dehydrogriseofulvin, about 1.4.

LIMITS

Using the chromatogram obtained with solution (3), calculate the ratio (R) of the area of the peak due to griseofulvin to the area of the peak due to the internal standard.

In the chromatogram obtained with solution (2):

the ratio of the area of any peak due to dechlorogriseofulvin to the area of the peak due to the internal standard is not greater than $0.6R$ (3%);

the ratio of the area of any peak due to dehydrogriseofulvin to the area of the peak due to the internal standard is not greater than $0.15R$ (0.75%).

ASSAY
To a quantity containing 35 mg of Griseofulvin add 60 mL of *ethyl acetate*, mix, heat to 60° and shake for 15 minutes. Allow to cool and dilute to 100 mL with *ethyl acetate*. Centrifuge and transfer two 5 mL aliquots of the clear supernatant liquid into separate 100 mL graduated flasks. To the first flask add 5.0 mL of a 13% v/v solution of *methanesulfonic acid* in *methanol*, allow to stand at 20° for 30 minutes and dilute to 100 mL with *methanol* (solution A). Dilute the contents of the second flask to 100 mL with *methanol* (solution B). To a third flask add 5.0 mL of the methanolic methanesulfonic acid solution and dilute to 100 mL with *methanol* (solution C). Measure the *absorbance* of each solution at 266 nm, Appendix II B. Calculate the content of $C_{17}H_{17}ClO_6$ from the difference between the absorbance obtained with solution A and the sum of the absorbances obtained with solutions B and C and from the difference obtained by repeating the operation using 35 mg of *griseofulvin BPCRS* in place of the preparation being examined and from the declared content of $C_{17}H_{17}ClO_6$ in *griseofulvin BPCRS*.

Ivermectin Injection

Action and use
Antihelminthic.

DEFINITION
Ivermectin Injection is a sterile solution of Ivermectin in a suitable non-aqueous vehicle.

The injection complies with the requirements stated under Parenteral Preparations and with the following requirements.

Content of ivermectin, calculated as the sum of component H_2B_{1a} ($C_{48}H_{74}O_{14}$) and component H_2B_{1b} ($C_{47}H_{72}O_{14}$)
95.0 to 105.0% of the stated amount.

The ratio of the contents H_2B_{1a} / (H_2B_{1a} + H_2B_{1b}) is at least 90.0%.

IDENTIFICATION
A. Carry out the method for *thin-layer chromatography*, Appendix III A, using a silica gel 60 F_{254} precoated plate (Merck silica gel 60 F_{254} plates are suitable) and a mixture of 1 volume of *concentrated ammonia R1*, 9 volumes of *methanol* and 90 volumes of *dichloromethane* as the mobile phase. Apply separately to the plate 2 μL of each of the following solutions. For solution (1) dissolve a volume of the injection in sufficient *methanol* to produce a solution containing 0.05% w/v of Ivermectin; filter if necessary. Solution (2)

contains 0.05% w/v of *ivermectin BPCRS* in *methanol*. After removal of the plate, allow it to dry in air and examine under *ultraviolet light (254 nm* and *366 nm)*. The principal spot in the chromatogram obtained with solution (1) is similar in position, colour and size to that in the chromatogram obtained with solution (2).

B. In the Assay, the chromatogram obtained with solution (1) shows two principal peaks with retention times similar to those of the two principal peaks in the chromatogram obtained with solution (2).

TESTS
Clarity and colour of solution
The injection is *clear*, Appendix IV A, and not more intensely coloured than *reference solution Y_4*, Appendix IV B, Method II.

Related substances
Carry out the method for *liquid chromatography*, Appendix III D, using the following solutions. For solution (1) dissolve a volume of the injection in sufficient *methanol* to produce a solution containing 0.04% w/v of Ivermectin. Solutions (2), (3) and (4) contain 0.04% w/v, 0.0004% w/v and 0.00002% w/v respectively of *ivermectin BPCRS* in *methanol*. Inject 20 μL of each solution.

The chromatographic procedure may be carried out using (a) a stainless steel column (25 cm × 4.6 mm) packed with *octadecylsilyl silica gel for chromatography* (5 μm) (Apex ODS 1 is suitable), (b) as the mobile phase at a flow rate of 1.5 mL per minute a mixture of 39 volumes of *water*, 55 volumes of *methanol* and 106 volumes of *acetonitrile* and (c) a detection wavelength of 245 nm.

The test is not valid unless, in the chromatogram obtained with solution (2), the *resolution factor* between the first peak (component H_2B_{1b}) and the second peak (component H_2B_{1a}) is at least 3.0.

In the chromatogram obtained with solution (1) the area of any peak with a retention time of 1.3 to 1.5 relative to that of the principal peak is not greater than 2.7 times the area of the principal peak in the chromatogram obtained with solution (3) (2.7%), the area of any other *secondary peak* is not greater than the area of the principal peak in the chromatogram obtained with solution (3) (1%) and the sum of the areas of any such peaks is not greater than 6 times the area of the principal peak in the chromatogram obtained with solution (3) (6%). Disregard any peak with an area less than the area of the principal peak in the chromatogram obtained with solution (4) (0.05%).

ASSAY
Carry out the method for *liquid chromatography*, Appendix III D, using the following solutions. For solution (1) dissolve a volume of the injection in sufficient *methanol* to produce a solution containing 0.04% w/v of Ivermectin. Solution (2) contains 0.04% w/v of *ivermectin BPCRS* in *methanol*. Inject 20 μL of each solution.

The chromatographic conditions described under Related substances may be used.

Calculate the content of ivermectin (H_2B_{1a} + H_2B_{1b}) in the injection and the ratio H_2B_{1a} / (H_2B_{1a} + H_2B_{1b}) using as the declared content the contents of $C_{48}H_{74}O_{14}$ (H_2B_{1a}) and $C_{47}H_{72}O_{14}$ (H_2B_{1b}) in *ivermectin BPCRS*.

Ivermectin Oral Solution

Action and use
Antihelminthic.

DEFINITION
Ivermectin Oral Solution is a solution of Ivermectin in a suitable vehicle.

The oral solution complies with the requirements stated under Oral Liquids and with the following requirements.

Content of ivermectin, calculated as the sum of component H_2B_{1a} ($C_{48}H_{74}O_{14}$) and component H_2B_{1b} ($C_{47}H_{72}O_{14}$)
95.0 to 105.0% of the stated amount.
The ratio of the contents H_2B_{1a} / (H_2B_{1a} + H_2B_{1b}) is at least 90.0%.

IDENTIFICATION
A. Carry out the method for *thin-layer chromatography*, Appendix III A, using the following solutions.

(1) Dilute a quantity of the oral solution with sufficient *methanol* to produce a solution containing 0.05% w/v of Ivermectin.

(2) 0.05% w/v of *ivermectin BPCRS* in *methanol*.

CHROMATOGRAPHIC CONDITIONS

(a) Use as the coating *silica gel F_{254}* (Merck silica gel 60 F_{254} plates are suitable).

(b) Use the mobile phase as described below.

(c) Apply 2 μL of each solution.

(d) Develop the plate to 15 cm.

(e) After removal of the plate, dry in air and examine under *ultraviolet light (254 nm)*.

MOBILE PHASE

1 volume of *concentrated ammonia R1*, 9 volumes of *methanol* and 90 volumes of *dichloromethane*.

CONFIRMATION

The principal spot in the chromatogram obtained with solution (1) corresponds in position, colour and size to that in the chromatogram obtained with solution (2).

B. In the Assay, the chromatogram obtained with solution (1) shows peaks with the same retention times as the peaks due to Ivermectin H_2B_{1a} and Ivermectin H_2B_{1b} in the chromatogram obtained with solution (2).

TESTS
Related substances
Prepare a 0.0002% w/v solution of *moxidectin BPCRS* (internal standard) in *acetonitrile* (solution A).

Carry out the method for *liquid chromatography*, Appendix III D, using the following solutions prepared immediately before use.

(1) Dilute a weighed quantity of the oral solution containing 4 mg of Ivermectin with about 190 mL of *acetonitrile*, mix, allow to cool to room temperature and add sufficient *acetonitrile* to produce 200 mL. Dilute 5 volumes of this solution to 50 volumes with solution A. Dry a portion of the resulting solution over *anhydrous sodium sulfate* and filter through a 0.45-μm filter.

(2) Dilute 2 volumes of a 0.02% w/v solution of *ivermectin BPCRS* in *acetonitrile* to 200 volumes with solution A.

(3) Dilute 2 volumes of solution (1) to 200 volumes with *acetonitrile*.

(4) Dilute 5 volumes of solution (3) to 50 volumes with *acetonitrile*.

Derivatise the solutions prior to analysis using the following method.

Transfer 300 μL of the solution being examined to a 2-mL HPLC vial and add 130 μL of *1-methylimidazole* and mix for 5 seconds using a vortex mixer, allow to settle and mix again for 5 seconds. Add 200 μL of a 50% v/v solution of *trifluoroacetic anhydride* in *acetonitrile* and mix for 5 seconds using a vortex mixer, allow to settle and mix again for 5 seconds.

CHROMATOGRAPHIC CONDITIONS

(a) Use a stainless steel column (10 cm × 3.0 mm) packed with *octadecylsilyl silica gel for chromatography* (2.5 μm) (Phenomenex Luna C18 HST is suitable).

(b) Use isocratic elution and the mobile phase described below.

(c) Use a flow rate of 1.2 mL per minute.

(d) Use a column temperature of 40°.

(e) Use a fluorescence detector with an excitation wavelength of 365 nm and an emission wavelength of 470 nm.

(f) Inject 20 μL of each solution.

MOBILE PHASE

To 120 mL of *water* add 1.2 mL of *orthophosphoric acid* and 1.2 mL of *triethylamine*. Add 1880 mL of *acetonitrile*, mix and filter through a 0.45-μm filter.

When the chromatograms are recorded under the prescribed conditions the retention times relative to ivermectin H_2B_{1a} (retention time, about 7 minutes) are: avermectin B1, about 0.6; ivermectin H_2B_{1b}, about 0.8; ivermectin H_4B_{1a}, about 1.2).

SYSTEM SUITABILITY

The test is not valid unless:

in the chromatogram obtained with solution (2), the *resolution factor* between the peaks due to ivermectin H_2B_{1a} and ivermectin H_2B_{1b} is at least 3.0;

in the chromatogram obtained with solution (4), the *signal-to-noise ratio* of the principal peak is at least 10.

LIMITS

In the chromatogram obtained with solution (1):

the area of any *secondary peak* is not greater than 2.5 times the area of the principal peak in the chromatogram obtained with solution (3) (2.5%);

the area of not more than one *secondary peak* is greater than the area of the principal peak in the chromatogram obtained with solution (3) (1%);

the sum of the areas of all the *secondary peaks* is not greater than 5 times the area of the principal peak in the chromatogram obtained with solution (3) (5%).

Disregard any peak with an area less than the area of the principal peak in the chromatogram obtained with solution (4) (0.1%).

ASSAY

Carry out the method for *liquid chromatography*, Appendix III D, using derivatised solutions (1) and (2) described under Related substances.

CHROMATOGRAPHIC CONDITIONS

The chromatographic conditions described under Related substances may be used.

SYSTEM SUITABILITY

The test is not valid unless, in the chromatogram obtained with solution (2), the *resolution factor* between the peaks due to ivermectin H_2B_{1a} and ivermectin H_2B_{1b} is at least 3.0.

DETERMINATION OF CONTENT

Determine the *weight per ml* of the oral solution, Appendix V G, and calculate the content of ivermectin $(H_2B_{1a} + H_2B_{1b})$, weight in volume, and the ratio H_2B_{1a} / $(H_2B_{1a} + H_2B_{1b})$ using as the declared content the contents of $C_{48}H_{74}O_{14}$ (H_2B_{1a}) and $C_{47}H_{72}O_{14}$ (H_2B_{1b}) in *ivermectin BPCRS*.

Ivermectin Veterinary Oral Paste

Ivermectin Veterinary Paste

Action and use
Anthelminthic.

DEFINITION

Ivermectin Veterinary Oral Paste contains Ivermectin in a suitable basis.

The veterinary oral paste complies with the requirements stated under Veterinary Oral Pastes and with the following requirements.

Content of ivermectin, calculated as the sum of component H_2B_{1a} ($C_{48}H_{74}O_{14}$) and component H_2B_{1b} ($C_{47}H_{72}O_{14}$)

95.0 to 110.0% of the stated amount.

The ratio of the contents H_2B_{1a} / $(H_2B_{1a} + H_2B_{1b})$ is at least 90.0%.

IDENTIFICATION

A. Carry out the method for *thin-layer chromatography*, Appendix III A, using a silica gel 60 F_{254} precoated plate (Merck silica gel 60 F_{254} plates are suitable) and a mixture of 1 volume of *concentrated ammonia R1*, 9 volumes of *methanol* and 90 volumes of *dichloromethane* as the mobile phase. Apply separately to the plate 2 μL of each of the following solutions. For solution (1) add 10 mL of *methanol* to a quantity of the oral paste containing 5 mg of Ivermectin and mix with the aid of ultrasound until completely dispersed. Solution (2) contains 0.05% w/v of *ivermectin BPCRS* in *methanol*. After removal of the plate, allow it to dry in air and examine under *ultraviolet light (254 nm and 366 nm)*. The principal spot in the chromatogram obtained with solution (1) is similar in position, colour and size to that in the chromatogram obtained with solution (2).

B. In the Assay, the chromatogram obtained with solution (1) shows two principal peaks with retention times similar to those of the two principal peaks in the chromatogram obtained with solution (2).

TESTS
Related substances
Carry out the method for *liquid chromatography*, Appendix III D, using the following solutions. For solution (1) disperse a quantity of the oral paste in *methanol* with the aid of ultrasound and add sufficient *methanol* to produce a solution containing 0.04% w/v of Ivermectin. Solutions (2), (3) and (4) contain 0.04% w/v, 0.0004% w/v and 0.00002% w/v respectively of *ivermectin BPCRS* in *methanol*. Inject 20 μL of each solution.

The chromatographic procedure may be carried out using (a) a stainless steel column (25 cm × 4.6 mm) packed with *octadecylsilyl silica gel for chromatography* (5 μm) (Apex ODS 1 is suitable), (b) as the mobile phase at a flow rate of 1.5 mL per minute a mixture of 39 volumes of *water*, 55 volumes of *methanol* and 106 volumes of *acetonitrile* and (c) a detection wavelength of 245 nm.

The test is not valid unless, in the chromatogram obtained with solution (2), the *resolution factor* between the first peak (component H_2B_{1b}) and the second peak (component H_2B_{1a}) is at least 3.0.

In the chromatogram obtained with solution (1) the area of any peak with a retention time of 1.3 to 1.5 relative to that of the principal peak is not greater than 3 times the area of the principal peak in the chromatogram obtained with solution (3) (3%), the area of any other *secondary peak* is not greater than the area of the principal peak in the chromatogram obtained with solution (3) (1%) and the sum of the areas of any such peaks is not greater than 6 times the area of the principal peak in the chromatogram obtained with solution (3) (6%). Disregard any peak with an area less than the area of the principal peak in the chromatogram obtained with solution (4) (0.05%).

ASSAY

Carry out the method for *liquid chromatography*, Appendix III D, using the following solutions. For solution (1) disperse a quantity of the oral paste in *methanol* with the aid of ultrasound and add sufficient *methanol* to produce a solution containing 0.04% w/v of Ivermectin. Solution (2) contains 0.04% w/v of *ivermectin BPCRS* in *methanol*. Inject 20 μL of each solution.

The chromatographic conditions described under Related substances may be used.

Calculate the content of ivermectin (H_2B_{1a} + H_2B_{1b}) in the oral paste and the ratio H_2B_{1a} / (H_2B_{1a} + H_2B_{1b}) using as the declared content the contents of $C_{48}H_{74}O_{14}$ (H_2B_{1a}) and $C_{47}H_{72}O_{14}$ (H_2B_{1b}) in *ivermectin BPCRS*.

Ivermectin Pour-on

Action and use
Antihelminthic.

DEFINITION

Ivermectin Pour-on is a *pour-on solution*. It contains Ivermectin in a suitable non-aqueous vehicle.

The pour-on complies with the requirements stated under Veterinary Liquid Preparations for Cutaneous Application and with the following requirements.

Content of ivermectin, calculated as the sum of component H_2B_{1a} ($C_{48}H_{74}O_{14}$) and component H_2B_{1b} ($C_{47}H_{72}O_{14}$)

95.0 to 105.0% of the stated amount.

The ratio of the contents H_2B_{1a} / (H_2B_{1a} + H_2B_{1b}) is at least 90.0%.

IDENTIFICATION

A. Carry out the method for *thin-layer chromatography*, Appendix III A, using a silica gel 60 F_{254} precoated plate (Merck silica gel 60 F_{254} plates are suitable) and a mixture of 1 volume of *concentrated ammonia R1*, 9 volumes of *methanol* and 90 volumes of *dichloromethane* as the mobile phase. Apply separately to the plate 2 μL of each of the following solutions. For solution (1) dissolve a quantity of the preparation being examined in sufficient *methanol* to produce a solution containing 0.05% w/v of Ivermectin. Solution (2)

contains 0.05% w/v of *ivermectin BPCRS* in *methanol*. After removal of the plate, allow it to dry in air and examine under *ultraviolet light (254 nm* and *366 nm)*. The principal spot in the chromatogram obtained with solution (1) is similar in position, colour and size to that in the chromatogram obtained with solution (2).

B. In the Assay, the chromatogram obtained with solution (1) shows two principal peaks with retention times similar to those of the two principal peaks in the chromatogram obtained with solution (2).

TESTS
Related substances

Carry out the method for *liquid chromatography*, Appendix III D, using the following solutions. For solution (1) dissolve a quantity of the preparation being examined in sufficient *methanol* to produce a solution containing 0.04% w/v of Ivermectin. Solutions (2), (3) and (4) contain 0.04% w/v, 0.0004% w/v and 0.00002% w/v respectively of *ivermectin BPCRS* in *methanol*. Inject 20 μL of each solution.

The chromatographic procedure may be carried out using (a) a stainless steel column (25 cm × 4.6 mm) packed with *octadecylsilyl silica gel for chromatography* (5 μm) (Apex ODS 1 is suitable), (b) as the mobile phase at a flow rate of 1.5 mL per minute a mixture of 39 volumes of *water*, 55 volumes of *methanol* and 106 volumes of *acetonitrile* and (c) a detection wavelength of 245 nm.

The test is not valid unless, in the chromatogram obtained with solution (2), the *resolution factor* between the first peak (component H_2B_{1b}) and the second peak (component H_2B_{1a}) is at least 3.0.

In the chromatogram obtained with solution (1) the area of any peak with a retention time of 1.3 to 1.5 relative to that of the principal peak is not greater than 2.7 times the area of the principal peak in the chromatogram obtained with solution (3) (2.7%), the area of any other *secondary peak* is not greater than the area of the principal peak in the chromatogram obtained with solution (3) (1%) and the sum of the areas of any such peaks is not greater than 6 times the area of the principal peak in the chromatogram obtained with solution (3) (6%). Disregard any peak with an area less than the area of the principal peak in the chromatogram obtained with solution (4) (0.05%).

ASSAY

Carry out the method for *liquid chromatography*, Appendix III D, using the following solutions. For solution (1) dissolve a quantity of the preparation being examined in sufficient *methanol* to produce a solution containing 0.04% w/v of Ivermectin. Solution (2) contains 0.04% w/v of *ivermectin BPCRS* in *methanol*. Inject 20 μL of each solution.

The chromatographic conditions described under Related substances may be used.

Calculate the content of ivermectin (H_2B_{1a} + H_2B_{1b}) in the preparation being examined and the ratio H_2B_{1a} / (H_2B_{1a} + H_2B_{1b}) using as the declared content the contents of $C_{48}H_{74}O_{14}$ (H_2B_{1a}) and $C_{47}H_{72}O_{14}$ (H_2B_{1b}) in *ivermectin BPCRS*.

Levamisole Injection

Action and use
Immunostimulant; antihelminthic.

DEFINITION
Levamisole Injection is a sterile solution of Levamisole Hydrochloride in Water for Injections. It may contain suitable colouring matter.

The injection complies with the requirements stated under Parenteral Preparations and with the following requirements.

Content of levamisole hydrochloride, $C_{11}H_{12}N_2S$,HCl
92.5 to 107.5% of the stated amount.

IDENTIFICATION
A. Carry out the method for *thin-layer chromatography*, Appendix III A, using *silica gel G* as the coating substance and a mixture of 100 volumes of *ethyl acetate*, 10 volumes of *methanol* and 1 volume of 13.5M *ammonia* as the mobile phase. Apply separately to the plate 1 µL of each of the following solutions in *methanol*. For solution (1) dilute a volume of the injection to produce a solution containing 1% w/v of Levamisole Hydrochloride. Solution (2) contains 1% w/v of *levamisole hydrochloride BPCRS*. After removal of the plate, allow it to dry in air and spray with *potassium iodoplatinate solution*. The principal spot in the chromatogram obtained with solution (1) corresponds to that in the chromatogram obtained with solution (2).

B. Dilute a volume of the injection containing 0.75 g of Levamisole Hydrochloride to 20 mL with *water* and add 6 mL of 1M *sodium hydroxide*. Extract with 20 mL of *dichloromethane*, discard the aqueous layer and wash the dichloromethane layer with 10 mL of *water*. Shake with *anhydrous sodium sulfate*, filter and evaporate the dichloromethane at room temperature. The *melting point* of the residue, after drying over *phosphorus pentoxide* at a pressure of 1.5 to 2.5 kPa at a temperature not exceeding 40°, is about 59°, Appendix V A.

C. The injection is laevorotatory.

D. Yields reaction B characteristic of *chlorides*, Appendix VI.

TESTS
Acidity
pH, 3.0 to 4.0, Appendix V L.

2,3-Dihydro-6-phenylimidazo[2,1-*b*]thiazole hydrochloride
Carry out the method for *thin-layer chromatography*, Appendix III A, using *silica gel G* as the coating substance and a mixture of 8 volumes of *glacial acetic acid*, 16 volumes of *methanol* and 90 volumes of *toluene* as the mobile phase. Apply separately to the plate 10 µL of each of the following two solutions. For solution (1) dilute a volume of the injection with *methanol* to produce a solution containing 5.0% w/v of Levamisole Hydrochloride. Solution (2) contains 0.021% w/v of *2,3-dihydro-6-phenylimidazo[2,1-b]thiazole BPCRS* in *methanol*. After removal of the plate, allow it to dry in air and spray with *potassium iodoplatinate solution*. Any spot in the chromatogram obtained with solution (1) corresponding to 2,3-dihydro-6-phenylimidazo[2,1-*b*]thiazole is not more intense than the spot in the chromatogram obtained with solution (2) (0.5%).

ASSAY
To a volume of the injection containing 0.75 g of Levamisole Hydrochloride add 50 mL of *water* and 15 mL of 2M *sodium hydroxide*, extract with three quantities, of 25, 20 and 15 mL,

of *chloroform* and wash the combined extracts with two 10 mL quantities of *water*. To the combined extracts add 50 mL of *anhydrous acetic acid* and carry out Method I for *non-aqueous titration*, Appendix VIII A, using *1-naphtholbenzein solution* as indicator. Each mL of 0.1M *perchloric acid VS* is equivalent to 24.08 mg of $C_{11}H_{12}N_2S$,HCl.

STORAGE
Levamisole Injection should be protected from light.

Levamisole Oral Solution

Action and use
Immunostimulant; antihelminthic.

DEFINITION
Levamisole Oral Solution is an aqueous solution of Levamisole Hydrochloride.

The oral solution complies with the requirements stated under Oral Liquids and with the following requirements.

Content of levamisole hydrochloride, $C_{11}H_{12}N_2S$,HCl
92.5 to 107.5% of the stated amount.

IDENTIFICATION
A. Carry out the method for *thin-layer chromatography*, Appendix III A, using *silica gel G* as the coating substance and a mixture of 1 volume of 13.5M *ammonia*, 10 volumes of *methanol* and 100 volumes of *ethyl acetate* as the mobile phase. Apply separately to the plate 1 µL of each of the following solutions. For solution (1) dilute a volume of the oral solution with *methanol* to produce a solution containing 1% w/v of Levamisole Hydrochloride. Solution (2) contains 1% w/v of *levamisole hydrochloride BPCRS* in *methanol*. After removal of the plate, allow it to dry in air and spray with *potassium iodoplatinate solution*. The principal spot in the chromatogram obtained with solution (1) corresponds to that in the chromatogram obtained with solution (2).

B. To a quantity of the oral solution containing 0.3 g of Levamisole Hydrochloride add 10 mL of *water* and 6 mL of 1M *sodium hydroxide*. Extract with 20 mL of *dichloromethane*, discard the aqueous layer and wash the dichloromethane layer with 10 mL of *water*. Shake with *anhydrous sodium sulfate*, filter and evaporate the dichloromethane at room temperature. The *melting point* of the residue, after drying over *phosphorus pentoxide* at a pressure of 1.5 to 2.5 kPa at a temperature not exceeding 40°, is about 59°, Appendix V A.

C. The oral solution is laevorotatory.

2,3-Dihydro-6-phenylimidazo[2,1-*b*]thiazole hydrochloride
Carry out the method for *thin-layer chromatography*, Appendix III A, using *silica gel G* as the coating substance and a mixture of 8 volumes of *glacial acetic acid*, 16 volumes of *methanol* and 90 volumes of *toluene* as the mobile phase. Apply separately to the plate 50 µL of solution (1) and 10 µL of solution (2). For solution (1) dilute a volume of the oral solution to produce a solution containing 1.0% w/v of Levamisole Hydrochloride. Solution (2) contains 0.021% w/v of *2,3-dihydro-6-phenylimidazo[2,1-b]thiazole BPCRS* in *methanol*. After removal of the plate, allow it to dry in air and spray with *potassium iodoplatinate solution*. Any spot in the chromatogram obtained with solution (1) corresponding to 2,3-dihydro-6-phenylimidazo[2,1-*b*]thiazole is not more

intense than the spot in the chromatogram obtained with solution (2) (0.5%).

ASSAY

To a volume of the oral solution containing 0.75 g of Levamisole Hydrochloride add 15 mL of 2M *sodium hydroxide*, extract with three quantities, of 25 mL, 20 mL and 15 mL, of *chloroform*, wash the combined extracts with two 10 mL quantities of *water* and discard the washings. To the clear chloroform solution, after drying with *anhydrous sodium sulfate* if necessary, add 50 mL of *anhydrous acetic acid*. Carry out Method I for *non-aqueous titration*, Appendix VIII A, using *1-naphtholbenzein solution* as indicator. Each mL of 0.1M *perchloric acid VS* is equivalent to 24.08 mg of $C_{11}H_{12}N_2S,HCl$.

Lincomycin Premix

Action and use
Lincosamide antibacterial.

DEFINITION

Lincomycin Premix contains Lincomycin Hydrochloride.

The premix complies with the requirements stated under Premixes and with the following requirements.

Content of lincomycin, $C_{18}H_{34}N_2O_6S$
90.0 to 105.0% of the stated amount.

IDENTIFICATION

In the Assay the chromatogram obtained with solution (2) shows a peak with the same retention time as the peak due to the trimethylsilyl derivative of lincomycin in the chromatogram obtained with solution (1).

TESTS
Lincomycin B

Examine solution (3) as described in the Assay but increasing the sensitivity by eight to ten times while recording the peak due to the trimethylsilyl derivative of lincomycin B, which is eluted immediately before the trimethylsilyl derivative of lincomycin.

LIMITS

The area of the peak due to the trimethylsilyl derivative of lincomycin B, when corrected for the sensitivity factor, is not more than 5% of the area of the peak due to the trimethylsilyl derivative of lincomycin.

ASSAY

Carry out the method for *gas chromatography*, Appendix III B, using the following solutions.

(1) Add 10 mL of a 0.8% w/w solution of *dotriacontane* (internal standard) in *chloroform* to 0.1 g of *lincomycin hydrochloride BPCRS*, dilute to 100 mL with a 2% w/v solution of *imidazole* in *chloroform*, shake to dissolve and filter. Place 4 mL of the filtrate in a 15 mL ground-glass-stoppered centrifuge tube, add 1 mL of a mixture of 99 volumes of N,O-*bis(trimethylsilyl)acetamide* and 1 volume of *trimethylchlorosilane* and swirl gently. Loosen the glass stopper and heat at 65° for 30 minutes.

(2) Prepare in the same manner as solution (1) but omitting the internal standard and using a quantity of the premix containing the equivalent of 90 mg of lincomycin in place of the *lincomycin hydrochloride BPCRS*.

(3) Prepare in the same manner as solution (1) but using a quantity of the premix containing the equivalent of 90 mg of lincomycin in place of the *lincomycin hydrochloride BPCRS*.

CHROMATOGRAPHIC CONDITIONS

(a) Use a glass column (1.5 m × 3 mm) packed with *acid-washed silanised diatomaceous support* impregnated with 3% w/w of phenyl methyl silicone fluid (50% phenyl) (OV-17 is suitable) and maintained at 260°.

(b) Use *helium* as the carrier gas at a flow rate of about 45 mL per minute.

(c) Use an inlet temperature of 260° to 290°.

(d) Use a flame ionisation detector at a temperature of 260° to 290°.

(e) Inject 1 µL of each solution.

DETERMINATION OF CONTENT

Calculate the content of $C_{18}H_{34}N_2O_6S$ in the premix using the declared content of $C_{18}H_{34}N_2O_6S$ in *lincomycin hydrochloride BPCRS*.

LABELLING

The quantity of active ingredient is stated in terms of the equivalent amount of lincomycin.

Lincomycin Tablets

Action and use
Lincosamide antibacterial.

DEFINITION

Lincomycin Tablets contains Lincomycin Hydrochloride.

The tablets comply with the requirements stated under Tablets and with the following requirements.

Content of lincomycin, $C_{18}H_{34}N_2O_6S$
90.0 to 105.0% of the stated amount.

IDENTIFICATION

A. Mix a quantity of the powdered tablets containing the equivalent of 0.2 g of lincomycin with 5 mL of a mixture of 4 volumes of *chloroform* and 1 volume of *methanol*, filter and evaporate the filtrate. Dissolve the oily residue in 1 mL of *water*, add *acetone* until precipitation begins and add a further 20 mL of *acetone*. Filter, wash with two 10-mL quantities of *acetone*, dissolve the residue in the chloroform-methanol mixture, evaporate to dryness and dry at 60° at a pressure of 2 kPa for 1 hour. The *infrared absorption spectrum* of the residue, Appendix II A, is concordant with the *reference spectrum* of lincomycin hydrochloride (*RSV 52*).

B. In the Assay, the chromatogram obtained with solution (2) shows a peak with the same retention time as the peak due to the trimethylsilyl derivative of lincomycin in the chromatogram obtained with solution (1).

TESTS
Lincomycin B

Examine solution (3) as described under the Assay but increasing the sensitivity by eight to ten times while recording the peak due to the trimethylsilyl derivative of lincomycin B, which is eluted immediately before the trimethylsilyl derivative of lincomycin.

LIMITS

The area of the peak due to the trimethylsilyl derivative of lincomycin B, when corrected for the sensitivity factor, is not

more than 5% of the area of the peak due to the
trimethylsilyl derivative of lincomycin.

ASSAY

Carry out the method for *gas chromatography*,
Appendix III B, using the following solutions.

(1) Add 10 mL of a 0.8% w/w solution of *dotriacontane*
(internal standard) in *chloroform* to 0.1 g of *lincomycin
hydrochloride BPCRS*, dilute to 100 mL with a 2% w/v
solution of *imidazole* in *chloroform*, shake to dissolve and filter.
Place 4 mL of the filtrate in a 15 mL ground-glass-stoppered
centrifuge tube, add 1 mL of a mixture of 99 volumes of
N,O-*bis(trimethylsilyl)acetamide* and 1 volume of
trimethylchlorosilane and swirl gently. Loosen the glass stopper
and heat at 65° for 30 minutes.

(2) Prepare in the same manner as solution (1) but omitting
the internal standard and using a quantity of the powdered
tablets containing the equivalent of 90 mg of lincomycin in
place of the *lincomycin hydrochloride BPCRS*.

(3) Prepare in the same manner as solution (1) but using a
quantity of the powdered tablets containing the equivalent of
90 mg of lincomycin in place of the *lincomycin
hydrochloride BPCRS*.

CHROMATOGRAPHIC CONDITIONS

(a) Use a glass column (1.5 m × 3 mm) packed with *acid-
washed silanised diatomaceous support* impregnated with 3%
w/w of phenyl methyl silicone fluid (50% phenyl) (OV-17 is
suitable) and maintained at 260°.

(b) Use *helium* as the carrier gas at a flow rate of about
45 mL per minute.

(c) Use an inlet temperature of 260° to 290°.

(d) Use a flame ionisation detector at a temperature of 260°
to 290°.

(e) Inject 1 μL of each solution.

DETERMINATION OF CONTENT

Calculate the content of $C_{18}H_{34}N_2O_6S$ in the tablets using
the declared content of $C_{18}H_{34}N_2O_6S$ in *lincomycin
hydrochloride BPCRS*.

LABELLING

The quantity of active ingredient is stated in terms of the
equivalent amount of lincomycin.

Meloxicam Injection

Action and use

Cyclo-oxygenase inhibitor; analgesic; anti-inflammatory.

DEFINITION

Meloxicam Injection is a sterile solution of Meloxicam in
Water for Injections.

*The injection complies with the requirements stated under
Parenteral Preparations and with the following requirements.*

Content of meloxicam, $C_{14}H_{13}N_3O_4S_2$

95.0 to 105.0% of the stated amount.

IDENTIFICATION

A. Carry out the method for *thin-layer chromatography*,
Appendix III A, using the following solutions.

(1) Dilute a volume of the injection containing 10 mg of
Meloxicam to 20 mL with *acetone*, stir for 15 minutes, filter
and use the filtrate.

(2) Dissolve 10 mg of *meloxicam BPCRS* in 10 mL of *acetone*,
add 2 mL of *water* and dilute to 20 mL with *acetone*.

CHROMATOGRAPHIC CONDITIONS

(a) Use a *silica gel F₅₄ plate* (Merck HPTLC plates are
suitable).

(b) Use the mobile phase described below.

(c) Apply 20 μL of each solution.

(d) Develop the plate to 8 cm.

(e) After removal of the plate, dry in air and examine under
ultraviolet light (254 nm).

MOBILE PHASE

1 volume of 13.5M *ammonia*, 20 volumes of *methanol* and
80 volumes of *dichloromethane*.

CONFIRMATION

The principal spot in the chromatogram obtained with
solution (1) corresponds to that in the chromatogram
obtained with solution (2).

B. In the Assay, the retention time of the principal peak in
the chromatogram obtained with solution (1) corresponds to
that of the principal peak in the chromatogram obtained with
solution (2).

TESTS

Alkalinity

pH, 7.5 to 9.1, Appendix V L.

Related substances

Carry out the method for *liquid chromatography*,
Appendix III D, using the following solutions.

(1) Add 0.3 mL of 0.4M *sodium hydroxide* to a volume of the
injection containing 40 mg of Meloxicam and dilute with
methanol (40%) to produce 10 mL.

(2) Dilute 1 mL of solution (1) to 100 mL with
methanol (40%).

(3) Add 0.3 mL of 0.4M *sodium hydroxide* to 40 mg of
meloxicam impurity standard BPCRS and dilute with
methanol (40%) to produce 10 mL.

CHROMATOGRAPHIC CONDITIONS

(a) Use a stainless steel column (10 cm × 4.0 mm) packed
with *octadecylsilyl silica gel for chromatography* (10 μm)
(Kromasil 100 C18 is suitable).

(b) Use gradient elution and the mobile phase described
below.

(c) Use a flow rate of 1.0 mL per minute.

(d) Use an ambient column temperature.

(e) Use detection wavelengths of 260 nm and 350 nm.

(f) Inject 10 μL of each solution.

MOBILE PHASE

Mobile phase A   0.1% w/v solution of *potassium dihydrogen
orthophosphate* adjusted to pH 6.0 with 2M *sodium hydroxide*.
Mobile phase B   methanol.

Time (Minutes)	Mobile phase A (% v/v)	Mobile phase B (% v/v)	Comment
0-2.5	60	40	isocratic
2.5-12	60→30	40→70	linear gradient
12-25	30	70	isocratic
25-26	30→60	70→40	linear gradient
26-30	60	40	re-equilibration

SYSTEM SUITABILITY

The chromatogram obtained with solution (3):

resembles that supplied with *meloxicam impurity standard BPCRS* at 260 nm and 350 nm and;

the *resolution* between the peaks due to meloxicam and impurity A at 350 nm is at least 3.0;

the *resolution* between the peaks due to impurity B and meloxicam at 260 nm is at least 3.0.

LIMITS

Identify any peaks in the chromatogram obtained with solution (1) corresponding to impurity A and impurity B using the chromatogram obtained with solution (3) and the chromatogram supplied with *meloxicam impurity standard BPCRS*.

In the chromatogram obtained with solution (1):

identify any peak corresponding to impurity A at 350 nm and multiply the area of this peak by a correction factor of 2.0;

the area of any peak corresponding to impurity B at 260 nm is not greater than twice the area of the principal peak in the chromatogram obtained with solution (2) (2.0%);

the area of any peak corresponding to impurity A at 350 nm is not greater than the area of the principal peak in the chromatogram obtained with solution (2) (1.0%).

In both the chromatograms obtained with solution (1) at 350 nm and at 260 nm:

the area of any other *secondary peak* is not greater than the area of the peak in the chromatogram obtained with solution (2) at that wavelength (1.0%).

The nominal total content of any such impurities is not greater than 3.5%.

Disregard any peak with an area less than 0.3 times the area of the principal peak in the chromatogram obtained with solution (2) at the same wavelength (0.3%).

ASSAY

Carry out the method for *liquid chromatography*, Appendix III D, using the following solutions.

(1) To a volume of the injection containing 40 mg of Meloxicam add 0.3 mL of 0.4M *sodium hydroxide* and add sufficient *methanol (40%)* to produce 10 mL. Dilute 1 mL of the resulting solution to 10 mL with *methanol (40%)*.

(2) 0.04% w/v of *meloxicam BPCRS* in *methanol (40%)*.

(3) Add 0.3 mL of 0.4M *sodium hydroxide* to 40 mg of *meloxicam impurity standard BPCRS* and dilute with *methanol (40%)* to produce 10 mL.

CHROMATOGRAPHIC CONDITIONS

The chromatographic procedure described under Related substances may be used but with a detection wavelength of 350 nm.

SYSTEM SUITABILITY

The test is not valid unless the chromatogram obtained with solution (3):

closely resembles the chromatogram supplied with *meloxicam impurity standard BPCRS* at 350 nm;

the *resolution* between the peaks due to meloxicam and impurity A at 350 nm is at least 3.0.

DETERMINATION OF CONTENT

Calculate the content of $C_{14}H_{13}N_3O_4S_2$ using the declared content of $C_{14}H_{13}N_3O_4S_2$ in *meloxicam BPCRS*.

IMPURITIES

The impurities limited by the requirements of this monograph include those listed under Meloxicam.

Meloxicam Oral Suspension

Action and use

Cyclo-oxygenase inhibitor; analgesic; anti-inflammatory.

DEFINITION

Meloxicam Oral Suspension is a suspension of Meloxicam in a suitable vehicle.

The oral suspension complies with the requirements stated under Oral Liquids and with the following requirements.

Content of meloxicam, $C_{14}H_{13}N_3O_4S_2$

95.0 to 105.0% of the stated amount.

IDENTIFICATION

A. Carry out the method for *thin-layer chromatography*, Appendix III A, using the following solutions.

(1) Dilute a quantity of the oral suspension containing 3 mg of Meloxicam to 10 mL with *acetone*, stir for 10 minutes, filter and use the filtrate.

(2) Dissolve 3 mg of *meloxicam BPCRS* in about 5 mL of *acetone*, add 0.5 mL of *water* and dilute to 10 mL with *acetone*.

CHROMATOGRAPHIC CONDITIONS

(a) Use as the coating high-performance *silica gel F_{254}* (Merck silica gel 60 F_{254} HPTLC plates are suitable).

(b) Use the mobile phase as described below.

(c) Apply 5 µL of each solution.

(d) Develop the plate to 8 cm.

(e) After removal of the plate, allow it to dry in air and examine under *ultraviolet light (254 and 365 nm)*.

MOBILE PHASE

1 volume of 13.5M *ammonia*, 20 volumes of *methanol* and 80 volumes of *dichloromethane*.

CONFIRMATION

By each method of visualisation the principal spot in the chromatogram obtained with solution (1) is similar in position, colour and size to that in the chromatogram obtained with solution (2).

B. Disperse a quantity of the oral suspension containing 1.5 mg of Meloxicam in 5 mL of 0.1M *sodium hydroxide*, dilute to 100 mL with *methanol* and filter. The *light absorption* of the filtrate, Appendix II B, in the range 340 to 450 nm exhibits a maximum at 362 nm.

ASSAY

Carry out the method for *liquid chromatography*, Appendix III D, using the following solutions.

(1) Mix a quantity of the oral suspension containing 15 mg of Meloxicam with sufficient of the mobile phase to produce 200 mL, mix with the aid of ultrasound for 30 minutes and filter.

(2) 0.0075% w/v of *meloxicam BPCRS* in the mobile phase.

CHROMATOGRAPHIC CONDITIONS

(a) Use a stainless steel column (10 cm × 4 mm) packed with *octadecylsilyl silica gel for chromatography* (10 µm) (Nucleosil C18 is suitable) and a pre-column 1-cm long packed with the same material.

(b) Use isocratic elution and the mobile phase described below.

(c) Use a flow rate of 0.8 mL per minute.

(d) Use a column temperature of 40°.

(e) Use a detection wavelength of 254 nm.

(f) Inject 20 μL of each solution and continue the chromatography for twice the retention time of the principal peak.

MOBILE PHASE

35 volumes of a mixture containing 10 parts of *propan-2-ol* and 65 parts of *methanol* and 65 volumes of a 0.2% w/v solution of *diammonium hydrogen orthophosphate* previously adjusted to pH 7.0 with *orthophosphoric acid*.

DETERMINATION OF CONTENT

Determine the *weight per mL* of the oral suspension, Appendix V G, and calculate the content of $C_{14}H_{13}N_3O_4S_2$, weight in volume, from the declared content of $C_{14}H_{13}N_3O_4S_2$ in *meloxicam BPCRS*.

Mepivacaine Injection

Action and use
Local anaesthetic.

DEFINITION

Mepivacaine Injection is a sterile solution of Mepivacaine Hydrochloride in Water for Injections.

The injection complies with the requirements stated under Parenteral Preparations and with the following requirements.

Content of mepivacaine hydrochloride, $C_{15}H_{22}N_2O_2$,HCl

95.0 to 105.0% of the stated amount.

IDENTIFICATION

A. Carry out the method for *thin-layer chromatography*, Appendix III A, using a *TLC silica gel F_{254} plate* and a mixture of 1 volume of 13.5M *ammonia*, 5 volumes of *methanol* and 100 volumes of *ether* as the mobile phase, but allowing the solvent front to ascend 12 cm above the line of application. Apply separately to the plate 10 μL of each of the following solutions. For solution (1) dilute a quantity of the injection with sufficient *ethanol (96%)* to produce a solution containing 0.4% w/v of Mepivacaine Hydrochloride. Solution (2) contains 0.4% w/v of *mepivacaine hydrochloride BPCRS* in *ethanol (96%)*. Solution (3) contains 0.4% w/v of each of *mepivacaine hydrochloride BPCRS* and *lidocaine hydrochloride BPCRS* in *ethanol (96%)*. After removal of the plate, allow it to dry in air and examine under *ultraviolet light (254 nm)*. The principal spot in the chromatogram obtained with solution (1) is similar in position and size to the principal spot in the chromatogram obtained with solution (2). The test is not valid unless the chromatogram obtained with solution (3) shows two clearly separated principal spots.

B. In the Assay, the chromatogram obtained with solution (1) shows a peak with the same retention time as the principal peak in the chromatogram obtained with solution (2).

TESTS

Acidity
pH, 4.5 to 6.0, Appendix V L.

2,6-Dimethylaniline

Carry out the method for *liquid chromatography*, Appendix III D, using the following solutions. For solution (1) dilute a quantity of the injection containing 0.1 g of Mepivacaine Hydrochloride to 100 mL with the mobile

phase. Solution (2) contains 0.0002% w/v of *2,6-dimethylaniline* in the mobile phase.

The chromatographic procedure described under Assay may be used.

In the chromatogram obtained with solution (1) the area of any peak corresponding to 2,6-dimethylaniline is not greater than the area of the principal peak in the chromatogram obtained with solution (2) (0.2% of the content of mepivacaine hydrochloride).

ASSAY

Carry out the method for *liquid chromatography*, Appendix III D, using the following solutions. For solution (1) dilute a quantity of the injection containing 0.1 g of Mepivacaine Hydrochloride to 100 mL with the mobile phase and dilute 1 volume of this solution to 20 volumes with the mobile phase. Solution (2) contains 0.005% w/v of *mepivacaine hydrochloride BPCRS* in the mobile phase.

The chromatographic procedure may be carried out using (a) a stainless steel column (25 cm × 3.2 mm) packed with *octadecylsilyl silica gel for chromatography* (5 μm) (Spherisorb ODS 1 is suitable), (b) as the mobile phase with a flow rate of 0.5 mL per minute a mixture of 1 volume of *triethylamine*, 400 volumes of *acetonitrile* and 600 volumes of a 0.2% w/v solution of *potassium dihydrogen orthophosphate*, the mixture adjusted to pH 4.0 with *orthophosphoric acid* and (c) a detection wavelength of 212 nm.

Calculate the content of $C_{15}H_{22}N_2O_2$,HCl in the injection using the declared content of $C_{15}H_{22}N_2O_2$,HCl in *mepivacaine hydrochloride BPCRS*.

Moxidectin Injection

Action and use
Antihelminthic; ectoparasiticide

DEFINITION

Moxidectin Injection is a sterile solution of Moxidectin. It is supplied as a ready-to-use solution.

The injection complies with the requirements stated under Parenteral Preparations and with the following requirements.

Content of moxidectin, $C_{37}H_{53}NO_8$
90.0 to 110.0% of the stated amount.

IDENTIFICATION

A. Carry out the method for *thin-layer chromatography*, Appendix III A, using the following solutions.

(1) Dilute a volume of the injection with sufficient *methanol* to produce a solution containing 0.04% w/v of Moxidectin.

(2) 0.04% w/v of *moxidectin BPCRS* in *methanol*.

CHROMATOGRAPHIC CONDITIONS

(a) Use as the coating *silica gel*.

(b) Use the mobile phase as described below.

(c) Apply 5 μL of each solution.

(d) Develop the plate to 15 cm.

(e) After removal of the plate, dry in air, spray with *anisaldehyde solution R1*, heat at 105° for 5 to 10 minutes and allow to cool.

MOBILE PHASE

8 volumes of a 15% w/v solution of *ammonium acetate* adjusted to pH 9.6 with *ammonia*, 19 volumes of *propan-2-ol* and 43 volumes of *ethyl acetate*.

CONFIRMATION

The principal spot in the chromatogram obtained with solution (1) corresponds in position, colour and size to that in the chromatogram obtained with solution (2).

B. In the Assay, the retention time of the principal peak in the chromatogram obtained with solution (1) is similar to that of the principal peak in the chromatogram obtained with solution (2).

ASSAY

Carry out the method for *liquid chromatography*, Appendix III D, using the following solutions in *acetonitrile*.

(1) Dilute a volume of the injection to produce a solution containing 0.1% w/v of Moxidectin. If the solution is cloudy, shake, allow to settle and use the supernatant.

(2) 0.1% w/v of *moxidectin BPCRS*.

(3) 0.1% w/v of *moxidectin for system suitability EPCRS*.

CHROMATOGRAPHIC CONDITIONS

(a) Use a stainless steel column (15 cm × 3.9 mm) packed with *end-capped octadecylsilyl silica gel for chromatography* (4 µm) (Waters Nova-Pak and Waters Pico-Tag are suitable).

(b) Use isocratic elution and the mobile phase described below.

(c) Use a flow rate of 2.5 mL per minute.

(d) Use a column temperature of 50°.

(e) Use a detection wavelength of 242 nm.

(f) Inject 10 µL of each solution.

MOBILE PHASE

40 volumes of a 1.925% w/v solution of *ammonium acetate* in *water*, adjusted to pH 4.8 with *glacial acetic acid*, and 60 volumes of *acetonitrile*.

When the chromatograms are recorded under the prescribed conditions the retention time of moxidectin is about 12 minutes and the retention time of impurity D relative to that of moxidection is about 0.94.

SYSTEM SUITABILITY

The test is not valid unless, in the chromatogram obtained with solution (3), the *peak-to-valley ratio* is at least 3.0 where H_p is the height above the baseline of the peak due to impurity D and H_v is the height above the baseline of the lowest point of the curve separating this peak from the peak due to moxidectin.

DETERMINATION OF CONTENT

Calculate the content of $C_{37}H_{53}NO_8$ in the injection using the declared content of $C_{37}H_{53}NO_8$ in *moxidectin BPCRS*.

Moxidectin Oral Solution

Moxidectin Oral Drench

Action and use

Antihelminthic; ectoparasiticide

DEFINITION

Moxidectin Oral Solution is a solution of Moxidectin in a suitable vehicle.

The oral solution complies with the requirements stated under Oral Liquids and with the following requirements.

Content of moxidectin, $C_{37}H_{53}NO_8$

90.0 to 110.0% of the stated amount.

IDENTIFICATION

A. Carry out the method for *thin-layer chromatography*, Appendix III A, using the following solutions.

(1) Dilute a quantity of the oral solution with sufficient *methanol* to produce a solution containing 0.04% w/v of Moxidectin.

(2) 0.04% w/v of *moxidectin BPCRS* in *methanol*.

CHROMATOGRAPHIC CONDITIONS

(a) Use as the coating *silica gel*.

(b) Use the mobile phase as described below.

(c) Apply 5 µL of each solution.

(d) Develop the plate to 15 cm.

(e) After removal of the plate, dry in air, spray with *anisaldehyde solution R1*, heat at 105° for 5 to 10 minutes and allow to cool.

MOBILE PHASE

8 volumes of a 15% w/v solution of *ammonium acetate* adjusted to pH 9.6 with *ammonia*, 19 volumes of *propan-2-ol* and 43 volumes of *ethyl acetate*.

CONFIRMATION

The principal spot in the chromatogram obtained with solution (1) corresponds in position, colour and size to that in the chromatogram obtained with solution (2).

B. In the Assay, the retention time of the principal peak in the chromatogram obtained with solution (1) is similar to that of the principal peak in the chromatogram obtained with solution (2).

ASSAY

Carry out the method for *liquid chromatography*, Appendix III D, using the following solutions in *acetonitrile*.

(1) Dilute a weighed quantity of the oral solution to produce a solution containing 0.05% w/v of Moxidectin, shake and allow to settle.

(2) 0.05% w/v of *moxidectin BPCRS*.

(3) 0.1% w/v of *moxidectin for system suitability EPCRS*.

CHROMATOGRAPHIC CONDITIONS

(a) Use a stainless steel column (15 cm × 3.9 mm) packed with *end-capped octadecylsilyl silica gel for chromatography* (4 µm) (Waters Nova-Pak and Waters Pico-Tag are suitable).

(b) Use isocratic elution and the mobile phase described below.

(c) Use a flow rate of 2.5 mL per minute.

(d) Use a column temperature of 50°.

(e) Use a detection wavelength of 242 nm.

(f) Inject 20 µL of each solution.

MOBILE PHASE

40 volumes of a 1.925% w/v solution of *ammonium acetate* in *water*, adjusted to pH 4.8 with *glacial acetic acid*, and 60 volumes of *acetonitrile*.

When the chromatograms are recorded under the prescribed conditions the retention time of moxidectin is about 12 minutes and the retention time of impurity D relative to that of moxidectin is about 0.94.

SYSTEM SUITABILITY

The test is not valid unless, in the chromatogram obtained with solution (3), the *peak-to-valley ratio* is at least 3.0 where H_p is the height above the baseline of the peak due to impurity D and H_v is the height above the baseline of the lowest point of the curve separating this peak from the peak due to moxidectin.

DETERMINATION OF CONTENT

Determine the *weight per ml* of the oral solution, Appendix V G, and calculate the content of $C_{37}H_{53}NO_8$, weight in volume, using the declared content of $C_{37}H_{53}NO_8$ in *moxidectin BPCRS*.

Moxidectin Oromucosal Gel

Moxidectin Oral Gel

Action and use
Antihelminthic; ectoparasiticide

DEFINITION
Moxidectin Oromucosal Gel is a solution of Moxidectin in a suitable water-miscible basis.

The oromucosal gel complies with the requirements stated under Oromucosal Preparations and with the following requirements.

Content of moxidectin, $C_{37}H_{53}NO_8$
90.0 to 110.0% of the stated amount.

IDENTIFICATION
A. Carry out the method for *thin-layer chromatography*, Appendix III A, using the following solutions.

(1) Disperse a quantity of the gel containing 10 mg of Moxidectin with sufficient *methanol* to produce a solution containing 0.04% w/v of Moxidectin.

(2) 0.04% w/v of *moxidectin BPCRS* in *methanol*.

CHROMATOGRAPHIC CONDITIONS

(a) Use as the coating *silica gel*.

(b) Use the mobile phase as described below.

(c) Apply 5 µL of each solution.

(d) Develop the plate to 15 cm.

(e) After removal of the plate, dry in air, spray with *anisaldehyde solution R1*, heat at 105° for 5 to 10 minutes and allow to cool.

MOBILE PHASE

8 volumes of a 15% w/v solution of *ammonium acetate* adjusted to pH 9.6 with *ammonia*, 19 volumes of *propan-2-ol* and 43 volumes of *ethyl acetate*.

CONFIRMATION

The principal spot in the chromatogram obtained with solution (1) corresponds in position, colour and size to that in the chromatogram obtained with solution (2).

B. In the Assay, the retention time of the principal peak in the chromatogram obtained with solution (1) is similar to that of the principal peak in the chromatogram obtained with solution (2).

ASSAY
Carry out the method for *liquid chromatography*, Appendix III D, using the following solutions in *acetonitrile*.

(1) Disperse a quantity of the gel containing 25 mg of Moxidectin in sufficient *acetonitrile* to produce a solution containing 0.1% w/v of Moxidectin and allow to settle.

(2) 0.1% w/v of *moxidectin BPCRS*.

(3) 0.1% w/v of *moxidectin for system suitability EPCRS*.

CHROMATOGRAPHIC CONDITIONS

(a) Use a stainless steel column (15 cm × 3.9 mm) packed with *end-capped octadecylsilyl silica gel for chromatography* (4 µm) (Waters Nova-Pak and Waters Pico-Tag are suitable).

(b) Use isocratic elution and the mobile phase described below.

(c) Use a flow rate of 2.5 mL per minute.

(d) Use a column temperature of 50°.

(e) Use a detection wavelength of 242 nm.

(f) Inject 10 µL of each solution.

MOBILE PHASE

40 volumes of a 1.925% w/v solution of *ammonium acetate* in *water*, adjusted to pH 4.8 with *glacial acetic acid*, and 60 volumes of *acetonitrile*.

When the chromatograms are recorded under the prescribed conditions the retention time of moxidectin is about 12 minutes and the retention time of impurity D relative to that of moxidectin is about 0.94.

SYSTEM SUITABILITY

The test is not valid unless, in the chromatogram obtained with solution (3), the *peak-to-valley ratio* is at least 3.0 where H_p is the height above the baseline of the peak due to impurity D and H_v is the height above the baseline of the lowest point of the curve separating this peak from the peak due to moxidectin.

DETERMINATION OF CONTENT

Calculate the content of $C_{37}H_{53}NO_8$ in the oromucosal gel using the declared content of $C_{37}H_{53}NO_8$ in *moxidectin BPCRS*.

Moxidectin Pour-on

Action and use
Antihelminthic; ectoparasiticide

DEFINITION
Moxidectin Pour-on is a *pour-on solution*. It contains Moxidectin in a suitable vehicle.

The pour-on complies with the requirements stated under Veterinary Liquid Preparations for Cutaneous Application and with the following requirements.

Content of moxidectin, $C_{37}H_{53}NO_8$
90.0 to 110.0% of the stated amount.

IDENTIFICATION
A. Carry out the method for *thin-layer chromatography*, Appendix III A, using the following solutions.

(1) Dilute a quantity of the pour-on solution, with shaking, in sufficient *methanol* to produce a solution containing 0.04% w/v of Moxidectin; filter a 5-mL portion through a 0.45-µm PTFE membrane filter and use the filtrate.

(2) 0.04% w/v of *moxidectin BPCRS* in *methanol*.

CHROMATOGRAPHIC CONDITIONS

(a) Use as the coating *silica gel*.

(b) Use the mobile phase as described below.

(c) Apply 5 µL of each solution.

(d) Develop the plate to 15 cm.

(e) After removal of the plate, dry in air, spray with *anisaldehyde solution R1*, heat at 105° for 5 to 10 minutes and allow to cool.

8 volumes of a 15% w/v solution of *ammonium acetate* adjusted to pH 9.6 with *ammonia*, 19 volumes of *propan-2-ol* and 43 volumes of *ethyl acetate*.

CONFIRMATION

The principal spot in the chromatogram obtained with solution (1) corresponds in position, colour and size to that in the chromatogram obtained with solution (2).

B. In the Assay, the retention time of the principal peak in the chromatogram obtained with solution (1) is similar to that of the principal peak in the chromatogram obtained with solution (2).

ASSAY

Carry out the method for *liquid chromatography*, Appendix III D, using the following solutions in *acetonitrile*.

(1) Dilute a weighed quantity of the pour-on solution to produce a solution containing 0.1% w/v of Moxidectin, shake and mix with the aid of ultrasound for 10 minutes. Allow to cool and filter the resulting solution through a 0.45-μm membrane filter, discarding the first few mL of filtrate.

(2) 0.1% w/v of *moxidectin BPCRS*.

(3) 0.1% w/v of *moxidectin for system suitability EPCRS*.

CHROMATOGRAPHIC CONDITIONS

(a) Use a stainless steel column (15 cm × 3.9 mm) packed with *end-capped octadecylsilyl silica gel for chromatography* (4 μm) (Waters Nova-Pak and Waters Pico-Tag are suitable).

(b) Use isocratic elution and the mobile phase described below.

(c) Use a flow rate of 2.5 mL per minute.

(d) Use a column temperature of 50°.

(e) Use a detection wavelength of 242 nm.

(f) Inject 10 μL of each solution.

MOBILE PHASE

40 volumes of a 1.925% w/v solution of *ammonium acetate* in *water*, adjusted to pH 4.8 with *glacial acetic acid*, and 60 volumes of *acetonitrile*.

When the chromatograms are recorded under the prescribed conditions the retention time of moxidectin is about 12 minutes and the retention time of impurity D relative to that of moxidectin is about 0.94.

SYSTEM SUITABILITY

The test is not valid unless, in the chromatogram obtained with solution (3), the *peak-to-valley ratio* is at least 3.0 where H_p is the height above the baseline of the peak due to impurity D and H_v is the height above the baseline of the lowest point of the curve separating this peak from the peak due to moxidectin.

DETERMINATION OF CONTENT

Determine the *weight per ml* of the pour-on solution, Appendix V G, and calculate the content of $C_{37}H_{53}NO_8$, weight in volume, using the declared content of $C_{37}H_{53}NO_8$ in *moxidectin BPCRS*.

Nandrolone Laurate Injection

Action and use
Anabolic steroid; androgen.

DEFINITION
Nandrolone Laurate Injection is a sterile solution of Nandrolone Laurate in Ethyl Oleate, or other suitable ester, in a suitable fixed oil or in any mixture of these.

The injection complies with the requirements stated under Parenteral Preparations and with the following requirements.

Content of nandrolone laurate, $C_{30}H_{48}O_3$
92.5 to 107.5% of the stated amount.

IDENTIFICATION
Carry out the method for *thin-layer chromatography*, Appendix III A, using a silica gel F_{254} precoated plate the surface of which has been modified by chemically-bonded octadecylsilyl groups (Whatman KC 18F plates are suitable) and a mixture of 20 volumes of *water*, 40 volumes of *acetonitrile* and 60 volumes of *propan-2-ol* as the mobile phase. Apply separately to the plate 5 μL of each of the following solutions. For solution (1) dilute the injection with *chloroform* to produce a solution containing 0.5% w/v of Nandrolone Laurate. Solution (2) contains 0.5% w/v of *nandrolone laurate BPCRS* in *chloroform*. For solution (3) mix equal volumes of solutions (1) and (2). After removal of the plate, allow it to dry in air until the solvent has evaporated and heat at 100° for 10 minutes. Allow to cool and examine under *ultraviolet light (254 nm)*. The principal spot in the chromatogram obtained with solution (1) corresponds to that in the chromatogram obtained with solution (2).

The principal spot in the chromatogram obtained with solution (3) appears as a single, compact spot.

ASSAY
To a volume containing 0.1 g of Nandrolone Laurate add sufficient *chloroform* to produce 100 mL. Dilute 3 mL to 50 mL with *chloroform*. To 5 mL add 10 mL of *isoniazid solution* and sufficient *methanol* to produce 20 mL. Allow to stand for 45 minutes and measure the *absorbance* of the resulting solution at the maximum at 380 nm, Appendix II B, using as the reference solution 5 mL of *chloroform* treated in the same manner. Calculate the content of $C_{30}H_{48}O_3$ from the *absorbance* obtained by repeating the operation using a suitable quantity of *nandrolone BPCRS* and from the declared content of $C_{18}H_{26}O_2$ in *nandrolone BPCRS*. Each mg of $C_{18}H_{26}O_2$ is equivalent to 1.664 mg of $C_{30}H_{48}O_3$.

STORAGE
Nandrolone Laurate Injection should be protected from light.

Nitroxinil Injection

Action and use
Antihelminthic.

DEFINITION
Nitroxinil Injection is a sterile solution of the N-ethylglucamine salt of Nitroxinil in Water for Injections.

The injection complies with the requirements stated under Parenteral Preparations and with the following requirements.

Content of nitroxinil, $C_7H_3IN_2O_3$
95.0 to 105.0% of the stated amount.

IDENTIFICATION

A. The *light absorption*, Appendix II B, in the range 240 to 350 nm of the solution obtained in the Assay exhibits a maximum only at 271 nm.

B. Heat 0.5 mL with 3 mL of *sulfuric acid*; iodine vapour is evolved.

TESTS

Acidity or alkalinity

pH, 5.0 to 7.0, Appendix V L, determined using a 20% w/v solution of N-*ethylglucamine hydrochloride BPCRS* in place of a saturated solution of *potassium chloride* as the liquid junction solution.

Inorganic iodide

Dilute a volume containing 0.4 g of Nitroxinil to 100 mL with *water*. To 10 mL add 4 mL of 1M *sulfuric acid* and extract with three 10 mL quantities of *chloroform*. Add to the aqueous extract 1 mL of *hydrogen peroxide solution (100 vol)* and 1 mL of *chloroform*, shake for 2 minutes and allow to separate. Any purple colour produced in the chloroform layer is not more intense than that obtained in a solution prepared in the following manner. Add 2 mL of a 0.0026% w/v solution of *potassium iodide* to a mixture of 4 mL of 1M *sulfuric acid* and 8 mL of *water*, add 10 mL of *chloroform*, shake for 2 minutes, add to the aqueous layer 1 mL of *hydrogen peroxide solution (100 vol)* and 1 mL of *chloroform*, shake for 2 minutes and allow to separate (0.1% w/v of iodide).

ASSAY

To a volume containing 1.7 g of Nitroxinil add sufficient 0.01M *sodium hydroxide* to produce 500 mL and dilute 20 mL of this solution to 500 mL with 0.01M *sodium hydroxide*. To 5 mL of this solution add sufficient 0.01M *sodium hydroxide* to produce 100 mL and measure the *absorbance* of the resulting solution at the maximum at 271 nm, Appendix II B. Calculate the content of $C_7H_3IN_2O_3$ taking 660 as the value of A(1%, 1 cm) at the maximum at 271 nm.

STORAGE

Nitroxinil Injection should be protected from light.

Oxfendazole Oral Suspension

Action and use

Antihelminthic.

DEFINITION

Oxfendazole Oral Suspension is an aqueous suspension of Oxfendazole.

The oral suspension complies with the requirements stated under Oral Liquids and with the following requirements.

Content of oxfendazole, $C_{15}H_{13}N_3O_3S$

90.0 to 110.0% of the stated amount.

IDENTIFICATION

Shake a quantity of the oral suspension containing 0.1 g of Oxfendazole with 50 mL of *methanol* for 15 minutes, centrifuge, evaporate the supernatant liquid to a volume of about 2 mL, cool and filter. Wash the residue with a little *water* and dry at 105° at a pressure not exceeding 2.7 kPa for 1 hour. The residue complies with the following tests.

A. The *infrared absorption spectrum*, Appendix II A, is concordant with the *reference spectrum* of oxfendazole *(RSV 32)*.

B. The *light absorption*, Appendix II B, in the range 220 to 350 nm of a 0.001% w/v solution in 1M *hydrochloric acid* exhibits three maxima, at 226, 284 and 291 nm.

TESTS

Acidity

pH, 4.3 to 5.3, Appendix V L.

Related substances

Carry out the method for *thin-layer chromatography*, Appendix III A, using *silica gel G* as the coating substance and a mixture of 5 volumes of *glacial acetic acid* and 95 volumes of *ethyl acetate* as the mobile phase. Apply separately to the plate 20 µL of each of the following solutions. For solution (1) shake a quantity of the oral suspension containing 0.1 g of Oxfendazole with 20 mL of a mixture of 4 volumes of *ethyl acetate* and 1 volume of *glacial acetic acid* and filter. For solution (2) dilute 1 volume of solution (1) to 50 volumes with the same solvent mixture. Solution (3) contains 0.005% w/v of *fenbendazole BPCRS*. After removal of the plate, allow it to dry in air and examine under *ultraviolet light (254 nm)*. Any spot in the chromatogram obtained with solution (1) corresponding to methyl 5-phenylthio-1*H*-benzimidazol-2-ylcarbamate is not more intense than the spot in the chromatogram obtained with solution (3) (1%) and any other *secondary spot* is not more intense than the spot in the chromatogram obtained with solution (2) (2%).

ASSAY

Disperse a quantity of the well-mixed oral suspension containing 0.1 g of Oxfendazole in 15 mL of *water*. Add 200 mL of *methanol* and mix with the aid of ultrasound for 15 minutes, cool, add sufficient *methanol* to produce 500 mL and filter. Dilute 4 mL of the filtrate to 100 mL with *methanol* and measure the *absorbance* of the resulting solution at the maximum at 296 nm, Appendix II B. Calculate the content of $C_{15}H_{13}N_3O_3S$ taking 550 as the value of A(1%, 1 cm) at the maximum at 296 nm.

Oxyclozanide Oral Suspension

Action and use

Antihelminthic.

DEFINITION

Oxyclozanide Oral Suspension is an aqueous suspension of Oxyclozanide containing suitable suspending and dispersing agents.

The oral suspension complies with the requirements stated under Oral Liquids and with the following requirements.

Content of oxyclozanide, $C_{13}H_6Cl_5NO_3$

95.0 to 105.0% of the stated amount.

IDENTIFICATION

In test A for Related substances the principal spot in the chromatogram obtained with 10 µL of solution (1) corresponds to that in the chromatogram obtained with solution (3).

Related substances

A. Carry out the method for *thin-layer chromatography*, Appendix III A, using *silica gel G* as the coating substance and a mixture of 5 volumes of *glacial acetic acid*, 20 volumes of *acetone* and 60 volumes of *petroleum spirit (boiling range, 60° to 80°)* as the mobile phase. Apply separately to the plate 40 µL and 10 µL of solution (1), 4 µL of solution (2) and 10 µL of solution (3). For solution (1) dilute the oral suspension with *acetone* to contain 1.0% w/v of Oxyclozanide, centrifuge and use the supernatant liquid. Solution (2) contains 0.050% w/v of *3,5,6-trichloro-2-hydroxybenzoic acid BPCRS* in *acetone*. Solution (3) contains 1.0% w/v of *oxyclozanide BPCRS* in *acetone*. After removal of the plate, allow it to dry in air and spray with a 3.0% w/v solution of *iron(III) chloride hexahydrate* in *methanol*. In the chromatogram obtained with 40 µL of solution (1) any spot corresponding to 3,5,6-trichloro-2-hydroxybenzoic acid is not more intense than the spot in the chromatogram obtained with solution (2) (0.5%).

B. Carry out the method for *thin-layer chromatography*, Appendix III A, using *silica gel G* as the coating substance and a mixture of 1 volume of 13.5M *ammonia* as the mobile phase, 10 volumes of *methanol* and 100 volumes of *ethyl acetate*. Apply separately to the plate 40 µL of solution (1) and 4 µL of solution (2). For solution (1) dilute the oral suspension with *acetone* to contain 1.0% w/v of Oxyclozanide, centrifuge and use the supernatant liquid. Solution (2) contains 0.050% w/v of *2-amino-4,6-dichlorophenol hydrochloride BPCRS* in *acetone*. After removal of the plate, allow it to dry in air and spray with *phosphomolybdotungstic reagent* . In the chromatogram obtained with solution (1) any spot corresponding to 2-amino-4,6-dichlorophenol is not more intense than the spot in the chromatogram obtained with solution (2) (0.4%).

ASSAY

Protect the solutions from light throughout the Assay. To a quantity of the oral suspension containing 60 mg of Oxyclozanide add 60 mL of *acidified methanol* and boil gently on a water bath. Shake continuously for 20 minutes, cool to 2° and dilute to 100 mL with *acidified methanol*. Filter, dilute 5 mL of the filtrate to 100 mL with *acidified methanol* and measure the *absorbance* of the resulting solution at the maximum at 300 nm, Appendix II B. Calculate the content of $C_{13}H_6Cl_5NO_3$ taking 254 as the value of A(1%, 1 cm) at the maximum at 300 nm.

Oxytetracycline Veterinary Oral Powder

Action and use
Tetracycline antibacterial.

DEFINITION
Oxytetracycline Veterinary Oral Powder is a mixture of Oxytetracycline Hydrochloride and Lactose Monohydrate or other suitable diluent.

Content of oxytetracycline hydrochloride, $C_{22}H_{24}N_2O_9,HCl$
90.0 to 110.0% of the stated amount.

The veterinary oral powder complies with the requirements stated under Veterinary Oral Powders and with the following requirements.

IDENTIFICATION
A. Carry out the method for *thin-layer chromatography*, Appendix III A, using the following solutions.

(1) Extract a quantity of the oral powder containing 10 mg of Oxytetracycline Hydrochloride with 20 mL of *methanol*, centrifuge and use the supernatant liquid.

(2) 0.05% w/v of *oxytetracycline hydrochloride BPCRS* in *methanol*.

(3) 0.05% w/v of each of *oxytetracycline hydrochloride BPCRS* and *demeclocycline hydrochloride BPCRS* in *methanol*.

CHROMATOGRAPHIC CONDITIONS

(a) Use a silica gel precoated plate (Merck silica gel 60 plates are suitable). Adjust the pH of a 10% w/v solution of *disodium edetate* to 7.0 with 10M *sodium hydroxide* and spray the solution evenly onto the plate (about 10 mL for a plate 100 mm × 200 mm). Allow the plate to dry in a horizontal position for at least 1 hour. Before use, dry the plate at 110° for 1 hour.

(b) Use the mobile phase as described below.

(c) Apply 1 µL of each solution.

(d) Develop the plate to 15 cm.

(e) After removal of the plate, dry it in a current of air and examine under *ultraviolet light (365 nm)*.

MOBILE PHASE

6 volumes of *water*, 35 volumes of *methanol* and 59 volumes of *dichloromethane*.

SYSTEM SUITABILITY

The test is not valid unless the chromatogram obtained with solution (3) shows two clearly separated spots.

CONFIRMATION

The principal spot in the chromatogram obtained with solution (1) is similar in position, colour and size to that in the chromatogram obtained with solution (2).

B. To a quantity of the powder containing 0.4 mg of Oxytetracycline Hydrochloride add 5 mL of a 1% w/v solution of *sodium carbonate*, shake and add 2 mL of *diazobenzenesulfonic acid solution*. A light brown colour is produced.

C. Shake a quantity of the powder containing 0.1 g of Oxytetracycline Hydrochloride with 10 mL of 2M *nitric acid* and filter. Decolourise the filtrate with *activated charcoal* and filter again. The filtrate yields the reactions characteristic of *chlorides*, Appendix VI.

ASSAY
Carry out the method for *liquid chromatography*, Appendix III D, using the following solutions.

(1) Dissolve a quantity of the oral powder in sufficient 0.01M *hydrochloric acid* to produce a solution containing 0.005% w/v of Oxytetracycline Hydrochloride.

(2) 0.005% w/v of *oxytetracycline BPCRS* in 0.01M *hydrochloric acid*.

(3) 0.1% w/v of *4-epioxytetracycline EPCRS* in 0.01M *hydrochloric acid*.

(4) 0.1% w/v of *tetracycline hydrochloride BPCRS* in 0.01M *hydrochloric acid*.

(5) Dilute a mixture containing 1.5 mL of a 0.1% w/v solution of *oxytetracycline BPCRS* in 0.01M *hydrochloric acid*, 1 mL of solution (3) and 3 mL of solution (4) to 25 mL with 0.01M *hydrochloric acid*.

CHROMATOGRAPHIC CONDITIONS

(a) Use a stainless steel column (25 cm × 4.6 mm) packed with *styrene-divinylbenzene copolymer* (8 to 10 µm) (Polymer Laboratories, PLRP-S 100A, is suitable).

(b) Use isocratic elution and the mobile phase described below.

(c) Use a flow rate of 1 mL per minute.

(d) Use a column temperature of 60°.

(e) Use a detection wavelength of 254 nm.

(f) Inject 20 µL of each solution.

MOBILE PHASE

To 50.0 g of *2-methylpropan-2-ol* add 200 mL of *water*, 60 mL of *0.33M phosphate buffer pH 7.5*, 50 mL of a 1.0% w/v solution of *tetrabutylammonium hydrogen sulfate* previously adjusted to pH 7.5 with 2M *sodium hydroxide* and 10 mL of a 0.04% w/v solution of *disodium edetate* previously adjusted to pH 7.5 with 2M *sodium hydroxide* and dilute to 1 litre with *water*.

SYSTEM SUITABILITY

The Assay is not valid unless, in the chromatogram obtained with solution (5):

the *resolution* between the first peak (4-epioxytetracycline) and the second peak (oxytetracycline) is at least 4.0;

the *resolution* between the second peak and the third peak (tetracycline) is at least 5.0 (if necessary reduce the content of 2-methylpropan-2-ol in the mobile phase to increase the resolution);

the *symmetry factor* of the peak due to oxytetracycline is not more than 1.25.

DETERMINATION OF CONTENT

Calculate the content of $C_{22}H_{24}N_2O_9,HCl$ in the oral powder using the declared content of $C_{22}H_{24}N_2O_9$ in *oxytetracycline BPCRS*. Each mg of $C_{22}H_{24}N_2O_9$ is equivalent to 1.079 mg of $C_{22}H_{24}N_2O_9,HCl$.

Pentobarbital Injection

Action and use

Barbiturate.

DEFINITION

Pentobarbital Injection is a sterile[1] solution of Pentobarbital Sodium in a suitable vehicle.

The injection complies with the requirements stated under Parenteral Preparations and with the following requirements.

Content of pentobarbital sodium, $C_{11}H_{17}N_2NaO_3$

95.0 to 105.0% of the stated amount.

CHARACTERISTICS

A clear, colourless or almost colourless solution.

IDENTIFICATION

A. The *infrared absorption spectrum* of the residue obtained in the Assay, Appendix II A, is concordant with the *reference spectrum* of pentobarbital *(RSV 34)*.

B. *Melting point* of the residue obtained in the Assay, about 128°, Appendix V A.

C. When introduced on a platinum wire into the flame of a Bunsen burner, imparts a yellow colour to the flame.

TESTS

Alkalinity

pH, 10.0 to 11.5, Appendix V L.

Isomer

To a volume containing 0.3 g of Pentobarbital Sodium diluted, if necessary, to 5 mL with *water*, add 0.3 g of *4-nitrobenzyl bromide* dissolved in 10 mL of *ethanol (96%)* and heat under a reflux condenser for 30 minutes. Cool to 25°, filter, wash the residue with four 5 mL quantities of *water*

and transfer as completely as possible to a small flask. Add 25 mL of *ethanol (96%)* and heat under a reflux condenser for 10 minutes. The residue, after drying at 105° for 30 minutes, melts completely between 136° and 155°.

ASSAY

To a volume containing 0.5 g of Pentobarbital Sodium diluted to 15 mL with *water* add 5 mL of 2M *hydrochloric acid*, extract with 50 mL of *ether* and then with successive 25 mL quantities of *ether* until complete extraction is effected. Wash the combined extracts with two 5 mL quantities of *water* and wash the combined aqueous washings with 10 mL of *ether*. Add the ether to the main ether extract, evaporate to low volume, add 2 mL of *absolute ethanol*, evaporate to dryness and dry the residue to constant weight at 105°. Each g of residue is equivalent to 1.097 g of $C_{11}H_{17}N_2NaO_3$.

When pentobarbitone injection is prescribed or demanded, Pentobarbital Injection shall be dispensed or supplied.

---

[1] *Solutions containing 20% w/v of Pentobarbital Sodium in 100 mL and 500 mL quantities are also available for purposes other than injection; such solutions are not necessarily sterile but comply with all the other requirements of the monograph; they may be coloured.*

Phenylbutazone Tablets

Action and use

Cyclo-oxygenase inhibitor; pyrazolone analgesic.

DEFINITION

Phenylbutazone Tablets contain Phenylbutazone. They are coated.

The tablets comply with the requirements stated under Tablets and with the following requirements.

Content of phenylbutazone, $C_{19}H_{20}N_2O_2$

95.0 to 105.0% of the stated amount.

IDENTIFICATION

Extract a quantity of the powdered tablets containing 0.2 g of Phenylbutazone with 40 mL of warm *acetone*, filter and evaporate the filtrate to dryness. The residue complies with the following tests.

A. The *infrared absorption spectrum*, Appendix II A, is concordant with the *reference spectrum* of phenylbutazone *(RSV 35)*.

B. To 0.1 g of the residue add 1 mL of *glacial acetic acid* and 2 mL of *hydrochloric acid* and heat on a water bath for 30 minutes. Cool, add 10 mL of *water* and filter. Add to the filtrate 3 mL of 0.1M *sodium nitrite*; a yellow colour is produced. Add 1 mL of this solution to 5 mL of *2-naphthol solution*; a brownish red precipitate is produced which dissolves on the addition of *ethanol (96%)* yielding a red solution.

TESTS

Dissolution

Comply with the requirements for Monographs of the British Pharmacopoeia in the *dissolution test for tablets and capsules*, Appendix XII B1.

TEST CONDITIONS

(a) Use Apparatus 1, rotating the basket at 100 revolutions per minute.

(b) Use 900 mL of a 0.68% w/v solution of *potassium dihydrogen orthophosphate* adjusted to pH 7.5 with 1M *sodium hydroxide*, at a temperature of 37°, as the medium.

PROCEDURE

After 45 minutes withdraw a 10 mL sample of the medium and measure the *absorbance* of the filtered sample, suitably diluted with the dissolution medium if necessary, at the maximum at 264 nm, Appendix II B using the dissolution medium in the reference cell.

DETERMINATION OF CONTENT

Calculate the total content of phenylbutazone, $C_{19}H_{20}N_2O_2$, in the medium taking 653 as the value of A(1%, 1 cm) at the maximum at 264 nm.

Related substances

Carry out the method for *thin-layer chromatography*, Appendix III A, using the following solutions.

(1) Shake a quantity of the powdered tablets containing 0.1 g of Phenylbutazone with 3 mL of *chloroform* containing 0.02% w/v of *butylated hydroxytoluene*, centrifuge and use the supernatant liquid.

(2) Dilute 1 volume of solution (1) with sufficient of the same solvent mixture to produce a solution containing 0.5 mg of Phenylbutazone per mL.

CHROMATOGRAPHIC CONDITIONS

(a) Use as the coating *silica gel GF$_{254}$* (Machery Nagel plates are suitable). Prior to applying solutions (1) and (2), pre-treat the plate with the mobile phase allowing the solvent front to ascend 4 cm, remove the plate and dry it in a current of cold air.

(b) Use fresh mobile phase as described below.

(c) Without delay and in an atmosphere of carbon dioxide apply 3 µL of each solution. Expose the plate to carbon dioxide for 2 minutes.

(d) Develop the plate to 10 cm.

(e) After removal of the plate, allow it to dry in air and examine under *ultraviolet light (254 nm)*.

MOBILE PHASE

10 volumes of *glacial acetic acid*, 40 volumes of *cyclohexane* and 50 volumes of *chloroform* containing 0.02% v/v of *butylated hydroxytoluene*.

LIMITS

Any *secondary spot* in the chromatogram obtained with solution (1) is not more intense than the spot in the chromatogram obtained with solution (2) (1.5%).

ASSAY

Weigh and powder 20 tablets. Extract a quantity of the powder containing 0.5 g of Phenylbutazone with successive 30-, 30-, 15- and 15-mL quantities of warm *acetone*. Filter the combined extracts, cool and titrate with 0.1M *sodium hydroxide VS* using *bromothymol blue solution R3* as indicator and continuing the titration until the blue colour persists for at least 30 seconds. Repeat the titration without the powdered tablets; the difference between the titrations represents the amount of alkali required by the phenylbutazone. Each mL of 0.1M *sodium hydroxide VS* is equivalent to 30.84 mg of $C_{19}H_{20}N_2O_2$.

Piperazine Citrate Tablets

Action and use
Antihelminthic.

DEFINITION

Piperazine Citrate Tablets contain Piperazine Citrate.

The tablets comply with the requirements stated under Tablets and with the following requirements.

Content of anhydrous piperazine citrate, $(C_4H_{10}N_2)_3, 2C_6H_8O_7$
81.6 to 96.8% of the stated amount of Piperazine Citrate.

IDENTIFICATION

Extract a quantity of the powdered tablets containing 1 g of Piperazine Citrate with 20 mL of *water* and filter. The filtrate complies with the following tests.

A. Dilute 1 mL to 5 mL with *water*, add 0.5 g of *sodium hydrogen carbonate*, 0.5 mL of *potassium hexacyanoferrate(III) solution* and 0.1 mL of *mercury*, shake vigorously for 1 minute and allow to stand for 20 minutes; a reddish colour slowly develops.

B. Mix 4 mL with 1 mL of *hydrochloric acid*, add 0.5 g of *sodium nitrite*, heat to boiling, cool in ice for 15 minutes, scratching the side of the container with a glass rod to induce crystallisation and filter. The *melting point* of the crystals, after washing with 10 mL of iced *water* and drying at 100° to 105°, is about 159°, Appendix V A, Method I.

C. Yield the reactions characteristic of *citrates*, Appendix VI.

ASSAY

Weigh and powder 20 tablets. Dissolve as completely as possible a quantity of the powder containing 0.2 g of Piperazine Citrate in 10 mL of *water*, filter and wash the filter with three 5 mL quantities of *water*. To the combined filtrate and washings add 3.5 mL of 0.5M *sulfuric acid* and 100 mL of *picric acid solution R1*, heat on a water bath for 15 minutes, allow to stand for 1 hour, filter, wash the residue with *piperazine dipicrate solution* until the washings are free from sulfate and dry the residue to constant weight at 105°. Each g of residue is equivalent to 0.3935 g of $(C_4H_{10}N_2)_3, 2C_6H_8O_7$.

STORAGE

Piperazine Citrate Tablets should be protected from light.

Procaine Benzylpenicillin Injection

Action and use
Penicillin antibacterial.

DEFINITION

Procaine Benzylpenicillin Injection is a sterile suspension of Procaine Benzylpenicillin in Water for Injections.

The injection complies with the requirements stated under Parenteral Preparations and with the following requirements.

Content of total penicillins, calculated as $C_{13}H_{20}N_2O_2, C_{16}H_{18}N_2O_4S, H_2O$
90.0 to 110.0% of the stated amount of Procaine Benzylpenicillin.

Content of procaine, $C_{13}H_{20}N_2O_2$
36.0 to 44.0% of the stated amount of Procaine Benzylpenicillin.

CHARACTERISTICS

A white suspension.

IDENTIFICATION

A. Dilute a volume of the well-shaken suspension containing 10 mg of Procaine Benzylpenicillin to 10 mL with *water* and add 0.5 mL of *neutral red solution*. Add sufficient 0.01M *sodium hydroxide* to produce a permanent orange colour and then add 1 mL of *penicillinase solution*. A red colour is produced rapidly.

B. Carry out the method for *thin-layer chromatography*, Appendix III A, using the following solutions.

(1) Shake a volume of the well-shaken suspension containing 50 mg of Procaine Benzylpenicillin with 5 mL of *methanol*, add a small quantity of *water* to dissolve any residue and dilute to 10 mL with *water*.

(2) 0.5% w/v of *procaine benzylpenicillin BPCRS* in *acetone*.

CHROMATOGRAPHIC CONDITIONS

(a) Use a *TLC silica gel silanised plate* (Merck silanised silica gel 60 plates are suitable).

(b) Use the mobile phase as described below.

(c) Apply 1 µL of each solution.

(d) Develop the plate to 15 cm.

(e) After removal of the plate, allow it to dry in air, expose to iodine vapour until spots appear and examine in daylight.

MOBILE PHASE

30 volumes of *acetone* and 70 volumes of a 15.4% w/v solution of *ammonium acetate* adjusted to pH 7.0 with 10M *ammonia*.

SYSTEM SUITABILITY

The test is not valid unless the chromatogram obtained with solution (2) shows two clearly separated spots.

CONFIRMATION

The two principal spots in the chromatogram obtained with solution (1) are similar in position, colour and size to those in the chromatogram obtained with solution (2).

C. Yields the reaction characteristic of *primary aromatic amines*, Appendix VI, producing a bright orange-red precipitate.

TESTS

Related substances

Carry out the method for *liquid chromatography*, Appendix III D, using the following solutions.

(1) To a quantity of the well-shaken suspension containing 70 mg of Procaine Benzylpenicillin add sufficient mobile phase to produce 50 mL, mix, filter and use the filtrate.

(2) Mix 1 mL of solution (1) and 1 mL of a 0.007% w/v solution of *4-aminobenzoic acid* and add sufficient mobile phase to produce 100 mL.

(3) Dissolve 4 mg of *4-aminobenzoic acid* in 25 mL of a solution containing 0.070% w/v of *procaine benzylpenicillin BPCRS* in the mobile phase.

CHROMATOGRAPHIC CONDITIONS

(a) Use a stainless steel column (25 cm × 4.6 mm) packed with *octadecylsilyl silica gel for chromatography* (5 µm) (Lichrospher ODS is suitable).

(b) Use isocratic elution and the mobile phase described below.

(c) Use a flow rate of 1.5 mL per minute.

(d) Use an ambient column temperature.

(e) Use a detection wavelength of 225 nm.

(f) Inject 20 µL of each solution.

(g) For solution (1) allow the chromatography to proceed for 1.5 times the retention time of the peak due to benzylpenicillin.

MOBILE PHASE

250 volumes of *acetonitrile*, 250 volumes of water and 500 volumes of a freshly prepared solution containing 1.4% w/v of *potassium dihydrogen orthophosphate* and 0.65% w/v of *tetrabutylammonium hydroxide*, adjusted to pH 7.0 with 1M *potassium hydroxide*. Adjust the pH of the mixture to 7.2 with 2M *orthophosphoric acid*, if necessary.

For solution (3), when the chromatogram is recorded under the prescribed conditions the substances elute in the following order: 4-aminobenzoic acid, procaine, benzylpenicillin.

SYSTEM SUITABILITY

The test is not valid unless, in the chromatogram obtained with solution (3), the *resolution factor* between the peaks due to 4-aminobenzoic acid and procaine is at least 2.0. If necessary, adjust the concentration of acetonitrile in the mobile phase.

LIMITS

In the chromatogram obtained with solution (1):

the area of any peak due to 4-aminobenzoic acid is not greater than 10 times the area of the corresponding peak in the chromatogram obtained with solution (2) (0.5%);

the area of any other *secondary peak* is not greater than the area of the peak corresponding to benzylpenicillin in the chromatogram obtained with solution (2) (1%).

Bacterial endotoxins

Carry out the *test for bacterial endotoxins*, Appendix XIV C, Method C. Dilute a quantity of the well-shaken suspension, if necessary, with *water BET* to produce a solution containing 3 mg of Procaine Benzylpenicillin per mL (solution A). The endotoxin limit concentration of solution A is 0.3 IU per mL. Carry out the test using a suitable dilution of solution A as described under Method C.

ASSAY

Carry out the method for *liquid chromatography*, Appendix III D, using the following solutions.

(1) Add to a quantity of the well-shaken suspension containing 70 mg of Procaine Benzylpenicillin sufficient mobile phase to produce 100 mL, mix, filter and use the filtrate.

(2) 0.07% w/v of *procaine benzylpenicillin BPCRS* in the mobile phase.

(3) Dissolve 4 mg of *4-aminobenzoic acid* in 25 mL of solution (2).

CHROMATOGRAPHIC CONDITIONS

The chromatographic conditions described under Related substances may be used.

For solution (3), when the chromatogram is recorded under the prescribed conditions the substances elute in the following order: 4-aminobenzoic acid, procaine, benzylpenicillin.

SYSTEM SUITABILITY

The Assay is not valid unless, in the chromatogram obtained with solution (3), the *resolution factor* between the peaks due to 4-aminobenzoic acid and procaine is at least 2.0. If necessary, adjust the concentration of acetonitrile in the mobile phase.

DETERMINATION OF CONTENT

Calculate the content of $C_{13}H_{20}N_2O_2$ and of $C_{13}H_{20}N_2O_2,C_{16}H_{18}N_2O_4S,H_2O$ in the injection from the chromatograms obtained and using the declared content of $C_{13}H_{20}N_2O_2$ and of $C_{13}H_{20}N_2O_2,C_{16}H_{18}N_2O_4S,H_2O$ in *procaine benzylpenicillin BPCRS*.

3 g of Procaine Benzylpenicillin is approximately equivalent to 2 g of benzylpenicillin.

Pyrethrum Extract

DEFINITION
Pyrethrum Extract is prepared from Pyrethrum Flower.

Extemporaneous preparation
Exhaust Pyrethrum Flower, in *coarse powder*, by percolation with a suitable hydrocarbon solvent; remove the solvent and concentrate at a low temperature. The resulting product may be decolourised by a suitable procedure. Determine the proportion of pyrethrins in a portion of the extract by the Assay. To the remainder add, if necessary, sufficient Light Liquid Paraffin or *deodorised kerosene* to produce an extract of the required strength.

The extract complies with the requirements for Labelling stated under Extracts and with the following requirements.

Content of pyrethrins
24.5% to 25.5% w/w, of which not less than half consists of pyrethrin I.

CHARACTERISTICS
A dark olive green or brown viscous liquid or, if decolourised, a pale amber liquid.

ASSAY
To 0.5 g of the well-mixed extract add 20 mL of 0.5M *ethanolic potassium hydroxide* and boil under a reflux condenser for 45 minutes. Transfer the solution to a beaker and wash the flask with sufficient hot *water*, adding the washings to the beaker, to produce a total volume of 200 mL. Boil until the volume is reduced to 150 mL, cool rapidly and transfer the solution to a stoppered flask, washing the beaker with three 20 mL quantities of *water* and transferring any gummy residue to the flask. Add 1 g of diatomaceous earth (Filtercel is suitable) and 10 mL of *barium chloride solution*, swirl gently and add sufficient *water* to produce 250 mL. Stopper the flask, shake vigorously until the separating liquid is clear and filter the suspension through a filter paper (Whatman No. 1 is suitable).

If the pyrethrum extract is coloured, carry out the following preliminary treatment. Transfer 0.5 g of the well-mixed extract to a stoppered flask, add 50 mL of *aromatic-free petroleum spirit (boiling range, 40° to 60°)*, swirl, add 1 g of diatomaceous earth (Filtercel is suitable), swirl to mix completely, stopper the flask and allow to stand at 20° to 22° for 16 hours. Mix the contents of the flask thoroughly, filter with gentle suction through a sintered-glass filter (ISO 4793, porosity grade 4, is suitable) and wash the residue with five 10 mL quantities of *aromatic-free petroleum spirit (boiling range, 40° to 60°)*. Remove the solvent from the combined filtrate and washings and evaporate to a volume of 1 to 2 mL. Add 20 mL of 0.5M *ethanolic potassium hydroxide* and boil under a reflux condenser for 45 minutes. Transfer the solution to a beaker and wash the flask with sufficient hot *water*, adding the washings to the beaker, to produce a total volume of 200 mL. Boil until the volume is reduced to

150 mL, cool rapidly and transfer the solution to a stoppered flask, washing the beaker with three 20 mL quantities of *water* and transferring any gummy residue to the flask. Add 1 g of diatomaceous earth (Filtercel is suitable) and 10 mL of *barium chloride solution*, swirl gently and add sufficient *water* to produce 250 mL. Stopper the flask, shake vigorously until the separating liquid is clear and filter the suspension through a filter paper (Whatman No. 1 is suitable).

For pyrethrin I
Transfer 200 mL of the filtrate to a separating funnel, rinsing the measuring vessel with two 5 mL quantities of *water*, and add 0.05 mL of *phenolphthalein solution R1*. Neutralise the solution by the drop wise addition of *hydrochloric acid* and add 1 mL of *hydrochloric acid* in excess. Add 5 mL of a saturated solution of *sodium chloride* and 50 mL of *aromatic-free petroleum spirit (boiling range, 40° to 60°)*, shake vigorously for 1 minute, allow to separate, remove and retain the lower layer. Filter the petroleum spirit extract through absorbent cotton into a second separating funnel containing 10 mL of *water*. Return the aqueous layer to the first separating funnel and repeat the extraction with 50 mL and then with 25 mL of *aromatic-free petroleum spirit (boiling range, 40° to 60°)*, reserving the aqueous layer for the assay of pyrethrin II, and filtering the petroleum spirit extracts through the same absorbent cotton into the second separating funnel. Shake the combined petroleum spirit extracts and water for about 30 seconds and allow to separate; remove the lower layer and add it to the aqueous liquid reserved for the assay of pyrethrin II. Wash the combined petroleum spirit extracts with a further 10 mL of *water*, adding the washings to the reserved aqueous liquid.

To the petroleum spirit extracts add 5 mL of 0.1M *sodium hydroxide*, shake vigorously for 1 minute, allow to separate and remove the clear lower layer, washing the stem of the separating funnel with 1 mL of *water*. Repeat the extraction by shaking for about 30 seconds with two quantities of 2.5 mL and 1.5 mL of 0.1M *sodium hydroxide* and add the extracts to the alkaline extract. Add to the flask 10 mL of *mercury(II) sulfate solution*, stopper, swirl and allow to stand in the dark at 25° ± 0.5° for exactly 60 minutes after the addition of the mercury(II) sulfate solution. Add 20 mL of *acetone* and 3 mL of a saturated solution of *sodium chloride*, heat to boiling on a water bath, allow the precipitate to settle and decant the supernatant liquid through a filter paper (Whatman No. 1 is suitable), retaining most of the precipitate in the flask. Wash the precipitate with 10 mL of *acetone*, again boil, allow to settle and decant through the same filter paper. Repeat the washing and decanting with three 10 mL quantities of hot *chloroform*. Transfer the filter paper to the flask, add 50 mL of a cooled mixture of three volumes of *hydrochloric acid* and two volumes of *water*, 1 mL of *strong iodine monochloride reagent* and 6 mL of *chloroform*. Titrate with 0.01M *potassium iodate VS*, running almost all the required volume of titrant into the flask in one portion. Continue the titration, shaking the flask vigorously for 30 seconds after each addition of the titrant, until the chloroform is colourless. Repeat the operation without the extract; the difference between the titrations represents the amount of potassium iodate required. Each mL of 0.01M *potassium iodate VS* is equivalent to 5.7 mg of pyrethrin I.

For pyrethrin II
Transfer the combined aqueous liquids reserved in the Assay for pyrethrin I to a beaker, cover with a watch glass and evaporate to 50 mL within 35 to 45 minutes. Cool, washing

the underside of the watch glass with not more than 5 mL of *water* and adding the washings to the beaker. Filter through absorbent cotton into a separating funnel, washing with successive quantities of 10, 7.5, 7.5, 5 and 5 mL of *water*. Saturate the aqueous liquid with *sodium chloride*, add 10 mL of *hydrochloric acid* and 50 mL of *ether*, shake for 1 minute, allow to separate, and remove the lower layer. Repeat the extraction successively with 50, 25 and 25 mL of *ether*. Wash the combined ether extracts with three 10 mL quantities of a saturated solution of *sodium chloride* and transfer the ether layer to a flask with the aid of 10 mL of *ether*. Remove the bulk of the ether by distillation and remove the remainder with a gentle current of air and dry the residue at 100° for 10 minutes, removing any residual acid fumes with a gentle current of air. Add 2 mL of *ethanol (96%)* previously neutralised to *phenolphthalein solution R1* and 0.05 mL of *phenolphthalein solution R1*, swirl to dissolve the residue, add 20 mL of *carbon dioxide-free water* and titrate rapidly with 0.02M *sodium hydroxide VS* until the colour changes to brownish pink and persists for 30 seconds, keeping the flask stoppered between additions of alkali. Repeat the operation using the aqueous liquid reserved for the repeat operation in the Assay for pyrethrin I. The difference between the titrations represents the volume of 0.02M *sodium hydroxide VS* required. Each mL of 0.02M *sodium hydroxide VS* is equivalent to 3.74 mg of pyrethrin II.

STORAGE
Pyrethrum Extract should be kept in a well-filled container, protected from light and should be thoroughly stirred before use.

Sodium Calcium Edetate Intravenous Infusion for Veterinary Use

Action and use
Chelating agent.

DEFINITION
Sodium Calcium Edetate Intravenous Infusion for Veterinary Use is a sterile solution of Sodium Calcium Edetate. It is prepared immediately before use by diluting Sterile Sodium Calcium Edetate Concentrate for Veterinary Use with a suitable diluent in accordance with the manufacturer's instructions.

The intravenous infusion complies with the requirements stated under Parenteral Preparations and with the following requirement.

LABELLING
The quantity of active ingredient is stated in terms of the equivalent amount of anhydrous sodium calcium edetate in a suitable dose-volume.

STERILE SODIUM CALCIUM EDETATE CONCENTRATE FOR VETERINARY USE

DEFINITION
Sterile Sodium Calcium Edetate Concentrate for Veterinary Use is a sterile solution of Sodium Calcium Edetate in Water for Injections containing the equivalent of 25.0% w/v of anhydrous sodium calcium edetate.

The concentrate complies with the requirements for Concentrates for Injections or Infusions stated under Parenteral Preparations and with the following requirements.

Content of anhydrous sodium calcium edetate, $C_{10}H_{12}CaN_2Na_2O_8$
22.5 to 27.5% w/v.

CHARACTERISTICS
A colourless solution.

IDENTIFICATION
A. Dilute 2.5 mL with 7.5 mL of *water*, make alkaline to *litmus paper* with 5M *ammonia* and add 5 mL of a 2.5% w/v solution of *ammonium oxalate*. Not more than a trace of precipitate is produced.

B. To 10 mL add 2 mL of a 10% w/v solution of *lead(II) nitrate*, shake and add 5 mL of *dilute potassium iodide solution*; no yellow precipitate is produced. Make alkaline to *litmus paper* with 5M *ammonia* and add 5 mL of a 2.5% w/v solution of *ammonium oxalate*; a white precipitate is produced.

C. Evaporate to dryness and ignite. The residue yields the reactions characteristic of *sodium salts* and of *calcium salts*, Appendix VI.

TESTS
Acidity or alkalinity
pH, 6.5 to 8.0, Appendix V L.

Bacterial endotoxins
Carry out the *test for bacterial endotoxins*, Appendix XIV C. The endotoxin limit concentration is not more than 0.125 IU per mg of sodium calcium edetate.

ASSAY
To 2.5 mL add 90 mL of *water*, 7 g of *hexamine* and 5 mL of 2M *hydrochloric acid* and titrate with 0.05M *lead nitrate VS* using *xylenol orange solution* as indicator. Each mL of 0.05M *lead nitrate VS* is equivalent to 18.71 mg of $C_{10}H_{12}CaN_2Na_2O_8$.

STORAGE
Sterile Sodium Calcium Edetate Concentrate for Veterinary Use should be kept in containers made from lead-free glass.

Sulfadimidine Injection

Action and use
Sulfonamide antibacterial.

DEFINITION
Sulfadimidine Injection is a sterile solution of sulfadimidine sodium in Water for Injections free from dissolved air. It is prepared by the interaction of Sulfadimidine and Sodium Hydroxide.

The injection complies with the requirements stated under Parenteral Preparations and with the following requirements.

Content of sulfadimidine sodium, $C_{12}H_{13}N_4NaO_2S$
95.0 to 105.0% of the stated amount.

IDENTIFICATION
A. Acidify a volume containing 0.1 g of sulfadimidine sodium with 6M *acetic acid*, filter, reserving the filtrate, wash the residue with *water* and dry at 105°. The *infrared absorption spectrum* of the residue, Appendix II A, is concordant with the *reference spectrum* of sulfadimidine *(RSV 50)*.

B. The residue obtained in test A yields the reaction characteristic of *primary aromatic amines*, Appendix VI, producing a bright orange-red precipitate.

TESTS
Alkalinity
pH, 10.0 to 11.0, Appendix V L.

Colour of solution
An injection containing 1 g of sulfadimidine sodium in 3 mL is not more intensely coloured than *reference solution Y_4*, Appendix IV B, Method I.

Related substances
Carry out the method for *thin-layer chromatography*, Appendix III A, using *silica gel H* as the coating substance and a mixture of 18 volumes of 10M *ammonia* and 90 volumes of *butan-1-ol* as the mobile phase. Apply separately to the plate 10 μL of each of the following solutions. For solution (1) use the injection being examined diluted with *water* to contain 0.20% w/v of sulfadimidine sodium. Solution (2) contains 0.0020% w/v of *sulfanilamide* in a mixture of 1 volume of 13.5M *ammonia* and 9 volumes of *ethanol (96%)*. After removal of the plate, heat it at 105° for 10 minutes and spray with a 0.1% w/v solution of *4-dimethylaminobenzaldehyde* in *ethanol (96%)* containing 1% v/v of *hydrochloric acid*. Any *secondary spot* in the chromatogram obtained with solution (1) is not more intense than the spot in the chromatogram obtained with solution (2) (1%).

ASSAY
Dilute a volume containing 0.5 g of sulfadimidine sodium to 75 mL with *water*, add 10 mL of *hydrochloric acid* and pass air slowly through the solution until the vapours do not turn moistened *starch iodate paper* blue. Add 3 g of *potassium bromide*, cool in ice and titrate slowly with 0.1M *sodium nitrite VS*, stirring constantly and determining the end point electrometrically. Each mL of 0.1M *sodium nitrite VS* is equivalent to 30.03 mg of $C_{12}H_{13}N_4NaO_2S$.

STORAGE
Sulfadimidine Injection should be protected from light.

LABELLING
The strength is stated as the amount of sulfadimidine sodium in a suitable dose-volume.

Sulfadoxine and Trimethoprim Injection

Action and use
Sulfonamide antibacterial.

DEFINITION
Sulfadoxine and Trimethoprim Injection is a sterile solution, in a suitable aqueous vehicle, containing Sulfadoxine and Trimethoprim in the proportion five parts to one part. The pH is adjusted to about 10 by the addition of Sodium Hydroxide. It may contain 0.1% w/v of Lidocaine Hydrochloride.

The injection complies with the requirements stated under Parenteral Preparations and with the following requirements.

Content of sulfadoxine, $C_{12}H_{14}N_4O_4S$
92.5 to 107.5% of the stated amount.

Content of trimethoprim, $C_{14}H_{18}N_4O_3$
92.5 to 107.5% of the stated amount.

CHARACTERISTICS
A clear, yellow solution.

IDENTIFICATION
A. Evaporate 50 mL of solution B obtained in the Assay for trimethoprim to about 10 mL, neutralise with 5M *sodium hydroxide* and then acidify with 2M *acetic acid*. Dissolve the precipitate by warming and adding a small volume of *ethanol (25%)*. Cool, recrystallise the precipitate from *ethanol (25%)*, wash with *water* and dry at 105°. The *infrared absorption spectrum* of the residue, Appendix II A, is concordant with the *reference spectrum* of sulfadoxine *(RSV 37)*.

B. Evaporate 100 mL of solution A obtained in the Assay for trimethoprim to about 4 mL, transfer to a test tube with the aid of about 4 mL of hot *water* and allow to cool. Wash the resulting crystals with *water* and dry at 105°. The *infrared absorption spectrum* of the residue, Appendix II A, is concordant with the *reference spectrum* of trimethoprim *(RSV 45)*.

C. Carry out the method for *thin-layer chromatography*, Appendix III A, using *silica gel G* as the coating substance and a mixture of 19 volumes of *chloroform* and 1 volume of *methanol* as the mobile phase. Apply separately to the plate 5 μL of each of the following solutions. For solution (1) dilute the injection with *methanol* to contain 2.5% w/v of Sulfadoxine. Solution (2) is a 0.040% w/v solution of *lidocaine hydrochloride BPCRS* in 0.1M *sodium hydroxide* in *methanol*. After removal of the plate, allow it to dry in air and spray with *potassium iodobismuthate solution*. For an injection labelled as containing Lidocaine Hydrochloride the chromatogram obtained with solution (1) exhibits a spot corresponding to the spot in the chromatogram obtained with solution (2); an injection not so labelled exhibits no such spot.

Alkalinity
pH, 9.0 to 10.5, when diluted with an equal volume of *carbon dioxide-free water*, Appendix V L.

ASSAY
For trimethoprim
Prepare an anion exchange column (Dowex 1-X1 is suitable) pre-treated in the following manner. Wash with 100 mL of *water*, rinse with 50 mL of 1M *sodium hydroxide*, wash with *water* until the washings are neutral, rinse with 70 mL of 0.1M *hydrochloric acid* in *methanol (70%)* and again wash with *water*, activate the column with 50 mL of 1M *sodium hydroxide*, again wash with *water* and finally moisten with *methanol (70%)*.

Apply to the anion-exchange column 20 mL of a dilution of the injection in *methanol (70%)* containing 50 mg of Trimethoprim and elute with *methanol (70%)* to a final elution volume of 200 mL (solution A). Elute the material remaining on the column with 150 mL of 0.1M *hydrochloric acid* in *methanol (70%)* and add sufficient 0.1M *hydrochloric acid* in *methanol (70%)* to produce 200 mL (solution B). Reserve solution B for the Assay for sulfadoxine and Identification test A. To 10 mL of solution A add 1 mL of 1M *sodium hydroxide* and sufficient *methanol (70%)* to produce 100 mL. Measure the *absorbance* of the resulting solution at the maximum at 288 nm, Appendix II B. Calculate the content of $C_{14}H_{18}N_4O_3$ taking 250 as the value of A(1%, 1 cm) at the maximum at 288 nm.

For sulfadoxine
To 2 mL of solution B obtained in the Assay for Trimethoprim add sufficient 0.1M *hydrochloric acid* in *methanol (70%)* to produce 250 mL. Measure the *absorbance*

of the resulting solution at the maximum at 267 nm, Appendix II B. Calculate the content of $C_{12}H_{14}N_4O_4S$ from the *absorbance* obtained by repeating the procedure using 2 mL of a 0.125% w/v solution of *sulfadoxine BPCRS* in 0.1M *hydrochloric acid* in *methanol (70%)* in place of solution B and using the declared content of $C_{12}H_{14}N_4O_4S$ in *sulfadoxine BPCRS*.

STORAGE

Sulfadoxine and Trimethoprim Injection should be protected from light.

LABELLING

The label states (1) the amount of Sulfadoxine and of Trimethoprim in a suitable dose-volume; (2) where applicable, that the injection contains Lidocaine Hydrochloride.

Tylosin Injection

Action and use

Macrolide antibacterial.

DEFINITION

Tylosin Injection is a sterile solution of Tylosin in a mixture of equal parts by volume of Propylene Glycol and Water for Injections.

The injection complies with the requirements stated under Parenteral Preparations and with the following requirements.

CHARACTERISTICS

A pale yellow to amber-coloured solution.

IDENTIFICATION

A. Dilute a volume containing 0.1 g of Tylosin with *water* to give a solution containing 0.02% w/v of Tylosin. To 5 mL of this solution add 10 mL of 0.1M *sodium hydroxide* and extract with 10 mL of *chloroform*. Separate the chloroform layer and extract it with 25 mL of 0.1M *hydrochloric acid*. Discard the chloroform, wash the aqueous layer with 3 mL of *chloroform*, discard the washings and filter. The *light absorption* of the filtrate, Appendix II B, in the range 230 to 350 nm, exhibits a maximum only at 290 nm. The *absorbance* at the maximum is about 0.94.

B. To 10 mL of the filtrate obtained in test A add 1 mL of 2M *sodium hydroxide*, heat on a water bath for 20 minutes and cool. The *light absorption*, Appendix II B, in the range 250 to 430 nm, exhibits a maximum at 332 nm.

TESTS

Composition

Carry out the method for *liquid chromatography*, Appendix III D, using the following freshly prepared solutions.

(1) Dilute the injection with sufficient of a mixture of equal volumes of *water* and *acetonitrile* to produce a solution containing 0.02% w/v of Tylosin.

(2) 0.02% w/v of *tylosin BPCRS* in a mixture of equal volumes of *water* and *acetonitrile*.

CHROMATOGRAPHIC CONDITIONS

(a) Use a stainless steel column (20 cm × 5 mm) packed with *octadecylsilyl silica gel for chromatography* (5 μm) (Nucleosil C18 is suitable).

(b) Use isocratic elution and the mobile phase described below.

(c) Use a flow rate of 1 mL per minute.

(d) Use an ambient column temperature.

(e) Use a detection wavelength of 290 nm.

(f) Inject 20 μL of each solution.

MOBILE PHASE

0.85M *sodium perchlorate* in a 40% v/v solution of *acetonitrile*, the solution being adjusted to pH 2.5 using 1M *hydrochloric acid*.

SYSTEM SUITABILITY

The chromatogram obtained with solution (2) shows similar resolution to the reference chromatogram supplied with *tylosin BPCRS*. If necessary adjust the molarity of the sodium perchlorate or raise the temperature of the column to a maximum of 50°. The order of elution of the six major components of *tylosin BPCRS* in the chromatogram obtained with solution (2) is: desmycinosyltylosin, tylosin C, tylosin B, tylosin D, an aldol impurity and tylosin A.

The *column efficiency*, determined using the peak due to tylosin A in the chromatogram obtained with solution (2), should be at least 22,000 theoretical plates per metre.

LIMITS

Calculate the percentage content of components by *normalisation*. In the chromatogram obtained with solution (1):

the content of tylosin A is not less than 80%;

the total content of tylosins A, B, C and D is not less than 90%.

Tyramine

Dilute a volume containing 0.1 g of Tylosin with 5 mL of 0.03M *orthophosphoric acid* in a 25 mL graduated flask, add 1 mL of *pyridine* and 2 mL of a saturated solution of *ninhydrin* (approximately 4% w/v). Close the flask by covering with a piece of aluminium foil and heat in a water bath at 85° for at least 20 minutes. Cool rapidly and add sufficient *water* to produce 25 mL. Measure the *absorbance* of the resulting solution without delay at 570 nm, Appendix II B, using in the reference cell a solution prepared in the same manner but omitting the injection being examined. The absorbance is not greater than that obtained by carrying out the procedure at the same time using 5 mL of a solution in 0.03M *orthophosphoric acid* containing 35 μg of *tyramine* per mL and beginning at the words 'add 1 mL...' (0.175%).

ASSAY

Carry out the *microbiological assay of antibiotics*, Appendix XIV A. The precision of the assay is such that the fiducial limits of error are not less than 95% and not more than 105% of the estimated potency.

Calculate the content of tylosin in the injection taking each 1000 IU found to be equivalent to 1 mg of tylosin.

The upper fiducial limit of error is not less than 97.0% and the lower fiducial limit of error is not more than 110.0% of the stated content.

STORAGE

Tylosin Injection should be kept in a cool place.

Monographs

Immunological Products

VETERINARY IMMUNOSERA

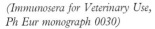

(Immunosera for Veterinary Use,
Ph Eur monograph 0030)

Veterinary Immunosera comply with the requirements of the European Pharmacopoeia monograph for Immunosera for Veterinary Use. These requirements are reproduced below.

The provisions of this monograph apply to the following immunosera.

Antitoxic sera

Clostridium Novyi Alpha Antitoxin⋆

Clostridium Perfringens Antitoxins

(incorporating Clostridium Perfringens Beta Antitoxin⋆

and Clostridium Perfringens Epsilon Antitoxin⋆)

Clostridium Tetani Antitoxin⋆

⋆ Monograph *of the European Pharmacopoeia*

Ph Eur _____

DEFINITION

Immunosera for veterinary use are preparations containing immunoglobulins, purified immunoglobulins or immunoglobulin fragments obtained from serum or plasma of immunised animals. They may be preparations of crude polyclonal antisera or purified preparations.

The immunoglobulins or immunoglobulin fragments have the power of specifically neutralising the antigen used for immunisation. The antigens include microbial or other toxins, bacterial and viral antigens, venoms of snakes and hormones. The preparation is intended for parenteral administration to provide passive immunity.

PRODUCTION
GENERAL PROVISIONS

Immunosera are obtained from the serum or plasma of healthy animals immunised by administration of one or more suitable antigens.

The production method shall have been shown to yield consistently batches of immunosera of acceptable safety (5.2.6) and efficacy (5.2.7).

DONOR ANIMALS

The animals used are exclusively reserved for production of immunoserum. They are maintained under conditions protecting them from the introduction of disease, as far as possible. The donor animals, and any animals in contact with them, are tested and shown to be free from a defined list of infectious agents and re-tested at suitable intervals. The list of agents for testing includes not only those agents that are relevant to the donor animal, but also those that are relevant to the recipient target species for the product. Where the donor animals have not been demonstrated to be free from a relevant pathogen, a justification must be provided and a validated inactivation or purification procedure must be included in the manufacturing procedure. The feed originates from a controlled source. Where the donor animals are chickens, use chickens from a flock free from specified pathogens (5.2.2). Where applicable for the species used, measures are taken to avoid contamination with agents of transmissible spongiform encephalopathies.

As far as possible, animals being introduced into the herd are from a known source and have a known breeding and rearing history. The introduction of animals into the herd follows specified procedures, including defined quarantine measures. During the quarantine period the animals are observed and tested to establish that they are free from the list of agents

relevant for the donor animals. It may be necessary to test the animals in quarantine for freedom from additional agents, depending on their known breeding and rearing history or any lack of information on their source.

Any routine or therapeutic medicinal treatment administered to the animals in quarantine or thereafter must be recorded.

IMMUNISING ANTIGEN

The principles described in the Production section of *Vaccines for veterinary use (0062)* are applied to the production of the immunogen. The antigen used is identified and characterised. The starting materials used for antigen preparation must be controlled to minimise the risk of contamination with extraneous agents. The antigen may be blended with a suitable adjuvant. The immunogen is produced on a batch basis. The batches must be prepared and tested in such a manner that assures that each batch will be equally safe and free from extraneous agents and will produce a satisfactory, consistent immune response.

IMMUNISATION

The donor animals are immunised according to a defined schedule. For each animal, the details of the dose of immunising antigen, route of administration and dates of administration are recorded. Animals are kept under general health surveillance and the development of specific antibodies are monitored at appropriate stages of the immunisation process.

COLLECTION OF BLOOD OR PLASMA

Animals are thoroughly examined before each collection. Only healthy animals may be used as a donor animal. Collection of blood is made by venepuncture or plasmapheresis. The puncture area is shaved, cleaned and disinfected. The method of collection and the volume to be collected on each occasion are specified. The blood or plasma is collected in such a manner as to maintain sterility of the product. If the serum or plasma is stored before further processing, precautions are taken to avoid microbial contamination.

The blood or plasma collection is conducted at a site separate from the area where the animals are kept or bred and the area where the immunoserum is further processed.

Clear criteria are established for determining the time between immunisation and first collection of blood or plasma as well as the time between subsequent collections and the length of time over which collections are made. The criteria applied must take into account the effect of the collections on the health and welfare of the animal as well as the effect on the consistency of production of batches of the finished product, over time.

The rate of clearance of any residues that may arise from the immunising antigen or medication given needs to be taken into account. In the case of the risk of residues from chemical substances, consideration could be given to the inclusion of a withdrawal period for the finished product. If the immunising agent consists of a live organism, the time between immunisation and collection may need to take into account the time required for the donor to eliminate the immunogen, particularly if any residual live organisms might be harmful to the recipient.

PREPARATION OF THE FINISHED PRODUCT

Several single plasma or serum collections from one or more animals may be pooled to form a bulk for preparation of a batch. The number of collections that may be used to produce a bulk and the size of the bulk are defined. Where pooling is not undertaken, the production procedure must be very carefully controlled to ensure that the consistency of the product is satisfactory.

The active substance is subjected to a purification and/or inactivation procedure unless omission of such a step has been justifed and agreed with the competent authority. The procedure applied must have been validated and be shown not to adversely impair the biological activity of the product. The validation studies must address the ability of the procedure to inactivate or remove any potential contaminants such as pathogens that could be transmitted from the donor to the recipient target species and infectious agents such as those that cause ubiquitous infections in the donor animals and cannot be readily eliminated from these donor animals.

For purified immunosera, the globulins containing the immune substances may be obtained from the crude immunoserum by enzyme treatment and fractional precipitation or by other suitable chemical or physical methods

Antimicrobial preservatives

Antimicrobial preservatives are used to prevent spoilage or adverse effects caused by microbial contamination occurring during use of a product. Antimicrobial preservatives are not included in freeze-dried products but, if justified, taking into account the maximum recommended period of use after reconstitution, they may be included in the diluent for multidose freeze-dried products. For single-dose liquid preparations, inclusion of antimicrobial preservatives is not normally acceptable, but may be acceptable, for example where the same product is filled in single-dose and multidose containers and is for use in non-food producing species. For multidose liquid preparations, the need for effective antimicrobial preservation is evaluated taking into account likely contamination during use and the maximum recommended period of use after broaching of the container.

During development studies the effectiveness of the antimicrobial preservative throughout the period of validity shall be demonstrated to the satisfaction of the competent authority.

The efficacy of the antimicrobial preservative is evaluated as described in chapter *5.1.3*; for a multidose preparation, additional samples are taken, to monitor the effect of the antimicrobial preservative over the proposed in-use shelf-life. If neither the A criteria nor the B criteria can be met, then in justified cases the following criteria are applied to antisera for veterinary use: bacteria, no increase at 24 h and 7 days, $3 \log_{10}$ reduction at 14 days, no increase at 28 days; fungi, no increase at 14 days and 28 days.

Addition of antibiotics as antimicrobial preservative is not acceptable.

Unless otherwise prescribed in the monograph, the final bulk is distributed aseptically into sterile, tamper-proof containers which are then closed so as to exclude contamination.

The preparation may be freeze-dried.

In-process tests Suitable tests are carried out in-process, such as on samples from collections before pooling to form a bulk.

BATCH TESTS

The tests that are necessary to demonstrate the suitability of a batch of a product will vary and are influenced by a number of factors, including the detailed method of production. The tests to be conducted by the manufacturer on a particular product are agreed with the competent authority. If a product is treated by a validated procedure for inactivation of extraneous agents, the test for extraneous

agents can be omitted on that product with the agreement of the competent authority. If a product is treated by a validated procedure for inactivation of mycoplasmas, the test for mycoplasmas can be omitted on that product with the agreement of the competent authority.

Only a batch that complies with each of the relevant requirements given below under Identification, Tests and Potency and/or in the relevant specific monograph may be released for use. With the agreement of the competent authority, certain tests may be omitted where in-process tests give an equal or better guarantee that the batch would comply or where alternative tests validated with respect to the Pharmacopoeia method have been carried out.

Certain tests, e.g. for antimicrobial preservatives, for foreign proteins and for albumin, may be carried out by the manufacturer on the final bulk rather than on the batch, batches or sub-batches of finished product prepared from it. In some circumstances, e.g. when collections are made into plasmapheresis bags and each one is, essentially, a batch, pools of samples may be tested, with the agreement of the competent authority.

It is recognised that, in accordance with General Notices (section 1.1. General statements), for an established antiserum the routine application of the safety test will be waived by the competent authority in the interests of animal welfare when a sufficient number of consecutive batches have been produced and found to comply with this test, thus demonstrating consistency of the manufacturing process. Significant changes to the manufacturing process may require resumption of routine testing to re-establish consistency. The number of consecutive batches to be tested depends on a number of factors such as the type of antiserum, the frequency of production of batches, and experience with the immunoserum during developmental safety testing and during application of the batch safety test. Without prejudice to the decision of the competent authority in the light of information available for a given antiserum, testing of 10 consecutive batches is likely to be sufficient for the majority of products. For products with an inherent safety risk, it may be necessary to continue to conduct the safety test on each batch.

Animal tests In accordance with the provisions of the European Convention for the Protection of Vertebrate Animals Used for Experimental and Other Scientific Purposes, tests must be carried out in such a way as to use the minimum number of animals and to cause the least pain, suffering, distress or lasting harm. The criteria for judging tests in monographs must be applied in the light of this. For example, if it is indicated that an animal is considered to show positive, infected etc. when typical clinical signs occur then as soon as sufficient indication of a positive result is obtained the animal in question shall be either euthanised or given suitable treatment to prevent unnecessary suffering. In accordance with the General Notices, alternative test methods may be used to demonstrate compliance with the monograph and the use of such tests is particularly encouraged when this leads to replacement or reduction of animal use or reduction of suffering.

pH (*2.2.3*)

The pH of crude and purified immunosera is shown to be within the limits set for the products.

Formaldehyde

If formaldehyde is used for production of immunoserum, a test for free formaldehyde is carried out as prescribed under Tests.

Other inactivating agents

When other inactivation methods are used, appropriate tests are carried out to demonstrate that the inactivating agent has been removed or reduced to an acceptable residual level.

Batch potency test

If a specific monograph exists for the product, the test described under Potency is not necessarily carried out for routine testing of batches of antiserum. The type of batch potency test to be carried out will depend on the claims being made for the product. Wherever possible, *in vitro* tests must be used. The type of test required may include measurement of antibodies against specific infectious organisms, determination of the type of antibody (e.g. neutralising or opsonising). All tests must be validated. The criteria for acceptance must be set with reference to a batch that has been shown to comply with the requirements specified under Potency if a specific monograph exists for the product, and which has been shown to have satisfactory efficacy, in accordance with the claims being made for the product.

Total immunoglobulins

A test for the quantities of total immunoglobulins and/or total gammaglobulins and/or specific immunoglobulin classes is carried out. The results obtained must be within the limits set for the product and agreed with the competent authority. The batch contains not more than the level shown to be safe in the safety studies and, unless the batch potency test specifically covers all appropriate immunoglobulins, the level in the batch is not less than that in the batch or batches shown to be effective in the efficacy studies.

Total protein

For products where claims are being made which relate to the protein content, as well as demonstrating that the batch contains not more than the stated upper limit, the batch shall be shown to contain not less than that in the batch or batches shown to be effective in the efficacy studies.

Extraneous agents

In addition to the test described under Tests, specific tests may be required depending on the nature of the preparation, its risk of contamination and the use of the product.

In particular, specific tests for important potential pathogens may be required when the donor and recipient species are the same and when these agents would not be detected reliably by the general screening test described under Tests.

Water

Where applicable, the freeze-drying process is checked by a determination of water and shown to be within the limits set for the product.

IDENTIFICATION

The identity of the product is established by immunological tests and, where necessary, by determination of biological activity. The potency test may also serve for identification.

TESTS

The following requirements refer to liquid immunosera and reconstituted freeze-dried immunosera.

Foreign proteins

When examined by precipitation tests with specific antisera against plasma proteins of a suitable range of species, only protein from the declared animal species is shown to be present.

Albumin

Purified immunosera comply with a test for albumin. Unless otherwise prescribed in the monograph, when examined electrophoretically, purified immunosera show not more than a trace of albumin, and the content of albumin is in any case not greater than 30 g/L of the reconstituted preparation, where applicable.

Total protein

Dilute the preparation to be examined with a 9 g/L solution of *sodium chloride R* to obtain a solution containing about 15 mg of protein in 2 mL. To 2 mL of this solution in a round-bottomed centrifuge tube add 2 mL of a 75 g/L solution of *sodium molybdate R* and 2 mL of a mixture of 1 volume of *nitrogen-free sulfuric acid R* and 30 volumes of *water R*. Shake, centrifuge for 5 min, discard the supernatant and allow the inverted tube to drain on filter paper. Determine the nitrogen in the residue by the method of sulfuric acid digestion (*2.5.9*) and calculate the content of protein by multiplying by 6.25. The results obtained are not greater than the upper limit stated on the label.

Antimicrobial preservative

Determine the amount of antimicrobial preservative by a suitable physicochemical method. The amount is not less than the minimum amount shown to be effective and is not greater than 115 per cent of that stated on the label.

Formaldehyde (*2.4.18*)

Where formaldehyde has been used in the preparation, the concentration of free formaldehyde is not greater than 0.5 g/L, unless a higher amount has been shown to be safe.

Sterility (*2.6.1*)

Immunosera for veterinary use comply with the test for sterility. When the volume of liquid in a container is greater than 100 mL, the method of membrane filtration is used wherever possible. If this method is used, incubate the media for not less than 14 days. Where the method of membrane filtration cannot be employed, the method of direct inoculation may be used. Where the volume of liquid in each container is at least 20 mL, the minimum volume to be used for each culture medium is 10 per cent of the contents of the container or 5 mL, whichever is the least. The appropriate number of items to be tested (*2.6.1*) is 1 per cent of the batch with a minimum of 4 and a maximum of 10.

Mycoplasmas (*2.6.7*)

Immunosera for veterinary use comply with the test for mycoplasmas.

Safety

A test is conducted in one of the species for which the product is recommended. Unless an overdose is specifically contraindicated on the label, twice the maximum recommended dose for the species used is administered by a recommended route. If there is a warning against administration of an overdose, a single dose is administered. For products to be used in mammals, use 2 animals of the minimum age for which the product is recommended. For avian products, use not fewer than 10 birds of the minimum age recommended. The birds are observed for 21 days. The other species are observed for 14 days. No abnormal local or systemic reaction occurs.

Extraneous agents

A test for extraneous agents is conducted by inoculation of cell cultures sensitive to pathogens of the species of the donor animal and into cells sensitive to pathogens of each of the recipient target species stated on the label (*2.6.25*). Observe the cells for 14 days. During this time, carry out at least one passage. The cells are checked daily for cytopathic effect and are checked at the end of 14 days for the presence of a haemadsorbing agent. The batch complies with the test if there is no evidence of the presence of an extraneous agent.

For immunosera of avian origin, if a test in cell culture is insufficient to detect potential extraneous agents, a test is conducted by inoculation of embryonated eggs from flocks free from specified pathogens (5.2.2) or by some other suitable method (polymerase chain reaction (PCR) for example).

POTENCY

Carry out a suitable test for potency.

Where a specific monograph exists, carry out the biological assay prescribed in the monograph and express the result in International Units per millilitre when such exist.

STORAGE

Protected from light, at a temperature of 5 ± 3 °C. Liquid immunosera must not be allowed to freeze.

LABELLING

The label states:
— that the preparation is for veterinary use;
— whether or not the preparation is purified;
— the minimum number of International Units per millilitre, where such exist;
— the volume of the preparation in the container;
— the indications for the product;
— the instructions for use including the interval between any repeat administrations and the maximum number of administrations that is recommended;
— the recipient target species for the immunoserum;
— the dose recommended for different species;
— the route(s) of administration;
— the name of the species of the donor animal;
— the maximum quantity of total protein;
— the name and amount of any antimicrobial preservative or any other excipient;
— any contra-indications to the use of the product including any required warning on the dangers of administration of an overdose;
— for freeze-dried immunosera:
— the name or composition and the volume of the reconstituting liquid to be added;
— the period within which the immunoserum is to be used after reconstitution.

Ph Eur

Clostridium Tetani Antitoxin

Tetanus Antitoxin (Veterinary)

(Tetanus Antitoxin for Veterinary Use, Ph Eur monograph 0343)

Ph Eur

DEFINITION

Tetanus antitoxin for veterinary use is a preparation containing principally the globulins that have the power of specifically neutralising the neurotoxin formed by *Clostridium tetani*. It consists of the serum or a preparation obtained from the serum of animals immunised against tetanus toxin.

PRODUCTION
CHOICE OF COMPOSITION

The antitoxin is shown to be satisfactory with respect to safety (5.2.6) and efficacy (5.2.7). For the latter, it shall be demonstrated, for each target species, that the product, when administered at the minimum recommended dose and according to the recommended schedule(s), provides a response or responses consistent with the claims made for the product. The ability of the product to neutralise the

neurotoxin formed by *C. tetani* must also be demonstrated, e.g. by conducting the test in mice as described below.

Demonstration of neurotoxin neutralisation

The ability of tetanus antitoxin to neutralise the neurotoxin of *C. tetani* is determined by establishing the dose necessary to protect mice (or guinea-pigs) against the toxic effects of a fixed dose of tetanus toxin. The test must be conducted in parallel with a test of a reference preparation of tetanus antitoxin, calibrated in International Units, using a quantity expected to give the same protection. The ability of the test antitoxin to neutralise the neurotoxin (potency) can then be expressed in International Units. For this study, a suitable preparation of tetanus toxin for use as a test toxin is required. The dose of the test toxin is determined in relation to the reference preparation; the potency of the antitoxin to be examined is determined in relation to the reference preparation using the test toxin.

Preparation of test toxin

Prepare the test toxin from a sterile filtrate of an 8-10 day culture in liquid medium of *C. tetani*. A test toxin may be prepared by adding this filtrate to *glycerol R* in the proportion of 1 volume of filtrate to 1 to 2 volumes of *glycerol R*. The solution of test toxin may be stored at or slightly below 0 °C. The toxin may also be dried by a suitable method. Select the test toxin by determining for mice the Lp/10 dose and the paralytic dose 50 per cent. A suitable toxin contains not less than 1000 times the paralytic dose 50 per cent in 1 Lp/10 dose.

Lp/10 dose (Limes paralyticum)

This is the smallest quantity of toxin which when mixed with 0.1 IU of antitoxin and injected subcutaneously into mice (or guinea-pigs) causes tetanic paralysis in the animals on or before the 4th day after injection.

Paralytic dose 50 per cent

This is the quantity of toxin which when injected subcutaneously into mice (or guinea-pigs) causes tetanic paralysis in one half of the animals on or before the 4th day after injection.

Determination of test dose of toxin

Reconstitute or dilute the reference preparation with a suitable liquid so that it contains 0.5 IU/mL. Measure or weigh a quantity of the test toxin and dilute with or dissolve in a suitable liquid. Prepare mixtures of the solution of the reference preparation and the solution of the test toxin so that each mixture will contain 0.1 IU of antitoxin in the volume chosen for injection and one of a series of graded volumes of the solution of the test toxin, separated from each other by steps of not more than 20 per cent and covering the expected end-point. Adjust each mixture with a suitable liquid to the same final volume (0.4 mL to 0.6 mL if mice are used for the test or 4.0 mL if guinea-pigs are used). Allow the mixtures to stand at room temperature for 60 min. Using not fewer than 2 animals for each mixture, inject the chosen volume subcutaneously into each animal. Observe the animals for 96 h and make daily records of the degree of tetanus developing in each group of animals. Repeat the test at least once and calculate the test dose as the mean of the different tests. The test dose of the toxin is the amount present in that mixture which causes tetanic paralysis in one half of the total number of animals injected with it.

Determination of the neutralising ability of the antitoxin to be examined

Preliminary test Measure or weigh a quantity of the test toxin and dilute with or dissolve in a suitable liquid so that the solution contains 5 test doses per millilitre (solution of the test toxin). Prepare mixtures of the solution of the test toxin and of the antitoxin to be examined so that for each mixture the volume chosen for injection contains the test dose of toxin and one of a series of graded volumes of the antitoxin to be examined. Adjust each mixture to the same final volume with a suitable liquid. Allow the mixtures to stand at room temperature for 60 min. Using not fewer than 2 animals for each mixture, inject the chosen volume subcutaneously into each animal. Observe the animals for 96 h and make daily records of the degree of tetanus developing in each group of animals. Using the results, select suitable mixtures for the final test.

Final test Prepare mixtures of the solution of the test toxin and of the antitoxin to be examined so that for each mixture the volume chosen for the injection contains the test dose of toxin and one of a series of graded volumes of the antitoxin to be examined, separated from each other by steps of not more than 20 per cent and covering the expected end-point as determined in the preliminary test. Prepare further mixtures with the same amount of test toxin and graded volumes of the reference preparation, centred on 0.1 IU in the volume chosen for injection, to confirm the test dose of the toxin. Adjust each mixture to the same final volume with a suitable liquid. Allow the mixtures to stand at room temperature for 60 min. Using not fewer than 2 animals for each mixture, inject the chosen volume subcutaneously into each animal. Observe the animals for 96 h and make daily records of the degree of tetanus developing in each group of animals. The test mixture which contains 0.1 IU in the volume injected is that mixture which causes tetanic paralysis in the same, or almost the same, number of animals as the reference mixture containing 0.1 IU in the volume injected. Repeat the determination at least once and calculate the mean of all valid estimates. Estimates are valid only if the reference preparation gives a result within 20 per cent of the expected value.

The confidence limits (P = 0.95) have been estimated to be:
— 85 per cent and 114 per cent when 2 animals per dose are used;
— 91.5 per cent and 109 per cent when 3 animals per dose are used;
— 93 per cent and 108 per cent when 6 animals per dose are used.

IDENTIFICATION
The antitoxin is shown, by a suitable immunochemical method (*2.7.1*), to react specifically with the neurotoxin formed by *C. tetani*. The potency test may also serve for identification.

POTENCY
Determine the titre of antibodies against the neurotoxin formed by *C. tetani* using a suitable immunochemical method (*2.7.1*) such as a toxin-binding-inhibition test (ToBI test) and a homologous reference serum, calibrated in International Units per millilitre.

The International Unit is the specific neutralising activity for tetanus toxin contained in a stated amount of the International Standard which consists of a quantity of dried immune horse serum. The equivalence in International Units of the International Standard is stated by the World Health Organization.

The potency of the finished product is expressed in International Units per millilitre and is shown to be not less than the minimum number stated on the label.

_____ *Ph Eur*

Veterinary Vaccines

(Vaccines for Veterinary Use,
Ph Eur monograph 0062)

Veterinary Vaccines comply with the requirements of the European Pharmacopoeia monograph for Vaccines for Veterinary Use. These requirements are reproduced below.

The provisions of this monograph apply to the following vaccines.

Inactivated Bacterial Vaccines

Bovine Leptospirosis Vaccine (Inactivated)★
Canine Leptospirosis Vaccine (Inactivated)★
Clostridium Botulinum Vaccine★
Clostridium Chauvoei Vaccine★
Clostridium Novyi Type B Vaccine★
Clostridium Perfringens Vaccines★
Clostridium Septicum Vaccine★
Clostridium Tetani Vaccines★
Feline Chlamydiosis Vaccine (Inactivated)★
Fowl Cholera Vaccine (Inactivated)★
Furunculosis Vaccine for Salmonids, Inactivated★
Mannheimia Vaccine (Inactivated) for Cattle★
Mannheimia Vaccine (Inactivated) for Sheep★
Mycoplasma Gallisepticum Vaccine (Inactivated)★
Pasteurella Vaccine (Inactivated) for Sheep★
Porcine Actinobacillosis Vaccine, Inactivated★
Porcine Enzootic Pneumonia Vaccine (Inactivated)★
Porcine E. Coli Vaccine, Inactivated★
Porcine Progressive Atrophic Rhinitis Vaccine, Inactivated★
Ruminant E. Coli Vaccine, Inactivated★
Salmonella Enteritidis Vaccine (Inactivated) for Chickens★
Salmonella Typhimurium Vaccine (Inactivated) for Chickens★
Swine Erysipelas Vaccine, Inactivated★
Vibriosis Vaccine for Salmonids, Inactivated, Cold-water★
Vibriosis Vaccine for Salmonids, Inactivated★

Living Bacterial Vaccines

Anthrax Vaccine, Living★
Brucella Melitensis (Strain Rev. 1) Vaccine, Living★
Coccidiosis Vaccine (Live) for Chickens★
Salmonella Dublin Vaccine, Living

Inactivated Viral Vaccines

Aujesky's Disease Vaccine, Inactivated★
Avian Infectious Bronchitis Vaccine, Inactivated★
Avian Paramyxovirus 3 Vaccine, Inactivated★
Bovine Viral Diarrhoea Vaccine (Inactivated)★
Calf Coronavirus Diarrhoea Vaccine (Inactivated)★
Calf Rotavirus Diarrhoea Vaccine (Inactivated)★
Canine Adenovirus Vaccine, Inactivated★
Canine Parvovirus Vaccine, Inactivated ★
Egg-drop Syndrome 76 (Adenovirus) Vaccine★
Equine Herpesvirus Vaccine, Inactivated★
Equine Influenza Vaccine★
Feline Calicivirus Vaccine, Inactivated★
Feline Infectious Enteritis Vaccine, Inactivated★
Feline Leukaemia Vaccine, Inactivated★
Feline Viral Rhinotracheitis Vaccine, Inactivated★

Foot and Mouth Disease (Ruminants) Vaccine★

Infectious Bursal Disease Vaccine, Inactivated★

Louping-ill Vaccine

Newcastle Disease Vaccine, Inactivated★

Ovine Enzootic Abortion Vaccine

Porcine Parvovirus Vaccine, Inactivated★

Rabbit Haemorrhagic Disease Vaccine (Inactivated)★

Rabies Veterinary Vaccine, Inactivated★

Swine Influenza Vaccine, Inactivated★

Living Viral Vaccines

Aujesky's Disease Vaccine, Living★

Avian Infectious Bronchitis Vaccine, Living★

Avian Viral Tenosynovitis Vaccine (Live)★

Bovine Parainfluenza Virus Vaccine, Living★

Bovine Respiratory Syncytial Virus Vaccine, Living★

Canine Adenovirus Vaccine, Living ★

Canine Distemper Vaccine, Living★

Canine Parainfluenza Virus Vaccine (Live)★

Canine Parvovirus Vaccine, Living★

Contagious Pustular Dermatitis Vaccine, Living

Duck Plague Vaccine (Live)★

Duck Viral Hepatitis Type I Vaccine (Live)★

Feline Calicivirus Vaccine, Living★

Feline Infectious Enteritis Vaccine, Living★

Feline Viral Rhinotracheitis Vaccine, Living★

Ferret and Mink Distemper Vaccine, Living★

Fowl Pox Vaccine, Living★

Infectious Avian Encephalomyelitis Vaccine, Living★

Infectious Bovine Rhinotracheitis Vaccine, Living★

Infectious Bursal Disease Vaccine, Living★

Infectious Chicken Anaemia Vaccine (Live)★

Laryngotracheitis Vaccine, Living★

Marek's Disease Vaccine, Living★

Myxomatosis Vaccine (Live) for Rabbits★

Newcastle Disease and Avian Infectious Bronchitis Vaccine, Living

Newcastle Disease Vaccine, Living★

Rabies Vaccine for Foxes, Living★

Swine-Fever Vaccine (Live, Prepared in Cell Cultures), Classical★

Helminth Vaccine

Lungworm (Dictyocaulus Viviparus) Oral Vaccine, Living

★*Monograph* of the European Pharmacopoeia

Ph Eur

In the case of combined vaccines, for each component that is the subject of a monograph in the Pharmacopoeia, the provisions of that monograph apply to that component, modified where necessary as indicated (see chapters 5.2.6. Evaluation of safety of veterinary vaccines and immunosera and 5.2.7. Evaluation of efficacy of veterinary vaccines and immunosera). If an immunological product for veterinary use is intended for minor use, certain tests may be excluded, subject to approval by the competent authority[1].

---

[1] NOTE: Guidance on data requirements for immunological veterinary medicinal products intended for minor use or minor species/limited markets (EMA/CVMP/IWP/123243/2006, including any subsequent revision of this document.

1 DEFINITION

Vaccines for veterinary use are preparations containing antigenic substances and are administered for the purpose of inducing a specific and active immunity against disease provoked by bacteria, toxins, viruses, fungi or parasites. The vaccines, live or inactivated, confer active immunity that may be transferred passively via maternal antibodies against the immunogens they contain and sometimes also against antigenically related organisms. Vaccines may contain bacteria, toxins, viruses or fungi, living or inactivated, parasites, or antigenic fractions or substances produced by these organisms and rendered harmless whilst retaining all or part of their antigenic properties; vaccines may also contain combinations of these constituents. The antigens may be produced by recombinant DNA technology. Suitable adjuvants may be included to enhance the immunising properties of the vaccines.

Terminology used in monographs on vaccines for veterinary use is defined in chapter *5.2.1.*

1-1 BACTERIAL VACCINES AND BACTERIAL TOXOIDS

Bacterial vaccines and bacterial toxoids are prepared from cultures grown on suitable solid or liquid media, or by other suitable means; the requirements of this section do not apply to bacterial vaccines prepared in cell cultures or in live animals. The strain of bacterium used may have been modified by genetic engineering. The identity, antigenic potency and purity of each bacterial culture used is carefully controlled.

Bacterial vaccines contain inactivated or live bacteria or their antigenic components; they are liquid preparations of various degrees of opacity or they may be freeze-dried.

Bacterial toxoids are prepared from toxins by diminishing their toxicity to a very low level or by completely eliminating it by physical or chemical means whilst retaining adequate immunising potency. The toxins are obtained from selected strains of specified micro-organisms grown in suitable media or are obtained by other suitable means, for example, chemical synthesis.

The toxoids may be:
— liquid;
— precipitated with alum or another suitable agent;
— purified and/or adsorbed on aluminium phosphate, aluminium hydroxide, calcium phosphate or another adsorbent prescribed in the monograph.

Bacterial toxoids are clear or slightly opalescent liquids. Adsorbed toxoids are suspensions or emulsions. Certain toxoids may be freeze-dried.

Unless otherwise indicated, statements and requirements given below for bacterial vaccines apply equally to bacterial vaccines, bacterial toxoids and products containing a combination of bacterial cells and toxoid.

1-2 VIRAL VACCINES

Viral vaccines are prepared by growth in suitable cell cultures (*5.2.4*), in tissues, in micro-organisms, in fertilised eggs or, where no other possibility is available, in live animals, or by other suitable means. The strain of virus used may have been modified by genetic engineering. They are liquid or freeze-dried preparations of one or more viruses or viral subunits or peptides.

Live viral vaccines are prepared from viruses of attenuated virulence or of natural low virulence for the target species.

Inactivated viral vaccines are treated by a validated procedure for inactivation of the virus and may be purified and concentrated.

1-3 VECTOR VACCINES

Vector vaccines are liquid or freeze-dried preparations of one or more types of live micro-organisms (bacteria or viruses) that are non-pathogenic or have low pathogenicity for the target species and in which have been inserted one or more genes encoding antigens that stimulate an immune response protective against other micro-organisms.

2 PRODUCTION
2-1 PREPARATION OF THE VACCINE

The methods of preparation, which vary according to the type of vaccine, are such as to maintain the identity and immunogenicity of the antigen and to ensure freedom from contamination with extraneous agents.

Substances of animal origin used in the production of vaccines for veterinary use comply with the requirements of chapter *5.2.5*. Other substances used in the preparation of vaccines for veterinary use comply with requirements of the Pharmacopoeia (where a relevant monograph exists) and are prepared in a manner that avoids contamination of the vaccine.

2-1-1 Substrates for production

Cell cultures used in the production of vaccines for veterinary use comply with the requirements of chapter *5.2.4*.

Where a monograph refers to chicken flocks free from specified pathogens (SPF), these flocks comply with the requirements prescribed in chapter *5.2.2*.

For production of inactivated vaccines, where vaccine organisms are grown in poultry embryos, such embryos are derived either from SPF flocks (*5.2.2*) or from healthy non-SPF flocks free from the presence of certain agents and their antibodies, as specified in the monograph. It may be necessary to demonstrate that the inactivation process is effective against specified potential contaminants. For the production of a master seed lot and for all passages of a micro-organism up to and including the working seed lot, eggs from SPF flocks (*5.2.2*) are used.

Where it is unavoidable to use animals or animal tissues in the production of veterinary vaccines, such animals shall be free from specified pathogens, as appropriate to the source species and the target animal for the vaccine.

2-1-2 Media used for seed culture preparation and for production

At least the qualitative composition must be recorded of media used for seed culture preparation and for production. The grade of each named ingredient is specified. Where media or ingredients are claimed as proprietary, this is indicated and an appropriate description recorded. Ingredients that are derived from animals are specified as to the source species and country of origin, and must comply with the criteria described in chapter *5.2.5*. Preparation processes for media used, including sterilisation procedures, are documented.

The addition of antibiotics during the manufacturing process is normally restricted to cell culture fluids and other media, egg inocula and material harvested from skin or other tissues.

2-1-3 Seed lots

2-1-3-1 Bacterial seed lots

2-1-3-1-1 General requirements. The genus and species (and varieties where appropriate) of the bacteria used in the vaccine are stated. Bacteria used in manufacture are handled

in a seed-lot system wherever possible. Each master seed lot is tested as described below. A record of the origin, date of isolation, passage history (including purification and characterisation procedures) and storage conditions is maintained for each master seed lot. Each master seed lot is assigned a specific code for identification purposes.

2-1-3-1-2 Propagation. The minimum and maximum number of subcultures of each master seed lot prior to the production stage are specified. The methods used for the preparation of seed cultures, preparation of suspensions for seeding, techniques for inoculation of seeds, titre and concentration of inocula and the media used, are documented. It shall be demonstrated that the characteristics of the seed material (for example, dissociation or antigenicity) are not changed by these subcultures. The conditions under which each seed lot is stored are documented.

2-1-3-1-3 Identity and purity. Each master seed lot is shown to contain only the species and strain of bacterium stated. A brief description of the method of identifying each strain by biochemical, serological and morphological characteristics and distinguishing it as far as possible from related strains is recorded, as is also the method of determining the purity of the strain. If the master seed lot is shown to contain living organisms of any kind other than the species and strain stated, then it is unsuitable for vaccine production.

2-1-3-2 Virus seed lots

2-1-3-2-1 General requirements. Viruses used in manufacture are handled in a seed-lot system. Each master seed lot is tested as described below. A record of the origin, date of isolation, passage history (including purification and characterisation procedures) and storage conditions is maintained for each seed lot. Each master seed lot is assigned a specific code for identification purposes. Production of vaccine is not normally undertaken using virus more than 5 passages from the master seed lot. In the tests on the master seed lot described below, the organisms used are not normally more than 5 passages from the master seed lot at the start of the tests, unless otherwise indicated.

Where the master seed lot is contained within a permanently infected master cell seed, the following tests are carried out on an appropriate volume of virus from disrupted master cell seed. Where relevant tests have been carried out on disrupted cells to validate the suitability of the master cell seed, these tests need not be repeated.

2-1-3-2-2 Propagation. The master seed lot and all subsequent passages are propagated on cells, on embryonated eggs or in animals that have been shown to be suitable for vaccine production (see above), and, where applicable, using substances of animal origin that meet the requirements prescribed in chapter *5.2.5*.

2-1-3-2-3 Identification. A suitable method to identify the vaccine strain and to distinguish it as far as possible from related strains must be used.

2-1-3-2-4 Bacteria and fungi. The master seed lot complies with the test for sterility (*2.6.1*).

2-1-3-2-5 Mycoplasmas (*2.6.7*). The master seed lot complies with the test for mycoplasmas (culture method and indicator cell culture method).

2-1-3-2-6 Absence of extraneous viruses. Monographs may contain requirements for freedom from extraneous agents, otherwise the requirements stated below apply.

Preparations of monoclonal or polyclonal antibodies containing high levels of neutralising antibody to the virus of the seed lot are made on a batch basis, using antigen that is not derived from any passage level of the virus isolate giving rise to the master seed virus. Each batch of serum is maintained at 56 °C for 30 min to inactivate complement. Each batch is shown to be free of antibodies to potential contaminants of the seed virus and is shown to be free of any non-specific inhibiting effects on the ability of viruses to infect and propagate within cells (or eggs, where applicable). If such a serum cannot be obtained, other methods are used to remove or neutralise the seed virus specifically.

If the seed lot virus would interfere with the conduct and sensitivity of a test for extraneous viruses, a sample of the master seed lot is treated with a minimum amount of the monoclonal or polyclonal antibody so that the vaccine virus is neutralised as far as possible or removed. The final virus-serum mixture shall, if possible, contain at least the virus content of 10 doses of vaccine per 0.1 mL for avian vaccines and per millilitre for other vaccines. For avian vaccines, the testing to be carried out on seed lots is given in chapter *2.6.24*. For mammalian vaccines, the seed lot or the mixture of seed lot and antiserum is tested for freedom from extraneous agents as follows.

The mixture is inoculated onto cultures of at least 70 cm^2 of the required cell types. The cultures may be inoculated at any suitable stage of growth up to 70 per cent confluency. At least 1 monolayer of each type must be retained as a control. The cultures must be monitored daily for a week. At the end of this period the cultures are freeze thawed 3 times, centrifuged to remove cell debris and re-inoculated onto the same cell type as above. This is repeated twice. The final passage must produce sufficient cells in appropriate vessels to carry out the tests below.

Cytopathic and haemadsorbing agents are tested for using the methods described in the relevant sections on testing cell cultures (*5.2.4*) and techniques such as immunofluorescence are used for detection of specific contaminants for the tests in cell cultures. The master seed lot is inoculated onto:
— primary cells of the species of origin of the virus;
— cells sensitive to viruses pathogenic for the species for which the vaccine is intended;
— cells sensitive to pestiviruses.

If the master seed lot is shown to contain living organisms of any kind, other than the virus of the species and strain stated, or foreign viral antigens, then it is unsuitable for vaccine production.

2-1-4 Inactivation
Inactivated vaccines are subjected to a validated inactivation procedure. The testing of the inactivation kinetics described below is carried out once for a given production process. The rest of this section applies to each production run. When conducting tests for inactivation, it is essential to take account of the possibility that under the conditions of manufacture, organisms may be physically protected from inactivant.

2-1-4-1 Inactivation kinetics. The inactivating agent and the inactivation procedure shall be shown, under conditions of manufacture, to inactivate the vaccine micro-organism. Adequate data on inactivation kinetics shall be obtained. Normally, the time required for inactivation shall be not more than 67 per cent of the duration of the inactivation process.

2-1-4-2 Aziridine. If an aziridine compound is used as the inactivating agent then it shall be shown that no inactivating agent remains at the end of the inactivation procedure. This may be accomplished by neutralising the inactivating agent with thiosulfate and demonstrating residual thiosulfate in the inactivated harvest at the completion of the inactivation procedure.

2-1-4-3 Formaldehyde. If formaldehyde is used as the inactivating agent, then a test for free formaldehyde is carried out as prescribed under Tests.

2-1-4-4 Other inactivating agents. When other inactivation methods are used, appropriate tests are carried out to demonstrate that the inactivating agent has been removed or reduced to an acceptable residual level.

2-1-4-5 Residual live virus/bacteria and/or detoxification testing. A test for complete inactivation and/or detoxification is performed immediately after the inactivation and/or detoxification procedure and, if applicable, the neutralisation or removal of the inactivating or detoxifying agent.

2-1-4-5-1 Bacterial vaccines. The test selected shall be appropriate to the vaccine bacteria being used and shall consist of at least 2 passages in production medium or, if solid medium has been used for production, in a suitable liquid medium or in the medium prescribed in the monograph. The product complies with the test if no evidence of any live micro-organism is observed.

2-1-4-5-2 Bacterial toxoids. The test selected shall be appropriate to the toxin or toxins present and shall be the most sensitive available.

2-1-4-5-3 Viral vaccines. The test selected shall be appropriate to the vaccine virus being used and must consist of at least 2 passages in cells, embryonated eggs or, where no other suitably sensitive method is available, in animals. The quantity of cell samples, eggs or animals shall be sufficient to ensure appropriate sensitivity of the test. For tests in cell cultures, not less than 150 cm^2 of cell culture monolayer is inoculated with 1.0 mL of inactivated harvest. The product complies with the test if no evidence of the presence of any live virus or other micro-organism is observed.

The final bulk vaccine is prepared by combining one or more batches of antigen that comply with all the relevant requirements with any auxiliary substances, such as adjuvants, stabilisers, antimicrobial preservatives and diluents.

2-2 CHOICE OF VACCINE COMPOSITION AND CHOICE OF VACCINE STRAIN
For the choice of vaccine composition and choice of vaccine strain, important aspects to be evaluated include safety, efficacy and stability. General requirements for evaluation of safety and efficacy are given in chapter *5.2.6* and chapter *5.2.7*. These requirements may be made more explicit or supplemented by the requirements of specific monographs.

For live vaccines, a maximum virus titre or bacterial count acceptable from the point of view of safety is established during development studies. This is then used as the maximum acceptable titre for each batch of vaccine at release.

2-2-1 Potency and immunogenicity
The tests given under the headings Potency and Immunogenicity in monographs serve 2 purposes:
— the Potency section establishes, by a well-controlled test in experimental conditions, the minimum acceptable vaccinating capacity for all vaccines within the scope of the definition, which must be guaranteed throughout the period of validity;
— well-controlled experimental studies are normally a part of the overall demonstration of efficacy of a vaccine (see chapter *5.2.7*); the test referred to in the section

Immunogenicity (to which the section Potency usually cross-refers) is suitable as a part of this testing.

2-2-2 Route of administration

During development of a vaccine, safety and immunogenicity are demonstrated for each route of administration to be recommended. The following is a non-exhaustive list of such routes of administration:
— intramuscular;
— subcutaneous;
— intravenous;
— ocular;
— oral;
— nasal;
— foot-stab;
— wing web;
— intradermal;
— intraperitoneal;
— *in ovo*.

2-2-3 Methods of administration

During development of a vaccine, safety and immunogenicity are demonstrated for each method of administration to be recommended. The following is a non-exhaustive list of such methods of administration:
— injection;
— drinking water;
— spray;
— eye-drop;
— scarification;
— implantation;
— immersion.

2-2-4 Categories of animal

Monographs may indicate that a given test is to be carried out for each category of animal of the target species for which the product is recommended or is to be recommended. The following is a non-exhaustive list of categories that are to be taken into account.
— *Mammals*:
　　— pregnant animals/non-pregnant animals;
　　— animals raised primarily for breeding/animals raised primarily for food production;
　　— animals of the minimum age or size recommended for vaccination.
— *Avian species*:
　　— birds raised primarily for egg production/birds raised primarily for production of meat;
　　— birds before point of lay/birds after onset of lay.
— *Fish*:
　　— broodstock fish/fish raised primarily for food production.

2-2-5 Antimicrobial preservatives

Antimicrobial preservatives are used to prevent spoilage or adverse effects caused by microbial contamination occurring during use of a vaccine which is expected to be no longer than 10 h after first broaching. Antimicrobial preservatives are not included in freeze-dried products but, if justified, taking into account the maximum recommended period of use after reconstitution, they may be included in the diluent for multi-dose freeze-dried products. For single-dose liquid preparations, inclusion of antimicrobial preservatives is not acceptable unless justified and authorised, but may be acceptable, for example where the same vaccine is filled in single-dose and multidose containers and is used in non-food-producing species. For multidose liquid preparations, the need for effective antimicrobial preservation is evaluated taking into account likely contamination during use and the maximum recommended period of use after broaching of the container.

During development studies the effectiveness of the antimicrobial preservative throughout the period of validity shall be demonstrated to the satisfaction of the competent authority.

The efficacy of the antimicrobial preservative is evaluated as described in chapter *5.1.3* and in addition samples are tested at suitable intervals over the proposed in-use shelf-life.

If neither the A criteria nor the B criteria can be met, then in justified cases the following criteria are applied to vaccines for veterinary use: bacteria, no increase from 24 h to 7 days, 3 $\log_{10}$ reduction at 14 days, no increase at 28 days; fungi, no increase at 14 days and 28 days.

Addition of antibiotics as antimicrobial preservative is generally not acceptable.

2-2-6 Stability

Evidence of stability is obtained to justify the proposed period of validity. This evidence takes the form of the results of virus titrations, bacterial counts or potency tests carried out at regular intervals until 3 months beyond the end of the shelf life on not fewer than 3 representative consecutive batches of vaccine kept under recommended storage conditions together with results from studies of moisture content (for freeze-dried products), physical tests on the adjuvant, chemical tests on substances such as the adjuvant constituents and preservatives, and pH, as appropriate.

Where applicable, studies on the stability of the reconstituted vaccine are carried out, using the product reconstituted in accordance with the proposed recommendations.

2-3 MANUFACTURER′S TESTS

Certain tests may be carried out on the final bulk vaccine rather than on the batch or batches prepared from it; such tests include those for antimicrobial preservatives, free formaldehyde and the potency determination for inactivated vaccines.

2-3-1 Residual live virus/bacteria and/or detoxification testing

For inactivated vaccines, where the auxiliary substances would interfere with a test for inactivation and/or detoxification, a test for inactivation or detoxification is carried out during preparation of the final bulk, after the different batches of antigen have been combined but before addition of auxiliary substances; the test for inactivation or detoxification may then be omitted on the final bulk and the batch.

Where there is a risk of reversion to toxicity, the test for detoxification performed at the latest stage of the production process at which the sensitivity of the test is not compromised (e.g. after the different batches of antigen have been combined but before the addition of auxiliary substances) is important to demonstrate a lack of reversion to toxicity.

2-3-2 Batch potency test

For most vaccines, the tests cited under Potency or Immunogenicity are not suitable for the routine testing of batches.

For live vaccines, the minimum acceptable virus titre or bacterial count that gives satisfactory results in the potency test and other efficacy studies is established during development. For routine testing it must be demonstrated for each batch that the titre or count at release is such that at the end of the period of validity, in the light of stability studies, the vaccine, stored in the recommended conditions, will contain not less than the minimum acceptable virus titre or bacterial count determined during development studies.

For inactivated vaccines, if the test described under Potency is not used for routine testing, a batch potency test is established during development. The aim of the batch potency test is to ensure that each batch of vaccine would, if tested, comply with the test described under Potency and Immunogenicity. The acceptance criteria for the batch potency test are therefore established by correlation with the test described under Potency. Where a batch potency test is described in a monograph, this is given as an example of a test that is considered suitable, after establishment of correlation with the potency test; other test models can also be used.

2-3-3 Batch

Unless otherwise prescribed in the monograph or otherwise justified and authorised, the final bulk vaccine is distributed aseptically into sterile, tamper-proof containers, with or without freeze-drying, which are then closed so as to exclude contamination.

Only a batch that complies with each of the requirements given below under 3 Batch tests or in the relevant individual monograph may be released for use. With the agreement of the competent authority, certain of the batch tests may be omitted where in-process tests give an equal or better guarantee that the batch would comply or where alternative tests validated with respect to the Pharmacopoeia method have been carried out. Under particular circumstances (i.e. significant changes to the manufacturing process, as well as reports of unexpected adverse reactions observed in the field or reports that the final batches do not comply with the former data provided during licensing), other tests, including tests on animals, may be needed on an *ad hoc* basis; they are carried out in agreement with or at the request of the competent authority. For safety testing, one or more of the tests described in chapter *5.2.6* may be carried out.

The identification test can often be conveniently combined with the batch potency test to avoid the unnecessary use of animals. For a given vaccine, a validated *in vitro* test can be used to avoid the unnecessary use of animals.

2-3-3-1 Animal tests. In accordance with the provisions of the European Convention for the Protection of Vertebrate Animals Used for Experimental and Other Scientific Purposes, tests must be carried out in such a way as to use the minimum number of animals and to cause the least pain, suffering, distress or lasting harm. The criteria for judging tests in monographs must be applied in light of this.

For example, if it is indicated that an animal is considered to be positive, infected etc. when typical clinical signs occur then as soon as it is clear that result will not be affected the animal in question shall be either euthanised or given suitable treatment to prevent unnecessary suffering. In accordance with the General Notices, alternative test methods may be used to demonstrate compliance with the monograph and the use of such tests is particularly encouraged when this leads to replacement or reduction of animal use or reduction of suffering.

2-3-3-2 Physical tests. A vaccine with an oily adjuvant is tested for viscosity by a suitable method and shown to be within the limits set for the product. The stability of the emulsion shall be demonstrated.

2-3-3-3 Chemical tests. Tests for the concentrations of appropriate substances such as aluminium and preservatives are carried out to show that these are within the limits set for the product.

2-3-3-4 pH. The pH of liquid products and diluents is measured and shown to be within the limits set for the product.

2-3-3-5 Water. Where applicable, the freeze-drying process is checked by a determination of water and shown to be within the limits set for the product.

3 BATCH TESTS

The monographs also indicate tests to be carried out on each particular vaccine.

All hen eggs, chickens and chicken cell cultures for use in quality control tests shall be derived from an SPF flock (*5.2.2*).

3-1 Identification

For inactivated vaccines, the identification prescribed in monographs is usually an antibody induction test since this is applicable to all vaccines.

3-2 Formaldehyde (*2.4.18*); use Method B if sodium metabisulfite has been used to neutralise excess formaldehyde)

Where formaldehyde has been used in the preparation, the concentration of free formaldehyde is not greater than 0.5 g/L, unless a higher amount has been shown to be safe.

3-3 Phenol (*2.5.15*)

When the vaccine contains phenol, the concentration is not greater than 5 g/L.

3-4 Sterility (*2.6.1*)

Vaccines comply with the test for sterility. Where the volume of liquid in a container is greater than 100 mL, the method of membrane filtration is used wherever possible. Where the method of membrane filtration cannot be used, the method of direct inoculation may be used. Where the volume of liquid in each container is at least 20 mL, the minimum volume to be used for each culture medium is 10 per cent of the contents or 5 mL, whichever is less. The appropriate number of items to be tested (*2.6.1*) is 1 per cent of the batch with a minimum of 4 and a maximum of 10.

For live bacterial and for live fungal vaccines, the absence of micro-organisms other than the vaccine strain is demonstrated by suitable methods such as microscopic examination and inoculation of suitable media.

For frozen or freeze-dried avian live viral vaccines produced in embryonated eggs, for non-parenteral use only, the requirement for sterility is usually replaced by requirements for absence of pathogenic micro-organisms and for a maximum of 1 non-pathogenic micro-organism per dose.

3-5 Extraneous agents

Monographs prescribe a set of measures that, taken together, give an acceptable degree of assurance that the final product does not contain infectious extraneous agents. These measures include:

1) production within a seed-lot system and a cell-seed system, wherever possible;

2) extensive testing of seed lots and cell seed for extraneous agents;

3) requirements for SPF flocks used for providing substrates for vaccine production;

4) testing of substances of animal origin, which must, wherever possible, undergo an inactivation procedure;

5) for live vaccines, testing of the final product for infectious extraneous agents; such tests are less extensive than those carried out at earlier stages because of the guarantees given by in-process testing.

— all the vaccinated pigs survive and the difference between the averages of the daily gains for the 2 groups is not less than 1.5 kg;

— the geometrical mean titres and the duration of excretion of the challenge virus are significantly lower in vaccinates than in controls.

2-3-2-2 Vaccines intended for passive immunisation. If the vaccine is intended for use in sows for the passive protection of piglets, the suitability of the strain for this purpose may be demonstrated by the following method.

Use for the test not fewer than 12 sows that do not have antibodies against Aujeszky's disease virus. Vaccinate not fewer than 8 sows, according to the schedule to be recommended. Maintain not fewer than 4 sows as controls. At 6-10 days of age, challenge the piglets from the sows with a sufficient quantity of virulent Aujeszky's disease virus. Observe the piglets at least daily for 21 days.

The test is not valid if the average number of piglets per litter for each group is less than 6. The vaccine complies with the test if not less than 80 per cent protection against mortality is found in the piglets from the vaccinated sows compared to those from the control sows.

2-4 MANUFACTURER'S TESTS

2-4-1 Residual live virus

The test for residual live virus is carried out using 2 passages in the same type of cell culture as that used in the production of the vaccine or cells shown to be at least as sensitive. The quantity of inactivated virus harvest used in the test is equivalent to not less than 25 doses of the vaccine. The inactivated virus harvest complies with the test if no live virus is detected.

2-4-2 Batch potency test

It is not necessary to carry out the potency test (section 3-5) for each batch of vaccine if it has been carried out using a batch of vaccine with a minimum potency. The test described under Potency is carried out for a given vaccine, on one or more occasions, as decided by or with the agreement of the competent authority. Where this test is not carried out, an alternative validated method is used, the criteria for acceptance being set with reference to a batch of vaccine that has given satisfactory results in the test described under Potency.

3 BATCH TESTS

3-1 Identification

In animals that do not have antibodies against Aujeszky's disease virus or against a fraction of the virus, the vaccine stimulates the production of specific antibodies against Aujeszky's disease virus or the fraction of the virus used in the production of the vaccine.

3-2 Bacteria and fungi

The vaccine, including where applicable the diluent supplied for reconstitution, complies with the test for sterility prescribed in the monograph *Vaccines for veterinary use (0062)*.

3-3 Residual live virus

Wherever possible, carry out a suitable test for residual live Aujeszky's disease virus using 2 passages in the same type of cell culture as used in the production of the vaccine or cells shown to be at least as sensitive. Otherwise, inject 1 dose of the vaccine subcutaneously into each of 5 healthy non-immunised rabbits. Observe the rabbits for 14 days after the injection. The vaccine complies with the test if no abnormal reaction (in particular a local rash) occurs. If the vaccine

strain is not pathogenic for the rabbit, carry out the test in 2 sheep.

3-4 Specified extraneous agents

Use not fewer than 2 pigs that do not have antibodies against Aujeszky's disease virus and against pestiviruses. Administer to each pig by a recommended route a double dose of the vaccine, then another dose after 14 days. 14 days after the last administration, carry out tests for antibodies. The vaccine complies with the test if it does not stimulate the formation of antibodies against pestiviruses.

3-5 Potency

The vaccine complies with the requirements of the test described below when administered by a recommended route and method.

Use for the test not fewer than 10 pigs weighing 15-35 kg and that do not have antibodies against Aujeszky's disease virus or against a fraction of the virus. The body mass of none of the pigs differs from the average body mass of the group by more than 25 per cent. Vaccinate not fewer than 5 pigs with 1 dose of the vaccine. Maintain not fewer than 5 pigs as controls. After 3 weeks, weigh each pig, then challenge them by the intranasal route with a sufficient quantity of virulent Aujeszky's disease virus. Weigh each animal 7 days after challenge or at the time of death if this occurs earlier and calculate the average daily gain as a percentage. For each group (vaccinated and controls), calculate the average of the average daily gains.

The test is invalid unless all the control pigs display signs of Aujeszky's disease and the average of their daily gains is less than −0.5 kg. The vaccine complies with the test if the vaccinated pigs survive and the difference between the averages of the daily gains for the 2 groups is not less than 1.1 kg.

4 LABELLING

The label states whether the vaccine strain is pathogenic for the rabbit.

———————————————————————— Ph Eur

Aujeszky's Disease Vaccine, Living

(Aujeszky's Disease Vaccine (Live) for Pigs for Parenteral Administration, Ph Eur monograph 0745)

Ph Eur ——————————————————————————

1 DEFINITION

Aujeszky's disease vaccine (live) for pigs for parenteral administration is a preparation of a suitable strain of Aujeszky's disease virus. This monograph applies to vaccines intended for the active immunisation of pigs and for passive protection of their progeny against Aujeszky's disease. The vaccine may be administered after mixing with an adjuvant.

2 PRODUCTION

2-1 PREPARATION OF THE VACCINE

The vaccine virus is grown in cell cultures.

2-2 SUBSTRATE FOR VIRUS PROPAGATION

2-2-1 Cell cultures

The cell cultures comply with the requirements for cell cultures for the production of veterinary vaccines (*5.2.4*).

2-3 CHOICE OF VACCINE VIRUS

The vaccine virus is shown to be satisfactory with respect to safety (5.2.6) and efficacy (5.2.7) for the pigs for which it is intended. The virus may have a genetic marker.

The following tests for safety (section 2-3-1), virus excretion (section 2-3-2), non-transmissibility, including transmission across the placenta and by semen (section 2-3-3), increase in virulence (section 2-3-4) and immunogenicity (section 2-3-5), may be used during the demonstration of safety and efficacy.

2-3-1 Safety

2-3-1-1 Safety test in piglets Carry out the test for each route and method of administration to be recommended for vaccination, using in each case piglets 3-4 weeks old. Use vaccine virus at the least attenuated passage level that will be present between the master seed lot and a batch of the vaccine.

For each test, use not fewer than 20 piglets that do not have antibodies against Aujeszky's disease virus. Administer to not fewer than 10 piglets a quantity of the vaccine virus equivalent to not less than 10 times the maximum virus titre likely to be contained in 1 dose of the vaccine. Maintain not fewer than 10 piglets as controls. Observe the piglets at least daily for at least 21 days.

The vaccine virus complies with the test if the weight curve of the vaccinated piglets does not differ significantly from that of the controls and if no piglet shows signs of disease or dies from causes attributable to the vaccine virus.

2-3-1-2 Safety of the pigs used in tests 2-3-5 for immunogenicity The pigs used in the tests for immunogenicity are also used to evaluate safety. Measure the body temperature of each vaccinated pig at the time of vaccination and 6 h, 24 h and 48 h later. Examine the injection site at slaughter for local reactions.

The vaccine virus complies with the test if no pig shows:
— a temperature rise greater than 1.5 °C and the number of pigs showing a temperature greater than 41 °C does not exceed 10 per cent of the group;
— other systemic reactions (for example, anorexia);
— abnormal local reactions attributable to the vaccine virus.

2-3-1-3 Safety in field studies The pigs used for field trials are also used to evaluate safety. Carry out a test in each category of pigs for which the vaccine is intended (sows, fattening pigs). Use not fewer than 3 groups, each of not fewer than 20 pigs, with corresponding groups of not fewer than 10 controls. Measure the body temperature of each pig at the time of vaccination and 6 h, 24 h and 48 h later. Examine the injection site at slaughter for local reactions.

The vaccine virus complies with the test if no pig shows:
— a temperature rise greater than 1.5 °C and the number of pigs showing a temperature greater than 41 °C does not exceed 25 per cent of the group;
— abnormal local reactions attributable to the vaccine virus.

2-3-1-4 Neurological safety Use for the test not fewer than 10 piglets, 3-5 days old and that do not have antibodies against Aujeszky's disease virus. Administer to each piglet by the intranasal route a quantity of the vaccine virus equivalent to not less than 10 times the maximum virus titre likely to be contained in 1 dose of the vaccine. Observe the piglets at least daily for at least 21 days.

The vaccine virus complies with the test if none of the piglets dies or shows signs of neurological disorder attributable to the vaccine virus.

2-3-1-5 Neurological safety for strains other than gE-negative This test is not necessary for gE-negative strains. Administer to not fewer than 5 piglets, 3-5 days old, by the intracerebral route, $10^{4.5}$ CCID$_{50}$ of vaccine virus.

The vaccine virus complies with the test if none of the piglets dies or shows signs of neurological disorder.

2-3-1-6 Absence of latent infections Use for the test not fewer than 10 piglets, 3-4 weeks old and that do not have antibodies against Aujeszky's disease virus. Administer to each piglet a daily injection of 2 mg of prednisolone per kilogram of body mass for 5 consecutive days. On the 3rd day administer to each piglet a quantity of vaccine virus equivalent to not less than the maximum virus titre likely to be contained in 1 dose of the vaccine by a route to be recommended. Antimicrobial agents may be administered to prevent aspecific signs. Observe the piglets at least daily for at least 21 days.

The vaccine virus complies with the test if no piglet shows signs of disease or dies from causes attributable to the vaccine virus.

2-3-1-7 Safety in pregnant sows and absence of transmission across the placenta Use for the test not fewer than 15 pregnant sows that do not have antibodies against Aujeszky's disease virus. Administer to not fewer than 5 sows, by a route to be recommended, a quantity of vaccine virus equivalent to not less than 10 times the maximum virus titre likely to be contained in 1 dose of the vaccine during the 4th or 5th week of gestation. Administer to not fewer than 5 other sows the same dose of the virus by the same route during the 10th or 11th weeks of gestation. Maintain not fewer than 5 other pregnant sows as controls. For the piglets from vaccinated sows: carry out tests for serum antibodies against Aujeszky's disease virus; carry out tests for Aujeszky's disease virus antigen in the liver and lungs of those piglets showing abnormalities and in a quarter of the remaining healthy piglets.

The vaccine virus complies with the test if:
— the number of piglets born to the vaccinated sows, any abnormalities in the piglets and the duration of gestation do not differ significantly from those of the controls;
— no Aujeszky's disease virus antigen is found in piglets born to the vaccinated sows;
— no antibodies against Aujeszky's disease virus are found in the serum taken before ingestion of the colostrum.

2-3-2 Virus excretion

Use for the test not fewer than 18 pigs, 3-4 weeks old and that do not have antibodies against Aujeszky's disease virus. Administer to not fewer than 14 pigs a quantity of the vaccine virus equivalent to not less than the maximum virus titre likely to be contained in 1 dose of the vaccine by a route and a site to be recommended. Maintain not fewer than 4 pigs as contact controls. Carry out suitably sensitive tests for the virus individually on the nasal and oral secretions as follows: collect nasal and oral swabs daily from the day before vaccination until 10 days after vaccination.

The vaccine complies with the test if the virus is not isolated from the secretions collected.

2-3-3 Non-transmissibility

Carry out the test on 4 separate occasions. Each time, administer to not fewer than 4 piglets, 3-4 weeks old and that do not have antibodies against Aujeszky's disease virus, by a route to be recommended, a quantity of the vaccine virus equivalent to not less than the maximum virus titre likely to be contained in 1 dose of the vaccine. After 1 day, keep not fewer than 2 other piglets of the same age and that do not have antibodies against Aujeszky's disease virus close together with them. After 5 weeks, test all the piglets for the presence of antibodies against Aujeszky's disease virus.

The test is not valid if any vaccinated piglet does not show an antibody response. The vaccine virus complies with the test if no antibodies against Aujeszky's disease virus are detected in any group of contact controls and if all the vaccinated piglets show an antibody response.

2-3-4 Increase in virulence

Carry out the test according to general chapter *5.2.6* using piglets 3-5 days old and that do not have antibodies against Aujeszky's disease virus. If the properties of the vaccine virus allow sequential passage through 5 groups via natural spreading, this method may be used, otherwise passage as described below is carried out.

Administer to each piglet of the 1st group by the intranasal route a quantity of the vaccine virus that will allow recovery of virus for the passages described below. After 3-5 days, prepare a suspension from the brain, lung, tonsils and local lymph glands of each piglet and pool the samples. Administer 1 mL of the suspension of pooled samples by the intranasal route to each piglet of the next group. Carry out this passage operation not fewer than 4 times, verify the presence of the virus at each passage. If the virus is not found at a passage level, repeat the passage by administration to a group of 10 animals.

If the 5th group of animals shows no evidence of an increase in virulence indicative of reversion during the observation period, further testing is not required. Otherwise, carry out an additional safety test and compare the clinical signs and any relevant parameters in a group of at least 8 animals receiving the material used for the 1st passage and another similar group receiving the virus at the final passage level.

The vaccine virus complies with the test if no indication of increased virulence of the virus recovered for the final passage compared with the material used for the 1st passage is observed. If virus is not recovered after an initial passage in 2 animals and a subsequent repeat passage in 10 animals, the vaccine virus also complies with the test.

2-3-5 Immunogenicity

A test is carried out for each route and method of administration to be recommended for vaccination.

The quantity of vaccine virus to be administered to each pig is not greater than the minimum virus titre to be stated on the label and the virus is at the most attenuated passage level that will be present in a batch of vaccine.

2-3-5-1 Vaccines intended for active immunisation Use for the test not fewer than 15 fattening pigs of the age to be recommended and that do not have antibodies against Aujeszky's disease virus. The body mass of none of the pigs differs from the average body mass of the group by more than 20 per cent. Vaccinate not fewer than 10 pigs, according to the schedule to be recommended. Maintain not fewer than 5 pigs as controls. At the end of the fattening period (80-90 kg), weigh and challenge each pig by the intranasal route with a sufficient quantity of virulent Aujeszky's disease virus (challenge with at least 10^6 CCID$_{50}$ of a virulent strain having undergone not more than 3 passages and administered in not less than 4 mL of diluent has been found to be satisfactory). Determine the titre of virus in swabs taken from the nasal cavity of each pig daily from the day before challenge until virus is no longer detected. Weigh each pig 7 days after challenge or at the time of death if this occurs earlier and calculate the average

daily gain as a percentage. For each group (vaccinated and controls), calculate the average of the average daily gains.

The test is invalid unless all the control pigs display signs of Aujeszky's disease and the average of their average daily gains is less than -0.5 kg. The vaccine complies with the test if:
— all the vaccinated pigs survive and the difference between the averages of the average daily gains for the 2 groups is not less than 1.5 kg;
— the geometrical mean titres and the duration of excretion of the challenge virus are significantly lower in vaccinates than in controls.

2-3-5-2 Vaccines intended for passive protection If the vaccine is intended for use in sows for the passive protection of piglets, the suitability of the vaccine virus for this purpose may be demonstrated by the following method.

Use for the test not fewer than 12 sows that do not have antibodies against Aujeszky's disease virus. Vaccinate not fewer than 8 sows, according to the schedule to be recommended. Maintain not fewer than 4 sows as controls. At 6-10 days of age, challenge the piglets from the sows with a sufficient quantity of virulent Aujeszky's disease virus. Observe the piglets at least daily for 21 days.

The test is not valid if the average number of piglets per litter for each group is less than 6.

The vaccine complies with the test if not less than 80 per cent protection against mortality is found in the piglets from the vaccinated sows compared to those from the control sows.

2-4 MANUFACTURER'S TESTS

2-4-1 Batch potency test

It is not necessary to carry out the Potency test (section 3-6) for each batch of the vaccine if it has been carried out on a representative batch using a vaccinating dose containing not more than the minimum virus titre stated on the label.

The test described under Potency is carried out for a given vaccine, on one or more occasions, as decided by or with the agreement of the competent authority. Where this test is not carried out, an alternative validated method is used, the criteria for acceptance being set with reference to a batch of vaccine that has given satisfactory results in the test described under Potency.

3 BATCH TESTS

3-1 Identification

The vaccine virus is identified by a suitable method, e.g. when mixed with a monospecific antiserum, the vaccine virus is no longer able to infect susceptible cell cultures into which it is inoculated.

3-2 Bacteria and fungi

The vaccine, including where applicable, the diluent supplied for reconstitution, complies with the test for sterility prescribed in the monograph *Vaccines for veterinary use (0062)*.

3-3 Mycoplasmas *(2.6.7)*

The vaccine complies with the test for mycoplasmas.

3-4 Extraneous agents

Neutralise the vaccine virus with a suitable monospecific antiserum or monoclonal antibodies against Aujeszky's disease virus and inoculate into cell cultures known for their susceptibility to viruses pathogenic for pigs and to pestiviruses. Carry out at least 1 passage and maintain the cultures for 14 days. The vaccine complies with the test if no cytopathic effect develops and there is no sign of the presence of haemadsorbing agents. Carry out a specific test for pestiviruses.

3-5 Virus titre

Titrate the vaccine virus in suitable cell cultures. The vaccine complies with the test if 1 dose contains not less than the minimum virus titre stated on the label.

3-6 Potency

The vaccine complies with the requirements of the test described below when administered by a recommended route and method.

Use not fewer than 10 pigs weighing 15-35 kg and that do not have antibodies against Aujeszky's disease virus. The body mass of none of the pigs differs from the average body mass of the group by more than 25 per cent. Vaccinate not fewer than 5 pigs with 1 dose of the vaccine. Maintain not fewer than 5 pigs as controls. After 3 weeks, weigh each pig, then challenge them by the intranasal route with a sufficient quantity of virulent Aujeszky's disease virus. Weigh each pig 7 days after challenge or at the time of death if this occurs earlier and calculate the average daily gain as a percentage. For each group (vaccinated and controls), calculate the average of the average daily gains.

The test is invalid unless all the control pigs display signs of Aujeszky's disease and the average of their average daily gains is less than -0.5 kg. The vaccine complies with the test if all the vaccinated pigs survive and the difference between the averages of the average daily gains for the 2 groups is not less than 1.6 kg.

_____ *Ph Eur*

Avian Infectious Bronchitis Vaccine (Inactivated)

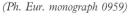

(Ph. Eur. monograph 0959)

CAUTION Accidental injection of oily vaccine can cause serious local reactions in man. Expert medical advice should be sought immediately and the doctor should be informed that the vaccine is an oil emulsion.

Ph Eur _____

1 DEFINITION

Avian infectious bronchitis vaccine (inactivated) is a preparation of one or more suitable strains of one or more serotypes of avian infectious bronchitis virus, inactivated while maintaining adequate immunogenic properties. This monograph applies to vaccines intended to protect birds against a drop in egg production or quality; for vaccines also intended for protection against respiratory signs, a demonstration of efficacy additional to that described under Potency is required.

2 PRODUCTION
2-1 PREPARATION OF THE VACCINE

The vaccine virus is propagated in fertilised hens' eggs or in cell cultures. The vaccine may be adjuvanted.

2-2 SUBSTRATE FOR VIRUS PROPAGATION
2-2-1 Embryonated hens' eggs

If the vaccine virus is grown in embryonated hens' eggs, they are obtained from healthy flocks.

2-2-2 Cell cultures

If the vaccine is grown in cell cultures, they comply with the requirements for cell cultures for production of veterinary vaccines *(5.2.4)*.

2-3 SEED LOTS
2-3-1 Extraneous agents

The master seed lot complies with the test for extraneous agents in seed lots *(2.6.24)*. In these tests on the master seed lot, the organisms used are not more than 5 passages from the master seed lot at the start of the test.

2-4 CHOICE OF VACCINE COMPOSITION

The vaccine is shown to be satisfactory with respect to safety *(5.2.6)* and efficacy *(5.2.7)* for the birds for which it is intended.

The following tests for safety (section 2-4-1) and immunogenicity (section 2-4-2) may be used during the demonstration of safety and efficacy.

2-4-1 Safety

The test is carried out for each route of administration to be recommended for vaccination and for each avian species for which the vaccine is intended. Use a batch of vaccine containing not less than the maximum potency that may be expected in a batch of vaccine.

For each test, use not fewer than 8 birds not older than the minimum age to be recommended for vaccination. In the case of chickens, use chickens from a flock free from specified pathogens (SPF) *(5.2.2)* and if the vaccine is used for species other than chickens, they have not been vaccinated and do not have antibodies against avian infectious bronchitis virus. Administer by a route to be recommended and method to each bird 1 dose of the vaccine. Observe the birds for at least daily for at least 14 days after the administration of the vaccine.

The test is not valid if non-specific mortality occurs. The vaccine complies with the test if no bird shows abnormal signs of disease or dies from causes attributable to the vaccine.

2-4-2 Immunogenicity

A test is carried out for each route and method of administration to be recommended, using in each case chickens from an SPF flock *(5.2.2)* and for each serotype in the vaccine. The vaccine administered to each chicken is of minimum potency.

Use for the test 4 groups of not fewer than 30 chickens treated as follows:
— group A: unvaccinated controls;
— group B: vaccinated with inactivated avian infectious bronchitis vaccine;
— group C: vaccinated with live avian infectious bronchitis vaccine and inactivated avian infectious bronchitis vaccine according to the schedule to be recommended;
— group D: vaccinated with live avian infectious bronchitis vaccine.

Monitor egg production and quality in all chickens from point of lay until at least 4 weeks after challenge. At the peak of lay, challenge all groups with a quantity of virulent avian infectious bronchitis virus sufficient to cause a drop in egg production or quality over 3 consecutive weeks during the 4 weeks following challenge. The test is invalid unless there is a drop in egg production in group A compared to the normal level noted before challenge of at least 35 per cent where challenge has been made with a Massachusetts-type strain; where it is necessary to carry out a challenge with a strain of another serotype for which there is documented evidence that the strain will not cause a 35 per cent drop in egg production, the challenge must produce a drop in egg production commensurate with the documented evidence and in any case not less than 15 per cent. The vaccine complies with the test if egg production or quality is significantly better in group C than in group D and significantly better in group B than in group A.

2-5 MANUFACTURER'S TESTS

2-5-1 Residual live virus
An amplification test for residual live avian infectious bronchitis virus is carried out on each batch of antigen immediately after inactivation and on the final bulk vaccine or, if the vaccine contains an adjuvant, on the bulk antigen or mixture of bulk antigens immediately before the addition of adjuvant; the test is carried out in embryonated hen eggs from SPF flocks (5.2.2) or in suitable cell cultures (5.2.4), whichever is the most sensitive for the vaccine strain. The quantity of inactivated virus harvest used in the test is equivalent to not less than 10 doses of vaccine. The vaccine complies with the test if no live virus is detected.

2-5-2 Batch potency test
It is not necessary to carry out the potency test (section 3-5) for each batch of vaccine if it has been carried out using a batch of vaccine with a minimum potency. Where the test is not carried out, an alternative validated method is used, the criteria for acceptance being set with reference to a batch of vaccine that has given satisfactory results in the test described under Potency. The following test may be used.

Administer 1 dose of vaccine by the intramuscular route to each of not fewer than 10 chickens, between 2 weeks of age and the minimum age stated for vaccination and from an SPF flock (5.2.2), and maintain 5 hatch mates as unvaccinated controls. Collect serum samples from each chicken just before administration of the vaccine and after the period defined when testing the reference vaccine; determine the antibody titre of each serum, for each serotype in the vaccine, by a suitable serological method, for example, serum neutralisation. The test is invalid unless the sera collected from the unvaccinated controls and from the chickens just before the administration of the vaccine are free from detectable specific antibody. The vaccine complies with the test if the antibody levels are not significantly less than those obtained with a batch that has given satisfactory results in the test described under Potency.

3 BATCH TESTS

3-1 Identification
When injected into chickens that do not have antibodies against each of the virus serotypes in the vaccine, the vaccine stimulates the production of such antibodies, detectable by virus neutralisation.

3-2 Bacteria and fungi
The vaccine, including where applicable the diluent supplied for reconstitution, complies with the test for sterility prescribed in the monograph *Vaccines for veterinary use (0062)*.

3-3 Residual live virus
A test for residual live virus is carried out to confirm inactivation of avian infectious bronchitis virus.

A. For vaccine prepared with embryo-adapted strains of virus, inject 2/5 of a dose into the allantoic cavity of ten 9- to 11-day-old embryonated hens' eggs from an SPF flock (5.2.2) and incubate. Observe for 5-6 days and pool separately the allantoic liquid from eggs containing live embryos and that from eggs containing dead embryos, excluding those that die within the first 24 h after injection. Examine for abnormalities all embryos which die after 24 h of injection or which survive 5-6 days. No death or abnormality attributable to the vaccine virus occurs. Inject

into the allantoic cavity of each of ten 9- to 11-day-old embryonated hens' eggs from an SPF flock (5.2.2) 0.2 mL of the pooled allantoic liquid from the live embryos and into each of 10 similar eggs 0.2 mL of the pooled liquid from the dead embryos and incubate for 5-6 days. Examine for abnormalities all embryos which die after 24 h of injection or which survive 5-6 days. If more than 20 per cent of the embryos die at either stage repeat the test from that stage. The vaccine complies with the test if there is no death or abnormality attributable to the vaccine virus.

B. For vaccine prepared with cell-culture-adapted strains of virus, inoculate 10 doses of the vaccine into suitable cell cultures. If the vaccine contains an oil adjuvant, eliminate it by suitable means. Incubate at 38 ± 1 °C for 7 days. Make a passage on another set of cell cultures and incubate at 38 ± 1 °C for 7 days. The vaccine complies with the test if none of the cultures show signs of infection.

3-4 Specified extraneous agents
Use 10 chickens, 14-28 days old, from an SPF flock (5.2.2). Vaccinate each chicken by a recommended route with a double dose of the vaccine. After 3 weeks, administer 1 dose by the same route. Collect serum samples from each chicken 2 weeks later and carry out tests for antibodies against the following agents by the methods prescribed in general chapter *5.2.2. Chicken flocks free from specified pathogens for the production and quality control of vaccines*: avian encephalomyelitis virus, avian leucosis viruses, egg-drop syndrome virus, avian infectious bursal disease virus, avian infectious laryngotracheitis virus, influenza A virus, Marek's disease virus, Newcastle disease virus.

The vaccine complies with the test if it does not stimulate the formation of antibodies against these agents.

3-5 Potency
The vaccine complies with the requirements of the test mentioned under Immunogenicity (section 2-4-2) when administered by a recommended route and method.

4 LABELLING
The label states whether the strain in the vaccine is embryo-adapted or cell-culture-adapted.

_____ *Ph Eur*

Avian Infectious Bronchitis Vaccine, Living

(Avian Infectious Bronchitis Vaccine (Live), Ph Eur monograph 0442)

Ph Eur _____

1 DEFINITION
Avian infectious bronchitis vaccine (live) is a preparation of one or more suitable strains of different types of avian infectious bronchitis virus. This monograph applies to vaccines intended for administration to chickens for active immunisation against respiratory disease caused by avian infectious bronchitis virus.

2 PRODUCTION

2-1 PREPARATION OF THE VACCINE
The vaccine virus is grown in embryonated hens' eggs or in cell cultures.

2-2 SUBSTRATE FOR VIRUS PROPAGATION

2-2-1 Embryonated hens' eggs

If the vaccine virus is grown in embryonated hens' eggs, they are obtained from flocks free from specified pathogens (SPF) (*5.2.2*).

2-2-2 Cell cultures

If the vaccine virus is grown in cell cultures, they comply with the requirements for cell cultures for production of veterinary vaccines (*5.2.4*).

2-3 SEED LOTS

2-3-1 Extraneous agents

The master seed lot complies with the tests for extraneous agents in seed lots (*2.6.24*). In these tests on the master seed lot, the organisms used are not more that 5 passages from the master seed lot at the start of the test.

2-4 CHOICE OF VACCINE VIRUS

The vaccine virus shall be shown to be satisfactory with respect to safety (*5.2.6*) and efficacy (*5.2.7*) for the chickens for which it is intended.

The following tests for safety (section 2-4-1), increase in virulence (section 2-4-2) and immunogenicity (section 2-4-3) may be used during the demonstration of safety and efficacy.

2-4-1 Safety

2-4-1-1 Safety for the respiratory tract and kidneys. Carry out the test in chickens not older than the minimum age to be recommended for vaccination. Use vaccine virus at the least attenuated passage level that will be present between the master seed lot and a batch of the vaccine.

Use not fewer than 15 chickens of the same origin and from an SPF flock (*5.2.2*). Administer to each chicken by the oculonasal route a quantity of the vaccine virus equivalent to not less than 10 times the maximum virus titre likely to be contained in 1 dose of the vaccine. On each of days 5, 7 and 10 after administration of the virus, euthanise not fewer than 5 of the chickens and take samples of trachea and kidney. Fix kidney samples for histological examination. Remove the tracheas and prepare 3 transverse sections from the upper part, 4 from the middle part and 3 from the lower part of the trachea of each chicken; examine all tracheal explants as soon as possible and at the latest 2 h after sampling by low-magnification microscopy for ciliary activity. Score for ciliostasis on a scale from 0 (100 per cent ciliary activity) to 4 (no activity, complete ciliostasis); calculate the mean ciliostasis score (the maximum for each trachea being 40) for the 5 chickens euthanised on each of days 5, 7 and 10.

The test is not valid if more than 10 per cent of the chickens die from causes not attributable to the vaccine virus.

The vaccine virus complies with the test if:
— no chicken shows notable clinical signs of avian infectious bronchitis or dies from causes attributable to the vaccine virus;
— any inflammatory lesions seen during the kidney histological examination are, at most, moderate.

A risk/benefit analysis is carried out, taking into account the average ciliostasis scores obtained and the benefits expected from the use of the vaccine.

2-4-1-2 Safety for the reproductive tract. If the recommendations for use state or imply that the vaccine may be used in females less than 3 weeks old that are subsequently kept to sexual maturity, it shall be demonstrated that there is no damage to the development of the reproductive tract when the vaccine is given to chickens of the minimum age to be recommended for vaccination.

The following test may be carried out: use not fewer than 40 female chickens from an SPF flock (*5.2.2*) that are not older than the minimum age to be recommended for vaccination; use the vaccine virus at the least attenuated passage level that will be present between the master seed lot and a batch of the vaccine; administer to each chicken by a route to be recommended a quantity of virus equivalent to not less than the maximum titre likely to be present in 1 dose of vaccine; at least 10 weeks after administration of the vaccine virus, euthanise the chickens and carry out a macroscopic examination of the oviducts. The vaccine virus complies with the test if abnormalities are present in not more than 5 per cent of the oviducts.

2-4-2 Increase in virulence

Carry out the test according to general chapter *5.2.6* using 2-week-old SPF chickens (*5.2.2*). If the properties of the vaccine virus allow sequential passage through 5 groups via natural spreading, this method may be used, otherwise, passage as described below is carried out.

Administer to each chicken of the 1st group by eye-drop a quantity of the vaccine virus that will allow recovery of virus for the passages described below. 2-4 days after administration of the vaccine virus, prepare a suspension from the mucosa of the trachea of each chicken and pool these samples. Administer 0.05 mL of the pooled samples by eye-drop to each chicken of the next group. Carry out this passage operation not fewer than 4 times; verify the presence of the virus at each passage. If the virus is not found at a passage level, repeat the passage by administration to a group of 10 chickens. Carry out the test for safety for the respiratory tract and kidneys (section 2-4-1-1) and, where applicable, the test for safety for the reproductive tract (section 2-4-1-2) using the material used for the 1st passage and the virus at the final passage level. Administer the virus by the route to be recommended for vaccination that is likely to be the least safe.

The vaccine virus complies with the test if no indication of an increase in virulence of the virus recovered for the final passage compared with the material used for the 1st passage is observed. If virus is not recovered after an initial passage in 5 animals and a subsequent repeat passage in 10 animals, the vaccine virus also complies with the test.

2-4-3 Immunogenicity

Immunogenicity is demonstrated for each strain of virus to be included in the vaccine. A test is carried out for each route and method of administration to be recommended using in each case chickens from an SPF flock (*5.2.2*) that are not older than the minimum age to be recommended for vaccination. The quantity of the vaccine virus administered to each chicken is not greater than the minimum virus titre to be stated on the label and the virus is at the most attenuated passage level that will be present in a batch of the vaccine.

Either or both of the tests below may be used during the demonstration of immunogenicity.

2-4-3-1 Ciliary activity of tracheal explants. Use not fewer than 25 chickens of the same origin and from an SPF flock (*5.2.2*). Vaccinate by a route to berecommended not fewer than 20 chickens. Maintain not fewer than 5 chickens as controls. Challenge each chicken after 21 days by eye-drop with a sufficient quantity of virulent avian infectious bronchitis virus of the same type as the vaccine virus to be tested. Euthanise the chickens 4-7 days after challenge and prepare 3 transverse sections from the upper part, 4 from the middle part, and 3 from the lower part of the trachea of each chicken. Examine all tracheal explants as soon as possible and at the latest 2 h after sampling by low-magnification microscopy for ciliary activity. For a given tracheal section, ciliary activity is considered as normal when at least 50 per cent of the internal ring shows vigorous ciliary movement. A chicken is considered not affected if not fewer than 9 out of 10 rings show normal ciliary activity.

The test is not valid if:
— fewer than 80 per cent of the control chickens show cessation or extreme loss of vigour of ciliary activity;
— and/or during the period between the vaccination and challenge, more than 10 per cent of vaccinated or control chickens show abnormal clinical signs or die from causes not attributable to the vaccine.

The vaccine virus complies with the test if not fewer than 80 per cent of the vaccinated chickens show normal ciliary activity.

2-4-3-2 Virus recovery from tracheal swabs. Use not fewer than 30 chickens of the same origin and from an SPF flock (*5.2.2*). Vaccinate by a route to be recommended not fewer than 20 chickens. Maintain not fewer than 10 chickens as controls. Challenge each chicken after 21 days by eye-drop with a sufficient quantity of virulent avian infectious bronchitis virus of the same type as the vaccine virus to be tested. Euthanise the chickens 4-7 days after challenge and prepare a suspension from swabs of the tracheal mucosa of each chicken. Inoculate 0.2 mL of the suspension into the allantoic cavity of each of 5 embryonated hens' eggs, 9-11 days old, from an SPF flock (*5.2.2*). Incubate the eggs for 6-8 days after inoculation. Eggs that after 1 day of incubation do not contain a live embryo are eliminated and considered as non-specific deaths. Record the other eggs containing a dead embryo and after 6-8 days' incubation examine each egg containing a live embryo for lesions characteristic of avian infectious bronchitis. Make successively 3 such passages. If 1 embryo of a series of eggs dies or shows characteristic lesions, the inoculum is considered to be a carrier of avian infectious bronchitis virus. The examination of a series of eggs is considered to be definitely negative if no inoculum concerned is a carrier.

The test is not valid if:
— the challenge virus is re-isolated from fewer than 80 per cent of the control chickens;
— and/or during the period between vaccination and challenge, more than 10 per cent of the vaccinated or control chickens show abnormal clinical signs or die from causes not attributable to the vaccine;
— and/or more than 1 egg in any group is eliminated because of non-specific embryo death.

The vaccine virus complies with the test if the challenge virus is re-isolated from not more than 20 per cent of the vaccinated chickens.

3 BATCH TESTS
3-1 Identification
3-1-1 Vaccines containing one type of virus. The vaccine, diluted if necessary and mixed with avian infectious bronchitis virus antiserum specific for the virus type, no longer infects embryonated hens' eggs from an SPF flock (*5.2.2*) or susceptible cell cultures (*5.2.4*) into which it is inoculated.

3-1-2 Vaccines containing more than one type of virus. The vaccine, diluted if necessary and mixed with type-specific antisera against each strain present in the vaccine except that to be identified, infects embryonated hens' eggs from an SPF flock (*5.2.2*) or susceptible cell cultures (*5.2.4*)

into which it is inoculated, whereas after further admixture with type-specific antiserum against the strain to be identified it no longer produces such infection.

3-2 Bacteria and fungi
Vaccines intended for administration by injection comply with the test for sterility prescribed in the monograph *Vaccines for veterinary use (0062)*.

Frozen or freeze-dried vaccines produced in embryonated eggs and not intended for administration by injection comply either with the test for sterility prescribed in the monograph *Vaccines for veterinary use (0062)* or with the following test: carry out a quantitative test for bacterial and fungal contamination; carry out identification tests for micro-organisms detected in the vaccine; the vaccine does not contain pathogenic micro-organisms and contains not more than 1 non-pathogenic micro-organism per dose.

Any diluent supplied for reconstitution of the vaccine complies with the test for sterility prescribed in the monograph *Vaccines for veterinary use (0062)*.

3-3 Mycoplasmas
The vaccine complies with the test for mycoplasmas (*2.6.7*).

3-4 Extraneous agents
The vaccine complies with the tests for extraneous agents in batches of finished product (*2.6.25*).

3-5 Virus titre
Titrate the vaccine virus by inoculation into embryonated hens' eggs from an SPF flock (*5.2.2*) or into suitable cell cultures (*5.2.4*). If the vaccine contains more than 1 strain of virus, titrate each strain after having neutralised the others with type-specific avian infectious bronchitis antisera.
The vaccine complies with the test if 1 dose contains for each vaccine virus not less than the minimum titre stated on the label.

3-6 Potency
The vaccine complies with the requirements of 1 of the tests prescribed under Immunogenicity (section 2-4-3) when administered according to the recommended schedule by a recommended route and method. It is not necessary to carry out the potency test for each batch of the vaccine if it has been carried out on a representative batch using a vaccinating dose containing not more than the minimum virus titre stated on the label.

Ph Eur

Avian Paramyxovirus 3 Vaccine for Turkeys, Inactivated

(Avian Paramyxovirus 3 Vaccine (Inactivated) for Turkeys, Ph. Eur. monograph 1392)

Ph Eur

1 DEFINITION
Avian paramyxovirus 3 vaccine (inactivated) for turkeys is a preparation of a suitable strain of avian paramyxovirus 3, inactivated while maintaining adequate immunogenic properties. This monograph applies to vaccines intended for protection of turkeys against a drop in egg production and loss of egg quality.

2 PRODUCTION
2-1 PREPARATION OF THE VACCINE
The vaccine virus is propagated in embryonated eggs or in cell cultures. The vaccine may be adjuvanted.

2-2 SUBSTRATE FOR VIRUS PROPAGATION

2-2-1 Embryonated eggs

If the vaccine virus is grown in embryonated eggs, they are obtained from healthy flocks.

2-2-2 Cell cultures

If the vaccine virus is grown in cell cultures, they comply with the requirements for cell cultures for production of veterinary vaccines (*5.2.4*).

2-3 SEED LOTS

2-3-1 Extraneous agents

The master seed lot complies with the tests for extraneous agents in seed lots (*2.6.24*). In these tests on the master seed lot, the organisms used are not more than 5 passages from the master seed lot at the start of the test.

2-4 CHOICE OF VACCINE COMPOSITION

The vaccine is shown to be satisfactory with respect to safety (*5.2.6*) and efficacy (*5.2.7*) for each category of turkeys for which it is intended.

The following tests for safety (section 2-4-1) and immunogenicity (section 2-4-2) may be used during the demonstration of safety and efficacy.

2-4-1 Safety

The test is carried out for each route of administration to be recommended for vaccination. Use a batch of vaccine containing not less than the maximum potency that may be expected in a batch of vaccine.

For each test, use not fewer than 8 turkeys not older than the minimum age to be recommended for vaccination, that have not been vaccinated and that do not have antibodies against avian paramyxovirus 3. Administer by a recommended route and method to each turkey 1 dose of the vaccine. If the schedule to be recommended requires a 2nd dose, administer 1 dose to each turkey after an interval of at least 14 days. Observe the turkeys at least daily for at least 14 days after the last administration of the vaccine.

The test is not valid if non-specific mortality occurs. The vaccine complies with the test if no turkey shows abnormal signs of disease or dies from causes attributable to the vaccine.

2-4-2 Immunogenicity

A test is carried out for each route and method of administration to be recommended, using in each case turkeys of the minimum age to be recommended for vaccination. The vaccine administered to each turkey is of minimum potency.

Use for the test 2 groups each of not fewer than 20 turkeys of the same origin and of the same age, that do not have antibodies against avian paramyxovirus 3. Vaccinate one group in accordance with the recommendations stated on the label. Maintain the other group as controls.

The test is not valid if serological tests carried out on serum samples obtained at the time of first vaccination show the presence of antibodies against avian paramyxovirus 3 in either vaccinates or controls or if tests carried out at the time of challenge show such antibodies in controls.

At the egg-production peak, challenge the 2 groups by the oculonasal route with a sufficient quantity of a virulent strain of avian paramyxovirus 3. For not less than 6 weeks after challenge, record the number of eggs laid weekly for each group, distinguishing between normal and abnormal eggs. The vaccine complies with the test if egg production and quality are significantly better in the vaccinated group than in the control group.

2-5 MANUFACTURER'S TESTS

2-5-1 Residual live virus

The test for residual live virus is carried out in embryonated eggs or suitable cell cultures (*5.2.4*), whichever is the most sensitive for the vaccine strain. The quantity of inactivated virus harvest used in the test is equivalent to not less than 10 doses of vaccine. The vaccine complies with the test if no live virus is detected.

2-5-2 Batch potency test

It is not necessary to carry out the potency test (section 3-5) for each batch of vaccine if it has been carried out using a batch of vaccine with a minimum potency. Where the test is not carried out, an alternative validated method is used, the criteria for acceptance being set with reference to a batch of vaccine that has given satisfactory results in the test described under Potency.

3 BATCH TESTS

3-1 Identification

When injected into animals that do not have antibodies against avian paramyxovirus 3, the vaccine stimulates the production of such antibodies.

3-2 Bacteria and fungi

The vaccine, including where applicable the diluent supplied for reconstitution, complies with the test for sterility prescribed in the monograph *Vaccines for veterinary use (0062)*.

3-3 Residual live virus

A test for residual live virus is carried out to confirm inactivation of avian paramyxovirus 3.

Inject 2/5 of a dose into the allantoic cavity of each of not fewer than 10 embryonated hen eggs 9-11 days old, from flocks free from specified pathogens (SPF) (*5.2.2*) and incubate. Observe for 6 days and pool separately the allantoic fluid from eggs containing live embryos, and that from eggs containing dead embryos, excluding those dying within 24 h of the injection. Examine embryos that die within 24 h of injection for the presence of avian paramyxovirus 3.

The vaccine does not comply with the test if avian paramyxovirus 3 is found.

Inject into the allantoic cavity of each of not fewer than ten 9- to 11-day-old fertilised hen eggs from an SPF flock (*5.2.2*), 0.2 mL of the pooled allantoic fluid from the live embryos and, into each of 10 similar eggs, 0.2 mL of the pooled fluid from the dead embryos, and incubate for 5-6 days. Test the allantoic fluid from each egg for the presence of haemagglutinins using chicken erythrocytes.

The vaccine complies with the test if there is no evidence of haemagglutinating activity and if not more than 20 per cent of the embryos die at either stage. If more than 20 per cent of the embryos die at one of the stages, repeat that stage; the vaccine complies with the test if there is no evidence of haemagglutinating activity and not more than 20 per cent of the embryos die at that stage.

Antibiotics may be used in the test to control extraneous bacterial infection.

3-4 Specified extraneous agents

Use 10 chickens, 14-28 days old, from an SPF flock (*5.2.2*). Vaccinate each chicken by a recommended route with a double dose of the vaccine. After 3 weeks, administer 1 dose by the same route. Collect serum samples from each chicken 2 weeks later and carry out tests for antibodies against the following agents by the methods prescribed in general chapter *5.2.2. Chicken flocks free from specified pathogens for the production and quality control of vaccines*: avian encephalomyelitis virus, avian infectious bronchitis virus, avian leucosis viruses, egg-drop syndrome virus, avian infectious bursal disease virus, avian infectious laryngotracheitis virus, influenza A virus, Marek's disease virus.

The vaccine complies with the test if it does not stimulate the formation of antibodies against these agents.

3-5 Potency
The vaccine complies with the requirements of the test mentioned under Immunogenicity (section 2-4-2) when administered by a recommended route and method.

Ph Eur

Avian Viral Tenosynovitis Vaccine (Live)

(Ph Eur monograph 1956)

Ph Eur

1 DEFINITION
Avian viral tenosynovitis vaccine (live) is a preparation of a suitable strain of avian tenosynovitis virus (avian orthoreovirus). This monograph applies to vaccines intended for administration to chickens for active immunisation.

2 PRODUCTION
2-1 PREPARATION OF THE VACCINE
The vaccine virus is grown in cell cultures.

2-2 SUBSTRATE FOR VIRUS PROPAGATION
2-2-1 Cell cultures
Cell cultures comply with the requirements for cell cultures for production of veterinary vaccines (5.2.4).

2-3 SEED LOTS
2-3-1 Extraneous agents
The master seed lot complies with the tests for extraneous agents in seed lots (2.6.24). In these tests on the master seed lot, the organisms used are not more than 5 passages from the master seed lot at the start of the tests.

2-4 CHOICE OF VACCINE VIRUS
The vaccine virus shall be shown to be satisfactory with respect to safety (5.2.6) and efficacy (5.2.7) for the chickens for which it is intended.

The following tests for safety (section 2-4-1), increase in virulence (section 2-4-2) and immunogenicity (section 2-4-3) may be used during the demonstration of safety and efficacy.

2-4-1 Safety
Carry out the test for each route and method of administration to be recommended for vaccination using in each case chickens not older than the minimum age to be recommended for vaccination and from a flock free from specified pathogens (SPF) (5.2.2). Use vaccine virus at the least attenuated passage level that will be present in a batch of the vaccine.

For each test performed in chickens younger than 3 weeks of age, use not fewer than 10 chickens. For each test performed in chickens older than 3 weeks of age, use not fewer than 8 chickens. Administer to each chicken a quantity of the vaccine virus equivalent to not less than 10 times the maximum virus titre likely to be contained in 1 dose of the vaccine. Observe the chickens at least daily for at least 21 days. Carry out histological examination of the joints and tendon sheaths of the legs and feet at the end of the

observation period (as a basis for comparison in the test for increase in virulence).

The test is not valid if more than 10 per cent of the chickens younger than 3 weeks of age show abnormal signs of disease or die from causes not attributable to the vaccine virus. For chickens older than 3 weeks of age, the test is not valid if non-specific mortality occurs.

The vaccine virus complies with the test if no chicken shows abnormal signs of disease or dies from causes attributable to the vaccine.

2-4-2 Increase in virulence
Carry out the test according to general chapter 5.2.6 using 1-day-old chickens from an SPF flock (5.2.2). If the properties of the vaccine virus allow sequential passage through 5 groups via natural spreading, this method may be used, otherwise passage as described below is carried out.

Administer to each chicken of the 1st group by a suitable route a quantity of the vaccine virus that will allow recovery of virus for the passages described below. Euthanise the chickens at the moment when the virus concentration in the most suitable material (for example, tendons, tendon sheaths and liquid exudates from the hock joints, spleen) is sufficient. Prepare a suspension from this material from each chicken and pool these samples. Administer 0.1 mL of the pooled samples by the route of administration most likely to lead to increase in virulence to each chicken of the next group. Carry out this passage operation not fewer than 4 times; verify the presence of the virus at each passage. If the virus is not found at a passage level, repeat the passage by administration to a group of 10 chickens.

If the 5th group of chickens shows no evidence of an increase in virulence indicative of reversion during the observation period, further testing is not required. Otherwise, carry out an additional safety test and compare the clinical signs and any relevant parameters in a group of at least 10 chickens receiving the material used for the 1st passage and another similar group receiving the virus at the final passage level.

The vaccine virus complies with the test if no indication of an increase in virulence of the virus at the final passage level compared with the material used for the 1st passage is observed. If the virus is not recovered after an initial passage in 5 chickens and a subsequent repeat passage in 10 chickens, the vaccine virus also complies with the test.

2-4-3 Immunogenicity
A test is carried out for each route and method of administration to be recommended for vaccination using in each case chickens not older than the minimum age to be recommended for vaccination. The quantity of the vaccine virus administered to each chicken is not greater than the minimum virus titre to be stated on the label and the virus is at the most attenuated passage level that will be present in a batch of the vaccine. Use not fewer than 30 chickens of the same origin and from an SPF flock (5.2.2). Administer the vaccine by a route to be recommended to not fewer than 20 chickens. Maintain not fewer than 10 chickens as controls. Challenge each chicken after 21 days by a suitable route with a sufficient quantity of virulent avian tenosynovitis virus. Observe the chickens at least daily for 21 days after challenge. Record the deaths and the surviving chickens that show clinical signs of disease. If the challenge is administered by the foot pad, any transient swelling of the foot pad during the first 5 days after challenge may be considered non-specific. At the end of the observation period, euthanise all the surviving chickens and carry out macroscopic and/or

microscopic examination for lesions of the joints and tendon sheaths of the legs and feet, e.g. exudate and swelling.

The test is not valid if:
— during the observation period after challenge fewer than 80 per cent of the control chickens die or show severe clinical signs of avian viral tenosynovitis or show macroscopical and/or microscopical lesions in the joints and tendon sheaths of the legs and feet,
— or if during the period between vaccination and challenge more than 10 per cent of the control or vaccinated chickens show abnormal clinical signs or die from causes not attributable to the vaccine.

The vaccine virus complies with the test if during the observation period after challenge not fewer than 90 per cent of the vaccinated chickens survive and show no notable clinical signs of disease or show macroscopical and/or microscopical lesions in the joints and tendon sheaths of the legs and feet.

3 BATCH TESTS
3-1 Identification
Carry out an immunostaining test in cell cultures to identify the vaccine virus.

3-2 Bacteria and fungi
Vaccines intended for administration by injection comply with the test for sterility prescribed in the monograph *Vaccines for veterinary use (0062)*.

Frozen or freeze-dried vaccines produced in embryonated eggs and not intended for administration by injection either comply with the test for sterility prescribed in the monograph *Vaccines for veterinary use (0062)* or with the following test: carry out a quantitative test for bacterial and fungal contamination; carry out identification tests for microorganisms detected in the vaccine; the vaccine does not contain pathogenic microorganisms and contains not more than 1 non-pathogenic microorganism per dose.

Any diluent supplied for reconstitution of the vaccine complies with the test for sterility prescribed in the monograph *Vaccines for veterinary use (0062)*.

3-3 Mycoplasmas
The vaccine complies with the test for mycoplasmas (2.6.7).

3-4 Extraneous agents
The vaccine complies with the tests for extraneous agents in batches of finished product (2.6.25).

3-5 Virus titre
Titrate the vaccine virus by inoculation into suitable cell cultures (5.2.4). The vaccine complies with the test if 1 dose contains not less than the minimum virus titre stated on the label.

3-6 Potency
The vaccine complies with the requirements of the test prescribed under Immunogenicity (section 2-4-3) when administered by a recommended route and method. It is not necessary to carry out the potency test for each batch of the vaccine if it has been carried out on a representative batch using a vaccinating dose containing not more than the minimum virus titre stated on the label.

Ph Eur

Bordetella Bronchiseptica Vaccine (live) for Dogs

(Ph. Eur. monograph 2525)

Ph Eur

1 DEFINITION
Bordetella bronchiseptica Vaccine (live) for dogs is a preparation of a suitable strain of *Bordetella bronchiseptica*. This monograph applies to vaccines intended for the active immunisation of dogs against respiratory disease caused by *B. bronchiseptica*.

2 PRODUCTION
2-1 PREPARATION OF THE VACCINE
The vaccine strain is grown in a suitable medium.

2-2 CHOICE OF VACCINE COMPOSITION
The vaccine strain is shown to be satisfactory with respect to safety (5.2.6) and efficacy (5.2.7) for the dogs for which it is intended.

The following tests for safety (section 2-2-1), excretion and transmission of the vaccine strain (section 2-2-2), increase in virulence (section 2-2-3) and immunogenicity (section 2-2-4) may be used during the demonstration of safety and efficacy.

2-2-1 Safety
Carry out the test for each route and method of administration to be recommended for vaccination using in each case dogs not older than the minimum age to be recommended for vaccination. The vaccine strain to be administered is at the least attenuated passage level that will be present in a batch of the vaccine.

For each test, use not fewer than 8 dogs, shown to be free from *B. bronchiseptica* and that do not have antibodies against *B. bronchiseptica*. Administer to each dog a quantity of the vaccine strain equivalent to not less than 10 times the maximum number of live bacteria likely to be contained in 1 dose of the vaccine. Observe the dogs at least daily for at least 14 days.

The vaccine strain complies with the test if no dog shows abnormal local or systemic reactions or dies from causes attributable to the vaccine strain.

2-2-2 Excretion and transmission of the vaccine strain
Use dogs not older than 10 weeks of age. Administer the strain by the route to be recommended for vaccination most likely to lead to excretion. The vaccine strain to be administered is at the least attenuated passage level that will be present in a batch of the vaccine.

For each test, use not fewer than 8 dogs, shown to be free from *B. bronchiseptica* and that do not have antibodies against *B. bronchiseptica*. Administer to not fewer than 4 dogs a quantity of the vaccine strain equivalent to not less than the maximum number of live bacteria likely to be contained in 1 dose of the vaccine. 2 days after vaccination add 4 dogs to the group of vaccinated dogs. Observe the animals for 70 days. Collect nasal swabs or washings from each dog at weekly intervals. Verify the presence of the excreted vaccine strain with a suitable method.

The vaccine strain complies with the test if no dog shows abnormal local or systemic reactions or dies from causes attributable to the vaccine strain.

The results are noted and used to formulate the label statement (whether the vaccinated strain is excreted, the period over which there is excretion and whether or not the vaccine strain spreads to in-contact dogs).

2-2-3 Increase in virulence

Carry out the test according to general chapter 5.2.6 using dogs not older than 10 weeks of age, which are free from *B. bronchiseptica* and that do not have antibodies against *B. bronchiseptica*. If the properties of the vaccine strain allow sequential passage through 5 groups via natural spreading, this method may be used, otherwise passage as described below is carried out.

Administer to each dog by a route to be recommended a quantity of the vaccine strain that will allow recovery of bacteria for the passages described below. Administer the strain by the route to be recommended for vaccination most likely to lead to reversion to virulence. On one occasion between 4 and 6 days after administration, collect nasal swabs or washings from each dog, verify the presence of bacteria and pool positive samples. Administer 1 mL of the pooled samples by a suitable route (for example, the intranasal route) to each dog of the next group. Carry out this passage operation not fewer than 4 times; verify the presence of the bacteria at each passage. If the bacteria are not found at a passage level, repeat the passage by administration to a group of 10 animals.

If the 5th group of animals shows no evidence of an increase in virulence indicative of reversion during the observation period, further testing is not required. Otherwise, carry out an additional safety test and compare the clinical signs and any relevant parameters in a group of at least 8 animals receiving the material used for the 1st passage and another similar group receiving the bacteria at the final passage level.

The vaccine strain complies with the test if no indication of increased virulence of the bacteria recovered for the final passage compared with the material used for the 1st passage is observed. If bacteria are not recovered after an initial passage in 2 animals and a subsequent repeat passage in 10 animals, the vaccine strain also complies with the test.

2-2-4 Immunogenicity

A test is carried out for each route and method of administration to be recommended for vaccination using in each case dogs of the minimum age to be recommended. The quantity of vaccine strain to be administered to each dog is not greater than the minimum number of live bacteria to be stated on the label and the strain is at the most attenuated passage level that will be present in a batch of vaccine.

Use for the test not fewer than 15 dogs which are free from *B. bronchiseptica* and that do not have antibodies against *B. bronchiseptica*. Vaccinate not fewer than 10 dogs, according to the schedule to be recommended. Maintain not fewer than 5 dogs as controls. Challenge each dog after 20-22 days by the intranasal route with a quantity of a suspension of virulent *B. bronchiseptica* sufficient to cause typical signs of respiratory disease in a dog that does not have antibodies against *B. bronchiseptica*. Observe the dogs at least daily for 14 days after challenge. Collect nasal swabs or washings from each dog daily from day 2 to 14 after challenge and determine the number of excreted *B. bronchiseptica* in each sample. Use a scoring system to record the signs of respiratory disease in each dog.

The test is invalid if more than 20 per cent of the controls show no typical signs of the disease.

The vaccine complies with the test if there is a significant decrease in the score for respiratory signs and in the number of *B. bronchiseptica* excreted in vaccinates compared to controls.

3 BATCH TESTS

3-1 Identification

The vaccine strain is identified by suitable methods.

3-2 Bacteria and fungi

Carry out the test by inoculation of suitable media. The vaccine complies with the test if it does not contain extraneous micro-organisms. Any diluent supplied for reconstitution of the vaccine complies with the test for sterility prescribed in the monograph *Vaccines for veterinary use (0062)*.

3-3 Live bacteria

Make a count of live bacteria on a solid medium suitable for the culture of *B. bronchiseptica*. The vaccine complies with the test if 1 dose contains not less than the minimum number of live *B. bronchiseptica* stated on the label.

3-4 Potency

The vaccine complies with the requirements of the test prescribed under Immunogenicity (section 2-2-4) when administered by a recommended route and method. It is not necessary to carry out the potency test for each batch of the vaccine if it has been carried out on a representative batch using a vaccinating dose containing not more than the minimum number of live *B. bronchiseptica* stated on the label.

4 LABELLING

The label states:
— where applicable, the period after vaccination during which the vaccine is excreted;
— where applicable, that the vaccine strain may be transmitted to other dogs.

Ph Eur

Bovine Parainfluenza Virus Vaccine, Living

(Bovine Parainfluenza Virus Vaccine (Live), Ph Eur monograph 1176)

Ph Eur ————————————————

1 DEFINITION

Bovine parainfluenza virus vaccine (live) is a preparation of a suitable strain of bovine parainfluenza 3 virus. This monograph applies to vaccines intended for the active immunisation of cattle against infection with bovine parainfluenza virus.

2 PRODUCTION

2-1 PREPARATION OF THE VACCINE

The vaccine virus is grown in cell cultures.

2-2 SUBSTRATE FOR VIRUS PROPAGATION

2-2-1 Cell cultures

The cell cultures comply with the requirements for cell cultures for production of veterinary vaccines (5.2.4).

2-3 CHOICE OF VACCINE VIRUS

The vaccine virus is shown to be satisfactory with respect to safety (5.2.6) and efficacy (5.2.7) for the cattle for which it is intended.

The following tests for safety (section 2-3-1), increase in virulence (section 2-3-2) and immunogenicity (2-3-3) may be used during the demonstration of safety and efficacy.

2-3-1 Safety

Carry out the test for each route and method of administration to be recommended for vaccination.

Use vaccine virus at the least attenuated passage level that will be present in a batch of the vaccine.

For each test, use not fewer than 5 calves of the minimum age to be recommended for vaccination and preferably that do not have antibodies against bovine parainfluenza 3 virus or, where justified, use calves with a very low level of such antibodies as long as they have not been vaccinated against bovine parainfluenza virus and administration of the vaccine does not cause an anamnestic response. Administer to each calf a quantity of the vaccine virus equivalent to not less than 10 times the maximum virus titre likely to be contained in 1 dose of the vaccine. Observe the calves at least daily for at least 14 days. Measure the body temperature of each calf on the day before vaccination, at the time of vaccination and for the 4 subsequent days.

The vaccine virus complies with the test if no abnormal effect on body temperature occurs and if no calf shows abnormal, local or systemic reactions or dies from causes attributable to the vaccine virus.

2-3-2 Increase in virulence

Carry out the test according to chapter *5.2.6. Evaluation of safety of veterinary vaccines and immunosera*, using calves that do not have antibodies against bovine parainfluenza 3 virus. If the properties of the vaccine virus allow sequential passage through 5 groups via natural spreading, this method may be used, otherwise passage as described below is carried out.

Administer to each calf of the 1st group by the intranasal route a quantity of the vaccine virus that will allow recovery of virus for the passages described below. On each of days 3 to 7 after administration of the virus, take nasal swabs from each calf and collect in not more than 5 mL of a suitable medium, which is then used to inoculate cell cultures to verify the presence of virus. Administer about 1 mL of the suspension from the swabs that contain the maximum amount of virus, as indicated by the titration of cell cultures, to each calf of the next group. Carry out this passage operation not fewer than 4 times; verify the presence of the virus at each passage. If the virus is not found at a passage level, repeat the passage by administration to a group of 10 animals.

If the 5th group of animals shows no evidence of an increase in virulence indicative of reversion during the observation period, further testing is not required. Otherwise, carry out an additional safety test and compare the clinical signs and any relevant parameters in a group of at least 8 animals receiving the material used for the 1st passage and another similar group receiving the virus at the final passage.

The vaccine virus complies with the test if no indication of increased virulence of the virus recovered for the final passage compared with the material used for the 1st passage is observed; account is taken of the titre of excreted virus in the nasal swabs. If virus is not recovered after an initial passage in 2 animals and a subsequent repeated passage in 10 animals, the vaccine virus also complies with the test.

2-3-3 Immunogenicity

A test is carried out for each route and method of administration to be recommended for vaccination using in each case calves of the minimum age to be recommended. The quantity of vaccine to be administered to each calf is not greater than the minimum virus titre to be stated on the label and the virus is at the most attenuated passage level that will be present in a batch of vaccine.

Use for the test not fewer than 10 calves that do not have antibodies against bovine parainfluenza 3 virus; calves having low levels of such antibodies may be used if it has been

demonstrated that valid results are obtained in these conditions. Collect sera from the calves before vaccination, 7 days and 14 days after the time of vaccination and just before challenge. Vaccinate not fewer than 5 calves, according to the schedule to be recommended. Maintain not fewer than 5 calves as controls. Challenge each calf after 20-22 days by a respiratory tract route with a sufficient quantity of a suspension of a low-passage virulent bovine parainfluenza 3 virus. Observe the calves at least daily for 14 days after challenge and monitor each of them for signs, in particular respiratory signs and virus shedding (by nasal swabs or tracheobronchial washing).

The test is not valid if tests for antibodies against bovine parainfluenza 3 virus on the sera indicate that there was intercurrent infection with the virus during the test or if, during the observation period after challenge, more than 2 of the 5 control calves show no excretion of the challenge virus, as shown by nasal swabs or samples harvested by tracheobronchial washing.

The vaccine virus complies with the test if, during the observation period after challenge, in vaccinated calves compared to controls there is a significant reduction in mean titre and in mean duration of virus excretion, and a notable reduction in general and local signs (if the challenge virus used produces such signs).

3 BATCH TESTS

3-1 Identification

Carry out an immunostaining test in suitable cell cultures, using a monospecific antiserum.

3-2 Bacteria and fungi

The vaccine, including where applicable the diluent supplied for reconstitution, complies with the test for sterility prescribed in the monograph *Vaccines for veterinary use (0062)*.

3-3 Mycoplasmas (2.6.7)

The vaccine complies with the test for mycoplasmas.

3-4 Extraneous agents

Neutralise the vaccine virus with a suitable monospecific antiserum against bovine parainfluenza 3 virus and inoculate into cell cultures known for their susceptibility to viruses pathogenic for cattle. Carry out at least 1 passage and maintain the cultures for 14 days.

The vaccine complies with the test if no cytopathic effect develops and there is no sign of the presence of haemadsorbing agents. Carry out a specific test for pestiviruses.

3-5 Virus titre

Titrate the vaccine virus in suitable cell cultures. The vaccine complies with the test if 1 dose contains not less than the minimum virus titre stated on the label.

3-6 Potency

The vaccine complies with the requirements of the test prescribed under Immunogenicity (section 2-3-3) when administered by a recommended route and method. It is not necessary to carry out the potency test for each batch of the vaccine if it has been carried out on a representative batch using a vaccinating dose containing not more than the minimum virus titre stated on the label.

Ph Eur

Bovine Respiratory Syncytial Virus Vaccine, Living

(Bovine Respiratory Syncytial Virus Vaccine (Live), Ph Eur monograph 1177)

Ph Eur

1 DEFINITION

Bovine respiratory syncytial virus vaccine (live) is a preparation of a suitable strain of bovine respiratory syncytial virus. This monograph applies to vaccines intended for the active immunisation of cattle against infection with bovine respiratory syncytial virus.

2 PRODUCTION
2-1 PREPARATION OF THE VACCINE
The vaccine virus is grown in cell cultures.

2-2 SUBSTRATE FOR VIRUS PROPAGATION
2-2-1 Cell cultures
The cell cultures comply with the requirements for cell cultures for production of veterinary vaccines (*5.2.4*).

2-3 CHOICE OF VACCINE VIRUS
The vaccine virus is shown to be satisfactory with respect to safety (*5.2.6*) and efficacy (*5.2.7*) for the cattle for which it is intended.

The following tests for safety (section 2-3-1), increase in virulence (section 2-3-2) and immunogenicity (section 2-3-3) may be used during the demonstration of safety and efficacy.

2-3-1 Safety
Carry out the test for each route and method of administration to be recommended for vaccination, using in each case calves of the minimum age to be recommended for vaccination. Use vaccine virus at the least attenuated passage level that will be present in a batch of the vaccine.

2-3-1-1 *Laboratory test* For each test, use not fewer than 5 calves that do not have antibodies against bovine respiratory syncytial virus. Administer to each calf a quantity of the vaccine virus equivalent to not less than 10 times the maximum virus titre likely to be contained in 1 dose of the vaccine. Observe the calves at least daily for at least 14 days. Measure the body temperature of each calf on the day before vaccination, at the time of vaccination and daily for the following 7 days.

The vaccine virus complies with the test if no abnormal effect on body temperature occurs and if no calf shows abnormal local or systemic reactions or dies from causes attributable to the vaccine virus.

2-3-1-2 *Field studies* The calves used for the field trials are also used to evaluate the incidence of hypersensitivity reactions in vaccinated calves following subsequent exposure to the vaccine or to wild virus. The vaccine complies with the test if it is not associated with an abnormal incidence of immediate hypersensitivity reactions.

2-3-2 Increase in virulence
Carry out the test according to chapter *5.2.6. Evaluation of safety of veterinary vaccines and immunosera*, using calves that do not have antibodies against bovine respiratory syncytial virus. If the properties of the vaccine virus allow sequential passage through 5 groups via natural spreading, this method may be used, otherwise passage as described below is carried out.

Administer to each calf of the 1st group by the intranasal route a quantity of the vaccine virus that will allow recovery of virus for the passages described below. On each of days

3 to 7 after administration of the virus, take nasal swabs from each calf and collect in not more than 5 mL of a suitable medium, which is then used to inoculate cell cultures to verify the presence of virus. Administer about 1 mL of the suspension from the swabs that contain the maximum amount of virus, as indicated by the titration of cell cultures, to each calf of the next group. Carry out this passage operation not fewer than 4 times; verify the presence of the virus at each passage. If the virus is not found at a passage level, repeat the passage by administration to a group of 10 animals.

If the 5th group of calves shows no evidence of an increase in virulence indicative of reversion during the observation period, further testing is not required. Otherwise, carry out an additional safety test and compare the clinical signs and any relevant parameters in a group of at least 8 animals receiving the material used for the 1st passage and another similar group receiving the virus at the final passage level.

The vaccine virus complies with the test if no calf shows signs attributable to the vaccine virus and no indication of increased virulence of the virus recovered for the final passage compared with the material used for the 1st passage is observed; account is taken of the titre of excreted virus in the nasal swabs. If virus is not recovered after an initial passage in 2 animals and a subsequent repeated passage in 10 animals, the vaccine virus also complies with the test.

2-3-3 Immunogenicity
A test is carried out for each route and method of administration to be recommended for vaccination using in each case calves of the minimum age to be recommended. The quantity of vaccine to be administered to each calf is not greater than the minimum virus titre to be stated on the label and the virus is at the most attenuated passage level that will be present in a batch of vaccine.

Use for the test not fewer than 10 calves that do not have antibodies against bovine respiratory syncytial virus. Collect sera from the calves before the time of vaccination, 7 and 14 days after the time of vaccination and just before challenge. Vaccinate not fewer than 5 calves, according to the schedule to be recommended. Maintain not fewer than 5 calves as controls. Challenge each calf after 20-22 days by a respiratory tract route with a sufficient quantity of a suspension of a low-passage virulent bovine respiratory syncytial virus. Observe the calves at least daily for 14 days after challenge and monitor each of them for signs, in particular respiratory signs and virus shedding (by nasal swabs or tracheobronchial washing).

The test is not valid if antibodies against bovine respiratory syncytial virus are detected in any sample from control calves before challenge or if more than 2 of the 5 control calves show no excretion of the challenge virus, as shown by nasal swabs or samples harvested by tracheobronchial washing.

The vaccine virus complies with the test if, during the observation period after challenge, there is a significant reduction in mean titre and in mean duration of virus excretion in vaccinates compared to controls, and a notable reduction in general and local signs in vaccinated calves (if the challenge virus used produces such signs).

3 BATCH TESTS
3-1 Identification
Identify the vaccine by an immunostaining test in suitable cell cultures using a monospecific antiserum.

3-2 Bacteria and fungi

The vaccine, including where applicable the diluent supplied for reconstitution, complies with the test for sterility prescribed in the monograph *Vaccines for veterinary use (0062)*.

3-3 Mycoplasmas *(2.6.7)*

The vaccine complies with the test for mycoplasmas.

3-4 Extraneous agents

Neutralise the vaccine virus with a suitable monospecific antiserum against bovine respiratory syncytial virus and inoculate into cell cultures known for their susceptibility to viruses pathogenic for cattle. Carry out at least one passage and maintain the cultures for 14 days.

The vaccine complies with the test if no cytopathic effect develops and there is no sign of the presence of haemadsorbing agents. Carry out a specific test for pestiviruses.

3-5 Virus titre

Titrate the vaccine virus in suitable cell cultures. The vaccine complies with the test if 1 dose contains not less than the minimum virus titre stated on the label.

3-6 Potency

The vaccine complies with the requirements of the test prescribed under Immunogenicity (section 2-3-3) when administered by a recommended route and method. It is not necessary to carry out the potency test for each batch of the vaccine if it has been carried out on a representative batch using a vaccinating dose containing not more than the minimum virus titre stated on the label.

———— Ph Eur

Bovine Viral Diarrhoea Vaccine (Inactivated)

(Ph. Eur. monograph 1952)

Ph Eur ————————————————————————

1 DEFINITION

Bovine viral diarrhoea vaccine (inactivated) is a preparation of one or more suitable strains of bovine diarrhoea virus inactivated while maintaining adequate immunogenic properties. This monograph applies to vaccines intended for the active immunisation of heifers and cows for protection of their progeny against transplacental infection.

2 PRODUCTION
2-1 PREPARATION OF THE VACCINE

The vaccine virus is grown in cell cultures. The viral suspensions of each vaccine virus are harvested separately and inactivated by a method that maintains immunogenicity. The viral suspensions may be purified and concentrated. The vaccine may be adjuvanted.

2-2 SUBSTRATE FOR VIRUS PROPAGATION
2-2-1 Cell cultures

The cell cultures comply with the requirements for cell cultures for production of veterinary vaccines *(5.2.4)*.

2-3 CHOICE OF VACCINE COMPOSITION

The vaccine is shown to be satisfactory with respect to safety *(5.2.6)* and efficacy *(5.2.7)* for the cattle for which it is intended.

The following tests for safety (section 2-3-1) and immunogenicity (section 2-3-2) may be used during the demonstration of safety and efficacy.

2-3-1 Safety

Carry out the test for each route and method of administration to be recommended for vaccination and in each category of cattle for which the vaccine is intended. Use a batch of vaccine containing not less than the maximum potency that may be expected in a batch of vaccine.

2-3-1-1 General safety. For each test, use not fewer than 8 cattle of the minimum age to be recommended for vaccination and that do not have bovine diarrhoea virus or antibodies against the virus. Administer to each animal 1 dose of the vaccine. If the schedule to be recommended requires a 2nd dose, administer another dose after an interval of at least 14 days. Observe the cattle at least daily for at least 14 days.

The vaccine complies with the test if no animal shows abnormal local or systemic reactions or dies from causes attributable to the vaccine.

2-3-1-2 Safety in pregnant cattle. If the vaccine is intended for use in pregnant cattle, use not fewer than 8 cattle at the beginning of each semester for which use is not contraindicated. Administer to each animal 1 dose of the vaccine. If the schedule to be recommended requires a 2nd dose, administer another dose after an interval of at least 14 days. Observe the cattle at least daily until calving.

The vaccine complies with the test if no animal shows abnormal local or systemic reactions or dies from causes attributable to the vaccine and if no adverse effects on gestation or the offspring are noted.

2-3-1-3 Examination of reproductive performance. If the vaccine is intended for administration shortly before or at insemination, absence of undesirable effects on conception rate must be demonstrated.

2-3-2 Immunogenicity

The following test is suitable to demonstrate the immunogenicity of the vaccine with respect to bovine diarrhoea virus of genotype 1; if protection against bovine diarrhoea virus of genotype 2 is claimed, an additional test, similar to that described below, but using bovine diarrhoea virus of genotype 2 for challenge, is carried out.

A test is carried out for each route and method of administration to be recommended. The vaccine administered to each heifer is of minimum potency.

Use for the test not fewer than 20 heifers free from bovine diarrhoea virus and that do not have antibodies against bovine diarrhoea virus. Vaccinate not fewer than 13 heifers according to the schedule to be recommended. Maintain not fewer than 7 heifers as controls. Keep all the animals as one group. Inseminate the heifers. Take a blood sample from non-vaccinated heifers shortly before challenge. The test is discontinued if fewer than 10 vaccinated heifers or 5 non-vaccinated heifers are pregnant at the time of challenge. Challenge each heifer between the 60th and 90th days of gestation. For both test models described (observation until calving and harvest of foetuses at 28 days), challenge may be made by the intranasal route with a sufficient quantity of a non-cytopathic strain of bovine diarrhoea virus or alternatively, where the heifers are observed until calving, challenge may be made by contact with a persistently viraemic animal. Observe the heifers clinically at least daily from challenge either until the end of gestation or until harvest of foetuses after 28 days. If abortion occurs, examine the aborted foetus for bovine diarrhoea virus by suitable methods. If cattle are observed until calving, immediately after birth and prior to ingestion of colostrum, examine all calves for viraemia and antibodies against bovine diarrhoea virus. If foetuses are harvested 28 days after challenge, examine the foetuses for bovine diarrhoea virus by suitable methods. Transplacental infection is considered to have occurred if virus is detected in foetal organs or in the blood of newborn calves or if antibodies are detected in precolostral sera of calves.

The test is not valid if any of the control heifers have neutralising antibody before challenge or if transplacental infection fails to occur in more than 10 per cent of the calves from the control heifers. The vaccine complies with the test if at least 90 per cent of the calves from the vaccinated heifers are protected from transplacental infection.

2-4 MANUFACTURER'S TESTS

2-4-1 Residual live virus

The test for residual live virus is carried out using a quantity of inactivated virus harvest equivalent to not less than 25 doses of vaccine in cells of the same type as those used for production of the vaccine or cells shown to be at least as sensitive; the cells are passaged after 7 days and observed for a total of not less than 14 days. The inactivated virus harvest complies with the test if no live virus is detected.

2-4-2 Batch potency test

It is not necessary to carry out the potency test (section 3-4) for each batch of vaccine if it has been carried out using a batch of vaccine with a minimum potency. Where the test is not carried out, an alternative validated method is used, the criteria for acceptance being set with reference to a batch of vaccine that has given satisfactory results in the test described under Potency. The following test may be used.

Use for the test 7 suitable laboratory animals or calves that do not have antibodies against bovine diarrhoea virus. Administer by the subcutaneous route to 5 animals a suitable dose of the vaccine. Maintain 2 animals as controls. A 2nd dose of vaccine may be administered after a suitable interval if this has been shown to provide a suitably discriminating test system. Collect blood samples before the 1st vaccination and at a given interval between 14 and 21 days after the last vaccination. Determine the antibody titres against bovine diarrhoea virus by seroneutralisation on suitable cell cultures.

The test is not valid if the control animals show antibodies against bovine diarrhoea virus. The vaccine complies with the test if the level of antibodies in the vaccinates is not lower than that found for a batch of vaccine that has given satisfactory results in the test described under Potency.

3 BATCH TESTS

3-1 Identification

When administered to animals that do not have specific neutralising antibodies against bovine diarrhoea virus, the vaccine stimulates the production of such antibodies.

3-2 Bacteria and fungi

The vaccine, including where applicable the diluent supplied for reconstitution, complies with the test for sterility prescribed in the monograph *Vaccines for veterinary use (0062)*.

3-3 Residual live virus

Carry out a test for residual live bovine diarrhoea virus by inoculating not less than 10 doses onto cells known to be sensitive to bovine diarrhoea virus; passage the cells after

7 days and observe the 2nd culture for not less than 7 days. The vaccine complies with the test if no live virus is detected. If the vaccine contains an adjuvant, separate the adjuvant if possible from the liquid phase by a method that does not interfere with the detection of possible live virus.

3-4 Potency

The vaccine complies with the requirements of the test prescribed under Immunogenicity (section 2-3-2) when administered by a recommended route and method.

_____ Ph Eur

Brucella Melitensis (Strain Rev. 1) Vaccine, Living

(Brucellosis Vaccine (Live) (Brucella Melitensis Rev. 1 Strain) for Veterinary Use, Ph. Eur. monograph 0793)

Ph Eur _____

1 DEFINITION

Brucellosis vaccine (live) (Brucella melitensis Rev. 1 strain) for veterinary use is a suspension of live *Brucella melitensis* Rev. 1 strain. The vaccine contains not fewer than 0.5×10^9 and not more than 4×10^9 live bacteria per dose. This monograph applies to vaccines intended for the active immunisation of sheep and goats against disease caused by *B. melitensis*.

2 PRODUCTION

2-1 PREPARATION OF THE VACCINE

B. melitensis Rev. 1 strain is cultured in a suitable medium. The method of culture is such as to avoid bacterial dissociation and thus maintain the smooth characteristic of the culture. The bacteria are suspended in a buffer solution that may contain a suitable stabiliser. The suspension is distributed into containers.

2-2 CHOICE OF VACCINE STRAIN

The vaccine strain is shown to be satisfactory with respect to safety *(5.2.6)* and efficacy *(5.2.7)* for the sheep and goats for which it is intended.

The following tests for safety (section 2-2-1), residual virulence (section 2-2-2), determination of dissociation phase of master seed lot (section 2-2-3) and immunogenicity in mice (section 2-2-4) may be used during the demonstration of safety and efficacy.

2-2-1 Safety

Use 8 sheep, 4-6 months old, that do not have antibodies against *B. melitensis*. Administer to each sheep by a route to be recommended 3 doses of the vaccine. Observe the sheep at least daily for at least 14 days.

The vaccine complies with the test if no sheep shows notable signs of disease or dies from causes attributable to the vaccine.

2-2-2 Residual virulence

The test is carried out on the master seed lot and on a representative batch of vaccine. If the quantity of the master seed sufficient for performing the test is not available, the lowest passage seed used for the production that is available in sufficient quantity may be used.

Use 32 female CD1 mice, 5-6 weeks old. Vaccinate each mouse by the subcutaneous route with a suspension (0.1 mL) containing 10^8 live bacteria. Euthanise the mice in groups of 8, selected at random, 3, 6, 9 and 12 weeks later.

Remove the spleens and homogenise individually and aseptically in 1 mL of *phosphate buffered saline pH 6.8 R*. Spread the entire suspension on plates containing a suitable culture medium (lower limit of detection: 1 bacterium per spleen). Carry out in parallel a similar test using a suitable reference strain of *Brucella melitensis* Rev. 1. Calculate the 50 per cent persistence time by the usual statistical methods (5.3) for probit analysis.

The product complies with the test if the 50 per cent persistence time for the vaccine strain does not differ significantly from that of the reference strain.

2-2-3 Determination of dissociation phase of the master seed lot

Examine not fewer than 200 colonies by a suitable technique. The culture of the vaccine strain is seen to be in the smooth (S) phase.

The seed lot complies with the test if not fewer than 99 per cent of the colonies are of the smooth type.

2-2-4 Immunogenicity in mice

The test is carried out on the master seed lot and on a representative batch of vaccine. If the quantity of the master seed sufficient for performing the test is not available, the lowest passage seed used for the production that is available in sufficient quantity may be used.

Use for the test healthy CD1 female mice, 5-7 weeks old and from the same stock. Distribute the mice into 3 groups of 6 mice. Dilute the vaccine strain and a suitable reference strain of *Brucella melitensis* Rev. 1 to a concentration of 10^6 CFU/mL.

Vaccinate by the subcutaneous route the mice of the 1st group with 0.1 mL of the diluted vaccine strain and the mice of the 2nd group with 0.1 mL of the diluted reference strain; keep the 3rd group as the unvaccinated control. After 30 days, challenge all the mice with 2×10^5 bacteria of *B. abortus* strain 544 (CO_2-dependent). Euthanise the mice 15 days later and remove the spleen for *B. abortus* isolation. Record the number of *B. abortus* per spleen (X) and transform this value to obtain $Y = \log_{10} (X/\log_{10} X)$. Then calculate the mean and standard deviation of each group.

The test is valid if:
— the mean of the unvaccinated control group is at least 4.5 (mean of Y);
— the mean of the group receiving the reference strain is lower than 2.5 (mean of Y); and
— the standard deviation of each group is lower than 0.8.

Carry out a statistical comparison of the immunogenicity values of the 3 groups using the least significant differences test. The vaccine strain complies with the test if:
— the immunogenicity value of the group receiving the vaccine strain is significantly lower than the immunogenicity value of the control group; and
— the immunogenicity value of the group receiving the vaccine strain is not significantly different from the immunogenicity value of the group receiving the reference strain.

3 BATCH TESTS

3-1 Identification

B. melitensis present in the vaccine is identified by suitable morphological, serological and biochemical tests and by culture: Rev. 1 strain is inhibited by addition to the suitable culture medium of either benzylpenicillin sodium (3 μg/mL), thionin (20 μg/mL) or basic fuchsin (20 μg/mL); the strain grows on agar containing 2.5 μg of streptomycin per millilitre.

3-2 Determination of dissociation phase

Examine not fewer than 200 colonies by a suitable technique. The culture of the vaccine strain is seen to be in the smooth (S) phase.

The vaccine complies with the test if not fewer than 95 per cent of the colonies are of the smooth type.

3-3 Bacteria and fungi

The vaccine complies with the test if it does not contain extraneous micro-organisms. Verify the absence of micro-organisms other than *B. melitensis* Rev. 1 strain as described in the test for sterility prescribed in the monograph *Vaccines for veterinary use (0062)*.

3-4 Live bacteria

Make a count of live bacteria on a solid medium suitable for the culture of *B. melitensis* Rev. 1 strain.

The vaccine complies with the test if it contains not fewer than 0.5×10^9 and not more than 4×10^9 live bacteria per dose.

4 LABELLING

The label states:
— that the vaccine may be dangerous for man;
— that the vaccine is not to be used in pregnant animals;
— that the vaccine may be dangerous for cattle and that they are not to be kept in contact with sheep or goats vaccinated less than 24 h previously.

Ph Eur

Calf Coronavirus Diarrhoea Vaccine (Inactivated)

(Ph. Eur. monograph 1953)

Ph Eur

1 DEFINITION

Calf coronavirus diarrhoea vaccine (inactivated) is a preparation of one or more suitable strains of bovine coronavirus, inactivated while maintaining adequate immunogenic properties. This monograph applies to vaccines intended for the active immunisation of dams for passive protection of their progeny against coronavirus diarrhoea during the first few weeks of life.

2 PRODUCTION

2-1 PREPARATION OF THE VACCINE

Each vaccine virus is grown separately in cell cultures. The viral suspensions of each vaccine virus are harvested separately and inactivated by a method that maintains immunogenicity. The viral suspensions may be purified and concentrated. The vaccine may be adjuvanted.

2-2 SUBSTRATE FOR VIRUS PROPAGATION

2-2-1 Cell cultures

The cell cultures comply with the requirements for cell cultures for production of veterinary vaccines (5.2.4).

2-3 CHOICE OF VACCINE COMPOSITION

The vaccine is shown to be satisfactory with respect to safety (5.2.6) and efficacy (5.2.7) for the pregnant cows for which it is intended.

The following tests for safety (section 2-3-1) and immunogenicity (section 2-3-2) may be used during the demonstration of safety and efficacy.

2-3-1 Safety in pregnant cows

Carry out the test for each route and method of administration to be recommended for vaccination, using in each case pregnant cows that have not been vaccinated against bovine coronavirus. Use a batch of vaccine containing not less than the maximum potency that may be expected in a batch of vaccine.

For each test, use not fewer than 8 cows per group at the stage or at different stages of pregnancy according to the schedule to be recommended. Administer to each pregnant animal 1 dose of the vaccine. If the schedule to be recommended requires a 2nd dose, administer another dose after an interval of at least 14 days. After each injection, measure the body temperature on the day of the injection and on the 4 following days. Observe the pregnant cows at least daily until calving.

The vaccine complies with the test if no pregnant cow shows abnormal local or systemic reactions or dies from causes attributable to the vaccine and if no adverse effects on gestation or the offspring are noted.

2-3-2 Immunogenicity

A test is carried out for each route and method of administration to be recommended. The vaccine administered to each cow is of minimum potency.

Use for the test not fewer than 15 pregnant cows, preferably that do not have antibodies against bovine coronavirus. Where such cows are not available, use cows that: have not been vaccinated against bovine coronavirus; come from a farm where there is no recent history of infection with bovine coronavirus; and have a low level of antibodies against bovine coronavirus, the levels being comparable in all cows. Vaccinate not fewer than 10 pregnant cows according to the schedule to be recommended. Maintain not fewer than 5 pregnant cows as controls. Starting at calving, take the colostrum and then milk from each cow and keep it in suitable conditions. Determine individually the protective activity of the colostrum and milk from each cow using calves born from healthy cows, and which may be born by Caesarean section, and maintained in an environment where they are not exposed to infection by bovine coronavirus. Feed colostrum and then milk to each calf every 6 h or according to the schedule to be recommended. At 5-7 days after birth, challenge each calf by the oral route with a sufficient quantity of a virulent strain of bovine coronavirus. Observe the calves at least daily for 7 days. Note the incidence, severity and duration of diarrhoea and the duration and quantity of virus excretion.

The vaccine complies with the test if there is a significant reduction in diarrhoea and virus excretion in calves given colostrum and milk from vaccinated cows compared to those given colostrum and milk from controls.

2-4 MANUFACTURER'S TESTS

2-4-1 Residual live virus

The test for residual live virus is carried out using 2 passages in cell cultures of the same type as those used for production or in cells shown to be at least as sensitive. The quantity of inactivated virus harvest used in the test is equivalent to not less than 10 doses of vaccine. The inactivated virus harvest complies with the test if no live virus is detected.

2-4-2 Batch potency test

It is not necessary to carry out the potency test (section 3-5) for each batch of vaccine if it has been carried out using a batch of vaccine with a minimum potency. Where the test is not carried out, an alternative validated method is used, the criteria for acceptance being set with reference to a batch of vaccine that has given satisfactory results in the test described under Potency. The following test may be used.

To obtain a valid assay, it may be necessary to carry out a test using several groups of animals, each receiving a different dose. For each dose required, carry out the test as follows. Use for the test not fewer than 7 animals of a suitable species and that do not have specific antibodies against bovine coronavirus. Vaccinate not fewer than 5 animals using 1 injection of a suitable dose. Maintain not fewer than 2 animals as controls. Where the recommended schedule requires a booster injection to be given, a booster vaccination may also be given in this test provided it has been demonstrated that this will still provide a suitably sensitive test system. At a given interval not less than 14 days after the last injection, collect blood from each animal and prepare serum samples. Use a suitable validated test to measure the antibody response. The vaccine complies with the test if the antibody level in the vaccinates is not significantly less than that obtained with a batch that has given satisfactory results in the test described under Potency and there is no significant increase in antibody titre in the controls.

3 BATCH TESTS

3-1 Identification

Injected into animals that do not have specific antibodies against bovine coronavirus, the vaccine stimulates the formation of such antibodies.

3-2 Bacteria and fungi

The vaccine, including where applicable the diluent supplied for reconstitution, complies with the test for sterility prescribed in the monograph *Vaccines for veterinary use (0062)*.

3-3 Residual live virus

Carry out a test for residual live virus using 10 doses of vaccine and 2 passages in cell cultures of the same type as those used for production of the vaccine or other cell cultures of suitable sensitivity. The vaccine complies with the test if no live virus is detected. If the vaccine contains an adjuvant that interferes with the test, separate it if possible from the liquid phase of the vaccine by a method that does not inactivate virus nor interfere in any other way with detection of live viruses.

3-4 Specified extraneous agents

Use 2 cattle not less than 6 months old and that do not have antibodies against bovine herpesvirus 1 (BHV1), bovine leukaemia virus (BLV) and bovine viral diarrhoea virus (BVDV). Administer to each animal by a recommended route a double dose of the vaccine, then another dose after 14 days. Observe the cattle at least daily until 14 days after the last administration. Take a blood sample at the end of the observation period. The vaccine complies with the test if it does not stimulate the formation of antibodies against bovine herpesvirus 1 (BHV1), bovine leukaemia virus (BLV) and bovine viral diarrhoea virus (BVDV).

3-5 Potency

The vaccine complies with the requirements of the test prescribed under Immunogenicity (section 2-3-2) when administered by a recommended route and method.

4 LABELLING

The label states the recommended schedule for administering colostrum and milk, *post-partum*.

Calf Rotavirus Diarrhoea Vaccine (Inactivated)

(Ph. Eur. monograph 1954)

Ph Eur

1 DEFINITION

Calf rotavirus diarrhoea vaccine (inactivated) is a preparation of one or more suitable strains of bovine rotavirus, inactivated while maintaining adequate immunogenic properties. This monograph applies to vaccines intended for the active immunisation of dams for passive protection of their progeny against rotavirus diarrhoea during the first few weeks of life.

2 PRODUCTION
2-1 PREPARATION OF THE VACCINE

Each vaccine virus is grown separately in cell cultures. The viral suspensions of each vaccine virus are harvested separately and inactivated by a method that maintains immunogenicity. The viral suspensions may be purified and concentrated. The vaccine may be adjuvanted.

2-2 SUBSTRATE FOR VIRUS PROPAGATION
2-2-1 Cell cultures

The cell cultures comply with the requirements for cell cultures for production of veterinary vaccines (*5.2.4*).

2-3 CHOICE OF VACCINE COMPOSITION

The vaccine is shown to be satisfactory with respect to safety (*5.2.6*) and efficacy (*5.2.7*) for the pregnant cows for which it is intended.

The following tests for safety (section 2-3-1) and immunogenicity (section 2-3-2) may be used during the demonstration of safety and efficacy.

2-3-1 Safety in pregnant cows

Carry out the test for each route and method of administration to be recommended for vaccination, using in each case pregnant cows that have not been vaccinated against bovine rotavirus. Use a batch of vaccine containing not less than the maximum potency that may be expected in a batch of vaccine.

For each test, use not fewer than 8 cows per group at the stage or at different stages of pregnancy according to the schedule to be recommended. Administer to each pregnant animal 1 dose of the vaccine. If the schedule to be recommended requires a 2nd dose, administer another dose after an interval of at least 14 days. After each injection, measure the body temperature on the day of the injection and on the 4 following days. Observe the pregnant cows at least daily until calving.

The vaccine complies with the test if no pregnant cow shows abnormal local or systemic reactions or dies from causes attributable to the vaccine and if no adverse effects on gestation or the offspring are noted.

2-3-2 Immunogenicity

A test is carried out for each route and method of administration to be recommended. The vaccine administered to each cow is of minimum potency.

Use for the test not fewer than 15 pregnant cows, preferably that do not have antibodies against bovine rotavirus. Where such cows are not available, use cows that: have not been vaccinated against bovine rotavirus; come from a farm where there is no recent history of infection with bovine rotavirus; and have a low level of antibodies against bovine rotavirus, the levels being comparable in all cows. Vaccinate not fewer than 10 pregnant cows according to the schedule to be

recommended. Maintain not fewer than 5 pregnant cows as controls. Starting at calving, take the colostrum and then milk from each cow and keep it in suitable conditions. Determine individually the protective activity of the colostrum and milk from each cow using calves born from healthy cows, and which may be born by Caesarean section, and maintained in an environment where they are not exposed to infection by bovine rotavirus. Feed colostrum and then milk to each calf every 6 h or according to the schedule to be recommended. At 5-7 days after birth, challenge each calf by the oral route with a sufficient quantity of a virulent strain of bovine rotavirus. Observe the calves at least daily for 7 days. Note the incidence, severity and duration of diarrhoea and the duration and quantity of virus excretion.

The vaccine complies with the test if there is a significant reduction in diarrhoea and virus excretion in calves given colostrum and milk from vaccinated cows compared to those given colostrum and milk from controls.

2-4 MANUFACTURER'S TESTS
2-4-1 Residual live virus

The test for residual live virus is carried out using 2 passages in cell cultures of the same type as those used for production or in cells shown to be at least as sensitive. The quantity of inactivated virus harvest used in the test is equivalent to not less than 100 doses of vaccine. The inactivated viral harvest complies with the test if no live virus is detected.

2-4-2 Batch potency test

It is not necessary to carry out the potency test (section 3-5) for each batch of vaccine if it has been carried out using a batch of vaccine with a minimum potency. Where the test is not carried out, an alternative validated method is used, the criteria for acceptance being set with reference to a batch of vaccine that has given satisfactory results in the test described under Potency. The following test may be used.

To obtain a valid assay, it may be necessary to carry out a test using several groups of animals, each receiving a different dose. For each dose required, carry out the test as follows. Use for the test not fewer than 7 animals of a suitable species and that do not have antibodies against bovine rotavirus. Vaccinate not fewer than 5 animals using 1 injection of a suitable dose. Maintain not fewer than 2 animals as controls. Where the recommended schedule requires a booster injection to be given, a booster vaccination may also be given in this test provided it has been demonstrated that this will still provide a suitably sensitive test system. At a given interval not less than 14 days after the last injection, collect blood from each animal and prepare serum samples. Use a suitable validated test to measure the antibody response. The vaccine complies with the test if the antibody level in the vaccinates is not significantly less than that obtained with a batch that has given satisfactory results in the test described under Potency and there is no significant increase in antibody titre in the controls.

3 BATCH TESTS
3-1 Identification

Injected into animals that do not have specific antibodies against bovine rotavirus, the vaccine stimulates the formation of such antibodies.

3-2 Bacteria and fungi

The vaccine, including where applicable the diluent supplied for reconstitution, complies with the test for sterility prescribed in the monograph *Vaccines for veterinary use (0062)*.

3-3 Residual live virus

Carry out a test for residual live virus using 10 doses of vaccine and 2 passages in cell cultures of the same type as those used for production of the vaccine or other cell cultures of suitable sensitivity. The vaccine complies with the test if no live virus is detected. If the vaccine contains an adjuvant that interferes with the test, separate it if possible from the liquid phase of the vaccine by a method that does not inactivate virus nor interfere in any other way with detection of live viruses.

3-4 Specified extraneous agents

Use 2 cattle not less than 6 months old and that do not have antibodies against bovine herpesvirus 1 (BHV1), bovine leukaemia virus (BLV) and bovine viral diarrhoea virus (BVDV). Administer to each animal by a recommended route a double dose of the vaccine, then another dose after 14 days. Observe the cattle at least daily until 14 days after the last administration. Take a blood sample at the end of the observation period. The vaccine complies with the test if it does not stimulate the formation of antibodies against bovine herpesvirus 1 (BHV 1), bovine leukaemia virus (BLV) and bovine viral diarrhoea virus (BVDV).

3-5 Potency

The vaccine complies with the requirements of the test prescribed under Immunogenicity (section 2-3-2) when administered by a recommended route and method.

4 LABELLING

The label states the recommended schedule for administering colostrum and milk, *post-partum*.

_____ *Ph Eur*

Canine Adenovirus Vaccine, Inactivated

(Canine Adenovirus Vaccine (Inactivated),
Ph Eur monograph 1298)

Ph Eur _____

1 DEFINITION

Canine adenovirus vaccine (inactivated) is a preparation of one or more suitable strains of canine adenovirus 1 (canine contagious hepatitis virus) and/or canine adenovirus 2, inactivated while maintaining adequate immunogenic properties. This monograph applies to vaccines intended for the active immunisation of dogs against canine contagious hepatitis and/or respiratory disease caused by canine adenovirus.

2 PRODUCTION
2-1 PREPARATION OF THE VACCINE

The vaccine virus is grown in cell cultures. The virus harvest is inactivated. The vaccine may be adjuvanted.

2-2 SUBSTRATE FOR VIRUS PROPAGATION
2-2-1 Cell cultures

The cell cultures comply with the requirements for cell cultures for production of veterinary vaccines (*5.2.4*).

2-3 CHOICE OF VACCINE COMPOSITION

The vaccine is shown to be satisfactory with respect to safety (*5.2.6*) and efficacy (*5.2.7*) for the dogs for which it is intended.

The following tests for safety (section 2-3-1) and immunogenicity (section 2-3-2) may be used during the demonstration of safety and efficacy.

2-3-1 Safety

Carry out the test for each route and method of administration to be recommended for vaccination. Use a batch of vaccine containing not less than the maximum potency that may be expected in a batch of vaccine.

For each test, use not fewer than 8 dogs of the minimum age to be recommended and that do not have antibodies against canine adenovirus 1 or 2. Administer to each dog 1 dose of the vaccine. If the schedule to be recommended requires a 2nd dose, administer 1 dose after an interval of at least 14 days. Observe the dogs at least daily for at least 14 days after the last administration.

The vaccine complies with the test if no dog shows abnormal local or systemic reactions or dies from causes attributable to the vaccine.

2-3-2 Immunogenicity

For vaccines intended to protect against hepatitis, the test described below is suitable for demonstration of immunogenicity. If the vaccine is indicated for protection against respiratory signs, a further test to demonstrate immunogenicity for this indication is also necessary.

A test is carried out for each route and method of administration to be recommended for vaccination, using in each case dogs of the minimum age to be recommended. The vaccine administered to each dog is of minimum potency.

Use for the test not fewer than 7 dogs that do not have antibodies against canine adenovirus. Vaccinate not fewer than 5 dogs, according to the schedule to be recommended. Maintain not fewer than 2 dogs as controls. Challenge each dog after 20-22 days by the intravenous route with a sufficient quantity of a suspension of pathogenic canine adenovirus. Observe the dogs at least daily for 21 days after challenge. Dogs displaying typical signs of serious infection with canine adenovirus are euthanised to avoid unnecessary suffering.

The test is not valid if, during the observation period after challenge, fewer than 100 per cent of the control dogs die from or show typical signs of serious infection with canine adenovirus. The vaccine complies with the test if, during the observation period, all the vaccinated dogs survive and show no signs of disease.

2-4 MANUFACTURER'S TESTS
2-4-1 Residual live virus

The test for residual live virus is carried out using a quantity of inactivated virus harvest equivalent to at least 10 doses of vaccine with 2 passages in cell cultures of the same type as those used for production or in cell cultures shown to be at least as sensitive. The inactivated viral harvest complies with the test if no live virus is detected.

2-4-2 Batch potency

It is not necessary to carry out the Potency test (section 3-4) for each batch of vaccine if it has been carried out using a batch of vaccine with a minimum potency. Where the test is not carried out, an alternative validated method is used, the criteria for acceptance being set with reference to a batch of vaccine that has given satisfactory results in the test described under Potency.

3 BATCH TESTS
3-1 Identification

When injected into animals that do not have specific antibodies against the type or types of canine adenovirus stated on the label, the vaccine stimulates the formation of such antibodies.

3-2 Bacteria and fungi

The vaccine, including where applicable the diluent supplied for reconstitution, complies with the test for sterility prescribed in the monograph *Vaccines for veterinary use (0062)*.

3-3 Residual live virus

Carry out a test for residual canine adenovirus using 10 doses of vaccine by inoculation into sensitive cell cultures; make a passage after 6-8 days and maintain the cultures for 14 days. The vaccine complies with the test if no live virus is detected. If the vaccine contains an adjuvant, separate the adjuvant from the liquid phase by a method that does not inactivate or otherwise interfere with the detection of live virus.

3-4 Potency

The vaccine complies with the requirements of the test mentioned under Immunogenicity (section 2-3-2) when administered by a recommended route and method.

Ph Eur

Canine Adenovirus Vaccine, Living

(Canine Adenovirus Vaccine (Live), Ph Eur monograph 1951)

Ph Eur

1 DEFINITION

Canine adenovirus vaccine (live) is a preparation of a suitable strain of canine adenovirus 2. This monograph applies to vaccines intended for the active immunisation of dogs against canine contagious hepatitis and/or respiratory disease caused by canine adenovirus.

2 PRODUCTION

2-1 PREPARATION OF THE VACCINE

The vaccine virus is grown in cell cultures.

2-2 SUBSTRATE FOR VIRUS PROPAGATION

2-2-1 Cell cultures

The cell cultures comply with the requirements for cell cultures for production of veterinary vaccines (5.2.4).

2-3 CHOICE OF VACCINE VIRUS

The vaccine virus is shown to be satisfactory with respect to safety (5.2.6) and efficacy (5.2.7) for the dogs for which it is intended.

The following tests for safety (section 2-3-1), increase in virulence (section 2-3-2) and immunogenicity (section 2-3-3) may be used during the demonstration of safety and efficacy.

2-3-1 Safety

Carry out the test for each route and method of administration to be recommended for vaccination. Use vaccine virus at the least attenuated passage level that will be present in a batch of the vaccine.

For each test, use not fewer than 5 dogs of the minimum age to be recommended for vaccination and that do not have antibodies against canine adenoviruses. Administer to each dog a quantity of the vaccine virus equivalent to not less than 10 times the maximum virus titre likely to be contained in 1 dose of the vaccine. Observe the dogs at least daily for at least 14 days.

The vaccine virus complies with the test if no dog shows abnormal local or systemic reactions, signs of disease or dies from causes attributable to the vaccine virus.

2-3-2 Increase in virulence

Carry out the test according to general chapter 5.2.6 using dogs 5-7 weeks old, that do not have antibodies against canine adenoviruses. If the properties of the vaccine virus allow sequential passage through 5 groups via natural spreading, this method may be used, otherwise passage as described below is carried out.

Administer to each dog of the 1st group by a route to be recommended a quantity of the vaccine virus that will allow recovery of virus for the passages described below. Administer the virus by the route to be recommended for vaccination most likely to lead to reversion of virulence. After 4-6 days, prepare a suspension from the nasal and pharyngeal mucosa, tonsils, lung, spleen and if they are likely to contain virus, liver and kidney of each dog and pool the samples. Administer 1 mL of the pooled samples by a suitable route – for example, the intranasal route – to each dog of the next group. Carry out this passage operation not fewer than 4 times; verify the presence of the virus at each passage. If the virus is not found at a passage level, repeat the passage by administration to a group of 10 animals.

If the 5th group of animals shows no evidence of an increase in virulence indicative of reversion during the observation period, further testing is not required. Otherwise, carry out an additional safety test and compare the clinical signs and any relevant parameters in a group of at least 8 animals receiving the material used for the 1st passage and another similar group receiving the virus at the final passage level.

The vaccine virus complies with the test if no indication of increased virulence of the virus recovered for the final passage compared with the material used for the 1st passage is observed. If virus is not recovered after an initial passage in 2 animals and a subsequent repeat passage in 10 animals, the vaccine virus also complies with the test.

2-3-3 Immunogenicity

A test is carried out for each route and method of administration to be recommended for vaccination using in each case dogs of the minimum age to be recommended. The quantity of vaccine virus to be administered to each dog is not greater than the minimum virus titre to be stated on the label and the virus is at the most attenuated passage level that will be present in a batch of vaccine.

2-3-3-1 Vaccines intended to protect against hepatitis. Use for the test not fewer than 7 dogs that do not have antibodies against canine adenoviruses. Vaccinate not fewer than 5 dogs, according to the schedule to be recommended. Maintain not fewer than 2 dogs as controls. Challenge each dog after 20-22 days by the intravenous route with a sufficient quantity of a suspension of virulent canine adenovirus 1 (canine contagious hepatitis virus). Observe the dogs at least daily for 21 days after challenge. Dogs displaying typical signs of serious infection with canine adenovirus are euthanised to avoid unnecessary suffering.

The test is not valid if during the observation period after challenge, fewer than 100 per cent of the control dogs die or show notable signs of canine adenovirosis.

The vaccine virus complies with the test if during the observation period after challenge, all the vaccinated dogs survive and show no signs of disease except for a possible transient elevated rectal temperature.

2-3-3-2 Vaccine intended to protect against respiratory signs. Use for the test not fewer than 20 dogs that do not have antibodies against canine adenoviruses. Vaccinate not fewer than 10 dogs, according to the schedule to be recommended. Maintain not fewer than 10 dogs as controls. Challenge each dog after 20-22 days by the intranasal route with a quantity of a suspension of virulent canine adenovirus 2 sufficient to cause typical signs of respiratory disease in a dog that does not have antibodies against canine adenoviruses. Observe the dogs at least daily for 10 days after challenge. Record the incidence of signs of respiratory and general disease in each dog (for example, sneezing, coughing, nasal and lachrymal discharge, loss of appetite). Collect nasal swabs or washings from each dog daily from days 2 to 10 after challenge and test these samples to determine the presence and titre of excreted virus.

The vaccine complies with the test if there is a notable decrease in the incidence and severity of signs and in virus excretion in vaccinates compared to controls.

3 BATCH TESTS
3-1 Identification
The vaccine mixed with monospecific antiserum against canine adenovirus 2 no longer infects susceptible cell cultures.

3-2 Bacteria and fungi
The vaccine, including where applicable the diluent supplied for reconstitution, complies with the test for sterility prescribed in the monograph *Vaccines for veterinary use (0062)*.

3-3 Mycoplasmas *(2.6.7)*
The vaccine complies with the test for mycoplasmas.

3-4 Extraneous agents
Neutralise the vaccine virus with a suitable monospecific antiserum against canine adenovirus 2 and inoculate into cell cultures known for their susceptibility to viruses pathogenic for the dog. Carry out a passage after 6-8 days and maintain the cultures for a total of 14 days.

The vaccine complies with the test if no cytopathic effect develops and there is no sign of the presence of haemadsorbing agents.

3-5 Virus titre
Titrate the vaccine virus in suitable cell cultures. The vaccine complies with the test if one dose contains not less than the minimum virus titre stated on the label.

3-6 Potency
The vaccine complies with the requirements of one or both of the tests prescribed under Immunogenicity (section 2-3-3) when administered by a recommended route and method. It is not necessary to carry out the potency test for each batch of the vaccine if it has been carried out on a representative batch using a vaccinating dose containing not more than the minimum virus titre stated on the label.

—————————————————————————— *Ph Eur*

Canine Distemper Vaccine, Living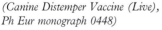

(Canine Distemper Vaccine (Live),
Ph Eur monograph 0448)

Ph Eur _____

1 DEFINITION
Canine distemper vaccine (live) is a preparation of a suitable strain of distemper virus. This monograph applies to vaccines intended for the active immunisation of dogs against canine distemper.

2 PRODUCTION
2-1 PREPARATION OF THE VACCINE
The vaccine virus is grown in embryonated hens' eggs or in cell cultures.

2-2 SUBSTRATE FOR VIRUS PROPAGATION
2-2-1 Embryonated hens' eggs
If the vaccine virus is grown in embryonated hens' eggs, they are obtained from flocks free from specified pathogens (SPF) *(5.2.2)*.

2-2-2 Cell cultures
If the vaccine virus is grown in cell cultures, they comply with the requirements for cell cultures for production of veterinary vaccines *(5.2.4)*.

2-3 CHOICE OF VACCINE VIRUS
The vaccine virus is shown to be satisfactory with respect to safety *(5.2.6)* and efficacy *(5.2.7)* for the dogs for which it is intended.

The following tests for safety (section 2-3-1), increase in virulence (section 2-3-2) and immunogenicity (section 2-3-3) may be used during the demonstration of safety and efficacy.

2-3-1 Safety
Carry out the test for each route and method of administration to be recommended for vaccination. Use vaccine virus at the least attenuated passage level that will be present in a batch of the vaccine.

For each test, use not fewer than 5 dogs of the minimum age to be recommended for vaccination and that do not have antibodies against canine distemper virus. Administer to each dog a quantity of the vaccine virus equivalent to not less than 10 times the maximum virus titre likely to be contained in 1 dose of the vaccine. Observe the dogs at least daily for 42 days.

The vaccine virus complies with the test if no dog shows abnormal local or systemic reactions, signs of disease or dies from causes attributable to the vaccine virus.

2-3-2 Increase in virulence
Carry out the test according to general chapter *5.2.6* using dogs 5-7 weeks old, that do not have antibodies against canine distemper virus. If the properties of the vaccine virus allow sequential passage through 5 groups via natural spreading, this method may be used, otherwise passage as described below is carried out.

Administer to each dog of the 1st group by a route to be recommended a quantity of the vaccine virus that will allow recovery of virus for the passages described below. Administer the virus by the route to be recommended for vaccination most likely to lead to reversion to virulence. After 5-10 days, prepare a suspension from the nasal mucosa, tonsils, thymus, spleen and the lungs and their local lymph nodes of each dog and pool the samples. Administer 1 mL of the pooled samples by the intranasal route to each dog of the next group. Carry out this passage operation not fewer than 4 times; verify the presence of the virus at each passage. If the virus is not found at a passage level, repeat the passage by administration to a group of 10 animals.

If the 5th group of animals shows no evidence of an increase in virulence indicative of reversion during the observation period, further testing is not required. Otherwise, carry out an additional safety test and compare the clinical signs and any relevant parameters in a group of at least 8 animals receiving the material used for the 1st passage and another similar group receiving the virus at the final passage level.

The vaccine virus complies with the test if no indication of increased virulence of the virus recovered for the final passage compared with the material used for the 1st passage is observed. If virus is not recovered after an initial passage in 2 animals and a subsequent repeat passage in 10 animals, the vaccine virus also complies with the test.

2-3-3 Immunogenicity

A test is carried out for each route and method of administration to be recommended for vaccination using in each case dogs 8-16 weeks old. The quantity of vaccine virus to be administered to each dog is not greater than the minimum virus titre to be stated on the label and the virus is at the most attenuated passage level that will be present in a batch of vaccine.

Use for the test not fewer than 7 dogs that do not have antibodies against canine distemper virus. Vaccinate not fewer than 5 dogs according to the schedule to be recommended. Maintain not fewer than 2 dogs as controls. Challenge each dog after 20-22 days by the intravenous route with a sufficient quantity of a suspension of virulent canine distemper virus. Observe the dogs at least daily for 21 days after challenge. Dogs displaying typical signs of serious infection with canine distemper virus are euthanised to avoid unnecessary suffering.

The test is not valid if during the observation period after challenge, fewer than 100 per cent of the control dogs die or show notable signs of canine distemper.

The vaccine virus complies with the test if during the observation period after challenge, all the vaccinated dogs survive and show no signs of disease.

3 BATCH TESTS

3-1 Identification

The vaccine mixed with a monospecific distemper antiserum against canine distemper virus no longer provokes cytopathic effects in susceptible cell cultures.

3-2 Bacteria and fungi

The vaccine, including where applicable the diluent supplied for reconstitution, complies with the test for sterility prescribed in the monograph *Vaccines for veterinary use (0062)*.

3-3 Mycoplasmas (*2.6.7*)

The vaccine complies with the test for mycoplasmas.

3-4 Extraneous agents

Neutralise the vaccine virus with a suitable monospecific antiserum against canine distemper virus and inoculate into cell cultures known for their susceptibility to viruses pathogenic for the dog. Carry out a passage after 6-8 days and maintain the cultures for 14 days.

The vaccine complies with the test if no cytopathic effect develops and there is no sign of the presence of haemadsorbing agents.

3-5 Virus titre

Titrate the vaccine virus in suitable cell cultures. The vaccine complies with the test if one dose contains not less than the minimum virus titre stated on the label.

3-6 Potency

The vaccine complies with the requirements of the test prescribed under Immunogenicity (section 2-3-3) when administered by a recommended route and method. It is not necessary to carry out the potency test for each batch of the vaccine if it has been carried out on a representative batch using a vaccinating dose containing not more than the minimum virus titre stated on the label.

Ph Eur

Canine Parainfluenza Virus Vaccine (Live)

(Ph. Eur. monograph 1955)

Ph Eur

1 DEFINITION

Canine parainfluenza virus vaccine (live) is a preparation of a suitable strain of parainfluenza virus of canine origin. This monograph applies to vaccines intended for the active immunisation of dogs against respiratory signs of infection with parainfluenza virus of canine origin.

2 PRODUCTION

2-1 PREPARATION OF THE VACCINE

The vaccine virus is grown in cell cultures.

2-2 SUBSTRATE FOR VIRUS PROPAGATION

2-2-1 Cell cultures

The cell cultures comply with the requirements for cell cultures for production of veterinary vaccines (*5.2.4*).

2-3 CHOICE OF VACCINE VIRUS

The vaccine virus is shown to be satisfactory with respect to safety (*5.2.6*) and efficacy (*5.2.7*) for the dogs for which it is intended.

The following tests for safety (section 2-3-1), increase in virulence (section 2-3-2) and immunogenicity (section 2-3-3) may be used during the demonstration of safety and efficacy.

2-3-1 Safety

Carry out the test for each route and method of administration to be recommended for vaccination. Use vaccine virus at the least attenuated passage level that will be present in a batch of the vaccine.

For each test, use not fewer than 5 dogs of the minimum age to be recommended for vaccination and that do not have antibodies against parainfluenza virus of canine origin. Administer to each dog a quantity of the vaccine virus equivalent to not less than 10 times the maximum virus titre likely to be contained in 1 dose of the vaccine. Observe the dogs at least daily for at least 14 days.

The vaccine virus complies with the test if no dog shows abnormal local or systemic reactions, signs of disease or dies from causes attributable to the vaccine virus.

2-3-2 Increase in virulence

Carry out the test according to general chapter *5.2.6* using dogs 5-7 weeks old, that do not have antibodies against parainfluenza virus of canine origin. If the properties of the vaccine virus allow sequential passage through 5 groups via natural spreading, this method may be used, otherwise passage as described below is carried out.

Administer to each dog of the 1st group by the intranasal route and by a route to be recommended a quantity of the vaccine virus that will allow recovery of virus for the passages described below. Administer the virus by the route to be recommended for vaccination most likely to lead to reversion to virulence. After 3-10 days, prepare a suspension from nasal swabs of each dog. Administer 1 mL of the suspension from the swabs that contain the maximum amount of virus by the intranasal route to each dog of the next group. Carry out this passage operation not fewer than 4 times; verify the presence of the virus at each passage. If the virus is not found at a passage level, repeat the passage by administration to a group of 10 animals.

If the 5th group of animals shows no evidence of an increase in virulence indicative of reversion during the observation period, further testing is not required. Otherwise, carry out an additional safety test and compare the clinical signs and any relevant parameters in a group of at least 8 animals receiving the material used for the 1st passage and another similar group receiving the virus at the final passage level.

The vaccine virus complies with the test if no indication of increased virulence of the virus recovered for the final passage compared with the material used for the 1st passage is observed. If virus is not recovered after an initial passage in 2 animals and a subsequent repeat passage in 10 animals, the vaccine virus also complies with the test.

2-3-3 Immunogenicity

A test is carried out for each route and method of administration to be recommended for vaccination, using in each case dogs of the minimum age to be recommended. The quantity of vaccine virus to be administered to each dog is not greater than the minimum virus titre to be stated on the label and the virus is at the most attenuated passage level that will be present in a batch of vaccine.

Use for the test not fewer than 15 dogs that do not have antibodies against parainfluenza virus of canine origin. Vaccinate not fewer than 10 dogs according to the schedule to be recommended. Maintain not fewer than 5 dogs as controls. Challenge each dog after not less than 20-22 days by the intratracheal or intranasal route with a sufficient quantity of a suspension of virulent parainfluenza virus of canine origin. Observe the dogs at least daily for 14 days after challenge. Collect nasal swabs or washings from each dog daily from day 2 to 10 after challenge and test these samples for the presence of excreted virus. Use a scoring system to record the incidence of coughing in each dog.

The test is not valid if more than 1 of the control dogs shows neither coughing nor the excretion of the challenge virus.

The vaccine complies with the test if the scores for coughing or virus excretion for the vaccinated dogs are significantly lower than in the controls.

3 BATCH TESTS

3-1 Identification

Carry out an immunofluorescence test in suitable cell cultures, using a monospecific antiserum.

3-2 Bacteria and fungi

The vaccine, including where applicable the diluent supplied for reconstitution, complies with the test for sterility prescribed in the monograph *Vaccines for veterinary use (0062)*.

3-3 Mycoplasmas (2.6.7)

The vaccine complies with the test for mycoplasmas.

3-4 Extraneous agents

Neutralise the vaccine virus with a suitable monospecific antiserum against parainfluenza virus of canine origin and inoculate into cell cultures known for their susceptibility to viruses pathogenic for the dog. Carry out a passage after 6-8 days and maintain the cultures for a total of 14 days.

The vaccine complies with the test if no cytopathic effect develops and there is no sign of the presence of haemadsorbing agents.

3-5 Virus titre

Titrate the vaccine virus in suitable cell cultures. The vaccine complies with the test if one dose contains not less than the minimum virus titre stated on the label.

3-6 Potency

The vaccine complies with the requirements of the test prescribed under Immunogenicity (section 2-3-3) when administered by a recommended route and method. It is not necessary to carry out the potency test for each batch of the vaccine if it has been carried out on a representative batch using a vaccinating dose containing not more than the minimum virus titre stated on the label.

_____ *Ph Eur*

Canine Parvovirus Vaccine, Inactivated

(Canine Parvovirosis Vaccine (Inactivated),
Ph Eur monograph 0795)

Ph Eur _____

1 DEFINITION

Canine parvovirosis vaccine (inactivated) is a preparation of a suitable strain of canine parvovirus inactivated while maintaining adequate immunogenic properties. This monograph applies to vaccines intended for the active immunisation of dogs against canine parvovirosis.

2 PRODUCTION
2-1 PREPARATION OF THE VACCINE

The vaccine virus is grown in cell cultures. The virus harvest is inactivated. The vaccine may be adjuvanted.

2-2 SUBSTRATE FOR VIRUS PROPAGATION
2-2-1 Cell cultures

The cell cultures comply with the requirements for cell cultures for production of veterinary vaccines (5.2.4).

2-3 CHOICE OF VACCINE COMPOSITION

The vaccine is shown to be satisfactory with respect to safety (5.2.6) and efficacy (5.2.7) for the dogs for which it is intended.

The following tests for safety (section 2-3-1) and immunogenicity (section 2-3-2) may be used during the demonstration of safety and efficacy.

2-3-1 Safety

Carry out the test for each route and method of administration to be recommended for vaccination. Use a batch of vaccine containing not less than the maximum potency that may be expected in a batch of vaccine.

For each test, use not fewer than 8 dogs not older than the minimum age to be recommended for vaccination and that do not have antibodies against canine parvovirus. Administer to each dog 1 dose of the vaccine. If the schedule to be recommended requires a 2nd dose, administer 1 dose after an interval of at least 14 days. Observe the dogs at least daily for at least 14 days after the last administration.

The vaccine complies with the test if no dog shows abnormal local or systemic reactions or dies from causes attributable to the vaccine.

2-3-2 Immunogenicity

A test is carried out for each route and method of administration to be recommended for vaccination using in each case dogs of the minimum age to be recommended. The vaccine administered to each dog is of minimum potency.

Use for the test not fewer than 7 dogs that do not have antibodies against canine parvovirus. Vaccinate not fewer than 5 dogs according to the schedule to be recommended. Maintain not fewer than 2 dogs as controls. Challenge each dog after 20-22 days by the oronasal route with a sufficient quantity of a suspension of pathogenic canine parvovirus.

Observe the dogs at least daily for 14 days after challenge. At the end of the observation period, carry out haemagglutination tests for and titration of the virus in the faeces.

The test is not valid if fewer than 100 per cent of the control dogs show notable signs of the disease or leucopenia and excretion of the virus. The vaccine complies with the test if all the vaccinated dogs survive and show no signs of disease nor leucopenia and if the maximum titre of virus excreted in the faeces is less than 1/100 of the geometric mean of the maximum titres found in the controls.

2-4 MANUFACTURER'S TESTS

2-4-1 Residual live virus
A test for residual live virus is carried out on the bulk harvest of each batch to confirm inactivation of the canine parvovirus. The quantity of inactivated virus harvest used in the test is equivalent to not less than 100 doses of the vaccine. The inactivated viral harvest is inoculated into suitable non-confluent cells; after incubation for 8 days, a subculture is made using trypsinised cells. After incubation for a further 8 days, the cultures are examined for residual live parvovirus by an immunofluorescence test.

The immunofluorescence test may be supplemented by a haemagglutination test or other suitable tests on the supernatant of the cell cultures. The inactivated viral harvest complies with the test if no live virus is detected.

3 BATCH TESTS

3-1 Identification
When injected into animals that do not have antibodies against canine parvovirus, the vaccine stimulates the production of such antibodies.

3-2 Bacteria and fungi
The vaccine, including where applicable the diluent supplied for reconstitution, complies with the test for sterility prescribed in the monograph *Vaccines for veterinary use (0062)*.

3-3 Potency
Carry out test 3-3-1 or test 3-3-2.

3-3-1 Test in guinea-pigs for haemagglutination-inhibiting antibodies. Use for the test not fewer than 5 guinea-pigs that do not have specific antibodies. Administer to each guinea-pig by the subcutaneous route half of the dose to be recommended. After 14 days, inject again half of the dose to be recommended. 14 days later, collect blood samples and separate the serum. Inactivate each serum by heating at 56 °C for 30 min. To 1 volume of each serum add 9 volumes of a 200 g/L suspension of *light kaolin R* in *phosphate buffered saline pH 7.4 R*. Shake each mixture for 20 min. Centrifuge, collect the supernatant and mix with 1 volume of a concentrated suspension of pig erythrocytes. Allow to stand at 4 °C for 60 min and centrifuge. The dilution of the serum obtained is 1:10. Using each serum, prepare a series of twofold dilutions. To 0.025 mL of each of the latter dilutions add 0.025 mL of a suspension of canine parvovirus antigen containing 4 haemagglutinating units. Allow to stand at 37 °C for 30 min and add 0.05 mL of a suspension of pig erythrocytes containing 30×10^6 cells per millilitre. Allow to stand at 4 °C for 90 min and note the last dilution of serum that still completely inhibits haemagglutination. The vaccine complies with the test if the median antibody titre of the sera collected after the second vaccination is not less than 1/80.

3-3-2 Test in dogs for virus-neutralising antibodies. Use for the test not fewer than 2 healthy dogs, 8-12 weeks old, that have antibody titres less than 4 ND_{50} per 0.1 mL of serum, measured by the method described below. Vaccinate each dog according to the recommended schedule. 14 days after vaccination, examine the serum of each dog as follows. Heat the serum at 56 °C for 30 min and prepare serial dilutions using a medium suitable for canine cells. Add to each dilution an equal volume of a virus suspension containing an amount of virus such that when the volume of serum-virus mixture appropriate for the assay system is inoculated into cell cultures, each culture receives approximately 10^4 $CCID_{50}$. Incubate the mixtures at 37 °C for 1 h and inoculate 4 canine cell cultures with a suitable volume of each mixture. Incubate the cell cultures at 37 °C for 7 days, passage and incubate for a further 7 days. Examine the cultures for evidence of specific cytopathic effects and calculate the antibody titre. The vaccine complies with the test if the mean titre is not less than 32 ND_{50} per 0.1 mL of serum. If one dog fails to respond, repeat the test using 2 more dogs and calculate the result as the mean of the titres obtained from all of the 3 dogs that have responded.

Ph Eur

Canine Parvovirus Vaccine, Living

*(Canine Parvovirosis Vaccine (Live),
Ph Eur monograph 0964)*

Ph Eur

1 DEFINITION
Canine parvovirosis vaccine (live) is a preparation of a suitable strain of canine parvovirus. This monograph applies to vaccines intended for the active immunisation of dogs against canine parvovirosis.

2 PRODUCTION

2-1 PREPARATION OF THE VACCINE
The vaccine virus is grown in cell cultures.

2-2 SUBSTRATE FOR VIRUS PROPAGATION

2-2-1 Cell cultures
The cell cultures comply with the requirements for cell cultures for production of veterinary vaccines *(5.2.4)*.

2-3 CHOICE OF VACCINE VIRUS
The vaccine virus is shown to be satisfactory with respect to safety *(5.2.6)* and efficacy *(5.2.7)* for the dogs for which it is intended.

The following tests for safety (section 2-3-1), increase in virulence (section 2-3-2) and immunogenicity (section 2-3-3) may be used during the demonstration of safety and efficacy.

2-3-1 Safety
Carry out the test for each route and method of administration to be recommended for vaccination, using in each case dogs of the minimum age to be recommended for vaccination. Use vaccine virus at the least attenuated passage level that will be present in a batch of the vaccine.

2-3-1-1 General safety. For each test, use not fewer than 5 dogs that do not have haemagglutination-inhibiting antibodies against canine parvovirus. A count of white blood cells in circulating blood is made on days 4, 2 and 0 before injection of the vaccine strain. Administer to each dog a quantity of the vaccine virus equivalent to not less than 10 times the maximum virus titre likely to be contained in 1 dose of the vaccine. Observe the dogs at least daily for at least 14 days. A count of white blood cells in circulating blood is made on days 3, 5, 7 and 10 after the injection.

The test is not valid if a diminution in the number of circulating white blood cells greater than 50 per cent of the initial number - determined as the average of the 3 values found before injection of the vaccine strain – is noted. The vaccine virus complies with the test if no dog shows abnormal local or systemic reactions, signs of disease or dies from causes attributable to the vaccine virus and if, for each dog and each blood count, after vaccination, the number of leucocytes is not less than 50 per cent of the initial value.

2-3-1-2 Effects on the thymus. For each test, use not fewer than 8 dogs that do not have haemagglutination-inhibiting antibodies against canine parvovirus. Administer to each of not fewer than 4 dogs a quantity of the vaccine virus equivalent to not less than 10 times the maximum virus titre likely to be contained in 1 dose of the vaccine. Maintain not fewer than 4 dogs as controls. Observe the dogs at least daily. After 14 days, euthanise 2 dogs from each group and after 21 days, the remaining dogs from each group. Carry out histological examination of the thymus of each dog.

The vaccine virus complies with the test if there is no more than slight hypoplasia of the thymus after 14 days and no damage is evident after 21 days.

2-3-2 Increase in virulence

Carry out the test according to general chapter *5.2.6* using dogs of the minimum age to be recommended for vaccination, that do not have haemagglutination-inhibiting antibodies against canine parvovirus. If the properties of the vaccine virus allow sequential passage through 5 groups via natural spreading, this method may be used, otherwise passage as described below is carried out.

Administer to each dog of the 1st group by a route to be recommended a quantity of the vaccine virus that will allow recovery of virus for the passages described below. Collect the faeces from each dog from the 2nd to the 10th day after administration of the virus, check them for the presence of the virus and pool the faeces containing virus. Administer 1 mL of the suspension of pooled faeces by the oronasal route to each dog of the next group. Carry out this passage operation not fewer than 4 times; verify the presence of the virus at each passage. If the virus is not found at a passage level, repeat the passage by administration to a group of 10 animals.

If the 5th group of animals shows no evidence of an increase in virulence indicative of reversion during the observation period, further testing is not required. Otherwise, carry out an additional safety test and compare the clinical signs and any relevant parameters in a group of at least 8 animals receiving the material used for the 1st passage and another similar group receiving the virus at the final passage level.

The vaccine virus complies with the test if no indication of increased virulence of the virus recovered for the final passage compared with the material used for the 1st passage is observed; account is taken, notably, of the count of white blood cells, of results of histological examination of the thymus and of the titre of excreted virus. If virus is not recovered after an initial passage in 2 animals and a subsequent repeat passage in 10 animals, the vaccine virus also complies with the test.

2-3-3 Immunogenicity

A test is carried out for each route and method of administration to be recommended using in each case dogs of the minimum age to be recommended for vaccination. The quantity of vaccine virus to be administered to each dog

is not greater than the minimum virus titre to be stated on the label and the virus is at the most attenuated passage level that will be present in a batch of vaccine.

Use for the test not fewer than 7 dogs that do not have haemagglutination-inhibiting antibodies against canine parvovirus. Vaccinate not fewer than 5 dogs. Maintain not fewer than 2 dogs as controls. Challenge each dog after 20-22 days by the oronasal route with a sufficient quantity of a suspension of virulent canine parvovirus. Observe the dogs at least daily for 14 days after challenge. At the end of the observation period, carry out a haemagglutination test for and titration of the virus in the faeces.

The test is not valid if fewer than 100 per cent of the control dogs show typical signs of the disease and/or leucopenia and excretion of the virus.

The vaccine virus complies with the test if all the vaccinated dogs survive and show no sign of disease nor leucopenia and if the maximum titre of virus excreted in the faeces is less than 1/100 of the geometric mean of the maximum titres found in the controls.

3 BATCH TESTS
3-1 Identification
The vaccine is grown in a susceptible cell line in a substrate suitable for presenting for fluorescent antibody or immunoperoxidase tests. Suitable controls are included. A proportion of the cells is tested with a monoclonal antibody specific for canine parvovirus and a proportion of the cells tested with a monoclonal antibody specific for feline parvovirus. Canine parvovirus antigen is detected but no feline parvovirus is detected in the cells inoculated with the vaccine.

3-2 Bacteria and fungi
The vaccine, including where applicable the diluent supplied for reconstitution, complies with the test for sterility prescribed in the monograph *Vaccines for veterinary use (0062)*.

3-3 Mycoplasmas *(2.6.7)*
The vaccine complies with the test for mycoplasmas.

3-4 Extraneous agents
Neutralise the vaccine virus with a suitable monospecific antiserum against canine parvovirus and inoculate into cell cultures known for their susceptibility to viruses pathogenic for the dog.

The vaccine complies with the test if no cytopathic effect develops and there is no sign of haemagglutinating or haemadsorbing agents and no other sign of the presence of extraneous viruses.

3-5 Virus titre
Titrate the vaccine virus by inoculation into suitable cell cultures. The vaccine complies with the test if one dose contains not less than the minimum virus titre stated on the label.

3-6 Potency
The vaccine complies with the requirements of the test prescribed under Immunogenicity (section 2-3-3) when administered by a recommended route and method. It is not necessary to carry out the potency test for each batch of the vaccine if it has been carried out on a representative batch using a vaccinating dose containing not more than the minimum virus titre stated on the label.

Clostridium Botulinum Vaccine

Botulinum Vaccine

*(Clostridium Botulinum Vaccine for Veterinary Use,
Ph Eur monograph 0360)*

When Clostridium Botulinum Vaccine or Botulinum Vaccine
is prescribed or demanded and the types to be present are
not stated, Clostridium Botulinum Vaccine prepared from
types C and D shall be dispensed or supplied.

Ph Eur

1 DEFINITION

Clostridium botulinum vaccine for veterinary use is prepared
from liquid cultures of suitable strains of *Clostridium
botulinum* type C or type D or a mixture of these types.
The whole culture or its filtrate or a mixture of the two is
inactivated to eliminate its toxicity while maintaining
adequate immunogenic properties. This monograph applies
to vaccines intended for active immunisation of animals
against botulism.

2 PRODUCTION

2-1 PREPARATION OF THE VACCINE

C. botulinum used for production is grown in an appropriate
liquid medium.

The preparation may be adsorbed, precipitated or
concentrated. It may be treated with a suitable adjuvant and
may be freeze-dried.

2-2 CHOICE OF VACCINE COMPOSITION

The vaccine is shown to be satisfactory with respect to safety
(5.2.6) and efficacy *(5.2.7)* for the animals for which it is
intended.

The following test for safety (section 2-2-1) may be used
during the demonstration of safety.

2-2-1 Safety

Carry out the tests for each route and method of
administration to be recommended for vaccination and where
applicable, in animals of each category for which the vaccine
is intended, using in each case animals not older than the
minimum age to be recommended for vaccination. Use a
batch of vaccine containing not less than the maximum
potency that may be expected in a batch of vaccine.

For each test, use not fewer than 8 animals that do not have
antibodies against *C. botulinum*. Administer to each animal
1 dose of the vaccine. If the schedule to be recommended
requires a 2nd dose, administer another dose after an interval
of at least 14 days. Observe the animals at least daily until
14 days after the last administration.

The vaccine complies with the test if no animal shows
abnormal local or systemic reactions or dies from causes
attributable to the vaccine.

2-3 MANUFACTURER'S TESTS

2-3-1 Batch potency test

It is not necessary to carry out the potency test (section 3-4)
for each batch of the vaccine if it has been carried out using
a batch of vaccine with a minimum potency. Where the test
is not carried out, an alternative validated method is used,
the criteria for acceptance being set with reference to a batch
of vaccine that has given satisfactory results in the test
described under Potency.

3 BATCH TESTS

*The identification, the tests and the determination of potency apply
to the liquid preparation and to the freeze-dried preparation
reconstituted as stated on the label.*

3-1 Identification

When injected into a healthy animal free from antibodies
against the type or types of *C. botulinum* from which the
vaccine was prepared, the vaccine stimulates the production
of such antibodies.

3-2 Bacteria and fungi

The vaccine, including where applicable the diluent supplied
for reconstitution, complies with the test for sterility
prescribed in the monograph *Vaccines for veterinary
use (0062)*.

3-3 Residual toxicity

Inject 0.5 mL of the vaccine by the subcutaneous route into
each of 5 mice, each weighing 17-22 g. Observe the animals
at least daily for 7 days.

The vaccine complies with the test if no animal shows
notable signs of disease or dies from causes attributable to
the vaccine.

3-4 Potency

Use for the test healthy white mice from a uniform stock,
each weighing 18-20 g. Use as challenge dose a quantity of a
toxin of *C. botulinum* of the same type as that used in the
preparation of the vaccine corresponding to 25 times the
paralytic dose 50 per cent, a paralytic dose 50 per cent being
the quantity of toxin that, when injected by the
intraperitoneal route into mice, causes paralysis in
50 per cent of the animals within an observation period of
7 days. If 2 types of *C. botulinum* have been used in the
preparation of the vaccine, carry out the potency
determination for each. Dilute the vaccine to be examined
8-fold using a 9 g/L solution of *sodium chloride R*. Inject
0.2 mL of the dilution subcutaneously into each of 20 mice.
After 21 days, inject the challenge dose by the intraperitoneal
route into each of the vaccinated mice and into each of 10
control mice. Observe the mice for 7 days and record the
number of animals that show signs of botulism.

The test is not valid unless all the control mice show signs of
botulism during the observation period. The vaccine
complies with the test if not fewer than 80 per cent of the
vaccinated mice are protected.

4 LABELLING

The label states:
— the type or types of *C. botulinum* from which the vaccine
  has been prepared;
— whether the preparation is a toxoid or a vaccine prepared
  from a whole inactivated culture or a mixture of the two.

Ph Eur

Clostridium Chauvoei Vaccine

Blackleg Vaccine

*(Clostridium Chauvoei Vaccine for Veterinary Use,
Ph Eur monograph 0361)*

Ph Eur

1 DEFINITION

Clostridium chauvoei vaccine for veterinary use is prepared
from liquid cultures of one or more suitable strains of
Clostridium chauvoei. The whole culture is inactivated to
eliminate its toxicity while maintaining adequate
immunogenic properties. This monograph applies to vaccines
intended for active immunisation of animals against disease
caused by *C. chauvoei*.

2 PRODUCTION
2-1 PREPARATION OF THE VACCINE
C chauvoei Used for production is grown in an appropriate liquid medium. Inactivated cultures may be treated with a suitable adjuvant.

2-2 CHOICE OF VACCINE COMPOSITION
The vaccine is shown to be satisfactory with respect to safety (*5.2.6*) and efficacy (*5.2.7*) for the animals for which it is intended.

The following test for safety (section 2-2-1) may be used during the demonstration of safety.

2-2-1 Safety
Carry out the tests for each route and method of administration to be recommended for vaccination and where applicable, in animals of each category for which the vaccine is intended, using in each case animals not older than the minimum age to be recommended for vaccination. Use a batch of vaccine containing not less than the maximum potency that may be expected in a batch of vaccine.

For each test, use not fewer than 8 animals that do not have antibodies against *C. chauvoei*. Administer to each animal 1 dose of the vaccine. If the schedule to be recommended requires a 2nd dose, administer another dose after an interval of at least 14 days. Observe the animals at least daily until 14 days after the last administration.

The vaccine complies with the test if no animal shows abnormal local or systemic reactions or dies from causes attributable to the vaccine.

3 BATCH TESTS
3-1 Identification
The vaccine protects susceptible animals against infection with *C. chauvoei*. The potency test may also serve for identification.

3-2 Bacteria and fungi
The vaccine, including where applicable the diluent supplied for reconstitution, complies with the test for sterility prescribed in the monograph *Vaccines for veterinary use (0062)*.

3-3 Potency
Use for the test not fewer than 10 healthy guinea-pigs, each weighing 350-450 g. Administer to each guinea-pig by the subcutaneous route a quantity of the vaccine not greater than the minimum dose stated on the label as the 1st dose. After 28 days, administer to the same animals a quantity of the vaccine not greater than the minimum dose stated on the label as the 2nd dose. 14 days after the 2nd vaccination, inoculate by the intramuscular route each of the vaccinated guinea-pigs and each of 5 control animals with a suitable quantity of a virulent culture, or of a spore suspension, of *C. chauvoei*, activated if necessary with an activating agent such as calcium chloride.

The vaccine complies with the test if not more than 10 per cent of the vaccinated guinea-pigs die from *C. chauvoei* infection within 5 days and all the control animals die from *C. chauvoei* infection within 48 h of challenge or within 72 h if a spore suspension was used for the challenge. If more than 10 per cent but not more than 20 per cent of the vaccinated animals die, repeat the test. The vaccine complies with the test if not more than 10 per cent of the 2nd group of vaccinated animals die within 5 days and all of the 2nd group of control animals die within 48 h of challenge or within 72 h if a spore suspension was used for the challenge. To avoid unnecessary suffering following virulent challenge, moribund animals are euthanised and are then considered to have died from *C. chauvoei* infection.

Ph Eur

Clostridium Novyi Type B Vaccine

Black Disease Vaccine

(Clostridium Novyi (Type B) Vaccine for Veterinary Use, Ph Eur monograph 0362)

Ph Eur

1 DEFINITION
Clostridium novyi (type B) vaccine for veterinary use is prepared from a liquid culture of a suitable strain of *Clostridium novyi* (type B).

The whole culture or its filtrate or a mixture of the two is inactivated to eliminate its toxicity while maintaining adequate immunogenic properties. This monograph applies to vaccines intended for active immunisation of animals and/or to protect passively their progeny against disease caused by *C. novyi* (type B).

2 PRODUCTION
2-1 PREPARATION OF THE VACCINE
C novyi (type B) used for production is grown in an appropriate liquid medium. Toxoids and/or inactivated cultures may be treated with a suitable adjuvant, after concentration if necessary.

2-2 CHOICE OF VACCINE COMPOSITION
The vaccine is shown to be satisfactory with respect to safety (*5.2.6*) and efficacy (*5.2.7*) for the animals for which it is intended. For the latter, it shall be demonstrated that for each target species the vaccine, when administered according to the schedule to be recommended, stimulates an immune response (for example, induction of antibodies) consistent with the claims made for the product.

The following test for safety (section 2-2-1) may be used during the demonstration of safety.

2-2-1 Safety
Carry out the tests for each route and method of administration to be recommended for vaccination and where applicable, in animals of each category for which the vaccine is intended, using in each case animals not older than the minimum age to be recommended for vaccination. Use a batch of vaccine containing not less than the maximum potency that may be expected in a batch of vaccine.

For each test, use not fewer than 8 animals that do not have antibodies against *C. novyi* (type B). Administer to each animal 1 dose of the vaccine. If the schedule to be recommended requires a 2nd dose, administer another dose after an interval of at least 14 days. Observe the animals at least daily until 14 days after the last administration.

The vaccine complies with the test if no animal shows abnormal local or systemic reactions or dies from causes attributable to the vaccine. If the test is carried out in pregnant animals, no adverse effects on gestation or the offspring are noted.

2-3 MANUFACTURER'S TESTS
2-3-1 Residual toxicity
A test for detoxification is carried out immediately after the detoxification process and, when there is risk of reversion, a 2nd test is carried out at as late a stage as possible during the

production process. The test for residual toxicity (section 3-3) may be omitted by the manufacturer.

2-3-2 Batch potency test

It is not necessary to carry out the potency test (section 3-4) for each batch of vaccine if it has been carried out using a batch of vaccine with a minimum potency.

Where the test is not carried out, an alternative validated method is used, the criteria for acceptance being set with reference to a batch of vaccine that has given satisfactory results in the test described under Potency and that has been shown to be satisfactory with respect to immunogenicity in the target species. The following test may be used after a satisfactory correlation with the test under Potency (section 3-4) has been established.

Vaccinate rabbits as described under Potency and prepare sera. Determine the level of antibodies against the alpha toxin of *C. novyi* in the individual sera by a suitable method such as an immunochemical method (*2.7.1*) or neutralisation in cell cultures. Use a homologous reference serum calibrated in International Units of *C. novyi* alpha antitoxin. *Clostridia (multicomponent) rabbit antiserum BRP* is suitable for use as a reference serum.

The vaccine complies with the test if the level of antibodies is not less than that found for a batch of vaccine that has given satisfactory results in the test described under Potency and that has been shown to be satisfactory with respect to immunogenicity in the target species.

3 BATCH TESTS

3-1 Identification

When injected into animals that do not have novyi alpha antitoxin, the vaccine stimulates the formation of such antitoxins.

3-2 Bacteria and fungi

The vaccine, including where applicable the diluent supplied for reconstitution, complies with the test for sterility prescribed in the monograph *Vaccines for veterinary use (0062)*.

3-3 Residual toxicity

Administer 0.5 mL of the vaccine by the subcutaneous route into each of 5 mice, each weighing 17-22 g. Observe the animals at least daily for 7 days.

The vaccine complies with the test if no animal shows notable signs of disease or dies from causes attributable to the vaccine.

3-4 Potency

Use for the test not fewer than 10 healthy rabbits, 3-6 months old. Administer to each rabbit by the subcutaneous route a quantity of vaccine not greater than the minimum dose stated on the label as the 1st dose. After 21-28 days, administer to the same animals a quantity of the vaccine not greater than the minimum dose stated on the label as the 2nd dose. 10-14 days after the 2nd injection, bleed the rabbits and pool the sera.

The vaccine complies with the test if the potency of the pooled sera is not less than 3.5 IU/mL.

The International Unit is the specific neutralising activity for *C. novyi* alpha toxin contained in a stated amount of the International Standard, which consists of a quantity of dried immune horse serum. The equivalence in International Units of the International Standard is stated by the World Health Organization.

The potency of the pooled sera obtained from the rabbits is determined by comparing the quantity necessary to protect mice or other suitable animals against the toxic effects of a fixed dose of *C. novyi* alpha toxin with the quantity of a reference preparation of Clostridium novyi alpha antitoxin, calibrated in International Units, necessary to give the same protection. For this comparison, a suitable preparation of *C. novyi* alpha toxin for use as a test toxin is required. The dose of the test toxin is determined in relation to the reference preparation; the potency of the serum to be examined is determined in relation to the reference preparation using the test toxin.

Clostridia (multicomponent) rabbit antiserum BRP is suitable for use as a reference serum.

3-4-1 Preparation of test toxin. Prepare the test toxin from a sterile filtrate of an approximately 5-day culture in liquid medium of *C. novyi* type B and dry by a suitable method. Select the test toxin by determining for mice the L+/10 dose and the LD_{50}, the observation period being 72 h.

A suitable alpha toxin contains not less than 1 L+/10 dose in 0.05 mg and not less than 10 LD_{50} in each L+/10 dose.

3-4-2 Determination of test dose of toxin. Prepare a solution of the reference preparation in a suitable liquid so that it contains 1 IU/mL. Prepare a solution of the test toxin in a suitable liquid so that 1 mL contains a precisely known amount such as 1 mg. Prepare mixtures of the solution of the reference preparation and the solution of the test toxin such that each mixture contains 1.0 mL of the solution of the reference preparation (1 IU), one of a series of graded volumes of the solution of the test toxin and sufficient of a suitable liquid to bring the total volume to 2.0 mL. Allow the mixtures to stand at room temperature for 60 min. Using not fewer than 2 mice, each weighing 17-22 g, for each mixture, inject a dose of 0.2 mL by the intramuscular or the subcutaneous route into each mouse. Observe the mice for 72 h. If all the mice die, the amount of toxin present in 0.2 mL of the mixture is in excess of the test dose. If none of the mice die, the amount of toxin present in 0.2 mL of the mixture is less than the test dose. Prepare fresh mixtures such that 2.0 mL of each mixture contains 1.0 mL of the solution of the reference preparation (1 IU) and one of a series of graded volumes of the solution of the test toxin separated from each other by steps of not more than 20 per cent and covering the expected end-point. Allow the mixtures to stand at room temperature for 60 min. Using not fewer than 2 mice for each mixture, inject a dose of 0.2 mL by the intramuscular or the subcutaneous route into each mouse. Observe the mice for 72 h. Repeat the determination at least once and combine the results of the separate tests that have been made with mixtures of the same composition so that a series of totals is obtained, each total representing the mortality due to a mixture of a given composition.

The test dose of toxin is the amount present in 0.2 mL of that mixture which causes the death of one half of the total number of mice injected with it.

3-4-3 Determination of the potency of the serum obtained from rabbits

Preliminary test Dissolve a quantity of the test toxin in a suitable liquid so that 1.0 mL contains 10 times the test dose (solution of the test toxin). Prepare a series of mixtures of the solution of the test toxin and of the serum to be examined such that each mixture contains 1.0 mL of the solution of the test toxin, one of a series of graded volumes of the serum to be examined and sufficient of a suitable liquid to bring the final volume to 2.0 mL. Allow the mixtures to stand at room temperature for 60 min. Using not fewer than 2 mice for each mixture, inject a dose of 0.2 mL by the intramuscular or the subcutaneous route into each mouse. Observe the mice for 72 h. If none of the mice die, 0.2 mL of the mixture contains more than 0.1 IU. If all the mice die, 0.2 mL of the mixture contains less than 0.1 IU.

Final test Prepare a series of mixtures of the solution of the test toxin and the serum to be examined such that 2.0 mL of each mixture contains 1.0 mL of the solution of the test toxin and one of a series of graded volumes of the serum to be examined, separated from each other by steps of not more than 20 per cent and covering the expected end-point as determined by the preliminary test. Prepare further mixtures of the solution of the test toxin and of the solution of the reference preparation such that 2.0 mL of each mixture contains 1.0 mL of the solution of the test toxin and one of a series of graded volumes of the solution of the reference preparation, in order to confirm the test dose of the toxin. Allow the mixtures to stand at room temperature for 60 min. Using not fewer than 2 mice for each mixture, proceed as described in the preliminary test.

The test mixture that contains 0.1 IU in 0.2 mL is that mixture which kills the same or almost the same number of mice as the reference mixture containing 0.1 IU in 0.2 mL. Repeat the determination at least once and calculate the average of all valid estimates. The test is valid only if the reference preparation gives a result within 20 per cent of the expected value.

The confidence limits ($P = 0.95$) have been estimated to be:
— 85 per cent and 114 per cent when 2 animals per dose are used;
— 91.5 per cent and 109 per cent when 4 animals per dose are used;
— 93 per cent and 108 per cent when 6 animals per dose are used.

4 LABELLING
The label states:
— whether the product is a toxoid, a vaccine prepared from a whole inactivated culture or a mixture of the two;
— for each target species, the immunising effect produced (for example, antibody production, protection against signs of disease or infection).

_____ *Ph Eur*

Clostridium Perfringens Vaccines

(Clostridium Perfringens Vaccine for Veterinary Use, Ph Eur monograph 0363)

The following titles may be used for appropriate vaccines:

Clostridium Perfringens Type B Vaccine; Lamb Dysentery Vaccine;

Clostridium Perfringens Type C Vaccine; Struck Vaccine;

Clostridium Perfringens Type D Vaccine; Pulpy Kidney Vaccine

Ph Eur _____

1 DEFINITION
Clostridium perfringens vaccine for veterinary use is prepared from liquid cultures of suitable strains of *Clostridium perfringens* type B, *C. perfringens* type C or *C. perfringens* type D or a mixture of these types.

The whole cultures or their filtrates or a mixture of the two are inactivated to eliminate their toxicity while maintaining adequate immunogenic properties. This monograph applies to vaccines intended for active immunisation of animals and/or to protect passively their progeny against disease caused by *C. perfringens*.

2 PRODUCTION
2-1 PREPARATION OF THE VACCINE
C perfringens Used for production is grown in an appropriate liquid medium. Toxoids and/or inactivated cultures may be treated with a suitable adjuvant.

2-2 CHOICE OF VACCINE COMPOSITION
The vaccine is shown to be satisfactory with respect to safety (*5.2.6*) and efficacy (*5.2.7*) for the animals for which it is intended. For the latter, it shall be demonstrated that for each target species the vaccine, when administered according to the schedule to be recommended, stimulates an immune response (for example, induction of antibodies) consistent with the claims made for the product.

The following test for safety (section 2-2-1) may be used during the demonstration of safety.

2-2-1 Safety
Carry out the tests for each route and method of administration to be recommended for vaccination and where applicable, in animals of each category for which the vaccine is intended, using in each case animals not older than the minimum age to be recommended for vaccination. Use a batch of vaccine containing not less than the maximum potency that may be expected in a batch of vaccine.

For each test, use not fewer than 8 animals that do not have antibodies against *C. perfringens*. Administer to each animal 1 dose of the vaccine. If the schedule to be recommended requires a 2nd dose, administer another dose after an interval of at least 14 days. Observe the animals at least daily until 14 days after the last administration.

The vaccine complies with the test if no animal shows abnormal local or systemic reactions or dies from causes attributable to the vaccine. If the test is carried out in pregnant animals, no adverse effects on gestation or the offspring are noted.

2-3 MANUFACTURER'S TESTS
2-3-1 Residual toxicity
A test for detoxification is carried out immediately after the detoxification process and, when there is risk of reversion, a 2nd test is carried out at as late a stage as possible during the production process. The test for residual toxicity (section 3-3) may be omitted by the manufacturer.

2-3-2 Batch potency test
It is not necessary to carry out the potency test (section 3-4) for each batch of vaccine if it has been carried out using a batch of vaccine with a minimum potency. Where the test is not carried out, an alternative validated method is used, the criteria for acceptance being set with reference to a batch of vaccine that has given satisfactory results in the test described under Potency and that has been shown to be satisfactory with respect to immunogenicity in the target species.

The following test may be used after a satisfactory correlation with the test under Potency (section 3-4) has been established.

Vaccinate rabbits as described under Potency and prepare sera. Determine the level of antibodies against the beta and/or epsilon toxins of *C. perfringens* in the individual sera by a suitable method such as an immunochemical method (*2.7.1*) or neutralisation in cell cultures. Use a homologous reference serum calibrated in International Units of *C. perfringens* beta and/or epsilon antitoxin. *Clostridia (multicomponent) rabbit antiserum BRP* is suitable for use as a reference serum.

The vaccine complies with the test if the level or levels of antibodies are not less than that found for a batch of vaccine that has given satisfactory results in the test described under Potency and that has been shown to be satisfactory with respect to immunogenicity in the target species.

3 BATCH TESTS

3-1 Identification

Type B When injected into animals that do not have beta and epsilon antitoxins, the vaccine stimulates the formation of such antitoxins.

Type C When injected into animals that do not have beta antitoxin, the vaccine stimulates the formation of such antitoxin.

Type D When injected into animals that do not have epsilon antitoxin, the vaccine stimulates the formation of such antitoxin.

3-2 Bacteria and fungi

The vaccine, including where applicable the diluent supplied for reconstitution, complies with the test for sterility prescribed in the monograph *Vaccines for veterinary use (0062)*.

3-3 Residual toxicity

Administer 0.5 mL of the vaccine by the subcutaneous route to each of 5 mice, each weighing 17-22 g. Observe the mice at least daily for 7 days.

The vaccine complies with the test if no animal shows notable signs of disease or dies from causes attributable to the vaccine.

3-4 Potency

Use for the test not fewer than 10 healthy rabbits, 3-6 months old. Administer to each rabbit by the subcutaneous route a quantity of vaccine not greater than the minimum dose stated on the label as the 1st dose. After 21-28 days, administer to the same animals a quantity of the vaccine not greater than the minimum dose stated on the label as the 2nd dose. 10-14 days after the 2nd injection, bleed the rabbits and pool the sera.

Type B The vaccine complies with the test if the potency of the pooled sera is not less than 10 IU of beta antitoxin and not less than 5 IU of epsilon antitoxin per millilitre.

Type C The vaccine complies with the test if the potency of the pooled sera is not less than 10 IU of beta antitoxin per millilitre.

Type D The vaccine complies with the test if the potency of the pooled sera is not less than 5 IU of epsilon antitoxin per millilitre.

3-4-1 International standard for Clostridium perfringens beta antitoxin

The International Unit is the specific neutralising activity for *C. perfringens* beta toxin contained in a stated amount of the International Standard, which consists of a quantity of dried immune horse serum. The equivalence in International Units of the International Standard is stated by the World Health Organization.

3-4-2 International standard for Clostridium perfringens epsilon antitoxin

The International Unit is the specific neutralising activity for *C. perfringens* epsilon toxin contained in a stated amount of the International Standard, which consists of a quantity of dried immune horse serum. The equivalence in International

Units of the International Standard, is stated by the World Health Organization.

The potency of the pooled sera obtained from the rabbits is determined by comparing the quantity necessary to protect mice or other suitable animals against the toxic effects of a fixed dose of *C. perfringens* beta toxin or *C. perfringens* epsilon toxin with the quantity of a reference preparation of Clostridium perfringens beta antitoxin or Clostridium perfringens epsilon antitoxin, as appropriate, calibrated in International Units, necessary to give the same protection. For this comparison, a suitable preparation of *C. perfringens* beta or epsilon toxin for use as a test toxin is required. The dose of the test toxin is determined in relation to the appropriate reference preparation; the potency of the serum to be examined is determined in relation to the appropriate reference preparation using the appropriate test toxin.

Clostridia (multicomponent) rabbit antiserum BRP is suitable for use as a reference serum.

3-4-3 Preparation of test toxin. Prepare the test toxin from a sterile filtrate of an early culture in liquid medium of *C. perfringens* type B, type C or type D as appropriate and dry by a suitable method. Use a beta or epsilon toxin as appropriate. Select the test toxin by determining for mice the L+ and the LD$_{50}$ for the beta toxin and the L+/10 dose and the LD$_{50}$ for the epsilon toxin, the observation period being 72 h.

A suitable beta toxin contains not less than 1 L+ in 0.2 mg and not less than 25 LD$_{50}$ in 1 L+ dose. A suitable epsilon toxin contains not less than 1 L+/10 dose in 0.005 mg and not less than 20 LD$_{50}$ in 1 L+/10 dose.

3-4-4 Determination of test dose of toxin. Prepare a solution of the reference preparation in a suitable liquid so that it contains 5 IU/mL for Clostridium perfringens beta antitoxin and 0.5 IU/mL for Clostridium perfringens epsilon antitoxin. Prepare a solution of the test toxin in a suitable liquid so that 1 mL contains a precisely known amount such as 10 mg for beta toxin and 1 mg for epsilon toxin. Prepare mixtures of the solution of the reference preparation and the solution of the test toxin such that each contains 2.0 mL of the solution of the reference preparation, one of a series of graded volumes of the solution of the test toxin and sufficient of a suitable liquid to bring the total volume to 5.0 mL. Allow the mixtures to stand at room temperature for 30 min. Using not fewer than 2 mice, each weighing 17-22 g, for each mixture, inject a dose of 0.5 mL by the intravenous or the intraperitoneal route into each mouse. Observe the mice for 72 h. If all the mice die, the amount of toxin present in 0.5 mL of the mixture is in excess of the test dose. If none of the mice die the amount of toxin present in 0.5 mL of the mixture is less than the test dose. Prepare fresh mixtures such that 5.0 mL of each mixture contains 2.0 mL of the solution of the reference preparation and one of a series of graded volumes of the solution of the test toxin separated from each other by steps of not more than 20 per cent and covering the expected end-point. Allow the mixtures to stand at room temperature for 30 min. Using not fewer than 2 mice for each mixture, inject a dose of 0.5 mL by the intravenous or the intraperitoneal route into each mouse. Observe the mice for 72 h. Repeat the determination at least once and add together the results of the separate tests that have been made with mixtures of the same composition so that a series of totals is obtained, each total representing the mortality due to a mixture of given composition.

The test dose of toxin is the amount present in 0.5 mL of that mixture which causes the death of one half of the total number of mice injected with it.

3-4-5 Determination of the potency of the serum obtained from rabbits

Preliminary test Dissolve a quantity of the test toxin in a suitable liquid so that 2.0 mL contains 10 times the test dose (solution of the test toxin). Prepare a series of mixtures of the solution of the test toxin and of the serum to be examined such that each contains 2.0 mL of the solution of the test toxin, one of a series of graded volumes of the serum to be examined and sufficient of a suitable liquid to bring the final volume to 5.0 mL. Allow the mixtures to stand at room temperature for 30 min. Using not fewer than 2 mice for each mixture, inject a dose of 0.5 mL by the intravenous or the intraperitoneal route into each mouse. Observe the mice for 72 h. If none of the mice die, 0.5 mL of the mixture contains more than 1 IU of beta antitoxin or 0.1 IU of epsilon antitoxin. If all the mice die, 0.5 mL of the mixture contains less than 1 IU of beta antitoxin or 0.1 IU of epsilon antitoxin.

Final test Prepare a series of mixtures of the solution of the test toxin and the serum to be examined such that 5.0 mL of each mixture contains 2.0 mL of the solution of the test toxin and one of a series of graded volumes of the serum to be examined separated from each other by steps of not more than 20 per cent and covering the expected end-point as determined by the preliminary test. Prepare further mixtures of the solution of the test toxin and of the solution of the reference preparation such that 5.0 mL of each mixture contains 2.0 mL of the solution of the test toxin and one of a series of graded volumes of the solution of the reference preparation, in order to confirm the test dose of the toxin. Allow the mixtures to stand at room temperature for 30 min. Using not fewer than 2 mice for each mixture proceed as described in the preliminary test.

Beta antitoxin The test mixture that contains 1 IU in 0.5 mL is that mixture which kills the same or almost the same number of mice as the reference mixture containing 1 IU in 0.5 mL.

Epsilon antitoxin The test mixture that contains 0.1 IU in 0.5 mL is that mixture which kills the same or almost the same number of mice as the reference mixture containing 0.1 IU in 0.5 mL. Repeat the determination at least once and calculate the average of all valid estimates. The test is valid only if the reference preparation gives a result within 20 per cent of the expected value.

The confidence limits ($P = 0.95$) have been estimated to be:
— 85 per cent and 114 per cent when 2 animals per dose are used;
— 91.5 per cent and 109 per cent when 4 animals per dose are used;
— 93 per cent and 108 per cent when 6 animals per dose are used.

4 LABELLING

The label states:
— whether the preparation is a toxoid or a vaccine prepared from a whole inactivated culture or a mixture of the two;
— for each target species, the immunising effect produced (for example, antibody production, protection against signs of disease or infection).

———————————— Ph Eur

Clostridium Septicum Vaccine

Braxy Vaccine

(Clostridium Septicum Vaccine for Veterinary Use, Ph Eur monograph 0364)

Ph Eur ————————————————————————

1 DEFINITION

Clostridium septicum vaccine for veterinary use is prepared from a liquid culture of a suitable strain of *Clostridium septicum*.

The whole culture or its filtrate or a mixture of the two is inactivated to eliminate its toxicity while maintaining adequate immunogenic properties. This monograph applies to vaccines intended for active immunisation of animals and/or to protect passively their progeny against disease caused by *C. septicum*.

2 PRODUCTION
2-1 PREPARATION OF THE VACCINE

C septicum used for production is grown in an appropriate liquid medium. Toxoid and/or inactivated cultures may be treated with a suitable adjuvant.

2-2 CHOICE OF VACCINE COMPOSITION

The vaccine is shown to be satisfactory with respect to safety *(5.2.6)* and efficacy *(5.2.7)* for the animals for which it is intended. For the latter, it shall be demonstrated that for each target species the vaccine, when administered according to the schedule to be recommended, stimulates an immune response (for example, induction of antibodies) consistent with the claims made for the product.

The following test for safety (section 2-2-1) may be used during the demonstration of safety.

2-2-1 Safety

Carry out the tests for each route and method of administration to be recommended for vaccination and where applicable, in animals of each category for which the vaccine is intended, using in each case animals not older than the minimum age to be recommended for vaccination. Use a batch of vaccine containing not less than the maximum potency that may be expected in a batch of vaccine.

For each test, use not fewer than 8 animals that do not have antibodies against *C. septicum*. Administer to each animal 1 dose of the vaccine. If the schedule to be recommended requires a 2nd dose, administer another dose after an interval of at least 14 days. Observe the animals at least daily until 14 days after the last administration.

The vaccine complies with the test if no animal shows abnormal local or systemic reactions or dies from causes attributable to the vaccine. If the test is carried out in pregnant animals, no adverse effects on gestation or the offspring are noted.

2-3 MANUFACTURER'S TESTS
2-3-1 Residual toxicity

A test for detoxification is carried out immediately after the detoxification process and, when there is risk of reversion, a 2nd test is carried out at as late a stage as possible during the production process. The test for residual toxicity (section 3-3) may be omitted by the manufacturer.

2-3-2 Batch potency test

It is not necessary to carry out the potency test (section 3-4) for each batch of vaccine if it has been carried out using a batch of vaccine with a minimum potency. Where the test is not carried out, an alternative validated method is used, the criteria for acceptance being set with reference to a batch of vaccine that has given satisfactory results in the test described under Potency and that has been shown to be satisfactory with respect to immunogenicity in the target species.

The following test may be used after a satisfactory correlation with the test under Potency (section 3-4) has been established.

Vaccinate rabbits as described under Potency and prepare sera. Determine the level of antibodies against the toxin of *C. septicum* in the individual sera by a suitable method such as an immunochemical method (*2.7.1*) or neutralisation in cell cultures. Use a homologous reference serum calibrated in International Units of *C. septicum* antitoxin. *Clostridia (multicomponent) rabbit antiserum BRP* is suitable for use as a reference serum. The vaccine complies with the test if the level of antibodies is not less than that found for a batch of vaccine that has given satisfactory results in the test described under Potency and that has been shown to be satisfactory with respect to immunogenicity in the target species.

3 BATCH TESTS

3-1 Identification
When injected into animals that do not have *C. septicum* antitoxin, the vaccine stimulates the formation of such antitoxin.

3-2 Bacteria and fungi
The vaccine, including where applicable the diluent supplied for reconstitution, complies with the test for sterility prescribed in the monograph *Vaccines for veterinary use (0062)*.

3-3 Residual toxicity
Inject 0.5 mL of the vaccine by the subcutaneous route into each of 5 mice, each weighing 17-22 g. Observe the mice at least daily for 7 days.

The vaccine complies with the test if no animal shows notable signs of disease or dies from causes attributable to the vaccine.

3-4 Potency
Use for the test not fewer than 10 healthy rabbits, 3-6 months old. Administer to each rabbit by the subcutaneous route a quantity of vaccine not greater than the minimum dose stated on the label as the 1st dose. After 21-28 days, administer to the same animals a quantity of the vaccine not greater than the minimum dose stated on the label as the 2nd dose. 10-14 days after the 2nd injection, bleed the rabbits and pool the sera.

The vaccine complies with the test if the potency of the pooled sera is not less than 2.5 IU/mL.

The International Unit is the specific neutralising activity for *C. septicum* toxin contained in a stated amount of the International Standard, which consists of a quantity of dried immune horse serum. The equivalence in International Units of the International Standard is stated by the World Health Organization.

The potency of the pooled sera obtained from the rabbits is determined by comparing the quantity necessary to protect mice or other suitable animals against the toxic effects of a dose of *C. septicum* toxin with the quantity of a reference preparation of Clostridium septicum antitoxin, calibrated in International Units, necessary to give the same protection. For this comparison, a suitable preparation of *C. septicum* toxin for use as a test toxin is required. The dose of the test toxin is determined in relation to the reference preparation; the potency of the serum to be examined is determined in relation to the reference preparation using the test toxin.

Clostridia (multicomponent) rabbit antiserum BRP is suitable for use as a reference serum.

3-4-1 Preparation of test toxin. Prepare the test toxin from a sterile filtrate of a 1- to 3-day culture of *C. septicum* in liquid medium and dry by a suitable method. Select the test toxin by determining for mice the L+/5 dose and the LD_{50}, the observation period being 72 h.

A suitable toxin contains not less than 1 L+/5 dose in 1.0 mg and not less than 10 LD_{50} in each L+/5 dose.

3-4-2 Determination of test dose of toxin. Prepare a solution of the reference preparation in a suitable liquid so that it contains 1.0 IU/mL. Prepare a solution of the test toxin in a suitable liquid so that 1 mL contains a precisely known amount, such as 4 mg. Prepare mixtures of the solution of the reference preparation and the solution of the test toxin such that each mixture contains 2.0 mL of the solution of the reference preparation (2 IU), one of a series of graded volumes of the solution of the test toxin and sufficient of a suitable liquid to bring the total volume to 5.0 mL. Allow the mixtures to stand at room temperature for 60 min. Using not fewer than 2 mice, each weighing 17-22 g, for each mixture, inject a dose of 0.5 mL by the intravenous or the intraperitoneal route into each mouse. Observe the mice for 72 h. If all the mice die, the amount of toxin present in 0.5 mL of the mixture is in excess of the test dose. If none of the mice die, the amount of toxin present in 0.5 mL of the mixture is less than the test dose. Prepare fresh mixtures such that 5.0 mL of each mixture contains 2.0 mL of the reference preparation (2 IU) and one of a series of graded volumes of the solution of the test toxin separated from each other by steps of not more than 20 per cent and covering the expected end-point. Allow the mixtures to stand at room temperature for 60 min. Using not fewer than 2 mice for each mixture, inject a dose of 0.5 mL by the intravenous or the intraperitoneal route into each mouse. Observe the mice for 72 h. Repeat the determination at least once and add together the results of the separate tests that have been made with mixtures of the same composition so that a series of totals is obtained, each total representing the mortality due to a mixture of a given composition.

The test dose of toxin is the amount present in 0.5 mL of that mixture which causes the death of one half of the total number of mice injected with it.

3-4-3 Determination of the potency of the serum obtained from rabbits

Preliminary test Dissolve a quantity of the test toxin in a suitable liquid so that 2.0 mL contains 10 times the test dose (solution of the test toxin). Prepare a series of mixtures of the solution of the test toxin and of the serum to be examined such that each contains 2.0 mL of the solution of the test toxin, one of a series of graded volumes of the serum to be examined and sufficient of a suitable liquid to bring the final volume to 5.0 mL. Allow the mixtures to stand at room temperature for 60 min. Using not fewer than 2 mice for each mixture, inject a dose of 0.5 mL by the intravenous or the intraperitoneal route into each mouse. Observe the mice for 72 h. If none of the mice die, 0.5 mL of the mixture contains more than 0.2 IU. If all the mice die, 0.5 mL of the mixture contains less than 0.2 IU.

Final test Prepare a series of mixtures of the solution of the test toxin and of the serum to be examined such that 5.0 mL of each mixture contains 2.0 mL of the solution of the test toxin and one of a series of graded volumes of the serum to be examined, separated from each other by steps of not more than 20 per cent and covering the expected end-point as determined by the preliminary test. Prepare further mixtures of the solution of the test toxin and of the solution of the reference preparation such that 5.0 mL of each mixture contains 2.0 mL of the solution of the test toxin and one of a series of graded volumes of the solution of the reference preparation to confirm the test dose of the toxin. Allow the mixtures to stand at room temperature for 60 min. Using not fewer than 2 mice for each mixture proceed as described in the preliminary test. The test mixture which contains 0.2 IU in 0.5 mL is that mixture which kills the same or almost the same number of mice as the reference mixture containing 0.2 IU in 0.5 mL. Repeat the determination at least once and calculate the average of all valid estimates. The test is valid only if the reference preparation gives a result within 20 per cent of the expected value.

The confidence limits ($P = 0.95$) have been estimated to be:
— 85 per cent and 114 per cent when 2 animals per dose are used;
— 91.5 per cent and 109 per cent when 4 animals per dose are used;
— 93 per cent and 108 per cent when 6 animals per dose are used.

4 LABELLING

The label states:
— whether the preparation is a toxoid or a vaccine prepared from a whole inactivated culture, or a mixture of the two;
— for each target species, the immunising effect produced (for example, antibody production, protection against signs of disease or infection).

Ph Eur

Clostridium Tetani Vaccines

Tetanus Toxoids (Veterinary)

(Tetanus Vaccine for Veterinary Use, Ph Eur monograph 0697)

The name Clostridium Tetani Vaccine for Equidae (Tetanus Toxoid for Equidae) may be used for vaccines with an appropriate potency.

When Tetanus Toxoid is demanded for veterinary use, Clostridium Tetani Vaccine shall be supplied.

Ph Eur

1 DEFINITION

Tetanus vaccine for veterinary use is a preparation of the neurotoxin of *Clostridium tetani* inactivated to eliminate its toxicity while maintaining adequate immunogenic properties. The vaccine may be used to induce active and/or passive immunity.

2 PRODUCTION
2-1 PREPARATION OF THE VACCINE

C. tetani used for production is grown in an appropriate liquid medium. The toxin is purified and then detoxified or it may be detoxified before purification. The antigenic purity is determined in Lf units of tetanus toxoid per milligram of protein and shown to be not less than the value approved for the particular product.

2-2 CHOICE OF VACCINE COMPOSITION

The vaccine is shown to be satisfactory with respect to safety (*5.2.6*) and efficacy (*5.2.7*) for the animals for which it is intended. The following tests for production of antigens (section 2-2-1), safety (section 2-2-2) and immunogenicity (section 2-2-3) may be used during demonstration of safety and efficacy.

The *C. tetani* strain used in the preparation of the vaccine is shown to be satisfactory with respect to the production of the neurotoxin.

2-2-1 Production of antigens
The production of the neurotoxin of *C. tetani* is verified by a suitable immunochemical method (*2.7.1*) carried out on the neurotoxin obtained from the vaccine strain under the conditions used for the production of the vaccine.

2-2-2 Safety
Carry out the test for each route and method of administration to be recommended for vaccination and where applicable, in animals of each category for which the vaccine is intended, using in each case animals not older than the minimum age to be recommended for vaccination and of the most sensitive category for the species. Use a batch of vaccine containing not less than the maximum potency that may be expected in a batch of vaccine.

For each test use not fewer than 8 animals, free from antitoxic antibodies. Administer to each animal 1 dose of vaccine. If the schedule to be recommended requires a 2nd dose, administer another dose after an interval of at least 14 days. Observe the animals at least daily until at least 14 days after the last administration.

The vaccine complies with the test if no animal shows abnormal local or systemic reactions or dies from causes attributable to the vaccine. If the test is carried out in pregnant animals, no adverse effects on gestation or the offspring are noted.

2-2-3 Immunogenicity
2-2-3-1 Immunogenicity test in the target species

It shall be demonstrated for each target species that the vaccine, when administered according to the schedule to be recommended and by the route to be recommended, stimulates an immune response (for example, induction of antitoxic antibodies or induction of protective levels of antitoxic antibodies) consistent with the claims made for the product.

2-2-3-2 Immunogenicity test in guinea-pigs

Administer 1 dose of vaccine by the subcutaneous route to each of at least 5 guinea-pigs that do not have antibodies against the neurotoxin of *C. tetani*. After 28 days, administer again to each guinea-pig 1 dose by the subcutaneous route. 14 days after the 2nd dose, collect blood from each guinea-pig and prepare serum samples. Determine for each serum the titre of antibodies against the neurotoxin of *C. tetani* using a suitable immunochemical method (*2.7.1*) such as a toxin-binding-inhibition test (ToBI test) and a homologous reference serum. Determine the average antibody titre of the serum samples.

Clostridium tetani guinea-pig antiserum for vaccines for veterinary use BRP is suitable for use as a reference serum.

Tetanus vaccine intended for use in animals other than horses complies with the test if the average antibody titre is not less than 7.5 IU/mL.

Tetanus vaccine intended for use in horses complies with the test if the average antibody titre is not less than 30 IU/mL.

For tetanus vaccine presented as a combined vaccine for use in animals other than horses, the above test may be carried out in susceptible rabbits instead of guinea-pigs. The vaccine complies with the test if the average antibody titre of the sera of the vaccinated rabbits is not less than 2.5 IU/mL.

Clostridia (multicomponent) rabbit antiserum BRP and *Clostridium tetani rabbit antiserum BRP* are suitable for use as reference sera.

2-3 MANUFACTURER'S TESTS
2-3-1 Absence of toxin and irreversibility of toxoid
Carry out a test for reversion to toxicity on the detoxified harvest using 2 groups of 5 guinea-pigs, each weighing 350-450 g; if the vaccine is adsorbed, carry out the test with the shortest practical time interval before adsorption. Prepare a dilution of the detoxified harvest so that the guinea-pigs each receive 10 times the amount of toxoid (measured in Lf units) that will be present in a dose of vaccine. Divide the dilution into 2 equal parts. Keep 1 part at 5 ± 3 °C and the other at 37 °C for 6 weeks. Attribute each dilution to a separate group of guinea-pigs and inject into each guinea-pig the dilution attributed to its group. Observe the animals at least daily for 21 days. The toxoid complies with the test if no guinea-pig shows signs of disease or dies from causes attributable to the neurotoxin of *C. tetani*.

2-3-2 Batch potency test
It is not necessary to carry out the potency test (section 3-4) for each batch of vaccine if it has been carried out using a batch of vaccine with a minimum potency. Where the test is not carried out, an alternative validated method is used, the criteria for acceptance being set with reference to a batch of vaccine that has given satisfactory results in the test described under Potency.

Where the test described under Potency is used as the batch potency test, the vaccine complies with the test if the antibody titre in International Units is not less than that found for a batch of vaccine shown to be satisfactory with respect to immunogenicity in the target species.

3 BATCH TESTS
3-1 Identification
If the nature of the adjuvant allows it, carry out test A. Otherwise carry out test B.

A. Dissolve in the vaccine sufficient *sodium citrate R* to give a 100 g/L solution. Maintain the solution at 37 °C for about 16 h and centrifuge until a clear supernatant is obtained. The supernatant reacts with a suitable tetanus antitoxin, giving a precipitate.

B. When injected into animals that do not have antibodies against the neurotoxin of *C. tetani*, the vaccine stimulates the production of such antibodies.

3-2 Bacteria and fungi
The vaccine, including where applicable the diluent supplied for reconstitution, complies with the test for sterility prescribed in the monograph *Vaccines for veterinary use (0062)*.

3-3 Residual toxicity
Administer 5 mL of the vaccine by the subcutaneous route, as 2 equal divided doses at separate sites, into each of 5 healthy guinea-pigs, each weighing 350-450 g, that have not previously been treated with any material that will interfere with the test. The vaccine complies with the test if no animal shows notable signs of disease or dies from causes attributable to the vaccine. If within 21 days of the injection any of the animals shows signs of or dies from tetanus, the vaccine does not comply with the test. If more than 1 animal dies from non-specific causes, repeat the test. If any animal dies in the 2nd test, the vaccine does not comply with the test.

3-4 Potency
The vaccine complies with the requirements of the test mentioned under Immunogenicity (section 2-2-3-2).

Ph Eur

Coccidiosis Vaccine (Live) for Chickens

(Ph. Eur. monograph 2326)

Ph Eur

1 DEFINITION
Coccidiosis vaccine (live) for chickens is a preparation of sporulated oocysts of a suitable line or lines of species of coccidial parasites (*Eimeria* spp.). This monograph applies to vaccines intended for administration to chickens for active immunisation.

2 PRODUCTION
2-1 *PREPARATION OF THE VACCINE*
Oocysts are produced in chickens from a flock free from specified pathogens (SPF) (*5.2.2*) or in embryonated hens' eggs from an SPF flock (*5.2.2*). The eggs must be subject to disinfection and/or incubation conditions validated to ensure the inactivation of any *Eimeria* that may be on the shells. The hatched chickens must then be reared in disinfected premises, in isolation conditions that ensure no infection with *Eimeria*. The chickens must not have been treated with coccidiostats. Oocysts are collected from faeces or contents of the intestinal tract of infected chickens during the patent period. Oocysts of different *Eimeria* lines are produced separately. Oocysts are isolated, purified, disinfected, sporulated and counted. The vaccine is produced by blending defined numbers of sporulated oocysts of each line in a suitable medium.

2-2 *SEED LOTS*
2-2-1 Identification
The identity of each *Eimeria* master seed is established from the characteristics of the coccidia produced from it, based on an appropriate selection of the following characteristics: size and shape of the oocyst; localisation of the developmental stages in the chicken intestine; pathognomonic lesions (*E. tenella*, *E. acervulina*, *E. necatrix*, *E. maxima* and *E. brunetti*) and lack of macroscopic lesions (*E. praecox* and *E. mitis*); size of schizonts in the intestinal mucosa; size of gametocytes in the mucosa; differences in the electrophoretic mobilities of certain isoenzymes, e.g. lactate dehydrogenase and glucose phosphate isomerase; and by the use of molecular biology techniques. Artificially attenuated lines may be distinguished from the parent strains by studying parameters appropriate to the method of attenuation.

2-2-2 Extraneous agents
Carry out tests 1-6 of chapter *2.6.24. Avian viral vaccines: tests for extraneous agents in seed lots*. General provisions *a-d*, *f* and *h* and section 7 of chapter *2.6.24* are also applicable. In these tests on the master seed lot, use organisms that are not more than 5 passages from the master seed lot at the start of the tests. Each master seed lot complies with the requirements of each test.

2-3 *CHOICE OF VACCINE COMPOSITION*
Only coccidial lines shown to be satisfactory with respect to residual pathogenicity and increase in virulence may be used in the preparation of the vaccine, and the tests described below (sections 2-3-2 and 2-3-3) may be used to demonstrate this. The vaccine shall be shown to be satisfactory with respect to safety (*5.2.6*) and efficacy (*5.2.7*) for the chickens for which it is intended. The following tests under Specific test for the safety of the vaccine composition (section 2-3-1) and Immunogenicity (section 2-3-4) may be used during the demonstration of safety and efficacy.

2-3-1 Specific test for the safety of the vaccine composition

Carry out the test with a preparation containing oocysts of each species at the least attenuated passage level that will be present in a batch of vaccine. Use not fewer than 10 chickens from an SPF flock (5.2.2). The chickens must be hatched and reared as described in section 2-1 and must not have been treated with coccidiostats. Use chickens of the category that is expected to be the most sensitive, i.e. 14-day-old chickens. During the test, chickens are housed in suitable conditions with the use of floor pens or cages with solid floors to favour reinfection with oocysts. Administer by gavage or another suitable route to each chicken a quantity of vaccinal oocysts consisting of the equivalent of not less than 10 times the maximum quantity of oocysts of each coccidial species likely to be contained in 1 dose of the vaccine. Observe the chickens at least daily for at least 14 days.

The test is not valid if more than 10 per cent of the vaccinated chickens die from causes not attributable to the vaccinal oocysts.

The vaccine complies with the test if no vaccinated chicken shows abnormal signs of disease or dies from causes attributable to the vaccine.

2-3-2 Test for residual pathogenicity

Carry out a separate test with each coccidial species and line to be included in the vaccine. Use in each case a preparation containing oocysts at the least attenuated passage level that will be present between the master seed lot and a batch of the vaccine. For each test use not fewer than 20 chickens from an SPF flock (5.2.2). The chickens must be hatched and reared as described in section 2-1 and must not have been treated with coccidiostats. Use chickens of the category that is expected to be the most sensitive, i.e. 14-day-old chickens. During the test, the chickens are placed in cages (or any other suitable accomodation that prevents reinfection and allows collection of faeces). Administer by gavage or another suitable route to each chicken the equivalent of not less than 10 times the maximum quantity of the vaccinal oocysts likely to be contained in 1 dose of the vaccine. Observe the chickens at least daily for 14 days. The test is not valid if more than 10 per cent of the chickens die from causes not attributable to the vaccinal oocysts. Collect faeces and determine oocyst production daily from day 3 until day 14. On one day between days 4 and 8, depending on the length of the pre-patent period, when lesions are expected to be maximal, and on day 14, euthanise not fewer than 9 chickens and examine the intestinal tract for specific lesions indicative of infection with the coccidial species or, for species known not to induce macroscopic lesions (*E. mitis* and *E. praecox*), microscopic evidence of infection such as demonstration of oocysts or developing oocysts in the intestinal contents or scrapings of the intenstinal wall. For species that have the potential to produce relevant macroscopic pathological changes if not attenuated, a scoring system with a scale from 0 to 4 is used to record the species-specific lesions visible in the intestine as follows.

Eimeria acervulina

0   No gross lesions.

1   Scattered, white, plaque-like lesions containing developing oocysts are confined to the duodenum. These lesions are elongated with the longer axis transversely oriented on the intestinal walls like the rungs of a ladder. They may be seen on either the serosal or mucosal intestinal surfaces. There may be up to a maximum of 5 lesions per square centimetre.

2   Lesions are much closer together, but not coalescent; lesions may extend as far posterior as 20 cm below the duodenum in 3-week-old birds. The intestinal walls show no thickening. Digestive tract contents are normal.

3   Lesions are numerous enough to cause coalescence with reduction in lesion size and give the intestine a coated appearance. The intestinal wall is thickened and the contents are watery. Lesions may extend as far posterior as the yolk sac diverticulum.

4   The mucosal wall is greyish with completely coalescent colonies. Congestion may be confined to small petechiae or, in extremely heavy infections, the entire mucosa may be bright red in colour. Individual lesions may be indistinguishable in the upper intestine. Typical ladder-like lesions appear in the middle part of the intestine. The intestinal wall is very much thickened and the intestine is filled with a creamy exudate, which may bear large numbers of oocysts. Birds dying of coccidiosis are scored as 4.

Eimeria brunetti

0   No gross lesions.

1   No gross lesions. In the absence of distinct lesions, the presence of parasites may go undetected unless scrapings from suspicious areas are examined microscopically.

2   The intestinal wall may appear grey in colour. The lower portion may be thickened and flecks of pink material sloughed from the intestine are present.

3   The intestinal wall is thickened and a blood-tinged catarrhal exudate is present. Transverse red streaks may be present in the lower rectum and lesions occur in the caecal tonsils. Soft mucous plugs may be present in this latter area.

4   Extensive coagulation necrosis of the mucosal surface of the lower intestine may be present. In some birds a dry necrotic membrane may line the intestine and caseous cores may plug the entrance to the caeca. Lesions may extend into the middle or upper intestine. Birds dying of coccidiosis are scored as 4.

Eimeria maxima

0   No gross lesions.

1   Small red petechiae may appear on the serosal side of the mid-intestine. There is no ballooning or thickening of the intestine, though small amounts of orange mucous may be present.

2   The serosal surface may be speckled with numerous red petechiae. The intestine may be filled with orange mucous, but there is little or no ballooning of the intestine. There is thickening of the wall.

3   The intestinal wall is ballooned and thickened. The mucosal surface is roughened. Intestinal contents are composed of pinpoint blood clots and mucous.

4   The intestinal wall may be ballooned for most of its length. It contains numerous blood clots and digested red blood cells giving a characteristic colour and putrid odour. The wall is greatly thickened. Birds dying of coccidiosis are scored as 4.

Eimeria necatrix

0   No gross lesions.

1   Small scattered petechiae and white spots are easily seen on the serosal surface. There is little, if any, damage apparent on the mucosal surface.

2   Numerous petechiae are seen on the serosal surface. Slight ballooning confined to the midgut area may be present.

3 There is extensive haemorrhage into the lumen of the intestine. The serosal surface is covered with red petechiae and/or white plaques, and is rough and thickened with many pinpoint haemorrhages. Normal intestinal contents are lacking. Ballooning extends over the lower half of the small intestine.

4 Extensive haemorrhage gives the intestine a dark colour, and the intestinal contents consist of red or brown mucous. Ballooning may extend throughout much of the length of the intestine. Birds dying of coccidiosis are scored as 4.

Eimeria tenella

0 No gross lesions.

1 Very few scattered petechiae are seen on the caecal wall, and there is no thickening of the caecal walls. Normal caecal contents are present.

2 Lesions are more numerous with noticeable blood in the caecal contents, and the caecal wall is somewhat thickened. Normal caecal contents are present.

3 Large amounts of blood or caecal cores are present, and the caecal walls are greatly thickened. There is little if any normal faecal content in the caeca.

4 The caecal wall is greatly distended with blood or large caseous cores. Faecal debris is lacking or included in the cores. Birds dying of coccidiosis are scored as 4.

The species and line comply with the test for attenuation if no more than mild coccidial lesions or limited signs of infection are observed; where the scoring system described above is appropriate, the average lesion score on the day of sampling between days 4 and 8 and on day 14 is not greater than 1.5 points and no individual score is greater than 3 points. The quantity and time of oocyst production is determined.

2-3-3 Increase in virulence

Carry out a separate test according to general chapter *5.2.6* with each coccidial species and line to be included in the vaccine. Use a preparation containing oocysts at the master seed lot level. If the quantity of the master seed sufficient for performing the test is not available, the lowest passage seed used for the production that is available in sufficient quantity may be used. For each test use 14-day-old chickens from an SPF flock (*5.2.2*). If the properties of the vaccinal oocysts allow sequential passage through 5 groups via natural spreading, this method may be used, otherwise, passage as described below is carried out. The chickens must be hatched and reared as described in section 2-1 and must not have been treated with coccidiostats. During the test, the chickens are placed in cages (or any other suitable accomodation that prevents reinfection and allows collection of faeces). Administer by gavage or another suitable route to each chicken of the 1st group a quantity of oocysts that will allow recovery of the oocysts for the passages described below. Collect faeces daily from day 2 to day 14 after infection and prepare a pooled suspension of sporulated oocysts from the 5 chickens. Administer a suitable quantity by gavage or another suitable route to each chicken of the next group. Carry out this passage operation not fewer than 4 times, verifying the presence of oocysts at each passage. If the vaccinal oocysts are not found at a passage level, repeat the passage by administration to a group of 10 chickens. Carry out the test for residual pathogenicity (section 2-3-2), using the material used for the 1st passage and the oocysts that have been recovered in the final passage. Compare the results obtained for signs of lesions or infection in the intestinal tract and oocyst output from administration of passaged and unpassaged oocysts.

The line complies with the test if no indication of an increase in virulence of the maximally passaged oocysts compared with the unpassaged oocysts is observed.

The test is not valid if oocysts are not recovered at any passage level.

2-3-4 Immunogenicity

The efficacy of each coccidial species and line included in the vaccine is determined in a separate study with an appropriate challenge strain. For each component, a test is carried out with vaccine administered by each route and method of administration to be recommended, using in each case chickens not older than the minimum age to be recommended for vaccination. The quantity of each of the components in the batch of vaccine administered to each chicken is not greater than the minimum number of oocysts to be stated on the label and the oocysts are at the most attenuated passage level that will be present in a batch of vaccine. Use for the test not fewer than 40 chickens from an SPF flock (*5.2.2*). The chickens must be hatched and reared as described in section 2-1 and must not have been treated with coccidiostats. Vaccinate not fewer than 20 chickens and maintain not fewer than 20 chickens as controls. For the evaluation of weight gain with *Eimeria* strains showing a low pathogenicity, the number of chickens used may be higher. The test may require different challenge doses for different test parameters and so may be assessed as separate challenge groups. For example, a lower challenge dose may be needed to determine the effect on oocyst output than the dose needed to determine the effect on weight gain and lesion scoring. After vaccination, the chickens are housed in suitable conditions with the use of floor pens or cages with solid floors to favour reinfection with oocysts. On a suitable day between days 14 and 21 after vaccination, weigh each chicken, move them to cages (or any other suitable accomodation that prevents reinfection and allows collection of faeces) and challenge each chicken by gavage or another suitable route with a sufficient quantity of virulent coccidia to induce in the unvaccinated controls signs of disease characteristic of the *Eimeria* challenge species. Observe the chickens at least daily until the end of the test. Record deaths and the number of surviving chickens that show clinical signs of disease. Collect faeces and determine oocyst production from day 3 after challenge until the end of the test. On an appropriate day between days 4 and 8 after challenge, depending on the length of the pre-patent period of the challenge species, weigh each chicken. Euthanise 10 chickens from each group and examine them for lesions in the intestinal tract. Where appropriate, record the specific lesions indicative of the coccidial challenge species (using the scoring system described in section 2-3-2). For species known not to induce macroscopic lesions (*E. mitis* and *E. praecox*), examine the chickens for microscopic evidence of infection such as demonstration of oocysts or developing oocysts in the intestinal contents or scrapings of the intestinal wall. On day 14 after challenge, weigh each of the remaining chickens.

The test is not valid if:

— during the period between vaccination and challenge, more than 10 per cent of the vaccinated or control chickens show abnormal clinical signs or die from causes not attributable to the vaccine;

— for challenges with *E. tenella*, *E. acervulina*, *E. necatrix*, *E. maxima* or *E. brunetti*, fewer than 80 per cent of the control chickens euthanised between days 4 and 8 have marked characteristic lesions of the challenge infection in

the intestine at post-mortem examination (e.g. lesion scores not less than 2);
— for challenges with *E. mitis* or *E. praecox*, fewer than 80 per cent of the control chickens euthanised between days 4 and 8 are infected.

The vaccine complies with the test if:
— for all the *Eimeria* challenge species, the production of the oocysts is significantly decreased in vaccinates compared with controls;
— for all the *Eimeria* challenge species, no vaccinated chicken dies due to the challenge infection;
— for challenge with *E. tenella*, *E. acervulina*, *E. necatrix*, *E. maxima* or *E. brunetti*, at least 80 per cent of the vaccinates show no more than mild signs of disease and these are less marked than those in the controls;
— for challenges with *E. tenella*, *E. acervulina*, *E. necatrix*, *E. maxima* or *E. brunetti*, at least 80 per cent of the vaccinates have no or minimal lesions in the intestine (e.g. mean lesion scores not greater than 1) and no bird has a lesion score of 4;
— for challenges with *E. tenella*, *E. acervulina*, *E. necatrix*, *E. maxima*, *E. brunetti*, *E. mitis*, or *E. praecox*, the growth rate in the vaccinates is significantly greater than in the controls.

2-4 *MANUFACTURER'S TESTS*

2-4-1 In-process test for sporulation rate and oocyst count
A sample of each oocyst bulk is examined microscopically after the sporulation step and before blending to determine the percentage of sporulated oocysts and the oocyst count. The values obtained are within the limits shown to allow preparation of a satisfactory vaccine.

2-4-2 Batch potency test for each *Eimeria* species in the vaccine
It is not necessary to carry out the potency test (section 3-6) for each batch of the vaccine if it has been carried out using a batch or batches of vaccine with minimum potency and sporulated oocyst content. Where the test is not carried out, an alternative validated method is used, the criteria for acceptance for each component being set with reference to a batch of vaccine that has given satisfactory results in the test described under Potency.

2-4-3 Freedom from extraneous agents
The disinfection method applied during the preparation of the final product from the harvested oocysts may be validated to show effective inactivation of certain potential extraneous agents. Where relevant validation data is available and where justified and authorised, some or all of the tests indicated under Extraneous agents (section 3-4) may be omitted as routine tests on each batch.

3 BATCH TESTS

3-1 Identification
3-1-1 Microscopical examination is used to confirm the presence of coccidial oocysts in the batch of vaccine.

3-1-2 The potency test (or batch potency test) is used to confirm the presence of oocysts of each of the *Eimeria* species stated on the label.

3-2 Bacteria and fungi
The vaccine, including where applicable the diluent supplied for reconstitution, complies with the test for sterility prescribed in the monograph *Vaccines for veterinary use (0062)* and comply with the test with a medium selective for *Campylobacter* spp.

3-3 Mycoplasmas
The vaccine complies with the test for mycoplasmas (*2.6.7*).

3-4 Extraneous agents
Carry out tests 1-6 of chapter *2.6.25. Avian live virus vaccines: tests for extraneous agents in batches of finished product.* General provisions *a-d*, *g* and *h* are also applicable. The vaccine complies with the requirements of each test.

3-5 Sporulated oocyst count
The sporulated oocysts content per dose is determined by counting the sporulated oocysts in a suitable counting chamber, under the microscope. The contents are not less than the minimum and not more than the maximum content of sporulated oocysts stated on the label.

3-6 Potency
The vaccine complies with the requirements of the test prescribed under Immunogenicity (section 2-3-4) using 1 dose of the vaccine administered by a recommended route.

4 LABELLING
The label states the minimum and maximum number of sporulated oocysts per dose.

Ph Eur

Contagious Pustular Dermatitis Vaccine, Living
Orf Vaccine

DEFINITION
Contagious Pustular Dermatitis Vaccine, Living is a preparation of a suitable strain of orf virus (contagious pustular dermatitis virus) for administration to sheep, by skin scarification.

PRODUCTION
The vaccinal organisms are obtained from the vesiculo-pustular lesions produced on the skin of lambs inoculated with the seed virus or prepared in suitable cell cultures (Appendix XV J(Vet) 1). If lambs are used for production, they are obtained from a flock known to be free from the natural disease, are healthy and have not been exposed previously to orf virus. Both the flock and the lambs are monitored for freedom from infectious diseases, the range of diseases in each case being agreed with the competent authority.

The harvested material may be freeze-dried. The finished preparation administered to the animals may contain glycerol and may contain an approved dye.

CHOICE OF VACCINE STRAIN
The vaccine strain is shown to be satisfactory with respect to safety and immunogenicity for the animals for which the vaccine is intended. The following tests may be used during the demonstration of safety, Appendix XV K(Vet) 1, reversion to virulence and immunogenicity, Appendix XV K(Vet) 2.

Safety   Carry out a test in each category of animal for which the vaccine is to be recommended. Vaccinate at least five animals that do not have antibodies to orf virus. Administer to each animal, by skin scarification of one site or a small number of contiguous sites, a quantity of virus containing not less than ten times the maximum virus titre likely to be contained in a dose of the vaccine. Observe the animals for 4 weeks. No systemic or local reactions occur except for mild localised lesions of orf which resolve in less than three weeks after vaccination to leave no more than a small area of scar tissue.

Reversion to virulence Administer by skin scarification a quantity of virus containing not less than one dose of the vaccine to each of two lambs of the minimum age to be recommended for vaccination and that do not have antibodies to orf virus. Six to eight days later, anaesthetise the lambs and remove, pool and homogenise the orf lesions in buffer containing suitable antibiotics and inoculate into two more lambs. Inoculate the homogenate into suitable cell cultures to verify the presence of the virus. Carry out this passage operation four times. If the virus disappears (no lesions develop) repeat the passage by administration to a group of 10 animals. Observe the lambs given the last passage material for 4 weeks. If the fifth group of animals shows no evidence of an increase in virulence indicative of reversion during the observation period, further testing is not required. Otherwise, materials used for the first passage and the final passage should be used in a separate experiment using at least 8 animals per group to directly compare the clinical signs and other relevant parameters. The vaccine complies with the test if the virus from the last passage produces no systemic reactions and the local reactions observed are no more severe than those seen in the lambs given the unpassaged material.

Immunogenicity Carry out a test in each category of animal for which the vaccine is to be recommended. Vaccinate, by skin scarification, at least five animals that do not have antibodies to orf virus, with a quantity of virus containing the minimum virus titre likely to be contained in a dose of vaccine. Maintain separately at least two animals of the same age and from the same source as unvaccinated controls. Eighteen to twenty four days later, challenge all the animals by skin scarification with a sufficient quantity of virulent strain of orf virus to cause disease in the controls. Observe the animals for 21 days and monitor and score the skin lesions. The test is not valid unless there are marked lesions of orf in both the control animals after challenge.

The vaccine complies with the test if, after challenge, there are no more than mild transient lesions of orf in the vaccinates.

BATCH TESTING
Extraneous bacteria and fungi:

A. Vaccines produced in lambs For each batch, the number of non-pathogenic organisms per dose shall be within the limits set for the product and shown to be safe.

B. Vaccines produced in cell cultures Each batch complies with the test described under Veterinary Vaccines.

Virus titre Where the nature of the vaccine strain allows a satisfactory test to be conducted *in vitro*, the test for Potency may be omitted as a routine control on each batch of vaccine. Where the Potency test is not carried out, an alternative validated *in vitro* test is conducted on each batch to measure the virus content. The batch complies with the tests if the titre of the batch is not less than the minimum titre stated on the label.

The vaccine complies with the requirements stated under Veterinary Vaccines with the following modifications.

IDENTIFICATION
Produces the characteristic lesions of contagious pustular dermatitis when applied to a scarified area of the skin of lambs.

TESTS
Extraneous bacteria and fungi
The vaccine is shown by appropriate methods to be free from pathogenic organisms.

Mycoplasmas
Complies with the test for absence of mycoplasmas, Appendix XVI B(Vet) 3.

Extraneous viruses
Neutralise the vaccine if necessary. Inoculate the vaccine onto suitable cell cultures that are susceptible to ovine viruses, make at least one passage and maintain the cultures for at least 14 days. No cytopathic effect develops. Conduct a test for freedom from haemadsorbing agents. The cell cultures show no signs of viral contamination.

POTENCY
Vaccinate each of no fewer than two healthy susceptible sheep, 6 to 12 months old, with serial dilutions of the vaccine applied to the scarified skin. Characteristic lesions of contagious pustular dermatitis appearing on the fourth to eighth day after inoculation are recorded. The vaccine contains not less than 100 MID (minimum infectious dose) in the dose stated on the label.

Duck Plague Vaccine (Live)

(Ph Eur monograph 1938)

―――――――――――――――――――――――――Ph Eur

1 DEFINITION
Duck plague vaccine (live) is a preparation of a suitable strain of duck plague virus (anatid herpesvirus 1). This monograph applies to vaccines intended for the active immunisation of ducks.

2 PRODUCTION
2-1 PREPARATION OF THE VACCINE
The vaccine virus is grown in embryonated hens' eggs or in cell cultures. The vaccine may be freeze-dried.

2-2 SUBSTRATE FOR VIRUS PROPAGATION
2-2-1 Embryonated hens' eggs
If the vaccine virus is grown in embryonated hens' eggs, they are obtained from flocks free from specified pathogens (SPF) (*5.2.2*).

2-2-2 Cell cultures
If the vaccine virus is grown in cell cultures, they comply with the requirements for cell cultures for production of veterinary vaccines (*5.2.4*).

2-3 SEED LOTS
2-3-1 Extraneous agents
The master seed lot complies with the test for extraneous agents in seed lots (*2.6.24*). In these tests on the master seed lot, the organisms used are not more than 5 passages from the master seed lot at the start of the tests.

2-4 CHOICE OF VACCINE VIRUS
The vaccine virus shall be shown to be satisfactory with respect to safety (*5.2.6*) and efficacy (*5.2.7*) for the ducks for which the vaccine is intended.

The following tests for safety (section 2-4-1), increase in virulence (section 2-4-2) and immunogenicity (section 2-4-3) may be used during demonstration of safety and efficacy.

2-4-1 Safety

Carry out the test for each route and method of administration to be recommended for vaccination, using in each case ducks from a species considered to be the most susceptible among the species to be recommended for vaccination, not older than the minimum age to be recommended for vaccination and that do not have antibodies against duck plague virus. Use vaccine virus at the least attenuated passage level that will be present in a batch of the vaccine.

For each test performed in ducks younger than 3 weeks of age, use not fewer than 10 susceptible ducks. For each test performed in ducks older than 3 weeks of age, use not fewer than 8 susceptible ducks. Administer to each duck a quantity of vaccine virus equivalent to not less than 10 times the maximum virus titre likely to be contained in 1 dose of the vaccine. Observe the ducks at least daily for at least 14 days.

The test is not valid if more than 10 per cent of the ducks younger than 3 weeks of age show abnormal signs of disease or die from causes not attributable to the vaccine. For ducks older than 3 weeks of age, the test is not valid if non-specific mortality occurs.

The vaccine virus complies with the test if no duck shows abnormal signs of disease or dies from causes attributable to the vaccine virus.

2-4-2 Increase in virulence

Carry out the test according to general chapter 5.2.6 using domestic ducks that do not have antibodies against duck plague virus and of an age suitable for the multiplication of the virus. If the properties of the vaccine virus allow sequential passage through 5 groups via natural spreading, this method may be used, otherwise passage as described below is carried out. Administer to each duck of the 1st group by a route to be recommended a quantity of the vaccine virus that will allow recovery of virus for the passages described below. 2 to 4 days later, take samples of liver and spleen from each duck and pool all samples. Administer 0.1 mL of the pooled suspension by the oro-nasal or a parenteral route to each duck of the next group. Carry out this passage operation not fewer than 4 times; verify the presence of the virus at each passage. If the virus is not found at a passage level, repeat the passage by administration to a group of 10 ducks.

If the 5th group of ducks shows no evidence of an increase in virulence indicative of reversion during the observation period, further testing is not required. Otherwise, carry out an additional safety test and compare the clinical signs and any relevant parameters in a group of at least 10 ducks receiving the material used for the 1st passage and another similar group receiving the virus at the final passage level.

The vaccine virus complies with the test if no indication of an increase in virulence of the virus at the final passage level compared with the material used for the 1st passage is observed. If virus is not recovered after an initial passage in 5 ducks and a subsequent repeat passage in 10 ducks, the vaccine virus also complies with the test.

2-4-3 Immunogenicity

A test is carried out for each route and method of administration to be recommended for vaccination, using in each case domestic ducks not older than the minimum age to be recommended for vaccination. The quantity of the vaccine virus administered to each duck is not greater than the minimum virus titre to be stated on the label and the virus is at the most attenuated passage level that will be present in a batch of the vaccine. For each test, use not fewer than

30 ducks of the same origin and that do not have antibodies against duck plague virus. Vaccinate by a route to be recommended not fewer than 20 ducks. Maintain not fewer than 10 ducks as controls. After 5 days, challenge each duck by a suitable route with a sufficient quantity of virulent duck plague virus. Observe the ducks at least daily for 14 days after challenge. Record the deaths and the number of surviving ducks that show clinical signs of disease.

The test is not valid if during the observation period after challenge fewer than 80 per cent of the control ducks die or show typical signs of duck plague and/or if during the period between the vaccination and challenge more than 10 per cent of control or vaccinated ducks show abnormal clinical signs of disease or die from causes not attributable to the vaccine.

The vaccine virus complies with the test if during the observation period after challenge not fewer than 80 per cent of the vaccinated ducks survive and show no notable clinical signs of duck plague.

3 BATCH TESTS

3-1 Identification

The vaccine, diluted if necessary and mixed with a monospecific duck plague virus antiserum, no longer infects embryonated hens' eggs from an SPF flock (5.2.2) or susceptible cell cultures (5.2.4) into which it is inoculated.

3-2 Bacteria and fungi

The vaccine, including where applicable the diluent supplied for reconstitution, complies with the test for sterility prescribed in the monograph *Vaccines for veterinary use (0062)*.

3-3 Mycoplasmas

The vaccine complies with the test for mycoplasmas (2.6.7).

3-4 Extraneous agents

The vaccine complies with the tests for extraneous agents in batches of finished product (2.6.25).

3-5 Virus titre

Titrate the vaccine virus by inoculation into embryonated hens' eggs from an SPF flock (5.2.2) or into suitable cell cultures (5.2.4). The vaccine complies with the test if 1 dose contains not less than the minimum virus titre stated on the label.

3-6 Potency

The vaccine complies with the test prescribed under immunogenicity (section 2-4-3), when administered by a recommended route and method. It is not necessary to carry out the potency test for each batch of the vaccine if it has been carried out on a representative batch using a vaccinating dose containing not more than the minimum virus titre stated on the label.

_____ Ph Eur

Duck Viral Hepatitis Type I Vaccine (Live)

(Ph. Eur. monograph 1315)

Ph Eur _____

1 DEFINITION

Duck viral hepatitis type I vaccine (live) is a preparation of a suitable strain of duck hepatitis virus type I. This monograph applies to vaccines intended for the active immunisation of breeder ducks in order to protect passively their progeny and/or for the active immunisation of ducklings.

2 PRODUCTION

2-1 PREPARATION OF THE VACCINE

The vaccine virus is grown in embryonated hens' eggs or in cell cultures.

2-2 SUBSTRATE FOR VIRUS PROPAGATION

2-2-1 Embryonated hens' eggs

If the vaccine virus is grown in embryonated hens' eggs, they are obtained from flocks free from specified pathogens (SPF) (*5.2.2*).

2-2-2 Cell cultures

If the vaccine virus is grown in cell cultures, they comply with the requirements for cell cultures for production of veterinary vaccines (*5.2.4*).

2-3 SEED LOTS

2-3-1 Extraneous agents

The master seed lot complies with the tests for extraneous agents in seed lots (*2.6.24*). In these tests on the master seed lot, the organisms used are not more than 5 passages from the master seed lot at the start of the tests.

2-4 CHOICE OF VACCINE VIRUS

The vaccine virus shall be shown to be satisfactory with respect to safety (*5.2.6*) and efficacy (*5.2.7*) for the ducks for which it is intended.

The following tests for safety (section 2-4-1), increase in virulence (section 2-4-2) and immunogenicity (section 2-4-3) may be used during demonstration of safety and efficacy.

2-4-1 Safety

Carry out the test for each route and method of administration to be recommended for vaccination using in each case susceptible domestic ducks (*Anas platyrhynchos*) not older than the minimum age to be recommended for vaccination and that do not have antibodies against duck hepatitis virus type I. Use vaccine virus at the least attenuated passage level that will be present in a batch of the vaccine.

For each test performed in ducklings younger than 3 weeks of age, use not fewer than 10 ducklings. For each test performed in ducklings older than 3 weeks of age, use not fewer than 8 ducklings. Administer to each duckling a quantity of vaccine virus equivalent to not less than 10 times the maximum virus titre likely to be contained in 1 dose of vaccine. Observe the ducklings at least daily for at least 14 days.

The test is not valid if more than 10 per cent of the ducklings younger than 3 weeks of age show abnormal signs of disease or die from causes not attributable to the vaccine. For ducklings older than 3 weeks of age, the test is not valid if non-specific mortality occurs.

The vaccine virus complies with the test if no duckling shows abnormal signs of disease or dies from causes attributable to the vaccine virus.

2-4-2 Increase in virulence

Carry out the test according to general chapter *5.2.6* using 1-day-old domestic ducklings that do not have antibodies against duck hepatitis virus type I. If the properties of the vaccine virus allow sequential passage through 5 groups via natural spreading, this method may be used, otherwise passage as described below is carried out.

Administer to each duckling of the 1st group by the oro-nasal route a quantity of vaccine virus that will allow recovery of virus for the passages described below. 2 to 4 days later, take samples of liver from each duckling and pool the samples. Administer 1 mL of the pooled liver suspension by the oro-nasal route to each duckling of the next group. Carry out this operation 4 times. Verify the presence of the virus at each passage. If the virus is not found at a passage level, repeat the passage by administration to a group of 10 ducklings. Observe the ducklings given the last passage at least daily for 21 days.

If the 5th group of ducklings shows no evidence of an increase in virulence indicative of reversion during the observation period, further testing is not required. Otherwise, carry out an additional safety test and compare the clinical signs and any relevant parameters in a group of at least 10 ducklings receiving the material used for the 1st passage and another similar group receiving the virus at the final passage level.

The vaccine virus complies with the test if no indication of an increase in virulence of the virus at the final passage level compared with the material used for the 1st passage is observed. If the virus is not recovered after an initial passage in 5 ducklings and a subsequent repeat passage in 10 ducklings, the vaccine virus also complies with the test.

2-4-3 Immunogenicity

A test is carried out for each route and method of administration to be recommended for vaccination, using in each case domestic ducks not older than the minimum age to be recommended for vaccination. The quantity of the vaccine virus administered to each bird is not greater than the minimum virus titre to be stated on the label and the virus is at the most attenuated passage level that will be present in a batch of the vaccine.

2-4-3-1 Vaccines for passive immunisation of ducklings. Use for the test not fewer than 15 laying ducks or ducks intended for laying, as appropriate, of the same origin and that do not have antibodies against duck hepatitis virus type I. Vaccinate by a route to be recommended not fewer than 10 ducks using the schedule to be recommended. Maintain not fewer than 5 ducks as controls. Starting from 4 weeks after onset of lay, collect embryonated eggs from vaccinated and control ducks and incubate them. Challenge not fewer than twenty 1-week-old ducklings representative of the vaccinated group and not fewer than 10 from the control group by the oro-nasal route with a sufficient quantity of virulent duck hepatitis virus type I. Observe the ducklings at least daily for 14 days after challenge. Record the deaths and the number of surviving ducklings that show clinical signs of disease.

The test is not valid if:
— during the observation period after challenge fewer than 70 per cent of the challenged ducklings from the control ducks die or show typical signs of the disease,
— and/or during the period between vaccination and collection of the eggs more than 10 per cent of the control or vaccinated ducks show abnormal clinical signs or die from causes not attributable to the vaccine.

The vaccine virus complies with the test if during the observation period after challenge the percentage relative protection calculated using the following expression is not less than 80 per cent:

$$\frac{V - C}{100 - C} \times 100$$

V = percentage of challenged ducklings from vaccinated ducks that survive to the end of the observation period without clinical signs of the disease;

C = percentage of challenged ducklings from unvaccinated control ducks that survive to the end of the observation period without clinical signs of the disease.

2-4-3-2 Vaccines for active immunisation of ducklings. Use for the test not fewer than 30 ducklings of the same origin and that do not have antibodies against duck hepatitis virus type I. Vaccinate by a route to be recommended not fewer than 20 ducklings. Maintain not fewer than 10 ducklings as controls. Challenge each duckling after at least 5 days by the oro-nasal route with a sufficient quantity of virulent duck hepatitis virus type I. Observe the ducklings at least daily for 14 days after challenge. Record the deaths and the number of surviving ducklings that show clinical signs of disease.

The test is not valid if:
— during the observation period after challenge fewer than 70 per cent of the control ducklings die or show typical signs of the disease;
— and/or during the period between vaccination and challenge more than 10 per cent of the control or vaccinated ducklings show abnormal clinical signs or die from causes not attributable to the vaccine.

The vaccine virus complies with the test if during the observation period after challenge the percentage relative protection calculated using the following expression is not less than 80 per cent:

$$\frac{V - C}{100 - C} \times 100$$

V = percentage of challenged vaccinated ducklings that survive to the end of the observation period without clinical signs of the disease;

C = percentage of challenged unvaccinated control ducklings that survive to the end of the observation period without clinical signs of the disease.

3 BATCH TESTS
3-1 Identification
The vaccine, diluted if necessary and mixed with a monospecific duck hepatitis virus type I antiserum, no longer infects embryonated hens' eggs from an SPF flock (5.2.2) or susceptible cell cultures (5.2.4) into which it is inoculated.

3-2 Bacteria and fungi
Vaccines intended for administration by injection comply with the test for sterility prescribed in the monograph *Vaccines for veterinary use (0062)*.

Frozen or freeze-dried vaccines produced in embryonated eggs and not intended for administration by injection either comply with the test for sterility prescribed in the monograph *Vaccines for veterinary use (0062)* or with the following test: carry out a quantitative test for bacterial and fungal contamination; carry out identification tests for micro-organisms detected in the vaccine; the vaccine does not contain pathogenic micro-organisms and contains not more than 1 non-pathogenic micro-organism per dose.

Any diluent supplied for reconstitution of the vaccine complies with the test for sterility prescribed in the monograph *Vaccines for veterinary use (0062)*.

3-3 Mycoplasmas
The vaccine complies with the test for mycoplasmas (2.6.7).

3-4 Extraneous agents
The vaccine complies with the tests for extraneous agents in batches of finished product (2.6.25).

3-5 Virus titre
Titrate the vaccine virus by inoculation into embryonated hens' eggs from an SPF flock (5.2.2) or into suitable cell cultures (5.2.4). The vaccine complies with the test if 1 dose contains not less than the minimum virus titre stated on the label.

3-6 Potency
Depending on the indications, the vaccine complies with 1 or both of the tests prescribed under Immunogenicity (section 2-4-3), when administered by a recommended route and method. It is not necessary to carry out the potency test for each batch of the vaccine if it has been carried out on a representative batch using a vaccinating dose containing not more than the minimum virus titre stated on the label.

4 LABELLING
If it has been found that the vaccine may show reversion to virulence, the label indicates the precautions necessary to avoid transmission of virulent virus to unvaccinated ducklings.

Ph Eur

Egg Drop Syndrome 76 (Adenovirus) Vaccine

(Egg Drop Syndrome '76 Vaccine (Inactivated), Ph Eur monograph 1202)

CAUTION *Accidental injection of oily vaccine can cause serious local reactions in man. Expert medical advice should be sought immediately and the doctor should be informed that the vaccine is an oil emulsion.*

Ph Eur

1 DEFINITION
Egg drop syndrome '76 vaccine (inactivated) is a preparation of a suitable strain of egg drop syndrome '76 virus (haemagglutinating avian adenovirus), inactivated while maintaining adequate immunogenic properties. This monograph applies to vaccines intended for protection of laying birds against a drop in egg production and/or for prevention of loss of egg quality.

2 PRODUCTION
2-1 PREPARATION OF THE VACCINE
The vaccine strain is propagated in embryonated hens' or ducks' eggs or in cell cultures. The vaccine may be adjuvanted.

2-2 SUBSTRATE FOR VIRUS PROPAGATION
2-2-1 Embryonated hens' or ducks' eggs
If the vaccine virus is grown in embryonated hens' or ducks' eggs, they are obtained from healthy flocks.

2-2-2 Cell cultures
If the vaccine virus is grown in cell cultures, they comply with the requirements for cell cultures for production of veterinary vaccines (5.2.4).

2-3 SEED LOTS
2-3-1 Extraneous agents
The master seed lot complies with the test for extraneous agents in seed lots (2.6.24). In these tests on the master seed lot, the organisms used are not more than 5 passages from the master seed lot at the start of the test.

2-4 CHOICE OF VACCINE COMPOSITION

The vaccine is shown to be satisfactory with respect to safety (5.2.6) and efficacy (5.2.7) for the birds for which it is intended.

The following tests for safety (section 2-4-1) and immunogenicity (section 2-4-2) may be used during the demonstration of safety and efficacy.

2-4-1 Safety

The test is carried out for each route of administration to be recommended for vaccination. Use a batch of vaccine containing not less than the maximum potency that may be expected in a batch of vaccine.

For each test, use not fewer than 8 hens not older than the minimum age to be recommended for vaccination and from a flock free from specified pathogens (SPF) (5.2.2). Administer by a route and method to be recommended to each hen 1 dose of the vaccine. Observe the hens at least daily for at least 14 days after the administration of the vaccine.

The test is not valid if non-specific mortality occurs. The vaccine complies with the test if no hen shows abnormal signs of disease or dies from causes attributable to the vaccine.

2-4-2 Immunogenicity

A test is carried out for each route and method of administration to be recommended, using in each case hens from an SPF flock (5.2.2) and of the age at which vaccination is recommended. The vaccine administered to each hen is of minimum potency.

Vaccinate each of 2 groups of 30 hens. Maintain 2 control groups one of 10 hens and the other of 30 hens, of the same age and from the same source as the vaccinates. Maintain individual egg production records from point of lay until 4 weeks after challenge. At 30 weeks of age, challenge each hen from 1 group of 30 vaccinates and the group of 10 control hens with a quantity of egg drop syndrome '76 virus sufficient to cause a well marked drop in egg production and/or quality. The test is invalid unless there is a well marked drop in egg production and/or quality in the control hens. The vaccine complies with the test if the vaccinated hens show no marked drop in egg production and/or quality.

When the second group of vaccinated hens and the group of 30 control hens are nearing the end of lay, challenge these hens, as before. The test is invalid unless there is a well marked drop in egg production and/or quality in the control hens. The vaccine complies with the test if the vaccinated hens show no marked drop in egg production and/or quality.

Carry out serological tests on serum samples obtained at the time of vaccination, 4 weeks later and just prior to challenge. The test is not valid if antibodies against egg drop syndrome '76 virus are detected in any sample from control hens.

2-5 MANUFACTURER'S TESTS

2-5-1 Residual live virus

The test for residual live virus is carried out in embryonated ducks' eggs from a flock free from egg drop syndrome '76 virus infection, or in embryonated hens' eggs from an SPF flock (5.2.2), or in suitable cell cultures, whichever is the most sensitive for the vaccine strain. The quantity of inactivated virus harvest used in the test is equivalent to not less than 10 doses of the vaccine. The inactivated virus harvest complies with the test if no live virus is detected.

2-5-2 Batch potency test

It is not necessary to carry out the potency test (section 3-5) for each batch of vaccine if it has been carried out using a

batch of vaccine with a minimum potency. Where the test is not carried out, an alternative validated method is used, the criteria for acceptance being set with reference to a batch of vaccine that has given satisfactory results in the test described under Potency. The following test may be used.

Vaccinate not fewer than ten 14- to 28-day-old chickens from an SPF flock (5.2.2) with 1 dose of vaccine by one of the recommended routes. 4 weeks later, collect serum samples from each bird and from 5 unvaccinated control birds of the same age and from the same source. Measure the antibody response in a haemagglutination (HA) inhibition test on each serum using 4 HA units of antigen and chicken erythrocytes. The test is not valid if there are specific antibodies in the sera of the unvaccinated birds. The vaccine complies with the test if the mean titre of the vaccinated group is not less than that found previously for a batch of vaccine that has given satisfactory results in the test described under Potency.

3 BATCH TESTS

3-1 Identification

When injected into chickens that do not have antibodies against egg drop syndrome '76 virus, the vaccine stimulates the production of such antibodies.

3-2 Bacteria and fungi

The vaccine, including where applicable the diluent supplied for reconstitution, complies with the test for sterility prescribed in the monograph *Vaccines for veterinary use (0062)*.

3-3 Residual live virus

A test for residual live virus is carried out to confirm inactivation of egg drop syndrome '76 virus.

A. For a vaccine prepared in eggs, carry out the test in embryonated ducks' eggs from a flock free from egg drop syndrome '76 virus infection or, if it is known to provide a more sensitive test system, in hens' eggs from an SPF flock (5.2.2). Inject 2/5 of a dose into the allantoic cavity of each of ten 10- to 14-day-old embryonated eggs that are free from parental antibodies to egg drop syndrome '76 virus. Incubate the eggs and observe for 8 days. Pool separately the allantoic fluid from eggs containing live embryos, and that from eggs containing dead embryos, excluding those that die from non-specific causes within 24 h of the injection. Inject into the allantoic cavity of each of ten 10- to 14-day-old embryonated eggs that do not have parental antibodies to egg drop syndrome '76 virus, 0.2 mL of the pooled allantoic fluid from the live embryos and into each of 10 similar eggs, 0.2 mL of the pooled allantoic fluid from the dead embryos and incubate for 8 days. Examine the allantoic fluid from each egg for the presence of haemagglutinating activity using chicken erythrocytes. If more than 20 per cent of the embryos die at either stage, repeat that stage. The vaccine complies with the test if there is no evidence of haemagglutinating activity and if, in any repeat test, not more than 20 per cent of the embryos die from non-specific causes.

Antibiotics may be used in the test to control extraneous bacterial infection.

B. For a vaccine adapted to growth in cell cultures, inoculate 10 doses into suitable cell cultures. If the vaccine contains an oily adjuvant, eliminate it by suitable means. Incubate the cultures at 38 ± 1 °C for 7 days. Make a passage on another set of cell cultures and incubate at 38 ± 1 °C for 7 days. Examine the cultures regularly and at the end of the incubation period examine the supernatant for the presence of haemagglutinating activity. The vaccine complies with the test if the cell cultures show no sign of infection and if there is no haemagglutinating activity in the supernatant.

3-4 Specified extraneous agents
Use 10 chickens, 14-28 days old, from an SPF flock (*5.2.2*). Vaccinate each chicken by a recommended route with a double dose of the vaccine. After 3 weeks, administer 1 dose by the same route. Collect serum samples from each chicken 2 weeks later and carry out tests for antibodies against the following agents by the methods prescribed in general chapter *5.2.2. Chicken flocks free from specified pathogens for the production and quality control of vaccines*: avian encephalomyelitis virus, avian leucosis viruses, infectious bronchitis virus, avian infectious bursal disease virus, avian infectious laryngotracheitis virus, influenza A virus, Marek's disease virus, Newcastle disease virus and, for vaccine produced in duck eggs, *Chlamydia* (by a complement-fixation test or agar gel precipitation test), duck hepatitis virus type I (by a fluorescent-antibody test or serum-neutralisation test) and Derzsy's disease virus (by a serum-neutralisation test).

The vaccine complies with the test if it does not stimulate the formation of antibodies against these agents.

3-5 Potency
The vaccine complies with the requirements of the test mentioned under Immunogenicity (section 2-4-2) when administered by a recommended route and method.

4 LABELLING
The label states whether the strain in the vaccine is duck- or hen-embryo-adapted or cell-culture-adapted.

_____ *Ph Eur*

Equine Herpesvirus Vaccine, Inactivated

*(Equine Herpesvirus Vaccine (Inactivated),
Ph Eur monograph 1613)*

Ph Eur _____

1 DEFINITION
Equine herpesvirus vaccine (inactivated) is a preparation of one or more suitable strains of equid herpesvirus 1 and/or equid herpesvirus 4, inactivated while maintaining adequate immunogenic properties or a suspension of an inactivated fraction of the virus. This monograph applies to vaccines intended for the active immunisation of horses against disease caused by equid herpesvirus 1 and/or equid herpesvirus 4.

2 PRODUCTION
2-1 PREPARATION OF THE VACCINE
Each strain of vaccine virus is grown separately in cell cultures. The viral suspensions may be purified and concentrated and are inactivated; they may be treated to fragment the virus and the viral fragments may be purified and concentrated. The vaccine may be adjuvanted.

2-2 SUBSTRATE FOR VIRUS PROPAGATION
2-2-1 Cell cultures
The cell cultures comply with the requirements for cell cultures for production of veterinary vaccines (*5.2.4*).

2-3 CHOICE OF VACCINE COMPOSITION
The vaccine is shown to be satisfactory with respect to safety (*5.2.6*) and efficacy (*5.2.7*) for the horses for which it is intended. Where a particular breed of horse is known to be especially sensitive to the vaccine, horses from that breed are included in the test for safety.

The following tests for safety (section 2-3-1) and immunogenicity (section 2-3-2) may be used during the demonstration of safety and efficacy.

2-3-1 Safety
Carry out the test for each route and method of administration to be recommended for vaccination and in horses of each category for which the vaccine is intended. Use a batch of vaccine containing not less than the maximum potency that may be expected in a batch of vaccine.

Use for the test not fewer than 8 horses that have not been previously vaccinated with an equine herpesvirus vaccine, that have at most a low antibody titre not indicative of recent infection and that do not excrete equid herpesvirus. Administer to each horse 1 dose of the vaccine, then another dose after 14 days. Observe the horses at least daily until at least 14 days after the last administration.

The vaccine complies with the test if no horse shows abnormal local or systemic reactions or dies from causes attributable to the vaccine during the 28 days of the test.

2-3-2 Immunogenicity
The type of immunogenicity test depends on the claims for the product. For vaccines intended to protect against the disease of the respiratory tract, carry out test 2-3-2-1, using equid herpesvirus 1 and/or equid herpesvirus 4 depending on the claims for protection. For vaccines intended to protect against abortion carry out test 2-3-2-2.

A test is carried out for each route and method of administration to be recommended, using in each case horses that have not been vaccinated with an equine herpesvirus vaccine, that have at most a low antibody titre not indicative of recent infection, and that do not excrete equid herpesvirus. To demonstrate that no recent infection occurs, immediately before vaccination: draw a blood sample from each horse and test individually for antibodies against equid herpesviruses 1 and 4; collect 10 mL of heparinised blood and test the washed leucocytes for equid herpesviruses 1 and 4; collect a nasopharyngeal swab and test for equid herpesviruses 1 and 4. There is no indication of an active infection. Immediately before challenge collect a nasopharyngeal swab and test for equid herpesviruses 1 and 4. If there is an indication of virus excretion remove the horse from the test. Keep the horses in strict isolation. The vaccine administered to each horse is of minimum potency.

2-3-2-1 Vaccines intended for protection against disease of the respiratory tract. Use for the test not fewer than 10 horses, not less than 6 months old. Vaccinate not fewer than 6 horses according to the schedule to be recommended. Maintain not fewer than 4 horses as controls. At least 2 weeks after the last vaccination, challenge each horse by nasal instillation with a quantity of equid herpesvirus 1 or 4, sufficient to produce in a susceptible horse characteristic signs of the disease such as pyrexia and virus excretion (and possibly nasal discharge and coughing). Observe the horses at least daily for 14 days. Collect nasopharyngeal swabs daily from each individual horse to isolate the virus.

The vaccine complies with the test if the vaccinated horses show no more than slight signs; the signs in vaccinates are less severe than in controls. The average number of days on which virus is excreted and the respective virus titres are significantly lower in vaccinated horses than in controls.

2-3-2-2 Vaccines intended for protection against abortion.
Use not fewer than 10 pregnant horses. In addition to the testing described above, 6, 4, 3, 2 and 1 month before the first vaccination draw a blood sample from each horse and

test individually for antibodies against equid herpesviries 1 and 4. There is no evidence of recent infection or virus excretion. Vaccinate not fewer than 6 horses according to the schedule to be recommended. Maintain not fewer than 4 horses as controls. Between day 260 and day 290 of pregnancy but not earlier than 3 weeks after the last vaccination, challenge each horse, by nasal instillation, with a quantity of equid herpesvirus 1 sufficient to produce abortion in susceptible horses. Observe the horses at least daily up to foaling or abortion. Collect samples of fetal lung and liver tissues from aborted fetuses and carry out tests for virus in cell cultures.

The test is not valid if more than one control horse gives birth to a healthy foal and if the challenge virus is not isolated from the aborted fetuses. The vaccine complies with the test if not more than one vaccinated horse aborts.

2-4 MANUFACTURER'S TESTS

2-4-1 Residual live virus
The test for residual live virus is carried out using 2 passages in the same type of cell culture as that used in the production or in cell cultures shown to be at least as sensitive. The quantity of inactivated virus harvest used in the test is equivalent to not less than 25 doses of the vaccine. The inactivated virus harvest complies with the test if no live virus is detected.

2-4-2 Batch potency test
It is not necessary to carry out the potency test (section 3-4) for each batch of vaccine if it has been carried out using a batch of vaccine with a minimum potency. Where the test is not carried out, an alternative validated method is used, the criteria for acceptance being set with reference to a batch of vaccine that has given satisfactory results in the test described under Potency. The following test may be used.

Vaccinate not fewer than 5 rabbits, guinea-pigs or mice with a single injection of a suitable dose. Where the recommended schedule requires a 2nd injection to be given, the recommended schedule may be used in laboratory animals provided it has been demonstrated that this will still provide a suitably sensitive test system. At a given interval within the range of 14-21 days after the last injection, collect blood from each animal and prepare serum samples. Use a suitable validated test such as an enzyme-linked immunosorbent assay to measure the response to each of the antigens stated on the label. The vaccine complies with the test if the antibody levels are not significantly less than those obtained with a batch that has given satisfactory results in the test described under Potency.

3 BATCH TESTS

3-1 Idenfication
In animals that do not have antibodies against equid herpesvirus 1 and equid herpesvirus 4 or a fraction of the viruses, the vaccine stimulates the production of specific antibodies against the virus type or types included in the product. The method used must distinguish between antibodies against equid herpesviruses 1 and 4.

3-2 Bacteria and fungi
The vaccine, including where applicable the diluent supplied for reconstitution, complies with the test for sterility prescribed in the monograph *Vaccines for veterinary use (0062)*.

3-3 Residual live virus
Carry out a test for residual live virus using not less than 25 doses of vaccine by inoculating cell cultures sensitive to equid herpesviruses 1 and 4; make a passage after 5-7 days

and maintain the cultures for 14 days. The vaccine complies with the test if no live virus is detected. If the vaccine contains an adjuvant, separate the adjuvant from the liquid phase, by a method that does not inactivate or otherwise interfere with the detection of live virus, or carry out a test for inactivation on the mixture of bulk antigens before addition of the adjuvant.

3-4 Potency
The vaccine complies with the requirements of the test mentioned under Immunogenicity (section 2-3-2) when administered by a recommended route and method.

————————————————————————— Ph Eur

Equine Influenza Vaccine, Inactivated

(Equine Influenza Vaccine (Inactivated), Ph Eur monograph 0249)

Ph Eur ————————————————————————————

1 DEFINITION
Equine influenza vaccine (inactivated) is a preparation of one or more suitable strains of equine influenza virus, inactivated while maintaining adequate immunogenic properties. Suitable strains contain both haemagglutinin and neuraminidase. This monograph applies to vaccines intended for the active immunisation of horses against equine influenza.

2 PRODUCTION
2-1 PREPARATION OF THE VACCINE
Each strain of virus is grown separately in embryonated hens' eggs or in cell cultures. The viral suspensions may be purified and concentrated. The antigen content of the vaccine is based on the haemagglutinin content of the viral suspensions determined as described under Manufacturer's tests; the amount of haemagglutinin for each strain is not less than that in the vaccine shown to be satisfactory in the test for potency. The vaccine may be adjuvanted.

2-2 SUBSTRATE FOR VIRUS PROPAGATION
2-2-1 Embryonated hens' eggs
If the vaccine virus is grown in embryonated hens' eggs, they are obtained from a healthy flock.

2-2-2 Cell cultures
If the vaccine virus is grown in cell cultures, they comply with the requirements for cell cultures for production of veterinary vaccines (*5.2.4*).

2-3 CHOICE OF VACCINE COMPOSITION
The choice of strains used in the vaccine is based on epidemiological data. The World Organisation for Animal Health (OIE, formerly the *Office international des épizooties*) reviews the epidemiological data periodically and if necessary recommends new strains corresponding to prevailing epidemiological evidence. Such strains are used in accordance with the regulations in force in the signatory states of the Convention on the Elaboration of a European Pharmacopoeia.

The vaccine is shown to be satisfactory with respect to safety (*5.2.6*) and efficacy (*5.2.7*) for the horses for which it is intended. Where a particular breed of horse is known to be especially sensitive to the vaccine, horses from that breed are included in the tests for safety.

The following tests for safety (section 2-3-1) and immunogenicity (section 2-3-2) may be used during the demonstration of safety and efficacy.

2-3-1 Safety

Carry out the test for each route and method of administration to be recommended for vaccination and in horses of each category for which the vaccine is intended. Use a batch of vaccine containing not less than the maximum potency that may be expected in a batch of vaccine.

Use for the test not fewer than 8 horses that preferably do not have antibodies against equine influenza virus or, where justified, use horses with a low level of such antibodies as long as they have not been vaccinated against equine influenza and administration of the vaccine does not cause an anamnestic response. Administer to each horse 1 dose of the vaccine, then another dose after at least 14 days. Observe the horses at least daily until at least 14 days after the last administration.

The vaccine complies with the test if no horse shows abnormal local or systemic reactions or dies from causes attributable to the vaccine during the 28 days of the test.

2-3-2 Immunogenicity

The test described under 2-3-2-1 is suitable to demonstrate the immunogenicity of the strains present in the vaccine.

A test with virulent challenge is carried out for at least one vaccine strain (see test under 2-3-2-1). For other strains in the vaccine, demonstration of immunogenicity may, where justified, be based on the serological response induced in horses by the vaccine (see tests under 2-3-2-2); justification for protection against these strains may be based on published data on the correlation of the antibody titre with protection against antigenically related strains.

Where serology is used, the test is carried out as described under 2-3-2-1 but instead of virulent challenge, a blood sample is drawn 2 weeks after the last vaccination and the antibody titre of each serum is determined by a suitable immunochemical method (*2.7.1*), such as the single radial haemolysis test or the haemagglutination-inhibition test shown below; a reference serum is used to validate the test. The acceptance criteria depend on the strain and are based on available data; for A/equine-2 virus, vaccines have usually been found satisfactory if the antibody titre of each serum is not less than 85 mm^2 where the single radial haemolysis test is used, or not less than 1:64 (before mixture with the suspension of antigen and erythrocytes) where the haemagglutination-inhibition test is used.

Equine influenza subtype 1 strain A/eq/Newmarket/77 horse antiserum BRP, equine influenza subtype 2 European-like strain A/eq/Newmarket/2/93 horse antiserum BRP, equine influenza subtype 2 American-like strain A/eq/Newmarket/1/93 horse antiserum BRP and *equine influenza subtype 2 American-like strain A/eq/South Africa/4/03 horse antiserum BRP* are suitable for use as reference sera for the single radial haemolysis test.

The claims for the product reflect the type of immunogenicity demonstrated (protection against challenge or antibody production).

2-3-2-1 Protection from signs of disease and reduction of virus excretion. Carry out the immunogenicity test using a challenge strain against which the vaccine is stated to provide protection. Use where possible a recent isolate.

A test is carried out for each route and method of administration to be recommended, using in each case horses

not less than 6 months old. The vaccine administered to each horse is of minimum potency.

Use for the test not fewer than 10 horses that do not have antibodies against equine influenza virus. Draw a blood sample from each horse and test individually for antibodies against equine influenza virus to determine seronegativity. Vaccinate not fewer than 6 horses according to the schedule to be recommended. Maintain not fewer than 4 horses as controls. Draw a second blood sample from each vaccinated horse 7 days after the first vaccination and test individually for antibodies against equine influenza virus, to detect an anamnestic sero-response. Horses showing sero-conversion at this stage are excluded from the test. At least 2 weeks after the last vaccination, challenge each horse by aerosol with a quantity of equine influenza virus sufficient to produce characteristic signs of disease such as fever, nasal discharge and coughing in a susceptible horse. Observe the horses at least daily for 14 days. Collect nasal swabs daily from each individual horse to isolate the virus.

The vaccine complies with the test if the vaccinated horses show no more than slight signs; the controls show characteristic signs. The average number of days on which virus is excreted and the respective virus titres are significantly lower in vaccinated horses than in control horses.

2-3-2-2 Presence of antibodies after vaccination

2-3-2-2-1 Single radial haemolysis. Heat each serum at 56 °C for 30 min. Perform tests on each serum using respectively the antigen or antigens prepared from the strain(s) used in the production of the vaccine. Mix 1 mL of sheep erythrocyte suspension in barbital buffer solution (1 volume of erythrocytes in 10 volumes of final suspension) with 1 mL of a suitable dilution of the influenza virus strain in barbital buffer solution and incubate the mixture at 4 °C for 30 min. To 2 mL of the virus/erythrocyte mixture, add 1 mL of a 3 g/L solution of *chromium(III) trichloride hexahydrate R*, mix and allow to stand for 10 min. Heat the sensitised erythrocytes to 47 °C in a water-bath. Mix 15 mL of a 10 g/L solution of *agarose for electrophoresis R* in barbital buffer solution, 0.7 mL of sensitised erythrocyte suspension and the appropriate amount of diluted guinea-pig complement in barbital buffer solution at 47 °C. Pour the mixture into Petri dishes and allow the agar to set. Punch holes in the agar layer and place in each hole 5 μL of the undiluted serum to be tested or the control serum. Incubate the Petri dishes at 37 °C for 18 h. Measure the diameter of the haemolysis zone and calculate its area, which expresses the antibody titre, in square millimetres.

Equine influenza subtype 1 strain A/eq/Newmarket/77 horse antiserum BRP, equine influenza subtype 2 European-like strain A/eq/Newmarket/2/93 horse antiserum BRP, equine influenza subtype 2 American-like strain A/eq/Newmarket/1/93 horse antiserum BRP and *equine influenza subtype 2 American-like strain A/eq/South Africa/4/03 horse antiserum BRP* are suitable for use as reference sera for the single radial haemolysis test.

2-3-2-2-2 Haemagglutination-inhibition test. Inactivate each serum by heating at 56 °C for 30 min. To 1 volume of each serum add 3 volumes of *phosphate buffered saline pH 7.4 R* and 4 volumes of a 250 g/L suspension of *light kaolin R* in the same buffer solution. Shake each mixture for 10 min. Centrifuge, collect the supernatant and mix with a concentrated suspension of chicken erythrocytes. Allow to stand at 37 °C for 60 min and centrifuge. The dilution of the serum obtained is 1:8. Perform tests on each serum using each antigen prepared from the strains used in the production of the vaccine. Using each diluted serum, prepare a series of 2-fold dilutions. To 0.025 mL of each of the latter dilutions add 0.025 mL of a suspension of antigen treated with *ether R* and containing 4 haemagglutinating units. Allow the mixture to stand for 30 min and add 0.05 mL of a suspension of chicken erythrocytes containing 2×10^7 erythrocytes/mL. Allow to stand for 1 h and note the last dilution of serum that still completely inhibits haemagglutination.

2-4 MANUFACTURER'S TESTS
2-4-1 Residual live virus
The test for residual live virus is carried out using method 2-4-1-1 or method 2-4-1-2, whichever is more sensitive. The quantity of inactivated virus harvest used is equivalent to not less than 10 doses of vaccine.

2-4-1-1 Test in cell cultures. Inoculate the vaccine into suitable cells; after incubation for 8 days, make a subculture. Incubate for a further 6-8 days. Harvest about 0.1 mL of the supernatant and examine for live virus by a haemagglutination test. If haemagglutination is found, carry out a further passage in cell culture and test for haemagglutination; the inactivated virus harvest complies with the test if no haemagglutination occurs.

2-4-1-2 Test in embryonated eggs. Inoculate 0.2 mL into the allantoic cavity of each of 10 embryonated eggs and incubate at 33-37 °C for 3-4 days. The test is invalid unless not fewer than 8 of the 10 embryos survive. Harvest 0.5 mL of the allantoic fluid from each surviving embryo and pool the fluids. Inoculate 0.2 mL of the pooled fluid into a further 10 embryonated eggs and incubate at 33-37 °C for 3-4 days. The test is invalid unless at least 8 of the 10 embryonated embryos survive. Harvest about 0.1 mL of the allantoic fluid from each surviving embryo and examine each individual harvest for live virus by a haemagglutination test. If haemagglutination is found for any of the fluids, carry out a further passage of that fluid in eggs and test for haemagglutination; the inactivated virus harvest complies with the test if no haemagglutination occurs.

2-4-2 Batch potency test
It is not necessary to carry out the potency test (section 3-4) for each batch of vaccine if it has been carried out using a batch of vaccine with a minimum potency. Where the test is not carried out, an alternative validated method is used, the criteria for acceptance being set with reference to a batch of vaccine that has given satisfactory results in the test(s) described under Potency. The following test may be used.

Use 5 guinea-pigs that do not have specific antibodies. Vaccinate each guinea-pig by the subcutaneous route with one dose of vaccine. 21 days later, collect blood samples and separate the serum. Carry out tests on the serum for specific antibodies by a suitable immunochemical method (*2.7.1*) such as single radial haemolysis or haemagglutination-inhibition, using reference sera to validate the test.

The vaccine complies with the test if the antibody titres are not significantly lower than those obtained in guinea-pigs with a reference batch of vaccine shown to have satisfactory potency in horses.

2-4-3 Bacterial endotoxins
For vaccines produced in eggs, the content of bacterial endotoxins is determined on the virus harvest to monitor production.

2-4-4 Haemagglutinin content
The content of haemagglutinin in the inactivated virus suspension, after purification and concentration where applicable, is determined by a suitable immunochemical method (*2.7.1*), such as single radial immunodiffusion, using a suitable haemagglutinin reference preparation; the inactivated virus suspension complies with the test if the content is shown to be within the limits shown to allow preparation of a satisfactory vaccine.

3 BATCH TESTS
3-1 Identification
In animals that do not have specific antibodies against equine influenza virus, the vaccine stimulates the production of such antibodies.

3-2 Bacteria and fungi
The vaccine, including where applicable the diluent supplied for reconstitution, complies with the test for sterility prescribed in the monograph *Vaccines for veterinary use (0062)*.

3-3 Residual live virus
Inoculate 0.2 mL of the vaccine into the allantoic cavity of each of 10 embryonated eggs and incubate at 33-37 °C for 3-4 days. The test is invalid unless at least 8 of the 10 embryos survive. Harvest 0.5 mL of the allantoic fluid from each surviving embryo and pool the fluids. Inoculate 0.2 mL of the pooled fluid into a further 10 embryonated eggs and incubate at 33-37 °C for 3-4 days. The test is invalid unless not fewer than 8 of the 10 embryos survive. Harvest about 0.1 mL of the allantoic fluid from each surviving embryo and examine each individual harvest for live virus by a haemagglutination test. If haemagglutination is found for any of the fluids, carry out for that fluid a further passage in eggs and test for haemagglutination; the vaccine complies with the test if no haemagglutination occurs.

3-4 Potency
The vaccine complies with the requirements of the test(s) mentioned under Immunogenicity (section 2-3-2) when administered by a recommended route and method.

Ph Eur

Feline Calicivirus Vaccine, Inactivated

(Feline Calicivirosis Vaccine (Inactivated), Ph Eur monograph 1101)

Ph Eur

1 DEFINITION
Feline calicivirosis vaccine (inactivated) is a preparation of one or more suitable strains of feline calicivirus inactivated while maintaining adequate immunogenic properties or of fractions of one or more strains of feline calicivirus with adequate immunogenic properties. This monograph applies to vaccines intended for the active immunisation of cats against feline calicivirosis.

2 PRODUCTION
2-1 PREPARATION OF THE VACCINE
The vaccine virus is grown in cell cultures. The virus harvest is inactivated; the virus may be disrupted and the fractions purified and concentrated. The vaccine may be adjuvanted.

2-2 SUBSTRATE FOR VIRUS PROPAGATION
2-2-1 Cell cultures
The cell cultures comply with the requirements for cell cultures for production of veterinary vaccines (5.2.4).

2-3 CHOICE OF VACCINE COMPOSITION
The vaccine is shown to be satisfactory with respect to safety (5.2.6) and efficacy (5.2.7) for the cats for which it is intended.

The following tests for safety (section 2-3-1) and immunogenicity (section 2-3-2) may be used during the demonstration of safety and efficacy.

2-3-1 Safety
Carry out the test for each route and method of administration to be recommended for vaccination. Use a batch of vaccine containing not less than the maximum potency that may be expected in a batch of vaccine.

For each test, use not fewer than 8 cats of the minimum age to be recommended for vaccination and that do not have antibodies against feline calicivirus. Administer to each cat 1 dose of the vaccine. If the schedule to be recommended requires a 2nd dose, administer 1 dose after an interval of at least 14 days after the last administration. Observe the cats at least daily for at least 14 days after the last administration.

The vaccine complies with the test if no cat shows abnormal local or systemic reactions or dies from causes attributable to the vaccine.

2-3-2 Immunogenicity
A test is carried out for each strain of feline calicivirus in the vaccine and for each route and method of administration to be recommended for vaccination, using in each case cats 8-12 weeks old. The vaccine administered to each cat is of minimum potency.

Use for the test not fewer than 20 cats that do not have antibodies against feline calicivirus. Vaccinate not fewer than 10 cats, according to the schedule to be recommended. Maintain not fewer than 10 cats as controls. Challenge each cat after 4 weeks by the intranasal route with a sufficient quantity of a suspension of virulent feline calicivirus. Observe the cats at least daily for 14 days after challenge. Collect nasal washings daily on days 2 to 14 to test for virus excretion. Note daily the body temperature and signs of disease using the scoring system shown below.

The test is not valid if during the observation period after challenge, fewer than 80 per cent of the control cats show notable signs of feline calicivirosis (hyperthermia, buccal ulcers, respiratory signs). The vaccine complies with the test if during the observation period after challenge, the score for the vaccinated cats is significantly lower than that for the controls.

Observed signs	Score
Death	10
Depressed state	2
Temperature ≥ 39.5 °C	1
Temperature ≤ 37 °C	2
Ulcer (nasal or oral)	
- small and few in number	1
- large and numerous	3
Nasal discharge	
- slight	1
- copious	2
Ocular discharge	1
Weight loss	2

Virus excretion (total number of days):

≤ 4 days	1
5-7 days	2
> 7 days	3

2-4 MANUFACTURER'S TESTS
2-4-1 Residual live virus
The test for residual live calicivirus is carried out using 2 passages in cell cultures of the same type as those used for preparation of the vaccine or in cell cultures shown to be at least as sensitive; the quantity of inactivated virus harvest used in the test is equivalent to not less than 25 doses of vaccine. The inactivated viral harvest complies with the test if no live virus is detected.

2-4-2 Batch potency test
It is not necessary to carry out the Potency test (section 3-4) for each batch of vaccine if it has been carried out using a batch of vaccine with a minimum potency. Where the test is not carried out, an alternative validated method is used, the criteria for acceptance being set with reference to a batch of vaccine that has given satisfactory results in the test described under Potency. The following test may be used.

Use for the test groups of 15 seronegative mice. Administer to each mouse half a dose of the vaccine and 7 days later, repeat the administration. After 21 days following the first injection, take blood samples and determine the level of antibodies against feline calicivirus by an immunofluorescence technique using pools of serum from groups of 3 mice. The vaccine complies with the test if the antibody levels are not significantly lower than those obtained with a batch of vaccine that has given satisfactory results in the test described under Potency.

3 BATCH TESTS
3-1 Identification
When injected into animals that do not have specific antibodies against feline calicivirus, the vaccine stimulates the formation of such antibodies.

3-2 Bacteria and fungi
The vaccine, including where applicable the diluent supplied for reconstitution, complies with the test for sterility prescribed in the monograph *Vaccines for veterinary use (0062)*.

3-3 Residual live virus
Carry out a test for residual live calicivirus using 10 doses of vaccine and 2 passages in cell cultures of the same type as those used for preparation of the vaccine or in cell cultures shown to be at least as sensitive. The vaccine complies with the test if no live virus is detected. If the vaccine contains an adjuvant that would interfere with the test, where possible separate the adjuvant from the liquid phase by a method that does not inactivate or otherwise interfere with detection of live virus.

3-4 Potency
The vaccine complies with the requirements of the test prescribed under Immunogenicity (section 2-3-2) when administered by a recommended route and method.

Feline Calicivirus Vaccine, Living

(Feline Calicivirosis Vaccine (Live),
Ph Eur monograph 1102)

Ph Eur _____

1 DEFINITION

Feline calicivirosis vaccine (live) is a preparation of one or more suitable strains of feline calicivirus. This monograph applies to vaccines intended for the active immunisation of cats against feline calicivirosis.

2 PRODUCTION

2-1 PREPARATION OF THE VACCINE

The vaccine virus is grown in cell cultures.

2-2 SUBSTRATE FOR VIRUS PROPAGATION

2-2-1 Cell cultures

The cell cultures comply with the requirements for cell cultures for production of veterinary vaccines (*5.2.4*).

2-3 CHOICE OF VACCINE VIRUS

The vaccine virus is shown to be satisfactory with respect to safety (*5.2.6*) and efficacy (*5.2.7*) for the cats for which it is intended.

The following tests for safety (section 2-3-1), increase in virulence (section 2-3-2) and immunogenicity (section 2-3-3) may be used during the demonstration of safety and efficacy.

2-3-1 Safety

Carry out the test for each route and method of administration to be recommended for vaccination.
Use vaccine virus at the least attenuated passage level that will be present in a batch of the vaccine.

For each test, use not fewer than 8 cats of the minimum age to be recommended for vaccination and that do not have antibodies against feline calicivirus. Administer to each cat a quantity of the vaccine virus equivalent to not less than 10 times the maximum virus titre likely to be contained in 1 dose of the vaccine. Observe the cats at least daily for at least 14 days.

The vaccine virus complies with the test if no cat shows abnormal local or systemic reactions, or dies from causes attributable to the vaccine virus.

2-3-2 Increase in virulence

Carry out the test according to general chapter *5.2.6* using cats that do not have antibodies against feline calicivirus.
If the properties of the vaccine virus allow sequential passage through 5 groups via natural spreading, this method may be used, otherwise passage as described below is carried out.

Administer to each cat of the 1st group by a route to be recommended a quantity of the vaccine virus that will allow recovery of virus for the passages described below.
Administer the virus by the route to be recommended for vaccination most likely to lead to reversion of virulence. After 5 days, remove the nasal mucus, tonsils and trachea of each cat. Mix, homogenise in 10 mL of buffered saline and allow the solids to settle. Administer the supernatant by the intranasal route to each cat of the next group. Carry out this passage operation 4 times; verify the presence of the virus at each passage. If the virus is not found at a passage level, repeat the passage by administration to a group of 10 animals.

If the 5th group of animals shows no evidence of an increase in virulence indicative of reversion during the observation period, further testing is not required. Otherwise, carry out an additional safety test and compare the clinical signs and any relevant parameters in a group of at least 8 animals receiving the material used for the first passage and another similar group receiving the virus at the final passage level.

The vaccine virus complies with the test if no indication of increased virulence of the virus recovered for the final passage compared with the material used for the first passage is observed. If virus is not recovered after an initial passage in 2 animals and a subsequent repeat passage in 10 animals, the vaccine virus also complies with the test.

2-3-3 Immunogenicity

A test is carried out for each strain of feline calicivirus in the vaccine, for each route and method of administration to be recommended for vaccination. The quantity of vaccine virus to be administered to each cat is not greater than the minimum virus titre to be stated on the label and the virus is at the most attenuated passage level that will be present in a batch of vaccine.

Use for the test not fewer than 20 cats, 8-12 weeks old, that do not have antibodies against feline calicivirus. Vaccinate not fewer than 10 cats, according to the schedule to be recommended. Maintain not fewer than 10 cats as controls. Challenge each cat after 4 weeks by the intranasal route with a sufficient quantity of a suspension of virulent feline calicivirus virus. Observe the cats at least daily for 14 days after challenge. Collect nasal washings daily on days 2 to 14 to test for virus excretion. Note daily the body temperature and signs of disease using the scoring system shown below.

The test is not valid if during the observation period after challenge, fewer than 80 per cent of the control cats show notable signs of feline calicivirosis (hyperthermia, buccal ulcers, respiratory signs).

The vaccine virus complies with the test if during the observation period after challenge, the score for the vaccinated cats is significantly lower than that for the controls.

Observed signs	Score
Death	10
Depressed state	2
Temperature $\geq 39.5\ °C$	1
Temperature $\leq 37\ °C$	2
Ulcer (nasal or oral)	
- small and few in number	1
- large and numerous	3
Nasal discharge	
- slight	1
- copious	2
Ocular discharge	1
Weight loss	2
Virus excretion (total number of days):	
≤ 4 days	1
5-7 days	2
> 7 days	3

3 BATCH TESTS

3-1 Identification

When neutralised by one or more monospecific antisera, the vaccine no longer infects susceptible cell cultures into which it is inoculated.

3-2 Bacteria and fungi

The vaccine, including where applicable the diluent supplied for reconstitution, complies with the test for sterility prescribed in the monograph *Vaccines for veterinary use (0062)*.

3-3 Mycoplasmas (*2.6.7*)

The vaccine complies with the test for mycoplasmas.

3-4 Extraneous agents

Neutralise the vaccine virus with one or more suitable monospecific antisera against feline calicivirus and inoculate into cell cultures known for their susceptibility to viruses pathogenic for the cat. Carry out at least 1 passage and maintain the cultures for 14 days. The vaccine complies with the test if no cytopathic effect develops and there is no sign of the presence of haemadsorbing agents.

3-5 Virus titre

Titrate the vaccine virus in suitable cell cultures at a temperature favourable to replication of the virus.

The vaccine complies with the test if one dose contains not less than the minimum virus titre stated on the label.

3-6 Potency

The vaccine complies with the requirements of the test prescribed under Immunogenicity (section 2-3-3) when administered by a recommended route and method. It is not necessary to carry out the potency test for each batch of the vaccine if it has been carried out on a representative batch using a vaccinating dose containing not more than the minimum virus titre stated on the label.

———————————————————— Ph Eur

Feline Chlamydiosis Vaccine (Inactivated)

(Ph. Eur. monograph 2324)

Ph Eur _____

1 DEFINITION

Feline chlamydiosis vaccine (inactivated) is a preparation of one or more suitable strains of *Chlamydophila felis*, which have been inactivated by a suitable method. This monograph applies to vaccines intended for administration to cats for active immunisation.

2 PRODUCTION

2-1 PREPARATION OF THE VACCINE

The seed material is cultured in embryonated hens' eggs from a healthy flock or in suitable cell cultures (*5.2.4*). If the vaccine contains more than one strain of bacterium, the different strains are grown and harvested separately. The bacterial harvests are inactivated using suitable and validated methods. The suspensions may be treated to fragment the micro-organisms and the fragments may be purified and concentrated. The vaccine may contain adjuvants.

2-2 CHOICE OF VACCINE COMPOSITION

The vaccine is shown to be satisfactory with respect to safety (*5.2.6*) and efficacy (*5.2.7*) in cats for which it is intended.

The following tests for safety (section 2-2-1) and immunogenicity (section 2-2-2) may be used during the demonstration of safety and efficacy.

2-2-1 Safety

Carry out the test for each route and method of administration to be recommended for vaccination. Use a batch of vaccine containing not less than the maximum potency that may be expected in a batch of vaccine.

For each test, use not fewer than 8 cats of the minimum age to be recommended for vaccination and that do not have antibodies against *C. felis*. Administer to each cat 1 dose of

the vaccine. If the schedule to be recommended requires a 2nd dose, administer 1 dose after an interval of at least 14 days.

Observe the cats at least daily for at least 14 days after the last administration.

The vaccine complies with the test if no cat shows abnormal local or systemic reactions or dies from causes attributable to the vaccine.

2-2-2 Immunogenicity

Carry out the test for each route and method of administration to be recommended for vaccination, using in each case cats not older than the minimum age to be recommended for vaccination. The vaccine to be administered to each cat is of minimum potency.

Vaccinate 10 cats that are free from antibodies against *C. felis* and keep 10 cats as controls. Not later than 4 weeks after the last administration of vaccine, administer by a suitable route to each cat a quantity of a virulent strain of *C. felis* sufficient to produce in susceptible cats typical signs of disease such as conjunctivitis and nasal discharge. Observe the cats for 28 days. Where reduction of chlamydophila excretion is to be claimed, collect nasal washings and/or conjunctival swabs on days 7, 14, 17, 21, 24 and 28 after challenge to test for chlamydophila excretion. The duration of excretion for the vaccinated animals is significantly lower than for the controls. Note daily the body temperature and signs of disease using a suitable scoring system. The vaccine complies with the test if the score for the vaccinated cats is significantly lower than that for the controls.

2-3 MANUFACTURER'S TESTS

2-3-1 Batch potency test

It is not necessary to carry out the potency test (section 3-4) for each batch of the vaccine if it has been carried out using a batch of vaccine with a minimum potency. Where the test is not carried out on a batch, an alternative validated method is used, the criteria for acceptance being set with reference to a batch of vaccine that has given satisfactory results in the potency test (section 3-4). The following test may be used.

Inject a suitable dose by a suitable route into each of 5 seronegative cats or another suitable species. Where the schedule stated on the label requires a booster injection to be given, a booster vaccination may also be given in this test provided it has been demonstrated that this will still provide a suitably sensitive test system. Before the vaccination and at a given interval usually within the range of 14-21 days after the last injection, collect blood from each animal and prepare serum samples. Determine individually for each serum the titre of antibodies against each strain stated on the label, using a suitable test such as enzyme-linked immunosorbent assay (*2.7.1*). The vaccine complies with the test if the antibody levels are not significantly lower than those obtained for a batch that has given satisfactory results in the potency test (section 3-4).

2-3-2 Bacterial endotoxins

A test for bacterial endotoxins (*2.6.14*) is carried out on the final lot or, where the nature of the adjuvant prevents performance of a satisfactory test, on the bulk antigen or the mixture of bulk antigens immediately before addition of the adjuvant. The maximum acceptable amount of bacterial endotoxins is that found for a batch of vaccine that has been shown to be satisfactory in the safety test (section 2-2-1). The method chosen for determining the maximum acceptable amount of bacterial endotoxins is subsequently used for the testing of each batch.

3 BATCH TESTS

3-1 Identification

When injected into seronegative animals, the vaccine stimulates the production of antibodies against each of the strains of *C. felis* present in the vaccine.

3-2 Residual live chlamydophila

The vaccine complies with a suitable test for residual live chlamydophila.

3-3 Bacteria and fungi

The vaccine, including where applicable the diluent supplied for reconstitution, complies with the test for sterility prescribed in the monograph *Vaccines for veterinary use (0062)*.

3-4 Potency

The vaccine complies with the test for immunogenicity (section 2-2-2).

_____ *Ph Eur*

Feline Infectious Enteritis Vaccine, Inactivated

Feline Panleucopenia Vaccine, Inactivated

(Feline Infectious Enteritis (Feline Panleucopenia) Vaccine (Inactivated), Ph Eur monograph 0794)

Ph Eur _____

1 DEFINITION

Feline infectious enteritis (feline panleucopenia) vaccine (inactivated) is a preparation of a suitable strain of feline panleucopenia virus or canine parvovirus inactivated while maintaining adequate immunogenic properties. This monograph applies to vaccines intended for the active immunisation of cats against feline infectious enteritis (feline panleucopenia).

2 PRODUCTION

2-1 PREPARATION OF THE VACCINE

The vaccine virus is grown in cell cultures. The virus harvest is inactivated. The vaccine may be adjuvanted.

2-2 SUBSTRATE FOR VIRUS PROPAGATION

2-2-1 Cell cultures

The cell cultures comply with the requirements for cell cultures for production of veterinary vaccines (*5.2.4*).

2-3 CHOICE OF VACCINE COMPOSITION

The vaccine is shown to be satisfactory with respect to safety (*5.2.6*) and efficacy (*5.2.7*) for the cats for which it is intended.

The following tests for safety (section 2-3-1) and immunogenicity (section 2-3-2) may be used during the demonstration of safety and efficacy.

2-3-1 Safety

Carry out the test for each route and method of administration to be recommended for vaccination. Use a batch of vaccine containing not less than the maximum potency that may be expected in a batch of vaccine.

For each test, use not fewer than 8 cats of the minimum age to be recommended for vaccination and that do not have antibodies against feline panleucopenia virus. Administer to each cat 1 dose of the vaccine. If the schedule to be recommended requires a 2nd dose, administer 1 dose after an interval of at least 14 days. Observe the cats at least daily for at least 14 days after the last administration.

The vaccine complies with the test if no cat shows abnormal local or systemic reactions or dies from causes attributable to the vaccine.

2-3-2 Immunogenicity

A test is carried out for each route and method of administration to be recommended for vaccination, using in each case cats 8-12 weeks old. The vaccine administered to each cat is of minimum potency.

Use for the test not fewer than 10 cats that do not have antibodies against feline panleucopenia virus and canine parvovirus. Vaccinate not fewer than 5 cats, according to the schedule to be recommended. Maintain not fewer than 5 cats as controls. Carry out leucocyte counts 8 days and 4 days before challenge and calculate the mean of the 2 counts to serve as the initial value. Challenge each cat after 20-22 days by the intraperitoneal route with a sufficient quantity of a suspension of virulent feline panleucopenia virus. Observe the cats at least daily for 14 days after challenge. Carry out leucocyte counts on the 4th, 6th, 8th and 10th days after challenge.

The test is not valid if during the observation period after challenge, fewer than 100 per cent of the control cats show on not fewer than one occasion a diminution in the number of leucocytes of at least 75 per cent of the initial value or die from panleucopenia. The vaccine complies with the test if during the observation period after challenge, all the vaccinated cats survive and show no signs of disease nor leucopenia; that is to say, the diminution in the number of leucocytes does not exceed, in any of the 4 counts, 50 per cent of the initial value.

2-4 MANUFACTURER'S TESTS

2-4-1 Residual live virus

The test for residual live virus is carried out using a quantity of inactivated virus harvest equivalent to not less than 100 doses of the vaccine by a validated method such as the following: inoculate into suitable non-confluent cells and after incubation for 8 days, make a subculture using trypsinised cells. After incubation for a further 8 days, examine the cultures for residual live parvovirus by an immunofluorescence test. The immunofluorescence test may be supplemented by a haemagglutination test or other suitable tests on the supernatant of the cell cultures. The inactivated viral harvest complies with the test if no live virus is detected.

2-4-2 Batch potency test

For routine testing of batches of vaccine, a test based on production of haemagglutination-inhibiting antibodies in guinea-pigs may be used instead of test 3-3-1 or 3-3-2 described under Potency if a satisfactory correlation with the test for immunogenicity has been established.

3 BATCH TESTS

3-1 Identification

When injected into animals, the vaccine stimulates the production of antibodies against the parvovirus present in the vaccine.

3-2 Bacteria and fungi

The vaccine, including where applicable the diluent supplied for reconstitution, complies with the test for sterility prescribed in the monograph *Vaccines for veterinary use (0062)*.

3-3 Potency

Carry out test 3-3-1 or test 3-3-2.

3-3-1 Test in cats for haemagglutination-inhibiting antibodies

Use for the test not fewer than 4 cats, 8-12 weeks old, that do not have antibodies against feline panleucopenia virus and canine parvovirus. Vaccinate not fewer than 2 cats with 1 dose of the vaccine. Maintain not fewer than 2 cats as controls. After 21 days, draw a blood sample from each cat and separate the serum from each sample. Inactivate each serum by heating at 56 °C for 30 min. To 1 volume of each serum add 9 volumes of a 200 g/L suspension of *light kaolin R* in *phosphate buffered saline pH 7.4 R*. Shake each mixture for 20 min. Centrifuge, collect the supernatant and mix with 1 volume of a concentrated suspension of pig erythrocytes. Allow to stand at 4 °C for 60 min and centrifuge. The dilution of the serum obtained is 1:10. Using each serum, prepare a series of twofold dilutions.

To 0.025 mL of each of the latter dilutions add 0.025 mL of a suspension of canine parvovirus or feline panleucopenia virus antigen containing 4 haemagglutinating units. Allow to stand at 37 °C for 30 min and add 0.05 mL of a suspension of pig erythrocytes containing 30×10^{6} cells per millilitre. Allow to stand at 4 °C for 90 min and note the last dilution of serum that still completely inhibits haemagglutination.

The test is not valid if either control cat develops antibodies against canine parvovirus or feline panleucopenia virus. The vaccine complies with the test if both vaccinated cats have developed titres of at least 1:20.

3-3-2 Test in cats for virus-neutralising antibodies

Use for the test not fewer than 2 cats, 8-12 weeks old, that have antibody titres less than $4ND_{50}$ per 0.1 mL of serum measured by the method described below. Vaccinate each cat according to the recommended schedule. 14 days after vaccination, examine the serum of each cat as follows. Heat the serum at 56 °C for 30 min and prepare serial dilutions using a medium suitable for feline cells. Add to each dilution an equal volume of a virus suspension containing an amount of virus such that when the volume of serum-virus mixture appropriate for the assay system is inoculated into cell cultures, each culture receives approximately 10^{4} $CCID_{50}$. Incubate the mixtures at 37 °C for 1 h and inoculate 4 feline cell cultures with a suitable volume of each mixture. Incubate the cell cultures at 37 °C for 7 days, passage and incubate for a further 7 days. Examine the cultures for evidence of specific cytopathic effects and calculate the antibody titre.

The vaccine complies with the test if the mean titre is not less than 32 ND_{50} per 0.1 mL of serum. If one cat fails to respond, repeat the test using 2 more cats and calculate the result as the mean of the titres obtained from all of the 3 cats that have responded.

Ph Eur

Feline Infectious Enteritis Vaccine, Living

Feline Panleucopenia Vaccine, Living

(Feline Infectious Enteritis (Feline Panleucopenia) Vaccine (Live), Ph Eur monograph 0251)

Ph Eur

1 DEFINITION

Feline infectious enteritis (feline panleucopenia) vaccine (live) is a preparation of a suitable strain of feline panleucopenia virus. This monograph applies to vaccines intended for the active immunisation of cats against feline infectious enteritis (feline panleucopenia).

2 PRODUCTION
2-1 PREPARATION OF THE VACCINE
The vaccine virus is grown in cell cultures.

2-2 SUBSTRATE FOR VIRUS PROPAGATION
2-2-1 Cell cultures
The cell cultures comply with the requirements for cell cultures for production of veterinary vaccines (*5.2.4*).

2-3 CHOICE OF VACCINE VIRUS
The vaccine virus is shown to be satisfactory with respect to safety (*5.2.6*) and efficacy (*5.2.7*) for the cats for which it is intended, including safety for pregnant queens if the vaccine may be used in such queens. If the virus is excreted in the faeces, the effect in pregnant queens must be documented.

The following tests for safety (section 2-3-1), increase in virulence (section 2-3-2) and immunogenicity (section 2-3-3) may be used during the demonstration of safety and efficacy.

2-3-1 Safety
Carry out the test for each route and method of administration to be recommended for vaccination. Use vaccine virus at the least attenuated passage level that will be present in a batch of the vaccine.

2-3-1-1 General safety. For each test, use not fewer than 5 cats of the minimum age to be recommended for vaccination and that do not have antibodies against feline panleucopenia virus and canine parvovirus. Make counts of leucocytes in circulating blood on days 8 and 4 before injection of the vaccine virus and calculate the mean of the 2 counts to serve as the initial value. Administer to each cat a quantity of the vaccine virus equivalent to not less than 10 times the maximum virus titre likely to be contained in 1 dose of the vaccine. Observe the cats at least daily for at least 14 days. Make leucocyte counts on the 4th, 6th, 8th and 10th days after inoculation.

The vaccine virus complies with the test if no cat shows abnormal local or systemic reactions, signs of disease or dies from causes attributable to the vaccine virus and if, for each cat and each blood count, the number of leucocytes is not less than 50 per cent of the initial value.

2-3-1-2 Safety in pregnant queens. If the vaccine is intended for use or may be used in pregnant queens, use not fewer than 5 queens per group, at the stage of pregnancy to be recommended or at a range of stages of pregnancy according to the schedule to be recommended. Administer to each queen a quantity of vaccine virus at least equivalent to the maximum virus titre likely to be contained in 1 dose of the vaccine. Observe the queens at least daily until 1 day after parturition and observe their kittens until at least the age of 3 weeks.

The vaccine virus complies with the test if no queen shows abnormal local or systemic reactions, signs of disease or dies from causes attributable to the vaccine virus and if no adverse effects on the pregnancy or the offspring, such as foetal resorption or ataxia in the kittens, are noted.

2-3-2 Increase in virulence
Carry out the test according to general chapter 5.2.6 using cats of the minimum age to be recommended for vaccination and that do not have antibodies against feline panleucopenia virus and canine parvovirus. If the properties of the vaccine virus allow sequential passage through 5 groups via natural spreading, this method may be used, otherwise passage as described below is carried out.

Administer to each cat of the 1st group by a route to be recommended a quantity of the vaccine virus that will allow recovery of virus for the passages described below. Collect the faeces from each cat from the 2nd to the 10th day after administration of the virus, check them for the presence of the virus and pool the faeces containing virus. Administer 1 mL of the suspension of pooled faeces by either the oral or the intranasal route to each cat of the next group. Carry out this passage operation not fewer than 4 times; verify the presence of the virus at each passage. If the virus is not found at a passage level, repeat the passage by administration to a group of 10 animals.

If the 5th group of animals shows no evidence of an increase in virulence indicative of reversion during the observation period, further testing is not required. Otherwise, carry out an additional safety test and compare the clinical signs and any relevant parameters (count of white blood cells, results of histological examination of the thymus and titre of excreted virus) in a group of at least 8 animals receiving the material used for the 1st passage and another similar group receiving the virus at the final passage level.

The vaccine virus complies with the test if no cat dies or shows signs attributable to the vaccine virus and no indication of increasing virulence of the virus recovered for the final passage compared with the material used for the 1st passage is observed. Account is taken, notably, of the count of white blood cells, of results of histological examination of the thymus and of the titre of excreted virus. If virus is not recovered after an initial passage in 2 animals and a subsequent repeat passage in 10 animals, the vaccine virus also complies with the test.

2-3-3 Immunogenicity

A test is carried out for each route and method of administration to be recommended for vaccination.
The quantity of vaccine virus to be administered to each cat is not greater than the minimum virus titre to be stated on the label and the virus is at the most attenuated passage level that will be present in a batch of vaccine.

Use for the test not fewer than 10 cats, 8-12 weeks old, that do not have antibodies against feline panleucopenia virus and canine parvovirus. Vaccinate not fewer than 5 cats, according to the schedule to be recommended. Maintain not fewer than 5 cats as controls. Carry out leucocyte counts 8 days and 4 days before challenge and calculate the mean of the 2 counts to serve as the initial value. Challenge each cat after 20-22 days by the intraperitoneal route with a sufficient quantity of a suspension of virulent feline panleucopenia virus. Observe the cats at least daily for 14 days after challenge. Carry out leucocyte counts on the 4th, 6th, 8th and 10th days after challenge.

The test is not valid if during the observation period after challenge, fewer than 100 per cent of the control cats show, on fewer than one occasion, a diminution in the number of leucocytes of at least 75 per cent of the initial value or die from feline panleucopenia. The vaccine virus complies with the test if during the observation period after challenge, all the vaccinated cats survive and show no signs of disease nor leucopenia; that is to say, the diminution in the number of leucocytes does not exceed, in any of the 4 counts, 50 per cent of the initial value.

3 BATCH TESTS
3-1 Identification

Carry out replication of the vaccine virus in a susceptible cell line in a substrate suitable for a fluorescent antibody test or peroxidase test. Prepare suitable controls. Test a proportion of the cells with monoclonal antibodies specific for feline panleucopenia virus and a proportion with monoclonal antibodies specific for canine parvovirus. Feline panleucopenia virus is detected but no canine parvovirus is detected in the cells inoculated with the vaccine.

3-2 Bacteria and fungi

The vaccine, including where applicable the diluent supplied for reconstitution, complies with the test for sterility prescribed in the monograph *Vaccines for veterinary use (0062)*.

3-3 Mycoplasmas *(2.6.7)*

The vaccine complies with the test for mycoplasmas.

3-4 Extraneous agents

Neutralise the vaccine virus with a suitable monospecific antiserum against feline panleucopenia virus and inoculate into cell cultures known for their susceptibility to viruses pathogenic for the cat. Carry out at least 1 passage and maintain the cultures for 14 days. The vaccine complies with the test if no cytopathic effect develops and there is no sign of the presence of haemadsorbing agents.

3-5 Virus titre

Titrate the vaccine virus in suitable cell cultures. The vaccine complies with the test if one dose contains not less than the minimum virus titre stated on the label.

3-6 Potency

The vaccine complies with the requirements of the test prescribed under Immunogenicity (section 2-3-3) when administered by a recommended route and method. It is not necessary to carry out the potency test for each batch of the vaccine if it has been carried out on a representative batch using a vaccinating dose containing not more than the minimum virus titre stated on the label.

Ph Eur

Feline Leukaemia Vaccine, Inactivated

(Feline Leukaemia Vaccine (Inactivated), Ph Eur monograph 1321)

Ph Eur

1 DEFINITION

Feline leukaemia vaccine (inactivated) is a preparation of immunogens from a suitable strain of feline leukaemia virus. This monograph applies to vaccines intended for the active immunisation of cats against feline leukaemia.

2 PRODUCTION
2-1 PREPARATION OF THE VACCINE

The immunogens consist either of a suitable strain of feline leukaemia virus inactivated while maintaining adequate immunogenic properties or of a fraction of the virus with adequate immunogenic properties; the immunogenic fraction may be produced by recombinant DNA technology.
The vaccine may be adjuvanted.

2-2 CHOICE OF VACCINE COMPOSITION

The vaccine is shown to be satisfactory with respect to safety *(5.2.6)* and efficacy *(5.2.7)* for the cats for which it is intended.

The following tests for safety (section 2-2-1) and immunogenicity (section 2-2-2) may be used during the demonstration of safety and efficacy.

2-2-1 Safety

Carry out the test for each route and method of administration to be recommended for vaccination. Use a batch of vaccine containing not less than the maximum potency that may be expected in a batch of vaccine.

2-2-1-1 General safety and immunosuppression. Use for the test not fewer than 15 cats of the minimum age to be recommended and that do not have antibodies against gp 70 antigen of feline leukaemia virus nor display viraemia or antigenaemia at the time of the test; absence of antibodies and antigen is demonstrated by enzyme-linked immunosorbent assay (*2.7.1*). Administer to each of not fewer than 10 cats 1 dose of the vaccine. If the schedule to be recommended requires a 2nd dose, administer 1 dose after an interval of at least 14 days. Maintain not fewer than 5 cats as controls. Record the body temperature of each cat on the day before each vaccination, at the time of vaccination, 4 h and 8 h later, and once per day during the 4 following days. Observe the cats at least daily for not less than 4 weeks after the last vaccination. 1, 2 and 4 weeks after the last vaccination, submit the cats to suitable tests for evidence of an immunosuppressive effect.

The vaccine complies with the test if no cat shows abnormal local or systemic reactions or dies from causes attributable to the vaccine and if no significant difference is observed in vaccinated cats compared with controls regarding immunosuppressive effect.

2-2-2 Immunogenicity

A test is carried out for each route and method of administration to be recommended, using in each case cats of the minimum age to be recommended for vaccination. The vaccine administered to each cat is of minimum potency.

Use for the test not fewer than 25 cats that do not have antibodies against the antigens of feline leukaemia virus and against the feline oncogene membrane antigen (anti-FOCMA antibodies), and showing no viraemia or antigenaemia at the time of the test. Vaccinate not fewer than 15 cats according to the schedule to be recommended. Maintain not fewer than 10 cats as controls. Challenge each cat after 14 days by the peritoneal or oronasal route, on one or several occasions, with a sufficient quantity of suspension of an epidemiologically relevant virulent strain of feline leukaemia virus, consisting predominantly of type A virus. Observe the cats at least daily for 15 weeks and, from the 3rd week onwards, test each week for viraemia or antigenaemia (p27 protein) by suitable methods such as immunofluorescence on circulating leucocytes or enzyme-linked immunosorbent assay. A cat is considered persistently infected if it shows positive viraemia or antigenaemia for 3 consecutive weeks or on 5 occasions, consecutively or not, between the 3rd and the 15th week.

The test is not valid if during the observation period after challenge, fewer than 80 per cent of the control cats show persistant viraemia or antigenaemia. The vaccine complies with the test if during the observation period after challenge, not fewer than 80 per cent of the vaccinated cats show no persistent infection.

2-3 IN-PROCESS CONTROL TESTS

During production, suitable immunochemical tests are carried out for the evaluation of the quality and purity of the viral antigens included in the vaccine composition. The values found are within the limits approved for the particular vaccine.

2-4 MANUFACTURER'S TESTS

2-4-1 Residual live virus

Where applicable, the test for residual live virus is carried out using a quantity of inactivated virus harvest equivalent to not less than 25 doses of vaccine and 2 passages in the same type of cell cultures as used for the production of the vaccine or in cell cultures shown to be at least as sensitive. The inactivated viral harvest complies with the test if no live virus is detected.

2-4-2 Batch potency test

It is not necessary to carry out the Potency test (section 3-4) for each batch of vaccine if it has been carried out using a batch of vaccine with a minimum potency. Where the test is not carried out, an alternative validated method is used, the criteria for acceptance being set with reference to a batch of vaccine that has given satisfactory results in the test described under Potency.

2-4-3 Bacterial endotoxins

For vaccines produced by recombinant DNA technology with a bacterial host cell such as *Escherichia coli*, a test for bacterial endotoxins (*2.6.14*) is carried out on each final lot or, where the nature of the adjuvant prevents performance of a satisfactory test, on the antigen immediately before addition of the adjuvant. The value found is within the limit approved for the particular vaccine and which has been shown to be safe for cats.

3 BATCH TESTS

3-1 Identification

When injected into healthy cats that do not have specific antibodies against the antigen or antigens stated on the label, the vaccine stimulates the production of such antibodies.

3-2 Bacteria and fungi

The vaccine, including where applicable the diluent supplied for reconstitution, complies with the test for sterility prescribed in the monograph *Vaccines for veterinary use (0062)*.

3-3 Residual live virus

If the vaccine contains inactivated virus, carry out a test for residual live feline leukaemia virus by making 2 passages on susceptible cell cultures. The vaccine complies with the test if no virus is detected. If the vaccine contains an adjuvant, if possible separate the adjuvant from the liquid phase by a method that does not inactivate the virus nor interfere in any other way with the detection of virus.

3-4 Potency

The vaccine complies with the requirements of the test prescribed under Immunogenicity (section 2-2-2) when administered by a recommended route and method.

_____ *Ph Eur*

Feline Viral Rhinotracheitis Vaccine, Inactivated

(Feline Viral Rhinotracheitis Vaccine (Inactivated), Ph Eur monograph 1207)

Ph Eur _____

1 DEFINITION

Feline viral rhinotracheitis vaccine (inactivated) is a preparation of a suitable strain of feline rhinotracheitis virus (feline herpesvirus 1), inactivated while maintaining adequate immunogenic properties, or of an inactivated fraction of the virus having adequate immunogenic properties. This monograph applies to vaccines intended for the active immunisation of cats against feline viral rhinotracheitis.

2 PRODUCTION

2-1 PREPARATION OF THE VACCINE

The vaccine virus is grown in cell cultures. The virus harvest is inactivated; the virus may be disrupted and the fractions purified and concentrated. The vaccine may be adjuvanted.

2-2 SUBSTRATE FOR VIRUS PROPAGATION

2-2-1 Cell cultures

The cell cultures comply with the requirements for cell cultures for production of veterinary vaccines (5.2.4).

2-3 CHOICE OF VACCINE COMPOSITION

The vaccine is shown to be satisfactory with respect to safety (5.2.6) and efficacy (5.2.7) for the cats for which it is intended.

The following tests for safety (section 2-3-1) and immunogenicity (section 2-3-2) may be used during the demonstration of safety and efficacy.

2-3-1 Safety

Carry out the test for each route and method of administration to be recommended for vaccination. Use a batch of vaccine containing not less than the maximum potency that may be expected in a batch of vaccine.

For each test, use not fewer than 8 cats of the minimum age to be recommended for vaccination and that do not have antibodies against feline herpesvirus 1 or against a fraction of the virus. Administer to each cat 1 dose of the vaccine.

If the schedule to be recommended requires a 2nd dose, administer 1 dose after an interval of at least 14 days after the last administration. Observe the cats at least daily for at least 14 days after the last administration. The vaccine complies with the test if no cat shows abnormal local or systemic reactions or dies from causes attributable to the vaccine.

2-3-2 Immunogenicity

A test is carried out for each route and method of administration to be recommended for vaccination, using in each case cats 8-12 weeks old. The vaccine administered to each cat is of minimum potency.

Use for the test not fewer than 20 cats that do not have antibodies against feline herpesvirus 1 or against a fraction of the virus. Vaccinate not fewer than 10 cats, according to the schedule to be recommended. Maintain not fewer than 10 cats as controls. Challenge each cat after 4 weeks by the intranasal route with a quantity of a suspension of virulent feline herpesvirus 1 sufficient to produce typical signs of the disease such as fever, nasal discharge and cough in a cat that does not have antibodies against feline herpesvirus 1 or a fraction of the virus. Observe the cats at least daily for 14 days after challenge. Collect nasal washings daily on days 2 to 14 after challenge to test for virus excretion. Note daily the body temperature and signs of disease using the scoring system shown below.

The vaccine complies with the test if the score for the vaccinated cats is significantly lower than that for the controls.

Sign	Score
Death	10
Depressed state	2
Temperature:	
39.5 °C - 40.0 °C	1
$\geq$ 40.0 °C	2
$\leq$ 37.0 °C	3

Glossitis	3
Nasal discharge, slight	1
Nasal discharge, copious	2
Cough	2
Sneezing	1
Sneezing, paroxysmal	2
Ocular discharge, slight	1
Ocular discharge, serious	2
Conjunctivitis	2
Weight loss $\geq$ 5.0 per cent	5
Virus excretion (total number of days):	
$\leq$ 4 days	1
5-7 days	2
> 7 days	3

2-4 MANUFACTURER'S TESTS

2-4-1 Residual live virus

The test for residual live virus is carried out using 2 passages in cell cultures of the same type as those used for preparation of the vaccine or in cell cultures shown to be at least as sensitive; the quantity of inactivated virus harvest used in the test is equivalent to not less than 25 doses of vaccine.
The inactivated viral harvest complies with the test if no live virus is detected.

2-4-2 Batch potency test

It is not necessary to carry out the Potency test (section 3-4) for each batch of vaccine if it has been carried out using a batch of vaccine with a minimum potency. Where the test is not carried out, an alternative validated method is used, the criteria for acceptance being set with reference to a batch of vaccine that has given satisfactory results in the test described under Potency. The following test may be used.

Use for the test a group of 15 seronegative mice. Administer to each mouse half a dose of the vaccine and, 7 days later, repeat the administration. 21 days after the first injection, take blood samples and determine the level of antibodies against feline herpesvirus 1 by a suitable immunochemical method (2.7.1), such as an immunofluorescence technique using pools of serum from groups of 3 mice. The vaccine complies with the test if the antibody levels are not significantly lower than those obtained with a batch of vaccine that has given satisfactory results in the test described under Potency.

3 BATCH TESTS

3-1 Identification

When administered to animals that do not have specific antibodies against feline herpesvirus 1 or against the fraction of the virus used to produce the vaccine, the vaccine stimulates the production of such antibodies.

3-2 Bacteria and fungi

The vaccine, including where applicable the diluent supplied for reconstitution, complies with the test for sterility prescribed in the monograph *Vaccines for veterinary use (0062)*.

3-3 Residual live virus

Carry out a test for residual live feline herpesvirus 1 using 10 doses of vaccine and 2 passages in cell cultures of the same type as those used for preparation of the vaccine, or in other suitably sensitive cell cultures. The vaccine complies with the test if no live virus is detected. If the vaccine contains an adjuvant that interferes with the test, where possible separate the adjuvant from the liquid phase by a method that does not inactivate or otherwise interfere with detection of live virus.

3-4 Potency

The vaccine complies with the requirements of the test prescribed under Immunogenicity (section 2-3-2) when administered by a recommended route and method.

_____ _Ph Eur_

Feline Viral Rhinotracheitis Vaccine, Living

(Feline Viral Rhinotracheitis Vaccine (Live),
Ph Eur monograph 1206)

Ph Eur _____

1 DEFINITION

Feline viral rhinotracheitis vaccine (live) is a preparation of a suitable strain of feline rhinotracheitis virus (feline herpesvirus 1). This monograph applies to vaccines intended for the active immunisation of cats against feline viral rhinotracheitis.

2 PRODUCTION
2-1 PREPARATION OF THE VACCINE

The vaccine virus is grown in cell cultures.

2-2 SUBSTRATE FOR VIRUS PROPAGATION
2-2-1 Cell cultures

The cell cultures comply with the requirements for cell cultures for production of veterinary vaccines (5.2.4).

2-3 CHOICE OF VACCINE VIRUS

The vaccine virus is shown to be satisfactory with respect to safety (5.2.6) and efficacy (5.2.7) for the cats for which it is intended.

The following tests for safety (section 2-3-1), increase in virulence (section 2-3-2) and immunogenicity (section 2-3-3) may be used during the demonstration of safety and efficacy.

2-3-1 Safety

Carry out the test for each route and method of administration to be recommended for vaccination. Use vaccine virus at the least attenuated passage level that will be present in a batch of the vaccine.

For each test, use not fewer than 8 cats of the minimum age to be recommended for vaccination and that do not have antibodies against feline herpesvirus 1. Administer to each cat a quantity of the vaccine virus equivalent to not less than 10 times the maximum virus titre likely to be contained in 1 dose of the vaccine. Observe the cats at least daily for at least 14 days.

The vaccine virus complies with the test if no cat shows abnormal local or systemic reactions or signs of disease, or dies from causes attributable to the vaccine virus.

2-3-2 Increase in virulence

Carry out the test according to general chapter 5.2.6 using cats that do not have antibodies against feline herpesvirus 1. If the properties of the vaccine virus allow sequential passage through 5 groups via natural spreading, this method may be used, otherwise passage as described below is carried out.

Administer to each cat of the 1st group by a route to be recommended a quantity of the vaccine virus that will allow recovery of virus for the passages described below. Administer the virus by the route to be recommended for vaccination most likely to lead to reversion of virulence. After 2-4 days, remove the nasal mucus, tonsils and local lymphatic ganglia and the trachea of each cat. Mix, homogenise in 10 mL of buffered saline and allow the solids

to settle. Administer 1 mL of the supernatant by the intranasal route to each cat of the next group. Carry out this passage operation not fewer than 4 times; verify the presence of the virus at each passage. If the virus is not found at a passage level, repeat the passage by administration to a group of 10 animals.

If the 5th group of animals shows no evidence of an increase in virulence indicative of reversion during the observation period, further testing is not required. Otherwise, carry out an additional safety test and compare the clinical signs and any relevant parameters in a group of at least 8 animals receiving the material used for the first passage and another similar group receiving the virus at the final passage level.

The vaccine virus complies with the test if no indication of increased virulence of the virus recovered for the final passage compared with the material used for the first passage is observed. If virus is not recovered after an initial passage in 2 animals and a subsequent repeat passage in 10 animals, the vaccine virus also complies with the test.

2-3-3 Immunogenicity

A test is carried out for each route and method of administration to be recommended for vaccination.
The quantity of vaccine virus to be administered to each cat is not greater than the minimum virus titre to be stated on the label and the virus is at the most attenuated passage level that will be present in a batch of vaccine.

Use for the test not fewer than 20 cats, 8-12 weeks old, that do not have antibodies against feline herpesvirus 1. Vaccinate not fewer than 10 cats, according to the schedule to be recommended. Maintain not fewer than 10 cats as controls. Challenge each cat after 4 weeks by the intranasal route with a quantity of a suspension of virulent feline herpesvirus 1 sufficient to cause typical signs of disease such as fever, nasal discharge and cough. Observe the cats at least daily for 14 days after challenge. Collect nasal washings daily on days 2 to 14 after challenge to test for virus excretion. Note daily the body temperature and signs of disease using the scoring system shown below.

The vaccine virus complies with the test if, during the observation period after challenge, the score for the vaccinated cats is significantly lower than that for the controls.

Sign	Score
Death	10
Depressed state	2
Temperature:	
39.5 °C - 40.0 °C	1
$\geq$ 40.0 °C	2
$\leq$ 37.0 °C	3
Glossitis	3
Nasal discharge, slight	1
Nasal discharge, copious	2
Cough	2
Sneezing	1
Sneezing, paroxysmal	2
Ocular discharge, slight	1
Ocular discharge, serious	2
Conjunctivitis	2
Weight loss $\geq$ 5.0 per cent	5
Virus excretion (total number of days):	
$\leq$ 4 days	1
5-7 days	2
> 7 days	3

3 BATCH TESTS
3-1 Identification
When mixed with a monospecific antiserum, the vaccine no longer infects susceptible cell cultures into which it is inoculated.

3-2 Bacteria and fungi
The vaccine, including where applicable the diluent supplied for reconstitution, complies with the test for sterility prescribed in the monograph *Vaccines for veterinary use (0062)*.

3-3 Mycoplasmas (*2.6.7*)
The vaccine complies with the test for mycoplasmas.

3-4 Extraneous agents
Neutralise the vaccine virus with a suitable monospecific antiserum against feline herpesvirus 1 and inoculate into cell cultures known for their susceptibility to viruses pathogenic for the cat. Carry out at least 1 passage and maintain the cultures for 14 days. The vaccine complies with the test if no cytopathic effect develops and there is no sign of the presence of haemadsorbing agents.

3-5 Virus titre
Titrate the vaccine virus in suitable cell cultures and at a temperature favourable to replication of the virus.
The vaccine complies with the test if 1 dose contains not less than the minimum virus titre stated on the label.

3-6 Potency
The vaccine complies with the requirements of the test prescribed under Immunogenicity (section 2-3-3) when administered by a recommended route and method. It is not necessary to carry out the potency test for each batch of the vaccine if it has been carried out on a representative batch using a vaccinating dose containing not more than the minimum virus titre stated on the label.

———————————————— Ph Eur

Ferret and Mink Distemper Vaccine, Living

(Distemper Vaccine (Live) for Mustelids, Ph Eur monograph 0449)

Ph Eur ———————————————————

1 DEFINITION
Distemper vaccine (live) for mustelids is a preparation of a suitable strain of distemper virus that is attenuated for ferrets, or for ferrets and minks. This monograph applies to vaccines intended for the active immunisation of ferrets, or ferrets and minks, against disease caused by distemper virus.

2 PRODUCTION
2-1 PREPARATION OF THE VACCINE
The vaccine virus is grown in embryonated hens' eggs or in cell cultures.

2-2 SUBSTRATE FOR VIRUS PROPAGATION
2-2-1 Embryonated hens' eggs
If the vaccine virus is grown in embryonated hens' eggs, they are obtained from flocks free from specified pathogens (SPF) (*5.2.2*).

2-2-2 Cell cultures
If the vaccine virus is grown in cell cultures, they comply with the requirements for cell cultures for production of veterinary vaccines (*5.2.4*).

2-3 CHOICE OF VACCINE VIRUS
The vaccine virus is shown to be satisfactory with respect to safety (*5.2.6*) and efficacy (*5.2.7*) for the ferrets, or for the ferrets and minks for which it is intended.

The following tests for safety (section 2-3-1) and immunogenicity (section 2-3-3) may be used during the demonstration of safety and efficacy. The tests are performed in each species for which the vaccine is intended.

2-3-1 Safety
Carry out the test for each route and method of administration to be recommended for vaccination.
Use vaccine virus at the least attenuated passage level that will be present in a batch of the vaccine.

For each test, use not fewer than 5 ferrets and/or minks of the minimum age to be recommended for vaccination and that do not have antibodies against distemper virus. Administer to each ferret and/or mink a quantity of the vaccine virus equivalent to not less than 10 times the maximum virus titre likely to be contained in 1 dose of the vaccine. Observe the animals at least daily for 42 days.

The vaccine complies with the test if no animal shows abnormal local or systematic reactions, signs of disease or dies from causes attributable to the vaccine.

2-3-2 Increase in virulence
Carry out the test according to general chapter *5.2.6* using animals of the most susceptible target species. Use animals that do not have antibodies against distemper virus. If the properties of the vaccine virus allow sequential passage through 5 groups via natural spreading, this method may be used, otherwise passage as described below is carried out.

Administer to each animal of the 1st group by a route to be recommended a quantity of the vaccine virus that will allow recovery of virus for the passages described below.
Administer the virus by the route to be recommended for vaccination most likely to lead to reversion to virulence. After 5-10 days, prepare a suspension from, for example, the nasal mucosa, tonsils, thymus, spleen and the lungs and their local lymph nodes of each animal and pool the samples.
Administer 1 mL of the pooled samples by the intranasal route to each animal of the next group. Carry out this passage operation not fewer than 4 times; verify the presence of the virus at each passage. If the virus is not found at a passage level, repeat the passage by administration to a group of 10 animals.

If the 5th group of animals shows no evidence of an increase in virulence indicative of reversion during the observation period, further testing is not required. Otherwise, carry out an additional safety test and compare the clinical signs and any relevant parameters in a group of at least 8 animals receiving the material used for the 1st passage and another similar group receiving the virus at the final passage level.

The vaccine virus complies with the test if no indication of an increased virulence of the virus recovered for the final passage compared with the material used for the 1st passage is observed. If virus is not recovered after an initial passage in 2 animals and a subsequent repeat passage in 10 animals, the vaccine virus also complies with the test.

2-3-3 Immunogenicity
A test is carried out for each route and method of administration to be recommended for vaccination using animals of the target species (ferrets and/or minks) for which the vaccine is intended. Use animals not older than the minimum age to be recommended for vaccination.
The quantity of the vaccine virus administered to each

animal is not greater than the minimum virus titre to be stated on the label and the virus is at the most attenuated passage level that will be present in a batch of vaccine.

Use for the test not fewer than 7 ferrets and/or minks that do not have antibodies against distemper virus. Vaccinate not fewer than 5 animals, according to the schedule to be recommended. Maintain not fewer than 2 animals as controls. Challenge each animal after 20-22 days by the intramuscular route with a quantity of a suspension of virulent distemper virus sufficient to cause the death of a ferret and/or a mink. Observe the animals at least daily for 21 days after challenge. Animals displaying typical signs of serious infection with distemper virus are euthanised to avoid unecessary suffering.

The test is not valid if 1 or both of the control animals do not die of distemper. The vaccine virus complies with the test if the vaccinated animals remain in normal health.

3 BATCH TESTS
3-1 Identification
The vaccine mixed with a specific distemper antiserum no longer provokes cytopathic effects in susceptible cell cultures or lesions on the chorio-allantoic membranes of fertilised hen eggs 9-11 days old.

3-2 Bacteria and fungi
The vaccine, including where applicable the diluent supplied for reconstitution, complies with the test for sterility prescribed in the monograph *Vaccines for veterinary use (0062)*.

3-3 Mycoplasmas *(2.6.7)*
The vaccine complies with the test for mycoplasmas.

3-4 Extraneous agents
Neutralise the vaccine virus with a suitable monospecific antiserum against distemper virus and inoculate into susceptible cell cultures. The vaccine complies with the test if no cytopathic effect develops and there is no sign of the presence of haemagglutinating or haemadsorbing agents.

3-5 Virus titre
Titrate the vaccine virus in suitable cell cultures or fertilised hens' eggs 9-11 days old. The vaccine complies with the test if one dose contains not less than the minimum virus titre stated on the label.

3-6 Potency
The vaccine complies with the requirements of the test prescribed under Immunogenicity (section 2-3-3) when administered by a recommended route and method. It is not necessary to carry out the potency test for each batch of the vaccine if it has been carried out on a representative batch using a vaccinating dose containing not more than the minimum virus titre stated on the label.

——— Ph Eur

Foot and Mouth Disease (Ruminants) Vaccine

(Foot-and-Mouth Disease (Ruminants) Vaccine (Inactivated), Ph Eur monograph 0063)

Ph Eur _____

1 DEFINITION
Foot-and-mouth disease (ruminants) vaccine (inactivated) is a preparation containing one or more suitable strains of foot-and-mouth disease virus inactivated while maintaining

adequate immunogenic properties. This monograph applies to vaccines intended for active immunisation of ruminants against foot-and-mouth disease.

2 PRODUCTION
2-1 PREPARATION OF THE VACCINE
The vaccine virus is grown in cell cultures and then separated from cellular material by filtration or other suitable procedures. The harvested virus is inactivated in suitable conditions and may be concentrated and purified. It is used for the preparation of vaccine immediately or after storage at a temperature shown to be consistent with antigen stability. The vaccine is prepared from inactivated virus by blending with one or more adjuvants. For a given strain, the quantity of 146S antigen blended in each batch of vaccine is not lower than that of a batch of vaccine that has been found satisfactory with respect to Immunogenicity.

2-2 SUBSTRATE FOR VIRUS PROPAGATION
2-2-1 Cell cultures
The cell cultures comply with the requirements for cell cultures for production of veterinary vaccines *(5.2.4)*.

2-3 VALIDATION OF THE INACTIVATION PROCEDURE
During inactivation, the virus titre is monitored by a sensitive and reproducible technique. The inactivation procedure is not satisfactory unless the decrease in virus titre, plotted logarithmically, is linear and extrapolation indicates that there is less than 1 infectious virus unit per 10^4 litres of liquid preparation at the end of inactivation.

2-4 CHOICE OF VACCINE COMPOSITION
The vaccine is shown to be satisfactory with respect to safety *(5.2.6)* and efficacy *(5.2.7)* for each species for which it is intended.

The following tests for safety (section 2-4-1) and immunogenicity (section 2-4-2) may be used during the demonstration of safety and efficacy.

2-4-1 Safety
Carry out the test for each route and method of administration to be recommended for vaccination and in each category of each species for which the vaccine is intended, using in each case animals of the minimum age to be recommended. Use a representative batch of vaccine containing not less than the maximum antigen content that may be expected in a batch of vaccine.

For each test, use not fewer than 8 animals that do not have antibodies against foot-and-mouth disease virus. Administer to each animal 1 dose of the vaccine. If the schedule to be recommended requires a 2nd dose, administer 1 dose after an interval of at least 14 days. Observe the animals at least daily for at least 14 days after the last administration.

The vaccine complies with the test if no animal shows abnormal local or systemic reactions, or dies from causes attributable to the vaccine.

2-4-2 Immunogenicity
Carry out an immunogenicity test for each strain of foot-and-mouth disease virus that may be included in the vaccine.

Each test is carried out for each route and method of administration to be recommended for vaccination, using in each case cattle not less than 6 months old. The vaccine administered to each cattle is of minimum antigen content.

Either of the following 2 tests is suitable to demonstrate immunogenicity of the vaccine for cattle.

2-4-2-1 PD_{50} challenge test. The potency of the vaccine is expressed as the number of 50 per cent cattle protective doses (PD_{50}) contained in the dose stated on the label. The PD_{50} is determined in cattle given primary vaccination and challenged by the inoculation of 10 000 ID_{50} of virulent bovine virus of the same strain as that used in the preparation of the vaccine in the conditions described below. The vaccine virus may be used for challenge.

Use for the test not fewer than 17 cattle obtained from areas free from foot-and-mouth disease, that have never been vaccinated against foot-and-mouth disease and do not have antibodies neutralising the different strains of foot-and-mouth disease virus. Vaccinate not fewer than 3 groups of not fewer than 5 cattle per group, using a different dose of the vaccine for each group. Administer the different doses by injecting different volumes of the vaccine and not by dilution of the vaccine. Maintain 2 cattle as controls. For example, if the label states that the injection of 2 mL corresponds to the administration of 1 dose of vaccine, a 1/4 dose of vaccine would be obtained by injecting 0.5 mL, and a 1/10 dose would be obtained by injecting 0.2 mL. Challenge all the cattle after 20-22 days by the intradermal route, into at least 2 sites on the upper surface of the tongue (0.1 mL per site), with a dose equivalent to approximately 10 000 ID_{50} of a suspension of a fully virulent virus, obtained from cattle and of the same strain as that used in the preparation of the vaccine. Observe the cattle at least daily for 8 days. In the interest of animal welfare, individual animals may be euthanised before the end of the observation period and considered as unprotected if a vaccinated animal shows lesions of foot-and-mouth disease on at least 1 foot or if a control animal shows lesions of foot-and-mouth disease on at least 3 feet. Unprotected cattle show lesions at sites other than the tongue. Protected cattle may display lingual lesions.

The test is not valid if both control cattle do not show lesions on at least 3 feet. From the number of protected cattle in each group, calculate the PD_{50} content of the vaccine.

The vaccine complies with the test if the potency is not less than that to be stated on the label; the minimum potency to be stated on the label is not less than 3 PD_{50} per dose for cattle.

2-4-2-2 PPG test. The following test could also be used to demonstrate immunogenicity of the vaccine for cattle (referred to as the 'Percentage of protection against generalised foot infection' (PPG test).

The potency of the vaccine is expressed as the percentage of cattle that do not show lesions on any feet. The PPG is determined in cattle given primary vaccination and challenged by the inoculation of 10 000 ID_{50} of virulent virus of the same strain as that used in the preparation of the vaccine under the conditions described below. The vaccine virus may be used for challenge. Use for the test not fewer than 18 cattle obtained from areas free from foot-and-mouth disease, that have never been vaccinated against foot-and-mouth disease and do not have antibodies neutralising the different strains of foot-and-mouth disease virus. Vaccinate not fewer than 16 cattle with 1 full dose. Maintain 2 cattle as controls. Challenge all the cattle after 20-22 days by the intradermal route, into at least 2 sites on the upper surface of the tongue (0.1 mL per site), with a dose equivalent to approximately 10 000 ID_{50} of a suspension of a fully virulent virus of the same strain as that used in the preparation of the vaccine. Observe the cattle at least daily for 8 days. In the interest of animal welfare, individual animals may be euthanised before the end of the observation period and considered as unprotected if a vaccinated animal shows lesions of foot-and-mouth disease on at least 1 foot or if a

control animal shows lesions of foot-and-mouth disease on at least 3 feet. Unprotected cattle show lesions at sites other than the tongue. Protected cattle may display lingual lesions.

The test is not valid if both control cattle do not show lesions on at least 3 feet. From the number of protected cattle in the vaccinated group, calculate the percentage of protected cattle.

The vaccine complies with the test if the potency is not less than that to be stated on the label; the minimum potency to be stated on the label is not less than 75 per cent.

2-5 MANUFACTURER'S TESTS
2-5-1 Identification
The bulk inactivated antigen is identified by a suitable immunochemical method (*2.7.1*).

2-5-2 Residual live virus
The limit of detection of the cell cultures to be used with respect to the virus to be tested is established by determining the number of $CCID_{50}$ and the 146S antigen content of a sample of live virus. The cells are not suitable if an amount of virus corresponding to 1 µg of 146S antigen has less than 10^6 $CCID_{50}$. A proportion of each batch of bulk inactivated antigen representing at least 200 doses is tested for freedom from live virus by inoculation into suitable cell cultures. A passage is made during culture of the cells. For this purpose, the sample of the inactivated antigen may be concentrated to allow testing of such large samples in cell cultures. It must be shown that the selected concentration and assay systems are not detrimental to detection of infectious virus within the test sample and that the concentrated inactivated antigen does not interfere with virus replication or cause toxic changes. A positive control is included in each test.

2-5-3 Antigen content
The 146S antigen content of each batch of bulk inactivated antigen is determined by an *in vitro* method (for example, by sucrose density gradient centrifugation and ultraviolet spectrophotometry at 259 nm).

2-5-4 Batch potency test
It is not necessary to carry out the potency test (section 3-3) for each batch of vaccine if it has been carried out using a batch of vaccine with a minimum antigen content. Where the test is not carried out, an alternative validated method is used, the criteria for acceptance being set with reference to a batch of vaccine that has given satisfactory results in the test described under Potency and has been shown to be satisfactory with respect to immunogenicity in the target species.

The following test may be used after a satisfactory pass level for a given strain has been established. Once a pass level has been established for a given strain, the same level of antigen may be used when this strain is formulated in combination with any other antigen provided that the formulation of the vaccine differs only in the strains included.

2-5-4-1 Vaccines for use in cattle. Use cattle of the minimum age recommended for vaccination obtained from areas free from foot-and-mouth disease, that have never been vaccinated against foot-and-mouth disease and do not have antibodies neutralising the different strains of foot-and-mouth disease virus. Vaccinate not fewer than 5 cattle by a recommended route. Use a suitable dose of the vaccine for each animal. After a defined period, not greater than 28 days following vaccination, draw a blood sample and determine individually in each serum the level of antibodies against each strain used in the preparation of the vaccine by a validated technique (e.g. sero-neutralisation test, ELISA). The vaccine complies with the test if the geometric mean of the antibody titre in cattle is not significantly lower than the pass level.

2-5-4-2 Vaccines for use in other ruminants. The potency of each batch shall be demonstrated in a suitable, validated test.

EMERGENCY USE: in situations of extreme urgency and subject to agreement by the competent authority, a batch of vaccine may be released before completion of the tests and the determination of potency if a test for sterility has been carried out on the bulk inactivated antigen and all other components of the vaccine and if the test for safety and the determination of potency have been carried out on a representative batch of vaccine prepared from the same bulk inactivated antigen. In this context, a batch is not considered to be representative unless it has been prepared with not more than the amount of antigen or antigens and with the same formulation as the batch to be released.

3 BATCH TESTS

3-1 Identification
The serum of an animal that did not have antibodies against foot-and-mouth disease virus prior to being immunised with the vaccine neutralises the strains of the virus used to prepare the vaccine, when tested by a suitably sensitive method.

3-2 Bacteria and fungi
The vaccine and, where applicable, the liquid supplied with it, comply with the test for sterility prescribed in the monograph *Vaccines for veterinary use (0062)*.

3-3 Potency
The vaccine complies with the requirements of the test mentioned under Immunogenicity (section 2-4-2) when administered by a recommended route and method.

——————————————————————— Ph Eur

Fowl Cholera Vaccine (Inactivated)

(Ph. Eur. monograph 1945)

Ph Eur _____

1 DEFINITION
Fowl cholera vaccine (inactivated) is a preparation of one or more suitable strains of one or more serovars of *Pasteurella multocida*, inactivated while maintaining adequate immunogenic properties. This monograph applies to vaccines intended for the active immunisation of chickens, turkeys, ducks and geese against acute fowl cholera.

2 PRODUCTION
2-1 PREPARATION OF THE VACCINE
The seed material is cultured in a suitable medium. If the vaccine contains more than one strain of bacterium, the different strains are grown and harvested separately. The bacterial harvests are inactivated. The vaccine may be adjuvanted.

2-2 CHOICE OF VACCINE COMPOSITION
The vaccine is shown to be satisfactory with respect to safety (5.2.6) and efficacy (5.2.7) for the species for which it is intended.

The following tests for safety (section 2-2-1) and immunogenicity (section 2-2-2) may be used during the demonstration of safety and efficacy.

2-2-1 Safety
The test is carried out for each route of administration to be recommended for vaccination and for each avian species for which the vaccine is intended. Use a batch of vaccine containing not less than the maximum potency that may be expected in a batch of vaccine.

For each test performed in birds younger than 3 weeks of age, use not fewer than 10 birds not older than the minimum age to be recommended for vaccination. For each test performed in birds older than 3 weeks of age, use not fewer than 8 birds not older than the minimum age to be recommended for vaccination. In the case of chickens, use chickens from a flock free from specified pathogens (SPF) (5.2.2) and in the case of turkeys, ducks or geese, use birds that have not been vaccinated and that do not have antibodies against *P. multocida*. Administer by a route and method to be recommended to each bird 1 dose of vaccine. If the schedule to be recommended requires a 2nd dose, administer 1 dose to each bird after an interval of at least 14 days. Observe the birds at least daily for at least 14 days for the last administration of the vaccine.

The test is not valid if more than 10 per cent of the birds younger than 3 weeks of age show abnormal signs of disease or die from causes not attributable to the vaccine. For birds older than 3 weeks of age, the test is not valid if non-specific mortality occurs.

The vaccine complies with the test if no bird shows abnormal signs of disease or dies from causes attributable to the vaccine.

2-2-2 Immunogenicity
The test is carried out for each route and method of administration to be recommended for vaccination, for each avian species for which the vaccine is intended and for each serovar of *P. multocida* against which protection is claimed. Use for each test not fewer than 30 birds not older than the minimum age to be recommended for vaccination. Use birds that have not been vaccinated and that are free from antibodies against *P. multocida*. For each test, administer to each of not fewer than 20 birds a quantity of the vaccine not greater than 1 dose. If re-vaccination is recommended, repeat this operation after the recommended interval. Maintain not fewer than 10 birds as controls. Challenge each of the birds of both groups 21 days after the last administration by the intramuscular route with a sufficient quantity of virulent *P. multocida*. Observe the birds for 14 days after challenge.

The test is not valid if during the observation period after challenge, fewer than 70 per cent of the control birds die or show signs of infection (such as either clinical signs or bacterial re-isolation in organs) or if during the period before challenge, more than 10 per cent of the birds from the control group or from the vaccinated group show abnormal signs of disease or die from causes not attributable to the vaccine.

The vaccine complies with the test if, at the end of the observation period after challenge, not fewer than 70 per cent of the birds from the vaccinated group survive and show no signs of disease. Mild signs that do not persist beyond the observation period may be tolerated.

2-3 MANUFACTURER'S TESTS
2-3-1 Batch potency test
It is not necessary to carry out the potency test (section 3-3) for each batch of vaccine if it has been carried out using a batch of vaccine with minimum potency. Where the test is not carried out, an alternative validated method is used, the criteria for acceptance being set with reference to a batch of vaccine that has given satisfactory results in the test described under Potency. The following test may be used.

Use not fewer than 15 SPF chickens (*5.2.2*), 3-4 weeks old. Collect serum samples from each vaccinated and control chicken just before vaccination and check for the absence of antibodies against each serovar of *P. multocida* in the vaccine. Administer to each of 10 chickens 1 dose of the vaccine by the subcutaneous route. Maintain 5 chickens as controls. Collect serum samples 5 weeks after vaccination from each vaccinated and control chicken. Measure the titres of serum antibodies against each serovar of *P. multocida* stated on the label using a suitable validated serological method. Calculate the mean titres for the group of vaccinates.

The test is not valid if specific *P. multocida* antibodies are found: before vaccination in 1 or more sera from chickens to be vaccinated or from controls; in 1 or more sera from control chickens 5 weeks after the time of administration of the vaccine.

The vaccine complies with the test if the mean antibody titres of the group of vaccinates are equal to or greater than the titres obtained with a batch that has given satisfactory results in the test described under Potency.

2-3-2 Bacterial endotoxins
A test for bacterial endotoxins (*2.6.14*) is carried out on the final lot or, where the nature of the adjuvant prevents performance of a satisfactory test, on the bulk antigen or the mixture of bulk antigens immediately before addition of the adjuvant. The maximum acceptable amount of bacterial endotoxins is that found for a batch of vaccine that has been shown satisfactory in safety test (section 2-2-1). The method chosen for determining the maximum acceptable amount of bacterial endotoxins is used subsequently for testing each batch.

3 BATCH TESTS
3-1 Identification
When injected into SPF chickens (*5.2.2*), the vaccine stimulates the production of antibodies against each of the serovars of *P. multocida* in the vaccine.

3-2 Bacteria and fungi
The vaccine, including where applicable the diluent supplied for reconstitution, complies with the test for sterility prescribed in the monograph *Vaccines for veterinary use (0062)*.

3-3 Potency
The vaccine complies with the requirements of the test mentioned under Immunogenicity (section 2-2-2) when administered by a recommended route and method.

LABELLING
The label states:
— the serovar(s) used to prepare the vaccine;
— the serovar(s) against which protection is claimed.

Ph Eur

Fowl Pox Vaccine, Living

(Fowl-pox Vaccine (Live), Ph Eur monograph 0649)

Ph Eur

1 DEFINITION
Fowl-pox vaccine (live) is a preparation of a suitable strain of avian pox virus. This monograph applies to vaccines intended for administration to chickens for active immunisation.

2 PRODUCTION
2-1 PREPARATION OF THE VACCINE
The vaccine virus is grown in embryonated hens' eggs or in cell cultures.

2-2 SUBSTRATE FOR VIRUS PROPAGATION
2-2-1 Embryonated hens' eggs
If the vaccine virus is grown in embryonated hens' eggs, they are obtained from flocks free from specified pathogens (SPF) (*5.2.2*).

2-2-2 Cell cultures
If the vaccine virus is grown in cell cultures, they comply with the requirements for cell cultures for production of veterinary vaccines (*5.2.4*).

2-3 SEED LOTS
2-3-1 Extraneous agents
The master seed lot complies with the tests for extraneous agents in seed lots (*2.6.24*). In these tests on the master seed lot, the organisms used are not more than 5 passages from the master seed lot at the start of the tests.

2-4 CHOICE OF VACCINE VIRUS
The vaccine virus shall be shown to be satisfactory with respect to safety (*5.2.6*) and efficacy (*5.2.7*) for the chickens for which it is intended.

The following tests for safety (section 2-4-1), increase in virulence (section 2-4-2) and immunogenicity (section 2-4-3) may be used during demonstration of safety and efficacy.

2-4-1 Safety
Carry out the test for each route and method of administration to be recommended for vaccination using in each case chickens not older than the minimum age to be recommended for vaccination from an SPF flock (*5.2.2*). Use vaccine virus at the least attenuated passage level that will be present in a batch of the vaccine.

For each test performed in chickens younger than 3 weeks of age, use not fewer than 10 chickens. For each test performed in chickens older than 3 weeks of age, use not fewer than 8 chickens. Administer to each chicken a quantity of the vaccine virus equivalent to not less than 10 times the maximum virus titre likely to be contained in 1 dose of the vaccine. Observe the chickens at least daily for at least 14 days.

The test is not valid if more than 10 per cent of the chickens younger than 3 weeks of age show abnormal signs of disease or die from causes not attributable to the vaccine.
For chickens older than 3 weeks of age, the test is not valid if non-specific mortality occurs.

The vaccine virus complies with the test if no chicken shows abnormal signs of disease or dies from causes attributable to the vaccine virus.

2-4-2 Increase in virulence
Carry out the test according to general chapter *5.2.6* using chickens not older than the minimum age to be recommended for vaccination and from an SPF flock (*5.2.2*). If the properties of the vaccine virus allow sequential passage through 5 groups via natural spreading, this method may be used, otherwise, passage as described below is carried out.

Administer to each chicken of the 1st group by a suitable route a quantity of the vaccine virus that will allow recovery of virus for the passages described below. Prepare 4-7 days after administration a suspension from the induced skin lesions of each chicken and pool these samples. Administer 0.2 mL of the pooled samples by cutaneous scarification of the comb or other unfeathered part of the body, or by another suitable method to each chicken of the next group.

Carry out this passage operation not fewer than 4 times; verify the presence of the virus at each passage. If the virus is not found at a passage level, repeat the passage by administration to a group of 10 chickens.

If the 5th group of chickens shows no evidence of an increase in virulence indicative of reversion during the observation period, further testing is not required. Otherwise, carry out an additional safety test and compare the clinical signs and any relevant parameters in a group of at least 10 chickens receiving the material used for the 1st passage and another similar group receiving the virus at the final passage level.

The vaccine virus complies with the test if no indication of increase in virulence of the virus at the final passage level compared with the material used for the 1st passage is observed. If virus is not recovered after an initial passage in 5 chickens and a subsequent repeat passage in 10 chickens, the vaccine virus also complies with the test.

2-4-3 Immunogenicity

A test is carried out for each route and method of administration to be recommended using in each case chickens not older than the minimum age to be recommended for vaccination. The quantity of the vaccine virus administered to each chicken is not greater than the minimum virus titre to be stated on the label and the virus is at the most attenuated passage level that will be present in a batch of the vaccine. Use for the test not fewer than 30 chickens of the same origin and from an SPF flock (5.2.2). Vaccinate by a route to be recommended not fewer than 20 chickens. Maintain not fewer than 10 chickens as controls. Challenge each chicken after 21 days by the feather-follicle route with a sufficient quantity of virulent fowl-pox virus. Observe the chickens at least daily for 21 days after challenge. Record the deaths and the number of surviving chickens that show clinical signs of disease. Examine each surviving chicken for macroscopic lesions: cutaneous lesions of the comb, wattle and other unfeathered areas of the skin and diphtherical lesions of the mucous membranes of the oro-pharyngeal area.

The test is not valid if:
— during the observation period after challenge fewer than 90 per cent of the control chickens die or show severe clinical signs of fowl pox, including notable macroscopical lesions of the skin or mucous membranes of the oro-pharyngeal area,
— and/or during the period between vaccination and challenge, more than 10 per cent of the control or vaccinated chickens show abnormal clinical signs or die from causes not attributable to the vaccine.

The vaccine virus complies with the test if during the observation period after challenge not less than 90 per cent of the vaccinated chickens survive and show no notable clinical signs of disease, including macroscopical lesions of the skin and mucous membranes of the oro-pharyngeal area.

3 BATCH TESTS

3-1 Identification

Carry out an immunostaining test in cell cultures to demonstrate the presence of the vaccine virus. For egg adapted strains, inoculate the vaccine into eggs and notice the characteristic lesions.

3-2 Bacteria and fungi

Vaccines intended for administration by injection, scarification or wing web piercing comply with the test for sterility prescribed in the monograph *Vaccines for veterinary use (0062)*.

Frozen or freeze-dried vaccines produced in embryonated eggs and not intended for administration by injection, scarification or wing web piercing either comply with the test for sterility prescribed in the monograph *Vaccines for veterinary use (0062)* or with the following test: carry out a quantitative test for bacterial and fungal contamination; carry out identification tests for microorganisms detected in the vaccine; the vaccine does not contain pathogenic microorganisms and contains not more than 1 non-pathogenic microorganism per dose.

Any diluent supplied for reconstitution of the vaccine complies with the test for sterility prescribed in the monograph *Vaccines for veterinary use (0062)*.

3-3 Mycoplasmas

The vaccine complies with the test for mycoplasmas (2.6.7).

3-4 Extraneous agents

The vaccine complies with the tests for extraneous agents in batches of finished product (2.6.25).

3-5 Virus titre

Titrate the vaccine virus by inoculation into embryonated hens' eggs from an SPF flock (5.2.2) or into suitable cell cultures (5.2.4). The vaccine complies with the test if 1 dose contains not less than the minimum virus titre stated on the label.

3-6 Potency

The vaccine complies with the requirements of the test prescribed under Immunogenicity (section 2-4-3) when administered according to the recommended schedule by a recommended route and method. It is not necessary to carry out the potency test for each batch of the vaccine if it has been carried out on a representative batch using a vaccinating dose containing not more than the minimum virus titre stated on the label.

_____ *Ph Eur6*

Furunculosis Vaccine for Salmonids, Inactivated

(Furunculosis Vaccine (Inactivated, Oil-Adjuvanted, Injectable) for Salmonids, Ph Eur monograph 1521)

Ph Eur _____

1 DEFINITION

Furunculosis vaccine (inactivated, oil-adjuvanted, injectable) for salmonids is prepared from cultures of one or more suitable strains of *Aeromonas salmonicida* subsp. *salmonicida*, inactivated while maintaining adequate immunogenic properties. This monograph applies to vaccines intended for the active immunisation of salmonids against furunculosis.

2 PRODUCTION

2-1 PREPARATION OF THE VACCINE

The strains of *A. salmonicida* are cultured and harvested separately. The harvests are inactivated by a suitable method. They may be purified and concentrated. Whole or disrupted cells may be used and the vaccine may contain extracellular products of the bacterium released into the growth medium. The vaccine contains an oily adjuvant.

2-2 CHOICE OF VACCINE STRAIN

The strains included in the vaccine are shown to be suitable with respect to the production of antigens of assumed protective importance. The vaccine is shown to be satisfactory with respect to safety (5.2.6) and efficacy (5.2.7) in the species of fish for which it is intended.

The following tests for safety (section 2-2-1) and immunogenicity (section 2-2-2) may be used during the demonstration of safety and efficacy.

2-2-1 Safety

2-2-1-1 Laboratory test. Carry out the test in each species of fish for which the vaccine is intended, using fish of the minimum body mass to be recommended for vaccination. Use a batch of vaccine containing not less than the maximum potency that may be expected in a batch of vaccine.

Use not fewer than 50 fish from a population that does not have specific antibodies against *A. salmonicida* subsp. *salmonicida* and has not been vaccinated against or exposed to furunculosis. The test is carried out in the conditions to be recommended for the use of the vaccine with a water temperature not less than 10 °C. Administer to each fish by the intraperitoneal route 1 dose of the vaccine. Observe the fish at least daily for 21 days.

The test is not valid if more than 6 per cent of the fish die from causes not attributable to the vaccine. The vaccine complies with the test if no fish shows abnormal local or systemic reactions or dies from causes attributable to the vaccine.

2-2-1-2 Field studies. Safety is also demonstrated in field trials by administering the intended dose to a sufficient number of fish in not fewer than 2 sets of premises. Samples of 30 fish are taken on 3 occasions (after vaccination, at the middle of the rearing period and at slaughter) and examined for local reactions in the body cavity. Moderate lesions involving localised adhesions between viscera or between viscera and the abdominal wall and slight opaqueness and/or sparse pigmentation of the peritoneum are acceptable. Extensive lesions including adhesions between greater parts of the abdominal organs, massive pigmentation and/or obvious thickening and opaqueness of greater areas of the peritoneum are unacceptable if they occur in more than 10 per cent of the fish in any sample. Such lesions include adhesions that give the viscera a 'one-unit' appearance and/or lead to manifest laceration of the peritoneum following evisceration.

2-2-2 Immunogenicity

Carry out the test according to a protocol defining limits of body mass for the fish, water source, water flow and temperature limits, and preparation of a standardised challenge. A test is carried out for the route and method of administration to be recommended. The vaccine administered to each fish is of minimum potency.

Use for the test not fewer than 60 fish from a population that does not have specific antibodies against *A salmonicida* subsp. *salmonicida* and has not been vaccinated against or exposed to furunculosis. Vaccinate not fewer than 30 fish according to the instructions for use. Perform mock vaccination on a control group of not fewer than 30 fish; mark vaccinated and control fish for identification. Keep all the fish in the same tank or mix equal numbers of controls and vaccinates in each tank if more than one tank is used. Where justified and when fish cannot be marked, non-marked fish may be used. Vaccinates and controls may then be kept in the same tank but physically separated (for example by fishing nets). Challenge each fish, by injection, at a fixed interval after vaccination corresponding to the onset of immunity claimed, with a sufficient quantity of a culture of *A salmonicida* subsp. *salmonicida* whose virulence has been verified. Observe the fish at least daily until the end of mortality is reached in the control group (no fish have died over a period of 2 days).

The test is not valid if the specific mortality is less than 60 per cent in the control group 21 days after the 1st death in the fish. Calculate the relative percentage survival (RPS) using the following expression:

$$\left(1 - \frac{V}{C}\right) \times 100$$

V = percentage of mortality in vaccinates;
C = percentage of mortality in controls.

The vaccine complies with the test if the RPS is not less than 70 per cent.

2-3 MANUFACTURER'S TESTS

2-3-1 Batch potency test

The potency test (section 3-3) may be carried out for each batch of vaccine, using fish of one of the species for which the vaccine is intended. Where the test is not carried out, an alternative validated method based on antibody response may be used, the criteria for acceptance being set with reference to a batch of vaccine that has given satisfactory results in the test described under Potency. The following test may be used.

Use not fewer than 35 fish from a population that does not have specific antibodies against *A salmonicida* subsp. *salmonicida* and that are within specified limits for body mass. Carry out the test at a defined temperature not less than 12 °C. Inject intraperitoneally into each of not fewer than 25 fish 1 dose of vaccine, according to the instructions for use. Perform mock vaccination on a control group of not fewer than 10 fish. Collect blood samples from vaccinates and controls at a defined time not less than 500 degree days after vaccination. Determine for each sample the level of specific antibodies against *A salmonicida* subsp. *salmonicida* by a suitable immunochemical method (*2.7.1*).

The test is not valid if the control group shows antibodies against *A. salmonicida* subsp. *salmonicida*.

The vaccine complies with the test if the mean level of antibodies in the vaccinates is not significantly lower than that found for a batch that gave satisfactory results in the test described under Potency.

3 BATCH TESTS

3-1 Identification

When injected into fish that do not have specific antibodies against *A. salmonicida*, the vaccine stimulates the production of such antibodies.

3-2 Bacteria and fungi

The vaccine, including where applicable the diluent supplied for reconstitution, complies with the test for sterility prescribed in the monograph Vaccines for veterinary use (0062).

3-3 Potency

The vaccine complies with the requirements of the test mentioned under Immunogenicity (section 2-2-2) when administered by the recommended route and method.

4 LABELLING

The label states information on the time needed for development of immunity after vaccination under the range of conditions corresponding to the recommended use.

Ph Eur

Infectious Avian Encephalomyelitis Vaccine, Living

Epidemic Tremor Vaccine, Living

*(Avian Infectious Encephalomyelitis Vaccine (Live),
Ph Eur monograph 0588)*

Ph Eur _____

1 DEFINITION

Avian infectious encephalomyelitis vaccine (live) is a preparation of a suitable strain of avian encephalomyelitis virus. This monograph applies to vaccines intended for administration to non-laying breeder chickens to protect passively their future progeny and/or to prevent vertical transmission of virus via the egg.

2 PRODUCTION
2-1 PREPARATION OF THE VACCINE

The vaccine virus is grown in embryonated hens' eggs or in cell cultures.

2-2 SUBSTRATE FOR VIRUS PROPAGATION
2-2-1 Embryonated hens' eggs

If the vaccine virus is grown in embryonated hens' eggs, they are obtained from flocks free from specified pathogens (SPF) (5.2.2).

2-2-2 Cell cultures

If the vaccine virus is grown in cell cultures, they comply with the requirements for cell cultures for production of veterinary vaccines (5.2.4).

2-3 SEED LOTS
2-3-1 Extraneous agents

The master seed lot complies with the tests for extraneous agents in seed lots (2.6.24). In these tests on the master seed lot, the organisms used are not more than 5 passages from the master seed lot at the start of the tests.

2-4 CHOICE OF VACCINE VIRUS

The vaccine virus shall be shown to be satisfactory with respect to safety (5.2.6) and efficacy (5.2.7) for the chickens for which it is intended.

The following tests for safety (section 2-4-1), increase in virulence (section 2-4-2) and immunogenicity (section 2-4-3) may be used during the demonstration of safety and efficacy.

2-4-1 Safety

Carry out the test for each route and method of administration to be recommended for vaccination using in each case non-laying breeder chickens not older than the minimum age to be recommended for vaccination.
Use vaccine virus at the least attenuated passage level that will be present in a batch of the vaccine.

For each test, use not fewer than 8 chickens from an SPF flock (5.2.2). Administer to each chicken a quantity of the vaccine virus equivalent to not less than 10 times the maximum virus titre likely to be contained in 1 dose of the vaccine. Observe the chickens at least daily for 21 days.

The test is not valid if non-specific mortality occurs.

The vaccine virus complies with the test if no chicken shows abnormal signs of disease or dies from causes attributable to the vaccine virus.

2-4-2 Increase in virulence

Carry out the test according to general chapter 5.2.6 using 1-day-old chickens from an SPF flock (5.2.2). If the properties of the vaccine virus allow sequential passage through 5 groups via natural spreading, this method may be used, otherwise passage as described below is carried out.

Administer to each chicken of the 1st group by a route and method to be recommended a quantity of the vaccine virus that will allow recovery of virus for the passages described below. 5-7 days later, prepare a suspension from the brain of each chicken and pool these samples. Administer a suitable volume of the pooled samples by the oral route to each chicken of the next group. Carry out this passage operation not fewer than 4 times; verify the presence of the virus at each passage. If the virus is not found at a passage level, repeat the passage by administration to a group of 10 chickens.

If the 5th group of chickens shows no evidence of an increase in virulence indicative of reversion during the observation period, further testing is not required. Otherwise, carry out an additional safety test and compare the clinical signs and any relevant parameters in a group of at least 10 chickens receiving the material used for the 1st passage and another similar group receiving the virus at the final passage level.

The vaccine virus complies with the test if no indication of an increase in virulence of the virus recovered for the final passage compared with the material used for the 1st passage is observed. If virus is not recovered after an initial passage in 5 chickens and a subsequent repeat passage in 10 chickens, the vaccine virus also complies with the test.

2-4-3 Immunogenicity

If the vaccine is recommended for passive protection of future progeny carry out test 2-4-3-1. If the vaccine is recommended for prevention of vertical transmission of virus via the egg, carry out test 2-4-3-2. A test is carried out for each route and method of administration to be recommended, using in each case chickens from an SPF flock (5.2.2) not older than the minimum age to be recommended for vaccination. The quantity of the vaccine virus administered to each chicken is not greater than the minimum titre to be stated on the label and the virus is at the most attenuated passage level that will be present in a batch of the vaccine.

2-4-3-1 Passive immunity in chickens. Vaccinate not fewer than 20 breeder chickens from an SPF flock (5.2.2). Maintain separately not fewer than 10 breeder chickens of the same age and origin as controls. At the peak of lay, hatch not fewer than 25 chickens from eggs from vaccinated breeder chickens and 10 chickens from non-vaccinated breeder chickens. At 2 weeks of age, challenge each chicken by the intracerebral route with a sufficient quantity of virulent avian encephalomyelitis virus. Observe the chickens at least daily for 21 days after challenge. Record the deaths and the number of surviving chickens that show clinical signs of disease.

The test is not valid if:
— during the observation period after challenge fewer than 80 per cent of the control chickens die or show severe clinical signs of avian infectious encephalomyelitis,
— and/or during the period between the vaccination and challenge more than 15 per cent of control or vaccinated chickens show abnormal clinical signs or die from causes not attributable to the vaccine.

The vaccine virus complies with the test if during the observation period after challenge not fewer than 80 per cent of the progeny of vaccinated chickens survive and show no notable clinical signs of disease.

2-4-3-2 Passive immunity in embryos. Vaccinate not fewer than 20 breeder chickens from an SPF flock (5.2.2). Maintain separately not fewer than 10 breeder chickens of the same age and origin as controls. At the peak of lay, incubate not fewer than 36 eggs from the 2 groups, vaccinated and controls, and carry out an embryo sensitivity test. On the sixth day of incubation inoculate 100 EID_{50} of the Van Roekel strain of avian encephalomyelitis virus into the yolk sacs of the eggs. 12 days after inoculation examine the embryos for specific lesions of avian encephalomyelitis (muscular atrophy). Deaths during the first 24 h are considered to be non-specific.

The test is not valid if fewer than 80 per cent of the control embryos show lesions of avian encephalomyelitis. The test is not valid if fewer than 80 per cent of the embryos can be given an assessment.

The vaccine virus complies with the test if not fewer than 80 per cent of the embryos in the vaccinated group show no lesions of avian encephalomyelitis.

3 BATCH TESTS

3-1 Identification
The vaccine, diluted if necessary and mixed with a monospecific avian encephalomyelitis virus antiserum, no longer infects embryonated hens' eggs from an SPF flock (5.2.2) or susceptible cell cultures (5.2.4) into which it is inoculated.

3-2 Bacteria and fungi
Vaccines intended for administration by injection comply with the test for sterility prescribed in the monograph *Vaccines for veterinary use (0062)*.

Frozen or freeze-dried vaccines produced in embryonated eggs and not intended for administration by injection either comply with the test for sterility prescribed in the monograph *Vaccines for veterinary use (0062)* or with the following test: carry out a quantitative test for bacterial and fungal contamination; carry out identification tests for microorganisms detected in the vaccine; the vaccine does not contain pathogenic microorganisms and contains not more than 1 non-pathogenic microorganism per dose.

Any diluent supplied for reconstitution of the vaccine complies with the test for sterility prescribed in the monograph *Vaccines for veterinary use (0062)*.

3-3 Mycoplasmas
The vaccine complies with the test for mycoplasmas (2.6.7).

3-4 Extraneous agents
The vaccine complies with the tests for extraneous agents in batches of finished product (2.6.25).

3-5 Virus titre
Titrate the vaccine virus by inoculation into embryonated hens' eggs from an SPF flock (5.2.2) or into suitable cell cultures (5.2.4). The vaccine complies with the test if 1 dose contains not less than the minimum virus titre stated on the label.

3-6 Potency
Depending on the indications, the vaccine complies with the requirements of 1 or both of the tests prescribed under Immunogenicity (section 2-4-3-1, 2-4-3-2), when administered by a recommended route and method. It is not necessary to carry out the potency test for each batch of the vaccine if it has been carried out on a representative batch using a vaccinating dose containing not more than the minimum virus titre stated on the label.

Ph Eur

Infectious Bovine Rhinotracheitis Vaccine, Living

(Infectious Bovine Rhinotracheitis Vaccine (Live), Ph Eur monograph 0696)

Ph Eur

1 DEFINITION
Infectious bovine rhinotracheitis vaccine (live) is a preparation of one or more suitable strains of infectious bovine rhinotracheitis virus (bovine herpesvirus 1). This monograph applies to vaccines intended for the active immunisation of cattle against bovine rhinotracheitis caused by bovine herpesvirus 1.

2 PRODUCTION

2-1 PREPARATION OF THE VACCINE
The vaccine virus is grown in cell cultures.

2-2 SUBSTRATE FOR VIRUS PROPAGATION

2-2-1 Cell cultures
The cell cultures comply with the requirements for cell cultures for production of veterinary vaccines (5.2.4).

2-3 CHOICE OF VACCINE VIRUS
The vaccine virus is shown to be satisfactory with respect to safety (5.2.6) and efficacy (5.2.7) for the cattle for which it is intended.

The following tests for safety (section 2-3-1), abortigenicity and passage through the placenta (section 2-3-2), increase in virulence (section 2-3-3) and immunogenicity (section 2-3-4) may be used during the demonstration of safety and efficacy.

2-3-1 Safety
Carry out the test for each route and method of administration to be recommended for vaccination. Use vaccine virus at the least attenuated passage level that will be present in a batch of the vaccine.

For each test, use not fewer than 5 calves, 3 months old or of the minimum age to be recommended for vaccination if this is less than 3 months, and that do not have antibodies against infectious bovine rhinotracheitis virus. Administer to each calf a quantity of the vaccine virus equivalent to not less than 10 times the maximum virus titre likely to be contained in 1 dose of the vaccine. Observe the calves at least daily for at least 14 days.

The vaccine virus complies with the test if no calf shows abnormal local or systemic reactions or dies from causes attributable to the vaccine virus.

2-3-2 Abortigenicity and passage through the placenta
Use not fewer than 24 pregnant cows that do not have antibodies against infectious bovine rhinotracheitis virus: 8 of the cows are in the 4th month of pregnancy, 8 in the 5th and 8 in the 6th or 7th month. Administer to each cow by a route to be recommended a quantity of the vaccine virus equivalent to not less than 10 times the maximum virus titre likely to be contained in 1 dose of the vaccine. Observe the cows at least daily until the end of pregnancy.

The vaccine virus complies with the test if:
— where abortion occurs, tests show that neither virus nor viral antigens are present in the foetus or placenta;
— on calves born at term before ingestion of colostrum, a test for antibodies against infectious bovine rhinotracheitis virus indicates no such antibodies are found.

2-3-3 Increase in virulence
Carry out the test according to chapter 5.2.6. *Evaluation of safety of veterinary vaccines and immunosera* using calves 3 months old or of the minimum age to be recommended for

vaccination if this is less than 3 months, and that do not have antibodies against infectious bovine rhinotracheitis virus.

If the properties of the vaccine virus allow sequential passage through 5 groups via natural spreading, this method may be used, otherwise passage as described below is carried out.

Take suitable samples from the calves used for the test for safety at a time when the vaccinal virus can be easily detected, verify the presence and titre of the virus in the samples and mix them. Administer to each calf of the 1st group by the intranasal route a quantity of the vaccine virus that will allow recovery of virus for the passages described below. Administer the virus by the intranasal route to each calf of the next group. Carry out this passage operation not fewer than 4 times; verify the presence of the virus at each passage. If the virus is not found at a passage level, repeat the passage by administration to a group of 10 animals.

If the 5th group of calves shows no evidence of an increase in virulence indicative of reversion during the observation period, further testing is not required. Otherwise, carry out an additional safety test and compare the clinical signs and any relevant parameters in a group of at least 8 animals receiving the material used for the 1st passage and another similar group receiving the virus at the final passage level.

The vaccine virus complies with the test if no indication of increased virulence of the virus recovered for the final passage compared with the material used for the 1st passage is observed. If virus is not recovered after an initial passage in 2 animals and a subsequent repeated passage in 10 animals, the vaccine virus also complies with the test.

2-3-4 Immunogenicity

A test is carried out for each route and method of administration to be recommended for vaccination using in each case calves 2-3 months old. The quantity of vaccine to be administered to each calf is not greater than the minimum virus titre to be stated on the label and the virus is at the most attenuated passage level that will be present in a batch of vaccine. Use for the test not fewer than 7 calves that do not have antibodies against infectious bovine rhinotracheitis virus. Vaccinate not fewer than 5 calves, according to the schedule to be recommended. Maintain not fewer than 2 calves as controls. Challenge each calf after 20-22 days by the intranasal route with a sufficient quantity of a virulent infectious bovine rhinotracheitis virus. Observe the calves at least daily for 21 days after challenge, in particular for respiratory signs and virus shedding (by nasal swabs or tracheobronchial washing).

The test is not valid if the controls do not show typical signs of disease such as fever, ocular and nasal discharge and ulceration of the nasal mucosa.

The vaccine virus complies with the test if, during the observation period after challenge:
— the vaccinated calves show no more than mild signs;
— in not fewer than 4 of the 5 vaccinated calves, the maximum virus titre found in the nasal mucus is at least 100 times lower than the average of the maximum titres found in the control calves; and
— the average number of days on which virus is excreted is at least 3 days less in vaccinated calves than in the control calves.

3 BATCH TESTS
3-1 Identification

3-1-1
When mixed with a suitable quantity of a monospecific antiserum, the vaccine is no longer able to infect susceptible cell cultures into which it is inoculated.

3-1-2
Any markers of the strain are verified.

3-2 Bacteria and fungi
The vaccine, including where applicable the diluent supplied for reconstitution, complies with the test for sterility prescribed in the monograph *Vaccines for veterinary use (0062)*.

3-3 Mycoplasmas (*2.6.7*)
The vaccine complies with the test for mycoplasmas.

3-4 Extraneous agents
Neutralise the vaccine virus with a suitable monospecific antiserum against bovine rhinotracheitis virus and inoculate into cell cultures known for their susceptibility to viruses pathogenic for cattle. Carry out 1 passage at 7 days and maintain the cultures for 14 days.

The vaccine complies with the test if no cytopathic effect develops and there is no sign of the presence of haemadsorbing agents.

3-5 Virus titre
Titrate the vaccine virus in susceptible cell cultures at a temperature favourable to replication of the virus.
The vaccine complies with the test if 1 dose contains not less than the minimum virus titre stated on the label.

3-6 Potency
The vaccine complies with the requirements of the test prescribed under Immunogenicity (section 2-3-4) when administered by a recommended route and method. It is not necessary to carry out the potency test for each batch of the vaccine if it has been carried out on a representative batch using a vaccinating dose containing not more than the minimum virus titre stated on the label.

Ph Eur

Infectious Bursal Disease Vaccine, Inactivated

Gumboro Disease Vaccine, Inactivated

(Avian Infectious Bursal Disease Vaccine (Inactivated), Ph Eur monograph 0960)

caution: *Accidental Injection of oily vaccine can cause serious local reactions in man. Expert medical advice should be sought immediately and the doctor should be informed that the vaccine is an oil emulsion.*

Ph Eur

1 DEFINITION
Avian infectious bursal disease vaccine (inactivated) is a preparation of a suitable strain of avian infectious bursal disease virus type 1, inactivated while maintaining adequate immunogenic properties. This monograph applies to vaccines intended for use in breeding chickens to protect their progeny from avian infectious bursal disease.

2 PRODUCTION
2-1 PREPARATION OF THE VACCINE
The vaccine virus is grown in embryonated hens' eggs or in cell cultures.

The vaccine may be adjuvanted.

2-2 SUBSTRATE FOR VIRUS PROPAGATION
2-2-1 Embryonated hens' eggs
If the vaccine virus is grown in embryonated hens' eggs, they are obtained from healthy flocks.

2-2-2 Cell cultures
If the vaccine is grown in cell cultures, they comply with the requirements for cell cultures for production of veterinary vaccines (5.2.4).

2-3 SEED LOTS
2-3-1 Extraneous agents
The master seed lot complies with the tests for extraneous agents in seed lots (2.6.24). In these tests on the master seed lot, the organisms used are not more than 5 passages from the master seed lot at the start of the test.

2-4 CHOICE OF VACCINE COMPOSITION
The vaccine is shown to be satisfactory with respect to safety (5.2.6) and efficacy (5.2.7) for the birds for which it is intended.

The following tests for safety (section 2-4-1) and immunogenicity (section 2-4-2) may be used during the demonstration of safety and efficacy.

2-4-1 Safety
The test is carried out for each route of administration to be recommended for vaccination. Use a batch of vaccine containing not less than the maximum potency that may be expected in a batch of vaccine.

For each test, use not fewer than 8 chickens not older than the minimum age to be recommended for vaccination and from a flock free from specified pathogens (SPF) (5.2.2). Administer by a route and method to be recommended to each chicken 1 dose of the vaccine. Observe the chickens at least daily for at least 14 days after the administration of the vaccine.

The test is not valid if non-specific mortality occurs. The vaccine complies with the test if no chicken shows abnormal signs of disease or dies from causes attributable to the vaccine.

2-4-2 Immunogenicity
A test is carried out for each route and method of administration to be recommended using in each case chickens from an SPF flock (5.2.2) and not older than the minimum age to be recommended for vaccination (close to the point of lay). The dose of vaccine administered to each chicken contains not more than the minimum potency to be stated on the label.

Where a challenge test is to be carried out, the following test may be used. Use 2 groups of not less than 20 hens treated as follows:
— group A: unvaccinated controls;
— group B: vaccinated with inactivated avian infectious bursal disease vaccine.

Serum samples are collected from each unvaccinated control (group A) hen just before administration of the vaccine, 4-6 weeks later, and at the time of egg collection for hatching. If a serological test is to be carried out for demonstration of immunogenicity by other routes, serum samples are also collected from each vaccinated (group B) hen at the time of egg collection for hatching. The antibody response is measured in a serum-neutralisation test.

Eggs are collected for hatching not less than 5 weeks after vaccination and the test described below is carried out with chickens at least 3 weeks old from that egg collection.

25 chickens from vaccinated (group B) hens and 10 control chickens of the same breed and age from unvaccinated (group A) hens are challenged with an eye-drop application of a quantity of a virulent strain of avian infectious bursal disease virus sufficient to produce severe signs of disease,

including lesions of the bursa of Fabricius, in all unvaccinated chickens. 3-4 days after challenge, the bursa of Fabricius is removed from each chicken. The bursae are examined for evidence of infection by histological examination and by testing for the presence of avian infectious bursal disease antigen by a suitable method. The vaccine complies with the test if 3 or fewer of the chickens from group B hens show evidence of avian infectious bursal disease. The test is invalid unless all the chickens from group A hens show evidence of avian infectious bursal disease.

Where there is more than one recommended route of administration, the test described under Potency is carried out in parallel with the above immunogenicity test, using different groups of birds for each recommended route. The serological response of the birds inoculated by routes other than that used in the immunogenicity test is not significantly less than that of the group vaccinated by that route.

2-5 MANUFACTURER'S TESTS
2-5-1 Residual live virus
An amplification test for residual live avian infectious bursal disease virus is carried out on each batch of antigen immediately after inactivation to confirm inactivation; the test is carried out in embryonated hens' eggs or in suitable cell cultures (5.2.4), whichever is the most sensitive for the vaccine strain; the quantity of inactivated virus harvest used in the test is equivalent to not less than 10 doses of the vaccine. The vaccine complies with the test if no live virus is detected.

2-5-2 Batch potency test
It is not necessary to carry out the potency test (section 3-5) for each batch of the vaccine if it has been carried out using a batch of vaccine with a minimum potency. Where the test is not carried out, an alternative validated method is used, the criteria for acceptance being set with reference to a batch of vaccine that has given satisfactory results in the test described under Potency. The following test may be used.

Vaccinate each of not fewer than 10 chickens, 14-28 days old and from an SPF flock (5.2.2), with 1 dose of vaccine by a recommended route. 4-6 weeks later, collect serum samples from each bird and 10 unvaccinated control birds of the same age and from the same source. Measure the antibody response in a serum-neutralisation test.

The test is not valid if there are specific antibodies in the sera of the unvaccinated birds. The vaccine complies with the test if the mean antibody titre in the sera from the vaccinated birds is equal to or greater than the titres obtained with a batch that has given satisfactory results in the test described under Potency.

3 BATCH TESTS
3-1 Identification
When injected into chickens that do not have antibodies against avian infectious bursal disease virus type 1, the vaccine stimulates the production of such antibodies.

3-2 Bacteria and fungi
The vaccine, including where applicable the diluent supplied for reconstitution, complies with the test for sterility prescribed in the monograph *Vaccines for veterinary use (0062)*.

3-3 Residual live virus
A test for residual live virus is carried out to confirm inactivation of avian infectious bursal disease type 1.

A. For vaccine prepared with embryo-adapted strains of virus, inject 2/5 of a dose into the allantoic cavity or onto the chorio-allantoic membrane of ten 9- to 11-day-old embryonated hen eggs from an SPF flock (5.2.2). Incubate the eggs and observe at least daily for 6 days. Pool separately the allantoic liquid or membranes from eggs containing live embryos, and that from eggs containing dead embryos, excluding those that die from non-specific causes within 24 h of the injection.

Inject into the allantoic cavity or onto the chorio-allantoic membrane of each of ten 9- to 11-day-old SPF eggs 0.2 mL of the pooled allantoic liquid or crushed chorio-allantoic membranes from the live embryos and, into each of 10 similar eggs, 0.2 mL of the pooled liquid or membranes from the dead embryos and incubate for 6 days. Examine each embryo for lesions of avian infectious bursal disease. If more than 20 per cent of the embryos die at either stage repeat that stage.

The vaccine complies with the test if there is no evidence of lesions of avian infectious bursal disease and if, in any repeat test, not more than 20 per cent of the embryos die from non-specific causes.

Antibiotics may be used in the test to control extraneous bacterial infection.

B. For vaccine prepared with cell-culture-adapted strains of virus, inoculate 10 doses of the vaccine into suitable cell cultures. If the vaccine contains an oil adjuvant, eliminate it by suitable means. Incubate at 38 $\pm$ 1 °C for 7 days. Make a passage on another set of cell cultures and incubate at 38 $\pm$ 1 °C for 7 days.

The vaccine complies with the test if the cultures show no signs of infection.

3-4 Specified extraneous agents
Use 10 chickens, 14-28 days old, from an SPF flock (5.2.2). Vaccinate each chicken by a recommended route with a double dose of the vaccine. After 3 weeks, administer 1 dose by the same route. Collect serum samples from each chicken 2 weeks later and carry out tests for antibodies against the following agents by the methods prescribed in general chapter 5.2.2. *Chicken flocks free from specified pathogens for the production and quality control of vaccines*: avian encephalomyelitis virus, avian leucosis viruses, egg-drop syndrome virus, avian infectious bronchitis virus, avian infectious laryngotracheitis virus, influenza A virus, Marek's disease virus, Newcastle disease virus.

The vaccine complies with the test if it does not stimulate the formation of antibodies against these agents.

3-5 Potency
The vaccine complies with the requirements of the test mentioned under Immunogenicity (section 2-4-2) when administered by a recommended route and method.

4 LABELLING
The label states whether the strain in the vaccine is embryo-adapted or cell-culture-adapted.

_____ *Ph Eur*

Infectious Bursal Disease Vaccine, Living

Gumboro Disease Vaccine, Living

(Avian Infectious Bursal Disease Vaccine (Live), Ph Eur monograph 0587)

Ph Eur _____

1 DEFINITION
Avian infectious bursal disease vaccine (live) [Gumboro disease vaccine (live)] is a preparation of a suitable strain of infectious bursal disease virus type 1. This monograph applies to vaccines intended for administration to chickens for active immunisation; it applies to vaccines containing strains of low virulence but not to those containing strains of higher virulence that may be needed for disease control in certain epidemiological situations.

2 PRODUCTION
2-1 PREPARATION OF THE VACCINE
The vaccine virus is grown in embryonated hens' eggs or in cell cultures.

2-2 SUBSTRATE FOR VIRUS PROPAGATION
2-2-1 Embryonated hens' eggs
If the vaccine virus is grown in embryonated hens' eggs, they are obtained from flocks free from specified pathogens (SPF) (5.2.2).

2-2-2 Cell cultures
If the vaccine virus is grown in cell cultures, they comply with the requirements for cell cultures for production of veterinary vaccines (5.2.4).

2-3 SEED LOTS
2-3-1 Extraneous agents
The master seed lot complies with the tests for extraneous agents in seed lots (2.6.24). In these tests on the master seed lot, the organisms used are not more than 5 passages from the master seed lot at the start of the tests.

2-4 CHOICE OF VACCINE VIRUS
The vaccine virus shall be shown to be satisfactory with respect to safety (5.2.6) and efficacy (5.2.7) for the chickens for which it is intended.

The following tests for safety (section 2-4-1), damage to the bursa of Fabricius (section 2-4-2), immunosuppression (section 2-4-3), increase in virulence (section 2-4-4) and immunogenicity (section 2-4-5) may be used during the demonstration of safety and efficacy.

2-4-1 Safety
Carry out the test for each route and method of administration to be recommended for vaccination using in each case chickens not older than the minimum age to be recommended for vaccination and from an SPF flock (5.2.2). Use vaccine virus at the least attenuated passage level that will be present in a batch of the vaccine.

For each test performed in chickens younger than 3 weeks of age, use not fewer than 10 chickens. For each test performed in chickens older than 3 weeks of age, use not fewer than 8 chickens. Administer to each chicken a quantity of the vaccine virus equivalent to not less than 10 times the maximum virus titre likely to be contained in 1 dose of the vaccine. Observe the chickens at least daily for at least 14 days.

The test is not valid if more than 10 per cent of the chickens younger than 3 weeks of age show abnormal signs of disease or die from causes not attributable to the vaccine.

For chickens older than 3 weeks of age, the test in not valid if non-specific mortality occurs.

The vaccine virus complies with the test if no chicken shows abnormal signs of disease or dies from causes attributable to the vaccine virus.

2-4-2 Damage to the bursa of Fabricius

Carry out the test for the route to be recommended for vaccination likely to be the least safe using chickens not older than the minimum age to be recommended for vaccination. Use virus at the least attenuated passage level that will be present between the master seed lot and a batch of the vaccine. Use not fewer than 20 chickens from an SPF flock (*5.2.2*). Administer to each chicken a quantity of the vaccine virus equivalent to 10 times the maximum titre likely to be contained in a dose of the vaccine. On each of days 7, 14, 21 and 28 after administration of the vaccine virus, euthanise not fewer than 5 chickens and prepare a section from the site with the greatest diameters of the bursa of Fabricius of each chicken. Carry out histological examination of the section and score the degree of bursal damage using the following scale.

0   No lesion, normal bursa.
1   1 per cent to 25 per cent of the follicles show lymphoid depletion (i.e., less than 50 per cent depletion in 1 affected follicle) influx of heterophils in lesions.
2   26 per cent to 50 per cent of the follicles show nearly complete lymphoid depletion (i.e., more than 75 per cent depletion in 1 affected follicle), affected follicles show necrosis and severe influx of heterophils may be detected.
3   51 per cent to 75 per cent of the follicles show lymphoid depletion; affected follicles show necrosis and severe influx of heterophils is detected.
4   76 per cent to 100 per cent of the follicles show nearly complete lymphoid depletion, hyperplasia and cyst structures are detected; affected follicles show necrosis and severe influx of heterophils is detected.
5   100 per cent of the follicles show nearly complete lymphoid depletion; complete loss of follicular structure, thickened and folded epithelium, fibrosis of bursal tissue.

Calculate the average score for each group of chickens. The vaccine virus complies with the test if:
— no chicken shows notable clinical signs of disease or dies from causes attributable to the vaccine virus,
— the average score for bursal damage 21 days after administration of the vaccine virus is less than or equal to 2.0 and 28 days after administration is less than or equal to 0.6,
— during the 21 days after administration a notable repopulation of the bursae by lymphocytes has taken place.

2-4-3 Immunosuppression

Carry out the tests for the route to be recommended for vaccination likely to be the least safe using chickens not older than the minimum age to be recommended for vaccination. Use vaccine virus at the least attenuated passage level that will be present between the master seed lot and a batch of the vaccine. Use not fewer than 30 chickens from an SPF flock (*5.2.2*). Divide them randomly into 3 groups each of not fewer than 10 and maintain the groups separately. Administer by eye-drop to each chicken of 1 group a quantity of the vaccine virus equivalent to not less than the maximum titre likely to be contained in 1 dose of the vaccine. At the time after administration when maximal bursal damage is likely to be present, as judged from the

results obtained in the test for damage to the bursa of Fabricius (section 2-4-2), administer to each vaccinated chicken and to each chicken of another group 1 dose of Hitchner B1 strain Newcastle disease vaccine (live). Determine the seroresponse of each chicken of the 2 groups to the Newcastle disease virus 14 days after administration. Challenge each chicken of the 3 groups by the intramuscular route with not less than 10^5 EID_{50} of virulent Newcastle disease virus and note the degree of protection in the 2 groups vaccinated with Hitchner B1 strain Newcastle vaccine compared with the non-vaccinated group.

The test is not valid if 1 or more of the non-vaccinated chickens does not die within 7 days of challenge. The degree of immunosuppression is estimated from the comparative seroresponses and protection rates of the 2 Hitchner B1 vaccinated groups.

The vaccine complies with the test if there is no significant difference between the 2 groups.

2-4-4 Increase in virulence

Carry out the test according to general chapter *5.2.6* using chickens from an SPF flock (*5.2.2*) and not older than the minimum age to be recommended for vaccination. If the properties of the vaccine virus allow sequential passage through 5 groups via natural spreading, this method may be used, otherwise passage as described below is carried out.

Administer to each chicken of the 1st group by eye-drop a quantity of the vaccine virus that will allow recovery of virus for the passages described below. Prepare 3 to 4 days after administration a suspension from the bursa of Fabricius of each chicken and pool these samples. Administer 0.05 mL of the pooled samples by eye-drop to each chicken of the next group. Carry out this passage operation not fewer than 4 times; verify the presence of the virus at each passage. If the virus is not found at a passage level, repeat the passage by administration to a group of 10 chickens.

Carry out the test for damage to the bursa of Fabricius (section 2-4-2) using the material used for the 1st passage and the virus at the final passage. Administer the virus by the route to be recommended for vaccination likely to be the least safe.

The vaccine virus complies with the test if no indication of increasing virulence of the virus recovered for the final passage compared with the material used for the 1st passage is observed. If virus is not recovered after an initial passage in 5 chickens and a subsequent repeat passage in 10 chickens, the vaccine virus also complies with the test.

2-4-5 Immunogenicity

A test is carried out for each route and method of administration to be recommended using in each case chickens not older than the minimum age to be recommended for vaccination. The quantity of vaccine virus administered to each chicken is not greater than the minimum virus titre to be stated on the label and the virus is at the most attenuated passage level that will be present in a batch of the vaccine. Use not fewer than 30 chickens of the same origin and from an SPF flock (*5.2.2*). Vaccinate by a route to be recommended not fewer than 20 chickens. Maintain not fewer than 10 chickens as controls. Challenge each chicken after 14 days by eye-drop with a sufficient quantity of virulent avian infectious bursal disease virus. Observe the chickens at least daily for 10 days after challenge. Record the deaths due to infectious bursal disease and the surviving chickens that show clinical signs of disease. At the end of the observation period, euthanise all the surviving chickens and carry out histological examination for lesions of the bursa of Fabricius.

The test is not valid if one or more of the following applies:

— during the observation period following challenge, fewer than 50 per cent of the control chickens show characteristic signs of avian infectious bursal disease;

— 1 or more of the surviving control chickens does not show degree 3 lesions of the bursa of Fabricius;

— during the period between the vaccination and challenge more than 10 per cent of the vaccinated or control chickens show abnormal clinical signs or die from causes not attributable to the vaccine.

The vaccine virus complies with the test if during the observation period after challenge not fewer than 90 per cent of the vaccinated chickens survive and show no notable clinical signs of disease nor degree 3 lesions of the bursa of Fabricius.

3 BATCH TESTS

3-1 Identification

The vaccine, diluted if necessary and mixed with a monospecific infectious bursal disease virus type 1 antiserum, no longer infects embryonated hens′ eggs from an SPF flock (5.2.2) or susceptible cell cultures (5.2.4) into which it is inoculated.

3-2 Bacteria and fungi

Vaccines intended for administration by injection comply with the test for sterility prescribed in the monograph *Vaccines for veterinary use (0062)*.

Frozen or freeze-dried vaccines produced in embryonated eggs and not intended for administration by injection either comply with the test for sterility prescribed in the monograph *Vaccines for veterinary use (0062)* or with the following test: carry out a quantitative test for bacterial and fungal contamination; carry out identification tests for microorganisms detected in the vaccine; the vaccine does not contain pathogenic microorganisms and contains not more than 1 non-pathogenic microorganism per dose.

Any diluent supplied for reconstitution of the vaccine complies with the test for sterility prescribed in the monograph *Vaccines for veterinary use (0062)*.

3-3 Mycoplasmas

The vaccine complies with the test for mycoplasmas (2.6.7).

3-4 Extraneous agents

The vaccine complies with the tests for extraneous agents in batches of finished product (2.6.25).

3-5 Virus titre

Titrate the vaccine virus by inoculation into embryonated hens′ eggs from an SPF flock (5.2.2) or into suitable cell cultures (5.2.4). The vaccine complies with the test if 1 dose contains not less than the minimum virus titre stated on the label.

3-6 Potency

The vaccine complies with the requirements of the test prescribed under Immunogenicity (section 2-4-5) when administered by a recommended route and method. It is not necessary to carry out the potency test for each batch of the vaccine if it has been carried out on a representative batch using a vaccinating dose containing not more than the minimum virus titre stated on the label.

———————————————————— *Ph Eur*

Infectious Chicken Anaemia Vaccine (Live)

(Ph. Eur. monograph 2038)

Ph Eur ————————————————————————————

1 DEFINITION

Infectious chicken anaemia vaccine (live) is a preparation of a suitable strain of chicken anaemia virus. This monograph applies to vaccines intended for administration to breeder chickens for active immunisation, to prevent excretion of the virus, to prevent or reduce egg transmission and to protect passively their future progeny.

2 PRODUCTION

2-1 PREPARATION OF THE VACCINE

The vaccine virus is grown in embryonated hens′ eggs or in cell cultures.

2-2 SUBSTRATE FOR VIRUS PROPAGATION

2-2-1 Embryonated hens′ eggs

If the vaccine virus is grown in embryonated hens′ eggs, they are obtained from flocks free from specified pathogens (SPF) (5.2.2).

2-2-2 Cell cultures

If the vaccine virus is grown in cell cultures, they comply with the requirements for cell cultures for production of veterinary vaccines (5.2.4).

2-3 SEED LOTS

2-3-1 Extraneous agents

The master seed lot complies with the test for extraneous agents in seed lots (2.6.24). In these tests on the master seed lot, the organisms used are not more than 5 passages from the master seed lot at the start of the tests.

2-4 CHOICE OF VACCINE VIRUS

The vaccine virus is shown to be satisfactory with respect to safety (5.2.6) and efficacy (5.2.7) for the chickens for which it is intended.

The following tests for safety (section 2-4-1), increase in virulence (section 2-4-2) and immunogenicity (section 2-4-3) may be used during the demonstration of safety and efficacy.

2-4-1 Safety

Carry out the test for each route and method of administration to be recommended for vaccination in chickens not older than the minimum age to be recommended for vaccination and from an SPF flock (5.2.2). Use vaccine virus at the least attenuated passage level that will be present in a batch of the vaccine.

2-4-1-1 General safety. For each test, use not fewer than 8 chickens. Administer to each chicken a quantity of the vaccine virus equivalent to not less than 10 times the maximum virus titre likely to be contained in 1 dose of the vaccine. 14 days after vaccination, collect blood samples from half of the chickens and determine the haematocrit value. Euthanise these chickens and carry out post-mortem examination. Note any pathological changes attributable to chicken anaemia virus, such as thymic atrophy and specific bone-marrow lesions. Observe the remaining chickens at least daily for at least 21 days.

The test is not valid if non-specific mortality occurs.

The vaccine virus complies with the test if during the observation period no chicken shows abnormal signs of disease or dies from causes attributable to the vaccine virus.

2-4-1-2 Safety for young chickens. Use not fewer than twenty 1-day-old chickens from an SPF flock (5.2.2). Administer to each chicken by the oculonasal route a quantity of the vaccine virus equivalent to not less than the maximum titre likely to be contained in 1 dose of the vaccine. Observe the chickens at least daily. Record the incidence of any signs attributable to the vaccine virus, such as depression, and any deaths. 14 days after vaccination, collect blood samples from half of the chickens and determine the haematocrit value. Euthanise these chickens and carry out post-mortem examination. Note any pathological changes attributable to chicken anaemia virus, such as thymic atrophy and specific bone marrow lesions. Observe the remaining chickens at least daily for at least 21 days. Assess the extent to which the vaccine strain is pathogenic for 1-day-old susceptible chickens from the results of the clinical observations and mortality rates and the proportion of chickens examined at 14 days that show anaemia (haematocrit value less than 27 per cent) and signs of infectious chicken anaemia on post-mortem examination. The results are used to formulate the label statement on safety for young chickens.

2-4-2 Increase in virulence

Carry out the test according to general chapter *5.2.6* using 1-day-old chickens from an SPF flock (*5.2.2*). If the properties of the vaccine virus allow sequential passage through 5 groups via natural spreading, this method may be used, otherwise passage as described below is carried out.

Administer to each chicken of the 1st group by the intramuscular route a quantity of the vaccine virus that will allow recovery of virus for the passages described below. Prepare 7-9 days after administration a suspension from the liver of each chicken and pool these samples. Depending on the tropism of the virus, other tissues such as spleen or bone marrow may be used. Administer 0.1 mL of the pooled samples by the intramuscular route to each chicken of the next group. Carry out this passage operation not fewer than 4 times; verify the presence of the virus at each passage. If the virus is not found at a passage level, repeat the passage by administration to a group of 10 chickens.

If the 5th group of chickens shows no evidence of an increase in virulence indicative of reversion during the observation period, further testing is not required. Otherwise, carry out an additional safety test and compare the clinical signs and any relevant parameters in a group of at least 10 chickens receiving the material used for the 1st passage and another similar group receiving the virus at the final passage level.

The vaccine virus complies with the test if no indication of increased virulence of the virus at the final passage level compared with the material used for the 1st passage is observed. If virus is not recovered after an initial passage in 5 chickens and a subsequent repeat passage in 10 chickens, the vaccine virus also complies with the test.

2-4-3 Immunogenicity

A test is carried out for each route and method of administration to be recommended for vaccination using chickens not older than the minimum age to be recommended for vaccination and from an SPF flock (*5.2.2*). The test for prevention of virus excretion is intended to demonstrate reduction of egg transmission through viraemia and virus excretion in the faeces. The quantity of the vaccine virus to be administered to each chicken is not greater than the minimum virus titre to be stated on the label and the virus is at the most attenuated passage level that will be present in a batch of vaccine.

2-4-3-1 Passive immunisation of chickens. Vaccinate according to the schedule to be recommended not fewer than 10 breeder chickens not older than the minimum age to be

recommended for vaccination and from an SPF flock (*5.2.2*); keep not fewer than 10 unvaccinated breeder chickens of the same origin and from an SPF flock (*5.2.2*) as controls. At a suitable time after excretion of vaccine virus has ceased, collect fertilised eggs from each vaccinated and control breeder chicken and incubate them. Challenge at least 3 randomly chosen 1-day-old chickens from each vaccinated and control breeder chicken by intramuscular administration of a sufficient quantity of virulent chicken anaemia virus. Observe the chickens at least daily for 14 days after challenge. Record the deaths and the surviving chickens that show signs of disease. At the end of the observation period determine the haematocrit value of each surviving chicken. Euthanise these chickens and carry out post-mortem examination. Note any pathological signs attributable to chicken anaemia virus, such as thymic atrophy and specific bone-marrow lesions.

The test is not valid if:
— during the observation period after challenge fewer than 90 per cent of the chickens of the control breeder chickens die or show severe signs of infectious chicken anaemia, including haematocrit value under 27 per cent, and/or notable macroscopic lesions of the bone marrow and thymus;
— and/or during the period between vaccination and egg collection more than 10 per cent of vaccinated or control breeder chickens show notable signs of disease or die from causes not attributable to the vaccine.

The vaccine complies with the test if during the observation period after challenge not fewer than 90 per cent of the chickens of the vaccinated breeder chickens survive and show no notable signs of disease and/or macroscopic lesions of the bone marrow and thymus.

2-4-3-2 Prevention of virus excretion. Vaccinate according to the schedule to be recommended not fewer than 10 chickens not older than the minimum age to be recommended for vaccination and from an SPF flock (*5.2.2*). Maintain separately not fewer than 10 chickens of the same age and origin as controls. At a suitable time after excretion of vaccine virus has ceased, challenge all the chickens by intramuscular administration of a sufficient quantity of virulent chicken anaemia virus. Collect blood samples from the chickens on days 3, 5 and 7 after challenge and faecal samples from the chickens on days 7, 14 and 21 after challenge and carry out a test for presence of virus to determine whether or not the chickens are viraemic and are excreting the virus.

The test is not valid if:
— fewer than 70 per cent of the control chickens are viraemic and excrete the virus at one or more times of sampling;
— and/or during the period between vaccination and challenge more than 10 per cent of control or vaccinated chickens show abnormal clinical signs or die from causes not attributable to the vaccine.

The vaccine complies with the test if not fewer than 90 per cent of the vaccinated chickens do not develop viraemia or excrete the virus.

3 BATCH TESTING
3-1 Identification
The vaccine, diluted if necessary and mixed with a monospecific chicken anaemia virus antiserum, no longer infects susceptible cell cultures or eggs from an SPF flock (*5.2.2*) into which it is inoculated.

3-2 Bacteria and fungi

Vaccines intended for administration by injection comply with the test for sterility prescribed in the monograph *Vaccines for veterinary use (0062)*.

Frozen or freeze-dried vaccines produced in embryonated eggs and not intended for administration by injection either comply with the test for sterility prescribed in the monograph *Vaccines for veterinary use (0062)* or with the following test: carry out a quantitative test for bacterial and fungal contamination; carry out identification tests for microorganisms detected in the vaccine; the vaccine does not contain pathogenic microorganisms and contains not more than 1 non-pathogenic microorganism per dose.

Any diluent supplied for reconstitution of the vaccine complies with the test for sterility prescribed in the monograph *Vaccines for veterinary use (0062)*.

3-3 Mycoplasmas

The vaccine complies with the test for mycoplasmas (*2.6.7*).

3-4 Extraneous agents

The vaccine complies with the tests for extraneous agents in batches of finished product (*2.6.25*).

3-5 Virus titre

Titrate the vaccine virus by inoculation into suitable cell cultures (*5.2.4*) or eggs from an SPF flock (*5.2.2*).
The vaccine complies with the test if 1 dose contains not less than the minimum virus titre stated on the label.

3-6 Potency

The vaccine complies with the requirements of the tests prescribed under Immunogenicity (sections 2-4-3-1 and 2-4-3-2) when administered by a recommended route and method. It is not necessary to carry out the potency test for each batch of the vaccine if it has been carried out on a representative batch using a vaccinating dose containing not more than the minimum virus titre stated on the label.

4 LABELLING

The label states to which extent the vaccine virus causes disease if it spreads to susceptible young chickens.

_____ *Ph Eur*

Laryngotracheitis Vaccine, Living

(Avian Infectious Laryngotracheitis Vaccine (Live), Ph Eur monograph 1068)

Ph Eur _____

1 DEFINITION

Avian infectious laryngotracheitis vaccine (live) is a preparation of a suitable strain of avian infectious laryngotracheitis virus (gallid herpesvirus 1). This monograph applies to vaccines intended for administration to chickens for active immunisation.

2 PRODUCTION
2-1 PREPARATION OF THE VACCINE

The vaccine virus is grown in embryonated hens' eggs or in cell cultures.

2-2 SUBSTRATE FOR VIRUS PROPAGATION
2-2-1 Embryonated hens' eggs

If the vaccine virus is grown in embryonated hens' eggs, they are obtained from flocks free from specified pathogens (SPF) (*5.2.2*).

2-2-2 Cell cultures

If the vaccine virus is grown in cell cultures, they comply with the requirements for cell cultures for production of veterinary vaccines (*5.2.4*).

2-3 SEED LOTS
2-3-1 Extraneous agents

The master seed lot complies with the tests for extraneous agents in seed lots (*2.6.24*). In these tests on the master seed lot, the organisms used are not more than 5 passages from the master seed lot at the start of the tests.

2-4 CHOICE OF VACCINE VIRUS

The vaccine virus shall be shown to be satisfactory with respect to safety (*5.2.6*) and efficacy (*5.2.7*) for the chickens for which it is intended.

The following tests for index of respiratory virulence (section 2-4-1), safety (section 2-4-2), increase in virulence (section 2-4-3) and immunogenicity (section 2-4-4) may be used during the demonstration of safety and efficacy.

2-4-1 Index of respiratory virulence

Use for the test not fewer than sixty 10-day-old chickens from an SPF flock (*5.2.2*). Divide them randomly into 3 groups, maintained separately. Prepare 2 tenfold serial dilutions starting from a suspension of the vaccine virus having a titre of 10^5 EID$_{50}$ or 10^5 CCID$_{50}$ per 0.2 mL or, if not possible, having the maximum attainable titre.
Use vaccine virus at the least attenuated passage level that will be present between the master seed lot and a batch of the vaccine. Allocate the undiluted virus suspension and the 2 virus dilutions each to a different group of chickens. Administer by the intratracheal route to each chicken 0.2 mL of the virus suspension attributed to its group. Observe the chickens for 10 days after administration and record the number of deaths. The index of respiratory virulence is the total number of deaths in the 3 groups divided by the total number of chickens. The vaccine virus complies with the test if its index of respiratory virulence is not greater than 0.33.

2-4-2 Safety

Carry out the test for each route and method of administration to be recommended for vaccination, using in each case chickens not older than the minimum age to be recommended for vaccination and from an SPF flock (*5.2.2*). Use vaccine virus at the least attenuated passage level that will be present in a batch of the vaccine. For each test performed in chickens younger than 3 weeks of age, use not fewer than 10 chickens. For each test performed in chickens older than 3 weeks of age, use not fewer than 8 chickens. Administer to each chicken a quantity of the vaccine virus equivalent to not less than 10 times the maximum virus titre likely to be contained in 1 dose of the vaccine. Observe the chickens at least daily for at least 14 days.

The test is not valid if more than 10 per cent of the chickens younger than 3 weeks of age show abnormal signs of disease or die from causes not attributable to the vaccine.
For chickens older than 3 weeks of age, the test is not valid if non-specific mortality occurs.

The vaccine virus complies with the test if no chicken shows abnormal signs of disease or dies from causes attributable to the vaccine virus.

2-4-3 Increase in virulence

Carry out the test according to general chapter *5.2.6* using chickens not more than 2 weeks old, from an SPF flock (*5.2.2*). If the properties of the vaccine virus allow sequential passage through 5 groups via natural spreading, this method may be used, otherwise passage as described below is carried out.

Administer to each chicken of the 1st group by eye-drop a quantity of the vaccine virus that will allow recovery of virus for the passages described below. After the period shown to correspond to maximum replication of the virus, prepare a suspension from the mucosae of suitable parts of the respiratory tract of each chicken and pool these samples. Administer 0.05 mL of the pooled samples by eye-drop to each 2 week-old SPF chicken (5.2.2) of the next group. Carry out this passage operation not fewer than 4 times; verify the presence of the virus at each passage. If the virus is not found at a passage level, repeat the passage by administration to a group of 10 chickens. Determine the index of respiratory virulence (section 2-4-1) using the material used for the 1st passage and the virus at the final passage level; if the titre of the final passaged virus is less than 10^5 EID_{50} or 10^5 $CCID_{50}$, prepare the tenfold, serial dilutions using the highest titre available.

The vaccine virus complies with the test if no indication of an increase in virulence of the virus recovered for the final passage compared with the material used for the 1st passage is observed. If virus is not recovered after an initial passage in 5 chickens and a subsequent repeat passage in 10 chickens, the vaccine virus also complies with the test.

2-4-4 Immunogenicity
A test is carried out for each route and method of administration to be recommended for vaccination using in each case chickens not older than the minimum age to be recommended for vaccination. The quantity of the vaccine virus administered to each chicken is not greater than the minimum virus titre to be stated on the label and the virus is at the most attenuated passage level that will be present in a batch of the vaccine. Use for the test not fewer than 30 chickens of the same origin and from an SPF flock (5.2.2). Vaccinate by a route to be recommended not fewer than 20 chickens. Maintain not fewer than 10 chickens as controls. Challenge each chicken after 21 days by the intratracheal route with a sufficient quantity of virulent infectious laryngotracheitis virus. Observe the chickens at least daily for 7 days after challenge. Record the deaths and the number of surviving chickens that show clinical signs of disease. At the end of the observation period euthanise all the surviving chickens and carry out examination for macroscopic lesions: mucoid, haemorrhagic and pseudomembraneous inflammation of the trachea and orbital sinuses.

The test is not valid if:
— during the observation period after challenge fewer than 90 per cent of the control chickens die or show severe clinical signs of avian infectious laryngotracheitis or notable macroscopic lesions of the trachea and orbital sinuses;
— or if during the period between the vaccination and challenge more than 10 per cent of the vaccinated or control chickens show notable clinical signs of disease or die from causes not attributable to the vaccine.

The vaccine virus complies with the test if during the observation period after challenge not fewer than 90 per cent of the vaccinated chickens survive and show no notable clinical signs of disease and/or macroscopical lesions of the trachea and orbital sinuses.

3 BATCH TESTS
3-1 Identification
The vaccine, diluted if necessary and mixed with a monospecific infectious laryngotracheitis virus antiserum, no

longer infects embryonated hens' eggs from an SPF flock (5.2.2) or susceptible cell cultures (5.2.4) into which it is inoculated.

3-2 Bacteria and fungi
Vaccines intended for administration by injection comply with the test for sterility prescribed in the monograph *Vaccines for veterinary use (0062)*.

Frozen or freeze-dried vaccines produced in embryonated eggs and not intended for administration by injection either comply with the test for sterility prescribed in the monograph *Vaccines for veterinary use (0062)* or with the following test: carry out a quantitative test for bacterial and fungal contamination; carry out identification tests for micro-organisms detected in the vaccine; the vaccine does not contain pathogenic micro-organisms and contains not more than 1 non-pathogenic micro-organism per dose.

Any diluent supplied for reconstitution of the vaccine complies with the test for sterility prescribed in the monograph *Vaccines for veterinary use (0062)*.

3-3 Mycoplasmas
The vaccine complies with the test for mycoplasmas (2.6.7).

3-4 Extraneous agents
The vaccine complies with the tests for extraneous agents in batches of finished product (2.6.25).

3-5 Virus titre
Titrate the vaccine virus by inoculation into embryonated hens' eggs from an SPF flock (5.2.2) or into suitable cell cultures (5.2.4). The vaccine complies with the test if 1 dose contains not less than the minimum titre stated on the label.

3-6 Potency
The vaccine complies with the requirements of the test prescribed under Immunogenicity (section 2-4-4) when administered according to the recommended schedule by a recommended route and method. It is not necessary to carry out the potency test for each batch of the vaccine if it has been carried out on a representative batch using a vaccinating dose containing not more than the minimum virus titre stated on the label.

—————— Ph Eur

Bovine Leptospirosis Vaccine (Inactivated)

(Ph. Eur. monograph 1939)

Ph Eur —————

1 DEFINITION
Bovine leptospirosis vaccine (inactivated) is a preparation of inactivated whole organisms and/or antigenic extract(s) of one or more suitable strains of one or more of *Leptospira borgpetersenii* serovar hardjo, *Leptospira interrogans* serovar hardjo or other *L. interrogans* serovars, inactivated while maintaining adequate immunogenic properties. This monograph applies to vaccines intended for the active immunisation of cattle against leptospirosis.

2 PRODUCTION
2-1 PREPARATION OF THE VACCINE
The seed material is cultured in a suitable medium; each strain is cultivated separately. During production, various parameters such as growth rate are monitored by suitable methods; the values are within the limits approved for the particular product. Purity and identity are verified on the

harvest using suitable methods. After cultivation, the bacterial harvest is inactivated by a suitable method. The antigen may be concentrated. The vaccine may be adjuvanted.

2-2 CHOICE OF VACCINE COMPOSITION

The vaccine is shown to be satisfactory with respect to safety (5.2.6) and efficacy (5.2.7) for the cattle for which it is intended.

The following tests for safety (section 2-2-1) and immunogenicity (section 2-2-2) may be used during the demonstration of safety and efficacy.

2-2-1 Safety

2-2-1-1 Laboratory tests. Carry out the test for each route and method of administration to be recommended for vaccination and in cattle of each category for which the vaccine is intended (for example, young calves, pregnant cattle). Use a batch of vaccine containing not less than the maximum potency that may be expected in a batch of vaccine.

For each test, use not fewer than 8 cattle that do not have antibodies against *L. borgpetersenii* serovar hardjo and the principal serovars of *L. interrogans* (icterohaemorrhagiae, canicola, grippotyphosa, sejroe, hardjo, hebdomonadis, pomona, australis and autumnalis). Administer to each animal 1 dose of the vaccine. If the schedule to be recommended requires a 2nd dose, administer another dose after an interval of at least 14 days. Observe the cattle at least daily for at least 14 days after the last administration. Record body temperatures the day before each vaccination, at vaccination, 4 h later and daily for 4 days.

The vaccine complies with the test if no animal shows abnormal local or systemic reactions, signs of disease, or dies from causes attributable to the vaccine.

2-2-1-2 Field studies. The cattle used for the field trials are also used to evaluate safety. Use not fewer than 3 groups of 20 cattle with corresponding groups of not fewer than 10 controls in 3 different locations. Examine the injection sites for local reactions after vaccination. Record body temperatures the day before vaccination, at vaccination and on the 2 days following vaccination.

The vaccine complies with the test if no animal shows notable signs of disease or dies from causes attributable to the vaccine. In addition, if the vaccine is for use in pregnant cattle, no adverse effects on the pregnancy and offspring are noted.

2-2-2 Immunogenicity

Carry out a separate test for each of the serovars for which a claim is made for a beneficial effect on the rates of infection and urinary excretion. If claims are to be made for protection against reproductive or production losses, further specific studies will be required.

Each test is carried out for each route and method of administration to be recommended, using in each case cattle of the minimum age to be recommended for vaccination. The vaccine administered to each animal is of minimum potency.

2-2-2-1 Immunogenicity against L. borgpetersenii serovar hardjo. Use not fewer than 15 cattle that do not have antibodies against *L. borgpetersenii* serovar hardjo and the principal serovars of *L. interrogans* (icterohaemorrhagiae, canicola, grippotyphosa, sejroe, hardjo, hebdomonadis, pomona, australis and autumnalis). Vaccinate not fewer than 10 cattle according to the schedule to be recommended. Maintain not fewer than 5 cattle as controls. 20-22 days after the last vaccination, challenge all the cattle by a suitable mucosal route with a sufficient quantity of a virulent strain of the

relevant serovar. Observe the cattle at least daily for a further 35 days. Collect urine samples from each animal on days 0, 14, 21, 28 and 35 post-challenge. Euthanise surviving cattle at the end of the observation period. Carry out post-mortem examination on any animal that dies and on those euthanised at the end of the observation period. In particular, examine the kidneys for macroscopic and microscopic signs of leptospira infection. A sample of each kidney is collected and each urine and kidney sample is tested for the presence of the challenge organisms by re-isolation or by another suitable method.

For the test conducted with *L. borgpetersenii* serovar hardjo, control cattle are regarded as infected if the challenge organisms are re-isolated from at least 2 samples. The test is not valid if infection has been established in fewer than 80 per cent of the control cattle.

The vaccine complies with the test if the challenge organisms are re-isolated from any urine or kidney sample from not more than 20 per cent of the vaccinated cattle.

2-2-2-2 Immunogenicity against other leptospira species. For leptospiral species other than *L. borgpetersenii* serovar hardjo, the test is conducted as described in section 2-2-2-1 but urine samples are collected on appropriate days, determined by the characteristics of the challenge model. In the case of serovars for which there is published evidence that the serovar has a lower tropism for the urinary tract, a lower rate of infection may be justified. Depending on their tissue tropism, for some leptospira serovars, samples from other tissues/body fluids can be used to establish whether the cattle are infected or not by the challenge organism.

2-3 MANUFACTURER'S TESTS

2-3-1 Batch potency test

It is not necessary to carry out the potency test (section 3-4) for each batch of vaccine if it has been carried out using a batch of vaccine with a minimum potency. Where the test is not carried out, an alternative validated method is used, the criteria for acceptance being set with reference to a batch of vaccine that has given satisfactory results in the test described under Potency. The following test may be used.

For each of the serovars for which protection is claimed, the antibody response from vaccinated animals is measured. Use not fewer than 12 guinea-pigs weighing 250-350 g that do not have antibodies against *L. borgpetersenii* serovar hardjo and the principal serovars of *L. interrogans* (icterohaemorrhagiae, canicola, grippotyphosa, sejroe, hardjo, hebdomonadis, pomona, australis and autumnalis) and that have been obtained from a regularly tested and certified leptospira-free source. The dose to be administered to the guinea-pigs is that fraction of a cattle dose which has been shown in the validation studies to provide a suitably sensitive test. Vaccinate each of 10 guinea-pigs with the suitable dose. Maintain not fewer than 2 guinea-pigs as controls. At a given interval within the range of 19-23 days after the injection, collect blood from each guinea-pig and prepare serum samples. Use a suitable validated method such as a micro-agglutination test to measure the antibodies in each sample.

The vaccine complies with the test if antibody levels are equal to or greater than those obtained with a batch that has given satisfactory results in the test described under Potency and there is no significant increase in antibody titre in the controls.

3 BATCH TESTS

3-1 Identification

When injected into healthy animals that do not have specific antibodies against the leptospira serovar(s) present in the vaccine, the vaccine stimulates the production of such antibodies.

3-2 Bacteria and fungi

The vaccine, including where applicable the diluent supplied for reconstitution, complies with the test for sterility prescribed in the monograph *Vaccines for veterinary use (0062)*.

3-3 Residual live bacteria

Carry out a test for live leptospirae by inoculation of a specific medium. Inoculate 1 mL of the vaccine into 100 mL of the medium. Incubate at 30 °C for 14 days, subculture into a further quantity of the medium and incubate both media at 30 °C for 14 days: the vaccine complies with the test if no growth occurs in either medium. At the same time, carry out a control test by inoculating a further quantity of the medium with the vaccine together with a quantity of a culture containing approximately 100 leptospirae and incubating at 30 °C: the test is not valid if growth of leptospirae does not occur within 14 days.

3-4 Potency

The vaccine complies with the requirements of the test mentioned under Immunogenicity (section 2-2-2) when administered by a recommended route and method.

_____ *Ph Eur*

Canine Leptospirosis Vaccine (Inactivated)

(Ph. Eur. monograph 0447)

Ph Eur _____

1 DEFINITION

Canine leptospirosis vaccine (inactivated) is a preparation of inactivated whole organisms and/or antigenic extract(s) of one or more suitable strains of one or more of *Leptospira interrogans* serovar canicola, serovar icterohaemorrhagiae or any other epidemiologically appropriate serovar, inactivated while maintaining adequate immunogenic properties. This monograph applies to vaccines intended for the active immunisation of dogs against leptospirosis.

2 PRODUCTION

2-1 PREPARATION OF THE VACCINE

The seed material is cultured in a suitable medium; each strain is cultivated separately. During production, various parameters such as growth rate are monitored by suitable methods; the values are within the limits approved for the particular product. Purity and identity are verified on the harvest using suitable methods. After cultivation, the bacterial harvests are collected separately and inactivated by a suitable method. The antigen may be concentrated. The vaccine may be adjuvanted.

2-2 CHOICE OF VACCINE COMPOSITION

The vaccine is shown to be satisfactory with respect to safety (*5.2.6*) and efficacy (*5.2.7*) for the dogs for which it is intended.

The following tests for safety (section 2-2-1) and immunogenicity (section 2-2-2) may be used during the demonstration of safety and efficacy.

2-2-1 Safety

Carry out the test for each route and method of administration to be recommended for vaccination and in dogs of each category for which the vaccine is to be intended, using in each case dogs not older than the minimum age to be recommended for vaccination. Use a batch of vaccine containing not less than the maximum potency that may be expected in a batch of vaccine.

For each test, use not fewer than 8 dogs that do not have antibodies against the principal *L. interrogans* serovars (icterohaemorrhagiae, canicola, grippotyphosa, sejroe, hardjo, hebdomonadis, pomona, australis and autumnalis). Administer to each dog 1 dose of the vaccine. If the schedule to be recommended requires a 2nd dose, administer 1 dose after the recommended interval. Observe the dogs at least daily for at least 14 days after the last administration. Record body temperatures the day before each vaccination, at vaccination, 4 h later and daily for 4 days.

The vaccine complies with the test if no dog shows abnormal local or systemic reactions, signs of disease or dies from causes attributable to the vaccine.

2-2-2 Immunogenicity

For each type of the serovars against which protective immunity is claimed on the label, carry out a separate test with a challenge strain representative of that serovar.

Each test is carried out for each route and method of administration to be recommended for vaccination, using in each case dogs of the minimum age to be recommended. The vaccine administered to each dog is of minimum potency.

Use for the test not fewer than 12 dogs that do not have antibodies against the principal serovars of *L. interrogans* (icterohaemorrhagiae, canicola, grippotyphosa, sejroe, hardjo, hebdomonadis, pomona, australis and autumnalis). Vaccinate not fewer than 6 dogs, according to the schedule to be recommended. Maintain not fewer than 6 dogs as controls. Challenge each dog after 25-28 days by the conjunctival and/or intraperitoneal route with a sufficient quantity of a suspension of the relevant pathogenic *L. interrogans* serovar. Observe the dogs at least daily for 28 days after challenge.

Examine the dogs daily and record and score clinical signs observed post-challenge and any deaths that occur. If a dog shows marked signs of disease, it is euthanised. Monitor body temperatures each day for the first week after challenge. Collect blood samples from each dog on days 0, 2, 3, 4, 5, 8 and 11 post challenge. Collect urine samples from each dog on days 0, 3, 5, 8, 11, 14, 21 and 28 post challenge. Euthanise surviving dogs at the end of the observation period. Carry out post-mortem examination on any dog that dies during the observation period and on the remainder when euthanised at the end of the observation period. In particular, examine the liver and kidneys for macroscopic and microscopic signs of leptospira infection. Take a sample of each kidney and test each blood, urine and kidney sample for the presence of challenge organisms by re-isolation or by another suitable method. Analyse blood samples to detect biochemical and haematological changes indicative of infection and score these.

The test is not valid if: samples give positive results on day 0; *L. interrogans* serovar challenge strain is re-isolated from or demonstrated by another suitable method to be present in fewer than 2 samples on fewer than 2 different days, to show infection has been established in fewer than 80 per cent of the control dogs.

The vaccine complies with the test if: at least 80 per cent of the vaccinates show no more than mild signs of disease (for example, transient hyperthermia) and, depending on the *L. interrogans* serovar used for the challenge, one or more of the following is also shown:

— where the vaccine is intended to have a beneficial effect against signs of disease, the clinical scores and haematological and biochemical scores are statistically lower for the vaccinates than for the controls,
— where the vaccine is intended to have a beneficial effect against infection, the number of days that the organisms are detected in the blood is statistically lower for the vaccinates than for the controls,
— where the vaccine is intended to have a beneficial effect against urinary tract infection and excretion, the number of days that the organisms are detected in the urine and the number of kidney samples in which the organisms are detected is statistically lower for the vaccinates than for the controls.

2-3 MANUFACTURER'S TESTS
2-3-1 Batch potency test
It is not necessary to carry out the Potency test (section 3-4) for each batch of the vaccine if it has been carried out using a batch of vaccine with a minimum potency. Where the test is not carried out, an alternative validated method is used, the criteria for acceptance being set with reference to a batch of vaccine that has given satisfactory results in the test described under Potency. The following tests may be used.

2-3-1-1 For vaccines with or without adjuvants. If leptospira from more than one serovar (for example *L. interrogans* serovar canicola and serovar icterohaemorrhagiae) has been used to prepare the vaccine, carry out a batch potency test for each serovar against which protective immunity is claimed on the label. Use for the test 10 healthy hamsters not more than 3 months old, that do not have antibodies against the principal serovars of *L. interrogans* (icterohaemorrhagiae, canicola, grippotyphosa, sejroe, hardjo, hebdomadis, pomona, australis and autumnalis) and which have been obtained from a regularly tested and certified leptospira-free source. Administer 1/40 of the dose for dogs by the subcutaneous route to 5 hamsters. Maintain 5 hamsters as controls. Challenge each hamster after 15-20 days by the intraperitoneal route with a sufficient quantity of a virulent culture of leptospirae of the serovar against which protective immunity is claimed on the label. The vaccine complies with the test if not fewer than 4 of the 5 control hamsters die showing typical signs of leptospira infection within 14 days of receiving the challenge suspension and if not fewer than 4 of the 5 vaccinated hamsters remain in good health for 14 days after the death of 4 control hamsters.

2-3-1-2 For vaccines with or without adjuvants. A suitable validated sero-response test may be carried out. Vaccinate each animal in a group of experimental animals with a suitable dose. Collect blood samples after a suitable, fixed time after vaccination. For each of the serovars present in the vaccine, an *in vitro* test is carried out on individual blood samples to determine the antibody response to one or more antigenic components which are indicators of protection and which are specific for that serovar. The criteria for acceptance are set with reference to a batch of vaccine that has given satisfactory results in the test described under Potency.

2-3-1-3 For vaccines without adjuvants. For each of the serovars present in the vaccine, a suitable validated *in vitro* test may be carried out to determine the content of one or more antigenic components which are indicators of protection and which are specific for that serovar.

The criteria for acceptance are set with reference to a batch of vaccine that has given satisfactory results in the test described under Potency.

3 BATCH TESTS
3-1 Identification
When injected into healthy animals that do not have specific antibodies against leptospira serovar(s) present in the vaccine, the vaccine stimulates the production of such antibodies. If test 2-3-1-3 is used for the batch potency test, it also serves to identify the vaccine.

3-2 Bacteria and fungi
The vaccine, including where applicable the diluent supplied for reconstitution, complies with the test for sterility prescribed in the monograph *Vaccines for veterinary use (0062)*.

3-3 Residual live bacteria
Carry out a test for live leptospirae by inoculation of a specific medium. Inoculate 1 mL of the vaccine into 100 mL of the medium. Incubate at 30 °C for 14 days, subculture into a further quantity of the medium and incubate both media at 30 °C for 14 days: the vaccine complies with the test if no growth occurs in either medium. At the same time, carry out a control test by inoculating a further quantity of the medium with the vaccine together with a quantity of a culture containing approximately 100 leptospirae and incubating at 30 °C: the test is not valid if growth of leptospirae does not occur within 14 days.

3-4 Potency
The vaccine complies with the requirements of the test mentioned under Immunogenicity (section 2-2-2) when administered by a recommended route and method.

Ph Eur

Louping-ill Vaccine
DEFINITION
Louping-ill Vaccine is a preparation of a suitable strain of louping-ill virus which has been inactivated in such a manner that immunogenic activity is retained.

PRODUCTION
The virus strain is grown in suitable cell cultures, Appendix XV J(Vet)1. The viral suspension is harvested and inactivated. A test for residual infectious louping-ill virus is carried out on each batch of antigen immediately after inactivation. A mouse inoculation test may provide a suitably sensitive test if there is no suitably sensitive *in vitro* test for the strain.

The vaccine contains an adjuvant.

CHOICE OF VACCINE COMPOSITION
This vaccine is shown to be satisfactory with respect to safety and immunogenicity for the animals for which the vaccine is intended. The following tests may be used during the demonstration of safety, Appendix XV J(Vet) 1 and immunogenicity, Appendix XV J(Vet) 2.

Safety
Carry out a test in each category of each species of animal for which the vaccine is to be recommended and by each recommended route of administration. Vaccinate at least five animals that do not have antibodies to louping-ill virus. Use for the test a batch of vaccine with the maximum

potency likely to be included in a dose of the vaccine. Administer a single dose of vaccine to each animal and observe them for two weeks. If the schedule to be recommended requires a single dose or primary vaccination series followed by booster vaccination, the primary vaccination regimen plus an additional dose should be used with an interval of 14 days between doses. No abnormal local or systemic reactions occur.

Immunogenicity
The tests to demonstrate immunogenicity are carried out in each category of each species of animal for which the vaccine is to be recommended and by each recommended route of administration and using a batch or batches with the minimum potency likely to be included in a dose of the vaccine. The efficacy claims made on the label reflect the type of data generated.

BATCH TESTING

Inactivation
Carry out a suitable validated test for residual louping-ill virus on the bulk antigen blend immediately before the addition of the adjuvant. No live virus is detected.

The vaccine complies with the requirements stated under Veterinary Vaccines with the following modifications.

IDENTIFICATION
When injected into healthy seronegative animals, the vaccine stimulates the production of specific haemagglutinating antibodies against louping-ill virus.

TESTS
Extraneous bacteria and fungi
The vaccine complies with the test for sterility described under Veterinary Vaccines.

POTENCY
Inject subcutaneously each of no fewer than six healthy sheep, free from louping-ill haemagglutination-inhibiting (HI) antibodies, with the dose stated on the label. Between 14 and 28 days after injection the serum of at least five of the sheep contains HI antibodies at dilutions of 1 in 20 or greater against 4 to 8 haemagglutinating units.

Lungworm (Dictyocaulus Viviparus) Oral Vaccine, Living

DEFINITION
Lungworm (Dictyocaulus Viviparus) Oral Vaccine, Living is an aqueous preparation containing approximately 1000 modified *Dictyocaulus viviparus* larvae per dose.

PRODUCTION
The vaccinal organisms are produced in calves. The calves used for production are obtained from a known, defined source that is monitored for freedom from certain diseases, as agreed with the competent authority. The calves are healthy, have not been exposed previously to *Dictyocaulus viviparus* and have been shown to be free from a range of infectious diseases, as agreed with the competent authority.

The third stage larvae are harvested from the faeces, purified, partially inactivated by ionising radiation, then diluted as necessary.

CHOICE OF VACCINE STRAIN
The suspension of irradiated vaccinal organisms is shown to be satisfactory with respect to safety and immunogenicity for the animals for which the vaccine is intended. The following

tests may be used during the demonstration of safety, Appendix XV K(Vet) 1 and immunogenicity, Appendix XV K(Vet) 2.

Safety
Carry out a test in at least five calves of the minimum age to be recommended for vaccination that do not have antibodies to *Dictyocaulus viviparus*. Administer orally, to each calf, a quantity of irradiated vaccinal organisms corresponding to twice the maximum number of organisms likely to be included in a dose of the vaccine. If the schedule to be recommended requires a single dose or primary vaccination series followed by booster vaccination, the primary vaccination regimen plus an additional dose should be used with an interval of 14 days between doses. Observe the calves for 6 weeks after the last administration. They remain in good health and show no more than transient respiratory signs approximately one week after vaccination. Collect faecal samples from each calf 4, 5 and 6 weeks after vaccination and examine separately for the presence of *D. viviparus* larvae. No larvae are detected.

Immunogenicity
The test described under Potency is suitable to demonstrate immunogenicity when carried out using the minimum number of organisms likely to be included in a dose of the vaccine.

BATCH TESTING
If Identification test B and the test for Potency have been carried out with satisfactory results on a representative batch of vaccine, these tests may be omitted as a routine control on other batches of vaccine subject to the agreement of the competent authority.

Extraneous bacteria
For each batch, the number of non-pathogenic organisms per dose is shown to be within the limits set for the product and shown to be safe.

The vaccine complies with the requirements stated under Veterinary Vaccines with the following modifications.

IDENTIFICATION
A. Produces petechial haemorrhages in the lungs of guinea-pigs within 48 hours of oral administration. Adult worms do not develop.

B. Protects calves against *D. viviparus* infection and does not cause parasitic bronchitis.

TESTS
Extraneous bacteria and fungi
The vaccine is shown by appropriate methods to be free from pathogenic organisms including *Brucella*, *Mycobacteria* and *Salmonella* species.

Extraneous viruses
Inoculate the vaccine onto suitable cell cultures susceptible to bovine viruses, make at least one passage and maintain the cultures for at least 14 days. No cytopathic effect develops.

Carry out a specific test for freedom from bovine viral diarrhoea. No evidence of bovine viral diarrhoea is found.

Carry out a test for freedom from haemadsorbing agents. The cell cultures show no signs of viral contamination.

Viable larvae
The number of viable larvae is not less than 1000 per dose determined by microscopic examination.

POTENCY
Use calves of the minimum age for vaccination recommended on the label and that do not have antibodies

to *D. viviparus*. Vaccinate at least ten calves as recommended on the label. Maintain at least five calves as unvaccinated controls. Seven weeks after vaccination challenge by oral administration of a sufficient quantity of stage 3 larvae. Observe the calves for 40 days and monitor and score the calves for signs of respiratory disease (e.g. increased respiratory rate, coughing). Carry out post-mortem examination of the lungs of any animal that dies during the observation period. At the end of the observation period, kill the surviving calves and examine the lungs. The test is not valid unless the control calves show typical signs of respiratory disease due to lungworm infection and, at post-mortem examination, there are noticeable, typical lesions in the lungs (e.g. areas of consolidation) and in calves submitted to post-mortem examination in the later stages, adult worms are present.

The vaccine complies with the test if the vaccinated calves show no more than very mild respiratory signs after challenge and, at post-mortem examination, there are no or only very limited lesions in the lungs (e.g. areas of consolidation) and no or very few adult worms are present.

Mannheimia Vaccine (Inactivated) for Cattle

(Ph. Eur. monograph 1944)

Ph Eur _____

1 DEFINITION

Mannheimia vaccine (inactivated) for cattle is a preparation from cultures of one or more suitable strains of *Mannheimia haemolytica* (formerly *Pasteurella haemolytica*), inactivated while maintaining adequate immunogenic properties. This monograph applies to vaccines intended for active immunisation of cattle of different ages against respiratory diseases caused by *M. haemolytica*.

2 PRODUCTION
2-1 PREPARATION OF THE VACCINE

Production of the vaccine is based on a seed-lot system. The seed material is cultured in a suitable medium; each strain is cultivated separately and identity is verified using a suitable method. During production, various parameters such as growth rate are monitored by suitable methods; the values are within the limits approved for the particular product. Purity and identity of the harvest are verified using suitable methods. After cultivation, the bacterial suspensions are collected separately and inactivated by a suitable method. The vaccine may be adjuvanted.

2-2 CHOICE OF VACCINE COMPOSITION

The choice of composition and the strains to be included in the vaccine is based on epidemiological data on the prevalence of the different serovars of *M. haemolytica* and on the claims being made.

The vaccine is shown to be satisfactory with respect to safety (5.2.6) and efficacy (5.2.7) for the cattle for which it is intended.

The following tests for safety (section 2-2-1) and immunogenicity (section 2-2-2) may be used during the demonstration of safety and efficacy.

2-2-1 Safety

2-2-1-1 Laboratory tests. Carry out the test for each route and method of administration to be recommended for vaccination and in cattle of each category for which the vaccine is intended (for example, young calves, pregnant cattle). Use a batch of vaccine containing not less than the maximum potency that may be expected in a batch of vaccine.

For each test, use not fewer than 8 cattle that preferably do not have antibodies against the serovars of *M. haemolytica* or against the leucotoxin present in the vaccine. Where justified, cattle with a known history of no previous mannheimia vaccination and with low antibody titres (measured in a sensitive test system such as ELISA) may be used. Administer to each animal 1 dose of the vaccine. If the schedule to be recommended requires a 2nd dose, administer another dose after an interval of at least 14 days. Observe the cattle at least daily for at least 14 days after the last administration. Record body temperature the day before vaccination, at vaccination, 2 h, 4 h and 6 h later and then daily for 4 days; note the maximum temperature increase for each animal.

The vaccine complies with the test if no animal shows abnormal local or systemic reactions or signs of disease, or dies from causes attributable to the vaccine, if the average body temperature increase for all cattle does not exceed 1.5 °C, and if no animal shows a rise greater than 2.0 °C.

2-2-1-2 Field studies. The cattle used for the field trials are also used to evaluate safety. Carry out a test in each category of cattle for which the vaccine is intended. Use not fewer than 3 groups of 20 cattle with corresponding groups of not fewer than 10 controls in 3 different locations. Examine the injection sites for local reactions after vaccination. Record body temperatures the day before vaccination, at vaccination and on the 2 days following vaccination.

The vaccine complies with the test if no animal shows abnormal local or systemic reactions or signs of disease, or dies from causes attributable to the vaccine. The average body temperature increase for all cattle does not exceed 1.5 °C and no animal shows a rise greater than 2.0 °C. In addition, if the vaccine is intended for use in pregnant cows, no significant effects on gestation or the offspring are demonstrated.

2-2-2 Immunogenicity

Carry out a test for each serovar for which protection is claimed on the label.

Each test is carried out for each route and method of administration to be recommended, using in each case cattle of the minimum age to be recommended for vaccination. The vaccine administered to each animal is of minimum potency.

Use not fewer than 16 cattle that do not have antibodies against *M. haemolytica* and against the leucotoxin of *M. haemolytica*. Vaccinate not fewer than 8 of the cattle according to the schedule to be recommended. Maintain not fewer than 8 cattle as controls. Challenge each animal 20-22 days after the last vaccination by the intratracheal route or by another appropriate route, with a sufficient quantity of a low-passage, virulent strain of a serovar of *M. haemolytica*. Observe the cattle at least daily for a further 7 days; to avoid unnecessary suffering, severely ill cattle are euthanised and are then considered to have died from the disease. During the observation period, examine the cattle for signs of disease (for example, increased body temperature, dullness, abnormal breathing) and record the mortality. Euthanise surviving cattle at the end of the observation period. Carry out post-mortem examination on any animal that dies and those euthanised at the end of the observation period. Examine the lungs and evaluate the extent of lung lesions due to mannheimiosis. Collect samples of lung tissue for re-isolation of the challenge organisms. Score the clinical observations and lung lesions and compare the results obtained for these parameters and the bacterial re-isolation results for the 2 groups.

The test is not valid if signs of *M. haemolytica* infection occur in less than 70 per cent of the control cattle. The vaccine complies with the test if there is a significant difference between the scores obtained for the clinical and post-mortem observations in the vaccinates compared to the controls. For vaccines with a claim for a beneficial effect on the extent of infection against the serovar, the results for the infection rates are also significantly better for the vaccinates compared to the controls.

2-3 MANUFACTURER'S TESTS

2-3-1 Batch potency test
It is not necessary to carry out the potency test (section 3-3) for each batch of vaccine if it has been carried out using a batch of vaccine with a minimum potency. Where the test is not carried out, an alternative validated method is used, the criteria for acceptance being set with reference to a batch of vaccine that has given satisfactory results in the test described under Potency.

2-3-2 Bacterial endotoxins
A test for bacterial endotoxins (*2.6.14*) is carried out on the final lot or, where the nature of the adjuvant prevents performance of a satisfactory test, on the bulk antigen or the mixture of bulk antigens immediately before addition of the adjuvant. The maximum acceptable amount of bacterial endotoxins is that found for a batch of vaccine that has been shown satisfactory in safety test 2-2-1-1 given under Choice of vaccine composition. The method chosen for determining the amount of bacterial endotoxin present in the vaccine batch used in the safety test for determining the maximum acceptable level of endotoxin is used subsequently for testing of each batch.

3 BATCH TESTS

3-1 Identification
When injected into healthy animals that do not have specific antibodies against the serovars of *M. haemolytica* and/or against the leucotoxin present in the vaccine, the vaccine stimulates the production of such antibodies.

3-2 Bacteria and fungi
The vaccine, including where applicable the diluent supplied for reconstitution, complies with the test for sterility prescribed in the monograph *Vaccines for veterinary use (0062)*.

3-3 Potency
The vaccine complies with the requirements of the test mentioned under Immunogenicity (section 2-2-2) when administered by a recommended route and method.

Ph Eur

Mannheimia Vaccine (Inactivated) for Sheep

(Ph. Eur. monograph 1946)

Ph Eur

1 DEFINITION
Mannheimia vaccine (inactivated) for sheep is a preparation of one or more suitable strains of *Mannheimia haemolytica* (formerly *Pasteurella haemolytica*), inactivated while

maintaining adequate immunogenic properties. This monograph applies to vaccines intended for the active immunisation of sheep and/or for the passive protection of their progeny against disease caused by *M. haemolytica*.

2 PRODUCTION

2-1 PREPARATION OF THE VACCINE
Production of the vaccine is based on a seed-lot system. The seed material is cultured in a suitable medium; each strain is cultivated separately and identity is verified using a suitable method. During production, various parameters such as growth rate are monitored by suitable methods; the values are within the limits approved for the particular product. Purity and identity of the harvest are verified using suitable methods. After cultivation, the bacterial suspensions are collected separately and inactivated by a suitable method. The vaccine may be adjuvanted.

2-2 CHOICE OF VACCINE COMPOSITION
The choice of composition and the strains to be included in the vaccine are based on epidemiological data on the prevalence of the different serovars of *M. haemolytica* and on the claims being made for the product, for example active and/or passive protection.

The vaccine is shown to be satisfactory with respect to safety (*5.2.6*) and efficacy (*5.2.7*) for the sheep for which it is intended.

The following tests for safety (section 2-2-1) and immunogenicity (section 2-2-2) may be used during the demonstration of safety and efficacy.

2-2-1 Safety
2-2-1-1 Laboratory tests. Carry out the tests for each route and method of administration to be recommended for vaccination and in sheep of each category for which the vaccine is intended (for example, young sheep, pregnant ewes). Use a batch of vaccine containing not less than the maximum potency that may be expected in a batch of vaccine.

For each test, use not fewer than 8 sheep that preferably do not have antibodies against the serovars of *M. haemolytica* or against the leucotoxin present in the vaccine. Where justified, sheep with a known history of no previous mannheimia vaccination and with low antibody titres (measured in a sensitive test system such as ELISA) may be used. Administer to each sheep 1 dose of the vaccine. If the schedule to be recommended requires a 2nd dose, administer another dose after an interval of at least 14 days. Observe the sheep at least daily for at least 14 days after the last administration. If the test is carried out in pregnant ewes, observe the ewes until 1 day after lambing. Record body temperature the day before vaccination, at vaccination, 2 h, 4 h and 6 h later and then daily for 4 days; note the maximum temperature increase for each sheep.

The vaccine complies with the test if:
— no sheep shows abnormal local reactions or notable signs of disease, or dies from causes attributable to the vaccine,
— the average body temperature increase for all sheep does not exceed 1.5 °C and no sheep shows a rise greater than 2.0 °C, and if
— no adverse effects on gestation or the offspring are noted if the test is carried out in pregnant ewes.

2-2-1-2 Field studies. The sheep used for the field trials are also used to evaluate safety. Carry out a test in each category of sheep for which the vaccine is intended. Use not fewer than 3 groups of 20 sheep with corresponding groups of not fewer than 10 controls in 3 different locations. Examine the injection sites for local reactions after vaccination. Record body temperatures the day before vaccination, at vaccination and on the 2 days following vaccination.

The vaccine complies with the test if no sheep shows abnormal local or systemic reactions or notable signs of disease, or dies from causes attributable to the vaccine. The average body temperature increase for all sheep does not exceed 1.5 °C and no sheep shows a rise greater than 2.0 °C. In addition, if the vaccine is intended for use in pregnant ewes, no adverse effects on the gestation or offspring are demonstrated.

2-2-2 Immunogenicity

2-2-2-1 Active immunisation. For vaccines with claims for active immunisation against mannheimiosis, carry out a test for each serovar of *M. haemolytica* for which protection is to be claimed on the label.

A test is carried out for each route and method of administration to be recommended, using in each case lambs of the minimum age to be recommended for vaccination. The vaccine administered to each lamb is of minimum potency.

Use not fewer than 20 lambs that do not have antibodies against *M. haemolytica* and against the leucotoxin of *M. haemolytica*. Vaccinate not fewer than 10 lambs according to the schedule to be recommended. Maintain not fewer than 10 lambs as controls. 20-22 days after the last vaccination, challenge each lamb by the intratracheal route or by another appropriate route, with a sufficient quantity of a low-passage, virulent strain of a serovar of *M. haemolytica*. Where necessary for a given serovar, prechallenge with parainfluenza type 3 (PI3) virus or another appropriate respiratory pathogen may be used. Observe the lambs for a further 7 days; to avoid unnecessary suffering, severely ill lambs are euthanised and are then considered to have died from the disease. During the observation period, examine the lambs for signs of disease (for example, increased body temperature, dullness, abnormal respiration) and record the mortality. Euthanise surviving lambs at the end of the observation period. Carry out post-mortem examination on any lamb that dies and those euthanised at the end of the observation period. Examine the lungs and evaluate the extent of lung lesions due to mannheimiosis. Collect samples of lung tissue for re-isolation of the challenge organisms. Score the clinical observations and lung lesions and compare the results obtained for these parameters and the bacterial re-isolation results for the 2 groups.

The test is not valid if signs of *M. haemolytica* infection occur in less than 70 per cent of the control lambs. The vaccine complies with the test if there is a significant difference between the scores obtained for the clinical and post-mortem observations in the vaccinates compared to the controls. For vaccines with a claim for a beneficial effect on the extent of infection against the serovar, the results for the infection rates are also significantly better for the vaccinates compared to the controls.

2-2-2-2 Passive protection. For vaccines with claims for passive protection against mannheimiosis carry out a test for each serovar of *M. haemolytica* for which protection is to be claimed on the label.

A test is carried out for each route and method of administration to be recommended for vaccination. The vaccine administered to each ewe is of minimum potency.

Use not fewer than 6 ewes that preferably do not have antibodies against the serovars of *M. haemolytica* or against

the leucotoxin present in the vaccine. Where justified, ewes with a known history of no previous mannheimia vaccination, from a source with a low incidence of respiratory disease and with low antibody titres (measured in a sensitive test system such as ELISA) may be used. Vaccinate the ewes at the stages of pregnancy and according to the schedule to be recommended. A challenge study is conducted with 20 newborn, colostrum-deprived lambs. 10 of these lambs are given colostrum from the vaccinated ewes and 10 control lambs are given colostrum or colostrum substitute without detectable antibodies to *M. haemolytica*. When the lambs are at the age to be claimed for the duration of the passive protection, challenge each by the intratracheal route with a sufficient quantity of a low-passage, virulent strain of a serovar of *M. haemolytica*. Observe the lambs for a further 7 days; to avoid unnecessary suffering, severely ill lambs are euthanised and are then considered to have died from the disease. Observe the lambs and assess the effect of the challenge on the offspring of the vaccinates and the controls as described in the test for active immunisation.

The test is not valid if signs or lesions of *M. haemolytica* infection occur in less than 70 per cent of the control lambs. The vaccine complies with the test if there is a significant difference between the scores obtained for the clinical and post-mortem observations in the lambs from the vaccinates compared to those from the controls. For vaccines with a claim for a beneficial effect on the extent of infection against the serovar, the results for the infection rates are also significantly better for the lambs from the vaccinates compared to those from the controls.

2-3 MANUFACTURER'S TESTS

2-3-1 Batch potency test

It is not necessary to carry out the relevant potency test or tests (section 3-3) for each batch of vaccine if they have been carried out using a batch of vaccine with a minimum potency. Where the relevant test or tests are not carried out, an alternative validated method is used, the criteria for acceptance being set with reference to a batch of vaccine that has given satisfactory results in the test(s) described under Potency.

2-3-2 Bacterial endotoxins

A test for bacterial endotoxins (*2.6.14*) is carried out on the final lot or, where the nature of the adjuvant prevents performance of a satisfactory test, on the bulk antigen or the mixture of bulk antigens immediately before addition of the adjuvant. The maximum acceptable amount of bacterial endotoxins is that found for a batch of vaccine that has been shown satisfactory in safety tests 2-2-1-1 given under Choice of vaccine composition. The method chosen for determining the amount of bacterial endotoxin present in the vaccine batch used in the safety test for determining the maximum acceptable level of endotoxin is used subsequently for testing of each batch.

3 BATCH TESTS

3-1 Identification

When injected into healthy animals that do not have specific antibodies against the serovars *M. haemolytica* and/or against the leucotoxin present in the vaccine, the vaccine stimulates the production of such antibodies.

3-2 Bacteria and fungi

The vaccine, including where applicable the diluent supplied for reconstitution, complies with the test for sterility prescribed in the monograph *Vaccines for veterinary use (0062)*.

3-3 Potency

The vaccine complies with the requirements of the test or test(s) mentioned under Immunogenicity (section 2-2-2) when administered by a recommended route and method.

_____ _Ph Eur_

Marek's Disease Vaccine, Living

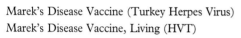

Marek's Disease Vaccine (Turkey Herpes Virus)

Marek's Disease Vaccine, Living (HVT)

(Marek's Disease Vaccine (Live), Ph Eur monograph 0589)

Ph Eur _____

1 DEFINITION

Marek's disease vaccine (live) is a preparation of a suitable strain or strains of Marek's disease virus (gallid herpesvirus 2 or 3) and/or turkey herpesvirus (meleagrid herpesvirus 1). This monograph applies to vaccines intended for administration to chickens and/or chicken embryos for active immunisation.

2 PRODUCTION

2-1 PREPARATION OF THE VACCINE

The vaccine virus is grown in cell cultures. If the vaccine contains more than one type of virus, the different types are grown separately. The vaccine may be freeze-dried or stored in liquid nitrogen.

2-2 SUBSTRATE FOR VIRUS PROPAGATION

2-2-1 Cell cultures

The cell cultures comply with the requirements for cell cultures for production of veterinary vaccines (5.2.4).

2-3 SEED LOTS

2-3-1 Extraneous agents

The master seed lot complies with the tests for extraneous agents in seed lots (2.6.24). In these tests on the master seed lot, the organisms used are not more than 5 passages from the master seed lot at the start of the tests.

2-4 CHOICE OF VACCINE VIRUS

The vaccine virus shall be shown to be satisfactory with respect to safety (5.2.6) and efficacy (5.2.7) for the chickens and/or chicken embryos for which it is intended.

The tests shown below for residual pathogenicity of the strain (section 2-4-1-1), increase in virulence (section 2-4-2) and immunogenicity (section 2-4-3) may be used during the demonstration of safety and efficacy. Additional testing may be needed to demonstrate safety in breeds of chickens known to be particularly susceptible to Marek's disease virus, unless the vaccine is to be contra-indicated.

2-4-1 Safety

2-4-1-1 Residual pathogenicity of the strain. Carry out the test for the route to be recommended for vaccination that is likely to be the least safe and in the category of chickens for which the vaccine is intended that is likely to be the most susceptible for Marek's disease.

Carry out the test in chickens if the vaccine is intended for chickens; carry out the test in chicken embryos if the vaccine is intended for chicken embryos; carry out the test in chickens and in chicken embryos if the vaccine is intended for both.

Use vaccine virus at the least attenuated passage level that will be present between the master seed lot and a batch of the vaccine.

Vaccines intended for use in chickens Use not fewer than 80 1-day-old chickens from a flock free from specified pathogens (SPF) (5.2.2). Divide them randomly into 2 groups of not fewer than 40 chickens and maintain the groups separately. Administer by a suitable route to each chicken of one group (I) a quantity of the vaccine virus equivalent to not less than 10 times the maximum virus titre likely to be contained in 1 dose of the vaccine. Administer by a suitable route to each chicken of the other group (II) a quantity of virulent Marek's disease virus that will cause mortality and/or severe macroscopic lesions of Marek's disease in not fewer than 70 per cent of the effective number of chickens within 70 days (initial number reduced by the number that die within the first 7 days of the test).

Vaccines intended for use in chicken embryos Use not fewer than 150 embryonated eggs from an SPF flock (5.2.2). Divide them randomly into 3 groups of not fewer than 50 embryonated eggs and maintain the groups separately but under identical incubation conditions. Not later than the recommended day of vaccination, administer by the method to be recommended to each embryonated egg of one group (I) a quantity of the vaccine virus equivalent to not less than 10 times the maximum virus titre likely to be contained in 1 dose of the vaccine. Administer by a suitable route to each embryonated egg of another group (II) a quantity of virulent Marek's disease virus that will cause mortality and/or severe macroscopic lesions of Marek's disease in not fewer than 70 per cent of the effective number of hatched chickens within 70 days (initial number reduced by the number that die within the first 7 days after hatching). Keep the last group (III) non-inoculated. The test is not valid if there is a significant difference in hatchability between groups I and III and the hatchability in any of the 3 groups is less than 80 per cent.

Provided that the chickens and chicken embryos are derived from the same flock, a common control group for _in ovo_ and parenteral administration can be used.

Irrespective of whether the vaccine was administered to chickens or chicken embryos, observe the chickens of group II at least daily for 70 days and those of group I at least daily for 120 days.

The test is not valid if one or more of the following apply:
— more than 10 per cent of the chickens in any of the 3 groups die within the first 7 days;
— fewer than 70 per cent of the effective number of chickens in group II show macroscopic lesions of Marek's disease;

The vaccine virus complies with the test if:
— no chicken of group I shows notable clinical signs or macroscopic lesions of Marek's disease or dies from causes attributable to the vaccine virus;
— at 120 days the number of surviving chickens of group I is not fewer than 80 per cent of the effective number.

2-4-2 Increase in virulence

The test for increase in virulence is required for Marek's disease virus vaccine strains but not for turkey herpesvirus vaccine strains, which are naturally apathogenic.

Carry out the test according to general chapter 5.2.6.

Vaccines intended for use in chickens Administer to each 1-day-old SPF chicken (5.2.2) by the intramuscular route a quantity of the vaccine virus that will allow recovery of virus for the passages described below.

Vaccines intended for use only in chicken embryos or intended for use in chickens and in chicken embryos Administer to each embryonated egg not later than the recommended day for vaccination by the *in ovo* route, using the recommended method, a quantity of the vaccine virus that will allow recovery of virus for the passages described below.

If the properties of the vaccine virus allow sequential passage through 5 groups via natural spreading, this method may be used, otherwise passage as described below is carried out.

5-7 days after administering the vaccine to chickens or 5-7 days after hatching when the vaccine has been administered *in ovo*, prepare a suspension of white blood cells from each chicken and pool these samples. Administer a suitable volume of the pooled samples by the intraperitoneal route to each 1-day-old SPF chicken (*5.2.2*) of the next group. Carry out this passage operation not fewer than 4 times; verify the presence of the virus at each passage. If the virus is not found at a passage level, repeat the passage by administration to a group of 10 animals. Carry out the test for residual pathogenicity (section 2-4-1-1) using the material used for the 1st passage and the virus at the final passage level. Administer the virus by the route to be recommended for vaccination that is likely to be the least safe for use in these chickens or chicken embryos.

The vaccine virus complies with the test if no indication of increase in virulence of the virus recovered for the final passage compared with the material used for the 1st passage is observed. If virus is not recovered after an initial passage in 5 chickens or chicken embryos and a subsequent repeat passage in 10 chickens or chicken embryos, the vaccine virus also complies with the test.

2-4-3 Immunogenicity

A test is carried out for each route and method of administration to be recommended, using in each case chickens of the minimum age to be recommended for vaccination or chicken embryos. The quantity of the vaccine virus administered to each chicken or chicken embryo is not greater than the minimum virus titre to be stated on the label and the virus is at the most attenuated passage level that will be present in a batch of the vaccine.

Vaccines intended for use in chickens Use not fewer than 60 chickens of the same origin and from an SPF flock (*5.2.2*). Vaccinate by a route to be recommended not fewer than 30 chickens. Maintain not fewer than 30 chickens as controls.

Vaccines intended for use in chicken embryos Use embryonated chickens of the same origin and from an SPF flock (*5.2.2*). Vaccinate by the *in ovo* route using the method to be recommended, 50 per cent of the embryonated eggs. Maintain 50 per cent of the embryonated eggs as controls. The test is not valid if any group consists of fewer than 30 hatched chicks.

Irrespective of whether the vaccine was administered to chickens or chicken embryos, challenge each chicken not later than 9 days after vaccination by a suitable route with a sufficient quantity of virulent Marek's disease virus. Observe the chickens at least daily for 70 days after challenge. Record the deaths and the number of surviving chickens that show clinical signs of disease. At the end of the observation period, euthanise all the surviving chickens and carry out an examination for macroscopic lesions of Marek's disease.

The test is not valid if:
— during the observation period after challenge, fewer than 70 per cent of the control chickens die or show severe clinical signs or macroscopic lesions of Marek's disease;
— and/or, during the period between the vaccination and challenge, more than 10 per cent of the control or

vaccinated chickens show abnormal clinical signs or die from causes not attributable to the vaccine.

The vaccine virus complies with the test if the relative protection percentage, calculated using the following expression, is not less than 80 per cent:

$$\frac{V - C}{100 - C} \times 100$$

V = percentage of challenged vaccinated chickens that survive to the end of the observation period without notable clinical signs or macroscopic lesions of Marek's disease;

C = percentage of challenged control chickens that survive to the end of the observation period without notable clinical signs or macroscopic lesions of Marek's disease.

3 BATCH TESTS

3-1 Identification

Carry out an immunostaining test in cell cultures using monoclonal antibodies to demonstrate the presence of each type of virus stated on the label.

3-2 Bacteria and fungi

The vaccine, including where applicable the diluent supplied for reconstitution, complies with the test for sterility prescribed in the monograph *Vaccines for veterinary use (0062)*.

3-3 Mycoplasmas

The vaccine complies with the test for mycoplasmas (*2.6.7*).

3-4 Extraneous agents

The vaccine complies with the tests for extraneous agents in batches of finished product (*2.6.25*).

3-5 Virus titre

3-5-1 Vaccines containing one type of virus. Titrate the vaccine virus by inoculation into suitable cell cultures (*5.2.4*). If the virus titre is determined in plaque-forming units (PFU), only primary plaques are taken into consideration. The vaccine complies with the test if one dose contains not less than the minimum virus titre stated on the label.

3-5-2 Vaccines containing more than one type of virus. For vaccines containing more than one type of virus, titrate each virus by inoculation into suitable cell cultures (*5.2.4*), reading the results by immunostaining using antibodies. The vaccine complies with the test if one dose contains for each vaccine virus not less than the minimum virus titre stated on the label.

3-6 Potency

The vaccine complies with the test for immunogenicity (section 2-4-3) when administered according to the recommended schedule by a recommended route and method. It is not necessary to carry out the potency test for each batch of the vaccine if it has been carried out on a representative batch using a vaccinating dose containing not more than the minimum virus titre stated on the label.

Ph Eur

Mycoplasma Gallisepticum Vaccine (Inactivated)

(Ph Eur monograph 1942)

Ph Eur _____

1 DEFINITION

Mycoplasma gallisepticum vaccine (inactivated) is a preparation of one or more suitable strains of *Mycoplasma gallisepticum* that have been inactivated while maintaining adequate immunogenic properties. This monograph applies to vaccines intended for the active immunisation of chickens and/or turkeys.

2 PRODUCTION
2-1 PREPARATION OF THE VACCINE

Production of the vaccine is based on a seed-lot system. The seed material is cultured in a suitable solid and/or liquid medium to ensure optimal growth under the chosen incubation conditions. Each strain is cultivated separately and identity is verified using a suitable method. During production, various parameters such as growth rate are monitored by suitable methods; the values are within the limits approved for the particular vaccine. Purity and identity of the harvest are verified using suitable methods. After cultivation, the mycoplasma suspensions are collected separately and inactivated by a suitable method.

The mycoplasma suspensions may be treated to fragment the mycoplasmas and the fragments may be purified and concentrated. The vaccine may contain an adjuvant.

2-2 CHOICE OF VACCINE COMPOSITION

The vaccine is shown to be satisfactory with respect to safety (*5.2.6*) and efficacy (*5.2.7*) in the target animals.

The following tests for safety (section 2-2-1) and immunogenicity (section 2-2-2) may be used during the demonstration of safety and efficacy. If the indications for the vaccine include protection against a drop in laying performance or protection against infectious sinusitis in turkeys, further suitable immunogenicity testing is necessary.

2-2-1 Safety

The test is carried out for each route of administration to be recommended for vaccination and for each avian species for which the vaccine is intended. Use a batch of vaccine containing not less than the maximum potency that may be expected in a batch of vaccine.

For each test performed in birds younger than 3 weeks of age, use not fewer than 10 birds not older than the minimum age to be recommended for vaccination. For each test performed in birds older than 3 weeks of age, use not fewer than 8 birds not older than the minimum age to be recommended for vaccination. In the case of chickens, use chickens from a flock free from specified pathogens (SPF) (*5.2.2*) and in the case of turkeys, use birds that have not been vaccinated and that do not have antibodies against *M. gallisepticum*. Administer by a route and method to be recommended to each bird 1 dose of vaccine. If the schedule to be recommended requires a 2nd dose, administer 1 dose to each bird after an interval of at least 14 days. Observe the birds at least daily for at least 14 days after the last administration of the vaccine.

The test is not valid if more than 10 per cent of the birds younger than 3 weeks of age show abnormal signs of disease or die from causes not attributable to the vaccine. For birds older than 3 weeks of age, the test is not valid if non-specific mortality occurs.

The vaccine complies with the test if no bird shows abnormal signs of disease or dies from causes attributable to the vaccine.

2-2-2 Immunogenicity

The test is carried out for each recommended route of administration and for each avian species for which the vaccine is intended. Use for each test not fewer than 40 birds not older than the minimum age to be recommended for vaccination. Use chickens from an SPF flock (*5.2.2*) or turkeys that have not been vaccinated and are free from antibodies against *M. gallisepticum*. For each test, administer to each of not fewer than 20 birds a quantity of the vaccine not greater than a single dose. If re-vaccination is recommended, repeat this operation after the recommended interval. Maintain not fewer than 20 birds as controls. Challenge each bird from both groups not more than 28 days after the last administration by a suitable route with a sufficient quantity of virulent *M. gallisepticum* (R-strain). Observe the birds at least daily for 14 days after challenge. Evaluation is carried out 14 days after challenge, at which point the birds are euthanised. Record the deaths and the number of surviving birds that show clinical signs of disease (e.g. respiratory distress, nasal discharge), and record air sac lesions.

The test is not valid if:
— during the observation period after challenge, fewer than 70 per cent of the controls die or show lesions or clinical signs of disease; and/or
— during the period between vaccination and challenge, more than 10 per cent of the birds from the control group or from the vaccinated group show abnormal clinical signs of disease or die from causes not attributable to the vaccine.

Thoracic and abdominal air sacs are evaluated individually on each side of the animal. The scoring system presented below may be used. The vaccine complies with the test if the score for the vaccinated birds is significantly lower than that for the controls and if the reduction is not less than 30 per cent.

0   no air sac lesions
1   in a limited area of 1 or 2 air sacs: cloudiness with slight thickening of the air sac membrane or flecks of yellowish exudate
2   in 1 air sac or portions of 2 air sacs: greyish or yellow, sometimes foamy exudate, with thickening of the air sac membrane
3   in 3 air sacs: extensive exudate, with clear thickening of most air sacs
4   severe air-sacculitis with considerable exudate and thickening of most air sacs.

2-3 MANUFACTURER'S TESTS
2-3-1 Batch potency test

It is not necessary to carry out the potency test (section 3-4) for each batch of the vaccine if it has been carried out using a batch of vaccine with a minimum potency. Where the test is not carried out on a batch, an alternative validated method is used, the criteria for acceptance being set with reference to a batch of vaccine that has given satisfactory results in the potency test (section 3-4). The following test may be used.

Use not fewer than 15 chickens, 3-4 weeks old, from an SPF flock (*5.2.2*) or not fewer than 15 turkeys, 3-4 weeks old, that have not been vaccinated against *M. gallisepticum*, do not have antibodies against *M. gallisepticum*, and are obtained from a healthy flock. Collect serum samples from each vaccinate and control bird just before vaccination and check for the absence of antibodies against *M. gallisepticum*. Administer to each of not fewer than 10 birds 1 dose of the vaccine by a recommended route. Maintain not fewer than 5 birds as controls. Collect serum samples 5 weeks after vaccination from each vaccinated and control bird. Measure the titres of serum antibodies against *M. gallisepticum* using a suitable method. Calculate the mean titres for the group of vaccinates. The test is not valid if specific *M. gallisepticum* antibodies are found in any serum samples from the control birds 5 weeks after the time of administration of the vaccine. The vaccine complies with the test if the mean antibody titres of the group of vaccinates are equal to or greater than the titres obtained with a batch that has given satisfactory results in the potency test (section 3-4).

3 BATCH TESTS

3-1 Identification
When injected into chickens from an SPF flock (*5.2.2*) or turkeys from healthy flocks, the vaccine stimulates the production of antibodies against one or more strains of *M. gallisepticum*.

3-2 Bacteria and fungi
The vaccine, including where applicable the diluent supplied for reconstitution, complies with the test for sterility prescribed in the monograph *Vaccines for veterinary use (0062)*.

3-3 Residual live mycoplasmas
A test for residual live mycoplasmas is carried out to confirm inactivation of *M. gallisepticum*. The vaccine complies with a validated test for residual live *M. gallisepticum* carried out by a culture method (see for example *2.6.7*, using media shown to be suitable for *M. gallisepticum*).

3-4 Potency
The vaccine complies with the test for immunogenicity (section 2-2-2).

Ph Eur

Myxomatosis Vaccine (Live) for Rabbits

(Ph Eur monograph 1943)

Ph Eur

1 DEFINITION
Myxomatosis vaccine (live) for rabbits is a preparation of a suitable strain of either myxoma virus that is attenuated for rabbits or Shope fibroma virus. This monograph applies to vaccines intended for the active immunisation of rabbits against myxomatosis.

2 PRODUCTION
2-1 PREPARATION OF THE VACCINE
The vaccine virus is grown in cell cultures. The viral suspension is harvested and titrated and may be mixed with a suitable stabilising solution.

2-2 SUBSTRATE FOR VIRUS PROPAGATION
2-2-1 Cell cultures
The cell cultures comply with the requirements for cell cultures for production of veterinary vaccines (*5.2.4*).

2-3 CHOICE OF VACCINE VIRUS
The vaccine virus is shown to be satisfactory with respect to safety (*5.2.6*) and efficacy (*5.2.7*) for the rabbits for which it is intended.

The following tests for safety (section 2-3-1), increase in virulence (section 2-3-2) and immunogenicity (2-3-3) may be used during the demonstration of safety and efficacy.

2-3-1 Safety
Carry out the test for each route and method of administration to be recommended for vaccination, using in each case rabbits of the minimum age to be recommended for vaccination. Use vaccine virus at the least attenuated passage level that will be present in a batch of the vaccine.

For each test, use not fewer than 8 rabbits that do not have antibodies against myxoma virus. Administer to each rabbit a quantity of the vaccine virus equivalent to not less than 10 times the maximum virus titre likely to be contained in 1 dose of the vaccine. Observe the rabbits at least daily for 28 days. Record the body temperature the day before vaccination, at vaccination, 4 h after vaccination and then daily for 4 days; note the maximum temperature increase for each rabbit.

The vaccine virus complies with the test if no rabbit shows notable signs of disease or dies from causes attributable to the vaccine virus; the average temperature increase does not exceed 1.0 °C and no rabbit shows a rise greater than 2.0 °C. A local reaction lasting less than 28 days may occur.

2-3-2 Increase in virulence
(This test is performed only for vaccines based on attenuated strains of myxoma virus). Carry out the test according to general chapter *5.2.6. Evaluation of safety of veterinary vaccines and immunosera*, using rabbits 5-7 weeks old that do not have antibodies against myxoma virus. If the properties of the vaccine virus allow sequential passage through 5 groups via natural spreading, this method may be used, otherwise passage as described below is carried out.

Administer to each rabbit by a route to be recommended a quantity of the vaccine virus that will allow recovery of virus for the passages described below. Administer the virus by the route to be recommended for vaccination most likely to lead to reversion of virulence. Euthanise the rabbits 5-10 days after inoculation and remove from each rabbit organs or tissues with sufficient virus to allow passage; homogenise the organs and tissues in a suitable buffer solution, centrifuge the suspension and use the supernatant for further passages. Inoculate the supernatant into suitable cell culture to verify the presence of virus. Administer by an appropriate route, at a suitable rate, a suitable volume of the supernatant to each rabbit of the next group. Carry out this passage operation not fewer than 4 times; verify the presence of the virus at each passage. If the virus is not found at a passage level, repeat the passage by administration to a group of 10 animals.

If the 5th group of animals shows no evidence of an increase in virulence indicative of reversion during the observation period, further testing is not required. Otherwise, carry out an additional safety test and compare the clinical signs and any relevant parameters in a group of at least 8 animals receiving the material used for the 1st passage and another similar group receiving the virus at the final passage level.

The vaccine virus complies with the test if no indication of increased virulence of the virus recovered for the final passage compared with the material used for the 1st passage is observed. If virus is not recovered after an initial passage in 2 animals and a subsequent repeat passage in 10 animals, the vaccine virus also complies with the test.

2-3-3 Immunogenicity
A test is carried out for each route and method of administration to be recommended for vaccination using in each case rabbits of the minimum age to be recommended.

The quantity of vaccine virus to be administered to each rabbit is not greater than the minimum virus titre to be stated on the label and the virus is at the most attenuated passage level that will be present in a batch of vaccine.

Use for the test not fewer than 15 rabbits that do not have antibodies against myxoma virus and are reared in suitable isolation conditions to ensure absence of contact with myxoma virus. Administer 1 dose of vaccine to each of not fewer than 10 of the rabbits according to the schedule to be recommended. Maintain not fewer than 5 rabbits as controls. Challenge each rabbit not less than 21 days after the last vaccination by a suitable route with a quantity of a virulent strain of myxoma virus sufficient to cause typical signs of myxomatosis in a rabbit. Observe the rabbits at least daily for a further 21 days after challenge and monitor each of them.

The test is not valid if fewer than 90 per cent of the control rabbits display typical signs of myxomatosis. A vaccine containing myxoma virus complies with the test if, during the observation period after challenge, not fewer than 90 per cent of vaccinated rabbits show no signs of myxomatosis.
A vaccine containing Shope fibroma virus complies with the test if, during the observation period after challenge, not fewer than 75 per cent of vaccinated rabbits show no signs of myxomatosis.

3 BATCH TESTS
3-1 Identification
Carry out an immunofluorescence test in suitable cell cultures, using a monospecific antiserum.

3-2 Bacteria and fungi
The vaccine, including where applicable the diluent supplied for reconstitution, complies with the test for sterility prescribed in the monograph *Vaccines for veterinary use (0062)*.

3-3 Mycoplasmas (2.6.7)
The vaccine complies with the test for mycoplasmas.

3-4 Specified extraneous agents
Use not fewer than 2 rabbits that are not older than the minimum age recommended for vaccination, that do not have antibodies against myxoma virus and rabbit haemorrhagic disease virus and that have been reared in suitable isolation conditions to avoid contact with myxoma virus. Administer to each rabbit by a recommended route 10 doses of the vaccine. Observe the rabbits at least daily for 14 days. At the end of the observation period administer by a recommended route to each rabbit a further 10 doses of vaccine. After 14 days take a blood sample from each rabbit and carry out a test for antibodies against rabbit haemorrhagic disease virus. The vaccine complies with the test if no antibodies are found.

3-5 Virus titre
Titrate the vaccine virus in suitable cell cultures. The vaccine complies with the test if 1 dose contains not less than the minimum virus titre stated on the label.

3-6 Potency
The vaccine complies with the requirements of the test prescribed under Immunogenicity (section 2-3-3) when administered by a recommended route and method. It is not necessary to carry out the potency test for each batch of the vaccine if it has been carried out on a representative batch using a vaccinating dose containing not more than the minimum virus titre stated on the label.

―――――――――――――――――――――――――――――――――――― Ph Eur

Newcastle Disease and Avian Infectious Bronchitis Vaccine, Living
DEFINITION
Newcastle Disease and Avian Infectious Bronchitis Vaccine, Living is a mixed preparation derived from separate groups of eggs infected with suitable strains of Newcastle disease virus and of avian infectious bronchitis virus. The Newcastle disease virus seed is either a modified strain, such as Hitchner B1 or La Sota, or a naturally occurring strain of low pathogenicity. The avian infectious bronchitis virus seed is an IB strain and it may be used at various levels of attenuation. The vaccine is prepared immediately before use by reconstitution from the dried vaccine with a suitable liquid.

PRODUCTION
For vaccine production the virus is propagated in embryonated eggs derived from chicken flocks free from specified pathogens. The final product is freeze dried.

Provided that the test for potency described below has been performed with satisfactory results on a representative batch of vaccine it may be omitted by the manufacturer as a routine control on other batches of vaccine prepared from the same seed lot, subject to the agreement of the competent authority.

Virus titre
For the Newcastle disease component   Neutralise the vaccine with monospecific avian infectious bronchitis virus antiserum. Inoculate serial dilutions of neutralised vaccine into the allantoic cavity of 10- to 11-day-old embryonated eggs derived from chicken flocks free from specified pathogens. Incubate the eggs for 3 days at $37°$ and then examine the embryos for evidence of virus infection, which is shown by the presence of chick red cell haemagglutinins. The vaccine contains not less than $10^{6.0}$ EID_{50} of virus per bird dose.

For the avian infectious bronchitis component   Neutralise the vaccine with monospecific Newcastle disease virus antiserum. Inoculate serial dilutions of neutralised vaccine into the allantoic cavity of 10- to 11-day-old embryonated eggs derived from chicken flocks free from specified pathogens. Incubate the eggs at $37°$ for 7 days and then examine the embryos for lesions typical of avian infectious bronchitis. The vaccine contains not less than $10^{3.5}$ EID_{50} of virus per bird dose.

The vaccine, reconstituted with a suitable liquid to provide a concentration appropriate to the particular test, complies with the requirements stated under Veterinary Vaccines with the following modifications.

IDENTIFICATION
When mixed with a mixture of monospecific Newcastle disease virus antiserum and avian infectious bronchitis virus antiserum, the vaccine no longer infects susceptible 10- to 11-day-old embryonated eggs.

TESTS
Mycoplasmas
Complies with the *test for absence of mycoplasmas*, Appendix XVI B(Vet) 3.

Sterility
Carry out the test described under Veterinary Vaccines using solid media in place of liquid media. The vaccine contains no pathogenic organisms and not more than one organism of a non-pathogenic species per bird dose.

Absence of extraneous pathogens

The neutralised vaccine complies with the *test for Avian Live Virus Vaccines: Tests for Extraneous Agents in Batches of Finished Product*, Appendix XVI B(Vet) 5.

POTENCY

For the Newcastle disease component

Vaccinate each of twenty-five 5- to 10-day-old chicks from flocks free from specified pathogens, by the nasal instillation of one dose of vaccine. Twenty-one days later challenge the vaccinated chicks as well as 10 control birds by the intramuscular inoculation of at least $10^{6.0}$ EID_{50} of Herts (Weybridge 33/56) strain of Newcastle disease virus and observe for 10 days. All the control birds die within 6 days and no fewer than 23 of the vaccinated birds survive the observation period without showing signs of Newcastle disease.

For the avian infectious bronchitis component

Vaccinate each of 10 healthy 3- to 4-week-old chickens from flocks free from specified pathogens, by nasal or ocular instillation such that each chicken receives one dose of vaccine. Twenty-one to twenty-eight days later challenge the vaccinated chickens, as well as 10 control birds that are kept separate from the vaccinated birds, by nasal or ocular instillation of $10^{3.0}$ to $10^{3.5}$. EID_{50} of the Massachusetts 41 strain of virulent infectious bronchitis virus.

Between the 4th and 7th day after challenge, take a tracheal swab from each bird. Place each swab in a test tube containing 3 mL of broth to which suitable antibiotics have been added to inhibit the growth of bacterial contaminants and test for the presence of infectious bronchitis virus by the inoculation of 0.2 mL of inoculum into the allantoic cavity of 9- to 11-day-old embryonated eggs using at least five eggs for each swab. A tracheal swab is positive if 20% or more of the embryos inoculated from it show lesions typical of infectious bronchitis virus. If more than one embryo but fewer than 20% of those inoculated from any one swab show lesions similar to those of infectious bronchitis, inoculate at least five additional embryonated eggs with allantoic fluid from each of the suspect embryos. The swab is positive if 20% or more of these additional embryos show lesions typical of infectious bronchitis virus.

Not less than 80% of the control birds give positive tracheal swabs, and no more than 20% of the vaccinated chickens give positive tracheal swabs.

LABELLING

The label states the names of the strains of virus used in the vaccine.

Newcastle Disease Vaccine, Inactivated

(Newcastle Disease Vaccine (Inactivated), Ph Eur monograph 0870)

Ph Eur _____

1 DEFINITION

Newcastle disease vaccine (inactivated) (also known as avian paramyxovirus 1 vaccine (inactivated) for vaccines intended for some species) is a preparation of a suitable strain of Newcastle disease virus (avian paramyxovirus 1), inactivated while maintaining adequate immunogenic properties. This monograph applies to vaccines intended for active immunisation of birds against Newcastle disease.

2 PRODUCTION
2-1 PREPARATION OF THE VACCINE

The vaccine virus is grown in embryonated hens' eggs or in cell cultures. The virus harvest is inactivated. The vaccine may be adjuvanted.

2-2 SUBSTRATE FOR VIRUS PROPAGATION
2-2-1 Embryonated hens' eggs

If the vaccine virus is grown in embryonated hens' eggs, they are obtained from healthy flocks.

2-2-2 Cell cultures

If the vaccine virus is grown in cell cultures, they comply with the requirements for cell cultures for production of veterinary vaccines (*5.2.4*).

2-3 SEED LOTS
2-3-1 Extraneous agents

The master seed lot complies with the test for extraneous agents in seed lots (*2.6.24*). In these tests on the master seed lot, the organisms used are not more than 5 passages from the master seed lot at the start of the test.

2-4 CHOICE OF VACCINE COMPOSITION

The vaccine is shown to be satisfactory with respect to safety (*5.2.6*) and efficacy (*5.2.7*) for each species and category of birds for which it is intended.

The following tests for safety (section 2-4-1) and immunogenicity (section 2-4-2) may be used during the demonstration of safety and efficacy.

2-4-1 Safety

The test is carried out for each route of administration to be recommended for vaccination and for each avian species for which the vaccine is intended. Use a batch of vaccine containing not less than the maximum potency that may be expected in a batch of vaccine.

For each test performed in birds younger than 3 weeks of age, use not fewer than 10 birds not older than the minimum age to be recommended for vaccination. For each test performed in birds older than 3 weeks of age, use not fewer than 8 birds not older than the minimum age to be recommended for vaccination. In the case of chickens, use chickens from a flock free from specified pathogens (SPF) (*5.2.2*) and if the vaccine is used for species other than chickens, they have not been vaccinated and do not have antibodies against Newcastle disease virus. Administer by a route and method to be recommended to each bird 1 dose of vaccine. Observe the birds at least daily for at least 14 days after the last administration of the vaccine.

The test is not valid if more than 10 per cent of the birds younger than 3 weeks of age show abnormal signs of disease or die from causes not attributable to the vaccine. For birds older than 3 weeks of age, the test is not valid if non-specific mortality occurs.

The vaccine complies with the test if no bird shows abnormal signs of disease or dies from causes attributable to the vaccine.

2-4-2 Immunogenicity

A test is carried out for each route and method of administration to be recommended; the vaccine administered to each bird is of minimum potency.

For chickens, the test for vaccines for use in chickens (section 2-4-2-1) is suitable for demonstrating immunogenicity. For other species of birds (for example, pigeons or turkeys), the test for vaccines for use in species other than the chicken (section 2-4-2-2) is suitable for demonstrating immunogenicity.

2-4-2-1 Vaccines for use in chickens. Use not fewer than 70 chickens, 21-28 days old, of the same origin and from an SPF flock (*5.2.2*). For vaccination, use not fewer than 3 groups, each of not fewer than 20 chickens. Choose a number of different volumes of the vaccine corresponding to the number of groups: for example, volumes equivalent to 1/25, 1/50 and 1/100 of a dose. Allocate a different volume to each vaccination group. Vaccinate each chicken by the intramuscular route with the volume of vaccine allocated to its group. Maintain not fewer than 10 chickens as controls. Challenge each chicken after 17-21 days by the intramuscular route with 6 $\log_{10}$ embryo LD_{50} of the Herts (Weybridge 33/56) strain of avian paramyxovirus 1. Observe the chickens at least daily for 21 days after challenge. At the end of the observation period, calculate the PD_{50} by standard statistical methods from the number of chickens that survive in each vaccinated group without showing any signs of Newcastle disease during the 21 days.

The test is invalid unless all the control birds die within 6 days of challenge.

The vaccine complies with the test if the smallest dose stated on the label corresponds to not less than 50 PD_{50} and the lower confidence limit is not less than 35 PD_{50} per dose. If the lower confidence limit is less than 35 PD_{50} per dose, repeat the test; the vaccine must be shown to contain not less than 50 PD_{50} in the repeat test.

2-4-2-2 Vaccines for use in species other than the chicken. Use not fewer than 30 birds of the target species, of the same origin and of the same age, that do not have antibodies against avian paramyxovirus 1. Vaccinate in accordance with the recommendations for use not fewer than 20 birds. Maintain not fewer than 10 birds as controls. Challenge each bird after 4 weeks by the intramuscular route with a sufficient quantity of virulent avian paramyxovirus 1.

The test is not valid if serum samples obtained at the time of the first vaccination show the presence of antibodies against avian paramyxovirus 1 in either vaccinates or controls, or if tests carried out at the time of challenge show such antibodies in controls.

The test is not valid if fewer than 70 per cent of the control birds die or show serious signs of Newcastle disease.

The vaccine complies with the test if not fewer than 90 per cent of the vaccinated birds survive and show no serious signs of avian paramyxovirus 1 infection.

2-5 MANUFACTURER'S TESTS
2-5-1 Residual live virus
The test is carried out in embryonated eggs or suitable cell cultures (*5.2.4*), whichever is the most sensitive for the vaccine strain. The quantity of inactivated virus harvest used in the test is equivalent to not less than 10 doses of vaccine. The vaccine complies with the test if no live virus is detected.

2-5-2 Batch potency test
It is not necessary to carry out the potency test (section 3-5) for each batch of vaccine if it has been carried out using a batch of vaccine with a minimum potency. Where the test is not carried out, an alternative validated method is used, the criteria for acceptance being set with reference to a batch of vaccine that has given satisfactory results in the test described under Potency. The following tests may be used. Wherever possible, carry out the test for antigen content (section 2-5-2-1) together with the test for adjuvant (section 2-5-2-2).

Vaccines for use in chickens The test for antigen content (section 2-5-2-1) together with the test for adjuvant (section 2-5-2-2) may be carried out; if the nature of the product does not allow valid results to be obtained with these tests, or if the vaccine does not comply, the test for serological assay (section 2-5-2-3) may be carried out. If the vaccine does not comply with the latter test, the test for vaccines for use in chickens (section 2-4-2-1) may be carried out. A test using fewer than 20 birds per group and a shorter observation period after challenge may be used if this has been shown to give a valid potency test.

Vaccines for use in species other than the chicken Carry out a suitable test for which a satisfactory correlation has been established with the test for vaccines for use in species other than the chicken (section 2-4-2-2), the criteria for acceptance being set with reference to a batch that has given satisfactory results in the latter test. A test in chickens from an SPF flock (*5.2.2*) consisting of a measure of the serological response to graded amounts of vaccine (for example, 1/25, 1/50 and 1/100 of a dose with serum sampling 17-21 days later) may be used. Alternatively, the test for antigen content (section 2-5-2-1) together with the test for adjuvant (section 2-5-2-2) may be conducted if shown to provide a valid potency test.

2-5-2-1 Antigen content. The relative antigen content is determined by comparing the content of haemagglutinin-neuraminidase antigen per dose of vaccine with a haemagglutinin-neuraminidase antigen reference preparation, by enzyme-linked immunosorbent assay (*2.7.1*). For this comparison, *Newcastle disease virus reference antigen BRP*, *Newcastle disease virus control antigen BRP*, *Newcastle disease virus coating antibody BRP* and *Newcastle disease virus conjugated detection antibody BRP* are suitable. Before estimation, the antigen may be extracted from the emulsion using *isopropyl myristate R* or another suitable method.

The vaccine complies with the test if the estimated antigen content is not significantly lower than that of a batch that has been found to be satisfactory with respect to immunogenicity (section 2-4-2).

2-5-2-2 Adjuvant. If the immunochemical assay (section 2-5-2-1) is performed and if the vaccine is adjuvanted, the adjuvant is tested by suitable physical and chemical methods. For oil-adjuvanted vaccines, the adjuvant is tested in accordance with the monograph *Vaccines for veterinary use (0062)*. If the adjuvant cannot be adequately characterised, the antigen content determination cannot be used as the batch potency test.

2-5-2-3 Serological assay. Use not fewer than 15 chickens, 21-28 days old, of the same origin and from an SPF flock (*5.2.2*). Vaccinate by the intramuscular route not fewer than 10 chickens with a volume of the vaccine equivalent to 1/50 of a dose. Maintain not fewer than 5 chickens as controls. Collect serum samples from each chicken after 17-21 days. Measure the antibody levels in the sera by the haemagglutination-inhibition (HI) test using the technique described below or an equivalent technique with the same numbers of haemagglutinating units and red blood cells. The test system used must include negative and positive control sera, the latter having an HI titre of 5.0 $\log_2$ to 6.0 $\log_2$. The vaccine complies with the test if the mean HI titre of the vaccinated group is equal to or greater than 4.0 $\log_2$ and that of the unvaccinated group is 2.0 $\log_2$ or less. If the HI titres are not satisfactory, carry out the test for vaccines for use in chickens (section 2-4-2-1).

Haemagglutination inhibition
Inactivate the test sera by heating at 56 °C for 30 min. Add 25 μL of inactivated serum to the first row of wells in a microtitre plate. Add 25 μL of a buffered 9 g/L solution of

sodium chloride R at pH 7.2-7.4 to the rest of the wells.
Prepare twofold dilutions of the sera across the plate.
To each well add 25 µL of a suspension containing
4 haemagglutinating units of inactivated Newcastle disease
virus. Incubate the plate at 4 °C for 1 h. Add 25 µL of a
1 per cent *V/V* suspension of red blood cells collected from
chickens that are 3-4 weeks old and free from antibodies
against Newcastle disease virus. Incubate the plate at 4 °C
for 1 h. The HI titre is equal to the highest dilution that
produces complete inhibition.

3 BATCH TESTS

3-1 Identification
When injected into animals that do not have antibodies
against Newcastle disease virus, the vaccine stimulates the
production of such antibodies.

3-2 Bacteria and fungi
The vaccine, including where applicable the diluent supplied
for reconstitution, complies with the test for sterility
prescribed in the monograph *Vaccines for veterinary
use (0062)*.

3-3 Specified extraneous agents
Use 10 chickens, 14-28 days old, from an SPF flock (*5.2.2*).
Vaccinate each chicken by a recommended route with a
double dose of the vaccine. After 3 weeks, administer 1 dose
by the same route. Collect serum samples from each chicken
2 weeks later and carry out tests for antibodies to the
following agents by the methods prescribed in general
chapter *5.2.2. Chicken flocks free from specified pathogens for the
production and quality control of vaccines*: avian
encephalomyelitis virus, avian infectious bronchitis virus,
avian leucosis viruses, egg-drop syndrome virus, avian
infectious bursal disease virus, avian infectious
laryngotracheitis virus, influenza A virus, Marek's disease
virus.

The vaccine complies with the test if it does not stimulate the
formation of antibodies against these agents.

3-4 Residual live virus
A test for residual live virus is carried out to confirm
inactivation of Newcastle disease virus.

Inject 2/5 of a dose into the allantoic cavity of each of 10
embryonated hen eggs that are 9-11 days old and from SPF
flocks (*5.2.2*) (SPF eggs), and incubate. Observe for 6 days
and pool separately the allantoic fluid from eggs containing
live embryos and that from eggs containing dead embryos,
excluding those dying within 24 h of the injection. Examine
embryos that die within 24 h of injection for the presence of
Newcastle disease virus: the vaccine does not comply with
the test if Newcastle disease virus is found.

Inject into the allantoic cavity of each of 10 SPF eggs,
9-11 days old, 0.2 mL of the pooled allantoic fluid from the
live embryos and, into each of 10 similar eggs, 0.2 mL of the
pooled fluid from the dead embryos and incubate for
5-6 days. Test the allantoic fluid from each egg for the
presence of haemagglutinins using chicken erythrocytes.

The vaccine complies with the test if there is no evidence of
haemagglutinating activity and if not more than 20 per cent
of the embryos die at either stage. If more than 20 per cent
of the embryos die at one of the stages, repeat that stage;
the vaccine complies with the test if there is no evidence of
haemagglutinating activity and not more than 20 per cent of
the embryos die at that stage.

Antibiotics may be used in the test to control extraneous
bacterial infection.

3-5 Potency
The vaccine complies with the requirements of the test
mentioned under Immunogenicity (section 2-4-2) when
administered by a recommended route and method.

Ph Eur

Newcastle Disease Vaccine, Living

*(Newcastle Disease Vaccine (Live),
Ph Eur monograph 0450)*

*The use of Newcastle Disease Vaccine, Living is restricted in the
United Kingdom by the Department for Environment, Food and
Rural Affairs.*

Ph Eur

1 DEFINITION
Newcastle disease vaccine (live) is a preparation of a suitable
strain of Newcastle disease virus (avian paramyxovirus 1).
This monograph applies to vaccines intended for
administration to chickens and/or other avian species for
active immunisation.

2 PRODUCTION
2-1 PREPARATION OF THE VACCINE
The vaccine virus is grown in embryonated hens' eggs or in
cell cultures.

2-2 SUBSTRATE FOR VIRUS PROPAGATION
2-2-1 Embryonated hens' eggs
If the vaccine virus is grown in embryonated hens' eggs, they
are obtained from flocks free from specified pathogens (SPF)
(*5.2.2*).

2-2-2 Cell cultures
If the vaccine virus is grown in cell cultures, they comply
with the requirements for cell cultures for production of
veterinary vaccines (*5.2.4*).

2-3 SEED LOTS
2-3-1 Extraneous agents
The master seed lot complies with the tests for extraneous
agents in seed lots (*2.6.24*). In these tests on the master seed
lot, the organisms used are not more than 5 passages from
the master seed lot at the start of the tests.

2-4 CHOICE OF VACCINE VIRUS
The vaccine virus shall be shown to be satisfactory with
respect to safety (*5.2.6*) and efficacy (*5.2.7*) for the birds for
which it is intended.

The following tests for intracerebral pathogenicity index
(section 2-4-1), amino-acid sequence (section 2-4-2), safety
(section 2-4-3), increase in virulence (section 2-4-4) and
immunogenicity (section 2-4-5) may be used during the
demonstration of safety and efficacy.

2-4-1 Intracerebral pathogenicity index
Use vaccine virus at the least attenuated passage level that
will be present between the master seed lot and a batch of
the vaccine. Inoculate the vaccine virus into the allantoic
cavity of embryonated hens' eggs, 9- to 11- days-old, from
an SPF flock (*5.2.2*). Incubate the inoculated eggs for a
suitable period and harvest and pool the allantoic fluids.
Use not fewer than ten 1-day-old chickens (i.e. more than
24 h but less than 40 h after hatching), from an SPF flock
(*5.2.2*). Administer by the intracerebral route to each chick
0.05 mL of the pooled allantoic fluids containing not less
than $10^{8.0}$ EID$_{50}$ or, if this virus quantity cannot be achieved,
not less than $10^{7.0}$ EID$_{50}$. Observe the chickens at least daily

for 8 days after administration and score them once every 24 h. A score of 0 is attributed to a chicken if it is clinically normal, 1 if it shows clinical signs of disease and 2 if it is dead. The intracerebral pathogenicity index is the mean of the scores per chicken per observation over the 8-day period.

If an inoculum of not less than $10^{8.0}$ EID_{50} is used, the vaccine virus complies with the test if its intracerebral pathogenicity index is not greater than 0.5; if an inoculum of not less than $10^{7.0}$ EID_{50} but less than $10^{8.0}$ EID_{50} is used, the vaccine virus complies with the test if its intracerebral pathogenicity index is not greater than 0.4.

2-4-2 Amino-acid sequence

Determine the sequence of a fragment of RNA from the vaccine virus containing the region encoding for the F0 cleavage site by a suitable method. The encoded amino-acid sequence is shown to be one of the following:

				F2			Cleavage site		F1	
Site		111	112	113	114	115	116	∨	117	118	119
		Gly	Gly	Lys	Gln	Gly	Arg		Leu	Ile	Gly
	or	Gly	Gly	Arg	Gln	Gly	Arg		Leu	Ile	Gly
	or	Gly	Glu	Arg	Gln	Glu	Arg		Leu	Val	Gly

or equivalent with leucine at 117 and no basic amino acids at sites 111, 112, 114 and 115.

2-4-3 Safety

Carry out the test for each route and method of administration to be recommended for vaccination and in each avian species for which the vaccine is intended, using in each case birds not older than the minimum age to be recommended for vaccination. If the test is performed in chickens, use chickens from an SPF flock (5.2.2). If the test is performed in birds other than chickens, use birds that do not have antibodies against Newcastle disease virus.

Use vaccine virus at the least attenuated passage level that will be present in a batch of the vaccine.

For each test performed in birds younger than 3 weeks of age, use not fewer than 10 birds. For each test performed in birds older than 3 weeks of age, use not fewer than 8 birds. Administer to each bird a quantity of the vaccine virus equivalent to not less than 10 times the maximum virus titre likely to be contained in 1 dose of the vaccine. Observe the birds at least daily for at least 14 days.

The test is not valid if more than 10 per cent of the birds younger than 3 weeks of age show abnormal signs of disease or die from causes not attributable to the vaccine virus. For birds older than 3 weeks of age, the test is not valid if non-specific mortality occurs.

The vaccine virus complies with the test if no bird shows abnormal signs of disease or dies from causes attributable to the vaccine.

2-4-4 Increase in virulence

Carry out the test according to general chapter 5.2.6 using birds not more than 2 weeks old. If the properties of the vaccine virus allow sequential passage through 5 groups via natural spreading, this method may be used, otherwise passage as described below is carried out. Carry out the test in a target species, using the chicken if it is one of the target species. For the test in chickens, use chickens from an SPF flock (5.2.2). For other species, carry out the test in birds that do not have antibodies against Newcastle disease virus. Administer to each bird of the 1st group by eye-drop a

quantity of the vaccine virus that will allow recovery of virus for the passages described below. Observe the birds for the period shown to correspond to maximum replication of the vaccine virus, euthanise them and prepare a suspension from the brain of each bird and from a suitable organ depending on the tropism of the strain (for example, mucosa of the entire trachea, intestine, pancreas); pool the samples. Administer 0.05 mL of the pooled samples by eye-drop to each bird of the next group. Carry out this passage operation not fewer than 4 times; verify the presence of the virus at each passage. If the virus is not found at a passage level, repeat the passage by administration to a group of 10 birds.

A. Carry out the test for intracerebral pathogenicity index (section 2-4-1) using the material used for the 1st passage and the virus at the final passage level.

B. Carry out the test for amino-acid sequence (section 2-4-2) using unpassaged vaccine virus the material used for the 1st passage and the virus at the final passage level.

C. Carry out the test for safety (section 2-4-3) using material used for the 1st passage and the virus at the final passage level.

Administer the virus by the route to be recommended for vaccination likely to be the least safe and to the avian species for which the vaccine is intended that is likely to be the most susceptible to Newcastle disease.

The vaccine virus complies with the test if, in the tests 2-4-4A, 2-4-4B and 2-4-4C, no indication of increase in virulence of the virus recovered for the final passage compared with the material used for the 1st passage is observed. If virus is not recovered after an initial passage in 5 birds and a subsequent repeat passage in 10 birds, the vaccine virus also complies with the test.

2-4-5 Immunogenicity

For each avian species for which the vaccine is intended, a test is carried out for each route and method of administration to be recommended using in each case birds not older than the minimum age to be recommended for vaccination. The quantity of the vaccine virus administered to each bird is not greater than the minimum titre to be stated on the label and the virus is at the most attenuated passage level that will be present in a batch of the vaccine.

2-4-5-1 Vaccines for use in chickens. Use not fewer than 30 chickens of the same origin and from an SPF flock (5.2.2). Vaccinate by a route to be recommended not fewer than 20 chickens. Maintain not fewer than 10 chickens as controls. Challenge each chicken after 21 days by the intramuscular route with not less than $10^{5.0}$ embryo LD_{50} of the Herts (Weybridge 33/56) strain of Newcastle disease virus. Observe the chickens at least daily for 14 days after challenge. Record the deaths and the number of surviving chickens that show clinical signs of disease.

The test is not valid if 6 days after challenge fewer than 100 per cent of the control chickens have died or if during the period between vaccination and challenge more than 10 per cent of the vaccinated or control chickens show abnormal clinical signs or die from causes not attributable to the vaccine.

The vaccine virus complies with the test if during the observation period after challenge not fewer than 90 per cent of the vaccinated chickens survive and show no notable clinical signs of Newcastle disease.

2-4-5-2 Vaccines for use in avian species other than the chicken. Use not fewer than 30 birds of the species for which the vaccine is intended for Newcastle disease, of the same origin and that do not have antibodies against avian paramyxovirus 1. Vaccinate by a route to be recommended not fewer than 20 birds. Maintain not fewer than 10 birds as controls. Challenge each bird after 21 days by the intramuscular route with a sufficient quantity of virulent avian paramyxovirus 1. Observe the birds at least daily for 21 days after challenge. Record the deaths and the surviving birds that show clinical signs of disease.

The test is not valid if:
— during the observation period after challenge fewer than 90 per cent of the control birds die or show severe clinical signs of Newcastle disease;
— or if during the period between the vaccination and challenge more than 10 per cent of the vaccinated or control birds show abnormal clinical signs or die from causes not attributable to the vaccine.

The vaccine virus complies with the test if during the observation period after challenge not fewer than 90 per cent of the vaccinated birds survive and show no notable clinical signs of Newcastle disease. For species where there is published evidence that it is not possible to achieve this level of protection, the vaccine complies with the test if there is a significant reduction in morbidity and mortality of the vaccinated birds compared with the control birds.

3 BATCH TESTS

3-1 Identification

3-1-1 Identification of the vaccine virus. The vaccine, diluted if necessary and mixed with a monospecific Newcastle disease virus antiserum, no longer provokes haemagglutination of chicken red blood cells or infects embryonated hens' eggs from an SPF flock (5.2.2) or susceptible cell cultures (5.2.4) into which it is inoculated.

3-1-2 Identification of the virus strain. The strain of vaccine virus is identified by a suitable method, for example using monoclonal antibodies.

3-2 Bacteria and fungi

Vaccines intended for administration by injection comply with the test for sterility prescribed in the monograph *Vaccines for veterinary use (0062)*.

Frozen or freeze-dried vaccines produced in embryonated eggs and not intended for administration by injection either comply with the test for sterility prescribed in the monograph *Vaccines for veterinary use (0062)* or with the following test: carry out a quantitative test for bacterial and fungal contamination; carry out identification tests for microorganisms detected in the vaccine; the vaccine does not contain pathogenic microorganisms and contains not more than 1 non-pathogenic microorganism per dose.

Any diluent supplied for reconstitution of the vaccine complies with the test for sterility prescribed in the monograph *Vaccines for veterinary use (0062)*.

3-3 Mycoplasmas

The vaccine complies with the test for mycoplasmas (2.6.7).

3-4 Extraneous agents

The vaccine complies with the tests for extraneous agents in batches of finished product (2.6.25).

3-5 Virus titre

Titrate the vaccine virus by inoculation into embryonated hens' eggs from an SPF flock (5.2.2) or into suitable cell cultures (5.2.4). The vaccine complies with the test if 1 dose contains not less than the minimum virus titre stated on the label.

3-6 Potency

Depending on the indications, the vaccine complies with 1 or both of the tests prescribed under Immunogenicity (section 2-4-5) when administered according to the recommended schedule by a recommended route and method. If the test in section 2-4-5-2 *Vaccine for use in avian species other than the chicken* is conducted and the vaccine is recommended for use in more than 1 avian species, the test is carried out with birds of that species for which the vaccine is recommended which is likely to be the most susceptible to avian paramyxovirus 1. It is not necessary to carry out the potency test for each batch of the vaccine if it has been carried out on a representative batch using a vaccinating dose containing not more than the minimum virus titre stated on the label.

_____ *Ph Eur*

Ovine Enzootic Abortion Vaccine, Inactivated

DEFINITION

Ovine Enzootic Abortion Vaccine, Inactivated is a suspension of one or more strains of the chlamydia organisms of ovine enzootic abortion which have been inactivated in such a manner that the immunogenic activity is retained.

PRODUCTION

The *Chlamydia psittaci* organisms are grown in either suitable cell cultures, Appendix XV J(Vet) 1, or in the yolk sacs of embryonated eggs derived from healthy chicken flocks. The organisms are harvested and inactivated. A validated, suitably sensitive test for residual chlamydia is carried out in tissue cultures, on each batch of antigen immediately after inactivation.

The vaccine contains an adjuvant.

CHOICE OF VACCINE COMPOSITION

The vaccine is shown to be satisfactory with respect to safety and immunogenicity for the animals for which the vaccine is intended. The following tests may be used during the demonstration of safety, Appendix XV K(Vet) 1, and immunogenicity, Appendix XV K(Vet) 2.

Safety

Carry out a test in each category of animal for which the vaccine is to be recommended and by each recommended route of administration. Vaccinate at least five animals that do not have antibodies to *Chlamydia psittaci*. Use for the test, a batch of vaccine with the maximum potency likely to be included in a dose of the vaccine. Administer a single dose of vaccine to each animal and observe them for two weeks. If the schedule to be recommended requires a single dose or primary vaccination series followed by booster vaccination, the primary vaccination regimen plus an additional dose should be used with an interval of 14 days between doses. No abnormal local or systemic reactions occur.

Immunogenicity

The tests to demonstrate Immunogenicity are carried out in each category of animal for which the vaccine is to be recommended and by each recommended route of administration and using a batch or batches with the minimum potency likely to be included in a dose of the vaccine. The efficacy claims made on the label (e.g. protection from abortion) reflect the type of data generated.

BATCH TESTING

Inactivation

Carry out a suitable validated test in tissue cultures for residual *Chlamydia psittaci* on the bulk antigen blend immediately before the addition of the adjuvant. No live organisms are detected.

CAUTION *Accidental injection of oil emulsion vaccines can cause serious local reactions in man. Expert medical advice should be sought immediately and the doctor should be informed that the vaccine is an oil emulsion.*

The vaccine complies with the requirements stated under Veterinary Vaccines with the following modifications.

IDENTIFICATION

When injected into healthy seronegative animals, the vaccine stimulates the production of specific antibodies against *Chlamydia psittaci.*

TESTS

Extraneous bacteria and fungi

The vaccine complies with the test for sterility described under Veterinary Vaccines.

POTENCY

Inject each of five healthy susceptible sheep according to the recommendations stated on the label. Maintain two unvaccinated sheep from the same source as the unvaccinated controls. Bleed all of the animals before vaccination and again not less than 28 days later. Using an appropriate serological test (complement-fixation or immunofluorescence is suitable) the serum of each sheep before vaccination is negative at a 2-fold dilution and, not less than 28 days after vaccination, the serum of no fewer than four of the vaccinated sheep gives a positive reaction at an 8-fold or greater dilution. The test is not valid if there is an increase in antibody levels in the controls.

Pasteurella Vaccine (Inactivated) for Sheep

(Ph. Eur. monograph 2072)

Ph Eur _____

1 DEFINITION

Pasteurella vaccine (inactivated) for sheep is a preparation of one or more suitable strains of *Pasteurella trehalosi*, inactivated while maintaining adequate immunogenic properties. This monograph applies to vaccines intended for the active immunisation of sheep against disease caused by *P. trehalosi.*

2 PRODUCTION
2-1 PREPARATION OF THE VACCINE

Production of the vaccine is based on a seed-lot system. The seed material is cultured in a suitable medium; each strain is cultivated separately and identity is verified using a suitable method. During production, various parameters such as growth rate are monitored by suitable methods; the values are within the limits approved for the particular product. Purity and identity of the harvest are verified using suitable methods. After cultivation, the bacterial suspensions are collected separately and inactivated by a suitable method. The vaccine may be adjuvanted.

2-2 CHOICE OF VACCINE COMPOSITION

The choice of composition and the strains to be included in the vaccine are based on epidemiological data on the prevalence of the different serovars of *P. trehalosi.*

The vaccine is shown to be satisfactory with respect to safety (5.2.6) and efficacy (5.2.7) for the sheep for which it is intended.

The following tests for safety (section 2-2-1) and immunogenicity (section 2-2-2) may be used during the demonstration of safety and efficacy.

2-2-1 Safety

2-2-1-1 Laboratory tests. Carry out the tests for each route and method of administration to be recommended for vaccination and in sheep of each category for which the vaccine is intended (for example, young sheep, pregnant ewes). Use a batch of vaccine containing not less than the maximum potency that may be expected in a batch of vaccine.

For each test, use not fewer than 8 sheep that preferably do not have antibodies against the serovars of *P. trehalosi* or against the leucotoxin present in the vaccine. Where justified, sheep with a known history of no previous pasteurella vaccination and with low antibody titres (measured in a sensitive test system such as ELISA) may be used. Administer to each sheep 1 dose of the vaccine. If the schedule to be recommended requires a 2nd dose, administer another dose after an interval of at least 14 days. Observe the sheep at least daily for at least 14 days after the last administration. Record body temperature the day before vaccination, at vaccination, 2 h, 4 h and 6 h later and then daily for 4 days; note the maximum temperature increase for each sheep.

The vaccine complies with the test if no sheep shows abnormal local reactions, notable signs of disease or dies from causes attributable to the vaccine, if the average body temperature increase for all sheep does not exceed 1.5 °C and no sheep shows a rise greater than 2.0 °C.

2-2-1-2 Field studies. The sheep used for the field trials are also used to evaluate safety. Carry out a test in each category of sheep for which the vaccine is intended. Use not fewer than 3 groups of 20 sheep with corresponding groups of not fewer than 10 controls in 3 different locations. Examine the injection sites for local reactions after vaccination. Record body temperatures the day before vaccination, at vaccination and on the 2 days following vaccination.

The vaccine complies with the test if no sheep shows abnormal local or systemic reactions, notable signs of disease or dies from causes attributable to the vaccine. The average body temperature increase for all sheep does not exceed 1.5 °C and no sheep shows a rise greater than 2.0 °C. In addition, if the vaccine is intended for use in pregnant ewes, no adverse effects on the pregnancy and offspring are demonstrated.

2-2-2 Immunogenicity

Carry out a test for each serovar of *P. trehalosi* for which protection is to be claimed on the label.

A test is carried out for each route and method of administration to be recommended, using in each case lambs of the minimum age to be recommended for vaccination. The vaccine administered to each lamb is of minimum potency.

Use not fewer than 20 lambs that do not have antibodies against *P. trehalosi* and against the leucotoxin of *P. trehalosi.* Vaccinate not fewer than 10 lambs according to the schedule to be recommended. Maintain not fewer than 10 lambs as controls. 20-22 days after the last vaccination, challenge each lamb by the subcutaneous or another suitable route, with a sufficient quantity of a low-passage, virulent strain of a serovar of *P. trehalosi*. Observe the lambs for a further 7 days; to avoid unnecessary suffering, severely ill lambs are euthanised and are then considered to have died from the disease. During the observation period, examine the lambs for any signs of disease (for example, severe dullness, excess salivation) and record the mortality. Euthanise surviving lambs at the end of the observation period. Carry out post-mortem examination on any lamb that dies and those euthanised at the end of the observation period. Examine the lungs, pleura, liver and spleen for haemorrhages and evaluate the extent of lung consolidation due to pasteurellosis. Collect samples of lung, liver and spleen tissue for re-isolation of the challenge organisms. Score the mortality, clinical observations and the post-mortem lesions and compare the results obtained for these parameters and the bacterial re-isolation results for the 2 groups.

The test is not valid if signs or lesions of *P. trehalosi* infection occur in less than 70 per cent of the control lambs.

The vaccine complies with the test if there is a significant difference between the scores obtained for the clinical and post-mortem observations in the vaccinates compared to the controls. For vaccines with a claim for a beneficial effect on the extent of infection against the serovar, the results for the infection rates are also significantly better for the vaccinates compared to the controls.

2-3 MANUFACTURER'S TESTS

2-3-1 Batch potency test
It is not necessary to carry out the potency test (section 3-3) for each batch of vaccine if it has been carried out using a batch of vaccine with a minimum potency. Where the test is not carried out, an alternative validated method is used, the criteria for acceptance being set with reference to a batch of vaccine that has given satisfactory results in the test described under Potency.

2-3-2 Bacterial endotoxins
A test for bacterial endotoxins (*2.6.14*) is carried out on the final lot or, where the nature of the adjuvant prevents performance of a satisfactory test, on the bulk antigen or the mixture of bulk antigens immediately before addition of the adjuvant. The maximum acceptable amount of bacterial endotoxins is that found for a batch of vaccine that has been shown satisfactory in safety tests 2-2-1-1 given under Choice of vaccine composition. The method chosen for determining the amount of bacterial endotoxin present in the vaccine batch used in the safety test for determining the maximum acceptable level of endotoxin is used subsequently for testing of each batch.

3 BATCH TESTS

3-1 Identification
When injected into healthy animals that do not have specific antibodies against the serovars of *P. trehalosi* and/or against the leucotoxin present in the vaccine, the vaccine stimulates the production of such antibodies.

3-2 Bacteria and fungi
The vaccine, including where applicable the diluent supplied for reconstitution, complies with the test for sterility prescribed in the monograph *Vaccines for veterinary use (0062)*.

3-3 Potency
The vaccine complies with the requirements of the test mentioned under Immunogenicity (section 2-2-2) when administered by a recommended route and method.

Porcine Actinobacillosis Vaccine, Inactivated

(Porcine Actinobacillosis Vaccine (Inactivated), Ph Eur monograph 1360)

Ph Eur _____

1 DEFINITION
Porcine actinobacillosis vaccine (inactivated) is a preparation which has one or more of the following components: inactivated *Actinobacillus pleuropneumoniae* of a suitable strain or strains; toxins, proteins or polysaccharides derived from suitable strains of *A. pleuropneumoniae*, and treated to render them harmless while maintaining adequate immunogenic properties; fractions of toxins derived from suitable strains of *A. pleuropneumoniae* and treated if necessary to render them harmless while maintaining adequate immunogenic properties. This monograph applies to vaccines intended for the active immunisation of pigs against actinobacillosis.

2 PRODUCTION
2-1 PREPARATION OF THE VACCINE
The seed material is cultured in a suitable medium; each strain is cultivated separately. During production, various parameters such as growth rate, protein content and quantity of relevant antigens are monitored by suitable methods; the values are within the limits approved for the particular product. Purity and identity are verified on the harvest using suitable methods. After cultivation, the bacterial harvests are collected separately and inactivated by a suitable method. They may be detoxified, purified and concentrated. The vaccine may be adjuvanted.

2-2 CHOICE OF VACCINE COMPOSITION
The choice of strains is based on epidemiological data. The vaccine is shown to be satisfactory with respect to safety (*5.2.6*) and efficacy (*5.2.7*) for the pigs for which it is intended.

The following tests for safety (section 2-2-1) and immunogenicity (section 2-2-2) may be used during the demonstration of safety and efficacy.

2-2-1 Safety
2-2-1-1 Laboratory tests Carry out the test for each route and method of administration to be recommended for vaccination and where applicable, in pigs of each category for which the vaccine is intended, using in each case pigs not older than the minimum age to be recommended for vaccination. Use a batch containing not less than the maximum potency that may be expected in a batch of vaccine.

For each test, use not fewer than 8 pigs that do not have antibodies against the serotypes of *A. pleuropneumoniae* or its toxins present in the vaccine. Administer to each pig 1 dose of the vaccine. If the schedule to be recommended requires a 2nd dose, administer another dose after an interval of at least 14 days. Observe the pigs at least daily until 14 days after the last administration. Record body temperature the day before vaccination, at vaccination, 2 h, 4 h and 6 h later and then daily for 4 days; note the maximum temperature increase for each pig.

The vaccine complies with the test if no pig shows abnormal local or systemic reactions or dies from causes attributable to the vaccine, and if the average temperature increase for all pigs does not exceed 1.5 °C and no pig shows a rise greater than 2.0 °C.

2-2-1-2 *Field studies* The pigs used for field trials are also used to evaluate safety. Carry out a test in each category of pigs for which the vaccine is intended. Use not fewer than 3 groups each of not fewer than 20 pigs with corresponding groups of not fewer than 10 controls. Examine the injection site for local reactions after vaccination. Record body temperature the day before vaccination, at vaccination, at the time interval after which a rise in temperature, if any, was seen in test 2-2-1-1, and daily during the 2 days following vaccination; note the maximum temperature increase for each pig.

The vaccine complies with the test if no pig shows abnormal local or systemic reactions or dies from causes attributable to the vaccine, and if the average temperature increase for all pigs does not exceed 1.5 °C and no pig shows a rise greater than 2.0 °C.

2-2-2 Immunogenicity

The challenge strain for the following test is chosen to ensure challenge with each Ap toxin[1] produced by the serotypes to be stated on the label; it may be necessary to carry out more than one test using a different challenge strain for each test.

Each test is carried out for each route and method of administration to be recommended. The vaccine administered to each pig is of minimum potency.

For each test, use not fewer than 14 pigs that do not have antibodies against *A. pleuropneumoniae* and Ap toxins. Vaccinate not fewer than 7 pigs according to the schedule to be recommended. Maintain not fewer than 7 pigs as controls. 3 weeks after the last vaccination, challenge all the pigs by the intranasal or intratracheal route or by aerosol with a sufficient quantity of a virulent serotype of *A. pleuropneumoniae*. Observe the pigs at least daily for 7 days; to avoid unnecessary suffering, severely ill control pigs are euthanised and are then considered to have died from the disease. Euthanise all surviving pigs at the end of the observation period. Carry out a post-mortem examination on all pigs. Examine the lungs, the tracheobronchial lymph nodes and the tonsils for the presence of *A. pleuropneumoniae*. Evaluate the extent of lung lesions at post-mortem examination. Each of the 7 lobes of the lungs is allotted a maximum possible lesion score[2] of 5. The area showing pneumonia and/or pleuritis of each lobe is assessed and expressed on a scale of 0 to 5 to give the pneumonic score per lobe (the maximum total score possible for each complete lung is 35). Calculate separately for the vaccinated and the control pigs the total score (the maximum score per group is 245, if 7 pigs are used per group).

The vaccine complies with the test if the vaccinated pigs, when compared with controls, show lower incidence of: mortality; typical signs (dyspnoea, coughing and vomiting); typical lung lesions; re-isolation of *A. pleuropneumoniae* from the lungs, the tracheobronchial lymph nodes and the tonsils. Where possible, the incidence is analysed statistically and shown to be significantly lower for vaccinates.

2-3 MANUFACTURER'S TESTS

2-3-1 Batch potency test

It is not necessary to carry out the potency test (section 3-4) for each batch of vaccine if it has been carried out using a batch of vaccine with a minimum potency. Where the test is not carried out, an alternative validated method is used, the criteria for acceptance being set with reference to a batch of vaccine that has given satisfactory results in the test described under Potency. The following test may be used.

Use 5 mice weighing 18-20 g and that do not have antibodies against the serotypes of *A. pleuropneumoniae* or its toxins present in the vaccine. Vaccinate each mouse by the subcutaneous route with a suitable dose. Where the recommended schedule requires a booster injection to be given, a booster vaccination may also be given in this test provided it has been demonstrated that this will still provide a suitably sensitive test system. Before the vaccination and at a given interval within the range of 14-21 days after the last injection, collect blood from each mouse and prepare serum samples. Determine individually for each serum the titre of specific antibodies against each antigenic component stated on the label, using a suitable validated test such as enzyme-linked immunosorbent assay (2.7.1). The vaccine complies with the test if the antibody levels are not significantly lower than those obtained for a batch that has given satisfactory results in the test described under Potency.

2-3-2 Bacterial endotoxins

A test for bacterial endotoxins (2.6.14) is carried out on the final bulk or, where the nature of the adjuvant prevents performance of a satisfactory test, on the bulk antigen or mixture of bulk antigens immediately before addition of the adjuvant. The maximum acceptable amount of bacterial endotoxins is that found for a batch of vaccine that has been shown satisfactory in safety test 2-2-1-1 described under Choice of vaccine composition or in the residual toxicity test described under Batch tests, carried out using 10 pigs. Where the latter test is used, note the maximum temperature increase for each animal; the vaccine complies with the test if the average temperature increase for all animals does not exceed 1.5 °C. The method chosen for determining the amount of bacterial endotoxin present in the vaccine batch used in the safety test for determining the maximum acceptable level of endotoxin is used subsequently for batch testing.

3 BATCH TESTS

3-1 Identification

When injected into healthy animals that do not have specific antibodies against the antigenic components of *A. pleuropneumoniae* stated on the label, the vaccine stimulates the production of such antibodies.

3-2 Bacteria and fungi

The vaccine, including where applicable the diluent supplied for reconstitution, complies with the test for sterility prescribed in the monograph *Vaccines for veterinary use (0062)*.

3-3 Residual toxicity

Use 2 pigs of the minimum age recommended for vaccination and that do not have antibodies against the serotypes of *A. pleuropneumoniae* or its toxins present in the vaccine. Administer to each pig by a recommended route a double dose of the vaccine. Observe the pigs at least daily for 14 days. Record body temperature the day before vaccination, at vaccination, 2 h, 4 h and 6 h later and then daily for 2 days.

It is recommended to use the mean temperature of the days before administration of the vaccine (e.g. day −3 to day 0) as the baseline temperature to have clear guidance for evaluation of the test.

The vaccine complies with the test if no pig shows notable signs of disease or dies from causes attributable to the vaccine; a transient temperature increase not exceeding 2.0 °C may occur.

3-4 Potency

The vaccine complies with the requirements of the test mentioned under Immunogenicity (section 2-2-2) when administered by a recommended route and method.

_____ *Ph Eur*

(1) The nomenclature of the toxins of A. pleuropneumoniae is described by J. Frey et al., Journal of General Microbiology, 1993, 139, 1723-1728.
(2) The system of lung scores is described in detail by P.C.T. Hannan, B.S. Bhogal, J.P. Fish, Research in Veterinary Science, 1982, 33, 76-88.

Porcine Enzootic Pneumonia Vaccine (Inactivated)

(Ph. Eur. monograph 2448)

Ph Eur _____

1 DEFINITION

Porcine enzootic pneumonia vaccine (inactivated) is a preparation of a suitable strain of *Mycoplasma hyopneumoniae* that has been inactivated while maintaining adequate immunogenic properties. This monograph applies to vaccines intended for the active immunisation of pigs against enzootic pneumonia caused by *M. hyopneumoniae*.

2 PRODUCTION
2-1 PREPARATION OF THE VACCINE

Production of the vaccine is based on a seed-lot system. The seed material is cultured in a suitable solid and/or liquid medium to ensure optimal growth under the chosen incubation conditions. The identity of the strain is verified using a suitable method.

During production, various parameters such as growth rate are monitored by suitable methods; the values are within the limits approved for the particular vaccine. Purity of the harvest is verified using a suitable method.

After cultivation, the mycoplasma suspension is collected and inactivated by a suitable method. The vaccine may contain an adjuvant.

2-2 CHOICE OF VACCINE COMPOSITION

The vaccine is shown to be satisfactory with respect to safety (5.2.6) and efficacy (5.2.7) for the pigs for which it is intended.

The following tests for safety (section 2-2-1) and immunogenicity (section 2-2-2) may be used during the demonstration of safety and efficacy.

2-2-1 Safety

2-2-1-1 Laboratory tests. Carry out the test for each route and method of administration to be recommended for vaccination and where applicable, in pigs of each category for which the vaccine is intended, using in each case pigs not older than the minimum age to be recommended for vaccination. Use a batch of vaccine containing not less than the maximum potency that may be expected in a batch of vaccine.

For each test, use not fewer than 8 pigs that do not have antibodies against *M. hyopneumoniae*. Administer to each pig 1 dose of the vaccine. If the schedule to be recommended requires a 2nd dose, administer another dose after an interval of at least 14 days. Observe the pigs at least daily until at least 14 days after the last administration. Record body temperature the day before vaccination, at vaccination, 4 h

later and then daily for 4 days; note the maximum temperature increase for each pig.

The vaccine complies with the test if no pig shows notable signs of disease or dies from causes attributable to the vaccine, and, in particular, if the average body temperature increase for all pigs does not exceed 1.5 °C and no pig shows a rise greater than 2.0 °C.

2-2-1-2 Field studies. The animals used for field trials are also used to evaluate safety. Carry out a test in each category of animals for which the vaccine is intended. Use not fewer than 3 groups each of not fewer than 20 animals with corresponding groups of not fewer than 10 controls. Examine the injection site for local reactions after vaccination. Record body temperature the day before vaccination, at vaccination, at the time interval after which a rise in temperature, if any, was seen in test 2-2-1-1, and daily during the 2 days following vaccination; note the maximum temperature increase for each animal.

The vaccine complies with the test if no animal shows notable signs of disease or dies from causes attributable to the vaccine, the average body temperature increase for all animals does not exceed 1.5 °C, and no animal shows a rise in body temperature greater than 2.0 °C.

2-2-2 Immunogenicity

A test is carried out for each route and method of administration to be recommended using in each case pigs not older than the minimum age to be recommended for vaccination. The vaccine to be administered to each pig is of minimum potency.

Use not fewer than 20 pigs that do not have antibodies against *M. hyopneumoniae* and that are from a herd or herds where there are no signs of enzootic pneumonia and that have not been vaccinated against *M. hyopneumoniae*. Vaccinate not fewer than 12 pigs according to the schedule to be recommended. Maintain not fewer than 8 non-vaccinated pigs as controls. Challenge each pig at least 14 days after the last vaccination by the intranasal or intratracheal route or by aerosol with a sufficient quantity of a virulent strain of *M. hyopneumoniae*. The challenge strain used is different from the vaccine strain. 21-30 days after challenge, euthanise the pigs. Conduct a post-mortem examination on each pig in order to evaluate the extent of lung lesions using a validated lung lesion scoring system that is adapted to the age of the animals. The following scoring system may be used.

A weighted score is allocated to each of the 7 lobes of the lungs according to the relative weight of the lung lobes.

Lobes	Left	Right
Apical	5	11
Cardiac	6	10
Diaphragmatic	29	34
Intermediate	5	

The vaccine complies with the test if the vaccinated pigs, when compared with controls, show a significant reduction in the lung lesion score.

2-3 MANUFACTURER'S TESTS
2-3-1 Batch potency test

It is not necessary to carry out the potency test (section 3-4) for each batch of the vaccine if it has been carried out using a batch of vaccine with a minimum potency. Where the test is not carried out, an alternative validated method is used, the criteria for acceptance being set with reference to a batch of vaccine that has given satisfactory results in the test described under Potency. A quantification of the antigen (i.e. an *in vitro* test using a reference vaccine that has given satisfactory results in the test described under Potency) together with a test for adjuvant quantification may be used as an alternative method provided the antigen that is measured has been proven to be protective and/or immunorelevant.

Alternatively, a test measuring induction of antibody response in laboratory animals may be used. The following method is given as an example.

Use at least 5 mice weighing 18-20 g and that do not have antibodies against *M. hyopneumoniae*. Vaccinate each mouse by the subcutaneous route with a suitable dose. Maintain not fewer than 5 mice as controls. Where the recommended schedule requires a booster injection to be given, a booster vaccination may also be given in this test provided it has been demonstrated that this will still provide a suitably sensitive test system. Before the vaccination and at a given interval within the range of 14-21 days after the last injection, collect blood from each mouse and prepare serum samples. Determine individually for each serum the titre of specific antibodies against each antigenic component stated on the label, using a suitable validated test such as enzyme-linked immunosorbent assay (*2.7.1*).

The vaccine complies with the test if the mean antibody levels are not significantly lower than those obtained for a batch that has given satisfactory results in the test described under Potency.

3 BATCH TESTS
3-1 Identification
When injected into healthy animals that do not have antibodies against *M. hyopneumoniae*, the vaccine stimulates the production of such antibodies. Suitable molecular methods such as nucleic acid amplification techniques (*2.6.21*) may also serve for identification.

3-2 Bacteria and fungi
The vaccine, including where applicable the diluent supplied for reconstitution, complies with the test for sterility prescribed in the monograph *Vaccines for veterinary use (0062)*.

3-3 Residual live mycoplasmas
A test for residual live mycoplasmas is carried out to confirm inactivation of *M. hyopneumoniae*. The vaccine complies with a validated test for residual live *M. hyopneumoniae* carried out by a culture method (see for example *2.6.7*, using media shown to be suitable for *M. hyopneumoniae*).

3-4 Potency
The vaccine complies with the requirements of the test mentioned under Immunogenicity (section 2-2-2) when administered by a recommended route and method.

Ph Eur

Porcine E. Coli Vaccine, Inactivated

Porcine Escherichia Coli Vaccine, Inactivated

(Neonatal Piglet Colibacillosis Vaccine (Inactivated), Ph Eur monograph 0962)

Ph Eur

1 DEFINITION
Neonatal piglet colibacillosis vaccine (inactivated) is a preparation from cultures of one or more suitable strains of *Escherichia coli*, carrying one or more adhesins or enterotoxins. This monograph applies to vaccines intended for the active immunisation of sows and gilts for passive protection of their newborn progeny against enteric forms of colibacillosis, administered by injection.

2 PRODUCTION
2-1 PREPARATION OF THE VACCINE
The *E. coli* strains used for production are cultured separately in a suitable medium. The cells or toxins are processed to render them safe while maintaining adequate immunogenic properties and are blended. The vaccine may be adjuvanted.

2-2 CHOICE OF VACCINE COMPOSITION
The *E. coli* strains used in the production of the vaccine are shown to be satisfactory with respect to expression of antigens and the vaccine is shown to be satisfactory with respect to safety (*5.2.6*) and efficacy (*5.2.7*) for the sows and gilts for which it is intended.

The following tests for expression of antigens (section 2-2-1), safety (section 2-2-2) and immunogenicity (section 2-2-3) may be used during the demonstration of safety and efficacy.

2-2-1 Expression of antigens
The expression of antigens that stimulate a protective immune response is verified by a suitable immunochemical method (*2.7.1*) carried out on the antigen obtained from each of the vaccine strains under the conditions used for the production of the vaccine.

2-2-2 Safety
2-2-2-1 Safety in pregnant sows. Carry out the test for each route and method of administration to be recommended for vaccination and in pregnant sows. Use a batch of vaccine containing not less than the maximum potency that may be expected in a batch of vaccine.

For each test, use not fewer than 8 pregnant sows per group that have not been vaccinated against colibacillosis, at the relevant stages of pregnancy in accordance with the schedule to be recommended or at different stages of pregnancy. Administer to each sow 1 dose of the vaccine. If the schedule to be recommended requires a 2nd dose, administer another dose after an interval of at least 14 days. Observe the sows at least daily until farrowing. Record body temperature the day before vaccination, at vaccination, 2 h, 4 h and 6 h later and then daily for 4 days; note the maximum temperature increase for each sow.

The vaccine complies with the test if:
— no sow shows abnormal local or systemic reactions or dies from causes attributable to the vaccine;
— the average temperature increase for all sows does not exceed 1.5 °C and no sow shows a rise greater than 2.0 °C; and
— no adverse effects on gestation or the offspring are noted.

2-2-2-2 Field studies. The pigs used for field trials are also used to evaluate safety. Use not fewer than 3 groups each of not fewer than 20 pigs with corresponding groups of not fewer than 10 controls. Examine the injection site for local reactions after vaccination. Record body temperature the day before vaccination, at vaccination, at the time interval after which a rise in temperature, if any, was seen in test 2-2-2-1, and daily during the 2 days following vaccination; note the maximum temperature increase for each pig.

The vaccine complies with the test if no pig shows abnormal local or systemic reactions or dies from causes attributable to the vaccine, the average temperature increase for all pigs does not exceed 1.5 °C, and no pig shows a rise greater than 2.0 °C.

2-2-3 Immunogenicity

Carry out the test with a challenge strain representing each type of antigen against which the vaccine is intended to protect: if a single strain with all the necessary antigens is not available, repeat the test using different challenge strains.

Each test is carried out for each route and method of administration to be recommended for vaccination. The vaccine administered to each gilt is of minimum potency.

Use not fewer than 8 gilts susceptible to *E. coli* infections and that do not have antibodies against the antigens to be stated on the label. Take not fewer than 4 at random and vaccinate these at the stage of pregnancy and according to the schedule to be recommended. Maintain not fewer than 4 gilts as controls. Within 12 h of their giving birth, take not fewer than 15 healthy piglets from the vaccinated gilts and 15 healthy piglets from the controls, taking at least 3 from each litter. Challenge each piglet by the oral route with a sufficient quantity of a virulent strain of *E. coli* before or after colostrum feeding and using the same conditions for vaccinated piglets and controls. The strain used must not be one used in the manufacture of the vaccine. Return the piglets to their dam and observe at least daily for 8 days.

On each day, note signs in each piglet and score using the following scale.

0   no signs
1   slight diarrhoea
2   marked diarrhoea (watery faeces)
3   dead

Calculate total scores for each piglet over 8 days.

The test is not valid if fewer than 40 per cent of the piglets from the control gilts die and more than 15 per cent of the piglets from the control gilts show no signs of illness. The vaccine complies with the test if there is a significant reduction in score in the group of piglets from the vaccinated gilts compared with the group from the unvaccinated controls.

For some adhesins (for example, F5 and F41), there is published evidence that high mortality cannot be achieved under experimental conditions. If challenge has to be carried out with a strain having such adhesins: the test is not valid if fewer than 70 per cent of the control piglets show signs expected with the challenge strain; the vaccine complies with the test if there is a significant reduction in score in the group of piglets from the vaccinated gilts compared with the group from the unvaccinated controls.

2-3 MANUFACTURER′S TESTS

2-3-1 Batch potency test

It is not necessary to carry out the potency test (section 3-3) for each batch of vaccine if it has been carried out using a batch of vaccine with a minimum potency. Where the test is not carried out, an alternative validated method is used, the criteria for acceptance being set with reference to a batch of

vaccine that has given satisfactory results in the test described under Potency. The following test may be used.

Use 7 pigs not less than 3 weeks old and that do not have antibodies against the antigens stated on the label. Vaccinate each of 5 pigs by the recommended route and according to the recommended schedule. Maintain 2 pigs as controls. Alternatively, if the nature of the antigens allows reproducible results to be obtained, a test in laboratory animals (for example, guinea-pigs, mice, rabbits or rats) may be carried out. To obtain a valid assay, it may be necessary to carry out a test using several groups of animals, each receiving a different dose. For each dose, carry out the test as follows. Vaccinate not fewer than 5 animals with a single injection of a suitable dose. Maintain not fewer than 2 animals as controls. Where the recommended schedule requires a booster injection to be given, a booster vaccination may also be given in this test provided it has been demonstrated that this will still provide a suitably sensitive test system. At a given interval within the range of 14-21 days after the last injection, collect blood from each animal and prepare serum samples. Use a suitable validated test such as an enzyme-linked immunosorbent assay (*2.7.1*) to measure the antibody response to each of the antigens stated on the label.

The vaccine complies with the test if the antibody levels in the vaccinates are not significantly less than those obtained with a batch that has given satisfactory results in the test described under Potency and there is no significant increase in antibody titre in the controls.

Where animals that do not have antibodies against the antigens stated on the label are not available, seropositive animals may be used in the above test. During the development of a test with seropositive animals, particular care will be required during the validation of the test system to establish that the test is suitably sensitive and to specify acceptable pass, fail and retest criteria. It will be necessary to take into account the range of possible prevaccination titres and establish the acceptable minimum titre rise after vaccination in relation to these.

2-3-2 Bacterial endotoxins

A test for bacterial endotoxins (*2.6.14*) is carried out on the final lot or, where the nature of the adjuvant prevents performance of a satisfactory test, on the bulk antigen or the mixture of bulk antigens immediately before addition of the adjuvant. The maximum acceptable amount of bacterial endotoxins is that found for a batch of vaccine that has been shown satisfactory in safety test 2-2-2-1 given under Choice of vaccine composition. The method chosen for determining the amount of bacterial endotoxin present in the vaccine batch used in the safety test for determining the maximum acceptable level of endotoxin is used subsequently for testing of each batch.

3 BATCH TESTS

3-1 Identification

In animals that do not have antibodies against the antigens stated on the label, the vaccine stimulates the production of such antibodies.

3-2 Bacteria and fungi

The vaccine, including where applicable the diluent supplied for reconstitution, complies with the test for sterility prescribed in the monograph *Vaccines for veterinary use (0062)*.

3-3 Potency

The vaccine complies with the requirements of the test mentioned under Immunogenicity (section 2-2-3) when administered by a recommended route and method.

_____ Ph Eur

Porcine Parvovirus Vaccine, Inactivated

(Porcine Parvovirosis Vaccine (Inactivated), Ph Eur monograph 0965)

Ph Eur _____

1 DEFINITION

Porcine parvovirosis vaccine (inactivated) is a preparation of a suitable strain of porcine parvovirus, inactivated while maintaining adequate immunogenic properties, or of a non infectious fraction of the virus. This monograph applies to vaccines intended for the active immunisation of sows and gilts for protection of their progeny against transplacental infection.

2 PRODUCTION
2-1 PREPARATION OF THE VACCINE

The vaccine virus is grown in cell cultures. The viral suspension is harvested; the virus is inactivated by a suitable method and may be fragmented (inactivation may be by fragmentation); the virus or viral fragments may be purified and concentrated at a suitable stage of the process. The vaccine may be adjuvanted.

2-2 SUBSTRATE FOR VIRUS PROPAGATION
2-2-1 Cell cultures

The cell cultures comply with the requirements for cell cultures for production of veterinary vaccines (*5.2.4*).

2-3 CHOICE OF VACCINE COMPOSITION

The vaccine is shown to be satisfactory with respect to safety (*5.2.6*) (including absence of adverse effects on fertility, gestation, farrowing or offspring) and efficacy (*5.2.7*) for the pigs for which it is intended.

The following tests for safety (section 2-3-1) and immunogenicity (section 2-3-2) may be used during the demonstration of safety and efficacy.

2-3-1 Safety

2-3-1-1 Laboratory tests. Carry out the tests for each route and method of administration to be recommended for vaccination and where applicable, in pigs of each category for which the vaccine is intended, using in each case pigs not older than the minimum age to be recommended for vaccination. Use a batch of vaccine containing not less than the maximum potency that may be expected in a batch of vaccine.

2-3-1-1-1 General safety. For each test, use not fewer than 8 pigs that do not have antibodies against porcine parvovirus or against a fraction of the virus. Administer to each pig 1 dose of the vaccine. If the schedule to be recommended requires a 2nd dose, administer another dose after an interval of at least 14 days. Observe the pigs at least daily until 14 days after the last administration.

The vaccine complies with the test if no pig shows notable signs of disease or dies from causes attributable to the vaccine during the test.

2-3-1-1-2 Safety in pregnant sows. If the vaccine is intended for use in pregnant sows, use for the test not fewer than

8 pregnant sows at the stage or at different stages of pregnancy according to the recommended schedule. Administer to each sow 1 dose of the vaccine. If the schedule to be recommended requires a 2nd dose, administer another dose after an interval of at least 14 days. Observe the sows at least daily until farrowing.

The vaccine complies with the test if no sow shows abnormal local or systemic reactions or dies from causes attributable to the vaccine and if no adverse effects on gestation or the offspring are noted.

2-3-1-1-3 Safety in the pigs used in test 2-3-2 for immunogenicity. The pigs used in the test for immunogenicity are also used to evaluate safety. Measure the body temperature of each vaccinated pig at the time of vaccination 24 h and 48 h later. Examine the injection site after vaccination and at slaughter for local reactions.

The vaccine complies with the test if no pig shows:
— abnormal body temperature;
— other systemic reactions (for example, anorexia);
— abnormal local reactions attributable to the vaccine.

2-3-1-2 Field studies. The pigs used for field trials are also used to evaluate safety. Carry out a test in each category of pigs for which the vaccine is intended (sows, gilts). Use not fewer than 3 groups each of not fewer than 20 pigs with corresponding groups of not fewer than 10 controls. Measure the body temperature of each vaccinated pig at the time of vaccination, 24 h and 48 h later. Examine the injection site after vaccination and at slaughter for local reactions.

The vaccine complies with the test if no pig shows:
— abnormal body temperature;
— abnormal local reactions attributable to the vaccine.

2-3-2 Immunogenicity

A test is carried out for each route and method of administration to be recommended, using in each case gilts of 5-6 months old. The vaccine administered to each gilt is of minimum potency.

Use for the test not fewer than 12 gilts that do not have antibodies against porcine parvovirus or against a fraction of the virus. Vaccinate not fewer than 7 gilts according to the schedule to be recommended. Maintain not less than 5 unvaccinated gilts of the same age as controls. The interval between vaccination and service is that to be recommended. Mate all the gilts on 2 consecutive days immediately following signs of oestrus. At about the 40th day of gestation, challenge each gilt with a suitable quantity of a virulent strain of porcine parvovirus. Euthanise the gilts at about the 90th day of gestation and examine their foetuses for infection with porcine parvovirus as demonstrated by the presence of either virus or antibodies.

The test is not valid if:
— fewer than 7 vaccinated gilts and 5 control gilts are challenged;
— fewer than 90 per cent of piglets from the control gilts are infected;
— and the average number of piglets per litter for the vaccinated gilts is fewer than 6.

The vaccine complies with the test if not fewer than 80 per cent of the total number of piglets from vaccinated gilts are protected from infection.

2-4 MANUFACTURER'S TESTS
2-4-1 Residual live virus

A test for residual live virus is carried out on each batch of antigen immediately after inactivation. The quantity of inactivated viral harvest used in the test is equivalent to not less than 100 doses of the vaccine. The bulk harvest is inoculated into suitable non-confluent cells; after incubation for 7 days, a subculture is made using trypsinised cells. After incubation for a further 7 days, the cultures are examined for residual live parvovirus by an immunofluorescence test. The inactivated viral harvest complies with the test if no live virus is detected.

2-4-2 Batch potency test

It is not necessary to carry out the potency test (section 3-5) for each batch of the vaccine if it has been carried out using a batch of vaccine with a minimum potency. Where the test is not carried out, an alternative validated method is used, the criteria for acceptance being set with reference to a batch of vaccine that has given satisfactory results in the test described under Potency. The following test may be used.

Use not fewer than 5 guinea-pigs, 5-7 weeks old and that do not have antibodies against porcine parvovirus or against a fraction of the virus. Vaccinate each guinea-pig by the subcutaneous route with a quarter of the prescribed dose volume. Take blood samples after the period corresponding to maximum antibody production and carry out tests on the serum for specific antibodies by a haemagglutination-inhibition test or other suitable test. The vaccine complies with the test if the level of antibodies is not lower than that found for a batch of vaccine that has given satisfactory results in the test described under Potency.

3 BATCH TESTS

3-1 Identification

When injected into animals that do not have specific antibodies against porcine parvovirus or the fraction of the virus used in the production of the vaccine, on one or, if necessary, more than one occasion, the vaccine stimulates the formation of such antibodies.

3-2 Bacteria and fungi

The vaccine, including where applicable the diluent supplied for reconstitution, complies with the test for sterility prescribed in the monograph *Vaccines for veterinary use (0062)*.

3-3 Residual live virus

Use a quantity of vaccine equivalent to 10 doses. If the vaccine contains an oily adjuvant, break the emulsion and separate the phases. If the vaccine contains a mineral adjuvant, carry out an elution to liberate the virus. Concentrate the viral suspension 100 times by ultrafiltration or ultracentrifugation. None of the above procedures must be such as to inactivate or otherwise interfere with detection of live virus. Carry out a test for residual live virus in suitable non-confluent cells; after incubation for 7 days, make a subculture using trypsinised cells. After incubation for a further 7 days, examine the cultures for residual live parvovirus by an immunofluorescence test. The vaccine complies with the test if no live virus is detected.

3-4 Specified extraneous agents

Use 2 pigs that do not have antibodies against porcine parvovirus or against a fraction of the virus, against Aujeszky's disease virus or against pestiviruses. Administer to each pig by a recommended route a double dose of the vaccine, then another dose after 14 days. 14 days after the last administration, carry out tests for antibodies. The vaccine complies with the test if it does not stimulate the formation of antibodies against pestiviruses and against Aujeszky's disease virus.

3-5 Potency

The vaccine complies with the requirements of the test mentioned under Immunogenicity (section 2-3-2) when administered by a recommended route and method.

———————————————— *Ph Eur*

Porcine Progressive Atrophic Rhinitis Vaccine, Inactivated

(Porcine Progressive Atrophic Rhinitis Vaccine (Inactivated), Ph Eur monograph 1361)

Ph Eur ————————————————————————

1 DEFINITION

Porcine progressive atrophic rhinitis vaccine (inactivated) is a preparation containing either the dermonecrotic exotoxin of *Pasteurella multocida*, treated to render it harmless while maintaining adequate immunogenic properties, or a genetically modified form of the exotoxin that has adequate immunogenic properties and that is free from toxic properties; the vaccine may also contain cells and/or antigenic components of one or more suitable strains of *P. multocida* and/or *Bordetella bronchiseptica*. This monograph applies to vaccines intended for the active immunisation of sows and gilts for passive protection of their progeny against porcine progressive atrophic rhinitis.

2 PRODUCTION

2-1 PREPARATION OF THE VACCINE

The bacterial strains used for production are cultured separately in suitable media. The toxins and/or cells are treated to render them safe. The vaccine may be adjuvanted.

2-2 DETOXIFICATION

A test for detoxification of the dermonecrotic exotoxin of *P. multocida* is carried out immediately after detoxification. The concentration of detoxified exotoxin used in the test is not less than that in the vaccine. The suspension complies with the test if no toxic dermonecrotic exotoxin is detected. The test for detoxification is not required where the vaccine is prepared using a toxin-like protein free from toxic properties, produced by expression of a modified form of the corresponding gene.

2-3 ANTIGEN CONTENT

The content of the dermonecrotic exotoxin of *P. multocida* in the detoxified suspension or the toxin-like protein in the harvest is determined by a suitable immunochemical method *(2.7.1)*, such as an enzyme-linked immunosorbent assay, and the value found is used in the formulation of the vaccine. The content of other antigens stated on the label is also determined *(2.7.1)*.

2-4 CHOICE OF VACCINE COMPOSITION

The strains used for the preparation of the vaccine are shown to be satisfactory with respect to the production of the dermonecrotic exotoxin and the other antigens claimed to be protective. The vaccine is shown to be satisfactory with respect to safety *(5.2.6)* and efficacy *(5.2.7)* for the sows and gilts for which it is intended.

The following tests for production of antigens (section 2-4-1), safety (section 2-4-2) and immunogenicity (section 2-4-3) may be used during the demonstration of safety and efficacy.

2-4-1 Production of antigens

The production of antigens claimed to be protective is verified by a suitable bioassay or immunochemical method

(*2.7.1*), carried out on the antigens obtained from each of the vaccine strains under the conditions to be used for the production of the vaccine.

2-4-2 Safety

2-4-2-1 Safety in pregnant sows Carry out the test for each route and method of administration to be recommended for vaccination using in each case pregnant sows or gilts that do not have antibodies against the components of the vaccine, from a herd or herds where there are no signs of atrophic rhinitis and that have not been vaccinated against atrophic rhinitis. Use a batch containing not less than the maximum potency that may be expected in a batch of vaccine.

Use not fewer than 8 pregnant sows or gilts per group, at the stage or at different stages of pregnancy according to the schedule to be recommended. Administer to each pregnant sow or gilt 1 dose of the vaccine. If the schedule to be recommended requires a 2nd dose, administer another dose after an interval of at least 14 days. Observe the pregnant sows or gilts at least daily until farrowing. Record body temperature the day before vaccination, at vaccination, 2 h, 4 h and 6 h later and then daily for 4 days; note the maximum temperature increase for each pregnant sow or gilt.

The vaccine complies with the test if no pregnant sow or gilt shows abnormal local or systemic reactions or dies from causes attributable to the vaccine, if the average temperature increase for all pregnant sows or gilts does not exceed 1.5 °C and no pregnant sow or gilt shows a rise greater than 2.0 °C, and if no adverse effects on gestation and offspring are noted.

2-4-2-2 Field studies The pigs used for field trials are also used to evaluate safety. Use not fewer than 3 groups each of not fewer than 20 pigs with corresponding groups of not fewer than 10 controls. Examine the injection site for local reactions after vaccination. Record body temperature the day before vaccination, at vaccination, at the time interval after which a rise in temperature, if any, was seen in test 2-4-2-1, and daily during the 2 days following vaccination; note the maximum temperature increase for each pig.

The vaccine complies with the test if no pig shows abnormal local or systemic reactions or dies from causes attributable to the vaccine and if the average temperature increase for all pigs does not exceed 1.5 °C and no pig shows a rise greater than 2.0 °C.

2-4-3 Immunogenicity

Each test is carried out for each route and method of administration to be recommended, using in each case pigs that do not have antibodies against the components of the vaccine, that are from a herd or herds where there are no signs of atrophic rhinitis and that have not been vaccinated against atrophic rhinitis. The vaccine administered to each pig is of minimum potency.

2-4-3-1 Vaccines containing dermonecrotic exotoxin of P. multocida (with or without cells of P. multocida) Use not fewer than 12 breeder pigs. Vaccinate not fewer than 6 randomly chosen pigs at the stage of pregnancy or non-pregnancy and according to the schedule to be recommended. Maintain not fewer than 6 pigs as controls. From birth allow all the piglets from the vaccinated and unvaccinated breeder pigs to feed from their own dam. Constitute from the progeny 2 challenge groups each of not fewer than 30 piglets chosen randomly, taking not fewer than 3 piglets from each litter. On the 2 consecutive days preceding challenge, the mucosa of the nasal cavity of the piglets may be treated by instillation of 0.5 mL of a solution of acetic acid (10 g/L C$_2$H$_4$O$_2$) in isotonic buffered saline pH 7.2.

Challenge each piglet at 10 days of age by the intranasal route with a sufficient quantity of a toxigenic strain of *P. multocida*. At the age of 42 days, euthanise the piglets of the 2 groups and dissect the nose of each of them transversally at premolar-1. Examine the ventral and dorsal turbinates and the nasal septum for evidence of atrophy or distortion and grade the observations on the following scales.

Turbinates

0   no atrophy
1   slight atrophy
2   moderate atrophy
3   severe atrophy
4   very severe atrophy with almost complete disappearance of the turbinate

The maximum score is 4 for each turbinate and 16 for the sum of the 2 dorsal and 2 ventral turbinates.

Nasal septum

0   no deviation
1   very slight deviation
2   deviation of the septum

The maximum total score for the turbinates and the nasal septum is 18.

The test is not valid if fewer than 80 per cent of the progeny of each litter of the unvaccinated breeder pigs have a total score of at least 10. The vaccine complies with the test if a significant reduction in the total score has been demonstrated in the group from the vaccinated breeder pigs compared to that from the unvaccinated breeder pigs.

2-4-3-2 Vaccines containing P. multocida dermonecrotic exotoxin (with or without cells of P. multocida) and cells and/or antigenic components of B. bronchiseptica Use not fewer than 24 breeder pigs. Vaccinate not fewer than 12 randomly chosen pigs at the stage of pregnancy or non-pregnancy and according to the schedule to be recommended. Maintain not fewer than 12 pigs as controls. From birth allow all the piglets from the vaccinated and unvaccinated breeder pigs to feed from their own dam. Using groups of not fewer than 6 pigs, constitute from their progeny 2 challenge groups from vaccinated pigs and 2 groups from control pigs each group consisting of not fewer than 30 piglets chosen randomly, taking not fewer than 3 piglets from each litter. On the 2 consecutive days preceding challenge, the mucosa of the nasal cavity of the piglets may be treated by instillation of 0.5 mL of a solution of acetic acid (10 g/L C$_2$H$_4$O$_2$) in isotonic buffered saline pH 7.2. For a group of piglets from not fewer than 6 vaccinated pigs and a group from not fewer than 6 controls, challenge each piglet by the intranasal route at 10 days of age with a sufficient quantity of a toxigenic strain of *P. multocida*. For the other group of piglets from not fewer than 6 vaccinated pigs and the other group from not fewer than 6 controls, challenge each piglet at 7 days of age by the intranasal route with a sufficient quantity of *B. bronchiseptica*. In addition, challenge each piglet at 10 days of age by the intranasal route with a sufficient quantity of a toxigenic strain of *P. multocida*. At the age of 42 days, euthanise the piglets of the 4 groups and dissect the nose of each of them transversally at premolar-1. Examine the ventral and dorsal turbinates and the nasal septum for evidence of atrophy or distortion and grade the observations on the scale described above.

The test is not valid if fewer than 80 per cent of the progeny of each litter of the unvaccinated breeder pigs have a total score of at least 10. The vaccine complies with the test if a significant reduction in the total score has been demonstrated in the groups from the vaccinated breeder pigs compared to the corresponding group from the unvaccinated breeder pigs.

2-5 MANUFACTURER'S TESTS

2-5-1 Batch potency test

It is not necessary to carry out the potency test (section 3-4) for each batch of vaccine if it has been carried out using a batch of vaccine with a minimum potency. Where the test is not carried out, an alternative validated method is used, the criteria for acceptance being set with reference to a batch of vaccine that has given satisfactory results in the test described under Potency. The following test may be used.

Use not fewer than 7 pigs not less than 3 weeks old and that do not have antibodies against the components of the vaccine. Vaccinate not fewer than 5 pigs by a recommended route and according to the recommended schedule. Maintain not fewer than 2 pigs of the same origin as controls under the same conditions. Alternatively, if the nature of the antigens allows reproducible results to be obtained, a test in laboratory animals that do not have antibodies against the components of the vaccine may be carried out. To obtain a valid assay, it may be necessary to carry out a test using several groups of animals, each receiving a different quantity of vaccine. For each quantity of vaccine, carry out the test as follows: vaccinate not fewer than 5 animals with a suitable quantity of vaccine. Maintain not fewer than 2 animals of the same species and origin as controls. Where the recommended schedule requires a booster injection to be given, a booster vaccination may also be given in this test provided it has been demonstrated that this will still provide a suitably sensitive test system. At a given interval within the range of 14-21 days after the last administration, collect blood from each animal and prepare serum samples. Use a validated test such as an enzyme-linked immunosorbent assay to measure the antibody response to each of the antigens stated on the label.

The test is not valid if there is a significant antibody titre in the controls. The vaccine complies with the test if the antibody responses of the vaccinated animals are not significantly less than those obtained with a batch of vaccine that has given satisfactory results in the test or tests (as applicable) described under Potency.

Where animals that do not have antibodies against the antigens stated on the label are not available, seropositive animals may be used in the above test. During the development of a test with seropositive animals, particular care will be required during the validation of the test system to establish that the test is suitably sensitive and to specify acceptable pass, fail and retest criteria. It will be necessary to take into account the range of prevaccination antibody titres and to establish the acceptable minimum antibody titre rise after vaccination in relation to these.

2-5-2 Bacterial endotoxins

A test for bacterial endotoxins (2.6.14) is carried out on the batch or, where the nature of the adjuvant prevents performance of a satisfactory test, on the bulk antigen or the mixture of bulk antigens immediately before addition of the adjuvant. The maximum acceptable amount of bacterial endotoxins is that found for a batch of vaccine shown satisfactory in safety test 2-4-2-1 given under Choice of vaccine composition or in the residual toxicity test described under Batch tests, carried out using 10 pigs. Where the latter test is used, note the maximum temperature increase for each pig; the vaccine complies with the test if the average temperature increase for all pigs does not exceed 1.5 °C.

The method chosen for determining the amount of bacterial endotoxin present in the vaccine batch used in the safety test for determining the maximum acceptable level of endotoxin is used subsequently for testing of each batch.

3 BATCH TESTS

3-1 Identification

In animals that do not have specific antibodies against the antigens stated on the label, the vaccine stimulates the production of such antibodies.

3-2 Bacteria and fungi

The vaccine, including where applicable the diluent supplied for reconstitution, complies with the test for sterility prescribed in the monograph *Vaccines for veterinary use (0062)*.

3-3 Residual toxicity

Use not fewer than 2 pigs that do not have antibodies against *P. multocida* and that preferably do not have antibodies against *B. bronchiseptica*. Administer to each pig by a recommended route a double dose of the vaccine. Observe the pigs at least daily for 14 days. Record body temperature the day before vaccination, at vaccination, 2 h, 4 h and 6 h later and then daily for 2 days.

It is recommended to use the mean temperature of the days before administration of the vaccine (e.g. day −3 to day 0) as the baseline temperature to have clear guidance for evaluation of the test.

The vaccine complies with the test if no pig shows notable signs of disease or dies from causes attributable to the vaccine; a transient temperature increase not exceeding 2.0 °C may occur.

3-4 Potency

The vaccine complies with the requirements of the tests mentioned under Immunogenicity (section 2-4-3) when administered by a recommended route and method.

————————————————————————— Ph Eur

Rabies Vaccine (Live, Oral) for Foxes and Raccoon Dogs

(Ph. Eur. monograph 0746)

Ph Eur ————————————————————————————

1 DEFINITION

Rabies vaccine (live, oral) for foxes (*Vulpes vulpes*) and raccoon dogs (*Nyctereutes procyonoides*) is a preparation of a suitable immunogenic strain of an attenuated rabies virus. The virus strain has one or more stable genetic markers that discriminates the vaccine strain from other rabies virus strains. The vaccine is incorporated in bait in such a manner as to enable the tests prescribed below to be performed aseptically. The bait casing, attractive to the target species, may contain a biomarker (e.g. tetracycline). This monograph applies to vaccines intended for the active immunisation of foxes, or foxes and raccoon dogs against rabies.

2 PRODUCTION

2-1 PREPARATION OF THE VACCINE

The vaccine virus is grown in cell cultures. The virus suspension is harvested on one or more occasions within 14 days of inoculation. Multiple harvests from a single cell lot may be pooled and considered as a single harvest. It may be mixed with a suitable stabiliser.

2-2 SUBSTRATE FOR VIRUS PROPAGATION
2-2-1 Cell cultures
The cell cultures comply with the requirements for cell cultures for production of veterinary vaccines (*5.2.4; if the cell cultures are of mammalian origin, they are shown to be free from rabies virus.*

2-3 CHOICE OF VACCINE VIRUS
The vaccine virus is shown to be satisfactory with respect to safety (*5.2.6*) for the target species and the non-target species, and efficacy (*5.2.7*) for the species for which it is intended. The vaccine strain is genetically characterised by gene sequencing.

The following tests for safety of the virus strain (section 2-3-1), stability of the genetic marker (section 2-3-2) and immunogenicity (2-3-3) may be used during the demonstration of safety and efficacy.

In natural and experimental conditions, the virus strain does not spread from one animal to another in wild rodents.

2-3-1 Safety of the virus strain
Administer the virus strain by the oral route. Use vaccine virus at the least attenuated passage level that will be present in a batch of the vaccine.

For each test performed in the target species (foxes, or foxes and raccoon dogs), use not fewer than 20 animals that do not have antibodies against rabies virus. Administer orally to each animal a quantity of the vaccine virus equivalent to not less than 10 times the maximum virus titre likely to be contained in 1 vaccine bait. Observe the animals at least daily for 180 days.

For each test performed in the non-target species (dogs, cats, and if appropriate, raccoon dogs), use not fewer than 10 animals that do not have antibodies against rabies virus. Administer orally to each animal a quantity of the vaccine virus equivalent to not less than 10 times the maximum virus titre likely to be contained in 1 vaccine bait. Observe the animals at least daily for 180 days.

The vaccine virus complies with the test if no animal shows signs of disease and if the presence of the vaccine virus is not demonstrated in the brain of any animal. The presence of rabies virus in the brain is tested using reference diagnostic tests (immunofluorescence test and cell-culture test).

2-3-2 Stability of the genetic marker
Carry out the test using suckling mice that have not been vaccinated against rabies. Passage the vaccine virus sequentially through 5 groups via the intracerebral route.

Inoculate each of the 5 mice of the 1st group with a quantity of the vaccine virus that will allow recovery of virus for the passages described below (e.g. not more than 0.02 mL). When the mice show signs of rabies, but not later than 14 days after inoculation, euthanise the mice and remove the brain of each mouse. Prepare a suspension from the brain of each mouse and pool the samples. Administer not more than 0.02 mL of the pooled samples to each mouse of the next group. Carry out this passage operation not fewer than 4 times; verify the presence of the virus at each passage. If the virus is not found at a passage level, repeat the passage by administration to a group of 10 animals.

Verify the genetic marker in the vaccine virus recovered from the last passage.

The vaccine virus complies with the test if the genetic marker remains stable.

2-3-3 Immunogenicity
A test is carried out for the oral route of administration and with the bait to be stated on the label using animals of the target species (foxes, or foxes and raccoon dogs) at least 3 months old. The quantity of vaccine virus to be administered to each fox, or fox and raccoon dog, is not greater than the minimum virus titre to be stated on the label and the virus is at the most attenuated passage level that will be present in a batch of vaccine.

Use for the test not fewer than 35 animals of each target species, that do not have antibodies against rabies virus. In each target species, apply the following protocol, validity criteria and acceptance limits.

Vaccinate not fewer than 25 animals, according to the schedule to be recommended. Maintain not fewer than 10 animals as controls. Observe the animals for 180 days after vaccination. The test is not valid if fewer than 25 vaccinated animals survive after this observation period. Challenge all the animals at least 180 days after vaccination by intramuscular injection of a sufficient quantity of a virulent rabies virus strain approved by the competent authority. Observe the animals at least daily for 90 days after challenge. Animals that die from causes not attributable to rabies are eliminated.

The test is not valid if the number of such deaths reduces the number of vaccinated animals in the test to fewer than 25 and the test is invalid unless at least 9 control animals (or a statistically equivalent number if more than 10 control animals are challenged) show signs of rabies and the presence of rabies virus in their brain is demonstrated by the immunofluorescence test or some other reliable method.

The vaccine virus complies with the test if not more than 2 of 25 vaccinated animals (or a statistically equivalent number if more than 25 vaccinated animals are challenged) show signs of rabies.

2-4 BAIT STABILITY
Incubate the bait at 25 °C for 5 days. Titrate the vaccine. The virus titre must be at least the minimum virus titre stated on the label. Heat the bait at 40 °C for 1 h. The bait casing complies with the test if it remains in its original shape and adheres to the vaccine container.

3 BATCH TESTS
3-1 Identification
3-1-1 The vaccine virus is identified by a suitable method, e.g. when mixed with a monospecific rabies antiserum, the vaccine is no longer able to infect susceptible cell cultures into which it is inoculated.

3-1-2 A test is carried out to demonstrate the presence of the genetic marker.

3-2 Bacteria and fungi
The vaccine complies with the test for sterility prescribed in the monograph *Vaccines for veterinary use (0062)*.

3-3 Mycoplasmas (*2.6.7*)
The vaccine complies with the test for mycoplasmas.

3-4 Extraneous agents
3-4-1 Neutralise the vaccine virus with a suitable monospecific neutralising rabies virus antiserum and inoculate into susceptible cell cultures. The vaccine complies with the test if it no longer provokes cytopathic effects in susceptible cell cultures, and it shows no evidence of haemagglutinating or haemadsorbing agents.

3-4-2 Inoculate 1 in 10 and 1 in 1000 dilutions of the vaccine into susceptible cell cultures. Incubate at 37 °C.

After 2, 4 and 6 days, stain the cells with a panel of monoclonal antibodies that do not react with the vaccine strain but that react with other strains of rabies vaccine (for example, street virus, Pasteur strain). The vaccine complies with the test if it shows no evidence of contaminating rabies virus.

3-5 Virus titre
Titrate the vaccine virus in suitable cell cultures. The vaccine complies with the test if 1 dose contains not less than the minimum virus titre stated on the label.

3-6 Potency
The vaccine complies with the requirements of the test prescribed under Immunogenicity (section 2-3-3) when administered by a recommended route and method. It is not necessary to carry out the potency test for each batch of the vaccine if it has been carried out on a representative batch using a vaccinating dose containing not more than the minimum virus titre stated on the label.

3-7 Biomarker
If the bait contains a biomarker, the stability of the biomarker is verified by a suitable method. When tetracycline is used, the vaccine complies with the test if chemical analysis of the bait casing shows less than 30 per cent conversion of the total amount of tetracycline into the epitetracycline isomer.

4 LABELLING
The label states:
— the nature of the genetic marker of the virus strain;
— where applicable, the nature of the biomarker of the bait.

———————————————————————————— Ph Eur

Rabies Veterinary Vaccine, Inactivated

(Rabies Vaccine (Inactivated) for Veterinary Use, Ph Eur monograph 0451)

Ph Eur _____

1 DEFINITION
Rabies vaccine (inactivated) for veterinary use is a preparation of a suitable strain of fixed rabies virus, inactivated while maintaining adequate immunogenic properties. This monograph applies to vaccines intended for the active immunisation of animals against rabies.

2 PRODUCTION
2-1 PREPARATION OF THE VACCINE
The vaccine is prepared from virus grown either in suitable cell lines or in primary cell cultures from healthy animals (5.2.4). The virus suspension is harvested on one or more occasions within 28 days of inoculation. Multiple harvests from a single production cell culture may be pooled and considered as a single harvest.

The virus harvest is inactivated. The vaccine may be adjuvanted.

2-2 SUBSTRATE FOR VIRUS PROPAGATION
2-2-1 Cell cultures
The cell cultures comply with the requirements for cell cultures for production of veterinary vaccines (5.2.4).

2-3 CHOICE OF VACCINE COMPOSITION
The vaccine virus is shown to be satisfactory with respect to safety (5.2.6) and efficacy (5.2.7) for the species for which it is intended.

The following tests for safety (section 2-3-1) and immunogenicity (section 2-3-2) may be used during the demonstration of safety and efficacy in cats and dogs.

The suitability of the vaccine with respect to immunogenicity (section 2-3-2) for carnivores (cats and dogs) is demonstrated by direct challenge. For other species, if a challenge test has been carried out for the vaccine in cats or dogs, an indirect test is carried out by determining the antibody level following vaccination of not fewer than 20 animals according to the schedule to be recommended; the vaccine is satisfactory if, after the period to be claimed for protection, the mean rabies virus antibody level in the serum of the animals is not less than 0.5 IU/mL and if not more than 10 per cent of the animals have an antibody level less than 0.1 IU/mL.

2-3-1 Safety
Carry out the test for each route and method of administration to be recommended for vaccination. Use a batch of vaccine containing not less than the maximum potency that may be expected in a batch of vaccine.

For each test, use not fewer than 8 animals of the minimum age to be recommended and that do not have antibodies against rabies virus. Administer to each animal 1 dose of the vaccine. If the schedule to be recommended requires a 2nd dose, administer 1 dose after an interval of at least 14 days. Observe the animals at least daily for at least 14 days after the last administration.

The vaccine complies with the test if no animal shows abnormal local or systemic reactions or dies from causes attributable to the vaccine.

2-3-2 Immunogenicity
Each test is carried out for each route and method of administration to be recommended, using in each case animals of the minimum age to be recommended for vaccination. The vaccine administered to each animal is of minimum potency.

Use for the test not fewer than 35 animals. Take a blood sample from each animal and test individually for antibodies against rabies virus to determine susceptibility. Vaccinate not fewer than 25 animals, according to the schedule to be recommended. Maintain not fewer than 10 animals as controls. Observe all the animals for a period equal to the claimed duration of immunity. No animal shows signs of rabies. On the last day of the claimed period for duration of immunity or later, challenge each animal by intramuscular injection with a sufficient quantity of virulent rabies virus of a strain approved by the competent authority. Observe the animals at least daily for 90 days after challenge. Animals that die from causes not attributable to rabies are eliminated. The test is not valid if the number of such deaths reduces the number of vaccinated animals in the test to fewer than 25 and the test is invalid unless at least 8 control animals (or a statistically equivalent number if more than 10 control animals are challenged) show signs of rabies and the presence of rabies virus in their brain is demonstrated by the fluorescent-antibody test or some other suitable method. The vaccine complies with the test if not more than 2 of the 25 vaccinated animals (or a statistically equivalent number if more than 25 vaccinated animals are challenged) show signs of rabies.

2-4 MANUFACTURER'S TESTS

2-4-1 Residual live virus

The test for residual live virus is carried out by inoculation of the inactivated virus into the same type of cell culture as that used in the production of the vaccine or a cell culture shown to be at least as sensitive. The quantity of inactivated virus harvest used is equivalent to not less than 25 doses of the vaccine. After incubation for 4 days, a subculture is made using trypsinised cells; after incubation for a further 4 days, the cultures are examined for residual live rabies virus by an immunofluorescence test. The inactivated virus harvest complies with the test if no live virus is detected.

2-4-2 Antigen content of the harvest

The content of rabies virus glycoprotein is determined by a suitable immunochemical method (2.7.1). The content is within the limits approved for the particular preparation.

2-4-3 Antigen content of the pooled harvest

The quantity of rabies virus glycoprotein per dose, determined by a suitable immunochemical method (2.7.1) on the pooled harvest immediately before blending, is not significantly lower than that of a batch of vaccine that gave satisfactory results in the test described under Potency.

2-4-4 Batch potency test

It is not necessary to carry out the potency test (section 3-4) for each batch of vaccine if it has been carried out using a batch of vaccine with a minimum potency. Where the test is not carried out, an alternative validated method is used, the criteria for acceptance being set with reference to a batch of vaccine that has given satisfactory results in the test described under Potency. In accordance with the provisions of the European Convention for the Protection of Vertebrate Animals Used for Experimental and Other Scientific Purposes, such an alternative validated method should preferably be used for routine testing. The following serological assay has been shown to be suitable and may be used provided the test for antigen content of the pooled harvest (section 2-4-3) has been carried out with satisfactory results.

Use groups of not fewer than 8 female mice (strain NMRI), each weighing 18-20 g. Prepare a 1 IU/mL suspension of *rabies vaccine (inactivated) for veterinary use BRP* using phosphate-buffered saline (PBS) for dilution. Vaccines with a minimum potency requirement of 1 IU/mL are used without further dilution. Vaccines with a minimum potency requirement of more than 1 IU/mL are diluted with PBS to contain approximately, but not less than, 1 IU/mL. Administer by the intraperitoneal route to each mouse of one group 0.2 mL of the vaccine, diluted where necessary, and to each mouse of another group 0.2 mL of the suspension of *rabies vaccine (inactivated) for veterinary use BRP*. Take blood samples 14 days after the injection and test the sera individually for rabies antibody using a suitable virus neutralisation test, for example the rapid fluorescent focus inhibition test (RFFIT) described for *Human rabies immunoglobulin (0723)* or a suitable validated modification of the RFFIT.[1]

The test is not valid if more than 2 mice injected with the suspension of *rabies vaccine (inactivated) for veterinary use BRP* show no antibodies in their serum.

Individual serum titres are determined with an appropriate anti-rabies immunoglobulin reference.

The antibody titre of mice receiving the suspension of *rabies vaccine (inactivated) for veterinary use BRP* is compared to the antibody titre of mice receiving the vaccine using a suitable statistical approach (5.3).

The vaccine complies with the test if the antibody titre of mice injected with the vaccine is significantly higher than that of mice injected with the suspension of *rabies vaccine (inactivated) for veterinary use BRP*.

3 BATCH TESTS

3-1 Identification

Administered to animals that do not have antibodies against rabies virus, the vaccine stimulates the production of such antibodies.

3-2 Bacteria and fungi

The vaccine, including where applicable the diluent supplied for reconstitution, complies with the test for sterility prescribed in the monograph *Vaccines for veterinary use (0062)*.

3-3 Residual live virus

Carry out the test using a pool of the contents of 5 containers.

For vaccines which do not contain an adjuvant, carry out a suitable amplification test for residual live virus using the same type of cell culture as that used in the production of the vaccine or a cell culture shown to be at least as sensitive. The vaccine complies with the test if no live virus is detected.

For vaccines that contain an adjuvant, inject intracerebrally into each of not fewer than 10 mice, each weighing 11-15 g, 0.03 mL of a pool of at least 5 times the smallest stated dose. To avoid interference from any antimicrobial preservative or the adjuvant, the vaccine may be diluted not more than 10 times before injection. In this case or if the vaccine strain is pathogenic only for unweaned mice, carry out the test on mice 1-4 days old. Observe the animals for 21 days. If more than 2 animals die during the first 48 h, repeat the test. The vaccine complies with the test if, from the 3rd to the 21st days following the injection, the animals show no signs of rabies and immunofluorescence tests carried out on the brains of the animals show no indication of the presence of rabies virus.

3-4 Potency

The potency of rabies vaccine is determined by comparing the dose necessary to protect mice against the clinical effects of the dose of rabies virus defined below, administered intracerebrally, with the quantity of a reference preparation, calibrated in International Units, necessary to provide the same protection.

The International Unit is the activity of a stated quantity of the International Standard. The equivalence in International Units of the International Standard is stated by the World Health Organization.

Rabies vaccine (inactivated) for veterinary use BRP is calibrated in International Units against the International Standard.

The test described below uses a parallel-line model with at least 3 points for the vaccine to be examined and the reference preparation. Once the analyst has experience with the method for a given vaccine, it is possible to carry out a simplified test using 1 dilution of the vaccine to be examined. Such a test enables the analyst to determine that the vaccine has a potency significantly higher than the required minimum but will not give full information on the validity of each individual potency determination. It allows a considerable reduction in the number of animals required for the test and should be considered by each laboratory in accordance with

[1] B. Kramer *et al.* The rapid fluorescenct focus inhibition test is a suitable method for batch potency testing of inactivated rabies vaccine. Biologicals 2009; 37: 119-126.

the provisions of the European Convention for the Protection of Vertebrate Animals Used for Experimental and Other Scientific Purposes.

Selection and distribution of the test animals Use in the test healthy female mice about 4 weeks old and from the same stock. Distribute the mice into at least 10 groups of not fewer than 10 mice.

Preparation of the challenge suspension Inoculate a group of mice intracerebrally with the CVS strain of rabies virus and when the mice show signs of rabies, but before they die, euthanise the mice and remove the brains and prepare a homogenate of the brain tissue in a suitable diluent. Separate gross particulate matter by centrifugation and use the supernatant as challenge suspension. Distribute the suspension in small volumes in ampoules, seal and store at a temperature below -60 °C. Thaw 1 ampoule of the suspension and make serial dilutions in a suitable diluent. Allocate each dilution to a group of mice and inject intracerebrally into each mouse 0.03 mL of the dilution allocated to its group. Observe the animals at least daily for 14 days and record the number in each group that, between the 5th and the 14th days, develop signs of rabies. Calculate the ID_{50} of the undiluted suspension.

Determination of potency of the vaccine to be examined Prepare at least 3 serial dilutions of the vaccine to be examined and 3 similar dilutions of the reference preparation. Prepare the dilutions such that those containing the largest quantity of vaccine may be expected to protect more than 50 per cent of the animals into which they are injected and those containing the smallest quantities of vaccine may be expected to protect less than 50 per cent of the animals into which they are injected. Allocate each dilution to a different group of mice and inject by the intraperitoneal route into each mouse 0.5 mL of the dilution allocated to its group. 14 days after the injection prepare a suspension of the challenge virus such that, on the basis of the preliminary titration, it contains about 50 ID_{50} in each 0.03 mL. Inject intracerebrally into each vaccinated mouse 0.03 mL of this suspension. Prepare 3 suitable serial dilutions of the challenge suspension. Allocate the challenge suspension and the 3 dilutions one to each of 4 groups of 10 unvaccinated mice and inject intracerebrally into each mouse 0.03 mL of the suspension or one of the dilutions allocated to its group. Observe the animals in each group at least daily for 14 days. The test is not valid if more than 2 mice of any group die within the first 4 days after challenge. Record the numbers in each group that show signs of rabies in the period 5 days to 14 days after challenge.

The test is invalid unless:
— for both the vaccine to be examined and the reference preparation the 50 per cent protective dose lies between the smallest and the largest dose given to the mice;
— the titration of the challenge suspension shows that 0.03 mL of the suspension contained at least 10 ID_{50};
— the confidence limits ($P = 0.95$) are not less than 25 per cent and not more than 400 per cent of the estimated potency; when this validity criteria is not met, the lower limit of the estimated potency must be at least 1 IU in the smallest prescribed dose;
— the statistical analysis shows a significant slope ($P = 0.95$) and no significant deviations from linearity or parallelism of the dose-response lines ($P = 0.99$).

The vaccine complies with the test if the estimated potency is not less than 1 IU in the smallest prescribed dose.

Application of alternative end-points Once a laboratory has established the above assay for routine use, the lethal end-point is replaced by an observation of clinical signs and application of an end-point earlier than death to reduce animal suffering. The following is given as an example.

The progress of rabies infection in mice following intracerebral injection can be represented by 5 stages defined by typical clinical signs:

Stage 1: ruffled fur, hunched back;

Stage 2: slow movements, loss of alertness (circular movements may also occur);

Stage 3: shaky movements, trembling, convulsions;

Stage 4: signs of paresis or paralysis;

Stage 5: moribund state.

Mice are observed at least twice daily from day 4 after challenge. Clinical signs are recorded using a chart such as that shown in Table 0451.-1. Experience has shown that using stage 3 as an end-point yields assay results equivalent to those found when a lethal end-point is used. This must be verified by each laboratory by scoring a suitable number of assays using both clinical signs and the lethal end-point.

Table 0451.-1. – *Example of a chart used to record clinical signs in the rabies vaccine potency test*

	Days after challenge							
Clinical signs	4	5	6	7	8	9	10	11
Ruffled fur Hunched back								
Slow movements Loss of alertness Circular movements								
Shaky movements Trembling Convulsions								
Paresis Paralysis								
Moribund state								

4. LABELLING

The label states:
— the type of cell culture used to prepare the vaccine and the species of origin;
— the minimum number of International Units per dose;
— the minimum period for which the vaccine provides protection.

Ph Eur

Rabbit Haemorrhagic Disease Vaccine (Inactivated)

(Ph. Eur. monograph 2325)

Ph Eur

1 DEFINITION

Rabbit haemorrhagic disease vaccine (inactivated) is a preparation of a suitable strain of rabbit haemorrhagic disease virus (RHDV), inactivated while maintaining adequate immunogenic properties. This monograph applies to vaccines intended for active immunisation of rabbits.

2 PRODUCTION

2-1 PREPARATION OF THE VACCINE

The vaccine virus is grown in rabbits. The rabbits must be healthy, not vaccinated against RHDV, free from antibodies against RHDV, not treated with antibiotics within at least 15 days of their use and from a healthy and monitored breeding unit. A suspension is prepared from a homogenate of suitable internal organs of those rabbits that are euthanised or that succumb to the infection within 120 h of inoculation. The virus in the suspension may be purified and concentrated, and is inactivated by a suitable method.

2-2 SEED LOTS

2-2-1 Extraneous agents

Each master seed lot complies with the tests for extraneous agents in seed lots prescribed in the monograph *Vaccines for veterinary use (0062)*.

2-3 CHOICE OF VACCINE COMPOSITION

The vaccine is shown to be satisfactory with respect to safety (*5.2.6*) and efficacy (*5.2.7*) for the rabbits for which it is intended.

The following tests for safety (section 2-3-1) and immunogenicity (section 2-3-2) may be used during the demonstration of safety and efficacy.

2-3-1 Safety

Carry out the test for each route and method of administration to be recommended for vaccination and in rabbits of each category for which the vaccine is intended. Use a batch of vaccine containing not less than the maximum potency that may be expected in a batch of vaccine.

For each test, use not fewer than 8 healthy rabbits from the same stock, not older than the minimum age to be recommended for vaccination and free from antibodies against RHDV. Administer to each rabbit 1 dose of the vaccine. If the schedule to be recommended requires a 2nd dose, administer 1 dose after an interval of at least 14 days. Observe the animals for at least 14 days after the last administration. Record the body temperature the day before vaccination, at vaccination, 4 h after vaccination and then daily for 4 days; note the maximum temperature increase for each animal.

The vaccine complies with the test if no rabbit shows abnormal local or systemic reactions or signs of disease, or dies from causes attributable to the vaccine, the average body temperature increase for all animals does not exceed 1.5 °C, and no animal shows a temperature rise greater than 2.0 °C.

2-3-2 Immunogenicity

A test is carried out for each route and method of administration to be recommended for vaccination.

The test is carried out using in each case rabbits not less than 10 weeks old. The vaccine administered to each rabbit is of minimum potency.

Use not fewer than 15 healthy, susceptible rabbits, free from antibodies against RHDV, from the same healthy stock, and reared in suitable isolation conditions to ensure absence of contact with RHDV. Administer 1 dose of vaccine to each of not fewer than 10 of the rabbits according to the instructions for use to be stated on the label. Maintain not fewer than 5 other rabbits as controls. Not less than 7 days after vaccination, challenge each rabbit by a suitable route with a quantity of a virulent strain of RHDV sufficient to cause signs of rabbit haemorrhagic disease (RHD) in a susceptible rabbit. Observe the rabbits for a further 14 days.

The test is not valid if fewer than 80 per cent of control rabbits die with typical signs of RHD within 120 h of challenge.

The vaccine complies with the test if not fewer than 90 per cent of vaccinated rabbits show no signs of RHD.

2-4 MANUFACTURER'S TESTS

2-4-1 Residual live virus

A test for residual live virus is carried out on the bulk harvest of each batch to confirm inactivation of the RHDV. The test for inactivation is carried out in healthy, susceptible rabbits, not less than 10 weeks old, free from antibodies against RHDV and from the same healthy stock. 5 rabbits are inoculated by a suitable parenteral route (subcutaneous or intramuscular) with at least a 5 mL dose of the suspension. The rabbits are observed for not less than 7 days. At the end of the observation period, the animals are euthanised and liver extracts are tested by a suitable method for freedom from RHDV.

The vaccine complies with the test if no rabbit dies and no RHDV antigen is detected in the livers.

2-4-2 Batch potency test

It is not necessary to carry out the potency test (section 3-4) for each batch of the vaccine if it has been carried out using a batch of vaccine with a minimum potency. Where the test is not carried out, an alternative validated method is used, the criteria for acceptance being set with reference to a batch of vaccine that has given satisfactory results in the test described under Potency.

The following method is given as an example. Administer 1 dose of vaccine intramuscularly to each of 5 healthy rabbits, 10 weeks old, free from antibodies against RHDV and from the same healthy stock. Maintain 2 rabbits as unvaccinated controls. Collect serum samples from each rabbit just before administration of the vaccine and after the period defined when testing the reference vaccine; determine the antibody titre of each serum by a suitable immunological method, for example, ELISA. The antibody levels are not significantly lower than those obtained with a batch that has given satisfactory results in the test described under Potency.

The test is not valid if the sera collected from the unvaccinated controls and from the rabbits just before the administration of the vaccine show detectable specific antibodies.

3 BATCH TESTS

3-1 Identification

When injected into susceptible animals, the vaccine stimulates the production of specific antibodies against RHDV, detectable by a haemagglutination-inhibition test or enzyme immunoassay.

3-2 Bacteria and fungi

The vaccine, including where applicable the diluent supplied for reconstitution, complies with the test for sterility prescribed in the monograph *Vaccines for veterinary use (0062)*.

3-3 Residual live virus

Use not fewer than 2 healthy rabbits, not less than 10 weeks old, free from antibodies against RHDV and from the same healthy stock. Administer by a recommended route to each rabbit 2 doses of vaccine. Observe the rabbits for 14 days.

The vaccine complies with the test if no rabbit shows notable signs of disease or dies from causes attributable to the vaccine.

3-4 Potency

The vaccine complies with the requirements of the test mentioned under Immunogenicity (section 2-3-2), when administered by a recommended route and method.

_____ Ph Eur

Ruminant E. Coli Vaccine, Inactivated

Ruminant Escherichia Coli Vaccine, Inactivated

(Neonatal Ruminant Colibacillosis Vaccine (Inactivated), Ph Eur monograph 0961)

Ph Eur _____

1 DEFINITION

Neonatal ruminant colibacillosis vaccine (inactivated) is a preparation from cultures of one or more suitable strains of _Escherichia coli_, carrying one or more adhesin factors or enterotoxins. This monograph applies to vaccines intended for the active immunisation of dams for passive protection of their newborn progeny against enteric forms of colibacillosis, administered by injection.

2 PRODUCTION
2-1 PREPARATION OF THE VACCINE

The _E. coli_ strains used for production are cultured separately in a suitable medium. The cells or toxins are processed to render them safe while maintaining adequate immunogenic properties and are blended. The vaccine may be adjuvanted.

2-2 CHOICE OF VACCINE COMPOSITION

The _E. coli_ strains used in the production of the vaccine are shown to be satisfactory with respect to expression of antigens and the vaccine is shown to be satisfactory with respect to safety (_5.2.6_) and efficacy (_5.2.7_) for the ruminants for which it is intended.

The following tests for expression of antigens (section 2-2-1), safety (section 2-2-2) and immunogenicity (section 2-2-3) may be used during the demonstration of safety and efficacy.

2-2-1 Expression of antigens

The expression of antigens that stimulate a protective immune response is verified by a suitable immunochemical method (_2.7.1_) carried out on the antigen obtained from each of the vaccine strains under the conditions used for the production of the vaccine.

2-2-2 Safety

2-2-2-1 Safety in pregnant animals. Carry out the test for each route and method of administration to be recommended for vaccination and in pregnant animals of each species for which the vaccine is intended. Use a batch of vaccine containing not less than the maximum potency that may be expected in a batch of vaccine.

For each test, use not fewer than 8 pregnant animals per group that have not been vaccinated against colibacillosis. Administer to each animal 1 dose of the vaccine. If the schedule to be recommended requires a 2nd dose, administer another dose after an interval of at least 14 days. Observe the animals at least daily until parturition. Record body temperature the day before vaccination, at vaccination, 2 h, 4 h and 6 h later and then daily for 4 days; note the maximum temperature increase for each animal.

The vaccine complies with the test if:
— no animal shows abnormal local or systemic reactions or dies from causes attributable to the vaccine;

— the average temperature increase for all animals does not exceed 1.5 °C and no animal shows a rise greater than 2.0 °C; and
— no adverse effects on gestation or the offspring are noted.

2-2-2-2 Field studies. Safety is demonstrated in field trials for each species for which the vaccine is intended. Administer the dose to be recommended to not fewer than 60 animals from 3 different stocks by the route and according to the schedule to be recommended. Assign not fewer than 30 animals from the same stocks to control groups. Observe the animals at least daily for 14 days after the last administration.

The vaccine complies with the test if no animal shows abnormal local or systemic reactions or dies from causes attributable to the vaccine and if no rise in temperature of more than 1.5 °C occurs within 2 days of administration of each dose of the vaccine.

2-2-3 Immunogenicity

Carry out the test with a challenge strain representing each type of antigen against which the vaccine is intended to protect: if a single strain with all the necessary antigens is not available, repeat the test using different challenge strains. Each test is carried out for each route and method of administration to be recommended for vaccination, using in each case animals of each species for which the vaccine is intended. The vaccine administered to each animal is of minimum potency.

For each test, use not fewer than 15 animals that do not have antibodies against the antigens to be stated on the label. Take not fewer than 10 at random and vaccinate these at the stage of pregnancy and according to the schedule to be recommended. Maintain not fewer than 5 animals as controls. Collect colostrum from all animals after parturition and store the samples individually in conditions that maintain antibody levels. Take not fewer than 15 newborn unsuckled animals and house them in an environment ensuring absence of enteric pathogens. Allocate a colostrum sample from not fewer than 10 vaccinated dams and not fewer than 5 controls to the offspring. After birth, feed the animals with the colostrum sample allocated to it. After feeding the colostrum and within 12 h of birth, challenge all the animals by the oral route with a sufficient quantity of a virulent strain of _E. coli_ and observe at least daily for 10 days. The strain must not be one used in the manufacture of the vaccine.

On each day, note daily signs in each animal and score using the following scale.
0   no signs
1   slight diarrhoea
2   marked diarrhoea (watery faeces)
3   dead

Calculate total scores for each animal over 10 days.

The test is not valid if fewer than 80 per cent of the animals given colostrum from the controls die or show severe signs of disease. The vaccine complies with the test if there is a significant reduction in score in the group of animals given colostrum from vaccinated dams compared with the group given colostrum from the unvaccinated controls.

2-3 MANUFACTURER'S TESTS
2-3-1 Batch potency test

It is not necessary to carry out the potency test (section 3-3) for each batch of vaccine if it has been carried out using a batch of vaccine with a minimum potency. Where the test is not carried out, an alternative validated method is used, the criteria for acceptance being set with reference to a batch of vaccine that has given satisfactory results in the test described under Potency. The following test may be used.

To obtain a valid assay, it may be necessary to carry out a test using several groups of animals, each receiving a different dose. For each dose required, carry out the test as follows. Use not fewer than 7 animals (for example rabbits, guinea-pigs, rats or mice) that do not have antibodies against the antigens stated on the label. Vaccinate not fewer than 5 animals, using 1 injection of a suitable dose. Maintain 2 animals as controls. Where the recommended schedule requires a booster injection to be given, a booster vaccination may also be given in this test provided it has been demonstrated that this will still provide a suitably sensitive test system. At a given interval within the range of 14-21 days after the last injection, collect blood from each animal and prepare serum samples. Use a suitable validated test such as an enzyme-linked immunosorbent assay (2.7.1) to measure the antibody response to each of the protective antigens stated on the label. The vaccine complies with the test if the antibody levels in the vaccinates are not significantly less than those obtained with a batch that has given satisfactory results in the test described under Potency and there is no significant increase in antibody titre in the controls.

Where animals that do not have antibodies against the antigens stated on the label are not available, seropositive animals may be used in the above test. During the development of a test with seropositive animals, particular care will be required during the validation of the test system to establish that the test is suitably sensitive and to specify acceptable pass, fail and retest criteria. It will be necessary to take into account the range of possible prevaccination titres and establish the acceptable minimum titre rise after vaccination in relation to these.

2-3-2 Bacterial endotoxins

A test for bacterial endotoxins (2.6.14) is carried out on the final lot or, where the nature of the adjuvant prevents performance of a satisfactory test, on the bulk antigen or the mixture of bulk antigens immediately before addition of the adjuvant. The maximum acceptable amount of bacterial endotoxins is that found for a batch of vaccine that has been shown satisfactory in safety test 2-2-2-1 given under Choice of vaccine composition. The method chosen for determining the amount of bacterial endotoxin present in the vaccine batch used in the safety test for determining the maximum acceptable level of endotoxins is used subsequently for testing of each batch.

3 BATCH TESTS
3-1 Identification

In animals that do not have antibodies against the antigens stated on the label, the vaccine stimulates the production of such antibodies.

3-2 Bacteria and fungi

The vaccine, including where applicable the diluent supplied for reconstitution, complies with the test for sterility prescribed in the monograph *Vaccines for veterinary use (0062)*.

3-3 Potency

The vaccine complies with the requirements of the test mentioned under Immunogenicity (section 2-2-3) when administered by a recommended route and method.

Ph Eur

Salmonella Dublin Vaccine, Living

Calf Paratyphoid Vaccine, Living

DEFINITION

Salmonella Dublin Vaccine, Living is a suspension of a suitably modified rough strain of *Salmonella dublin*. The vaccine is prepared immediately before use by reconstitution from the dried vaccine with a suitable liquid.

PRODUCTION

The vaccine may be prepared using suitable cultures grown in solid or liquid media. The final product is freeze dried.

Safety

Carry out a test in each category of animal for which the vaccine is to be recommended. Vaccinate at least five animals that, as far as possible, are free from antibodies to *Salmonella* spp. Administer to each animal a quantity of bacteria containing not less than ten times the maximum titre likely to be contained in a dose of the vaccine. Observe the animals for 2 weeks. No abnormal local or systemic reactions occur.

The reconstituted vaccine complies with the requirements stated under Veterinary Vaccines, with the following modifications.

IDENTIFICATION

Consists of a suspension of Gram-negative bacilli having the morphological, cultural and serological characteristics of rough strains of *S. dublin*.

TESTS
Extraneous micro-organisms

Does not contain extraneous micro-organisms. Verify the absence of micro-organisms other than *Salmonella dublin* as described in the test for sterility under Veterinary Vaccines.

Viable count

The batch complies with the test if the titre of the batch is not less than the titre stated on the label, determined by plate counts.

Salmonella Enteritidis Vaccine (Inactivated) for Chickens

(Ph. Eur. monograph 1947)

Ph Eur

1 DEFINITION

Salmonella Enteritidis vaccine (inactivated) for chickens is a preparation of a suitable strain or strains of *Salmonella enterica* Enteritidis, inactivated while maintaining adequate immunogenic properties. This monograph applies to vaccines intended for administration to chickens for reducing *S. enterica* Enteritidis colonisation and faecal excretion of *S. enterica* Enteritidis.

2 PRODUCTION
2-1 PREPARATION OF THE VACCINE

The seed material is cultured in a suitable medium; each strain is cultivated separately. During production, various parameters such as growth rate are monitored by suitable methods; the values are within the limits approved for the particular vaccine. Purity of the cultures and identity are verified on the harvest using suitable methods. After cultivation, the bacterial harvests are collected separately, inactivated by a suitable method, and blended. The vaccine may contain adjuvants.

2-2 CHOICE OF VACCINE COMPOSITION

The vaccine is shown to be satisfactory with respect to safety (*5.2.6*) and efficacy (*5.2.7*) for the birds for which it is intended.

The following tests for safety (section 2-2-1) and immunogenicity (section 2-2-2) may be used during the demonstration of safety and efficacy.

2-2-1 Safety

The test is carried out for each route of administration to be recommended for vaccination, using in each case chickens not older than the minimum age to be recommended for vaccination and from a flock free from specified pathogens (SPF) (*5.2.2*). Use a batch of vaccine containing not less than the maximum potency that may be expected in a batch of vaccine.

For each test performed in chickens younger than 3 weeks of age, use not fewer than 10 chickens. For each test performed in chickens older than 3 weeks of age, use not fewer than 8 chickens. Administer by a route and method to be recommended to each chicken 1 dose of the vaccine. If the schedule to be recommended requires a 2nd dose, administer 1 dose to each chicken after an interval of at least 14 days. Observe the chickens at least daily for at least 14 days after the last administration of the vaccine.

The test is not valid if more than 10 per cent of the chickens younger than 3 weeks of age show abnormal signs of disease or die from causes not attributable to the vaccine.

For chickens older than 3 weeks of age, the test is not valid if non-specific mortality occurs.

The vaccine complies with the test if no chicken shows abnormal signs of disease or dies from causes attributable to the vaccine.

2-2-2 Immunogenicity

A test is carried out for each route and method of administration to be recommended for vaccination.

The vaccine administered to each animal is of minimum potency.

Use for the test not fewer than 60 SPF chickens (*5.2.2*) not older than the minimum age to be recommended for vaccination. Vaccinate not fewer than 30 chickens with no more than the minimum recommended number of doses of vaccine. Maintain not fewer than 30 chickens as controls for each group of vaccinates. Challenge both groups, 4 weeks after the last administration of vaccine, by oral administration to each chicken of a sufficient quantity of a strain of *S. enterica* Enteritidis that is able to colonise chickens. Take blood samples from control chickens on the day before challenge. Observe the chickens at least daily for 4 weeks. Take individual fresh faeces samples on day 1 after challenge and at least twice weekly (including day 7) until 14 days after challenge. Test the fresh faeces samples for the presence of *S. enterica* Enteritidis by direct plating. Euthanise all surviving chickens at the end of the observation period, take samples of liver and spleen and test for the presence of *S. enterica* Enteritidis by an appropriate method.

The test is not valid if antibodies against *S. enterica* Enteritidis are found in any control chicken before challenge.

The vaccine complies with the test if:

— the number of *S. enterica* Enteritidis in fresh faeces samples from vaccinated chickens after challenge at the different days of sampling is significantly lower in vaccinates than in controls and remains lower until the end of the test;

— the number of positive samples of liver and spleen is significantly lower in vaccinates than in controls.

2-3 MANUFACTURER′S TEST

2-3-1 Batch potency test

It is not necessary to carry out the potency test (section 3-3) for each batch of the vaccine if it has been carried out using a batch of vaccine with a minimum potency. Where the test is not carried out, an alternative validated method is used, the criteria for acceptance being set with reference to a batch of vaccine that has given satisfactory results in the test described under Potency. The following test may be used.

Use not fewer than 15 SPF chickens (*5.2.2*). Maintain not fewer than 5 SPF chickens as controls. Administer to each of 10 chickens 1 dose of vaccine by a recommended route. Where the schedule stated on the label requires a booster injection to be given, a booster vaccination may also be given in this test provided it has been demonstrated that this will still provide a suitably sensitive test system. At a given interval after the last injection, collect blood from each vaccinated and control chicken and prepare serum samples. Measure the titre of antibodies against *S. enterica* Enteritidis in each serum sample using a suitable validated serological method. Calculate the titre for the group of vaccinates.

The test is not valid if specific *S. enterica* Enteritidis antibodies are found in 1 or more sera from control chickens at a given interval after the time of administration of the vaccine in the vaccinated group.

The vaccine complies with the test if the antibody titres of the group of vaccinates at a given interval after each vaccination, where applicable, are not significantly lower than the value obtained with a batch that has given satisfactory results in the test described under Potency (section 3-3).

3 BATCH TESTS

3-1 Identification

In animals that do not have antibodies against *S. enterica* Enteritidis, the vaccine stimulates the production of such antibodies.

3-2 Bacteria and fungi

The vaccine, including where applicable the diluent supplied for reconstitution, complies with the test for sterility prescribed in the monograph *Vaccines for veterinary use (0062)*.

3-3 Potency

The vaccine complies with the requirements of the test mentioned under Immunogenicity (section 2-2-2) when administered by a recommended route and method.

Ph Eur

Salmonella Enteritidis Vaccine (Live, Oral) for Chickens

(*Ph. Eur. monograph 2520*)

Ph Eur

1 DEFINITION

Salmonella Enteritidis vaccine (live, oral) for chickens is a preparation of a suitable strain of live *Salmonella enterica* Enteritidis. This monograph applies to vaccines intended for the active immunisation of chickens against colonisation by and faecal excretion of *S. enterica* Enteritidis.

2 PRODUCTION
2-1 PREPARATION OF THE VACCINE

The vaccine strain is cultured in a suitable medium. During production, various parameters such as growth rate are monitored by suitable methods; the values are within the limits approved for the particular vaccine. Purity and identity of the cultures are verified on the harvest using a combination of methods such as morphological, serological and biochemical methods and culture on appropriate selective media. Suitable test(s) are conducted to confirm the presence of relevant marker(s). The harvests are shown to be pure and the results obtained from the tests for identity are in accordance with the documented characteristics of the strain.

2-2 CHOICE OF VACCINE STRAIN

The vaccine strain is shown to be satisfactory with respect to safety (*5.2.6*) and efficacy (*5.2.7*) for the chickens for which it is intended. During development, the safety of the vaccine for the persons handling the vaccine or vaccinated chickens has to be addressed as well as, in accordance with the requirements of general chapter *5.2.6*, the safety of the spread of the vaccine to other susceptible species. The strain has a stable marker or markers to distinguish it from wild-type strains.

The following tests described under General safety (section 2-2-1-1), Excretion, duration of excretion and survival in the environment (section 2-2-1-2), Spread of the vaccine strain (section 2-2-1-3), Dissemination and survival of the vaccine strain in vaccinated chickens after each vaccination (section 2-2-1-4), Increase in virulence (section 2-2-1-5), Field trials (section 2-2-1-6), and Immunogenicity (sections 2-2-2-1 and 2-2-2-2) may be used during the demonstration of safety and efficacy.

For vaccines intended to prevent and/or reduce colonisation by and faecal excretion of *S. enterica* Enteritidis, the test for immunogenicity (section 2-2-2-1) is suitable to demonstrate that the vaccine is suitably immunogenic.

When the vaccine is recommended for use in laying chickens, the continuing immunogenicity of the vaccine until the end of the laying period has to be demonstrated and the test for immunogenicity at the end of the laying period (section 2-2-2-2) is suitable.

2-2-1 Safety

Unless otherwise indicated below, carry out each test by the oral route of administration, using chickens from a flock free from specified pathogens (SPF) (*5.2.2*) not older than the minimum age to be recommended for vaccination and that are free from antibodies against *Salmonella* spp. Where the vaccine is recommended for administration to 1-day-old chickens, the vaccine is administered before food is provided. Use vaccine bacteria at the least attenuated passage level that will be present in a batch of vaccine.

Measures taken to ensure absence of contamination by *Salmonella* spp. from the environment before the start of the test and on a regular ongoing basis are described and justified.

Whenever possible, items taken into the facilities are sterilised.

For re-isolation of the vaccine strain, suitably sensitive validated methods that are optimal for the vaccine strain concerned are used. The presence of relevant markers is confirmed to demonstrate that the organisms isolated are vaccine-derived and not wild-type contaminants.

2-2-1-1 General safety. For each test performed in chickens younger than 3 weeks of age, use not fewer than 10 chickens that are free from antibodies against *Salmonella* spp. Administer orally to each chicken a quantity of the vaccine strain equivalent to not less than 10 times the maximum titre(s) likely to be contained in 1 dose of the vaccine. Observe the chickens at least daily for at least 14 days.

The test is not valid if more than 10 per cent of the chickens younger than 3 weeks of age show abnormal signs or die from causes not attributable to the vaccine.

The vaccine complies with the test if no chicken shows notable signs of disease or dies from causes attributable to the vaccine.

2-2-1-2 Excretion, duration of excretion and survival in the environment. The same animals can be used for the test for spread of the vaccine strain (section 2-2-1-3) provided they are of the minimum age to be recommended for vaccination. Use for the test not fewer than 10 chickens. Administer orally to each chicken a quantity of the vaccine equivalent to not less than the maximum titre of the strain under study likely to be contained in 1 dose of the vaccine. Samples are collected for re-isolation of vaccine from cloacal swabs from each chicken and floor faeces on days 3, 7, 10 and 14 after vaccination and then weekly until 3 consecutive negative weekly samples are obtained from all vaccinated chickens. Samples are collected for re-isolation of the vaccine strain from the caeca of vaccinates at the end of the test.

The test is not valid if more than 10 per cent of vaccinated chickens show abnormal clinical signs or die from causes not attributable to the vaccine. The results are noted and used to formulate the label statement on the length of time of excretion of the vaccine strain.

2-2-1-3 Spread of the vaccine strain. The same animals can be used for the test for excretion, duration of excretion and survival in the environment (section 2-2-1-2). Use for the test not fewer than 10 chickens of the minimum age to be recommended for vaccination. Use 10 chickens as controls.

Administer orally to each chicken a quantity of the vaccine strain equivalent to not less than the maximum titre of the strain likely to be contained in 1 dose of the vaccine. 1 day after vaccination, mix the 10 vaccinates with at least 10 non-vaccinated chickens of the same age and source. Samples are collected for the re-isolation of the vaccine strain from cloacal swabs from each chicken and floor faeces on days 3, 7, 10 and 14 after vaccination and then weekly until 3 consecutive negative weekly samples are obtained from all chickens. Collect samples of the caeca and spleens for re-isolation of the vaccine strain from 10 in-contact control chickens at the end of the test. The results are noted and used to formulate the label statement on the extent to which the vaccine spreads to in-contact non-vaccinated chickens.

2-2-1-4 Dissemination and survival of the vaccine strain in vaccinated chickens after each vaccination. Conduct the test after each vaccination as prescribed by the vaccination schedule to be recommended in chickens of each category for which the vaccine is intended with oral administration of the test preparation. Use a sufficient number of chickens to conduct the sampling described below, the number of chickens required being dependent on the number of vaccinations to be recommended, the interval between vaccinations and the length of time chickens are maintained after the last vaccination. Administer to each chicken a quantity of the vaccine strain equivalent to not less than the maximum titre of the strain under study likely to be contained in 1 dose of the vaccine. Collect cloacal swabs from each chicken for re-isolation of the vaccine strain on days 7 and 14 after each vaccination and at later appropriate stages and with sufficient frequency to determine the duration of dissemination.

For example, for broilers, samples are collected from 5 chickens for re-isolation of the vaccine strain on days 7 and 14 after each vaccination and weekly until 8 weeks of age. At the 7- and 14-day sampling points, samples are taken from the liver, caecum and spleen of 5 chickens.

In the case of chickens intended for laying, samples are collected from 5 chickens on days 7 and 14 after each vaccination and weekly until 3 consecutive negative weekly samples are obtained or the time of the next vaccination is reached, whichever is the sooner. At the 7- and 14-day sampling points, samples are taken from the liver, caecum and spleen of 5 chickens. In addition, samples are collected from ovaries and oviducts where dissemination in vaccinated future layers is being investigated.

The test is not valid if more than 10 per cent of vaccinated chickens in any group show abnormal clinical signs or die from causes not attributable to the vaccine. The results are noted and used to formulate the label statement on the length of time the vaccine strain survives in the body and to define a suitable withdrawal period.

2-2-1-5 Increase in virulence. Carry out the test according to general chapter *5.2.6* using SPF chickens (*5.2.2*) not older than the minimum age to be recommended for vaccination.

Administer orally to each chicken of the 1st group a quantity of the vaccine strain of the strain under study that will allow recovery of bacteria for the passages described below. 4 to 7 days after administration of the vaccine strain, prepare a suspension from the liver, spleen and caecum of chickens and pool these samples. Administer pooled samples orally to each chicken of the next group. Carry out this passage operation not fewer than 4 times; verify the presence of the bacteria at each passage. If the bacteria are not found at a passage level, repeat the passage by administration to a group of 10 chickens. Any mortalities are investigated for the presence of the vaccine strain and the properties of any re-isolated vaccine strain determined.

Carry out the test for excretion, duration of excretion and survival in the environment (section 2-2-1-2) and, if the last group of birds from which the bacteria was recovered shows evidence of an increase in virulence indicative of reversion during the observation period, carry out the test for general safety (section 2-2-1-1), using the material used for the 1st passage and the bacteria at the last passage level where it was recovered. Test the bacteria recovered for the final passage for the presence and stability of the marker(s).

The vaccine strain complies with the test if no indication of increased virulence of the bacteria recovered for the final passage compared with the material used for the 1st passage is observed and the presence of the marker(s) is confirmed in the bacteria recovered for the final passage and remains identical to the material used for the 1st passage. If the bacteria are not recovered after an initial passage in 5 animals and a subsequent repeat passage in 10 animals, the vaccine also complies with the test.

2-2-1-6 Field trials. The chickens used for field trials are also used to evaluate safety. A trial is carried out in each category of chickens for which the vaccine strain is intended, in not fewer than 2 sets of premises. Samples are taken from a significant number of chickens for re-isolation of bacteria to provide information on the persistence, dissemination and spread of the bacteria, which can be used, with the data from

the laboratory studies, to formulate the statements on the label. The samples include cloacal swabs, floor faeces, spleen and liver and, in laying chickens, samples of ovaries and oviducts. Environmental samples are also tested at regular intervals.

2-2-2 Immunogenicity

The tests described in section 2-2-2-1 and, if appropriate, in section 2-2-2-2 are carried out using chickens not older than the minimum age to be recommended for vaccination and that are free from antibodies against *Salmonella* spp.

The quantity of the vaccine strain to be administered orally to each chicken is not greater than the minimum titre to be stated on the label.

Measures taken to ensure absence of contamination by *Salmonella* spp. from the environment before the start of the test and on a regular ongoing basis are described and justified.

Whenever possible, items taken into the facilities are sterilised.

Suitably sensitive validated methods are used for re-isolation of bacteria derived from the challenge and for distinguishing these from the vaccine strain.

2-2-2-1 Immunogenicity. Use for the test not fewer than 40 chickens of the same origin and from an SPF flock (*5.2.2*). Vaccinate according to the schedule to be recommended not fewer than 20 chickens with a single dose of vaccine. Maintain not fewer than 20 chickens as controls. Challenge each chicken after 14 days by a suitable route with a sufficient quantity of a virulent strain of *S. enterica* Enteritidis to give a valid test. Collect cloacal swabs from vaccinates and controls on days 3, 5, 7, 10 and 14 post-challenge. Samples of caecum, liver and spleen are collected from 10 chickens of each group on days 7 and 14 post-challenge for re-isolation of challenge bacteria. Collect the same samples of internal organs from any chicken that dies. Examine the samples for the presence of the challenge organisms using a suitable sensitive culture medium and compare results for vaccinates and controls.

The test is not valid if, during the observation period, fewer than 80 per cent of the control chickens die or challenge organisms are re-isolated from fewer than 80 per cent of the control chickens.

The vaccine complies with the test if there is a significant reduction in the total number of cloacal swabs from vaccinates containing challenge organisms compared with the number from the controls and there is a significant reduction in the number of samples from internal organs from vaccinates containing challenge bacteria compared with the number from the controls.

2-2-2-2 Immunogenicity at the end of the laying period. Use for the test not fewer than 40 chickens of the same origin and from an SPF flock (*5.2.2*). Vaccinate not fewer than 20 chickens according to the schedule to be recommended. Maintain not fewer than 20 chickens as controls. At the end of the laying period, take serum samples and cloacal swabs from the chickens and environmental samples from the housing area. Test each serum sample individually for the presence of antibodies to *S. enterica* Enteritidis and each cloacal swab and environmental sample for the presence of *Salmonella* spp. Challenge each chicken by a suitable route with a sufficient quantity of a virulent strain of *S. enterica* Enteritidis to give a valid test. Collect cloacal swabs from vaccinates and controls on days 3, 5, 7, 10 and 14 post-challenge. Samples of caecum, liver, spleen, ovaries and oviducts are collected from 10 chickens of each group for re-isolation of challenge bacteria on days 7 and 14 post-challenge. Collect the same samples of internal organs from any chicken that dies during the observation period. Examine the samples for the presence of the challenge organisms with growth in a suitable medium and compare results for vaccinates and controls.

The test is not valid if, before the challenge, antibodies to *Salmonella* spp. are found in the serum of the controls or *Salmonella* spp. bacteria are isolated from any of the chickens. The test is also not valid if the challenge organisms are re-isolated from fewer than 80 per cent of the control chickens.

The vaccine complies with the test if there is a significant reduction in the number of cloacal swabs from vaccinates containing challenge organisms compared with the number from the controls and there is a significant decrease in the number of samples of internal organs from vaccinates containing challenge bacteria compared with the number from the controls.

3 BATCH TESTS
3-1 Identification
The strain present in the vaccine is identified by a combination of methods such as morphological, serological and biochemical methods and culture on appropriate selective media. Suitable test(s) are conducted to confirm the presence of the relevant marker(s).

3-2 Bacteria and fungi
Carry out the test by microscopic examination and by inoculation of suitable media, or verify the absence of micro-organisms other than the vaccine strain present in the vaccine as described in the test for sterility prescribed in the monograph *Vaccines for veterinary use (0062)*. The vaccine complies with the test if it does not contain extraneous micro-organisms.

Any diluent supplied for reconstitution of the vaccine complies with the test for sterility prescribed in the monograph *Vaccines for veterinary use (0062)*.

3-3 Live bacteria
Titrate the vaccine strain using a suitable medium for the culture of the strain. The vaccine complies with the test if it contains not less than the titre stated on the label.

3-4 Potency
The vaccine complies with the requirements of the test prescribed under Immunogenicity (section 2-2-2-1) when administered by a recommended route and method. It is not necessary to carry out the potency test for each batch of the vaccine if it has been carried out on a representative batch using a vaccinating dose containing not more than the minimum titre stated on the label.

4 LABELLING
The label states:
— the nature of the markers allowing the vaccine to be distinguished from wild-type strains;
— the extent to which the vaccine spreads and is transmitted to non-vaccinated chickens and the time over which this could occur;
— the time that the vaccine survives in the body;
— the length of time of excretion and the time that the vaccine survives in the environment;
— the potential for spread to other susceptible species including humans;
— the withdrawal period.

Ph Eur ⎯⎯⎯⎯

Salmonella Typhimurium Vaccine (Inactivated) for Chickens

(Ph. Eur. monograph 2361)

Ph Eur ⎯⎯⎯⎯

1 DEFINITION
Salmonella Typhimurium vaccine (inactivated) for chickens is a preparation of a suitable strain or strains of *Salmonella enterica* Typhimurium, inactivated while maintaining adequate immunogenic properties. This monograph applies to vaccines intended for administration to chickens for reducing *S. enterica* Typhimurium colonisation and faecal excretion of *S. enterica* Typhimurium.

2 PRODUCTION
2-1 PREPARATION OF THE VACCINE
The seed material is cultured in a suitable medium; each strain is cultivated separately. During production, various parameters such as growth rate are monitored by suitable methods; the values are within the limits approved for the particular vaccine. Purity of the cultures and identity are verified on the harvest using suitable methods. After cultivation, the bacterial harvests are collected separately, inactivated by a suitable method, and blended. The vaccine may contain adjuvants.

2-2 CHOICE OF VACCINE COMPOSITION
The vaccine is shown to be satisfactory with respect to safety (*5.2.6*) and efficacy (*5.2.7*) for the birds for which it is intended.

The following tests for safety (section 2-2-1) and immunogenicity (section 2-2-2) may be used during the demonstration of safety and efficacy.

2-2-1 Safety
The test is carried out for each route of administration to be recommended for vaccination, using in each case chickens not older than the minimum age to be recommended for vaccination and from a flock free from specified pathogens (SPF) (*5.2.2*). Use a batch of vaccine containing not less than the maximum potency that may be expected in a batch of vaccine.

For each test performed in chickens younger than 3 weeks of age, use not fewer than 10 chickens. For each test performed in chickens older than 3 weeks of age, use not fewer than 8 chickens. Administer by a route and method to be recommended to each chicken 1 dose of the vaccine. If the schedule to be recommended requires a 2nd dose, administer 1 dose to each chicken after an interval of at least 14 days. Observe the chickens at least daily for at least 14 days after the last administration of the vaccine.

The test is not valid if more than 10 per cent of the chickens younger than 3 weeks of age show abnormal signs of disease or die from causes not attributable to the vaccine.
For chickens older than 3 weeks of age, the test is not valid if non-specific mortality occurs.

The vaccine complies with the test if no chicken shows abnormal signs of disease or dies from causes attributable to the vaccine.

2-2-2 Immunogenicity
A test is carried out for each route and method of administration to be recommended for vaccination.
The vaccine administered to each animal is of minimum potency.

Use for the test not fewer than 60 SPF chickens (*5.2.2*) not older than the minimum age to be recommended for vaccination. Vaccinate not fewer than 30 chickens with no more than the minimum number of doses of vaccine to be recommended. Maintain not fewer than 30 chickens as controls for each group of vaccinates. Challenge both groups, 4 weeks after the last administration of vaccine, by oral administration to each chicken of a sufficient quantity of a strain of *S. enterica* Typhimurium that is able to colonise chickens. Take blood samples from control chickens on the day before challenge. Observe the chickens at least daily for 4 weeks. Take individual fresh faeces samples on day 1 after challenge and at least twice weekly (including day 7) until 14 days after challenge. Test the fresh faeces samples for the presence of *S. enterica* Typhimurium by direct plating. Euthanise all surviving chickens at the end of the observation period, take samples of liver and spleen and test for the presence of *S. enterica* Typhimurium by an appropriate method.

The test is not valid if antibodies against *S. enterica* Typhimurium are found in any control chicken before challenge.

The vaccine complies with the test if:
— the number of *S. enterica* Typhimurium in fresh faeces samples from vaccinated chickens after challenge at the different days of sampling is significantly lower in vaccinates than in controls and remains lower until the end of the test;
— the number of positive samples of liver and spleen is significantly lower in vaccinates than in controls.

2-3 MANUFACTURER'S TEST
2-3-1 Batch potency test
It is not necessary to carry out the potency test (section 3-3) for each batch of the vaccine if it has been carried out using a batch of vaccine with a minimum potency. Where the test is not carried out, an alternative validated method is used, the criteria for acceptance being set with reference to a batch of vaccine that has given satisfactory results in the test described under Potency. The following test may be used.

Use not fewer than 15 SPF chickens (5.2.2). Maintain not fewer than 5 SPF chickens as controls. Administer to each of 10 chickens 1 dose of vaccine by a recommended route. Where the schedule stated on the label requires a booster injection to be given, a booster vaccination may also be given in this test provided it has been demonstrated that this will still provide a suitably sensitive test system. At a given interval after the last injection, collect blood from each vaccinated and control chicken and prepare serum samples. Measure the titre of antibodies against *S. enterica* Typhimurium in each serum sample using a suitable validated serological method. Calculate the titre for the group of vaccinates.

The test is not valid if specific *S. enterica* Typhimurium antibodies are found in 1 or more sera from control chickens at a given interval after the time of administration of the vaccine in the vaccinated group.

The vaccine complies with the test if the antibody titres of the group of vaccinates at a given interval after each vaccination, where applicable, are not significantly lower than the value obtained with a batch that has given satisfactory results in the test described under Potency (section 3-3).

3 BATCH TESTS
3-1 Identification
In animals that do not have antibodies against *S. enterica* Typhimurium, the vaccine stimulates the production of such antibodies.

3-2 Bacteria and fungi
The vaccine, including where applicable the diluent supplied for reconstitution, complies with the test for sterility prescribed in the monograph *Vaccines for veterinary use (0062)*.

3-3 Potency
The vaccine complies with the requirements of the test mentioned under Immunogenicity (section 2-2-2) when administered by a recommended route and method.

_____ *Ph Eur*

Salmonella Typhimurium Vaccine (Live, Oral) for Chickens

(Ph. Eur. monograph 2521)

Ph Eur _____

1 DEFINITION
Salmonella Typhimurium vaccine (live, oral) for chickens is a preparation of a suitable strain of live *Salmonella enterica* Typhimurium. This monograph applies to vaccines intended for the active immunisation of chickens against colonisation by and faecal excretion of *S. enterica* Typhimurium.

2 PRODUCTION
2-1 PREPARATION OF THE VACCINE
The vaccine strain is cultured in a suitable medium. During production, various parameters such as growth rate are monitored by suitable methods; the values are within the limits approved for the particular vaccine. Purity and identity of the cultures are verified on the harvest using a combination of methods such as morphological, serological and biochemical methods and culture on appropriate selective media. Suitable test(s) are conducted to confirm the presence of relevant marker(s). The harvests are shown to be pure and the results obtained from the tests for identity are in accordance with the documented characteristics of the strain.

2-2 CHOICE OF VACCINE STRAIN
The vaccine strain is shown to be satisfactory with respect to safety (5.2.6) and efficacy (5.2.7) for the chickens for which it is intended. During development, the safety of the vaccine for the persons handling the vaccine or vaccinated chickens has to be addressed as well as, in accordance with the requirements of general chapter 5.2.6, the safety of the spread of the vaccine to other susceptible species. The strain has a stable marker or markers to distinguish it from wild-type strains.

The following tests described under General safety (section 2-2-1-1), Excretion, duration of excretion and survival in the environment (section 2-2-1-2), Spread of the vaccine strain (section 2-2-1-3), Dissemination and survival of the vaccine strain in vaccinated chickens after each vaccination (section 2-2-1-4), Increase in virulence (section 2-2-1-5), Field trials (section 2-2-1-6), Immunogenicity (sections 2-2-2-1 and 2-2-2-2) may be used during the demonstration of safety and efficacy.

For vaccines intended to prevent and/or reduce colonisation by and faecal excretion of *S. enterica* Typhimurium, the test for immunogenicity (section 2-2-2-1) is suitable to demonstrate that the vaccine is suitably immunogenic.

When the vaccine is recommended for use in laying chickens, the continuing immunogenicity of the vaccine until the end of the laying period has to be demonstrated and the test for immunogenicity at the end of the laying period (section 2-2-2-2) is suitable.

2-2-1 Safety

Unless otherwise indicated below, carry out each test by the oral route of administration, using chickens from a flock free from specified pathogens (SPF) (5.2.2) not older than the minimum age to be recommended for vaccination and that are free from antibodies against *Salmonella* spp. Where the vaccine is recommended for administration to 1-day-old chickens, the vaccine is administered before food is provided. Use vaccine bacteria at the least attenuated passage level that will be present in a batch of vaccine.

Measures taken to ensure absence of contamination by *Salmonella* spp. from the environment before the start of the test and on a regular ongoing basis are described and justified.

Whenever possible, items taken into the facilities are sterilised.

For re-isolation of the vaccine strain, suitably sensitive validated methods that are optimal for the vaccine strain concerned are used. The presence of relevant markers is confirmed to demonstrate that the organisms isolated are vaccine-derived and not wild-type contaminants.

2-2-1-1 General safety. For each test performed in chickens younger than 3 weeks of age, use not fewer than 10 chickens that are free from antibodies against *Salmonella* spp. Administer orally to each chicken a quantity of the vaccine strain equivalent to not less than 10 times the maximum titre(s) likely to be contained in 1 dose of the vaccine. Observe the chickens at least daily for at least 14 days.

The test is not valid if more than 10 per cent of the chickens younger than 3 weeks of age show abnormal signs or die from causes not attributable to the vaccine.

The vaccine complies with the test if no chicken shows abnormal signs of disease or dies from causes attributable to the vaccine.

2-2-1-2 Excretion, duration of excretion and survival in the environment. The same animals can be used for the test for spread of the vaccine strain (section 2-2-1-3) provided they are of the minimum age to be recommended for vaccination. Use for the test not fewer than 10 chickens. Administer orally to each chicken a quantity of the vaccine equivalent to not less than the maximum titre of the strain under study likely to be contained in 1 dose of the vaccine. Samples are collected for reisolation of vaccine from cloacal swabs from each chicken and floor faeces on days 3, 7, 10 and 14 after vaccination and then weekly until 3 consecutive negative weekly samples are obtained from all vaccinated chickens. Samples are collected for re-isolation of the vaccine strain from the caeca of vaccinates at the end of the test.

The test is not valid if more than 10 per cent of vaccinated chickens show abnormal clinical signs or die from causes not attributable to the vaccine. The results are noted and used to formulate the label statement on the length of time of excretion of the vaccine strain.

2-2-1-3 Spread of the vaccine strain. The same animals can be used for the test for excretion, duration of excretion and survival in the environment (section 2-2-1-2). Use for the test not fewer than 10 chickens of the minimum age to be recommended for vaccination. Use 10 chickens as controls. Administer orally to each chicken a quantity of the vaccine strain equivalent to not less than the maximum titre of the strain likely to be contained in 1 dose of the vaccine. 1 day

after vaccination, mix the 10 vaccinates with at least 10 non-vaccinated chickens of the same age and source. Samples are collected for the re-isolation of the vaccine strain from cloacal swabs from each chicken and floor faeces on days 3, 7, 10 and 14 after vaccination and then weekly until 3 consecutive negative weekly samples are obtained from all chickens. Collect samples of the caeca and spleens for re-isolation of the vaccine strain from 10 in-contact control chickens at the end of the test. The results are noted and used to formulate the label statement on the extent to which the vaccine spreads to in-contact non-vaccinated chickens.

2-2-1-4 Dissemination and survival of the vaccine strain in vaccinated chickens after each vaccination. Conduct the test after each vaccination as prescribed by the vaccination schedule to be recommended in chickens of each category for which the vaccine is intended with oral administration of the test preparation. Use a sufficient number of chickens to conduct the sampling described below, the number of chickens required being dependent on the number of vaccinations recommended, the interval between vaccinations and the length of time chickens are maintained after the last vaccination. Administer to each chicken a quantity of the vaccine strain equivalent to not less than the maximum titre of the strain under study likely to be contained in 1 dose of the vaccine. Collect cloacal swabs from each chicken for re-isolation of vaccinal bacteria on days 7 and 14 after each vaccination and at later appropriate stages and with sufficient frequency to determine the duration of dissemination.

For example, for broilers, samples are collected from 5 chickens for re-isolation of the vaccine strain on days 7 and 14 after each vaccination and weekly until 8 weeks of age. At the 7- and 14-day sampling points, samples are taken from the liver, caecum and spleen of 5 chickens.

In the case of chickens intended for laying, samples are collected from 5 chickens on days 7 and 14 after each vaccination and weekly until 3 consecutive negative weekly samples are obtained or the time of the next vaccination is reached, whichever is the sooner. At the 7- and 14- day sampling points, samples are taken from the liver, caecum and spleen of 5 chickens. In addition, samples are collected from ovaries and oviducts where dissemination in vaccinated future layers is being investigated.

The test is not valid if more than 10 per cent of vaccinated chickens in any group show abnormal clinical signs or die from causes not attributable to the vaccine. The results are noted and used to formulate the label statement on the length of time the vaccine strain survives in the body and to define a suitable withdrawal period.

2-2-1-5 Increase in virulence. Carry out the test according to general chapter 5.2.6 using SPF chickens (5.2.2) not older than the minimum age to be recommended for vaccination.

Administer orally to each chicken of the 1st group a quantity of the vaccine strain under study that will allow recovery of bacteria for the passages described below. 4 to 7 days after administration of the vaccine strain, prepare a suspension from the liver, spleen and caecum of chickens and pool these samples. Administer pooled samples orally to each chicken of the next group. Carry out this passage operation not fewer than 4 times; verify the presence of the bacteria at each passage. If the bacteria are not found at a passage level, repeat the passage by administration to a group of 10 chickens. Any mortalities are investigated for the presence of the vaccine strain and the properties of any re-isolated vaccine strain determined.

Carry out the test for excretion, duration of excretion and survival in the environment (section 2-2-1-2) and, if the last group of birds from which the bacteria was recovered shows evidence of an increase in virulence indicative of reversion during the observation period, carry out the test for general safety (section 2-2-1-1), using the material used for the 1st passage and the bacteria at the last passage level where it was recovered. Test the bacteria recovered for the final passage for the presence and stability of the marker(s).

The vaccine strain complies with the test if no indication of increased virulence of the bacteria recovered for the final passage compared with the material used for the 1st passage is observed and the presence of the marker(s) is confirmed in the bacteria recovered for the final passage and remains identical to the material used for the 1st passage. If the bacteria are not recovered after an initial passage in 5 animals and a subsequent repeat passage in 10 animals, the vaccine also complies with the test.

2-2-1-6 Field trials. The chickens used for field trials are also used to evaluate safety. A trial is carried out in each category of chickens for which the vaccine strain is intended, in not fewer than 2 sets of premises. Samples are taken from a significant number of chickens for re-isolation of bacteria to provide information on the persistence, dissemination and spread of the bacteria, which can be used, with the data from the laboratory studies, to formulate the statements on the label. The samples include cloacal swabs, floor faeces, spleen and liver and, in laying chickens, samples of ovaries and oviducts. Environmental samples are also tested at regular intervals.

2-2-2 Immunogenicity

The tests described in section 2-2-2-1 and, if appropriate, in section 2-2-2-2, are carried out using chickens not older than the minimum age to be recommended for vaccination and that are free from antibodies against *Salmonella* spp.

The quantity of the vaccine strain to be administered orally to each chicken is not greater than the minimum titre to be stated on the label.

Measures taken to ensure absence of contamination by *Salmonella* spp. from the environment before the start of the test and on a regular ongoing basis are described and justified.

Suitably sensitive validated methods are used for re-isolation of bacteria derived from the challenge and for distinguishing these from the vaccine strain.

2-2-2-1 Immunogenicity. Use for the test not fewer than 40 chickens of the same origin and from an SPF flock (5.2.2). Vaccinate according to the schedule to be recommended not fewer than 20 chickens with a single dose of vaccine. Maintain not fewer than 20 chickens as controls. Challenge each chicken after 14 days by a suitable route with a sufficient quantity of a virulent strain of *S. enterica* Typhimurium to give a valid test. Collect cloacal swabs from vaccinates and controls on days 3, 5, 7, 10 and 14 post-challenge. Samples of caecum, liver and spleen are collected from 10 chickens of each group on days 7 and 14 post-challenge for re-isolation of challenge bacteria. Collect the same samples of internal organs from any chicken that dies. Examine the samples for the presence of the challenge organisms using a suitable sensitive culture medium and compare results for vaccinates and controls.

The test is not valid if, during the observation period, fewer than 80 per cent of the control chickens die or challenge organisms are re-isolated from fewer than 80 per cent of the control chickens.

The vaccine complies with the test if there is a significant reduction in the number of cloacal swabs from vaccinates containing challenge organisms compared with the number from the controls and there is a significant reduction in the number of samples from internal organs from vaccinates containing challenge bacteria compared with the number from the controls.

2-2-2-2 Immunogenicity at the end of the laying period. Use for the test not fewer than 40 chickens of the same origin and from an SPF flock (5.2.2). Vaccinate not fewer than 20 chickens according to the schedule to be recommended. Maintain not fewer than 20 chickens as controls. At the end of the laying period, take serum samples and cloacal swabs from the chickens and environmental samples from the housing area. Test each serum sample individually for the presence of antibodies to *S. enterica* Typhimurium and each cloacal swab and fresh environmental sample for the presence of *Salmonella* spp. Challenge each chicken by a suitable route with a sufficient quantity of a virulent strain of *S. enterica* Typhimurium to give a valid test. Collect cloacal swabs from vaccinates and controls on days 3, 5, 7, 10 and 14 post-challenge. Samples of caecum, liver, spleen, ovaries and oviducts are collected from 10 chickens of each group for re-isolation of challenge bacteria on days 7 and 14 post-challenge. Collect the same samples of internal organs from any chicken that dies during the observation period. Examine the samples for the presence of the challenge organisms with growth in a suitable medium and compare results for vaccinates and controls.

The test is not valid if, before the challenge, antibodies to *Salmonella* spp. are found in the serum of the controls or *Salmonella* spp. bacteria are isolated from any of the chickens. The test is also not valid if the challenge organisms are re-isolated from fewer than 80 per cent of the control chickens.

The vaccine complies with the test if there is a significant reduction in the number of cloacal swabs from vaccinates containing challenge organisms compared with the number from the controls and there is a significant decrease in the number of samples of internal organs from vaccinates containing challenge bacteria compared with the number from the controls.

3 BATCH TESTS

3-1 Identification

The strain present in the vaccine is identified by a combination of methods such as morphological, serological and biochemical methods and culture on appropriate selective media. Suitable test(s) are conducted to confirm the presence of the relevant marker(s).

3-2 Bacteria and fungi

Carry out the test by microscopic examination and by inoculation of suitable media, or verify the absence of micro-organisms other than the vaccine strain present in the vaccine as described in the test for sterility prescribed in the monograph *Vaccines for veterinary use (0062)*. The vaccine complies with the test if it does not contain extraneous micro-organisms.

Any diluent supplied for reconstitution of the vaccine complies with the test for sterility prescribed in the monograph *Vaccines for veterinary use (0062)*.

3-3 Live bacteria

Titrate the vaccine strain using a suitable medium for the culture of the strain. The vaccine complies with the test if it contains not less than the titre stated on the label.

3-4 Potency

The vaccine complies with the requirements of the test prescribed under Immunogenicity (section 2-2-2-1) when administered by a recommended route and method. It is not necessary to carry out the potency test for each batch of the vaccine if it has been carried out on a representative batch using a vaccinating dose containing not more than the minimum titre stated on the label.

4 LABELLING

The label states:

— the nature of the markers allowing the vaccine to be distinguished from wild-type strains;

— the extent to which the vaccine spreads and is transmitted to non-vaccinated chickens and the time over which this could occur;

— the time that the vaccine survives in the body;

— the length of time of excretion and the time that the vaccine survives in the environment;

— the potential for spread to other susceptible species including humans;

— the withdrawal period.

_____ *Ph Eur*

Swine Erysipelas Vaccine, Inactivated

*(Swine Erysipelas Vaccine (Inactivated),
Ph Eur monograph 0064)*

Ph Eur _____

1 DEFINITION

Swine erysipelas vaccine (inactivated) is a preparation of one or more suitable strains of *Erysipelothrix rhusiopathiae*, inactivated while maintaining adequate immunogenic properties. This monograph applies to vaccines intended for the active immunisation of pigs against swine erysipelas.

2 PRODUCTION

The vaccine may be adjuvanted.

2-1 CHOICE OF VACCINE COMPOSITION

The vaccine is shown to be satisfactory with respect to safety (*5.2.6*) and efficacy (*5.2.7*) for the pigs for which it is intended.

The following test for safety (section 2-1-1) and immunogenicity (section 2-1-2) may be used during the demonstration of safety and efficacy.

2-1-1 Safety

Carry out the test for each route and method of administration to be recommended for vaccination and where applicable, in pigs of each category for which the vaccine is intended, using in each case pigs not older than the minimum age to be recommended for vaccination. Use a batch of vaccine containing not less than the maximum potency that may be expected in a batch of vaccine.

For each test, use not fewer than 8 pigs that do not have antibodies against swine erysipelas. Administer to each pig 1 dose of the vaccine. If the schedule to be recommended requires a 2nd dose, administer another dose after an interval of at least 14 days. Observe the pigs at least daily until at least 14 days after the last administration. Record body temperatures the day before each vaccination, at vaccination, 2 h, 4 h and 6 h later and daily for 4 days; note the maximum temperature increase for each pig.

The vaccine complies with the test if no pig shows abnormal local or systemic reactions or signs of disease, or dies from causes attributable to the vaccine, if the average body temperature increase for all pigs does not exceed 1.5 °C, and if no pig shows a rise greater than 2.0 °C.

2-1-2 Immunogenicity

The test described below is suitable to demonstrate immunogenicity of the vaccine with respect to *E. rhusiopathiae* serotypes 1 and 2. If claims are made concerning another serotype, then a further test to demonstrate immunogenicity against this serotype is necessary.

If the vaccine contains more than 1 serotype, a test for 2 serotypes may be carried out on a single group by injecting each challenge serotype on different flanks of the pigs. Validation and acceptance criteria are applied separately to the respective injection sites. If the vaccine contains more than 1 serotype, the immunogenicity test may also be carried out using a separate group for each serotype.

A test is carried out for each route and method of administration to be recommended, using in each case pigs not less than 12 weeks old and weighing not less than 20 kg. The vaccine administered to each pig is of minimum potency.

For each test, use not fewer than 15 pigs that do not have antibodies against swine erysipelas. Divide the pigs into 2 groups. Vaccinate a group of not fewer than 10 pigs according to the schedule to be recommended. Maintain a group of not fewer than 5 pigs as controls. Challenge each pig 3 weeks after vaccination by the intradermal route by separate injections of 0.1 mL of a virulent strain of each of serotype 1 and serotype 2 of *E. rhusiopathiae*. Observe the pigs at least daily for 7 days.

The test is not valid if fewer than 80 per cent of control pigs show typical signs of disease, i.e. diamond skin lesions at the injection sites. The vaccine complies with the test if not fewer than 90 per cent of the vaccinated pigs remain free from diamond skin lesions at the injection site.

Swine erysipelas bacteria serotype 1 BRP and *swine erysipelas bacteria serotype 2 BRP* are suitable for use as challenge strains.

2-2 MANUFACTURER'S TESTS

2-2-1 Batch potency test

It is not necessary to carry out the potency test (section 3-3) for each batch of vaccine if it has been carried out using a batch of vaccine with a minimum potency. Where the test is not carried out, an alternative validated method is used, the criteria for acceptance being set with reference to a batch of vaccine that has given satisfactory results in the test described under Potency. The following test may be used.

Use 10 mice of a suitable strain (for example, NMRI) weighing 17-20 g, from a uniform stock and that do not have antibodies against swine erysipelas. Vaccinate each mouse by the subcutaneous route with a suitable dose (usually 1/10 of the pig dose). At a given interval (for example, 21-28 days), depending on the vaccine to be examined, bleed the mice under anaesthesia. Pool the sera, using an equal volume from each mouse. Determine the level of antibodies by a suitable immunochemical method (*2.7.1*), for example, enzyme-linked immunosorbent assay with *erysipelas ELISA coating antigen BRP*. The vaccine complies with the test if the antibody level is not significantly less than that obtained with a batch that has given satisfactory results in the test described under Potency.

3 BATCH TESTS

3-1 Identification
Injected into animals that do not have antibodies against *E. rhusiopathiae*, the vaccine stimulates the production of such antibodies.

3-2 Bacteria and fungi
The vaccine, including where applicable the diluent supplied for reconstitution, complies with the test for sterility prescribed in the monograph *Vaccines for veterinary use (0062)*.

3-3 Potency
The vaccine complies with the requirements of the tests mentioned under Immunogenicity (section 2-1-2) when administered by a recommended route and method.

Ph Eur

Swine-Fever Vaccine (Live, Prepared in Cell Cultures), Classical

(Ph Eur monograph 0065)

Ph Eur

1 DEFINITION
Classical swine-fever vaccine (live, prepared in cell cultures) is a preparation obtained from a strain of classical swine-fever virus that has lost its pathogenicity for the pig by *in vivo* and/or *in vitro* passage and has been adapted to growth in cell cultures.

2 PRODUCTION

2-1 PREPARATION OF THE VACCINE
The vaccine virus is grown in cell cultures.

2-2 SUBSTRATE FOR VIRUS PROPAGATION
Cell cultures
Cell cultures comply with the requirements for cell cultures for production of veterinary vaccines (*5.2.4*).

2-3 CHOICE OF VACCINE VIRUS
The vaccine virus is shown to be satisfactory with respect to safety (*5.2.6*) and efficacy (*5.2.7*) for the swine for which it is intended.

The following tests described under Safety test in piglets (section 2-3-1), Safety test in pregnant sows and test for transplacental transmission (section 2-3-2), Non-transmissibility (section 2-3-3), Increase in virulence (section 2-3-4) and Immunogenicity (section 2-3-5) may be used during the demonstration of safety and immunogenicity.

2-3-1 Safety test in piglets
Carry out the test for each route to be recommended using in each case piglets not older than the minimum age to be recommended for vaccination. Use vaccine virus at the least attenuated passage level that will be present in a batch of the vaccine.

Use not fewer than 8 healthy piglets that do not have antibodies against pestiviruses. Administer to not fewer than 8 piglets a quantity of the vaccine virus equivalent to not less than 10 times the maximum virus titre likely to be contained in 1 dose of the vaccine. Observe the piglets at least daily for at least 14 days. The body temperature of each vaccinated piglet is measured on at least the 3 days preceding administration of the vaccine, at the time of administration, 4 h after and then daily for at least 14 days. The vaccine

complies with the test if the average body temperature increase for all piglets does not exceed 1.5 °C, no piglet shows a temperature rise greater than 1.5 °C for a period exceeding 3 days, and no piglet shows notable signs of disease or dies from causes attributable to the vaccine.

2-3-2 Safety test in pregnant sows and test for transplacental transmission
Carry out the test by a route to be recommended using not fewer than 8 healthy sows or gilts of the same age and origin, between the 55th and 80th days of gestation, and that do not have antibodies against pestiviruses. Use vaccine virus at the least attenuated passage level that will be present in a batch of the vaccine.

Administer to not fewer than 8 sows or gilts a quantity of the vaccine virus equivalent to not less than the maximum virus titre likely to be contained in 1 dose of the vaccine. Record the body temperature on at least the 3 days preceding administration of the vaccine, at the time of administration, 4 h after and then daily for at least 15 days. Observe until farrowing.

Carry out tests for serum antibodies against classical swine-fever virus. No antibodies against classical swine-fever virus are found in sera taken from the newborn piglets before ingestion of colostrum. The test is not valid if the vaccinated sows do not seroconvert. The vaccine virus complies with the test if no abnormalities in the gestation or in the piglets are noted, no sow or gilt shows a temperature rise greater than 1.5 °C for a period exceeding 5 days, and no sow or gilt shows notable signs of disease or dies from causes attributable to the vaccine.

2-3-3 Non-transmissibility
Keep together for the test not fewer than 12 healthy piglets, 6-10 weeks old and of the same origin, and that do not have antibodies against pestiviruses. Use vaccine virus at the least attenuated passage level that will be present between the master seed lot and a batch of the vaccine. Administer by a route to be recommended to not fewer than 6 piglets a quantity of the vaccine virus equivalent to not less than the maximum virus titre likely to be contained in 1 dose of the vaccine. Maintain not fewer than 6 piglets as contact controls. The mixing of vaccinated piglets and contact piglets is done 24 h after vaccination.

After 45 days, euthanise all piglets. Carry out appropriate tests on the piglets to detect antibodies to classical swine-fever. Carry out appropriate tests on the control piglets to detect classical swine-fever virus in the tonsils. The vaccine complies with the test if antibodies are found in all vaccinated piglets and if no antibodies and no virus are found in the control piglets.

2-3-4 Increase in virulence
Carry out the test according to chapter *5.2.6. Evaluation of safety of veterinary vaccines and immunosera*, using piglets 6-10 weeks old that do not have antibodies against pestiviruses. If the properties of the vaccine virus allow sequential passage through 5 groups via natural spreading, this method may be used, otherwise passage as described below is carried out.

Administer to each piglet of the 1st group by a route to be recommended a quantity of the vaccine virus equivalent to not less than the maximum virus titre likely to be contained in 1 dose of the vaccine. Collect an appropriate quantity of blood from each piglet daily between day 2 and day 7 after administration of the vaccine virus, and pool the samples taken on the same day. Administer 2 mL of the pooled blood with the highest virus titre by a route to be recommended to each piglet of the next group. Carry out this passage operation not fewer than 4 times, verifying the presence of the virus at each passage. If no virus is found, repeat the test once. If virus is found, carry out a 2nd series of passages by administering 2 mL of positive blood by a route to be recommended to each piglet of a group of 10 animals.

If the 5th group of animals shows no evidence of an increase in virulence indicative of reversion during the observation period, further testing is not required. Otherwise, carry out an additional safety test and compare the clinical signs and any relevant parameters in a group of at least 8 animals receiving the material used for the 1st passage and another similar group receiving the virus at the final passage level.

The vaccine virus complies with the test if no indication of increasing virulence of the virus recovered for the final passage compared with the material used for the 1st passage is observed. If virus is not recovered after an initial passage in 2 animals and a subsequent repeat passage in 10 animals, the vaccine virus also complies with the test.

2-3-5 Immunogenicity

2-3-5-1 *Protective dose* The efficacy of the vaccine is expressed by the number of 50 per cent protective doses (PD$_{50}$) for pigs contained in the vaccinal dose as indicated on the label. The vaccine contains at least 100 PD$_{50}$ per dose.

Use 1 or more groups of piglets aged 6-10 weeks and that do not have antibodies against pestiviruses, and use an additional group of piglets of the same age and origin as controls. Each group of piglets is vaccinated with 1 dilution of the vaccine dose. 14 days after the single injection of vaccine, challenge the piglets by a suitable route with a suitable strain of virulent virus and a dose that kills not fewer than 50 per cent of the non-vaccinated piglets in less than 21 days. Observe the piglets for 21 days and record the body temperature 3 days before challenge and daily after challenge for 21 days. The PD$_{50}$ is calculated by the usual statistical methods (for example, 5.3), taking into account the surviving piglets that have no clinical signs of swine fever, including cutaneous lesions or an increase in body temperature.

The test is not valid if fewer than 50 per cent of the control piglets display typical signs of serious infection with swine-fever virus, including cutaneous lesions, or die, and if fewer than 100 per cent of the control piglets show clinical signs of disease within the 21 days following challenge. The vaccine complies with the test if the minimum dose stated on the label corresponds to not less than 100 PD$_{50}$.

2-3-5-2 *Protection against transplacental infection* Use at least 8 sows that do not have antibodies against pestiviruses, randomly allocated to either the vaccine group ($n = 6$) or the control group ($n = 2$).

Between the 40th and 50th day of gestation, all sows allocated to the vaccine group are vaccinated once with 1 dose of vaccine containing not more than the minimum titre stated on the label. On day 60 of gestation, all sows are challenged by a route to be recommended with a suitable strain of virulent virus. Just before farrowing and about 5-6 weeks after challenge, the sows are euthanised and their foetuses are examined for classical swine-fever virus. Serum samples from sows and foetuses are tested for the presence of antibodies against classical swine-fever virus. Isolation of classical swine-fever virus is carried out from blood of the sows (collected 7 and 9 days after challenge and at euthanasia), and from homogenised organ material (spleen, kidneys, lymph nodes) of the foetuses.

The test is not valid if one or more of the vaccinated sows do not seroconvert after the vaccination and the control sows do not seroconvert after the challenge, or if no virus is found in more than 50 per cent of the foetuses from the control sows (excluding mummified foetuses).

The vaccine complies with the test if no virus is found in the blood of vaccinated sows and in foetuses from the vaccinated sows, and no antibodies against classical swine-fever virus are found in the serum of the foetuses from the vaccinated sows.

3 BATCH TESTS

3-1 Identification

Specific classical swine-fever monoclonal antibodies are used to identify the vaccinal strain.

3-2 Bacteria and fungi

The vaccine, including where applicable, the diluent supplied for reconstitution, complies with the test for sterility prescribed in the monograph *Vaccines for veterinary use (0062)*.

3-3 Mycoplasmas (2.6.7)

The vaccine complies with the test for mycoplasmas.

3-4 Extraneous agents

Neutralise the vaccine virus using monoclonal antibodies to the vaccine virus. Inoculate into cell cultures known to be sensitive to viruses pathogenic for pigs and to pestiviruses. Maintain these cultures for not less than 14 days and carry out at least 3 passages during this period.

The vaccine complies with the test if no cytopathic effect is produced and if the cells show no evidence of the presence of haemadsorbing agents.

Use monoclonal antibodies that can identify possible contamination with pestiviruses. No virus is detected by an appropriate method.

3-5 Virus titre

Titrate the vaccine virus in suitable cell cultures (5.2.4). The vaccine complies with the test if 1 dose contains not less than the minimum virus titre stated on the label.

3-6 Potency

The vaccine complies with the requirements of the test prescribed under Immunogenicity (section 2-3-5) when administered by a recommended route and method. It is not necessary to carry out the potency test for each batch of the vaccine if it has been carried out on a representative batch using a vaccinating dose containing not more than the minimum virus titre stated on the label.

_____ *Ph Eur*

Swine Influenza Vaccine, Inactivated

(Porcine Influenza Vaccine (Inactivated), Ph Eur monograph 0963)

Ph Eur _____

1 DEFINITION

Porcine influenza vaccine (inactivated) is a preparation of one or more suitable strains of swine or human influenza virus inactivated while maintaining adequate immunogenic properties. Suitable strains contain both haemagglutinin and neuraminidase. This monograph applies to vaccines intended for the active immunisation of pigs against porcine influenza.

2 PRODUCTION

2-1 PREPARATION OF THE VACCINE

The vaccine virus is grown in embryonated hens' eggs or in cell cultures. Each virus strain is cultivated separately. After cultivation, the viral suspensions are collected separately and inactivated by a suitable method. If necessary, they may be purified. The vaccine may be adjuvanted.

2-2 SUBSTRATE FOR VIRUS PROPAGATION

2-2-1 Embryonated hens' eggs

If the vaccine virus is grown in embryonated hens' eggs, they are obtained from a healthy flock.

2-2-2 Cell cultures

If the vaccine virus is grown in cell cultures, they comply with the requirements for cell cultures for production of veterinary vaccines (5.2.4).

2-3 CHOICE OF VACCINE COMPOSITION

The choice of strains is based on the antigenic types and sub-types observed in Europe. The vaccine is shown to be satisfactory with respect to safety (5.2.6) and efficacy (5.2.7) for the pigs for which it is intended.

The following tests for safety (section 2-3-1) and immunogenicity (section 2-3-2) may be used during the demonstration of safety and efficacy.

2-3-1 Safety

2-3-1-1 Laboratory tests. Carry out the tests for each route and method of administration to be recommended for vaccination and where applicable, in pigs of each category for which the vaccine is intended (sows, fattening pigs), using in each case pigs not older than the minimum age to be recommended for vaccination. Use a batch of vaccine containing not less than the maximum potency that may be expected in a batch of vaccine.

2-3-1-1-1 General safety. For each test, use not fewer than 8 pigs that do not have antibodies against swine influenza virus. Administer to each pig 1 dose of the vaccine. If the schedule to be recommended requires a 2nd dose, administer another dose after an interval of at least 14 days. Observe the pigs at least daily until 14 days after the last administration.

The vaccine complies with the test if no pig shows abnormal local or systemic reactions or dies from causes attributable to the vaccine during the test.

2-3-1-1-2 Safety in the pigs used in test 2-3-2 for immunogenicity. The pigs used in the test for immunogenicity are also used to evaluate safety. Measure the body temperature of each vaccinated pig at the time of vaccination and 24 h and 48 h later. Examine the injection site at slaughter for local reactions.

The vaccine complies with the test if no pig shows:
— abnormal body temperature;
— other systemic reactions (for example, anorexia);
— abnormal local reactions attributable to the vaccine.

2-3-1-2 Field studies. The pigs used for field trials are also used to evaluate safety. Carry out a test in each category of pigs for which the vaccine is intended (sows, fattening pigs). Use not fewer than 3 groups each of not fewer than 20 pigs in at least 2 locations with corresponding groups of not fewer than 10 controls. Measure the body temperature of each vaccinated pig at the time of vaccination and 24 h and 48 h later. Examine the injection site at slaughter for local reactions.

The vaccine complies with the test if no pig shows:
— abnormal body temperature;
— abnormal local reactions attributable to the vaccine.

2-3-2 Immunogenicity

The following test carried out using an epidemiologically relevant challenge strain or strains is suitable to demonstrate the immunogenicity of the vaccine. It is carried out for each subtype used in the preparation of the vaccine.

A test is carried out for each route and method of administration to be recommended, using in each case pigs of the minimum age to be recommended for vaccination. The vaccine administered to each pig is of minimum potency.

Use for the test not fewer than 20 pigs that do not have antibodies against swine influenza virus. Vaccinate not fewer than 10 pigs according to the schedule to be recommended. Maintain not fewer than 10 pigs as controls. Take a blood sample from all control pigs immediately before challenge. 3 weeks after the last administration of vaccine, challenge all the pigs by the intratracheal route with a sufficient quantity of a virulent influenza field virus. Euthanise half of the vaccinated and control pigs 24 h after challenge and the other half 72 h after challenge. For each pig, measure the quantity of influenza virus in 2 lung tissue homogenates, one from the left apical, cardiac and diaphragmatic lobes, and the other from the corresponding right lung lobes. Take equivalent samples from each pig.

The test is not valid if antibodies against influenza virus are found in any control pig immediately before challenge. The vaccine complies with the test if, at both times of measurement, the mean virus titre in the pooled lung tissue samples of vaccinated pigs is significantly lower than that for control pigs, when analysed by a suitable statistical method such as the Wilcoxon Mann-Whitney test.

2-4 MANUFACTURER'S TESTS

2-4-1 Residual live virus

An amplification test for residual live virus is carried out on each batch of antigen immediately after inactivation by passage in the same type of substrate as that used for production (eggs or cell cultures) or a substrate shown to be at least as sensitive. The quantity of inactivated virus harvest used in the test is equivalent to not less than 10 doses of the vaccine. The inactivated viral harvest complies with the test if no live virus is detected.

2-4-2 Batch potency test

It is not necessary to carry out the potency test (section 3-5) for each batch of vaccine if it has been carried out using a batch of vaccine with a minimum potency. Where the test is not carried out, an alternative validated method is used, the criteria for acceptance being set with reference to a batch of vaccine that has given satisfactory results in the test described under Potency. The following test may be used.

Use 5 guinea-pigs, 5-7 weeks old and that do not have antibodies against swine influenza virus. Vaccinate each guinea-pig by the subcutaneous route with a quarter of the recommended dose. Collect blood samples before the vaccination and 21 days after vaccination. Determine for each sample the level of specific antibodies against each virus subtype in the vaccine by haemagglutination-inhibition or another suitable test. The vaccine complies with the test if the level of antibodies is not lower than that found for a batch of vaccine that gave satisfactory results in the potency test in pigs (see Potency).

2-4-3 Bacterial endotoxins

For vaccines produced in eggs, the content of bacterial endotoxins is determined on the virus harvest to monitor production.

3 BATCH TESTS

3-1 Identification

When injected into healthy animals that do not have specific antibodies against the influenza virus subtypes included in the vaccine, the vaccine stimulates the production of such antibodies. The antibodies may be detected by a suitable immunochemical method (*2.7.1*).

3-2 Bacteria and fungi

The vaccine, including where applicable the diluent supplied for reconstitution, complies with the test for sterility prescribed in the monograph *Vaccines for veterinary use (0062)*.

3-3 Residual live virus

3-3-1 Vaccines prepared in eggs. If the vaccine has been prepared in eggs, inoculate 0.2 mL into the allantoic cavity of each of 10 fertilised hen eggs, 9-11 days old. Incubate at a suitable temperature for 3 days. The death of any embryo within 24 h of inoculation is considered as non-specific mortality and the egg is discarded. The test is not valid if fewer than 80 per cent of the eggs survive. Collect the allantoic fluid of each egg, pool equal quantities and carry out a 2nd passage on fertilised eggs in the same manner. Incubate for 4 days; the vaccine complies with the test if the allantoic fluid of these eggs shows no haemagglutinating activity.

3-3-2 Vaccines prepared in cell cultures. If the vaccine has been prepared in cell cultures, carry out a suitable test for residual live virus using 2 passages in the same type of cell culture as used in the production of vaccine. The vaccine complies with the test if no live virus is detected. If the vaccine contains an oily adjuvant that interferes with this test, where possible separate the aqueous phase from the vaccine by means that do not diminish the capacity to detect residual infectious influenza virus.

3-4 Specified extraneous agents

Use not fewer than 2 pigs that do not have antibodies against swine influenza virus, against Aujeszky's disease virus and against pestiviruses. Administer to each pig by a recommended route a double dose of the vaccine, then another dose after 14 days. 14 days after the last administration, carry out tests for antibodies. The vaccine complies with the test if it does not stimulate the formation of antibodies against pestiviruses and Aujeszky's disease virus.

3-5 Potency

The vaccine complies with the requirements of the test mentioned under Immunogenicity (section 2-3-2) when administered by a recommended route and method.

Ph Eur

Turkey Infectious Rhinotracheitis Vaccine (Live)

(Ph. Eur. monograph 2461)

Ph Eur

1 DEFINITION

Turkey infectious rhinotracheitis vaccine (live) is a preparation of a suitable strain of turkey rhinotracheitis virus. This monograph applies to vaccines intended for administration to turkeys for active immunisation against turkey infectious rhinotracheitis.

2 PRODUCTION

2-1 PREPARATION OF THE VACCINE

The vaccine virus is grown in cell cultures.

2-2 SUBSTRATE FOR VIRUS PROPAGATION

2-2-1 Cell cultures

The vaccine virus is grown in cell cultures that comply with the requirements for cell cultures for production of veterinary vaccines (*5.2.4*).

2-3 SEED LOTS

2-3-1 Extraneous agents

The master seed lot complies with the tests for extraneous agents in seed lots (*2.6.24*). In these tests on the master seed lot, the organisms used are not more than 5 passages from the master seed lot at the start of the test.

2-4 CHOICE OF VACCINE VIRUS

The vaccine virus shall be shown to be satisfactory with respect to safety (*5.2.6*) and efficacy (*5.2.7*) for the turkeys for which it is intended.

The following tests for safety (section 2-4-1), increase in virulence (section 2-4-2) and immunogenicity (section 2-4-3) may be used during the demonstration of safety and efficacy.

2-4-1 Safety

Safety for the respiratory tract Carry out the test using turkeys not older than the minimum age to be recommended for vaccination and free from antibodies against turkey rhinotracheitis virus. Use vaccine virus at the least attenuated passage level that will be present in a batch of vaccine.

For each test performed in turkeys younger than 3 weeks of age, use not fewer than 10 turkeys. For each test performed in turkeys older than 3 weeks of age, use not fewer than 8 turkeys. Administer to each turkey, by the oculonasal route, a quantity of the vaccine virus equivalent to not less than 10 times the maximum virus titre likely to be contained in 1 dose of the vaccine. Observe the turkeys at least daily for at least 14 days and monitor clinical signs individually by a suitable scoring system. Mortality should be taken into account when calculating clinical scores. Record the death of any turkey and check for lesions of the respiratory tract.

The test is not valid if more than 10 per cent of the turkeys younger than 3 weeks of age show abnormal signs of disease or die from causes not attributable to the vaccine virus. For turkeys older than 3 weeks of age, the test is not valid if non-specific mortality occurs.

The vaccine virus complies with the test if no vaccinated turkey shows notable signs of disease or dies from causes attributable to the vaccine virus.

The clinical scores are used in the test described under 2-4-2.

2-4-2 Increase in virulence

Carry out the test according to general chapter *5.2.6* using turkeys younger than 3 weeks of age and free from antibodies against turkey rhinotracheitis virus. If the properties of the vaccine virus allow sequential passage through 5 groups via natural spreading, this method may be used, otherwise, passage as described below is carried out.

Administer to each turkey of the 1st group, by the oculonasal route, a quantity of the vaccine virus that will allow recovery of virus for the passages described below. 2-6 days after administration of the vaccine virus, prepare a suspension from the mucosa of the turbinates or the upper trachea, or from an oro-pharyngal or tracheal swab from not less than 5 inoculated turkeys and pool these samples. Administer 0.1 mL of the pooled samples by the oculonasal route to each turkey of the next group. Carry out this passage operation not fewer than 4 times; verify the presence of the virus at each passage. If the virus is not found at a passage level, repeat the passage by administration to a group of 10 turkeys.

If the 5th group of turkeys shows no evidence of an increase in virulence during the observation period, further testing is not required. Otherwise, carry out an additional safety test for the respiratory tract and compare the clinical signs and any relevant parameters in a group of at least 10 turkeys receiving the material used for the 1st passage and another similar group receiving the virus at the final passage level.

The vaccine virus complies with the test if no indication of an increased virulence of the virus at the final passage level compared with the material used for the 1st passage is observed or a slight increase in virulence of the virus at the final passage level may be observed for a vaccine which complies with the safety test (section 2-4-1). If virus is not recovered after an initial passage in 5 turkeys and a subsequent repeat passage in 10 turkeys, the vaccine virus also complies with the test.

2-4-3 Immunogenicity

A test is carried out for each route and method of administration to be recommended using turkeys not older than the minimum age to be recommended for vaccination and that are free from antibodies against turkey rhinotracheitis virus. The quantity of vaccine virus to be administered to each turkey is not greater than the minimum virus titre to be stated on the label and the virus is at the most attenuated passage level that will be present in a batch of the vaccine.

Clinical protection against virulent challenge Use not fewer than 30 turkeys of the same origin and free from antibodies against turkey rhinotracheitis virus. Vaccinate by a route to be recommended not fewer than 20 turkeys according to the schedule to be recommended. Maintain not fewer than 10 turkeys as controls. Challenge each turkey after 21 days by the oculonasal route with a sufficient quantity of a suitable strain of virulent turkey rhinotracheitis virus. Observe the turkeys at least daily for 10 days and monitor clinical signs individually. Record the death of any turkey and check for lesions of the respiratory tract.

The test is not valid if one or more of the following applies:
— fewer than 80 per cent of the unvaccinated turkeys show typical signs of respiratory disease following challenge with the virulent turkey rhinotracheitis virus;
— during the period between vaccination and challenge, more than 10 per cent of vaccinated or control turkeys show abnormal clinical signs or die from causes not attributable to the vaccine.

The vaccine virus complies with the test if during the observation period after challenge not fewer than 90 per cent of the vaccinated turkeys survive and show no typical clinical signs or lesions of an infection with turkey rhinotracheitis virus.

3 BATCH TESTS

3-1 Identification

The vaccine, diluted if necessary and mixed with turkey rhinotracheitis virus antiserum specific for the virus subgroup, no longer infects susceptible cell cultures (*5.2.4*) into which it is inoculated. The vaccine may also be identified using appropriate molecular biology techniques (for example RT-PCR).

3-2 Bacteria and fungi

Vaccines intended for administration by injection comply with the test for sterility prescribed in the monograph *Vaccines for veterinary use (0062)*.

Any diluent supplied for reconstitution of the vaccine complies with the test for sterility prescribed in the monograph *Vaccines for veterinary use (0062)*.

3-3 Mycoplasmas

The vaccine complies with the test for mycoplasmas (*2.6.7*).

3-4 Extraneous agents

The vaccine complies with the tests for extraneous agents in batches of finished product (*2.6.25*).

3-5 Virus titre

Titrate the vaccine virus by inoculation into suitable cell cultures (*5.2.4*). The vaccine complies with the test if 1 dose contains not less than the minimum titre of vaccine virus stated on the label.

3-6 Potency

The vaccine complies with the requirements of the test prescribed under Immunogenicity (section 2-4-3) when administered according to the recommended schedule by a recommended route and method. It is not necessary to carry out the potency test for each batch of the vaccine if it has been carried out on a representative batch using a vaccinating dose containing not more than the minimum virus titre stated on the label.

———————————————————— Ph Eur

Cold-water Vibriosis Vaccine for Salmonids, Inactivated

(Vibriosis (Cold-water) Vaccine (Inactivated) for Salmonids, Ph Eur monograph 1580)

Ph Eur _____

1 DEFINITION

Cold-water vibriosis vaccine (inactivated) for salmonids is prepared from cultures of one or more suitable strains of *Vibrio salmonicida*, inactivated while maintaining adequate immunogenic properties. This monograph applies to vaccines intended for administration by injection or immersion for the active immunisation of salmonids against cold-water vibriosis.

2 PRODUCTION
2-1 PREPARATION OF THE VACCINE

The strains of *V. salmonicida* are cultured and harvested separately. The harvests are inactivated by a suitable method. They may be purified and concentrated. Whole or disrupted cells may be used and the vaccine may contain extracellular products of the bacterium released into the growth medium.

2-2 CHOICE OF VACCINE COMPOSITION

The strain or strains of *V. salmonicida* used are shown to be suitable with respect to production of antigens of assumed protective importance. The vaccine is shown to be satisfactory with respect to safety (*5.2.6*) and efficacy (*5.2.7*) in the species of fish for which it is intended.

The following tests for safety (section 2-2-1) and immunogenicity (section 2-2-2) may be used during the demonstration of safety and efficacy.

2-2-1 Safety

2-2-1-1 Laboratory tests. Safety is tested using test 2-2-1-1-1, test 2-2-1-1-2, or both, depending on the recommendations for use.

Carry out the test in each species of fish for which the vaccine is intended, using fish of the minimum body mass to be recommended for vaccination. Use a batch of vaccine containing not less than the maximum potency that may be expected in a batch of vaccine. The test is carried out in the conditions to be recommended for use of the vaccine with a water temperature not less than 10 °C.

2-2-1-1-1 Vaccines intended for administration by injection. Use not fewer than 50 fish from a population that does not have specific antibodies against *V. salmonicida* and has not been vaccinated against or exposed to cold-water vibriosis. Administer to each fish by the intraperitoneal route 1 dose of the vaccine. Observe the fish at least daily for 21 days.

The test is not valid if more than 6 per cent of the fish die from causes not attributable to the vaccine. The vaccine complies with the test if no fish shows abnormal local or systemic reactions or dies from causes attributable to the vaccine.

2-2-1-1-2 Vaccines intended for administration by immersion. Use not fewer than 50 fish from a population that does not have specific antibodies against *V. salmonicida* and has not been vaccinated against or exposed to cold-water vibriosis. Prepare an immersion bath at twice the concentration to be recommended. Bathe the fish for twice the time to be recommended. Observe the fish at least daily for 21 days.

The test is not valid if more than 6 per cent of the fish die from causes not attributable to the vaccine. The vaccine complies with the test if no fish shows abnormal local or systemic reactions or dies from causes attributable to the vaccine.

2-2-1-2 Field studies. Safety is demonstrated in addition in field trials by administering the dose to be recommended to a sufficient number of fish distributed in not fewer than 2 sets of premises.

The vaccine complies with the test if no fish shows abnormal reactions or dies from causes attributable to the vaccine.

2-2-2 Immunogenicity

Carry out a separate test for each fish species and each strain included in the vaccine, according to a protocol defining water source, water flow, temperature limits, and preparation of a standardised challenge. Each test is carried out for each route and method of administration to be recommended. The vaccine administered to each fish is of minimum potency.

Use for the test not fewer than 60 fish of the minimum body mass to be recommended for vaccination, from a population that does not have specific antibodies against *V. salmonicida* and has not been vaccinated against or exposed to cold-water vibriosis. Vaccinate not fewer than 30 fish according to the instructions for use. Perform mock vaccination on a control group of not fewer than 30 fish; mark vaccinated and control fish for identification. Keep all the fish in the same tank or mix equal numbers of controls and vaccinates in each tank if more than 1 tank is used. Where justified and when fish cannot be marked, non-marked fish may be used. Vaccinates and controls may then be kept in the same tank but physically separated (for example by fishing nets). Challenge each fish at a fixed interval after vaccination, corresponding to the onset of immunity claimed, by a suitable route, with a sufficient quantity of a culture of *V. salmonicida* whose virulence has been verified. Observe the fish at least daily until at least 60 per cent specific mortality is reached in the control group. Plot for both vaccinates and controls a curve of specific mortality against time from challenge and determine by interpolation the time corresponding to 60 per cent specific mortality in controls.

The test is not valid if the specific mortality is less than 60 per cent in the control group 21 days after the 1st death in the fish. Read from the curve for vaccinates the mortality (M) at the time corresponding to 60 per cent mortality in controls. Calculate the relative percentage survival (RPS) using the following expression:

$$\left(1 - \frac{M}{60}\right) \times 100$$

The vaccine complies with the test if the RPS is not less than 60 per cent for vaccines administered by immersion and 90 per cent for vaccines administered by injection.

2-3 MANUFACTURER'S TESTS
2-3-1 Batch potency test
The potency test (section 3-3) may be carried out for each batch of vaccine using fish of one of the species for which the vaccine is intended. Where the test is not carried out, an alternative validated method based on antibody response may be used, the criteria for acceptance being set with reference to a batch of vaccine that has given satisfactory results in the test described under Potency. The following test may be used.

Use not fewer than 35 fish from a population that does not have specific antibodies against *V. salmonicida* and that are within specified limits for body mass. Carry out the test at a defined temperature. Inject into each of not fewer than 25 fish 1 dose of vaccine, according to the instructions for use. Perform mock vaccination on a control group of not fewer than 10 fish. Collect blood samples at a defined time after vaccination. Determine for each sample the level of specific antibodies against *V. salmonicida* by a suitable immunochemical method (*2.7.1*). The test is not valid if the control group shows antibodies against *V. salmonicida*. The vaccine complies with the test if the mean level of antibodies in the vaccinates is not significantly lower than that found for a batch that gave satisfactory results in the test described under Potency.

3 BATCH TESTS
3-1 Identification
When injected into fish that do not have specific antibodies against *V. salmonicida*, the vaccine stimulates the production of such antibodies.

3-2 Bacteria and fungi
The vaccine, including where applicable the diluent supplied for reconstitution, complies with the test for sterility prescribed in the monograph *Vaccines for veterinary use* (*0062*).

3-3 Potency
The vaccine complies with the requirements of the test mentioned under Immunogenicity (section 2-2-2) when administered by a recommended route and method.

4 LABELLING
The label states information on the time needed for development of immunity after vaccination under the range of conditions corresponding to the recommended use.

_____ *Ph Eur*

Vibriosis Vaccine for Salmonids, Inactivated

(Vibriosis Vaccine (Inactivated) for Salmonids, Ph Eur monograph 1581)

Ph Eur _____

1 DEFINITION
Vibriosis vaccine (inactivated) for salmonids is prepared from cultures of one or more suitable strains or serovars of *Listonella anguillarum* (*Vibrio anguillarum*), inactivated while

maintaining adequate immunogenic properties; the vaccine may also include *Vibrio ordalii*. This monograph applies to vaccines intended for administration by injection or immersion for the active immunisation of salmonids against vibriosis.

2 PRODUCTION
2-1 PREPARATION OF THE VACCINE

The strains of *L. anguillarum* and *V. ordalii* are cultured and harvested separately. The harvests are inactivated by a suitable method. They may be purified and concentrated. Whole or disrupted cells may be used and the vaccine may contain extracellular products of the bacterium released into the growth medium.

2-2 CHOICE OF VACCINE COMPOSITION

The strains of *L. anguillarum* and *V. ordalii* used are shown to be suitable with respect to production of antigens of assumed protective importance. The vaccine is shown to be satisfactory with respect to safety (*5.2.6*) and efficacy (*5.2.7*) in the species of fish for which it is intended.

The following tests for safety (section 2-2-1) and immunogenicity (section 2-2-2) may be used during the demonstration of safety and efficacy.

2-2-1 Safety

2-2-1-1 Laboratory tests. Safety is tested using test 2-2-1-1-1, test 2-2-1-1-2, or both, depending on the recommendations for use.

Carry out the test in each species of fish for which the vaccine is intended, using fish of the minimum body mass to be recommended for vaccination. Use a batch of vaccine containing not less than the maximum potency that may be expected in a batch of vaccine. The test is carried out in the conditions to be recommended for use of the vaccine with a water temperature not less than 10 °C.

2-2-1-1-1 Vaccines intended for administration by injection. Use not fewer than 50 fish from a population that does not have specific antibodies against *L. anguillarum* or where applicable *V. ordalii* and has not been vaccinated against or exposed to vibriosis. Administer to each fish by the intraperitoneal route 1 dose of the vaccine. Observe the fish at least daily for 21 days.

The test is not valid if more than 6 per cent of the fish die from causes not attributable to the vaccine. The vaccine complies with the test if no fish shows abnormal local or systemic reactions or dies from causes attributable to the vaccine.

2-2-1-1-2 Vaccines intended for administration by immersion. Use not fewer than 50 fish from a population that does not have specific antibodies against *L. anguillarum* or where applicable *V. ordalii* and has not been vaccinated against or exposed to vibriosis. Prepare an immersion bath at twice the concentration to be recommended. Bathe the fish for twice the time to be recommended. Observe the fish at least daily for 21 days.

The test is not valid if more than 6 per cent of the fish die from causes not attributable to the vaccine. The vaccine complies with the test if no fish shows abnormal local or systemic reactions or dies from causes attributable to the vaccine.

2-2-1-2 Field studies. Safety is demonstrated in addition in field trials by administering the dose to be recommended to a sufficient number of fish distributed in not fewer than 2 sets of premises.

The vaccine complies with the test if no fish shows abnormal reactions or dies from causes attributable to the vaccine.

2-2-2 Immunogenicity

Carry out a separate test for each fish species and each serovar included in the vaccine, according to a protocol defining water source, water flow and temperature limits, and preparation of a standardised challenge. Each test is carried out for each route and method of administration to be recommended. The vaccine administered to each fish is of minimum potency.

Use for the test not fewer than 60 fish of the minimum body mass to be recommended for vaccination, from a population that does not have specific antibodies against *L. anguillarum* or where applicable *V. ordalii* and has not been vaccinated against or exposed to vibriosis. Vaccinate not fewer than 30 fish according to the instructions for use. Perform mock vaccination on a control group of not fewer than 30 fish; mark vaccinated and control fish for identification. Keep all the fish in the same tank or mix equal numbers of controls and vaccinates in each tank if more than 1 tank is used. Where justified and when fish cannot be marked, non-marked fish may be used. Vaccinates and controls may then be kept in the same tank but physically separated (for example by fishing nets). Challenge each fish at a fixed interval after vaccination, corresponding to the onset of immunity claimed, by a suitable route with a sufficient quantity of cultures of *L. anguillarum* or *V. ordalii* whose virulence has been verified. Observe the fish at least daily until at least 60 per cent specific mortality is reached in the control group. Plot for both vaccinates and controls a curve of specific mortality against time from challenge and determine by interpolation the time corresponding to 60 per cent specific mortality in controls.

The test is not valid if the specific mortality is less than 60 per cent in the control group 21 days after the 1st death in the fish. Read from the curve for vaccinates the mortality (M) at the time corresponding to 60 per cent mortality in controls. Calculate the relative percentage survival (RPS) using the following expression:

$$\left(1 - \frac{M}{60}\right) \times 100$$

The vaccine complies with the test if the RPS is not less than 60 per cent for vaccines administered by immersion and 75 per cent for vaccines administered by injection.

2-3 MANUFACTURER'S TESTS
2-3-1 Batch potency test

The potency test (section 3-3) may be carried out for each batch of vaccine, using fish of one of the species for which the vaccine is intended. Where the test is not carried out, an alternative validated method based on antibody response may be used, the criteria for acceptance being set with reference to a batch of vaccine that has given satisfactory results in the test described under Potency. The following test may be used.

Use not fewer than 35 fish from a population that does not have specific antibodies against *L. anguillarum* included in the vaccine and where applicable against *V. ordalii*, and that are within specified limits for body mass. Carry out the test at a defined temperature. Inject into each of not fewer than 25 fish 1 dose of vaccine, according to the instructions for use. Perform mock vaccination on a control group of not fewer than 10 fish. Collect blood samples at a defined time after vaccination. Determine for each sample the level of specific antibodies against *L. anguillarum* included in the vaccine and where applicable against *V. ordalii*, by a suitable immunochemical method (*2.7.1*). The test is not valid if the control group shows antibodies against *L. anguillarum* or, where applicable, against *V. ordalii*. The vaccine complies with the test if the mean level of antibodies in the vaccinates is not significantly lower than that found for a batch that gave satisfactory results in the test described under Potency.

3 BATCH TESTS
3-1 Identification
When injected into fish that do not have specific antibodies against *L. anguillarum* and, where applicable, *V. ordalii*, the vaccine stimulates the production of such antibodies.

3-2 Bacteria and fungi
The vaccine, including where applicable the diluent supplied for reconstitution, complies with the test for sterility prescribed in the monograph *Vaccines for veterinary use (0062)*.

3-3 Potency
The vaccine complies with the requirements of the test mentioned under Immunogenicity (section 2-2-2) when administered by a recommended route and method.

4 LABELLING
The label states information on the time needed for the development of immunity after vaccination under the range of conditions corresponding to the recommended use.

——————————————————————— *Ph Eur*

Enteric Redmouth Disease Vaccine for Rainbow Trout (Inactivated)

Yersiniosis Vaccine (Inactivated) for Salmonids (Ph. Eur. monograph 1950)

Ph Eur ————————

1 DEFINITION
Yersiniosis vaccine (inactivated) for salmonids is prepared from cultures of serovars 1 or 2 of *Yersinia ruckeri*, inactivated while maintaining adequate immunogenic properties. This monograph applies to vaccines intended for administration by injection or immersion for the active immunisation of salmonids against yersiniosis.

2 PRODUCTION
2-1 PREPARATION OF THE VACCINE
The strains of *Y. ruckeri* are harvested and inactivated by a suitable method. They may be purified and concentrated. Whole or disrupted cells may be used and the vaccine may contain extracellular products of the bacterium released into the growth medium.

2-2 CHOICE OF VACCINE COMPOSITION
The strains of *Y. ruckeri* used are shown to be suitable with respect to the production of antigens of assumed protective importance. The vaccine is shown to be satisfactory with respect to safety (*5.2.6*) and efficacy (*5.2.7*) in the species of fish for which it is intended.

The following tests for safety (section 2-2-1) and immunogenicity (section 2-2-2) may be used during the demonstration of safety and efficacy.

2-2-1 Safety
2-2-1-1 Laboratory tests. Safety is tested using test 2-2-1-1-1, test 2-2-1-1-2, or both, depending on the recommendations for use.

Carry out the test in each species of fish for which the vaccine is intended, using in each case fish of the minimum body mass to be recommended for vaccination. Use a batch of vaccine containing not less than the maximum potency that may be expected in a batch of vaccine. The test is carried out in the conditions to be recommended for use of the vaccine with a water temperature not less than 10 °C.

2-2-1-1-1 Vaccines intended for administration by injection. Use not fewer than 50 fish from a population that does not have specific antibodies against the relevant serovars of *Y. ruckeri* and has not been vaccinated against or exposed to yersiniosis. Where the size of the fish for the test is such that a blood sample cannot be removed for antibody testing, a number of larger fish may be kept with the group for this purpose. Administer to each fish by the intraperitoneal route 1 dose of the vaccine. Observe the fish at least daily for 21 days.

The test is not valid if more than 6 per cent of the fish die from causes not attributable to the vaccine. The vaccine complies with the test if no fish shows abnormal local or systemic reactions or dies from causes attributable to the vaccine.

2-2-1-1-2 Vaccines intended for administration by immersion. Use not fewer than 50 fish from a population that does not have specific antibodies against the relevant serovars of *Y. ruckeri* and has not been vaccinated against or exposed to yersiniosis. Where the size of the fish for the test is such that a blood sample cannot be removed for antibody testing, a number of larger fish may be kept with the group for this purpose. Prepare an immersion bath at twice the concentration to be recommended. Bathe the fish for twice the time to be recommended. Observe the fish at least daily for 21 days.

The test is not valid if more than 6 per cent of the fish die from causes not attributable to the vaccine. The vaccine complies with the test if no fish shows abnormal local or systemic reactions or dies from causes attributable to the vaccine.

2-2-2 Immunogenicity
Carry out a separate test for each fish species and each serovar included in the vaccine, according to a protocol defining water source, water flow and temperature limits, and preparation of a standardised challenge. Each test is carried out for each route and method of administration to be recommended. Where the size of the fish for the test is such that a blood sample cannot be removed for antibody testing, a number of larger fish of the same origin may be selected for this purpose. The vaccine administered to each fish is of minimum potency.

Use for the test not fewer than 60 fish of the minimum body mass to be recommended for vaccination, from a population that does not have specific antibodies against the relevant serovars of *Y. ruckeri* and has not been vaccinated against or exposed to yersiniosis. Vaccinate not fewer than 30 fish according to the instructions for use. Perform mock vaccination on a control group of not fewer than 30 fish; mark vaccinated and control fish for identification. Keep all the fish in the same tank or mix equal numbers of controls and vaccinates in each tank if more than 1 tank is used. Where justified and when fish cannot be marked, non-marked fish may be used. Vaccinates and controls may then be kept in the same tank but physically separated (for example by fishing nets). Challenge each fish at a fixed interval after vaccination, corresponding to the onset of immunity claimed, by injection or immersion, with a sufficient quantity of cultures of *Y. ruckeri* whose virulence has been verified or, where all fish are kept in the same tank, with a sufficient challenge by cohabitation. Observe the fish at least daily until at least 60 per cent specific mortality is reached in the control group. Plot for both vaccinates and controls a curve of specific mortality against time and determine by interpolation the time corresponding to 60 per cent specific mortality in controls.

The test is not valid if the specific mortality is less than 60 per cent in the control group 21 days after the 1st death in the fish. Read from the curve for vaccinates the mortality (*M*) at the time corresponding to 60 per cent mortality in controls. Calculate the relative percentage survival (RPS) using the following expression:

$$\left(1 - \frac{M}{60}\right) \times 100$$

For serovar 1 vaccines, the vaccine complies with the test if the RPS is not less than 75 per cent for vaccines administered by immersion and 90 per cent for vaccines administered by injection.

For serovar 2 vaccines, the vaccine complies with the test if the RPS is not less than 60 per cent for vaccines administered by immersion and 85 per cent for vaccines administered by injection.

2-3 MANUFACTURER'S TESTS
2-3-1 Batch potency test
The potency test (section 3-3) may be carried out for each batch of the vaccine, using fish of one of the species for which the vaccine is intended. Where the test is not carried out, an alternative validated method based on antibody response in fish or other vertebrate animals may be used, the criteria for acceptance being set with reference to a batch of vaccine that has given satisfactory results in the test described under Potency. The following test may be used.

Use not fewer than 25 fish from a population that does not have specific antibodies against the relevant serovars of *Y. ruckeri* and that are within specified limits for body mass. Carry out the test at a defined temperature. Inject into each of not fewer than 20 fish 1 dose of vaccine, according to the instructions for use. Perform mock vaccination on a control group of not fewer than 5 fish. Collect blood samples at a defined time after vaccination. Determine for each sample the level of specific antibodies against the relevant serovars of *Y. ruckeri* included in the vaccine by a suitable immunochemical method (*2.7.1*).

The test is not valid if the control group shows antibodies against the relevant serovars of *Y. ruckeri*. The vaccine complies with the test if the mean level of antibodies in the vaccinates is not significantly lower than that found for a batch that gave satisfactory results in the test described under Potency.

3 BATCH TESTS
3-1 Identification
When injected into animals that do not have specific antibodies against the relevant serovars of *Y. ruckeri*, the vaccine stimulates the production of such antibodies or protects against virulent challenge with *Y. ruckeri*.

3-2 Bacteria and fungi
The vaccine, including where applicable the diluent supplied for reconstitution, complies with the test for sterility prescribed in the monograph *Vaccines for veterinary use (0062)*.

3-3 Potency
The vaccine complies with the requirements of the test mentioned under Immunogenicity (section 2-2-2) when administered by a recommended route and method.

4 LABELLING
The label states information on the time needed for development of immunity after vaccination under the range of conditions corresponding to the recommended use.

_____ *Ph Eur*

DIAGNOSTIC PREPARATIONS

Avian Tuberculin Purified Protein Derivative

Avian Tuberculin P.P.D.

(Ph. Eur. monograph 0535)

Ph Eur _____

DEFINITION

Avian tuberculin purified protein derivative (avian tuberculin PPD) is a preparation obtained from the heat-treated products of growth and lysis of *Mycobacterium avium* capable of revealing a delayed hypersensitivity in an animal sensitised to micro-organisms of the same species.

PRODUCTION

It is obtained from the water-soluble fractions prepared by heating in free-flowing steam and subsequently filtering cultures of *M. avium* grown in a liquid synthetic medium. The active fraction of the filtrate, consisting mainly of protein, is isolated by precipitation, washed and re-dissolved. An antimicrobial preservative that does not give rise to false positive reactions, such as phenol, may be added. The final sterile preparation, free from mycobacteria, is distributed aseptically into sterile tamper-proof glass containers, which are then closed so as to prevent contamination.

The preparation may be freeze-dried.

The identification, the tests and the determination of potency apply to the liquid form and to the freeze-dried form after reconstitution as stated on the label.

IDENTIFICATION

Inject a range of graded doses intradermally at different sites into suitably sensitised albino guinea-pigs, each weighing not less than 250 g. After 24-28 h, reactions appear in the form of oedematous swellings with erythema, with or without necrosis, at the points of injection. The size and severity of the reactions vary according to the dose. Unsensitised guinea-pigs show no reactions to similar injections.

TESTS

pH *(2.2.3)*

6.5 to 7.5.

Phenol *(2.5.15)*

Maximum 5 g/L, if the preparation to be examined contains phenol.

Sensitising effect

Use a group of 3 guinea-pigs that have not been treated with any material that will interfere with the test. On 3 occasions at intervals of 5 days, inject intradermally into each guinea-pig a dose of the preparation to be examined equivalent to 500 IU in 0.1 mL. 15-21 days after the 3rd injection, inject the same dose (500 IU) intradermally into these animals and into a control group of 3 guinea-pigs of the same mass, which have not previously received injections of tuberculin. 24-28 h after the last injections, the reactions of the 2 groups are not significantly different.

Toxicity

Use 2 guinea-pigs, each weighing not less than 250 g, that have not previously been treated with any material that will interfere with the test. Inject subcutaneously into each guinea-pig 0.5 mL of the preparation to be examined. Observe the animals for 7 days. No abnormal effects occur during the observation period.

Sterility

It complies with the test for sterility prescribed in the monograph *Vaccines for veterinary use (0062)*.

POTENCY

The potency of avian tuberculin purified protein derivative is determined by comparing the reactions produced in sensitised guinea-pigs by the intradermal injection of a series of dilutions of the preparation to be examined with those produced by known concentrations of a reference preparation calibrated in International Units.

The International Unit is the activity contained in a stated amount of the International Standard. The equivalence in International Units of the International Standard is stated by the World Health Organization.

Sensitise not fewer than 8 albino guinea-pigs, each weighing 400-600 g, by the deep intramuscular injection of a suitable dose of inactivated or live *M. avium*. Not less than 4 weeks after the sensitisation of the guinea-pigs, shave their flanks to provide space for not more than 4 injection sites on each side. Prepare dilutions of the preparation to be examined and of the reference preparation using isotonic phosphate-buffered saline (pH 6.5-7.5) containing 0.005 g/L of *polysorbate 80 R*. Use not fewer than 3 doses of the reference preparation and not fewer than 3 doses of the preparation to be examined. Choose the doses such that the lesions produced have a diameter of not less than 8 mm and not more than 25 mm. Allocate the dilutions randomly to the sites, for example using a Latin square design. Inject each dose intradermally in a constant volume of 0.1 mL or 0.2 mL. Measure the diameters of the lesions after 24-28 h and calculate the results of the test using the usual statistical methods (for example, *5.3*) and assuming that the diameters of the lesions are directly proportional to the logarithm of the concentration of the tuberculins.

The test is not valid unless the confidence limits ($P = 0.95$) are not less than 50 per cent and not more than 200 per cent of the estimated potency. The estimated potency is not less than 75 per cent and not more than 133 per cent of the stated potency. The stated potency is not less than 20 000 IU/mL.

STORAGE

Protected from light, at a temperature of 5 ± 3 °C.

LABELLING

The label states:

— the potency in International Units per millilitre;

— the name and quantity of any excipient;

— for freeze-dried preparations:

    — the name and volume of the reconstituting liquid to be added;

    — that the product is to be used immediately after reconstitution.

_____ *Ph Eur*

Bovine Tuberculin Purified Protein Derivative

Bovine Tuberculin P.P.D.

(Ph. Eur. monograph 0536)

Ph Eur

DEFINITION

Bovine tuberculin purified protein derivative (bovine tuberculin PPD) is a preparation obtained from the heat-treated products of growth and lysis of *Mycobacterium bovis* capable of revealing a delayed hypersensitivity in an animal sensitised to micro-organisms of the same species.

PRODUCTION

It is obtained from the water-soluble fractions prepared by heating in free-flowing steam and subsequently filtering cultures of *M. bovis* grown in a liquid synthetic medium. The active fraction of the filtrate, consisting mainly of protein, is isolated by precipitation, washed and re-dissolved. An antimicrobial preservative that does not give rise to false positive reactions, such as phenol, may be added. The final sterile preparation, free from mycobacteria, is distributed aseptically into sterile, tamper-proof glass containers, which are then closed so as to prevent contamination.
The preparation may be freeze-dried.

The identification, the tests and the determination of potency apply to the liquid form and to the freeze-dried form after reconstitution as stated on the label.

IDENTIFICATION

Inject a range of graded doses intradermally at different sites into suitably sensitised albino guinea-pigs, each weighing not less than 250 g. After 24-28 h, reactions appear in the form of oedematous swellings with erythema, with or without necrosis, at the points of injection. The size and severity of the reactions vary according to the dose. Unsensitised guinea-pigs show no reactions to similar injections.

TESTS

pH *(2.2.3)*
6.5 to 7.5.

Phenol *(2.5.15)*
Maximum 5 g/L, if the preparation to be examined contains phenol.

Sensitising effect

Use a group of 3 guinea-pigs that have not been treated with any material that will interfere with the test. On 3 occasions at intervals of 5 days, inject intradermally into each guinea-pig a dose of the preparation to be examined equivalent to 500 IU in 0.1 mL. 15-21 days after the 3rd injection, inject the same dose (500 IU) intradermally into these animals and into a control group of 3 guinea-pigs of the same mass, which have not previously received injections of tuberculin. 24-28 h after the last injections, the reactions of the 2 groups are not significantly different.

Toxicity

Use 2 guinea-pigs, each weighing not less than 250 g, that have not previously been treated with any material that will interfere with the test. Inject subcutaneously into each guinea-pig 0.5 mL of the preparation to be examined. Observe the animals for 7 days. No abnormal effects occur during the observation period.

Sterility

It complies with the test for sterility prescribed in the monograph *Vaccines for veterinary use (0062)*.

POTENCY

The potency of bovine tuberculin purified protein derivative is determined by comparing the reactions produced in sensitised guinea-pigs by the intradermal injection of a series of dilutions of the preparation to be examined with those produced by known concentrations of a reference preparation calibrated in International Units.

The International Unit is the activity contained in a stated amount of the International Standard. The equivalence in International Units of the International Standard is stated by the World Health Organization.

Sensitise not fewer than 8 albino guinea-pigs, each weighing 400-600 g, by the deep intramuscular injection of 0.0001 mg of wet mass of living *M. bovis* of strain AN5 suspended in 0.5 mL of a 9 g/L solution of *sodium chloride R*. Not less than 4 weeks after the sensitisation of the guinea-pigs, shave their flanks to provide space for not more than 4 injection sites on each side. Prepare dilutions of the preparation to be examined and of the reference preparation using isotonic phosphate-buffered saline (pH 6.5-7.5) containing 0.005 g/L of *polysorbate 80 R*. Use not fewer than 3 doses of the reference preparation and not fewer than 3 doses of the preparation to be examined. Choose the doses such that the lesions produced have a diameter of not less than 8 mm and not more than 25 mm. Allocate the dilutions randomly to the sites, for example using a Latin square design. Inject each dose intradermally in a constant volume of 0.1 mL or 0.2 mL. Measure the diameters of the lesions after 24-28 h and calculate the results of the test using the usual statistical methods (for example, *5.3*) and assuming that the diameters of the lesions are directly proportional to the logarithm of the concentration of the tuberculins.

The test is not valid unless the confidence limits ($P = 0.95$) are not less than 50 per cent and not more than 200 per cent of the estimated potency. The estimated potency is not less than 66 per cent and not more than 150 per cent of the stated potency. The stated potency is not less than 20 000 IU/mL.

STORAGE

Protected from light, at a temperature of $5 \pm 3\ °C$.

LABELLING

The label states:
— the potency in International Units per millilitre;
— the name and quantity of any excipient;
— for freeze-dried preparations:
— the name and volume of the reconstituting liquid to be added;
— that the product is to be used immediately after reconstitution.

Ph Eur

Mallein Purified Protein Derivative

Mallein P.P.D.

DEFINITION

Mallein Purified Protein Derivative is a preparation of the heat treated products of growth and lysis of *Pseudomonas mallei*. It contains not less than 0.95 mg per mL and not more than 1.05 mg per mL of purified protein derivative.

PRODUCTION

It is prepared from the water-soluble fractions obtained by heating in free-flowing steam and subsequently filtering cultures of the glanders bacillus grown in a liquid synthetic medium. The active fraction of the filtrate, which is predominantly protein, is isolated by precipitation, washed and redissolved in phosphate buffered saline at neutral pH. It is then distributed in sterile containers that are inert towards the contents and sealed so as to exclude micro-organisms. A suitable preservative may be added.

CAUTION *Mallein P.P.D. is not dangerous to man, but the organism from which it is prepared is pathogenic to man and may be fatal if an infection is untreated. If an infection is suspected treatment should begin without delay.*

IDENTIFICATION

Inject small doses intradermally into suitable guinea-pigs that have been sensitised with killed *P. mallei* in oily adjuvant. Oedematous swellings occur at the point of injection after 48 hours.

TESTS

Acidity or alkalinity
pH, 6.5 to 7.5, Appendix V L.

Phenol
For preparations containing phenol as a preservative, not more than 0.5% w/v, determined by the method described under Veterinary Antisera.

Sterility
Complies with the *test for sterility,* Appendix XVI A, using Method I: Membrane filtration, whenever possible and particularly when the volume in a container is greater than 100 mL, with the following modifications.

Incubate the media for not less than 14 days at 30° to 35° in the test intended to detect bacteria and at 20° to 25° in the test intended to detect fungi.

Use the quantities stated under Application of the test to injectable preparations except that when the quantity in each container[1] is 20 mL or more of a liquid, the minimum quantity to be used for each medium is 10% of the contents or 5 mL, whichever is the less.

Abnormal toxicity
Inject 0.5 mL subcutaneously into each of two guinea-pigs. Neither shows a significant local or systemic reaction within 7 days.

ASSAY

To 2.5 mL add 2.5 mL of *water* and 2.5 mL of a 40% w/v solution of *trichloroacetic acid*, mix, allow to stand for 30 minutes and centrifuge for 15 minutes. Discard the supernatant liquid and dissolve the residue in 0.5 mL of 5M *sodium hydroxide.* Transfer the solution to a Kjeldahl flask with the aid of 6 mL of *water* and add about 0.1 g of a mixture of 100 parts of *potassium sulfate*, 10 parts of *copper(II) sulfate* and 5 parts of *selenium dioxide* and 1 mL of *nitrogen-free sulfuric acid.* Evaporate the water and continue heating until a brown deposit appears. Dissolve the deposit by the addition of 0.5 mL of *hydrogen peroxide solution (100 vol)*, continue heating until white fumes of sulfur trioxide appear and boil rapidly for at least 10 minutes. (If while heating a brown deposit again appears, add a further 0.5 mL of *hydrogen peroxide solution (100 vol)*. Transfer to an ammonia distillation apparatus with the aid of 5 mL of *water* and add 5 mL of a 50% w/v solution of *sodium hydroxide* to form a lower layer. Distil for 3 minutes, collecting the distillate in a mixture of 5 mL of a 2% w/v solution of *boric acid* and 0.05 mL of a solution containing 0.066% w/v of *methyl red* and 0.033% w/v of *bromocresol green* in *ethanol (96%)* and titrate with 0.00447M *sulfuric acid VS* (prepared by diluting 89.3 mL of 0.05M *sulfuric acid VS* to 1000 mL with *water*).

Repeat the operation using 2.5 mL of *water* in place of the preparation being examined. The difference between the titrations represents the ammonia liberated by the substance being tested. Each mL of 0.00447M *sulfuric acid VS* is equivalent to 0.875 mg of purified protein derivative.

STORAGE

Mallein Purified Protein Derivative should be protected from light and stored at a temperature between 2° and 8°. Under these conditions it may be expected to retain its potency for not less than 6 months.

LABELLING

The label states (1) the volume of the contents; (2) the date after which the preparation is not intended to be used; (3) that the preparation is to be used for animals only; (4) the conditions under which it should be stored; (5) the name and percentage of any added preservative; (6) the dose.

ANNEX

Guidance to manufacturers performing the test for sterility. In determining the number of containers to be tested, the manufacturer should have regard to the environmental conditions of manufacture, the volume of preparation per container and any other special considerations applying to the preparation concerned. With respect to diagnostic preparations for veterinary use, 1% of the containers in a batch, with a minimum of three and a maximum of 10 is considered a suitable number assuming that the preparation has been manufactured under appropriately validated conditions designed to exclude contamination.

---

[1] Guidance to manufacturers on the number of containers is provided in the Annex to this monograph.

Monographs

Surgical Materials

SUTURES

Sterile Catgut in Distributor

(Catgut, Sterile, in Distributor for Veterinary Use,
Ph Eur monograph 0660)

Ph Eur _____

DEFINITION
Sterile catgut in distributor for veterinary use consists of
strands prepared from collagen taken from the intestinal
membranes of mammals. After cleaning, the membranes are
split longitudinally into strips of varying width, which, when
assembled in small numbers, according to the diameter
required, are twisted under tension, dried, polished, selected
and sterilised. The strands may be treated with chemical
substances such as chromium salts to prolong absorption and
glycerol to make them supple, provided such substances do
not reduce tissue acceptability.

The strand is presented in a distributor that allows the
withdrawal and use of all or part of it in aseptic conditions.
The design of the distributor is such that with suitable
handling the sterility of the content is maintained even when
part of the strand has been withdrawn. It may be stored dry
or in a preserving liquid to which an antimicrobial
preservative but not an antibiotic may be added.

TESTS
If stored in a preserving liquid, remove the strand from the
distributor and measure promptly and in succession the length,
diameter and breaking load If stored in the dry state, immerse the
strand in alcohol R or a 90 per cent V/V solution of
2-propanol R for 24 h and proceed with the measurements as
indicated above.

Length
Measure the length without applying to the strand more
tension than is necessary to keep it straight. The length is not
less than 95 per cent of the length stated on the label. If the
strand consists of several sections joined by knots, the length
of each section is not less than 2.5 m.

Diameter
Carry out the test using a suitable instrument capable of
measuring with an accuracy of at least 0.002 mm and having
a circular pressor foot 10 mm to 15 mm in diameter.
The pressor foot and the moving parts attached to it are
weighted so as to apply a total load of 100 ± 10 g to the
strand being tested. When making the measurements, lower
the pressor foot slowly to avoid crushing the strand. Make not
fewer than one measurement per 2 m of length. If the strand
consists of several sections joined by knots, make not fewer
than three measurements per section. In any case make not
fewer than twelve measurements. Make the measurements at
points evenly spaced along the strand or along each section.
The strand is not subjected to more tension than is necessary
to keep it straight during measurement. The average of the
measurements carried out on the strand being tested and not
less than two-thirds of the individual measurements are within
the limits given in the column under A in Table 0660.-1 for
the gauge number concerned. None of the measurements is
outside the limits given in the columns under B in
Table 0660.-1 for the gauge number concerned.

Minimum breaking load
The minimum breaking load is determined over a simple
knot formed by placing one end of a strand held in the right
hand over the other end held in the left hand, passing one
end over the strand and through the loop so formed (see
Figure 0660.-1) and pulling the knot tight.

Figure 0660.-1. – *Simple knot*

Make not fewer than one measurement per 2 m of length.
If the strand consists of several sections joined by knots,
make not fewer than three measurements per section and, in
any case, not fewer than one measurement per 2 m of length
at points evenly spaced along the strand or along each
section. Determine the breaking load using a suitable
tensilometer. The apparatus has two clamps for holding the
strand, one of which is mobile and is driven at a constant
rate of 30 cm per minute. The clamps are designed so that
the strand being tested can be attached without any
possibility of slipping. At the beginning of the test the length
of strand between the clamps is 12.5 cm to 20 cm and the
knot is midway between the clamps. Set the mobile clamp in
motion and note the force required to break the strand. If the
strand breaks in a clamp or within 1 cm of it, the result is
discarded and the test repeated on another part of the strand.
The average of all the results, excluding those legitimately
discarded, is equal to or greater than the value in column C
and no value is less than that given in column D in
Table 0660.-1 for the gauge number concerned.

Table 0660.-1. – *Diameters and breaking loads*

Gauge number	Diameter (millimetres)				Breaking load (newtons)	
	A		B		C	D
	min.	max.	min.	max.		
1	0.100	0.149	0.085	0.175	1.8	0.4
1.5	0.150	0.199	0.125	0.225	3.8	0.7
2	0.200	0.249	0.175	0.275	7.5	1.8
2.5	0.250	0.299	0.225	0.325	10	3.8
3	0.300	0.349	0.275	0.375	12.5	7.5
3.5	0.350	0.399	0.325	0.450	20	10
4	0.400	0.499	0.375	0.550	27.5	12.5
5	0.500	0.599	0.450	0.650	38.4	20.0
6	0.600	0.699	0.550	0.750	45.0	27.5
7	0.700	0.799	0.650	0.850	60.0	38.0
8	0.800	0.899	0.750	0.950	70.0	45.0

Soluble chromium compounds

Place 0.25 g in a conical flask containing 1 mL of *water R* per 10 mg of catgut. Stopper the flask, allow to stand at 37 ± 0.5 °C for 24 h, cool and decant the liquid. Transfer 5 mL to a small test tube and add 2 mL of a 10 g/L solution of *diphenylcarbazide R* in *alcohol R* and 2 mL of *dilute sulfuric acid R*. The solution is not more intensely coloured than a standard prepared at the same time using 5 mL of a solution containing 2.83 μg of *potassium dichromate R* per millilitre, 2 mL of *dilute sulfuric acid R* and 2 mL of a 10 g/L solution of *diphenylcarbazide R* in *alcohol R* (1 ppm of Cr).

Sterility (2.6.1)

It complies with the test for sterility as applied to catgut and other surgical sutures. Carry out the test on three sections, each 30 cm long, cut off respectively from the beginning, the centre and the end of the strand.

STORAGE

Store protected from light and heat.

LABELLING

The label states:
— the gauge number,
— the length in centimetres or in metres.

Ph Eur

Sterile Non-absorbable Strands in Distributor

(Strands, Sterile Non-absorbable, in Distributor for Veterinary Use, Ph Eur monograph 0605)

Ph Eur

DEFINITION

The statements in this monograph are intended to be read in conjunction with the individual monographs on sterile non-absorbable strands in distributor for veterinary use in the Pharmacopoeia The requirements do not necessarily apply to sterile non-absorbable strands which are not the subject of such monographs.

Sterile non-absorbable strands in distributor for veterinary use are strands which, when introduced into a living organism, are not metabolised by that organism. Sterile non-absorbable strands vary in origin, which may be animal, vegetable or synthetic. They occur as cylindrical monofilaments or as multifilament strands. Multifilament strands consist of elementary fibres which are assembled by twisting, cabling or braiding. Such strands may be sheathed. Sterile non- absorbable strands may be treated to render them non-capillary, and they may be coloured with colouring matter or pigments authorised by the competent authority. The strands are sterilised.

They are presented in a suitable distributor that allows the withdrawal and use of all or part of the strand in aseptic conditions. The design of the distributor is such that with suitable handling the sterility of the content is maintained even when part of the strand has been removed. They may be stored dry or in a preserving liquid to which an antimicrobial preservative but not an antibiotic may be added.

TESTS

Remove the strand from the distributor and measure promptly and in succession the length, diameter and minimum breaking load.

Length

Measure the length in the condition in which the strand is presented and without applying more tension than is necessary to keep it straight. The length of the strand is not less than 95 per cent of the length stated on the label.

Diameter

Unless otherwise prescribed, measure the diameter by the following method using the strand in the condition in which it is presented. Use a suitable instrument capable of measuring with an accuracy of at least 0.002 mm and having a circular pressor foot 10 mm to 15 mm in diameter. The pressor foot and the moving parts attached to it are weighted so as to apply a total load of 100 ± 10 g to the strand being tested. When making the measurements, lower the pressor foot slowly to avoid crushing the strand. Make not fewer than one measurement per 2 m of length and in any case not fewer than 12 measurements at points evenly spaced along the strand. During the measurement submit monofilament strands to a tension not greater than that required to keep them straight. Submit multifilament strands to a tension not greater than one-fifth of the minimum breaking load shown in column C of Table 0605.-1 appropriate to the gauge number and type of material concerned or 10 N whichever is less. For multifilament strands of gauge number above 1.5 make two measurements at each point, the second measurement being made after rotating the strand through 90°. The diameter of that point is the average of the two measurements. The average of the measurements carried out on the strand being tested and not less than two-thirds of the individual measurements are within the limits given in the columns under A in Table 0605.-1 for the gauge number concerned. None of the measurements is outside the limits given in the columns under B in Table 0605.-1 for the gauge number concerned.

Table 0605.-1. – *Diameters and minimum breaking loads*

Gauge number	Diameter (millimetres)				Minimum breaking load (newtons)			
	A		B		Linen thread		All other non-absorbable strands	
	min.	max.	min.	max.	C	D	C	D
0.5	0.050	0.069	0.045	0.085	-	-	1.0	0.35
0.7	0.070	0.099	0.060	0.125	1.0	0.3	1.5	0.60
1	0.100	0.149	0.085	0.175	2.5	0.6	3.0	1.0
1.5	0.150	0.199	0.125	0.225	5.0	1.0	5.0	1.5
2	0.200	0.249	0.175	0.275	8.0	2.5	9.0	3.0
2.5	0.250	0.299	0.225	0.325	9.0	5.0	13.0	5.0
3	0.300	0.349	0.275	0.375	11.0	8.0	15.0	9.0
3.5	0.350	0.399	0.325	0.450	15.0	9.0	22.0	13.0
4	0.400	0.499	0.375	0.550	18.0	11.0	27.0	15.0
5	0.500	0.599	0.450	0.650	26.0	15.0	35.0	22.0
6	0.600	0.699	0.550	0.750	37.0	18.0	50.0	27.0
7	0.700	0.799	0.650	0.850	50.0	26.0	62.0	35.0
8	0.800	0.899	0.750	0.950	65.0	37.0	73.0	50.0

Minimum breaking load

Unless otherwise prescribed, determine the minimum breaking load by the following method using the strand in the condition in which it is presented. The minimum breaking load is determined over a simple knot formed by placing one end of a strand held in the right hand over the other end held in the left hand, passing one end over the strand and through the loop so formed (see Figure 0605.-1) and pulling the knot tight.

Make not fewer than one measurement per 2 m of length at points evenly spaced along the strand. Determine the breaking load using a suitable tensilometer. The apparatus has two clamps for holding the strand, one of which is mobile and is driven at a constant rate of 30 cm per minute. The clamps are designed so that the strand being tested can be attached with-out any possibility of slipping. At the beginning of the test the length of strand between the clamps is 12.5 cm to 20 cm and the knot is midway between the clamps. Set the mobile clamp in motion and note the force required to break the strand. If the strand breaks in a clamp or within 1 cm of it, the result is discarded and the test repeated on another part of the strand. The average of all the results, excluding those legitimately dis-carded, is equal to or greater than the value in column C and no value is less than that given in column D in Table 0605.-1 for the gauge number and type of material concerned.

Figure 0605.-1. – *Simple knot*

Sterility (*2.6.1*)
They comply with the test for sterility as applied to catgut and other surgical sutures. Carry out the test on three sections each 30 cm long, cut off respectively from the beginning, the centre and the end of the strand.

Extractable colour
Strands that are dyed and intended to remain so during use comply with the test for extractable colour. Place 0.25 g of the strand to be examined in a conical flask, add 25.0 mL of *water R* and cover the mouth of the flask with a short-stemmed funnel. Boil for 15 min, cool and adjust to the original volume with *water R*. Depending on the colour of the strand, prepare the appropriate reference solution as described in Table 0605.-2 using the primary colour solutions (*2.2.2*).

Table 0605.-2. – *Colour reference solutions*

Colour of strand	Composition of reference solution (parts by volume)			
	Red primary solution	Yellow primary solution	Blue primary solution	Water
Yellow - brown	0.2	1.2	–	8.6
Pink - red	1.0	–	–	9.0
Green - blue	–	–	2.0	8.0
Violet	1.6	–	8.4	–

The test solution is not more intensely coloured than the appropriate reference solution.

STORAGE
Store protected from light and heat.

LABELLING
The label states:
— the gauge number,
— the length in centimetres or in metres,
— where appropriate, that the strand is coloured and intended to remain so during use.

_____ *Ph Eur*

Sterile Linen Thread in Distributor

(Linen Thread, Sterile, in Distributor for Veterinary Use, Ph Eur monograph 0608)

Ph Eur _____

DEFINITION
Sterile linen thread in distributor for veterinary use consists of the pericyclic fibres of the stem of *Linum usitatissimum* L. The elementary fibres, 2.5 cm to 5 cm long, are assembled in bundles 30 cm to 80 cm long and spun into continuous lengths of suitable diameter. The thread may be creamy-white or may be coloured with colouring matter authorised by the competent authority. The thread is sterilised.

IDENTIFICATION
A. Dissect the end of a thread, using a needle or fine tweezers, to isolate a few individual fibres. Examined under a microscope, the fibres are seen to be 12 µm to 31 µm wide and, along the greater part of their length, have thick walls, sometimes marked with fine longitudinal striations, and a narrow lumen. The fibres gradually narrow to a long, fine point. Sometimes there are unilateral swellings with transverse lines.

B. Impregnate isolated fibres with *iodinated zinc chloride solution R*. The fibres are coloured violet-blue.

TESTS
It complies with the tests prescribed in the monograph on *Strands, sterile non-absorbable, in distributor for veterinary use (0605)*.

If stored in a dry state, expose to an atmosphere with a relative humidity of 65 ± 5 per cent at 20 ± 2 °C for 4 h immediately before measuring the diameter and for the determination of minimum breaking load immerse in water R at room temperature for 30 min immediately before carrying out the test.

STORAGE
See the monograph on *Strands, sterile non-absorbable, in distributor for veterinary use (0605)*.

LABELLING
See the monograph on *Strands, sterile non-absorbable, in distributor for veterinary use (0605)*.

_____ *Ph Eur*

Sterile Poly(ethylene terephthalate) Suture in Distributor

(Poly(ethylene terephthalate) Suture, Sterile, in Distributor for Veterinary Use, Ph Eur monograph 0607)

Ph Eur —————————————————————

DEFINITION

Sterile poly(ethylene terephthalate) suture in distributor for veterinary use is obtained by drawing poly(ethylene terephthalate) through a suitable die. The suture is prepared by braiding very fine filaments in suitable numbers, depending on the gauge required. It may be whitish in colour, or may be coloured with authorised colouring matter or pigments authorised by the competent authority. The suture is sterilised.

CHARACTERS

It is practically insoluble in most of the usual organic solvents, but is attacked by strong alkaline solutions. It is incompatible with phenols.

IDENTIFICATION

A. It dissolves with difficulty when heated in *dimethylformamide R* and in *dichlorobenzene R*.

B. To about 50 mg add 10 mL of *hydrochloric acid R1*. The material remains intact even after immersion for 6 h.

TESTS

It complies with the tests prescribed in the monograph on *Strands, sterile non-absorbable, in distributor for veterinary use (0605)*.

STORAGE

See the monograph on *Strands, sterile non-absorbable, in distributor for veterinary use (0605)*.

LABELLING

See the monograph on *Strands, sterile non-absorbable, in distributor for veterinary use (0605)*.

————————————————————— *Ph Eur*

Sterile Polyamide 6 Suture in Distributor

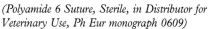

(Polyamide 6 Suture, Sterile, in Distributor for Veterinary Use, Ph Eur monograph 0609)

NOTE: The name Nylon 6 as a synonym for Polyamide 6 may be used freely in many countries, including Great Britain and Northern Ireland, but exclusive proprietary rights in this name are claimed in certain other countries.

Ph Eur —————————————————————

DEFINITION

Sterile polyamide 6 suture in distributor for veterinary use is obtained by drawing through a suitable die a synthetic plastic material formed by the polymerisation of ε-caprolactam. It consists of smooth, cylindrical monofilaments or braided filaments, or lightly twisted strands sheathed with the same material. It may be coloured with colouring matter authorised by the competent authority. The suture is sterilised.

CHARACTERS

It is practically insoluble in the usual organic solvents; it is not attacked by dilute alkaline solutions (for example a

100 g/L solution of sodium hydroxide) but is attacked by dilute mineral acids (for example 20 g/L sulfuric acid), by hot glacial acetic acid and by 70 per cent *m/m* formic acid.

IDENTIFICATION

A. Heat about 50 mg with 0.5 mL of *hydrochloric acid R1* in a sealed glass tube at 110 °C for 18 h and allow to stand for 6 h. No crystals appear.

B. To about 50 mg add 10 mL of *hydrochloric acid R1*. The material disintegrates in the cold and dissolves completely within a few minutes.

C. It dissolves in a 70 per cent *m/m* solution of *anhydrous formic acid R*.

TESTS

It complies with the tests prescribed in the monograph on *Strands, sterile non-absorbable, in distributor for veterinary use (0605)* and with the following test:

Monomer and oligomers

In a continuous-extraction apparatus, treat 1.00 g with 30 mL of *methanol R* at a rate of at least three extractions per hour for 7 h. Evaporate the extract to dryness, dry the residue at 110 °C for 10 min, allow to cool in a desiccator and weigh. The residue weighs not more than 20 mg (2 per cent).

STORAGE

See the monograph on *Strands, sterile non-absorbable, in distributor for veterinary use (0605)*.

LABELLING

See the monograph on *Strands, sterile non-absorbable, in distributor for veterinary use (0605)*.

The label states whether the suture is braided, monofilament or sheathed.

————————————————————— *Ph Eur*

Sterile Polyamide 6/6 Suture in Distributor

(Polyamide 6/6 Suture, Sterile, in Distributor for Veterinary Use, Ph Eur monograph 0610)

NOTE: The name Nylon 6/6 as a synonym for Polyamide 6/6 may be used freely in many countries including Great Britain and Northern Ireland, but exclusive proprietary rights in this name are claimed in certain other countries.

Ph Eur —————————————————————

DEFINITION

Sterile polyamide 6/6 suture in distributor for veterinary use is obtained by drawing through a suitable die a synthetic plastic material formed by the polycondensation of hexamethylene-diamine and adipic acid. It consists of smooth, cylindrical monofilaments or braided filaments, or lightly twisted strands sheathed with the same material. It may be coloured with authorised colouring matter or pigments authorised by the competent authority. The suture is sterilised.

CHARACTERS

It is practically insoluble in the usual organic solvents; it is not attacked by dilute alkaline solutions (for example a 100 g/L solution of sodium hydroxide) but is attacked by dilute mineral acids (for example 20 g/L sulfuric acid), by hot glacial acetic acid and by 80 per cent *m/m* formic acid.

IDENTIFICATION

A. In contact with a flame it melts and burns, forming a hard globule of residue and gives off a characteristic odour resembling that of celery.

B. Place about 50 mg in an ignition tube held vertically and heat gently until thick fumes are evolved. When the fumes fill the tube, withdraw it from the flame and insert a strip of *nitrobenzaldehyde paper R*. A violet-brown colour slowly appears on the paper and fades slowly in air; it disappears immediately on washing with *dilute sulfuric acid R*.

C. To about 50 mg add 10 mL of *hydrochloric acid R1*. The material disintegrates in the cold and dissolves within a few minutes.

D. It does not dissolve in a 70 per cent *m/m* solution of *anhydrous formic acid R* but dissolves in an 80 per cent *m/m* solution of *anhydrous formic acid R*.

TESTS

It complies with the tests prescribed in the monograph on *Strands, sterile non-absorbable, in distributor for veterinary use (0605)*.

STORAGE

See the monograph on *Strands, sterile non-absorbable, in distributor for veterinary use (0605)*.

LABELLING

See the monograph on *Strands, sterile non-absorbable, in distributor for veterinary use (0605)*.

The label states whether the suture is braided, monofilament or sheathed.

_____ *Ph Eur*

LABELLING

See the monograph on *Strands, sterile non-absorbable, in distributor for veterinary use (0605)*.

_____ *Ph Eur*

Sterile Braided Silk Suture in Distributor

(Silk Suture, Sterile, Braided, in Distributor for Veterinary Use, Ph Eur monograph 0606)

Ph Eur _____

DEFINITION

Sterile braided silk suture in distributor for veterinary use is obtained by braiding a variable number of threads, according to the diameter required, of degummed silk obtained from the cocoons of the silkworm *Bombyx mori* L. It may be coloured with colouring matter authorised by the competent authority. The suture is sterilised.

IDENTIFICATION

A. Dissect the end of a strand, using a needle or fine tweezers, to isolate a few individual fibres. The fibres are sometimes marked with very fine longitudinal striations parallel to the axis of the strand. Examined under a microscope, a cross-section is more or less triangular or semi-circular, with rounded edges and without a lumen.

B. Impregnate isolated fibres with *iodinated potassium iodide solution R*. The fibres are coloured pale yellow.

TESTS

It complies with the tests prescribed in the monograph on *Strands, sterile non-absorbable, in distributor for veterinary use (0605)*.

STORAGE

See the monograph on *Strands, sterile non-absorbable, in distributor for veterinary use (0605)*.

Infrared Reference Spectra

All spectra presented in this section were recorded using either a Perkin-Elmer model 682 dispersive infrared spectrophotometer or a Perkin Elmer model 16PC Fourier transform infrared spectrophotometer.

Pressed discs, 13 mm in diameter, were prepared using potassium bromide or potassium chloride. Liquid paraffin mulls and thin films were prepared between potassium bromide plates, and gas and solution spectra were prepared using cells with potassium bromide windows. Solution spectra were prepared against a solvent reference and all other spectra were recorded against air.

For solution spectra the regions of the spectrum within which the solvent shows strong absorption should be disregarded. Solvent 'cut-offs' in the reference spectra may be recorded as horizontal straight lines or may appear as blank regions on the spectrum.

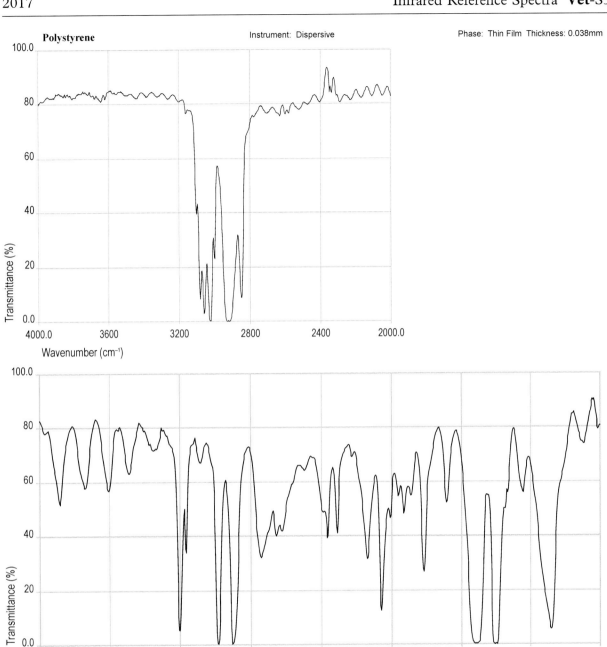

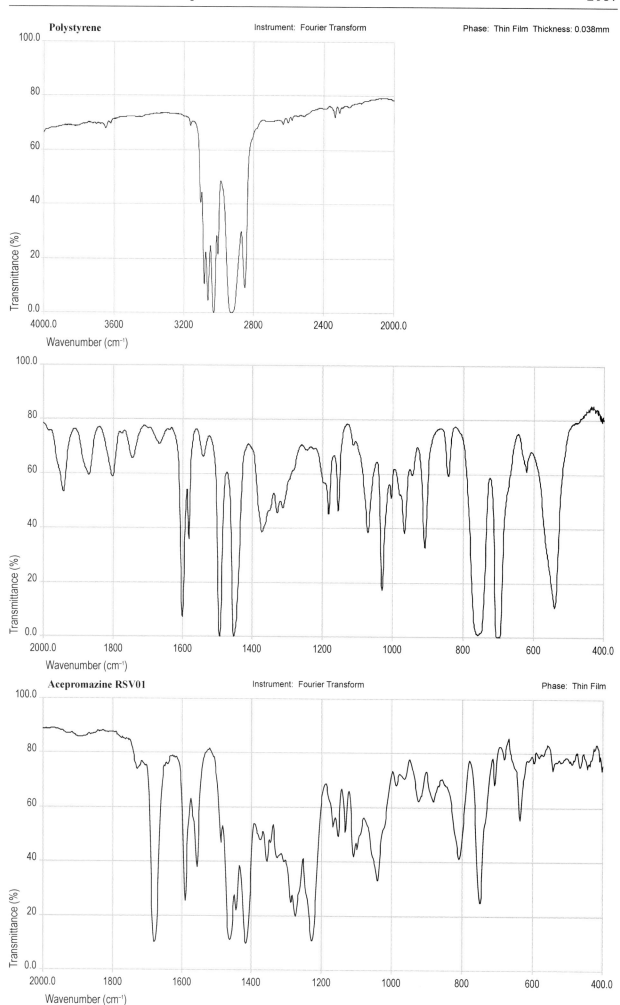

Polystyrene   Instrument: Fourier Transform   Phase: Thin Film Thickness: 0.038mm

Acepromazine RSV01   Instrument: Fourier Transform   Phase: Thin Film

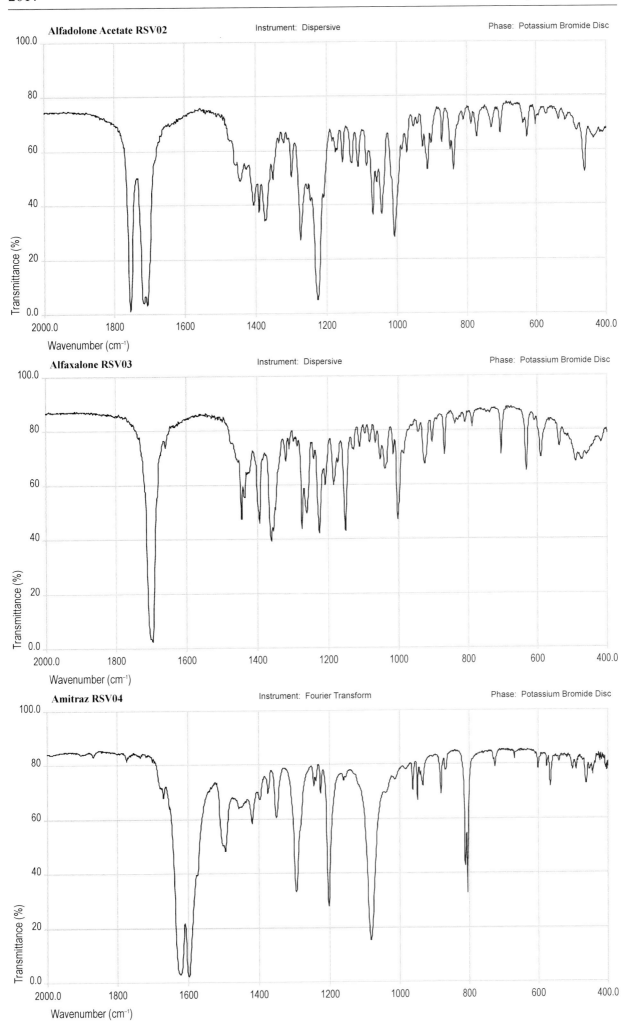

Alfadolone Acetate RSV02   Instrument: Dispersive   Phase: Potassium Bromide Disc

Alfaxalone RSV03   Instrument: Dispersive   Phase: Potassium Bromide Disc

Amitraz RSV04   Instrument: Fourier Transform   Phase: Potassium Bromide Disc

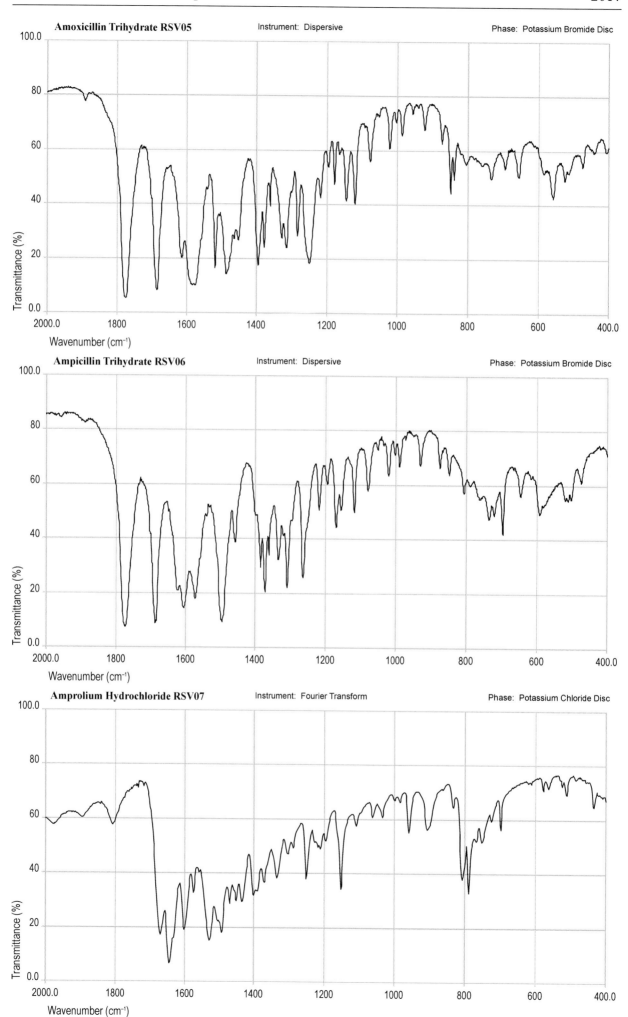

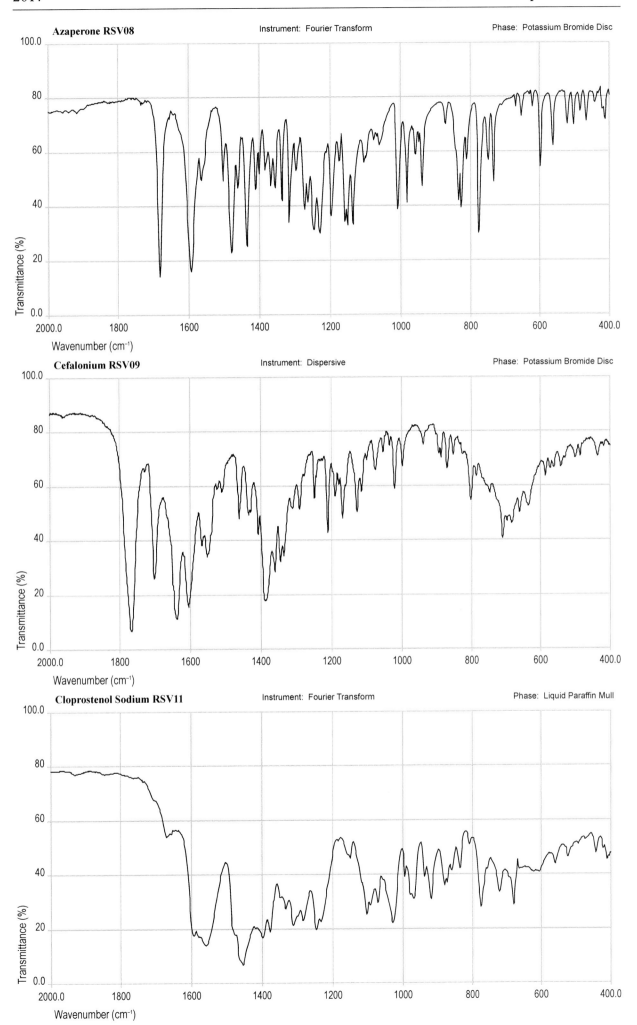

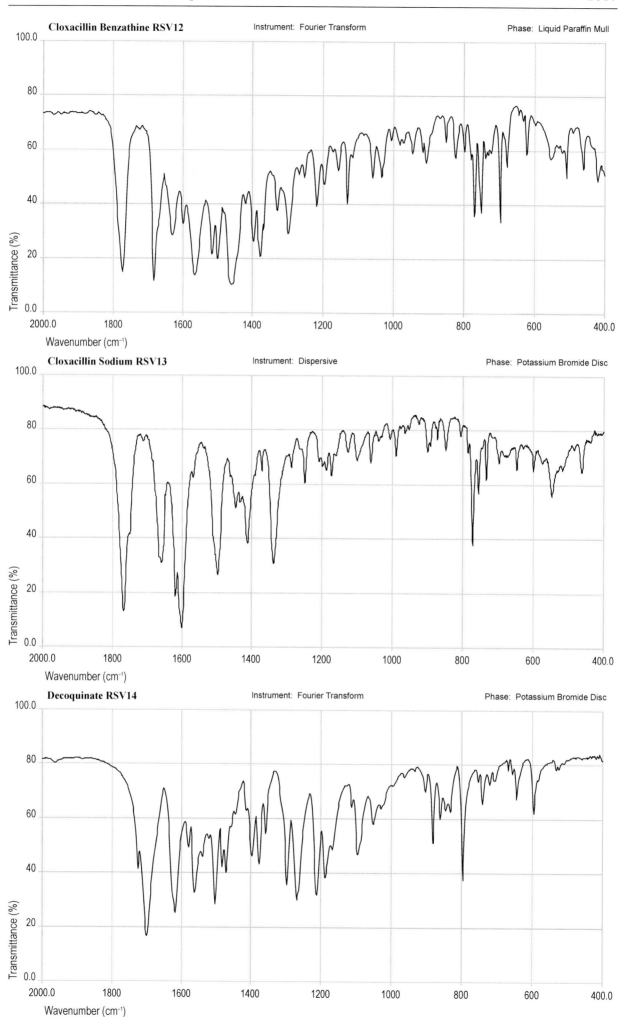

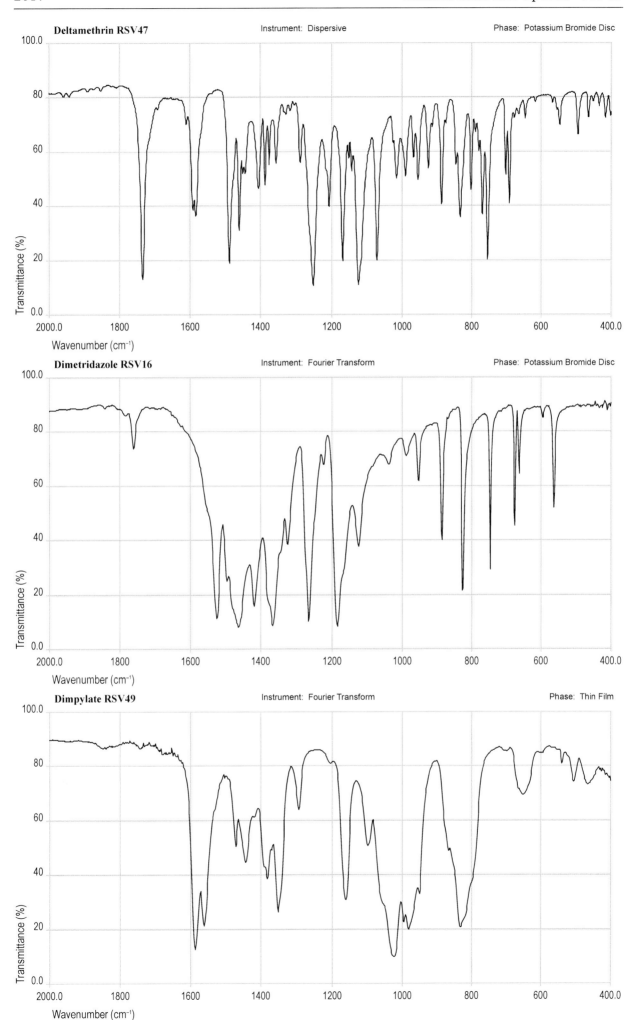

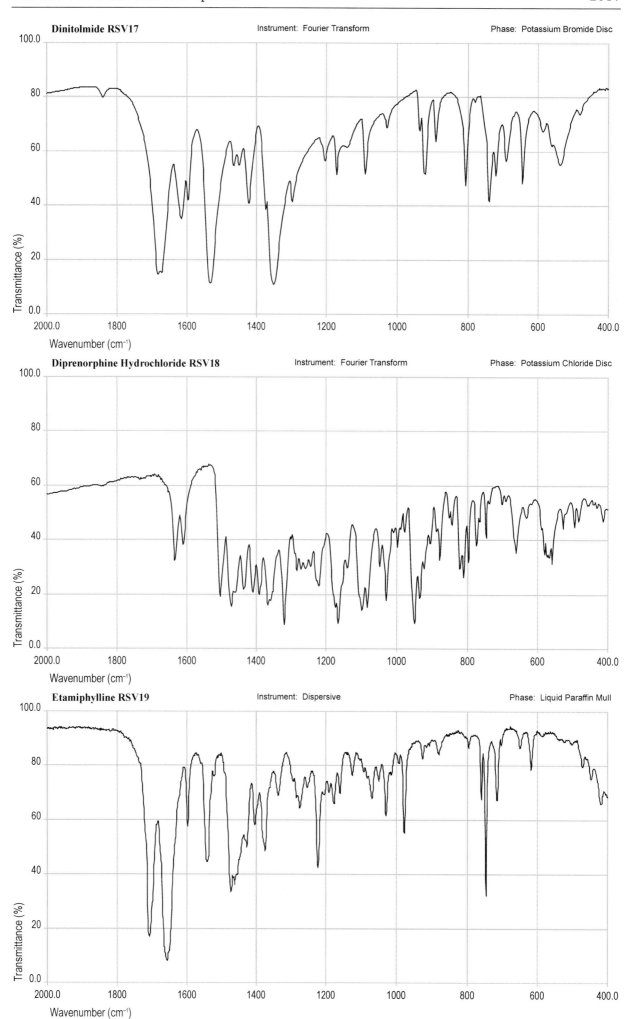

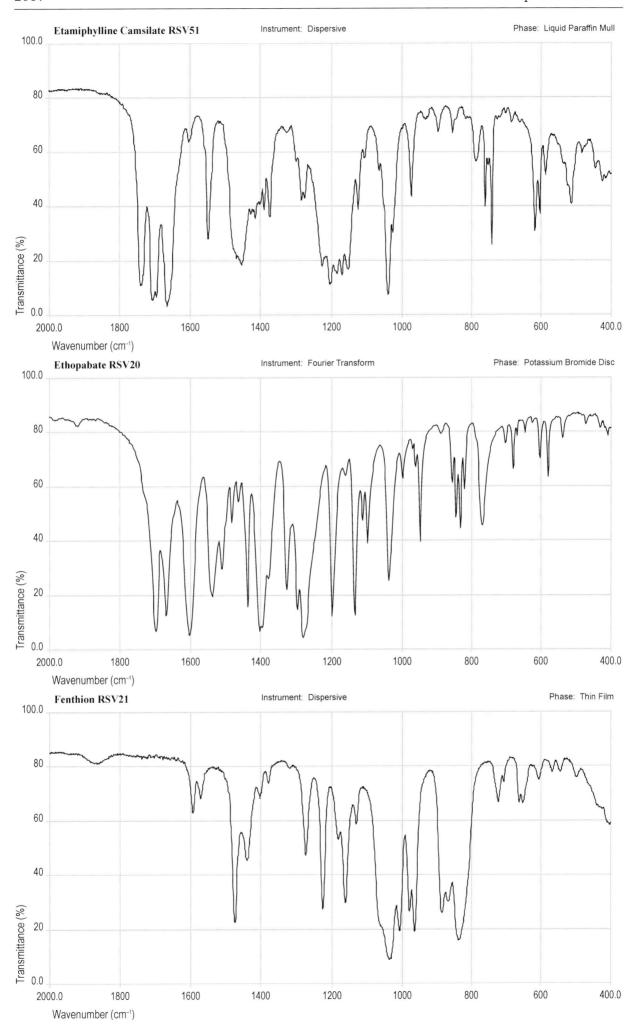

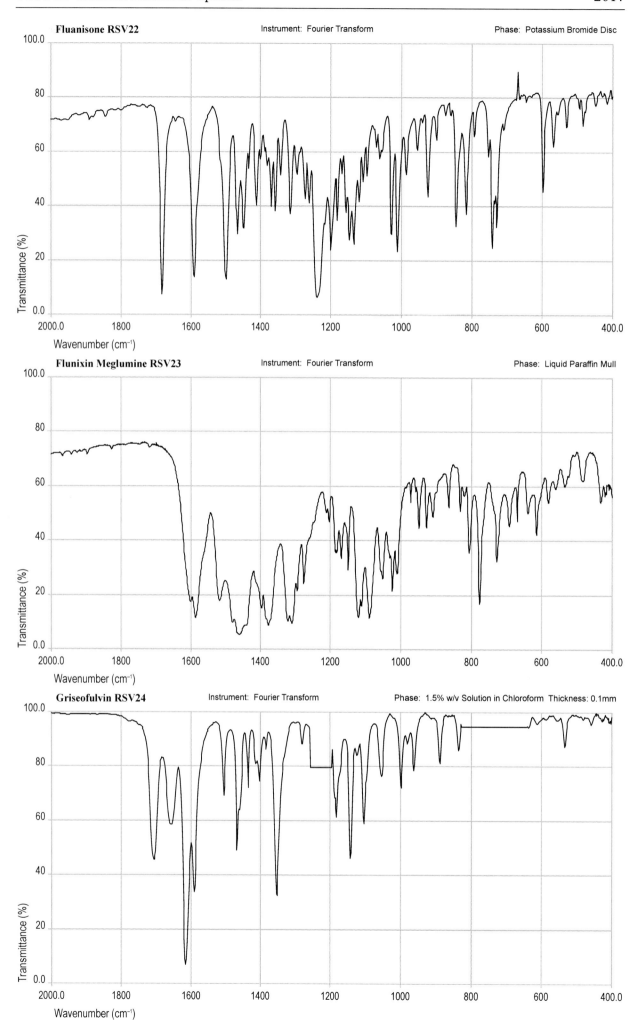

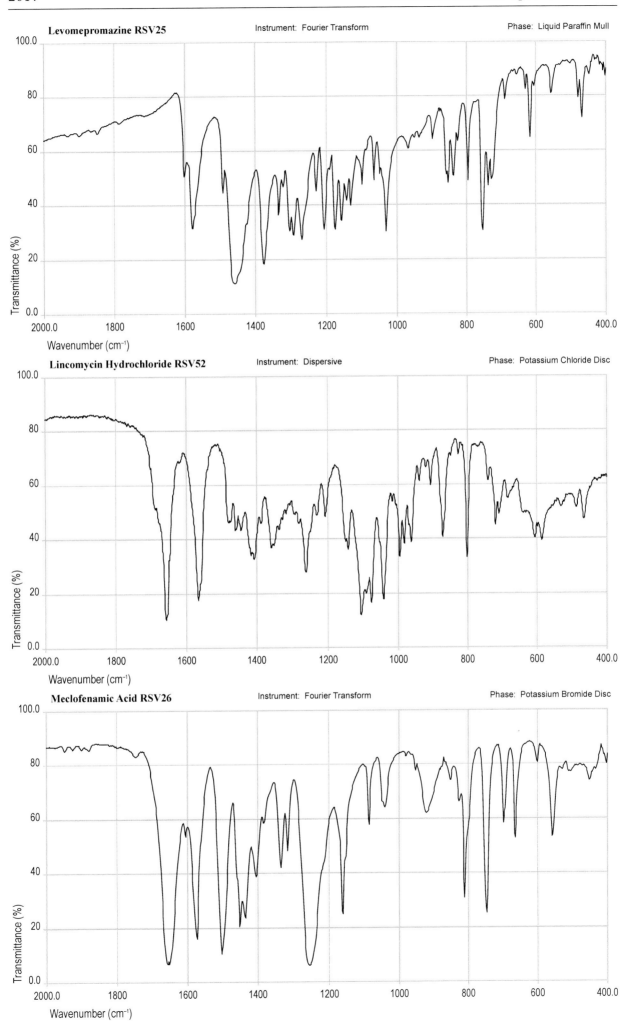

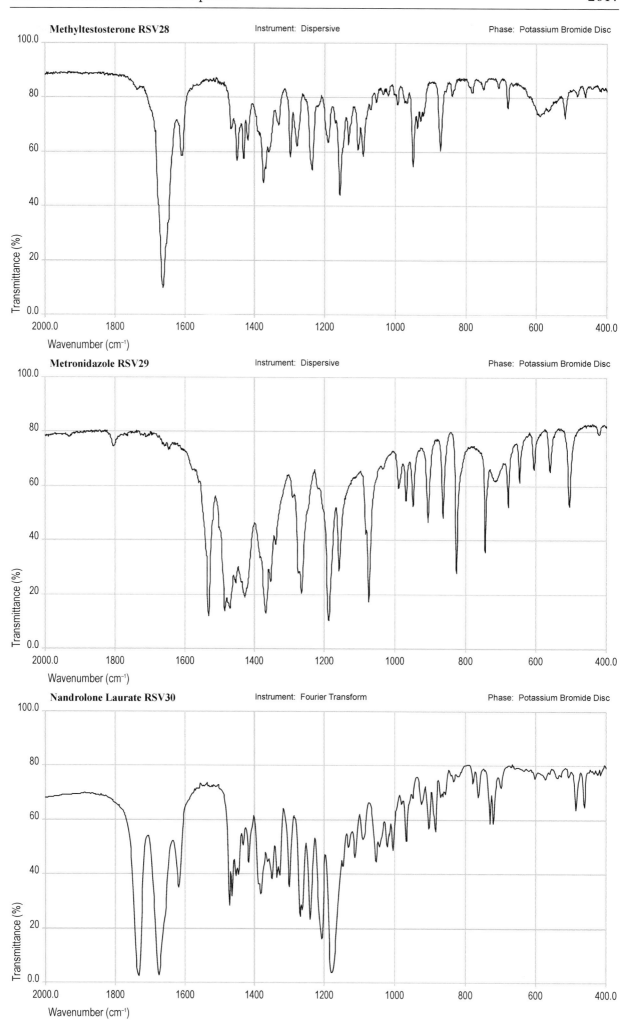

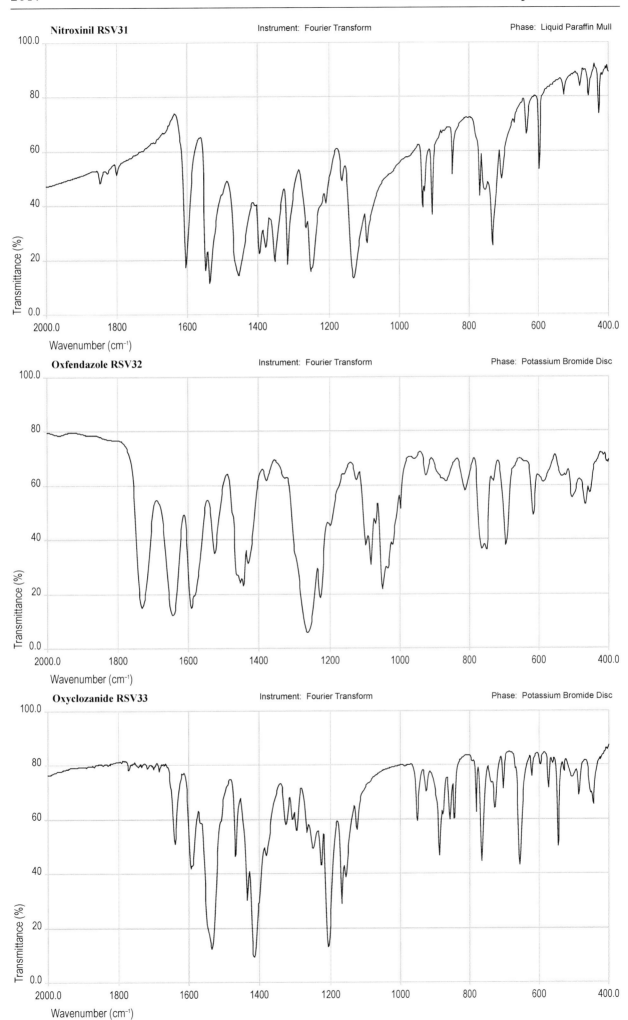

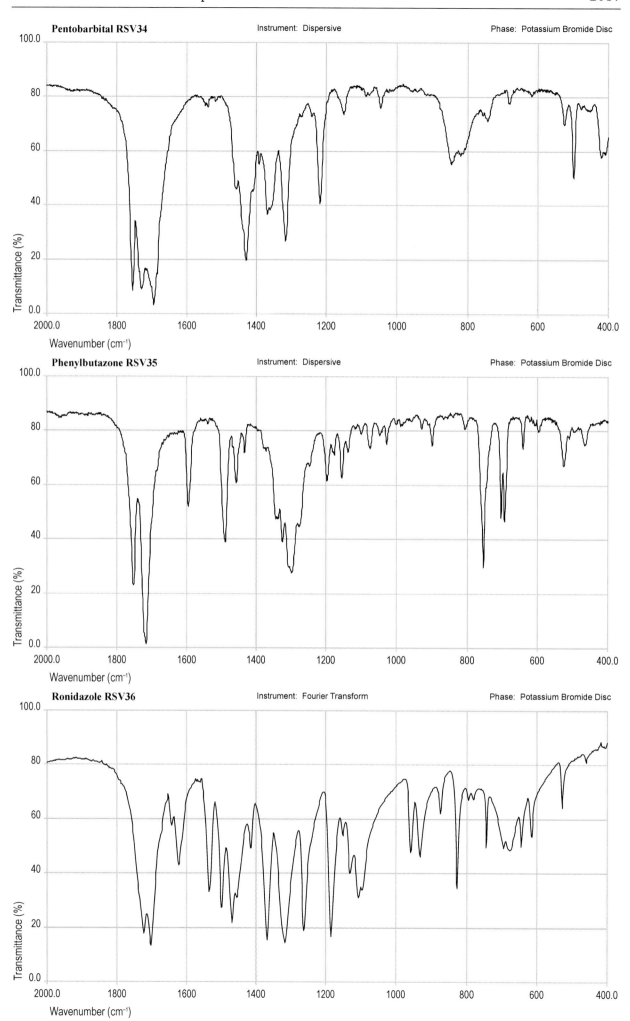

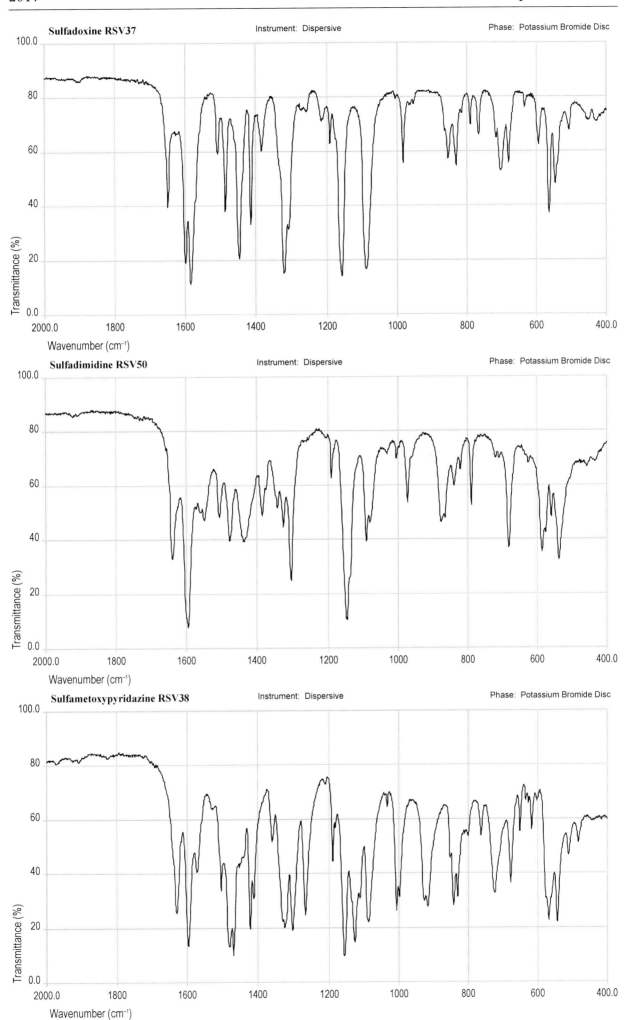

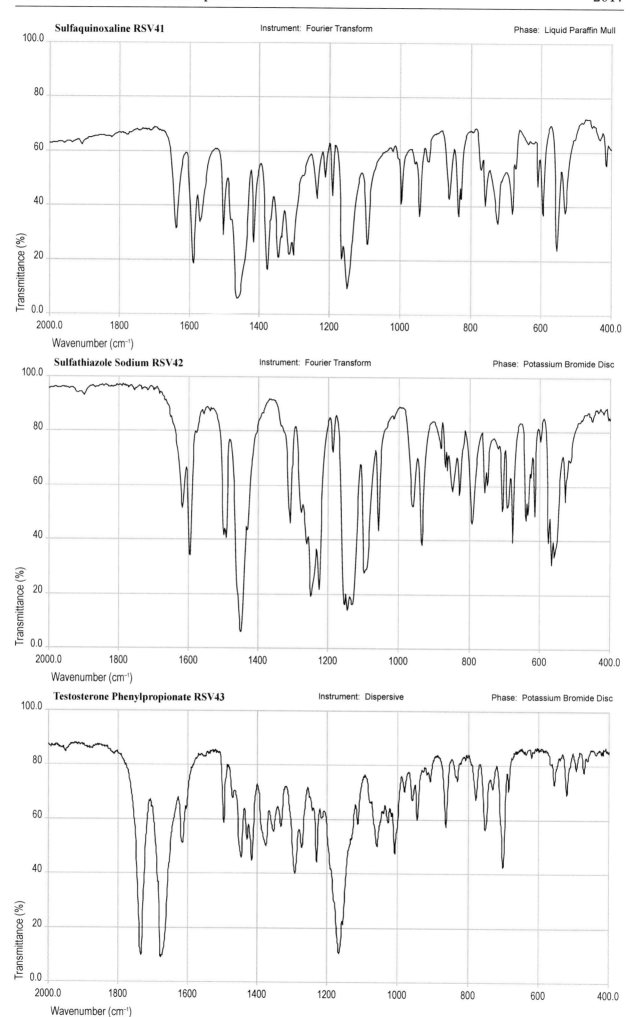

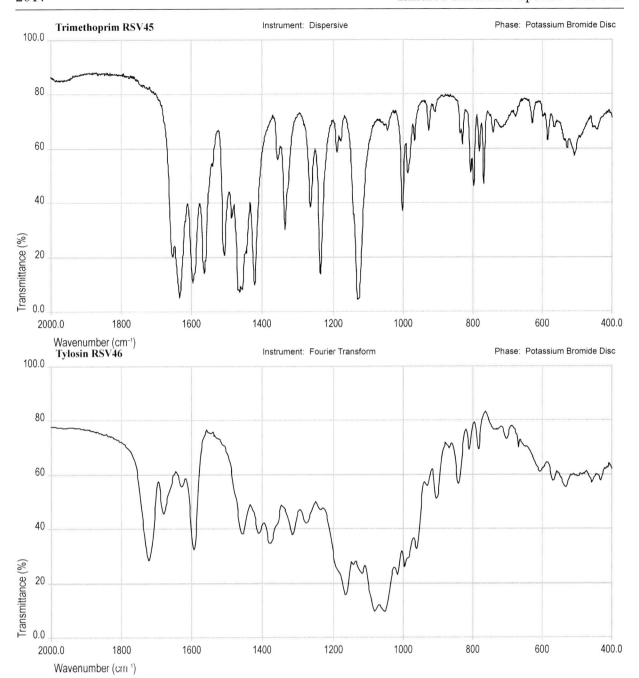

Appendices

Contents of the Appendices

When a method, test or other matter described in an appendix is invoked in a monograph reproduced from the European Pharmacopoeia, Part III of the General Notices applies. When a method, test or other matter described in an appendix is invoked in any other monograph, Part II of General Notices applies.

Any reference to an appendix that is not contained within this edition of the British Pharmacopoeia (Veterinary) is to be construed as a reference to the said appendix contained within the *British Pharmacopoeia 2011* modified as necessary by amendments.

The following appendices are included in this section of the British Pharmacopoeia (Veterinary).

European Pharmacopoeia Equivalent Texts

In monographs reproduced from the European Pharmacopoeia the analytical methods, tests and other supporting texts are invoked by means of the reference number of the text in the General Chapters of the European Pharmacopoeia. The table below lists the contents of the General Chapters of the European Pharmacopoeia and gives the British Pharmacopoeia or British Pharmacopoeia (Veterinary) equivalents. It is provided for information but it is emphasised that, for texts of the European Pharmacopoeia, in cases of doubt or dispute the text published by the Council of Europe is authoritative. Appendices of the British Pharmacopoeia (Veterinary) are identified by inclusion of '(Vet)' after the Appendix letter, for example, Appendix XV J (Vet) 1.

Ph. Eur.	Subject of text	British Pharmacopoeia reference
1	General Notices	†
2.1.1	Droppers	Appendix I A
2.1.2	Sintered-glass Filters	Appendix XVII B2
2.1.3	UV lamps	Appendix III A
2.1.4	Sieves	Appendix XVII B1
2.1.5	Tubes for Comparative Tests	Appendix VII
2.1.6	Gas detector tubes	Appendix IX K
2.2.1	Clarity and Degree of Opalescence of Liquids	Appendix IV A
2.2.2	Degree of Coloration of Liquids	Appendix IV B
2.2.3	Potentiometric Determination of pH	Appendix V L
2.2.4	Approximate pH of Solutions	Appendix V K
2.2.5	Relative Density	Appendix V G
2.2.6	Refractive Index	Appendix V E
2.2.7	Optical Rotation	Appendix V F
2.2.8	Viscosity	Appendix V H
2.2.9	Capillary Viscometer Method	Appendix V H, Method II
2.2.10	Rotating Viscometer Method	Appendix V H, Method III
2.2.11	Distillation Range	Appendix V C
2.2.12	Boiling Point	Appendix V D
2.2.13	Water by Distillation Range	Appendix IX C, Method II
2.2.14	Melting point: Capillary Method	Appendix V A, Method I
2.2.15	Melting point: Open Capillary Method	Appendix V A, Method IV
2.2.16	Melting point: Instantaneous Method	Appendix V A, Method V
2.2.17	Drop Point	Appendix V A, Method III
2.2.18	Freezing Point	Appendix V B
2.2.19	Amperometric Titration	Appendix VIII B
2.2.20	Potentiometric Titration	Appendix VIII B
2.2.21	Fluorimetry	Appendix II E
2.2.22	Atomic Emission Spectrometry	Appendix II D
2.2.23	Atomic Absorption Spectrometry	Appendix II D
2.2.24	Infrared Spectrophotometry	Appendix II A
2.2.25	Visible and Ultraviolet Spectrophotometry	Appendix II B
2.2.26	Paper Chromatography	Appendix III E
2.2.27	Thin-layer Chromatography	Appendix III A
2.2.28	Gas Chromatography	Appendix III B
2.2.29	Liquid Chromatography	Appendix III D
2.2.30	Size-exclusion Chromatography	Appendix III C
2.2.31	Electrophoresis	Appendix III F
2.2.32	Loss on Drying	Appendix IX D
2.2.33	Nuclear Magnetic Resonance Spectrometry	Appendix II C
2.2.34	Thermogravimetry	Appendix V M
2.2.35	Osmolality	Appendix V N
2.2.36	Ion-selective Potentiometry	Appendix VIII E
2.2.37	X-ray Fluorescent Spectrophotometry	Appendix II F
2.2.38	Conductivity	Appendix V O
2.2.39	Molecular Mass Distribution in Dextrans	Appendix III C
2.2.40	Near-Infrared Spectroscopy	Appendix II A

† *Reproduced in full as Part III of the General Notices of the British Pharmacopoeia and British Pharmacopoeia (Veterinary).*

3.2.2	Plastic Containers and Closures	Appendix XIX C
3.2.2.1	Plastic Containers for Aqueous Solutions for Parenteral Infusions	Appendix XIX C1
3.2.3	Sterile Plastic Containers for Blood and Blood Components	Appendix XIX D1
3.2.4	Empty Sterile Plastic Containers for Blood and Blood Components	Appendix XIX D2
3.2.5	Sterile Plastic Containers with Anticoagulant for Blood and Blood Components	Appendix XIX D3
3.2.6	Sets for the Transfusion of Blood and Blood Components	Appendix XIX F
3.2.7	*Vacant*	
3.2.8	Sterile Single-Use Plastic Syringes	Appendix XIX G
3.2.9	Rubber Closures for Containers for Aqueous Preparations for Parenteral Use	Appendix XIX E
4.1.1	Reagents	Appendix I A
4.1.2	Standard Solutions	Appendix I C
4.1.3	Buffer Solutions	Appendix I D
4.2.1	Reference Substances for Volumetric Solutions	Appendix I B
4.2.2	Volumetric Solutions	Appendix I B
5.1.1	Methods of Preparation of Sterile Products	Appendix XVIII
5.1.2	Biological Indicators (sterilisation)	Appendix XVIII
5.1.3	Efficacy of Antimicrobial Preservation	Appendix XVI C
5.1.4	Microbiological Quality of Non-sterile Pharmaceutical Preparations and Substances for Pharmaceutical Use	Appendix XVI D
5.1.5	F_0 Concept (sterilisation)	Appendix XVIII
5.1.6	Alternative Methods for Control of Microbiological Quality	Supplementary Chapter IV L
5.1.7	Viral Safety	Appendix XXII A
5.1.8	Microbiological Quality of Herbal Medicinal Products for Oral Use and Extracts used in their Preparation	Appendix XVI G
5.1.9	Guidelines for using the Test for Sterility	Supplementary Chapter IV P
5.1.10	Guidelines for using the test for bacterial endotoxins	Supplementary Chapter I C
5.2.1	Terminology: Vaccines	Appendix XV A *and* Appendix XV A(Vet)
5.2.2	SPF Chicken Flocks	Appendix XV H *and* Appendix XV H(Vet)
5.2.3	Cell Substrates for the Production of Vaccines for Human Use	Appendix XV J
5.2.4	Cell Cultures (Veterinary Vaccine Production)	Appendix XV J(Vet)1
5.2.5	Substances of Animal Origin for the Production of Immunological Veterinary Medicinal Products	Appendix XV J(Vet)2
5.2.6	Safety: Veterinary Vaccines	Appendix XV K(Vet)1
5.2.7	Efficacy: Veterinary Vaccines	Appendix XV K(Vet)2
5.2.8	Minimising the Risk of Transmitting Animal Spongiform Encephalopathy Agents via Medicinal Products	Appendix XXII B
5.2.9	Evaluation of Safety of Each Batch of Immunosera for Veterinary Use	Appendix XV K(Vet)3
5.2.11	Carrier Proteins for the Production of Conjugated Polysaccharide Vaccines for Human Use	Appendix XV K
5.3	Statistical Analysis of Biological Assays and Tests	Supplementary Chapter IV G
5.4	Residual Solvents	Supplementary Chapter IV D
5.5	Alcoholimetric Tables	Supplementary Chapter IV E
5.6	Assay of Interferons	Appendix XIV M1
5.7	Physical Characteristics of Radionuclides	Radiopharmaceutical Preparations
5.8	Pharmacopoeial Harmonisation	Supplementary Chapter IV F
5.9	Polymorphism	Appendix I F
5.10	Control of Impurities in Substances for Pharmaceutical Use	Supplementary Chapter IV J
5.11	Characters Section in Monographs	Supplementary Chapter IV K
5.12	Reference Standards	Supplementary Chapter IV M
5.14	Gene Transfer Medicinal Products for Human Use	Supplementary Chapter IV N
5.16	Crystallinity	Appendix XVII U
5.17.1	Recommendations on dissolution testing	Appendix XII B1
5.19	Extemporaneous Preparation of Radiopharmaceuticals	Radiopharmaceutical Preparations
5.20	Metal Catalyst or Metal Reagent Residues	Supplementary Chapter IV Q
5.21	Chemometric Methods Applied to Analytical Data	Supplementary Chapter IV R
5.22	Names of Herbal Drugs Used in Traditional Chinese Medicine	Supplementary Chapter VII B
5.23	Monographs on Herbal Drug Extracts (Information Chapter)	Supplementary Chapter VII C

Appendix XV
Production and testing of Vaccines

A (Vet). Terminology used in Monographs on Biological Products

(Ph. Eur. method 5.2.1)

For some items, alternative terms commonly used in connection with veterinary vaccines are shown in parenthesis.

Seed-lot system A seed-lot system is a system according to which successive batches of a product are derived from the same master seed lot. For routine production, a working seed lot may be prepared from the master seed lot. The origin and the passage history of the master seed lot and the working seed lot are recorded.

Master seed lot A culture of a micro-organism distributed from a single bulk into containers and processed together in a single operation in such a manner as to ensure uniformity and stability and to prevent contamination. A master seed lot in liquid form is usually stored at or below -70 °C. A freeze-dried master seed lot is stored at a temperature known to ensure stability.

Working seed lot A culture of a micro-organism derived from the master seed lot and intended for use in production. Working seed lots are distributed into containers and stored as described above for master seed lots.

Cell-bank system (Cell-seed system) A system whereby successive final lots (batches) of a product are manufactured by culture in cells derived from the same master cell bank (master cell seed). A number of containers from the master cell bank (master cell seed) are used to prepare a working cell bank (working cell seed). The cell-bank system (cell-seed system) is validated for the highest passage level achieved during routine production.

Master cell bank (Master cell seed) A culture of cells distributed into containers in a single operation, processed together and stored in such a manner as to ensure uniformity and stability and to prevent contamination. A master cell bank (master cell seed) is usually stored at -70 °C or lower.

Working cell bank (Working cell seed) A culture of cells derived from the master cell bank (master cell seed) and intended for use in the preparation of production cell cultures. The working cell bank (working cell seed) is distributed into containers, processed and stored as described for the master cell bank (master cell seed).

Primary cell cultures Cultures of cells obtained by trypsination of a suitable tissue or organ. The cells are essentially identical to those of the tissue of origin and are no more than 5 *in vitro* passages from the initial preparation from the animal tissue.

Cell lines Cultures of cells that have a high capacity for multiplication *in vitro*. In diploid cell lines, the cells have essentially the same characteristics as those of the tissue of origin. In continuous cell lines, the cells are able to multiply indefinitely in culture and may be obtained from healthy or tumoral tissue. Some continuous cell lines have oncogenic potential under certain conditions.

Production cell culture A culture of cells intended for use in production; it may be derived from one or more containers of the working cell bank (working cell seed) or it may be a primary cell culture.

Control cells A quantity of cells set aside, at the time of virus inoculation, as uninfected cell cultures. The uninfected cells are incubated under similar conditions to those used for the production cell cultures.

Single harvest Material derived on one or more occasions from a single production cell culture inoculated with the same working seed lot or a suspension derived from the working seed lot, incubated, and harvested in a single production run.

Monovalent pooled harvest Pooled material containing a single strain or type of micro-organism or antigen and derived from a number of eggs, cell culture containers etc. that are processed at the same time.

Final bulk vaccine Material that has undergone all the steps of production except for the final filling. It consists of one or more monovalent pooled harvests, from cultures of one or more species or types of micro-organism, after clarification, dilution or addition of any adjuvant or other auxiliary substance. It is treated to ensure its homogeneity and is used for filling the containers of one or more final lots (batches).

Final lot (Batch) A collection of closed, final containers or other final dosage units that are expected to be homogeneous and equivalent with respect to risk of contamination during filling or preparation of the final product. The dosage units are filled, or otherwise prepared, from the same final bulk vaccine, freeze-dried together (if applicable) and closed in one continuous working session. They bear a distinctive number or code identifying the final lot (batch). Where a final bulk vaccine is filled and/or freeze-dried on several separate sessions, there results a related set of final lots (batches) that are usually identified by the use of a common part in the distinctive number or code; these related final lots (batches) are sometimes referred to as sub-batches, sub-lots or filling lots.

Combined vaccine A multicomponent preparation formulated so that different antigens are administered simultaneously. The different antigenic components are intended to protect against different strains or types of the same organism and/or different organisms. A combined vaccine may be supplied by the manufacturer either as a single liquid or freeze-dried preparation or as several constituents with directions for admixture before use.

H (Vet). Chicken Flocks Free from Specified Pathogens for the Production and Quality Control of Vaccines

(Ph. Eur. method 5.2.2)

Where specified, chickens, embryos or cell cultures used for the production or quality control of vaccines are derived from eggs produced by chicken flocks free from specified pathogens (SPF). The SPF status of a flock is ensured by means of the system described below. The list of micro-organisms given is based on current knowledge and will be updated as necessary.

A flock is defined as a group of birds sharing a common environment and having their own caretakers who have no contact with non-SPF flocks. Once a flock is defined, no non-SPF birds are added to it.

Each flock is housed so as to minimise the risk of contamination. The facility in which the flock is housed must

Table 5.2.2.-1

Agent	Test to be used**	Vertical transmission	Rapid/slow spread
Avian adenoviruses, group 1	AGP, EIA	yes	slow
Avian encephalomyelitis virus	AGP, EIA	yes	rapid
Avian infectious bronchitis virus	HI, EIA	no	rapid
Avian infectious laryngotracheitis virus	VN, EIA	no	slow
Avian leucosis viruses	EIA for virus, VN, EIA for antibody	yes	slow
Avian nephritis virus	IS	no	slow
Avian orthoreoviruses	IS, EIA	yes	slow
Avian reticuloendotheliosis virus	AGP, IS, EIA	yes	slow
Chicken anaemia virus	IS, EIA, VN	yes	slow
Egg drop syndrome virus	HI, EIA	yes	slow
Infectious bursal disease virus	Serotype 1: AGP, EIA, VN Serotype 2: VN	no	rapid
Influenza A virus	AGP, EIA, HI	no	rapid
Marek's disease virus	AGP	no	rapid
Newcastle disease virus	HI, EIA	no	rapid
Turkey rhinotracheitis virus	EIA	no	slow
Mycoplasma gallisepticum	Agg and HI to confirm a positive test, EIA, HI	yes	slow
Mycoplasma synoviae	Agg and HI to confirm a positive test, EIA, HI	yes	rapid
Salmonella pullorum	Agg	yes	slow

Agg: agglutination
AGP: agar gel precipitation; the technique is suitable where testing is carried out weekly
EIA: enzyme immunoassay

HI: haemagglutination inhibition
IS: immunostaining
VN: virus neutralisation

**Subject to agreement by the competent authority, other types of test may be used provided they are at least as sensitive as those indicated and of appropriate specificity.

not be sited near to any non-SPF flocks of birds with the exception of flocks that are in the process of being established as SPF flocks and that are housed in facilities and conditions appropriate to SPF flocks. The SPF flock is housed within an isolator or in a building with filtered air under positive pressure. Appropriate measures are taken to prevent entry of rodents, wild birds, insects and unauthorised personnel.

Personnel authorised to enter the facility must have no contact with other birds or with agents potentially capable of infecting the flock. It is advisable for personnel to shower and change clothing or to wear protective clothing before entering the controlled facility.

Wherever possible, items taken into the facility are sterilised. In particular it is recommended that the feed is suitably treated to avoid introduction of undesirable micro-organisms and that water is at least of potable quality, for example from a chlorinated supply. No medication is administered to birds within the flock that might interfere with detection of any disease.

A permanent record is kept of the general health of the flock and any abnormality is investigated. Factors to be monitored include morbidity, mortality, general physical condition, feed consumption, daily egg production and egg quality, fertility and hatchability. Records are maintained for a period of at least 5 years. Details of any deviation from normal in these

performance parameters or detection of any infection are notified to the users of the eggs as soon as practicable.

The tests or combination of tests described below must have suitable specificity and sensitivity with respect to relevant serotypes of the viruses. Samples for testing are taken at random.

A positive result for chicken anaemia virus (CAV) does not necessarily exclude use of material derived from the flock, but live vaccines for use in birds less than 7 days old shall be produced using material from CAV-negative flocks. Inactivated vaccines for use in birds less than 7 days old may be produced using material from flocks that have not been shown to be free from CAV, provided it has been demonstrated that the inactivation process inactivates CAV.

Establishment of an SPF flock

A designated SPF flock is derived from chickens shown to be free from vertically-transmissible agents listed in Table 5.2.2-1. This is achieved by testing of 2 generations prior to the designated SPF flock. A general scheme for the procedure to be followed in establishing and maintaining an SPF flock is shown diagrammatically in Table 5.2.2.-2. In order to establish a new SPF flock, a series of tests must be conducted on 3 generations of birds. All birds in the 1st generation must be tested at least once before the age of 20 weeks for freedom from avian leucosis group-antigen and tested by an enzyme immunoassay (EIA) or by virus

Table 5.2.2-2. – *Schematic description of the establishment and maintenance of SPF flocks*

NEW STOCK	Establish freedom from vertically-transmissible agents
	Test all birds for avian leucosis antigen and antibodies prior to 20 weeks of age
	Test for *Salmonella* spp. and perform general clinical observation from 8 weeks of age
	Carry out routine testing for specified agents from 20 weeks of age
2nd GENERATION	Test all birds for avian leucosis antigen and antibodies prior to 20 weeks of age
	Test for *Salmonella* spp. and perform general clinical observation from 8 weeks of age
	Carry out routine testing for specified agents from 20 weeks of age
3rd GENERATION	Test all birds for avian leucosis antigen and antibodies prior to 20 weeks of age
	Test for *Salmonella* spp. and perform general clinical observation from 8 weeks of age
DESIGNATE FLOCK AS SPF IF ALL TESTS ARE SATISFACTORY	
3rd GENERATION	Carry out routine testing for specified agents from 20 weeks of age
	Carry out post-lay testing for vertically-transmissible agents
SUBSEQUENT GENERATIONS	Test two 5 per cent samples for avian leucosis antigen and for antibodies against specified agents between 12 and 20 weeks of age
	Test for *Salmonella* spp. and perform general clinical observation from 8 weeks of age
	Carry out routine testing for specified agents from 20 weeks of age
	Carry out post-lay testing for vertically-transmissible agents

neutralisation (VN) for freedom of antibodies to avian leucosis virus subtypes A, B and J. All birds must also be tested for freedom from antibodies to the vertically-transmissible agents listed in Table 5.2.2-1. From the age of 8 weeks the flock is tested for freedom from *Salmonella*. Clinical examination is carried out on the flock from 8 weeks of age and the birds must not exhibit any signs of infectious disease. The test methods to be used for these tests are given in the table and further guidance is also given in the section below on routine testing of designated SPF flocks. From 20 weeks of age, the flock is tested as described under Routine testing of designated SPF flocks. All stages of this testing regime are also applied to the subsequent 2 generations, except the testing of every bird before lay for vertically-transmissible agents. All test results must indicate freedom from pathogens in all 3 generations for the flock consisting of the 3rd generation to be designated as SPF.

SPF embryos derived from another designated SPF flock contained within a separate facility on the same site may be introduced. From 8 weeks of age, these replacement birds are regarded as a flock and are tested in accordance with test procedures described above.

Initial testing requirements for subsequent generations derived from a designated SPF flock

Where a replacement flock is derived exclusively from a fully established SPF flock the new generation is tested prior to being designated as SPF. In addition to the tests for *Salmonella* and monitoring of the general health and performance of the flock, further specific testing from the age of 8 weeks is required. Tests are performed on two 5 per cent samples of the flock (minimum 10, maximum 200 birds) taken with an interval of at least 4 weeks between the ages of 12-16 weeks and 16-20 weeks.

All samples are collected and tested individually. Blood samples for antibody tests and suitable samples for testing for leucosis antigen are collected. The test methods to be used are as described under Routine testing of designated SPF flocks. Only when all tests have confirmed the absence of infection may the new generation be designated as SPF.

Routine testing of designated SPF flocks

General examination and necropsy

Clinical examination is carried out at least once per week throughout the life of the flock in order to verify that the birds are free from fowl-pox virus and signs of any other infection. In the event of mortality exceeding 0.2 per cent per week, necropsy is performed on all available carcasses to verify that there is no sign of infection. Where appropriate, histopathological and/or microbiological/virological studies are performed to confirm diagnosis. Specific examination for tuberculosis lesions is carried out and histological samples from any suspected lesions are specifically stained to verify freedom from *Mycobacterium avium*. Caecal contents of all available carcasses are examined microbiologically for the presence of *Salmonella* spp. using the techniques described below. Where appropriate, caecal samples from up to 5 birds may be pooled.

Cultural testing for Salmonella spp

Cultural testing for *Salmonella* spp. is performed either by testing samples of droppings or cloacal swabs or by testing of drag swabs. Where droppings or cloacal swabs are tested, a total of 60 samples within each 4-week period is tested throughout the entire life of the flock. Tests may be performed on pools of up to 10 samples. Where drag swabs are tested, a minimum of 2 drag swabs are tested during each 4-week period throughout the entire life of the flock. Detection of *Salmonella* spp. in these samples is performed by pre-enrichment of the samples followed by culture using *Salmonella*-selective media.

Tests for avian leucosis antigen

Prior to the commencement of laying, cloacal swabs or blood samples (using buffy coat cultivation) are tested for the presence of group-specific leucosis antigen. A total of 5 per cent (minimum 10, maximum 200) of the flock is sampled during each 4-week period. During lay, albumen samples from 5 per cent (minimum 10, maximum 200) of the eggs are tested in each 4-week period. Tests are performed by EIA for group-specific antigen using methods that are capable of detecting antigen from subgroups A, B and J.

Test for antibodies to other agents

Tests for antibodies to all agents listed in Table 5.2.2.-1 are performed throughout the laying period of the flock. In each 4-week period, samples are taken from 5 per cent (minimum 10, maximum 200) of the flock. It is recommended that 1.25 per cent of the flock is sampled each week since some test methods for some agents must be conducted on a weekly basis. Table 5.2.2.-1 classifies the agents into those that spread rapidly through the flock and those that spread slowly or may not infect the entire flock. For those agents listed as slowly spreading, each sample is tested individually.

For those agents listed as rapidly spreading, at least 20 per cent of the samples collected in each 4-week period are tested individually or, where serum neutralisation or ELISA tests are employed, all of the samples may be tested individually or by preparing pools of 5 samples, collected at the same time.

Suitable methods to be used for detection of the agents are shown in Table 5.2.2.-1. Subject to agreement by the competent authority, other test methods may be used provided they are shown to be at least as sensitive as those indicated and of appropriate specificity.

Tests to be conducted at the end of the laying period

Following the last egg collection, final testing to confirm the absence of vertically-transmissible agents indicated in Table 5.2.2.-1 is performed. After the last egg collection, a minimum of 5 per cent of the flock (minimum 10, maximum 200) is retained for at least 4 weeks. Blood samples are collected from every bird in the group during the 4-week period with at least 1.25 per cent of the birds (25 per cent of the sample) being bled not earlier than 4 weeks after the final egg collection. Serum samples are tested for vertically-transmissible agents (as defined by Table 5.2.2.-1) using the methods indicated. Where sampling is performed on a weekly basis, at least 1.25 per cent of the birds (25 per cent of the sample) are tested each week during this period.

Alternatively, within 4 weeks of the final egg collection blood and/or other suitable sample materials are collected from at least 5 per cent of the flock and tested for the presence of vertically-transmissible agents using validated nucleic acid amplification techniques (*2.6.21*).

Action to be taken in the event of detection of a specified agent

If evidence is found of contamination of the flock by an agent listed as slowly spreading in Table 5.2.2.-1, all materials derived from the flock during the 4-week period immediately preceding the date on which the positive sample was collected are considered unsatisfactory. Similarly, if evidence is found of contamination of the flock by an agent listed as rapidly spreading in Table 5.2.2.-1, all materials derived from the flock during the 2-week period immediately preceding the date on which the positive sample was collected are considered unsatisfactory. Any product manufactured with such materials, and for which the use of SPF materials is required, is considered unsatisfactory and must be discarded; any quality control tests conducted using the materials are invalid.

Producers must notify users of all eggs of the evidence of contamination as soon as possible following the outbreak.

Any flock in which an outbreak of any specified agent is confirmed may not be redesignated as an SPF flock. Any progeny derived from that flock during or after the 4-week period prior to the last negative sample being collected may not be designated as SPF.

J (Vet) 1. Cell Cultures for the Production of Veterinary Vaccines

(Ph. Eur. general texts 5.2.4)

Cell cultures for the production of vaccines for veterinary use comply with the requirements of this section. It may also be necessary that cell cultures used for testing of vaccines for veterinary use also comply with some or all of these requirements.

For most mammalian viruses, propagation in cell lines is possible and the use of primary cells is then not acceptable.

Permanently infected cells used for production of veterinary vaccines comply with the appropriate requirements described below. The cells shall be shown to be infected only with the agent stated.

CELL LINES

Cell lines are normally handled according to a cell-seed system. Each master cell seed is assigned a specific code for identification purposes. The master cell seed is stored in aliquots at $-70\ ^\circ$C or lower. Production of vaccine is not normally undertaken on cells more than twenty passages from the master cell seed. Where suspension cultures are used, an increase in cell numbers equivalent to approximately three population doublings is considered equivalent to one passage. If cells beyond twenty passage levels are to be used for production, it shall be demonstrated, by validation or further testing, that the production cell cultures are essentially similar to the master cell seed with regard to their biological characteristics and purity and that the use of such cells has no deleterious effect on vaccine production.

The history of the cell line shall be known and recorded in detail (for example, origin, number of passages and media used for multiplication, storage conditions).

The method of storing and using the cells, including details of how it is ensured that the maximum number of passages permitted is not exceeded during product manufacture, are recorded. A sufficient quantity of the master cell seed and each working cell seed are kept for analytical purposes.

The tests described below are carried out (as prescribed in Table 5.2.4.-1) on a culture of the master cell seed and the working cell seed or on cell cultures from the working cell seed at the highest passage level used for production and derived from a homogeneous sample demonstrated to be representative.

Characteristics of culture

The appearance of cell monolayers, before and after histological staining, is described. Information, if possible numerical data, is provided especially on the speed and rate of growth. Similarly, the presence or absence of contact inhibition, polynucleated cells and any other cellular abnormalities are specified.

Karyotype

A chromosomal examination is made of not fewer than fifty cells undergoing mitosis in the master cell seed and at a passage level at least as high as that to be used in production. Any chromosomal marker present in the master cell seed must also be found in the high passage cells and the modal number of chromosomes in these cells must not be more than 15 per cent higher than of cells of the master cell seed. The karyotypes must be identical. If the modal number exceeds the level stated, if the chromosomal markers are not found in the working cell seed at the highest level used for production or if the karyotype differs, the cell line shall not be used for manufacture.

Table 5.2.4.-1. – *Cell culture stage at which tests are carried out*

	Master cell seed	Working cell seed	Cell from working cell seed at highest passage level
General microscopy	+	+	+
Bacteria and fungi	+	+	–
Mycoplasmas	+	+	–
Viruses	+	+	–
Retroviruses	+	–	+
Identification of species	+	–	+
Karyotype	+	–	+
Tumorigenicity	+	–	–

Identification of the species

It shall be shown, by one validated method, that the master cell seed and the cells from the working cell seed at the highest passage level used for production come from the species of origin specified. When a fluorescence test is carried out and the corresponding serum to the species of origin of cells is used and shows that all the tested cells are fluorescent, it is not necessary to carry out other tests with reagents able to detect contamination by cells of other species.

Bacterial and fungal contamination

The cells comply with the test for sterility (*2.6.1*). The sample of cells to be examined consists of not less than the number of cells in a monolayer with an area of 70 cm^2 or, for cells grown in suspension, an approximately equivalent number of cells. The cells are maintained in culture for at least 15 days without antibiotics before carrying out the test.

Mycoplasmas (*2.6.7*)

The cells comply with the test for mycoplasmas. The cells are maintained in culture for at least 15 days without antibiotics before carrying out the test.

Absence of contaminating viruses

The cells must not be contaminated by viruses; suitably sensitive tests, including those prescribed below, are carried out.

The monolayers tested shall have an area of at least 70 cm^2, and shall be prepared and maintained using medium and additives, and grown under similar conditions to those used for the preparation of the vaccine. The monolayers are maintained in culture for a total of at least 28 days. Subcultures are made at 7-day intervals, unless the cells do not survive for this length of time, when the subcultures are made on the latest day possible. Sufficient cells, in suitable containers, are produced for the final subculture to carry out the tests specified below.

The monolayers are examined regularly throughout the incubation period for the possible presence of cytopathic effects and at the end of the observation period for cytopathic effects, haemadsorbent viruses and specific viruses by immuno-fluorescence and other suitable tests as indicated below.

Detection of cytopathic viruses

Two monolayers of at least 6 cm^2 each are stained with an appropriate cytological stain. The entire area of each stained monolayer is examined for any inclusion bodies, abnormal numbers of giant cells or any other lesion indicative of a cellular abnormality which might be attributable to a contaminant.

Detection of haemadsorbent viruses

Monolayers totalling at least 70 cm^2 are washed several times with an appropriate buffer and a sufficient volume of a suspension of suitable red blood cells added to cover the surface of the monolayer evenly. After different incubation times cells are examined for the presence of haemadsorption.

Detection of specified viruses

Tests are carried out for freedom from contaminants specific for the species of origin of the cell line and for the species for which the product is intended. Sufficient cells on suitable supports are prepared to carry out tests for the agents specified. Suitable positive controls are included in each test. The cells are subjected to suitable tests, for example using fluorescein-conjugated antibodies or similar reagents.

Tests in other cell cultures

Monolayers totalling at least 140 cm^2 are required. The cells are frozen and thawed at least three times and then centrifuged to remove cellular debris. Inoculate aliquots onto the following cells at any time up to 70 per cent confluency:
— primary cells of the source species;
— cells sensitive to viruses pathogenic for the species for which the vaccine is intended;
— cells sensitive to pestiviruses.

The inoculated cells are maintained in culture for at least 7 days, after which freeze-thawed extracts are prepared as above and inoculated onto sufficient fresh cultures of the same cell types to allow for the testing as described below. The cells are incubated for at least a further 7 days. The cultures are examined regularly for the presence of any cytopathic changes indicative of living organisms.

At the end of this period of 14 days, the inoculated cells are subjected to the following checks:
— freedom from cytopathic and haemadsorbent organisms, using the methods specified in the relevant paragraphs above,
— absence of pestiviruses and other specific contaminants by immunofluorescence or other validated methods as indicated in the paragraph above on Detection of Specified Viruses.

Retroviruses

A validated *in vitro* test is carried out to detect the presence of retroviruses in cell lines. If the presence of retrovirus is known or established by testing such as an endpoint product-enhanced reverse transcriptase (PERT) assay (*2.6.21*), then infectivity assays should be carried out. A PERT assay may be suitable to detect infective retrovirus after passage on permissive cells.

Since the sensitivity of PERT assays is very high, interpretation of a positive signal may be equivocal.

Cell seeds that show the presence of infectious retroviruses are not acceptable for the production of vaccines. In exceptional cases of positive or equivocal result in the infectivity assay, it may be justified and authorised to use such cells. Such a justification is based on a risk assessment including all available data and any down stream processing steps until the final product stage. The results of the risk assessment must demonstrate that the risk associated with the presence of infectious retroviruses is negligible in the final product.

Tumorigenicity

The risk of a cell line for the target species must be evaluated and, if necessary, tests are carried out.

PRIMARY CELLS

For most mammalian vaccines, the use of primary cells is not acceptable for the manufacture of vaccines since cell lines can be used. If there is no alternative to the use of primary cells, the cells are obtained from a herd or flock free from specified pathogens, with complete protection from introduction of diseases (for example, disease barriers, filters on air inlets, suitable quarantine before introduction of animals). Chicken flocks comply with the requirements prescribed in general chapter *5.2.2. Chicken Flocks Free from Specified Pathogens for the Production and Quality Control of Vaccines.* For all other species, the herd or flock is shown to be free from relevant specified pathogens. All the breeding stock in the herd or flock intended to be used to produce primary cells for vaccine manufacture is subject to a suitable monitoring procedure including regular serological checks carried out at least twice a year and two supplementary serological examinations performed in 15 per cent of the breeding stock in the herd between the two checks mentioned above.

Wherever possible, particularly for mammalian cells, a seed-lot system is used with, for example, a master cell seed formed after less than five passages, the working cell seed being no more than five passages from the initial preparation of the cell suspension from the animal tissues.

Each master cell seed, working cell seed and cells of the highest passage of primary cells are checked in accordance with Table 5.2.4.-2 and the procedure described below. The sample tested shall cover all the sources of cells used for the manufacture of the batch. No batches of vaccine manufactured using the cells may be released if any one of the checks performed produces unsatisfactory results.

Table 5.2.4.-2. – *Cell culture stage at which tests are carried out*

	Master cell seed	Working cell seed	Highest passage level
General microscopy	+	+	+
Bacteria and fungi	+	+	−
Mycoplasmas	+	+	−
Viruses	+	+	−
Retroviruses	+	+	−
Identification of species	+	−	−

Characteristics of cultures

The appearance of cell monolayers, before and after histological staining, is described. Information, if possible numerical data, is recorded, especially on the speed and rate of growth. Similarly, the presence or absence of contact inhibition, polynucleated cells and any other cellular abnormalities are specified.

Identification of species

It shall be demonstrated by one validated test that the master cell seed comes from the specified species of origin.

When a fluorescence test is carried out and the corresponding serum to the species of origin of cells is used and shows that all the tested cells are fluorescent, it is not necessary to carry out other tests with reagents able to detect contamination by cells of other species.

Bacterial and fungal sterility

The cells comply with the test for sterility (*2.6.1*).

The sample of cells to be examined consists of not less than the number of cells in a monolayer with an area of 70 cm^2 or for cells grown in suspension an approximately equivalent number of cells. The cells are maintained in culture for at least 15 days without antibiotics before carrying out the test.

Mycoplasmas (*2.6.7*)

The cells comply with the test for mycoplasmas. The cells are maintained in culture for at least 15 days without antibiotics before carrying out the test.

Absence of contaminating viruses

The cells must not be contaminated by viruses; suitably sensitive tests, including those prescribed below are carried out.

The monolayers tested shall be at least 70 cm^2, and shall be prepared and maintained in culture using the same medium and additives, and under similar conditions to those used for the preparation of the vaccine.

The monolayers are maintained in culture for a total of at least 28 days or for the longest period possible if culture for 28 days is impossible. Subcultures are made at 7-day intervals, unless the cells do not survive for this length of time when the subcultures are made on the latest day possible. Sufficient cells, in suitable containers are produced for the final subculture to carry out the tests specified below.

The monolayers are examined regularly throughout the incubation period for the possible presence of cytopathic effects and at the end of the observation period for cytopathic effects, haemadsorbent viruses and specific viruses by immunofluorescence and other suitable tests as indicated below.

Detection of cytopathic viruses

Two monolayers of at least 6 cm^2 each are stained with an appropriate cytological stain. Examine the entire area of each stained monolayer for any inclusion bodies, abnormal numbers of giant cells or any other lesion indicative of a cellular abnormality that might be attributable to a contaminant.

Detection of haemadsorbent viruses

Monolayers totalling at least 70 cm^2 are washed several times with a suitable buffer solution and a sufficient volume of a suspension of suitable red blood cells added to cover the surface of the monolayer evenly. After different incubation times, examine cells for the presence of haemadsorption.

Detection of specified viruses

Tests are be carried out for freedom of contaminants specific for the species of origin of the cells and for the species for which the product is intended.

Sufficient cells on suitable supports are prepared to carry out tests for the agents specified. Suitable positive controls are included in each test. The cells are subjected to suitable tests using fluorescein-conjugated antibodies or similar reagents.

Tests in other cell cultures

Monolayers totalling at least 140 cm^2 are required. The cells are frozen and thawed at least three times and then centrifuged to remove cellular debris. Aliquots are inoculated onto the following cells at any time up to 70 per cent confluency:

— primary cells of the source species;
— cells sensitive to viruses pathogenic for the species for which the vaccine is intended;
— cells sensitive to pestiviruses.

The inoculated cells are maintained in culture for at least 7 days, after which freeze-thawed extracts are prepared as above, and inoculated onto sufficient fresh cultures of the same cell types to allow for the testing as described below. The cells are incubated for at least a further 7 days.

All cultures are regularly examined for the presence of any cytopathic changes indicative of living organisms.

At the end of this period of 14 days, the inoculated cells are subjected to the following checks:
— freedom from cytopathic and haemadsorbent organisms is demonstrated using the methods specified in the relevant paragraphs above;
— relevant substrates are tested for the absence of pestiviruses and other specific contaminants by immunofluorescence or other validated methods as indicated in the paragraph above on Detection of Specified Viruses.

Retroviruses

A validated *in vitro* test is carried out to detect the presence of retroviruses in primary cells. If the presence of retrovirus is known or established by testing such as an endpoint product-enhanced reverse transcriptase (PERT) assay *(2.6.21)*, then infectivity assays should be carried out. A PERT assay may be suitable to detect infective retrovirus after passage on permissive cells.

Since the sensitivity of PERT assays is very high, interpretation of a positive signal may be equivocal.

Primary cells that show the presence of infectious retroviruses are not acceptable for the production of vaccines.

In exceptional cases of positive or equivocal result in the infectivity assay, it may be justified and authorised to use such cells. Such a justification is based on a risk assessment including all available data and any down stream processing steps until the final product stage. The results of the risk assessment must demonstrate that the risk associated with the presence of infectious retroviruses is negligible in the final product.

J (Vet) 2. Substances of Animal Origin for the Production of Immunological Veterinary Medicinal Products

(Ph Eur general texts 5.2.5)

1. SCOPE

Substances of animal origin (for example serum, trypsin and serum albumin) may be used during the manufacture of immunological veterinary medicinal products.

The requirements set out in this chapter apply to substances of animal origin produced on a batch basis, for use at all stages of manufacture, for example in culture media or as added constituents of products during blending. These requirements are not intended for the control of seed materials or substrates of animal origin that are covered by requirements in other pharmacopoeial texts such as the monograph *Vaccines for veterinary use (0062)* and chapter *5.2.4. Cell cultures for the production of veterinary vaccines.*

2. GENERAL PRINCIPLES AND REQUIREMENTS

Substances of animal origin comply with the requirements of the European Pharmacopoeia (where a relevant monograph exists).

Restrictions are placed on the use of substances of animal origin because of safety concerns associated with pathogens that may be present in them and epidemiological and/or regulatory concerns associated with the presence of particular antigens (either live or inactivated).

General principles:
— it is recommended to minimise, wherever practicable, the use of substances of animal origin;
— unless otherwise justified, the use of substances of animal origin as constituents in the formulation of medicinal products is not acceptable except where such substances are subject to a treatment validated for the inactivation of live extraneous agents.

General requirements:
— any batch of substance (after inactivation and/or processing, if relevant) found to contain or suspected of containing any living extraneous agent shall be discarded or used only in exceptional and justified circumstances; to be accepted for use, further processing must be applied that will ensure elimination and/or inactivation of the extraneous agent, and it shall then be demonstrated that the elimination and/or inactivation has been satisfactory;
— any batch of substance that, as concluded from the risk assessment, may induce an unacceptable detectable immune response in the target species as a consequence of contamination with inactivated extraneous agents, must not be used for the manufacture of that particular immunological veterinary medicinal product.

3. RISK MANAGEMENT

No single measure or combination of measures can guarantee the safety of the use of substances of animal origin, but they can reduce the risk from such use. It is therefore necessary for the manufacturer of immunological veterinary medicinal products to take account of this when choosing a substance of animal origin to use in manufacture, and to conduct a risk assessment, taking into account the origin of the substance and the manufacturing steps applied to it.

In addition, risk management procedures must be applied. Any residual risk must be evaluated in relation to the potential benefits derived from the use of the substance for the manufacture of the immunological veterinary medicinal product.

3-1 RISK ASSESSMENT

The risk assessment must take account of the animal diseases occurring in the country of origin of the animals used as a source of the substance, the potential infectious diseases occurring in the source species and the likely infectivity in the source organ or tissue. From this information, as part of the risk assessment, a list can be prepared of the extraneous agents that may be present in the substance.

The risk of contamination of the substance and the resultant immunological veterinary medicinal product with living extraneous agents needs to be assessed. The risk of contamination of the substance and the resultant immunological veterinary medicinal product with inactivated extraneous agents may also need to be taken into account. This would be the case if, for example, the contaminant was one from which a European country is officially free and/or is the subject of a specific disease control program in a European country and where the presence of the inactivated agent could lead to the stimulation of a detectable immune response in recipient animals.

As part of the risk assessment, the presence in the substance of antibodies that can interfere with the detection and/or inactivation of living extraneous agents must also be taken into account.

The risk assessment may need to be repeated and the risk management steps described below re-evaluated and revised in order to take account of changes:
— in the incidence of diseases occurring in the country or countries of origin of animals used as the source for the substance, including emerging diseases (new pathogens);

— in the incidence of diseases and of disease control measures applied in the European countries in which immunological veterinary medicinal products manufactured with the substance are used.

3-2 RISK CONTROL

For each of the potential extraneous agents identified by the risk assessment, and taking into account the proposed use of the substance, the risk must be controlled by the use of one or a combination of the followings measures:
— placing restrictions on the source of the material and auditing this;
— using validated inactivation procedures;
— demonstrating the ability of a production step to remove or inactivate extraneous agents;
— testing for extraneous agents.

4. CONTROL MEASURES
4-1 SOURCE

All substances of animal origin used in the manufacture (including blending) of immunological veterinary medicinal products must be from a known and documented source (including species of origin and country of origin of source animals and tissues).

4-2 PREPARATION

Substances of animal origin are prepared from a homogeneous bulk designated with a batch number. A batch may contain substances derived from as many animals as desired but once defined and given a batch number, the batch is not added to or contaminated in any way.

The production method used to prepare the substance of animal origin from the raw material may contribute to the removal and/or inactivation of extraneous agents (see section 4-3).

4-3 INACTIVATION AND/OR OTHER PROCESSING STEPS FOR REMOVAL OF EXTRANEOUS AGENTS

The inactivation procedure and/or other processing steps chosen shall have been validated and shown to be capable of reducing the titre of potential extraneous agents described below in the substance concerned by a factor of at least 10^6.

If this reduction in titre cannot be shown experimentally, a maximum pre-treatment titre of the extraneous agent must be set, taking into account the reduction in titre afforded by the inactivation/processing step and including a safety margin factor of 100; each batch of substance must be tested to determine the pre-treatment starting titre and confirm it is no greater than the specified limit, unless proper risk assessment, based on valid and suitable data, shows that titres will always be at least 100-fold below the titre that can effectively be inactivated.

The validation of the procedure(s) is conducted with a suitable representative range of viruses covering different types and sizes (enveloped and non-enveloped, DNA and RNA, single- and double-stranded, temperature- and pH-resistant), including test viruses with different degrees of resistance, taking into account the type of procedure(s) to be applied and the viruses that may be present in the material. The evidence for the efficacy of the procedure may take the form of references to published literature and/or experimental data generated by the manufacturer, but must be relevant to the conditions that will be present during the production and inactivation/processing of the substance.

For inactivated immunological veterinary medicinal products, the method used for inactivation of the active ingredient may also be validated for inactivation of possible contaminants from substances of animal origin used in the manufacture of this active ingredient.

4-4 TESTS

Depending on the outcome of the risk assessment and the validation data available for any procedure applied, tests for extraneous agents may be conducted on each batch before and/or after the application of an inactivation/processing step. For examination of the substance for freedom from extraneous agents, any solids are dissolved or suspended in a suitable medium to provide a suitable preparation for testing. A sufficient quantity of the preparation is tested to give a suitably sensitive test, as established in the validation studies.

As well as tests for living extraneous agents, tests may need to be conducted for the presence of inactivated extraneous agents, depending on the risks identified.

Freedom from living extraneous viruses

A sample from each batch of the substance is tested for extraneous viruses by general and specific tests. These tests are validated with respect to sensitivity and specificity for detection of a suitable range of potential extraneous viruses. Suitably sensitive cell cultures are used for the tests for extraneous viruses, including primary cells from the same species as the substance to be examined.

General test The inoculated cell cultures are observed regularly for 21 days for cytopathic effects. At the end of each 7-day period, a proportion of the original cultures is fixed, stained and examined for cytopathic effects, and a proportion is tested for haemadsorbing agents.

Specific tests A proportion of the cells available at the end of the general test is tested for specific viruses. The specific viruses to be tested for are potential extraneous viruses that are identified through the risk assessment and that would not be detected by the general test. A test for pestiviruses is conducted if the source species is susceptible to these.

Bacteria and fungi

Before use, substances are tested for sterility (*2.6.1*), or sterilised to inactivate any bacterial or fungal contaminants.

Mycoplasma

Before use, substances are tested for freedom from mycoplasma (*2.6.7*), or sterilised to inactivate any mycoplasmal contaminants.

K (Vet) 1. Evaluation of Safety of Veterinary Vaccines and Immunosera

Safety Veterinary Vaccines and Immunosera

(Ph Eur general texts 5.2.6)

The term 'product' means either a vaccine or an immunoserum throughout the text.

During development, safety tests are carried out in the target species to show the risks from use of the product.

Immune status for tests on vaccines The immune status of animals to be used for the safety test is specified in the specific monograph. For most monographs, 1 of the 3 following categories is specified:

1) the animals must be free from antibodies against the virus/bacterium/toxin etc. contained in the vaccine;

2) the animals are preferably free from antibodies against the virus/bacterium/toxin etc. contained in the vaccine, but animals with a low level of antibody may be used as long as the animals have not been vaccinated and the administration of the vaccine does not cause an anamnestic response;

3) the animals must not have been vaccinated against the disease that the vaccine is intended to prevent.

As a general rule, category 1 is specified for live vaccines. For other vaccines, category 2 is usually specified, but where most animals available for use in tests would comply with category 1, this may be specified for inactivated vaccines also. Category 3 is specified for some inactivated vaccines where determination of antibodies prior to testing is unnecessary or impractical. For poultry vaccines, as a general rule the use of specified-pathogen-free (SPF) birds is specified.

For avian vaccines, the safety test is generally carried out using SPF chickens (5.2.2), except that for vaccines not recommended for use in chickens it is carried out using birds of one of the species for which the vaccine is recommended, the birds being free from antibodies against the disease agent for which the vaccine is intended to provide protection.

Vaccines In laboratory tests, 'dose' means that quantity of the product to be recommended for use and containing the maximum titre or potency likely to be contained in production batches. Live vaccines are prepared only from strains of organisms that have been shown to be safe. For live vaccines, use a batch or batches of vaccine containing virus/bacteria at the least attenuated passage level that will be present in a batch of vaccine.

For combined vaccines, the safety shall be demonstrated; for live components of combined vaccines, compliance with the special requirements for live vaccines stated below shall be demonstrated separately for each vaccine strain.

For inactivated vaccines, safety tests carried out on the combined vaccine may be regarded as sufficient to demonstrate the safety of the individual components.

Immunosera In the tests, 'dose' means the maximum quantity of the product to be recommended for use and containing the maximum potency and maximum total protein likely to be contained in production batches. In addition, if appropriate, the dose tested also contains maximum quantities of immunoglobulin or gammaglobulin.

The tests described below, modified or supplemented by tests described in the Production section of a monograph, may be carried out as part of the tests necessary during development to demonstrate the safety of the product.

1 LABORATORY TESTS
1-1 SAFETY OF THE ADMINISTRATION OF 1 DOSE

For each of the recommended routes of administration, administer 1 dose of product to animals of each species and category for which use of the product is to be recommended. This must include animals of the youngest recommended age and pregnant animals, if appropriate.

For vaccines intended for use in mammals, in general 8 animals per group are used unless otherwise justified or specified in a specific monograph.

For fish vaccines administered by immersion, bathe the fish for twice the recommended time using a bath at twice the recommended concentration.

For vaccines intended for use in fish, in general 50 fish per group are used unless otherwise justified or specified in a specific monograph.

For vaccines intended for use in birds older than 3 weeks, in general 8 birds per group are used unless otherwise justified or specified in a specific monograph. For vaccines intended for use in birds younger than 3 weeks, in general 10 birds per group are used unless otherwise justified or specified in a specific monograph.

The animals are observed and examined at least daily for signs of abnormal local and systemic reactions. Where appropriate, these studies shall include detailed post-mortem macroscopic and microscopic examinations of the injection site. Other objective criteria are recorded, such as body temperature (for mammals) and performance measurements. The body temperatures are recorded on at least the day before and at the time of administration of the product, 4 h later and on the following 4 days. The animals are observed and examined at least daily until reactions may no longer be expected but, in all cases, the observation and examination period extends at least until 14 days after administration.

Unless otherwise prescribed in a specific monograph or, in the absence of a specific monograph, unless otherwise justified and authorised, the vaccine complies with the test if no animal shows abnormal local or systemic reactions or signs of disease, or dies from causes attributable to the vaccine.

1-2 SAFETY OF 1 ADMINISTRATION OF AN OVERDOSE

Overdose testing is required only for live vaccines. An overdose of the product is administered by each recommended route of administration to animals of the categories of the target species that are expected to be the most sensitive, such as animals of the youngest age. If multiple routes and methods of administration are specified for the product concerned, administration by all routes is recommended. If 1 route of administration has been shown to cause the most severe effects, this single route may be selected as the only one for use in the study.

The overdose normally consists of 10 doses of a live vaccine. For freeze-dried live vaccines, the 10 doses shall be reconstituted in a suitable volume of diluent for the test. For vaccines intended for use in mammals, in general 8 animals per group are used unless otherwise justified or specified in a specific monograph. For vaccines intended for use in fish, in general 50 fish per group are used unless otherwise justified or specified in a specific monograph. For vaccines intended for use in birds older than 3 weeks, in general 8 birds per group are used unless otherwise justified or specified in a specific monograph. For vaccines intended for use in birds younger than 3 weeks, in general 10 birds per group are used unless otherwise justified or specified in a specific monograph. The animals are observed and examined at least daily for signs of local and systemic reactions. Other objective criteria are recorded, such as body temperature (for mammals) and performance measurements. The animals are observed and examined for at least 14 days after administration.

Unless otherwise prescribed in a specific monograph or, in the absence of a specific monograph, unless otherwise justified and authorised, the vaccine complies with the test if no animal shows abnormal local or systemic reactions or signs of disease, or dies from causes attributable to the vaccine.

1-3 SAFETY OF THE REPEATED ADMINISTRATION OF 1 DOSE

Repeated administration of 1 dose may be required to reveal any adverse effects induced by such administration. These tests are particularly important where the product, notably an immunoserum, may be administered on several occasions over a relatively short period of time. These tests are carried out on the most sensitive categories of the target species, using each recommended route of administration. If multiple routes and methods of administration are specified for the product concerned, administration by all routes is recommended. If 1 route of administration has been shown to cause the most severe effects, this single route may be selected as the only one for use in the study. The number of administrations must be not less than the maximum number recommended; for vaccines, this shall take account of the number of administrations for primary vaccination and the 1st re-vaccination; for immunosera, it shall take account of the number of administrations required for treatment. The interval between administrations shall be suitable (e.g. period of risk or required for treatment) and appropriate to the recommendations of use. Although, for convenience, as far as vaccines are concerned, a shorter interval may be used in the study than that recommended in the field, an interval of at least 14 days must be allowed between administrations for the development of any hypersensitivity reaction. For immunosera, however, administration shall follow the recommended schedule. For vaccines intended for use in mammals, in general 8 animals per group are used unless otherwise justified or specified in a specific monograph. For vaccines intended for use in fish, in general 50 fish per group are used unless otherwise justified or specified in a specific monograph. For vaccines intended for use in birds older than 3 weeks, in general 8 birds per group are used unless otherwise justified or specified in a specific monograph. For vaccines intended for use in birds younger than 3 weeks, in general 10 birds per group are used unless otherwise justified or specified in a specific monograph. The animals are observed and examined at least daily for at least 14 days after the last administration for signs of systemic and local reactions. Other objective criteria are recorded, such as body temperature and performance measurements.

Unless otherwise prescribed in a specific monograph or, in the absence of a specific monograph, unless otherwise justified and authorised, the product complies with the test if no animal shows abnormal local or systemic reactions or signs of disease, or dies from causes attributable to the product.

1-4 EXAMINATION OF REPRODUCTIVE PERFORMANCE

When the vaccine is recommended for use or may be used in pregnant animals or laying birds, carry out a test for safety in this category of animals. If the reproductive safety studies are not performed, an exclusion statement appears on the label, unless a scientific justification for absence of risk is provided. Examination of reproductive performance must also be considered when data suggest that the starting material from which the product is derived may be a risk factor. Where appropriate, reproductive performance of males and females and harmful effects on the progeny, including teratogenic or abortifacient effects, are investigated by each of the recommended routes of administration. If multiple routes and methods of administration are specified for the product concerned, administration by all routes is recommended. If 1 route of administration has been shown to cause the most severe effects, this single route may be selected as the only one for use in the study.

For vaccines intended for use in mammals, in general 8 animals per group are used unless otherwise justified or

specified in a specific monograph. Vaccines recommended for use or that may be used in pregnant animals, are tested in each of the specific periods of gestation recommended for use on the label. An exclusion statement will be required for those gestation periods not tested.

The observation period is extended to parturition, to examine any harmful effects during gestation or on progeny, unless otherwise justified or specified in a specific monograph.

The following protocol is given as an example of an appropriate test for vaccines.

Safety in pregnant animals Use not fewer than 8 animals per group, at the recommended stage of gestation or at a range of stages of gestation according to the recommended schedule. Not fewer than 8 animals are used for each stage of pregnancy (i.e. 24 animals for 3 trimesters of pregnancy in cattle). Administer to each animal a recommended dose of the vaccine. If the recommended schedule requires a 2nd dose, administer another dose after an interval of at least 14 days. Unless otherwise prescribed in a specific monograph, observe the animals at least daily until 1 day after parturition. Unless otherwise prescribed in a specific monograph, or, in the absence of a specific monograph, unless otherwise justified and authorised, the vaccine complies with the test if no animal shows abnormal local or systemic reactions or signs of disease, or dies from causes attributable to the vaccine, and if no adverse effects on the pregnancy or the offspring are noted.

1-5 RESIDUES

In the case of live vaccines for well-established zoonotic diseases, the determination of residual vaccine organisms at the injection site may be required, in addition to the studies of dissemination described below.

1-6 ADVERSE EFFECTS ON IMMUNOLOGICAL FUNCTIONS

Where the product might adversely affect the immune response of the animal to which the product is administered or of its progeny, suitable tests on the immunological functions are carried out.

1-7 ADVERSE EFFECTS FROM INTERACTIONS

Studies are undertaken to show a lack of adverse effect on the safety of the product when simultaneous administration is recommended or where administration of the product is recommended as part of a schedule of administration of products within a short period of time.

1-8 SPECIAL REQUIREMENTS FOR LIVE VACCINES

The following laboratory tests must also be carried out with live vaccines.

For the following tests except for the test for increase in virulence (section 1-8-3), use the vaccine strain at the least attenuated passage level that will be present between the master seed lot and a batch of vaccine.

1-8-1 Spread of the vaccine strain Spread of the vaccine strain from vaccinated to unvaccinated target animals is investigated using the recommended route of administration most likely to result in spread. Moreover, it may be necessary to investigate the safety of spread to non-target species that could be highly susceptible to a live vaccine strain.

An assessment must be made of how many animal-to-animal passages are likely to be sustainable under normal circumstances together with an assessment of the likely consequences.

1-8-2 Dissemination in vaccinated animal Faeces, urine, milk, eggs, and oral, nasal and other secretions shall be tested for the presence of the organism as appropriate. Moreover, studies may be required of the dissemination of the vaccine strain in the body, with particular attention being paid to the predilection sites for replication of the organism. In the case of live vaccines for well-established zoonotic diseases for food-producing animals, these studies are obligatory and shall particularly take into account the persistence of the strain at the injection site.

1-8-3 Increase in virulence Unless otherwise prescribed in a specific monograph or, in the absence of a specific monograph, unless otherwise justified and authorised, the following applies. This test is carried out using the master seed lot. If the quantity of the master seed lot sufficient for performing the test is not available, the lowest passage material used for the production that is available in sufficient quantity may be used. At the time of inoculation, the animals in all groups are of an age suitable for recovery of the strain. Serial passages are carried out in target animals using 5 groups of animals, unless there is justification to carry out more passages or unless the strain disappears from the test animal sooner. *In vitro* propagation may not be used to expand the passage inoculum.

The passages are carried out using animals most appropriate to the potential risk being assessed.

The initial administration is carried out using the recommended route of administration most likely to lead to reversion to virulence, using an initial inoculum containing the maximum release titre. After this, not fewer than 4 further serial passages through animals of the target species are undertaken. The passages are undertaken by the route of administration most likely to lead to reversion to virulence. If the properties of the strain allow sequential passage via natural spreading, this method may be used, otherwise passage as described in each specific monograph is carried out and the micro-organisms that have been recovered at the final passage are tested for increase in virulence. For the first 4 groups, a minimum of 2 animals is used for mammalian vaccines, and a minimum of 5 birds is used for avian vaccines. The last group consist of a minimum of 8 mammals or 10 birds. At each passage, the presence of living vaccine-derived micro-organisms in the material used for passage is demonstrated. Care must be taken to avoid contamination by micro-organisms from previous passages. When the micro-organism is not recovered from any intermediate *in vivo* passage, repeat the passage in 10 animals using *in vivo* passaged material from the last passage in which the micro-organism was recovered. The micro-organism recovered is used as the inoculum for the next passage. If the target micro-organism is not recovered, the experiment is considered to be completed with the conclusion that the target micro-organism does not show an increase in virulence.

General clinical observations are made during the study. Animals in the last group are observed for 21 days unless otherwise justified. These observations include all relevant parameters typical for the disease that could indicate increase in virulence. Compare the clinical signs and other relevant parameters with those observed in the animals used in the test for safety of the administration of 1 dose (section 1-1). If the last group of animals shows no evidence of an increase in virulence, further testing is not required. Otherwise, material used for the 1st passage and the microorganisms recovered at the final passage level are used in a separate experiment using at least 8 animals per group for mammal

vaccines and at least 10 birds per group for avian vaccines, to compare directly the clinical signs and other relevant parameters. This study is carried out using the route of administration that was used for previous passages. An alternative route of administration may be used if justified.

Unless otherwise justified and authorised, the product complies with the test if no animal dies or shows signs attributable to the vaccine strain and no indication of increased virulence is observed in the animals of the last group.

1-8-4 Biological properties of the vaccine strain Other tests may be necessary to determine as precisely as possible the intrinsic biological properties of the vaccine strain (for example, neurotropism). For vector vaccines, evaluation is made of the risk of changing the tropism or virulence of the strain and where necessary specific tests are carried out. Such tests are systematically carried out where the product of a foreign gene is incorporated into the strain as a structural protein.

1-8-5 Recombination or genomic reassortment of strain The probability of recombination or genomic reassortment with field or other strains shall be considered.

2 FIELD STUDIES

Results from laboratory studies shall normally be supplemented with supportive data from field studies. Provided that laboratory tests have adequately assessed the safety and efficacy of a product under experimental conditions using vaccines of maximum and minimum titre or potency respectively, a single batch of product may be used to assess both safety and efficacy under field conditions. In these cases, a typical routine batch of intermediate titre or potency may be used.

For food-producing mammals, the studies include measurement of the body temperatures of a sufficient number of animals, before and after administration of the product; for other mammals, such measurements are carried out if the laboratory studies indicate that there might be a problem. The size and persistence of any local reaction and the proportion of animals showing local or systemic reactions are recorded. Performance measurements are made, where appropriate.

Performance measures for broilers include weekly mortality, feed conversion ratios, age at slaughter and weight, down grading and rejects at the processing plant. For vaccines for use in laying birds or in birds that may be maintained to lay, the effect of the vaccine on laying performance and hatchability is investigated, as appropriate.

3 ECOTOXICITY

An assessment is made of the potential harmful effects of the product for the environment and any necessary precautionary measures to reduce such risks are identified. The likely degree of exposure of the environment to the product is assessed, taking into account: the target species and mode of administration; excretion of the product; and disposal of unused product. If these factors indicate that there will be significant exposure of the environment to the product, the potential ecotoxicity is evaluated, taking into account the properties of the product.

K (Vet) 2. Evaluation of Efficacy of Veterinary Vaccines and Immunosera

(Ph Eur general texts 5.2.7)

The term 'product' means either a vaccine or an immunoserum throughout the text.

During development of the product, tests are carried out to demonstrate that the product is efficacious when administered by each of the recommended routes and methods of administration and using the recommended schedule to animals of each species and category for which use of the product is to be recommended. The type of efficacy testing to be carried out varies considerably depending on the particular type of product.

As part of tests carried out during development to establish efficacy, the tests described in the Production section of a monograph may be carried out; the following must be taken into account.

The dose to be used is that quantity of the product to be recommended for use and containing the minimum titre or potency expected at the end of the period of validity.

For live vaccines, use vaccine containing virus/bacteria at the most attenuated passage level that will be present in a batch of vaccine.

For immunosera, if appropriate, the dose tested also contains minimum quantities of immunoglobulin or gammaglobulin and/or total protein.

The efficacy evidence must support all the claims being made. For example, claims for protection against respiratory disease must be supported at least by evidence of protection from clinical signs of respiratory disease. Where it is claimed that there is protection from infection this must be demonstrated using re-isolation techniques. If more than one claim is made, supporting evidence for each claim is required.

Vaccines The influence of passively acquired and maternally derived antibodies on the efficacy of a vaccine is adequately evaluated. Any claims, stated or implied, regarding onset and duration of protection shall be supported by data from trials.

Claims related to duration of immunity are supported by evidence of protection. The test model described under Immunogenicity and/or Potency is not necessarily used to support claims regarding the duration of immunity afforded by a vaccine.

The efficacy of each of the components of multivalent and combined vaccines shall be demonstrated using the combined vaccine.

Immunosera Particular attention must be paid to providing supporting data for the efficacy of the regime that is to be recommended. For example, if it is recommended that the immunoserum needs only to be administered once to achieve a prophylactic or therapeutic effect then this must be demonstrated. Any claims, stated or implied, regarding onset and duration of protection or therapeutic effect must be supported by data from trials. For example, the duration of the protection afforded by a prophylactic dose of an antiserum must be studied so that appropriate guidance for the user can be given on the label.

Studies of immunological compatibility are undertaken when simultaneous administration is recommended or where it is a part of a usual administration schedule. Wherever a product is recommended as part of an administration scheme, the priming or booster effect or the contribution of the product to the efficacy of the scheme as a whole is demonstrated.

LABORATORY TESTS

In principle, demonstration of efficacy is undertaken under well-controlled laboratory conditions by challenge of the target animal under the recommended conditions of use.

In so far as possible, the conditions under which the challenge is carried out shall mimic the natural conditions for infection, for example with regard to the amount of challenge organism and the route of administration of the challenge.

Vaccines Unless otherwise justified, challenge is carried out using a strain different from the one used in the production of the vaccine.

If possible, the immune mechanism (cell-mediated/humoral, local/general, classes of immunoglobulin) that is initiated after the administration of the vaccine to target animals shall be determined.

Immunosera Data are provided from measurements of the antibody levels achieved in the target species after administration of the product, as recommended. Where suitable published data exist, references are provided to relevant published literature on protective antibody levels and challenge studies are avoided.

Where challenges are required, these can be given before or after administration of the product, in accordance with the indications and specific claims to be made.

FIELD TRIALS

In general, results from laboratory tests are supplemented with data from field trials, carried out, unless otherwise justified, with untreated control animals. Provided that laboratory tests have adequately assessed the safety and efficacy of a product under experimental conditions using vaccines of maximum and minimum titre or potency respectively, a single batch of product could be used to assess both safety and efficacy under field conditions. In these cases, a typical routine batch of intermediate titre or potency may be used. Where laboratory trials cannot be supportive of efficacy, the performance of field trials alone may be acceptable.

K (Vet) 3. Evaluation of Safety of each Batch of Immunosera for Veterinary Use

(Ph Eur general texts 5.2.9)

Definition of abnormal reactions During development studies, the type and degree of reactions expected after administration of the immunoserum are defined in the light of safety testing. This definition of normal or abnormal local and systemic reactions is then used as part of the operation procedure for the batch safety test to evaluate acceptable and unacceptable reactions.

Amount to be administered in the test In the tests, 'dose' means the quantity of the immunoserum to be recommended for use and containing the titre or potency within the limits specified for production batches. The amount to be administered in the test is usually defined in a number of doses.

Route of administration The immunoserum is administered by a recommended route. In principle, preference should be given to the application route with the higher possibility to detect reactions.

Target animal species and category of animals Use animals of the most sensitive species and of the minimum age recommended for administration of the immunoserum, unless otherwise justified and authorised.

Animal numbers The number of animals to be used for the test is prescribed in the general monograph *Immunosera for veterinary use (0030)*.

Identification of animals Unless otherwise justified and authorised, all animals are marked in a suitable way to ensure individual documentation of data for the whole observation period.

Observation period Where objective criteria such as body temperature are to be recorded as described below, the animals are examined and observed for at least 3 days prior to administration of the immunoserum. After administration of the immunoserum, the animals are observed and examined at least once every day for a period of at least 14 days for signs of local and systemic reactions. On the day of administration of the immunoserum, at least 1 additional inspection is necessary after 4 h or at intervals as specified in the monograph. Where there is a 2nd administration of the immunoserum the period usually ends 14 days after the 2nd administration.

Local and systemic reactions Animals showing severe abnormal local or systemic reactions are euthanised. All dead animals undergo a post-mortem with macroscopic examination. Additional microscopic and microbiological investigations may be indicated.

The animals are observed and examined for signs of local and systemic reactions. Where it is known to be a useful indicator, other criteria are recorded, such as body temperature, body mass, other performance measurements and food intake.

Local reactions As far as appropriate and possible, the size and persistence of any local reaction (including incidence of painful reactions) and the proportion of animals showing local reactions are recorded.

Systemic reactions Body temperature and, if appropriate, body mass are documented as general indicators of systemic effects of administration of the immunoserum. In addition, all clinical signs are recorded.

Body temperature For mammals, the studies include measurement of body temperature during the observation period. The body temperatures are recorded beginning at least 3 days before administration of the immunoserum, at the time of administration, 4 h after and at suitable intervals. The body temperature before administration of the immunoserum has to be within the physiological range. At least for immunosera where a significant increase in body temperature may be expected or where an increase in body temperature is specified in an individual monograph, it is recommended to use the mean temperature of the days before administration of the immunoserum (e.g. day −3 to day 0) as the baseline temperature to have clear guidance for evaluation of the test.

Body mass and food intake Where it is known to be a reliable and useful indicator of safety, for example in young growing animals, the body mass is measured and documented shortly before administration of the immunoserum and during the observation period. The food intake is monitored and documented as an indicator of the effect of administering the immunoserum. In most cases, it will be sufficient to record the daily ration has been consumed or partly or wholly rejected but, in some cases it may be necessary to record the actual weight of food consumed, if this is a relevant indicator of the safety of the immunoserum.

Clinical signs All expected and unexpected clinical signs of a general nature are recorded, including changes in health status and behaviour changes.

Score sheets The score sheets are prepared for each immunoserum in the light of expected signs. All parameters and data are recorded in score sheets. The score sheets contain general parameters but are also adapted for each kind of immunoserum to list clinical signs that might be more evident for a given immunoserum.

Criteria for repeating the test If an abnormal sign occurs, the responsible veterinarian determines, based on post-mortem examination if necessary, whether this was due to the immunoserum or not. If it is not clear what caused the abnormal sign or where an animal is withdrawn for reasons unrelated to the immunoserum, the test may be repeated. If in the 2nd test there is the same abnormal sign as in the 1st test, the immunoserum does not comply with the test. Any treatment administered to an animal during the observation period is recorded. If the treatment may interfere with the test, the test is invalid.

Appendix XVI

B (Vet) 3. Test for Absence of Mycoplasmas

(Ph. Eur. method 2.6.7 as applied to vaccines for human use)

Where the test for mycoplasmas is prescribed for a master cell bank, for a working cell bank, for a virus seed lot or for control cells, both the culture method and the indicator cell culture method are used. Where the test for mycoplasmas is prescribed for a virus harvest, for a bulk vaccine or for the final lot (batch), the culture method is used. The indicator cell culture method may also be used, where necessary, for screening of media.

Nucleic acid amplification techniques (NAT) may be used as an alternative to one or both of the other methods after suitable validation.

Culture method

CHOICE OF CULTURE MEDIA

The test is carried out using a sufficient number of both solid and liquid media to ensure growth in the chosen incubation conditions of small numbers of mycoplasmas that may be present in the product to be examined. Liquid media must contain phenol red. The range of media chosen is shown to have satisfactory nutritive properties for at least the micro-organisms shown below. The nutritive properties of each new batch of medium are verified for the appropriate micro-organisms in the list. When testing for mycoplasmas in the product to be examined, at least 1 of the following species will be included as a positive control:

— *Acholeplasma laidlawii* (vaccines for human and veterinary use where an antibiotic has been used during production);
— *Mycoplasma gallisepticum* (where avian material has been used during production or where the vaccine is intended for use in poultry);
— *Mycoplasma hyorhinis* (non-avian veterinary vaccines);
— *Mycoplasma orale* (vaccines for human and veterinary use);
— *Mycoplasma pneumoniae* (vaccines for human use) or other suitable species of D-glucose fermenter such as *Mycoplasma fermentans*;
— *Mycoplasma synoviae* (where avian material has been used during production or where the vaccine is intended for use in poultry).

The test strains are field isolates having undergone a limited number of subcultures (not more than 15), and are stored frozen or freeze-dried. After cloning, the strains are identified as being of the required species by comparison with type cultures, for example:

A. laidlawii	NCTC 10116	CIP 75.27	ATCC 23206
M. gallisepticum	NCTC 10115	CIP 104967	ATCC 19610
M. fermentans	NCTC 10117	CIP 105680	ATCC 19989
M. hyorhinis	NCTC 10130	CIP 104968	ATCC 17981
M. orale	NCTC 10112	CIP 104969	ATCC 23714
M. pneumoniae	NCTC 10119	CIP 103766	ATCC 15531
M. synoviae	NCTC 10124	CIP 104970	ATCC 25204

Acholeplasma laidlawii BRP, Mycoplasma fermentans BRP, Mycoplasma hyorhinis BRP, Mycoplasma orale BRP and *Mycoplasma synoviae BRP* are suitable for use as low-passage reference strains.

INCUBATION CONDITIONS

Incubate liquid media in tightly stoppered containers at 35-38 °C. Incubate solid media in microaerophilic conditions (nitrogen containing 5-10 per cent of carbon dioxide and sufficient humidity to prevent desiccation of the agar surface) at 35-38 °C.

NUTRITIVE PROPERTIES

Carry out the test for nutritive properties for each new batch of medium. Inoculate the chosen media with the appropriate test micro-organisms; use not more than 100 CFU (colony-forming units) per 60 mm diameter plate containing 9 mL of solid medium and per 100 mL container of liquid medium; use a separate plate and container for each species of micro-organism. Incubate the media and make subcultures from 0.2 mL of liquid medium to solid medium at the specified intervals (see below under Test for mycoplasmas in the product to be examined). The solid medium complies with the test if adequate growth is found for each test micro-organism (growth obtained does not differ by a factor greater than 5 from the value calculated with respect to the inoculum). The liquid medium complies with the test if growth on agar plates subcultured from the broth is found for at least 1 subculture for each test micro-organism.

INHIBITORY SUBSTANCES

The test for inhibitory substances is carried out once for a given product and is repeated whenever there is a change in production method that may affect the detection of mycoplasmas.

To demonstrate absence of inhibitory substances, carry out the test for nutritive properties in the presence and absence of the product to be examined. If growth of a test micro-organism occurs more than 1 subculture sooner in the absence of the product to be examined than in its presence, or if plates directly inoculated with the product to be examined have fewer than 1/5 of the number of colonies of those inoculated without the product to be examined, inhibitory substances are present and they must be neutralised or their effect otherwise countered, for example by passage in substrates not containing inhibitors or dilution in a larger volume of medium before the test. If dilution is used, larger medium volumes may be used or the inoculum volume may be divided among several 100 mL flasks.

The effectiveness of the neutralisation or other process is checked by repeating the test for inhibitory substances after neutralisation.

TEST FOR MYCOPLASMAS IN THE PRODUCT TO BE EXAMINED

Inoculate 10 mL of the product to be examined per 100 mL of each liquid medium. If it has been found that a significant pH change occurs upon the addition of the product to be examined, the liquid medium is restored to its original pH value by the addition of a solution of either sodium hydroxide or hydrochloric acid. Inoculate 0.2 mL of the product to be examined on each plate of each solid medium. Incubate liquid media for 20-21 days. Incubate solid media for not less than 14 days, except those corresponding to the 20-21 day subculture, which are incubated for 7 days. At the same time incubate an uninoculated 100 mL portion of each liquid medium and agar plates, as a negative control. On days 2-4 after inoculation, subculture each liquid medium by inoculating 0.2 mL on at least 1 plate of each solid medium. Repeat the procedure between the 6th and 8th days, again between the 13th and 15th days and again between the 19th and 21st days of the test. Observe the liquid media every 2 or 3 days and if a colour change occurs, subculture. If a liquid medium shows bacterial or fungal contamination, the test is invalid. The test is valid if at least 1 plate per medium and per inoculation day can be read. Include in the test positive controls prepared by inoculation of not more than 100 CFU of at least 1 test micro-organism on agar medium or into broth medium. Where the test for mycoplasmas is carried out regularly and where possible, it is recommended to use the test micro-organisms in regular rotation. The test micro-organisms used are those listed under Choice of culture media.

INTERPRETATION OF RESULTS

At the end of the prescribed incubation period, examine all inoculated solid media microscopically for the presence of mycoplasma colonies. The product complies with the test if growth of typical mycoplasma colonies has not occurred. The product does not comply with the test if growth of typical mycoplasma colonies has occurred on any of the solid media. The test is invalid if 1 or more of the positive controls do not show growth of mycoplasmas on at least 1 subculture plate. The test is invalid if 1 or more of the negative controls show growth of mycoplasmas. If suspect colonies are observed, a suitable validated method may be used to determine whether they are due to mycoplasmas.

The following section is published for information.

Recommended media for the culture method

The following media are recommended. Other media may be used, provided that their ability to sustain the growth of mycoplasmas has been demonstrated on each batch in the presence and absence of the product to be examined.

HAYFLICK MEDIA (RECOMMENDED FOR THE GENERAL DETECTION OF MYCOPLASMAS)

Liquid medium

Beef heart infusion broth (1)	90.0 mL
Horse serum (unheated)	20.0 mL
Yeast extract (250 g/L)	10.0 mL
Phenol red (0.6 g/L solution)	5.0 mL
Penicillin (20 000 IU/mL)	0.25 mL
Deoxyribonucleic acid (2 g/L solution)	1.2 mL

Adjust to pH 7.8.

Solid medium

Prepare as described above replacing beef heart infusion broth by beef heart infusion agar containing 15 g/L of agar.

FREY MEDIA (RECOMMENDED FOR THE DETECTION OF M. SYNOVIAE)

Liquid medium

Beef heart infusion broth (1)	90.0 mL
Essential vitamins (2)	0.025 mL
Glucose monohydrate (500 g/L solution)	2.0 mL
Swine serum (inactivated at 56 °C for 30 min)	12.0 mL
β-Nicotinamide adenine dinucleotide (10 g/L solution)	1.0 mL
Cysteine hydrochloride (10 g/L solution)	1.0 mL
Phenol red (0.6 g/L solution)	5.0 mL
Penicillin (20 000 IU/mL)	0.25 mL

Mix the solutions of β-nicotinamide adenine dinucleotide and cysteine hydrochloride and after 10 min add to the other ingredients. Adjust to pH 7.8.

Solid medium

Beef heart infusion broth (1)	90.0 mL
Agar, purified (3)	1.4 g

Adjust to pH 7.8, sterilise by autoclaving then add:

Essential vitamins (2)	0.025 mL
Glucose monohydrate (500 g/L solution)	2.0 mL
Swine serum (unheated)	12.0 mL
β-Nicotinamide adenine dinucleotide (10 g/L solution)	1.0 mL
Cysteine hydrochloride (10 g/L solution)	1.0 mL
Phenol red (0.6 g/L solution)	5.0 mL
Penicillin (20 000 IU/mL)	0.25 mL

FRIIS MEDIA (RECOMMENDED FOR THE DETECTION OF NON-AVIAN MYCOPLASMAS)

Liquid medium

Hanks' balanced salt solution (modified) (4)	800 mL
Distilled water	67 mL
Brain heart infusion (5)	135 mL
PPLO Broth (6)	248 mL
Yeast extract (170 g/L)	60 mL
Bacitracin	250 mg
Meticillin	250 mg
Phenol red (5 g/L)	4.5 mL
Horse serum	165 mL
Swine serum	165 mL

Adjust to pH 7.40-7.45.

Solid medium

Hanks' balanced salt solution (modified) (4)	200 mL
DEAE-dextran	200 mg
Agar, purified (3)	15.65 g

Mix well and sterilise by autoclaving. Cool to 100 °C. Add to 1740 mL of liquid medium as described above.

(1) *Beef heart infusion broth*

Beef heart (for preparation of the infusion)	500 g
Peptone	10 g
Sodium chloride	5 g
Distilled water	to 1000 mL

Sterilise by autoclaving.

(2) *Essential vitamins*

Biotin	100 mg
Calcium pantothenate	100 mg
Choline chloride	100 mg
Folic acid	100 mg
i-Inositol	200 mg
Nicotinamide	100 mg
Pyridoxal hydrochloride	100 mg
Riboflavine	10 mg
Thiamine hydrochloride	100 mg
Distilled water	to 1000 mL

(3) *Agar, purified*

A highly refined agar for use in microbiology and immunology, prepared by an ion-exchange procedure that results in a product having superior purity, clarity and gel strength. It contains about:

Water	12.2 per cent
Ash	1.5 per cent
Acid-insoluble ash	0.2 per cent
Chlorine	0
Phosphate (calculated as P_2O_5)	0.3 per cent
Total nitrogen	0.3 per cent
Copper	8 ppm
Iron	170 ppm
Calcium	0.28 per cent
Magnesium	0.32 per cent

(4) *Hanks' balanced salt solution (modified)*

Sodium chloride	6.4 g
Potassium chloride	0.32 g
Magnesium sulfate heptahydrate	0.08 g
Magnesium chloride hexahydrate	0.08 g
Calcium chloride, anhydrous	0.112 g
Disodium hydrogen phosphate dihydrate	0.0596 g
Potassium dihydrogen phosphate, anhydrous	0.048 g
Distilled water	to 800 mL

(5) *Brain heart infusion*

Calf-brain infusion	200 g
Beef-heart infusion	250 g
Proteose peptone	10 g
Glucose monohydrate	2 g
Sodium chloride	5 g
Disodium hydrogen phosphate, anhydrous	2.5 g
Distilled water	to 1000 mL

(6) *PPLO broth*

Beef-heart infusion	50 g
Peptone	10 g
Sodium chloride	5 g
Distilled water	to 1000 mL

Indicator cell culture method

Cell cultures are stained with a fluorescent dye that binds to DNA. Mycoplasmas are detected by their characteristic particulate or filamentous pattern of fluorescence on the cell surface and, if contamination is heavy, in surrounding areas. Mitochondria in the cytoplasm may be stained but are readily distinguished from mycoplasmas.

If for viral suspensions the interpretation of results is affected by marked cytopathic effects, the virus may be neutralised using a specific antiserum that has no inhibitory effects on mycoplasmas or a cell culture substrate that does not allow growth of the virus may be used. To demonstrate the absence of inhibitory effects of serum, carry out the positive control tests in the presence and absence of the antiserum.

VERIFICATION OF THE SUBSTRATE

Use Vero cells or another cell culture (for example, the production cell line) that is equivalent in effectiveness for detecting mycoplasmas. Test the effectiveness of the cells to be used by applying the procedure shown below and inoculating not more than 100 CFU or CFU-like micro-organisms of suitable reference strains of *M. hyorhinis* and *M. orale*. The following strains have been found to be suitable:

M. hyorhinis	ATCC 29052
M. orale NCTC 10112 CIP 104969	ATCC 23714

The cells are suitable if both reference strains are detected. The indicator cells must be subcultured without an antibiotic before use in the test.

TEST METHOD

1. Seed the indicator cell culture at a suitable density (for example, 2×10^4 to 2×10^5 cells/mL, 4×10^3 to 2.5×10^4 cells/cm^2) that will yield confluence after 3 days of growth. Inoculate 1 mL of the product to be examined into the cell culture vessel and incubate at 35-38 °C.

2. After at least 3 days of incubation, when the cells have grown to confluence, make a subculture on cover slips in suitable containers or on some other surface (for example, chambered slides) suitable for the test procedure. Seed the cells at low density so that they reach 50 per cent confluence after 3-5 days of incubation. Complete confluence impairs visualisation of mycoplasmas after staining and must be avoided.

3. Remove the medium and rinse the indicator cells with *phosphate buffered saline pH 7.4 R,* then add a suitable fixing solution (a freshly prepared mixture of 1 volume of *glacial acetic acid R* and 3 volumes of *methanol R* is suitable when *bisbenzimide R* is used for staining).

4. Remove the fixing solution and wash the cells with *sterile water R.* Dry the slides completely if they are to be stained more than 1 h later (particular care is needed for staining of slides after drying owing to artefacts that may be produced).

5. Add a suitable DNA stain and allow to stand for a suitable time (*bisbenzimide working solution R* and a standing time of 10 min are suitable).

6. Remove the stain and rinse the monolayer with *water R.*

7. Mount each coverslip, where applicable (a mixture of equal volumes of *glycerol R* and *phosphate-citrate buffer solution pH 5.5 R* is suitable for mounting). Examine by fluorescence (for bisbenzimide stain a 330 nm/380 nm excitation filter and an LP 440 nm barrier filter are suitable) at 400 × magnification or greater.

8. Compare the microscopic appearance of the test cultures with that of the negative and positive controls, examining for extranuclear fluorescence. Mycoplasmas produce pinpoints or filaments over the indicator cell cytoplasm. They may also produce pinpoints and filaments in the intercellular spaces. Multiple microscopic fields are examined according to the protocol established during validation.

INTERPRETATION OF RESULTS

The product to be examined complies with the test if fluorescence typical of mycoplasmas is not present. The test is invalid if the positive controls do not show fluorescence typical of mycoplasmas. The test is invalid if the negative controls show fluorescence typical of mycoplasmas.

Nucleic acid amplification techniques (NAT)

NAT (*2.6.21*) may be used for detection of mycoplasmas by amplification of nucleic acids extracted from a test sample with specific primers that reveal the presence of the target nucleic acid. NAT indicate the presence of a particular nucleic acid sequence and not necessarily the presence of viable mycoplasmas. A number of different techniques are available. This general chapter does not prescribe a particular method for the test. The procedure applied must be validated as described, taking account of the guidelines presented at the end of this section. Where a commercial kit is used, certain elements of the validation may be carried out by the manufacturer and information provided to the user but it must be remembered that full information on the primers may not be available and that production of the kit may be modified or discontinued.

NAT are applied where prescribed in a monograph. They may also be used instead of the culture method and the indicator cell culture method after suitable validation.

Direct NAT Can be applied in the presence of cytotoxic material and where a rapid method is needed.

Cell-culture enrichment followed by NAT The test sample and a suitable cell substrate (as described under the indicator cell-culture method) are cultured together for a suitable period; the nucleic acids are then extracted from cells and supernatant and used for detection by NAT.

VALIDATION

Reference standards are required at various stages during validation and for use as controls during routine application of the test. The reference standards may be mycoplasmas or nucleic acids.

For validation of the limit of detection, the following species represent an optimal selection in terms of the frequency of occurrence as contaminants and phylogenetic relationships:
— *A. laidlawii;*
— *M. fermentans;*
— *M. hyorhinis* (where cell-culture enrichment is used, a fastidious strain such as ATCC 29052 is included);
— *M. orale;*
— *M. pneumoniae* or *M. gallisepticum;*
— *M. synoviae* (where there is use of or exposure to avian material during production);
— *Mycoplasma arginini;*
— *Spiroplasma citri* (where there is use of or exposure to insect or plant material during production).

Demonstration of specificity requires the use of a suitable range of bacterial species other than mycoplasmas. Bacterial genera with close phylogenetic relation to mycoplasmas are most appropriate for this validation; these include *Clostridium*, *Lactobacillus* and *Streptococcus*.

Comparability studies for use of NAT as an alternative method For each mycoplasma test species:
— as an alternative to the culture method: the NAT test system must be shown to detect 10 CFU/mL;
— as an alternative to the indicator cell culture method: the NAT test system must be shown to detect 100 CFU/mL;

or an equivalent limit of detection in terms of the number of copies of mycoplasma nucleic acid in the test sample (using suitable reference standards of mycoplasma nucleic acid).

CONTROLS

Internal controls Internal controls are necessary for routine verification of absence of inhibition. The internal control may contain the primer binding-site, or some other suitable sequence may be used. It is preferably added to the test material before isolating the nucleic acid and therefore acts as an overall control (extraction, reverse transcription, amplification, detection).

External controls The external positive control contains a defined number of target-sequence copies or CFUs from 1 or more suitable species of mycoplasma chosen from those used during validation of the test conditions. 1 of the positive controls is set close to the positive cut-off point to demonstrate that the expected sensitivity is achieved.

The external negative control contains no target sequence but does not necessarily represent the same matrix as the test article.

INTERPRETATION OF RESULTS

The primers used may also amplify non-mycoplasmal bacterial nucleic acid, leading to false positive results. Procedures are established at the time of validation for dealing with confirmation of positive results, where necessary.

The following section is published for information.

Validation of nucleic acid amplification techniques (NAT) for the detection of mycoplasmas : guidelines

1 SCOPE

Nucleic acid amplification techniques (NAT) are either qualitative or quantitative tests for the presence of nucleic acid. For the detection of mycoplasma contamination of various samples such as vaccines and cell substrates, qualitative tests are adequate and may be considered to be limit tests.

These guidelines describe methods to validate qualitative nucleic acid amplification analytical procedures for assessing mycoplasma contamination. They may also be applicable for real-time NAT used as limit tests for the control of contaminants.

The 2 characteristics regarded as the most important for validation of the analytical procedure are the specificity and the detection limit. In addition, the robustness of the analytical procedure should be evaluated.

For the purpose of this document, an analytical procedure is defined as the complete procedure from extraction of nucleic acid to detection of the amplified products.

Where commercial kits are used for part or all of the analytical procedure, documented validation points already covered by the kit manufacturer can replace validation by the user. Nevertheless, the performance of the kit with respect to its intended use has to be demonstrated by the user (e.g. detection limit, robustness, cross-detection of other classes of bacteria).

NAT may be used as:
— a complementary test (for example, for cytotoxic viral suspensions) or for in-process control purposes;
— an alternative method to replace an official method (indicator cell culture method or culture method).

These guidelines will thus separate these 2 objectives by presenting first a guideline for the validation of the NAT themselves, and second, a guideline for a comparability study between NAT and official methods.

2 GUIDELINE FOR MYCOPLASMA NAT VALIDATION

3 parameters should be evaluated: specificity, detection limit and robustness.

2-1 Specificity Specificity is the ability to unequivocally assess target nucleic acid in the presence of components that may be expected to be present.

The specificity of NAT is dependent on the choice of primers, the choice of probe (for analysis of the final product) and the stringency of the test conditions (for both the amplification and detection steps).

The ability of the NAT to detect a large panel of mycoplasma species will depend on the choice of primers, probes and method parameters. This ability should be demonstrated using characterised reference panels (e.g. reference strains provided by the EDQM). Since NAT systems are usually based on a mix of primers, the theoretical analysis of primers and probes by comparison with databases is not recommended, because interpretation of the results may be quite complex and may not reflect the experimental results.

Moreover, as it is likely that the primers will detect other bacterial species, the potential cross-detection should be documented in the validation study. Bacterial genera such as gram-positive bacteria with close phylogenetic relation to mycoplasmas are most appropriate for this validation; these include *Clostridium*, *Lactobacillus* and *Streptococcus*. However, this is not an exhaustive list and species to be tested will depend on the theoretical ability (based on primers/probes sequences) of the NAT system to detect such other species.

Based on the results from this validation of the specificity, if a gap in the specificity of the method is identified (such as detection of non-mycoplasmal bacterial nucleic acid), an appropriate strategy must be proposed in the validation study to allow interpretation of positive results on a routine basis. For example, a second test may be performed using an alternative method without this specificity gap or using an official method.

2-2 Detection limit. The detection limit of an individual analytical procedure is the lowest amount of target nucleic acid in a sample that can be detected but not necessarily quantitated as an exact value.

For establishment of the detection limit, a positive cut-off point should be determined for the nucleic acid amplification analytical procedure. The positive cut-off point (as defined in general chapter *2.6.21*) is the minimum number of target sequence copies per volume of sample that can be detected in 95 per cent of test runs. This positive cut-off point is influenced by the distribution of mycoplasmal genomes in the individual samples being tested and by factors such as enzyme efficiency, and can result in different 95 per cent cut-off values for individual analytical test runs.

To determine the positive cut-off point, a dilution series of characterised and calibrated (either in CFUs or nucleic acid copies) in-house working strains or EDQM standards should be tested on different days to examine variation between test runs.

For validation of the limit of detection, the following species represent an optimal selection in terms of the frequency of occurrence as contaminants and phylogenetic relationships:
— *A. laidlawii;*
— *M. fermentans;*
— *M. hyorhinis;*
— *M. orale;*
— *M. pneumoniae* or *M. gallisepticum;*
— *M. synoviae* (where there is use of or exposure to avian material during production);
— *M. arginini;*
— *S. citri* (where there is use of or exposure to insect or plant material during production).

For each strain, at least 3 independent 10-fold dilution series should be tested, with a sufficient number of replicates at each dilution to give a total number of 24 test results for each dilution, to enable a statistical analysis of the results.

For example, a laboratory may test 3 dilution series on different days with 8 replicates for each dilution, 4 dilution series on different days with 6 replicates for each dilution, or 6 dilution series on different days with 4 replicates for each dilution. In order to keep the number of dilutions at a manageable level, a preliminary test should be performed to obtain a preliminary value for the positive cut-off point (i.e. the highest dilution giving a positive signal). The range of dilutions can then be chosen around the predetermined

preliminary cut-off point. The concentration of mycoplasmas (CFUs or copies) that can be detected in 95 per cent of test runs can then be calculated using an appropriate statistical evaluation.

These results may also serve to evaluate the variability of the analytical procedure.

2-3 Robustness The robustness of an analytical procedure is a measure of its capacity to remain unaffected by small but deliberate variations in method parameters, and provides an indication of its reliability during normal usage.

The evaluation of robustness should be considered during the development phase. It should show the reliability of the analytical procedure with respect to deliberate variations in method parameters. For NAT, small variations in the method parameters can be crucial. However, the robustness of the method can be demonstrated during its development when small variations in the concentrations of reagents (e.g. $MgCl_2$, primers or deoxyribonucleotides) are tested. Modifications of extraction kits or extraction procedures as well as different thermal cycler types may also be evaluated.

Finally, robustness of the method can be evaluated through collaborative studies.

3 GUIDELINE FOR COMPARABILITY STUDY
NAT may be used instead of official methods (indicator cell culture method and/or culture method). In this case a comparability study should be carried out. This comparability study should include mainly a comparison of the respective detection limits of the alternative method and official methods. However, specificity (mycoplasma panel detected, putative false positive results) should also be considered.

For the detection limit, acceptability criteria are defined as follows:
— if the alternative method is proposed to replace the culture method, the NAT system must be shown to detect 10 CFU/mL for each mycoplasma test species described in paragraph 2-2;
— if the alternative method is proposed to replace the indicator cell culture method, the NAT system must be shown to detect 100 CFU/mL for each mycoplasma test species described in paragraph 2-2

For both cases, suitable standards calibrated for the number of nucleic acid copies and the number of CFUs may be used for establishing that these acceptability criteria are reached. The relation between CFUs and nucleic acid copies for the reference preparations should be previously established to compare the performance of the alternative NAT method with the performance of the official methods.

1 of the following 2 strategies can be used to perform this comparability study:
— perform the NAT alternative method in parallel with the official method(s) to evaluate simultaneously the detection limit of both methods using the same samples of calibrated strains;
— compare the performance of the NAT alternative method using previously obtained data from official method validation. In this case, calibration of standards used for both validations as well as their stabilities should be documented carefully.

Comparability study reports should describe all the validation elements described in section 2 (specificity, limit of detection and variability, as well as robustness) in order to assess all the advantages and/or disadvantages of the alternative NAT method compared to official methods.

B (Vet) 4. Avian Viral Vaccines: Tests for Extraneous Agents in Seed Lots

(Ph. Eur. method 2.6.24)

GENERAL PROVISIONS

a) In the following tests, chickens and/or chicken material such as eggs and cell cultures shall be derived from chicken flocks free from specified pathogens (SPF) (*5.2.2*).

b) Cell cultures for the testing of extraneous agents comply with the requirements for the master cell seed of general chapter *5.2.4. Cell cultures for the production of veterinary vaccines*, with the exception of the karyotype test and the tumorigenicity test, which do not have to be carried out.

c) In tests using cell cultures, precise specifications are given for the number of replicates, monolayer surface areas and minimum survival rate of the cultures. Alternative numbers of replicates and cell surface areas are possible as well, provided that a minimum of 2 replicates are used, the total surface area and the total volume of test substance applied are not less than that prescribed here and the survival rate requirements are adapted accordingly.

d) For a freeze-dried preparation, reconstitute using a suitable liquid. Unless otherwise stated or justified, the test substance must contain a quantity of virus equivalent to at least 10 doses of vaccine in 0.1 mL of inoculum.

e) If the virus of the seed lot would interfere with the conduct and sensitivity of the test, neutralise the virus in the preparation with a monospecific antiserum.

f) Monospecific antiserum and serum of avian origin used for cell culture or any other purpose, in any of these tests, shall be free from antibodies against and free from inhibitory effects on the organisms listed hereafter under 7 Antibody specifications for sera used in extraneous agents testing.

g) Where specified in a monograph or otherwise justified, if neutralisation of the virus of the seed lot is required but difficult to achieve, the tests described below are adapted, as required, to provide the necessary guarantees of freedom from contamination with an extraneous agent.

h) Other types of tests than those indicated may be used, provided they are at least as sensitive as those indicated and of appropriate specificity. Nucleic acid amplification techniques (*2.6.21*) give specific detection for many agents and can be used after validation for sensitivity and specificity.

1 TEST FOR EXTRANEOUS AGENTS USING EMBRYONATED HENS′ EGGS

Use a test substance, diluted if necessary, containing a quantity of neutralised virus equivalent to at least 10 doses of vaccine in 0.2 mL of inoculum. Suitable antibiotics may be added. Inoculate the test substance into 3 groups of 10 embryonated hens′ eggs as follows:

— group 1: 0.2 mL into the allantoic cavity of each 9- to 11-day-old embryonated egg;

— group 2: 0.2 mL onto the chorio-allantoic membrane of each 9- to 11-day-old embryonated egg;

— group 3: 0.2 mL into the yolk sac of each 5- to 6-day-old embryonated egg.

Candle the eggs in groups 1 and 2 daily for 7 days and the eggs in group 3 daily for 12 days. Discard embryos that die during the first 24 h as non-specific deaths; the test is not valid unless at least 6 embryos in each group survive beyond the first 24 h after inoculation. Examine macroscopically for abnormalities all embryos that die more than 24 h after inoculation, or that survive the incubation period. Examine also the chorio-allantoic membranes of these eggs for any abnormality and test the allantoic fluids for the presence of haemagglutinating agents.

Carry out a further embryo passage. Pool separately material from live and from the dead and abnormal embryos. Inoculate each pool into 10 eggs for each route as described above, chorio-allantoic membrane material being inoculated onto chorio-allantoic membranes, allantoic fluids into the allantoic cavity and embryo material into the yolk sac. For eggs inoculated by the allantoic and chorio-allantoic routes, candle the eggs daily for 7 days, proceeding and examining the material as described above. For eggs inoculated by the yolk sac route, candle the eggs daily for 12 days, proceeding and examining the material as described above.

The seed lot complies with the test if no test embryo shows macroscopic abnormalities or dies from causes attributable to the seed lot and if examination of the chorio-allantoic membranes and testing of the allantoic fluids show no evidence of the presence of any extraneous agent.

2 TEST IN CHICKEN KIDNEY CELLS

Prepare 7 monolayers of chicken kidney cells, each monolayer having an area of about 25 cm^2. Maintain 2 monolayers as negative controls and treat these in the same way as the 5 monolayers inoculated with the test substance, as described below. Remove the culture medium when the cells reach confluence. Inoculate 0.1 mL of the test substance onto each of the 5 monolayers. Allow adsorption for 1 h, add culture medium and incubate the cultures for a total of at least 21 days, subculturing at 4- to 7-day intervals. Each passage is made with pooled cells and fluids from all 5 monolayers after carrying out a freeze-thaw cycle. Inoculate 0.1 mL of pooled material onto each of 5 recently prepared monolayers of about 25 cm^2 each, at each passage. For the last passage, grow the cells also on a suitable substrate so as to obtain an area of about 10 cm^2 of cells from each of the monolayers for test A. The test is not valid if less than 80 per cent of the monolayers survive after any passage.

Examine microscopically all the cell cultures frequently throughout the entire incubation period for any signs of cytopathic effect or other evidence of the presence of contaminating agents in the test substance. At the end of the total incubation period, carry out the following procedures.

A. Fix and stain (with Giemsa or haematoxylin and eosin) about 10 cm^2 of confluent cells from each of the 5 monolayers. Examine the cells microscopically for any cytopathic effect, inclusion bodies, syncytial formation, or other evidence of the presence of contaminating agents from the test substance.

B. Drain and wash about 25 cm^2 of cells from each of the 5 monolayers. Cover these cells with a 0.5 per cent suspension of washed chicken erythrocytes (using at least 1 mL of suspension for each 5 cm^2 of cells). Incubate the cells at 4 °C for 20 min and then wash gently in phosphate buffered saline pH 7.4. Examine the cells microscopically for haemadsorption attributable to the presence of a haemadsorbing agent in the test substance.

C. Test individual samples of the fluids from each cell culture using chicken erythrocytes for haemagglutination attributable to the presence of a haemagglutinating agent in the test substance.

The test is not valid if there are any signs of extraneous agents in the negative control cultures. The seed lot complies with the test if there is no evidence of the presence of any extraneous agent.

3 TEST FOR AVIAN LEUCOSIS VIRUSES

Prepare at least 13 replicate monolayers of either DF-1 cells or primary or secondary chick embryo fibroblasts from the tissues of 9- to 11-day-old embryos that are known to be genetically susceptible to subgroups A, B and J of avian leucosis viruses and that support the growth of exogenous but not endogenous avian leucosis viruses (cells from C/E strain chickens are suitable). Each replicate shall have an area of about 50 cm^2.

Remove the culture medium when the cells reach confluence. Inoculate 0.1 mL of the test substance onto each of 5 of the replicate monolayers. Allow adsorption for 1 h, and add culture medium. Inoculate 2 of the replicate monolayers with subgroup A avian leucosis virus (not more than 10 CCID$_{50}$ in 0.1 mL), 2 with subgroup B avian leucosis virus (not more than 10 CCID$_{50}$ in 0.1 mL) and 2 with subgroup J avian leucosis virus (not more than 10 CCID$_{50}$ in 0.1 mL) as positive controls. Maintain not fewer than 2 non-inoculated replicate monolayers as negative controls.

Incubate the cells for a total of at least 9 days, subculturing at 3- to 4-day intervals. Retain cells from each passage level and harvest the cells at the end of the total incubation period. Wash cells from each passage level from each replicate and resuspend the cells at 10^7 cells per millilitre in barbital-buffered saline for subsequent testing by a Complement Fixation for Avian Leucosis (COFAL) test or in phosphate buffered saline for testing by Enzyme-Linked Immunosorbent Assay (ELISA). Then, carry out 3 cycles of freezing and thawing to release any group-specific antigen and perform a COFAL test or an ELISA test on each extract to detect group-specific avian leucosis antigen if present.

The test is not valid if group-specific antigen is detected in fewer than 5 of the 6 positive control replicate monolayers or if a positive result is obtained in any of the negative control monolayers, or if the results for both of the 2 negative control monolayers are inconclusive. If the results for more than 1 of the test replicate monolayers are inconclusive, then further subcultures of reserved portions of the fibroblast monolayers shall be made and tested until an unequivocal result is obtained. If a positive result is obtained for any of the test monolayers, then the presence of avian leucosis virus in the test substance has been detected.

The seed lot complies with the test if there is no evidence of the presence of any avian leucosis virus.

4 TEST FOR AVIAN RETICULOENDOTHELIOSIS VIRUS

Prepare 11 monolayers of primary or secondary chick embryo fibroblasts from the tissues of 9- to 11-day old chick embryos or duck embryo fibroblasts from the tissues of 13- to 14-day-old embryos, each monolayer having an area of about 25 cm^2.

Remove the culture medium when the cells reach confluence. Inoculate 0.1 mL of the test substance onto each of 5 of the monolayers. Allow adsorption for 1 h, and add culture medium. Inoculate 4 of the monolayers with avian reticuloendotheliosis virus as positive controls (not more than 10 CCID$_{50}$ in 0.1 mL). Maintain 2 non-inoculated monolayers as negative controls.

Incubate the cells for a total of at least 10 days, subculturing twice at 3- to 4-day intervals. The test is not valid if fewer

than 3 of the 4 positive controls or fewer than 4 of the 5 test monolayers or neither of the 2 negative controls survive after any passage.

For the last subculture, grow the fibroblasts on a suitable substrate so as to obtain an area of about 10 cm^2 of confluent fibroblasts from each of the original 11 monolayers for the subsequent test: test about 10 cm^2 of confluent fibroblasts derived from each of the original 11 monolayers by immunostaining for the presence of avian reticuloendotheliosis virus. The test is not valid if avian reticuloendotheliosis virus is detected in fewer than 3 of the 4 positive control monolayers or in any of the negative control monolayers, or if the results for both of the 2 negative control monolayers are inconclusive. If the results for more than 1 of the test monolayers are inconclusive then further subcultures of reserved portions of the fibroblast monolayers shall be made and tested until an unequivocal result is obtained.

The seed lot complies with the test if there is no evidence of the presence of avian reticuloendotheliosis virus.

5 TEST FOR CHICKEN ANAEMIA VIRUS

Prepare eleven 20 mL suspensions of the MDCC-MSBI cell line or another cell line of equivalent sensitivity in 25 cm^2 cell culture flasks containing about 5 $\times$ 10^5 cells/mL. Inoculate 0.1 mL of the test substance into each of 5 flasks. Inoculate 4 of the suspensions with 10 CCID$_{50}$ chicken anaemia virus as positive controls. Maintain not fewer than 2 non-inoculated suspensions. Maintain all the cell cultures for a total of at least 24 days, subculturing 8 times at 3- to 4-day intervals. During the subculturing the presence of chicken anaemia virus may be indicated by a metabolic colour change in the infected cultures, the culture fluids becoming red in comparison with the control cultures. Examine the cells microscopically for cytopathic effect. At this time or at the end of the incubation period, centrifuge the cells from each flask at low speed and resuspend at about 10^6 cells/mL and place 25 μL in each of 10 wells of a multi-well slide. Examine the cells by immunostaining.

The test is not valid if chicken anaemia virus is detected in fewer than 3 of the 4 positive controls or in any of the non-inoculated controls. If the results for more than 1 of the test suspensions are inconclusive, then further subcultures of reserved portions of the test suspensions shall be made and tested until an unequivocal result is obtained.

The seed lot complies with the test if there is no evidence of the presence of chicken anaemia virus.

6 TEST FOR EXTRANEOUS AGENTS USING CHICKS

Inoculate each of at least 10 chicks with the equivalent of 100 doses of vaccine by the intramuscular route and with the equivalent of 10 doses by eye-drop. Chicks that are 2 weeks of age are used in the test except that if the seed virus is pathogenic for birds of this age, older birds may be used, if required and justified. In exceptional cases, for inactivated vaccines, the virus may be neutralised by specific antiserum if the seed virus is pathogenic for birds at the age of administration. Repeat these inoculations 2 weeks later. Observe the chicks for a period of 5 weeks from the day of the first inoculation. No antimicrobial agents shall be administered to the chicks during the test period. The test is not valid if fewer than 80 per cent of the chicks survive to the end of the test period.

Collect serum from each chick at the end of the test period. Test each serum sample for antibodies against each of the agents listed below (with the exception of the virus type of the seed lot) using one of the methods indicated for testing for the agent.

Clinical signs of disease in the chicks during the test period (other than signs attributable to the virus of the seed lot) and the detection of antibodies in the chicks after inoculation (with the exception of antibodies to the virus of the seed lot), are classed as evidence of the presence of an extraneous agent in the seed lot.

It is recommended that sera from these birds is retained so that additional testing may be carried out if requirements change.

A. Standard tests

Agent	Type of test
Avian adenoviruses, group 1	SN, EIA, AGP
Avian encephalomyelitis virus	AGP, EIA
Avian infectious bronchitis virus	EIA, HI
Avian infectious laryngotracheitis virus	SN, EIA, IS
Avian leucosis viruses	SN, EIA
Avian nephritis virus	IS
Avian orthoreoviruses	IS, EIA
Avian reticuloendotheliosis virus	AGP, IS, EIA
Chicken anaemia virus	IS, EIA, SN
Egg drop syndrome virus	HI, EIA
Avian infectious bursal disease virus	Serotype 1: AGP, EIA, SN Serotype 2: SN
Influenza A virus	AGP, EIA, HI
Marek's disease virus	AGP
Newcastle disease virus	HI, EIA
Turkey rhinotracheitis virus	EIA
Salmonella pullorum	Agg

Agg: agglutination
AGP: agar gel precipitation
EIA: enzyme immunoassay (e.g. ELISA)
HI: haemagglutination inhibition
IS: immunostaining (e.g. fluorescent antibody)
SN: serum neutralisation

B. Additional tests for turkey extraneous agents

If the seed virus is of turkey origin or was propagated in turkey substrates, tests for antibodies against the following agents are also carried out.

Agent	Type of test
Chlamydia spp.	EIA
Avian infectious haemorrhagic enteritis virus	AGP
Avian paramyxovirus 3	HI
Avian infectious bursal disease virus type 2	SN

A test for freedom from turkey lympho-proliferative disease virus is carried out by intraperitoneal inoculation of twenty 4-week-old turkey poults. Observe the poults for 40 days. The test is not valid if more than 20 per cent of the poults die from non-specific causes. The seed lot complies with the test if sections of spleen and thymus taken from 10 poults 2 weeks after inoculation show no macroscopic or

microscopic lesions (other than those attributable to the seed lot virus) and no poult dies from causes attributable to the seed lot.

C. Additional tests for duck extraneous agents

If the seed virus is of duck origin or was propagated in duck substrates, tests for antibodies against the following agents are also carried out.

Agent	Type of test
Chlamydia spp.	EIA
Duck and goose parvoviruses	SN, EIA
Duck enteritis virus	SN
Duck hepatitis virus type I	SN

The seed lot complies with the test if there is no evidence of the presence of any extraneous agent.

D. Additional tests for goose extraneous agents

If the seed virus is of goose origin or was prepared in goose substrates, tests for the following agents are also carried out.

Agent	Type of test
Duck and goose parvovirus	SN, EIA
Duck enteritis virus	SN
Goose haemorrhagic polyomavirus	test in goslings shown below or another suitable test

Inoculate subcutaneously the equivalent of at least 10 doses to each of ten 1-day-old susceptible goslings. Observe the goslings for 28 days. The test is not valid if more than 20 per cent of the goslings die from non-specific causes. The seed virus complies with the test if no gosling dies from causes attributable to the seed lot.

7 ANTIBODY SPECIFICATIONS FOR SERA USED IN EXTRANEOUS AGENTS TESTING

All batches of serum to be used in extraneous agents testing, either to neutralise the vaccine virus (seed lot or batch of finished product) or as a supplement for cell culture media, shall be shown by suitably sensitive tests to be free from antibodies against and free from inhibitory effects on the following micro-organisms - except for one type, namely, antibodies against the virus that they are supposed to neutralise.

Avian adenoviruses

Avian encephalomyelitis virus

Avian infectious bronchitis viruses

Avian infectious bursal disease virus types 1 and 2

Avian infectious haemorrhagic enteritis virus

Avian infectious laryngotracheitis virus

Avian leucosis viruses

Avian nephritis virus

Avian paramyxoviruses 1 to 9

Avian orthoreoviruses

Avian reticuloendotheliosis virus

Chicken anaemia virus

Duck enteritis virus

Duck hepatitis virus type I

Egg drop syndrome virus

Fowl pox virus

Influenza viruses

Marek's disease virus

Turkey herpesvirus

Turkey rhinotracheitis virus

Non-immune serum for addition to culture media can be assumed to be free from antibodies against any of these viruses if the agent is known not to infect the species of origin of the serum and it is not necessary to test the serum for such antibodies. Monospecific antisera for virus neutralisation can be assumed to be free from the antibodies against any of these viruses if it can be shown that the immunising antigen could not have been contaminated with antigens derived from that virus and if the virus is known not to infect the species of origin of the serum; it is not necessary to test the serum for such antibodies. It is not necessary to retest sera obtained from birds from SPF chicken flocks (5.2.2).

Batches of sera prepared for neutralising the vaccine virus must not be prepared from any passage level derived from the virus isolate used to prepare the master seed lot or from an isolate cultured in the same cell line.

B (Vet) 5. Avian Live Virus Vaccines: Tests for Extraneous Agents in Batches of Finished Product

(Ph. Eur. method 2.6.25)

GENERAL PROVISIONS

a) In the following tests, chickens and/or chicken material such as eggs and cell cultures shall be derived from chicken flocks free from specified pathogens (SPF) (5.2.2).

b) Cell cultures for the testing of extraneous agents comply with the requirements for the master cell seed of general chapter 5.2.4. *Cell cultures for the production of veterinary vaccines*, with the exception of the karyotype test and the tumorigenicity test, which do not have to be carried out.

c) In tests using cell cultures, precise specifications are given for the number of replicates, monolayer surface areas and minimum survival rate of the cultures. Alternative numbers of replicates and cell surface areas are possible as well, provided that a minimum of 2 replicates are used, the total surface area and the total volume of vaccine test applied are not less than that prescribed here and the survival rate requirements are adapted accordingly.

d) In these tests, use the liquid vaccine or reconstitute a quantity of the freeze-dried preparation to be tested with the liquid stated on the label or another suitable diluent such as water for injections. Unless otherwise stated or justified, the test substance contains the equivalent of 10 doses in 0.1 mL of inoculum.

e) If the vaccine virus would interfere with the conduct and sensitivity of the test, neutralise the virus in the preparation with a monospecific antiserum.

f) Monospecific antiserum and serum of avian origin used for cell culture and any other purpose, in any of these tests, shall be free of antibodies against and free from inhibitory effects on the organisms listed under 7 Antibody specifications for sera used in extraneous agents testing (2.6.24).

g) Where specified in a monograph or otherwise justified, if neutralisation of the vaccine virus is required but difficult to achieve, the tests described below are adapted, as required,

to provide the necessary guarantees of freedom from contamination with an extraneous agent.

If the vaccine virus cannot be completely neutralised – using monospecific antiserum – for the yolk sac inoculation test, the following tests may be performed:

— for enveloped viruses such as Newcastle disease virus: perform the test for extraneous agents using embryonated hens' eggs by the yolk sac route with prior inactivation of enveloped vaccine viruses with lipid solvents,

— for avian encephalomyelitis virus and avian nephritis viruses: perform appropriate tests to detect these viruses. For avian nephritis virus, the test in chicken kidney cells described in section 2 of general chapter 2.6.24. *Avian viral vaccines: tests for extraneous agents in seed lots* may be used.

If the vaccine virus cannot be completely neutralised – using monospecific antiserum – for the other tests below, alternatively or in addition to *in vitro* tests conducted on the batch, a test for extraneous agents may be conducted on chick sera obtained from testing the batch of vaccine, as described under 6 Test for extraneous agents using chicks in general chapter 2.6.24. *Avian viral vaccines: tests for extraneous agents in seed lots.*

h) Other types of tests than those indicated may be used, provided they are at least as sensitive as those indicated and of appropriate specificity. Nucleic acid amplification techniques (2.6.21) give specific detection for many agents and can be used after validation for sensitivity and specificity.

1 TEST FOR EXTRANEOUS AGENTS USING EMBRYONATED HENS' EGGS

Prepare the test vaccine, diluted if necessary, to contain neutralised virus equivalent to 10 doses of vaccine in 0.2 mL of inoculum. Suitable antibiotics may be added. Inoculate the test vaccine into 3 groups of 10 embryonated hens' eggs as follows:

— group 1: 0.2 mL into the allantoic cavity of each 9- to 11-day-old embryonated egg,

— group 2: 0.2 mL onto the chorio-allantoic membrane of each 9- to 11-day-old embryonated egg,

— group 3: 0.2 mL into the yolk sac of each 5- to 6-day-old embryonated egg.

Candle the eggs in groups 1 and 2 daily for 7 days and the eggs in group 3 for 12 days. Discard embryos that die during the first 24 h as non-specific deaths; the test is not valid unless at least 6 embryos in each group survive beyond the first 24 h after inoculation. Examine macroscopically for abnormalities all embryos which die more than 24 h after inoculation, or which survive the incubation period. Examine also the chorio-allantoic membranes of these eggs for any abnormality and test the allantoic fluids for the presence of haemagglutinating agents.

Carry out a further embryo passage. Pool separately material from live and from the dead and abnormal embryos. Inoculate each pool into 10 eggs for each route as described above, chorio-allantoic membrane material being inoculated onto chorio-allantoic membranes, allantoic fluids into the allantoic cavity and embryo material into the yolk sac. For eggs inoculated by the allantoic and chorio-allantoic routes, candle the eggs daily for 7 days, proceeding and examining the material as described above. For eggs inoculated by the yolk sac route, candle the eggs daily for 12 days, proceeding and examining the material as described above.

The batch of vaccine complies with the test if no test embryo shows macroscopic abnormalities or dies from causes attributable to the vaccine and if examination of the chorio-allantoic membranes and testing of the allantoic fluids show no evidence of the presence of extraneous agents.

As previously mentioned under General provisions (paragraph g), if neutralisation of the virus is not possible and as a consequence the yolk sac inoculation cannot be evaluated, suitable tests other than those indicated may be carried out to provide the necessary guarantees of freedom from contamination with an extraneous agent; in particular other tests to detect avian encephalomyelitis and avian nephritis viruses may be carried out. In this case, justification to use other tests must be provided, and the vaccine complies if there is no evidence of the presence of avian encephalomyelitis virus or avian nephritis virus.

2 TEST IN CHICKEN EMBRYO FIBROBLAST CELLS

Prepare 7 monolayers of primary or secondary chicken embryo fibroblasts, from the tissues of 9- to 11-day-old embryos, each monolayer having an area of about 25 cm^2. Maintain 2 monolayers as negative controls and treat these in the same way as the 5 monolayers inoculated with the test vaccine, as described below. Remove the culture medium when the cells reach confluence. Inoculate 0.1 mL of test vaccine onto each of 5 of the monolayers. Allow adsorption for 1 h and add culture medium. Incubate the cultures for a total of at least 21 days, subculturing at 4- to 5-day intervals. Each passage is made with pooled cells and fluids from all 5 monolayers after carrying out a freeze-thaw cycle. Inoculate 0.1 mL of pooled material onto each of 5 recently prepared monolayers of chicken embryo fibroblast cells, each monolayer having an area of about 25 cm^2 each as before. For the last passage, grow the cells also on a suitable substrate so as to obtain an area of about 10 cm^2 of cells from each of the monolayers, for test A. The test is not valid if less than 80 per cent of the test monolayers, or neither of the 2 negative control monolayers survive after any passage.

Examine microscopically all the cell cultures frequently throughout the entire incubation period for any signs of cytopathic effect or other evidence of the presence of contaminating agents in the test vaccine. At the end of the total incubation period, carry out the following procedures.

A. Fix and stain (with Giemsa or haematoxylin and eosin) about 10 cm^2 of confluent cells from each of the 5 original monolayers. Examine the cells microscopically for any cytopathic effect, inclusion bodies, syncytial formation, or any other evidence of the presence of a contaminating agent from the test vaccine.

B. Drain and wash about 25 cm^2 of cells from each of the 5 monolayers. Cover these cells with a 0.5 per cent suspension of washed chicken red blood cells (using at least 1 mL of suspension for each 5 cm^2 of cells). Incubate the cells at 4 °C for 20 min and then wash gently in phosphate buffered saline pH 7.4. Examine the cells microscopically for haemadsorption attributable to the presence of a haemadsorbing agent in the test vaccine.

C. Test individually samples of the fluid from each cell culture using chicken red blood cells for haemagglutination attributable to the presence of a haemagglutinating agent in the test vaccine.

The test is not valid if there are any signs of extraneous agents in the negative control cultures. The batch of vaccine complies with the test if there is no evidence of the presence of any extraneous agent.

3 TEST FOR EGG DROP SYNDROME VIRUS

Prepare 11 monolayers of chicken embryo liver cells, from the tissues of 14- to 16-day-old embryos, each monolayer having an area of about 25 cm^2. Remove the culture medium when the cells reach confluence. Inoculate 0.1 mL of test vaccine onto each of 5 of the monolayers (test monolayers). Allow adsorption for 1 h, add culture medium. Inoculate 4 of the monolayers with a suitable strain of egg drop syndrome virus (not more than 10 CCID$_{50}$ in 0.1 mL) to serve as positive control monolayers. Maintain 2 non-inoculated monolayers as negative control monolayers.

Incubate the cells for a total of at least 21 days, subculturing every 4-5 days. Each passage is made as follows: carry out a freeze-thaw cycle; prepare separate pools of the cells plus fluid from the test monolayers, from the positive control monolayers and from the negative control monolayers; inoculate 0.1 mL of the pooled material onto each of 5, 4 and 2 recently prepared monolayers of chicken embryo liver cells, each monolayer having an area of about 25 cm^2 as before. The test is not valid if fewer than 4 of the 5 test monolayers or fewer than 3 of the 4 positive controls or neither of the 2 negative control monolayers survive after any passage.

Examine microscopically all the cell cultures at frequent intervals throughout the entire incubation period for any signs of cytopathic effect or other evidence of the presence of a contaminating agent in the test vaccine. At the end of the total incubation period, carry out the following procedure: test separately, cell culture fluid from the test monolayers, positive control monolayers and negative control monolayers, using chicken red blood cells, for haemagglutination attributable to the presence of haemagglutinating agents.

The test is not valid if egg drop syndrome virus is detected in fewer than 3 of the 4 positive control monolayers or in any of the negative control monolayers, or if the results for both of the 2 negative control monolayers are inconclusive. If the results for more than 1 of the test monolayers are inconclusive then further subcultures of reserved portions of the monolayers shall be made and tested until an unequivocal result is obtained.

The batch of vaccine complies with the test if there is no evidence of the presence of egg drop syndrome virus or any other extraneous agent.

4 TEST FOR MAREK'S DISEASE VIRUS

Prepare 11 monolayers of primary or secondary chick embryo fibroblasts from the tissues of 9- to 11-day-old embryos, each monolayer having an area of about 25 cm^2. Remove the culture medium when the cells reach confluence. Inoculate 0.1 mL of test vaccine onto each of 5 of the monolayers (test monolayers). Allow adsorption for 1 h, and add culture medium. Inoculate 4 of the monolayers with a suitable strain of Marek's disease virus (not more than 10 CCID$_{50}$ in 0.1 mL) to serve as positive controls. Maintain 2 non-inoculated monolayers as negative controls.

Incubate the cultures for a total of at least 21 days, subculturing at 4- to 5-day intervals. Each passage is made as follows: trypsinise the cells, prepare separate pools of the cells from the test monolayers, from the positive control monolayers and from the negative control monolayers. Mix an appropriate quantity of each with a suspension of freshly prepared primary or secondary chick embryo fibroblasts and prepare 5, 4 and 2 monolayers, as before. The test is not valid if fewer than 4 of the 5 test monolayers or fewer than 3 of the 4 positive controls or neither of the 2 negative control monolayers survive after any passage.

Examine microscopically all the cell cultures frequently throughout the entire incubation period for any signs of cytopathic effect or other evidence of the presence of a contaminating agent in the test vaccine.

For the last subculture, grow the cells on a suitable substrate so as to obtain an area of about 10 cm^2 of confluent cells from each of the original 11 monolayers for the subsequent test: test about 10 cm^2 of confluent cells derived from each of the original 11 monolayers by immunostaining for the presence of Marek's disease virus. The test is not valid if Marek's disease virus is detected in fewer than 3 of the 4 positive control monolayers or in any of the negative control monolayers, or if the results for both of the 2 negative control monolayers are inconclusive.

The batch of vaccine complies with the test if there is no evidence of the presence of Marek's disease virus or any other extraneous agent.

5 TESTS FOR TURKEY RHINOTRACHEITIS VIRUS

A. In chicken embryo fibroblasts

NOTE: this test can be combined with Test 2 by using the same test monolayers and negative controls, for all stages up to the final specific test for turkey rhinotracheitis virus on cells prepared from the last subculture.

Prepare 11 monolayers of primary or secondary chick embryo fibroblasts from the tissues of 9- to 11-day-old embryos, each monolayer having an area of about 25 cm^2. Remove the culture medium when the cells reach confluence. Inoculate 0.1 mL of test vaccine onto each of 5 of the monolayers (test monolayers). Allow adsorption for 1 h, and add culture medium. Inoculate 4 of the monolayers with a suitable strain of turkey rhinotracheitis virus as positive controls (not more than 10 CCID$_{50}$ in 0.1 mL). Maintain 2 non-inoculated monolayers as negative controls.

Incubate the cultures for a total of at least 21 days, subculturing at 4- to 5-day intervals. Each passage is made as follows: carry out a freeze-thaw cycle; prepare separate pools of the cells plus fluid from the test monolayers, from the positive control monolayers and from the negative control monolayers; inoculate 0.1 mL of the pooled material onto each of 5, 4 and 2 recently prepared monolayers of chicken embryo fibroblasts cells, each monolayer having an area of about 25 cm^2 as before. The test is not valid if fewer than 4 of the 5 test monolayers or fewer than 3 of the 4 positive controls or neither of the 2 negative control monolayers survive after any passage.

For the last subculture, grow the cells on a suitable substrate so as to obtain an area of about 10 cm^2 of confluent cells from each of the original 11 monolayers for the subsequent test: test about 10 cm^2 of confluent cells derived from each of the original 11 monolayers by immunostaining for the presence of turkey rhinotracheitis virus. The test is not valid if turkey rhinotracheitis virus is detected in fewer than 3 of the 4 positive control monolayers or in any of the negative control monolayers, or if the results for both of the 2 negative control monolayers are inconclusive. If the results for both of the 2 test monolayers are inconclusive then further subcultures of reserved portions of the fibroblasts shall be made and tested until an unequivocal result is obtained.

The batch of vaccine complies with the test if there is no evidence of the presence of turkey rhinotracheitis virus or any other extraneous agent.

B. In Vero cells

Prepare 11 monolayers of Vero cells, each monolayer having an area of about 25 cm^2. Remove the culture medium when the cells reach confluence. Inoculate 0.1 mL of test vaccine onto each of 5 of the monolayers (test monolayers). Allow adsorption for 1 h, and add culture medium. Inoculate 4 of the monolayers with a suitable strain of turkey rhinotracheitis virus (not more than 10 CCID$_{50}$ in 0.1 mL) to serve as positive controls. Maintain 2 non-inoculated monolayers as negative controls.

Incubate the cultures for a total of at least 21 days, subculturing at 4- to 5-day intervals. Each passage is made as follows: carry out a freeze-thaw cycle. Prepare separate pools of the cells plus fluid from the test monolayers, from the positive control monolayers and from the negative control monolayers. Inoculate 0.1 mL of the pooled material onto each of 5, 4 and 2 recently prepared monolayers of Vero cells, each monolayer having an area of about 25 cm^2 as before. The test is not valid if fewer than 4 of the 5 test monolayers or fewer than 3 of the 4 positive controls or neither of the 2 negative controls survive after any passage.

For the last subculture, grow the cells on a suitable substrate so as to obtain an area of about 10 cm^2 of confluent cells from each of the original 11 monolayers for the subsequent test: test about 10 cm^2 of confluent cells derived from each of the original 11 monolayers by immunostaining for the presence of turkey rhinotracheitis virus. The test is not valid if turkey rhinotracheitis virus is detected in fewer than 3 of the 4 positive control monolayers or in any of the negative control monolayers, or if the results for both of the 2 negative control monolayers are inconclusive. If the results for more than 1 of the test monolayers are inconclusive then further subcultures of reserved portions of the monolayers shall be made and tested until an unequivocal result is obtained.

The batch of vaccine complies with the test if there is no evidence of the presence of turkey rhinotracheitis virus or any other extraneous agent.

6 TEST FOR CHICKEN ANAEMIA VIRUS

Prepare eleven 20 mL suspensions of the MDCC-MSB1 cell line or another cell line of equivalent sensitivity in 25 cm^2 flasks containing about 5×10^5 cells/mL. Inoculate 0.1 mL of test vaccine into each of 5 of these flasks. Inoculate 4 other suspensions with 10 CCID$_{50}$ chicken anaemia virus as positive controls. Maintain not fewer than 2 non-inoculated suspensions. Maintain all the cell cultures for a total of at least 24 days, subculturing 8 times at 3- to 4-day intervals. During the subculturing the presence of chicken anaemia virus may be indicated by a metabolic colour change in the infected cultures, the culture fluids becoming red in comparison with the control cultures. Examine the cells microscopically for cytopathic effect. At this time or at the end of the incubation period, centrifuge the cells from each flask at low speed, resuspend at about 10^6 cells per millilitre and place 25 μL in each of 10 wells of a multi-well slide. Examine the cells by immunostaining.

The test is not valid if chicken anaemia virus is detected in fewer than 3 of the 4 positive controls or in any of the non-inoculated controls. If the results for more than 1 of the test suspensions are inconclusive then further subcultures of reserved portions of the test suspensions shall be made and tested until an unequivocal result is obtained.

The batch of vaccine complies with the test if there is no evidence of the presence of chicken anaemia virus.

7 TEST FOR DUCK ENTERITIS VIRUS

This test is carried out for vaccines prepared on duck or goose substrates.

Prepare 11 monolayers of primary or secondary Muscovy duck embryo liver cells, from the tissues of 21- or 22-day-old embryos, each monolayer having an area of about 25 cm^2. Remove the culture medium when the cells reach confluence. Inoculate 0.1 mL of test vaccine onto each of 5 of the monolayers (test monolayers). Allow adsorption for 1 h and add culture medium. Inoculate 4 of the monolayers with a suitable strain of duck enteritis virus (not more than 10 CCID$_{50}$ in 0.1 mL) to serve as positive controls. Maintain 2 non-inoculated monolayers as negative controls.

Incubate the cultures for a total of at least 21 days, subculturing at 4- to 5-day intervals. Each passage is made as follows: trypsinise the cells and prepare separate pools of the cells from the test monolayers, from the positive control monolayers and from the negative control monolayers. Mix a portion of each with a suspension of freshly prepared primary or secondary Muscovy duck embryo liver cells to prepare 5, 4 and 2 monolayers, as before. The test is not valid if fewer than 4 of the 5 test monolayers or fewer than 3 of the 4 positive controls or neither of the 2 negative controls survive after any passage.

For the last subculture, grow the cells on a suitable substrate so as to obtain an area of about 10 cm^2 of confluent cells from each of the original 11 monolayers for the subsequent test: test about 10 cm^2 of confluent cells derived from each of the original 11 monolayers by immunostaining for the presence of duck enteritis virus. The test is not valid if duck enteritis virus is detected in fewer than 3 of the 4 positive control monolayers or in any of the negative control monolayers, or if the results for both of the 2 negative control monolayers are inconclusive. If the results for more than 1 of the test monolayers are inconclusive then further subcultures of reserved portions of the monolayers shall be made and tested until an unequivocal result is obtained.

The batch of vaccine complies with the test if there is no evidence of the presence of duck enteritis virus or any other extraneous agent.

8 TEST FOR DUCK AND GOOSE PARVOVIRUSES

This test is carried out for vaccines prepared on duck or goose substrates.

Prepare a suspension of sufficient primary or secondary Muscovy duck embryo fibroblasts from the tissues of 16- to 18-day-old embryos, to obtain not fewer than 11 monolayers, each having an area of about 25 cm^2. Inoculate 0.5 mL of test vaccine into an aliquot of cells for 5 monolayers and seed into 5 replicate containers to form 5 test monolayers. Inoculate 0.4 mL of a suitable strain of duck parvovirus (not more than 10 CCID$_{50}$ in 0.1 mL) into an aliquot of cells for 4 monolayers and seed into 4 replicate containers to form 4 positive control monolayers. Prepare 2 non-inoculated monolayers as negative controls.

Incubate the cultures for a total of at least 21 days, subculturing at 4- to 5-day intervals. Each passage is made as follows: carry out a freeze-thaw cycle. Prepare separate pools of the cells plus fluid from the test monolayers, from the positive control monolayers and from the negative control monolayers. Inoculate 0.5 mL, 0.4 mL and 0.2 mL of the pooled materials into aliquots of a fresh suspension of sufficient primary or secondary Muscovy duck embryo fibroblast cells to prepare 5, 4 and 2 monolayers, as before. The test is not valid if fewer than 4 of the 5 test monolayers or fewer than 3 of the 4 positive controls or neither of the 2 negative controls survive after any passage.

For the last subculture, grow the cells on a suitable substrate so as to obtain an area of about 10 cm^2 of confluent cells from each of the original 11 monolayers for the subsequent test: test about 10 cm^2 of confluent cells derived from each of the original 11 monolayers by immunostaining for the presence of duck or goose parvovirus. The test is not valid if duck parvovirus is detected in fewer than 3 of the 4 positive control monolayers or in any of the negative control monolayers, or if the results for both of the 2 negative control monolayers are inconclusive.

The batch of vaccine complies with the test if there is no evidence of the presence of duck (or goose) parvovirus or any other extraneous agent.

Appendix XXI

B (Vet). Approved Synonyms

Where the English title at the head of a monograph in the European Pharmacopoeia is different from that at the head of the text incorporated into the British Pharmacopoeia or the British Pharmacopoeia (Veterinary), an Approved Synonym (or Approved Synonyms) is created on the recommendation of the British Pharmacopoeia Commission.

In accordance with the General Notice on Titles, the name or names given in the right-hand column of the list below are Approved Synonyms for the name at the head of the monograph of the European Pharmacopoeia given in the left-hand column. Where there is more than one entry in the right-hand column, the first entry is used as the title of the monograph in the British Pharmacopoeia or the British Pharmacopoeia (Veterinary) and the remaining entries are included as subsidiary titles.

Approved Synonyms and subsidiary titles have the same significance as the main title and are thus official titles.

Names made by changing the order of the words in an Approved Synonym, with the addition of a preposition when necessary, are also Approved Synonyms.

Where square brackets are used in a title these may be replaced by round brackets, and *vice versa*. The words 'per cent' may be replaced by the symbol '%'.

Where the word 'Injection' appears in the title or synonym of a monograph in the European Pharmacopoeia, the abbreviation 'Inj.' is declared to be an Approved Synonym for that part of the title.

A consolidated list of all Approved Synonyms is included in Appendix XXI B of the British Pharmacopoeia.

EUROPEAN PHARMACOPOEIA TITLE	APPROVED SYNONYM
Medicinal Substances and Formulated Preparations	
Azaperone for Veterinary Use	Azaperone
Carprofen for Veterinary Use	Carprofen
Clazuril for Veterinary Use	Clazuril
Closantel Sodium Dihydrate for Veterinary Use	Closantel Sodium Dihydrate
Dembrexine Hydrochloride Monohydrate for Veterinary Use	Dembrexine Hydrochloride Monohydrate
Detomidine Hydrochloride for Veterinary Use	Detomidine Hydrochloride
Diclazuril for Veterinary Use	Diclazuril
Difloxacin Hydrochloride Trihydrate for Veterinary Use	Difloxacin Hydrochloride Trihydrate
Dihydrostreptomycin Sulfate for Veterinary Use	Dihydrostreptomycin Sulfate
Enilconazole for Veterinary Use	Enilconazole
Enrofloxacin for Veterinary Use	Enrofloxacin
Equine Serum Gonadotrophin for Veterinary Use	Serum Gonadotrophin
Febantel for Veterinary Use	Febantel
Fenbendazole for Veterinary Use	Fenbendazole
Flunixin Meglumine for Veterinary Use	Flunixin Meglumine
Levamisole for Veterinary Use	Levamisole
Lufenuron for Veterinary Use	Lufenuron
Marbofloxacin for Veterinay Use	Marbofloxacin
Morantel Hydrogen Tartrate for Veterinary Use	Morantel Tartrate
Moxidectin for Veterinary Use	Moxidectin
Orbifloxacin for Veterinary Use	Orbifloxacin
Oxfendazole for Veterinary Use	Oxfendazole
Selamectin for Veterinary Use	Selamectin
Spectinomycin Sulfate Tetrahydrate for Veterinary Use	Spectinomycin Sulfate Tetrahydrate
Sulfadimethoxine Sodium for Veterinary Use	Sulfadimethoxine Sodium
Sulfamethoxypyridazine for Veterinary Use	Sulfametoxypyridazine
Tiamulin for Aveterinary Use	Tiamulin
Tiamulin Hydrogen Fumarate for Veterinary Use	Tiamulin Hydrogen Fumarate
Triclabendazole for Veterinary Use	Triclabendazole
Tylosin For Veterinary Use	Tylosin

EUROPEAN PHARMACOPOEIA TITLE	APPROVED SYNONYM
Tylosin Phosphate Bulk Solution for Veterinary Use	Tylosin Phosphate
Tylosin Tartrate For Veterinary Use	Tylosin Tartrate
Valnemulin Hydrochloride for Veterinary Use	Valnemulin Hydrochloride
Vedaprofen for Veterinary Use	Vedaprofen
Xylazine Hydrochloride for Veterinary Use	Xylazine Hydrochloride

EUROPEAN PHARMACOPOEIA TITLE	APPROVED SYNONYM
Immunological Products (Veterinary)	
Anthrax Spore Vaccine (Live) for Veterinary Use	Anthrax Vaccine, Living
Aujeszky's Disease Vaccine (Inactivated) for Pigs	Aujeszky's Disease Vaccine, Inactivated
Aujeszky's Disease Vaccine (Live) for Pigs for Parenteral Administration	Aujeszky's Disease Vaccine, Living
Avian Infectious Bronchitis Vaccine (Live)	Avian Infectious Bronchitis Vaccine, Living
Avian Infectious Bursal Disease Vaccine (Inactivated)	Infectious Bursal Disease Vaccine, Inactivated Gumboro Disease Vaccine, Inactivated
Avian Infectious Bursal Disease Vaccine (Live)	Infectious Bursal Disease Vaccine, Living Gumboro Disease Vaccine, Living
Avian Infectious Encephalomyelitis Vaccine (Live)	Infectious Avian Encephalomyelitis Vaccine, Living Epidemic Tremor Vaccine, Living
Avian Infectious Laryngotracheitis Vaccine (Live)	Laryngotracheitis Vaccine, Living
Avian Paramyxovirus 3 Vaccine (Inactivated) for Turkeys	Avian Paramyxovirus 3 Vaccine for Turkeys, Inactivated
Bovine Parainfluenza Virus Vaccine (Live)	Bovine Parainfluenza Virus Vaccine, Living
Bovine Respiratory Syncytial Virus Vaccine (Live)	Bovine Respiratory Syncytial Virus Vaccine, Living
Infectious Bovine Rhinotracheitis Vaccine (Live)	Infectious Bovine Rhinotracheitis Vaccine, Living
Brucellosis Vaccine (Live) (Brucella Melitensis Rev. 1 Strain) for Veterinary Use	Brucella Melitensis (Strain Rev. 1) Vaccine, Living
Canine Adenovirus Vaccine (Inactivated)	Canine Adenovirus Vaccine, Inactivated
Canine Adenovirus Vaccine (Live)	Canine Adenovirus Vaccine, Living
Canine Distemper Vaccine (Live)	Canine Distemper Vaccine, Living
Canine Parvovirosis Vaccine (Inactivated)	Canine Parvovirus Vaccine, Inactivated
Canine Parvovirosis Vaccine (Live)	Canine Parvovirus Vaccine, Living
Clostridium Botulinum Vaccine for Veterinary Use	Clostridium Botulinum Vaccine Botulinum Vaccine
Clostridium Chauvoei Vaccine for Veterinary Use	Clostridium Chauvoei Vaccine Blackleg Vaccine
Clostridium Novyi (Type B) Vaccine for Veterinary Use	Clostridium Novyi Type B Vaccine Black Disease Vaccine
Clostridium Perfringens Vaccine for Veterinary Use Type B Type C Type D	Clostridium Perfringens Vaccines Clostridium Perfringens Type B Vaccine Lamb Dysentery Vaccine Clostridium Perfringens Type C Vaccine Struck Vaccine Clostridium Perfringens Type D Vaccine Pulpy Kidney Vaccine
Clostridium Septicum Vaccine for Veterinary Use	Clostridium Septicum Vaccine Braxy Vaccine
Distemper Vaccine (Live) for Mustelids	Ferret and Mink Distemper Vaccine, Living
Egg Drop Syndrome '76 Vaccine (Inactivated)	Egg Drop Syndrome 76 (Adenovirus) Vaccine
Equine Herpesvirus Vaccine (Inactivated)	Equine Herpesvirus Vaccine, Inactivated
Equine Influenza Vaccine (Inactivated)	Equine Influenza Vaccine, Inactivated
Feline Calicivirosis Vaccine (Inactivated)	Feline Calicivirus Vaccine, Inactivated
Feline Calicivirosis Vaccine (Live)	Feline Calicivirus Vaccine, Living
Feline Infectious Enteritis (Feline Panleucopenia) Vaccine (Inactivated)	Feline Infectious Enteritis Vaccine, Inactivated Feline Panleucopenia Vaccine, Inactivated

EUROPEAN PHARMACOPOEIA TITLE	APPROVED SYNONYM
Feline Infectious Enteritis (Feline Panleucopenia) Vaccine (Live)	Feline Infectious Enteritis Vaccine, Living Feline Panleucopenia Vaccine, Living
Feline Leukaemia Vaccine (Inactivated)	Feline Leukaemia Vaccine, Inactivated
Feline Viral Rhinotracheitis Vaccine (Inactivated)	Feline Viral Rhinotracheitis Vaccine, Inactivated
Feline Viral Rhinotracheitis Vaccine (Live)	Feline Viral Rhinotracheitis Vaccine, Living
Foot-and-Mouth Disease (Ruminants) Vaccine (Inactivated)	Foot and Mouth Disease (Ruminants) Vaccine
Fowl-pox Vaccine (Live)	Fowl Pox Vaccine, Living
Furunculosis Vaccine (Inactivated, Oil-adjuvanted, Injectable) for Salmonids	Furunculosis Vaccine for Salmonids, Inactivated
Marek's Disease Vaccine (Live)	Marek's Disease Vaccine, Living Marek's Disease Vaccine (Turkey Herpes Virus) Marek's Disease Vaccine, Living (HVT)
Neonatal Piglet Colibacillosis Vaccine (Inactivated)	Porcine E. Coli Vaccine, Inactivated Porcine Escherichia Coli Vaccine, Inactivated
Neonatal Ruminant Colibacillosis Vaccine (Inactivated)	Ruminant E. Coli Vaccine, Inactivated Ruminant Escherichia Coli Vaccine, Inactivated
Newcastle Disease Vaccine (Inactivated)	Newcastle Disease Vaccine, Inactivated
Newcastle Disease Vaccine (Live)	Newcastle Disease Vaccine, Living
Porcine Actinobacillosis Vaccine (Inactivated)	Porcine Actinobacillosis Vaccine, Inactivated
Porcine Influenza Vaccine (Inactivated)	Swine Influenza Vaccine, Inactivated
Porcine Parvovirosis Vaccine (Inactivated)	Porcine Parvovirus Vaccine, Inactivated
Porcine Progressive Atrophic Rhinitis Vaccine (Inactivated)	Porcine Progressive Atrophic Rhinitis Vaccine, Inactivated
Rabies Vaccine (Inactivated) for Veterinary Use	Rabies Veterinary Vaccine, Inactivated
Swine Erysipelas Vaccine (Inactivated)	Swine Erysipelas Vaccine, Inactivated
Tetanus Antitoxin for Veterinary Use	Clostridium Tetani Antitoxin Tetanus Antitoxin (Veterinary)
Tetanus Vaccine for Veterinary Use	Clostridium Tetani Vaccines Tetanus Toxoids (Veterinary) *The following titles may be used for vaccines with an appropriate potency:* Clostridium Tetani Vaccine for Equidae Tetanus Toxoid for Equidae
Vibriosis (Cold-water) Vaccine (Inactivated) for Salmonids	Cold-water Vibriosis Vaccine for Salmonids, Inactivated
Vibriosis Vaccine (Inactivated) for Salmonids	Vibriosis Vaccine for Salmonids, Inactivated
Yersiniosis Vaccine (Inactivated) for Salmonids	Enteric Redmouth Disease Vaccine for Rainbow Trout, Inactivated

Supplementary Chapters

Supplementary Chapters contain no standards, tests or assays nor any other mandatory specifications with respect to any Pharmacopoeial article. They comprise explanatory and other ancillary texts and are provided for the assistance and information of users of the Pharmacopoeia.

Contents of the Supplementary Chapters

Supplementary Chapter I

A. Monograph Development: Mechanism

The following Supplementary Chapter provides an outline of the mechanism by which monographs are selected and developed for inclusion in the British Pharmacopoeia (Veterinary).

The British Pharmacopoeia Commission will not usually develop monographs for drug substances or excipients. These will usually be elaborated by the European Pharmacopoeia Commission.

The British Pharmacopoeia Commission will consider a monograph for inclusion in the British Pharmacopoeia (Veterinary) in the following circumstances:

1. The formulation is widely used (for example: top 100 products identified following a survey of wholesale dealers in the United Kingdom; veterinary products identified by the members of the Panel of Experts for Veterinary Medicines).

2. The innovator product is approaching or past its patent expiry date (monographs will usually only be prepared in the two years preceding patent expiry. However there may be circumstances where it is justified to prepare a monograph at an earlier stage. These will be considered by the British Pharmacopoeia Commission individually).

3. There is a particular need based on the therapeutic category and/or the importance of the material concerned; the latter being particularly relevant to small patient populations.

4. The product falls within a "family" of product presentations, of which there are already published monographs and/or monographs on the work programme.

5. Drug substances or excipients which are not on the European Pharmacopoeia work programme, but for which there is a specific UK need.

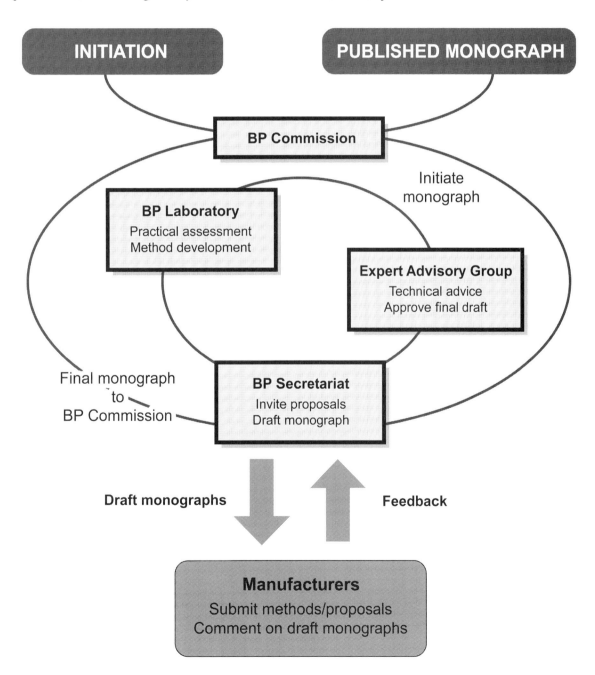

6. A request is received from the Competent Authority [Veterinary Medicines Directorate (VMD)].

7. A request is received from a manufacturer for one of their own products.

8. Support for relevant EC directives.

9. A request is received from official bodies [such as the World Health Organization (WHO)].

10. Other circumstances considered on a case-by-case basis.

It should be noted that compliance with any of the above criteria will not necessarily mean that a monograph will be included in the British Pharmacopoeia (Veterinary).

The British Pharmacopoeia Commission may decide not to elaborate a monograph for a number of reasons, including a lack of interest from stakeholders, resource limitations or other circumstances, decided on a case-by-case basis.

The diagram provides a simplified, schematic representation of the development of a monograph for a medicinal substance or an associated formulated preparation.

Index

Page numbers in **bold type** relate to monograph titles.

Pages – Vol VI: i – xxiv,   (Preliminaries and Introduction)
1 – 338,   (General Notices and Monographs)
S1 – S20,   (Spectra)
A1 – A44,   (Appendices; Supplementary Chapters)

V

W

X

Y

British Pharmacopoeia

MHRA
151 Buckingham Palace Road
London SW1W 9SZ
Telephone: +44 (0)20 3080 6561
E-mail: bpcom@mhra.gsi.gov.uk
Web site: www.pharmacopoeia.com

CUSTOMER FEEDBACK

Monographs of the British Pharmacopoeia are reviewed regularly. To ensure that the standards are up-to-date, users of the BP are invited to let us know where difficulties exist in any of the monographs published. Supporting data will be required for your request.

We are also keen to receive your views on how the BP can be improved. Take the time to tell us. You can either use the form below or respond via the BP website www.pharmacopoeia.com

---

MONOGRAPH TITLE:

Review Request

Reason:
- ☐ Error (Typographical or Technical)
- ☐ Analytical improvement
- ☐ Impurity not controlled
- ☐ BP Material not available
- ☐ Apparatus not available
- ☐ New source available
- ☐ Other
- ☐ Reagent not available
- ☐ Reference Material not available

REQUIREMENT TO BE REVIEWED

- ☐ Title
- ☐ Tests
- ☐ Other
- ☐ Definition
- ☐ Assay
- ☐ Identification
- ☐ Impurities

SUPPORTING DATA

- ☐ Batch
- ☐ Other
- ☐ Validation
- ☐ Chromatogram

COMMENTS AND SUGGESTIONS

Usability

Functionality (Website and Download)

New Monograph Proposal

New Appendix Proposal

New Supplementary Chapter Proposal

Compliment

Complaint

CUSTOMER DETAILS

Name and Address

Tel No:

Fax No:

Post Code: e-mail address: